117894

The

Renaissance

New

Testament

Randolph O. Yeager

VOLUME NINE

Mark 16:14—20
Luke 24:33—53
John 20:19—21:25
Acts 1:1—10:33

PELICAN PUBLISHING COMPANY

GRETNA 1982

Library of Congress Cataloging in Publication Data

Yeager, Randolph O.
    The Renaissance New Testament.

    Volumes 1-4 originally published in 1976-1978 by
Renaissance Press, Bowling Green, Ky.
    1. Bible. N.T.—Concordances, Greek. 2. Greek
language, Biblical. I. Title.
BS2302.Y4   1981   225.4'8'0321   79-28652
ISBN: 0-88289-858-2 (v. 9)

Manufactured in the United States of America

Published by Pelican Publishing Company, Inc.
1101 Monroe Street, Gretna, Louisiana 70053

Introduction

Lucifer, Eve, Baal, Zoroaster, Philo, Mani, Plotinus, Origen, Thomas Aquinas,

the Secular Humanists and some Amillenialists.

"Feathered biped vertebrates tend to be gregarious according to their respective plumage."

What do these distinguished people have in common? Some to a great, others to a less, but all to some extent tend to be afflicted with gnosticism. And what is a Gnostic?

Let us begin with a passage of scripture. Isaiah had just said that we should "seek the Lord, while he may be found and call upon him while he is near." The wicked is admonished to ". . . forsake his way, and the unrighteous man his thoughts." Rather we are to "return to the Lord, that He may have mercy on (us) and to our God, for He will abundantly pardon."

Note that this call unto repentance involves both our ethics and our philosophy. The wicked are walking in a path which they must forsake and the unrighteous man is indulging thoughts which he should abandon. Paul pointed out that bad philosophy corrupts ethics (1 Corinthians 15:33).

Why this call to repentance?

Isaiah tells us why in verses eight and nine - "For my thoughts are not your thoughts, neither are your ways my ways, says the Lord. For as the heavens are higher than the earth, so are my ways higher than your ways and my thoughts than your thoughts."

There follows in verses ten and eleven an analogous application of the principle that God thinks on one level and we on another lower level. Thus, His Word is like the rain and snow, without the moisture of which upon the earth, seed sown in hopes of a harvest would not germinate and there would be neither seed to the sower (the farmer would not even get his seed wheat back) nor bread to the eater.

Then God promises, "So shall my Word be that goes forth from my mouth. It shall not return to me empty, but it shall accomplish that which I purpose, and prosper in the thing for which I sent it."

The parable of the sower in Matthew 13 suggests that when the sower sows the seed of the Word of God, the germination ratio is three to one, although only one third of that which germinates develops in profitable fruit bearing.

Why then do we not see greater harvest results from our evangelistic seed sowing? Because Gnosticism has spoiled the seeding process. The Gnostics resent the thought that God knows more than they do, particularly in view of the fact that Isaiah implies that that will always be so. The heavens are a long distance above the earth, and God's knowledge is to the same extent higher than ours. The Gnostics do not like that.

The epistemological question has occupied the minds of philosophers for centuries. Materialists with their empiricism stand in diametric opposition to Idealists with their rationalism. Thus Democritus and Lucretius opposed Plato and Augustine while Aristotle and Thomas Aquinas sought middle ground between the two extremes. In modern times Locke, Hume and Berkeley opposed DesCartes, Leibniz and Spinoza, while Kant and Hegel sought the middle ground. It was Leibniz who countered Locke's *tabula rasa* notion that "there is nothing in the mind except what was first in the senses," by the retort, "nothing, except the intellect itself." Kant added, "Perceptions without conceptions are blind." There was little profit in this battle of the frogs and mice for anyone except the printer. Hume destroyed the human mind as thoroughly as Berkeley destroyed matter. As Will Durant has said, "Nothing was left; and philosophy found itself in the midst of ruins of its own making. No wonder that a wit advsied the abandonment of the controversy, saying: 'No matter, never mind.' " (Will Durant, *The Story of Philosophy*, 281).

Kant began with the stimulus of the senses, but he argued that sensation is stimulus without organization and needs perception to organize it. Organized perception is conception, which produces science which is organized knowledge, which leads to wisdom which is life organized at its highest possible level. "Each is a greater degree of order, and sequence, and unity." (*Ibid.,* 296).

But Kant, for all of his idealism with its devastating impact upon the empiricism of Locke, Berkeley and Hume, was forced to admit that since the intellectual process which leads to certitude begins with sense perception, there is no certitude for the Christian theologian, since only the Christians of the first century experienced the facts relating to the time/space experiences of Jesus of Nazareth. The rest of us know of Jesus and His life, miracles, death, resurrection and ascension only as we read about Him in a book which cannot be said to provide empirical evidence of truth. Thus, for Kant, religious "truth" was in the eye of the beholder and believer - not based on solid evidence. It is scant wonder that the Lutheran preachers in Northern Germany named their dogs after Immanual Kant.

Georg Wilhelm Friedrich Hegel sought to provide the certitude in spiritual matters which Kant considered unattainable, but failed, even if his readers could have understood him in the ten volumes which he wrote. Intellectuals have read Hegel and pseudointellectuals have endured the long ordeal of looking out and pronouncing all of the words, but even Hegel admitted that "only one man understands me and even he does not." Critics have challanged the authenticity of this story, but it is probable that few of Hegel's students really knew what he meant. It was something like this: progress toward certitude is the result of the *Zeitgeist*, the "Spirit of the Age." There is a spirit moving in society that directs debate between a thesis and its antithesis and brings an accommodation which Hegel called a synthesis. The synthesis, a conceptual child of its parents, the thesis and antithesis, is purer truth than either of them. The synthesis is then subjected to another accommodation process which produces another synthesis, which is even more pure. This process goes on and on until spiritual truths, unavailable under the Kantian system, are understood. Hegel thought that this spiritual dialectical process moved forward in history most effeciently in the Rhine River valley of Germany, the heartland of the Eurasian landmass, and thus he concluded that the German culture was the most sophisticated of all and should be looked to for world leadership. Nowhere else on earth did enlightened debate purify truth and banish error.

One might be impressed with the Hegelian system if it were not for the fact that Karl Marx took his method to the left to give us Communism and Adolf Hitler took his method to the right to give us Fascism.

Auguste Comte, the father of Logical Positivism, born in Montpellier in 1798 was so impressed with Benjamin Franklin that he called him a modern Socrates. Comte said, "You know that at five-and-twenty (Franklin) formed the design of becoming perfectly wise, and that he fulfilled his design. I have dared to undertake the same thing though I am not yet twenty." His ambitious quest for omniscience should be a warning to other teenagers not "to think more highly of themselves than they ought to think." Comte and his view that only empiricism provided certitude, although metaphysics had some value, concluded that Christian theology was based upon nothing more than superstition. The Vienna Circle in the twentieth century have carried on his work.

In recent times Bultmann, Tillich, Niebuhr and even Karl Barth have based Christian faith upon individual experience rather than upon the propositional revelation of Jesus in his time/space relationships.

Gnostics demonstrate that they know it all, by the simple expedients, either of denigrating to insignificance that which they cannot understand or of interpreting language into allegorical forms that they can understand. Agnostics go to the opposite extreme and boast that their intellectual sophistication is so lofty that they have now come to understand clearly that no one will ever understand anything clearly. Thus, happily resigned to universal and eternal ignorance they have resigned from the human race and spend their time playing bridge. It is significant however that they have chosen the Greek form for "One who knows nothing" rather than the Latin form which still carries connotations which are not flattering. The cocktail party goers in the drawing rooms may frequently hear, "I am an Agnostic." They never hear, "I am an Ignoramus." One wonders why not?

But Gnostics know it all or if they do not, give them another six weeks. They will never accept an intellectual status inferior to that of the Creator. Jesus said that the intellectually poverty stricken would inherit the Kingdom of Heaven (Mt.5:3), and that if we do not become like the little child He held on His lap we would never go to heaven (Mt.18:3). He thanked the Father one day that it served the divine purpose well that the mysteries should be hidden from the Gnostics and revealed rather to babes (Mt.11:25).

Paul looked over the lower middle class congregation in Corinth and observed that "not many mighty were called." Thank God he did not say, "Not any" but he did say, "Not many." The first thing that the Holy Spirit does when He calls the elect to Christ, whether he be mighty or not, is to say to him that relatively speaking the mighty are just as far below God's thoughts as those who are less heavily endowed. It is just as impossible for the Ph.D. as it is for Alfred J. Neumann to fathom the profundity of God's thoughts and to understand why or how He does what He does. But the Gnostics do not think so. They are determined to know it all or else.

There are two ways to achieve what they desire with such ardor. They can plumb the Greek New Testament to its magnificant and awesome depths, with such amazing objectivity and exhausting comprehension that they do in fact know all that God knows. This plan will not work. If it did, what Isaiah said would not be true. We can indeed come to understand all that God has revealed in the Greek New Testament. To say otherwise is to say that God deliberately wrote material beyond our comprehension, and it is to deny Jesus' statement to the Apostles in John 16:13-15. But God has not revealed in the Greek New Testament everything that He knows. He has revealed there all that we need to know in order to be saved. His divine reticence is His way of keeping His children in their proper place before His throne.

But there is an alternative method for the Gnostic. If the Word of God plainly says what he does not understand, he can abandon objective exegesis and employ an allegorical method of interpretation which allows him to pull God's message down to his own earth-bound level. And then he does understand it. This process of denigration of the Divine message does not yield the mind of God, but it satisfies the Gnostic ego.

The Gnostic reasons something like this:

Gnostic: "Did God create everything *ex nihilo?*"
The Babe: "That is what the Bible says."
Gnostic: "Is God good?"
The Babe: "Indubitably."
The Gnostic: "Does evil exist?"
The Babe: "Unfortunately yes. The Bible speaks of it as having objective existence."
The Gnostic: "Then God created evil."
The Babe: "It is a problem."
The Gnostic: "What is the answer?"
The Babe: "I do not know."
The Gnostic: "I am going to find out."
The Babe: "You cannot touch that problem with a ten foot pole."
The Gnostic: "Then I will get an eleven foot pole."
The Babe: "Is it not better to be a little agnostic about it?"
The Gnostic: "Never!"

Thus Spake Zarathustra and thus also spake Lucifer, who was perfect in all of his ways until iniquity was found in him (Ezekiel 28:15). Where did the iniquity come from if God created him? He determined to find out and said, "I will ascend into heaven, I will exalt my throne above the stars of God: I will sit also upon the mount of the congregation, in the sides of the north: I will ascend above the heights of the clouds: I will be like the most High." (Isaiah 14:13,14). To which God replied, "Yet thou shalt be brought down to hell" (Isaiah 14:15). Thus Lucifer was the first Gnostic. He could not live without the answer to every question. He would know as much as God.

The Satanic *coup d' etat* failed. The Son of God threw him out of heaven and watched him all of the way down (Luke 10:18) until he splattered upon the earth, probably somewhere in Texas - West Texas! Or it may have been in Iran! But Satan was still a Gnostic, for Gnostics never learn, by virtue of the fact that they do not believe that there is anything left for them to learn. When one knows it all one stops studying and starts congratulating himself.

Satan told Eve that if she would assert her independence and eat of the forbidden fruit she would be as Elohim, and thus would know the difference between good and evil. She hesitated, although she was enamored and intrigued with the idea that it would be great to understand the problem of evil. As she toyed with the idea, the devil read to her Ralph Waldo Emerson's essay on *Self Reliance*. That did it. The fruit was good to eat, pleasant to the eye and designed to make her wise. Thus Satan and his hellish Gnosticism appeals to the naive. John later warned that we are not to love that in the world which consists of the "lust of the flesh, the lust of the eye and the pride of life" (1 John 2:15,16). Eve was assailed by all three of these inducements. The fruit was delicious; it was pretty and it possessed a magical ability to make her as wise as God. Or at least so she thought. She ate. We all know the result.

Pagan idolatry was Gnostic. Judaism, with its pure monotheism, left the prophets with some unanswered questions. That is why Isaiah wrote as he did (Isaiah 55:6-11). The pagans had to have a god that they could understand, and since the God of Abraham, Moses and the Prophets had some secrets which He did not choose to divulge they made their own gods - like Aaron's golden calf. No trouble understanding Baal or Ra or Moloch or any other god if he is the product of your own brain and hands. Since they could not understand all of the Lord's message, presented to them by Moses and the Prophets, they made their own gods who gave them messages that they could understand. The idolatrous message was on an ethical level that offered no limitation upon the desires of the worshipper. Ahab could not in conscience kill Naboth and take his vineyard so long as he worshipped the God of the Hebrews, but after he converted to Baal it was easy.

Zoroaster, a Persian probably contemporary with Homer and Hesiod, could not live with his ignorance about the problem of evil, so he solved it to his own satisfaction. God was good and evil was not good. God was light and evil was darkness. God was love and peace and evil was hatred and war. Since God, who is good and light and love and peace could not therefore have created evil and darkness, hatred and war, it followed for the Persian that the kingdom of darkness is also eternal - that it is coexistent with God and good. What then is it? Since God is a Spirit, the evil must be matter. Thus God was fire, before Whose flames matter is destroyed. Thus Zoroaster and his fire worshipping Parsees.

vii

To be sure, the writer of Hebrews says that ". . . our God is a consuming fire" (Heb.12:29) but he did not mean it in Zoroastrian terms. In *Thus Spake Zarathrustra* Nietsche puts into the mouth of the prophet these words, "All that I am not, God and virtue is."

Alexander the Great went too far East. Aristotle, his tutor was asked by the young king what he would like to have as a present from the Orient. He replied, "Bring me a philosopher." Alexander did not come back but his army did and they brought back the Gnostic philosophy of Zoroaster. Back in Greece, Zoroastrian Gnosticism found some compatibility with Plato's extreme idealism, although Plato would probably have objected to it if he had been alive. Aristotle also would have objected, to be sure, since his "Golden Mean" moderation views were even at odds to some extent with Plato, his great teacher, but Aristotle outlived Alexander by only one year.

With both Plato and Aristotle dead, no convincing voice successfully resisted Gnosticism during the Hellenistic period and the Neo-Platonists who carried Plato further in the direction of idealism than he would have wished established the great schools of Gnosticism in Alexandria, in Antioch and even in Rome, where Plotinus taught his Gnostic Neo-Platonism.

The Gnostic, Mani, born about A.D. 202 came to Rome, preaching that the problem of evil was no problem to him. God did not create evil for evil was never created. It was as eternal as God. God is Spirit; evil is matter. Anything material is therefore evil. That included Mani. He did not hesitate to admit it. His evil, because material body was a part of the kingdom of darkness, hatred, lust and war, and it was in an endless fight against God (good, spirit, love, peace, light, etc.). Matter stinks. So did Mani who lived in a climate that was too warm and a culture that had not yet developed shower baths and deodorant. Mani is the founder of Manichaeism which produced the ascetics of the Middle Ages, including Simeon Stylite who sat atop a pole, sixty feet high, for thirty years.

Plotinus was a Gnostic who apologized to his students because his soul had a body. One of his students was Origen (c A.D.185 - c.254). Highly regarded by some church historians as a brilliant mind he nevertheless had a screw loose. His attempt to improve the Greek translation of the Hebrew text of the Old Testament which was produced in Alexandria 400 years before was a disaster. Driven by an ambition to know it all and faced with Scripture which resisted his attempts to plumb to its depths and scale its heights, Origen resorted to the strategem discussed above. If he could not understand what the Bible said when subjected to objective exegesis he would apply to it his own system of allegorical interpretation. Thus he brought God's thoughts, which Isaiah had said were as high above ours as the heavens are high above the earth, down to his human level. Unable to scale the heights of divine knowledge he pulled the divine message down to his level. Unable to deify his own thinking he humanized God. Otherwise he would have been forced to admit that there was something that he neither did nor could know. Of course such an admission is unthinkable for a Gnostic. So for Origen little in Scripture was to be taken at face value. Literal interpretation was taboo, since the Bible, when taken literally, asks us to believe unreasonable, if not impossible things.

We offer the evaluation of Origen from the pen of Mosheim, the great Lutheran church

After the encomiums we have given to Origen, who has an undoubted right to the first place among the interpreters of the Scripture in this century, it is not without deep concern that we are obliged to add, that he also, by an unhappy method, opened a secure retreat for all sorts of errors that a wild and irregular imagination could bring forth. Having entertained a notion that it was extremely difficult, if not impossible, to defend everything contained in the sacred writings from the cavils of heretics and infidels, so long as they were explained literally, according to the real import of the terms he had recourse to the fecundity of a lively imagination, and maintained, that they were to be interpreted in the same allegorical manner in which the Platonists explained the history of the gods. In consequence of this pernicious rule of interpretation, he alleged that the words of Scripture were, in many places, absolutely void of sense; and that though in others there were, indeed, certain notions conveyed under the outward terms according to their literal force and import yet it was not in these that the true meanings of the sacred writers were to be sought, but in a mysterious and hidden sense arising from the nature of the things themselves. This hidden sense he endeavours to investigate throughout his commentaries, neglecting and despising, for the most part, the outward letters; and in this devious path he displays the most ingenious strokes of fancy, though generally at the expense of truth, whose divine simplicity is rarely discernible through the cobweb veil of allegory.

Origen, in his **Stromata**, *book X, expresses himself in the following manner: 'The source of many evils lies in adhering to the carnal or external part of Scripture. Those who do so, shall not attain to the kingdom of God. Let us, therefore, seek after the spirit and the substantial fruit of the word, which are hidden and mysterious.' And again, 'The Scriptures are of little use to those who understand them as they are written.' One would think it impossible that such expressions should drop from the pen of a wise man. But the philosophy, which this great man embraced with such zeal, was one of the sources of his delusion. He could not find in the Bible the opinions he had adopted, as long as he interpreted that sacred book according to its literal sense. But Plato, Aristotle, Zeno, and, indeed, the whole philosophical tribe, could not fail to object for their sentiments, a place in the Gospel, when it was interpreted by the wanton inventions of fancy, and upon the supposition of a hidden sense, to which it was possible to give all sorts of forms. Hence all who desired to model Christianity according to their fancy, or their favorite system of philosophy, embraced Origen's method of interpretation."*

Mosheim, *Ecclesiastical History*, 66.

Origen is thus seen as the father of the allegorical system of Scripture interpretation - a system that serves admirably to this day by which modern Gnostics, who think themselves too sophisticated to believe what the Bible plainly says, tell us that since it does not mean what it says, it means what they say it means. Superior intelligence is not required to see that if we are free to interpret Scripture allegorically, the Bible can be made to teach whatever the interpreter wishes. When one has seen one allegory he has seen them all. Thus Mary who was not a virgin gave birth to Jesus whose human father, if not Joseph the carpenter, is unknown, and the passage that says that she conceived by the Holy Spirit means that she "conceived the idea of God." And the mist that arose from the rivers in the Garden of Eden was not water; it was mis(t)understanding, which refers to the confusion

ix

in theological matters of all those who have not read Mary Baker Eddy's book. And since, as amillenialists have told us and told us and told us and told us, *ad infinitum, ad nauseam* that one cannot bind the devil with a literal chain it follows that the verse which says "a thousand years" which occurs six times in the first seven verses of Revelation 20 does not mean "a thousand years." Since the truth of the Scripture is not in the text with its diction, its grammar and syntax, but in the eye of the allegorical interpreter, the Bible therefore teaches everything generally which is the same thing as saying that it teaches nothing specifically. According to Origen, whom Mosheim castigated so eloquently and with such eclat and aplomb, and according to all those who have decided that the Holy Spirit wrote a book too difficult for ordinary mortals to understand until its meaning is revealed first to them and then set forth in their commentaries, the Gospel of Jesus Christ, with its plan of salvation and guide to good ethics means only whatever ten thousand butchers and bakers and candestick makers say its means.

The evidence that Origen, for all of his highly touted ability, rode in an intellectual elevator that did not go to the top floor is found in the fact that after saying that "the Scriptures are of little use to those who understand them as they are written" he chose to take very seriously the one verse which he should have taken in another light. Jesus, in a subtle attack upon the Gnostic philosophy that held Origen himself in thrall, said that some feared the flesh so much that they made themselves eunuchs for the sake of the Kingdom of the Heavens, as though sex was always sin and that there was no place for it under divinely constituted conditions. This verse Origen decided should be taken "as it was written." Accordingly he indulged in the fantastic act of autoemasculation, little realizing that the illicit act is only the physical implementation of the illicit thought which Jesus said originates in the heart. If Origen had been the exegete that he has been described as being he would have cut out his heart, since apparently he did not understand the teaching of the New Testament that regeneration gives the believer a new heart immediately and a new body eventually.

Lucifer, the first Gnostic, has never gotten over his desire to know as much as God. Unable to achieve omniscience himself he nevertheless recognizes that his hellish ambition is a good tool to use to deceive others. We have seen how he used it to deceive Eve, Ahab, Zoroaster, Philo, Mani, Plotinus and Origen. And he used Origen to establish a school of allegorical interpretation which has been followed since by the Scholastics of whom Thomas Aquinas was chief.

Aquinas could not believe that a mind as great as his could be depraved - his will, yes, and his emotions, definitely, but not his mind. Thus the human system of rationalism which is the heart of Jesuit theology.

Not all the theology of the Middle Ages however was Thomist. The Jansenists, of whom Blaise Pascal was representative, were not contaminated, and hence continued in the Augustinian tradition, as had Calvin and Luther. Modern Jesuit theology is essentially Gnostic.

The field of eschatology has not escaped the infection and contamination of Gnosticism. For two hundred years the early church was chiliastic. The Apostles took literally the statements that Jesus Christ would sit on David's throne. John told us six times that the reign of Messiah would begin at His second coming, continue for one thousand years, and, after the unsuccessful *coup d'etat* of Satan and the creation of new heavens and a new earth, continue throughout the eternal ages of the ages. Why not, if that is what God wants? It is all right with me. Who am I to object? Do the amillenialists have a better idea? But Origen said that that doesn't make sense. So plain language must mean something other than what it says. Since Origen's day we have had our amillenial brethren with us. They are indeed our brothers in Christ, for many of them are Calvinists and thus closer to the New Testament message than the Pelagian premillenialists. There are, of course, others who have compounded theological felonies *in extremis*, with their soteriological Pelagianism, their eschatalogical amillenialism and their charismatic doctrine of the Holy Spirit. God be thanked that though some have reserved the right to explain away whatever seems to them to make no sense with reference to the Kingdom of the Heavens, they have not departed from the faith with reference to the plan of salvation.

Is it not better to occupy with Aristotle an epistemological "golden mean?" The mature Christian is neither a Gnostic nor an Agnostic. John's gospel is written that we might "know" but there are some things which we do not know. Paul could not explain why Pharaoh was treated as he was. His only remark was to the effect that Gnostics have no moral right to pry into God's business. The Bible clearly teaches predestination, election, total depravity, effectual call and limited atonement, but no one can give satisfactory explanations that will satisfy either his own mind or that of his critics. If Paul was a "fool for Christ" why should the rest of us refuse to bear "the offence of the cross?"

I do not know why God created a universe in which He permitted evil. It is enough for me to know that the Creator is greater than all He created and that there is no doubt that evil will be judged and that God and His good, life, love, peace, joy *et al* will prevail eternally.

I do not know how an axe head swam or how a dead man arose, but I am not ashamed to say that I do not know, nor am I ashamed to say that I believe all that the Bible says about God, His Son, His Spirit and His works.

But we must face the question of whether or not there is any figurative language in the Bible. Must we take it all literally? Of course not. For the Bible writers were also artists and poets. When Isaiah said, "For ye shall go out with joy, and be led forth with peace: the mountains and the hills shall break forth before you into singing, and all the trees of the field shall clap their hands" (Isaiah 55:12), he expected normal people to understand that that was his poetic way of saying that all of nature was glorifying God. No one in his right mind believes that the giant redwoods in northern California clapped two hands together to applaud the mountains and hills who had just sung Pagliacci. Where do we draw the line? A safe rule would seem to be that no Scripture is to be taken allegorically unless it is manifestly impossible to take it literally. We ought not to expect the miraculous unless divine power is involved. When the plain statements of Scripture make sense, seek no other sense. If the Bible said Peter walked on the water I would not believe it, but the same Bible that tells me that Jesus did, also tells me who Jesus is.

God's Word is like the rain and snow from heaven which comes down to water the earth so that the miracle of life can occur. It will always do what God has in mind for it. It is always successful. It is "living and operative." This is true only because it is the message about Him, Whose thoughts are as much beyond human thoughts as the heavens are higher than the earth. And it is this last idea that no Gnostic, beginning with Lucifer and ending with the last allegoricist can abide. Groucho Marx once said that he would not care to join a club with standards of excellence low enough to allow its members to invite him to join! In the same spirit I will have no faith in a system of truth every part of which is within the reach of my unaided intellect. If I can understand my religion in every one of its parts then my religion is no loftier than if I had designed it myself.

Who would trust a religious philosophy like that?

The Christian escapes the perils of Gnosticism because the New Testament holds out to him a challenge to understand the eternal verities which it is his delight to accept. It is the very fact that he does not know it all that makes the Christian experience so exciting and rewarding. He also escapes the perils of Agnosticism because, although he does not know it all, he knows with postive certitude a part. Those who look in upon the Tonight Show occasionally are familiar with the question which always follows a statement in the opening monologue such as "It was hot today." Immediately the announcer asks, "How hot was it?" When Isaiah said that God's thoughts are higher than our thoughts, we might well ask, "How high are they?" And the answer is as high as the heavens are above the earth. That is high!

That is where our resurrected Lord now sits while the Holy Spirit makes His enemies His footstool (Psalm 110:1). He is in the superheavenlies, ". . . far above all principality and power and might and dominion and every name that is named, not only in this world, but also in that which is to come" (Eph.1:21). God has given to Him a name that is above every name, at the mention of which every knee will bow and every tongue will admit that He is Lord, to the glory of God the Father (Phil.2:9-11).

He sits in repose (Heb.1:3) because His redemptive work is done, and in Him ". . . are hid all the treasures of wisdom and knowledge" (Col.2:3).

Meanwhile, as the Source of all Wisdom and Knowledge, the living embodiment of Philosophy and Science, sits at the Father's right hand the human quest for wisdom and knowledge goes on down here upon the earth beneath, as the battle of the frogs and mice rages. The unsaved are ever learning and never able to come to a knowledge of the truth (2 Tim.3:7). Neither text nor context, so far as I am able to determine, reveals whether Pilate's question was asked in sincerity or in derision. What is truth? (John 18:38). The Christian knows. He knows some of it now and he is destined to know more of it, though I personally doubt that he will ever in the coming ages of the ages know it all. What does the verse mean when John says, "We shall see Him and we shall be like Him for we shall see Him as He is" ? (1 John 3:2). We shall be like Him physically, to be sure, for in resurrection the Holy Spirit will make our bodies like His glorified body (Rom.8:11). Interred as natural bodies, subject to biodegradability, they will be raised as bodies dominated totally by the Holy Spirit and therefore eternal (1 Cor.15:44). But we will not become Ph.D.'s in every field of knowledge ". . . in a moment, in the twinkling of an eye, at the last trump" (1 Cor.15:52). That instantaneous transformation refers to bodies, not to intellects.

Speaking of transformation, Pauls tell us how, as victorious Christians, in a world that has never lost its way by simple virtue of the fact that it has not yet found it, we can escape its corruption. "Be ye not conformed to this world, but be ye transformed . . . " How? "by the renewing of your mind." Why should we, and if we do what is the result? "that you may prove what is that good, and acceptable, and perfect will of God" (Rom. 12:2). There is no security like that enjoyed by one who knows that he is walking day by day in the perfect will of God.

Daniel spoke of a day when men and women would run to and fro (Dan. 12:4). If you doubt that try to find a place to park at National Airport. If you are fortunate enough to find a place within a mile, sit in the waiting room and watch. Those who are not running to are running fro. They do it safely too. Statistical chances that you will be killed in an airplane are one in several million. Run over by a Washington D.C. taxicab? Too close to call.

Daniel added that knowledge would be increased. Has it ever! How brilliant we are. The Columbia blasted off on time at Cape Canaveral and two or three days later touched down in a California desert within seconds of the time that the engineers predicted. Not every course in the college catalogue is worth the candle, but most are. Twenty years ago I figured that if I went to Chicago University for 100 years on a trimester basis and took four three-hour courses each term I could take every course listed in their catalogue. Yes, science has done very well. We know a great deal collectively and a few people know a lot on an individual basis, but we do not know the truth. We sit like drunken hoot owls on a rotten limb of a dead tree, stare with open eyes straight at the sun and hoot, "Where is it?"

Where is the Son of Righteousness? Psalm 110:1 says that He is at the Father's right hand. The last time the world saw Him, His lifeless body sagged upon a Roman gibbet. There was no beauty in Him that we should desire Him (Isa. 53:2). He was despised and rejected of men - a man of sorrows, thoroughly acquainted with a load of grief as the divine rebuke broke His heart. In disgust men turned away, walked across Kedron to Jerusalem to the red-light districts with the observation that they would not be annoyed again with anymore Galilean carpenters turned preacher.

The unregenerate, in possession of a great number of facts, have no wisdom or knowledge because someone has taken away the key of knowledge (Luke 11:52). The Greek word for key, $\kappa\lambda\epsilon\iota\varsigma$ occurs only six times (Mt. 16:19; Lk. 11:52; Rev. 1:18; 3:7; 9:1; 20:1) in the New Testament. "Christ has the key of hell and death" whatever that means. Jesus gave to Peter the key of the kingdom of heaven. He used it first at Pentecost and opened the door of knowledge to 3000 Jews. He used it again in Caesarea, when a Roman army officer found Christ. Philip, a deacon, went to Samaria and opened the door of knowledge for a large group of social outcasts called Samaritans. One of them tried to buy it and Peter told him to go to the devil. Philip then went down into the Gaza strip and unlocked the door of salvation for a black man who carried it with him in his chariot to Ethiopia and Abysinnia where he probably founded the Coptic Church.

What is this key without which we can never open the door that leads to true knowledge?

We have attacked the Gnostic philosophy that assumes that all knowledge is attainable. Let us now examine the Agnostic philosophy that assumes that no knowledge is attainable. Unsaved philosophers deride the Christian quest for certitude. But knowledgeable Christians are not deterred. John said, "These things are written that ye might believe that Jesus is the Christ, the Son of God; and that believing ye might have life through his name" (John 20:31). One need only consult the list of passages where γινώσκω occurs (#131 in *The Renaissance New Testament*, I, 94,95) to be convinced that the Christian faith is based not upon conjecture, but upon certitude. To be sure sophisticated Christians are turned off by the gnostic fundamentalism that often appears too smug and self assured, but though some may have settled for too little knowledge too soon, there is no denying that the regenerated children of God know Him Whom they have believed and they are persuaded that He is able to guard their commitment to Him against the day of judgment (2 Timothy 1:12).

It is proper to rejoice with the child of God who enjoys his certitude, even though he may have arranged some of the cups in his intellectual cupboard on the wrong shelves, but it is difficult to avoid the boredom that quickly reaches the "Ho Hum" stage when we listen to the nihilistic existentialist who arrogates to himself an intellectual sophistication that he does not possess and proudly tells you that he is so smart that he has come to realize that he knows nothing at all, except, of course one thing - he is sure that he knows nothing. Furthermore he will tell you if you do not excuse yourself and walk out on him that you do not know anything either, since knowledge is impossible of attainment.

And I agree! Knowledge is not possible for those who do not have the key.

What is this key? It is humility. Like that of the little child who sat upon Jesus' knee, to whom our Lord referred when He said, "Except you become like this little child you will not enter the kingdom of heaven" (Matthew 18:3). Like the babies our Lord mentioned when He said, "I thank thee, O Father, Lord of heaven and earth, because thou hast hid these things from the wise and prudent, and hast revealed them unto babes. Even so, Father: for so it seemed good in thy sight" (Mt.11:25,26). That is why there are more Mortimer Snerds at prayer meeting than Ph.D.'s.

What does it take to be as humble as a little child? What are the prerequisites for repentance? The intellectual right-about-face, the one hundred, eighty degree turn that the New Testament calls repentance can never take place as long as the patient thinks that his mind-set is proper. Whatever he thinks he knows or does not know, if he is sure he knows or does not know it, he will not repent. And if he does not repent he cannot believe. And if he does not believe he cannot be saved. The Gnostic who knows it all and is so inordinately proud of it will go and spend eternity with the rest of the know-it-alls. He will go where no one ever learns anything, for if one already knows it all there is nothing left to learn.

Maturity? Who wants to be mature? I seem to recall that Oswald Spengler pointed out that the next step after maturity is senility and after that biodegradability.

Nor will the Agnostic who knows nothing ever repent, because for him knowledge is unattainable and a mind shift will only move him into a different area of ignorance. He may as well remain ignorant where he is. The amazing thing is that he is proud of it. So he too will go to Hell with the others, half of whom know it all and the other half of whom know nothing. Total mental stagnation will pervade the place - a condition far more hellish than the heat.

Humility? It is the state of mind and heart of one who has come to realize that we can look neither to reason nor experience if we wish the certitude that provides rest and peace.

Humility? It is the intellectual poverty that understands that whether we depend upon reason or upon experience, we shall never attain certitude.

The epistemological questions are these: "What can I know for certain?" "How can I be sure?" "Indeed, is knowledge possible?" Philosophers have struggled with these questions for centuries and the field of battle is strewn with the decomposing carrion fit only for the vultures. Parmenides was sure that "All is Being" and Heraclitus was just as sure that "All is Becoming." If all is Being then there is no change. If all is Becoming then there is nothing but change. For Parmenides the task lay in correct analysis of the universe which lay before him, ready for his examination. He was sure that what was would always be - that it would never become something different in the future. For Heraclitus the universe was in a state of constant flux. Nothing at the moment had ever been before, nor would ever be again. It was idle therefore to think about it because in the moment that is required to reach a conclusion about the nature of things the things have moved on in the constant round of change and the conclusion was not true any more. If chemistry is always changing there is no point in shaking up chemicals in a test tube or mixing air and gas in a Bunsen burner, because in the time that it takes to turn away from the experiment, pick up a pencil and record the observed results in a notebook the world has gone on, and what you have written is not true anymore. One can only record what *was* true, never what *is* true.

A third school of epistemological thought has sought intermediate ground between Parmenides and Heraclitus. Thus Kant sought middle ground between Locke, Hume and Berkeley on the empirical front and DesCartes, Leibniz and Spinoza, who stood on the side of reason. For Kant the solution lay in a combination of experience and reason. As we have seen the environmental stimulus provided only a sensation which needed intellect to be perceived in relation to time and space, without which perception there could be no concept which could in turn become the ground for science and the good life. Thus the order was stimulus, sensation, perception, conception, knowledge and the good life. That was as far as Kant could go in his *Critique of Pure Reason* and although he sought diligently for a guide to morals in his *Critique of Practical Reason* and *Groundwork of the Metaphysic of Morals*, in which his purpose was "to seek out and establish the supreme principle of morality" he could arrive at nothing better than Jesus' principle so clearly stated in the Sermon on the Mount. "All things whatsoever ye would that men should do to you, do ye even so to them: for this is the law and the prophets." This Golden Rule Kant called the Categorical Imperative. When Kant pondered the ethical question, which, simply stated is "What shall I do?" he had only to ask himself the simple question whether or not he could will that the maxim that guided his decision should become a universal law, which would govern, not only the action which he then contemplated, but the actions of all men everywhere, in every time and place of similar circumstance. Thus Kant restated Jesus' Golden Rule, although he did not give Him a footnote.

If, as Heraclitus and the empiricists argue there is nothing but change then we can set the dogs of philosophical warfare upon him and his followers as Plato did in his *Theaetetus*. I am indebted to Edward John Carnell for his condensed statement of Plato's observations in *An Introduction to Christian Apologetics*.

Heraclitus was the metaphysician and Protagoras was the epistemologist. We cannot separate these two disciplines. They go together ". . . like Scarlatti and the harpsichord.

Where you find the one, you immediately think of the other." (Carnell, *Ibid.*, 34).

Plato objected to the metaphysics of Heraclitus and the epistemology of Protagoras on the grounds that

1. Empiricism makes man the author of reality. If knowledge is sensation, then qualities are created by the mind, for the perception of qualities depends upon the physiological state of the observer, as in color blindness. The person who sees red and the person who sees green are equally qualified to report on what the color in *rerum natura* is. The real color is both, for knowledge is a report of the real and sensation is knowledge. This is metaphysical skepticism.

2. All judgments are true. If all sensations are knowledge, all are true. Then he who thinks that Protagoras is wrong, is making a true judgment. Being wrong, we may dismiss the claims of Protagoras to truth.

3. All judgments are false. Since true and false are correlatives, that is, each depends upon the other for its meaning, it follows that all being true, there is no true. If there is no true, then all is just as false as it is true. Once again Protagoras' philosophy is false.

4. Changeless criteria are impossible. If all is in flux, then even the proposition, 'all is in flux,' is in flux, and nothing has meaning. "Inasmuch as truth is the same today, tomorrow, and forever, there can be no certain and final knowledge if everything perceived by the senses constantly changes." (Weber, *History of Philosophy*, 35, as cited in *Ibid.*, 36). Without changeless criteria, all meaning is destroyed.

5. Society is impossible. "Epicharmos already made fun of it by putting it as an argument into the mouth of a debtor who did not wish to pay. How could he be liable, seeing he is not the same man that contracted the debt?" (Burnet, *Greek Philosophy,* Part I, 63, as cited in *Ibid.*).

6. Significant speech is impossible. No word can adequately describe reality, since before the word can be gotten out of the mouth, reality has changed. *Panta rei!* If words cannot be chosen because they fit the facts, then, they must be chosen for aesthetic reasons. But further, "all answers. . . to any question are equally correct. But all are inexact, for the very words used, even the words 'this' and 'thus,' imply some sort of stability and definiteness which the theory rules out." (Martin, *et al, History of Philosophy*, 96, as cited in *Ibid.*).

7. Involves subjectivism. Unless truth is changeless, there is no use arguing about anything, for one can never rise above opinion. When we speak of truth, goodness, and beauty, we are just describing how we feel. "For, if subjectivism is true, the arguments will not succeed in making any pronouncement on the subject to which they purport to relate; they will only succeed in telling us something about the opinions of subjectivists who use them. Thus, if the conclusions which subjectivism asserts are correct, there can be no arguments for them, since the truth both of the argument and of their conclusion must be subjective. Hence, to affirm that subjectivism is true will mean merely that it suits some people, those, namely, who maintain subjectivist views, to believe in it." (Joad, *God and Evil*, 186, as cited in *Ibid.*, 36,37. When subjective, truth exists *for us.* This is skepticism. "Truth is a relative thing, a matter of taste, temperament, and education. Metaphysical controversies are therefore utterly vain." (Weber, *History of Philosophy*, 35, as cited in *Ibid.*, 36, 37).

Is significant speech ever possible? Can we add to a sensible subject a sensible predicate? Suppose we join a noun to an adjective by means of a copula? This is the eternal problem of "The one and the many." If I say, "The paper is white" it seems simple enough. But unless you are a sophomore you know that you are up to your ears, nay, over your head, in philosophical difficulty. The statement, "The paper is white" fairly crawls with questions for which there are no answers. What I mean is "This particular instance of paperness, of which there are many, is of a color that is subsumed under the category called white." And there is only one such category. What you should ask, if you want to be difficult, is "How white is it?" If I fall into your trap and try to tell you how white it is, then it isn't white at all. It is some shade of grey. And there are a billion shades of grey. If all of the light that strikes it is reflected from it, so that it retains no light at all, then it is white. If none does, but is absorbed by it, then it is black. If some light is retained while the rest of the light is reflected, then it is grey. "Well then," you say with a diabolical gleam in your eye, "how grey is it?" That depends upon its ability to reflect or absorb light. It should be clear, therefore, if you have both your intellectual oars in the water, that I cannot really predicate at all about this piece of paper. I cannot say anything about it that is socially significant. I can say, "This piece of paper is a piece of paper," but that is about as helpful as saying that three *times* three is nine or that three *plus* three is six. In these two mathematical examples I have only repeated in the predicate what I said in the subject. Three times three is the same as nine. Look what happens when I change one word from *times* to *plus*. Three plus three is the same as six.   "A rose is a rose is a rose. . . . "

If knowledge exists only as a result of experience then no one knows what white is because all of the paper that we have ever seen reflects some but not all of the light that strikes it. So I cannot say anything about it. And if I cannot say anything about it, I had better stop talking.

Intelligible conversation is not possible until we have solved the problem of the one and the many. Heraclitus was certain that "Nothing is Being" but that "All is Becoming." Protagoras therefore said, "Since that is true, you have nothing to say." A sign painter in Norman, Oklahoma advertizes his business with the slogan, "Before I could talk, I made signs." But if one cannot talk he had not better make signs. That is the conclusion to which Cratylus arrived after he thought about the metaphysics of Heraclitus and the epistemology of Protagoras. For sign making is only a silent form of communication. Some of the most vivid and, in some cases, insulting forms of communication have been used by the mute who was incapable of uttering a syllable.

Plato, Zeno, Parmenides, Pythogoras, Aquinas, DesCartes, Leibniz, Spinoza — these men depended upon reason. Heraclitus, Protagoras, Locke, Hume, Berkeley, Sartes, Camus, Kierkegard, Tillich, Barth — they depended upon experience. The former said, "We know because we think." The latter said, "We know because we experience." The Christian says, "I know because I believe, as a result of which commitment by faith I have had an experience which I think about in the light of the propositional revelation of the infallible Word of God."

If it were true that *Nihil in intellectu prius nisi in sensu* then we must conclude that all knowledge is grounded in sensation. If I cannot see it, hear it, taste it, smell it or touch and feel it, then I cannot know it. Locke's baby was born *tabula rasa* - that is, with a psyche like a blank tablet, with no innate ability to think, but subject only to the imprints made upon it from the environment over which it had no control. Thus a good environment would make proper impressions upon the *tabula rasa* and the baby would grow up to be a good person. Ergo - environmental determinism, Darwin, Herbert Spencer, William Graham Sumner, sociology and situation ethics. Suppose the environment is bad instead of good? Then the baby is made a bad person and when he breaks the law he should not be punished because he could not help doing what he did. What I would like to know is how the first environment became evil? Or perhaps there is no real distinction between evil and good?!! Adam was neither profane nor vulgar in the Garden of Eden. He did not have a mother to teach him these things! Let the evolutionists answer.

If we learn only by experience then it follows that we know only that which is in the past. But since everything is Becoming - in constant flux, changing from what it is into what it is not, every new experience will be unlike the last and I cannot predict, except within the limits of statistical probability. It is statistically probable that my car will start the next time I crank it. It always has. But for all I know for sure, the next time I turn the ignition key it will bake a cake or sing a song or perhaps disappear into thin air. Thus honest people who would like to say what they think to be true will not say that the paper is white, although sense perception will allow them to say that one piece of paper is greyer than another. Our adjectives must become comparative. We must shun the positive and the superlative, unless we wish to obfuscate. Honest people eschew obfuscation!

Fortunately statistical probability is good enough to permit life to go on. A pound of beef for four dollars may not weign precisely sixteen ounces but we cannot afford to spend valuable time quibbling about it with the meat cutter. The chances are just as good that what you buy is overweight and thus that you are getting something for nothing as that it is underweight and that you are paying money for something which you did not get. The flight leaves Washington at *about* half past the hour, but you plan to be there five minutes early anyway. So life goes on. Who needs precision?

Since we cannot trust sense perception as a basis for prediction and the well ordered life since it is true that we have no idea what the next sense perception is going to be, it is not true that "To see is to believe." When I was teaching at Ouachita College a magician manifested his mighty and wondrous works. He called a coed - one of my students - from the audience and seated her on a bench before a large grand piano and asked her to play a hymn. As she played the magician stood aside and motioned with his hand. The grand piano, the bench, the coed and the hymn book slowly rose. It may or may not be significant that she was playing, "Love Lifted Me," although I doubt that her emotions had much to do with it. As several hundred spectators - students and "townies" gave rapt attention the piano and the girl on the bench attained a height of perhaps ten feet. The magician then passed a large hoop over, under and around to dispel any doubts that I might have had. Apparently there were no hidden supports arising from the floor nor wires suspended from the ceiling. Then the man with only a circular motion of his hand turned the phenomenon over in the air. At one point the piano, the piano bench and the girl appeared to be upside down. I saw it! And I am prepared to resist all contentions to the contrary. Then the man gently lowered the piano and the girl to the floor. The coed later said that she was not aware that anything unusual had occurred. Did he really do it? Of course he did not! But I saw it. Even if he had done it, he couldn't do it again since for the empiricist we live in a world of change and the scientific principles by which he fooled us the first time would no longer apply.

The magician was challenged by CBS to perform this stunt on the Gary Moore show, on the theory that what could fool an audience could not fool television cameras which were placed at strategic angles to insure total observation. He did and his secret was not disclosed.

Experience does not provide certitude because we cannot trust the testimonies of sense perceptors.

Can we trust reason? Plato thought so, within limits at least, although Plato was not a Gnostic and would have deplored the Gnosticism of the Neo-Platonists had he lived. His illustration of the sailor crossing the ocean on a raft, buoyant enough to support him, but not buoyant enough to keep his feet and ankles out of the water makes Plato's point. The perfect crossing could be made only "if God would send us the Word" - a passage that leads some of us to think that perhaps Plato looked forward in faith to ῾Ο Λόγος of John 1:1,14. Reason is better than experience without reason as Kant, DesCartes and Leibniz insisted, in reply to Locke, Hume and Berkeley, but reason alone cannot provide certitude.

But Pythogaras thought so, because everything in the universe is mathematical. He assumed that all mathematical relations are harmonious and he concluded that since the universe operated on principles consistent with mathematics, (1) the harmony of the spheres existed, and (2) they were discernible by man, subject only to his understanding of mathematics. But Pythagoras did not understand his mathematics. He knew nothing about irrational numbers. The current crop of urchins learn their whole numbers in kindergarten. They find out about fractions a grade or two later. Pythagoras apparently knew little or nothing about fractions. The Pythogorean theorem is not always true. The square on the hypotenuse of a right angle triangle is not always equal to the sum of the squares on the other two sides. Suppose that the sum of the squares on the two sides is a number of which you cannot take the square root without accepting an irrational number? We cannot take the square root of two. The only whole numbers of which the square root is also a whole number are those which result when we multiply a number by itself. Thus four (2 X 2), nine (3 X 3), sixteen (4 X 4), twenty-five, thirty-six, forty-nine, sixty-four, eighty-one, one hundred, etc.,are numbers which yield a square root which are also whole numbers. Suppose a right-angle triangle has sides which are six inches long. The square of six is thirty-six. The sum of the squares of the two sides is seventy-two. And we cannot extract the square root of seventy-two without accepting an irrational number, *i.e.* a fraction that is never resolved. The hypotenuse of such a triangle cannot be determined with certitude. It is somewhere between 8.4852 and 8.4853. Square the former and you get 71.998619, which is too little. Square the latter and you get 72.000316, which is too much. Carry out the square root extraction process as long as you will, the result is an irrational number - a number with a string of positive integers after the decimal point that would reach from here to Philadelphia and back.

So Pythagoras was not so smart. He did not understand irrationality in the field of research which is supposed to be very rational indeed. Nobody knows exactly what the area of any given circle is. Even if we had measuring sticks that yielded total precision, which we do not, and could find the radius of the circle, we would then be compelled to square the radius and then multiply it by π. But π is an irrational number. It is something more than 3.14159265. How much more? Who cares? Who wants to know what the precise area of a circle is? Who cares what the precise area of the square on the hypotenuse is? We know *about* what it is and for all practical purposes that is good enough.

But musicians with absolute pitch care a great deal when the village choir sings off pitch on a quiet Sunday morning or some overweight dowager with delusions of grandeur, who imagines herself the successor of Madame Ernestine Schumann-Heink, volunteers to edify the local P.T.A. No such problems of tonality would result if Pythagoras had been correct that mathematics is an exact science and that all interrelations in the universe are harmonious. If the temperature registers at the proper specified point and air pressure is at sea level the first A above middle C will vibrate, if you strike it, 440 times per second. The next A, one octave higher is tuned to vibrate 880 times per second. Thus it is the same note one octave higher. Thus the mathematics of tonality dictates that the root, third and fifth of a chord are consonant. Even the untrained ear reacts favorably when these notes are sounded. But the mathematics of sound, which Pythagoras thought was always harmonious, also dictates that if one strikes the tonic and the supertonic together the result is a dissonance. Those with only average capacity for music appreciation may break out in hives and musicians with absolute pitch will rush out of the door and throw up. Thus tonic-supertonic, mediant-subdominant, subdominant-dominant, dominant-submediant, submediant-leading tone and leading tone-tonic combinations belong in the "no no" class, which may help to explain why parents have been known to leave home when Junior began to take lessons on the violin. If the universe is totally harmonious, and that harmony can be expressed with precision in mathematical terms, as Pythagoras supposed, then there could be no such thing as a dissonance. It would make no difference which string Junior scraped (!) or when he scraped it, for the result would always be a beautiful tone poem.

Zeno, the Eleatic metaphysician, was a favorite disciple of Parmenides who accepted the dogma that everything is constant. There is no such thing as change. He had no faith in experience. All he wanted to do was think. And he proved that you cannot hit the ground with your hat. His argument has not been refuted to this day. The hat must first fall half of the distance from the point of its release to the ground; and then it must fall half of the remaining distance, and then half of the remaining distance, ... remaining distance, . . . distance, ... dis. . . . . tance. Now, since you can always divide a positive number by two and still get a positive number (greater than zero), your hat will never reach the ground. Do you follow me? Let us go over it again! But you and I know from experience that we can hit the ground with our hat.

Zeno also proved that the fleet footed Achilles couldn't catch the tortoise which moves ahead with only slightly greater speed than that achieved by the prudent snail. The proof is as follows: the tortoise starts at point B and Achilles at point A, some distance behind. While Achilles runs from A to B, the tortoise moves from B, his starting point, to C. To be sure, the distance is not a mile, but he is still ahead. As Achilles now runs from B to C, the tortoise moves on to point D. And so on *ad infinitum, ad frustratum.* It is self evident. Only fools or madmen will disagree. But I disagree. Why? Because I have caught several turtles in my time. I caught one only recently as I was mowing my lawn and gave it to a little neighbour girl, only three years old, with instructions as to what to feed it. Her mother has not spoken to me since, although I cannot imagine why? I never knew Achilles, though I had a fraternity brother by that name, but I doubt that it was the same fellow.

Experience says that you can catch a turtle. Reason says you cannot. Experience says that a man raised a grand piano off the floor, turned it over in the air, without touching it, and then let it down softly. But reason says that he did not.

So neither reason nor sense perception yields certitude about anything in this world. Kant was to show that when we put them together, the result is enough certitude that life can go on, despite the fact that it has degenerated into a dog and pony show in peacetime and the battle of the frogs and mice after diplomacy breaks down. But Kant could not give us certitude about the elements of our Christian faith, because only the Christians of the first century could speak from experience about the time and space relationships of the historical Jesus. The rest of us must take it all by faith in the only book that tells us about them. Suppose that the Christian's *a priori* commitment that the propositional revelation which we call the inspired Word of God is not founded upon reality. One can prove anything from a logical deduction following a given - an *a priori* statement. President Lincoln once bemused his cabinet, during a dark Civil War hour, by asking, "If you call a tail a leg, how many legs does a sheep have?" Secretary of State Seward, who was not in the mood for riddles responded impulsively by saying, "Five," to which Lincoln responded by saying that the correct answer was four, not five, and then added that a tail is not a leg regardless of what we call it. Seward was not amused, but Lincoln had pointed out that logical deduction from a false premise does not lead to valid conclusion. Thus reason is not the road to certitude. Nor is experience, for the reasons which we have advanced. And yet the Christian enjoys some certitude. We can say with Paul that we *know* whom we have belived and *we are persuaded* that he is able to keep faith with us, until, on and after the day of judgment (2 Tim.1:12).

When and why does the Christian receive this assurance, which is unavailable to scientists and philosophers? Why should God reveal to intellectual babes what He has chosen to withhold from the Ph.D.'s? (Mt.11:25-27). How does one get the key of knowledge? (Lk.11:52). It is only when we come to realize that neither reason nor sense perception, the only two approaches to the epistemological problem available to unregenerate man, give us the precise certitude which is characteristic of the knowledge of God, the Father, God, the Logos and God the Holy Spirit. It is then that we repent - then that we change our minds - then that we are willing to admit that we are of all men most miserable, and that we very much need to know. It is then that we become like the little boy on Jesus' knee. God will not refuse to give the key of knowledge when we get like that.

Paul learned this lesson on the road to Damascus when a bigoted know-it-all had evidence that the cause which he was determined to wipe out was the cause of a Galilean carpenter whom he thought was dead. He relearned it on his way down the mountain trail as he trudged along from Athens to Corinth. He had failed miserably on Mars Hill and, as he thought about it, he discovered why. In Athens he had yielded to the temptation to prove to a sophisticated Athenian audience that he too was a scholar. A graduate level lawyer who had studied with Gamaliel was determined to impress his audience. The result was a magnificant statement - the most scholarly speech in the New Testament. He probed the depths of Athenian philosophy. He challenged their most advanced thinkers, but he did not preach the gospel of Christ. He left out the incarnation and the cross. His sermon flattered the intelligence of his audience, but he did not ask them to believe something stupid. His was an appeal to reason and to experience. That they understood. But they had heard it all before. There was no demand that they take the leap of faith.

Paul came to realize this. If one wishes to be a scholar and prove his erudition to the lost, let him talk like a scholar, but he will not win many souls for Christ. But if he wishes to be a successful evangelist he must stand before unsaved people and talk like a fool. So, as he later wrote to the Corinthians, he had made a decision by the time he got to town. "When I came to you, I came not with excellency of speech or of wisdom, declaring unto you the testimony of God. For I determined not to know any thing among you save Jesus Christ, and him crucified. And I was with you in weakness, and in fear, and in much trembling. And my speech and my preaching was not with enticing words of man's wisdom, but in demonstration of the Spirit and of power. That your faith should not stand in the wisdom of men, but in the power of God." (1 Cor.2:1-5). All he did in Corinth was what he failed to do in Athens. He told the Corinthians an absurd story and dared them to believe it. A virgin had a baby. He was the eternal Son of God, the Creator of the universe, the long promised Messiah, King David's Greater Son, the only hope for national Israel. He had become incarnate in human flesh to save a world that could not save itself. An apprentice carpenter He never went to school a day in His life. He earned no degrees. He was elected to no public office. He commanded no troops in battle, though He saved thousands who later proved their devotion by dying for Him. The only thing He ever wrote was an I.O.U. to God in payment for the sins of a prostitute. Misunderstood by all and rejected by most He died on a cross between two thieves and was buried in a borrowed tomb. But on the third day He arose. Forty days after that He sat down at the right hand of the throne of God. He will remain there until His story, which men call History has run its course according to His scenario. When those for whom He died have been called by the Holy Spirit into membership in His body, He will return and take the throne that belongs to Him. Plato's Philosopher-King will come and a world society of peace and abundance will result. For the first time society will be viable, because He will have forever solved the problem of evil, which the Gnostics thought they had solved, but had not, and which the Agnostics ignored since for them the solution was beyond their scope. This Paul preached in Corinth. And the result was a great revival that continued for two and one-half years. Paul did not argue with the Corinthians. He told them. He did not try to convince them. He dared them to believe it. He said that "Eye hath not seen" (the scientific method) "nor ear heard" (the scientific method) "neither hath it entered into the heart of man" (the philosophic method) "the things that God has prepared for them that love Him. But God has revealed them unto us by His Spirit" (the theological method) (1 Cor.2:9,10).

Some of them thought that he was a fool. And so he was, from their point of view. And so am I. And so are you if you believe the Bible. But we know something. And we are saved.

Midway between Gnosticism and Agnosticism there is the position of the Christian who is sure about some things and confused about the rest. Gnostics, since St. Thomas Aquinas have broken with Augustine and Anselm who said *Credo ut intelligam* - "I believe in order that I may understand." They also disavow Tertullian's *Credo quia absurdum* - "I believe that which is absurd." Aquinas, who argued that Adam's fall did not affect the intellect, has taught the Jesuits and other Gnostics to say *Intelligo ut credam* - "I understand in order that I may believe."

If I cannot believe in something that I do not first understand, then I cannot believe the Bible, for the Bible is full of stories that I do not understand. I do not understand how a virgin could have a baby. I do not understand how a dead man could rise from the grave. I do not know how a man could rebuke a tornado, or walk upon the water, or feed thousands of hungry people with five small loaves and two small fish. If understanding is prerequisite to faith then I must confess that I have no faith in the Word of God. Most of all I cannot solve the problem of evil. If God was going to create all things, why did He have to create evil? The Bible teaches that God is against sin, but the same Bible says that he works "all things after the counsel of His own will" (Eph.1:11). Surely that does not make God the author of my sins. Arminians want to know too much. I would like also to know how the freedom of the will comports with the view that God is sovereign in His universe. If evil is as strong as good and darkness is as strong as light, then from whence comes the optimism of Christianity that seems to teach that the story of the human race on this planet is going to have a happy ending? Is it not just as probable that the darkness and sin will win the fight and human history will end with an agonizing shriek of despair instead of a triumphant shout of joy? The Christian, like the little child, can only look up into the face of a risen Christ and trust His word. He has "need of patience, that after he has done the will of God, he might receive the promise." He need not wait long, "for yet a little while, and he that shall come will come, and will not tarry" (Heb.10:36,37) and when He comes we who have believed what to us now is absurd will understand, precisely because we did believe.

Little children will believe anything you tell them, even if it is false. Christians are not asked to believe what is false, but they are asked to believe that which at the time appears to be absurd. If it is in the Bible it is true, even if I now, with my present mental capacity, find it difficult to accept. Has God lied to us? If so either there is no God or else He is a vicious mendacious bully. If there is no God then death ends all and we could look with Hamlet upon "a consummation devoutly to be wished. To die, to sleep; To sleep: perchance to dream: ay, there's the rub; For in that sleep of death what dreams may come When we have shuffled off this mortal coil, must give us pause." So the question remains: "Whether 'tis nobler in the mind, to suffer the slings and arrows of outrageous fortune, Or to take arms against a sea of troubles, and by opposing end them?" (Shakespeare, *Hamlet*, III, 1).

Thanks be to God, I am like the little boy sitting on Jesus' knee, looking up into His face and believing everything He has said. A fig for "the slings and arrows of outrageous fortune" that had Hamlet in distress. "Thanks be to God which giveth us the victory through our Lord Jesus Christ" (1 Cor.15:57). I am not an Agnostic. Some things I know. But, thank God, I am not a Gnostic. There are some things that I do not know. God has not chosen to reveal it all in His word. Lucifer tried to "be like the Most High." He is no relation to me. Eve tried to "be as Elohim, knowing good and evil." She was deceived. I am not deceived. I will respect the divine reticence. When our Lord wants us to know more He will reveal it to us. Meanwhile, "I know whom I have believed, and am persuaded that He is able to keep that which I have committed unto Him against that day" (2 Tim.1:12). That is all the certitude that anyone needs.

Fourth: The Report of the Emmaus Disciples, and the News of the Appearance to Simon Peter

(Luke 24:33-35)

Luke 24:33 - "And they rose up the same hour and returned to Jerusalem, and found the eleven gathered together, and them that were with them."

καὶ ἀναστάντες αὐτῇ τῇ ὥρᾳ ὑπέστρεφαν εἰς Ἰερουσαλήμ, καὶ εὗρον ἠθροισμένους τοὺς ἕνδεκα καὶ τοὺς σὺν αὐτοῖς,

καὶ (continuative conjunction) 14.
ἀναστάντες (aor.act.part.nom.pl.masc.of ἀνίστημι, temporal) 789.
αὐτῇ (loc.sing.fem.of αὐτός, in agreement with ὥρᾳ) 16.
τῇ (loc.sing.fem.of the article in agreement with ὥρᾳ) 9.
ὥρᾳ (loc.sing.fem.of ὥρα, time point) 735.
ὑπέστρεφαν (3d.per.pl.aor.act.ind.of ὑποστρέφω, ingressive) 1838.
εἰς (preposition with the accusative of extent) 140.
Ἰερουσαλήμ (acc.sing.neut.of Ἰεροσολύμων, extent) 141.
καὶ (adjunctive conjunction, joining verbs) 14.
εὗρον (3d.per.pl.2d.aor.act.ind.of εὑρίσκω, constative) 79.

#2911 ἠθροισμένους (perf.pass.part.acc.pl.masc.of ἀθροίζω, adjectival).

gathered together - Luke 24:33.

Meaning: α privative plus θρόος - "a noisy crowd." Hence, ἀθροίζω means the quiet assembling of persons who wished to remain in secret for any reason. In this context the reason for the stealth was the fear of the Jews - Luke 24:33.

τοὺς (acc.pl.masc.of the article in agreement with ἕνδεκα) 9.
ἕνδεκα (indeclin.direct object of εὗρον) 1693.
καὶ (adjunctive conjunction joining substantives) 14.
τοὺς (acc.pl.masc.of the article, direct object of εὗρον) 9.
σὺν (preposition with the instrumental of association) 1542.
αὐτοῖς (instru.pl.masc.of αὐτός, association) 16.

Translation - "And they got up immediately and started back to Jerusalem, and found the eleven, assembled secretly, and those with them."

Comment: The Emmaus disciples returned immediately (αὐτῇ τῇ ὥρᾳ) and started back (ingressive aorist in ὑπέστρεφαν) to Jerusalem, despite the facts that darkness had fallen and it was another seven miles on the same day. Doubtless, under different circumstances fourteen miles on the same day, would have exhausted them, but now they had wonderful news to bear. They knew where to find the disciples and the others of their group. The Jerusalem disciples had assembled furtively "for fear of the Jews" (John 20:19). Cf.#291.

Did the fact that some knew that Jesus was alive remove the fear? Apparently not. Though the eleven were not yet convinced there is little doubt that some of the women who were there with them were those who had seen Jesus. The boldness with which the early Christians witnessed in the face of the persecution that resulted in their deaths, was the result of the filling of the Holy Spirit.

Verse 34 - ". . . saying, the Lord is risen indeed, and hath appeared to Simon."

λέγοντας ὅτι ὄντως ἠγέρθη ὁ κύριος καὶ ὤφθη Σίμωνι.

λέγοντας (pres.act.part.acc.pl.fem.of λέγω, restrictive) 66.

ὅτι (conjunction introducing indirect discourse) 211.
ὄντως (adverbial) 2386.
ἠγέρθη (3d.per.sing.aor.pass.ind.of ἐγείρω, culminative) 125.
ὁ (nom.sing.masc.of the article in agreement with κύριος) 9.
κύριος (nom.sing.masc.of κύριος, subject of ἠγέρθη and ὤφθη) 97.
καὶ (adjunctive conjunction joining verbs) 14.
ὤφθη (3d.per.sing.1st.aor.pass.ind.of ὁράω, culminative) 144.
Σίμωνι (dat.sing.masc.of Σίμων, personal advantage) 386.

Translation - "... saying that the Lord had truly been raised and that He had appeared to Simon."

Comment: The participles ἠθροισμένους (vs.33) and λέγοντας (vs.34) are adjectival, the first modifying τοὺς ἕνδεκα and the second, which is feminine apparently referring to the women in the group. The eleven were those who had secretly assembled with the group and the women in the group announced to the Emmas disciples, as soon as they arrived that Jesus had risen and had been seen by Simon Peter. Peter was present and had told the group that he too had seen the Lord. This comports with 1 Cor.15:5. Paul says that Peter saw Jesus before He appeared to the other disciples.Therefore since the ten (excluding Peter) had not yet seen Him, although they were to see Him momentarily (vs.36), it follows that Peter had seen Him also. Thomas did not see Him with the other ten until eight days later and Paul, the twelfth, saw Him on the Damascus road much later. Paul does not deny that Jesus was also seen by Mary, the other women and by the two on the Emmaus road. The Emmaus disciples may have been surprized to learn that they were not bringing the startling news to the disciples to confirm what the women had already told them, since Peter had already confirmed their story. They told their story in

Verse 35 - "And they told what things were done in the way, and how he was known to them in breaking of bread."

καὶ αὐτοὶ ἐξηγοῦντο τὰ ἐν τῇ ὁδῷ καὶ ὡς ἐγνώσθη αὐτοῖς ἐν τῇ κλάσει τοῦ ἄρτου.

καὶ (continuative conjunction) 14.
αὐτοὶ (nom.pl.masc.of αὐτός, subject of ἐξηγοῦντο) 16.
ἐξηγοῦντο (3d.per.pl.imperfect act.ind.of ἐξηγέομαι) 1703.
τὰ (acc.pl.neut.of the article, direct article of ἐξηγοῦντο) 9.
ἐν (preposition with the locative of place where) 80.
τῇ (loc.sing.fem.of the article in agreement with ὁδῷ) 9.
ὁδῷ (loc.sing.fem.of ὁδός, place where) 199.
καὶ (adjunctive conjunction joining a phrase to a clause) 14.
ὡς (particle in a comparative clause) 128.
ἐγνώσθη (3d.per.sing.aor.pass.ind.of γινώσκω, culminative) 131.
αὐτοῖς (dat.pl.masc.of αὐτός, personal advantage) 16.
ἐν (preposition with the instrumental of manner) 80.
τῇ (instru.sing.fem.of the article in agreement with κλάσει) 9.

ὁδῷ (loc.sing.fem.of ὁδός, place where) 199.

καὶ (adjunctive conjunction joining a substantive with a comparative clause) 14.

ὡς (adverb introducing a comparative clause) 128.

ἐγνώσθη (3d.per.sing.aor.pass.ind.of γινώσκω, constative) 131.

αὐτοῖς (dat.pl.masc.of αὐτός, personal advantage) 16.

ἐν (preposition with the instrumental of manner) 80.

τῇ (instru.sing.fem.of the article in agreement with κλάσει) 9.

#2912 κλάσει (instru.sing.fem.of κλάσις, manner).

breaking - Luke 24:35; Acts 2:42.

Meaning: Cf. κλάω (#1121). A breaking. Followed in Luke 24:35 and Acts 2:42 by the genitive of description τοῦ ἄρτου. In the Emmas home - Luke 24:35; in the Jerusalem church with reference to the Lord's Supper - Acts 2:42.

τοῦ (gen.sing.masc.of the article in agreement with ἄρτου) 9.

ἄρτου (gen.sing.masc.of ἄρτος, description) 338.

Translation - "And these were telling about what happened on the road and how He was made known to them by the breaking of bread."

Comment: αὐτοὶ refers to the Emmaus disciples of verse 33. They gave a full account. Note the meaning of #1703, plus the fact that it is in the imperfect tense. Their excitement is reflected in Luke's omission of a substantive and a verb after τὰ - "the things *that happened* on the road." ὡς here in indirect question. Note the instrumental of manner in ἐν τῇ κλάσει τοῦ ἄρτου.

As the spirited discussion went on, each telling and perhaps retelling what facts he could offer from his own experience, Jesus suddenly appeared in the room.

Fifth: To Ten Apostles in a House

(Mark 16:14; Luke 24:36-43; John 19:19-25)

Mark 16:14 - "Afterward he appeared unto the eleven as they sat at meat, and upbraided them with their unbelief and hardness of heart, because they believed not them which had seen him after he was risen."

Ὕστερον (δὲ) ἀνακειμένοις αὐτοῖς τοῖς ἕνδεκα ἐφανερώθη, καὶ ὠνείδισεν τὴν ἀπιστίαν αὐτῶν καὶ σκληροκαρδίαν ὅτι τοῖς θεασαμένοις αὐτὸν ἐγηγερμένον οὐκ ἐπίστευσαν.

Ὕστερον (acc.sing.neut.of ὕστερος, adverbial) 334.

δὲ (continuative conjunction) 11.

ἀνακειμένοις (pres.mid.part.dat.pl.masc.of ἀνάκειμαι, adjectival, in agreement with αὐτοῖς) 790.

αὐτοῖς (dat.pl.masc.of αὐτός, personal advantage) 16.

τοῖς (dat.pl.masc.of the article in agreement with ἕνδεκα) 9.

ἕνδεκα (dat.pl.masc.indeclin. personal advantage) 1693.

ἐφανερώθη (3d.per.sing.aor.pass.ind.of φανερόω, constative) 1960.

καὶ (continuative conjunction) 14.

ὠνείδισεν (3d.per.sing.aor.act.ind.of ὀνειδίζω, ingressive) 437.

τὴν (acc.sing.fem.of the article in agreement with ἀπιστίαν and σκληροκαρδίαν) 9.

ἀπιστίαν (acc.sing.fem.of ἀπιστία, direct object of ὠνείδισεν) 1103.

αὐτῶν (gen.pl.masc.of αὐτός, possession) 16.

καὶ (adjunctive conjunction joining nouns) 14.

σκληροκαρδίαν (acc.sing.fem.of σκληροκαρδία, direct object of ὠνείδισεν) 1293.

ὅτι (conjunction introducing a subordinate causal clause) 211.

τοῖς (dat.pl.masc.of the article in agreement with θεασαμένοις) 9.

θεασαμένοις (aor.mid.part.dat.pl.masc.of θεάομαι, substantival, person) 556.

αὐτὸν (acc.sing.masc.of αὐτός, direct object ofd θεασαμένοις) 16.

ἐγηγερμένον (perf.pass.part.acc.sing.masc.of ἐγείρω, adjectival, restrictive, in agreement with αὐτὸν) 125.

οὐκ (summary negative conjunction with the indicative) 130.

ἐπίστευσαν (3d.per.pl.aor.act.ind.of πιστεύω, constative) 734.

Translation - "And afterward He appeared to the eleven sitting at the table, and He began to criticize their unbelief and hardness of heart because they did not believe those who had seen Him Who had been resurrected."

Comment: The writer is not being very specific about the time. ὕστερον is safe, if all you wish to do is to keep the chronological order of events straight. The fact that our text says the eleven, rather than the ten, indicates that this appearance was eight days later, when Thomas was present, as recorded in John 20:26-29. If the writer intended to describe Jesus' appearance on the evening of resurrection day, he is wrong about the number of disciples, since Thomas was absent then (John 20:24), Judas Iscariot was dead and Paul was not yet appointed. Note #437, the same word used in Matthew 11:20 when Jesus castigated the Pharisees. But here His remarks are directed, not against the disciples directly, but against their unbelief and hardness of heart. Why? The ὅτι clause follows. They had not believed those who saw Him alive. The passage teaches that one can err by refusing the pragmatic approach to truth as much as by depending too much upon it. Normally Christians are criticized for believing too strongly in their deductively established system, while they ignore contrary evidence. Here were eleven men who believed too much that Jesus was dead, with the evidence that he was alive, being attested by eye witnesses, being ignored. Jesus' basis for the attack was that even when eye witnesses said that they had seen Jesus in His resurrected body, the disciples rejected the testimony on the basis of a theory that such could not be the case. The scientific world is suppose to believe what honest people say they saw.

Luke 24:36 - "And as they thus spoke, Jesus himself stood in the midst of them,
and saith unto them, Peace be unto you."

Ταῦτα δὲ αὐτῶν λαλούντων αὐτὸς ἔστη ἐν μέσῳ αὐτῶν καὶ λέγει αὐτοῖς,
Εἰρήνη ὑμῖν.

Ταῦτα (acc.pl.neut.of οὗτος, direct object of λαλούντων) 93.

δὲ (continuative conjunction) 11.

αὐτῶν (gen.pl.masc.of αὐτός, genitive absolute) 16.

λαλούντων (pres.act.part.gen.pl.masc.of λαλέω, genitive absolute,
contemporaneous time) 815.

αὐτὸς (nom.sing.masc.of αὐτός, subject of ἔστη and λέγει) 16.

ἔστη (3d.per.sing.2d.aor.act.ind.of ἵστημι, constative) 180.

ἐν (preposition with the locative of place where) 80.

μέσῳ (loc.sing.neut.of μέσος, place where) 873.

αὐτῶν (gen.pl.masc.of αὐτός, description) 16.

καὶ (adjunctive conjunction joining verbs) 14.

λέγει (3d.per.sing.pres.act.ind.of λέγω, historical) 66.

αὐτοῖς (dat.pl.masc.of αὐτός, indirect object of λέγει) 16.

Εἰρήνη (nom.sing.fem.of εἰρήνη, nominative absolute) 865.

ὑμῖν (dat.pl.masc.of σύ, indirect object of the verb supplied) 104.

Translation - "And as they were telling about these things He stood in their midst
and He said, 'Peace to you.' "

Comment: There is considerable doubt about the text here. Metzger, speaking
for the Committee of the United Bible Society says, "The words ἐγώ εἰμι, μὴ
φοβεῖσθε, either before εἰρήνη ὑμῖν (as in W 579) or after (as in G P itc vg syrp,h,pal
cop bo mss arm eth geo Diatessaron a,i,n) are undoubtedly a gloss, perhaps derived
from Jo.6,20. The Committee was less sure concerning the origin of the words
καὶ λέγει αὐτοῖς, Εἰρήνη ὑμῖν, which, as the regular form of Semitic greeting,
might well be expected on this occasion. When the passage is compared with
Jn.20.19ff, the question arises: have the two evangelists depended upon a
common tradition, or have copyists expanded Luke's account by adding the
salutation from John's account? A majority of the Committee, impressed by the
presence of numerous points of contact between Luke and John in their Passion
and Easter accounts, preferred to follow the preponderance of external
attestation and to retain the words in the text." (Metzger, *A Textual*
Commentary on the Greek New Testament, 186,187).

As in the case of most variant textual readings, the exegesis if not materially
affected. If Jesus added ἐγώ εἰμι μὴ φοβεῖσθε, that is fine, since He certainly is
the Great I AM (Exodus 3:14) and they had nothing to fear. If He did not, we
have the same material from other passages.

Ταῦτα refers to the account being given by the disciples from Emmaus in verse
35. The genitive absolute participle is in the present tense, which indicates that
Jesus appeared while they were telling about their experiences on the road and in
their home. What dramatic support for their story. It is difficult to assess the

feelings of the disciples on this occasion. Modern Christians are conditioned to think of the resurrection of Jesus only in terms of great joy. Our task, if we are to understand the disciples is to achieve *zeitgeist*. We must put ourselves in the place of the disciples, huddled together in a secret room, with Jerusalem swarming with hostile Jews who had only two days before murdered their leader. Ten country peasants from Galilee, surrounded by a little band of friends, men and women, who have become identified with Jesus. They have been torn between their desire to believe that He was alive and their natural inclination to think that resurrection from the dead is not possible. Despite all of this, we are somewhat shocked to learn of their reaction in

Verse 37 - "But they were terrified and affrighted, and supposed that they had seen a spirit."

πτοηθέντες δὲ καί ἔμφοβοι γενόμενοι ἐδόκουν πνεῦμα θεωρεῖν.

πτοηθέντες (1st.aor.pass.part.nom.pl.masc. of πτοέω, adverbial, circumstantial) 2719.
δὲ (adversative conjunction) 11.
καὶ (adjunctive conjunction joining participles) 14.
ἔμφοβοι (nom.pl.masc. of ἔμφοβος, predicate adjective) 2890.
γενόμενοι (aor.mid.part.nom.pl.masc. of γίνομαι, adverbial, circumstantial) 113.
ἐδόκουν (3d.per.pl.imp.act.ind. of δοκέω, inceptive) 287.
πνεῦμα (acc.sing.neut. of πνεῦμα, direct object of θεωρεῖν) 83.
θεωρεῖν (pres.act.inf. of θεωρέω, epexegetical) 1667.

Translation - "But shocked and terror stricken, they began to think that they were seeing a ghost."

Comment: δὲ of course is adversative. The peace, which was Jesus' bequest (vs.36). was furthest from their thoughts. Luke uses two circumstantial participles, one with a predicate adjective, to describe the reaction of the disciples, as a result of which they began to think (inceptive imperfect in ἐδόκουν) that they were seeing a ghost. πτοέω (#2719) and ἔμφοβος (#2890) cannot be precisely synonymous, although they do not differ greatly. Both terms are used to describe the terror of the unsaved during the tribulation period (Rev.11:13; Lk.21:9). Scientists who love so much to attack the certitude that comes from God-given faith and to extol the certitude that derives from sense perception should be interested in this scene. Here is doubt and unbelief that seduced the disciples into a false conclusion, even though sensory perception was available. Jesus was standing there in their presence. They saw Him. They heard His voice. But experience did not serve to overthrow their unbelief in His bodily resurrection. Instead they reached a false conclusion. They thought that they were seeing a ghost!

Verse 38 - "And he said unto them, Why are ye troubled: And why do thoughts arise in your hearts?"

καὶ εἶπεν αὐτοῖς, Τί τεταραγμένοι ἐστέ, καὶ διὰ τί διαλογισμοὶ ἀναβαίνουσιν ἐν τῇ καρδίᾳ ὑμῶν;

καὶ (inferential conjunction) 14.

εἶπεν (3d.per.sing.aor.act.ind.of εἶπον, constative) 155.

αὐτοῖς (dat.pl.masc.of αὐτός, indirect object of εἶπεν) 16.

τί (acc.sing.neut.of τίς, interrogative pronoun, cause, with διά understood) 281.

τεταραγμένοι (perf.pass.part.nom.pl.masc.of ταράσσω, perfect periphrastic) 149.

ἐστέ (2d.per.pl.pres.ind.of εἰμί, perfect periphrastic) 86.

καὶ (continuative conjunction) 14.

διὰ (preposition with the accusative, cause) 118.

τί (acc.sing.neut.of τίς, interrogative pronoun, cause) 281.

διαλογισμοὶ (nom.pl.masc.of διαλογισμός, subject of ἀναβαίνουσιν) 1165.

ἀναβαίνουσιν (3d.per.pl.pres.act.ind.of ἀναβαίνω, aoristic) 323.

ἐν (preposition with the locative of place where) 80.

τῇ (instru.sing.fem.of the article in agreement with καρδίᾳ) 9.

καρδίᾳ (instru.sing.fem.of καρδία, cause) 432.

ὑμῶν (gen.pl.masc.of σύ, possession) 104.

Translation - "Therefore He said to them, 'Why are you upset, and why are doubts arising in your minds?' "

Comment: There is no difference between τί ("why?") and διὰ τί ("because/on account of what?"). διά with the accusative indicates cause. Cf.#281 for a list of each. Here we have them in the same sentence. The perfect periphrastic indicates present unrest as a result of an extended period when the disciples have been struggling with the question as to whether or not they could believe the stories of His resurrection. The first question deals with their emotions - the second with their intellectual difficulties. They were disputing with themselves, seeking one minute to believe it and entertaining doubts the next. This is the basic meaning of διαλογισμός (#1165). It is purely an intellectual process, but it was going on because of what was in their hearts. What we tend to think is often dictated by our emotions. Wishes and prejudices dictate how we think and, in the case of the Emmaus disciples, even our eyesight. Thus Jesus put His finger on the source of their intellectual difficulty. They were locked into a position which the *felt* was correct. Jesus was dead and that was that. They would therefore interpret all phenomena to the contrary in terms of illusion. It was the same error of the Emmaus disciples. It is the same fallacy of the unregenerate who says, "I wish that I could believe what you believe," which in reality is his patronizing way of saying that unfortunately he is smarter than you are and therefore is condemned to live with his misery - a misery which you do not share because of your low mental capacity. The truth is that he does not believe because he does not want to believe. His doubts, like those of the disciples, arise by means of/because of his heart. "If any man will do His will, He shall know. . . " (John 7:17).

Verse 39 - "Behold my hands and my feet, that it is I myself: handle me, and see: for a spirit hath not flesh and bones, as ye see me have."

ἴδετε τὰς χεῖράς μου καὶ τοὺς πόδας μου ὅτι ἐγώ εἰμι αὐτός, ψηλαφήσατέ με καὶ ἴδετε, ὅτι πνεῦμα σάρκα καὶ ὀστέα οὐκ ἔχει καθὼς ἐμὲ θεωρεῖτε ἔχοντα.

ἴδετε (2d.per.pl.aor.act.impv.of ὁράω, command) 144.
τὰς (acc.pl.fem.of the article in agreement with χεῖράς) 9.
χεῖράς (acc.pl.fem.of χείρ, direct object of ἴδετε) 308.
μου (gen.sing.masc.of ἐγώ, possession) 123.
καὶ (adjunctive conjunction joining nouns) 14.
τοὺς (acc.pl.masc.of the article in agreement with πόδας) 9.
πόδας (acc.pl.masc.of πούς, direct object of ἴδετε) 353.
μου (gen.sing.masc.of ἐγώ, possession) 123.
ὅτι (conjunction introducing an object clause in indirect discourse) 211.
ἐγώ (nom.sing.masc.of ἐγώ, subject of εἰμι) 123.
εἰμι (1st.per.sing.pres.ind.of εἰμί, static) 86.
αὐτός (nom.sing.masc.of αὐτός, intensive) 16.

#2913 ψηλαφήσατέ (2d.per.pl.aor.act.impv.of ψηλαφάω, command).

feel after - Acts 17:27.

handle - Luke 24:39; 1 John 1:1.
that might be touched - Heb.12:18.

Meaning: to handle, touch, feel. In a physical sense - Jesus' disciples handled Him - Luke 24:39; 1 John 1:1. In Heb.12:18 it is used to differentiate Mount Sinai, the earthly mountain, from the spiritual Mount Zion - *Cf.* Heb.12:18 with Heb.12:22-24. To make the same distinction between the Athenians deities and the true God in Acts 17:27.

με (acc.sing.masc.of ἐγώ, direct object of ψηλαφήσατέ) 123.
καὶ (adjunctive conjunction joining verbs) 14.
ἴδετε (2d.per.pl.aor.act.impv.of ὁράω, command) 144.
ὅτι (conjunction introducing a subordinate causal clause) 211.
πνεῦμα (nom.sing.neut.of πνεῦμα, subject of ἔχει) 83.
σάρκα (acc.sing.fem.of σάρξ, direct object of ἔχει) 1202.
καὶ (adjuntive conjunction joining nouns) 14.
ὀστέα (acc.pl.neut.of ὀστέον, direct object of ἔχει) 1466.
οὐκ (summary negative conjunction with the indicative) 130.
ἔχει (3d.per.sing.pres.act.ind.of ἔχω, customary) 82.
καθὼς (relative adverb introducing a comparative clause) 1348.
ἐμὲ (acc.sing.masc.of ἐγώ, direct object of θεωρεῖτε) 123.
θεωρεῖτε (2d.per.pl.pres.act.ind.of θεωρέω, aoristic) 1667.
ἔχοντα (pres.act.part.acc.sing.masc.of ἔχω, adverbial, circumstantial) 82.

Translation - "Look at my hands and my feet and see that I AM, myself. Handle me and see for yourselves, because a ghost does not have flesh and bones as you see that I have."

Comment: Jesus insisted upon a thorough empirical examination. They had not said what was in their minds, *viz.* that He was only a phantasmagoria, but of course, He knew what they were thinking. This is why He invited inspection. Hands and feet. Flesh and bones. The first ὅτι follows ἴδετε, and introduces an object clause in indirect discourse. If Jesus had introduced Himself in addition to bidding them have peace (vs.36), He would have said what He had said to Moses on Mount Sinai (Exodus 3:14) and then added the intensive αὐτός -'Ἐγώ εἰμι, αὐτός' "I AM, Himself." This is the designation He had given Himself on many former occasions. *Cf.* the list in our comment on John 4:26. Since indirect discourse follows the direct in tense, we have the present tense in the object clause. The second ὅτι, unlike the first, follows, not a verb of seeing (ὁράω) but ψηλαφήσατε and introduces a subordinate causal clause. Since they thought that He was a ghost, they could disprove that theory quickly by feeling His body, because (causal ὅτι) a ghost does not have flesh and bones, as they would discover that He had. The "handling test" was thus a valid procedure. We may say, in an aside that no empirical test is totally valid, without the use of the reasoning process. The conclusion that Jesus was not a ghost would depend (a) upon the empirical fact that He had flesh and bones, (b) upon the theory that ghosts are not so endowed, and (c) therefore, that Jesus was not a ghost. The third step in the reasoning is not experience but reason. Hence the radical empiricist who repudiates reason totally and depends only upon experience, cannot evaluate any experience which he has and must conclude with the existentialists that nothing means anything.

It has been suggested by some who build their theology on isolated proof texts that it is significant that Jesus did not mention His blood. Flesh and bones, yes, but not blood. This significant fact (!) is then linked with 1 Cor.15:50 which declares that "flesh and *blood* cannot inherit the kingdom of God." From the hermeneutical concatenation of these two Scriptures they conclude that the resurrection bodies of Jesus and the glorified saints will be bloodless! To which we reply that resurrection glorification applied to the flesh and bones of Jesus, tortured upon the cross and that the same could apply to His blood. The conclusion would be that the glorified body does not function like the perfect human body that God created in the Garden of Eden and that the biological systems of the body - skeletal, neurological, histological, digestive, excretory and respiratory will not function in heaven. At the risk of spending too much time and space on this silly theory we will only say that, (a) if that is true then God's statement that His first creation was "Good" is wrong and that He would be required to improve upon it when He takes us to heaven. The heavenly body will be "better" than the earthly body only in that it will be forever free from the corruption of sin, which is what Paul meant in 1 Cor.15:50, as is clear when we note that he ended his statement by adding, ". . . neither does corruption inherit incorruption" (1 Cor.15:50b). The miracle of glorification which will take place when we are "changed" (1 Cor.50:51,52; Phil.3:21; 1 John 3:2) will change our bodies as they are now constructed, but which are biodegradable because of sin, into non-biodegradable bodies. This means of course that we will eat when we get to heaven. Why not? There won't be any gnostics there to complain!

Verse 40 - "And when he had thus spoken, he showed them his hands and his feet."

καὶ τοῦτο εἰπὼν ἔδειξεν αὐτοῖς τὰς χεῖρας καὶ τοὺς πόδας.

καὶ (continuative conjunction) 14.

τοῦτο (acc.sing.neut.of οὗτος, direct object of εἰπὼν) 93.

εἰπὼν (aor.act.part.nom.sing.masc.of εἶπον, adverbial, temporal) 155.

ἔδειξεν (3d.per.sing.aor.act.ind.of δείκνυμι, constative) 359.

αὐτοῖς (dat.pl.masc.of αὐτός, indirect object of ἔδειξεν) 16.

τὰς (acc.pl.fem.of the article in agreement with χεῖρας) 9.

χεῖρας (acc.pl.fem.of χείρ, direct object of ἔδειξεν) 308.

καὶ (adjunctive conjunction joining nouns) 14.

τοὺς (acc.pl.masc.of the article in agreement with πόδας) 9.

πόδας (acc.pl.masc.of ποῦς, direct object of ἔδειξεν) 353.

Translation - "And when He had said this, He showed them His hands and His feet."

Comment: The antecedent of τοῦτο is the statement of verse 39. The Westcott/Hort text include verse 40 in double brackets, indicating great doubt that it is a part of the original text, but Metzger says, "Was ver.40 omitted by certain Western witnesses (D ita,b,d,e,ff2,l,rl syrc,s, Marcion) because it seemed superfluous after ver.39? Or is it a gloss introduced by copyists in all other witnesses from Jn.20.20, with a necessary adaptation (the passage in John refers to Christ's hands and side; this passage refers to his hands and feet)? A minority of the Committee preferred to omit the verse as an interpolation . . . ; the majority, however, was of the opinion that, had the passage been interpolated from the Johannine account, copyists would probably have left some trace of its origin by retaining τὴν πλευράν in place of τοὺς πόδας (either here only, or in ver.39 also)." (Metzger, *A Textual Commentary on the Greek New Testament,* 187).

That which is apprehended by faith can also be substantiated by sense perception. Ultimately sight will justify our faith, just as realization will justify our hope. There is nothing better than charity (1 Cor.13:13).

With reference again to the theory that the resurrected body of Jesus was without blood, proponents have asked, "If Jesus had blood in His body, why did He not mention it in verse 40?" He was inviting the disciples to conduct an investigation by feeling Him. They could see and feel His flesh, and they could feel His bones. Does anyone imagine that Peter would have been gauche enough to have insisted that Jesus also show them His blood?!

The disciples were beginning to believe it, but there was still some doubt, as we see in

Verse 41 - "And while they yet believed not for joy, and wondered, he said unto them, Have ye here any meat?"

ἔτι δὲ ἀπιστούντων αὐτῶν ἀπὸ τῆς χαρᾶς καὶ θαυμαζόντων εἶπεν αὐτοῖς, Ἔχετέ τι βρώσιμον ἐνθάδε;

ἔτι (temporal adverb) 448.

δέ (adversative conjunction) 11.

ἀπιστούντων (pres.act.part.gen.pl.masc.of ἀπιστέω, genitive absolute, adverbial, causal) 2893.

αὐτῶν (gen.pl.masc.of αὐτός, genitive absolute) 16.

ἀπό (preposition with the ablative, cause) 70.

τῆς (abl.sing.fem.of the article in agreement with χαρᾶς) 9.

χαρᾶς (abl.sing.fem.of χαρά, cause) 183.

καί (adjunctive conjunction joining participles) 14.

θαυμαζόντων (pres.act.part.gen.pl.masc.of θαυμάζω, genitive absolute, adverbial, causal) 726.

εἶπεν (3d.per.sing.aor.act.ind.of εἶπον, constative) 155.

αὐτοῖς (dat.pl.masc.of αὐτός, indirect object ofd εἶπεν) 16.

ἔχετε (2d.per.pl.pres.act.ind.of ἔχω, direct question) 82.

τι (acc.sing.neut.of τις, indefinite pronoun, in agreement with βρώσιμον) 486.

#2914 βρώσιμον (acc.sing.neut.of βρώσιμος, direct object of ἔχετε).

meat - Luke 24:41.

Meaning: Cf. βρῶσις (#594) and βρῶμα (#1118). Anything edible - Luke 24:41.

ἐνθάδε (local adverb) 2010.

Translation - "*But because they still continued to doubt and be amazed because of the joy, He said to them, 'Do you have anything here to eat?'*"

Comment: δέ is adversative. Despite the evidence presented to them the disciples were still in doubt. Their doubts however were mixed with joy and wonder. The temporal adverb ἔτι strengthens the durative force of the present participles in the genitive absolute constructions. The mixture of joy and doubt indicates that they wanted to believe it, but it seemed too good to be true. And yet . . . θαυμαζόντων - wonder, amazement, doubt, furtive joy. Jesus knew that they needed more proof. His next demonstration should settle the question. Did they have any food available?

Verse 42 - "*And they gave him a piece of broiled fish, and an honeycomb.*"

οἱ δέ ἐπέδωκαν αὐτῷ ἰχθύος ὀπτοῦ μέρος.

οἱ (nom.pl.masc.of the article, subject of ἐπέδωκαν) 9.

δέ (continuative conjunction) 11.

ἐπέδωκαν (3d.per.pl.aor.act.ind.of ἐπιδίδωμι, constative) 656.

αὐτῷ (dat.sing.masc.of αὐτός, indirect object of ἐπέδωκαν) 16.

ἰχθύος (gen.sing.masc.of ἰχθύς, description) 657.

#2915 ὀπτοῦ (gen.sing.masc.of ὀπτός, in agreement with ἰσθυός).

broiled - Luke 24:42.

Meaning: Cf.ὀπτάω - "to broil,cook." Hence, an adjective - cooked or broiled - Luke 24:42.

μέρος (acc.sing.neut.of μέρος, direct object of ἐπέδωκαν) 240.

Translation - "And they gave Him a piece of broiled fish."

Comment: The words μέρος καὶ ἀπὸ μελισσίου κηρίου are added by X Θ f₁₃ 1195ₘₘ 1242 1365 1546 it₍ₐ₎, aur,(b),(c), f, ff2, l (q), rl vg geo? Cyril-Jerusalem. *Cf. Aland, et al.* These words "("and from a honeycomb") in many of the later manuscripts (followed by the Textus Receptus) are an obvious interpolation, for it is not likely that they would have fallen out of so many of the best representatives of the earlier text-types. Since in parts of the ancient church honey was used in the celebration of the Eucharist and in the baptismal liturgy, copyists may have added the reference here in order to provide scriptural sanction for liturgical practice." (Metzger, *Textual Commentary*, 187,8).

In response to Jesus' question the disciples, still in doubt, but by now very much wanting to believe, quickly placed in His hands a piece of fish and watched eagerly to see the experiment.

Verse 43 - "And he took it, and did eat before them."

καὶ λαβὼν ἐνώπιον αὐτῶν ἔφαγεν.

καὶ (continuative conjunction) 14.
λαβὼν (aor.act.part.nom.sing.masc.of λαμβάνω, adverbial, temporal) 533.
ἐνώπιον (improper preposition with the genitive of place description) 1798.
αὐτῶν (gen.pl.masc.of αὐτός, place description) 16.
ἔφαγεν (3d.per.sing.aor.act.ind.of ἐσθίω, constative) 610.

Translation - "And He took it and ate it before their eyes."

Comment: It is a little annoying to read the lengthy dissertations by the pedants from early Church Fathers down to the present who wish to discuss how a material body that could be handled, examined, seen and heard and that was capable of chewing and swallowing food, nevertheless could vanish and appear in an instant. Thus the doubters still try to peddle the poison that a *material* body cannot, at the same time, be a *spiritual* body, as though πνευματικός can be thought of only in terms of something immaterial. Was Jesus' resurrected body spiritual? Without a doubt. *Cf.* 1 Cor.15:44. Does this mean that it had no material substance? To him who thinks that it does we suggest that he look at Gal.6:1. Study πνευματικός (#3791) very carefully. The attributes of spirituality have nothing whatever to do with the attributes of corporeity. To say with Hahn that Jesus assumed materiality only for a moment in order to convince the disciples is to charge Jesus with deceit. Did the body in which Jesus suffered leave the tomb or not? Was it stolen and disposed of surreptitiously? If so, by whom? Friends or enemies? Did He have it when Mary saw Him? The Emmaus disciples? The ten? The eleven? On Mount Olivet? (Acts 1:9). Sometimes after reading the German Higher Critics one wonders if Luther's reformation ever really touched the soul of Germany. Why do we castigate the inexpressibly iniquitous Adolph Hitler as the most wicked German of them all? Perhaps his philosophy and conduct is only the logical result for those who reject the propositional revelation of the Word of God.

John Reports the Sunday Night Visit

(John 20:19-25)

John 20:19 - *"Then the same day at evening, being the first day of the week, when the doors were shut where the disciples were assembled for fear of the Jews, came Jesus and stood in the midst, and saith unto them, Peace be unto you."*

Οὔσης οὖν ὀφίας τῇ ἡμέρᾳ ἐκείνῃ τῇ μιᾷ σαββάτων καὶ τῶν θυρῶν κεκλεισμένων ὅπου ἦσαν οἱ μαθηταὶ διὰ τὸν φόβον τῶν Ἰουδαίων, ἦλθεν ὁ Ἰησοῦς καὶ ἔστη εἰς τὸ μέσον καὶ λέγει αὐτοῖς, Εἰρήνη ὑμῖν.

Οὔσης (pres.part.gen.sing.fem.of εἰμί, genitive absolute) 86.
οὖν (continuative conjunction) 68.
ὀφίας (gen.sing.fem.of ὄφιος, genitive absolute) 739.
τῇ (loc.sing.fem.of the article in agreement with ἡμέρᾳ) 9.
ἡμέρᾳ (loc.sing.fem.of ἡμέρα, time point) 135.
ἐκείνῃ (loc.sing.fem.of ἐκεῖνος, in agreement with ἡμέρᾳ) 246.
τῇ (loc.sing.fem.of the article in agreement with μιᾷ) 9.
μιᾷ (loc.sing.fem.of εἷς, in apposition with ἡμέρᾳ) 469.
σαββάτων (gen.pl.neut.of σάββατον, partitive genitive) 962.
καὶ (adjunctive conjunction joining participial clauses) 14.
τῶν (gen.pl.fem.of the article in agreement with θυρῶν) 9.
θυρῶν (gen.pl.fem.of θύρα, genitive absolute) 571.
κεκλεισμένων (perf.pass.part.gen.pl.fem.of κλείω, genitive absolute) 570.
ὅπου (local adverb introducing a local clause) 592.
ἦσαν (3d.per.pl.imp.ind.of εἰμί, progressive description) 86.
οἱ (nom.pl.masc.of the article in agreement with μαθηταὶ) 9.
μαθηταὶ (nom.pl.masc.of μαθητής, subject of ἦσαν) 421.
διὰ (preposition with the accusative, cause) 118.
τὸν (acc.sing.masc.of the article in agreement with φόβον) 9.
φόβον (acc.sing.masc.of φόβος, cause) 1131.
τῶν (gen.pl.masc.of the article in agreement with Ἰουδαίων) 9.
Ἰουδαίων (gen.pl.masc.of Ἰουδαῖος, description) 143.
ἦλθεν (3d.per.sing.aor.act.ind.of ἔρχομαι, constative) 146.
ὁ (nom.sing.masc.of the article in agreement with Ἰησοῦς) 9.
Ἰησοῦς (nom.sing.masc.of Ἰησοῦς, subject of ἦλθεν, ἔστη and λέγει) 3.
καὶ (adjunctive conjunction joining verbs) 14.
ἔστη (3d.per.sing.2d.aor.act.ind.of ἵστημι, constative) 180.
εἰς (preposition with the accusative, static, locative use) 140.
τὸ (acc.sing.neut.of the article in agreement with μέσον) 9.

μέσον (acc.sing.neut.of μέσος, place where) 873.
καί (adjunctive conjunction joining verbs) 14.
λέγει (3d.per.sing.pres.act.ind.of λέγω, historical) 66.
αὐτοῖς (dat.pl.masc.of αὐτός, indirect object of λέγει) 16.
Εἰρήνη (nom.sing.fem.of εἰρήνη, nominative absolute) 865.
ὑμῖν (dat.pl.masc.of σύ, indirect object of the verb understood) 104.

Translation - "And when evening came on that the first day of the week and the doors had been closed where the disciples were, because of fear of the Jews, Jesus came and stood among them and said to them, 'Peace be with you.' "

Comment: We have a double genitive absolute. The first - Οὔσης ὀψίας - "it was evening" and the second τῶν θυρῶν κεκλεισμένων - "and the doors had been shut". The second is a perfect participle indicating that the disciples had locked the doors earlier. John tells us why. The disciples were afraid that the Jews would seek them out and possibly have them killed as well. The disciples had spent the day there (imperfect tense in ἦσαν). Thus John has set the scene long before he introduced the main clause - "Jesus came, . . . stood. . . and said. . . " He told us the hour of the day, the day of the week, the circumstances with reference to the locked doors, why they were locked and that the disciples had been there all day. And yet John did it all with one perfectly constructed Greek sentence. Mark probably would have broken up the material into a series of short paratactic clauses, joined together with καί. *Cf.* Mark 16:14; Luke 24:36,37. The Mark passage errs in saying that there were eleven disciples present. Thomas was absent and Judas was dead...There were only ten of the Apostles, plus others, including the women and the two from Emmaus. It is well to remember that Mark 16:9-20 are believed by textual critics to have been added much later. We need not be seriously concerned therefore with what they have to say. It is as likely that they contain error as it is that anything written without the benefit of divine inspiration would. We can therefore disregard the contents of these last twelve verses, especially verses 16-18 which provide the basis for baptismal regeneration and the snake handling cults.

Verse 20 - "And when he had so said, he shewed unto them his hands and his side. Then were the disciples glad when they saw the Lord."

     καὶ τοῦτο εἰπὼν ἔδειξεν τὰς χεῖρας καὶ τὴν πλευρὰν αὐτοῖς. ἐχάρησαν οὖν οἱ μαθηταὶ ἰδόντες τὸν κύριον.

καί (continuative conjunction) 14.
τοῦτο (acc.sing.neut.of οὗτος, direct object of εἰπών) 93.
εἰπών (aor.act.part.nom.sing.masc.of εἶπον, adverbial, temporal) 155.
ἔδειξεν (3d.per.sing.aor.act.ind.of δείκνυμι, constative) 359.
τάς (acc.pl.fem.of the article in agreement with χεῖρας) 9.
χεῖρας (acc.pl.fem.of χείρ, direct object of ἔδειξεν) 308.
καί (adjunctive conjunction joining nouns) 14.
τήν (acc.sing.fem.of the article in agreement with πλευράν) 9.

πλευρὰν (acc.sing.fem.of πλευρά, direct object of ἔδειξεν) 1660.
αὐτοῖς (dat.pl.masc.of αὐτός, indirect object of ἔδειξεν) 16.
ἐχάρησαν (3d.per.pl.aor.act.ind.of χαίρω, ingressive) 182.
οὖν (inferential conjunction) 68.
οἱ (nom.pl.masc.of the article in agreement with μαθηταὶ) 9.
μαθηταὶ (nom.pl.masc.of μαθητής, subject of ἐχάρησαν) 421.
ἰδόντες (aor.act.part.nom.pl.masc.of ὁράω, adverbial, temporal/causal) 144.
τὸν (acc.sing.masc.of the article in agreement with κύριον) 9.
κύριον (acc.sing.masc.of κύριος, direct object of ἰδόντες) 97.

Translation - "And having said this He showed His hands and His side to them. Therefore the disciples were seized with joy when (because) they saw the Lord."

Comment: εἰπών is a temporal participle, which has a slight time element in it, but we should not give too much emphasis to the aorist tense with its completed action. John is only saying that Jesus made the statement of verse 19 - εἰρήνη ὑμῖν, referred to here by τοῦτο, and then displayed His hands and side for inspection. Since we already know that Jesus said εἰρήνη ὑμῖν to them εἰπών is really pleonastic. The time element in the participle is sometimes vital to the exegesis, in which case we ought to make the most of it, but in a passage like ἀποκριθεὶς εἶπεν, the participle is totally unnecessary. Not all of the examples are as flagrant as that, but the exegete must always look for the main thrust of the participle, be it time, manner, means, cause, purpose, condition, concession or circumstance. If it suggests only time then the question is how important is it in the overall grasp of the passage to know the chronological sequence? Sometimes the participle is a pure case of pleonasm which is only a characteristic of the κοινή.

ἰδόντες, the participle in the last clause is causal, and, of course, also temporal, since cause must precede result. Note the ingressive aorist in ἐχάρησαν, with the emphasis upon the beginning of the reaction. This time Jesus convinced them that He was truly alive, and they were seized with joy at the realization of the fact. *Cf.* Luke 24:39,40,41. Luke agrees (vs.41) that they rejoiced, but adds that they still disbelieved until He ate the piece of broiled fish. John telescopes the story. Mark's statement in Mk.16:14 that Jesus upbraided the disciples because of their skepticism does not comport with the stories told by John and Luke. It is likely that if the Holy Spirit had been superintending the writer of the Mark 16:9-20 passage, He would have directed the writer to use a softer word than ὀνειδίζω (#437).

Verse 21 - "Then said Jesus to them again, Peace be unto you: as my Father hath sent me, even so send I you."

εἶπεν οὖν αὐτοῖς πάλιν, Εἰρήνη ὑμῖν. καθὼς ἀπέσταλκέν με ὁ πατήρ, κἀγὼ πέμπω ὑμᾶς.

εἶπεν (3d.per.sing.aor.act.ind.of εἶπον, constative) 155.
οὖν (continuative conjunction) 68.

αὐτοῖς (dat.pl.masc.of αὐτός, indirect object of εἶπεν) 16.

πάλιν (adverbial) 355.

Εἰρήνη (nom.sing.fem.of εἰρήνη, nominative absolute) 865.

ὑμῖν (dat.pl.masc.of σύ, indirect object of the verb understood) 104.

καθώς (particle in a comparative clause) 1348.

ἀπέσταλκέν (3d.per.sing.perf.act.ind.of ἀποστέλλω, consummative) 215.

με (acc.sing.masc.of ἐγώ, direct object of ἀπέσταλκέν) 123.

ὁ (nom.sing.masc.of the article in agreement with πατήρ) 9.

πατήρ (nom.sing.masc.of πατήρ, subject of ἀπέσταλκέν) 238.

κἀγώ (crasis, adjunctive καί and nom.sing.masc.of ἐγώ, subject of πέμπω) 178.

πέμπω (1st.per.sing.pres.act.ind.of πέμπω, futuristic) 169.

ὑμᾶς (acc.pl.masc.of σύ, direct object ofd πέμπω) 104.

Translation - "Then He said to them again, 'Peace be with you. As the Father has sent me, I also am going to send you.' "

Comment: οὖν is continuative, not inferential. Verse 20 tells us that the disciples were seized with joy when they saw the pierced hands of Jesus and the scar tissue upon His side. Their joy does not necessarily infer that Jesus repeated His Εἰρήνη ὑμῖν, in order to comfort them. But when we read Luke's account (Lk.24:40-43) and learn that, though they were joyous, they were also still in doubt, it can be argued that Jesus' second blessing (John 20:21) was given in order to dispel any lingering shred of doubt, in which case οὖν is inferential and should be translated "therefore."

καθώς introduces the comparative clause. Note the consummative force of the perfect ἀπέσταλκέν με. The Father had sent Jesus into the world. He came in incarnation, lived for thirty-three years here and now His redemptive work is finished. He has only to look forward to ascension to the Father's right hand and a seat in glory as He awaits the completion of His worldwide missionary enterprise. In the same way that the Father sent Jesus, He then announced to the disciples that He was going to send them. His mission was to provide the redemptive basis for man's salvation. Their mission was to go into all the world and tell about it. Their mission is as enduring and unending as His. He will always be the Man, Christ Jesus (1 Tim.2:5). The perfect tense in ἀπέσταλκεν joined to καθώς and κἀγώ is all the grammatical evidence we need to show that when Jesus sent His servants on the evangelistic mission, it was a permanent assignment, and all Christians, lay as well as clerical, had better not forget it.

The work of publicizing the fact that the Son of God died to provide salvation for the elect is as important as the work He accomplished when He provided it. Faith comes by hearing, and hearing by the Word of God, but how shall they hear without a preacher? (Rom.10:13-17). Since we, the members of His body, the Church are charged with a responsibility of such great importance and since the task of telling the entire world is so great we need the supernatural endowment of power which comes only with the indwelling and infilling of the Holy Spirit. They received the Holy Spirit in verse 22. They were not filled with Him until Pentecost. This is why we have taken πέμπω as a futuristic present.

Jesus did not send them out to begin their witness that day. Thirty-eight days later, He told them to wait ten more days (Acts 1:6-8). When, at Pentecost, the era of the Holy Spirit, the third Person of the Godhead, began the disciples needed no urging. Not even the police could keep them from witnessing (Acts 4 - 5, with special attention to Acts 5:29).

Verse 22 - "And when he had said this, he breathed on them, and saith unto them, Receive ye the Holy Ghost."

καὶ τοῦτο εἰπὼν ἐνεφύσησεν καὶ λέγει αὐτοῖς, Λάβετε πνεῦμα ἅγιον.

καὶ (continuative conjunction) 14.
τοῦτο (acc.sing.neut.of οὗτος, direct object of εἰπὼν) 93.
εἰπὼν (aor.act.part.nom.sing.masc.of εἶπον, adverbial, temporal) 155.

#2916 ἐνεφύσησεν (3d.per.sing.aor.act.ind.of ἐμφυσάω, constative).

breathe on - John 20:22.

Meaning: A combination of ἐν (#80) and φυσάω - "to blow, breathe, exhale." Hence, to breathe upon. With reference to Jesus' action in giving the gift of the Holy Spirit to the ten disciples - John 20:22.

καὶ (adjunctive conjunction joining verbs) 14.
λέγει (3d.per.sing.pres.act.ind.ofd λέγω, historical) 66.
αὐτοῖς (dat.pl.masc.of αὐτός, indirect object of λέγει) 16.
Λάβετε (2d.per.pl.aor.act.impv.of λαμβάνω, command) 533.
πνεῦμα (acc.sing.neut.of πνεῦμα, direct object of Λάβετε) 83.
ἅγιον (acc.sing.neut.of ἅγιος, in agreement with πνεῦμα) 84.

Translation - "And having said this He breathed upon and said to them, 'Receive the Holy Spirit.' "

Comment: The sovereign order was given and the Holy Spirit indwelt those who were present. This passage, if we will allow it, will correct a great deal of false teaching about the Holy Spirit. It is often said that the Holy Spirit *came* on the day of Pentecost. In the first place the Holy Spirit cannot *come* anywhere because He is God and He is already omnipresent. It is true that He changed His personal relationship with the disciples. *Cf.* John 14:17 and comment. Previous to this event on the evening of resurrection day, He was *by their side* as a Paraclete. Now He is *in them* (as of John 20:22). He is no longer Paraclete (called to stand parallel to them) but Enclete (called inside of them, though we have had to coin the word in order to express the relation). It is also said erroneously that this *coming* of the Holy Spirit was at Pentecost. The event of John 20:22 was 48 days before Pentecost. Another mistaken statement is that the believers *received* the Holy Spirit at Pentecost. They received Him on the evening of the day when He arose. They were *filled with* the Holy Spirit at Pentecost (Acts 2:4). It is significant that between resurrection evening, when they received the Holy Spirit and Pentecost, 48 days later, when they were filled with the One Who had indwelt them since the resurrection, the disciples did nothing noteworthy. In contrast we have only to see what they did on and after Pentecost day.

This passage also contradicts the notion, popular in some circles that the New Testament Church *began* on the day of Pentecost. A group of disciples, eleven or more, had the Holy Spirit and a commission in the secret room in Jerusalem on resurrection evening. Indeed if the necessary definition of a church involves a group (two or more) of Christians who are filled with the Spirit, there are few if any *churches* in the world at present. The New Testament church began, at least at Luke 6:13 (Eph.2:20).

The personnel of the Body of Christ whom the Apostles and those who have followed them for two thousand years, in obedience to the command of the great commission, are foreseen, though not specifically named in

Verse 23 - "Whose soever sins ye remit, they are remitted unto them; and whose soever sins ye retain, they are retained."

ἄν τινων ἀφῆτε τὰς ἁμαρτίας ἀφέωνται αὐτοῖς, ἄν τινων κρατῆτε κεκράτηνται.

ἄν (contingent particle in a third-class condition) 205.
τινων (gen.pl.masc.of τις, indefinite pronoun, possession) 486.
ἀφῆτε (2d.per.pl.aor.act.subj.of ἀφίημι, third-class condition) 319.
τὰς (acc.pl.fem.of the article in agreement with ἁμαρτίας) 9.
ἁμαρτίας (acc.pl.fem.of ἁμαρτία, direct object of ἀφῆτε) 111.
ἀφέωνται (3d.per.pl.perf.pass.ind.of ἀφίημι, consummative) 319.
αὐτοῖς (dat.pl.masc.of αὐτός, personal advantage) 16.
ἄν (contingent particle in a third-class condition) 205.
τινων (gen.pl.masc.of τις, indefinite pronoun, possession) 486.
κρατῆτε (2d.per.pl.pres.act.subj.of κρατέω, third-class condition) 828.
κεκράτηνται (3d.per.pl.perf.pass.ind.of κρατέω, consummative) 828.

Translation - "If you forgive the sins of anyone, they have already been forgiven for them. If you retain the sins of anyone they have already been retained."

Comment: It is not surprizing that this passage in the hands of sacerdotalists would be tortured into a grammatical form consistent with their position that God's decisions in heaven are contingent upon the decisions of men on earth. The Committee of the United Bible Society, with its usual commendable objectivity, however has restored the text which John wrote.

"Although the perfect tense ἀφέωνται could be regarded as a secondary assimilation to κεκράτηνται at the end of the sentence, a majority of the Committee interpreted the present tense ἀφίενται and the future ἀφεθήσεται as scribal simplifications which weaken the sense. To the external evidence supporting ἀφέωνται (Sinaiticus_c A D (L) X 050 *f₁f₁₃* 33vid 565 *al*) should perhaps be added B*, which reads ἀφείονται (ιο being written for ω). (Metzger, *Textual Commentary,* 255). On a scale of A — D, the Committee indicated a B degree of certitude for their decision to write the perfect, rather than the present form into the text.

The two perfect passive forms, each in the apodosis of a third-class condition, indicate action prior to the action of the verb in the protasis, as a result of which completed action a present and linear (durative) condition now and will prevail. Thus at the time that the Christian witness remits or retains a sinner's sins, those sins in question are the ones that have already been forgiven or retained as a result of the previous completed action. Thus the action of the preacher is only a ratifying action of a situation that has already been fixed and which therefore currently prevails.

The grammatical and syntactical problem in John 20:23 is essentially the same as that presented in Matthew 16:19; 18:18. *Cf.*comment in *The Renaissance New Testament,* 2, 545-548; 631-633. In those passages the apodoses have future perfect passive periphrastic constructions, instead of the perfect passives of John 20:23, but this difference does not affect the conclusions which are the same for all three passages.

"In the first extant copy of Origen's Commentary on Matthew he wrote that all Christians are rocks (πέτροι) and that we are to ratify God's will, rather than God ratifying ours." (J.R.Mantey in a letter to the author, March 6, 1972). *Cf.*J.R.Mantey, "Perfect Tenses Ignored in Matthew XVI, 19, XVIII, 18 and John XX, 23," (Expositor, Nicoll, 1922, 1, 470-72, and a reply by Henry J. Cadbury, "The Meaning of John 20:23, Matthew 16:19 and Matthew 18:18, *Journal of Biblical Literature*, 58, 1939, 251-54). Cadbury's rebuttal has some merit on the basis of a strict grammatical exegesis, and might be considered valid, but for the fact that Mantey's position is clearly taught in other passages of Scripture, *e.g.* Acts 13:48; Eph.2:1-10; 1 Peter 1:2; Rev.10:7; Jude 1, etc. *q.v.en.loc.* Cadbury does not contradict Mantey's interpretation of the perfect tense in the apodosis. "One may grant at the outset that Professor Mantey is right in contending that the various perfect tenses usually indicate a situation already existent at some time contemplated in the sentence." He only suggests that the perfect in the apodosis does not *always* (our emphasis) ". . . indicate an action or condition prior to the time of the apodosis." He cites 1 John 2:5; James 2:10; Romans 14:23 and Romans 13:8 as exceptions to the rule. That Cadbury chose very poor examples to indicate simultaneity of the time of the perfect in the apodosis with that of the protasis, thus to show that the conclusion of the apodosis in contingent upon the action in the protasis will be seen when we discuss each of these verses *en .loc.*

When Mantey says, "New Testament grammarians cite no instances of a perfect implying future action" (Cadbury, *Ibid.,*251), if indeed Cadbury is quoting Mantey outside quotation marks correctly, he goes too far, since Cadbury procedes to cite Blass-Debrunner, Moulton and Robertson, who thinks that James 2:10; Romans 13:8; 14:23 may be anticipatory, Burton, who agrees with Robertson *in re* James 2:10 and Winer, who also agrees *in re* Romans 14:23; 13:8. In fact Mantey did not say what Cadbury alleges in the article cited *supra.*

But the appeal to what great grammarians have said is an appeal to authority unworthy of an honest student of the New Testament. After all has been said, none of the distinguished grammarians here mentioned would have claimed or do now claim that they are infallible. Mantey's interpretation of John 20:23; Mt.16:19; 18:18 is based upon the normal rule for the exegesis of the perfect tense. The alleged exceptions to the rule are not clearly supported. Therefore we have translated John 20:23 accordingly and suggest that those who object are doing so out of a prejudice against the elective and predestinating decrees of a sovereign God.

Dr.Wilber Dayton, who wrote his doctoral dissertation for the degree of Doctor of Theology at Northern Baptist Theological Seminary, on the subject, "The Greek Perfect Tense In Relation to John 20:23; Matthew 16:19 and Matthew 18:18" says,

Since the perfect tense is used, there is certainly a past action implied as reckoned from some point, and that point would, from a grammatical standpoint, normally be the time of the speaker. Thus the implications of a literal translation would seem to rule out the origination of the forgiveness in the human agent and demand that the forgiveness be an already accomplished fact (at least in the Divine purpose) at the time of Jesus' speaking. In other words, the human agent must treat as forgiven none except those whom God had already forgiven previous to the declaration of Jesus. The forgiveness then would be a Divine act simply proclaimed by the human agent but not in any real sense accomplished by him. That is, by treating as forgiven only those whom God had already forgiven, they would be simply interpreting and applying the will of God to man instead of intruding into the mediatorial office of Christ and deciding man's salvation. As Christian scribes and interpreters they were thus warned only to apply the Divine will, but they were not given the power to initiate acts at their own discretion which heaven must ratify.

Or if one were to grant the figurative translation to the extent of a proleptical perfect, this interpretation would not be altered materially. Then the passage would simply correspond to the future perfects of the passages in Matthew's Gospel and declare that at the time when the disciples shall treat the sins as forgiven, they will already have been forgiven. That would simply mean that the whole unit of thought would be projected into the future and the completed action would simply be figured from the point in the future. Therefore, at the point that mattered, the disciples would not be originating the activity but would find the sins of their hearers already remitted by a Divine act, at least in the purpose and plan of God as designed according to Divine foreknowlege and wisdom. But since the proleptical use is rare and so highly figurative and even then no more favorable to sacerdotalism than the literal use, further consideration need not be given to it at present.

One need not study language long to learn that more is involved in translation than vocabulary and syntax. Dr. Cadbury says truly, "The case against sacerdotalism, as indeed the case for it, does not rest on disputable points of Greek grammar." (Henry J. Cadbury, "The Meaning of John 20:23, Matthew 16:19, and Matthew 18:18", *Journal of Biblical Literature,* LVIII (1939), p.254). That is, it does not rest solely on grammar, though grammar does have a definite determining function. No translation is certain until it has been tested by logic, by its immediate environment and by life as a whole. In the Scriptures that means that a translation must first be possible logically, then agree with the immediate context, and finally not contradict any other clear teaching of Scripture or fact of life. (*f.n.* Of course the latter consideration would not be granted by one who denies the supernatural origin and nature of the Bible, but such objections are of little account to those who have the inner assurance that God has spoken.). And it might be said in passing that all these considerations received their due attention in Dr. Mantey's study of the present problem. It would certainly be unfair to imply that his whole argument was based on grammar.

Submitting the literal translation and interpretation to the test of logic, one finds nothing logically impossible about it, provided, of course, that he grants the supernatural. What logical reason could be adduced to make the view impossible that God has already, in his eternal purpose, forgiven the sins of those whom he foreknows as truly penitent? This is the same sort of problem that one finds in the expressions "Knowing this, that our old man was crucified with him" (Romans 6:6) and "the Lamb slain from the foundation of the world." (Revelation 13:8). All these may properly be treated as undertaken and potentially accomplished by God in eternity on the basis of his foreknowledge and applied to man in the fullness of time — that is, at the earliest moment that man is ready.

In the case of forgiveness, it is not logical that God would wait to inform his human representative as a vicar or mediator before applying forgiveness to the penitent soul. Nor would God wait for a human agent to make the decision and forgive the penitent. He would do it himself directly on the basis of his perfect knowledge and matchless grace. The most that man could logically be expected to do is to act as an "ambassador to treat of peace and a herald to proclaim it." (Matthew Henry, *Commentary*, John 20:23). As such it is logical that their remitting of sin and retaining of sin would, as prophetically ministerial acts, rest upon corresponding acts of God, already accomplished in the Spirit." (Lange, *Commentary*, John 20:23). As John Wesley says, "Are not the sins of one who truly repents and unfeignedly believes in Christ, remitted without sacerdotal absolution? And are not the sins of one who does not repent or believe, retained even with it?" (John Wesley, *Notes*, John 20:23). Man, as a representative of God is entrusted with the message of salvation and states the terms of salvation but God himself forgives and makes known his forgiveness. At least no logical necessity refutes such a conclusion. Then it is normal logically to concede the literal translation and interpretation which would place the act of forgiveness as past to the speaker (*f.n.* Jesus in this instance) in the eternal purpose of God or at least, if a proleptical element were allowed at all, the forgiveness would still be actually accomplished in the past in relation to the human agent who represented Christ in carrying the terms of reconciliation. In either case, the forgiveness would have to be a Divine act accomplished before the proclamation of the human representative. Either view would adequately dispose of any possibility of an authorization of sacerdotalism as found in the words of Jesus.

Not only grammatically and logically but also theologically, the literal use is, on the face of it, in harmony with certain facts that would dispose one to favorable consideration of it.

In the first place, one of the most persistent and troublesome abuses of Jesus' day was the false traditionalism of the scribes that asserted authority over the law of God. Jesus repeatedly had to rebuke the scribes and Pharisees as hypocrites. Care must be taken in the training and equipping of the disciples that these abuses be not perpetuated by those whom he would send forth to teach and preach. Might it not be reasonable to say that it was, in part at least, to this end that Jesus breathed on them and said, "Receive ye the

Holy Ghost" and then immediately cautioned them not to use their power presumptuously? (John 20:22,23).

Furthermore the caprice and error of human judgment seem to have little room in such passages as Romans 8:28-30 where the Christian's security seems to rest in the fact of the perfect, inerrant work of God. Note how hard it would be to harmonize a sacerdotal interpretation with the above passage:

And we know that all things work together for good to them that love God, to them who are the called according to his purpose.

For whom he did foreknow, he also did predestinate to be conformed to the image of his Son, that he might be the firstborn among many brethren.

Moreover whom he did predestinate, them he also called, and whom he called, them he also justified, and whom he justified, them he also glorified.

Though this does not deny the cooperation of human agency, it certainly does make any idea that would give fallible man final authority in the forgiveness of his fellows seem unreasonable indeed. The idea of foregiveness is God's; the purpose is God's; the knowledge is God's; the predestination is an act of God; the pattern is God's; justification and glorification are acts of God. All is of God in a final sense. Though man does have a function of proclamation, it is God's gospel that has the final authority. As Matthew Henry says, "God will never alter this rule of judgment, nor vary from it; those whom the gospel acquits shall be acquitted, and those whom the gospel condemns shall be condemned." (Matthew Henry, *Commentary*, John 20:23).

(Wilber Thomas Dayton, *The Greek Perfect Tense In Relation to John 20:23; Matthew 16:19 And Matthew 18:18,* unpublished doctoral dissertation, Northern Baptist Theological Seminary, Lombard, Illinois, 1943, 101-107).

Following this passage, Dr. Dayton went on to examine and demolish, with Christian grace, eclat and aplomb the objections which the sacerdotalists have offered to his exegesis of the passages, one of which suggested that the use of the perfect tense by the New Testament writers was not to be found in the writings of profane Greek authors, to which Dayton responds,

In a somewhat detailed study of the *Hellenistic Greek Reader* and Strabo's *Geography,* Vol.I, the above conclusions were tested and confirmed. . . In harmony with the true meaning of the perfect tense in both classical and koine literature John 20:23 was translated as follows:

Whose soever sins ye forgive, they have been forgiven; whose soever sins ye retain, they have been retained."

This rendering implies that the Divine act of forgiveness was already accomplished (at least in the Divine purpose) at the time of the speaker (Jesus) and that the human agents were to forgive only those who were already forgiven. As human representatives, the apostles were to proclaim the gospel message of salvation and declare the terms of forgiveness but were not authorized to exceed such authority and, on their own initiative, open and close the doors of heaven to man. Their ministry must ever be an obedient and careful interpretation and application of the Divine will to man. No provision would thus be made for God's ratifying decisions based on the caprice of human ideas or even on sober judgments of finite man, as the Roman Catholics claims for their prelates." (*Ibid.*,191,192).

If our interpretation appears to be sacerdotal because it implies that forgiveness for sin or the lack thereof rests in the hands of the Apostles and their successors, so that the eternal fate of sinners hinges upon what human preachers do, we can reply that God's decrees are implemented in historic time, not by human instrumentalities, but by the Holy Spirit who indwells true believers. As Mantey points out, "The key to understanding John 20:23 seems to be the introductory statement, *"Receive the Holy Spirit."* (*supra*, 471,2). When one of God's servants, indwelt and filled by the Holy Spirit, Who is also Sovereign Deity, preaches the word of God, the Holy Spirit effectuates in time and thus brings to actuality what the triune God decreed from before the foundation of the world. The work is done, not by the church as a purely human institution, however sincere and ethically pure it motives, but by the Holy Spirit Who must do what He does through the instrumentality of imperfect human beings. When Jesus said, "As the Father sent me, I also send you," He was talking to a group of men and women to whom He said in the next breath, "Receive the Holy Spirit."

Those to whom the treasures of the Gospel of Christ were first entrusted were not sophisticated scholars in the formal sense. They were not scientists, philosophers or theologians, although they possessed at least average human intelligence. Since the Holy Spirit is the One Who witnesses the truths of the Gospel to the lost, the human instrument whom He chooses to use need not be highly qualified, however desireable we may think that to be. A deaf mute in a small village in west Texas, who was known in the community as "Dummy" was led to Christ in a brush arbor meeting by a Christian who could communicate to him with sign language. His regeneration resulted in such fulness of joy, depth of peace, radiance of countenance and sparkle of eye that he became one of the best soul winners in the community. His method was simple. He would point to a verse of scripture, point to his head and to his heart and smile, and the Holy Spirit did the hard part. A preacher in Missouri was mightily used of the Holy Spirit in the winning of the lost, despite the fact that he was reported to have preached on one occasion about the ten *leapers* who were cleansed, only one of whom returned to thank the Lord, while the other nine *leapers* went on their way without giving thanks! The Holy Spirit can use brains in the Christians whom He chooses to use to witness for Christ, but He has not shut Himself up to that policy.

It seems significant that upon the occasion of the dispatching of the Apostles to proclaim the gospel, by the risen Lord and Head of His church, He should have given such a clear statement of the Calvinistic theology which was to be her message - a theology which others have alleged was superimposed upon the teaching of Jesus by the Apostle Paul.

Verse 24 - "But Thomas, one of the twelve, called Didymus, was not with them when Jesus came."

Θωμᾶς δὲ εἷς ἐκ τῶν δώδεκα, ὁ λεγόμενος Δίδυμος, οὐκ ἦν μετ' αὐτῶν ὅτε ἦλθεν Ἰησοῦς.

Θωμᾶς (nom.sing.masc.of Θωμᾶς, subject of ἦν) 847.

δὲ (adversative conjunction) 11.

εἷς (nom.sing.masc.of εἷς, in apposition to Θωμᾶς) 469.

ἐκ (preposition with the partitive genitive) 19.

τῶν (gen.pl.masc.of the article, in agreement with δώδεκα) 9.

δώδεκα (numeral, indeclin., partitive genitive) 820.

ὁ (nom.sing.masc.of the article in agreement with λεγόμενος) 9.

λεγόμενος (pres.pass.part.nom.sing.masc.of λέγω, substantival, in apposition to Θωμᾶς) 66.

Δίδυμος (nom.sing.masc.of Δίδυμος, appellation) 2599.

οὐκ (summary negative conjunction with the indicative) 130.

ἦν (3d.per.sing.imp.ind.of εἰμί, progressive description) 86.

μετ' (preposition with the agenitive of accompaniment) 50.

αὐτῶν (gen.pl.masc.of αὐτός, accompaniment) 16.

ὅτε (adverb introducing a definite temporal clause, contemporaneous time) 703.

ἦλθεν (3d.per.sing.aor.ind.of ἔρχομαι, constative, definite temporal clause) 146.

Ἰησοῦς (nom.sing.masc.of Ἰησοῦς, subject of ἦλθεν) 3.

Translation - "But Thomas, one of the Twelve, who was called The Twin, was not with them when Jesus came."

Comment: Thus the episode described in vss.25-29 became necessary.

Verse 25 - "The other disciples therefore said unto him, We have seen the Lord. But he said unto them, Except I shall see in his hands the print of the nails, and put my finger into the print of the nails, and thrust my hand into his side, I will not believe."

ἔλεγον οὖν αὐτῷ οἱ ἄλλοι μαθηταί, Ἑωράκαμεν τὸν κύριον. ὁ δὲ εἶπεν αὐτοῖς, Ἐὰν μὴ ἴδω ἐν ταῖς χερσὶν αὐτοῦ τὸν τύπον τῶν ἥλων καὶ βάλω τὸν δάκτυλόν μου εἰς τὸν τύπον τῶν ἥλων καὶ βάλω μου τὴν χεῖρα εἰς τὴν πλευρὰν αὐτοῦ, οὐ μὴ πιστεύσω.

ἔλεγον (3d.per.pl.imp.act.ind.of λέγω, inceptive) 66.

οὖν (inferential conjunction) 68.

αὐτῷ (dat.sing.masc.of αὐτός, indirect object of ἔλεγον) 16.

οἱ (nom.pl.masc.of the article in agreement with μαθηταί) 9.

ἄλλοι (nom.pl.masc.of ἄλλος, in agreement with μαθηταί) 198.

μαθηταί (nom.pl.masc.of μαθητής, subject of ἔλεγον) 421.

Ἑωράκαμεν (1st.per.sing.perf.act.ind.of ὁράω, dramatic) 144.

τὸν (acc.sing.masc.of the article in agreement with κύριον) 9.

κύριον (acc.sing.masc.of κύριος, direct object of Ἑωράκαμεν) 97.

ὁ (nom.sing.masc.of the article, subject of εἶπεν) 9.

δὲ (adversative conjunction) 11.

εἶπεν (3d.per.sing.aor.act.ind.of εἶπον, constative) 155.

αὐτοῖς (dat.pl.masc.of αὐτός indirect object of εἶπεν) 16.

Ἐὰν (conditional particle in a negative third-class condition) 363.

μὴ (qualified negative conjunction with the subjunctive, in a third-class condition) 87.

ἴδω (1st.per.sing.aor.act.subj.of ὁράω, third-class condition) 144.

ἐν (preposition with the locative of place where) 80.

ταῖς (loc.pl.fem.of the article in agreement with χερσὶν) 9.

χερσὶν (loc.sing.fem.of χείρ, place where) 308.

αὐτοῦ (gen.sing.masc.of αὐτός, possession) 16.

τὸν (acc.sing.masc.of the article in agreement with τύπον) 9.

#2917 τύπον (acc.sing.masc.of τύπος, direct object of ἴδω).

ensample - Phil.3:17; 1 Thess.1:7; 2 Thess.3:9; 1 Peter 5:3.
example - 1 Cor.10:6; 1 Timothy 4:12.
fashion - Acts 7:44.
figure - Acts 7:43; Romans 5:14.
form - Romans 6:17.
manner - Acts 23:25.
pattern - Titus 2:7; Heb.8:5.
print - John 20:25,25.

Meaning: A likeness, pattern, example, similar form, etc. Seven clearly different concepts are found: (1). One Christian's life should be an example of how others ought to live - 1 Cor.10:11 (τυπικῶς); Phil.3:17; 1 Thess.1:7; 2 Thess.3:9; 1 Peter 5:3; 1 Timothy 4:12; Titus 2:7. (2) a tragedy occurred to Israel as a warning to Christians that something comparable would happen to the backslidden - 1 Cor.10:6. (3).An architectural pattern; a blueprint - Acts 7:44; Heb.8:5. (3a) -a design of an idol to represent a pagan God - Acts 7:43. (4) Adam is a type of Christ, *i.e.* there are parallel applications of truth that can be drawn from the life of each - Rom.5:14. (5) a certain philosophy is called a type of teaching - Rom.6:17. (6) a written form for a letter - Acts 23:25. (7) the imprint of a nail that leaves a scar of the same shape - John 20:25,25.

τῶν (gen.pl.masc.of the article in agreement with ἥλων) 9.

#2918 ἥλων (gen.pl.masc.of ἥλος, description).

nail - John 20:25,25.

Meaning: a nail - John 20:25,25.

καὶ (adjunctive conjunction joining verbs) 14.

βάλω (1st.per.sing.aor.act.subj.of βάλλω, third-class condition) 299.

τὸν (acc.sing.masc.of the article in agreement with δάκτυλόν) 9.

δάκτυλόν (acc.sing.masc.of δάκτυλος, direct object of βάλω) 1434.

μου (gen.sing.masc.of ἐγώ, possession) 123.

εἰς (preposition with the accusative of extent) 140.

τὸν (acc.sing.masc.of the article in agreement with τύπον) 9.

τύπον (acc.sing.masc.of τύπος, extent) 2917.

τῶν (gen.pl.masc.of the article in agreement with ἥλων) 9.

ἥλων (gen.pl.masc.of ἧλος, description) 2918.

καὶ (adjunctive conjunction joining verbs) 14.

βάλω (1st.per.sing.2d.aor.act.subj.of βάλλω, third-class condition) 299.

μου (gen.sing.masc.of ἐγώ, possession) 123.

τὴν (acc.sing.fem.of the article in agreement with χεῖρα) 9.

χεῖρα (acc.sing.fem.of χείρ, direct object of βάλω) 308.

εἰς (preposition with the accusative of extent) 140.

τὴν (acc.sing.fem.of the article in agreement with πλευρὰν) 9.

πλευρὰν (acc.sing.fem.of πλευρά, extent) 1660.

αὐτοῦ (gen.sing.masc.of αὐτός, possession) 16.

οὐ (summary negative conjunction with the indicative) 130.

μὴ (qualified negative conjunction with οὐ with the indicative, intensive negative) 87.

πιστεύσω (1st.per.sing.fut.act.ind.of πιστεύω, prediction) 734.

Translation - "Therefore the other disciples began to say to him, 'We have seen the Lord!' But he said to them, 'If I do not see in His hands the print of the nails and put my finger into the print of the nails, and put my hand into His side, I will never believe.' "

Comment: Thomas' absence when Jesus first appeared to the ten disciples (vs.19) of course resulted in their great desire to tell him about it as soon as he appeared. The disciples were so excited about it that they began (inceptive imperfect) and continued to tell him, 'We have seen the Lord.' (Note the dramatic perfect). But (adversative δὲ) Thomas was a skeptic, although no more so than the other disciples who also had not believed it until they were treated to the same empirical evidence which Thomas now demanded. His statement in the form of a third-class condition has three subjunctive verbs in the protasis, and an emphatic negative prediction in the apodosis. He demanded to see the nail scars in Jesus' hands, put his finger into the scars and his finger into the side of Jesus. If this could not be done he announced that he would never believe it (οὐ μὴ πιστεύσω).

This is all of the empirical evidence that the most extreme logical positivist should need.

The spike used by the Romans to drive through Jesus' hand was large enough to leave a hole of sufficient diameter to permit a literal implementation of Thomas' plan. Note the use of εἰς, not ἐπί, with the accusative. "Into" not "upon." Thus Thomas delivered his tough minded ultimatum and implied that his colleagues in their tender minded naviete had been gulled. As we shall see when Thomas had the chance he forgot all about his painstaking anatomical research!

(3). Appearance of Jesus After the Resurrection Day

Sixth: To the Eleven Apostles in a House

(John 20:26-31).

John 20:26 - *"And after eight days again his disciples were within and Thomas with them: then came Jesus, the doors being shut and stood in the midst, and said, Peace be unto you."*

Καὶ μεθ᾽ ἡμέρας ὀκτὼ πάλιν ἦσαν ἔσω οἱ μαθηταὶ αὐτοῦ καὶ Θωμᾶς μετ᾽ αὐτῶν. ἔρχεται ὁ Ἰησοῦς τῶν θυρῶν κεκλεισμένων, καὶ ἔστη εἰς τὸ μέσον καὶ εἶπεν, Εἰρήνη ὑμῖν.

Καὶ (continuative conjunction) 14.
μεθ᾽ (preposition with the accusative of time extent) 50.
ἡμέρας (acc.pl.fem.of ἡμέρα, time extent) 135.
ὀκτὼ (numeral) 1886.
πάλιν (adverbial) 355.
ἦσαν (3d.per.pl.imp.ind.of εἰμί, progressive description) 86.
ἔσω (adverb of place) 1601.
οἱ (nom.pl.masc.of the article in agreement with μαθηταὶ) 9.
μαθηταὶ (nom.pl.masc.of μαθητής, subject of ἦσαν) 421.
αὐτοῦ (gen.sing.masc.of αὐτός, relationship) 16.
καὶ (continuative conjunction) 14.
Θωμᾶς (nom.sing.masc.of Θωμᾶς, subject of ἦν understood) 847.
μετ᾽ (preposition with the genitive of accompaniment) 50.
αὐτῶν (gen.pl.masc.of αὐτός, accompaniment) 16.
ἔρχεται (3d.per.sing.pres.ind.of ἔρχομαι, historical) 146.
ὁ (nom.sing.masc.of the article in agreement with Ἰησοῦς) 9.
Ἰησοῦς (nom.sing.masc.of Ἰησοῦς, subject of ἔρχεται) 3.
τῶν (gen.pl.fem.of the article in agreement with θυρῶν) 9.
θυρῶν (gen.pl.fem.of θύρα, genitive absolute) 571.
κεκλεισμένων (perf.pass.part.gen.pl.fem.of κλείω, genitive absolute, adverbial, concessive) 570.
καὶ (adjunctive conjunction joining verbs) 14.
ἔστη (3d.per.sing.2d.aor.act.ind.of ἵστημι, ingressive) 180.
εἰς (preposition with the accusative, original static locative use) 140.
τὸ (acc.sing.neut.of the article in agreement with μέσον) 9.
μέσον (acc.sing.neut.of μέσος, place where, locative static use) 873.
καὶ (adjunctive conjunction joining verbs) 14.
εἶπεν (3d.per.sing.aor.act.ind.of εἶπον, constative) 155.
Εἰρήνη (nom.sing.fem.of εἰρήνη, nominative absolute) 865.
ὑμῖν (dat.pl.masc.of σύ, personal advantage) 104.

Translation - *"And eight days later, His disciples were inside (the house) again and Thomas was with them. Jesus came, although the doors had been shut and took His stand in the midst of them and said, 'Peace be with you.' "*

Comment: Eight days after the resurrection brings us to Monday of the second week. Jesus' disciples, this time with Thomas present, were still secreted behind locked doors, obviously for the same reason as before (John 20:19). Note μετά first with the accusative of time extension and then with the genitive of accompaniment. The genitive absolute construction has a concessive participle. "Although (despite the fact that) the doors had been locked, Jesus came . . . κ.τ.λ." Locked doors, however securely fastened, cannot keep the sovereign resurrected Christ out. They locked the doors against those whom they feared, not against Him Whom they worshipped. He took His stand among them (ingressive aorist in ἔστη) and repeated what He had said eight days before.

The history of the intervening eight days is passed over in silence, except for the implication that the disciples remained in Jerusalem and stayed under cover. Where Jesus went and what He did the text does not reveal.

It is interesting to speculate about how Thomas must have felt when Jesus suddenly appeared in the room. The other disciples, of course, were overjoyed to see Jesus again, but . . . Thomas, the skeptic? Did he reproach himself since his dogmatic statement of verse 25 for his doubts or congratulate himself for his superior mentality that refused to accept what could not be demonstrated? Did he indulge in total despair, since Jesus, His Lord was dead, or did he perhaps develop the "theology of hope" which has become so popular with modernists who do not believe anything anymore but nevertheless console themselves with the "confident despair" which for them is the hallmark of intellectual maturity! Maybe Thomas anticipated these modern skeptics with a view that after all it would all turn out for the best, heaven only knows how!

Verse 27 - *"Then saith he to Thomas, Reach hither thy finger, and behold my hands; and reach hither thy hand, and thrust it into my side: and be not faithless but believing."*

εἶτα λέγει τῷ Θωμᾷ, Φέρε τὸν δάκτυλόν σου ὧδε καὶ ἴδε τὰς χεῖράς μου, καὶ φέρε τὴν χεῖρά σου καὶ βάλε εἰς τὴν πλευράν μου, καὶ μὴ γίνου ἄπιστος ἀλλὰ πιστός.

εἶτα (temporal adverb) 2185.
λέγει (3d.per.sing.pres.act.ind.of λέγω, historical) 66.
τῷ (dat.sing.masc.of the article in agreement with Θωμᾷ) 9.
Θωμᾷ (dat.sing.masc.of Θωμᾶς, indirect object of λέγει) 847.
Φέρε (2d.per.sing.pres.act.impv.of φέρω, command) 683.
τὸν (acc.sing.masc.of the article in agreement with δάκτυλόν) 9.
δάκτυλόν (acc.sing.masc.of δάκτυλος, direct object of Φέρε) 1434.
σου (gen.sing.masc.of σύ, possession) 104.
ὧδε (local adverb) 766.
καὶ (adjunctive conjunction joining verbs) 14.
ἴδε (2d.per.sing.2d.aor.act.impv.of ὁράω, command) 144.

τὰς (acc.pl.fem.of the article in agreement with χεῖράς) 9.

χεῖράς (acc.pl.fem.of χείρ, direct object of ἴδε) 308.

μου (gen.sing.masc.of ἐγώ, possession) 123.

καὶ (adjunctive conjunction joining verbs) 14.

φέρε (2d.per.sing.pres.act.impv.of φέρω, command) 683.

τὴν (acc.sing.fem.of the article in agreement with χεῖρά) 9.

χεῖρά (acc.sing.fem.of χείρ, direct object of φέρε) 308.

σου (gen.sing.masc.of σύ, possession) 104.

καὶ (adjunctive conjunction joining verbs) 14.

βάλε (2d.per.sing.aor.act.impv.of βάλλω, command) 299.

εἰς (preposition with the accusative of extent) 140.

τὴν (acc.sing.fem.of the article in agreement with πλευράν) 9.

πλευράν (acc.sing.fem.of πλευρά, extent) 1660.

μου (gen.sing.masc.of ἐγώ, possession) 123.

καὶ (adjunctive conjunction joining verbs) 14.

μὴ (qualified negative conjunction with the imperative in a prophibition) 87.

γίνου (2d.per.sing.pres.impv.of γίνομαι, prohibition) 113.

ἄπιστος (nom.sing.masc.of ἄπιστος, predicate adjective) 1231.

ἀλλὰ (alternative conjunction) 342.

πιστός (nom.sing.masc.of πιστός, predicate adjective) 1522.

Translation - "*Then He said to Thomas, 'Reach out your finger here and see my hands, and hold out your hand and place it upon my side, and stop being skeptical but believe.'*"

Comment: Note that Jesus' invitation to Thomas does not follow the precise form of Thomas' challenge. Thomas had said καὶ βάλω τὸν δάκτυλόν μου εἰς τὸν τύπον τῶν ἥλων. Jesus suggested that Thomas inspect His palm, but does not suggest the insertion of the finger "into the print." Does this imply that Jesus' hand now had scar tissue? However Jesus did not object to the other experiment which Thomas had suggested. Of course, Thomas did not actually do either of these things. That this was the same body in which Jesus had suffered should be clear from this passage. Note the pun at the end. μὴ ἄπιστος ἀλλὰ πιστός. For the faithless who will believe only upon the basis of sense perception there is hope, since the empirical evidence will some day be available (Rev.1:7). *Cf.* also Zech.14:4; 13:6; Lk.21:27. But unlike Thomas, they will not believe, though they will be forced to admit "that Jesus Christ is Lord to the glory of God the Father" (Phil.2:10-11). He who believes only when he has been shown is not the "babe" to whom God reveals His truth (Mt.11:25-26). The empiricist will congratulate Thomas for his tough-minded objectivity. Jesus did not congratulate him. There is a tone of patronage in Jesus' remark.

Verse 28 - "*And Thomas answered and said unto him, My Lord and my God.*"

ἀπεκρίθη Θωμᾶς καὶ εἶπεν αὐτῷ, Ὁ κύριός μου καὶ ὁ θεός μου.

ἀπεκρίθη (3d.per.sing.aor.mid.ind.of ἀποκρίνομαι, constative) 318.

Θωμᾶς (nom.sing.masc.of Θωμᾶς, subject of ἀπεκρίθη and εἶπεν) 847.

καὶ (adjunctive conjunction joining verbs) 14.
εἶπεν (3d.per.sing.aor.act.ind.of εἶπον, constative) 155.
αὐτῷ (dat.sing.masc.of αὐτός, indirect object of εἶπεν) 16.
Ὁ (nom.sing.masc.of the article in agreement with κύριός) 9.
κύριός (nom.sing.masc.of κύριος, exclamation) 97.
μου (gen.sing.masc.of ἐγώ, relationship) 123.
καὶ (adjunctive conjunction joining nouns) 14.
ὁ (nom.sing.masc.of the article in agreement with θεός) 9.
θεός (nom.sing.masc.of θεός, exclamation) 124.
μου (gen.sing.masc.of ἐγώ, relationship) 123.

Translation - "Thomas said to Him, 'My Lord and my God!'"

Comment: A clear case of pleonasm in ἀπεκρίθη. Robertson argues at length for the conclusion that Ὁ κύριός μου καὶ ὁ θεός μου is vocative, and not exclamatory, and that Thomas is not only recognizing that Jesus is Lord and God, by virtue of the evidence of His resurrection, but that he was also confessing his personal faith in Jesus as his saviour. He cites Rev.6:10, ὁ δεσπότης ὁ ἅγιος καὶ ἀληθινός as vocative. Also ὁ καταλύων (Mt.27:40) and οἱ ἐμπεπλησμένοι νῦν in Luke 6:25. "In Rev.4:11 we have also the vocative case in ὁ κύριος καὶ ὁ θεός. In Jo.20:28 Thomas addresses Jesus as ὁ κύριός μου καὶ ὁ θεός μου, the vocative like those above. Yet, strange to say, Winer calls this exclamation rather than address, apparently to avoid the conclusion that Thomas was satisfied as to the deity of Jesus by his appearance to him after the resurrection. Dr. E.A.Abbott follows suit also in an extended argument to show that κύριε ὁ θεός is the LXX way of addressing God, not ὁ κύριος καὶ ὁ θεός. But after he had written he appends a note to p.95 to the effect that "this is not quite satisfactory. For xiii. 13, φωνεῖτέ με ὁ διδάσκαλον καὶ ὁ κύριος, and Rev.4:11 ἄξιος εἶ, ὁ κύριος καὶ ὁ θεὸς ἡμῶν, ought to have been mentioned above." This is a manly retraction, and he adds: "John may have used it here exceptionally" Leave out "exceptionally" and the conclusion is just. If Thomas used Aramaic he certainly used the article. It is no more exceptional in Jo.20:28 than in Rev.4:11" (E.A.Abbott, *Johannine Grammar*, 93 ff. and Winer-Thayer, 183, as cited in Robertson, *Grammar*, 465, 466).

Verse 29 - "Jesus saith unto him, Thomas, because thou hast seen me, thou hast believed: blessed are they that have not seen, and yet have believed."

λέγει αὐτῷ ὁ Ἰησοῦς, Ὅτι ἑώρακάς με πεπίστευκας; μακάριοι οἱ μὴ ἰδόντες καὶ πιστεύσαντες.

λέγει (3d.per.sing.pres.act.ind.of λέγω, historical) 66.
αὐτῷ (dat.sing.masc.of αὐτός, indirect object of λέγει) 16.
ὁ (nom.sing.masc.of the article in agreement with Ἰησοῦς) 9.
Ἰησοῦς (nom.sing.masc.of Ἰησοῦς, subject of λέγει) 3.
Ὅτι (conjunction introducing a subordinate causal clause) 211.
ἑώρακάς (2d.per.sing.perf.act.ind.of ὁράω, consummative) 144.

με (acc.sing.masc.of ἐγώ, direct object of ἑώρακάς) 123.

πεπίστευκας (2d.per.sing.perf.act.ind.of πιστεύω, intensive) 734.

μακάριοι (nom.pl.masc.of μακάριος, predicate adjective) 422.

οἱ (nom.pl.masc.of the article, subject of ἰδόντες and πιστεύσαντες) 9.

μὴ (qualified negative conjunction with the participle) 87.

ἰδόντες (aor.act.part.nom.pl.masc.of ὁράω, adverbial, concessive) 144.

καὶ (emphatic conjunction) 14.

πιστεύσαντες (aor.act.part.nom.pl.masc.of πιστεύω, substantival, subject of εἰσίν, understood) 734.

Translation - *"Jesus said to him, 'Because you saw me you have come to believe? Those who have believed despite the fact that they have not seen are indeed fortunate.' "*

Comment: Jesus' statement is really a rhetorical question. Was Thomas' faith based upon sensory perception? ἰδόντες is concessive, and καὶ is emphatic. If Thomas was fortunate enough to have the empirical evidence of the resurrection of Jesus available, in order that he could believe, how much more fortunate are those who, although they have not seen (concessive ἰδόντες) have nevertheless believed? They are indeed (emphatic καὶ) fortunate (happy, blessed).

This means that those who have come to Christ in more recent times, and who have never seen Jesus personally are more blessed than the Apostles and other first century Christians. This is supported by 2 Peter 1:15-21. After boasting that he had only reported what he saw (vss.16-18) Peter tells us that we have a "more sure word (vss.19-21). Once the Christian makes his *a priori* commitment to accept the Word of God as infallible authority, he is on surer ground than that provided by eye, ear and finger tip. Our senses can be deceived; so why trust them? But an *a priori* assumption, if it is true, is a solid foundation for a deductive superstructure. So let us stop envying the Apostles. They needed sense perception to give them certitude. Unfortunate creatures! We too will some day see Jesus as they did (Rev.1:7). But physical sight on that great day when He comes again will add nothing to the assurance which we already have. The true regenerate believes *now* that Jesus Christ is alive in the same body in which He suffered, with the same certitude that he will have when we have the experience of Thomas.

John pursues this line of thought in the last two verses of the chapter.

The Purpose of the Book

(John 20:30,31)

John 20:30 - *"And many other signs truly did Jesus in the presence of his disciples, which are not written in this book, . . . "*

Πολλὰ μὲν οὖν καὶ ἄλλα σημεῖα ἐποίησεν ὁ Ἰησοῦς ἐνώπιον τῶν μαθητῶν (αὐτοῦ), ἃ οὐκ ἔστιν γεγραμμένα ἐν τῷ βιβλίῳ τούτῳ,

Πολλὰ (acc.pl.neut.of πολύς, in agreement with σημεῖα) 228.

μὲν (correlative affirmative conjunction, with δὲ) 300.

οὖν (adversative conjunction) 68.

καὶ (adjunctive conjunction) 14.

ἄλλα (acc.pl.neut.of ἄλλος, in agreement with σημεῖα) 198.

σημεῖα (acc.pl.neut.of σημεῖον, direct object of ἐποίησεν) 1005.

ἐποίησεν (3d.per.sing.aor.act.ind.of ποιέω, constative) 127.

ὁ (nom.sing.masc.of the article in agreement with Ἰησοῦς) 9.

Ἰησοῦς (nom.sing.masc.of Ἰησοῦς, subject of ἐποίησεν) 3.

ἐνώπιον (improper preposition with the genitive of place description) 1798.

τῶν (gen.pl.masc.of the article in agreement with μαθητῶν) 9.

μαθητῶν (gen.pl.masc.of μαθητής, place description) 421.

ἃ (nom.pl.neut.of ὅς, subject of γεγραμμένα) 65.

οὐκ (summary negative conjunction with the indicative) 130.

ἔστιν (3d.per.sing.pres.ind.of εἰμί, perfect periphrastic) 86.

γεγραμμένα (perfect pass.part.acc.pl.neut.of γράφω, perfect periphrastic) 156.

ἐν (preposition with the locative of place where) 80.

τῷ (loc.sing.neut.of the article in agreement with βιβλίῳ) 9.

βιβλίῳ (loc.sing.neut.of βιβλίον, place where) 1292.

τούτῳ (loc.sing.neut.of οὗτος, in agreement with βιβλίῳ) 93.

Translation - "*However Jesus in fact performed many other miracles in the presence of His disciples which have not been recorded in this book, . . .* "

Comment: The affirmative particle μὲν here correlates with δὲ in verse 31. I have taken οὖν here as adversative, despite the fact that it is against the advice of my mentor, Dr. Julius R. Mantey, with whom I do not often argue. In his doctoral disseration, *The Meaning of* Οὖν *in John's Writings,* written at the Southern Baptist Theological Seminary, Mantey regards οὖν as intensive and translates it "to be sure." That is good because it does no violence to the context, but I submit that the adversative "however/but" fits the context better and offer the following argument. Thomas had made an unseemly boast about what sort of evidence it would take to convince him that Jesus was alive (vs.25). Eight days later Jesus appeared and offered to Thomas his evidence and implied a rebuke (vs.29a), which He followed with a statement about the superiority of the faith of those who believe without visible evidence (vs.29b). In this spirit, John adds in verse 30, "However (οὖν) despite the fact that Jesus wants disciples who can believe by faith alone, and who do not therefore require the kind of evidence which Thomas demanded, He did condescend to perform some other miracles also (adjunctive καὶ) in the presence of His disciples, but I have not included them in this little book, since the superior believer does not base his faith upon signs but upon the proposition that Jesus of Nazareth is the Messiah, the Son of God." He adds in verse 31 that he did include the hands and feet episode and the broiled fish story — these as a concession to future doubting Thomas's. The perfect periphrastic ἔστιν γεγραμμένα is interesting. ἔστιν is singular to go with the neuter plural subject σημεῖα, which is good Greek, but the participle is accusative plural, in agreement with σημεῖα. Having explained by inference, why he did not parade before us in his gospel record the other signs which Jesus did for His disciples, John then tells us why, since he did not report them all, he should indeed have reported any of them. By the "many other miracles" which Jesus performed in the presence of His disciples, which he has not included in his book, does John mean others that He performed that night in the secret room, as Jesus went to greater lengths than Scripture records to convince His disciples, or to all of the other miracles which Jesus performed in the course of His public ministry?

John had not given us all, for he says with pardonable hyperbole that had he done so, the world would not hold the books (John 21:25), but he did give us some, and he tells us why in

Verse 31 - "But these are written that ye might believe that Jesus is the Christ, the Son of God; and that, believing ye might have life through His name."

ταῦτα δὲ γέγραπται ἵνα πιστεύσητε ὅτι Ἰησοῦς ἐστιν ὁ Χριστὸς ὁ υἱὸς τοῦ θεοῦ, καὶ ἵνα πιστεύοντες ζωὴν ἔχητε ἐν τῷ ὀνόματι αὐτοῦ.

ταῦτα (nom.pl.neut.of οὗτος, subject of γέγραπται) 93.

δὲ (adversative conjunction) 11.

γέγραπται (3d.per.sing.perf.pass.ind.of γράφω, consummative) 156.

ἵνα (conjunction introducing the subjunctive in a sub-final clause) 114.

πιστεύητε (2d.per.pl.pres.act.subj.of πιστεύω, purpose/result) 734.

ὅτι (conjunction introducing an object clause in indirect discourse) 211.

Ἰησοῦς (nom.sing.masc.of Ἰησοῦς, subject of ἐστιν) 3.

ἐστιν (3d.per.sing.pres.ind.of εἰμί, static) 86.

ὁ (nom.sing.masc.of the article in agreement with Χριστὸς) 9.

Χριστὸς (nom.sing.masc.of Χριστός, predicate nominative) 4.

ὁ (nom.sing.masc.of the article in agreement with υἱὸς) 9.

υἱὸς (nom.sing.masc.of υἱός, in apposition with Χριστὸς) 5.

τοῦ (gen.sing.masc.of the article in agreement with θεοῦ) 9.

θεοῦ (gen.sing.masc.of θεός, designation) 124.

καὶ (adjunctive conjunction joining a sub-final and a consecutive clause) 14.

ἵνα (conjunction with the subjunctive in a consecutive clause) 114.

πιστεύοντες (pres.act.part.nom.pl.masc.of πιστεύω, adverbial, modal) 734.

ζωὴν (acc.sing.fem.of ζωή, direct object of ἔχητε) 668.

ἔχητε (2d.per.pl.pres.act.subj.of ἔχω, result) 82.

ἐν (preposition with the instrumental of means) 80.

τῷ (instru.sing.neut.of the article in agreement with ὀνόματι) 9.

ὀνόματι (instru.sing.neut.of ὄνομα, means) 108.

αὐτοῦ (gen.sing.masc.of αὐτός, possession) 16.

Translation - "But these have been written in order (and with the result) that you may believe that Jesus is the Messiah, the Son of God, and with the result that, by believing you will have life by means of His name."

Comment: δὲ completes the μὲν ... δὲ sequence, which began in verse 30. Why did John write his gospel? ἵνα introduces a sub-final and a consecutive clause.

We have called the first subjunctive clause sub-final because where the action of God is involved the only difference between purpose and result is the passage of time. God's purpose is always God's result. Thus both the divine purpose and the inevitable result for the writing of John's gospel was that some would believe. The consecutive clause follows. The result of John's having written his book is that the believers will have life, by means of His name. The participle πιστεύοντες is modal, an idea also expressed by the instrumental in ἐν τῷ ὀνόματι αὐτοῦ. Goodspeed translates the last phrase, "as his followers."

God's purpose is that we believe when we read the Gospel of John. Believe what? This is an important question since Satan has propagated the nonesense that the fact of believing is what saves not the content of what is believed. John leaves no doubt about what we are to believe if we are to have eternal life. The ὅτι clause is the object in indirect discourse. We are to believe that Jesus of Nazareth is the Messiah, the Son of God. This proposition is the sole ground for saving faith. Whatever else we may believe or disbelieve, the *sine qua non* of Christianity is acceptance of the proposition that the historic Jesus of Nazareth is the Messiah of Israel, the ever living fulfillment of God's promise to David (2 Samuel 7:12-14) and of Gabriel's promise to the virgin Mary (Luke 1:30-33). He is also the Son of God, as the apposition phrase appends. Those who roundly damn Jesus with praise that is so faint that one can scarcely hear it, by listing Him with other great philosophers, teachers, humanitarians and public spirited reformers, will never see life until they segregate Jesus from the common herd and elevate Him to the unique position which is His. To say that Jesus was a great philosopher like Plato, or a great mathematician like Bertrand Russell or a great scientist like Charles Darwin, or a great preacher like Charles H. Spurgeon or a great physician like the Brothers Mayo or a great warrior like Napoleon or a great statesman like Winston Churchill or a great saint like St. Francis of Assisi is like saying that Caspar Milquetoast was a great football player like Mean Joe Green of the Pittsburg Steelers! If these blind leaders of blind followers who apparently hope that they can ingratiate themselves with Jesus by lavishing their silly praise upon Him were honest they would not insult Plato by comparing him to Jesus, for Plato would never have said that he was the Son of God. Far from it. If Plato had claimed for himself the status that Jesus claimed for Himself, we would say either that he was the biggest liar in all of Greece or in a more considerate vein that the hot sunshine of the Grecian islands had gotten to him.

Once we are told by John in his gospel who Jesus is, what is the ground for our possession of eternal life? Obviously it is believing what we have been told. Therefore in order to help some wandering empiricist, with an inflated conception of his tough-minded objectivity, who has determined not to be gulled, but rather to demand good solid intellectual grounds for his commitment, John did condescend to include in his little book the story about Jesus, Thomas and the ten, along with the pierced hands, feet and side and the broiled fish. These eleven Galilean peasants, who behaved as though they had taken their doctorates in Education under John Dewey at Columbia University, were finally convinced that Jesus was the Messiah. Oh, the manifold grace of our Soverign God! And yet, John's literary efforts are to no avail, because a consistent logical positivist recognizes that John's story is not real evidence to a 20th century skeptic, because we must accept by faith the proposition that John told the truth. Anyone can write a book and fill it with the record of wondrous deeds, but few people can write a book that tells the truth and only one under the supervision of the Holy Spirit could write a book that told the truth all of the time. Hence, it all finally comes down to whether or not we believe that the New Testament is the inspired Word of God.

Empiricists since the day when Jesus ascended to Heaven (Acts 1:9) are without hope for so long time as they cling to their epistemological system, since He Who is their only hope for salvation is seated at the Father's right hand, there to remain until His enemies have been made His footstool (Psalm 110:1). Then He will return and the empirical evidence will be available, for every eye shall see Him (Rev.1:7) as Thomas and his friends did, but unfortunately it will be too late. Consistent with their view that only by seeing is believing possible, they will see and believe but not to accept Him as Thomas did. Rather they will *admit* that He is Lord, "to the glory of God the Father." (Phil.2:11).

Seventh: To Seven Apostles by the Sea of Galilee
A Miraculous Draught of Fishes

(John 21:1-14)
John 21:1 - "After these things Jesus showed himself again to the disciples at the sea of Tiberius: and on this wise showed he himself."

Μετὰ ταῦτα ἐφανέρωσεν ἑαυτὸν πάλιν ὁ Ἰησοῦς τοῖς μαθηταῖς ἐπὶ τῆς θαλάσσης τῆς Τιβεριάδος. ἐφανέρωσεν δὲ οὕτως.

Μετὰ (preposition with the accusative of time extent) 50.
ταῦτα (acc.pl.neut.of οὗτος, time extent) 93.
ἐφανέρωσεν (3d.per.sing.aor.act.ind.of φανερόω, constative) 1960.
ἑαυτὸν (acc.sing.masc.of ἑαυτός, direct object of ἐφανέρωσεν) 288.
πάλιν (adverbial) 355.
ὁ (nom.sing.masc.of the article in agreement with Ἰησοῦς) 9.
Ἰησοῦς (nom.sing.masc.of Ἰησοῦς, subject of ἐφανέρωσεν) 3.
τοῖς (dat.pl.masc.of the article in agreement with μαθηταῖς) 9.
μαθηταῖς (dat.pl.masc.of μαθητής, indirect object of ἐφανέρωσεν) 421.
ἐπὶ (preposition with the genitive of place description) 47.
τῆς (gen.sing.fem.of the article in agreement with θαλάσσης) 9.
θαλάσσης (gen.sing.fem.of θάλασσα, place description) 374.
τῆς (gen.sing.fem.of the article in agreement with Τιβεριάδος) 9.
Τιβεριάδος (gen.sing.fem.of Τιβέριος, designation) 1929.
ἐφανέρωσεν (3d.per.sing.aor.act.ind.of φανερόω, constative) 1960.
δὲ (explanatory conjunction) 11.
οὕτως (demonstrative adverb) 74.

Translation - "At a later time Jesus again showed Himself to the disciples at the

Seat of Tiberius. Now it happened like this: . . . "

Comment: There is nothing in the text to tell how how long after His resurrection this incident occurred. It was the third time that He appeared to the disciples after His resurrection (vs.14). The preposition does not always mean "upon" in a physical sense, either with the accusative of extent or the genitive of description. The context alone can tell us. Here it means "upon the Sea of Tiberius" in the sense of "upon the sea-shore" or "by the sea." We might use ἐπί with either the accusative or genitive to say that Louisville, Kentucky on "on the Ohio River" but we would not be misunderstood to mean that the city was floating around atop the water. *Cf.*ἐπὶ τῆς ὁδοῦ in Mt.21:19 which means, not that the fig-tree was in the middle of the road, but that it was by the side of the road. *Cf.*Mt.14:25 (ἐπὶ with the accusative) and John 6:19 (ἐπὶ with the genitive), in both of which passages Jesus was walking "upon/atop" the water, not "by the side of" the water. No hard and fast rule can be formulated for the preposition, either with the genitive or accusative, except that it means "upon" in some sense made clear by the context.

Not all of the Twelve were present on this occasion. Five are named and two others are unidentified as we see in

Verse 2 - "There were together Simon Peter, and Thomas called Didymus, and Nathanael of Cana in Galilee, and the sons of Zebedee, and two other of his disciples."

ἦσαν ὁμοῦ Σίμων Πέτρος καὶ Θωμᾶς ὁ λεγόμενος Δίδυμος καὶ Ναθαναὴλ ὁ ἀπὸ Κανὰ τῆς Γαλιλαίας καὶ οἱ τοῦ Ζεβεδαίου καὶ ἄλλοι ἐκ τῶν μαθητῶν αὐτοῦ δύο.

ἦσαν (3d.per.pl.imp.ind.of εἰμί, progressive description) 86.
ὁμοῦ (adverbial) 2015.
Σίμων (nom.sing.masc.of Σίμων, subject of ἦσαν) 386.
Πέτρος (nom.sing.masc.of Πέτρος, in apposition) 387.
καὶ (adjunctive conjunction joining nouns) 14.
Θωμᾶς (nom.sing.masc.of Θωμᾶς, subject of ἦσαν) 847.
ὁ (nom.sing.masc.of the article in agreement with λεγόμενος) 9.
λεγόμενος (pres.pass.part.nom.sing.masc.of λέγω, substantival, in apposition to Θωμᾶς) 66.
Δίδυμος (nom.sing.masc.of Δίδυμος, appellation) 2599.
καὶ (adjunctive conjunction joining nouns) 14.
Ναθαναὴλ (nom.sing.masc.of Ναθαναήλ, subject of ἦσαν) 1966.
ὁ (nom.sing.masc.of the article in apposition) 9.
ἀπὸ (preposition with the ablative of source) 70.
Κανὰ (abl.sing.fem.of Κανά, source) 1968.
τῆς (gen.sing.fem.of the article in agreement with Γαλιλαίας) 9.
Γαλιλαίας (gen.sing.fem.of Γαλιλαία, description) 241.
καὶ (adjunctive conjunction joining nouns) 14.
οἱ (nom.pl.masc.of the article, in agreement with υἱοί, understood) 9.

τοῦ (gen.sing.masc.of the article in agreement with Ζεβεδαίου) 9.
Ζεβεδαίου (gen.sing.masc.of Ζεβεδαῖος, relationship) 398.
καὶ (adjunctive conjunction joining substantives) 14.
ἄλλοι (nom.pl.masc.of ἄλλος,subject of ἦσαν) 198.
ἐκ (preposition with the partitive genitive) 19.
τῶν (gen.pl.masc.of the article in agreement with μαθητῶν) 9.
μαθητῶν (gen.pl.masc.of μαθητής, partitive genitive) 421.
αὐτοῦ (gen.sing.masc.of αὐτός, relationship) 16.
δύο (numeral) 385.

Translation - *"Simon Peter and Thomas, nicknamed 'Twin' and Nathanael, from Cana of Galilee and the sons of Zebedee and two other of His disciples were all together."*

Comment: Seven men in all. Simon Peter, James and John were fishermen by trade before Jesus called them. Some scholars believe Nathanael to be the same man as Bartholomew (#846). Thomas, the empiricist was in the group. The other two were not named, although they are said to be two of Jesus' disciples.

Verse 3 - *"Simon Peter saith unto them, I go a fishing. They say unto him, We also go with thee. They went forth and entered into a ship immediately: and that night they caught nothing."*

λέγει αὐτοῖς Σίμων Πέτρος, Ὑπάγω ἁλιεύειν. λέγουσιν αὐτῷ, Ἐρχόμεθα καὶ ἡμεῖς σὺν σοί. ἐξῆλθον καὶ ἐνέβησαν εἰς τὸ πλοῖον, καὶ ἐν ἐκείνῃ τῇ νυκτὶ ἐπίασαν οὐδέν.

λέγει (3d.per.sing.pres.act.ind.of λέγω, historical) 66.
αὐτοῖς (dat.pl.masc.of αὐτός, indirect object of λέγει) 16.
Σίμων (nom.sing.masc.of Σίμων, subject of λέγει and Ὑπάγω) 386.
Πέτρος (nom.sing.masc.of Πέτρος, in apposition) 387.
Ὑπάγω (1st.per.sing.pres.act.ind.of ὑπάγω, futuristic) 364.

#2919 ἁλιεύειν (pres.act.inf.of ἁλιεύω, dative, purpose).

go a fishing - John 21:3.

Meaning: Cf.ἁλιεύς (#390). To fish. With reference to the disciples after the resurrection - John 21:3.

λέγουσιν (3d.per.pl.pres.act.ind.of λέγω, historical) 66.
αὐτῷ (dat.sing.masc.of αὐτός, indirect object of λέγουσιν) 16.
Ἐρχόμεθα (1st.per.pl.pres.mid.ind.of ἔρχομαι, futuristic) 146.
καὶ (adjunctive conjunction joining pronouns) 14.
ἡμεῖς (nom.pl.masc.of ἐγώ, subject of Ἐρχόμεθα) 123.
σὺν (preposition with the instrumental of accompaniment) 1542.
σοί (instru.sing.masc.of σύ, accompaniment) 104.
ἐξῆλθον (3d.per.pl.aor.mid.ind.of ἐξέρχομαι, ingressive) 161.
καὶ (adjunctive conjunction joining verbs) 14.

ἐνέβησαν (3d.per.pl.aor.act.ind.of ἐμβαίνω, constative) 750.
εἰς (preposition with the accusative of extent) 140.
τό (acc.sing.neut.of the article in agreement with πλοῖον) 9.
πλοῖον (acc.sing.neut.of πλοῖον, extent) 400.
καὶ (adversative conjunction) 14.
ἐν (preposition with the locative of time point) 80.
ἐκείνῃ (loc.sing.fem.of ἐκεῖνος, in agreement with νυκτὶ) 246.
τῇ (loc.sing.fem.of the article in agreement with νυκτὶ) 9.
μυκτὶ (loc.sing.fem.of νύξ, time point) 209.
ἐπίασεν (3d.per.pl.aor.act.ind.of πιάζω, constative) 2371.
οὐδέν (acc.sing.neut.of οὐδείς, direct object of ἐπίασεν) 446.

Translation - *"Simon Peter said to them, 'I am going fishing.' They said to him, 'We also are coming with you.' They started out and got into the boat, but they caught nothing that night."*

Comment: John is using historical presents again in λέγει and λέγουσιν, and futuristic presents in Ὑπάγω and Ἐρχόμεθα. There are many futuristic presents in the New Testament, *e.g.* John 14:2 - πορεύομαι. The complementary infinitive of purpose ἁλιεύειν is in the dative case. The locative case occurs with ἐν and the articular infinitive as in ἐν τῷ εὐλογεῖν (Luke 24:51), "but with the dative it is different. There is no instance of the dative infinitive with a preposition, but the original dative is clear in all examples of purpose without τοῦ or a preposition." (Robertson, *Grammar*, 1062). *e.g.* we have Mt.5:17 - οὐκ ἦλθον καταλῦσαι, ἀλλὰ πληρῶσαι - "(I came not for destroying, but for fulfilling.") Also Luke 12:58, δὸς ἐργασίαν ἀπηλλάχθαι, "give diligence for being reconciled." With Mt.7:11; 16:3 οἶδα and γινώσκω occurs. But in Mt.2:2, ἤλθομεν προσκυνῆσαι - "we came for worshipping." So here in John 21:3, Ὑπάγω ἁλιεύειν - "I will go for (the purpose of) fishing." They other six disciples announced their intention to go along, although only James and John had had professional experience. "On that night" not "during the night" which would have been expressed by the accusative of time extent, "they caught nothing."

They should not have gone fishing. Did Peter mean that even though he was now convinced that Jesus was alive, nevertheless he saw his Messianic hopes dashed, and therefore that there was nothing in his own future professionally except to return to his former occupation? And does the ready acquiescence of the other six indicate a similar sad resignation on their part? The answers to these questions can only be inferred in ways that come out in the story. Certainly there is nothing sinful about a fishing trip, even for an Apostle of Jesus Christ, unless he intends to make it a way of life. There is a possibility that the disciples were in need of money. There is no record that any of them had been employed since the crucifixion. We saw them last in a secret room in Jerusalem, eight days after the resurrection. Perhaps they felt a little safer from persecution in Galilee than in Judea. One thing is certain. They had forgotten how to fish.

Verse 4 - *"But when the morning was now come, Jesus stood on the shore: but the disciples knew not that it was Jesus."*

πρωτας δὲ ἤδη γενομένης ἐστη Ἰησοῦς εἰς τὸν αἰγιαλόν, οὐ μέντοι ᾔδεισαν οἱ μαθηταὶ ὅτι Ἰησοῦς ἐστιν.

πρωτας (gen.sing.fem.of πρωῖος, gen. absolute) 1615.

δὲ (explanatory conjunction) 11.

ἤδη (temporal adverb) 291.

γινομένης (pres.mid.part.gen.sing.fem.of γίνομαι, genitive absolute, adverbial, temporal) 113.

ἐστη (3d.per.sing.2d.aor.act.ind.of ἵστημι, constative) 180.

Ἰησοῦς (nom.sing.masc.of Ἰησοῦς, subject of ἐστη) 3.

εἰς (preposition with the accusative, original static use, like a locative) 140.

τὸν (acc.sing.masc.of the article in agreement with αἰγιαλόν) 9.

αἰγιαλόν (acc.sing.masc.of αἰγιαλός, place where) 1026.

οὐ (summary negative conjunction with the indicative) 130.

μέντοι (adversative particle) 2013.

ᾔδεισαν (3d.per.pl.pluperfect ind.of οἶδα, intensive) 144.

οἱ (nom.pl.masc.of the article in agreement with μαθηταὶ) 9.

μαθηταὶ (nom.pl.masc.of μαθητής, subject of ᾔδεισαν) 421.

ὅτι (conjunction introducing an object clause in indirect discourse) 211.

Ἰησοῦς (nom.sing.masc.of Ἰησοῦς, subject of ἐστιν) 3.

ἐστιν (3d.per.sing.pres.ind.of εἰμί, aoristic, indirect discourse) 86.

Translation - "Now soon after daylight Jesus took His place upon the beach, but the disciples had not been aware that it was Jesus."

Comment: The participle in the genitive absolute construction is aorist and indicates that the dawning of a new day was antecedent to the action of the verb ἐστη. The Westcott/Hort reading γινομένης accounts for Goodspeed's translation, ". . . but just as dawn was breaking." Since it is aorist it is supported, albeit pleonastically by ἤδη. Jesus, of course knew that they had been out on the lake all night and that they had caught no fish. One need not be the Son of God to imagine the mood of the impulsive Big Fisherman, who was all too easily subject to fits of petulance. Our Lord appeared to teach them a valuable lesson. Intent upon the frustrations of repeated and always futile castings of the nets, the disciples had no idea who the stranger was. Peter may have asked, "Who is it?" to which the others replied, "We do not know." The indirect discourse would indicate that if they had known they would have said, "It is Jesus." It is a dramatic picture. Here we have seven tired, sleepy, hungry, disappointed, frustrated and disgusted men, who have cast the nets again and again throughout a long night, and they have not one single fish to reward their efforts. There may have been a lingering subliminal accusation in their minds that they had no business to be out there on the lake in the first place in view of their commission (John 20:21). Now they see the stranger! "Who is it?" "Who cares?"

Verse 5 - "Then Jesus saith unto them, Children, have ye any meat? They answered him, No."

λέγει οὖν αὐτοῖς (ὁ)'Ιησοῦς, Παιδία, μή τι προσφάγιον ἔχετε; ἀπεκρίθησαν αὐτῷ, Οὔ.

λέγει (3d.per.sing.pres.act.ind.of λέγω, historical) 66.
οὖν (continuative conjunction) 68.
αὐτοῖς (dat.pl.masc.of αὐτός, indirect object of λέγει) 16.
(ὁ) (nom.sing.masc.of the article in agreement with 'Ιησοῦς) 9.
'Ιησοῦς (nom.sing.masc.of 'Ιησοῦς, subject of λέγει) 3.
Παιδία (voc.pl.neut.of παιδίον, address) 174.
μή (qualified negative conjunction in direct question, expecting a negative reply) 87.
τι (acc.sing.neut.of τις, in agreement with προσφάγιον) 486.

#2920 προσφάγιον (acc.sing.neut.of προσφάγιον, direct object of ἔχετε) .

meat - John 21:5.

Meaning: A combination of πρός (#197), which, in composition adds the idea of "besides" to the concept and φάγω (#610). Hence, something *extra* to eat - John 21:5.

ἔχετε (2d.per.pl.pres.act.ind.of ἔχω, direct question) 82.
ἀπεκρίθησαν (3d.per.pl.aor.mid.ind.of ἀποκρίνομαι, constative) 318.
αὐτῷ (dat.sing.masc.of αὐτός, indirect object of ἀπεκρίθησαν) 16.
Οὔ (summary negative conjunction, with the indicative understood) 130.

Translation - "Then Jesus said to them, 'Little boys, you do not have anything extra to eat, do you?' They answered Him, 'No!' "

Comment: *Cf.*#174 for the meaning of παιδίον. The divine sarcasm is delightful! Here were seven grown men, divinely selected by the sovereign Creator of the universe to proclaim to all the world that Jesus died for the sins of the world and rose again. Their risen Lord finds them out on the lake in a boat with nothing to show for a long night of fishing except frustration. Jesus calls them "Little boys" - less than seven years old - according to Hypocrates, still with their baby teeth! When grown men, who become too interested in fishing, (unless they are called of God to fish for a living), indulge their hobby in excess, it is well to remember Jesus' epithet! His question has μή with the indicative. It is rhetorical which assumes as untrue what is asked and therefore expects a negative reply. And that is what Jesus got - a laconic "No." *Cf.*#2920 and our comments about πρός in composition. It is possible that Jesus meant, "You did not take a lunch with you, did you?" or He may have meant, "You do not have anything to eat beside what you catch, do you?" or perhaps simply, "You haven't caught any fish have you?" Jesus was teasing them, since experienced fishermen like Peter, James and John would disdain the suggestion that they should take a lunch in the event that they caught no fish. Wives sometimes tease their husbands, when they go fishing by asking if they should put a skillet on the stove? It seems that this is the sense of Jesus' innocent (!) question. If so, it reveals His skillful use of gentle sarcasm to teach a deep spiritual lesson. Because, as we shall see, though Peter had nothing to eat (verse 3), Jesus did (verse 9).

Verse 6 - "And he said unto them, Cast the net on the right side of the ship, and ye shall find. They cast therefore, and now they were not able to draw it for the multitude of fishes."

ὁ δὲ εἶπεν αὐτοῖς, Βάλετε εἰς τὰ δεξιὰ μέρη τοῦ πλοίου τὸ δίκτυον, καὶ εὑρήσετε. ἔβαλον οὖν, καὶ οὐκέτι αὐτὸ ἑλκύσαι ἴσχυον ἀπὸ τοῦ πλήθους τῶν ἰχθύων.

ὁ (nom.sing.masc.of the article, subject of εἶπεν) 9.
δὲ (continuative conjunction) 11.
εἶπεν (3d.per.sing.aor.act.ind.of εἶπον, constative) 155.
αὐτοῖς (dat.pl.masc.of αὐτός, indirect object of εἶπεν) 16.
Βάλετε (2d.per.pl.aor.act.impv.of βάλλω, command) 299.
εἰς (preposition with the accusative of extent) 140.
τὰ (acc.pl.neut.of the article in agreement with δεξιὰ) 9.
δεξιὰ (acc.pl.neut.of δεξιός, in agreement with μέρη) 502.
μέρη (acc.pl.neut.of μέρος, extent) 240.
τοῦ (gen.sing.neut.of the article in agreement with πλοίου) 9.
πλοίου (gen.sing.neut.of πλοῖον, description) 400.
τὸ (acc.sing.neut.of the article in agreement with δίκτυον) 9.
δίκτυον (acc.sing.neut.of δίκτυον, direct object of Βάλετε) 393.
καὶ (continuative conjunction) 14.
εὑρήσετε (2d.per.pl.fut.act.ind.of εὑρίσκω, predictive) 79.
ἔβαλον (3d.per.pl.aor.act.ind.of βάλλω, ingressive) 299.
οὖν (inferential conjunction) 68.
καὶ (adjunctive conjunction joining verbs) 14.
οὐκέτι (temporal adverb of denial) 1289.
αὐτὸ (acc.sing.neut.of αὐτός, direct object of ἑλκύσαι) 16.
ἑλκύσαι (aor.act.inf.of ἑλκύω, epexegetical) 2289.
ἴσχυον (3d.per.pl.imp.ind.of ἰσχύω, progressive description) 447.
ἀπὸ (preposition with the ablative of cause) 70.
τοῦ (abl.sing.masc.of the article in agreement with πλήθους) 9.
πλήθους (abl.sing.masc.of πλῆθύς, cause) 1792.
τῶν (gen.pl.masc.of the article in agreement with ἰχθύων) 9.
ἰχθύων (gen.pl.masc.of ἰχθύς, description) 657.

Translation - "And He said to them, 'Cast the net at the right side of the ship and you will catch some. So they cast and they could not draw it in because of the vast number of fish."

Comment: Note again the idiomatic plural in δεξιὰ (#502). οὖν obviously is inferential as the disciples obey the command of the stranger on the shore. Now comes an extended effort on the part of seven men to pull the net back into the ship - extended as the imperfect tense in ἴσχυον indicates. They struggled and struggled, sweating, panting, grunting, their efforts punctuated by shouts of jubilation and amazement. The imperfect is the "moving-picture show" tense (Robertson, *Grammar*, 883). All one needs to do is to use a little imagination.

Jesus had once said to Peter, "from now on you are going to catch men" (Luke 5:10), on a similar occasion after Peter had toiled at the nets all night for nothing, but who, upon Jesus' suggestion had let down the net one more time. That time he caught so many fish that the net was broken and another ship which came to their rescue was filled also. Both ships were swamped by the weight of the cargo. Peter reacted to that miracle with a confession that he was too sinful for Jesus and a suggestion that Jesus have no more to do with him. But he was told that from that moment on he was to fish for men (Mt.4:19), not fish. Now, three years and a great deal of experience later - experience that should have brought Peter to the point where he knew better, he seems to have forgotten his commission. He was about to learn a new lesson. It was only with Jesus' help that Peter could fish. Peter is an example of a good fisherman who, despite his expertise, could not fish as well as Jesus. That was true three years before (Luke 5:5,6) and it was still true three years later (John 21:3-6). When Peter fished by himself there was no profit. His input was great. His production was zero. All night long, casting and drawing the net again and again - nothing. But when he fished at Jesus' direction he was unable to draw the fish into the boat.

But Peter's inability to draw the fish is no problem. It is not his job to draw them. Only God can land the fish (John 6:44; 12:31). Both the Father (John 6:44) and the Son land the fish (John 12:31). Note that these verses use the same verb, ἑλκύω, used here in John 21:6. It was Peter's job to net them, not land them.

Neither Peter nor any other fisherman can draw the fish. Let the crowd psychologists, who by some unfortunate quirk of public relations have been miscalled "evangelists" take notice! The press often speaks of the "drawing power" of some noted evangelists. To be sure they draw great crowds to their meetings, but only God can draw men to Christ. Biblical evangelists are witnesses, not drawers. They are to tell what the Bible says about Christ. God will do whatever drawing is consistent with His eternal purpose.

The ablative of cause with ἀπό is a subtle application of the basic idea of the ablative which is source. The source (cause) of the disciples' inability to draw the net to the ship was τοῦ πλήθους τῶν ἰχθύων. There were 153 of them and John is careful to point out that they were all "keepers." How much did the lot weigh? Keep in mind that seven men could not pull them in. If they averaged three pounds the total weight, counting the nets approached 500 pounds.

Just as Jesus' act of blessing, breaking and serving bread had opened the eyes of the Emmaus disciples, as they remembered that Jesus had done the same thing on a previous occasion (Luke 24:30; Matthew 14:19), so now His fishing directive with its fantastic results reminded John of the previous similar episode (Luke 5:4-8), and thus he recognized the Stranger on the beach, in

Verse 7 - "Therefore that disciples whom Jesus loved saith unto Peter, It is the Lord. Now when Simon Peter heard that it was the Lord, he girt his fisher's coat

unto him, (for he was naked) and did cast himself into the sea."

λέγει οὖν ὁ μαθητὴς ἐκεῖνος ὃν ἠγάπα ὁ Ἰησοῦς τῷ Πέτρῳ, Ὁ κύριός ἐστιν.
Σίμων οὖν Πέτρος, ἀκούσας ὅτι ὁ κύριός ἐστιν, τὸν ἐπενδύτην διεζώσατο, ἦν
γὰρ γυμνός, καὶ ἔβαλεν ἑαυτὸν εἰς τὴν θάλασσαν.

λέγει (3d.per.sing.pres.act.ind.of λέγω, historical) 66.

οὖν (inferential conjunction) 68.

ὁ (nom.sing.masc.of the article in agreement with μαθητὴς) 9.

μαθητὴς (nom.sing.masc.of μαθητής, subject of λέγει) 421.

ἐκεῖνος (nom.sing.masc.of ἐκεῖνος, in agreement with μαθητὴς) 246.

ὃν (acc.sing.masc.of ὅς, direct object of ἠγάπα) 65.

ἠγάπα (3d.per.sing.imp.act.ind.of ἀγαπάω, progressive description) 540.

ὁ (nom.sing.masc.of the article in agreement with Ἰησοῦς) 9.

Ἰησοῦς (nom.sing.masc.of Ἰησοῦς, subject of ἠγάπα) 3.

τῷ (dat.sing.masc.of the article in agreement with Πέτρῳ) 9.

Πέτρῳ (dat.sing.masc.of Πέτρος, indirect object of λέγει) 387.

Ὁ (nom.sing.masc.of the article in agreement with κύριός) 9.

κύριός (nom.sing.masc.of κύριος, predicate nominative) 97.

ἐστιν (3d.per.sing.pres.ind.of εἰμί, aoristic, direct discourse) 86.

Σίμων (nom.sing.masc.of Σίμων, subject of διεζώσατο and ἔβαλεν) 386.

οὖν (inferential conjunction) 68.

Πέτρος (nom.sing.masc.of Πέτρος, in apposition) 387.

ἀκούσας (aor.act.part.nom.sing.masc.of ἀκούω, adverbial, temporal/causal) 148.

ὅτι (conjunction introducing an object clause in indirect discourse) 211.

ὁ (nom.sing.masc.of the article in agreement with κύριός) 9.

κύριός (nom.sing.masc.of κύριος, predicate nominative) 97.

ἐστιν (3d.per.sing.pres.ind.of εἰμί, aoristic, indirect discourse) 86.

τὸν (acc.sing.masc.of the article in agreement with ἐπενδύτην) 9.

#2921 ἐπενδύτην (acc.sing.masc.of ἐπενδύτης, direct object of διεζώσατο).

fishers' coat - John 21:7.

Meaning: Cf. ἐπενδύομαι (#4306). An upper garment, from ἐπί (#47) and ἐνδύω - "to clothe." Thayer adds, "where it seems to denote a kind of linen blouse or frock, which fishermen used to wear at their work." - John 21:7. Liddell and Scott say, a "robe of garment worn over another." If this is true, Peter was improperly dressed, since without the garment he was naked.

διεζώσατο (3d.per.sing.aor.mid.ind.of διαζώννυμι, constative) 2759.

ἦν (3d.per.sing.imp.ind.of εἰμί, progressive description) 86.

γὰρ (causal conjunction) 105.

γυμνός (nom.sing.masc.of γυμνός, predicate adjective) 1548.

καὶ (adjunctive conjunction joining verbs) 14.

ἔβαλεν (3d.per.sing.aor.act.ind.of βάλλω, constative) 299.

ἑαυτὸν (acc.sing.masc.of ἑαυτοῦ, direct object of ἔβαλεν) 288.

εἰς (preposition with the accusative of extent) 140.
τὴν (acc.sing.fem.of the article in agreement with θάλασσαν) 9.
θάλασσαν (acc.sing.fem.of θάλασσα, extent) 374.

*Translation - "So that disciple whom Jesus loved said to Peter, 'It is the Lord.'
Therefore when Simon Peter heard that it was the Lord, he wrapped his blouse
around him, for he was unclothed, and dived into the sea."*

Comment: Apparently Peter was so delighted with the catch, or so afraid that
the fish would get away, that he did not make the thought connection that
occurred to John. He had to be told that the Stranger on the beach was Jesus.
Both uses of οὖν then are inferential, since John's recognition of Jesus was the
result of the miraculous catch. That the second οὖν is also inferential is clear
from the causal adverbial participle ἀκούσας. Note the indirect discourse with
ὅτι following the direct discourse in the same terms. Once aware of the identity
of Jesus, however, Peter could not wait to get to shore. He did pause to put on his
blouse. *Cf.*#1548. Peter was naked, physically and spiritually. Jesus knew where
he was, what he was doing, and all about his discouragement, which of course,
was the result of his materialistic point of view. Why should a divinely appointed
"fisher of men" care whether or not he caught any fish? *Cf.* γυμνός in Heb.4:13;
Rev.3:17; 16:15. It is well for all Christians to realize that we can hide nothing
from the resurrected Christ. Those who recognize now that we are naked
(Heb.4:13) may not be naked (Rev.3:17) but have the blessing of being clothed
(Rev.16:15) at His appearing. Compare Peter's behavior on this occasion with
the way he reacted on the former occasion (Luke 5:6-9).
     It must be said to the credit of the Big Fisherman that as soon as he recognized
Jesus, he forgot all about the fish. One minute he was struggling with might and
main, along with six other men to prevent the loss of one of the two biggest
catches he had ever made. The next moment he forgot about the fish. What
mattered it about the fish, now that Jesus was there? Peter's act of diving into the
water and swimming to shore is the evidence that he had just had an axiological
revival. Often Christians get their sense of values out of line. How many repent
as quickly as Peter did?

*Verse 8 - "And the other disciples came in a little ship; (for they were not far from
land, but as it were two hundred cubits,) dragging the nets with fishes."*

οἱ δὲ ἄλλοι μαθηταὶ τῷ πλοιαρίῳ ἦλθον, οὐ γὰρ ἦσαν μακρὰν ἀπὸ τῆς γῆς
ἀλλὰ ὡς ἀπὸ πηχῶν διακοσίων, σύροντες τὸ δίκτυον τῶν ἰχθύων.

οἱ (nom.pl.masc.of the article in agreement with μαθηταὶ) 9.
δὲ (adversative conjunction) 11.
ἄλλοι (nom.pl.masc.of ἄλλος, in agreement with μαθηταὶ) 198.
μαθηταὶ (nom.pl.masc.of μαθητής, subject of ἦλθον and ἦσαν) 421.
τῷ (instru.sing.neut.of the article in agreement with πλοιαρίῳ) 9.
πλοιαρίῳ (instru.sing.neut.of πλοιαρίῳ, means) 2112.
ἦλθον (3d.per.pl.aor.act.ind.of ἔρχομαι, constative) 146.

οὐ (summary negative conjunction with the indicative) 130.
γάρ (causal conjunction) 105.
ἦσαν (3d.per.pl.imp.ind.of εἰμί, progressive description) 86.
μακρὰν (local adverb) 768.
ἀπό (preposition with the ablative of separation) 70.
τῆς (abl.sing.fem.of the article in agreement with γῆς) 9.
γῆς (abl.sing.fem.of γῆ, separation) 157.
ἀλλά (emphatic conjunction) 342.
ὡς (comparative particle) 128.
ἀπό (preposition with the ablative of comparison) 70.
πηχῶν (abl.pl.masc.of πῆχυς, comparison) 623.
διακοσίων (abl.pl.masc.of διακόσιοι, in agreement with πηχῶν) 2265.

#2922 σύροντες (pres.act.part.nom.pl.masc.of σύτω, adverbial, circumstantial).

drag - John 21:8.
draw - Acts 14:19; 17:6; Rev.12:4.
hale - Acts 8:3.

Meaning: Cf.κατασύρω (#2496). To drag. Physically - a net full of fish - John 21:8; the unconscious body of Paul - Acts 14:19; to conduct forcibly as with a subpoena and police power - Acts 8:3; 17:6. In a metaphorical sense, probably with seduction or undue influence - Rev.12:4.

τό (acc.sing.neut.of the article in agreement with δίκτυον) 9.
δίκτυον (acc.sing.neut.of δίκτυον, direct object of σύροντες) 393.
τῶν (gen.pl.masc.of the article in agreement with ἰχθύων) 9.
ἰχθύων (gen.pl.masc.of ἰχθύς, description) 657.

Translation - "But the other disciples came in the little boat, for they were not far from the shore, in fact only about three hundred feet, dragging the net full of fish."

Comment: δέ is adversative. The other disciples did not emulate Peter in his headlong, precipitous and unorthodox approach to the problem. τῷ πλοιαρίῳ can be either locative - "in the little boat" or instrumental - "by the little boat." Robertson thinks that "we have a pure locative" (Robertson, *Grammar*, 521), but concedes that "it may be either locative or instrumental" (*Ibid.,* 533). In fact it is both locative and instrumental. To say that they came "by ship" meaning that they used a naval mode of transportation, is also to say that they came "in a ship" in the locative sense.

ἀλλά is confirmatory, intensive or emphatic, not adversative or alternative. The idiom ὡς ἀπό occurs also in John 11:18, while in Rev.14:20 we have ἀπό with the ablative of separation, though without ὡς the comparative particle. The participle σύροντες is circumstantial. John had said in verse 3 that they had boarded a ship (πλοῖον) while now he calls it a little ship (πλοιάριον). That πλοιάριον is also πλοῖον is obvious, but it may suggest that John has not told us the entire story. Did they travel to the fishing site in a larger vessel and then transfer to a smaller craft which would allow them to come closer to the shore? From where on the Sea of Tiberius did the disciples come? How far was it to the site of our story? The text does not tell us. Could a ship (πλοῖον) be brought to a point only one hundred yards from the shore? That would depend upon how much larger a πλοῖον is than a πλοιάριον. Again the text does not tell us. The disciples, three of whom at least were experienced fishermen, may have tried both deep water fishing from a ship (πλοῖον) earlier in the evening and then, later moved to a smaller craft which would allow them to fish nearer the shore. All fishermen know that the secret of success lies in finding the fish as well as catching them.

Verse 9 - "As soon then as they were come to land, they saw a fire of coals there, and fish laid thereon, and bread."

ὡς οὖν ἀπέβησαν εἰς τὴν γῆν βλέπουσιν ἀνθρακιὰν κειμένην καὶ ὀψάριον ἐπικείμενον καὶ ἄρτον.

ὡς (particle introducing a temporal clause, contemporaneous time) 128.
οὖν (continuative conjunction) 68.
ἀπέβησαν (3d.per.pl.aor.act.ind.of ἀποβαίνω, culminative) 2042.
εἰς (preposition with the accusative of extent) 140.
τὴν (acc.sing.fem.of the article in agreement with γῆν) 9.
γῆν (acc.sing.fem.of γῆ, extent) 157.
βλέπουσιν (3d.per.pl.pres.act.ind.of βλέπω, historical) 499.
ἀνθρακιὰν (acc.sing.fem.of ἀνθρακιά, direct object of βλέπουσιν) 2820.
κειμένην (pres.pass.part.acc.sing.fem.of κεῖμαι, adjectival, restrictive, in agreement with ἀνθρακιὰν) 295.
καὶ (adjunctive conjunction joining nouns) 14.
ὀψάριον (acc.sing.neut.of ὀψάριον, direct object of βλέπουσιν) 2277.
ἐπικείμενον (pres.pass.part.acc.sing.neut.of ἐπίκειμαι, adjectival, restrictive, in agreement with ὀψάριον) 2040.
καὶ (adjunctive conjunction joining nouns) 14.
ἄρτον (acc.sing.masc.of ἄρτος, direct object of βλέπουσιν) 338.

Translation - "Then when they had arrived at the shore they saw a bed of burning coals and a small fish lying upon it and some bread."

Comment: The aorist ἀπέβησαν is culminative, *i.e.* the emphasis is upon the result of the completed action. In English we would use the pluperfect - "When they had arrived at the shore."

The irony of the situation is beautiful. Jesus had told them on resurrection evening that He was going to send them out to represent Him in the same way that the Father had sent Him. Then He bestowed upon them the Holy Spirit in conformity with His promise (John 14:17; 20:21-23), so that they would never be without at least one personality of the Godhead. Despite all of this, Peter was so concerned about material values, or perhaps bored with forced inactivity that he went fishing. But all his efforts availed nothing until Jesus, Who had a right to ask him what business he had out there anyway, told him how to fish. Here is a carpenter telling a professional Izaak Walton how to fish! Was Peter perspicacious enough to sense the irony in all of this and feel the barb of the divine rebuke? Then when he and his friends got to shore they found that Jesus had more food on the fire than Peter would have had if Jesus had not come to his rescue. "Seek ye first . . . κ.τ.λ." (Matthew 6:33).

The experience of the disciples illustrates the difference between the life of the believer in whom the Holy Spirit is resident and that of the believer in whom He is regnant. Peter and his friends took the Holy Spirit with them when they went fishing, because the indwelling Holy Spirit goes where the believer goes whether He wants to or not (1 Cor.6:19,20). But when the indwelling Holy Spirit also fills the believer, as He did the Christians at Pentecost, they forget all about fishing, unless of course that is the service to which the Lord has appointed them. We do not hear that Peter ever again wasted any time fishing after Pentecost, unless there was some special reason why God in His wisdom directed it. This is not to say that it is a sin for a Spirit filled Christian to fish, but it is to suggest that it is a sin for an Apostle of Jesus Christ to spend his time with a fishing rod in his hands.

Verse 10 - "Jesus saith unto them, Bring of the fish which ye have now caught."

λέγει αὐτοῖς ὁ Ἰησοῦς, Ἐνέγκατε ἀπὸ τῶν ὀφαρίων ὧν ἐπιάσατε νῦν.

λέγει (3d.per.sing.pres.act.ind.of λέγω,historical) 66.
αὐτοῖς (dat.pl.masc.of αὐτός, indirect object of λέγει) 16.
ὁ (nom.sing.masc.of the article in agreement wit Ἰησοῦς) 9.
Ἰησοῦς (nom.sing.masc.of Ἰησοῦς, subject of λέγει) 3.
Ἐνέγκατε (2d.per.pl.aor.act.impv.of φέρω, command) 683.
ἀπὸ (preposition with the ablative of source) 70.
τῶν (abl.pl.neut.of the article in agreement with ὀφαρίων) 9.
ὀφαρίων (abl.pl.neut.of ὀφάριον, source) 2277.
ὧν (abl.pl.neut.of ὅς, case attraction to ὀφαρίων) 65.
ἐπιάσατε (2d.per.pl.aor.act.ind.of πιάζω, culminative) 2371.
νῦν (temporal adverbial) 1497.

Translation - "Jeses said to them, 'Bring some of the little fish which you have just caught.' "

Comment: Jesus is giving the disciples the credit for the catch. Could there have been a mischevious grin on His face? Note also that He called them "little fish" (ὀφάριον). When John described them he called them ἰχθύων μεγάλων - "big fish." Note too that Jesus did not suggest that they bring all 153 of them. The temporal adverb νῦν supports the culminative aorist in ἐπιάσατε. They were "little fish" when compared in importance to the sinners that the disciples would later "catch" for Christ (Luke 5:10). Peter had begun to have a little of the grace of humility. He obeyed. It is a wonder that he did not start arguing with Jesus.

Verse 11 - "Simon Peter went up, and drew the net to land, full of great fishes, an hundred and fifty and three: and for all there were so many, yet was not the net broken."

ἀνέβη οὖν Σίμων Πέτρος καὶ εἵλκυσεν τὸ δίκτυον εἰς τὴν γῆν μεστὸν ἰχθύων μεγάλων ἑκατὸν πεντήκοντα τριῶν, καὶ τοσούτων ὄντων οὐκ ἐσχίσθη τὸ δίκτυον.

ἀνέβη (3d.per.sing.aor.act.ind.of ἀναβαίνω, constative) 323.
οὖν (inferential conjunction) 68.
Σίμων (nom.sing.masc.of Σίμων, subject of ἀνέβη and εἵλκυσεν) 386.
Πέτρος (nom.sing.masc.of Πέτρος, apposition) 387.
καὶ (adjunctive conjunction joining verbs) 14.
εἵλκυσεν (3d.per.sing.aor.act.ind.of ἑλκύω, ingressive) 2289.
τὸ (acc.sing.neut.of the article in agreement with δίκτυον) 9.
δίκτυον (acc.sing.neut.of δίκτυον, direct object of εἵλκυσεν) 393.
εἰς (preposition with the accusative of extent) 140.
τὴν (acc.sing.fem.of the article in agreement with γῆν) 9.
γῆν (acc.sing.fem.of γῆ, extent) 157.
μεστὸν (acc.sing.neut.of μεστός, in agreement with δίκτυον, predicate adjective) 1468.
ἰχθύων (gen.pl.masc.of ἰχθύς, description) 657.
μεγάλων (gen.pl.masc.of μέγας, in agreement with ἰχθύων) 184.
ἑκατὸν (acc.sing.neut.of ἑκατός, numerical extent) 1035.
πεντήκοντα (numeral) 2172.
τριῶν (gen.pl.masc of τρεῖς, in agreement with ἰχθύων) 1010.
καὶ (adversative conjunction) 14.
τοσούτων (gen.pl.masc.of τοσοῦτος, genitive absolute) 727.
ὄντων (pres.part.gen.pl.masc.of εἰμί, genitive absolute, adverbial, concessive) 86.
οὐκ (summary negative conjunction with the indicative) 130.
ἐσχίσθη (3d.per.sing.aor.pass.ind.of σχίζω, culminative) 1662.
τὸ (nom.sing.neut.of the article in agreement with δίκτυον) 9.
δίκτυον (nom.sing.neut.of δίκτυον, subject of ἐσχίσθη) 393.

Translation - *"So Peter went and started to pull up the net, filled with one hundred fifty three big fish, to the shore, but despite the fact that there were so many, the net was not broken."*

Comment: ἀναβαίνω (#323) is generally used when referring to "going up" to the sea, as a concession to the illusion of ascent one gets when standing on the shore and looking out to sea. Under the inspiration of our Lord's command Peter at least tried (ingressive aorist in εἵλκυσεν) to drag the net ashore, despite its great weight. Contrary to what one might expect (adversative καὶ) the net did not break despite the fact that it was full of big fish numbering 153 (concessive adverbial participle in the genitive absolute ὄντων). The concessive participle introduces an adversative idea into the context. The net full of big fish is a variation on the theme of which the "twelve baskets full" of Mt.14:20 is a part. Our Lord is not parsimonious. He knows little of an economy of scarcity (Ps.24:1; Eph.3:20).

Verse 12 - "Jesus saith unto them, Come and dine. And none of the disciples durst ask him, Who art thou? knowing that it was the Lord."

λέγει αὐτοῖς ὁ Ἰησοῦς Δεῦτε ἀριστήσατε. οὐδεὶς δὲ ἐτόλμα τῶν μαθητῶν ἐξετάσαι αὐτόν, Σὺ τίς εἶ; εἰδότες ὅτι ὁ κύριός ἐστιν.

λέγει (3d.per.sing.pres.act.ind.of λέγω, historical) 66.

αὐτοῖς (dat.pl.masc.of αὐτός, indirect object of λέγει) 16.

ὁ (nom.sing.masc.of the article in agreement with Ἰησοῦς) 9.

Ἰησοῦς (nom.sing.masc.of Ἰησοῦς, subject of λέγει) 3.

Δεῦτε (particle of exhortation, incitement, etc.) 391.

ἀριστήσατε (2d.per.pl.aor.act.impv.of ἀριστάω, command) 2461.

οὐδεὶς (nom.pl.masc.of οὐδείς, subject of ἐτόλμα) 446.

ἐτόλμα (3d.per.sing.imp.act.ind.of τολμάω, tendential) 1430.

τῶν (gen.pl.masc.of the article in agreement with μαθητῶν) 9.

μαθητῶν (gen.pl.masc.of μαθητής, partitive genitive) 421.

ἐξετάσαι (aor.act.inf.of ἐξετάζω, epexegetical) 171.

αὐτόν (acc.sing.masc.of αὐτός, direct object of ἐξετάσαι) 16.

Σὺ (nom.sing.masc.of σύ, subject of εἶ, direct question) 104.

τίς (nom.sing.masc.of τίς, interrogative pronoun, predicate nominative) 281.

εἶ (2d.per.sing.pres.ind.of εἰμί, aoristic, direct question) 86.

εἰδότες (pres.act.part.nom.pl.masc.of οἶδα, adverbial, causal) 144.

ὅτι (conjunction introducing an object clause in indirect discourse) 211.

ὁ (nom.sing.masc.of the article in agreement with κύριός) 9.

κύριός (nom.sing.masc.of κύριος, predicate nominative) 97.

ἐστιν (3d.per.sing.pres.ind.of εἰμί, indirect discourse) 86.

Translation - "Jesus said to them, 'Come! Breakfast is served!' And not one of the disciples dared to ask Him, 'Who are you?' because they knew that it was the Lord."

Comment: Jesus was enjoying this to the full, with the knowledge, of course that it was at the disciples' expense and that they were beginning to get the point. With a jaunty tone the announcement came that breakfast was ready. He prepared to serve them the food without which they would have gone hungry (verse 5) - food which was available only because of His miraculous power over His own creation. Had He not appeared to rescue them from their ill conceived fishing trip, they would have gone home tired, hungry, discouraged, despondent disgusted and ashamed. Anyone who ever went fishing, when he knew that he should not have gone, fished all night, caught nothing and failed to take along his breakfast, knows how the disciples felt. Add to their situation the fact that their Lord, Who had died on the cross for them and then risen from the dead, and Who had told them that they were to spend the rest of their lives in His service, found them in their disobedience and frustration and graciously served their breakfast, and we have the total picture. The tendential imperfect in ἐτόλμα admirably expresses their feeling. "The lack of a sense of attainment in the imperfect may be emphasized to the point of a positive implication that the end was not attained, but was only attempted, or that action tended toward realization." (Mantey, *Manual*, 189). Robertson calls it a negative imperfect, although he admits that "This is not a very happy piece of nomenclature ... and yet it is the best one can do." Gildersleeve says, "The negative imperfect commonly denotes resistance to pressure or disappointment." (Gildersleeve, *Syntax*, 97, as cited in Robertson, *Grammar*, 885). *Cf.* Mt.18:30; Lk.15:16,28; John 2:24; 7:1; Acts 19:30; Lk.1:59; Mt.3:14; Acts 7:26. The disciples wanted to ask Jesus who He was. As the pressure built up within them, they were also conscious of the fact that they were ashamed to ask the question, since they already knew that it was He. This is the force of the causal participle εἰδότες. Thus the ambivalence. They knew who He was, or at least thought they did. Yet they were not certain and would have been happy to ask Him and be assured. So, both knowing and doubting at the same time, they were on the point of asking Him, yet did not. One wonders if they enjoyed their breakfast?

We have anacoluthon in Σὺ τίς εἶ. The direct question interrupts the smooth flow of οὐδεὶς ἐτόλμα ... ἐξετάσαι αὐτόν ... εἰδότες ... κ.τ.λ. εἰδότες agrees in case with οὐδείς and in number with μαθητῶν! The sentence closes with indirect discourse.

It was a tense moment. The disciples had been caught red-handed. The clear implication of the circumstances of their being out there in a boat fishing was that they were washing their hands of the entire Jesus episode and going back to their old life. After all, one must be practical and face the exigencies of life. Jesus was indeed alive. Of this they had become convinced. But for all practical purposes how did that fact, as stupendous as it was, affect them? They still had to eat. It was all very well for Jesus to die for them, rise from the dead in triumph and then go back to the glory. They had to stay on this earth in an economy of scarcity. Scarcity creates competition and competition in its advanced form becomes conflict. Conflict threatens personal survival. Self preservation is, for people without faith, the first law of nature. There may have been some resentment in their hearts. Only twice before had He appeared to them (vs.14). Perhaps subconsciously they were thinking, "Why don't you go back to Heaven and let us alone?" And yet Peter was famished and that little fish on the fire smelled delicious. So they stood in silence, casting furtive glances in His direction. Should they apologize for their lack of faith? Was this man really the same Man they had followed for three years?

The disappointing performance of the disciples can be explained by the fact that although they had received the Holy Spirit (John 20:22) and He resided in their bodies, they were not yet filled with Him (Acts 2:4). After all they were not greatly different from the average backslidden Christian.

Jesus broke the tension by acting as the butler in

Verse 13 - "Jesus then cometh, and taketh bread, and giveth them, and fish likewise."

ἔρχεται Ἰησοῦς καὶ λαμβάνει τὸν ἄρτον καὶ δίδωσιν αὐτοῖς, καὶ τὸ ὀφάριον ὁμοίως.

ἔρχεται (3d.per.sing.pres.ind.of ἔρχομαι, historical) 146.

Ἰησοῦς (nom.sing.masc.of Ἰησοῦς, subject of ἔρχεται, λαμβάνει and δίδωσιν) 3.

καὶ (adjunctive conjunction joining verbs) 14.

λαμβάνει (3d.per.sing.pres.act.ind.of λαμβάνω, historical) 533.

τὸν (acc.sing.masc.of the article in agreement with ἄρτον) 9.

ἄρτον (acc.sing.masc.of ἄρτος, direct object of λαμβάνει and δίδωσιν) 338.

καὶ (adjunctive conjunction joining verbs) 14.

δίδωσιν (3d.per.sing.pres.act.ind.of δίδωμι, historical) 362.

αὐτοῖς (dat.pl.masc.of αὐτός, indirect object of δίδωσιν) 16.

καὶ (adjunctive conjunction joining nouns) 14.

τὸ (acc.sing.neut.of the article in agreement with ὀψάριον) 9.

ὀψάριον (acc.sing.neut.of ὀψάριον, direct object of δίδωσιν) 2277.

ὁμοίως (adverbial) 1425.

Translation - *"Jesus came and took the bread and gave to them, and also the fish."*

Comment: Robertson accuses John of pleonasm with his ἔρχεται . . . καὶ λαμβάνει, but adds that this is not a linguistic vice. All vernacular language is guilty of redundancy. As a language grows, words, once emphatic, lose their emphasis and now need repetition if emphasis is desired. The richness of color of the Oriental language shows up clearly in the idiom which a technical purist would be inclined to call pleonasm. Let us remember that the Holy Spirit has a minimal body of essential certitude which He wishes to convey to the reader. This He has done despite the linguistic peculiarities of the men whom He chose as amenuenses. If this minimum body of truth is clear to the exegete the purpose of divine and plenary inspiration has been served. The Holy Spirit, Who is God is of course a superb writer, and He probably winced when His writers wrote ἀποκριθεὶς εἶπεν - "when he had answered he said" or καὶ ἐγένετο ἦλθον - "and it came to pass that he went," just as Jesus must have winced when one of His disciples picked his nose or tried to eat peas with his knife. When God revealed Himself to men He could do so only by getting closer to man with his boorish manners than He with His divine standards cared to get. The Holy Spirit's task of revealing God, not only in a man, but also in a book had the same problem. So when the New Testament writers blundered grammatically and syntactically, we do not blame the Holy Spirit. He knew better, but He chose to reveal His message in the only idiom that His writers could use.

Jesus moved about the little group serving bread and fish. The disciples ate with the evident relish of healthy men who had worked hard all night long in the invigorating atmosphere of Lake Tiberius. While the men finished eating, John slipped in a sentence for the reader in

Verse 14 - *"This is now the third time that Jesus shewed himself to his disciples, after that he was risen from the dead."*

τοῦτο ἤδη τρίτον ἐφανερώθη Ἰησοῦς τοῖς μαθηταῖς ἐγερθεὶς ἐκ νεκρῶν.

τοῦτο (acc.sing.neut.of οὗτος, in agreement with τρίτον) 93.
ἤδη (temporal adverb) 291.
τρίτον (acc.sing.neut.of τρίτος, measure) 1209.
ἐφανερώθη (3d.per.sing.aor.pass.ind.of φανερόω, constative) 1960.
Ἰησοῦς (nom.sing.masc.of Ἰησοῦς, subject of ἐφανερώθη) 3.
τοῖς (dat.pl.masc.of the article in agreement with μαθηταῖς) 9.
μαθηταῖς (dat.pl.masc.of μαθητής, indirect object of ἐφανερώθη) 421.
ἐγερθεὶς (aor.pass.part.nom.sing.masc.of ἐγείρω, adverbial, temporal) 125.
ἐκ (preposition with the ablative of separation) 19.
νεκρῶν (abl.pl.masc.of νεκρός, separation) 749.

Translation - *"This was the third time that Jesus was seen by the disciples after He had risen from the dead."*

Comment: *Cf.*#1209 for a list of usages similar to τοῦτο τὸ τρίτον, with the substantive to be supplied. ἐγερθεὶς is clearly temporal here. The first time was on resurrection day evening in Jerusalem, with Thomas absent. The second time it was eight days later, again in Jerusalem with Thomas now present with the other ten. And now here in Galilee to the seven, five of whom are identified (vs.2). Thus Jesus kept His promise (Mt.26:32; Mk.14:28) and also the directive of the messenger in the garden (Mk.16:7; Mt.28:7). On the first occasion He presented them with His peace, evidence of His literal bodily resurrection and the Holy Spirit and charged them with a permanent commission to preach (John 20:19-23). The second time again He gave them His peace, offered Thomas the evidence that he had demanded and demonstrated again in various ways not revealed in the text the literality of His corporeal resurrection. On this third occasion, although He did not rebuke them verbally, His suggestion, with its mixed elements of tenderness, sarcasm and subtle humor that they intended to revert to their former life style must have hit them like a bombshell.

His early morning lesson by the seaside was delivered in three parts. First He pointed out to them the futility of a return to the fishing business. A fish merchant who couldn't fish any better than they had would starve to death. Second, He demonstrated His own superior ability to catch fish. This was a repeat lesson of the one they had had three years before. Third, in verses 15-23 He taught Peter that he had a ministry which was far too important for him to waste any more time vainly trying to outwit a fish.

The Fishers

Alone upon the shore there stood a man —
The man who'd said He was the Son of God;
And to His riven side the fishers ran
To tread again the paths that He had trod.

They'd seen Him dead, and to their nets had gone,
Tortured with unbelief and cowed by fear.
Was not His voice the sound that spurred us on?
Did not His presence bring the heavens near?

But He is dead and we cannot believe
The promise that He once again shall live.
Back to the reeking nets! We will retrieve
The fortunes He had said that we should give.

Men since have not believed that He arose,
And failing to believe have lived in sin —
The sin of sordidness. In darkness gross
Have groped amid the bloody battle's din.

But wheresoe'er the message has gone forth —
The message of the cross, the empty grave,
From southern sunkissed fields to icy north,
The message of the cross has power to save.

Jesus and Peter

(John 21:15-19)

John 21:15 - "So when they had dined, Jesus saith to Simon Peter, Simon, son of Jonas, lovest thou me more than these? He saith unto him, Yea, Lord; thou knowest that I love thee. He saith unto him, Feed my lambs."

Ὅτε οὖν ἠρίστησαν λέγει τῷ Σίμωνι Πέτρῳ ὁ Ἰησοῦς, Σίμων Ἰωάννου, ἀγαπᾷς με πλέον τούτων; λέγει αὐτῷ, Ναί, κύριε, σὺ οἶδας ὅτι φιλῶ σε. λέγει αὐτῷ, Βόσκε τὰ ἀρνία μου.

Ὅτε (conjunction introducing a definite temporal clause, contemporaneous time) 703.

οὖν (continuative conjunction) 68.

ἠρίστησαν (3d.per.pl.aor.act.ind.of ἀριστάω, culminative) 2461.

λέγει (3d.per.sing.pres.act.ind.of λέγω, historical) 66.

τῷ (dat.sing.masc.of the article in agreement with Σίμωνι) 9.

Σίμωνι (dat.sing.masc.of Σίμων, indirect object of λέγει) 386.

Πέτρῳ (dat.sing.masc.of Πέτρος, in apposition) 387.

ὁ (nom.sing.masc.of the article in agreement with Ἰησοῦς) 9.

Ἰησοῦς (nom.sing.masc.of Ἰησοῦς, subject of λέγει) 3.

Σίμων (voc.sing.masc.of Σίμων, address) 386.

Ἰωάννου (gen.sing.masc.of Ἰωάννης, relationship) 1963.

ἀγαπᾷς (2d.per.sing.pres.act.ind.of ἀγαπάω, direct question) 540.

με (acc.sing.masc.of ἐγώ, direct object of ἀγαπᾷς) 123.

πλέον (acc.sing.neut.of πλείων, measure) 474.

τούτων (abl.pl.neut.of οὗτος, comparison) 93.

λέγει (3d.per.sing.pres.act.ind.of λέγω, historical) 66.

αὐτῷ (dat.sing.masc.of αὐτός, indirect object of λέγει) 16.

Ναί (affirmative particle) 524.

κύριε (voc.sing.masc.of κύριος, address) 97.

σὺ (nom.sing.masc.of σύ, subject of οἶδας) 104.

οἶδας (2d.per.sing.pres.act.ind.of οἶδα, static) 144.

ὅτι (conjunction introducing an object clause in indirect discourse) 211.

φιλῶ (1st.per.sing.pres.act.ind.of φιλέω, aoristic) 566.

σε (acc.sing.masc.of σύ, direct object of φιλῶ) 123.

λέγει (3d.per.sing.pres.act.ind.of λέγω, historical) 66.

αὐτῷ (dat.sing.masc.of αὐτός, indirect object of λέγει) 16.

Βόσκε (2d.per.sing.pres.act.impv.of βόσκω, command) 770.

τὰ (acc.pl.neut.of the article in agreement with ἀρνία) 9.

#2923 ἀρνία (acc.pl.neut.of ἀρνίον, direct object of βόσκε).

lamb - John 21:15; Rev.5:6,8,12,13; 6:1,16; 7:9,10,14,17; 12:11; 13:8,11; 14:1,4,4,10; 15:3; 17:14,14; 19:7,9; 21:9,14,22,23,27; 22:1,3.

Meaning: lamb. *Cf.* ἀρνή (#2411) - a little lamb. With reference to the Christian believer - John 21:15. With reference to the animal - Rev.13:11. Elsewhere in Revelation with reference to Christ in His glorified state as crucified, resurrected, ascended and ruling Sovereign.

μου (gen.sing.masc.of ἐγώ, possession) 123.

Translation - "Then when they had eaten Jesus said to Simon Peter, 'Simon, son of Jonah, do you love me more than these?' He said to Him, 'Yes, Lord. You know that I like you.' He said to him, 'Feed my little lambs.' "

Comment: The temporal clause with ὅτε, indicates a time point contemporaneous with that of the verb ἠρίστησαν, which is culminative. Thus this dialogue began after they had finished eating. Peter was no longer interested in food. *Cf.*#'s 540 and 566. The difference between these two verbs, both of which mean "to love" must derive from the contexts in which they appear. In the context before us it is apparent that ἀγαπάω, the word used by Jesus, means love of such an intensity that it results in personal sacrifice on the part of the lover for the loved, while φιλέω indicates love of a less intensive quality, and can be translated "am fond of" or "like." That ἀγαπάω always refers to a love of a high ethical character, such as the love of God, is forbidden by Luke 11:43; John 3:19; 12:43; 2 Tim.4:10; 2 Peter 2:15; 1 John 2:15b, in which passages ἀγαπάω refers to chief seats in the synagogue, darkness, the praise of men, this present evil world, the wages of unrighteousness and the world. In all of these contexts it is the degree of intensity, not the ethical character of the devotion which is in view. A review of #566 reveals that φιλέω is often used of the love of God, but that it is also used in an evil sense in Mt.6:5; 23:6; Lk.20:46 (ostentation) and Rev.22:15 (falsehood). Thus we see that both a holy God and unholy men are capable of love both in the ἀγαπάω and φιλέω, sense of the words. In some contexts apparently there is no difference in the intensity of the emotion involved regardless of which word is used. That Peter was never willing to use Jesus' term and that Jesus in His third question accommodated to Peter's term would seem to indicate that, *in this context,* φιλέω means love of something less than the intensity that is willing to make personal sacrifices.

In this context ἀγαπάω refers to love which demands and receives self sacrifice. Jesus was asking Peter if he loved Him enough to devote his life in sacrificial service in keeping with his commission (Lk.22:32; John 20:21). This love would demand that Peter would forget about fishing for fish and devote himself to fishing for men, even though great personal sacrifice, financially and personally, was involved. Jesus' "follow me" of three years before meant that Peter forsook the fishing nets. Note the ablative of comparison following πλέον in τούτων. It is possible that τούτων means the other six disciples and that Jesus is asking Peter if his love for Jesus was greater than that of the other six men present. Thus Goodspeed translated, ". . . are you more devoted to me than these others are?" But it is also possible from a grammatical point of view to relate τούτων to the 153 big fish in the net, in which case the question was, "Do you love me enough to forsake a lucrative fishing business?" It is in this sense that I have translated, ". . . do you love me more than these?" - *i.e.* "more than these things?" Williams has, ". . . are you more devoted to me than you are to these things?" with an appended footnote, "That is, more devoted to me than you are to boats, nets, etc."

Each commentator will decide for himself which is correct. It seems to me to fit the context better to adopt the latter interpretation. Peter's reply advoided ἀγαπάω, but he did say that he was fond of Jesus (φιλέω, #566) - "I like you, Lord," with the implication, "but don't ask me for too many sacrifices." Once before Peter had boasted beyond his powers to deliver about his devotion to Jesus (Mark 14:29; Matthew 26:33; Luke 22:33; John 13:37). Perhaps now he has learned his lesson. He was trying to be honest by saying, in effect, "At least, Lord, I am fond of you. You are dear to me. I like you." Now comes Jesus' repeated commission - "Feed my little lambs." This is the charge that Jesus gave to Peter once before (Luke 22:32). *Cf.* Rev.7:17 - "the Lamb himself will shepherd the sheep."
Jesus decided to try again.

Verse 16 - "He saith to him again the second time, Simon, son of Jonas, lovest thou me? He saith unto him, Yea, Lord, thou knowest that I love thee. He saith unto him, Feed my sheep."

λέγει αὐτῷ πάλιν δεύτερον, Σίμων Ἰωάννου, ἀγαπᾷς με; λέγει αὐτῷ, Ναί, κύριε, σὺ οἶδας ὅτι φιλῶ σε. λέγει αὐτῷ Ποίμαινε τὰ πρόβατά μου.

λέγει (3d.per.sing.pres.act.ind.of λέγω, historical) 66.
αὐτῷ (dat.sing.masc.of αὐτός, indirect object of λέγει) 16.
πάλιν (adverbial) 355.
δεύτερον (acc.sing.neut.of δεύτερος, adverbial) 1371.
Σίμων (voc.sing.masc.of Σίμων, address) 386.
Ἰωάννου (gen.sing.masc.of Ἰωάννης, relationship) 1963.
ἀγαπᾷς (2d.per.sing.pres.act.ind.of ἀγαπάω, direct question) 540.
με (acc.sing.masc.of ἐγώ, direct object of ἀγαπᾷς) 123.
λέγει (3d.per.sing.pres.act.ind.of λέγω, historical) 66.

αὐτῷ (dat.sing.masc.of αὐτός, indirect object of λέγει) 16.

Ναί (affirmative particle) 524.

κύριε (voc.sing.masc.of κύριος, address) 97.

σύ (nom.sing.masc.of σύ, subject of οἶδας) 104.

οἶδας (2d.per.sing.pres.act.ind.of οἶδα, static) 144.

ὅτι (conjunction introducing an object clause in indirect discourse) 211.

φιλῶ (1st.per.sing.pres.act.ind.of φιλέω, aoristic) 566.

σε (acc.sing.masc.of σύ, direct object of φιλῶ) 104.

λέγει (3d.per.sing.pres.act.ind.of λέγω, historical) 66.

αὐτῷ (dat.sing.masc.of αὐτός, indirect object of λέγει) 16.

Ποίμαινε (2d.per.sing.pres.act.impv.of ποιμαίνω, command) 164.

τά (acc.pl.neut.of the article in agreement with πρόβατά) 9.

πρόβατά (acc.pl.neut.of πρόματον, direct object of Ποίμαινε) 671.

μου (gen.sing.masc.of ἐγώ, possession) 123.

Translation - "He said to him again a second time, 'Simon, son of Jonas, do you love me?' He said to Him, 'Yes, Lord. You know that I am fond of you.' He said to him, 'Shepherd my sheep.' "

Comment: Again Jesus asked Peter for his expression of a deep and abiding self-sacrifical love. Once again Peter confessed that he could go not further than to say that he liked Jesus. The commission is a little different, though essentially the same - "Shepherd (take good care of) my sheep." (Rev.7:17). This commission to shepherd made an impression on Peter's mind which is expressed in his epistles (1 Peter 2:25; 5:2,3,4).

The point of the story comes out in verse 17 when Jesus, on His third attempt, adapted His question to Peter's word.

Verse 17 - "He saith unto him a third time, Simon, son of Jonas, lovest thou me? Peter was grieved because he said unto him the third time, Lovest thou me? And he said unto him, Lord, thou knowest all things; thou knowest that I love thee. Jesus saith unto him, Feed my sheep."

λέγει αὐτῷ τὸ τρίτον, Σίμων Ἰωάννου, φιλεῖς με; ἐλυπήθη ὁ Πέτρος ὅτι εἶπεν αὐτῷ τὸ τρίτον, Φιλεῖς με; καὶ λέγει αὐτῷ, Κύριε, πάντα σὺ οἶδας, σὺ γινώσκεις ὅτι φιλῶ σε. λέγει αὐτῷ, Βόσκε τὰ προβατά μου.

λέγει (3d.per.sing.pres.act.ind.of λέγω, historical) 66.

αὐτῷ (dat.sing.masc.of ἀτός, indirect object of λέγει) 16.

τὸ (acc.sing.neut.of the article in agreement with τρίτον) 9.

τρίτον (acc.sing.neut.of τρίτος, adverbial) 1209.

Σίμων (voc.sing.masc.of Σίμων, address) 386.

Ἰωάννου (gen.sing.masc.of Ἰωάννης, relationship) 1963.

φιλεῖς (2d.per.sing.pres.act.ind.of φιλέω, aoristic, direct question) 566.

με (acc.sing.masc.of ἐγώ, direct object of φιλεῖς) 123.

ἐλυπήθη (3d.per.sing.aor.pass.ind.of λυπέω, ingressive) 1113.

ὁ (nom.sing.masc.of the article in agreement with Πέτρος) 9.

Πέτρος (nom.sing.masc.of Πέτρος, subject of ἐλυπήθη) 386.

ὅτι (conjunction introducing a subordinate causal clause) 211.

εἶπεν (3d.per.sing.aor.act.ind.of εἶπον, constative) 155.

αὐτῷ (dat.sing.masc.of αὐτός, indirect object of εἶπεν) 16.

τό (acc.sing.neut.of the article in agreement with τρίτον) 9.

τρίτον (acc.sing.neut.of τρίτος, adverbial) 1209.

Φιλεῖς (2d.per.sing.pres.act.ind.of φιλέω, direct question) 566.

με (acc.sing.masc.of ἐγώ, direct object of Φιλεῖς) 123.

καὶ (adjunctive conjunction joining verbs) 14.

λέγει (3d.per.sing.pres.act.ind.of λέγω, historical) 66.

αὐτῷ (dat.sing.masc.of αὐτός, indirect object of λέγει) 16.

Κύριε (voc.sing.masc.of κύριος, address) 97.

πάντα (acc.pl.neut.of πᾶς, direct object of οἶδας) 67.

σύ (nom.sing.masc.of σύ, subject of οἶδας) 104.

οἶδας (2d.per.sing.pres.act.ind.of οἶδα, static) 144.

σύ (nom.sing.masc.of σύ, subject of γινώσκεις) 104.

γινώσκεις (2d.per.sing.pres.act.ind.of γινώσκω static) 131.

ὅτι (conjunction introducing an object clause in indirect discourse) 211.

φιλῶ (1st.per.sing.pres.act.ind.of φιλέω, aoristic) 566.

σε (acc.sing.masc.of σύ, direct object of φιλῶ) 104.

λέγει (3d.per.sing.pres.act.ind.of λέγω, historical) 66.

αὐτῷ (dat.sing.masc.of αὐτός, indirect object of λέγει) 16.

Βόσκε (2d.per.sing.pres.act.impv.of βόσκω, command) 770.

τά (acc.pl.neut.of the article in agreement with πρόβατά) 9.

πρόβατά (acc.pl.neut.of πρόβατον, direct object of Βόσκε) 671.

μου (gen.sing.masc.of ἐγώ, possession) 123.

Translation - "He said to him the third time, 'Simon, son of Jonas, are you fond of me?' Peter lost heart because He said to him the third time, "Are you fond of me?' and he said to Him, 'Lord, you understand all about me. You know that I like you.' He said to him, 'Feed my sheep.' "

Comment: Twice Peter had been honest about it. He was not certain that he loved Jesus (ἀγαπάω). There was a time when he thought he did - on the night that Jesus was arrested. But before that night had passed he learned that he did not. It had been a bitter experience (Luke 22:62). Now he longed to say, Κύριε ἀγαπάω σε, but he was afraid to make a statement which once more might turn out to be an idle boast. So he had confined himself to a statement that he was sure was true. Φιλῶ σε was the truth. "Lord, I want to love you (ἀγαπάω) but I am certain that I like you (φιλέω)." So much for Peter's honesty up to this point. Then Jesus gave him the extreme test - Φιλεῖς με; "Do you even like me?" Can anyone who refuses to say that he loves Jesus enough to be totally faithful to Him, truthfully say that he likes Jesus? This is the question. Peter's feelings were hurt to think that Jesus doubted that he even liked Him. But of two things, Peter was certain: (1) that Jesus understood everything. Note πάντα in emphasis, ahead of σύ οἶδας. Peter was talking to the Lord of Creation Who had just redeemed the elect and risen from the dead. Jesus did not need to ask questions in order to gain information. He already had all of the answers. Then why was Jesus asking Peter, first, "Do you love me?" and now "Do you like me?" A spirit of impatience, born out of the sadness that Jesus doubted him and born also out of shame for his own past wretched performance may have possessed him. Almost with asperity Peter said to Jesus, "Why are you asking me these things? You already know the answers. And one of the things that you know is that I like you very much. (φιλῶς σε). I do not know whether I love you (ἀγαπάω) or not. I once thought I did when I did not. But I know now and you know too that I am fond of you (φιλέω). If that does not please you, at least give me credit for being honest about it." And by thinking all of this, which, if he did, was the same thing as saying it aloud to Jesus, Peter passed the test that Jesus was giving him. Hence, Jesus continued to offer to Peter his commission, "Feed my sheep." The pastor of a Christian church ought at least to have demonstrated that he can be honestly and severely introspective.

How could Peter have failed the Lord's test? In two ways: (1) Either by saying again, as he had on the night that Jesus was arrested, "I love you." or (2) by denying that he was fond of Jesus. The first mistake would have been the same overconfidence that he felt before. The last would have been (a) dishonest and (b) a craven and false self-deprecation. Some have a false humility which they love to put on parade as they whine and say to Jesus, 'Lord, I do not know whether I even like you. I am so inconstant." Not Peter. He did not know that he loved Jesus so he refused to say that he did, but he did know that he liked Him, and nobody, not even Jesus, was going to get him to say that he did not. The fact was that Peter both liked (φιλέω) and loved (ἀγαπάω) Jesus. His only problem was that, though he had all of the Holy Spirit (John 20:22) the Holy Spirit did not have all of him, as later He was to have (Acts 2:4). After Pentecost Peter gave all of the evidence that he loved Jesus (ἀγαπάω). In fact he loved his Lord enough to pass the supreme test - "Greater love hath no man than this, that a man lay down his life for his friends" (John 15:13).

This is the subject that Jesus took up next.

Peter scored big in another way in this exchange. He recognized the fact that one cannot be less than honest with Jesus and get away with it. Peter was still naked (John 21:7, γυμνός, Heb.4:13) and he knew it. *Cf.* 1 Cor.2:11 for another verse where οἶδα and γινώσκω are thrown together. What Peter is saying is that Jesus, being God, understands everything (οἶδας). He is therefore able to evaluate with precision on the basis of His experience with Peter (γινώσκω) what Peter's behavior means. γινώσκω means to know by observation and experience. οἶδα means to understand even in the absence of sensory data. It was in this sense that Jesus did not need for anyone to tell Him about man (John 2:25). Peter understood this very well. Jesus knew perfectly well that Peter's present honesty would work for his future spiritual development, and that it was therefore safe to trust him with the keys of the kingdom which He had already given to him (Mt.16:19). He also knew that Peter's fidelity to His Lord would result in his martyrdom.

Verse 18 - "Verily, verily, I say unto thee, When thou wast young, thou girdest thyself, and walkedest whither thou wouldest: but when thou shalt be old, thou shalt stretch forth thy hands, and another shall gird thee, and carry thee whither thou wouldest not."

ἀμὴν ἀμὴν λέγω σοι, ὅτε ἦς νεώτερος, ἐζώννυες σεαυτὸν καὶ περιεπάτεις ὅπου ἤθελες, ὅταν δὲ γηράσῃς, ἐκτενεῖς τὰς χεῖράς σου, καὶ ἄλλος σε ζώσει καὶ οἴσει ὅπου οὐ θέλεις.

ἀμὴν (explicative) 466.
ἀμὴν (explicative) 466.
λέγω (1st.per.sing.pres.act.ind.of λέγω, aoristic) 66.
σοι (dat.sing.masc.of σύ, indirect object of λέγω) 104.
ὅτε (conjunction introducing a definite temporal clause, contemporaneous time) 703.
ἦς (2d.per.sing.imp.ind.of εἰμί, progresseive description) 86.
νεώτερος (nom.sing.masc.of νεώτερος, predicate adjective) 2543.

#2924 ἐζώννυες (2d.per.sing.imp.act.ind.of ζώννυμι, iterative).

gird - John 21:18,18; Acts 12:8.

Meaning: Cf. ζώνη (#263). To clothe; to put on clothing. Followed by σεαυτόν in John 21:18a; followed by σε in John 21:18b. Absolutely in Acts 12:8.

σεαυτὸν (acc.sing.masc.of σεαυτοῦ, direct object of ἐζώννυες) 347.
καὶ (adjunctive conjunction joining verbs) 14.
περιεπάτεις (2d.per.sing.imp.act.ind.of περιπατέω, iterative) 384.
ὅπου (adverb introducing a local clause) 592.
ἤθελες (2d.per.sing.imp.act.ind.of θέλω, local clause) 88.
ὅταν (temporal adverb with the subjunctive in an indefinite temporal clause) 436.
δὲ (adversative conjunction) 11.

#2925 γηράσῃς (2d.per.sing.aor.act.subj.of γηράσκω, indefinite temporal clause).

be old - John 21:18.
wax old - Heb.8:13

Meaning: to grow old. With reference to Peter - John 21:18. The old covenant of the law is obsolete *vis a vis* the covenant of grace - Heb.8:13.

ἐκτενεῖς (2d.per.sing.fut.act.ind.of ἐκτείνω, predictive) 710.
τὰς (acc.pl.fem.of the article in agreement with χεῖρας) 9.
χεῖράς (acc.pl.fem.of χείρ, direct object of ἐκτενεῖς) 308.
σου (gen.sing.masc.of σύ, possession) 104.
καὶ (continuative conjunction) 14.
ἄλλος (nom.sing.masc.of ἄλλος, subject of ζώσει) 198.
ζώσει (3d.per.sing.fut.act.ind.of ζώννυμι, predictive) 2924.

σε (acc.sing.masc.of σύ, direct object of ζώσει) 104.
καὶ (adjunctive conjunction joining verbs) 14.
οἴσει (3d.per.sing.fut.act.ind.of φέρω, predictive) 683.
ὅπου (adverb introducing a local clause) 592.
οὐ (summary negative conjunction with the indicative) 130.
θέλεις (2d.per.sing.pres.act.ind.of θέλω, futuristic) 88.

Translation - "Truly, truly I am telling you (that) when you were young you used to dress yourself and you went wherever you wished, but when you get old you are going to stretch out your hands, and another is going to dress you and take you where you do not want to go."

Comment: Here is a thumbnail sketch of Peter's life in retrospect and a glimpse into his future. The two descriptions are centered about two temporal clauses, the first definite, and, of course the one picturing Peter's future, indefinite. ὅτε ἦς νεώτερος - "when you were a young man" - and ὅταν δὲ γηράσῃς - "when you get old" (indefinite). In his youth Peter had his own way. He chose his own wardrobe, needed no help in dressing himself and went wherever he chose to go. Note the iterative imperfect tenses. This was his life style. He did what he pleased and went where he pleased. We have observed that Peter chose to depart the Garden of Gethsemane when Jesus was arrested and procede elsewhere, where there was less danger (Mk.14:50). It is a picture of a selfish man. The other part of the picture speaks of a helpless old man. He will be clothed by others and conducted to places where he would rather not have gone, - to the Roman Colosseum for example, if tradition is to be believed, where Peter gave the overwhelming proof that he really did love Jesus more than the fishing business or anything else. Thus Jesus was telling him that although now he could only say Φιλῶ σε, κύριε, on that day he would say, Ἀγαπῶ σε, κύριε. Jesus, Who knew everything (verse 17) therefore knew that Peter loved Him though he was too uncertain of himself to say so. That Jesus was predicting Peter's martyrdom is clear from verse 19. Peter, now lacking in the self-confidence required to say in all honesty that he loved the Lord would later demonstrate a holy boldness to say it with a ministry of preaching that led to his death. The difference was the Holy Spirit's fullness, which Peter and the other Apostles received at Pentecost (Acts 2:4).

Verse 19 - "This spake he, signifying by what death he should glorify God. And when he had spoken this, he saith unto him, Follow me."

τοῦτο δὲ εἶπεν σημαίνων ποίῳ θανάτῳ δοξάσει τὸν θεόν. καὶ τοῦτο εἰπὼν λέγει αὐτῷ, Ἀκολούθει μοι.

τοῦτο (acc.sing.neut.of οὗτος, direct object of εἶπεν) 93.
δὲ (explanatory conjunction) 11.
εἶπεν (3d.per.sing.aor.act.ind.of εἶπον, constative) 155.
σημαίνων (pres.act.part.nom.sing.masc.of σημαίνω, adverbial, telic) 2708.
ποίῳ (instrumental sing.masc.of ποῖος, in agreement with θανάτῳ) 1298.

θανάτῳ (instru.sing.masc.of θάνατος, manner) 381.
δοξάσει (3d.per.sing.fut.act.ind.of δοξάζω, indirect question) 461.
τόν (acc.sing.masc.of the article in agreement with θεόν) 9.
θεόν (acc.sing.masc.of θεός, direct object of δοξάσει) 124.
καὶ (continuative conjunction) 14.
τοῦτο (acc.sing.neut.of οὗτος, direct object of εἰπών) 93.
εἰπών (aor.act.part.nom.sing.masc.of εἶπον, adverbial, temporal) 155.
λέγει (3d.per.sing.pres.act.ind.of λέγω, historical) 66.
αὐτῷ (dat.sing.masc.of αὐτός, indirect object of λέγει) 16.
'Ακολούθει (2d.per.sing.pres.act.impv.of ἀκολουθέω, command) 394.
μοι (dat.sing.masc.of ἐγώ, association) 123.

Translation - "Now He said this in order to point to the manner of death by which he would glorify God. And then He added, 'Follow me.' "

Comment: τοῦτο refers to the last half of verse 18. σημαίνων is telic. Jesus' purpose was to give some indication (foretoken, preindication, prefigure, type, sign) of the manner in which Peter was to die. That martyrdom was indicated seems clear from οἴσει ὅπου οὐ θέλεις, but there is nothing in the language to hint at crucifixion, or any other method of killing (burning, wild beasts, gladiators, *et al*). Note here the future indicative in indirect question. τοῦτο εἰπών τοῦτο is pleonasm. We have tried to cover it up with the translation.

Peter's love for Jesus was great enough to enable him to give his life for His Lord, although he was not certain that this was so at the time, and therefore he refused to say so, but Jesus knew, so He prophesied Peter's martyrdom and then added, "Follow me," even though to do so means death. Jesus had said that before on more than one occasion - Mt.16:24,25; 10:38; Mk.8:34; Lk.9:23; 14:27.

Other correlative passages that relate in homiletical ways to John 21:19 can be found by referring to #'s 899 (σταυρός) and 394 (ἀκολουθέω)

Jesus and the Beloved Disciple

(John 21:20-25)

John 21:20 - "Then Peter, turning about, seeth the disciple whom Jesus loved following; which also leaned on his breast at supper, and said, Lord, which is he that betrayeth thee?"

'Επιστραφεὶς ὁ Πέτρος βλέπει τὸν μαθητὴν ὃν ἠγάπα ὁ Ἰησοῦς ἀκολουθοῦντα, ὃς καὶ ἀνέπεσεν ἐν τῷ δείπνῳ ἐπὶ τὸ στῆθος αὐτοῦ καὶ εἶπεν, Κύριε, τίς ἐστιν ὁ παραδιδούς σε;

'Επιστραφεὶς (aor.act.part.nom.sing.masc.of ἐπιστρέφω, adverbial, temporal) 866.
ὁ (nom.sing.masc.of the article in agreement with Πέτρος) 9.
Πέτρος (nom.sing.masc.of Πέτρος, subject of βλέπει) 387.
βλέπει (3d.per.sing.pres.act.ind.of βλέπω, historical) 499.
τόν (acc.sing.masc.of the article in agreement with μαθητήν) 9.

μαθητὴν (acc.sing.masc.of μαθητής, direct object of βλέπει) 421.

ὅν (acc.sing.masc.of ὅς, direct attraction to μαθητὴν) 65.

ἠγάπα (3d.per.sing.imp.act.ind.of ἀγαπάω, progressive duration) 540.

ὁ (nom.sing.masc.of the article in agreement with Ἰησοῦς) 9.

Ἰησοῦς (nom.sing.masc.of Ἰησοῦς, subject of ἠγάπα) 3.

ἀκολουθοῦντα (pres.act.part.acc.sing.masc.of ἀκολουθέω, adverbial, circumstantial) 394.

ὅς (nom.sing.masc.of ὅς, subject of ἀνέπεσεν and εἶπεν) 65.

καὶ (adjunctive conjunction joining relative clauses) 14.

ἀνέπεσεν (3d.per.sing.aor.act.ind.of ἀναπίπτω, constative) 1184.

ἐν (preposition with the locative of time point) 80.

τῷ (loc.sing.neut.of the article in agreement with δείπνῳ) 9.

δείπνῳ (loc.sing.neut.of δεῖπνον, time point) 1440.

ἐπὶ (preposition with the accusative, place) 47.

τὸ (acc.sing.neut.of the article in agreement with στῆθος) 9.

στῆθος (acc.sing.neut.of στῆθος, place) 2631.

αὐτοῦ (gen.sing.masc.of αὐτός, possession) 16.

καὶ (adjunctive conjunction joining verbs) 14.

εἶπεν (3d.per.sing.aor.act.ind.of εἶπον, constative) 155.

Κύριε (voc.sing.masc.of κύριος, address) 97.

τίς (nom.sing.masc.of τίς, predicate nominative) 281.

ἐστιν (3d.per.sing.pres.ind.of εἰμί, direct question) 86.

ὁ (nom.sing.masc.of the article in agreement with παραδιδούς) 9.

παραδιδούς (pres.act.part.nom.sing.masc.of παραδίδωμι, substantival, subject of ἐστιν) 368.

σε (acc.sing.masc.of σύ, direct object of παραδιδούς) 104.

Translation - *"Peter turned around and saw the disciple whom Jesus always loved following - the one who also sat down with Him at the supper, near His side and said, 'Lord, who is the one who is going to betray you?'"*

Comment: ἐπιστραφεὶς is temporal and ἀκολουθοῦντα is circumstantial. *After* Peter turned he saw John as John was coming along behind them. Here we have something not revealed before in the text. After the breakfast Jesus had led them from the spot. This conversation took place as they walked along. John identified himself for his readers with the two relative clauses. He was the disciple for whom Jesus had always had a special fondness. He was also the one who asked the question at the last supper. Note the locative of time point phrase with ἐν and the accommodated use of ἐπὶ with the accusative of place - not "upon" Jesus breast, but "near/ next to" it.

When Peter saw John following he was induced to intrude a question into an area that was really none of his business, as he quickly discovered.

Verse 21 - "Peter seeing him saith to Jesus, Lord, and what shall this man do?"

τοῦτον οὖν ἰδὼν ὁ Πέτρος λέγει τῷ Ἰησοῦ, Κύριε, οὗτος δὲ τί;

τοῦτον (acc.sing.masc.of οὗτος, direct object of ἰδών) 93.

οὖν (inferential conjunction) 68.

ἰδών (aor.act.part.nom.sing.masc.of ὁράω, adverbial, temporal/causal) 144.

ὁ (nom.sing.masc.of the article in agreement with Πέτρος) 9.

Πέτρος (nom.sing.masc.of Πέτρος, subject of λέγει) 387.

λέγει (3d.per.sing.pres.act.ind.of λέγω, historical) 66.

τῷ (dat.sing.masc.of the article in agreement with Ἰησοῦ) 9.

Ἰησοῦ (dat.sing.masc.of Ἰησοῦς, indirect object of λέγει) 3.

Κύριε (voc.sing.masc.of κύριος, address) 97.

οὗτος (nom.sing.masc.of οὗτος, subject of γενήσεται, understood) 93.

δὲ (continuative conjunction) 11.

τί (acc.sing.neut.of τίς, interrogative pronoun, direct object of γενήσεται, understood) 281.

Translation - "So when Peter saw him he said to Jesus, 'Lord, this man - what about him?' "

Comment: The participle ἰδών is both temporal and causal, as cause is always antecedent to result. Inferential οὖν therefore in redundant. The sight of John following them triggered Peter's question. We must supply γενήσεται in οὗτος δὲ τί. τοῦτον is anaphoric, pointing to τὸν μαθητὴν of verse 20. οὗτος is deictic, although we trust not contemptuous! Peter pointed to John. Was he remembering that John had also fled from the scene of the arrest in the garden, and did he entertain the same doubts about John's courage and fidelity to Jesus that he felt for himself? The text only hints at it, if indeed it does that.

Peter was out of bounds with this question and Jesus rebuked him. *The Expositors' Greek Testament* (I, 872) reminds us of Thomas a Kempis *(De Imit. Christi,* II,3), who wrote that a man "neglects his duty musing on all that other men are bound to do." It is typical of our carnality that we grade our own performance in Christian service against the standard of what other Christian's do. If we are *average* with our service for Christ we are content. If above *average* we are conceited. If below, perhaps a little ashamed. Peter was probably thinking that since he was scheduled to die for Christ, it would be gratifying to know that his record would at least equal if not surpass that of John. There is sometimes a wicked feeling of gratification when we hear of the downfall of other Christians, since that tends to excuse us when we fail.

The golfer who is content to beat his partner will never be a great linksman. Professional golfers constantly try to beat par. So Christians ought never to even think about what John is going to do. They should be thinking about whether or not they are doing all that Christ, the Head over all things to His church (Eph.1:22,23) has cut out for them to do. The truth was that John would not suffer martyrdom as Peter did, but that does not prove that John was less devoted to Christ or that he was a bigger coward than Peter. It only proves that martyrdom was not in John's blueprint (Eph.2:10) as it was in Peter's. How much more harmoniously synchronized the movements within the Body of Christ would be if every member in it would abandoned his self-appointed role as Judge and mind his own business.

Verse 22 - "Jesus saith unto him, If I will that he tarry till I come, what is that to thee? Follow thou me."

λέγει αὐτῷ ὁ Ἰησοῦς, Ἐὰν αὐτὸν θέλω μένειν ἕως ἔρχομαι, τί πρὸς σέ; σύ μοι ἀκολούθει.

λέγει (3d.per.sing.pres.act.ind.of λέγω, historical) 66.

αὐτῷ (dat.sing.masc.of αὐτος, indirect object of λέγει) 16.

ὁ (nom.sing.masc.of the article in agreement with Ἰησοῦς) 9.

Ἰησοῦς (nom.sing.masc.of Ἰησοῦς, subject of λέγει) 3.

Ἐὰν (condition particle in a third-class condition) 363.

αὐτὸν (acc.sing.masc.of αὐτός, general reference) 16.

θέλω (1st.per.sing.pres.act.subj.of θέλω, third-class condition) 88.

μένειν (pres.act.inf.of μένω, accusative, object of θέλω) 864.

ἕως (conjunction introducing a temporal clause) 71.

ἔρχομαι (1st.per.sing.pres.ind.of ἔρχομαι, temporal clause - "until") 146.

τί (nom.sing.neut.of τίς, subject of ἐστιν understood) 281.

πρὸς (preposition with the accusative, general reference) 197.

σέ (acc.sing.masc.of σύ, general reference) 104.

σύ (nom.sing.masc.of σύ, subject of ἀκολούθει, emphatic) 104.

μοι (dat.sing.masc.of ἐγώ, association) 123.

ἀκολούθει (2d.per.sing.pres.act.impv.of ἀκολουθέω, command) 394.

Translation - "Jesus said to him, 'If I want him to stay (on earth) until I come, how does that concern you? You are always to follow me!' "

Comment: Jesus did not say that He wanted John to live until the second coming. It is a third-class condition. The premise in the protasis is in doubt. We know, only from history, not from this passage, that it was not our Lord's will for John to live on earth for 1900 years, although he did outlive all of the other apostles and died only when he was nearing 100 years of age. But let us suppose that Jesus had decreed that John should live until the rapture. What possible concern should Peter have had about that? The apodosis is a rhetorical question that expects the answer to be, "None at all." It was Jesus' polite way to tell Peter that it was none of his business. Jesus also did not divulge whether or not John would die a martyr's death. That also need be of no concern to Peter. The fact is that although John died at the close of the first century of the Christian era, he was given a preview of the last seven years of the Gentile age and witnessed the projection of scenes of "the day of the Lord" when Jesus will in fact return to earth. But Peter was not told that John would see and write the description of the scenes in the Revelation. Jesus' only point was that Peter should spend more time devoting his own energies to the task of following his Lord and less time worryig about what was going to happen to John. Every child of God has a blueprint of activity assigned to him (Eph.2:10). Our task is to do in this life all that has been assigned to us. Note the durative nature of the present imperative in ἀκολούθει. Peter, smarting under the rebuke of Jesus, did not quite learn his lesson. He had to go out and talk about it. And thus he started a false rumor!

Verse 23 - "Then went this saying abroad among the brethren, that that disciple should not die: yet Jesus said not unto him, He shall not die: but if I will that he tarry till I come, what is that to thee.?"

ἐξῆλθεν οὖν οὗτος ὁ λόγος εἰς τοὺς ἀδελφοὺς ὅτι ὁ μαθητὴς ἐκεῖνος οὐκ ἀποθνῄσκει. οὐκ εἶπεν δὲ αὐτῷ ὁ Ἰησοῦς ὅτι οὐκ ἀποθνῄσκει, ἀλλ᾽, Ἐὰν αὐτὸν θέλω μένειν ἕως ἔρχομαι (, τί πρὸς σέ);

ἐξῆλθεν (3d.per.sing.aor.act.ind.of ἐξέρχομαι, ingressive) 161.
οὖν (continuative conjunction) 68.
οὗτος (nom.sing.masc.of οὗτος, in agreement with λόγος) 93.
ὁ (nom.sing.masc.of the article in agreement with λόγος) 9.
λόγος (nom.sing.masc.of λόγος, subject of ἐξῆλθεν) 510.
εἰς (preposition with the accusative of extent) 140.
τοὺς (acc.pl.masc.of the article in agreement with ἀδελφοὺς) 9.
ἀδελφοὺς (acc.pl.masc.of ἀδελφός, extent) 15.
ὅτι (conjunction introducing a clause in apposition in indirect discourse) 211.
ὁ (nom.sing.masc.of the article in agreement with μαθητὴς) 9.
μαθητὴς (nom.sing.masc.of μαθητὴς, subject of ἀποθνῄσκει) 421.
ἐκεῖνος (nom.sing.masc.of ἐκεῖνος, in agreement with μαθητὴς) 246.
οὐκ (summary negative conjunction with the indicative) 130.
ἀποθνῄσκει (3d.per.sing.pres.ind.of ἀποθνῄσκω, futuristic) 774.
οὐκ (summary negative conjunction with the indicative) 130.
εἶπεν (3d.per.sing.aor.act.ind.of εἶπον, constative) 155.
δὲ (adversative conjunction) 11.
αὐτῷ (dat.sing.masc.of αὐτός, indirect object of εἶπεν) 16.
ὁ (nom.sing.masc.of the article in agreement with Ἰησοῦς) 9.
Ἰησοῦς (nom.sing.masc.of Ἰησοῦς, subject of εἶπεν) 3.
ὅτι (conjunction introducing an object clause in indirect discourse) 211.
οὐκ (summary negative conjunction with the indicative) 130.
ἀποθνῄσκει (3d.per.sing.pres.act.ind.of ἀποθνῄσκω, futuristic) 774.
ἀλλ᾽ (alternative conjunction) 342.
Ἐὰν (conditional particle in a third-class condition) 363.
αὐτὸν (acc.sing.masc.of αὐτός, general reference) 16.
θέλω (1st.per.sing.pres.act.subj.of θέλω, third-class condition) 88.
μένειν (pres.act.inf.of μένω, accusative, object of θέλω) 864.
ἕως (conjunction introducing a temporal clause) 71.
ἔρχεται (1st.per.sing.pres.ind.of ἔρχομαι, temporal clause) 146.
(τί (nom.sing.neut.of τίς, subject of ἐστιν, understood) 281.
πρὸς (preposition with the accusative, reference) 197.
σέ) (acc.sing.masc.of σύ, general reference) 104.

Translation - "Then this rumor began to circulate among the brethren that that disciple was not going to die. But Jesus did not say to him that he was not going to die, but, 'If I want him to remain until I come, how does that concern you?'"

Comment: Note οὗτος with ὁ λόγος, as opposed to ὁ μαθητὴς ἐκεῖνος - "this rumor . . . that disciple." Indirect discourse following ὅτι in both cases, although in the first the object clause seems to be in apposition with λόγος - "this rumor, *viz.* that that disciple would not die. . . "

This part of the story is so true to life. So the rumor spread among all of the brethren? We wonder who started it?! Peter had just been told that what happened to John was none of his business and that he was to concentrate upon his own "followship." But Peter may have read into Jesus' statement a tacit endorsement from the Lord of the popular feeling among the disciples that His return to earth would occur very soon, and thus the good news which he assumed that Jesus was giving was too good to keep. If John is to live until the second coming of Christ, at which time Messiah will bring to fulfillment all of their nationalistic dreams, then His coming must be soon - at least within the next one or two hundred years. So Peter made it his business to talk about something that was none of his business and also something that he knew nothing about. The verb ἐξῆλθεν is ingressive. All Peter needed to do was to get the rumor started. It did not stop until it had reached the entire Christian community. John hastens to correct the misunderstanding. Jesus did not say what Peter said He said.

Though εἰς with the accusative normally means "into", after a verb of motion, the context often makes "into" impossible, in which case, depending upon the context "unto," "to", "towards", "on" or "upon" results. Here "into" is impossible since it is followed by τοὺς ἀδελφούς. So we translate "among the brethren." Communication facilities in A.D.29 necessarily limited the spread of this false rumor to the area which could be canvassed on foot or, at best, by slow moving mail service. In the 20th century false rumors travel at the speed of fast cars, on the wings of jet airplanes and in instantanous transmission of ether waves and quasar. Thus what is whispered in the ear in Mississippi is announced forthwith in Texas and California. The "fellowship of kindred minds" which is said to be "like that above" seems more akin to "the Harper Valley P.T.A."

Verse 24 - "This is the disciple which testifieth of these things, and wrote these things: and we know that his testimony is true."

Οὗτός ἐστιν ὁ μαθητὴς ὁ μαρτυρῶν περὶ τούτων καὶ γράψας ταῦτα, καὶ οἴδαμεν ὅτι ἀληθής αὐτοῦ ἡ μαρτυρία ἐστίν.

Οὗτός (nom.sing.masc.of οὗτος, predicate nominative) 93.

ἐστιν (3d.per.sing.pres.ind.of εἰμί, aoristic) 86.

ὁ (nom.sing.masc.of the article in agreement with μαθητής) 9.

μαθητὴς (nom.sing.masc.of μαθητής, subject of ἐστιν) 421.

ὁ (nom.sing.masc.of the article in agreement with μαρτυρῶν) 9.

μαρτυρῶν (pres.act.part.nom.sing.masc.of μαρτυρέω, substantival, in apposition with Οὗτός) 1471.

περὶ (preposition with the genitive of reference) 173.

τούτων (gen.pl.neut.of οὗτος, reference) 93.

καὶ (adjunctive conjunction joining participles) 14.

ὁ (nom.sing.masc.of the article in agreement with γράψας) 9.

γράψας (aor.act.part.nom.sing.masc.of γράφω, substantival, in apposition with Οὗτός) 156.

ταῦτα (acc.pl.neut.of οὗτος, direct object of γράφας) 93.
καὶ (continuative conjunction) 14.
οἴδαμεν (1st.per.pl.pres.act.ind.of οἶδα, aoristic) 144.
ὅτι (conjunction introducing an object clause in indirect discourse) 211.
ἀληθής (nom.sing.fem.of ἀληθής, predicate adjective) 1415.
αὐτοῦ (gen.sing.masc.of αὐτός, possession) 16.
ἡ (nom.sing.fem.of the article in agreement with μαρτυρία) 9.
μαρτυρία (nom.sing.fem.of μαρτυρία, subject of ἐστίν) 1695.
ἐστίν (3d.per.sing.pres.ind.of εἰμί, static) 86.

Translation - "This man is the disciple who is still telling about these things and he has already written them down, and we know that his testimony is true."

Comment: Two substantival participles (acting as nouns) are in apposition with Ουτός, the deictic pronoun in the predicate, joined with ὁ μαϑητής, the subject of ἐστιν. Ουτός in turn refers to the disciple of whom Jesus was speaking in verse 23. Thus Ουτός, means John, the author of the fourth gospel. He was said, at the time of the writing of verse 24, to be still telling about these things, an obvious reference to the events related in the gospel. So at the time that verse 24 was written, the Apostle John was still living and still preaching. He was also said to have been, at the time of the writing of verse 24, the one who had written the gospel. This is clear from the aorist participle in γράφας. The writing περὶ τούτων - "about these things" was already finished, but the aged Apostle was still able to tell about them. Now comes a testimony in the first person *plural* that "*we* know that his testimony is the truth." There is no agreement among scholars as to whether οἴδαμεν is an editorial plural, which John used to refer to himself, or whether verse 24 was written by someone else - possibly by some of John's brethren in the church at Ephesus, where he had pastored for the past thirty years. It is believed by some that the good Greek grammar of the gospel, as contrasted with the grammar of the Revelation, was the result of the grammatical polish which the Ephesians applied to John's manuscript. This could never be demonstrated and need not be seriously considered, particularly in view of the fact that it is very likely that during those thirty years in Ephesus John was able to refine his own literary style without the help of others. If the Revelation was written at the time of the Neronian persecutuions we would expect it to be less polished that what he was to write thirty years later. Some have thought that John could have written better Greek in the Revealtion than he did, but was so excited by the nature of the visions which he saw and which he described in the Apocalypse that he was not careful about his grammar and syntax. This last idea seems fanciful to me. To be sure, John was excited as he watched the Apocalyptic display, but this should not have hampered his literary ability.

It seems plausible that verses 24 and 25 were added by some other hand as the Ephesian brethren wished to add their testimony with regard to the reliability of John's witness.

Verse 25 - "And there are also many other things which Jesus did, the which, if they should be written, every one, I suppose that even the world itself could not contain the books that should be written. Amen."

Ἔστιν δὲ καὶ ἄλλα πολλὰ ἃ ἐποίησαν ὁ Ἰησοῦς, ἅτινα ἐὰν γράφηται καθ' ἕν,
οὐδ' αὐτὸν οἶμαι τὸν κόσμον χωρῆσαι τὰ γραφόμενα βιβλία.

Ἔστιν (3d.per.sing.pres.ind.of εἰμί, aoristic) 86.

δὲ (adversative conjunction) 11.

καὶ (adjunctive conjunction joining substantives) 14.

ἄλλα (nom.pl.neut.of ἄλλος, subject of ἔστιν) 198.

πολλὰ (nom.pl.neut.of πολύς, in agreement with ἄλλα) 228.

ἃ (acc.pl.neut.of ὅς, direct object of ἐποίησεν) 65.

ἐποίησεν (3d.per.sing.aor.act.ind.of ποιέω, constative) 127.

ὁ (nom.sing.masc.of the article in agreement with Ἰησοῦς) 9.

Ἰησοῦς (nom.sing.masc.of Ἰησοῦς, subject of ἐποίησεν) 3.

ἅτινα (nom.pl.neut.of ὅστις, direct attraction to ἄλλα) 163.

ἐὰν (conditional particle in a third-class condition) 363.

γράφηται (3d.per.sing.pres.pass.subj.of γράφω, third-class condtion) 156.

καθ' (preposition with the accusative, distributive) 98.

ἕν (acc.sing.neut.of εἷς, distributive) 469.

οὐδ' (disjunctive particle) 452.

αὐτὸν (acc.sing.masc.of αὐτός, in agreement with κόσμον, intensive) 16.

#2926 οἶμαι (1st.per.sing.pres.ind.of οἴομαι, aoristic).

think - James 1:7.
suppose - John 21:25; Phil.1:17.

Meaning: to suppose, think, assume. Followed by an accusative with infinitive
in John 21:25; by the infinitive in Phil.1:17; by ὅτι in James 1:7.

τὸν (acc.sing.masc.of the article in agreement with κόσμον) 9.

κόσμον (acc.sing.masc.of κόσμον, general reference) 360.

χωρῆσαι (aor.act.infinitive of χωρέω, in indirect discourse) 1162.

τὰ (acc.pl.neut.of the article in agreement with βιβλία) 9.

γραφόμενα (pres.pass.part.acc.pl.neut.of γράφω, adjectival, ascriptive, in
agreement with βιβλία) 156.

βιβλία (acc.pl.neut.of βιβλίον, direct object of χωρῆσαι) 1292.

*Translation - "But there are also many other things which Jesus did, but I do not
think that if they are written one by one the world itself would contain the books
that would be written."*

Comment: δὲ is adversative. If we can assume that οἴδαμεν in verse 24 is not
editorial but grammatical plural, and thus that other Ephesian writers wrote
verse 24, in testimony to John's credibility, it is easy to see John taking the quill
and writing the last verse. Note the singular in οἶμαι after οἴδαμεν in verse 24.
John seems to be saying, "Of course, what I have written is true, but (adversative
δὲ) I could have written much more." His protasis ἐὰν γράφηται καθ' ἕν does

not fit the apodosis, τὸν κόσμον . . . βιβλία. οὐδ᾽ is joined to οἶμαι, not to χωρῆσαι. Some manuscripts have χωρήσειν instead of χωρῆσαι. If it were the original reading, it would be one of the rare future infinitives in indirect discourse, in this case after οἶμαι, standing for the future indicative. "In the papyri Moulton notes that the future infinitive is sometimes used in the κοινή as equivalent to the aorist or even the present, since the sense of the future was vanishing. Cf.χωρήσειν in Jo.21:25 (Sinaiticus BC), while the other later MSS. give χωρῆσαι. In the O.T. the future infinitive (anarthrous always) occurs only 14 times and only 6 in the N.T." (Moulton, *Prolegomena*, 204, as cited in Robertson, *Grammar*, 1082.)

γραφόμενα is a participial adjective in the attributive position, ascriptively modifying βιβλία. John's hyperbole is obvious. The point is that under the Holy Spirit's guidance, John selected his material. Note the distributive accusative with καθ᾽ ἕν - "one at a time," "one by one," or "one after another."

Eighth — To 500 Disciples in Galilee

(Matthew 28:16-20; Mark 16:15-18; 1 Corinthians 15:6, q.v. en loc)

Mark 16:15 - "And he said unto them, Go ye into all the world, and preach the gospel to every creature."

καὶ εἶπεν αὐτοῖς, Πορευθέντες εἰς τὸν κόσμον ἅπαντα κηρύξατε τὸ εὐαγγέλιον πάσῃ τῇ κτίσει.

καὶ (continuative conjunction) 14.

εἶπεν (3d.per.sing.aor.act.ind.of εἶπον, constative) 155.

αὐτοῖς (dat.pl.masc.of αὐτός, indirect object of εἶπεν) 16.

Πορευθέντες (aor.mid.part.nom.pl.masc.of πορεύομαι, adverbial, temporal) 170.

εἰς (preposition with the accusative of extent) 140.

τὸν (acc.sing.masc.of the article in agreement with κόσμον) 9.

ἅπαντα (acc.sing.masc.of ἅπας, in agreement with κόσμον) 639.

κηρύξατε (2d.per.pl.aor.act.impv.of κηρύσσω, command) 249.

τὸ (acc.sing.neut.of the article in agreement with εὐαγγέλιον) 9.

εὐαγγέλιον (acc.sing.neut.of εὐαγγέλιον, direct object of κηρύξατε) 405.

πάσῃ (dat.sing.fem.of πᾶς, in agreement with κτίσει) 67.

τῇ (dat.sing.fem.of the article in agreement with κτίσει) 9.

κτίσει (dat.sing.fem.of κτίσις, indirect object of κηρύξατε) 2633.

Translation - "And He said to them, 'When you have gone into all the world, tell the good news to the entire creation.' "

Comment: The participle is temporal. Obviously one must go before he can tell. Note ἅπαντα with its α intensive. κτίσει means the entire creation, inanimate as well as human.

Mark 16:16 - "He that believeth and is baptized shall be saved, but he that believeth not shall be damned."

ὁ πιστεύσας καὶ βαπτισθεὶς σωθήσεται, ὁ δὲ ἀπιστήσας κατακριθήσεται.

ὁ (nom.sing.masc.of the article in agreement with πιστεύσας) 9.

πιστεύσας (aor.act.part.nom.sing.masc.of πιστεύω, substantival, subject of σωθήσεται) 734.

καὶ (adjunctive conjunction joining participles) 14.

βαπτισθεὶς (aor.pass.part.nom.sing.masc.of βαπτίζω, substantival, subject of σωθήσεται) 273.

σωθήσεται (3d.per.sing.fut.pass.ind.of σώζω, predictive) 109.

ὁ (nom.sing.masc.of the article in agreement with ἀπιστήσας) 9.

δὲ (adversative conjunction) 11.

ἀπιστήσας (aor.act.part.nom.sing.masc.of ἀπιστέω, substantival, subject of κατακριθήσεται) 2893.

κατακριθήσεται (3d.per.sing.fut.pass.ind.of κατακρίνω, predictive) 1012.

Translation - "The one who has believed and has been immersed will be saved, but the one who has disbelieved will be condemned."

Comment: It is obvious that the Holy Spirit exercised no control over the man that wrote that! The verse is full of internal evidence that it does not belong in Mark's contribution to the canon of New Testament Scripture. The participial substantives (πιστεύσας, βαπτισθεὶς and ἀπιστήσας) are all aorist while the verbs with which they are associated (σωθήσεται and κατακριθήσεται) are predictive future passives. The passage is talking about two kinds of people. The first has already believed and he has already been immersed in water. Those two experiences are for him in the past. Nothing is said about his present condition, although the passage predicts that at some future time he will be saved. The unbeliever also has done his rejecting. It is in his past, but he also, at the present time is neither saved or damned, although he will be damned in the future. The contrast with John 5:24 makes the point. There John says that the present hearer and the present believer is also the present possessor of eternal life - ὁ ἀκούων καὶ πιστεύων . . . ἔχει ζωὴν αἰώνιον. Everything there is present tense. The Mark passage points to man's side of the bargain, faith and baptism, as completed events, while the result is predicted, but not implemented. Thus he is in a sort of middle limbo. Further this is the only scripture that makes water baptism a prerequisite to salvation. Rom.6:3 and Gal.3:27 are not talking about water. Some Roman Catholic prelate, devoid of the superintendence of the Holy Spirit added these verses to the divine record to support the sacerdotal system of the papal authorities. Mark 16:16 is a prominent foundation stone in the theological system of a small group of malcontents who came together in the southern mountain country of the United States in the 19th century, who openly proclaim the universal damnation of all constituents of all Christian denominational bodies except themselves. Regeneration as a result of immersion in water (or sprinkling/pouring) was widely taught by the Roman Church in the Middle

Ages at the time when textual critics think verses 9-20 of Mark 16 were added. The earliest extant manuscript that contains Mark 16:9-20 is A, which dates from the 5th century. The message of grace through a finished blood redemption which is universally taught through the New Testament is utterly inconsistent with baptismal regeneration.

Verse 17 - "And these signs shall follow them that believe; In my name shall they cast out devils; they shall speak with new tongues."

σημεῖα δὲ τοῖς πιστεύσασιν ταῦτα παρακολουθήσει. ἐν τῷ ὀνόματί μου δαιμόνια ἐκβαλοῦσιν, γλώσσαις λαλήσουσιν καιναῖς.

σημεῖα (nom.pl.neut.of σημεῖον, subject of παρακολουθήσει) 1005.
δὲ (continuative conjunction) 11.
τοῖς (dat.pl.masc.of the article in agreement with πιστεύσασιν) 9.
πιστεύσασιν (aor.act.part.dat.pl.masc.of πιστεύω, substantival, accompaniment) 734.
παρακολουθήσει (3d.per.sing.fut.act.ind.of παρακολουθέω, predictive) 1710.
ταῦτα (nom.pl.neut.of οὗτος, in agreement with σημεῖα) 93.
ἐν (preposition with the instrumental of means) 80.
τῷ (instru.sing.neut.of the article in agreement with ὀνόματι) 9.
ὀνόματί (instru.sing.neut.of ὄνομα, means) 108.
μου (gen.sing.masc.of ἐγώ, possession) 123.
διαμόνια (acc.pl.neut.of δαιμόνιον, direct object of ἐκβαλοῦσιν) 686.
ἐκβαλοῦσιν (3d.per.pl.fut.act.ind.of ἐκβάλλω, predictive) 649.
γλώσσαις (instru.pl.fem.of γλῶσσα, means) 1846.
λαλήσουσιν (3d.per.pl.fut.act.ind.of λαλέω, predictive) 815.
καιναῖς (instru.pl.fem.of καινός, in agreement with γλώσσαις) 812.

Translation - "And these signs shall accompany those who have believed: in my name they will cast out demons; they will speak with foreign languages."

Comment: These sign gifts, which were given to the Apostles in the first century, in the period before the New Testament canon was complete were withdrawn when the perfect revelation was finished. *Cf.* our comment on 1 Cor.13:8-13. The sign gifts served to prove the authenticity of the divine message in the mouths of the apostles, until the message had been written. When the literature of the New Testament was complete, with the writings of John (the gospel and the epistles) any further manifestation of miracle working power in the church would have led to supplements of the New Testament message, as the modern so-called "tongues movement" which is charactertistic of Pentecostalism does. This is also claimed by the Mormons. γλώσσαις means, not the unintelligible and inarticulate gibberish which is currently being produced in some circles but "language" like French, German, English, Russian, Chinese *et al.* γλώσσιας καιναῖς, therefore means "foreign languages." Everyone who is speaking in a language that one cannot understand is speaking in a *foreign* language.

Verse 18 - "They shall take up serpents: and if they drink any deadly thing, it shall not hurt them; they shall lay their hands on the sick, and they shall recover."

(καὶ ἐν ταῖς χερσὶν) ὄφεις ἀροῦσιν, κἄν θανάσιμόν τι πίωσιν οὐ μὴ αὐτοὺς βλάψη, ἐπὶ ἀρρώστους χεῖρας ἐπιθήσουσιν καὶ καλῶς ἕξουσιν.

(καὶ (continuative conjunction) 14.
ἐν (preposition with the locative of place where) 80.
ταῖς (loc.pl.fem.of the article in agreement with χερσὶν) 9.
χερσὶν) (loc.pl.fem.of χείρ, place where) 308.
ὄφεις (acc.pl.masc.of ὄφις, direct object of ἀροῦσιν) 658.
ἀροῦσιν (3d.per.pl.fut.act.ind.of αἴρω, predictive) 350.
κἄν (conditional particle, continuative καί, and ἄν, crasis, in a third-class condition) 1370.

#2927 θανάσιμόν (acc.sing.neut.of θανάσιμος, direct object of πίωσιν).

deadly thing - Mark 16:18.

Meaning: Cf.θανατόω (#879), θάνατος (#381) and θανατηφόρος (#5130). An adjective - deadly, conductive to death, fatal. Liquid poison in Mark 16:18.

τι (acc.sing.neut.of τις, indefinite pronoun, in agreement with θανάσιμόν) 486.
πίωσιν (3d.per.pl.2d.aor.act.subj.of πίνω, third-class condition) 611.
οὐ (summary negative conjunction with μὴ and the subjunctive, emphatic negation) 130.
μὴ (qualified negative conjunction with οὐ and the subjunctive, emphatic negation) 87.
βλάψη (3d.per.sing.aor.act.subj.of βλάπτω, emphatic negation) 2063.
ἐπὶ (preposition with the accusative of extent) 47.
ἀρρώστους (acc.pl.masc.of ἄρρωστος, extent) 1117.
χεῖρας (acc.pl.fem.of χείρ, direct object of ἐπιθήσουσιν) 308.
ἐπιθήσουσιν (3d.per.pl.ft.act.ind.of ἐπιτίθημι, predictive) 818.
καὶ (continuative conjunction) 14.
καλῶς (adverbial) 977.
ἕξουσιν (3d.per.pl.fut.act.ind.of ἔχω, predictive) 82.

Translation - "And they will take up snakes in their hands, and if they drink any poison it will never hurt them. They will lay their hands upon sick people and they will recover."

Comment: The reference to snakes is a presumptuous attempt on the part of the writer to suggest that the supernatural deliverance of Paul (Acts 28:1-5) was to be extended to other Christians after the canon of Scripture was complete. If I allowed a deadly snake to bite me and then shook it off my hand and suffered no harm, like Paul did, I would write another book for the New Testament and make a million dollars. Why the reference to drinking poison? What Apostle ever did this? The snake handlers are still with us in some sequestered regions.

Unlike the Apostle Paul who was bitten while he was putting wood of a fire, these modern "apostles" deliberately pick up snakes as pulpit demonstrations before church audiences that they are the anointed of the Lord, as a result of which some have been killed.

Although the miracle of healing is still possible, when the procedure is followed according to James 5:14-16 and if/when it is God's will to heal the sick, the "dog and pony show" healing service, which normally procedes the taking of the offering, which is characteristic of some electronic evangelism, was never carried on by the early church. Usually people who are sick are either at home or they go home, or to the hospital as soon as possible. The elders of the church are to visit them - not the other way around. The result is that prayer and anointing for healing is normally done in the home or hospital room. Not all prayers for healing are answered. Paul prayed for healing three times before the Lord told him to say no more about it. If the statement on healing in Mark 16:18 were a part of the divine text and therefore true, no one could ever die and go to heaven, and doctors, surgeons and funeral directors would be out of a job. The usual public healing service is generally punctuated with admonitions from the "healer" to the "patient" to believe. Thus the healer is always a winner. If the patient gets well after the prayer, the healer takes the credit and the money in the offering plate. If the patient dies it can always be said that he did not have enough faith. How can the healer lose? He can - at the judgment seat of Christ.

On the subject of divine healing it can be said that in a sense all healing is divine. The application of medical science is only an application of the knowledge which it has pleased the Lord to give to some doctors and surgeons. There are cases on record of those who were so ill as to be beyond medical help, but who were healed. The author was a participant in one such case in Grape Creek, Illinois, in which the doctor, who was not a Christian testified that the patient was dying of pneumonia when the pastor and the author prayed for her. Burning with fever at 9:00 p.m. with all medical possibilities for a recovery exhausted, she was completely healthy except for weakness by the testimony of the same doctor at 2:00 a.m. She lived to bear several children and see them grow to adulthood.

Hypochondriacs who enjoy ill health and would be miserable if they felt good are helped in "healing" meetings and often testify that they are healed after the anointing and prayer. This is easily explained by the simple fact that they were not sick in the first place.

Much confusion would be dispelled in the church today if the practices suggested in Mark 16:9-20 were recognized as being unauthorized additions to the inspired text by persons who were born hundreds of years after the Holy Spirit had directed the writing of that which Paul called, "that which is perfect" (1 Cor.13:10). The warning of Revelation 22:18,19 should be taken very seriously by the "unknown tongue" experts, the snake handlers, the poison drinkers and the "divine" healers.

Ninth. To James His Brother

(1 Corinthians 15:7, q.v. en loc.)

Tenth. To the Eleven in Jerusalem and on Olivet

(Luke 24:44-49)

Luke 24:44 - "And he said unto them, These are the words which I spake unto you, while I was yet with you, that all things must be fulfilled, which were written in the law of Moses, and in the prophets, and in the psalms, concerning me."

Εἶπεν δὲ πρὸς αὐτούς, Οὗτοι οἱ λόγοι μου οὓς ἐλάλησα πρὸς ὑμᾶς ἔτι ὢν σὺν ὑμῖν, ὅτι δεῖ πληρωθῆναι πάντα τὰ γεγραμμένα ἐν τῷ νόμῳ Μωϋσέως καὶ τοῖς προφήταις καὶ φαλμοῖς περὶ ἐμοῦ.

Εἶπεν (3d.per.sing.aor.act.ind.of εἶπον, constative) 155.

δὲ (continuative conjunction) 11.

πρὸς (preposition with the accusative of extent after a verb of speaking) 197.

αὐτούς (acc.pl.masc.of αὐτός, extent after a verb of speaking) 16.

Οὗτοι (nom.pl.masc.of οὗτος, predicate nominative) 93.

οἱ (nom.pl.masc.of the article in agreement with λόγοι) 9.

λόγοι (nom.pl.masc.of λόγος, subject of εἰσίν, understood) 510.

μου (gen.sing.masc.of ἐγώ, possession) 123.

οὓς (acc.pl.masc.of ὅς, direct object of ἐλάλησα) 65.

ἐλάλησα (1st.per.sing.aor.act.ind.of λαλέω, constative) 815.

πρὸς (preposition with the accusative of extent, after a verb of speaking) 197.

ὑμᾶς (acc.pl.masc.of σύ, extent after a verb of speaking) 104.

ἔτι (temporal adverb) 448.

ὢν (pres.part.nom.sing.masc.of εἰμί, adverbial, temporal) 86.

σὺν (preposition with the instrumental of association) 1542.

ὑμῖν (instru.pl.masc.of σύ, association) 104.

ὅτι (conjunction introducing an apposition clause in indirect discourse) 211.

δεῖ (3d.per.sing.pres.act.ind.imper.of δεῖ, indirect discourse) 1207.

πληρωθῆναι (aor.pass.inf.of πληρόω, epexegetical) 115.

πάντα (acc.pl.neut.of πᾶς, in agreement with γεγραμμένα) 67.

τὰ (acc.pl.neut.of the article in agreement with γεγραμμένα) 9.

γεγραμμένα (perf.pass.part.acc.pl.neut.of γράφω, substantival, general reference) 156.

ἐν (preposition with the locative of place where) 80.

τῷ (loc.sing.masc.of the article in agreement with νόμῳ) 9.

νόμῳ (loc.sing.masc.of νόμος, place where) 464.

Μωϋσέως (gen.sing.masc.of Μωϋσῆς, description) 715.

καὶ (adjunctive conjunction joining nouns) 14.

τοῖς (loc.pl.masc.of the article in agreement with προφήταις) 9.

προφήταις (loc.pl.masc.of προφήτης, place where) 119.

καὶ (adjunctive conjunction joining nouns) 14.

φαλμοῖς (loc.pl.masc.of φαλμός, place where) 2703.

περὶ (preposition with the genitive of reference) 173.

ἐμοῦ (gen.sing.masc.of ἐγώ, reference) 123.

Translation - "And He said to them, 'These are my words which I spoke to you when I was still with you - that it was necessary that all those things which are written be fulfilled, in the Mosaic law and the prophets and the psalms about me.' "

Comment: The definite relative οὕς is the object of ἐλάλησεν. Its antecedent is λόγοι, while the antecedent of Οὗτοι is the story that the Emmaus disciples had just told to the ten disciples in Jerusalem, the recital of which Jesus had interrupted with His sudden appearance. The topic of discussion was the exposition which Jesus had given on the road to Emmaus. The relative clause more closely identifies what messages (οἱ λόγοι) Jesus was talking about. What messages? "Those which He had spoken unto them." When? ἔτι ὢν σὺν ὑμῖν - a temporal clause with the present temporal adverbial participle ὢν and the temporal adverb ἔτι. He had been with (σὺν ὑμῖν) for three years and had told them again and again about His death and resurrection. What messages? The ὅτι clause with its indirect discourse is really in apposition. The assurance was that the prophecies would be fulfilled. They were found in the Mosaic law, in the messages of the Old Testament prophets and in the Psalms. And these prophecies were about Him (περὶ ἐμοῦ). The necessity to which δεῖ alludes is that of #1207, (5). Now Jesus defines more clearly than He did in Luke 24:27 what specific Old Testament Scriptures He means. Not those ἐν πάσαις ταῖς γραφαῖς, but in all that speak directly of Him, which are found in the Mosaic Law *i.e.* Genesis, Exodus, Leviticus, Numbers and Deuteronomy, the Prophets and the Psalms. *Cf.* comment on Luke 24:27. The time of the passage before us is Resurrection Day evening. *Cf.* John 20:19-25. Jesus is saying the same things to the ten Apostles and the two Emmaus disciples (and any others who may have been present) that He had said earlier that afternoon on the Emmasus road.

Verse 45 - "Then opened he their understanding, that they might understand the scriptures."

τότε διήνοιξεν αὐτῶν τὸν νοῦν τοῦ συνιέναι τὰς γραφάς.

τότε (temporal adverb) 166.
διήνοιξεν (3d.per.sing.aor.act.ind.of διανοίγω, ingressive) 1888.
αὐτῶν (gen.pl.masc.of αὐτός, possession) 16.
τὸν (acc.sing.masc.of the article in agreement with νοῦν) 9.

#2928 νοῦν (acc.sing.masc.of νοῦς, direct object of διήνοιξεν).

understanding - Luke 24:45; Rev.13:18; 1 Cor.14:14,15,15; Phil.4:7.
mind - Rev.17:9; 1 Cor.14:19; Rom.1:28; 7:23; Eph.4:17; 1 Tim.6:5; 2 Tim.3:8; Tit.1:15; Rom.7:25; Eph.4:23; Rom.12:2; 2 Thess.2:2; Rom.14:5; 1 Cor.1:10; Rom.11:34; 1 Cor.2:16,16; Col.2:18; 2 Cor.3:14; 4:4.

Meaning: The faculty for understanding in an intellectual way; the thinking process which enables us to construct a *rationale* by which we come to logical conclusions and make decisions for action. Human capacity to think straight -

Luke 24:45; Phil.4:7; Titus 1:15, where νοῦν is joined with συνείδησις; Rom.7:25; Eph.4:23; 2 Cor.3:14; 4:4. Where the capacity to think is not so much in view, but the *rationale* which it has provided - one's intellectual model; schematic system, theory, based on assumptions which permit certain conclusions - as we say, "According to my view (νοῦς) this conclusion should be reached . . κ.τ.λ.." *Cf.* also Rev.13:18; 17:9; 1 Cor.14:14,15,15,19; 2:16,16; Rom.1:28; 7:23; Eph.4:17; 1 Tim.6:5; 2 Tim.3:8; Rom.12:2; 2 Thess.2:2; Rom.14:5; 1 Cor.1:10; Rom.11:34; Col.2:18.

τοῦ (gen.sing.neut.of the article, articular infinitive, purpose) 9.
συνιέναι (pres.act.inf.of συνίημι, purpose) 1039.
τὰς (acc.pl.fem.of the article in agreement with γραφάς) 9.
γραφάς (acc.pl.fem.of γραφή, direct object of συνιέναι) 1389.

Translation - "Then He began to open their minds in order that they might understand the Scriptures."

Comment: *Cf.*#2928. Here it means the mind itself, not the rationale which the mind produces and holds. He stimulated and enlightened their thinking processes with a view to giving them the perception so that they might construct a proper *rationale* with reference to the specific passages of Scripture which He had expounded from Moses, the Prophets and the Psalms. They had the same prejudices that the Emmaus disciples had had that same day, earlier in the afternoon. *Cf.* our comment on Luke 24:16.

Verse 46 - "And said unto them, Thus it is written, and thus it behoved Christ to suffer, and to rise from the dead, the third day."

καὶ εἶπεν αὐτοῖς ὅτι Οὕτως γέγραπται παθεῖν τὸν Χριστὸν καὶ ἀναστῆναι ἐκ νεκρῶν τῇ τρίτῃ ἡμέρᾳ,

καὶ (adjunctive conjunction joining verbs) 14.
εἶπεν (3d.per.sing.aor.act.ind.of εἶπον, constative) 155.
αὐτοῖς (dat.pl.masc.of αὐτός, indirect object of εἶπεν) 16.
ὅτι (conjunction introducing an object clause in indirect discourse) 211.
Οὕτως (demonstrative adverb) 14.
γέγραπται (3d.per.sing.perf.pass.ind.of γράφω, intensive) 156.
παθεῖν (2d.aor.inf.of πάσχω, subject of γέγραπται, in indirect discourse) 1208.
τὸν (acc.sing.masc.of the article in agreement with Χριστὸν) 9.
Χριστὸν (acc.sing.masc.of Χριστός, general reference) 4.
καὶ (adjunctive conjunction joining infinitives) 14.
ἀναστῆναι (2d.aor.inf.of ἀνίστημι, subject of γέγραπται, indirect discourse, timeless aorist) 789.
ἐκ (preposition with the ablative of separation) 19.
νεκρῶν (abl.pl.masc.of νεκρός, separation) 749.
τῇ (loc.sing.fem.of the article in agreement with ἡμέρᾳ) 9.
τρίτῃ (loc.sing.fem.of τρίτος, in agreement with ἡμέρᾳ) 1209.

ἡμέρᾳ (loc.sing.fem.of ἡμέρα, time point) 135.

Translation - "And He said to them that thus the suffering of Christ and His resurrection from the dead have been recorded."

Comment: The ὅτι clause is the object of εἶπεν and it introduces indirect discourse, with two timeless aorist infinitives. They are timeless because at the time when the prophecies of the death and resurrection of Christ were recorded the events to which they pointed were in the future. One of the evidences of the supernatural in the revelation of the Word of God is the fact that centuries before the fact the writers of the Old Testament recorded it. This can be explained only by postulating a view of God that includes His perfect knowledge of all future events, and His control of those events of human history of which the prophecies have previously spoken. "Known unto God are all His works from the beginning of the world" (Acts 15:18) and He ". . . worketh all things after the counsel of His own will" (Eph.1:11b). This does not mean that God actively intervenes in every detail of the human history story. If the known results that flow from known causes are in harmony with the divine will, He does not interfere, but allows scientific laws to dictate the flow of events. But those results, (such as the regeneration of a depraved soul) which cannot flow from natural causes, are actively brought about by God, even when He uses human tools to carry out His purpose. Thus, Judas Iscariot betrayed Jesus, in fulfillment of Old Testament prophecies and also the predictions of our Lord Himself, without any awareness that he was acting under any compulsion other than his own. Peter, or any of the other disciples, or my reader or I could have betrayed Jesus to His murderers, and might very well have done so if the Holy Spirit had not intervened in our lives to direct us to loftier causes.

"The future infinitive echoes the expectation of a verb like ἐλπίζω (or μέλλω) or as the infinitive represents a future indicative in indirect discourse." (Robertson, *Grammar*, 1080). Here the infinitives (timeless aorists) pointed forward to Calvary and the resurrection when they were recorded in Old Testament times, but at the time that Jesus was speaking, these events had occurred and were now history.

Verse 47 - "And that repentance and remission of sins should be preached in his name among all nations, beginning at Jerusalem."

καὶ κηρυχθῆναι ἐπὶ τῷ ὀνόματι αὐτοῦ μετάνοιαν καὶ ἄφεσιν ἁμαρτιῶν εἰς πάντα τὰ ἔθνη — ἀρξάμενοι ἀπὸ Ἰερουσαλήμ.

καὶ (adjunctive conjunction joining infinitives) 14.
κηρυχθῆναι (2d.aor.pass.inf.of κηρύσσω, timeless aorist, subject of γέγραπται) 249.
ἐπὶ (preposition with the instrumental, agency) 47.
τῷ (instru.sing.neut.of the article in agreement with ὀνόματι) 9.
ὀνόματι (instru.sing.neut.of ὄνομα, agency) 108.
αὐτοῦ (gen.sing.masc.of αὐτός, possession) 16.

μετάνοιαν (acc.sing.fem.of μετάνοια, general reference) 286.

εἰς (preposition with the accusative, purpose) 140.

ἄφεσιν (acc.sing.fem.of ἄφεσις, purpose) 1576.

ἁμαρτιῶν (gen.pl.fem.of ἁμαρτία, description) 111.

εἰς (preposition with the accusative, original static use, like a locative) 140.

πάντα (acc.pl.neut.of πᾶς, in agreement with ἔθνη) 67.

τὰ (acc.pl.neut.of the article in agreement with ἔθνη) 9.

ἔθνη (acc.pl.neut.of ἔθνος, place where, original static use of εἰς with the accusative, like a locative) 376.

ἀρξάμενοι (aor.mid.part.nom.pl.masc.of ἄρχω, anacoluthon) 383.

ἀπὸ (preposition with the ablative of source) 70.

Ἰερουσαλήμ (abl.sing.neut.of Ἰεροσόλυμα, source) 141.

Translation - ". . . also the proclamation in His name of repentance unto forgiveness of sins among all the nations, beginning at Jerusalem."

Comment: Verse 47 is joined to γέγραπται of verse 46 in the same way as the infinitives of verse 46. The indirect discourse is still going on with a third timeless aorist infinitive in κηρυχθῆναι, another subject of γέγραπται. The Old Testament foretold Christ's death and resurrection, plus the fact that as a result of His sacrifice at Calvary and victory over death, the message of repentance and forgiveness of sins would be preached not only to the Jews, but also among all the Gentile nations. This is a blow to the Plymouth Brethren hyper-dispensationalism that says that there is nothing in the Old Testament about the evangelism of the Gentiles during what they refer to as "the church age." Repentance is here said to be prerequisite to and therefore for the purpose of remission of sins. The missionary enterprise is to be worldwide in its scope (Mt.28:18-20; Acts 1:8).

Luke's Greek in verses 46 and 47 becomes rather classically sophisticated, perhaps to be regarded as a foregleam of what we can expect in the Acts. We emphasize that the thrust of the passage is that the New Testament program, beginning with the incarnation of the Son of God, followed by His life, death, resurrection and ascension and not to be completed until the story of the gospel has been proclaimed unto the ends of the earth, was all foretold in the Old Testament writings.

Jesus then pointed out that death, burial and resurrection of the Son of God, which are the fundamental foundations of the entire plan of redemption, had been personally observed by the Apostles, so that, when they went out to preach, they could point to the Old Testament prophecies which foretold these events and then say, "I personally saw the fulfillment of these prophecies." A study of their preaching in the Acts of the Apostles reveals that that is exactly what they preached.

Verse 48 - "And ye are witnesses of these things."

ὑμεῖς μάρτυρες τούτων.

ὑμεῖς (nom.pl.masc.of σύ, subject of ἔσεσθε understood) 104.
μάρτυρες (nom.pl.masc.of μάρτος, predicate nominative) 1263.
τούτων (gen.pl.neut.of οὗτος, definition) 93.

Translation - "You are going to be witnesses of these things."

Comment: The participle ἀρξάμενοι is an anacoluthon, any way you look at it. It agrees with ὑμεῖς in case, number and gender. Whether it is a part of the body of Old Testament prophecy which was written (γέγραπτια) or is to be taken as a part of verse 48 is impossible to tell, but the interpretation is the same in any case. The worldwide mission enterprise was to begin at Jerusalem and that is where the witnesses first preached (Acts 2:14-40). ἀρξάμενοι could not join verse 46 or 47, since there is nothing there with which it can agree in case, number and gender. We must supply the future ἔσεσθε after ὑμεῖς, as Jesus predicted the ministry of the Apostles, which would begin only ten days after His ascension.

If the Apostles and other first century Christians were to carry the heavy responsibility of preaching the gospel to the entire world, they would need the supernatural help of the Holy Spirit, since human flesh, even that of regenerated people "profits nothing" whereas it is "the Spirit that makes alive" (John 6:63). It is appropriate therefore that Jesus should follow His announcement that the Apostles were to begin their ministry of witnessing to a gainsaying world by His promise of the fullness of the Holy Spirit, in

Verse 49: "And behold, I send the promise of my Father upon you: but tarry ye in the city of Jerusalem, until ye be endued with power from on high."

καὶ (ἰδοὺ) ἐγὼ ἀποστέλλω τὴν ἐπαγγελίαν τοῦ πατρός μου ἐφ' ὑμᾶς. ὑμεῖς δὲ καθίσατε ἐν τῇ πόλει ἕως οὗ ἐνδύσησθε ἐξ ὕψους δύναμιν.

καὶ (inferential conjunction) 14.
(ἰδοὺ) (exclamation) 95.
ἐγὼ (nom.sing.masc.of ἐγώ, subject of ἀποστέλλω) 123.
ἀποστέλλω, (1st.per.sing.pres.act.ind.of ἀποστέλλω, futuristic) 215.
τὴν (acc.sing.fem.of the article in agreement with ἐπαγγελίαν) 9.

#2929 ἐπαγγελίαν (acc.sing.fem.of ἐπαγγελία, direct object of ἀποστέλλω).

promise - Luke 24:49; Acts 1:4; 2:33,39; 7:17; 13:23,32; 23:21; 26:6; Rom.4:13,14,16,20; 9:4,8,9; 15:8; 2 Cor.1:20; 7:1; Gal.3:14,16,17,18,18,21,22,29; 4:23,28; Eph.1:13; 2:12; 3:6; 6:2; 1 Tim.4:8; 2 Tim.1:1; Heb.4:1; 6:12,15,17; 7:6; 8:6; 9:15; 10:36; 11:9,9,13,17,33,39; 2 Peter.3:4.

Meaning: Promise; assurance that something will be done. (1) A Roman officer's promise to deliver a prisoner - Acts 23:21. Elsewhere in the New Testament of God's promises to the Elect. (2) That the Holy Spirit would fill the early Christians - Luke 24:49; Acts 1:4; 2:33,39; Gal.3:14. (3) With reference to the covenant promises of God to Abraham and his descendants, as they related, both to Israel as a nation and to the elect for salvation - Acts 7:17; 13:23,32; 26:6; Rom.4:13,14,16,20; 9:4,8,9; 15:8; Gal.3:16,17,18,18,21,22,29; 4:23,28; Eph.3:6;

Heb.6:12,15,17; 7:6; 8:6; 9:15; 10:36; 11:9,9,13,17,39. (4) All of the promises of God - 2 Cor.1:20; 7:1. (5) The promise of longevity - Eph.6:2. (6) The promise τῆς παρουσίας αὐτοῦ - 2 Peter 3:4,9. (7) See also 1 Tim.4:8, followed by ζωῆς τῆς νῦν καὶ τῆς μελλούσης; 2 Tim.1:1, followed by ζωῆς τῆς ἐν Χριστῷ Ἰησοῦ; Heb.4:1, followed by the infintive; 1 John 2:2, followed by τὴν ζωὴν τὴν αἰώνιον. (8) Generally - Heb.11:33. *Cf.* also ἐγαγγελίας as a genitive of description in Eph.1:13; 2:12. Followed by ἐκπίστεως Ἰησοῦ Χριστοῦ - Gal.3:22.

τοῦ (gen.sing.masc.of the article in agreement with πατρός) 9.

πατρός (gen.sing.masc.of πατήρ, description) 238.

μου (gen.sing.masc.of ἐγώ, relationship) 123.

ἐφ' (preposition with the accusative of extent) 47.

ὑμᾶς (acc.pl.masc.of σύ, extent) 104.

ὑμεῖς (nom.pl.masc.of σύ, subject of καθίσατε) 104.

δὲ (adversative conjunction) 11.

καθίσατε (2d.per.pl.aor.act. impv.of καθίζω, command) 420.

ἐν (preposition with the locative of place where) 80.

τῇ (loc.sing.fem.of the article in agreement with πόλει) 9.

πόλει (loc.sing.fem.of πόλις, place where) 243.

ἕως (conjunction in a temporal clause, with the genitive, "until") 71.

οὗ (gen.sing.neut.of ὅς, time description in a temporal clause) 65.

ἐνδύσησθε (2d.per.pl.aor.mid.subj.of ἐνδύω, indefinite temporal clause) 613.

ἐξ (preposition with the ablative of source) 19.

ἕφους (abl.sing.masc.of ὕφος, source) 1858.

δύναμιν (acc.sing.fem.of δύναμις, predicate accusative) 687.

Translation - *"And behold, I am going to send forth the promise of My Father upon you; but you must remain in the city, until such time as you are equipped with power from on high."*

Comment: Note the futuristic present in ἀποστέλλω. The filling of the Holy Spirit here promised came ten days after Jesus made this promise to them. The promise of the Father was given in Joel 2:28. The predicate accusative in δύναμιν is adverbial. Luke could have written δυνάμει, - "clothed by means of power." Jesus command that they should remain in the city until they were clothed with the supernatural power of the Holy Spirit suggests the futility of every attempt to serve the Lord without His power. (Zech.4:6; Eph.6:13-17; 2 Cor.4:7; Acts 5:32). Though every Christian should "go" with the good news, he should not go until he has waited for the power. However, since Pentecost we do not have to wait long - only as long as it takes us to ask the Father for His fullness (Luke 11:13). *Cf.* Romans 13:14; Gal.3:27. *Cf.*#613 for other spiritual uses of ἐνδύω. "Clothes make the man!"

The Last Commission and the Ascension

(Mark 16:19,20; Luke 24:50-53; Acts 1:3-12 q.v.en loc)

Mark 16:19 - "So then after the Lord had spoken unto them, he was received up into heaven, and sat on the right hand of God."

'Ο μὲν οὖν κύριος (Ἰησοῦς) μετὰ τὸ λαλῆσαι αὐτοῖς ἀνελήμφθη εἰς τὸν οὐρανὸν καὶ ἐκάθισεν ἐκ δεξιῶν τοῦ θεοῦ.

'Ο (nom.sing.masc.of the article in agreement with κύριος) 9.
μὲν (particle of affirmation) 300.
οὖν (continuative conjunction) 68.
κύριος (nom.sing.masc.of κύριος, subject of ἀνελήμφθη and ἐκάθισεν) 97.
(Ἰησοῦς) (nom.sing.masc.of Ἰησοῦς, apposition) 3.
μετὰ (preposition with the accusative of time extent) 50.
τὸ (acc.sing.neut.of the article, articular infinitive, time extent) 9.
λαλῆσαι (aor.act.inf.of λαλέω, noun use, time extent) 815.
αὐτοῖς (dat.pl.masc.of αὐτός, indirect object of λαλῆσαι) 16.

#2930 ἀνελήμφθη (3d.per.sing.1st.aor.pass.ind.of ἀναλαμβάνω, constative).

receive up - Mark 16:19; Acts 10:16; 1 Tim.3:16.
take in - Acts 7:43; 23:31; Eph.6:13,16; 2 Tim.4:11.
take unto - Acts 20:13,14.
take up - Acts 1:2,11,22.

Meaning: A combination of ἀνά (#1059) and λαμβάνω (#533). Hence, to take up. With reference to the ascension of Jesus - Mark 16:19; 1 Tim.3:16; Acts 1:2,11,22. The sheet in Peter's dream - Acts 10:16; with reference to taking a passenger on board a ship - Mark, 2 Tim.4:11; Paul - Acts 20:13,14. Of the arrest and custody of Paul - Acts 23:31. Metaphorically of the Christian's taking of the spiritual weaponry of God - Eph.6:13,16. To erect a tabernacle - Acts 7:43.

εἰς (preposition with the accusative of extent) 140.
τὸν (acc.sing.masc.of the article in agreement with οὐρανὸν) 9.
οὐρανὸν (acc.sing.masc.of οὐρανός, extent) 254.
καὶ (adjunctive conjunction joining verbs) 14.
ἐκάθισεν (3d.per.sing.aor.act.ind.of καθίζω, constative) 420.
ἐκ (preposition with the ablative of place description) 19.
δεξιῶν (abl.pl.masc.of δελξιός, idiomatic plural, place) 502.
τοῦ (gen.sing.masc.of the article in agreement with θεοῦ) 9.
θεοῦ (gen.sing.masc.of θεός, description) 124.

Translation - "Then in fact after the Lord Jesus spoke to them, He was taken up into heaven and He sat down at the right hand of God."

Comment: The affirmative particle μὲν correlates with δὲ in verse 20. Jesus, in fact (μὲν) went back to heaven, but (δὲ, verse 20) the disciples stayed on earth and started out to preach the gospel. The student may wish to research the question as to how many times in the New Testament, particularly in Mark's gospel, μετὰ is followed by an articular infinitive in the accusative case to indicate time extent. We have the accusative in time extent after μετὰ often, but with the articular infinitive? This *may be* evidence of a later hand than Mark's. (*Note:* In the supplemental volume of *The Renaissance New Testament*, these data will be available.) *Cf.*#2930 for other uses of the verb to apply to our Lord's ascent to glory. *Cf.* Heb.1:3. *Cf.*#420 for καθίζω in the same sense. *Cf.*Acts 1:9-11.

Verse 20 - "And they went forth and preached everywhere, the Lord working with them, and confirming the word with signs following. Amen."

ἐκεῖνοι δὲ ἐξελθόντες ἐκήρυξαν πανταχοῦ, τοῦ κυρίου συνεργοῦντος καὶ τὸν λόγον βεβαιοῦντος διὰ τῶν ἐπακολουθούντων σημείων.

ἐκεῖνοι (nom.pl.masc.of ἐκεῖνος, subject of ἐκήρυξαν) 246.
δὲ (adversative conjunction) 11.
ἐξελθόντες (aor.mid.part.nom.pl.masc.of ἐξέρχομαι, adverbial, temporal) 161.
ἐκήρυξαν (3d.per.pl.aor.act.ind.of κηρύσσω, ingressive) 249.
πανταχοῦ (adverbial) 2062.
τοῦ (gen.sing.masc.of the article in agreement with κυρίου) 9.
κυρίου (gen.sing.masc.of κύριος, genitive absolute) 97.

#2931 συνεργοῦντος (pres.act.part.gen.sing.masc.of συνεργέω, genitive absolute, contemporaneous).

help with - 1 Cor.16:16.
work together - James 2:22.
worker together - 2 Cor.6:1.
work with - Mark 16:20; Rom.8:28.

Meaning: A combination of σύν (#1542) and ἔργον (#460). *Cf.* also συνεργός (#4066). To work together; to cooperate. The cooperation between the early Christians and the Lord - Mark 16:20; the Corinthian saints and God - 2 Cor.6:1; the saints with one another - 1 Cor.16:16; faith and works works work together in complementary roles - James 2:22; events in general work in harmonious cooperation for good for the elect - Romans 8:28.

καὶ (adjunctive conjunction joining participles) 14.
τὸν (acc.sing.masc.of the article in agreement with λόγον) 9.
λόγον (acc.sing.masc.of λόγος, direct object of βεβαιοῦντος) 510.

#2932 βεβαιοῦντος (pres.act.part.gen.sing.masc.of βεβαιόω, genitive absolute, contemporaneous).

confirm - Mark 16:20; Romans 15:8; 1 Cor.1:6,8; Heb.2:3.
establish - Heb.13:9.
stablish - 2 Cor.1:21; Col.2:7.

Meaning: To make sure; make firm; establish; confirm. The Lord confirmed the word of the early Christians, *i.e.* He proved that the testimony which they gave was valid - Mark 16:20. With reference to the establishment of the Abrahamic covenant - Romans 15:8; among the Corinthians - 1 Cor.1:6,8. With reference to the confirmation of the Apostles of Christ's message - Heb.2:3; of the solidity of the faith of a mature Christian - Heb.13:9; Col.2:7; 2 Cor.1:21.

διά (preposition with the genitive of means) 118.

τῶν (gen.pl.neut.of the article in agreement with σημείων) 9.

#2933 ἐπακολουθούντων (pres.act.part.gen.pl.neut.of ἐπακολουθέω, adjectival, attributive position, ascriptive, in agreement with σημείων).

follow - Mark 16:20; 1 Tim.5:10; 1 Peter 2:21; 1 Tim.5:24.

Meaning: A combination of ἐπί (#47) and ἀκολουθέω (#394). Hence, to follow upon; to follow closely. Chronologically - Mark 16:20; to follow the example of Christ closely (*i.e.* with exactitude) - 1 Peter 2:21; to pursue a consistent course of good works - 1 Tim.5:10; to follow in the sense that the effects of sin are felt later - 1 Tim.5:24.

σημείων (gen.pl.neut.of σημεῖον, means) 1005.

Translation - "But these went out and began to preach everywhere, while the Lord worked with them and confirmed their message by means of the signs which followed."

Comment: ἐξελθόντες is a temporal participle. Note the ingressive aorist - "They *began* to preach." And the preaching of the good news has never ceased, nor will it, until the end of the millenium. After that we will talk about it throughout eternity! The two genitive absolute participles, συνεργοῦντες and βεβαιοῦντος are in the present tense, thus indicating contemporaneity with the action of the main verb ἐκήρυξαν. *While* they preached the Lord worked with (and through) them and provided the empirical evidence for the audience that what they said was true. How did He do this? The διά phrase with the genitive indicates means. It was by means of the following signs. The participle ἐπακολουθούντων is an adjective, joined ascriptively in the attributive position to σημείων. The reference to signs is to those of verses 17,18. Luke's story of the early church in Acts does not support the statement that *all* of the early Christians who went out preaching saw the signs described in verses 17,18, which adds weight to the conviction of most textual critics that verses 9-20 of Mark 16 were added by a later hand, who was born after the first century and was not describing events as an eye witness or, as in Luke's case, on the basis of his interviews with eye witnesses. Also, since the writer did not restrict the signs to the ministry of the apostles, it can be inferred that the signs continued after the New Testament canon was completed and the Apostles were dead, an inference, widely used by Pentecostalists and other ecstatic groups now, but which is definitely controverted by 1 Cor.13:8-13. It is obvious that Mark did not write the last twelve verses of his gospel. We turn now to Luke's account of the ascension.

The Ascension of Jesus

(Mark 16:19-20; Luke 24:50-53; Acts 1:9-11 q.v. en loc)

Luke 24:50 - "And he led them out as far as to Bethany, and he lifted up his hands and blessed them."

Ἐξήγαγεν δὲ αυτοὺς (ἔξω) ἕως πρὸς Βηθανίαν, καὶ ἐπάρας τὰς χεῖρας αὐτοῦ εὐλόγησεν αὐτούς.

Ἐξήγαγεν (3d.per.sing.aor.act.ind.of ἐξάγω, constative) 2316.

δὲ (continuative conjunction) 11.

αὐτοὺς (acc.pl.masc.of αὐτός, direct object of ἐξήγαγεν) 16.

(ἔξω) (adverbial) 71.

ἕως (preposition with another preposition πρὸς) 71.

πρὸς (preposition with the accusative of extent) 197.

Βηθανίαν (acc.sing.fem.of Βηθανία, extent) 1363.

καὶ (adjunctive conjunction joining verbs) 14.

ἐπάρας (aor.act.part.nom.sing.masc.of ἐπαίρω, adverbial, temporal) 1227.

τὰς (acc.pl.fem.of the article in agreement with χεῖρας) 9.

χεῖρας (acc.pl.fem.of χείρ, direct object of ἐπάρας) 308.

αὐτοῦ (gen.sing.masc.of αὐτός, possession) 16.

εὐλόγησεν (3d.per.sing.aor.act.ind.of εὐλογέω, constative) 1120.

αὐτούς (acc.pl.masc.of αὐτός, direct object of εὐλόγησεν) 16.

Translation - "And He led them out until (they came) near to Bethany, and having lifted His hands, He blessed them."

Comment: *Cf.* John 10:3. The Good Shepherd led His sheep out. His last act on earth, until He comes again, was to lead the disciples out to Olivet, near to Bethany, so that they could receive His last earthly blessing and witness His ascension. "Four times ἕως occurs with another preposition, like ἕως πρός (Lk.24:50), ἕως ἐπί (Acts 17:14), ἕως ἔξω (21:5). In Mark 14:54 note ἕως ἔσω εἰς. Once (cf.Demosthenes, Aristotle, LXX) we find it with the article and the infinitive ἕως τοῦ ἐλθεῖν (Acts 8:40). (Robertson, *Grammar*, 643). Note our translation. We supply ἦλθαν. Jesus led them until (ἕως) they came to a place which is defined as being πρὸς Βηθανίαν - "near Bethany." Note the pleonasm in ἔξω, following ἐξ in composition in the verb. Specifically the place was the Mount of Olives (Acts 1:12). The words of our Lord's blessing for the people are not recorded. It was during the benediction that He began His ascent into heaven.

Verse 51 - "And it came to pass, while he blessed them, he was parted from them, and carried up into heaven."

καὶ ἐγένετο ἐν τῷ εὐλογεῖν αὐτὸν αὐτοὺς διέστη ἀπ' αὐτῶν καὶ ἀνεφέρετο εἰς τὸν οὐρανόν.

καὶ (continuative conjunction) 14.

ἐγένετο (3d.per.sing.aor.ind.of γίνομαι, constative) 113.

ἐν (preposition with the locative of time point) 80.

τῷ (loc.sing.neut.of the article, time point) 9.

εὐλογεῖν (pres.act.inf.of εὐλογέω, articular infinitive, time point) 1120.

αὐτὸν (acc.sing.masc.of αὐτός, general reference) 16.

αὐτοὺς (acc.pl.masc.of αὐτός, direct object of εὐλογεῖν) 16.

διέστη (3d.per.sing.aor.act.ind.of διίστημι, constative) 2818.

ἀπ' (preposition with the ablative of separation) 70.

αὐτῶν (abl.pl.masc.of αὐτός, separation) 16.

καὶ (adjunctive conjunction joining verbs) 14.

ἀνεφέρετο (3d.per.sing.imp.pass.ind.of ἀναφέρω, inceptive) 1221.

εἰς (preposition with the accusative of extent) 140.

τὸν (acc.sing.masc.of the article in agreement with οὐρανόν) 9.

οὐρανόν (acc.sing.masc.of οὐρανός, extent) 254.

Translation - "And it happened that while He was blessing them He stepped away from them and began to be lifted up into heaven."

Comment: The verb ἐγένετο adds nothing to the thought; however, out of deference to the text we have included it in the translation. The articular infinitive introduced by ἐν suggests time point. It is in the present tense, hence it denotes contemporaneity with the time of the main verbs διέστη and ἀνεφέρετο. The imperfect is inceptive - "He began to be lifted up into heaven." It was not a sudden disappearance. He ascended slowly. This is borne out by Acts 1:9, comment upon which see *en loc*. First Jesus moved away from them slightly. *Cf.*#2818 where διά in composition appears. διά, is related to δύο (#385) and implies some type of duality. Jesus stepped away so that He stood in one spot of two, in the other of which stood the disciples. Thus we see the precision of the Greek idiom. When διά (#118) occurs, alone or in composition, we always look for two of something. His ascent, once begun was continuous, as βλεπόντων αὐτῶν in Acts 1:9 indicates. ἀναφέρω (#1221) is used of lifting up an offering to God. It is altogether appropriate therefore to find it in Heb.9:28; 1 Peter 2:24; Heb.7;27b, as well as in Luke 24:51. God's perfectly acceptable offering for sin was lifted up from Olivet to the Father's right hand (Psalm 110:1; Eph.1:19-23; Phil.2:9-11). *Cf.* Mt.28:18-20; Acts 1:9-11.

Verse 52 - "And they worshipped Him, and returned to Jerusalem with great joy."

καὶ αὐτοὶ προσκυνήσαντες αὐτὸν ὑπέστρεφαν εἰς Ἰερουσαλὴμ μετὰ χαρᾶς μεγάλης.

καὶ (continuative conjunction) 14.

αὐτοὶ (nom.pl.masc.of αὐτός, subject of ὑπέστρεφαν) 16.

προσκυνήσαντες (aor.act.part.nom.pl.masc.of προσκυνέω, adverbial, temporal) 147.

αὐτὸν (acc.sing.masc.of αὐτός, direct object of προσκυνήσαντες) 16.

ὑπέστρεφαν (3d.per.pl.aor.act.ind.of ὑποστρέφω, ingressive) 1838.
εἰς (preposition with the accusative of extent) 140.
Ἰερουσαλήμ (acc.sing.of Ἰεροσολύμων, extent) 141.
μετὰ (preposition with the genitive, adverbial) 50.
χαρᾶς (gen.sing.fem.of χαρά, adverbial) 183.
μεγάλης (gen.sing.fem.of μέγας, in agreement with χαρᾶς) 184.

Translation - "And after they had worshipped Him, they began the trip back to Jerusalem with great joy."

Comment: The disciples did not return to Jerusalem immediately - only after they had spent some time upon Olivet worshipping their risen and ascended Lord. Thus the first worship service was held in contemplation of the glorification of Jesus Christ and the promise that He would return (Acts 1:11). The nature of the worship - prayer, praise, testimony, confession, singing - is not revealed. It is likely that all of these elements were included. No doubt a great many were ashamed of their previous doubts about His resurrection. It is likely that Peter vowed never to touch another fish net. Though they were not yet filled with the Holy Spirit, He Who indwelt them made it clear to them that though Jesus was now absent in a corporeal, visible and spatial sense, He was not absent from them in a real spiritual sense, any more than He is for any Christian. Hence, as they started the short trip back to Jerusalem and walked down the mountain, across Kedron and up the hill to the gate of the city, they were overflowing with joy. *Contra* Mt.9:15. The Bridegroom was not really gone - only to those empircists who suffer under the unfortunate restraint of a false epistemology.

Verse 53 - "And were continuously in the temple, praising and blessing God. Amen."

καὶ ἦσαν διὰ παντὸς ἐν τῷ ἱερῷ εὐλογοῦντες τὸν θεόν.

καὶ (adjunctive conjunction joining verbs) 14.
ἦσαν (3d.per.pl.imp.ind.of εἰμί, imperfect periphrastic) 86.
διὰ (preposition with the genitive of time description) 118.
παντὸς (gen.sing.masc.of πᾶς, in agreement with χρονοῦ, understood) 67.
ἐν (preposition with the locative of place where) 80.
τῷ (loc.sing.neut.of the article in agreement with ἱερῷ) 9.
ἱερῷ (loc.sing.neut.of ἱερόν, place where) 346.
εὐλογοῦντες (pres.act.part.nom.pl.masc.of εὐλογέω, imperfect periphratic) 1120.
τὸν (acc.sing.masc.of the article in agreement with θεόν) 9.
θεόν (acc.sing.masc.of θεός, direct object of εὐλογοῦντες) 124.

Translation - "And they were in the temple continually, praising God constantly."

Comment: We do not know precisely what to supply in the ellipsis following παντὸς. χρονοῦ is a good suggestion. "through all time" or continually (constantly). Perhaps καιροῦ is better - "on every occasion." We have used the adverbs "continually" and "constantly" in the translation to represent the true situation. The disciples did not spend their total time, without interruption, in the temple. Common sense dictates that, even if the record in the Acts did not contradict it. "**Continual** and **continuous** are not exact synonyms. *Continual* emphasizes recurrence at regular or frequent intervals: *Dancing requires continual practice. Continuous* means extending uninterruptedly in space of time: *a continuous procession of cars.* (The World Book Dictionary, I, 450). The adverb **constantly**, has the secondary definition: "continually happening; repeated often or again and again." (*Ibid.,* 444). The point is that the disciples allowed nothing to stop their constant praise to God. Under any and all conditions and from time to time they came to the temple, always with a testimony upon their lips. The previous fear of the Jews was evidently gone (John 20:19). There was nothing secret about their behavior now. Their witness was given in the presence of the Jewish Establishment, and among those who had crucified their Lord and would soon persecute them. But not today. This was their day. They believed without reservation that Jesus was the Son of God, their Messiah, that He died for their sins, although they did not understand the theology of atonement as well as they would later understand it when Paul wrote, that He was literally alive. They had just witnessed His ascent to heaven and heard the promise that some day He would come back again to fulfill all of their nationalistic hopes. In the meantime they were under marching orders to begin a worldwide missionary enterprise that would require all of their time and effort till their death or His return. *Cf.*Acts 1:3-12.

This completes the gospel records of Matthew, Mark, Luke and John. They contain 3779 verses. The remainder of the New Testament record contains 4085 verses, for a total of 7864 verses. For the remainder of the work, which may fill eight or nine more volumes, I will continue to follow the English text of the King James Version, since the concordance phase of the study is based upon it. However since beginning this phase of the study on June 15, 1944, more than thirty-seven years ago, advances in textual criticism have resulted in a better edition of the critical text than that of Westcott and Hort, with which we began in 1944. Accordingly we have chosen to follow the Greek text, edited by Kurt Aland, Matthew Black, Carlo M.Martini, Bruce M. Metzger and Allen Wikgren in cooperation with the Institute for New Testament Textual Research. We are still using the Second Edition, although a third edition is now available. Departures from the Westcott/Hort and Nestle texts are not extreme. Notable departures that might affect the exegesis will be discussed *en loc* with explanatory notes by Dr.Meztger in his *A Textual Commentary on the Greek New Testament.*

In the light of John 14:25,26; 16:12-15; 1 Cor.13:10; Eph.3:1-11 it is clear that progress from the exposition of the Gospels into and through the remainder of the New Testament revelation is analogous to graduation from undergraduate college and matriculation into graduate school. It is therefore that we face the next few months with eager anticipation and boundless joy. What is yet to be revealed in the Acts and beyond will never be contradictory to what has gone before - only superstructural.

The Acts of the Apostles

(More accurately The Acts of the Holy Spirit Through the Apostles)

So effective was the witness of the early Christians after Pentecost that there were few in the Mediterranean world who had not heard that Jesus of Nazareth was the Messiah of Israel and that He had come to die, not only for the sins of His people Israel, but for the sins of the entire world, and that He had risen from the dead and had gone back to heaven. The gospel message also promised that He would return to earth at some unannounced time and set up a kingdom of peace and justice which would never be destroyed.

Justin Martyr who wrote before A.D.150 said that ". . . there existed not a people, whether Greek or barbarian, whether they dwelt in tents or wandered about in covered waggons, among whom prayers were not offered up in the name of a crucified Jesus, to the Father and Creator of all things. (Justin Martyr, *Dial. cum Trypho*, 117, as cited in *The Pulpit Commentary, 16, The Gospel According to St. Luke*, i). Tertullian, the Christian polemicist of Carthage, who wrote a few years after Justin Martyr told the heathen that ". . . his brethren were to be found filling the camp, the assemblies, the palace, the senate." (Tertullian, *Apologia*, 37, as cited in *Ibid.*).

Before the close of the second century Irenaeus in Gaul, Clement in Alexandria and Tertullian told of the general acceptance of the books composing the New Testament canon. (*Ibid.*) Among these was the Gospel according to Luke.

Irenaeus succeeded Pothinus as the Bishop of Lyons about A.D.177. He had known Polycarp when he was a child. Polycarp was for many years the pastor of the church at Smyrna. He suffered martyrdom about 155 or 156. (Albert Henry Newman, *A Manual of Church History*, I, 232). He had known the Apostle John in his youth and related to Irenaeus many of his experiences with John. Irenaeus did not refer in his writings to any book of the New Testament by name, "but we meet with such striking coincidences of language and thought with many of those books, that it is perfectly certain he was intimately acquainted with them. St. Luke's gospel was one of these." (*Pulpit Commentary, 16, Luke, ii*).

The heretical writer Valentinus was teaching in Rome beginning about A.D.139. Fragments of his writings have been preserved. He cites among other New Testament books, the Gospel of St. Luke and calls it Scripture. (*Ibid.,*iii).

Archbishop Thomson of York says, "At the opening of the second century *(i.e.* A.D.100) the words of the Lord were quoted with unmistakable resemblance to passages of our Gospels, which, however, are quoted loosely without any reference to names of authors, and with a throwing together of passages from all three (synoptical) Gospels." (Archbishop of York in "Introduction to Gospel of St. Luke," in *Speaker's Commentary,* as cited in *Ibid.,*vii). Thus it is evident that in the last decade of the first century of the

Christian era, the Gospel accounts of Matthew, Mark and Luke were extant. It was also in this decade, perhaps about A.D.95 that John added his Gospel.

That Luke, the author of the Gospel, was also the author of the Acts of the Apostles is clear when we examine Luke 1:3 and Acts 1:1. He dedicated both books to Theophilus and specifically mentions "the former treatise" which he had written - Τὸν μὲν πρῶτον λόγον ἐποιησάμην περὶ πάντων . . . ὧν ἤρξατο ὁ Ἰησοῦς ποιεῖν τε καὶ διδάσκειν - Its subject matter was"all that which Jesus began both to do and teach."

It is significant that Luke closes his account of the Acts abruptly with his statement that Paul spent his last two years in Rome. He probably finished the writing early in the year A.D.63, shortly before Paul was martyred. During the two years of Paul's imprisonment he had the leisure to write up his notes which he had probably taken as he travelled with Paul on his previous missionary journeys. Now with Paul's help the work was finished. What Jesus began in His public ministry, the Holy Spirit, in keeping with His promise carried on. And He will continue to carry it on until the Body of Christ is complete.

The Promise of the Holy Spirit
(Acts 1:1-5)

Acts 1:1 - "The former treatise have I made, O Theophilus, of all that Jesus began both to do and teach"

Τὸν μὲν πρῶτον λόγον ἐποιησάμην περὶ πάντων, ὁ Θεόφιλε, ὧν ἤρξατο ὁ Ἰησοῦς ποιεῖν τε καὶ διδάσκειν

Τὸν (acc.sing.masc.of the article in agreement with λόγον) 9.
μὲν (particle of affirmation) 300.
πρῶτον (acc.sing.masc.of πρῶτος, in agreement with λόγον) 487.
λόγον (acc.sing.masc.of λόγος, direct object of ἐποιησάμην) 510.
ἐποιησάμην (1st.per.sing.1st.aor.mid.ind.of ποιέω, culminative) 127.
περὶ (preposition with the genitive of reference) 173.
πάντων (gen.pl.neut.of πᾶς, reference) 67.
ὦ (exclamation) 1177.
Θεόφιλε (voc.sing.masc.of Θεόφιλος, address) 1713.
ὧν (gen.pl.neut.of ὅς, attraction to πάντων) 65.
ἤρξατο (3d.per.sing.aor.mid.ind.of ἄρχω, ingressive) 383.
ὁ (nom.sing.masc.of the article in agreement with Ἰησοῦς) 9.
Ἰησοῦς (nom.sing.masc.of Ἰησοῦς, subject of ἤρξατο) 3.
ποιεῖν (pres.act.inf.ofd ποιέω, epexegetical) 127.
τε (correlative conjunction) 1408.
καὶ (adjunctive conjunction joining infinitives) 14.

διδάσκειν (pres.act.inf.of διδάσκω, epexegetical) 403.

Translation - *"I wrote the first account, O Theophilus, about everything that Jesus began both to do and to teach, . . . "*

Comment: Luke's use of πρῶτος (#487), the ordinal number, rather than the adjective πρότερος (#2293), which means "former" or "the one before" does not imply δεύτερος (#1371) and τρίτος (#1209) — "the first, second and third" as though he was projecting a series of studies of which the Gospel and the Acts were the first two, to be followed by others. μὲν implies contrast between the former work and the present. It does not require δέ or ἀλλά.

He delimits his subject matter with the phrase περὶ πάντων. . . ὧν ἤρξατο ὁ Ἰησοῦς ποιεῖν τε καὶ ποιεῖν. The genitive of reference in πάντων with the relative clause tells us that the Gospel was limited to everything that Jesus did and said. The ingressive ἤρξατο, followed by the two explanatory infinitives ποιεῖν τε καὶ διδάσκειν is an example of Luke's breviloquence. His pen was running ahead of his mind. Robertson suggests that ἤρξατο implies the addition of καὶ διετέλει between it and the infinitives — "all that Jesus began *and continued* to do and teach. . . κ.τ.λ." We are not to suppose that Luke intended to write that Jesus began good works which He was unable to finish. Luke gave equal attention both to what Jesus did and what He taught. τε καὶ - "both . . . and" where the two infinitives are coordinate or of equal importance.

We still need a chronological delimitation of Luke's work in the Gospel which he provides in verse 2. Jesus began in a personal way in the Gospel account what He proceeded to carry on through the Holy Spirit, working through the Apostles in the Acts. That work was not finished at the close of the apostolic period, but is still being done through the members of the Body of Christ. It will not be finished until the end of this age (Rev.10:7). "Luke would have gone on to say that this second book of his contained the story of what Jesus went on to do and teach after He was 'taken up,' if he had been strictly accurate, or had carried out his first intention, as shown by the mold of his introductory sentence; but he is swept on into the full stream of his narrative, and we have to infer the contrast between his two volumes from his statement of the contents of the first." (Alexander Maclaren, *Expositions of the Holy Scripture. Acts of the Apostles*, 2). However, it is more accurante to say that the Holy Spirit continued the ministry that Jesus began. Just as God the Father spoke in the Old Testament age to the fathers by the prophets (Heb.1:1), and God the Son spoke to us in His incarnation in the Gospels (Heb.1:2), so the Holy Spirit has spoken and is still speaking to the world in the period covered by the Acts and the years since. The Father and the Son, having spoken in their turn, there remained only one other personality in the Godhead to speak. If the world rejects Him, as they did the Father in the Old Testament, with their murder of the prophets and as they did in the Gospel period with the crucifixion of the Son, there is no fourth divine Person to witness. This is why the rejection of the witness of the Holy Spirit is called the unpardonable sin (Mt.12:31,32). This, in part, is what the parable of Matthew 21:33-43 is talking about, with its story of Israel's rejection of God's messengers in the Old Testament and her murder of His Son in the Gospels, with the hint in verse 41 that Gentiles would be offered the gospel after the death, burial and resurrection of Christ, which is the story of the work of the Holy Spirit through the chuch in the Acts.

To say, with Maclaren that the Lord Jesus continued to be active after His ascension is to ignore the fact that He has a seated position at the right hand of God (Heb.1:3; Psalm 110:1). His work was finished at Calvary (John 19:30). Just as He worked in creation for six days and rested on the seventh because nothing further in creation needed to be done, so He worked during the first thirty-three years of His incarnation in redemption and, having finished His work is now at rest during the interim period while the Holy Spirit is busy making His enemies His footstool (Psalm 110:1). Believers "enter into (His) rest" (Heb.3:11,18; 4:10,11). There is no rest for the believer to enter if our Lord is not now at rest. Indeed He is. It is the Holy Spirit Who is working. Jesus began to work and to teach and He continued working and teaching until He had fulfilled the part designated for Him in the division of labor in the Godhead. What He did was preparatory and indispensable for the finishing work of the Holy Spirit.

In Luke 1:3, Luke addressed his correspondent as κράτιστε Θεόφιλε, indicating a patrician status, while the adjective is omitted in Acts 1:1. Had Luke come to know Theophilus better and thus now felt free to address him more informally? Or had Theophilus now become a Christian and cared less for the more honorable title? The opening verses of the Gospel do not indicate with clarity whether Theophilus was a Christian, although it is clear that he had been given the basic facts of the gospel (Luke 1:4) and perhaps doubted that some of them were true. This is why Luke researched the story and wrote the former document. Perhaps Luke himself had been elevated to the peerage, successful physician that he was and could write to his peer in an informal way without impropriety. All of this is speculative. Who Theophilus was and what his status in society may have been the text does not tell us. Of course we respect the divine reticence.

Verse 2 - ". . . until the day in which he was taken up, after that he through the Holy Ghost, had given commandments unto the apostles whom he had chosen."

ἄχρι ἧς ἡμέρας ἐντειλάμενος τοῖς ἀποστόλοις διὰ πνεύματος ἁγίου οὓς ἐξελέξατο ἀνελήμφθη.

ἄχρι (improper preposition/conjunction with the genitive of time description) 1517.

ἧς (gen.sing.fem.of ὅς, relative pronoun in a temporal phrase) 65.

ἡμέρας (gen.sing.fem.of ἡμέρα, time description) 135.

ἐντειλάμενος (1st.aor.mid.part.nom.sing.masc.of ἐντέλλομαι, adverbial, temporal) 349.

τοῖς (dat.pl.masc.of the article in agreement with ἀποστόλοις) 9.

ἀποστόλοις (dat.pl.masc.of ἀπόστολος, indirect object of ἐντειλάμενος) 844.

διὰ (preposition with the genitive of intermediate agency) 118.

πνεύματος (gen.sing.neut.of πνεῦμα, intermediate agency) 83.

ἁγίου (gen.sing.neut.of ἅγιος, in agreement with πνεύματος) 84.

οὕς (acc.pl.masc.of ὅς, direct object of ἐξελέξατο) 65.

ἐξελέξατο (3d.per.sing.aor.mid.ind.of ἐκλέγω, culminative) 2119.

ἀνελήμφθη (3d.per.sing.aor.pass.ind.of ἀναλαμβάνω, constative) 2930.

Translation - " . . . until a day on which, after He had commissioned the Apostles whom through the Holy Spirit He had selected, He was taken up."

Comment: The improper preposition ἄχρι with the genitive of time description serves also as a conjunction here since it is involved in the relative temporal phrase. *Cf.*Mt.24:38; Acts 7: 18. The relative clause specifies the day on which the ministry of Jesus as a miracle worker and a teacher ended. Thus Luke focuses our attention upon a day. What day? When He was taken up (Luke 24:51; Acts 1:9). But before His ascension, Jesus had one last task to perform. He gave the great commission (Mt.28:18-20; Acts 1:8) to the Apostles whom He had selected, with the help of the Holy Spirit. Luke had written before (Luke 6:12-16) about the consultation which the incarnate Son of God had sought from the Father and the Holy Spirit before He chose the twelve disciples whom He then also called Apostles. It was after a long night of prayer on a mountain top that Jesus, Who in His *kenosis* felt His need of divine guidance, made His announcement. Now Luke tells us that it was through the indirect agency of the Holy Spirit that the choice was made. He selected them; He taught them; He died for their sins and rose again; He proved to them that His resurrection was real and finally He gave them the commission in the execution of which they pursued their ministry as the Acts records. We who have also been selected, not as Apostles in the special sense in which Jesus chose the eleven, but as members of His body, are also charged with the same commission, in obedience to which the church, albeit with greater leisure than our risen Lord could wish, have carried on the missionary enterprise to the ends of the earth. Note that the verb ἐκλέγω (#22119) is the same word used to describe the elelction of the saints.

Jesus gave a temporary commission to the Apostles on the day that He selected them (Matthew 10:5-7), but that is not the commission to which Luke refers now.   Acts 1:2 is speaking of the marching orders which Jesus gave to the church only moments before the ascension. Note the antecedent action in the aorist participle ἐντειλάμενος. Jesus chose the Apostles perhaps two years or more before (Luke 6; Matthew 10) and gave them orders to announce to Israel that her Messiah had arrived and was ready to establish His earthly kingdom, contingent of course upon her acceptance of Him. This, of course, Jesus did with the complete foreknowledge of the course of events. Had He told the Apostles then to preach His message of death, burial and resurrection to Israel they would have had what, for them, was a valid reason to reject His Messianic claim. *Cf.* our discussion of this in *The Renaissance New Testament*, I, 189-193. Now, at the close of His earthly ministry it has been made clear that before Jesus' Messianic ministry is begun at His second coming, the Holy Spirit will "visit the Gentiles to take out of them a people for His name" (Acts 15:14).

Verse 3 - ". . . to whom also he showed himself alive after his passion by many infallible proofs, having been seen of them forty days, and speaking of the things pertaining to the kingdom of God."

οἷς καὶ παρέστησεν ἑαυτὸν ζῶντα μετὰ τὸ παθεῖν αὐτὸν ἐν πολλοῖς τεκμηρίοις, δι' ἡμερῶν τεσσαράκοντα ὀπτανόμενος αὐτοῖς καὶ λέγων τὰ περὶ τῆς βασιλείας τοῦ θεοῦ.

οἷς (loc.pl.masc.of ὅς, place where, with persons, with παρά in composition) 65.

καὶ (adjunctive conjunction joining verbs) 14.

παρέστησεν (3d.per.sing.aor.act.ind.of παρίστημι, constative) 1596.

ἑαυτὸν (acc.sing.masc.of ἑαυτοῦ, direct object of παρέστησεν) 288.

ζῶντα (pres.act.part.acc.sing.masc.of ζάω, adverbial,circumstantial) 340.

μετὰ (preposition with the accusative of time extent) 50.

τὸ (acc.sing.neut.of the article in an articular infinitive construction, time) 9.

παθεῖν (aor.act.articular inf.of πάσχω, time expression) 1208

αὐτὸν (acc.sing.masc.of αὐτός, general reference) 16.

ἐν (preposition with the instrumental of manner) 80.

πολλοῖς (instr.pl.neut.of πολύς, in agreement with τεκμηρίοις) 228.

#2934 τεκμηρίοις (instru.pl.neut.of τεκμήριον, manner).

infallible proof - Acts 1:3.

*Meaning: Cf.*τέκμαρ - "sign;" τεκμαίρω - "to prove by a sign/demonstration." Hence, an infallible proof. Empirical evidence. With reference to the bodily resurrection of Jesus - Acts 1:3.

δι' (preposition with the genitive of time duration) 118.

ἡμερῶν (gen.pl.fem.of ἡμέρα, time duration description) 135.

τεσσαράκοντα (numeral) 333.

#2935 ὀπτανόμενος (pres.pass.part.nom.sing.masc.of ὀπτάνομαι, adverbial, modal).

see - Acts 1:3.

*Meaning: Cf.*ὄπτω - "to see; look at; in the passive to be seen; to be visible." With reference to Jesus' appearances to the Christians after His resurrection - Acts 1:3.

αὐτοῖς (instru.pl.masc.of αὐτός, agent) 16.

καὶ (adjunctive conjunction joining participles) 14.

λέγων (pres.act.part.nom.sing.masc.of λέγω, circumstantial, modal) 66.

τὰ (acc.pl.neut.of the article, direct object of λέγων) 9.

περὶ (preposition with the genitive of reference) 173.

τῆς (gen.sing.fem.of the article in agreement with βασιλείας) 9.

βασιλείας (gen.sing.fem.of βασιλεία, reference) 253.

τοῦ (gen.sing.masc.of the article in agreement with θεοῦ) 9.

θεοῦ (gen.sing.masc.of θεός, description) 124.

Translation - "In the presence of whom He took His place, alive, after His death and (presented) many empirical proofs, throughout a forty day period, by being seen by them and by speaking of the things about the kingdom of God."

Comment: In verse 2 Luke used ἐξελέξατο, an aorist, to indicate time antecedent to the time expressed by the aorist participle ἐντειλάμενος. It is the context, and our general knowledge of the events in the ministry of Jesus that tells us that ἐξελέξατο should be translated as a pluperfect. Winer was quite correct when he said that the tenses are not to be interchanged, so when he said "In narration the aorist is used for the pluperfect" (Winer-Moulton, *A Treatise of the Grammar of New Testament Greek*, 343, as cited in Robertson, *Grammar*, 840) he meant the German pluperfect. Burton (*New Testament Moods and Tenses,* 22), in Section #48, which he entitled **The Aorist For The (English) Pluperfect** says, "The Aorist Indicative is frequently used in narrative passages of a past event which precedes another past event mentioned or implied in the context. In English it is common in such a case to indicate the real order of events by the use of a Pluperfect for the earlier event" *e.g. cf.* John 19:30; Mt.14:3. Gildersleeve deals with the same problem by adding the word "translated" (*Syntax of Attic Greek,* 109, as cited in Robertston, *Grammar,* 840). Goodwin "adds more exactly that the aorist indicative merely refers the action to the past 'without the more exact specification' which the past perfect would give." (*Ibid.*) Robertson concurs with "The speaker or writer did not always care to make this more precise specification. He was content with the mere narrative of the events without the precision that we moderns like. We are therefore in constant peril of reading back into the Greek aorist our English or German translation. All that one is entitled to say is that the aorist sometimes occurs where the context 'implies completion before the main action' (Monro, *Homeric Greek,* 47) where in English we prefer the past perfect. (*Ibid.*). The antecedence of ἐξελέξατο in relation to ἐντειλάμενος in verse 2 is not expressed by a pluperfect, but the antecedence is there. *Cf.* Mark 8:14; Luke 1:1; 2:39; 7:1; 8:27; 24:1; John 2:9; 4:1,50; 5:13; 6:16; 9:18,35; 11:30; 13:12; 21:9; Rom.8:29.

In verse 3, I have translated παρέστησεν literally. "He stood Himself by their side/in their presence" (John 20:19,26; Luke 24:15). He was alive (circumstantial participle in ζῶντα). Jesus was no ghost, although the disciples at first thought so. This is why Luke adds ἐν πολλοῖς τεκμηρίοις. Luke seems to have anticipated the hallucination theory (that Jesus' post-resurrection appearances could be explained as psychic phenomena) by adding that these appearances occurred between (διὰ) the beginning and the end of a period of 40 days. They were chronologically *et passim*. "Now and again, from time to time, across a 40 day period. *Cf.* 1 Cor.15:5-8. The disciples not' only saw, handled, fished and ate with Jesus, but they also heard Him telling them more about the kingdom of God. Note that in His last instructions to them, Jesus said nothing more about the Kingdom of the Heavens, but He told them to go and preach the Kingdom of God.

Verse 4 - "And being assembled together with them, commanded them that they

should not depart from Jerusalem, but wait for the promise of the Father, which,
saith he, ye have heard of me."

καὶ συναλιζόμενος παρήγγειλεν αὐτοῖς ἀπὸ Ἱεροσολύμων μὴ χωρίζεσθαι,
ἀλλὰ περιμένειν τὴν ἐπαγγειλίαν τοῦ πατρὸς ἣν ἠκούσατέ μου.

καὶ (adjunctive conjunction joining verbs) 14.

#2936 συναλιζόμενος (pres.pass.part.nom.sing.masc.of συναλίζω, adverbial,
temporal).

be assembled together with - Acts 1:4.

Meaning: A combination of σύν (#1542) and ἁλής - "crowded; assembled *en*
masse" - Acts 1:4.

παρήγγειλεν (3d.per.sing.aor.act.ind.of παραγγέλλω, constative) 855.
αὐτοῖς (dat.pl.masc.of αὐτός, indirect object of παρήγγειλεν) 16.
ἀπό (preposition with the ablative of separation) 70.
Ἱεροσολύμων (abl.sing.of Ἱεροσολύμων, separation) 141.
μή (qualified negative conjunction with the infinitive) 87.
χωρίζεσθαι (pres.mid.inf.of χωρίζω, object clause in indirect discourse) 1291.
ἀλλά (alternative conjunction) 342.

#2937 περιμένειν (pres.act.inf.of περιμένω, object clause in direct discourse).

wait for - Acts 1:4.

Meaning: A combination of περί (#173) and μένω (#864). Hence, to remain
longer. Since περί basically means "around," that which is "around" is also
"beyond." Hence περί in composition means "more" or in the context of Acts 1:4
"longer." *Cf.* περίεργος (#3470), περιεργάζομαι (#4684), περιλείπω (#4665),
περιούσιος (#4899), περισσός (#525) and περισσεύω (#473). περιμένω therefore
means to remain longer; to wait. With reference to Jesus' orders to the disciples
to remain in Jerusalem for the Holy Spirit's fullness - Acts 1:4.

τήν (acc.sing.fem.of the article in agreement with ἐπαγγελίαν) 9.
ἐπαγγελίαν (acc.sing.fem.of ἐπαγγελία, direct object of περιμένειν) 2929.
τοῦ (abl.sing.masc.of the article in agreement with πατρός) 9.
πατρός (abl.sing.masc.of πατήρ, source) 238.
ἥν (acc.sing.fem.of ὅς, direct object of ἠκούσατέ) 65.
ἠκούσατέ (2d.per.pl.aor.act.ind.of ἀκούω, culminative) 148.
μου (abl.sing.masc.of ἐγώ, source) 123.

Translation - "And while they were gathered together He ordered them not to
leave Jerusalem, but (He said) 'wait for the promise from the Father which you
have heard from me.' "

Comment: In Luke 5:14 we have a typical change from indirect to direct
discourse as we have it here in παρήγγειλεν . . . μὴ χωρίζεσθαι, ἀλλὰ

περιμένειν τὴν ἐπαγγελίαν ... κ.τ.λ. Meyer, *en loc.* thought the etymology of συναλιζόμενος connected it with ἅλς - "salt." Hence "to eat together." So Goodspeed, Williams, Montgomery, RSV mgn. *et al.* But Moulton & Milligan demur. "We can cite no ex. of this rare verb from our sources, but reference should be made to Professor H. J. Cadbury's careful study in JBL xlv. (1926), p.310 ff., where he sets aside both the ordinary interpretations of the verb in Ac I₄ — συναλίζω, "eat with," and συναλίζομαι, "gather" (transitive or intransitive), and regards συναλιζόμενος as simply another spelling for συναυλιζόμενος, with the consequent meaning "live with" in the sense of spending the night together. Such an orthographic change of α for αυ is, as he shows, common in the Κοινή... ." (Moulton & Milligan, *The Vocabulary of the Greek Testament*, 601). Note the ablatives of source, both in τοῦ πατρὸς and μου. The promise was "from the Father" but they heard it from Jesus. Luke is talking about his earlier story in Luke 24:59. The direct discourse which begins with περιμένειν τὴν ἐπαγγελίαν continues through verse 5. *Cf.* comment on Luke 24:49. (Joel 2:28; Isa.44:3; Ezek.36:26).

Verse 5 - "For John truly baptized with water: but ye shall be baptized with the Holy Ghost, not many days hence."

ὅτι Ἰωάννης μὲν ἐβάπτισεν ὕδατι, ὑμεῖς δὲ ἐν πνεύματι βαπτισθήσεσθε ἁγίῳ οὐ μετὰ πολλὰς ταύτας ἡμέρας.

ὅτι (conjunction introducing a subordinate causal clause) 211.
Ἰωάννης (nom.sing.masc.of Ἰωάννης, subject of ἐβάπτισεν) 247.
μὲν (particle of affirmation) 300.
ἐβάπτισεν (3d.per.sing.aor.act.ind.of βαπτίζω, constative) 273.
ὕδατι (loc.sing.neut.of ὕδωρ, place) 301.
ὑμεῖς (nom.pl.masc.of σύ, subject of βαπτισθήσεσθε) 104.
δὲ (adversative conjunction) 11.
ἐν (preposition with the instrumental of means) 80.
πνεύματι (instru.sing.neut.of πνεῦμα, means) 83.
βαπτισθήσεσθε (2d.per.pl.fut.pass.ind.of βαπτίζω, predictive) 273.
ἁγίῳ (instru.sing.neut.of ἅγιος, in agreement with πνεύματι) 84.
οὐ (summary negative conjunction with the indicative) 130.
μετὰ (preposition with the accusative of time extension) 50.
πολλὰς (acc.pl.fem.of πολύς, in agreement with ἡμέρας) 228.
ταύτας (acc.pl.fem.of οὗτος, in agreement with ἡμέρας) 93.
ἡμέρας (acc.pl.fem.of ἡμέρα, time extent) 135.

Translation - "Because although John in fact immersed in water, you are going to be overwhelmed with the Holy Spirit not many days from now."

Comment: ὅτι is causal as Jesus hastens to explain why they are to wait for Pentecost. They had already received John's baptism in water, and they may have thought that they were sufficiently endowed with the power to witness for Christ. That such was not the case is clear from the distinction which He makes between the immersion in water at the hands of John the Baptist and the overwhelming experience with the Holy Spirit which they would experience ten days hence. We may read a concessive idea into the context. Note the μὲν . . . δὲ sequence - "in fact. . . but. . . " One cannot decide the baptism question on the basis of the grammatical use of ὕδατι or of the prepositional phrase ἐν πνεύματι ἁγίῳ. ὕδατι can be either locative or instrumental. If the former "in" and if the latter "by means of." ἐν can be followed by the locative or the instrumental with the same resultant translations. Pedobaptists indeed might argue that sprinkling can be practiced "in" water, as the candidate is led out into the water, sprinkled and led "out of" (ἐκ) the water. So we tend to adjust the Word of God in conformity with our sacrosanct ideas. The immersionist case is made on the meaning of the verb (#273). "Overwhelm" conveys the basic idea, since it means to be surrounded by something until immersion or submersion is the result. At Pentecost the Holy Spirit filled (surrounded, overwhelmed, totally dominated) the believers. Jesus was overwhelmed with sorrow and the righteous judgment of God upon the cross. Thus the fact that the preposition is lacking before ὕδατι in Acts 1:5 allows us to take it as either locative or instrumental. To be submerged/immersed *in* water (locative) is to be surrounded/overwhelmed *by* water (instrumental).

Jesus' point here is not the physical manner in which baptism is administered, but the results which flowed from John's baptism, which were negligible, in terms of divine power in the candidate's life, as contrasted with the baptism of the Holy Spirit, the results of which were dynamic. Immersion in water is mandated by the Great Commission (Mt.28:18-20) but it is only a symbol. The baptism of the Holy Spirit, which is also referred to as the filling of the Holy Spirit, which occurred at Pentecost was a vital personal experience that transformed the early Christians from common cowards into fearless, flaming evangels of a crucified and risen Saviour.

οὐ μετὰ πολλὰς ταύτας ἡμέρας presents a problem. It is obviously litotes (a rhetorical figure in which an affirmation (soon) is expressed by the negative of its contrary statement (not many days after). *e.g.* - Acts 21:39 - "a citizen of no mean city" which means "a citizen of a great city."). But Acts 1:5 does not follow the usual order for litotes. Normally it would read οὐ πολλὰς ἡμέρας μετὰ ταύτας - "not many days after these days." As it stands "It is literally 'after not many days these" as a starting point (from these). 'not many days hence' is essentially correct" (Robertson, *Grammar*, 702). How many days? Ten. οὐ μετὰ πολλὰς ταύτας ἡμέρας also means μετὰ ὀλίγα ἡμέρας - "after a few days." *Cf.* John 14:16; 15:25; 16:13,14. It is clear that the reception of the Holy Spirit, which occurred for the disciples on the evening of resurrection day (John 20:22) is not to be confused with the baptism of the Holy Spirit of Acts 1:5, which took place ten days after His ascension. Peter recalled Jesus' statement (Acts 11:16) as did Paul (Acts 19:4). The fact that Acts 2:4 refers to the Pentecost experience as a filling does not preclude the fact that Jesus also called it a baptism. The two ideas are not greatly different.

The Ascension of Jesus

(Acts 1:6-11)

Verse 6 - "When they therefore were come together, they asked him, saying, Lord, wilt thou at this time restore again the kingdom to Israel?"

Οἱ μὲν οὖν συνελθόντες ἠρώτων αὐτὸν λέγοντες, Κύριε, εἰ ἐν τῷ χρόνῳ τούτῳ ἀποκαθιστάνεις τὴν βασιλείαν τῷ Ἰσραήλ;

Οἱ (nom.pl.masc.of the article, in agreement with συνελθόντες) 9.

μὲν (affirmative particle) 300.

οὖν (continuative conjunction) 68.

συνελθόντες (aor.mid.part.nom.pl.masc.of συνέρχομαι,substantival, subject of ἠρώτων) 78.

ἠρώτων (3d.per.pl.imp.act.ind.of ἐρωτάω, inceptive) 1172.

αὐτὸν (acc.sing.masc.of αὐτός, direct object of ἠρώτων) 16.

λέγοντες (pres.act.part.nom.pl.masc.of λέγω, recitative) 66.

Κύριε (voc.sing.masc.of κύριος, address) 97.

εἰ (particle in a first-class elliptical condition) 337.

ἐν (preposition with the locative of time point) 80.

τῷ (loc.sing.masc.of the article in agreement with χρόνῳ) 9.

χρόνῳ (loc.sing.masc.of χρόνος, time point) 168.

τούτῳ (loc.sing.masc.of οὗτος, in agreement with χρόνῳ) 93.

#2938 ἀποκαθιστάνεις (2d.per.sing.pres.act.ind.of ἀποκαθιστάων, indirect question).

restore again - Acts 1:6.

*Meaning: Cf.*ἀποκαθίστημι (#978), of which it is a variant form, with essentially the same meaning. In Acts 1:6 with reference to the restoration of hegemony to Israel under the terms of the Davidic covenant.

τὴν (acc.sing.fem.of the article in agreement with βασιλείαν) 9.

βασιλείαν (acc.sing.fem.of βασιλεία, direct object of ἀποκαθιστάνεις) 253.

τῷ (dat.sing.masc.of the article in agreement with Ἰσραήλ) 9.

Ἰσραήλ (dat.sing.masc.of Ἰσραήλ, indirect object of ἀποκαθιστάνεις) 165.

Translation - "Then those who had come together began to ask Him, 'Lord, tell us if at this time you are going to restore the kingdom for Israel.' "

Comment: When εἰ occurs in a question it is elliptical. We either have a conditional sentence with the apodosis omitted or we have indirect question. The disciples were saying, "If you are going to restore the kingdom to Israel at this time" (the protasis) "tell us' (the apodosis). Note the urgency in the minds and hearts of the disciples, indicated by the inceptive imperfect in ἠρώτων - "they began (and continued) to ask Him." It was important for them to know. It is probable that their question was an effort to verify a rumor that had circulated among them since the conversation between Peter and Jesus of John 21:20-23. Jesus did not say that John would live until the second coming, but that interpretation was put upon His remarks and John did not correct it until the end of the century, more than 60 years after the ascension. Luke spotlights the fact that as the early Christians followed Jesus out to Olivet, now thoroughly convinced that He was in fact alive, the thought uppermost in their minds was whether or not He would now act in His Messianic capacity, occupy the throne of David (2 Sam.7:10-17), mobilize a Jewish army, drive out the Romans and take over the world. They were now to receive a commission to carry the gospel to the ends of the earth, and once they understood the scenario of the divine plot they did not shrink to carry it out, although the church in the past two hundred years has not been so zealous. But this commission came to them in verse 8. Their question at the moment, oft repeated and coming to Jesus from more than one of them, had to do with the social and political conditions which they might properly expect in the immediate future.

The Apostles had asked this question in a slightly different form once before (Matthew 24:1-3) and had been told in a general way what world history would be like, but there was nothing definite in Jesus' reply at that time as to the length of time between His first and second comings. Indeed He pointed them to a specific event (Matthew 24:15) which, when correlated with Daniel 9:24-27 and the Book of Revelation, which at that time had not yet been written, would tell him who read and understood precisely when He would return. Matthew 24:15 is our Lord's response to their request for "the sign of thy coming and the end of the age" (Matthew 24:3). But that event had not yet taken place, nor has it yet, at the time of this writing (5 February 1981). When it does Christians still on earth who understand their Bibles will become date setters like Noah was seven days before it began to rain. Of course there are many sincere students of the Word who believe that the church will have been raptured three and one half years before that event . In my opinion they are mistaken about this - sincere, no doubt, but sincerity is not a substitute for good hermeneutics.

When our Lord, Who alone can lay legal claim to the throne rights vested in David, returns to begin His reign of universal righteousness, there will still be evangelistic work to do and it will be done under the ideal kingdom conditions, as preachers tell the same story of the cross and empty tomb that we now tell, to those who will be born in the Millenium to parents who survived the catastrophes of the tribulation period. That unsaved adults will in fact survive Armageddon and continue to live into the kingdom age is clear from Revelation 20:7-9. The nations which will be deceived by Satan at the end of the Millenium certainly will not be composed of glorified saints.

The question of verse 6 provides the background for Jesus' reply in verses 7 and 8.

Verse 7 - "And he said unto them, It is not for you to know the times or the seasons, which the Father hath put in his own power."

εἶπεν δὲ πρὸς αὐτούς, Οὐχ ὑμῶν ἐστιν γνῶναι χρόνους ἢ καιροὺς οὓς ὁ πατὴρ ἔθετο ἐν τῇ ἰδίᾳ ἐξουσίᾳ.

εἶπεν (3d.per.sing.aor.act.ind.of εἶπον, constative) 155.
δὲ (adversative conjunction) 11.
πρὸς (preposition with the accusative of extent, after a verb of speaking) 197.
αὐτούς (acc.pl.masc.of αὐτός, extent, after a verb of speaking) 16.
Οὐχ (summary negative conjunction with the indicative) 130.
ὑμῶν (gen.pl.masc.of σύ, predicate genitive) 104.
ἐστιν (3d.per.sing.pres.ind.of εἰμί, static) 86.
γνῶναι (2d.aor.act.inf.of γινώσκω, noun use, nominative case, subject of ἐστιν) 131.
χρόνους (acc.pl.masc.of χρόνος, direct object of γνῶναι) 168.
ἢ (disjunctive particle) 465.
καιροὺς (acc.pl.masc.of καιρός, direct object of γνῶναι) 767.
οὓς (acc.pl.masc.of ὅς, direct object of ἔθετο) 65.
ὁ (nom.sing.masc.of the article in agreement with πατὴρ) 9.
πατὴρ (nom.sing.masc.of πατήρ, subject of ἔθετο) 238.
ἔθετο (3d.per.sing.2d.aor.mid.ind.of τίθημι, culminative) 455.
ἐν (preposition with the locative of sphere) 80.
τῇ (loc.sing.fem.of the article in agreement with ἐξουσίᾳ) 9.
ἰδίᾳ (loc.sing.fem.of ἴδιος, in agreement with ἐξουσίᾳ) 778.
ἐξουσίᾳ (loc.sing.fem.of ἐξουσία, sphere) 707.

Translation - "But He said to them, 'It is not yours to know about dates and events, which the Father has placed under His control.' "

Comment: δὲ is adversative . Jesus did not choose to give them the information for which they asked. Rather He explained to them why their repeated questions were inappropriate. The subject of the static present ἐστιν is the infinitive γνῶναι, in its noun use in the nominative case. The predicate genitive logically follows. "To know . . . is not yours." If we interpret Jesus' statement in the light of *zeitgeist* ἐστιν is static. It is obvious that those who asked the question would not know *in their lifetime.* That generation and many generations of Christians since died with no precise knowledge about dates and prophetic events. Thus Jesus could have meant ἐστιν in the futuristic sense - "You (*i.e.* those to whom He was speaking then) will never know . . . κ.τ.λ." or "If will never be yours to know. . ." But Jesus did not say that the precise knowledge for which they asked would be denied to those Christians who will live to see the fulfillment of Matthew 24:15/Daniel 9:27/2 Thess.2:3-5.

Our Lord was a bit more gentle on this occasion than He had been with Peter when he had asked about John. Then, in effect, Peter had been told that it was none of his business - "What concern is it of yours?" This is the essence of what Jesus said in our verse, although it was phrased more diplomatically. The information for which they asked could have been given to them by the Father if He had chosen to do so, because He certainly knew, but He did not choose to divulge it. The chronological extent (χρόνους) of dispensations, and the events (καιρὸς) which provide check-points to reveal to the perceptive Christian where we are on God's clock, is information which God had determined to keep under His control, and, although it would be revealed at the proper time, that time would not come during the lifetime of the disciples in the first century. Thus it was none of their business and they were as much out of line with their questions as Peter had been with his (John 21:21). These matters are God's business. They were placed by sovereign decree in His eternal past (culminative aorist in ἔθετο) within the sphere of His own discretion. At that time Jesus did not even know the answer to their question although it was given to Him after His ascension (Rev.1:1). Christians in the late 20th century still do not know the chronological limits of the church age, nor the date when Daniel's 70th week will begin. Thus the dates for future events (tribulation, rise of Antichrist, mark of the beast, second coming, kingdom age, eternal state) cannot be set, because the scriptural guide lines depend upon events which have not yet occurred. There is no objection to date setting, if it is done scripturally, but no one at present (2/5/1981) can mark out the schedule with precision. The Watchtower Bible and Tract Society, which refers to its dupes as "Jehovah's Witnesses" has an amazing record of fumbling with their date setting, and has long since earned the title of False Prophet. As the program of the Holy Spirit moves ahead in the world in keeping with the divine decree some have been anxious to terminate it, albeit without success. Signs carried on the streets in 1848, 1874, 1914, 1917, 1925 and 1975 which read **"The End is Near"** can be revised with little expense now to read **"The End Was Near."** We now learn that the rapture of the church is to occur in 1982. Indeed! This time the sign was not painted by a Jehovah's Witness. It was printed in a book. There are no royalties available to sign painters.

Pretribulation rapture teachers insist that the next event, the translation of the church, is unannounced and imminent, and that it will announce to the unsaved who remain upon the earth the beginning of seven years of tribulation at the end of which Christ will return to take His throne and establish the Kingdom of the Heavens. *Cf.* our comments in the proper contexts. *Cf.*#168, specifically Acts 3:21; 7:17; 17:30; Gal.4:4; 1 Thess.5:1; 1 Peter 1:20; Jude 18; 2 Tim.1:9 for χρόνος in this sense. Also *cf.*#767 - Luke 1:20; Mark 1:15; Luke 12:56; 21:24; Acts 17:26; 2 Cor.6:2,2; Eph.1:10; 1 Peter 1:11. All of these passages shed light on the point that God is the heavenly Dispatcher of events. Rather than expend scarce time and nervous energy trying to figure out God's time clock, the disciples would do better to be patient until they receive the divine power that would come with the fulness of the Holy Spirit, so essential to the successful implementation of their commission to preach the gospel throughout the world. Some preachers seem so anxious to tell the lost world that God is going to judge it "in flaming fire" (2 Thess.1:8) at His second coming, that they have forgotten that we are ordered to tell them that God loved them and died for them in His first coming.

Verse 8 - "But ye shall receive power after that the Holy Ghost is come upon you: and ye shall be witnesses unto me both in Jerusalem, and in all Judea, and in Samaria, and unto the uttermost part of the earth."

ἀλλὰ λήμφεσθε δύναμιν ἐπελθόντος τοῦ ἁγίου πνεύματος ἐφ' ὑμᾶς, καὶ
ἔσεσθέ μου μάρτυρες ἔν τε Ἰερουσαλὴμ καὶ ἐν πάσῃ τῇ Ἰουδαίᾳ καὶ Σαμαρείᾳ
καὶ ἕως ἐσχάτου τῆς γῆς.

ἀλλὰ (alternative conjunction) 342.

λήμφεσθε (2d.per.pl.fut.act.ind.of λαμβάνω, predictive) 533.

δύναμιν (acc.sing.fem.of δύναμις, direct object of λήμφεσθε) 687.

ἐπελθόντος (aor.mid.part.gen.sing.neut.of ἐπέρχομαι, genitive absolute)
1814.

τοῦ (gen.sing.neut.of the article in agreement with πνεύματος) 9.

ἁγίου (gen.sing.neut.of ἅγιος, in agreement with πνεύματος) 84.

πνεύματος (gen.sing.neut.of πνεῦμα, genitive absolute) 83.

ἐφ' (preposition with the accusative of extent) 47.

ὑμᾶς (acc.pl.masc.of σύ, extent) 104.

καὶ (adjunctive conjunction joining verbs) 14.

ἔσεσθέ (2d.per.pl.fut.ind.of εἰμί, predictive) 86.

μου (gen.sing.masc.of ἐγώ, description) 123.

μάρτυρες (nom.pl.masc.of μάρτυς, predicate nominative) 1263.

ἐν (preposition with the locative of place) 80.

τε (correlative particle) 1408.

Ἰερουσαλὴμ (loc.sing.masc.of Ἰεροσολύμων, place where) 141.

καὶ (adjunctive conjunction joining prepositional phrases) 14.

ἐν (prepositional with the locative of place) 80.

πάσῃ (loc.sing.fem.of πᾶς, in agreement with Ἰουδαίᾳ) 67.

Ἰουδαίᾳ (loc.sing.fem.of Ἰουδαῖος, place where) 134.

καὶ (adjunctive conjunction joining nouns) 14.

Σαμαρείᾳ (loc.sing.fem.of Σαμάρεια, place where) 1998.

καὶ (adjunctive conjunction joining prepositional phrases) 14.

ἕως (preposition with the genitive of place description) 71.

ἐσχάτου (gen.sing.masc.of ἔσχατος, place description) 496.

τῆς (gen.sing.fem.of the article in agreement with γῆς) 9.

γῆς (gen.sing.fem.of γῆ, description) 157.

Translation - *"Rather you will receive power when (and as a result of the fact
that) the Holy Spirit has come upon you, and you will be my witnesses both in
Jerusalem and in all Judea and Samaria, and unto the end of the earth."*

Comment: Matthew likes to put his genitive absolutes at the beginning of the
sentence. Luke has it here following the main verb. ἀλλὰ is alternative. Not
knowledge about when the kingdom will come, but rather (instead) power to
preach the gospel. Prophetic Bible conferences which feature the date setters are
not likely to have much evangelistic power to win the lost. The priority here is
clear. God needed the Apostles and their other Christian brothers and sisters as
witnesses for Christ, not as prophets of the date of the end of the world. The
supreme importance of the power of the Holy Spirit soon to be received is
contrasted with the insignificance of the value of precise knowledge of
eschatalogical details. The disciples were majoring in the minor. As a matter of
fact they were putting result ahead of cause. The filling of the Holy Spirit with

His consequent endowment of divine power resulted in the launch of the worldwide missionary enterprise (vs.8) which began to ". . . visit the Gentiles, to take out of them a people for His name (Acts 15:14). Thus the mystery, made known to Paul, which in the Old Testament had not been revealed as clearly as it was revealed to him (Eph.3:3-9) began to be unfolded. It is only after the mystery is finished (Rev.10:7) that Messiah will return and establish the rule of divine law upon the earth that the disciples were so eager to see in the first century. If Christians truly love His appearing (2 Tim.4:8) they should exert every effort to evangelize the lost. Time spent at a "prophetic Bible conference" might better be spent at a conference on how to win the remaining elect who as yet have not been saved. Christ will return to earth when the Father wishes - on a day which He set in eternity past. The specific day has not been revealed, either to the disciples on Mount Olivet or to us 1900 years later. We do not know when it will be. There is a possibility that He will come very soon. There is also a possibility that He will tarry for several hundred years. The last generation of Christians in this age who understand their Bibles will know, but of this we can be certain - the coming of the King follows the completion of the great commission (Rev.10:7). There have been dark moments in history before, when social scientists were unduly convinced that the second coming of Christ alone could prevent a total reduction of human society on this planet to chaos. They were wrong. Human society, for all of its faults, foibles and failures is remarkably resilient. We survived the Black Death in the 14th century and the Nazi horrors of Germany after that otherwise sophisticated nation yielded to the seductions of Adolf Hitler. The pendulum swings from extreme right to extreme left and back again. Periods of moderation give world society a new temporary lease on life. Revivals of true religion with their accompanying return to the moral standards of the Bible have given new opportunities for progress. Though the ultimate destiny of this age is chaos, no one can say when world society will descend to the levels of barbarity from which only the second coming of our Lord can rescue it. On this all Bible students can depend: God will keep civilization alive on earth until someone in the Body of Christ has reached the last elect soul for whom Christ died with the good news of the gospel.

The genitive absolute participle ἐπελθόντος is both causal and temporal. When and because of the fact that He came upon the Christian they received His power. Here is an example of an aorist participle which may be thought to express simultaneous time with the time of the main verb, instead of antecedent time. *Cf.*#1814, especially in its use in Luke 1:35. Just as the Holy Spirit "came upon" Mary to impregnate her with the incarnate Λόγος, so He came upon the church to supercharge her with His sovereign power, thus to equip her to produce the Body of Christ. The same Holy Spirit who generated the body of the historic Jesus also generates the members of His body. Note that the order of the commission is chronological, geographical and ethnic: first in Jerusalem and to the Jews only; then extending into the outlying regions of Judea, beyond the city limits of Jerusalem, but still for the Jews only; further geographic expansion to include Samaria and the beginning of ethnic expansion as the hybrid Samaritans were to be evangelized. Finally all barriers are down as the church was ordered to go to the ends of the earth and preach the good news to every people, tongue, race, tribe, color, kindred and culture (Rev.5:9).

Verse 9 - "And when he had spoken these things, while they beheld, he was taken up; and a cloud received him out of their sight."

καὶ ταῦτα εἰπὼν βλεπόντων αὐτῶν ἐπήρθη, καὶ νεφέλη ὑπέλαβεν αὐτὸν ἀπὸ τῶν ὀφθαλμῶν αὐτῶν.

καὶ (continuative conjunction) 14.
ταῦτα (acc.pl.neut.of οὗτος, direct object of εἰπὼν) 93.
εἰπὼν (aor.act.part.nom.sing.masc.of εἶπον, adverbial, temporal) 155.
βλεπόντων (pres.act.part.gen.pl.masc.of βλέπω, genitive absolute) 499.
αὐτῶν (gen.pl.masc.of αὐτός, genitive absolute) 16.
ἐπήρθη (3d.per.sing.aor.pass.ind.of ἐπαίρω, constative) 1227.
καὶ (continuative conjunction) 14.
νεφέλη (nom.sing.fem.of νεφέλη, subject of ὑπέλαβεν) 1225.
ὑπέλαβεν (3d.per.sing.aor.act.ind.of ὑπολαμβάνω, constative) 2173.
αὐτὸν (acc.sing.masc.of αὐτός, direct object of ὑπέλαβεν) 16.
ἀπὸ (preposition with the ablative of separation) 70.
τῶν (abl.pl.masc.of the article in agreement with ὀφθαλμῶν) 9.
ὀφθαλμῶν (abl.pl.masc.of ὀφθαλμός, separation) 501.
αὐτῶν (gen.pl.masc.of αὐτός, possession) 16.

Translation - "And when He had said these things, while they were watching, He was lifted up and a cloud took him from their sight."

Comment: The first participle is aorist. Jesus had finished His statement of verses 7 and 8 before the action of the main verb in the first clause, ἐπήρθη, began. Jesus spoke and then He was taken up. The second participle in the genitive absolute is present tense, indicating that they watched Him as He was being lifted up to heaven and did not cease to see Him until the action of the main verb of the second clause had taken place. The grammar conforms to Luke's previous description of the ascension in Luke 24:51, where he put his verb ἀνεφέρετο in the imperfect tense to show the slow, dignified and majestic ascension - slow enough for the people on the ground to continue to watch it. Since #2173 means "to take under" we must understand it from the point of view of one standing on earth and looking up at the cloud. Thus He went "behind a cloud." We often say "under a cloud" when in fact the object is atop (above,beyond) the cloud. The ablative phrase ἀπὸ τῶν ὀφθαλμῶν αὐτῶν - "separated from their view" makes the point clear.

The ascension of our Lord was not an instantaneous transference from earth to the right hand of God in heaven. Nor will the rapture of the church at the end of the age be sudden. The "twinkling of an eye" reference in 1 Cor.15:51,52 refers not to the act of being caught up but to the glorification of our bodies. *Cf.* our comment on 1 Cor.15:51,52.

Cf.#1225 and note the prominence of clouds in both Christ's ascension and also in His second coming. It will be a cloudy day when our Lord returns. *Cf.*

Psalm 110:1; Heb.1:3; Heb.12:2. Jesus came from a place πρὸς τὸν πατέρα (1 John 1:2) and He went back πρὸς τὸν πατέρα (John 20:17).

The adopted text of Aland *et al* is supported by Sinaiticus ͨ A B (except that B has εἰπὼν αὐτῶν βλεπόντων) ᾿C E Ψ, three number uncials and many miniscules, while Augustine and D and a few others have εἰπόντος αὐτοῦ νεφέλη ὑπέλαβεν αὐτὸν καὶ ἀπήρθη, except that D, through a copyist's error misplaced both the β and the λ in the verb to show ὑπέβαλεν, which means that the cloud *knocked him down!*. The Aland editors are quite confident that the text we are following is correct. The only change in interpretation is that the Augustine reading makes His speech of verse 8 simultaneous with the obscuring of the cloud and the ascension, which is highly unlikely.

"Accordings to one form of the Western text, preserved in Augustine and the Sahidic version, a cloud enveloped Jesus on earth before his ascension, and then he was lifted up (nothing is said of the disciples' watching his ascension). The only Greek witness to this form of text is codex Bezae, with καυτὰ εἰπόντος αὐτοῦ νεφέλη ὑπέλαβεν αὐτόν, καὶ ἀπήρθη, but it goes on, by conflation from the ordinary text, with the incongruous ἀπὸ ὀφθαλμῶν αὐτῶν.

According to Plooij, it appears that "the 'Western' Reviser did not want to make an explicit statement as to *how* and in which form of existence Jesus ascended to heaven. After the resurrection Jesus had a body somehow, or whatever kind it might be. But he did not want to say that the apostles *saw* him ascending to heaven in that body: before he was taken away from them he was enveloped by the cloud." (D. Plooij, *The Ascension in the 'Western' Textual Tradition* (Mededeelingen der koninklijke Akademie von Wetenschappen, *Afdeeling letterkunde, Deel 67, Serie A, no.2; Amsterdam, 1929, p. 17,* as cited in Metzger, *A Textual Commentary on the Greek New Testament,* 282).

Verse 10 - "And while they looked steadfastly toward heaven as he went up, behold, two men stood by them in white apparel, . . "

καὶ ὡς ἀτενίζοντες ἦσαν εἰς τὸν οὐρανὸν πορευομένου αὐτοῦ, καὶ ἰδοὺ ἄνδρες δύο παρειστήκεισαν αὐτοῖς ἐν ἐσθήσεσι λευκαῖς,

καὶ (continuative conjunction) 14.

ὡς (conjunction introducing a definite temporal clause, simultaneous action) 128.

ἀτενίζοντες (pres.act.part.nom.pl.masc.of ἀτενίζω, imperfect periphrastic) 2028.

ἦσαν (3d.per.pl.imp.ind.of εἰμί, imperfect periphrastic) 86.

εἰς (preposition with the accusative of extent) 140.

τὸν (acc.sing.masc.of the article in agreement with οὐρανὸν) 9.

οὐρανὸν (acc.sing.masc.of οὐρανός, extent) 254.

πορευομένου (pres.mid.part.gen.sing.masc.of πορεύομαι, genitive absolute) 170.

αὐτοῦ (gen.sing.masc.of αὐτός, genitive absolute) 16.

καὶ (emphatic conjunction) 14.

ἰδοὺ (exclamation) 95.

ἄνδρες (nom.pl.masc.of ἀνήρ, subject of παρειστήκεισαν) 63.

δύο (numeral) 385.

παρειστήκεισαν (3d.per.pl.pluperfect act.ind.of παρίστημι, intensive) 1596.

αὐτοῖς (loc.pl.masc.of αὐτός, with παρά in composition, place where with persons) 16.

ἐν (preposition with the instrumental of manner) 80.

#2939 ἐσθήσεσι (instru.sing.fem.of ἔσθησις, manner).

apparel - Acts 1:10.

Meaning: Cf.ἐσθής (#2831). Clothing. The white clothing of the two heavenly visitors at the ascension of Jesus - Acts 1:10.

λευκαῖς (instru.pl.fem.of λευκός, in agreement with ἐσθήσεσι) 522.

Translation - "And as they stood with eyes riveted upon the sky, as He was on His way up — Look! Two men had taken their stand by them (dressed) in white clothing."

Comment: ὡς in the definite temporal clause means simultaneous time with that of the main verb παρειστήκεισαν. The imperfect periphrastic in the temporal clause indicates the passage of some time that they stood gazing, with attention, totally rapt, as they watched Jesus during the time that (present tense in the genitive absolute πορευομένου αὐτοῦ) He was on His way up. Both the present tense in πορευομένου and the durative action of the imperfect periphrastic support the idea that our Lord's ascent was not something sudden. So totally engrossed in the sight that was unfolding before their eyes, the disciples did not see the two men who appeared and stood beside them. Luke makes this point beautifully with his use of the pluperfect in παρειστήκεισαν - "two men *had* come and taken their stand by them." It was not until Jesus disappeared behind a cloud that they saw the two men. We can well imagine their surprise, which Luke indicates with the emphatic conjunction καί and the exclamatory ἰδού.

In order to picture the episode let us review it carefully. It began when Jesus began to lead them out toward Bethany (Luke 24:50). He paused and they gathered about Him. They began to ask Him about His plans. Would He now become their King? He replied in the negative, and added that instead they were to forget their present curiosity about eschatology and concern themselves with their obvious lack of spiritual power - a lack that would be supplied at some undisclosed time, not too far in the future. In the meantime they were to remain in Jerusalem. When the promised filling of the Holy Spirit occurred they were to begin their ministry of witnessing to the world - first, in Jerusalem, and then in ever widening circles, to Judea and Samaria and ultimately to the far corners of the earth. They were to preach the good news of salvation to all men, without the discrimination against Gentiles which they had been taught. Then He blessed them and began His slow ascent into the clouds - a sight which they watched with such enraptured interest that they did not notice the sudden appearance of the two men. Finally they could see Jesus no more and as they looked about them we can well imagine their shock to see the heavenly visitors. One wonders if the men were the same who presided at His empty tomb (Luke 24:4). Were they Moses and Elijah who appeared with Him upon the Mount of Transfiguration? Will they appear again in the great tribulation period to announce again His second coming, as they do in verse 11? (Rev.11:3-12). If the Holy Spirit had been pleased to tell us all that we want to know we would be robbed of the joy of finding out when we experience these events. *Cf.* 1 Timothy 3:16 - ἀνελήμφθη ἐν δόξῃ.

The two men did not tell the disciples *when* Messiah would restore the kingdom to Israel, but they did tell them *that* He would do so, in

Verse 11 - ". . . which also said, Ye men of Galilee, why stand ye gazing up into heaven? This same Jesus, which is taken up from you into heaven, shall so come, in like manner, as ye have seen him go into heaven."

οἳ καὶ εἶπαν, Ἄνδρες Γαλιλαῖοι, τί ἐστήκατε βλέποντες εἰς τὸν οὐρανόν; οὗτος ὁ Ἰησοῦς ὁ ἀναλημφθεὶς ἀφ' ὑμῶν εἰς τὸν οὐρανὸν οὕτως ἐλεύσεται ὃν τρόπον ἐθεάσασθε αὐτὸν πορευόμενον εἰς τὸν οὐρανόν.

οἳ (nom.pl.masc.of ὅς, subject of εἶπαν) 65.

καὶ (adjunctive conjunction joining verbs) 14.

εἶπαν (3d.per.sing.aor.act.ind.of εἶπον, constative) 155.

Ἄνδρες (voc.pl.masc.of ἀνήρ, address) 63.

Γαλιλαῖοι (voc.pl.masc.of Γαλιλαῖος, in agreement with Ἄνδρες) 2016.

τί (acc.sing.neut.of τίς, cause, direct question) 281.

ἐστήκατε (2d.per.pl.perf.act.ind.of ἵστημι, intensive) 180.

βλέποντες (pres.act.part.nom.pl.masc.of βλέπω, adverbial, complementary) 499.

εἰς (preposition with the accusative of extent) 140.

τὸν (acc.sing.masc.of the article in agreement with οὐρανόν) 9.

οὐρανόν (acc.sing.masc.of οὐρανός, extent) 254.

οὗτος (nom.sing.masc.of οὗτος, in agreement with Ἰησοῦς, deictic) 93.

ὁ (nom.sing.masc.of the article in agreement with Ἰησοῦς) 9.

Ἰησοῦς (nom.sing.masc.of Ἰησοῦς, subject of ἐλεύσεται) 3.

ὁ (nom.sing.masc.of the article in agreement with ἀναλημφθεὶς) 9.

ἀναλημφθεὶς (aor.pass.part.nom.sing.masc.of ἀναλαμβάνω, substantival, in apposition with Ἰησοῦς) 2930.

ἀφ' (preposition with the ablative of separation) 70.

ὑμῶν (abl.pl.masc.of σύ, separation) 104.

εἰς (preposition with the accusative of extent) 140.

τὸν (acc.sing.masc.of the article in agreement with οὐρανὸν) 9.

οὐρανὸν (acc.sing.masc.of οὐρανός, extent) 254.

οὕτως (demonstrative adverb) 74.

ἐλεύσεται (3d.per.sing.fut.mid.ind.of ἔρχομαι, predictive) 146.

ὃν (acc.sing.masc.of ὅς, in agreement with τρόπον) 65.

τρόπον (acc.sing.masc.of τρόπος, adverbial accusative in a comparative clause) 1477.

ἐθεάσασθε (2d.per.pl.1st.aor.mid.ind.of θεάομαι, culminative, in a comparative clause) 556.

αὐτὸν (acc.sing.masc.of αὐτός, direct object of ἐθεάσασθε) 16.

πορευόμενον (pres.mid.part.acc.sing.masc.of πορεύομαι, adverbial, circumstantial) 170.

εἰς (preposition with the accusative of extent) 140.

τὸν (acc.sing.masc.of the article in agreement with οὐρανόν) 9.

οὐρανόν (acc.sing.masc.of οὐρανός, extent) 254.

Translation - " . . . who also said, 'Men of Galilee, why have you been standing here gazing into the sky? This same Jesus, the One Who has just been taken up from you into heaven will so come in the same manner as you have seen Him going into heaven."

Comment: οἵ has its antecedent in ἄνδρες of verse 10. The perfect ἑστήκατε relates the immediate past to the present. They had stood there, rooted to the spot, with eyes only for their Lord as He arose, slowly into heaven - so engrossed that they had failed to see the two men who had suddenly appeared and were standing there with them. Now Jesus has gone from their sight and they are aware of their visitors. The present participle βλέποντες reinforces the intensive force of the perfect. οὗτος is deictic and emphatic. "This very same Jesus" - none other. The participle in apposition strengthens the emphasis in οὗτος. What about Him? He will come again. How? And here every misguided commentator who has the compulsive urge to take symbolically every passage which, if taken literally, offends him (!) - (as if it made any difference what does and does not offend people like that) take note. He will come back οὕτως - He will come back as He went away. As if οὕτως, the demonstrative were insufficient to make the point, they added the adverbial accusative introducing the comparative clause, ὃν τρόπον - "in the same way." Cf.#1477 for other ὃν τρόπον constructions. "He will *so* come *in like manner* as you have seen Him go into heaven." How had they seen Him go? Indeed had they seen Him? Note βλεπόντων (vs.9); ἀτενίζοντες (vs.10); βλέποντες and ἐθάσασθε (vs.11). There is no doubt that they saw Him. How? Personally, physically, bodily and visibly. He went up with clouds. He will come back with clouds, physically, personally, visibly. He will even come to the same spot from which He left (Rev.1:7; Zech.14:1).

It is strange indeed that some who have no difficulty accepting His bodily resurrection feel it incredible that He should come again. Once we have swallowed the story of His bodily resurrection why should we doubt the rest of the story?

Many unchristian social scientists are extremely pessimistic about the viability of human society upon this planet for another generation. The computers have digested the data and have predicted not more than one more century. Leaky, the famous British archeologist thinks that we have no more than forty years. The Christian, who is also at home in the social sciences is also pessimistic when he views the current scene as a scientist. His pessimism however gives way to the rosiest of optimistic prospects in view of his faith in the sure return of Jesus Christ, Who will not permit God's experiment upon this planet to fail.

A somewhat balanced view between optimistic and pessimistic examinations of the prospects for future world peace and prosperity can be found in Alvin Toffler, *Future Shock* and *The Third Wave*, which offers hope for the future, based, not upon theism but upon human solutions, and Jeremy Rifkin, *Entropy*, which is somewhat less optimistic because the solution suggested must be considered unrealistic. The reaction of the Christian to Rifkin's book is that it takes less faith to believe in the second coming of Christ than it does to believe that late 20th century world society will return to the standard of living and consequent life styles which prevailed two hundred years ago. The logic of Rifkin's study is that nothing that man can do will forestall forever the death of the planet.

The Choice of Judas' Successor
(Acts 1:12-26)

Acts 1:12 - *"Then returned they unto Jerusalem from the mount called Olivet, which is from Jerusalem a sabbath day's journey."*

Τότε ὑπέστρεφαν εἰς Ἰερουσαλὴμ ἀπὸ ὄρους τοῦ καλουμένου Ἐλαιῶνος, ὅ ἐστιν ἐγγὺς Ἰερουσαλὴμ σαββάτου ἔχον ὁδόν.

Τότε (continuative conjunction) 166.

ὑπέστρεφαν (3d.per.pl.aor.act.ind.of ὑποστρέφω, constative) 1838.

εἰς (preposition with the accusative of extent) 140.

Ἰερουσαλὴμ (acc.sing.masc.of Ἰεροσολύμων, extent) 141.

ἀπὸ (preposition with the ablative of separation) 70.

ὄρους (abl.sing.neut.of ὄρος, separation) 357.

τοῦ (abl.sing.neut.of the article in agreement with καλουμένου) 9.

καλουμένου (pres.pass.part.abl.sing.neut.of καλέω, substantival, in apposition with ὄρους) 107.

Ἐλαιῶνος (nom.sing.fem.of ἐλαία, appellation) 1341.

ὅ (nom.sing.neut.of ὅς, subject of ἐστιν) 65.

ἐστιν (3d.per.sing.pres.ind.of εἰμί, aoristic) 86.

ἐγγὺς (nom.sing.neut.of ἐγγύς, predicate adjective) 1512.

Ἰερουσαλὴμ (acc.sing.masc.of Ἰεροσολύμων, extent, adverbial accusative) 141.

σαββάτου (gen.sing.neut.of σάββατον, description) 962.

ἔχον (pres.act.part.acc.sing.neut.of ἔχω, adverbial, causal) 82.

ὁδόν (acc.sing.fem.of ὁδός, extent) 199.

Translation - *"They they returned to Jerusalem from the mountain called Olivet which is less than a mile away."*

Comment: *Cf.* comment on "a sabbath day's journey" in Matthew 24:20.

Verse 13 - "And when they were come in, they went up into an upper room, where abode both Peter and James, and John, and Andrew, Phillip, and Thomas, Bartholemew, and Matthew, James, the son of Alphaeus, and Simon Zelotes, and Judas, the brother of James."

καὶ ὅτε εἰσῆλθον, εἰς τὸ ὑπερῷον ἀνέβησαν οὗ ἦσαν καταμένοντες, ὅ τε Πέτρος καὶ Ἰωάννης καὶ Ἰάκωβος καὶ Ἀνδρέας, Φίλιππος καὶ Θωμᾶς, Βαρθολομαῖος καὶ Μαθθαῖος, Ἰάκωβος, Ἀλφαίου καὶ Σίμων ὁ ζηλωτὴς καὶ Ἰούδας Ἰακώβου.

καὶ (continuative conjunction) 14.

ὅτε (conjunction introducing a definite temporal clause, simultaneous time) 703.

εἰσῆλθον (3d.per.pl.aor.mid.ind.of εἰσέρχομαι, definite temporal clause) 234.

εἰς (preposition with the accusative of extent) 140.

τό (acc.sing.neut.of the article in agreement with ὑπερῷον) 9.

#2940 ὑπερῷον (acc.sing.neut.of ὑπερῷος, extent).

upper chamber - Acts 9:37,39; 20:8.
upper room - Acts 1:13.

Meaning: Cf.ὑπέρ (#545). An upper room. Thayer says, ". . . the highest part of the house, the upper rooms or story where the women resided. . . a room in the upper part of a house sometimes built upon the flat roof of a house whither Orientals were wont to retire in order to sup, meditate, pray etc." Cf. 2 Kings 23:12. The upper room where the disciples lived before Pentecost - Acts 1:13; where Dorcas died in Joppa - Acts 9:37,39; where Paul preached in Troas - Acts 20:8. ". . . used of a pigeon-house, τὸν ὑπερῷον τόπον τῆς ὑπαρχούσης αὐτῷ ἐν Μουχινὺρ οἰκίας, O.P.1127, 5-7 (A.D. 183), (Robertson, *Grammar*, xii).

ἀνέβησαν (3d.per.pl.aor.act.ind.of ἀναβαίνω, constative) 323.
οὗ (gen.sing.neut.of ὅς, place description) 65.
ἦσαν (3d.per.pl.imp.ind.of εἰμί, imperfect periphrastic) 86.

#2941 καταμένοντες (pres.act.part.nom.pl.masc.of καταμένω, imperfect periphrastic).

abide - Acts 1:13.

Meaning: A combination of κατά (#98) and μένω (#864). Thayer translates "to remain permanently" but Moulton & Milligan cite P Fay 24 (A.D.158) to show it as a temporary residence. Cf. also P Ryl II. 112 (b) 5 (A.D. 250), about a man belonging to the village but at the moment residing in another. However, P Oxy VIII, 1121₁₇ (A.D. 295) Σωτᾶς τις καὶ παποντῶς καταμένοντες ἐν τῇ αὐτῇ οἰκίᾳ ἔνθα ἡ μήτηρ μου ᾤκει - "a certain Swtas and Papontas, who are my neighbours in the same house where my mother lived." But this does not say that Swtas and Papontas lived there permanently. In Acts 1:13 it was obviously a temporary arrangement. Could the prefix κατά be taken in its basic meaning -

"down" - thus to support the idea that the disciples were "keeping down," *i.e.* remaining out of sight for fear of the Jews? *Cf.contra. Luke 24:53.*

ὁ (nom.sing.masc.of the article in agreement with Πέτρος and other proper names) 9.

τε (correlative particle with καὶ in the remainder of the verse) 1408.

(Note: The proper names which follow are all nom.sing.masc., subject of ἦσαν unless otherwise indicated. καὶ in each case is adjunctive).

Πέτρος - 387.
καὶ - 14.
Ἰωάννης - 399.
καὶ - 14.
Ἰάκωβος - 397.
καὶ - 14.
Ἀνδρέας - 388.
καὶ - 14.
Φίλιππος - 845.
καὶ - 14.
Θωμᾶς - 847.
καὶ - 14.
Βαρθολομαῖος - 846.
καὶ - 14.
Μαθθαῖος - 788.
καὶ - 14.
Ἰάκωβος - 848.
Ἀλφαίου (gen.sing.masc.of Ἀλφαῖος, relationship) 849.
καὶ - 14.
Σίμων - 851.
ὁ (nom.sing.masc.of the article in agreement with ζηλωτής) 9.
ζηλωτής (nom.sing.masc.of ζηλωτής, in apposition with Σίμων) 2120.
καὶ - 14.
Ἰούδας - 2121.
Ἰακώβου (gen.sing.masc.of Ἰάκωβος, relationship) 848.

Translation - "And when they arrived in the city, they went up to the upper room where they were staying temporarily - both Peter and John and James and Andrew, Philip and Thomas, Bartholomew and Matthew, James, the son of Alphaeus and Simon, the Zealot and Judas, the brother of James the Younger."

Comment: We may supply τὴν πόλιν after εἰσῆλθον. They entered the city gate, went immediately to the upper room (#2940). It is likely that they had sought out this place where they could stay, pending developments in their relation with Jesus, Who for the past forty days was known by them to be alive, but Who had not, until now given precise instructions to them. There is some evidence that during these forty days the disciples had some trepidation about the Jews. Luke

24:53 refers to the period *after* the ascension, not to the forty days between the resurrection and ascension. This upper room may have been a hideout, during the time that they had no specific instructions from Jesus. They now understand that there is a be a waiting period of undisclosed duration. Jesus did not tell them that it would be ten days, although He did say that the baptism of the Holy Spirit would occur soon (vs.5). We know from knowledge after the fact that it was ten days. The Apostles were all there, except, of course Judas Iscariot who had committed suicide six weeks before. We learn in verse 14 that the mother and half-brothers of Jesus and some other women were also with them.

Verse 14 - "There all continued with one accord in prayer and supplication, with the women, and Mary the mother of Jesus, and with his brethren."

οὗτοι πάντες ἦσαν προσκαρτεροῦντες ὁμοθυμαδὸν τῇ προσευχῇ σὺν γυναιξὶν καὶ Μαριὰμ τῇ μητρὶ τοῦ Ἰησοῦ καὶ τοῖς ἀδελφοῖς αὐτοῦ.

οὗτοι (nom.pl.masc.of οὗτος, subject of ἦσαν) 93.

πάντες (nom.pl.masc.of πᾶς, in agreement with οὗτοι) 67.

ἦσαν (3d.per.pl.imp.ind.of εἰμί, imperfect periphrastic) 86.

προσκαρτεροῦντες (pres.act.part.nom.pl.masc.of προσκαρτερέω, imperfect periphrastic, progressive description) 2113.

#2942 ὁμοθυμαδὸν (adverbial).

with one accord - Acts 1:14.
with one mind - Acts 2:46; 4:24; 5:12; 7:57; 8:6; 12:20; 15:25; 18:12; 19:29; Rom.15:6.

Meaning: Cf. ὁμόθυμος, ὁμός and θυμός (#2034); ὁμοῦ (#2015). The idea of intellectual unanimity is present plus the notion of heightened emotional agreement (θυμός). Thus with enthusiastic accord - Of the early Christians - Acts 1:14; 2:46; 4:24; 5:12; Rom.15:6; in the church council in Jerusalem - Acts 15:25; with reference to Stephen's enemies - Acts 7:57; Samaritans listening to Philip's sermon - Acts 8:6; resident of Tyre and Sidon - Acts 12:20; of Jews against Paul - Acts 18;12; Ephesians against Paul's companions - Acts 19:29.

τῇ (loc.sing.fem.of the article in agreement with προσευχῇ) 9.

προσευχῇ (loc.sing.fem.of προσευχή, sphere) 1238.

σὺν (preposition with the instrumental of association) 1542.

γυναιξὶν (instr.pl.fem.of γυνή, association) 103.

καὶ (adjunctive conjunction joining nouns) 14.

Μαριὰμ (indeclin.instru.sing.fem.of Μαρία, association) 64.

τῇ (instru.sing.fem.of the article in agreement with μητρὶ) 9.

μητρὶ (instru.sing.fem.of μήτηρ, in apposition with Μαριὰμ) 76.

τοῦ (gen.sing.masc.of the article in agreement with Ἰησοῦ) 9.

Ἰησοῦ (gen.sing.masc.of Ἰησοῦς, relationship) 3.

καὶ (adjunctive conjunction joining nouns) 14.

τοῖς (instru.pl.masc.of the article in agreement with ἀδελφοῖς) 9.

ἀδελφοῖς (instr.pl.masc.of ἀδελφός, association) 15.
αὐτοῦ (gen.sing.masc.of αὐτός, relationship) 16.

Translation - "These all continued with one accord in prayer and supplication, with the women, and Mary the mother of Jesus, and with his brethren."

Comment: The antecedent of οὗτοι is the list of disciples named in verse 13. Total and enthusiastic unanimity characterized their behavior. The imperfect periphrastic adds its concept of emphatic duration to the meaning of the participle. With great determination and consistency they continued together in prayer. The locative of sphere limits their unanimity, although it is likely that they also were of the same mind in other spheres of activity and attitude. πρός in composition with κατερέω is perfective or intensive. Thus προσκαρτερέω itself (#2113) carries the idea of fideltiy, strength of purpose, steadfastness and consistent application. Note also #2942, with its emotional as well as intellectual rapport. There were thus no less than five indications of the unity of purpose and feeling, manifesting itself in common action among the early Christians. What a contrast to the Christians in Germany during the Thirty Years War who were so lacking in unanimity that they fought each other until both sides were exhausted, after which they still failed to find fellowship. The Peace of Westphalia in 1648 was not theological accord, but only the temporary cesstion of war which could no be longer waged due to lack of weaponry and manpower.

When an attitude of common purpose prevails prayer is the result. When prayer is employed the unity of the Body of Christ is enhanced. Thus there is a mutual and direct cause and result relationship between harmony and action. Note that there was no feeling of special privilege or status. The eleven Apostles did not refuse to fellowship as peers, either with the women or with Jesus' half-brothers, who previously had had their doubts about Jesus' sanity. The women, among others and in addition to Mary, the mother of Jesus, probably included Mary Magdalene, Mary the wife of Cleophas, Joanna, Salome and Jesus' sisters whose names were never given. His brothers were James (#1098), Joses (#1099), Simon (#1100) and Judas (#1101). There is never a need for a women's liberation or civil rights movement when the Holy Spirit indwells and inspires truly regenerate Christians. Since democracies are not necessarily dominated by Christians and guided therefore by the principles of Christian ethics, pressure groups demanding their rights are not *ipso facto* improper. No spirit filled Christian needs a governmental decree to direct him to treat others in a way consistent with Matthew 7:12. The application of this principle, referred to as "The Golden Rule," which Immanuel Kant called the categorical imperative would make all political efforts to assure equal rights for minorities and other second-class citizens unnecessary. It is ironical in the extreme that some of the worst discrimination against minorities is practised by those who profess the purest concepts and policies of the Christian ethic.

Verse 15 - "And in those days Peter stood up in the midst of the disciples, and said (the number of names together were about an hundred and twenty)."

Καὶ ἐν ταῖς ἡμέραις ταύταις ἀναστὰς Πέτρος ἐν μέσῳ τῶν ἀδελφῶν εἶπεν (ἦν τε ὄχλος ὀνομάτων ἐπὶ τὸ αὐτὸ ὡς ἑκατὸν εἴκοσι),

Καὶ (continuative conjunction) 14
ἐν (preposition with the locative of time point) 80.
ταῖς (loc.pl.fem.of the article in agreement with ἡμέραις) 9.
ἡμέραις (loc.pl.fem.of ἡμέρα, time point) 135.
ταύταις (loc.pl.fem.of οὗτος, in agreement with ἡμέραις) 93.
ἀναστὰς (aor.act.part.nom.sing.masc.of ἀνίστημι, adverbial, temporal) 789.
Πέτρος (nom.sing.masc.of Πέτρος, subject of εἶπεν) 387.
ἐν (preposition with the locative of place) 80.
μέσῳ (loc.sing.neut.of μέσος, place) 873.
τῶν (gen.pl.masc.of the article in agreement with ἀδελφῶν) 9.
ἀδελφῶν *(gen.pl.masc.of ἀδελφός, description)* 15.
εἶπεν (3d.per.sing.aor.act.ind.of εἶπον, constative) 155.
(ἦν (3d.per.sing.imp.ind.of εἰμί, progressive description) 86.
τε (correlative particle introducing the parenthesis) 1408.
ὄχλος (nom.sing.masc.of ὄχλος, subject of ἦν) 418.
ὀνομάτων (gen.pl.neut.of ὄνομα, description) 108.
ἐπὶ (preposition with the accusative of extent) 47.
τὸ (acc.sing.neut.of the article in agreement with αὐτό) 9.
αὐτό (acc.sing.neut.of αὐτός, accusative of extent) 16.
ὡς (particle in a comparative phrase) 128.
ἑκατὸν (numeral) 1035.
εἴκοσι (numeral) 2283.

Translation - "*And in those days Peter stood up in the midst of the brethren and said, (now the crowd was estimated all together at about one hundred twenty).*"

Comment: ἐν ταῖς ἡμέραις ταύταις is a locative of time point construction. In the period between the ascension and Pentecost. Peter assumed the position of leadership, not only because of his personal assumption of the role, a fact that is apparent in the gospel records, but also apparently by common consent. Jesus had implied as much (Mt.16:19). The primacy of Peter seems to be taught in Scripture though the Roman Catholics have carried it too far. τε here is explanatory,without καί or other particles,used to introduce the parenthesis.*Cf.* #1408. ὀνομάτων - is a genitive of description or designation. "The crowd by number" or "The crowd was named (estimated, put at) about 120" or "The crowd added up to 120." ἐπὶ τὸ αὐτό - an interesting example of the extremely varied use that the New Testament put to ἐπί with its basic idea of "upon." Robertson, (*Grammar,* 600) speaks of "the manifoldness of resultant uses true of no other preposition" due to the simple fact that ἐπί means "upon." αὐτό here means "the total number" so that "all together" the number was estimated at about 120. This was not the "charter membership" of the church since the church as the Body of Christ includes all regenerate persons of whatever dispensation. The first souls saved, Adam and Eve, when they believed God's redemptive promise of Genesis 3:15 and were given bloody cloaks of the skins of the sacrificial animals which gave up their lives in order that Adam and Eve might have covering for their nakedness, were the first members of the church. In Matthew 16:18 Jesus in essence said, "The foundation rock of my Deity, about which you have just spoken, is the foundation of my church and I will go on building upon it." Peter was just another little stone (πέτρος, as distinct from πέτρα). There had been many before him and there have been many since his conversion, and there will be many more until the last stone is in place upon the foundation rock (Rev.10:7). The future tense in οἰκοδομήσω (Mt.16:18) cannot be pushed to say that Jesus had not yet laid the foundation nor erected upon it the first stone. His deity, the foundation, is eternal. Peter was not a rock at all. He was not even the first stone, although he was one of them, just as every believer is. Tacitly named to assume leadership among the early Christians (Luke 22:32), Peter took the initiative upon this occasion. But he did so without the benefit of the fulness of the Holy Spirit which was to be his ten days later, and, as a result in his first policy conference here recorded in Acts 1:15-26 he gave the group some bad advice, which resulted in an act that was in no sense authorized by the resurrected Christ, Who alone is Head over all things to His church (Eph.1:22,23). Unfortunately Peter's presumption was not the last time that some self appointed leader, who thought more highly of himself than he ought (Rom.12:3) has led some unsuspecting flock of God's sheep down some blind alley or along a primrose path to confusion.

Here is Peter's speech in

Verse 16 - "Men and brethren this scripture must needs have been fulfilled, which the Holy Ghost by the mouth of David spake before concerning Judas, which was guide to them that took Jesus."

Ἄνδρες ἀδελφοί, ἔδει πληρωθῆναι τὴν γραφὴν ἣν προεῖπεν τὸ πνεῦμα τὸ ἅγιον διὰ στόματος Δαυὶδ περὶ Ἰούδα τοῦ γενομένου ὁδηγοῦ τοῖς συλλαβοῦσιν Ἰησοῦν,

Ἄνδρες (voc.pl.masc.of ἀνήρ, address) 63.

ἀδελφοί (voc.pl.masc.of ἀδελφός, address) 15.

ἔδει (3d.per.sing.imp.ind.of δέω, progressive description) 1207.

πληρωθῆναι (aor.pass.inf.of πληρόω, noun use, subject of ἔδει) 115.

τὴν (acc.sing.fem.of the article in agreement with γραφὴν) 9.

γραφὴν (acc.sing.fem.of γραφή, general reference) 1389.

ἣν (acc.sing.fem.of ὅς, direct object of προεῖπεν) 65.

προεῖπεν (3d.per.sing.aor.act.ind.of προεῖπον, constative) 1501.

τὸ (nom.sing.neut.of the article in agreement with πνεῦμα) 9.

πνεῦμα (nom.sing.neut.of πνεῦμα, subject of προεῖπεν) 83.

τὸ (nom.sing.neut.of the article in agreement with πνεῦμα) 9.

ἅγιον (nom.sing.neut.of ἅγιος, in agreement with πνεῦμα) 84.

διὰ (preposition with the genitive, intermediate agent) 118.

στόματος (gen.sing.neut.of στόμα, intermediate agent) 344.

Δαυὶδ (gen.sing.masc.of Δαυίδ, possession) 6.

περὶ (preposition with the genitive of reference) 173.

Ἰούδα (gen.sing.masc.of Ἰούδας, reference) 853.

τοῦ (gen.sing.masc.of the article in agreement with ὁδηγοῦ) 9.

γενομένου (aor.mid.part.gen.sing.masc.of γίνομαι, adjectival, ascriptive, in agreement with ὁδηγοῦ) 113.

ὁδηγοῦ (gen.sing.masc.of ὁδηγός, in apposition with Ἰούδα) 1155.

τοῖς (dat.pl.masc.of the article in agreement with συλλαβοῦσιν) 9.

συλλαβοῦσιν (aor.act.part.dat.pl.masc.of συλλαμβάνω, substantival, personal advantage) 1598.

Ἰησοῦν (acc.sing.masc.of Ἰησοῦς, direct object of συλλαβοῦσιν) 3.

Translation - "Men, brethren, it was necessary that the Scripture which the Holy Spirit inspired through the mouth of David about Judas, who became a guide for those who arrested Jesus, be fulfilled."

Comment: We can regard ἀδελφοί as in apposition to Ἄνδρες, the vocative or we can think of them both in terms of address. This time Peter left the women out of it. ἀνήρ means a man between the ages of 29 and 49 (*cf.#'s* 63 and 1300). The infinitive in its use as a noun is the subject of ἔδει, with τὴν γραφὴν an accusative of general reference. Not all of that which is written to predict events must be fulfilled. Witness the predictions of the false prophets. But the predictions written by the Holy Spirit *must* be fulfilled. This is the force of ἔδει. This Old Testament passage which David wrote concerned Judas, although it did not name him (Psalm 41:9). In apposition to Ἰούδα we have ὁδηγοῦ modified by the adjectival participle γενομένου. The participles γενομένους and συλλαβοῦσιν, though aorist describe events which were future in relation to the time represented by προεῖπεν. The prediction came before the events predicted. If Luke had used ὅτι and indirect discourse, rather than περὶ and the genitive of reference, the participles would have been future, the tense of direct discourse, so that it would have read, "The Holy Spirit foretold by David's mouth that Judas will become a guide to those who will arrest Jesus." Peter is correct in his remarks thus far. He had in mind Psalm 41:9 and it is indeed inevitable that what God says in Holy Scripture must be fulfilled. Indeed all of Peter's introductory remarks through verse 20 are factual and proper. It is only in his policy suggestion of verses 20,21 that he went astray. If Peter had not given so much thought to the failings of a former colleague, whose sin of betrayal was not greatly different from his own sin of denial, he might not have presumed to offer a solution to the problem, as though the sovereign Christ had overlooked this detail and had no solution of His own to offer in His own good time. Peter should have been spending his time reflecting upon his own miserable shortcomings - an exercise that would have done much to develop his humility, a spiritual grace for which he was not known, until after Pentecost. After that Peter gave a good account of himself, as any Christian will when he has been filled with the dynamic power of the Holy Spirit.

Verse 17 - "For he was numbered with us, and had obtained part of this ministry.

ὅτι κατηριθμημένος ἦν ἐν ἡμῖν καὶ ἔλαχεν τὸν κλῆρον τῆς διακονίας ταύτης.

ὅτι (conjunction introducing a subordinate causal clause) 211.

#2943 κατηριθμημένος (perf.pass.part.nom.sing.masc.of καταριθμέω, pluperfect periphrastic).

number - Acts 1:17.

Meaning: A combination of κατά (#98) and ἀριθμέω (#894). Hence, to number along with. κατά in a distributive sense. Judas was one of the twelve Apostles — Acts 1:17.

ἦν (3d.per.sing.imp.ind.of εἰμί, pluperfect periphrastic, consummative) 86.
ἐν (preposition with the locative - "among" with a plural pronoun) 80.
ἡμῖν (loc.pl.masc.of ἐγώ, association) 123.
καί (adjunctive conjunction joining verbs) 14.
ἔλαχεν (3d.per.sing.2d.aor.act.ind.of λαγχάνω, constative) 1790.
τόν (acc.sing.masc.of the article in agreement with κλῆρον) 9.
κλῆρον (acc.sing.masc.of κλῆρος, direct object of ἔλαχεν) 1648.
τῆς (gen.sing.fem.of the article in agreement with διακονίας) 9.
διακονίας (gen.sing.fem.of διακονία, description) 2442.
ταύτης (gen.sing.fem.of οὗτος, in agreement with διακονίας) 93.

Translation - ". . . because he has been one of our number and he obtained his share of this ministry."

Comment: The ὅτι clause is causal. The main thought of verse 16 is that the prophecy about Judas must be fulfilled. Indeed it had been fulfilled. There was nothing left for anyone to do about fulfilling it. The scripture referred to in verse 20 declares Judas' post vacant and directs that another take his place, but it does not say that the other eleven Apostles were to be given the responsibility of conducting a lottery in order to fill the position. Judas had been with them from the beginning (Matthew 10:1-4; Luke 6:13-16) and continued for three years to be numbered among them, during which time he had received his full share of participation in the ministry which Jesus had given to the Twelve. Then Judas' ministry ceased as recorded in verse 18. τῆς διακονίας ταύτης refers not to discipleship, but to Apostleship. There are only twelve Apostles in this specially favored group, although the word ἀπόστολος (#844) is found in contexts in which a broader application is made. The Twelve Apostles are to be rewarded richly in the Kingdom of the Heavens and charged with special judicial responsibilities (Mt.19:28).

Verse 18 - "Now this man purchased a field with the reward of iniquity, and falling headlong, he burst asunder in the midst and all his bowels gushed out."

Οὗτος μὲν οὖν ἐκτήσατο χωρίον ἐκ μισθοῦ τῆς ἀδικίας, καὶ πρηνὴς γενόμενος ἐλάκησεν μέσος, καὶ ἐξεχύθη πάντα τὰ σπλάγχνα αὐτοῦ.

Οὗτος (nom.sing.masc.of οὗτος, subject of ἐκτήσατο and ἐλάκησεν, contemptuous) 93.
μέν (affirmative particle) 300.

οὖν (continuative conjunction) 68.

ἐκτήσατο (3d.per.sing.aor.mid.ind.of κτάομαι, constative) 859.

χωρίον (acc.sing.neut.of χωρίον, direct object of ἐκτήσατο) 1583.

ἐκ (preposition with the ablative of means) 19.

μισθοῦ (abl.sing.masc.of μισθός means) 441.

τῆς (gen.sing.fem.of the article in agreement with ἀδικίας) 9.

ἀδικίας (gen.sing.fem.of ἀδικία, description) 2367.

καὶ (adjunctive conjunction joining verbs) 14.

#2944 πρηνής (nom.sing.masc.of πρηνής, predicate adverb).

headlong - Acts 1:18.

Meaning: prone; headlong - Judas - Acts 1:18.

γενόμενος (2d.aor.part.nom.sing.masc.of γίνομαι, adverbial, temporal) 113.

#2945 ἐλάκησεν (3d.per.sing.aor.act.ind.of λακέω, ingressive).

burst asunder - Acts 1:18.

Meaning: to crack or burst open - Acts 1:18.

μέσος (nom.sing.masc.of μέσος, predicate adverb) 873.

καὶ (continuative conjunction) 14.

ἐξεχύθη (3d.per.sing.1st.aor.pass.ind.of ἐκχέω, ingressive) 811.

πάντα (nom.pl.neut.of πᾶς, in agreement with σπλάγχνα) 67.

τὰ (nom.pl.neut.of the article in agreement with σπλάγχνα) 9.

σπλάγχνα (nom.pl.neut.of σπλάγχνα, subject of ἐξεχύθη) 1857.

αὐτοῦ (gen.sing.masc.of αὐτός, possession) 16.

Translation - "And this fellow in fact bought a field with the payment (he received for his) unrighteousness, and after he had fallen prostrate, he began to burst open in the middle and all his intestines began to be poured out."

Comment: The contemptuous use of οὗτος and emphatic μὲν indicates the mood of Peter as he tells about Judas' fate. The story of Judas' death was told in Matthew 27:3-10. Peter had his facts wrong. He said that Judas bought the field. Matthew says that the chief priests bought it with the money that Judas threw upon the floor in the temple. Luke's account is accurate. He is reporting what Peter said. The mistake was Peter's. After Judas had hanged himself, someone cut down the body but did not bury it. The corpse lay exposed in the hot sunshine and began to burst and his intestines began to emerge. It is not a pretty picture. Judas was not an attractive figure. One wonders whether any of the ladies present fainted or rushed out to throw up as Peter gave his graphic description? Most all that Peter did manifested overabundant and imaginative vitality.

Verse 19 - "And it was known unto all the dwellers at Jerusalem, insomuch as that field is called in their proper tongue, Aceldama, that is to say, The field of blood."

καὶ γνωστὸν ἐγένετο πᾶσι τοῖς κατοικοῦσιν Ἰερουσαλήμ, ὥστε κληθῆναι τὸ χωρίον ἐκεῖνο τῇ (ἰδίᾳ) διαλέκτῳ αὐτῶν Ἀκελδαμάχ, τοῦτ' ἐστιν Χωρίον Αἵματος.

καὶ (emphatic conjunction) 14.

γνωστὸν (acc.sing.neut.of γνωστός, predicate adjective) 1917.

ἐγένετο (3d.per.sing.aor.ind.of γίνομαι, ingressive) 113.

πᾶσι (dat.pl.masc.of πᾶς, in agreement with κατοικοῦσιν) 67.

τοῖς (dat.pl.masc.of the article in agreement with κατοικοῦσιν) 9.

κατοικοῦσιν (pres.act.part.dat.pl.masc.of κατοικέω, substantival, personal interest) 242.

Ἰερουσαλήμ (gen.sing.masc.indeclin.of Ἰεροσολύμων, description) 141.

ὥστε (conjunction with the infinitive introducing a consecutive clause) 752.

κληθῆναι (aor.pass.inf.of καλέω, result) 107.

τὸ (acc.sing.neut.of the article in agreement with χωρίον) 9.

χωρίον (acc.sing.neut.of χωρίον, general reference) 1583.

ἐκεῖνο (acc.sing.neut.of ἐκεῖνος, in agreement with χωρίον) 246.

τῇ (loc.sing.fem.of the article in agreement with διαλέκτῳ) 9.

ἰδίᾳ (loc.sing.fem.of ἴδιος, in agreement with διαλέκτῳ) 778.

#2946 διαλέκτῳ (loc.sing.fem.of διάλεκτος, sphere).

language - Acts 2:6.
tongue - Acts 1:19; 2:8; 21:40; 22:2; 26:14.

Meaning: A combination of διά (#118) and λέγω (#66). *Cf.* διαλέγω (#2349). Medium of communication whether spoken or written; language; dialect. Form of speech used normally by the people of a given culture. Of the Hebrew (which Robertson believes is the Aramaic) tongue. In Acts 1:19 the language of Jerusalem. Paul used it in his speech of defense in Jerusalem - Acts 21:40; 22:2. Jesus spoke it to Paul at his conversion on the Damascus road - Acts 26:14. Native language - Acts 2:6,8.

αὐτῶν (gen.pl.masc.of αὐτός, description) 16.

#2947 Ἀκελδαμάχ (appellation).

Aceldama - Acts 1:19.

Meaning: Aramaic for Χωρίον Αἵματος, the Greek for the English, "Field of Blood." - Acts 1:19 for the place where Judas Iscariot died.

τοῦτ' (nom.sing.neut.of οὗτος, subject of ἐστιν) 93.

ἐστιν (3d.per.sing.pres.ind.of εἰμί, static) 86.

Χωρίον (nom.sing.masc.of Χωρίον, predicate nominative) 1583.

Αἵματος (gen.sing.neut.of αἷμα, description) 1203.

Translation - "In fact it came to be known to everyone who lives in Jerusalem, with the result that that field is called in their own dialect 'Aceldama' which translates to 'Bloody Field.' "

Comment: καὶ is emphatic. ἐκεῖνο, modifying τὸ χωρίον is deictic. τοῦτ' ἐστιν - "that is," "that is to say," or "that translates into . . . " in this case Greek. *Cf.* comments on Matthew 27:3-8. Judas Iscariot, a stranger to the covenant of grace, died by his own hand, was disgraced both before and after he died and was never buried, although his body decomposed in a burial ground reserved for strangers. Thus other strangers find their way into the family of God, to a position of such dignity that Christ is not ashamed to call them His brethren (Hebrews 2:11,12).

Indirectly Judas bought the field as Peter said in Acts 1:18 since he refunded the money. Actually the Jewish religious Establishment negotiated the sale and consummated the deal. The money was the price of Judas' condemnation. This was no secret matter. The story was circulated all over Jerusalem. As a result Ἀκελδαμάχ became a household word - "Bloody Field," where a traitor who died by his own hand was left to rot and feed the buzzards and jackals.

Having enthralled his audience with a story that he admitted was already well known throughout the community, Peter now goes to a loftier theme, as he points to the biblical prediction of the Judas story, before he makes the unwarranted suggestion of verses 21-22.

Verse 20 - "For it is written in the book of Psalms, Let his habitation be desolate, and let no man dwell therein: and his bishopric let another take."

Γέγραπται γὰρ ἐν βίβλῳ φαλμῶν, Γενηθήτω ἡ ἐπαυλις αὐτοῦ ἔρημος καὶ μὴ ἔστω ὁ κατοικῶν ἐν αὐτῇ, καὶ Τὴν ἐπισκοπὴν αὐτοῦ λαβέτω ἔτερος.

Γέγραπται (3d.per.sing.perf.pass.ind.of γράφω, intensive) 156.
γὰρ (causal conjunction) 105.
ἐν (preposition with the locative of place) 80.
βίβλῳ (loc.sing.masc.of βίβλος, place) 1.
φαλμῶν (gen.pl.masc.of φαλμός, description) 2703.
Γενηθήτω (3d.per.sing.aor.pass.impv.of γίνομαι, command) 113.
ἡ (nom.sing.fem.of the article in agreement with ἐπαυλις) 9.

#2948 ἐπαυλις (nom.sing.fem.of ἐπαυλις, subject of γενηθήτω).

habitation - Acts 1:20.

Meaning: A combination of ἐπί (#47) and αὖλις - "tent." *Cf.* αὐλή (#1554). Cottage, country house or cabin; temporary dwelling. Used of military bivouacs. With reference to Judas' home - Acts 1:20.

αὐτοῦ (gen.sing.masc.of αὐτός, possession) 16.
ἔρημος (nom.sing.fem.of ἔρημος, predicate adjective) 250.
καὶ (continuative conjunction) 14.
μὴ (qualified negative conjunction with the imperative) 87.
ἔστω (3d.per.sing.pres.impv.of εἰμί, prohibition) 86.

ὁ (nom.sing.masc.of the article in agreement with κατοικῶν) 9.

κατοικῶν (pres.act.part.nom.sing.masc.of κατοικέω, substantival, subject of ἔστω) 242.

ἐν (preposition with the locative of place) 80.

αὐτῇ (loc.sing.fem.of αὐτός, place) 16.

καὶ (adjunctive conjunction joining quotations) 14.

Τὴν (acc.sing.fem.of the article in agreement with ἐπισκοπὴν) 9.

ἐπισκοπὴν (acc.sing.fem.of ἐπισκοπή, direct object of λαβέτω) 2679.

αὐτοῦ (gen.sing.masc.of αὐτός, possession) 16.

λαβέτω (3d.per.sing.aor.act.impv.of λαμβάνω, command) 533.

ἕτερος (nom.sing.masc.of ἕτερος, subject of λαβέτω) 605.

Translation - *"Because it stands, written in the Psalter, 'His house shall be deserted and no one shall ever live in it' and 'Some other man shall take his directorate."*

Comment: γὰρ is causal for the same reason that ὅτι is in verse 17. *Cf.* comment. The scripture about Judas must be fulfilled. This was Peter's statement in verse 16. Why? Because, said Peter (vs.17) "he was one of us." Also (vs.20) because (causal γὰρ) Psalm 69:25 says, γενηθήτω ἡ . . . ἔρημος. . . k.t.l." Also (adjunctive καὶ) Psalm 109:8 says, Τὴν . . . ἕτερος, . . . κ.τ.λ." Thus Peter built a logical case. The Big Fisherman had been doing his home work. One wonders how Peter became aware of these scriptures and how he had the insight to connect them to Judas and his apostasy? The LXX for Psalm 109:8 has the optative λάβοι rather than the imperative λαβέτω as Luke wrote it. Thus Judas' house and real estate possessions were to be permanently vacated and his position as co-administrator of the church was to be given to another. It is clear that Paul was the divine choice as the twelfth Apostle. But Peter, impetuous and compulsive as always, assumed that at least they could perform one needed function while they were waiting for the fulness of the Holy Spirit which the Lord had promised. They could fill the vacancy left by Judas' downfall, in keeping with the command of Psalm 109:8. It did not occur to Peter that the Apostles needed the filling of the Holy Spirit in order to perform this function as much as they did to preach the gospel. It is interesting that after Pentecost, the Spirit filled Christians did not mention this matter again and we never hear again of poor Matthias, who did not ask for the job and was apparently too polite (confused, afraid, embarrassed, humble) to challenge the wisdom of what Peter was suggesting. One wonders what his reactions to this entire procedure were? Did anyone in the company suggest that perhaps they ought to wait until after Pentecost, or that they ought not to presume at all that it was their job to fill the vacancy? By taking affairs into his own hands, Peter induced the Apostles to make their first major wrong decision.

Verse 21 - *"Wherefore of these men which have companied with us all the time that the Lord Jesus went in and out among us, . . . "*

δεῖ οὖν τῶν συνελθόντων ἡμῖν ἀνδρῶν ἐν παντὶ χρόνῳ ᾧ εἰσῆλθεν καὶ ἐξῆλθεν ἐφ᾽ ἡμᾶς ὁ κύριος Ἰησοῦς, δεῖ (3d.per.sing.impersonal ind.of δέω) 1207.

οὖν (inferential conjunction) 68.

τῶν (gen.pl.masc.of the article in agreement with συνελθόντων) 9.

συνελθόντων (aor.mid.part.gen.pl.masc.of συνέρχομαι, adjectival, restrictive, in agreement with ἀνδρῶν) 78.

ἡμῖν (instru.pl.masc.of ἐγώ, association) 123.

ἀνδρῶν (gen.pl.masc.of ἀνήρ, partitive) 63.

ἐν (preposition with the locative of time point) 80.

παντὶ (loc.sing.masc.of πᾶς, in agreement with χρόνῳ) 67.

χρόνῳ (loc.sing.masc.of χρόνος, time period) 168.

ᾧ (loc.sing.masc.of ὅς, relative to its antecedent χρόνῳ) 65.

εἰσῆλθεν (3d.per.sing.aor.mid.ind.of εἰσέρχομαι, constative) 234.

καὶ (adjunctive conjunction joining verbs) 14.

ἐξῆλθεν (3d.per.sing.aor.mid.ind.of ἐξέρχομαι, constative) 161.

ἐφ' (preposition with the accusative, physical place) 47.

ἡμᾶς (acc.pl.masc.of ἐγώ, place) 123.

ὁ (nom.sing.masc.of the article in agreement with κύριος) 9.

κύριος (nom.sing.masc.of κύριος, subject of εἰσῆλθεν and ἐξῆλθεν) 97.

Ἰησοῦς (nom.sing.masc.of Ἰησοῦς, in apposition with κύριος) 3.

(Note: The syntax of verses 21 and 22 ties them together in one long and involved sentence. Translation of both will be given after verse 22).

Verse 22 - ". . . beginning from the baptism of John, unto that same day that he was taken up from us, must one be ordained to be a witness with us of his resurrection."

ἀρξάμενος ἀπὸ τοῦ βαπτίσματος Ἰωάννου ἕως τῆς ἡμέρας ἧς ἀνελήμφθη ἀφ' ἡμῶν, μάρτυρα τῆς ἀναστάσεως αὐτοῦ σὺν ἡμῖν γενέσθαι ἕνα τούτων

ἀρξάμενος (aor.mid.part.nom.sing.masc.of ἄρχω, adverbial, circumstantial) 383.

ἀπὸ (preposition with the ablative of time separation) 70.

τοῦ (abl.sing.masc. of the article in agreement with βαπτίσματος) 9.

βαπτίσματος (abl.sing.masc.of βάπτισμα, time separation) 278.

Ἰωάννου (gen.sing.masc.of Ἰωάννης, description) 247.

ἕως (conjunction introducing a definite temporal clause) 71.

τῆς (gen.sing.fem.of the article in agreement with ἡμέρας) 9.

ἡμέρας (gen.sing.fem.of ἡμέρα, time description) 135.

ἧς (gen.sing.fem.of ὅς, relative temporal clause, case attraction from locative to genitive) 65.

ἀνελήμφθη (3d.per.sing.aor.pass.ind.of ἀναλαμβάνω, constative) 2930.

ἀφ' (preposition with the ablative of separation) 70.

ἡμῶν (abl.pl.masc.of ἐγώ, separation) 123.

μάρτυρα (acc.sing.masc.of μάρτυς, predicate accusative) 1263.

τῆς (gen.sing.fem.of the article in agreement with ἀναστάσεως) 9.

ἀναστάσεως (gen.sing.fem.of ἀνάστασις, description) 1423.

αὐτοῦ (gen.sing.masc.of αὐτός, possession) 16.

σύν (preposition with the instrumental of association) 1542.
ἡμῖν (instru.pl.masc.of ἐγώ, association) 123.
γενέσθαι (aor.mid.inf.of γίνομαι, epexegetical, explains δεῖ - vs.21) 113
ἕνα (acc.sing.masc.of εἷς, general reference) 469.
τούτων (gen.pl.masc.of οὗτος, in agreement with ἀνδρῶν) 93.

Translation - *"Therefore it is necessary that one of these men who have been associated with us throughout all of time in which the Lord Jesus went in and came out among us, beginning at the baptism of John and continuing until the day on which He was taken up from us, be a witness with us of His resurrection."*

Comment: (verses 21-22). This long and involved sentence is really grammatically and syntactically simple, although the circumstantial participle ἀρξάμενος should agree in case with χρόνῳ. Participles sometimes lend themselves to anacoluthon. οὖν is inferential, showing that Peter thought his analysis of the history of Judas' ministry and his interpretation of the prophetic scriptures which he cited, authorized him to make the statement of verses 21,22. "In the light of the foregoing (vss.16-20)," Peter was saying, "it is therefore necessary to elect an apostle!" δεῖ is completed by γενέσθαι, at the end of verse 22. One is reminded by the convoluted syntax of Peter's statement of the two volume *History of Bismarck*, written in German, in which the verb was in the second volume! Thus γενέσθαι is the subject of δεῖ and ἕνα is an accusative of general reference. ἕνα is joined with the partitive genitive ἀνδρῶν, modified by τούτων. "One of these men. . . " What men? Those defined by the restrictive participle τῶν συνελθόντων ἡμῖν - one of the men who had been associating with the eleven disciples. During what period of time? The time period involved included all of the time as defined by a relative temporal clause, ᾧ εἰσῆλθεν . . . Ἰησοῦς, and by the temporal clause beginning with the circumstantial participle ἀρξάμενος (which should read ἀρξαμένῳ, to agree with χρόνῳ) and closing with ἡμέρας, which, in turn is clarified by another relative temporal clause ἧς . . . ἡμῶν. The day when Jesus was taken up from them was the last day of the time which began with His baptism. It was during all of this time that Jesus went in and came out, in association with the eleven disciples. Thus the men are identified. One of them must be chosen, Peter said. For what purpose? To be a witness along with the witness of the other eleven. A witness to what? His resurrection. So much for the grammar and syntax.

What was Peter emphasizing? (1) That the candidate's experience must go back, along with the other disciples, to the ministry of John the Baptist. It must include the entire three years with Jesus. That was the important point in Peter's thinking. Only could such a man fulfill the function of corroborating the testimony of the other eleven. The candidate must have been an eye witness of Jesus' resurrection, as were the eleven. Otherwise his witness would be based upon hearsay, which normally is not admissible as evidence in a court room. Peter sounds like a lawyer.

What was the error in Peter's thinking? He assumed that since Jesus had gone back to heaven a teacher of His philosophy and an eye witness to His resurrection must come from the group before him. It did not occur to Peter that Jesus could appear to Saul of Tarsus and convince him that He was alive or that He could rapture Paul up to the third heaven (2 Cor. 12:1-4) and give him a crash course in Christian theology that would equip Paul for the obligations of Apostleship as well or better than Peter and the other ten were equipped. On one occasion Paul found it necessary to rebuke Peter publicly for his failure to conduct himself in keeping with the new insights into theology that both of them had come to understand (Gal.2:11-14). (2) Peter was also emphasizing the fact that such a witness as would be required could come only from the group to whom he spoke. (3) He seemed to imply that those who had been with Jesus from the beginning understood everything about the new Christian revelation, although at that point he did not know that the gospel would be received by the Gentiles and that Gentile Christians would occupy the same position in the Body of Christ as did the Jews. This revelation came to him in the home of Cornelius (Acts 10:9-35).

Of course we could not expect Peter to understand all of this, since it was the later events that were to demonstrate that he had acted with presumption when he chaired the meeting that elected Matthias to a position to which God had not chosen him.

Saul of Tarsus, ultimately chosen by the resurrected Christ who paid scant respect to a liberal show of democracy among misguided people, did not possess a single qualification listed by Peter on this occasion as essential. Matthias and Joseph Barsabas Justus had every one. But neither of them were Christ's choice. Peter seems to have implied that Jesus had been guilty of an oversight when He neglected to attend to this vital matter before He ascended to heaven - an oversight which he felt it his duty to take care of without further delay. The sovereign God Who predicted Judas' downfall (John 6:70,71; 13:9,10,21-27; 17:12) and Who had said that ultimately there would be twelve Apostles (Mt.19:28) was not likely to overlook the mathematical discrepancy and thus neglect to provide a means to replace Judas Iscariot. He did not need the help of eleven men, as yet devoid of the fulness and guidance of the Holy Spirit. Our condolence both to Matthias and Joseph Barsabas Justus, neither of whom had asked for the appointment. Joseph Justus, although nominated must have felt an additional slight when it appeared that the Lord had chosen Matthias instead of him. Neither he nor Matthias, who probably felt congratulated had any way of knowing that the court of heaven had ignored the entire procedure. It is not likely that Matthias, like a politician drafted against his will, ever really wanted to be an Apostle.

Verse 23 - "And they appointed two, Joseph called Barsabas, who was surnamed Justus, and Matthias."

καὶ ἔστησαν δύο Ἰωσὴφ τὸν καλούμενον Βαρσαββᾶν, ὃς ἐπεκλήθη Ἰοῦστος, καὶ Ματθίαν.

καὶ (continuative conjunction) 14.
ἔστησαν (3d.per.pl.aor.act.ind.of ἵστημι, constative) 180.
δύο (numeral) 385.

#2949 Ἰωσὴφ (acc.sing.masc.of Ἰωσήφ, direct object of ἔστησαν).

Joseph - Acts 1:23.

Meaning: A nominee for the vacated apostleship of Judas Iscariot - Acts 1:23.

τὸν (acc.sing.masc.of the article in agreement with καλούμενον) 9.
καλούμενον (pres.pass.part.acc.sing.masc.of καλέω, in apposition) 107.

#2950 Βαρσαββᾶν (acc.sing.masc.of Βαρσαββᾶς, direct object of καλούμενον).

Barsabbas - Acts 1:23.

Meaning: another name for Ἰωσήφ (#2949) - Acts 1:23. Surname for Ἰούδας - Acts 15:22.

ὅς (nom.sing.masc.of ὅς, subject of ἐπεκλήθη) 65.
ἐπεκλήθη (3d.per.sing.aor.pass.ind.of ἐπικαλέω, constative) 884.

#2951 Ἰοῦστος (nom.sing.masc.of Ἰοῦστος, appellation).

Justus - Acts 1:23; 18:7; Col.4:11.

Meaning: Justus, another name for Ἰωσὴφ Βαρσαββᾶν (#'s 2949,2950) - Acts 1:23. A Corinthian christian proselyte - Acts 18:7; a Jewish Christian - Col.4:11.

καὶ (adjunctive conjunction joining nouns) 14.

#2952 Μαθθίαν (acc.sing.masc.of Μαθθίας, direct object of ἔστησαν).

Matthias - Acts 1:23,26.

Meaning: An early disciple, associated from the earliest period with Jesus and the Twelve. Selected by the Eleven to succeed Judas Iscariot - Acts 1:23,26.

Translation - "So they nominated two - Joseph, the one called Barsabbas, who was nicknamed Justus, and Matthias."

Comment: According to Peter's arbitrary qualification guidelines, not a single one of the Eleven could qualify, if by "John's baptism" he meant the day that John the Baptist immersed Jesus (Mt.3). Peter himself was excluded by his own guideline. He was asking for one who was better qualified than he. Note also that they limited the field of choice to two before they prayed about it. Thus they tended to restrict the choice which God would have if He answered their prayer.

Verse 24 - "And they prayed, and said, Thou Lord, which knowest the hearts of all men, shew whether of these two thou hast chosen."

καὶ προσευξάμενοι εἶπαν, Σὺ κύριε καρδιογνῶστα πάντων, ἀνάδειξον ὃν
ἐξελέξω ἐκ τούτων τῶν δύο ἕνα

καὶ (continuative conjunction) 14.

προσευξάμενοι (aor.mid.part.nom.pl.masc.of προσεύχομαι, adverbial,
temporal) 544.

εἶπαν (3d.per.pl.aor.act.ind.of εἶπον, constative) 155.

Σὺ (voc.sing.masc.of σύ, address) 104.

κύριε (voc.sing.masc.of κύριος, address) 97.

#2953 καρδιογνῶστα (voc.sing.masc.of καρδιογνώστης, in agreement with
κύριε).

which knoweth the hearts - Acts 1:24; 15:8.

Meaning: A combination of καρδία (#432) and γινώσκω (#131). *Cf.*also
γνώστης (#3652). An expert. One who is knowledgeable about the affairs of the
heart. Heart specialist. Cardiologist in the medical sense, although the word was
probably not applied in that sense in New Testament times. Only in an ethical
and psychological sense. Applied to God in Acts 1:24; 15:8 as one who knows
what men are thinking and feeling.

πάντων (gen.pl.masc.of πᾶς, description) 67.

ἀνάδειξον (2d.per.sing.aor.act.impv.of ἀναδείκνυμι, entreaty) 2409.

ὃν (acc.sing.masc.of ὅς, attracted to ἕνα) 65.

ἐξελέξω (2d.per.sing.1st.aor.mid.ind.of ἐκλέγω, constative) 2119.

ἐκ (preposition with the partitive genitive) 19.

τούτων (gen.pl.masc.of οὗτος, in agreement with δύο) 93.

τῶν (gen.pl.masc.of the article in agreement with δύο, partitive) 9.

δύο (numeral) 385.

ἕνα (acc.sing.masc.of εἷς, direct object ofd ἐξελέξω) 469.

Translation - "*And as they prayed they said, 'You, Lord, who knows all hearts,
show us which one of these two men you have chosen'* "

Comment: Since the language of the direct discourse is clearly that of prayer,
προσευξάμενοι is pleonastic. Note Σὺ in emphasis. *Cf.*#2409 for meaning. The
prayer was that the Lord would indicate by some unmistakable evidence whom
He chose. The disciples were asking the Lord to point him out. It did not seem to
occur to the brethren that the Lord indeed knows the hearts of all, including
theirs, and that while He understood why they were doing this, He was out of
sympathy with the whole procedure. It is interesting to note that when a
Christian steps outside the will of God for his life, he is always eager to pray
about it. Thus we plead with God to put the stamp of His approval upon our
plans, which we have every intension of carrying to completion whether God
likes it or not. This show of sanctity on parade is not very different from that
which our Lord condemned in the Pharisees (Mt.23:14).

Verse 25 - "*. . . that he may take part of this ministry and apostleship, from which*

Judas by transgression fell, that he might go to his own place."

λαβεῖν τὸν τόπον τῆς διακονίας ταύτης καὶ ἀποστολῆς, ἀφ᾽ ἧς παρέβη
Ἰούδας πορευθῆναι εἰς τὸν τόπον τὸν ἴδιον.

λαβεῖν (2d.aor.act.inf.of λαμβάνω, purpose) 533.
τὸν (acc.sing.masc.of the article in agreement with τόπον) 9.
τόπον (acc.sing.masc.of τόπος, direct object of λαβεῖν) 1019.
τῆς (gen.sing.fem.of the article in agreement with διακονίας) 9.
διακονίας (gen.sing.fem.of διακονία, description) 2442.
ταύτης (gen.sing.fem.of οὗτος, in agreement with διακονίας) 93.
καὶ (adjunctive conjunction joining nouns) 14.

#2954 ἀποστολῆς (gen.sing.fem.of ἀποστολή, description).

apostleship - Acts 1:25; Rom.1:5; 1 Cor.9:2; Gal.2:8.

Meaning: the office of being an apostle. The position of the Twelve Apostles.
Offered to Matthias - Acts 1:25; of Paul - Rom.1:5; 1 Cor.9:2. Peter, followed by
a genitive of description, τῆς περιτομῆς - *i.e.* Peter's special ministry was
directed to Jews while Paul was sent principally to the Gentiles - Gal.2:8.

ἀφ᾽ (preposition with the ablative of separation) 70.
ἧς (abl.sing.fem.of ὅς, separation) 65.
παρέβη (3d.per.sing.2d.aor.act.ind.of παραβαίνω, constative) 1139.
Ἰούδας (nom.sing.masc.of Ἰούδας, subject of παρέβη) 853.
πορευθῆναι (aor.mid.inf.of πορεύομαι, result) 170.
εἰς (preposition with the accusative of extent) 140.
τὸν (acc.sing.masc.of the article in agreement with τόπον) 9.
τόπον (acc.sing.masc.of κτόπος, extent) 1019.
τὸν (acc.sing.masc.of the article in agreement with τόπον) 9.
ἴδιον (acc.sing.masc.of ἴδιος, in agreement with τόπον) 778.

*Translation - ". . . to take the place in this ministry and apostleship from which
Judas fell by the wayside with the result that he went unto his own place.' "*

Comment: The verse continues the sentence begun in the prayer in verse 24.
λαβεῖν indicates purpose. τὸν τόπον (some MSS. read κλῆρον) is defined by
two descriptive genitives, διακονίας καὶ ἀποστολῆς. The former, the ministry, is
open to all Christians. The latter, apostleship is open only to twelve divinely
chosen men. It is also defined by the relative clause with the ablative of
separation. It was the place "from which Judas fell." The infinitive πορευθῆναι
can be either purpose or result. We need not push the Calvinistic theology to the
point that we call it purpose. God did not make Judas fall by the wayside in order
that He might damn him. This is the supralapsarianism of the fanatics. But the
result of his fall was his descent to his own place.

There is more emphasis on τὸν τόπον τὸν ἴδιον than is proper. It is true that
Judas went to his own place of punishment, but it was not proper for the

apostles to emphasize the fact in prayer. They should have realized, as indeed later they came to realize, that but for the grace of God, they too, along with all of the human race, would be in that place into which Judas fell. There is a subtle warning here for the Christian who has overlooked John 5:22 and thus sometimes imagines that his place in the economy of God is that of the judge upon the bench in heaven's court. It is when we preempt the position of Jesus Christ Who is the only One in the universe Who has a moral right to judge others, since He alone has done anything positive to help others, that we make stupid suggestions such as Peter had just made and pray the Pharisaical prayer which they did. Such attitudes and conduct is characteristic of the Christian who has the Holy Spirit in residence, but in whom the Holy Spirit is not regnant. It really did not make much difference what the disciples prayed on this occasion. God was not listening.

Having restricted the freedom of choice of the Lord to two men, and having instructed Him that when He voted He must vote for one of the two and for no other, they implied that God was a democrat (small d). If they intended to insult Him they may as well have called Him a Republican (capital R). That God is not impressed with the collective will of the majority of sinners, even saved sinners, even when such will is expressed upon the same day between sunrise and sundown, is evident from the fact that He did not choose to vote in this election which Peter conducted. God had His own man in mind for the job that the disciples were trying to fill. One wonders what the reaction in that upper room would have been if God had replied to their request that He tell them whether it be Matthias or Justus by thundering from the heavens, "I don't want either one of them, stupid!" But He said nothing, since He had advised them once that it is not proper to cast genuine pearls before genuine swine. Few people who pray about the outcome of an election stop to listen for an answer to their prayer. Rather they rush out to the polls to cast the ballot that they had intended to cast all of the time. This is what the disciples did. They voted.

Verse 26 - "And they gave forth their lots; and the lot fell upon Matthias; and he was numbered with the eleven apostles."

καὶ ἔδωκαν κλήρους αὐτοῖς, καὶ ἔπεσεν ὁ κλῆρος ἐπὶ Μαθθίαν, καὶ συγκατεφηφίσθη μετὰ τῶν ἕνδεκα ἀποστόλων.

καὶ (continuative conjunction) 14.
ἔδωκαν (3d.per.pl.aor.act.ind.of δίδωμι, constative) 362.
κλήρους (acc.pl.masc.of κλῆρος, direct object of ἔδωκαν) 1648.
αὐτοῖς (dat.pl.masc.of αὐτός, reference) 16.
καὶ (continuative conjunction) 14.
ἔπεσεν (3d.per.sing.aor.act.ind.of πίπτω, constative) 187.
ὁ (nom.sing.masc.of the article in agreement with κλῆρος) 9.
κλῆρος (nom.sing.masc.of κλῆρος, subject of ἔπεσεν) 1648.
ἐπὶ (preposition with the accusative of place, metaphorical) 47.
Μαθθίαν (acc.sing.masc.of Μαθθίας, metaphorical place) 2952.
καὶ (inferential conjunction) 14.

#2955 συγκατεφηφίσθη (3d.per.sing.1st.aor.pass.ind.of συγκαταφηφίζω, constative).

number with - Acts 1:26.

Meaning: A combination of σύν (#1542), κατά (#98) and φηφίζω (#2532). *Cf.* also φῆφος (#3659) and συμφηφίζω (#3471). Hence, to be associated with (σύν) someone as a result of the number of ballots (φῆφος) dropped down (κατά) in a ballot box. With reference to Matthias' election to the apostolate - Acts 1:26.

μετὰ (preposition with the genitive of association) 50.
τῶν (gen.pl.masc.of the article in agreement with ἀποστόλων) 9.
ἔνδεκα (numeral) 1693.
ἀποστόλων (gen.pl.masc.of ἀπόστολος, association) 844.

Translation - *"And they cast ballots with reference to them, and the lot fell to Matthias; so he was declared elected to the apostolate."*

Comment: "Instead of αὐτοῖς, which is well attested by Sinaiticus A B C 33 81 1739 vg cop₍ₛₐ,bo₎ *al*, the Textus Receptus, following D* E Ψ most minuscules, reads αὐτῶν. In the opinion of a majority of the Committee, the ambiguity of αὐτοῖς (is it intended as indirect object, "they gave lots *to* them," or as ethical dative, "they cast lots *for* them"?) prompted copyists to replace it with the easier αὐτῶν," (Metzger, *A Textual Commentary on the Greek New Testament,* 289). We suggest, in addition to Metzger's dative of indirect object or ethical dative of personal advantage, the possibility that αὐτοῖς can be taken as a dative of reference - "they cast lots *with reference* to them." We must avoid the error of overrefinement. The truth in the New Testament is divine, but the linguistic medium (ever Greek) is human. The point is that they voted by identifying the κλῆρος in some way, either for Matthias or Joseph Justus (*cf.* #1648). The first lot that fell out had Matthias' name on it. Hence he was considered, for a short time at least, until Jesus countermanded their decision by choosing Paul, one of the Apostles along with the eleven. This Ouija Board method of ascertaining divine wisdom borders upon paganism. It speaks of a random universe, where anything can happen, or, at the other extreme, a block universe where everything is determined by environment operating on the basis of natural law. The Christian who prays for a message from the Lord and then allows the Bible to open at random, may discover that the book opens as it does due to the stiffness of the binding. It is not likely, as Einstein observed, that God is playing a game of chance with human history.

The Filling of the Holy Spirit

(Acts 2:1-13)
Acts 2:1 - "And when the day of Pentecost was fully come, they were all with one accord in one place."

Καὶ ἐν τῷ συμπληροῦσθαι τὴν ἡμέραν τῆς πεντηκοστῆς ἦσαν πάντες ὁμου ἐπὶ τὸ αὐτό.

Καὶ (continuative conjunction) 14.
ἐν (preposition with the locative of time point) 80.
τῷ (loc.sing.neut.of the article, time point) 9.
συμπληροῦσθαι (pres.pass.inf.of συμπληρόω, articular infinitive, time point) 2211.
τὴν (acc.sing.fem.of the article in agreement with ἡμέραν) 9.
ἡμέραν (acc.sing.fem.of ἡμέρα, general reference) 135.
τῆς (gen.sing.fem.of the article in agreement with πεντηκοστῆς) 9.

#2956 πεντηκοστῆς (gen.sing.fem.of πεντηκοστή, description).

Pentecost - Acts 2:1; 20:16; 1 Cor.16:8.

Meaning: Cf. πεντήκοντα (#2172). Pentecost. The 50th day after the resurrection of our Lord. On this day the early Christians were baptized (Acts 1:5) and filled (Acts 2:4) with the Holy Spirit. It is a day to be observed by the churches since that time. Always in the New Testament as a genitive of description - Acts 20:16; 1 Cor.16:8. The Jews also celebrate it as the 7th week after the Passover.

ἦσαν (3d.per.pl.imp.ind.of εἰμί, progressive description) 86.
πάντες (nom.pl.masc.of πᾶς, subject of ἦσαν) 67.
ὁμοῦ (adverbial) 2015.
ἐπὶ (preposition with the accusative of place) 47.
τὸ (acc.sing.neut.of the article in agreement with αὐτό) 9.
αὐτό (acc.sing.neut.of αὐτός, in agreement with τόπον understood) 16.

Translation - "And when the day of Pentecost came all were together at the same place."

Comment: The articular infinitive in the locative case, introduced by ἐν indicates a time point. It was Pentecost - fifty days after the resurrection of our Lord. Literally, when the number of days required to reach Pentecost (fifty) were fulfilled. *Cf.*#2211. *Cf.*#2015. In John 4:36 ὁμοῦ occurs in a context that requires togetherness in the psychological sense, while the other references indicate physical proximity as in John 20:4; 21:2. The Christians on the day of Pentecost were together physically, and perhaps also in terms of internal social and intellectual harmony, but this point can be pushed too far. In this verse ὁμοῦ simply means that 120 people were in the same room. ἐπὶ τὸ αὐτό needs a substantive to complete it, such as τόπον. ὁ αὐτός, with the pronoun in the attributive position is like the Latin *ipse* and *idem*. It means "the same." The idiom is found often in the New Testament. *Cf.*Rom.10:12;1 Cor.15:39; Heb.10:11 and in Mt.5:47, as in Acts 2:1, with the substantive understood. See also Heb.2:14 and Luke 6:23. The context sometimes is needed to supply the substantive as in Phil.2:18 where we supply "cause" and Mt.27:44 where the thieves crucified with Jesus were saying the same things as were said by the others who stood near the cross.

ὁμοῦ, interpreted in the physical sense - "they were all together" and ἐπὶ τὸ αὐτό - "at the same place" thus add up to redundancy. Luke did not need to write both, since each conveys the thought. We can rescue Luke from this charge of pleonasm if we interpret ὁμοῦ as in John 4:36, *viz.* that the disciples were united in their feelings toward each other and in their theological views. If it is psychological, social and theoretical harmony that is in view, then we have 120 people who agree upon everything who are gathered together in the same room.

But this solution creates a problem which is greater than that of Luke's pleonasm, for it says that Christians who have the Holy Spirit resident, to be sure, but who do not have His fulness are capable of achieving unity through social contact alone. The truth is that unity within the Body of Christ cannot exist as long as there is one member of that body who is not filled with the Holy Spirit. Carnality is a problem with all of us (Rom.7:14-25; Gal.5:16-26) "Unity . . . in the bond of peace" (Eph.4:3-6) is the fruit of the Holy Spirit, not of the flesh. That the 120 Christians who came together physically in that upper room were also united in their theological views and in their unselfish love for each other, despite the fact that the Holy Spirit had not yet filled them, is a denial of too much scripture for us to accept it. Far better to charge Luke with redundancy. It was *after* they were filled with the Holy Spirit that they were united intellectually and spiritually, and this unity existed even after they separated in a spatial sense. We have already seen that Peter's ill-advised business meeting in which Matthias was "elected" to become God's replacement for the fallen Judas Iscariot was not in harmony with the will of God. Yet these men who cast their lot had received the Holy Spirit fifty days before (John 20:22). He was resident, to be sure, but He was not regnant. If He had been Peter, if he felt it necessary to say anything (!) would have said that at some time, known but to God, He would select someone, known but to Him, to take the vacant seat in the apostolate.

This point is more important than it may appear to be on the surface, since some groups of Christians have pointed to ὁμοῦ and said that the *reason why* the Holy Spirit filled the Christians at Pentecost was that they were already united in their theology. Then they point to themselves and to their own unity of doctrinal position, since they have left the organizations to which they formally belonged and with whom they had fellowship, and say that since the cleavage which they brought about in keeping with 2 Cor.6:14-18, the are the modern models of the Christians at Pentecost. Yet close examination of these groups reveals unfortunately that they manifest few if any more evidences of the fulness of the Holy Spirit than the theologically corrupt organizations from which they seceded. Their power in evangelism is little if any greater than that of others and their own fellowship is still marred by hair-splitting divisions, to which they give great status, such as whether or not women should be allowed to speak in a public worship service, whether we should drink wine or grape juice at the Lord's Table or whether or not we should observe Christmas? So it can be safely concluded that the "unity" which such groups possess is not the unity (ὁμοῦ) that the 120 had *after* the Holy Spirit had filled them. It is only the physical unity which is present even when 120 atheists assemble. Let us not confuse cause with result. The spiritual unity which the disciples manifested after Pentecost (Acts 2:41-47) was the *result* of Pentecost. The Holy Spirit did not fill them *because* they were already united. They were later united *because* He filled them. Spirit filled Christians enjoy His fruits, some of which are love, longsuffering, gentleness, meekness and temperance (Gal.5:22-23). These qualities stand the Body of Christ in good stead as we observe that some of our brethren are not "sound in the faith." The question is not whether he agrees with all of our views, but whether he is regenerated. If he is he is a member of the Body of Christ, and as important in the divine scheme of things, as administered by the Head in heaven, as any other. If he is heterodox, there must be a reason. Maybe he is stupid! And, if so, that is not his fault. Morons cannot be expected to understand all of the fine points of Christian theology. He needs love and patient understanding.

This analysis cannot be applied in cases in which the heretic is not a Christian. The Christian is under no biblical obligation to fellowship with the unsaved. This is clear from 2 Cor.6:14-16. I will play golf with a secular humanist but I cannot worship with him. In that sphere we have nothing in common, since our premises stand in diametric opposition. But if a brother in Christ be "overtaken in a fault," someone who is filled with the Holy Spirit should restore him with proper dependence upon the meekness and humility which can come only from the Holy Spirit (Gal.6:1). Fundamentalists, whose fundamentalism extends a little further than the virgin birth, should give some attention to Galatians 6:1. Superior members of the Body of Christ have an obligation to help weaker members of the same body. The psychology of individual differences, the fact that not all Christians were reared in the same social and economic environments and that there are varying degrees of intelligence among us, militates against the notion that any group of Christians are going to be united in every respect. Does this mean that the Holy Spirit will not fill them with His presence and power to enable them to do His perfect will and evangelize the world as the Christians did in Jerusalem on that 50th day? Must the Holy Spirit wait until all Christians have exactly the same points of view in matters of theology? It did not mean that on the day of Pentecost. He filled them, with all of their faults because it was His sovereign will to do so.

Lest we be misunderstood, let it be said again that the Holy Spirit is not going to fill anyone who willfully rejects Jesus Christ. He will not fill them because He has not even indwelt them. If He had they would have called Jesus their Lord (1 Cor.12:3).

Verse 2 - "And suddenly there came a sound from heaven as of a rushing mighty wind, and it filled all the house where they were sitting."

καὶ ἐγένετο ἄφνω ἐκ τοῦ οὐρανοῦ ἦχος ὥσπερ φερομένης πνοῆς βιαίας καὶ ἐπλήρωσεν ὅλον τὸν οἶκον οὗ ἦσαν καθήμενοι.

καὶ (continuative conjunction) 14.
ἐγένετο (3d.per.sing.aor.mid.ind.of γίνομαι, constative) 113.

#2957 ἄφνω (adverbial).

suddenly - Acts 2:2; 16:26; 28:6.

Meaning: suddenly. *Cf.*αἴφνης - "suddenly." *Cf.*αἰνίδιος (#2737). The Pentecost experience - Acts 2:2; the earthquake - Acts 16:26; Paul's anticipated reaction to snakebite - Acts 28:6.

ἐκ (preposition with the ablative of source) 19.
τοῦ (abl.sing.masc.of the article in agreement with οὐρανοῦ) 9.
οὐρανοῦ (abl.sing.masc.of οὐρανός, source) 254.
ἦχος (nom.sing.masc.of ἦχος, subject of ἐγένετο) 2064.
ὥσπερ (intensive particle introducing a comparative clause) 560.
φερομένης (pres.mid.part.abl.sing.fem.of φέρω, adjectival, ascriptive, in agreement with πνοῆς) 683.

#2958 πνοῆς (abl.sing.fem.of πνοή, comparison).

breath - Acts 17:25.
wind - Acts 2:2.

Meaning: *Cf.*πνέω (#697). The breath of life - Acts 17;25. Wind, in the meteorological sense, in an ablative of compaison - Acts 2:2.

#2959 βιαίας (abl.sing.fem.of βίαιος, in agreement with πνοῆς).

mighty - Acts 2:2.

Meaning: violent, forcible, strong, tempestuous, tornadic. *Cf.*βία (#3063), βιαστής (#919), βιάζομαι (#918). Descriptive of the wind at Pentecost - Acts 2:2.

καὶ (adjunctive conjunction) 14.
ἐπλήρωσεν (3d.per.sing.aor.act.ind.of πληρόω, constative) 115.
ὅλον (acc.sing.masc.of ὅλος, in agreement with οἶκον) 112.
τὸν (acc.sing.masc.of the article in agreement with οἶκον) 9.
οἶκον (acc.sing.masc.of οἶκος, direct object of ἐπλήρωσεν) 784.
οὗ (gen.sing.masc.of ὅς, relative adverb to introduce a local clause) 65.
ἦσαν (3d.per.pl.imp.ind.of εἰμί, imperfect periphrastic) 86.
καθήμενοι (pres.mid.part.nom.pl.masc.of κάθημαι, imperfect periphrastic) 377.

Translation - "*And suddenly it happened! Out of heaven a sound exactly like a tornado and it filled the whole house where they were sitting.*"

Comment: Suddenly there was a sound. It came out of the sky, if one wishes to interpret οὐρανοῦ in this sense, which is proper (#254), but it also came ἐκ τοῦ οὐρανοῦ in the sense of heaven as the locus of the throne of God. Here is a context in which οὐρανοῦ can properly be interpreted in all three senses in which it is used in the New Testament. From the throne of God, the sound came down through the stellar and atmospheric heavens and filled the entire house where they were sitting. There was no wind. Luke only says that the sound was exactly like the sound of a transporting wind of violent force - tornadic in its intensity. Note the intensive περ suffix on ὥσπερ.. The participle in the attributive position, φερομένης, is an adjective modifying πνοῆς, which is also modified by βιαίας (#2959). Thus it was tempestuous , destructive, tornadic. An approaching tornado has a hum or a whine, which, as it approaches, rises in a crescendo until it sounds like a rushing freight train. Thus Luke describes the sound.

It has been too often said that the Holy Spirit "came" on the day of Pentecost. A prominent edition of the New Testament has a title over Chapter 2 which says, "The Coming of the Holy Spirit." The English translation says that the day came (Acts 2:1) and that the sound came (Acts 2:2), although the Greek verbs do not support "came" in English. The days were "fulfilled" (vs.1) and the sound "happened" (vs.1). Since the Holy Spirit is God and therefore omnipresent He cannot "come" or "go" anywhere. Verse three says that the tongues that looked like fire "appeared." Nowhere does the text say that the Holy Spirit "came." He was by their side (John 14:17a) and He entered into them (John 14:17b; 20:22) on the evening of resurrection day, fifty days before. Now, He Who had been for fifty days resident is now to become president. It is the difference between indwelling and infilling or overwhelming (Acts 1:5). He Who formerly resided, now presides. Residence is one thing and it is good, but when the resident begins to be regnant that is better.

The sound, not the wind, filled the entire house. Note the use of ὅλον, not πάντα is used, although D, (Codex Bezae) has πάντα. A sound such as Luke describes would certainly fill the entire house, which is what ὅλον demands (#112). ἦχος is associated with θαλάσσης in Luke 21:25. What mariner has not heard the sound of the roaring sea? What Kansas farmer has not heard the sound of a roaring tornado?

Verse 3 - "And there appeared unto them cloven tongues like as of fire, and it sat upon each of them."

καὶ ὤφθησαν αὐτοῖς διαμεριζόμεναι γλῶσσαι ὡσεὶ πυρός, καὶ ἐκάθισεν ἐφ' ἕνα ἕκαστον αὐτῶν,

καὶ (continuative conjunction) 14.
ὤφθησαν (3d.per.pl.aor.pass.ind.of ὁράω, constative) 144.
αὐτοῖς (dat.pl.masc.of αὐτός, personal interest) 16.
διαμεριζόμεναι (pres.pass.part.nom.pl.fem.of διαμερίζω, adjectival, ascriptive, in agreement with γλῶσσαι) 1647.
γλῶσσαι (nom.pl.fem.of γλῶσσα, subject of ὤφθησαν) 1846.
ὡσεὶ (particle introducing a comparative phrase) 325.
πυρός (abl.sing.neut.of πῦρ, comparison) 298.
καὶ (continuative conjunction) 14.
ἐκάθισεν (3d.per.sing.aor.act.ind.of καθίζω, constative) 420.
ἐφ' (preposition with the accusative of place) 47.
ἕνα (acc.sing.masc.of εἷς, extent) 469.
ἕκαστον (acc.sing.masc.of ἕκαστος, in agreement with ἕνα) 1217.
αὐτῶν (gen.pl.masc.of αὐτός, partitive genitive) 16.

Translation - "And there appeared unto them tongues like flames which separated and settled upon each one of them."

Comment: We cannot translate that "each tongue settled upon each one of them," since ἕκαστον is masculine singular and cannot therefore be joined to γλῶσσαι, which is feminine plural. It is an accusative singular masculine, joined to ἕνα. The phenomena which appeared looked like flaming tongues which separated, each from the others and each tongue found its place upon one of the disciples. διαμεριζόμεναι is not an adjective joined to a single tongue, but to the group of tongues. Note that both the adjectival participle and the noun γλῶσσαι are plural. The tongues separated - not each tongue. Hence, "cloven" ("split") tongues is not a correct translation, artistic representations of the event to the contrary notwithstanding. The picture which Luke draws has the tongues suddenly appearing, each one intact (not split), although coming in a group in sufficient number (120) that there is one for each person in the room. They approached, divided and each tongue went its way to sit or settle upon one person. They were not fiery tongues, any more than the sound was a rushing wind. They looked like fire, just as the sound sounded like a tornado.

The purpose of all of this audible and visible phenomena is revealed in

Verse 4 - "And they were all filled with the Holy Ghost, and began to speak with other tongues, as the spirit gave them utterance."

καὶ ἐπλήσθησαν πάντες πνεύματος ἁγίου, καὶ ἤρξαντο λαλεῖν ἑτέραις γλώσσαις καθὼς τὸ πνεῦμα ἐδίδου ἀποφθέγγεσθαι αὐτοῖς.

καὶ (continuative conjunction) 14.

ἐπλήσθησαν (3d.per.pl.aor.pass.ind.of πίμπλημι, constative) 1409.

πάντες (nom.pl.masc.of πᾶς, subject of ἐπλήσθησαν) 67.

πνεύματος (abl.sing.neut.of πνεῦμα, means) 83.

ἁγίου (abl.sing.neut.of ἅγιος, in agreement with πνεύματος) 84.

καὶ (adjunctive conjunction joining verbs) 14.

ἤρξαντο (3d.per.pl.aor.mid.ind.of ἄρχω, ingressive) 383.

λαλεῖν (pres.act.inf.of λαλέω, epexegetical) 815.

ἑτέραις (instru.pl.fem.of ἕτερος, in agreement with γλώσσαις) 605.

γλώσσαις (instru.pl.fem.of γλῶσσα, means) 1846.

καθὼς (adverb introducing a comparative clause) 1348.

τὸ (nom.sing.neut.of the article in agreement with πνεῦμα) 9.

πνεῦμα (nom.sing.neut.of πνεῦμα, subject of ἐδίδου) 83.

ἐδίδου (3d.per.sing.imp.act.ind.of δίδωμι, progressive description) 362.

#2960 ἀποφθέγγεσθαι (pres.mid.inf.of ἀποφθέγγομαι, object of ἐδίδου).

say - Acts 2:14.
speak forth - Acts 26:25.
utterance - Acts 2:4.

Meaning: A combination of ἀπό (#70) and φθέγγομαι (#3036). Hence, to speak from a source of great wisdom and sophistication. φθέγγομαι is not the word for everyday ordinary speech. Rather it is the speech of philosophers, kings and prophets - men of high repute. The Greeks called the saying of philosophers ἀποφθέγματα. With reference to Peter's inspired words after the miraculous language miracle - Acts 2:14; of the utterances themselves - Acts 2:4; of Paul's defense before Agrippa - Acts 26:25. Speech which normally might not be expected, considering the native abilities of the speaker. *Cf.* 2 Peter 2:16,18.

αὐτοῖς (dat.pl.masc.of αὐτός, indirect object of ἐδίδου) 16.

Translation - "And all were filled by the Holy Spirit and they began to speak in other languages whatever the Spirit gave them to say."

Comment: *Cf.*#1409 and its use in similar situations - *e.g.* Luke 1:15,41,67; 4:8,31; 9:17; 13:9. These people individually were overwhelmed (filled to the top, overflowed, submerged, immersed) and thus totally dominated by the Holy Spirit (Acts 1:5). The ablative is not ordinarily the case to express means, but is used when the idea of source is also present as in this case. Jesus called this a baptism (Acts 1:5), as indeed it was, since they were filled up and covered (totally surrounded) by the Holy Spirit. The natural tendencies and tastes were thus brought under subjection to the divine will. *Cf.* 1 Cor.12:13 and comment *en loc* for the baptism of the Holy Spirit in connection with regeneration. The result was that each one began to say what the Holy Spirit dictated and in the dialect that the Holy Spirit chose for him. They also spoke at a level of sophistication higher than what their natural resources would have dictated. The depth, sweep, scope, eloquence, cogency and trenchant qualities, sincereity, earnestness - in short, all of those qualities necessary for convincing and commanding communication were there as the audience stood dumbfounded. Note the continuing influence of the Holy Spirit in the imperfect tense in ἐδίδου. This was a notable demonstration of the power that Jesus promised (Acts 1:8; John 16:7-14).

"In the Four Gospels there is no reference whatsoever to a gift of tongues in any clear and precise form. There is no reference in the Gospels to Jesus or the Apostles ever speaking in tongues, promising such an ability or gift, or commanding, exhorting or encouraging anyone to seek, expect, or believe such a thing. In the disputed long ending of Mark (16:17) is a reference that has sometimes been misinterpreted to refer to such a gift. The word 'tongues' is, as always, simply the old English for 'languages.' Mark does predict that in the process of world missions, the evangelists will speak with 'new languages.' This has been abundantly fulfilled in the 2000 or so languages in which the gospel has been preached. In any case, no reference is made to a gift of tongues nor is it clear that any kind of so-called tongues-speaking is in evidence.

"There is a major difference between the Gospels and Acts in one respect. Though there is still no promise nor encouragement to seek a gift of tongues, there are three historical incidents of supernaturally transcending the language barrier (Acts 2:4; 10:46; 19:6). As far as the record goes, there was no seeking of tongues and no such expectation. It came as a surprise in each case. No explanation is given of its significance or value. Nor is there any mention of a 'gift' of tongues. Nor is there any suggestions that any of those so affected ever again exercised the ability or ever sought a continuance or renewal. At Pentecost the languages were one of three signs that accompanied the dispensational beginning. The language barrier which began in response to man's sin at the Tower of Babel will end at the gates of Heaven. In the meantime, the liberating Gospel is proclaimed at Pentecost in the power of the Holy Spirit, who partially and temporarily lifted the witnessing believers above the language barrier. None of the signs at Pentecost was elaborated beyond the few basic facts. It was made clear that 'tongues' meant intelligible languages known to people present and so capable of being understood without the services of an interpreter. The ability to speak inlanguages of a different kind (ἑτέραις - not ἄλλαις) was certainly not an 'unknown tongue' or incoherent sounds. The word is languages and ἑτέραις simply points out a difference within the category of languages. The speaking was communicating. They spoke and were heard in languages which the Galileans had never learned. This kind of tongues (languages) did not restrict communication. It expanded it. No interpreter was needed."

Wilber T. Dayton, *Charismatics and the New Testament*, 7,8.

Verse 5 - "And there were dwelling at Jerusalem Jews, devout men, out of every nation under heaven."

Ἦσαν δὲ ἐν Ἰερουσαλὴμ κατοικοῦντες Ἰουδαῖοι, ἄνδρες εὐλαβεῖς ἀπὸ παντὸς ἔθνους τῶν ὑπὸ τὸν οὐρανόν.

Ἦσαν (3d.per.pl.imp.ind.of εἰμί, imperfect periphrastic) 86.

δὲ (explanatory conjunction) 11.

ἐν (preposition with the locative of place) 80.

Ἰερουσαλὴμ (loc.sing.masc.of Ἰεροσολύμων, place) 141.

κατοικοῦντες (pres.act.part.nom.pl.masc. of κατοικέω, imperfect periphastic, durative) 242.

Ἰουδαῖοι (nom.pl.masc.of Ἰουδαῖος, subject of ἦσαν) 143.

ἄνδρες (nom.pl.masc.of ἀνήρ, in apposition) 63.

εὐλαβεῖς (nom.pl.masc.of εὐλαβής, in agreement with ἄνδρες) 1894.

ἀπὸ (preposition with the ablative of source) 70.

παντὸς (abl.sing.neut.of πᾶς, in agreement with ἔθνους) 67.

ἔθνους (abl.sing.neut.of ἔθνος, source) 376.

τῶν (gen.pl.neut.of the article in agreement with ἐθνῶν understood) 9.

ὑπὸ (preposition with the accusative of physical place, "under.") 117.

τὸν (acc.sing.masc.of the article in agreement with οὐρανόν) 9.

οὐρανόν (acc.sing.masc.of οὐρανός, physical place) 254.

Translation - "Now there were Jews living in Jerusalem - conscientious men from all over the world."

Comment: δὲ is explanatory, as Luke prepares to introduce a new phase of the story. The durative action of the immediate past is indicated by the imperfect periphrastic. A continuous residence in Jerusalem that extended into the remote past would have required a pluperfect periphrastic. These men lived in various parts of the then known world, beyond the confines of Palestine, but they had come to Jerusalem, probably for the Passover Feasts, 50 days before, and had remained for the Pentecost (Jewish) Celebration. They were "godly" in the Jewish sense, but εὐλαβής (#1894) does not mean "godly.'Anyone who "takes hold well" is εὐλαβής. An atheist can be conscientious in that the tasks he undertakes are pursued with skill and devoted attention to detail. This is all that the word denotes. This characteristic is revealed in the men in question by the fact that each had left his home and travelled to Jerusalem to spend the fifty day period of religious celebration required of all orthodox Jews. That they still entertained, in part at least, a faith in the nationalistic hopes of the nation, and looked for Messiah, may, no doubt be inferred. At any rate our sovereign Lord had arranged for them to be present on this occasion, with the results which follow. τῶν, following ἔθνους is plural, hence it cannot modify ἔθνους. We supply ἐθνῶν and it becomes a partitive genitive. ". . . from every nation (singular) out of all the nations under the heaven." This, of course means every nation where Jews, scattered abroad, following the Babylonian captivity lived. Luke did not mean to imply that someone was present at Pentecost from Peoria.

Verse 6 - "Now when this was noised abroad, the multitude came together, and were confounded, because that every man heard them speak in his own language."

γενομένης δὲ τῆς φωνῆς ταύτης συνῆλθεν τὸ πλῆθος καὶ συνεχύθη, ὅτι ἤκουον εἰς ἕκαστος τῇ ἰδίᾳ διαλέκτῳ λαλούντων αὐτῶν.

γενομένης (aor.part.gen.sing.fem.of γίνομαι, genitive absolute, adverbial, temporal/causal) 113.

δὲ (continuative conjunction) 11.

τῆς (gen.sing.fem.of the article in agreement with φωνῆς) 9.

φωνῆς (gen.sing.fem.of φωνή, genitive absolute) 222.

ταύτης (gen.sing.fem.of οὗτος, in agreement with φωνῆς) 93.

συνῆλθεν (3d.per.sing.aor.mid.ind.of συνέρχομαι, ingressive) 78.

τὸ (nom.sing.neut.of the article in agreement with πλῆθος) 9.

πλῆθος (nom.sing.neut.of πλῆθος, subject of συνῆλθεν and συνεχύθη) 1792.

καὶ (adjunctive conjunction joining verbs) 14.

#2961 συνεχύθη (3d.per.sing.aor.pass.ind.of συγχέω, constative).

        confound - Acts 2:6; 9:22.
        confuse - Acts 19:32.
        stir up - Acts 21:27.
        be in an uproar - Acts 21:31.

Meaning: A combination of σύν (#1542) and χέω - "pour." Hence, to pour together; to mix. In a psychological sense to disturb by presenting for one's consideration disparate elements in a way that defies rational analysis. We say, "I am mixed up!" meaning "I am confused, or disturbed." With reference to the

Jews at Pentecost - Acts 2:6. Saul's impact upon the Jews in Damascus, *i.e.* they could not resist his logic and were impelled to a position which was contrary to their previous belief - Acts 9:22. Of the Ephesian confusion - Acts 19;32; in Jerusalem - Acts 21:27,31.

ὅτι (conjunction introducing a subordinate causal clause) 211.

ἤκουον (3d.per.pl.imp.act.ind.of ἀκούω, progressive description) 148.

εἷς (nom.sing.masc.of εἷς, subject of ἤκουον) 469.

ἔκαστος (nom.sing.masc.of ἔκαστος, in agreement with εἷς) 1217.

τῇ (loc.sing.fem.of the article in agreement with διαλέκτῳ) 9.

ἰδίᾳ (loc.sing.fem.of ἴδιος, in agreement with διαλέκτῳ) 778.

διαλέκτῳ (loc.sing.fem.of διάλεκτος, sphere) 2946.

λαλούντων (pres.act.part.gen.pl.masc.of λαλέω, genitive absolute, simultaneous time) 815.

αὐτῶν (gen.pl.masc.of αὐτός, genitive absolute) 16.

Translation - "And when the sound was heard the crowd assembled and they were confused because as they were speaking each man was hearing in his own dialect."

Comment: Luke uses a genitive absolute both to begin and to conclude his sentence, the former in the aorist tense denoting antecedent time relative to the time of the main verb and the latter in the present tense with its simultaneous time. The sound that resembled the wind was heard beyond the confines of the house. We may be sure that a sound loud enough to fill an entire house would be heard beyond the limits of the house. The crowd assembled and the men were immediately confused (literally, "mixed up" *cf.*#2961), because (causal ὅτι) as the Christians were speaking every man heard (progressive description in ἤκουον) what they were saying in his own dialect (locative of sphere). The Christians were communicating perfectly. There was no need for the services of an interpreter. The KJV implies that a rumor circulated in Jerusalem about the Christians speaking in various languages, and that it was the rumor that brought the crowd together. To which we object, first, because by the time the rumor would have got around, the meeting of the Christians most probably would have ended. This view would demand that the speaking in languages other than their own continued for a long time, an idea that the text does not support. Also φωνή (#222) can mean "sound" as well as the human voice circulating a rumor. The Christians were alone in the room when the meeting began, while before it ended Peter's audience was very large, 3000 of whom were saved (vs.41). They were attracted by what they thought was the roaring of a great wind storm. Note that εἷς ἔκαστος - "every man" or "each one" is singular, but that the verb adjoined is collectively plural. They all heard but each man heard the sound of the voices in a dialect with which he was totally familiar, since it was the language that he used all of the time. It is probable that that since they were orthodox Jews each men also understood Aramaic, but the Christians were not speaking Aramaic, although when Peter preached he probably either spoke Aramaic or κοινή Greek which was the universal language of the Mediterranean world, from which the audience had come to Jerusalem.

This was a notable miracle, to be explained only by the fact that the Holy Spirit, Who, being God, speaks all dialects fluently, had filled (baptized, immersed, overwhelmed, submerged, surrounded) and thus controlled each of the Christians. Thus they were speaking both with linguistic and philosophical abilities beyond their own unaided natural scope (#2960).

With reference to the modern so-called glossalalia movement, which has made some inroads even into and among the more sophisticated and well educated segments of 20th century Christendom, it should be noted that what the visitors in Jerusalem heard that day was not incoherent gibberish, nor some heavenly patois to be understood only within the realms of glory, but dialects which were in common use in some one or more of the areas in the Meditteranean littoral listed in vss.9-11. And it should also be noted that there was a very practical reason why the language miracle occurred at Pentecost. Every man present heard the truths of the gospel of Christ uttered in a dialect that he understood and with a cogent clarity and trenchant depth that made a deep impression. The modern exercise of "tongues" in the 20th century is not for that purpose. The languages at Pentecost were not unknown, and no where does the Scripture use the adjective "unknown" to describe them. A visitor at the United Nations in New York would hear languages unknown perhaps to him, but not to all those present. The Germanic people who live in the Faeroes need no interpreter when Faeroese is being spoken and a Frenchman needs no help to understand French. Interpreters are needed only when someone present cannot understand what is being spoken as in the case of the Corinthian church meetings, in which visitors, of whom Corinth had a great many, due to the fact that the city was a prominent entrepot in the Mediterranean world of commerce, spoke in the church meetings in the only dialect which they could command, as a result of which others in the audience needed interpretation. Otherwise there would be no edification for those who could not understand. "Unknown tongues" speaking Christians now are not justified in their views because of the situation that existed in the Corinthian church. There are few folk in Pennsylvania who do not understand English, although some of them also speak "Pennsylvania Deutsche" which is not to be confused with the "Dutch" which is heard around Holland, Michigan, in which city the people also speak English. So if one wishes to edify those in Pennsylvania or Michigan, let him speak English, or in Paris, let him speak French. Paul spoke a great many different languages which he had occasion to use in his travels through the Mediterranean world, because otherwise he would not have been understood when he witnessed to the marvelous grace of God in the gospel, but he was not a showoff. "Unknown tongues" addicts in the United States should examine their motives. Finally there is no evidence that $\gamma\lambda\hat{\omega}\sigma\sigma\alpha$ (#1846) ever means a jargon that cannot be understood at all, anywhere in the world except by one who has the gift of interpreting what is alleged to be a heavenly language. More on the subject *en loc* when the text demands (Acts 10:46; 19;6; 1 Cor.12-14).

Verse 7 - "And they were all amazed and marvelled saying one to another, Behold, are not all these which speak Galileans?"

ἐξίσταντο δὲ καὶ ἐθαύμαζον λέγοντες, Οὐχ ἰδοὺ ἅπαντες οὗτοί εἰσιν οἱ λαλοῦντες Γαλιλαῖοι;

ἐξίσταντο (3d.per.pl.imp.mid.ind.of ἐξίστημι, inceptive) 992.
δὲ (continuative conjunction) 11.
καὶ (inferential conjunction) 14.
ἐθαύμαζον (3d.per.pl.imp.act.ind.of θαυμάζω, inceptive) 726.
λέγοντες (pres.act.part.nom.pl.masc.of λέγω, recitative) 66.
Οὐχ (summary negative conjunction with the indicative in rhetorical question expecting an affirmative reply) 130.
ἰδοὺ (exclamation) 95.
ἅπαντες (nom.pl.masc.of ἅπας, in agreement with οὗτοί) 693.
οὗτοί (nom.pl.masc.of οὗτος, in agreement with λαλοῦντες) 93.
εἰσιν (3d.per.pl.pres.ind.of εἰμί, rhetorical question) 86.
οἱ (nom.pl.masc.of the article in agreement with λαλοῦντες) 9.
λαλοῦντες (pres.act.part.nom.pl.masc.of λαλέω, substantival, subject of εἰσιν) 815.
Γαλιλαῖοι (nom.pl.masc.of Γαλιλαῖος, predicate nominative) 2016.

Translation - "And so they were awestricken and they began to wonder, saying, 'Look! All of these who are speaking are Galileans, are they not?' "

Comment: The visitors were seized with a fantastic confusion (inceptive imperfect in ἐξίσταντο #992). Before them stood a group of Galilean rustics, replete with crock haircuts and all other accouterments of plebeian origin, who normally spoke with an accent that identified them with the northern hinterlands (Mt.26:73), but who now manifested a linguistic and theological prowess beyond belief. The visitors began (inceptive imperfect in ἐθαύμαζον) to try to figure it out. Their question is rhetorical, put in the form that expects an affirmative reply. Note the intensive ἅπαντες, instead of the normal πάντες. That anyone in Jerusalem, be he chief priest, scribe, pharisee or lawyer, or anyone in Judea should speak with such ability, would be amazing! But these culturally deprived northern Galileans? Their next question is not rhetorical. These men wanted help.

Verse 8 - "And how hear we every man in our own tongue, wherein we were born?"

καὶ πῶς ἡμεῖς ἀκούομεν ἕκαστος τῇ ἰδίᾳ διαλέκτῳ ἡμῶν ἐν ᾗ ἐγεννήθημεν;

καὶ (inferential conjunction) 14.
πῶς (interrogative conjunction in direct question) 627.
ἡμεῖς (nom.pl.masc.of ἐγώ, subject of ἀκούομεν) 123.
ἀκούομεν (1st.per.pl.pres.act.ind.of ἀκούω, direct question) 148.
ἕκαστος (nom.sing.masc.of ἕκαστος, subject of ἀκούομεν) 1217.
τῇ (loc.sing.fem.of the article in agreement with διαλέκτῳ) 9.
ἰδίᾳ (loc.sing.fem.of ἴδιος, in agreement with διαλέκτῳ) 778.
διαλέκτῳ (loc.sing.fem.of διάλεκτος, sphere) 2946.

ἡμῶν (gen.pl.masc.of ἐγώ, description) 123.
ἐν (preposition with the locative of sphere) 80.
ᾗ (loc.sing.fem.of ὅς, sphere) 65.
ἐγεννήθημεν (1st.per.pl.aor.pass.ind.of γεννάω, constative) 8.

Translation - "So how (is it that) every man hears in his own dialect in which he was born?"

Comment: καί is inferential. The obvious fact that the disciples were Galileans makes the incredulous question logical. Galileans who could not even speak Aramaic or κοινή Greek properly were now giving eloquent expression in the native dialects of the various areas listed in verses 9-11. Note again, as in verse 6 that ἕκαστος, a singular substantive is joined to a plural verb ἀκούομεν and also to a plural descriptive genitive ἡμῶν. A literal translation would read, "Each man hears in *their* own dialect" - bad English grammar. The list that follows is long, diverse and impressive. It resembles a cultural and geographical atlas of the Mediterranean area.

Verse 9 - "Parthians, and Medes, and Elamites, and the dwellers in Mesopotamia, and in Judea, and Cappadocia, in Pontus, and Asia, . . . "

Πάρθοι καὶ Μῆδοι καὶ Ἐλαμῖται, καὶ οἱ κατοικοῦντες τὴν Μεσοποταμίαν, Ἰουδαίαν τε καὶ Καππαδοκίαν, Πόντον καὶ τὴν Ἀσίαν,

#2962 Πάρθοι (nom.pl.masc.of Πάρθος, nominative absolute).

Parthians - Acts 2:9.

Meaning: Residents of Parthia in Asia Minor. Bounded on the north by Hyrcania, on the east by Ariana, on the south by Carmania Deserta and on the west by Media - Acts 2:9, present at Pentecost.

καί (adjunctive conjunction joining nouns) 14.

#2963 Μῆδοι (nom.pl.masc.of Μῆδος, nominative absolute).

Medes - Acts 2:9.

Meaning: inhabitants of Media in Asia Minor. Chief city was Ecbatana. Present at Pentecost - Acts 2:9.

καί (adjunctive conjunction joining nouns) 14.

#2964 Ἐλαμῖται (nom.pl.masc.of Ἐλαμίτης, nominative absolute).

Elamites - Acts 2:9.

Meaning: from Elymais, north of the Persian Gulf. Present at Pentecost - Acts 2:9.

καί (adjunctive conjunction joining substantives) 14.

οἱ (nom.pl.masc.of the article in agreement with κατοικοῦντες) 9.

κατοικοῦντες (pres.act.part.nom.pl.masc.of κατοικέω, substatival, nominative absolute) 242.

τὴν (acc.sing.fem.of the article in agreement with Μεσοποταμίαν) 9.

#2965 Μεσοποταμίαν (acc.sing.fem.of Μεσοποταμία, adverbial accusative).

Mesopotamia - Acts 2:9; 7:2.

Meaning: Mesopotamia, a region from which Abraham came (Acts 7:2) between the Tigris and the Euphrates rivers. Men from this region were present at Pentecost - Acts 2:9.

Ἰουδαίαν (acc.sing.fem.of Ἰουδαίας, adverbial) 134.
τε (correlative particle) 1408.
καὶ (adjunctive conjunction joining nouns) 14.

#2966 Καππαδοκίαν (acc.sing.fem.of Καππαδοκία, adverbial).

Meaning: An Asia Minor province, bounded on the north by Pontus, on the east by Armenia Minor, on the south by Cilicia and Commagene and on the west by Lycaonia and Galatia. Cappadocians were present at Pentecost - Acts 2:9. Peter addressed his epistle to them - 1 Peter 1:1.

#2967 Πόντον (acc.sing.masc.of Πόντος, adverbial).

Pontus - Acts 2:9; 1 Peter 1:1.

Meaning: A territory in Eastern Asia Minor on the Black Sea and otherwise bounded by Armenia, Cappadocia, Galatia and Paphlagonia. Men from Pontus were present at Pentecost - Acts 2:9. *cf.* also 1 Peter 1:1.

καὶ (adjunctive conjunction joining nouns) 14.
τὴν (acc.sing.fem.of the article in agreement with Ἀσίαν) 9.

#2968 Ἀσίαν (acc.sing.fem.of Ἀσία, adverbial).

Asia - Acts 2:9; 6:9; 16:6; 19:10,22,26,27; 20:16,18; 21:27; 24:18; 1 Peter 1:1; Rev.1:4; 1 Cor.1:8; 2 Tim.1:15; Rom.16:5; 1 Cor.16:19.

Meaning: A region in proconsular Asia including Mysia, Lydia and Caria - Rom.16:5; Acts 2:9. Thayer thinks that in Acts 6:9; 16:6; 19:10,22,26,27; 1 Pet.1:1; Rev.1:4; Acts 20:16,18; 21:27; 24:18; 27:2; 2 Cor.1:8; 2 Tim. 1:15; 1 Cor.16:19 a larger region in Asia is meant.

Translation - "Parthians and Medes and Elamites, and the inhabitants of Mesopotamia, Judea and both Cappadocia and Pontus and the Asia province.

Comment: The article with Asia probably indicates the province in proconsular Asia rather than the entire area of Asia Minor, since all the regions mentioned are in Asia Minor.

Verse 10 - "Phrygia, and Pamphylia, in Egypt, and in the parts of Libya about Cyrene and strangers of Rome, Jews and proselytes."

Φρυγίαν τε καὶ Παμφυλίαν, Αἴγυπτον καὶ τὰ μέρη τῆς Λιβύης τῆς κτὰ Κυρήνην, καὶ οἱ ἐπιδημοῦντες Ῥωμαῖοι,

#2969 Φρυγίαν (acc.sing.fem.of Φρυγία, adverbial).

Phrygia - Acts 2:10; 16:6; 18:23.

Meaning: a region in Asia Minor, surrounded by Bithynia, Galatia, Lycaonia Pisidia, Lydia and Mysia. New Testament cities in Phrygia are Laodicea, Hierapolis and Colossae - Acts 2:10; 16:6; 18:23.

τε (correlative particle) 1408.
καὶ (adjunctive conjunction joining nouns) 14.

#2970 Παμφυλίαν (acc.sing.fem.of Παμφυλία, adverbial).

Pamphylia - Acts 2:10; 13:13; 14:24; 15:38; 27:5.

Meaning: a territory west of Cilicia, east of Lycia and Phrygia Minor, south of Galatia and Cappadocia and north of the Mediterranean Sea, now called the Gulf of Adalia. Inhabitants were present at Pentecost - Acts 2:10. Paul visited here - Acts 13:13; 14:24; 15:38; 27:5.

Αἴγυπτον (acc.sing.of Αἴγυπτον, adverbial) 203.
καὶ (adjunctive conjunction joining nouns) 14.
τὰ (acc.pl.neut.of the article in agreement with μέρη) 9.
μέρη (acc.pl.neut.of μέρος, adverbial) 240.
τῆς (gen.sing.fem.of the article in agreement with Λιβύης) 9.

#2971 Λιβύης (gen.sing.fem.of Λιβύς, description).

Libya - Acts 2:10.

Meaning: An area in North Africa, on the coast, west of Egypt. The region having Cyrene as its capital is called Libya Cyrenaica. Jews from this area were present at Pentecost - Acts 2:10.

τῆς (gen.sing.fem.of the article, description) 9.
κατὰ (preposition with the accusative, distributive) 98.

#2972 Κυρήνην (acc.sing.fem.of Κυρήνη, adverbial).

Cyrene - Acts 2:10.

Meaning: A large city of Libya Cyrenaica (Pentapolitana). Eleven miles south of the coast. Ptolemy I brought many Jews to Cyrene, and gave them citizenship - Acts 2:10.

καὶ (adjunctive conjunction joining substantives) 14.

οἱ (nom.pl.masc.of the article in agreement with ἐπιδημοῦντες) 9.

#2973 ἐπιδημοῦντες (pres.act.part.nom.pl.masc.of ἐπιδημέω, substantival, nominative absolute).

be there - Acts 17:21.
stranger - Acts 2:10.

Meaning: Cf.ἐπίδημος - "sojourners," "visitors," "temporary residents." Tourists who were in Rome temporarily, but who came to Jerusalem at the Passover-Pentecost season - Acts 2:10. Visitors to Athens - Acts 17:21.

Ῥωμαῖοι (nom.pl.masc.of Ῥωμαῖος, in agreement with ἐπιδημοῦντες) 2849.

Translation - "Both Phrygia and Pamphylia, Egypt and the area of Libya in the vicinity of Cyrene and the Roman tourists."

Comment: Note the τε καί sequence. χώρας (#201) can be supplied before κατά to agree with τῆς. Ῥωμαῖοι in the nominative case really modifies the participle ἐπιδημοῦντες. Verse nine describes the territory north of Jerusalem to the Black Sea and east to the Tigris-Euphrates valley. Verse 10 mentions two more Asia Minor areas and then carries us south to Egypt, west along the African coast and to Rome. Verse 11 describes two culture types of Jews and returns to give us two more geographic areas - Crete, in the Mediterranean and the desert country, east of the Jordan, Arabia.

Verse 11 - "Jews and proselytes, Cretes and Arabians, we do hear them speak in our tongues the wonderful works of God."

Ἰουδαῖοί τε καὶ προσήλυτοι, Κρῆτες καὶ Ἄραβες, ἀκούομεν λαλούντων αὐτῶν ταῖς ἡμετέραις γλώσσαις τὰ μεγαλεῖα τοῦ θεοῦ.

Ἰουδαῖοί (nom.pl.masc.of Ἰουδαῖος, nominative absolute) 143.
τε (correlative particle) 1408.
καί (adjunctive conjunction joining nouns) 14.
προσήλυτοι (nom.pl.masc.of προσήλυτος, nominative absolute) 1445.

#2974 Κρῆτες (nom.pl.masc.of Κρής, nominative absolute).

Cretes - Acts 2:11.
Cretians - Titus 1:12.

Meaning: An inhabitant of the island of Crete - Acts 2:11; Titus 1:12.

καί (adjunctive conjunction joining nouns) 14.

#2975 Ἄραβες (nom.pl.masc.of Ἀράβιος, nominative absolute).

Arabian - Acts 2:11.

Meaning: A citizen of Arabia, the land between the Jordan and the Tigris-

Euphrates valley. Present at Pentecost - Acts 2:11.

ἀκούομεν (1st.per.pl.pres.act.ind.of ἀκούω, aoristic) 148.
λαλούντων (pres.act.part.gen.pl.masc.of λαλέω, adverbial, circumstantial) 815.
αὐτῶν (gen.pl.masc.of αὐτός, description after a verb of hearing) 16.
ταῖς (loc.pl.fem.of the article in agreement with γλώσσαις) 9.
ἡμετέραις (loc.pl.fem.of ἡμέτερος, in agreement with γλώσσαις) 2571
γλώσσαις (loc.pl.fem.of γλῶσσα, sphere) 1846.
τὰ (acc.pl.neut.of the article in agreement with μεγαλεῖα) 9.

#2976 μεγαλεῖα (acc.pl.neut.of μεγαλεῖος, direct object of λαλούντων).

wonderful work - Acts 2:11.

Meaning: magnificant, splended, wonderful. In the neuter plural and followed by a genitive of description - τοῦ θεοῦ - Acts 2:11.

τοῦ (gen.sing.masc.of the article in agreement with θεοῦ) 9.
θεοῦ (gen.sing.masc.of θεός, description) 124.

Translation - ". . . both Jews and prosylytes, Cretes and Arabians - we are hearing them as they speak in our languages the wonderful works of God."

Comment: The list includes regions scattered roughly over the eastern half of the Augustan Empire, and included both Jews and prosylytes. Note the genitive of description after a verb of sensation.

Verse 12 - "And they were all amazed, and were in doubt, saying one to another, What meaneth this?"

ἐξίσταντο δὲ πάντες καὶ διηπόρουν, ἄλλος πρὸς ἄλλον λέγοντες, Τί θέλει τοῦτο εἶναι.

ἐξίσταντο (3d.per.pl.imp.mid.ind.of ἐξίστημι, progressive description) 992.
δὲ (continuative conjunction) 11.
πάντες (nom.pl.masc.of πᾶς, subject of ἐξίσταντο and διηπόρουν) 67.
καὶ (adjunctive conjunction joining verbs) 14.
διηπόρουν (3d.per.pl.imp.act.ind.of διαπορέω, progressive description) 2262.
ἄλλος (nom.sing.masc.of ἄλλος, reciprocal pronoun) 198.
πρὸς (preposition with the accusative of extent after a verb of speaking) 197.
ἄλλον (acc.sing.masc.of ἄλλος, extent after a verb of speaking) 198.
λέγοντες (pres.act.part.nom.pl.masc.of λέγω, adverbial, complementary) 66.
Τί (acc.sing.neut.of τίς, predicate accusative) 281.
θέλει (3d.per.sing.pres.act.ind.of θέλω, indirect question) 88.
τοῦτο (acc.sing.neut.of οὗτος, general reference) 93.
εἶναι (pres.inf.of εἰμί, indirect question) 86.

Translation - "*And they all continued to be agitated and in doubt as they said to one another, 'What is the purpose of this?'* "

Comment: The progressive descriptions in the two imperfect tenses give graphic pictures of the reaction of those present. #992 has elements of fear, confusion, excitement and thrill. Of course they were in doubt as they had never seen anything like this before. ἄλλος πρὸς ἄλλον is a Latinism common in Classical Greek. It reveals Luke's linguistic capability. *Cf.* also Acts 19;32; 21:34. It is almost reciprocal like ἀλλήλων (#1487). Τί θέλει τοῦτο εἶναι (*Cf.* Acts 17:20) - "what does this intend to be?" or "what is the purpose of this?"

Verse 13 - "Others mocking said, These men are full of new wine."

ἕτεροι δὲ διαχλευάζοντες ἔλεγον ὅτι Γλεύκους μεμεστωμένοι εἰσίν.

ἕτεροι (nom.pl.masc.of ἕτερος, subject of ἔλεγον) 605.
δὲ (adversative conjunction) 11.

#2977 διαχλευάζοντες (pres.act.part.nom.pl.masc.of διαχλευάζω, adverbial, telic).

mock - Acts 2:13.

*Meaning: Cf.*χλευάω (#3424). The addition of διά heightens the intensity of the scorn of the reaction of some of the Pentecost observers - Acts 2:13.

ἔλεγον (3d.per.pl.imp.act.ind.of λέγω, iterative) 66.
ὅτι (recitative) 211.

#2978 Γλεύκους (gen.sing.neut.of γλεῦκος, description).

new wine - Acts 2:13.

Meaning: The sweet unfermented (but in the process of fermentation) juice pressed from the grape. Highly intoxicating if taken in large quantities.

#2979 μεμεστωμένοι (perf.pass.part.nom.pl.masc.of μεστόω, perfect periphrastic).

be full - Acts 2:13.

*Meaning: Cf.*μεστός (#1468). To be full - Acts 2:13 in the accommodated sense of over indulgence.

εἰσίν (3d.per.pl.pres.ind.of εἰμί, perfect periphrastic) 86.

Translation - "But others in order to make fun were repeating, They are full of new wine.' "

Comment: The attitude of the men who spoke in verse 12 was not scorn. On the contrary (adversative δὲ) others found the sight amusing and in their desire to ridicule (telic participle in διαλευάζοντες) they moved through the crowd repeating their charge that the disciples were intoxicated. The perfect periphrastic has intensive force - "having drunk too much new wine these men are now drunk." Their remark gave Peter his chance to speak. This is the first gospel sermon after the Holy Spirit filled the Christians. It should be a model for all others to follow.

Peter's Sermon at Pentecost

(Acts 2:14-42)

Verse 14 - "But Peter, standing up with the eleven, lifted up his voice, and said unto them, Ye men of Judea, and all ye that dwell at Jerusalem, be this known unto you, and hearken to my words."

Σταθεὶς δὲ ὁ Πέτρος σὺν τοῖς ἕνδεκα ἐπῆρεν τὴν φωνὴν αὐτοῦ καὶ ἀπεφθέγξατο αὐτοῖς, Ἄνδρες Ἰουδαῖοι καὶ οἱ κατοικοῦντες Ἰερουσαλὴν πάντες, τοῦτο ὑμῖν γνωστὸν ἔστω καὶ ἐνωτίσασθε τὰ ῥήματά μου.

Σταθεὶς (aor.mid.part.nom.sing.masc.of ἵστημι, adverbial, temporal) 180.

δὲ (adversative conjunction) 11.

ὁ (nom.sing.masc.of the article in agreement with Πέτρος) 9.

Πέτρος (nom.sing.masc.of Πέτρος, subject of ἐπῆρεν and ἀπεφθέγξατο) 387.

σὺν (preposition with the instrumental of association) 1542.

τοῖς (instru.pl.masc.of the article, association) 9.

ἕνδεκα (numeral, with ἀποστόλοις understood) 1693.

ἐπῆρεν (3d.per.sing.aor.act.ind.of ἐπαίρω, constative) 1227.

τὴν (acc.sing.fem.of the article in agreement with φωνὴν) 9.

φωνὴν (acc.sing.fem.of φωνή, direct object of ἐπῆρεν) 222.

αὐτοῦ (gen.sing.masc.of αὐτός, possession) 16.

καὶ (adjunctive conjunction joining verbs) 14.

ἀπεφθέγξατο (3d.per.sing.aor.mid.ind.of ἀποφθέγγομαι, ingressive) 2960.

αὐτοῖς (dat.pl.masc.of αὐτός, indirect object of ἀπεφθέγξατο) 16.

Ἄνδρες (voc.pl.masc.of ἀνήρ, address) 63.

Ἰουδαῖοι (voc.pl.masc.of Ἰουδαῖος, in agreement with ἄνδρες) 143.

καὶ (adjunctive conjunction joining substantives) 14.

οἱ (voc.pl.masc.of the article in agreement with κατοικοῦντες) 9.

κατοικοῦντες (pres.act.part.voc.pl.masc.of κατοικέω, substantival, address) 242.

Ἰερουσαλήμ (indeclin. in agreement with κατοικοῦντες) 141.

πάντες (voc.pl.masc.of πᾶς, in agreement with κατοικοῦντες) 67.

τοῦτο (acc.sing.neut.of οὗτος, direct object of ἔστω) 93.

ὑμῖν (dat.pl.masc.of σύ, personal advantage) 104.

γνωστὸν (acc.sing.neut.of γνωστός, predicate adjective) 1917.

ἔστω (3d.per.sing.pres.impv.of εἰμί, command) 86.

καὶ (adjunctive conjunction joining verbs) 14.

#2980 ἐνωτίσασθε (2d.per.pl.1st.aor.mid.impv.of ἐνωτίζομαι, command).

hearken to - Acts 2:14.

Meaning: A combination of ἐν (#80), ὠτίον (#1595) and δέχομαι (#867). Hence, to receive in the ear. To listen. Pay attention to - with reference to Peter's sermon at Pentecost - Acts 2:14.

τὰ (acc.pl.neut.of the article in agreement with ῥήματά) 9.
ῥήματά (acc.pl.neut.of ῥῆμα, direct object of ἐνωτίσασθε) 343.
μου (gen.sing.masc.of ἐγώ, possession) 123.

Translation - "But Peter stood up with the Eleven, raised his voice and spoke to them: 'Men of Judea and all who are now living in Jerusalem, be advised of this and listen further to what I am going to say.'"

Comment: What ever happened to Matthias? The Eleven took their stand (Σταθεὶς) before the people, some of whom were genuinely impressed by the phenomenon, while others, perhaps in order to conceal their own amazement and concern tried to make a joke out of it. It takes moral and physical courage to "take your stand" before a crowd like that and the Apostles, now filled with the Holy Spirit, were equal to the occasion. *Cf.* Acts 13:16. Paul also had courage. *Cf.*#1227. Peter had to shout in order to be heard by those at the edges of the crowd which numbered more than 3000 (vs.41). *Cf.*#2960. The words were not his own, but far greater in sophistication and power than he could have uttered in his own strength, which was another result of the filling of the Holy Spirit. (Luke 22:15). Peter was about to experience the first delivery of the promise of John 16:12-15. Contrast the fallible human wisdom of Peter's remarks before he was filled with the Holy Spirit (Acts 1:15-26). τοῦτο probably refers to the glossalalia - "Understand this," or "Do not misinterpret this miracle," as some were doing by explaining it in terms of intoxication. He added that he would not only explain the fact that every man present had just heard the gospel of Christ in his own dialect, but that he was going to deliver a fuller exposition of the Word of God.

The student who has pored faithfully over the pages of the Gospels has had opened to him a door that leads into a larger revelation of the Word of God which begins at Pentecost. The Gospel accounts of Matthew, Mark, Luke and John provide the curriculum for undergraduate school. The Acts of the Holy Spirit through the early Christians, the epistles of Paul, Peter, James, Jude, John and the epistle to the Hebrews and the Revelation provide the curriculum for graduate school. The superstructure of revelation which began at Pentecost and closed with the completion of the New Testament canon is solidly and consistently erected upon the foundational substructure of the Gospels. Jesus promised that the material which He did not tell them, because they were as yet not ready for it, would be revealed to them by the Holy Spirit. There are no contradictions between what the Holy Spirit told them and what Jesus had told them in the Gospels. Paul and the other New Testament writers did not subvert Jesus.

Verse 15 - "For these are not drunken, as ye suppose, seeing it is but the third hour of the day."

οὐ γὰρ ὡς ἡμεῖς ὑπολαμβάνετε οὗτοι μεθύουσιν, ἔστιν γὰρ ὥρα τρίτη τῆς ἡμέρας,

οὐ (summary negative conjunction with the indicative) 130.

γὰρ (causal conjunction) 105.

ὡς (particle introducing a comparative clause) 128.

ὑμεῖς (nom.pl.masc.of σύ, subject of ὑπολαμβάνετε) 104.

ὑπολαμβάνετε (2d.per.pl.pres.act.ind.of ὑπολαμβάνω, aoristic) 2173.

οὗτοι (nom.pl.masc.of οὗτος, subject of μεθύουσιν) 93.

μεθύουσιν (3d.per.pl.pres.act.ind.of μεθύω, aoristic) 1527.

ἔστιν (3d.per.sing.pres.ind.of εἰμί, aoristic) 86.

γὰρ (causal conjunction) 105.

ὥρα (nom.sing.fem.of ὥρα, subject of ἔστιν) 735.

τρίτη (nom.sing.fem.of τρίτος, in agreement with ὥρα) 1209.

τῆς (gen.sing.fem.of the article in agreement with ἡμέρας) 9.

ἡμέρας (gen.sing.fem.of ἡμέρα, description) 135.

Translation - "Because, contrary to what you think, these people are not drunk, because it is (only) nine o'clock in the morning."

Comment: γὰρ is causal in both clauses. Note that Peter emphasized ὡς ὑμεῖς ὑπολαμβάνετε, calling attention first to their mistaken explanation of the strange performance of the Christians. This is the priority of verse 14. Some of his audience had no idea what was going on. Others had a theory which was wrong. First Peter must explain the miraculous use of the languages. (Note that I am assiduously avoiding referring to them as "tongues.") His argument was well understood by those in the audience. How can you get that drunk by nine in the morning, unless, of course you got up early?

Sunday School superintendants who are trying to build better attendance might point out that the Christians who come to church at nine o'clock in the morning are the ones who receive the blessings of the fulness of the Holy Spirit!

Peter's negative argument about how the performance was not to be explained has been made. Now he turns to a positive explanation of it in

Verse 16 - "But this is that which was spoken by the prophet Joel."

ἀλλὰ τοῦτο ἐστιν τὸ εἰρημένον διὰ τοῦ προφήτου Ἰωήλ,

ἀλλὰ (alternative conjunction) 342.

τοῦτο (nom.sing.neut.of οὗτος, subject of ἐστιν) 93.

ἐστιν (3d.per.sing.pres.ind.of εἰμί, aoristic) 86.

τὸ (nom.sing.neut.of the article in agreement with εἰρημένον) 9.

εἰρημένον (perf.pass.part.nom.sing.neut.of ῥέω, substantival, predicate nominative) 116

διὰ (preposition with the genitive, indirect agent) 118.

τοῦ (gen.sing.masc.of the article in agreement with προφήτου) 9.

προφήτου (gen.sing.masc.of προφήτης, indirect agent) 119.

#2981 Ἰωήλ (gen.sing.masc.of Ἰωήλ, apposition) .

Joel - Acts 2:16.

Meaning: Joel, the Old Testament prophet. The word means, "whose God is Jehovah." He prophesied during the reign of Uzziah. Cited by Peter - Acts 2:16.

Translation - "Rather this is that which has been spoken by the prophet Joel."

Comment: ἀλλά is the alternative conjunction - "not what you think, but something else." The perfect passive participle, τὸ εἰρημένον speaks of something prophesied in the past which still stands written in the Old Testament record. The reference is to Joel 2:28-32. Peter said, "This is that. . . " but he did not say, "This is *all of that . . .* " Joel's entire prophecy is quoted by Peter in Acts 2:17-21. The material in verses 17,18 had a fulfillment on the day of Pentecost. The remainder of the prophecy will be fulfilled on the last day of the church age, when the Lord returns again. The antecedent of τοῦτο, as it occurs both in verses 14 and 16 is the phenomenon of languages. The meteorological phenomena of verses 19,20 did not occur at Pentecost. The fact that a chronological gap may occur in an Old Testament passage, which takes no notice of it, has been noted before. *Cf.* Luke 1:30-33, with the church age covered by the colon after "Highest" in verse 32. *Cf.* also Luke 4:18, together with Isa.61:1,2, where Jesus stopped reading abruptly in the middle of Isa.61:2. *Cf.* comment *en loc.* If Peter had said that everything that Joel said was to be fulfilled at Pentecost, we would be in trouble. Joel covered both the beginning and the end of the period which he called "the last days" with a prophecy that describes events which were to take place sometime during that period which began to Pentecost and will end with the second coming of Christ. He did not say that every day in the "last days" would see the language miracle and/or the events of verses 19,20. The use of languages, other than their own, but understood without interpretation by others, such as occurred at Pentecost does not occur now, even though every day since Pentecost has been one of the "last days." Nor are the meteorological signs occurring now, but they will occur on the last day of the "last days." The modern so-called "tongues" movement apologists point to the Joel prophecy to justify the incomprehensible gibberish which they produce publicly, with or without the services of an "interpreter" who understands what was said no more than anyone else present. Thus we get additions to the revelation of the Holy Spirit in the New Testament, a book which Paul said was to be completed, at which time the sign gifts would be needed no longer, and thus would be phased out. *Cf.* our comments on 1 Cor.13:8-13 and the connection of these verses with 1 Cor.12:1-14:40.

Verse 17 -'"And it shall come to pass in the last days, saith God, I will pour out of my spirit upon all flesh: and your sons and your daughters shall prophesy, and your young men shall see visions, and your old men shall dream dreams."

Καὶ ἔσται ἐν ταῖς ἐσχάταις ἡμέραις, λέγει ὁ θεός, ἐκχεῶ ἀπὸ τοῦ πνεύματός

μου ἐπὶ πᾶσαν σάρκα, καὶ προφητεύσουσιν οἱ υἱοὶ ὑμῶν καὶ αἱ θυγατέρες
ὑμῶν, καὶ οἱ νεανίσκοι ὑμῶν ὁράσεις ὄψονται, καὶ οἱ πρεσβύτεροι ὑμῶν
ἐνυπνίοις ἐνυπνιασθήσονται,

καὶ (continuative conjunction) 14.
ἔσται (3d.per.sing.fut.ind.of εἰμί, predictive) 86.
ἐν (preposition with the locative of time point) 80.
ταῖς (loc.pl.fem.of the article in agreement with ἡμέραις) 9.
ἐσχάταις (loc.pl.fem.of ἔσχατος, in agreement with ἡμέραις) 496.
ἡμέραις (loc.pl.fem.of ἡμέρα, time point) 135.
λέγει (3d.per.sing.pres.act.ind.of λέγω, aoristic) 66.
ὁ (nom.sing.masc.of the article in agreement with θεός) 9.
θεός (nom.sing.masc.of θεός, subject of λέγει) 124.
ἐκχεῶ (1st.per.sing.fut.act.ind.of ἐκχέω, predictive) 811.
ἀπὸ (preposition with the ablative of source) 70.
τοῦ (abl.sing.neut.of the article in agreement with πνεύματός) 9.
πνεύματός (abl.sing.neut.of πνεῦμα, source) 83.
μου (gen.sing.masc.of ἐγώ, possession) 123.
ἐπὶ (preposition with the accusative of extent, place) 47.
πᾶσαν (acc.sing.fem.of πᾶς, in agreement with σάρκα) 67.
σάρκα (acc.sing.fem.of σάρξ, extent, place) 1202.
καὶ (continuative conjunction) 14.
προφητεύσουσιν (3d.per.pl.fut.act.ind.of προφητεύω, predictive) 685.
οἱ (nom.pl.masc.of the article in agreement with υἱοὶ) 9.
υἱοὶ (nom.pl.masc.of υἱός, subject of προφητεύσουσιν) 5.
ὑμῶν (gen.pl.masc.of σύ, relationship) 104.
καὶ (adjunctive conjunction joining nouns) 14.
αἱ (nom.pl.fem.of the article in agreement with θυγατέρες) 9.
θυγατέρες (nom.pl.fem.of θυγάτηρ, subject of προφητεύσουσιν) 817.
ὑμῶν (gen.pl.masc.of σύ, relationship) 104.
καὶ (continuative conjunction) 14.
οἱ (nom.pl.masc.of the article in agreement with νεανίσκοι) 9.
νεανίσκοι (nom.pl.masc.of νεανίσκος, subject of ὄψονται) 1300.
ὑμῶν (gen.pl.masc.of σύ, relationship) 104.

#2982 ὁράσεις (acc.pl.fem.of ὅρασις, direct object of ὄψονται).

sight - Rev.4:3.
vision - Acts 2:17; Rev.9:17.
look upon - Rev.4:3.

Meaning: Cf. ὅραμα (#1228), ὁράω (#144), ὁρατός (#4602). That which is seen. Appearance. Visible form. There is nothing in the word to indicate that what is seen is the result of extra-sensory experience brought about by divine help, although the context in each case seems to indicate this. With reference to what John saw in Rev.4:3,3; 9:17. Of young men upon the earth - Acts 2:17.

ὄψονται (3d.per.pl.fut.act.ind.of ὁράω, predictive) 144.

καὶ (continuative conjunction) 14.

οἱ (nom.pl.masc.of the article in agreement with πρεσβύτεροι) 9.

πρεσβύτεροι (nom.pl.masc.of πρεσβύτερος, subject of ἐνυπνιασθήσονται) 1141.

ὑμῶν (gen.pl.masc.of σύ, relationship) 104.

#2983 ἐνυπνίοις (instrumental pl.neut.of ἐνύπνιον, cognate instrumental).

dream - Acts 2:17.

Meaning: A combination of ἐν (#80) and ὕπνος (#126). Hence, that which appears during sleep - a dream - Acts 2:17.

#2984 ἐνυπνιασθήσονται (3d.per.pl.fut.mid.ind.of ἐνυπνιάζομαι, predictive).

dream - Acts 2:17.
filthy dreamer - Jude 8.

Meaning: Cf.ἐνύπνιον (#2983). To dream - Acts 2:17. Metaphorically in Jude 8.

Translation - " 'And it shall be in the last days,' God said, 'I will pour out of my Spirit upon all flesh, and your sons and your daughters will prophesy, and your young men will see visions, and your old men will dream dreams.' "

Comment: The New Testament idiom often employs the cognate accusative, *e.g.* ἀγῶνα ἠγώνισμαι (2 Tim.4:7). For other examples *cf.* Mt.2:10; 1 John 5:16; Luke 2:8; 1 Cor.9:7; John 7:24; Col.2:19, etc. But in ἐνυπνίοις ἐνυπνιασθήσονται we have the cognate idea, but in the instrumental. "There is one usage in the N.T. that has caused some trouble. It is called 'Hebraic' by some of the grammarians." (Moulton, *Prolegomena*, 75, as cited in Robertson, *Grammar*, 531). "The instances are rather numerous in the N.T., though nothing like so common as in the LXX. (Conybeare and Stock, *Selections from the LXX. A Grammatical Introduction,* 60f, as cited in *Ibid.*). Conybeare and Stock quote Plato to show that it is, however, an idiom in accordance with the genius of the Greek language. Thus λόγῳ λέγειν, φεύγων φυγῇ, φύσει πεφυκυῖαν,etc. They call it the 'cognate dative.' That will do if instrumental is inserted in the place of dative." (*Ibid.*) Robertson then lists some other examples: Mt.13:14; Acts 23:14; Acts 2:17; Luke 22:15; Mt.15:4; Acts 2:30; Mk.5:42; Acts 5:28; James 5:17; John 3:29; 1 Peter 1:8; John 18:32; John 21:19.

All of the experiences listed in verses 17-21 are predicted to occur within (during the time span of) a period which Joel called "the last days." If the text had used διά with the genitive, as in Mark 5:5 - διὰ παντὸς νυκτὸς καὶ ἡμέρας - "throughout every night and day," we would be justified in saying that the signs described here - supernatural use of languages, prophecies, visions, dreams, wonders in the sky and on earth, blood, fire, etc. - would occur throughout the period described as "the last days." This would support the contention of the Pentecostalists that their "tongues gift" is a fulfillment of Joel's prophecy. But the text describes the time period when these things will occur with ἐν ταῖς ἐσχάταις ἡμέραις. This is time point locative, not time description genitive.

The miracle that elevated the Apostles above the language barrier occured at the beginning of the "last days." The events of verses 19,20 will occur on the last day of the "last days." Thus all can be said to have occurred, and to yet occur "in the last days." These "last days" included Pentecost and will close with the second coming. Joel described miracles at the beginning and at the end. He did not say that these miracles would occur *throughout* the last days. The phrase "last days" have been interpreted incorrectly to apply only to the last days of the "last days" such as Daniel's 70th week or the Great Tribulation of three and one-half years duration, or of some period which is being considered as very close to the end of the age. That this is wrong is clear from Peter's statement that what happened at Pentecost, happened "in the last days." In what sense can all of the days since Pentecost, plus all future days unto the second coming of Christ be called "the last days." They are "last" in the sense that they represent the period during which the Agent of the Godhead Who is dealing with the human problem upon earth is the Holy Spirit. The Old Testament period could be called "the first days." During that time God, the Father spoke to the fathers through the prophets (Heb.1:1). The period of our Lord's incarnation upon earth might be called "the last days" also, since in those days God, the Father spoke to us through His Son (Heb.1:2). Now, since the ascension of Christ, God the Father is speaking unto us by the Holy Spirit. Thus Pentecost occurred on a day within the "last days." It is a fallacy to apply the phrase "the last days" *only* to the last seven years (or the last three and one-half years) of the church age. We have been living in the "last days" since Jesus began His public ministry at the Jordan River. It was then that God began to speak unto us through His Son. Before these days are over all that Joel prophesied will take place, supernatural language gifts at Pentecost and supernatural movements in the heavens at the end of this age.

ἀπὸ τοῦ πνεύματός μου is a Hebraism. We have called it an ablative of source. Robertson called it a partitive genitive, which is probably a little closer to the idea.

Note that the Holy Spirit, with His supernatural gifts, was to be poured out ἐπὶ πᾶσαν σάρκα - without respect to race, color, national origin, or religious affiliation. If the gift of communication in a language not previously known, as demonstrated currently is genuine, why is it not bestowed upon all the saints? Why upon only those identified with certain religious groups who are noted for their ecstatic experiences, unless the "tongues" people are willing to say that they are the only ones who are truly regenerate? Language skills are not the only results of this outpouring of the Holy Spirit. The visions of the young men, the dreams of the old men and the prophesies of the servants are also to be included. Perhaps as the last days approach the end, it will be necessary for these gifts to be bestowed again in order that the remainder of the task of the worldwide missionary enterprise, may be completed. But we can be sure that if this takes place, Christians will be going to parts of the world where a dialect is spoken in which they are not competent, and that what they say will be understood by the native populations. There will be no need for an interpreter. The miracle will be granted, not for the emotional titillation of the speaker, but for the spiritual enlightenment of those in the audience, with the result that God will also take them out from among the Gentiles as people for His name (Acts 15:14). The last days are those during which the missionary enterprise, begun at Pentecost will witness the presentation of the gospel of Christ on a universal basis. *Cf.*Luke 3:6; John 17:2. The results are set forth: sons and daughters will preach (*cf.*#685). The word does not necessarily mean to foretell future events, but to *forthtell* the good news of the gospel. The visions of the young and the dreams of the aged will contribute in some way to the completion of the work of the gospel. This is the purpose for all of the gifts of the Holy Spirit (1 Cor.12:1-31; Eph.4:11-13). *Cf.*#811 for ἐκχύω in other contexts. In this sense in Acts 2:17, 18, 33; Titus 3:6. Peter is thus announcing to the world that during these last days God's last appeal to the world will be made, this time through the agency of the Holy Spirit, working through the members of the Body of Christ who are filled with His presence and power. The elect will be saved now or never. Israel rejected the prophets in the Old Testament age. They murdered His Son in the gospel period, which was the beginning of the "last days." If they reject the Holy Spirit's witness during the remainder of the "last days" there will be no fourth member of the Godhead to make a further appeal. And there will be remedy but judgment.

Much confusion results when we identify the "last days" with the "church age", as though the elect called to salvation between Pentecost and the "rapture" which they put seven years before the second coming, are a special group of saints. If, in keeping with Hebrews 1:2 and Acts 2:17, we define the "last days" as the period from the baptism of Jesus to His second coming, we can include Old Testament and Gospel age saints in the church, and escape the snares of hyperdispensationalism.

Verse 18 - *"And on my servants and on my handmaidens I will pour out in those days of my Spirit; and they shall prophesy."*

καί γε ἐπὶ τοὺς δούλους μου καὶ ἐπὶ τὰς δούλας μου ἐν ταῖς ἡμέραις ἐκείναις ἐκχεῶ ἀπὸ τοῦ πνεύματός μου καὶ προφητεύσουσιν.

καὶ (continuative conjunction) 14.
γε (intensive particle) 2449.
ἐπὶ (preposition with the accusative of extent) 47.
τοὺς (acc.pl.masc.of the article in agreement with δούλους) 9.
δούλους (acc.pl.masc.of δοῦλος, extent, place where) 725.
μου (gen.sing.masc.of ἐγώ, relationship) 123.
καὶ (adjunctive conjunction joining prepositional phrases) 14.
ἐπὶ (preposition with the accusative of extent, place) 47.
τὰς (acc.pl.fem.of the article in agreement with δούλας) 9.
δούλας (acc.pl.fem.of δούλη, place where) 1817.
μου (gen.sing.masc.of ἐγώ, relationship) 123.
ἐν (preposition with the locative of time point) 80.
ταῖς (loc.pl.fem.of the article in agreement with ἡμέραις) 9.
ἡμέραις (loc.pl.fem.of ἡμέρα, time point) 135.

ἐκείναις (loc.pl.fem.of ἐκεῖνος, in agreement with ἡμέραις) 246.
ἐκχεῶ (1st.per.sing.fut.act.ind.of ἐκχέω, predictive) 811.
ἀπό (preposition with the partitive genitive) 70.
τοῦ (gen.sing.neut.of the article in agreement with πνεύματός) 9.
πνεύματός (gen.sing.neut.of πνεῦμα, partitive) 83.
μου (gen.sing.masc.of ἐγώ, possession) 123.
καὶ (continuative conjunction) 14.
προφητεύσουσιν (3d.per.pl.fut.act.ind.of προφητεύω, predictive) 685.

Translation - "And even upon my slaves, both men and women, in those days, will I pour out of my spirit and they will prophesy."

Comment: γε here with καί serves to heighten the force of καί. Thus our ascensive translation. Note the crescendo effect in continuative καί, adjunctive καί and ascensive καί. - "And I will . . . also I will . . . I will even . . . κ.τ.λ." Thus Joel gives us a further definition of πᾶσαν σάρκα of verse 17. There will be no discrimination on the basis of skin color, nationality, sex or social and economic status. The menials, both men and women will have their part in the ministry, as directed by the Holy Spirit. Thus God, in electing grace, knows nothing of humanly contrived social division.

The extreme egalitarianism of the Holy Spirit is revealed here in verses 17,18 and recalls Luke 1:52,53, with its political, social and economic revolutions.

There are to be other supernatural manifestations of the power of God, described in some detail in the Revelation, at the extreme end of the age, in addition to this outpouring of the Holy Spirit upon the members of the Body of Christ, as we see in

Verse 19 - "And I will shew wonders in heaven above, and signs in the earth beneath; blood, and fire, and vapour of smoke."

καὶ δώσω τέρατα ἐν τῷ οὐρανῷ ἄνω καὶ σημεῖα ἐπὶ τῆς γῆς κάτω, αἷμα καὶ πῦρ καὶ ἀτμίδα καπνοῦ,

καὶ (continuative conjunction) 14.
δώσω (1st.per.sing.fut.act.ind.of δίδωμι, predictive) 362.
τέρατα (acc.pl.neut.of τέρας, direct object of δώσω) 1500.
ἐν (preposition with the locative of place) 80.
τῷ (loc.sing.masc.of the article in agreement with οὐρανῳ) 9.
οὐρανῳ (loc.sing.masc.of οὐρανός, place where) 254.
ἄνω (adverbial) 1973.
καὶ (adjunctive conjunction joining nouns) 14.
σημεῖα (acc.pl.neut.of σημεῖον, direct object of δώσω) 1005.
ἐπὶ (preposition with the genitive of place description) 47.
τῆς (gen.sing.fem.of the article in agreement with γῆς) 9.
γῆς (gen.sing.fem.of γῆ, place description) 157.
κάτω (adverbial) 348.
αἷμα (acc.sing.fem.of αἷμα, in apposition to τέρατα) 1203.

καὶ (adjunctive conjunction joining nouns) 14.

πῦρ (acc.sing.neut.of πῦρ, in apposition to τέρατα) 298.

καὶ (adjunctive conjunction joining nouns) 14.

#2985 ἀτμίδα (acc.sing.fem.of ἀτμίς, in apposition to τέρατα).

vapour - Acts 2:19; James 4:14.

Meaning: vapour. Literally, followed by a genitive of description - Acts 2:19. illustratively in James 4:14.

#2986 καπνοῦ (gen.sing.masc.of καπνός, description).

smoke - Acts 2:19; Rev.8:4; 9:2,2,3,17,18; 14:11; 15:8; 18:9,18; 19:3.

Meaning: Smoke. Connected with God's judgments upon the earth at the end of the last days - Acts 2:19; Rev.9:2,2,3,17,18; 14:11 (gehenna).. Of the destruction of Babylon - Rev.18:9,19; 19:3. The smoke from burning incense, used in worship of God - Rev.8:4; the smoke of the holy temple of God - Rev.15:8.

Translation - "And I will show wonders in the sky above and signs throughout the earth beneath - blood and fire and smoky vapour."

Comment: δώσω (#362) properly means "to give." The context here indicates something for people to observe, such as τέρατα (#1500) and σημεῖα (#1005). Note ἐπί with the accusative of extent to show place in verses 17 and 18, while in verse 19 we have ἐπί with the genitive of place description. Joel is describing events which will take place also in "the last days" as defined in comment on verse 17, but these events and those of verse 20 are to be seen at the very close of the last days. It is not necessary to suppose that the phenomena of verses 19 and 20 occurred at Pentecost when the outpouring of the Holy Spirit bestowed upon the Apostles the linguistic abilities described. The language gifts were necessary, the wonders, signs, blood, fire and smoky vapour was not. Without the language miracle the Apostles could not have preached the gospel to the assembled visitors in a comprehensible manner. The Jews from the areas mentioned in verses 9-11 heard the good news of the gospel and each carried it back to his area. Thus the gospel seed was scattered (Matthew 13:3) and the work began by which the Holy Spirit took out "of the Gentiles a people for His name" (Acts 15:14). The mystery, already in action since the Garden of Eden and indistinctly revealed in the Old Testament, but clearly revealed to Paul (Eph.3:3-7) and to Peter (Acts 10:9-35), was advanced. When the mystery is finished at the time of the last trump (Rev.10:7) God's judgment upon the unsaved world will begin and will be characterized by the signs of verses 19,20. But throughout the entire period, whether at Pentecost or at the last moment before Christ returns, the promise of verse 21 holds.

Some have supposed that ἐπὶ πᾶσαν σάρκα verse 17, coming at this time from Peter's mouth, could not be taken universally, but must apply only to the Jews of the διασπορά. While Peter at Pentecost did not yet understand that Gentiles were to be included in the Body of Christ, since that revelation did not come to him until Acts 10:1-48, it should be pointed out that Peter was not speaking from his own wisdom at Pentecost, but as the Holy Spirit gave Him utterance. Also he was quoting Joel, who "spake as (he) was moved by the Holy Spirit" (2 Peter 1:21), even though he also did not grasp the full significance of what he said (1 Peter 1:10-12).

Verse 20 - "The sun shall be turned into darkness and the moon into blood, before that great and notable day of the Lord come."

ὁ ἥλιος μεταστραφήσεται εἰς σκότος καὶ ἡ σελήνη εἰς αἷμα πρὶν ἐλθεῖν ἡμέραν κυρίου τὴν μεγάλην (καὶ ἐπιφανῆ).

ὁ (nom.sing.masc.of the article in agreement with ἥλιος) 9.
ἥλιος (nom.sing.masc.of ἥλιος, subject of μεταστραφήσεται) 546.

#2987 μεταστραφήσεται (3d.per.sing.fut.pass.ind.of μεταστρέφω, predictive).

pervert - Gal.1:7.
turn - Acts 2:20; James 4:9.

Meaning: A combination of μετά (#50) and στρέφω (#530). To turn one thing into another. With reference to the sun - Acts 2:20; ideologically, of the gospel - Gal.1:7. Psychologically, of one's emotions - James 4:9.

εἰς (preposition with the accusative, predicate usage) 140.
σκότος (acc.sing.masc.of σκότος, predicate accusative, adverbial) 602.
καὶ (continuative conjunction) 14.
ἡ (nom.sing.fem.of the article in agreement with σελήνη) 9.
σελήνη (nom.sing.fem.of σελήνη, subject of μεταστραφήσεται) 1505.
εἰς (preposition with the accusative, predicate usage) 140.
αἷμα (acc.sing.fem.of αἷμα, predicate accusative, adverbial) 1203.
πρὶν (conjunction introducing a temporal clause with the infinitive, antecedent time) 77
ἐλθεῖν (aor.act.inf.of ἔρχομαι, temporal clause, antecedent time) 146.
ἡμέραν (acc.sing.fem.of ἡμέρα, general reference) 135.
κυρίου (gen.sing.masc.of κύριος, description) 97.
τὴν (acc.sing.fem.of the article in agreement with ἡμέραν) 9.
μεγάλην (acc.sing.fem.of μέγας, in agreement with ἡμέραν) 184.
(καὶ (adjunctive conjunction joining adjectives) 14.

#2988 ἐπιφανῆ) (acc.sing.fem.of ἐπιφανής, in agreement with ἡμέραν).

notable - Acts 2:20.

Meaning: A combination of ἐπί (#47) and φαίνω (#100). *Cf.* ἐπιφαίνω (#1859). That which appears and is seen without difficulty. Outstanding, notable, that which attracts attention. Something that cannot be overlooked. The day of the second coming of Christ - Acts 2:20.

Translation - "The sun will be turned into darkness and the moon into blood before the great and conspicuous day of the Lord comes."

Comment: We have πρίν with the infinitive in a temporal clause meaning "before." This is one of only 13 places in the New Testament where it occurs. We have chosen "conspicuous" as the best translation of ἐπιφανῆ (#2988). Any word that indicates that the day, when it comes, cannot be overlooked or ignored will do. *Cf.* Rev.6:12-18; 11:15-19; 16:17-21; 19:11-16, for descriptions of the sixth seal, seventh trumpet, seventh vial and a close-up of the return of the King of Kings and Lord of Lords. No one is going to overlook that.

These heavenly and earthly wonders are associated with the events in the last seven years of the church age (Daniel 9:27). Note that they are antecedent to the Day of the Lord which is the last day, on which Christ returns to earth. *Cf.* Rev.8:4,12; 9:2,3,17,18; 18:9,18. Peter, speaking with wisdom not his own has given in verses 14-20 an outline of the "last days." They began with the incarnation miracle when Ὁ Λόγος became flesh (John 1:14) and began a temporary visit on earth (Heb.1:2), and they continued with Pentecost, when the Holy Spirit, pursuant to our Lord's promise (John 14:16,17; 16:7-15; Acts 1:8) filled (baptized) the early Christians. They will continue until the day when Christ sets foot again upon this earth. The sign gifts - supernatural language ability, prophecies, healing *et al* as listed in 1 Cor.12 - were the Holy Spirit's gifts to the Body of Christ to enable her to do her work of establishing the churches in the first century during the time that the New Testament literature was being written, at the conclusion of which period they were phased out (1 Cor.13). We do not need them now, since we have the perfect revelation of God's works, will and ways in the New Testament. Indeed, if anyone did possess these gifts, he would be in a position to add to the New Testament literature and have his witness accepted on the basis of his prestige as a miracle worker. Peter, Paul and the other Apostles were believed and their writings were accepted into the canon because they did possess these gifts. When Antichrist comes Satan will give him power to perform miracles upon the basis of which he will deceive the world temporarily (Rev.13:13-15). When an evangelist today performs mighty works or "speaks in tongues" or announces that he has seen God and heard His voice, discretion would counsel prudence. He is about to sell you the Brooklyn Bridge or give some startling new revelation which adds to the New Testament and distorts the perfect coherence, consistency and correspondance to reality which it now possesses. Not all of the new prophets come from Salt Lake City. One can see and hear them on most any television channel.

The signs and wonders at the end of the age are the manifestations of the power, not of the Holy Spirit, but of the Judge of all the earth (John 5:22) Who will be preparing to return and take His place upon David's throne. Verses 17-18 describe the functions of the Holy Spirit. Verses 19-20 predict the judgments of the Lord Jesus Christ. The Holy Spirit's mission was to equip the church for the missionary enterprise (Mt.28:18-20). Every Christian since Pentecost can be equipped for Christian service (Luke 11:13; Eph.5:18), although His equipment will not include the sign gifts, for the reasons which I have outlined above. Once the church's task is completed (Rev.10:7; Eph.3:3-6) and the last elect soul is saved, the sole remaining function is judgment. That is not the work of the Holy Spirit, but of the Messiah. He will carry it out in connection with His return to take His place upon David's eternal throne. We are not to look for the Day of the Lord, in the sense in which the phrase is used here (*i.e.* the actual day of Christ's return), before the events of verses 19 and 20 have been observed. The darkened sun and bloody moon come on the same day that He will appear. It will indeed be a notable day (Rev.1:7; Mt.24:29-31; Rev.19:11-21). It will be the last day of "the last days" of which the day of the birth of Jesus was the first, and the day of Pentecost was another. Joel has one more thing to say about this era in

Verse 21 - "And it shall come to pass that whosoever shall call onthe name of the Lord shall be saved."

καὶ ἔσται πᾶς ὃς ἐὰν ἐπικαλέσηται τὸ ὄνομα κυρίου σωθήσεται.

καὶ (continuative conjunction) 14.

ἔσται (3d.per.sing.fut.ind.of εἰμί, predictive) 86.

πᾶς (nom.sing.masc.of πᾶς, subject of σωθήσεται) 67.

ὃς (nom.sing.masc.of ὅς, subject of ἐπικαλέσηται, in a more probable condition relative clause with the subjunctive) 65.

ἐὰν (conditional particle in a more probable condition relative clause with the subjunctive) 363.

ἐπικαλέσηται (3d.per.sing.aor.mid.subj.of ἐπικαλέω, more probable condition) 884.

τὸ (acc.sing.neut.of the article in agreement with ὄνομα) 9.

ὄνομα (acc.sing.neut.of ὄνομα, direct object of ἐπικαλέσηται) 108.

κυρίου (gen.sing.masc.of κύριος, description) 97.

σωθήσεται (3d.per.sing.fut.pass.ind.of σώζω, predictive) 109.

Translation - "And it shall be that everyone who calls upon the regal name will be saved."

Comment: κυρίου, without the article is descriptive, not possessive. Hence our translation. "Where the contingent or indefinite idea is supplied by the context, or the context and the nature of the relative, the subjunctive is used." This Mantey calls a "more probable condition. The protasis of a more probable future condition may be expressed by the use of a relative pronoun with ἄν" (Mantey, *Manual*, 273). The condition is determined as unfulfilled, but with a more probable prospect of fulfillment. Some are going to call upon the name of the Lord. When they do, there is no doubt that they will be saved. Here, again, Peter is using Joel's prophecy to teach a universal offer of salvation, something which was, at that time unclear to him, although later revealed, both to him (Acts 10:9ff) and to Paul (Eph.3:3-6). That critics, who approach the New Testament with the premise that there is nothing supernatural about its production, should overlook the supernatural direction of Peter's remarks by the Holy Spirit and thus analyze his thoughts on a humanistic basis is indeed both sad and disgusting. The Christian understands as well as any infidel that neither Joel nor Peter could have understood the full implication of the prophet's statement, either at the time when Joel uttered or Peter quoted it. They were fully conditioned to the idea that the nation Israel was to be the sole recipient of the blessings of the Lord's salvation, and that Gentiles could participate in it only by becoming prosylyte Jews. But the Christian has his commitment on file. Joel and Peter were only the mouthpieces of the Holy Spirit, Who, as God knows about all of His works "from the beginning of the world" (Acts 15:18; Eph.1:11). Paul who wrote much later also quoted Joel 2:32 in Romans 10:13 with a full understanding of the passage, because in the meantime He had received the revelation of the mystery (Eph.3:3-6).

The promise extends to "all flesh" (verse 17) of whatever social status (verse 18) in every day of "the last days." Peter later emphasized the universality of the invitation in verse 39. The promise that to call upon the Kingly Name is to be saved will hold until the last elect member of the Body of Christ has done so. That will be ". . . in the days of the voice of the seventh angel when he is about to trumpet. . . " (Rom.10:7). That is the "last trump" (1 Cor.15:51,52; 1 Thess.4:16,17) when the dead in Christ will rise and the living saints will be caught up. The "last trump" occurs when the "kingdoms of the world become the kingdoms of our Lord and of His Christ" (Rev.11:15), and that cannot occur until the last day of "the last days." On the day before the last day the kingdoms of this world will belong to the Beast (Rev.13:5). Pretribulation rapturists of course respond to this by insisting that Paul's "last trump" of 1 Cor.15:52 is not the same last trump as the last of the seven trumps of Revelation 11. If it is not and they are correct that the trumpet of 1 Thess.4:16 will sound seven years (or three and one-half years) before the last trump of the seven in Revelation 11, then Paul is guilty of having said that the "last trump" will sound before the seven trumpets, of which the seventh will be the last! Since to agree with the pretribulation rapture position makes it necessary to impugn the veracity of the Apostle Paul, it would appear that few Christians are likely to be troubled with that decision. Let Paul be true and every man . . . . !

Having expounded Joel's prophecy in order to explain the miracle of the languages, predict the gift of prophecy and the events at the end of the age, Peter then went on with his great statement. His κήρυγμα (#1013) is the perfect model for all preaching of those preachers who would come after him. What did Peter talk about? What did he leave unsaid? What was his approach to the audience? What were his results? What contrast, if any does this sermon offer to the evangelistic preaching to which the world is subjected today? If there is a contrast, at whose expense is the odious comparison? What should modern preachers do about it?

Verse 22 - "Ye men of Israel, hear these words: Jesus of Nazareth, a man approved of God among you by miracles and wonders and signs, which God did by him in the midst of you, as ye yourselves also know:"

Ἄνδρες Ἰσραηλῖται, ἀκούσατε τοὺς λόγους τούτους. Ἰησοῦν τὸν Ναζωραῖον, ἄνδρα ἀποδεδειγμένον ἀπὸ τοῦ θεοῦ εἰς ἡμᾶς δυνάμεσι καὶ τέρασι καὶ σημείοις οἷς ἐποίησεν δι' αὐτοῦ ὁ θεὸς ἐν μέσῳ ὑμῶν, καθὼς αὐτοὶ οἴδατε,

Ἄνδρες (voc.pl.masc.of ἀνήρ, address) 63.
Ἰσραηλῖται (voc.pl.masc.of Ἰσραλίτης, in agreement with ἄνδρες) 1967.
ἀκούσατε (2d.per.pl.aor.act.impv.of ἀκούω, command) 148.
τοὺς (acc.pl.masc.of the article in agreement with λόγους) 9.
λόγους (acc.pl.masc.of λόγος, direct object of ἀκούσατε) 510.
τούτους (acc.pl.masc.of οὗτος, in agreement with λόγους) 93.
Ἰησοῦν (acc.sing.masc.of Ἰησοῦς, direct object of ἀνείλατε) 3.
τὸν (acc.sing.masc.of the article in agreement with Ναζωραῖον) 9.
Ναζωραῖον (acc.sing.masc.of Ναζωραῖος, in apposition) 245.
ἄνδρα (acc.sing.masc.of ἀνήρ, in apposition) 63.

#2989 ἀποδεδειγμένον (perf.pass.part.acc.sing.masc.of ἀποδείκνυμι, adjectival, in agreement with ἄνδρα, restrictive).

approve - Acts 2:22.
prove - Acts 25:7.
set forth - 1 Cor.4:9.
show - 2 Thess.2:4.

Meaning: A combination of ἀπό (#70) and δείκνυμι (#359). To show from or by means of oneself. In the passive, to be shown. To exhibit, expose to view, point out, demonstrate; vindicate through one's actions - Jesus proved to be God's Son - Acts 2:22; to prove a point in court - Acts 25:7. To expose to view - the Apostles in their ministry, as objects of contempt before the world - 1 Cor.4:9. With reference to the attempt of Antichrist to prove that he is God - 2 Thess.2:4.

ἀπό (preposition with the ablative of direct agent) 70.
τοῦ (abl.sing.masc.of the article in agreement with θεοῦ) 9.
θεοῦ (abl.sing.masc.of θεός, direct agent) 124.
εἰς (preposition with the accusative in its original static use, like a locative) 140.
ὑμᾶς (acc.pl.masc.of σύ, locative use) 104.
δυνάμεσι (instru.pl.fem.of δύναμις, means) 687.
καὶ (adjunctive conjunction joining nouns) 14.
τέρασι (instru.pl.neut.of τέρας means) 1500.
καὶ (adjunctive conjunction joining nouns) 14.
σημείοις (instru.pl.neut.of σημεῖον, means) 1005.
οἷς (instru.pl.neut.of ὅς, case attraction of the relative to σημείοις) 65.
ἐποίησεν (3d.per.sing.aor.act.ind.of ποιέω, constative) 127.
δι' (preposition with the genitive of indirect agency) 118.
αὐτοῦ (gen.sing.masc.of αὐτός, indirect agency) 16.
ὁ (nom.sing.masc.of the article in agreement with θεὸς) 9.
θεὸς (nom.sing.masc.of θεός, subject of ἐποίησεν) 124.
ἐν (preposition with the locative of place where) 80.

μέσῳ (loc.sing.masc.of μέσος, place where) 873.

ὑμῶν (gen.pl.masc.of σύ, description) 104.

καθώς (adverbial) 1348.

αὐτοὶ (nom.pl.masc.of αὐτός, subject of οἴδατε, intensive) 16.

οἴδατε (2d.per.pl.pres.act.ind.of οἶδα, aoristic) 144.

Translation - *"Men of Israel, hear these words. Jesus, the Nazarene, a man proved worthy of trust by God among you by miracles and wonders and signs, which God performed through Him in your midst, as you yourselves know —"*

Comment:Ἰησοῦν is the object of ἀνείλατε at the end of verse 23. The simple sentence is, "You killed Jesus." The rest of the long complex sentence, which extends through verse 23, with its various subordinate clauses, sketches the history of the ministry of Jesus which had just been terminated by His death. ἄνδρα, in apposition with Ἰησοῦν is defined by the restrictive adjectival participle ἀποδεδειγμένον. Jesus was the only one (restrictive adjective) Whose claims to be the Son of God were adequately supported (attested, confirmed, substantiated, validated, certified, borne out) by the direct action of God, by means of the miracles which He did in their presence. These miracles to which Peter pointed were the ones that those in his audience had seen. Peter was not speaking of Jesus' resurrection from the dead and ascension into heaven, as these miracles were not witnessed by anyone in his audience except his fellow Christians. He will declare that Jesus arose from the dead, but he is not pointing to the resurrection as something that they had seen.

Thus the subject of Peter's sermon is introduced. He is Jesus. Then His public record, the events of which had been seen by the audience and could not therefore be denied, is passed in review. Jesus' history on earth was one of a constant round of evidences from God that this Nazarene carpenter was the incarnate Son of God. These miracles to which Peter alluded were not performed in a corner. They were a matter of public record, and the subject matter of long discussions in which some believed that they were true while other people sought to discredit Him.

Peter, having gotten himself into syntactical difficulty with this long sentence, began over with a resumptive pronoun in

Verse 23 - ". . . Him, being delivered by the determinate counsel and foreknowledge of God, ye have taken, and by wicked hands have crucified and slain."

τοῦτον τῇ ὡρισμένῃ βουλῇ καὶ προγνώσει τοῦ θεοῦ ἔκδοτον διὰ χειρὸς ἀνόμων προσπήξαντες ἀνείλατε,

τοῦτον (acc.sing.masc.of οὗτος, in agreement with Ἰησοῦν, resumptive) 93.

τῇ (instru.sing.fem.of the article in agreement with βουλῇ) 9.

ὡρισμένῃ (perf.pass.part.instru.sing.fem.of ὁρίζω, adjectival, ascriptive, in agreement with βουλῇ) 2764.

βουλῇ (instru.sing.fem.of βουλή, cause) 2163.

καὶ (adjunctive conjunction joining nouns) 14.

#2990 προγνώσει (instru.sing.fem.of πρόγνωσις, cause).

foreknowledge - Acts 2:23; 1 Peter 1:2.

Meaning: A combination of πρό (#442) and γνῶσις (#1856). *Cf.* προγινώσκω (#3655). Forethought. The state of knowing the future. Perfect foreknowledge precludes surprize. Associated with τῇ ὡρισμένῃ βουλῇ in Acts 2:23, with reference to the death of Jesus Christ. With ἐκλεκτοῖς and ἁγιασμῷ in 1 Peter 1:2 with reference to the salvation of souls.

τοῦ (gen.sing.masc.of the article in agreement with θεοῦ) 9.
θεοῦ (gen.sing.masc.of θεός, possession) 124.

#2991 ἔκδοτον (acc.sing.masc.of ἔκδοτος, in agreement with Ἰησοῦν).

being delivered - Acts 2:23.

Meaning: A combination of ἐκ (#19) and δίδωμι (#362). To be given over; given up to the will of another. With reference to the arrest, trial and crucifixion of Jesus - Acts 2:23.

διὰ (preposition with the genitive of agency) 118.
χειρὸς (gen.sing.fem.of χείρ, agency) 308.
ἀνόμων (gen.pl.masc.of ἄνομος, description) 2772.

#2992 προσπήξαντες (aor.act.part.nom.pl.masc.of προσπήγνυμι, adverbial, modal).

crucify - Acts 2:23.

Meaning: A combination of πρός (#197) and πήγνυμι (#4997). Hence to fasten to; in the case of crucifixion, with nails. To crucify - Acts 2:23.

ἀνείλατε (2d.per.pl.aor.act.ind.of ἀναιρῶ, constative) 216.

Translation - ". . . *this man, because of the firmly established plan and foreknowledge of God, betrayed by the hand of the wicked, you murdered by impaling Him to a cross."*

Comment: τοῦτον is deictic and resumptive. It refers to Ἰησοῦν of verse 22 and points definitely to Him. The instrumental of cause in τῇ ὡρισμένῃ βουλῇ καὶ προγνώσει involves God in the scenario. Thus Peter charges his audience with murder, but adds the thought that the scenario was played out in keeping with a divine plan. Jesus was delivered because of the counsel (plan) (#2163) of God and in full conformity to His foreknowledge (#2990). The adjectival perfect passive participle ὡρισμένη is intensive. God's established plan dates from eternity - "Having been established by God's decree in the past, it was still in force when Christ was crucified. Note that Christ's death was according to God's eternal counsel and foreknowledge and yet Peter charges his audience with the crime and says that they murdered Him with the hands of lawless men. Peter was not wrong in this accusation, John 10:17,18 to the contrary notwithstanding, because they certainly tried to kill Him and thus they were morally responsible for His death. That Christ was foreordained to die cannot be denied, but the men who killed Him are responsible to God (Luke 22:22).

Peter wasted no time in an attempt to harmonize predestination and free will, although the implications of what he said could certainly open the door for this kind of discussion. It is important to remember that we are studying the sermon of a man who was full of the Holy Spirit. If we are to learn how to preach it is well to note, not only what he did say, but what the Holy Spirit did not permit him to say. He was not permitted to lose himself and his audience in the trackless maze into which philosophers are enticed and in which they go round and round until they have forgotten the gate wherein they entered and care little about the gate from which they hope sometime to emerge. Aristotle pointed out that compulsion and freedom of the will can coexist, but if Peter even knew who Aristotle was, which he probably did not, he did not think a discussion of the philosophical problem was worth the candle. The facts were that some of the men in his audience that day had stood before Pilate's judgment throne and demanded that Jesus be crucified.

Christ, ordained to die (ὡρίζω #2764) is also ordained to judge the world (Acts 10:42; 17:31) *Cf.* Romans 1:4. *Cf.*#2163 for similar uses of βουλή as it relates to God's eternal plan of salvation.

If the people in Peter's audience who consented to the murder of God's Son had been given no chance to repent and be saved, we would have a problem. How can moral responsibility be charged against one who is party to that which by iron necessity has been predetermined, and who has been given no offer of forgiveness? But these men did repent. They were saved and they found pardon, forgiveness and justification. If Peter had yielded to the temptation to descend into the morass of philosophical speculation it is likely that the men would have gone from the meeting with some sort of idea that they had only done what God wanted done and had decreed should be done, and that they could not therefore be held responsible for it. They found, instead, in the death of the One Whom they had helped to murder, the only payment for their sins that the court of heaven was in a position to accept.

In verse 22 Jesus of Nazareth was presented with all of His credentials.

In verse 23 man's crime against God is discussed in all of its insane depravity.

In verse 24 God's reaction to the death of His Son is described.

Verse 24 - ". . . whom God hath raised up, having loosed the pains of death: because it was not possible that he should be holden of it."

δν ὁ θεὸς ἀνέστησεν λύσας τὰς ὠδῖνας τοῦ θανάτου, καθότι οὐκ ἦν δυνατὸν κρατεῖσθαι αὐτὸν ὑπ' αὐτοῦ.

δν (acc.sing.masc.of ὅς, direct object of ἀνέστησεν) 65.

ὁ (nom.sing.masc.of the article in agreement with θεὸς) 9.

θεὸς (nom.sing.masc.of θεός, subject of ἀνέστησεν) 124.
ἀνέστησεν (3d.per.sing.aor.act.ind.of ἀνίστημι, culminative) 789.
λύσας (aor.act.part.nom.sing.masc.of λύω, adverbial, modal) 471.
τὰς (acc.pl.fem.of the article in agreement with ὠδῖνας) 9.
ὠδῖνας (acc.pl.fem.of ὠδίν, direct object of λύσας) 1486.
τοῦ (gen.sing.masc.of the article in agreement with θανάτου) 9.
θανάτου (gen.sing.masc.of θάνατος, description) 381.
καθότι (particle introducing a subordinate causal clause) 1783.
οὐκ (summary negative conjunction with the indicative) 130.
ἦν (3d.per.sing.imp.ind.of εἰμί, progressive description) 86.
δυνατὸν (acc.sing.neut.of δυνατός, predicate adjective) 1311.
κρατεῖσθαι (pres.pass.inf.of κρατέω, noun use, subject of ἦν) 828.
αὐτὸν (acc.sing.masc.of αὐτός, general reference) 16.
ὑπ' (preposition with the ablative of direct agent) 117.
αὐτοῦ (abl.sing.masc.of αὐτός, direct agent) 16.

Translation - ". . . Whom God raised up by putting an end to the pains of death, because that He should continue to be dominated by it was not possible."

Comment: The participle λύσας is modal. It tells us how God raised Jesus from the dead. The infinitive κρατεῖσθαι in the nominative case is the subject of ἦν. That Christ, Who is the resurrection and the life (John 1:4; 11:25) could be held bondage to death, which he deliberately accepted on the cross, after demonstrating that He could not be made its victim, is preposterous. He proved before He died in the physical sense that death was not great enough to take Him without His consent. The death that paid the wages for sin and redeemed the elect was the spiritual death which He suffered for three hours as the Father cast Him out in total loneliness, forsaken by God and man. When that was finished, there remained only physical death, which Jesus could have forestalled forever. Thus His victory over physical death was gained upon the cross and the impossibility that He could be held in its clutches and pains was demonstrated there, not at the empty tomb. *Cf.* our comments on John 10:17,18; Mt.27:50. The same predetermined plan that He should die decreed His resurrection from the dead. (Psalm 16:10).

Peter did not argue with his audience about Jesus' miracles, signs and wonders. They had witnessed those personally and had to admit that the miracles of Jesus were genuine. But note also that he did not argue about whether or not resurrection from the dead was possible. They had not seen that for Jesus revealed Himself after His resurrection only to His disciples. Peter did not seek to prove it. He only stated that it was true and dared the people to believe it. Before he told them that he and the other Christians present were ready to testify that they had seen Jesus alive after His death,(verse 32) he demonstrated that the resurrection of Christ was in fulfillment of Old Testament scripture (vss.25-31). It is obvious that if Jesus had not been alive as Peter said, the preacher should have been accused either of mendacity or insanity.

Verse 25 - "For David speaketh concerning him, I foresaw the Lord always before my face, for he is on my right hand, that I should not be moved."

Δαυὶδ γὰρ λέγει εἰς αὐτόν, Προορώμην τὸν κύριον ἐνώπιόν μου διὰ παντός, ὅτι ἐκ δεξιῶν μού ἐστιν ἵνα μὴ σαλευθῶ.

Δαυὶδ (nom.sing.masc.of Δαυίδ, subject of λέγει) 6.
γὰρ (explanatory conjunction) 105.
λέγει (3d.per.sing.pres.act.ind.of λέγω, historical) 66.
εἰς (preposition with the accusative, like a dative of reference) 140.
αὐτόν (acc.sing.masc.of αὐτός, like a dative of reference) 16.

#2993 προορώμην (1st.per.sing.imp.mid.ind.of προοράω, progressive duration).

see before - Acts 21:29.
foresee - Acts 2:25,31; Gal.3:8.

Meaning: A combination of πρό (#442) and ὁράω (#144). To see before the time; to foresee; to exercise προγνῶσις. With reference to David's prophecy in Psalm 16:8-11, cited by Peter in Acts 2:25,31. To read the future accurately and to take appropriate action - Gal.3:8. Properly with reference to a previous experience of seeing Paul - Acts 21:29.

τὸν (acc.sing.masc.of the article in agreement with κύριον) 9.
κύριον (acc.sing.masc.of κύριος, direct object of προορώμην) 97.
ἐνώπιόν (improper preposition with the genitive of place description) 1798.
μου (gen.sing.masc.of ἐγώ, place description) 123.
διὰ (preposition with the genitive of time description) 118.
παντός (gen.sing.neut.of πᾶς, time description) 67.
ὅτι (conjunction introducing a subordinate causal clause) 211.
ἐκ (preposition with the genitive of place description) 19.
δεξιῶν (gen.pl.neut.of δεξιός, place, idiomatic plural) 502.
μού (gen.sing.masc.of ἐγώ, place description) 123.
ἐστιν (3d.per.sing.pres.ind.of εἰμί, static) 86.
ἵνα (conjunction with the subjunctive, negative result) 114.
μὴ (qualified negative conjunction with the subjunctive, negative result) 87.
σαλευθῶ (1st.per.sing.1st.aor.pass.subj.of σαλεύω, negative result) 911.

Translation - "Now David spoke about Him: 'I always foresaw the Lord before my face at all times, because He is at my right hand, with the result that I will not be removed.' "

Comment: I have taken γὰρ in an explanatory sense, as Peter moves to a new phase in his sermon, in which he will show the connection between the history of Jesus' ministry and the Old Testament prophecy that predicted it.

Expository preaching is inadequate if it fails to present the written Word of God as well as the Living Word. Both the living Λόγος and the written Λόγος are supernaturally conceived, brought to birth and delivered by the Holy Spirit in cooperation with selected human beings. The Holy Spirit visited Mary and His power overshadowed her with the result that her son was called the Son of God (Luke 1:35). Thus the hypostatic union of the human and the divine in the incarnate Christ, when Jesus was born. God saw in Him an ideal man, and man sees in Him the ideal God. The same union of human and divine was involved when the Written Word was produced. The prophecies of the Old Testament were not devised by human wisdom, ". . . but holy men of God spake as they were moved by the Holy Spirit" (2 Peter.1:21). Just as the Holy Spirit fathered the human nature of Jesus in the womb of the virgin, to produce a dual natured Saviour, "the man Christ Jesus" (1 Tim.2:5), so He authored the literature of the Old and New Testaments in the minds of the authors to produce a written revelation which is human, in that it reveals the human literary characteristics of the men who wrote it, but which is also divine, in that its message is inerrant. The dignity and worth of the Written Word is not to be denigrated in comparison to the homage which we pay to the Living Word. It is only writing that is "God breathed" that is profitable, said Paul, as he warned Timothy against the written propaganda of incipient gnosticism and fully developed Judaistic legalism that was being circulated in Ephesus (2 Timothy 3:16,17). If only the scripture that has the breath of the living God as its Author is profitable, then we can safely ignore the Sears-Roebuck catalogue, the telephone directory, Plato's Republic, Norman Mailer and the editorial page of the Chicago Tribune. But we cannot safely ignore the Bible.

Our Lord spoke of Himself as "the Way, *THE TRUTH* and the Life" (John 14:6) and so He is. The same can be said for the Written Word. Had Jesus not gone back to heaven the New Testament would never have been written. He went back to glory in order that the Holy Spirit could fill the early Christians and inspire the Apostles and Luke to write the message which completed the revelation of God's truth which Jesus did not complete while He was here (John 16:12-15). Thus the revelation of the New Testament is a more complete revelation of divine truth than that which we have from the lips of Jesus.

Truth is characterized by its consistency, coherence and correspondence to reality. Jesus Christ was consistent, coherent and He was real. The same things can be said about the Bible. Error, propagated by the "father of lies" (John 8:44) is inconsistent, incoherent and unreal. The Bible is the only book that can set us straight. Since the Holy Spirit is the Author of both the Old and New Testaments, we may be certain that His personal traits of consistency, coherence and reality have been transmitted to the writings which He has inspired. These traits come through to the diligent student of the Word despite the human frailties of the authors through whose minds and pens the words were inscribed. Just as Jesus revealed the human characteristics of his mother, in all respects apart from sin, but also clearly revealed the evidence that He was God in human flesh, so the Written Word, reveals its deity, both in origin and impact upon the reader, while not concealing the literary idiosyncracies of the human authors. Consistency demands that what the Old Testament predicts, the New Testament records as history. It has often been said that "The New is in the Old contained and the Old is in the New explained." Evolution of religion in the Darwinian sense is a Satanic attack upon the supernatural origin of the Bible, but if by the evolution of religion is meant the gradual unfolding of the various components of the divine revelation the Christian is in full agreement. Even God could not reveal it all to us at once, not because of any limitation of His own but because of the limitation of the human mind to receive it all at once. The limitations of the student automatically constitute the same limitations of the teacher. No teacher can teach what his student cannot learn, however well he understands it himself. It is a problem in communication. Thus God chose to reveal the package of truth which now, since the completion of the New Testament (1 Cor.13:10), is the subject matter of the entire Word of God (Old and New Testaments) in keeping with His own formula - "first the blade, then the ear, after that the full corn in the ear" (Mark 4:28). Thus His Word does not return unto Him void of the results for which He gave it. The rain and snow falls and waters the earth. The sower sows the seed; thanks to the moisture in the soil the seed germinates and grows. The grain matures, is harvested, ground into flour and baked into bread. The bread is eaten. The entire process is accomplished beginning with the winter snows and the spring rains and ending with the digestive process of the eater and the strength which he derives from what he eats (Isa.55:8-11). There is continuity of purpose in the entire process. The rain and snow falls for the same reason that the sower sows, the thresher harvests, the miller grinds, the baker bakes and the eater eats. All of this is said to illustrate the fact that God's thoughts, purposes, policies and procedures are as superior to our own as the heavens is higher than the earth. The problem that God faced in revealing His truth to man was the same problem that He faced in arranging in creation the manner in which he would feed a hungry man a slice of toast for breakfast. The process unfolds a step at a time. No step can be omitted if the end is to be attained. All are of equal importance. "So shall my Word be . . . " (Isa.55:11).

The Holy Spirit Who is the divine Author of the Bible of course understands this principle completely. Thus Peter at Pentecost, filled with the power and presence of the Author of the Book which he was expounding pointed out to his audience the consistency, coherence and correspondance to reality of both the Living Word, Whom they had crucified, and the Written Word, only portions of which they had come to understand. The Bible is as supernatural as the Lord Jesus Christ. They had seen evidences that the Living Word was abundantly certified to be all that He claimed to be. Peter had challenged them to deny what they had seen of the miracles of Jesus and they had not accepted the challenge. Now it remained for them to understand that the same supernatural reality of the person and works of Jesus the carpenter from Nazareth was to be found in the Scriptures. Only God can predict with the amazing attention to even the smallest details events four hundred years before they occur, or in the case of the prophecy which Peter quotes on this occasion one thousand years. One inconsistency in the testimony of any part of the Bible with that of any other part — one clear case of incoherence, or one assertion that unreality is real, and the Holy Spirit stands convicted of having written a book that sensible men cannot accept. What He revealed to Abraham was supplemental to what He revealed to Adam and Eve but it was not contradictory. As the process of unfolding the perfect revelation went forward each new concept added to the completion of the symmetrical design of the whole, just as the gradual unfolding of the rose bud reveals the beauty of form and the ravishing aroma arising from balanced proportions. As God moved in human history to reveal His Word to man, each new revelation added to the accumulation already revealed, but without destroying its consistency or coherence. An onion that develops normally adds layer upon layer until its development is complete. No extraneous growths, which do not belong, develop. A perfectly constructed building erected upon a foundation will tolerate no stud, sill, rafter, bit of sheathing or siding that is asymmetrical. The perfect building is built like "the house of God," which is "built upon the foundation of the apostles and prophets, Jesus Christ himself being the chief corner stone, in whom all the building fitly framed together groweth unto an holy temple in the Lord, in Whom (Gentile Christians) also are builded together for an habitation of God through the Spirit" (Eph.2:19-22). Paul teaches the same thing with a different figure when he adds that when we speak the truth in love the church will ". . . grow up into him in all things, which is the head, even Christ, from whom the whole body fitly joined together and *compacted by that which every joint supplieth,* according to the effectual working in the measure of every part, maketh increase of the body unto the edifying of itself in love" (Eph.4:16-17). The idea is that as the revelation approaches completion — "when that which is complete has come" (1 Cor.13:10) — the entire structure becomes more compact until it achieves a solidity that is eternally viable, and that every new addition to the building, every two-by-four, every floor joist, every rafter, or, to change the figure, every organ of the body, contributes to this solidity. That is why though heaven and earth may pass away, God's Word will never pass away (Mt.24:35) Why? Because it is consistent, coherent and real. It contains nothing asymmetrical. There is no inner eccentricity. There is no civil war among or between its component parts. Jesus Christ is also the Truth (John 14:6). That is why He is the same, "yesterday, today and forever" (Heb.13:8).

It is even more important for modern preachers of the gospel to extol the supernatural perfection of the Bible than for Peter, because he had an advantage that is denied to us. He spoke to an audience who had seen and heard the Living Word. That the deity of Jesus was attested by God through His signs, wonders and miracles could not be denied by any man present. They had seen and heard Him. Peter took pains to point that out to them. The modern audience has not seen or heard Jesus personally. The generation that did is long since dead. So, just as Peter challenged his audience to believe in the resurrection of Jesus on faith, since none of them had witnessed it or seen Him after He arose, so we must challenge our audiences to believe not only in the resurrection of Christ, but also in the miracles which He performed and the philosophy of life which He taught. And how can we do that? Only by an appeal to the only book that contains these stories. The commitment of the sinner who has come to Christ for salvation in every age since the apostolic period comes down to this: is the Word of God true? Can what we read in the Bible be depended upon? The only reason that I believe that Jesus Christ raised Lazarus from the dead, turned water to wine and fed a multitude with a little boy's lunch and that He arose from the dead, is that the

Bible is true. This is my "leap of faith" commitment. I cannot ask Lazarus about his experience. I cannot ask the disciples if Jesus really walked upon the water. But I can examine a book, all of which was written at least 400 years before His birth and the rest written during the sixty five years following His death, resurrection and ascension. I can observe the manner in which it gradually unfolded a system of truth which is miraculously consistent, coherent and in touch with reality. I can see that parts of it which foretold specific events in minute detail hundreds of years before they happened are followed by other parts written centuries later which record the history of those same events replete with the same minute details. This is a miracle, as great as the resurrection of Lazarus or the feeding of a hungry multitude.

But for many audiences in the modern institutional church there is not this understanding, nor even the invitation to conduct such research, because the sermons which they hear are not Biblical expositions such as Peter preached at Pentecost. Rather they are religious lectures in which the opinions of the preacher are substituted for the precepts of the Bible, with only an occasional and in many cases totally inapt allusion to some remote Old Testament passage of scripture. Peter was saying, "Christ is risen from the dead, and you should have been expecting it, since it was prophesied in your Bible one thousand years ago." Of course, Peter did not know it either, any more than those in his audience on the day that it occurred, but since then He had seen Jesus, talked with Him, had breakfast with Him when they ate fish that Peter couldn't catch and above all been filled with the Holy Spirit which did a great deal to "stir up (his) pure mind(s) by way of remembrance" (2 Peter 3:1). If we are to look to Peter's sermon at Pentecost as a guide to what Spirit inspired preaching is and how we can preach effectively, we must note that Peter connected the message of the Old Testament with that of the New in a way that demonstrated the same hypostatic union of deity and humanity in the Written Word that is seen in the Living Word.

God's decrees are firmly established and unchangeable. His foreknowledge is total. That Jesus should therefore rise from the dead following His death, which was decreed for the purpose of redemption, was inevitable since, in the nature of the case, it was impossible for Jesus to remain in the tomb. He engaged in physical death by an exercise of His own will (Mt.27:50; John 10:17,18) and thereby proved that He was not unwillingly victimized by it. Physical death has never been greater than Jesus Christ. Why, then should it be thought incredible "that God should raise the dead?" (Acts 26:8). What is incredible about it? Since these are facts and God's plans suffer no frustration David, under inspiration wrote the 16th Psalm. His prophecy was the result of the logic of the problem, given the premises with which the Christian begins. The Son of God must die. The Son of God is greater than physical death. Therefore the Son of God must rise from the dead. The third statement must follow logically from the first two. But we can also say that David's prophecy was the cause of Jesus' resurrection, since David was speaking under guidance of the Holy Spirit Who cannot misstate the facts of history nor falsely predict the facts of the future. In other words, God raised Jesus from the dead because God had inspired David to write that He would. The history that is written under divine inspiration is accurate and the prophecy written under divine inspiration is certain to be fulfilled. God wrote Psalm 16 because His foreknowledge made the fulfillment certain. It was certain because it was a part of His plan. It was also certain because the Eternal Λόγος is greater than physical death.

The problem we mortals face in an analysis of this sort lies in the fact that we are subject to the categories of time and space, to which categories God is not subject. It is impossible for us to think of cause and result relationships without also assigning to them points in time. Result must always follow cause, in the nature of the case. And when we use the word "follow" we inject into our thought the passage of time. Thus results come *after* causes. But God is not subject to the time category. He knows nothing of time in the sense in which we think of it. God never waits; nor does He ever hasten. Such words are meaningless to the One Who lives forever in the Eternal Present tense. God has neither watch, nor sundial nor calendar. He does not know what *time* it is. Thus the prophecy that Jesus would not continue to suffer the pains of death and the fact that He did not are all one and the same event to God, although for us they are separated by a thousand years.

The speaker in Psalm 16:8-11 is not David, but Christ. He says that He has always foreseen the Lord before Him through every exigency and/or untoward circumstance. Note Mt.18:10; Mk.5:5; Lk.24:53 for other instances of διὰ παντός in a temporal sense, meaning, "throughout all times." This statement could not have been made if Messiah had been consigned to eternal death, since such death would have meant an end to His eternal vision. Why are the two always in the presence of each other? Because God is always at His right hand. With what result? That Christ should not be removed from His ascended position in glory (Ps.110:1). Was Jesus ever worried about it? Never, because of His continuous prevision of the unbroken fellowship between Him and the Father that transcended even the agony of His death. The results of His eternal prescience is found in verse 26.

Note ἵνα here with the subjunctive in a result clause. "Grammarians have been reluctant to admit this use of ἵνα. But J. H. Moulton and A. T. Robertson, who at first stood against admitting the consecutive force of ἵνα, came to do so later. . . Again we find ἵνα used in result clauses, when it is translatable *so that*, but this usage is rare and it is a late Koine development (*cf.* Jn.9:2, 'Rabbi, who sinned, this man or his parents, *so that* he was born blind?' Rev.3:9, 'Behold I will make them ἵνα ἥξουσιν καὶ προσκυνήσουσιν ἐνώπιον τῶν ποδῶν σου, *so that they will come and worship before thy feet*' (see also Gal.5:17; 1 Jn. 1:9; Rev.9:20). We agree with Abbott-Smith's statement in his *Lexicon:* 'In late writers, ecbatic, denoting result equals ὥστε, *that, so that:* Rom.11:11; 1 Cor.7:29; 1 Ths.5:4; al.; so with the formula referring to the fulfillment of prophecy, ἵνα πληρωθῇ; Mt.1:22; 2:14; 4:14; Jn.13:8.' " (Mantey, *Manual*, 286, 249). "The use of ἵνα has been sharply disputed (*i.e.* to indicate pure result) but gradually modern grammarians have come to admit the actual ecbatic use of ἵνα in the New Testament like the Latin *ut* and as is certainly true in modern Greek." (Robertson, *Short Grammar,* 10th Edition, 346). *Cf.* also Robertson, *Grammar*, 997,998.

Verse 26 - "Therefore did my heart rejoice, and my tongue was glad; moreover also my flesh shall rest in hope."

διὰ τοῦτο ηὐφράνθη ἡ καρδία μου καὶ ἠγαλλιάσατο ἡ γλῶσσά μου, ἔτι δὲ καὶ ἡ σάρξ μου κατασκηνώσει ἐπ᾽ ἐλπίδι,

διὰ (preposition with the accusative, cause) 118.
τοῦτο (acc.sing.neut.of οὗτος, cause) 93.
ηὐφράνθη (3d.per.sing.1st.aor.pass.ind.of εὐφραίνω, constative) 2479.
ἡ (nom.sing.fem.of the article in agreement with καρδία) 9.
καρδία (nom.sing.fem.of καρδία, subject of ηὐφράνθη) 432.
μου (gen.sing.masc.of ἐγώ, possession) 123.
καὶ (continuative conjunction) 14.
ἠγαλλιάσατο (3d.per.sing.aor.mid.ind.of ἀγαλλιάω, constative) 440.
ἡ (nom.sing.fem.of the article in agreement with γλῶσσά) 9.
γλῶσσά (nom.sing.fem.of γλῶσσα, subject of ἠγαλλιάσατο) 1846.
μου (gen.sing.masc.of ἐγώ, possession) 123.
ἔτι (temporal adverb) 448.
δὲ (continuative conjunction) 11.
καὶ (ascensive conjunction) 14.
ἡ (nom.sing.fem.of the article in agreement with σάρξ) 9.
σάρξ (nom.sing.fem.of σάρξ, subject of κατασκηνώσει) 1202.
μου (gen.sing.masc.of ἐγώ, possession) 123.
κατασκηνώσει (3d.per.sing.fut.act.ind.of κατασκηνόω, predictive) 1070.
ἐπ᾽ (preposition with the instrumental of cause) 47.

#2994 ἐλπίδι (instru.sing.fem.of ἐλπίς, cause).

hope - Acts 2:26; 16:19; 23:6; 24:15; 26:6,7; 27:20; 28:20; Rom.4:18,18; 5:2,4,5; 8:20,24,24,24; 12:12; 15:4,13,13; 1 Cor.9:10,10; 13:13; 2 Cor.1:7; 3:12; 10:15; Gal.5:5; Eph.1;18; 2:12; 4:4; Phil.1:20; Col.1:5,23,27; 1 Thess.1:3; 2:19; 4:13; 5:8; 2 Thess.2:16; 1 Tim.1:1; Titus 1:2; 2:13; 3:7; Heb.3:6; 6:11,18; 7:19; 1 Peter 1:3,21; 3:15; 1 John 3:3.
faith - Heb.10:23.

Meaning: Cf.ἐλπίζω (#991). Assurance. Confident expectation. Related to πίστις (#728) and in some contexts apparently synonymous with it, but joined with πίστις, and therefore not synonymous in 1 Cor.13:13; 1 Thess.1:3; 5:8; 1 Pet.1:21. I. Followed by a genitive of description and meaning (1) money - Acts 16:19; (2) the resurrection of the body - Acts 23:6; 1 John 3:3; (3) Jewish nationalism - Acts 26:6,7; 28:20; (4) the glory of God - Rom.5:2; Col.1:21; (5) imputed righteousness - Gal.5:5; (6) the fulfillment of God's calling - Eph.1:18; 4:4; (7) the gospel - Col.1:23; (8) eternal life - Titus 1:2; 3:7; (9) salvation - 1 Thess.5:8. II. Followed by the infinitive - (1) of the resurrection - Acts 24:15; (2) of rescue from drowning - Acts 27:20; (3) of receiving money - 2 Cor.10;15. III. Followed by ὅτι and joined to ἀποκαραδοκίαν (#3938) - Phil.1:20; IV. With the instrumental case - Acts 2:26; Rom.4:18b; 8:20 (resurrection), 24a; 12:12; 15:13b;

174   *The Renaissance New Testament*   Acts 2:26,27

1 Cor.9:10a,b. V. As a direct object - Rom.5:4; 15:4; 2 Cor.3:12; Eph.2:12; Col.1:5; 1 Thess.1:3; 4:13; Heb.6:18; 2 Thess.2:16; Tit.2:13; 1 John 3:3. With παρά - Rom.4:18a. VI. as subject or predicate nominative and indicating a confident expectation that grows out of saving faith - Rom.5:5; 8;24b,c; 1 Cor.13:13 (where it occurs with πίστις); 2 Cor.1:7, where it refers to Paul's confidence in the Corinthian saints - 1 Thess.2:19; 4:13 (where it is clearly synonymous with πίστις); 1 Tim.1:1; 1 Peter 1:21; 3:15. VII. As a genitive of description - Rom.15:13a; Heb.3:6; 6:11; 7:19; Heb.10:23. VIII. Followed by εἰς - "unto a living hope" - 1 Peter 1:3.

Translation - "Because of this my heart was filled with joy and my tongue was glad; and even my flesh will live because of hope."

Comment: διὰ τοῦτο is causal, as Christ points back to the assurances of verse 25 as the reason for the joy in His heart, the gladness of His tongue and the hope for His flesh. The eternal purpose of God, which planned the death of His Son, in order to achieve redemption for the members of His body, will not be frustrated by permanent death. When Christ was buried He was armed with this assurance and thus his burial was only a temporary "bedding down." *Cf.*#1070. Faith in the inevitable execution of God's will brings joy in the heart, praise to the tongue and hope that gives rest to the flesh. Verse 27 now gives us the basis for His hope.

Verse 27 - "Because thou wilt not leave my soul in hell, neither wilt thou suffer thine Holy One to see corruption."

ὅτι οὐκ ἐγκαταλείψεις τὴν ψυχήν μου εἰς ᾅδην, οὐδὲ δώσεις τὸν ὅσιόν σου ἰδεῖν διαφθοράν.

ὅτι (conjunction introducing a subordinate causal clause) 211.
οὐκ (summary negative conjunction with the indicative) 130.
ἐγκαταλείψεις (2d.per.sing.fut.act.ind.of ἐγκαταλείπω, predictive) 1654.
τὴν (acc.sing.fem.of the article in agreement with ψυχήν) 9.
ψυχήν (acc.sing.fem.of ψυχή, direct object of ἐγκαταλείψεις) 233.
μου (gen.sing.masc.of ἐγώ, possession) 123.
εἰς (preposition with the accusative, like a locative of place) 140.
ᾅδην (acc.sing.fem.of ᾅδης, locative use, place) 947.
οὐδὲ (disjunctive particle) 452.
δώσεις (2d.per.sing.fut.act.ind.of δίδωμι, predictive) 362.
τὸν (acc.sing.masc.of the article in agreement with ὅσιόν) 9.

#2995 ὅσιόν (acc.sing.masc.of ὅσιος, general reference).

holy - 1 Tim.2:8; Tit.1:8; Heb.7:26; Rev.15:4.
Holy One - Acts 2:27; 13:35.
mercies - Acts 13:34.
not translated - Rev.16:5.

Meaning: As an adjective - holy. As a noun - Holy One. As a predicate adjective, describing God - Rev.15:4; Christ - Heb.7:26; bishops - Titus 1:8. As an attributive adjective - 1 Tim.2:8; As a noun in a reference to Christ - Acts 2:27; 13:34,34; Rev.16:5.

σου (gen.sing.masc.of σύ, relationship) 104.

ἰδεῖν (aor.act.inf.of ὁράω, epexegetical) 144.

#2996 διαφθοράν (acc.sing.fem.of διαφθορά, direct object of ἰδεῖν).

corruption - Acts 2:27,31; 13:34,35,36,37.

Meaning: A combination of διά (#118) and φθορά(#3942). *Cf.* also διαφθείρω (#2485). The total chemical disintegration of the human body after death. Biodegradability. David's body suffered it - Acts 13:36; Jesus did not - Acts 2:27,31; 13:34,35,37.

Translation - "Because you will not forsake my soul in Hades, neither will you allow your Holy One to experience decomposition."

Comment: The ὅτι clause is causal. This is why Jesus relaxed during His brief stay in Paradise. *Cf.*#1654. God did forsake Him on the cross (Mt.27:46; Mk.15:34), but He did not forsake Him in Paradise. Had Jesus not paid the extreme penalty for sin upon the cross, He would not have been taken out of Paradise and His body would have decomposed in the tomb. "He was delivered because of our sin and He was raised again because of our justification" (Rom.4:25). Note the οὐκ . . . οὐδὲ sequence. Jesus was indeed God's Holy One. *cf.* Heb.7:26 and many other passages supporting the sinlessness of Jesus. Paul used the same argument, here advanced by Peter in Acts 13:34,35,36,37. David's body did decompose, but the body of Jesus did not. Some have pointed out that Lazarus' body had begun to decompose as he had been dead four days (John 11:39). It was approximately 39 hours from the time of the death of Jesus to the time of His resurrection.

The Jews who heard Peter that day were familiar with the 16th Psalm but they had never heard it expounded like that. One wonders what they thought the language meant?

Verse 28 - "Thou hast made known to me the ways of life; thou shalt make me full of joy with thy countenance."

ἐγνώρισάς μοι ὁδοὺς ζωῆς, πληρώσεις με εὐφροσύνης μετὰ τοῦ προσώπου σου.

ἐγνώρισάς (2d.per.sing.1st.aor.act.ind.of γνωρίζω, culminative) 1882.

μοι (dat.sing.masc.of ἐγώ, indirect object of ἐγνώρισάς) 123.

ὁδοὺς (acc.pl.fem.of ὁδός, direct object of ἐγνώρισάς) 199.

ζωῆς (gen.sing.fem.of ζωή, description) 668.

πληρώσεις (2d.per.sing.fut.act.ind.of πληρόω, predictive) 115.

με (acc.sing.masc.of ἐγώ, direct object of πληρώσεις) 123.

#2997 εὐφροσύνης (abl.sing.fem.of εὐφροσύνη, source).

gladness - Acts 14:17.
joy - Acts 2:28.

Meaning: Cf.εὔφρων - "well disposed mentally." "cheerful." Hence, good cheer, joy, gladness. With reference to Jesus - Acts 2:28. Of pagan nations - Acts 14:17.

μετὰ (preposition with the ablative of means) 50.
τοῦ (abl.sing.neut.of the article in agreement with προσώπου) 9.
προσώπου (abl.sing.neut.of πρόσωπον, means) 588.
σου (gen.sing.masc.of σύ, possession) 104.

Translation - "*You revealed to me living paths; you will fill me out of your joy by means of your countenance.*"

Comment: A past and future tense action by the Father. He had already revealed to Him the living ways and He will always fill Him with joy because Christ will always be in the presence of the Father. No one but God really knows anything about life and the paths in which it can be found. Adam's race knows only of death, misery and gloom. There is joy only in the presence of God. The living ways are known to us only as God reveals them.

Peter must now show that David was not speaking of himself, but of Jesus. That David did not rise from the dead, but rather suffered decomposition was obvious, as Peter goes on to show in

Verse 29 - "*Men and brethren, let me freely speak unto you of the patriarch David, that he is both dead and buried, and his sepulchre is with us unto this day.*"

Ἄνδρες ἀδελφοί, ἐξὸν εἰπεῖν μετὰ παρρησίας πρὸς ὑμᾶς περὶ τοῦ πατριάρχου Δαυίδ, ὅτι καὶ ἐτελεύτησεν καὶ ἐτάφη καὶ τὸ μνῆμα αὐτοῦ ἐστιν ἐν ἡμῖν ἄρχι τῆς ἡμέρας ταύτης.

Ἄνδρες (voc.pl.masc.of ἀνήρ, address) 63.
ἀδελφοί (voc.pl.masc.of ἀδελφός, address) 15.
ἐξὸν (pres.part.imper.nom.sing.neut.of ἔξεστι, aoristic) 966.
εἰπεῖν (aor.act.inf.of εἶπον, epexegetical) 155.
μετὰ (preposition with the genitive of means) 50.
παρρησίας (gen.sing.fem.of παρρησία, means) 2319.
πρὸς (preposition with the accusative of extent, after a verb of speaking) 197.
ὑμᾶς (acc.pl.masc.of σύ, extent after a verb of speaking) 104.
περὶ (preposition with the genitive of reference) 173.
τοῦ (gen.sing.masc.of the article in agreement with πατριάρχου) 9.

#2998 πατριάρχου (gen.sing.masc.of πατριάρχης, reference).

patriarch - Acts 2:29; 7:8,9; Heb.7:4.

Meaning: Cf. πατρία (#1870) and ἄρχω (#383). Hence the ruler of a family. Clan leader. With reference to David - Acts 2:29; the twelve sons of Jacob - Acts 7:8,9. Abraham - Heb.7:4.

Δαυίδ (gen.sing.masc.of Δαυίδ, in apposition) 6.
ὅτι (conjunction introducing an object clause in indirect discourse) 211.
ἐτελεύτησεν (3d.per.sing.aor.act.ind.of τελευτάω, culminative) 231.
ἐτελεύτησεν (3d.per.sing.aor.act.ind.of τελευτάω, culminative) 231.
καὶ (correlative conjunction) 14.
ἐτάφη (3d.per.sing.2d.aor.pass.ind.of θάπτω, culminative) 748.
καὶ (continuative conjunction) 14.
τὸ (nom.sing.neut.of the article in agreement with μνῆμα) 9.
μνῆμα (nom.sing.neut.of μνῆμα, subject of ἔστιν) 2876.
αὐτοῦ (gen.sing.masc.of αὐτός, possession) 16.
ἔστιν (3d.per.sing.pres.ind.of εἰμί, aoristic) 86.
ἐν (preposition with the locative with plural pronouns, place where) 80.
ἡμῖν (loc.pl.masc.of ἐγώ, place where) 123.
ἄχρι (preposition with the genitive of time description) 1517.
τῆς (gen.sing.fem.of the article in agreement with ἡμέρας) 9.
ἡμέρας (gen.sing.fem.of ἡμέρα, time description) 135.
ταύτης (gen.sing.fem.of οὗτος, in agreement with ἡμέρας) 93.

Translation - "Men and brethren, it is necessary for me to tell you without reservation with reference to David that he is both dead and buried and his crypt is with us unto this day."

Comment: ὅτι with the object clause in indirect discourse. Peter wishes to be understood clearly as he talks about David. μετὰ παρρησίας - "without reservation" or "with clarity." David is both dead and buried. No one in the audience was likely to doubt that part of Peter's sermon. In verse 30, Peter builds his case. David was dead, but David was in possession of a promise — an unconditional covenant that could be fulfilled only if Christ arose from the dead.

Verse 30 - "Therefore being a prophet, and knowing that God had sworn with an oath to him, that of the fruit of his loins, according to the flesh, he would raise up Christ to sit on his throne."

προφήτης οὖν ὑπάρχων, καί εἰδὼς ὅτι ὅρκῳ ὤμοσεν αὐτῷ ὁ θεὸς ἐκ καρποῦ τῆς ὀσφύος αὐτοῦ καθίσαι ἐπὶ τὸν θρόνον αὐτοῦ,

προφήτης (nom.sing.masc.of προφήτης, predicate nominative) 119.
οὖν (adversative conjunction) 68.
ὑπάρχων (pres.act.part.nom.sing.masc.of ὑπάρχω, adverbial, causal) 1303.
καὶ (adjunctive conjunction joining participles) 14.
εἰδὼς (pres.act.part.nom.sing.masc.of οἶδα, adverbial, causal) 144.
ὅτι (conjunction introducing an object clause in indirect discourse) 211.
ὅρκῳ (instru.sing.masc.of ὅρκος, means) 515.
ὤμοσεν (3d.per.sing.aor.act.ind.of ὄμνυμι, culminative) 516.
αὐτῷ (dat.sing.masc.of αὐτός, indirect object of ὤμοσεν) 16.

ὁ (nom.sing.masc.of the article in agreement with θεὸς) 9.
θεὸς (nom.sing.masc.of θεός, subject of ὤμοσεν) 124.
ἐκ (preposition with the partitive genitive) 19.
καρπου (gen.sing.masc.of καρπός, partitive) 284.
τῆς (gen.sing.fem.of the article in agreement with ὀσφύος) 9.
ὀσφύος (abl.sing.fem.of ὀσφύς, source) 265.
αὐτοῦ (gen.sing.masc.of αὐτός, possession) 16.
καθίσαι (aor.act.inf.of καθίζω, epexegetical) 420.
ἐπὶ (preposition with the accusative, place) 47.
τὸν (acc.sing.masc.of the article in agreement with θρόνον) 9.
θρόνον (acc.sing.masc.of θρόνος, extent, place) 519.
αὐτοῦ (gen.sing.masc.of αὐτός, possession) 16.

Translation - "However, since he was a prophet and because he knew that God had sworn to him with an oath to select one of his descendants to sit upon his throne . . . "

Comment: "The Hebraic use of the phrase ἐκ καρποῦ as a noun, the object of καθίσαι, is extremely harsh in Greek and has given rise to various explanatory expansions (derived perhaps from 2 Sm 7.12). Thus, before καθίσαι D_gr* inserts κατὰ σάρκα ἀναστῆσαι τὸν Χριστὸν καί, and the Textus Receptus, following P 049 056 0142 most minuscules *Lect* it_d syr_h cop G67 *al*, reads τὸ κατὰ σάρκα ἀναστήσειν τὸν Χριστόν." (Metzger, *A Textual Commentary on the Greek New Testament*, 299). That the one who is described as ὁ καρπὸς τῆς ὀσφύος αὐτοῦ is Christ is clear when we compare 2 Samuel 7:14 with Heb.1:5, so it was not necessary for the editors to write explanations into the text which the more ancient manuscripts did not have. In many cases the Word of God is in more danger in the hands of its friends than in the hands of its enemies.

The thought is this: David, the author of the 16th Psalm, which contains the promise of the resurrection of Christ, which Peter has already cited, had his own covenant promise from the Lord (2 Sam.7:12-17; Ps.132:11) about the perpetuity of his throne and the eternal reign of David's Son Who would sit upon it (2 Sam.7:12-14; Heb.1:5; Luke 1:30-33). But (adversative οὖν) although David was dead and buried (vs.29) (a) he was a prophet and (b) he was aware of the covenant promise of 2 Samuel 7, as a sworn oath from God to him. Thus, though David knew that he would not live to sit forever upon his own throne, since his own death was mentioned in 2 Samuel 7:12, he knew that someone of his heirs, though He would first die for our sins (2 Sam.7:14,15) would be raised again from the dead. Otherwise the kingly dynasty, vested in David and in his seed, would have ended when the Jewish Establishment killed Jesus, and the throne rights of David would have been lost for the want of a legitimate heir to inherit them. The only legitimate heir to David's throne was Jesus, who died without issue. Since Israel crucified her King (John 19:15) before He could marry and pass the throne rights down to His firstborn son, the nation would never have a King and the nationalistic hopes for a future Israel were forevcer forfeited, unless God intervened and raised Jesus from the dead. The two participles are causal. ὅτι and the object clause in indirect discourse. Here is another of Luke's "cognate instrumentals." *Cf.* our discussion of it in comment on Acts 2:17. ἐκ καρποῦ τῆς ὀσφύος αὐτοῦ - a Hebraism - "one of his descendants." David had a great many descendants, but the problem arose when the only One with a valid legal claim to the throne did not marry and was murdered on a cross. In that case the only solution, if God's promise to David was to be kept, was resurrection from the dead. David was not only a prophet. He was also a logician. He faced the same problem as that confronting Abraham when he was told to kill Isaac, when the boy was too young to have a son. Abraham thought that through just as David later did and did not hesitate to carry out the order because he knew that God was able to raise him from the dead (Heb.11:17-19). We have, not only the word of the author of Hebrews for this, but Abraham's word as well, for he said to his servants, "Abide ye here with the ass, and I and the lad will go yonder and worship and come again to you." (Genesis 22:5) The verbs "go," "worship" and "come again" are all plural. Abraham said, "Two of us will go; two of us will worship and *two of us* will come back to you."

We can state the problem in a different way. One set of God's prophetic oaths to Old Testament patriarchs has Messiah reigning forever in righteousness as the Seed of Abraham, Isaac, Jacob, Judah and David, upon David's throne. Another set of God's promises has Messiah being offered at Calvary for the sins of the race. Since a dead Messiah and an eternally reigning Messiah constitute conflicting ideas, the dilemma must be resolved. And so it was, by the resurrection of Messiah from the dead. This is precisely what Peter added in

Verse 31 - "He, seeing this before, spoke of the resurrection of Christ, that his soul was not left in hell, neither his flesh did see corruption."

προϊδὼν ἐλάλησεν περὶ τῆς ἀναστάσεως τοῦ Χριστοῦ ὅτι οὔτε ἐγκατελείφθη εἰς ᾅδην οὔτε ἡ σὰρξ αὐτοῦ εἶδεν διαφθοράν.

προϊδὼν (2d.aor.act.part.nom.sing.masc.of προοράω, adverbial, causal) 2993.

ἐλάλησεν (3d.per.sing.aor.act.ind.of λαλέω, constative) 815.

περὶ (preposition with the genitive of reference) 173.

τῆς (gen.sing.fem.of the article in agreement with ἀναστάσεως) 9.

ἀναστάσεως (gen.sing.fem.of ἀνάστασις, reference) 1423.

τοῦ (gen.sing.masc.of the article in agreement with Χριστοῦ) 9.

Χριστοῦ (gen.sing.masc.of Χριστός, designation) 3.

ὅτι (recitative) 211.

οὔτε (negative correlative conjunction) 598.

ἐγκατελείφθη (3d.per.sing.aor.pass.ind.of ἐγκαταλείπω, culminative) 1654.

εἰς (preposition with the accusative, like a locative of place) 140.

ᾅδην (acc.sing.fem.of ᾅδης, like a locative) 947.

οὔτε (negative correlative conjunction) 598.

ἡ (nom.sing.fem.of the article in agreement with σάρξ) 9.

σὰρξ (nom.sing.fem.of σάρξ, subject of εἶδεν) 1202.

αὐτοῦ (gen.sing.masc.of αὐτός, possession) 16.

εἶδεν (3d.per.sing.aor.act.ind.of ὁράω, culminative) 144.

διαφθοράν (acc.sing.fem.of διαφθορά, direct object of εἶδεν) 2996.

Translation - "Because he foresaw this he spoke about the resurrection of Christ, 'He was neither deserted in Hades, nor did His flesh decompose.' "

Comment: The aorist participle is causal. It was because David foresaw the trend of events which grew with deductive logic out of the other elements in the picture that He spoke about the resurrection of Christ in Psalm 16:8-11. The promise of the eternal reign of Messiah upon his throne was clearer to David than his foresight into Messiah's death. The former he had from the mouth of the prophet Nathan in 2 Samuel 7:10-17. Although there is a veiled reference to Messiah's death and resurrection in verses 14,15 it is not likely that David understood that part of the prophecy as well as he did verses 12,13. David's Psalm 22 prophesies Christ's death with amazing detail, and David may have wondered what all of that language meant. So we cannot decide how much of David's conclusion that Messiah would rise from the dead was the result of his analyticial reasoning arrived at discursively, and to what extent he spoke at direct divine inspiration, without understanding the import of what he said (1 Peter 1:10-12). David probably did not understand how the divine *gestalt* fit together as well as Peter did, since Peter had the advantage of hindsight just as we do today. A little empirical evidence goes a long way to make us see what we should have been able to see before the prophecy was fulfilled. The story is an apt illustration of how the deductive and inductive methods complement each other. As William James said, "Truth happens to an idea." *Cf.* John Dewey, "The Process of Scientific Thinking," from Chapters 6, 7 and 11 of *How We Think*, revised edition, 1933. The Neo-Platonists carried discursion too far (*e.g.* Dionysius the Areopagite, *The Divine Names and The Mystical Theology*, Rolt translation) while the radical empiricists have gone too far in the direction of the opposite extreme, as a result of their wholesale misunderstanding of Dewey's thought. (*Cf.* J. Oliver Buswell, Jr., *The Philosophies of F. R. Tennant and John Dewey*. New York: Philosophical Library).

Peter told his audience that Psalm 16 is the logical outgrowth of all of the elements contained in 2 Samuel 7:11-17.   David had the help of divine inspiration. The prophet Nathan was inspired when he gave the covenant promise to David, and David was inspired when He wrote Psalms 11 and 22, among others. Peter also was inspired at Pentecost, as a result of the filling of the Holy Spirit. Thus he had supernatural help plus the advantage of hindsight to which we have referred. His exposition is brilliantly deductive. Now the question arises — did what must occur actually occur? Empirical expression must happen to a true idea. False predictions do not happen. True predictions do. It is logical to expect Jesus to die (2 Samuel 7:14,15) and to rise again (2 Samuel 7:12). Did He, in historic fact, arise? How does a scientist validate an empirical fact? Sense perception. Witnesses! Peter is ready with the evidence in

Verse 32 - "This Jesus hath God raised up, whereof we all are witnesses."

τοῦτον τὸν Ἰησοῦν ἀνέστησεν ὁ θεός, οὗ πάντες ἡμεῖς ἐσμεν μάρτυρες.

τοῦτον (acc.sing.masc.of οὗτος, in agreement with Ἰησοῦν) 93.

τὸν (acc.sing.masc.of the article in agreement with Ἰησοῦν) 9.

Ἰησοῦν (acc.sing.masc.of Ἰησοῦς, direct object of ἀνέστησεν) 3.

ἀνέστησεν (3d.per.sing.aor.act.ind.of ἀνίστημι, culminative) 789.

ὁ (nom.sing.masc.of the article in agreement with θεός) 9.

θεός (nom.sing.masc.of θεός, subject of ἀνέστησεν) 124.

οὗ (gen.sing.neut.of ὅς, reference) 65.

πάντες (nom.pl.masc.of πᾶς, in agreement with ἡμεῖς) 67.

ἡμεῖς (nom.pl.masc.of ἐγώ, subject ofd ἐσμεν) 123.

ἐσμεν (1st.per.pl.pres.ind.of εἰμί, aoristic) 86.

μάρτυρες (nom.pl.masc.of μάρτυς, predicate nominative) 1263.

Translation - "This Jesus God raised up, with reference to which fact all of us are witnesses."

Comment: τοῦτον is deictic. It points us back to Ἰησοῦν of verse 22. Peter emphasized the identity of the One resurrected ahead of the fact of resurrection itself. The definite relative οὗ can be taken as a genitive of possession (descriptiopn, designation) and in reference to Ἰησοῦν, as Goodspeed has translated - ". . . and to whose resurrection we are all witnesses" or it can be taken as a genitive of reference in reference to the fact of the resurrection. The pronoun must agree with its antecedent in number and gender. Since οὗ is both masculine and neuter the point cannot be decided. If masculine its antecedent is Ἰησοῦν. If neuter it refers to the fact of the resurrection, which supports our translation. In either case the interpretation is the same. Peter and his Christian friends of whom more than 500 could be assembled were ready to testify that they had seen Jesus dead and had later seen Him alive. With this the audience must either take Peter's word for it or reject it, since Peter could not produce the resurrected Jesus whom they had seen - not because He was not resurrected, but because He was not available, having taken His place at God's right hand ten days before. The people who were saved that day had seen some or all of Jesus' miracles and they had heard Him preach, but no one converted that day could testify that he had seen Jesus alive after His crucifixion. That they were compelled to accept as a result of Peter's witness. And that is precisely what good preaching does. It witnesses to what the preacher knows by experience as well as by faith. And in that way faith is granted to the elect. "Faith comes by hearing, and hearing by the Word of God." (Rom.10:17).The testimony of experience is stronger than the conclusions of faulty logic. The story is told of Parmenides, who had no faith in experience but total faith in reason, that he heard the Apostle John say, "And I saw a mighty angel come down from heaven . . . and he set his right foot upon the sea, and his left foot on the earth" (Rev.10:1,2) and rejected John's statement on the ground that it was not reasonable that an angel could set one foot upon the land and the other upon the sea. But when John remonstrated, "But I saw it!" Parmenides said, "Very well. If you *saw* it, it must have happened."

Up to this point Peter had confined his remarks to an exposition of the story of the supernatural life of Jesus (vs.22) and its connection with Psalm 16:8-11 and 2 Samuel 7:11-17. Aside from the fact that he was speaking with a verve, eclat and aplomb that would have put the best educated scribe in Jerusalem to shame, there was nothing really startling about it until he said, "Jesus is alive, just as Psalm 16 predicted and we know it because there are 120 of us here today who saw Him alive after His death." And he could have added that if that did not convince them, he could go out and find more than 380 more witnesses who also had seen Him. This bold declaration that the people in the audience were not dealing with a dead hero but with a living Saviour and/or Judge gave them pause. If Jesus is dead then all of the adoration and adulation which we bring to His tomb and dedicate to His memory cannot help us solve our problem of soul sorrow, nor need we fear His judgment if we spit on His grave. The Kuklux Klan and other Nazi disciples can get no help from Adolf Hitler, and the decent people in the world who opposed him can forget about any possible retribution which he might exact. Because Adolf Hitler is dead. He shot himself in the mouth as Russian shells were falling upon his underground bunker in Berlin on 30 April 1945 and then blasted what was left of the charred remains of his carcass into bits as his valet S. S. Sturmbannfuehrer Heinz Linge, and an orderly carried his body out to the garden of the Chancellery. An Army field-gray blanket concealed the shattered face. (William L. Shirer, *The Rise and Fall of the Third Reich*, 1133,1134). It was twelve years and three months to a day "since he had become Chancellor of Germany and had instituted the Third Reich. It would survive him but a week." Dead men tell no tales and give vent to no revenge. But the One Who is greater than death and Who proved it by surviving it, never again to die (Romans 6:9,10) had better be taken into account if one is interested in personal viability under conditions that please him. Peter's audience showed great interest in what Peter said from the beginning. The element of godly fear suggested itself to them when Peter spoke of the resurrection. The preacher who cannot tell his audience that Jesus Christ is alive has nothing really unique to say, and had better be gracious enough to stop boring them.

Our Lord's resurrection and ascension to glory was connected with the filling of the Holy Spirit which the Christians had received, the results of which filling included the miraculous language demonstration which they had witnessed. This is the thought of

Verse 33 - "Therefore being by the right hand of God exalted, and having received of the Father the promise of the Holy Ghost, he hath shed forth this, which ye now see and hear."

τῇ δεξιᾷ οὖν τοῦ θεοῦ ὑφωθεὶς τήν τε ἐπαγγελίαν τοῦ πνεύματος τοῦ ἁγίου λαβὼν παρὰ τοῦ πατρὸς ἐξέχεεν τοῦτο ὃ ὑμεῖς (καὶ) βλέπετε καὶ ἀκούετε.

τῇ (loc.sing.fem.of the article in agreement with δεξιᾷ) 9.
δεξιᾷ (loc.sing.fem.of δεξιός, place) 502.
οὖν (inferential conjunction) 68.
τοῦ (gen.sing.masc.of the article in agreement with θεοῦ) 9.

θεοῦ (gen.sing.masc.of θεός, possession) 124.

ὑφωθείς (aor.pass.part.nom.sing.masc.of ὑφόω, adverbial, temporal, causal) 946.

τήν (acc.sing.fem.of the article in agreement with ἐπαγγελίαν) 9.

τε (adjunctive particle joining participles) 1408.

ἐπαγγελίαν (acc.sing.fem.of ἐπαγγελία, direct object of λαβών) 2929.

τοῦ (gen.sing.neut.of the article in agreement with πνεύματος) 9.

πνεύματος (gen.sing.neut.of πνεῦμα, description) 83.

τοῦ (gen.sing.neut.of the article in agreement with ἁγίου) 9.

ἁγίου (gen.sing.neut.of ἅγιος, in agreement with πνεύματος) 84.

λαβών (aor.act.part.nom.sing.masc.of λαμβάνω, adverbial, temporal/causal) 533.

παρά (preposition with the ablative with persons, "by the side of") 154.

τοῦ (abl.sing.masc.of the article in agreement with πατρός) 9.

πατρός (abl.sing.masc.of πατήρ, "by the side of") 238.

ἐξέχεεν (3d.per.sing.1st.aor.act.ind. of ἐκχέω, culminative) 811.

τοῦτο (acc.sing.neut.of οὗτος, direct object of ἐξέχεεν) 93.

ὅ (acc.sing.neut.of ὅς, direct object of βλέπετε and ἀκούετε) 65.

ὑμεῖς (nom.pl.masc.of σύ, subject of βλέπετε and ἀκούετε) 104.

(καί) (correlative conjunction) 14.

βλέπετε (2d.per.pl.pres.act.ind.of βλέπω, aoristic) 499.

καί (adjunctive conjunction joining verbs) 14.

ἀκούετε (2d.per.pl.pres.act.ind.of ἀκούω, aoristic) 148.

Translation - "Therefore since (and because) He has been lifted up to the right hand of God and since (and because) He has received the promise of the Holy Spirit at the Father's side, He has poured forth this which you both see and hear."

Comment: τῇ δεξιᾷ (we should supply χειρί) can be either locative, instrumental or dative. All three ideas apply. Jesus was exalted to (locative), by means of (instrumental) and for the advantage of (dative) the Father's right hand. *Cf.*#946. He was lifted up on a cross (John 3:14b; 8:28; 12:32,34) and therefore also lifted up in exaltation to the Father's right hand. In Phil.2:8,9 the same idea is expressed. The promise of the Holy Spirit (Luke 24:49; Acts 1:4) was made by Jesus to the Apostles at the last supper (John 14:16,17; 16:7-11). Note in John 16:7 that the giving of the Holy Spirit was contingent upon His exaltation. This is Peter's emphasis as the two participles reveal. It was both after (temporal) and because He was lifted up to God's right hand and also both after and because Jesus received the promise of the Holy Spirit that He in turn sent the Spirit to fill the Christians. He ascended to heaven, received the promise of the Holy Spirit as He sat at God's right hand (παρά τοῦ πατρός) and then poured out upon the 120 the fullness of the Holy Spirit, the audible and visible results of Whose fullness the people in the audience saw and heard.

Thus Peter's argument has swung full circle. He began by explaining the language miracle as a partial fulfillment of the prophecy of Joel. Then he introduced Jesus' works and deeds, phenomena with which they were already familiar, after which he expounded David's connection with all of this from 2 Samuel 7 and Psalm 16. Dead, but resurrected, Christ was now exalted and had redeemed His promise to send the Holy Spirit to fill the Christians, one result of which was their ability to preach the gospel in languages not their own, as the people in Peter's audience had seen. So we are back to the language miracle where Peter started. *Cf.*Titus 3:5,6. We can reason in reverse and say that the language miracle which they saw and heard was the result of the filling of the Holy Spirit which the Christians had received, which was contingent upon Jesus having received the promise as He sat at His Father's right hand, which was contingent upon His ascension, which was contingent upon His resurrection, which was contingent upon His death, which was contingent upon the Davidic covenant. Thus Peter tied the Old Testament Scriptures to the events of the New Testament. To whom did the Davidic covenant apply? To Jesus Christ. How do we know that? 120 Christians witnessed it. Just as David was not speaking of himself in Psalm 16, so he was not speaking of himself, but of Jesus in Psalm 110:1, as Peter went on to point out in verse 34.

The least important event at Pentecost was the miracle of multi-lingual communication, which was only the means to a greater end, *viz.* the spreading of the gospel of Christ. The important thing that happened that day was the baptism of the Holy Spirit, as He filled them and gave power to their witness - a power which convinced 3000 lost sinners that day. This is what the Holy Spirit came into the world to do (John 16:7-11), as His ministry relates to the world. He also came to inspire the writing of the New Testament literature (John 16:12-15) and to empower the Christians to preach the gospel of Christ (Acts 1:8). We can trust a group of unregenerates to major on the minor matters. The thing in which they were most interested was the miracle by reason of which each man heard the gospel in his own dialect. After Peter had finished preaching, 3000 of them discovered that there was something far more important — the work of the Holy Spirit which enabled them to call upon the name of Jesus as Lord (1 Cor.12:3). It is not surprizing that Pentecostalists and other groups who major on ecstasy as an evidence of God's presence are more concerned about the "tongues" they speak, however esoteric they may be and however unintelligible they are to the unenlightened, than in the number of souls that are saved. One wonders whether the souls reported as having been "saved" in such meetings are converted to an appreciation of the righteousness of Jesus Christ and the reliability of His Word or to the thrill of an ecstatic experience, which is subject to social environment and even to the digestive process, when we are not prudent about what we eat or drink. Satan can work on our emotions, but he cannot change the Word of God (Mt.24:35; Heb.13:8).

Having related David's prophecies to the resurrection of Jesus, Peter now goes on to relate them to His ascension in

Verse 34 - "For David is not ascended into the heavens: but he saith himself, The Lord said unto my Lord, Sit thou on my right hand. . . . "

οὐ γὰρ Δαυὶδ ἀνέβη εἰς τοὺς οὐρανούς, λέγει δὲ αὐτός, Εἶπεν κύριος τῷ κυρίῳ μου, Κάθου ἐκ δεξιῶν μου

οὐ (summary negative conjunction with the indicative) 130.
γὰρ (explanatory conjunction) 105.
Δαυὶδ (nom.sing.masc.of Δαυίδ, subject of ἀνέβη) 6.
ἀνέβη (3d.per.sing.aor.act.ind.of ἀναβαίνω, constative) 323.
εἰς (preposition with the accusative of extent) 140.
τοὺς (acc.pl.masc.of the article in agreement with οὐρανούς) 9.
οὐρανούς (acc.pl.masc.of οὐρανός, extent) 254.
λέγει (3d.per.sing.pres.act.ind.of λέγω, historical) 66.
δὲ (adversative conjunction) 11.
αὐτός (nom.sing.masc.of αὐτός, subject of λέγει) 16.
Εἶπεν (3d.per.sing.aor.act.ind.of εἶπον, constative) 155.
κύριος (nom.sing.masc.of κύριος, subject of εἶπεν) 97.
τῷ (dat.sing.masc.of the article in agreement with κυρίῳ) 9.
κυρίῳ (dat.sing.masc.of κύριος, indirect object of λέγει) 97.
μου (gen.sing.masc.of ἐγώ, relationship) 123.
Κάθου (2d.per.sing.pres.act.impv.of κάθημαι, command) 377.
ἐκ (preposition with the genitive of place description) 19.
δεξιῶν (gen.pl.fem.of δεξιός, idiomatic plural, place description) 502.
μου (gen.sing.masc.of ἐγώ, possession) 123.

Translation - "Now David did not ascend into the heavens, but he said, 'The Lord said to my Lord, 'Sit at my right hand . . . ' ' "

Comment: γὰρ is explanatory, as Peter, having given a thorough explanation of Psalm 16 and 2 Samuel 7, now procedes to teach them further from Psalm 110. Thus, as we study this model sermon, which was the result of the filling of the Holy Spirit and can therefore be regarded as the kind of preaching that He wants us to do, we see that good preaching involves us in teaching something, as well as exhorting people to behave. David had not personally experienced a resurrection from the dead, but he spoke of the resurrection of His heir who would sit forever upon his throne. Nor had David personally experienced an ascension, but he prophesied in Psalm 110:1 about the ascension of his heir, Who was the subject of David's previous comment. "The Lord (God) said to my Lord (Jesus), 'Sit at my right hand . . . κ.τ.λ.' "

But Christ will not sit forever at the right hand of the Father. This we learn as verse 35 has the rest of the sentence.

Verse 35 - ". . . until I make thy foes thy footstool."

ἕως ἂν θῶ τοὺς ἐχθρούς σου ὑποπόδιον τῶν ποδῶν σου.

ἕως (conjunction with the subjunctive in an indefinite temporal clause) 71.
ἂν (contingent particle in an indefinite temporal clause) 206.
θῶ (1st.per.sing.aor.act.subj.of τίθημι, indefinite temporal clause) 455.
τοὺς (acc.pl.masc.of the article in agreement with ἐχθρούς) 9.
ἐχθρούς (acc.pl.masc.of ἐχθρός, direct object of θῶ) 543.

σου (gen.sing.masc.of σύ, relationship) 104.

ὑποπόδιον (acc.sing.neut.of ὑποπόδιον, predicate accusative) 520.

τῶν (gen.pl.masc.of the article in agreement with ποδῶν) 9.

ποδῶν (gen.pl.masc.of πούς, description) 353.

σου (gen.sing.masc.of σύ, possession) 104.

Translation - ". . . *until such time as I make your enemies a footstool for your feet.*"

Comment: The temporal clause introduced by ἕως has the subjunctive θῶ with ἄν. Thus the precise time when Christ's enemies will be made His footstool is not definitely revealed. There is a precise time, known but to God. But the fact that Christ's enemies will be subdued is not indefinite - only the time of their subjugation. That God knows when that will be is clear from Acts 1:7. In the meantime, between the day of His ascension and the day of His return to earth, Christ will occupy His exalted position in heaven at the Father's right hand. (Heb.1:3; 12:2; Col.3:1, *et al cf*.#377 for a complete list). During this time the great commission (Acts 1:8; Mt.28:18-20) will be completed and at the end of the age Christ's enemies will be judged. An interesting detail that should not surprize those of us who believe that the Bible has been carefully produced is that the tares are to be gathered out of the world and burned in judgment before the sheaves of wheat are gathered into God's barn (Mt.13:30). This comports with Psalm 110:1 which also suggests that the subjugation of Christ's enemies (tares) is to precede His return to earth, at which time His angels will gather His elect ". . . from the four winds, from one end of heaven to the other" (Mt.24:31) Some angels will gather and burn tares. Others will gather are store wheat. This angelic division of labor will result in the fulfillment of Psalm 110:1.

Some sermons never mention the second coming of our Lord. Indeed in some pulpits such an idea is rejected. But in Peter's sermon, directed as it was by the Holy Spirit, the second coming of Messiah is the last point, toward which the earlier portions of the sermon pointed and without which it would not have been complete. Jesus will not sit forever at the right hand of the throne of God in a place as remote as the heavens. The heavens are "high above the earth"(Isa.55:9), but Messiah will rule upon this earth, not high above it. God did not promise David that his son and heir would occupy a throne in heaven. He did promise the king that his son would occupy his throne which was always in Jerusalem, an earthly city. *Cf*.#455 for all of the verses that allude to Psalm 110:1. Jesus did not occupy David's throne when He ascended ten days before Pentecost. He will occupy it when He returns to earth. *Cf*. Psalm 8:6. Note especially Heb.10:12,13. Peter here was only repeating what He had heard Jesus say (Mt.22:44; Mk.12:36; Lk.20:43).

Thus Peter added the final element in his description of Jesus, which included His ministry with its signs, wonders and miracles by which He was given God's endorsement (vs.22), His crucifixion (vs.23), His resurrection (vss.24-28), David's prophecies of all this (vss.29-31), the witness of the Christians present to His bodily resurrection (vs.32), His ascension (vs.33), the reception of the promise of the Father and the manifestation of the Holy Spirit on earth (vs.33), His tenure in glory and the purpose for the interim period and finally His triumphant return to earth (vss.34-35). This was Peter's Spirit-filled sermon. I have just read it aloud and it took just three minutes and five seconds, with an additional fifteen seconds for his invitation, following their question, "Men and brethren, what shall we do?" After the sermon was finished he did linger to discuss it with them with "many other words" of testimony and exhortation (vs.40). Three thousand people responded to the invitation. Here was a sermon judged on the basis of the quality of its subject matter and upon the degree of its spiritual power.

Peter was now ready to state his conclusion toward which he had been pointing since his sermon began, three minutes before.

Verse 36 - "Therefore, let all the house of Israel know assuredly, that God hath made that same Jesus, whom ye have crucified, both Lord and Christ."

ἀσφαλῶς οὖν γινωσκέτω πᾶς οἶκος Ἰσραὴλ ὅτι καὶ κύριον αὐτὸν καὶ Χριστὸν ἐποίησεν ὁ θεός, τοῦτον τὸν Ἰησοῦν ὃν ὑμεῖς ἐσταυρώσατε.

ἀσφαλῶς (adverbial) 2801.
οὖν (inferential conjunction) 68.
γινωσκέτω (3d.per.sing.pres.act.impv.of γινώσκω, command) 131.
πᾶς (nom.sing.masc.of πᾶς, in agreement with οἶκος) 67.
οἶκος (nom.sing.masc.of οἶκος, subject of γινωσκέτω) 784.
Ἰσραὴλ (gen.sing.masc.of Ἰσραὴλ, designation) 165.
ὅτι (conjunction introducing an object clause in indirect discourse) 211.
καὶ (correlative conjunction) 14.
κύριον (acc.sing.masc.of κύριος, predicate adjective) 97.
αὐτὸν (acc.sing.masc.of αὐτός, direct object of ἐποίησεν) 16.
καὶ (adjunctive conjunction joining nouns) 14.
Χριστὸν (acc.sing.masc.of Χριστός, predicate adjective) 4.
ἐποίησεν (3d.per.sing.aor.act.ind.of ποιέω, culminative) 127.
ὁ (nom.sing.masc.of the article in agreement with θεός) 9.
θεός (nom.sing.masc.of θεός, subject of ἐποίησεν) 124.
τοῦτον (acc.sing.masc.of οὗτος, in agreement with Ἰησοῦν) 93.
τὸν (acc.sing.masc.of the article in agreement with Ἰησοῦν) 9.
Ἰησοῦν (acc.sing.masc.of Ἰησοῦς, in apposition with αὐτόν) 3.
ὃν (acc.sing.masc.of ὅς, direct object of ἐσταυρώσατε) 65.
ὑμεῖς (nom.pl.masc.of σύ, subject of ἐσταυρώσατε) 104.
ἐσταυρώσατε (2d.per.pl.aor.act.ind.of σταυρόω, constative) 1328.

Translation - "So let all the house of Israel know without a doubt that God has anointed Him, this man Jesus Whom you crucified, both Lord and King."

Comment: οὖν is inferential as Peter draws his conclusion on the basis of all that had gone before, beginning in verse 14. Earlier in the sermon Peter had accused them of murdering Jesus (vs.23) and he repeated the accusation in the last sentence.

How did God react to the murderous fury of His chosen people, poured out at Calvary upon His beloved Son? He has made "this man Jesus whom you crucified" both Sovereign Lord, destined to sit upon a judgment throne (John 5:22) and their anointed Messiah, Israel's King, and in the process Jesus had also become the personal Saviour of all who felt the tug of the Holy Spirit upon heart and mind. Israel hated Him. God loved Him. Israel rejected Him. God anointed Him King. Israel murdered Him. God approved of His sacrifice on the cross, raised Him from the dead, seated Him at His right hand, declared that Jesus was His Son (Psalm 2:7), made Him the only priest whose priestly intercession would be acceptable (Ps.110:4) and invited Him to pray for the salvation of the heathen as His inheritance and the uttermost parts of the earth as His possession (Ps.2:8). He gave to Jesus the name which is above every name and made Him to be Head over all things to His church (Phil.2:9; Eph.1:22).

Good evangelistic preaching as demonstrated by Peter's first use of the keys of the kingdom must be Bible based, expository in method and didactic in style. It must exalt Jesus Christ and degrade man. Sinners must be made to realize the wide gulf between God, Christ and the Holy Spirit on the one hand and themselves on the other - a gulf, however that can be bridged, but only by the grace of God, the supernatural power of the Holy Spirit and the sacrifice of Jesus Christ.

The Holy Spirit taught Peter a great many things that he had never known before during the course of that brief three minutes (John 16:12-15). He also convinced three thousand lost sinners that everything that Peter had said was true and that they were committing the sin that would forever separate them from God if they persisted in it. Further He convinced them that Jesus Christ, Whom they had crucified was righteous and finally He convinced them that their father, the devil, was already sitting on death row, awaiting the day of his execution. It is no wonder that they cried out for help, in

Verse 37 - "Now when they heard this, they were pricked in their heart, and said unto Peter and to the rest of the apostles, Men and brethren, what shall we do?"

᾽Ακούσαντες δὲ κατενύγησαν τὴν καρδίαν, εἰπόν τε πρὸς τὸν Πέτρον καὶ τοὺς λοιποὺς ἀποστόλους, Τί ποιήσωμεν, ἄνδρες ἀδελφοί;

᾽Ακούσαντες (aor.act.part.nom.pl.masc.of ἀκούω, adverbial, temporal/causal) 148.

δὲ (continuative conjunction) 11.

#2999 κατενύγησαν (3d.per.pl.2d.aor.pass.ind.of κατανύσσω, constative).

prick - Acts 2:37.

Meaning: A combination of κατά (#98) and νύσσω (#1659). To pierce or prick down or against. To wound or agitate mentally in Acts 2:37, where followed by an accusative of general reference, τὴν καρδίαν. In keeping with John 16:8-11, the passage in context means that they were convinced/convicted of the truth of what Peter had said, concerned about their own guilt and desirous to find salvation.

τὴν (acc.sing.fem.of the article in agreement with καρδίαν) 9.

καρδίαν (acc.sing.fem.of καρδία, predicate accusative, adverbial) 432.

εἶπον (3d.per.pl.aor.act.ind.of εἶπον, constative) 155.

τε (correlative conjunction) 1408.

πρὸς (preposition with the accusative of extent after a verb of speaking) 197.

τὸν (acc.sing.masc.of the article in agreement with Πέτρον) 9.

Πέτρον (acc.sing.masc.of Πέτρος, extent, after a verb of speaking) 387.

καὶ (adjunctive conjunction joining substantives) 14.

τοὺς (acc.pl.masc.of the article in agreement with ἀποστόλους) 9.

λοιποὺς (acc.pl.masc.of λοιπός, in agreement with ἀποστόλους) 1402.

ἀποστόλους (acc.pl.masc.of ἀπόστολος, extent after a verb of speaking) 844.

Τί (acc.sing.neut.of τίς, interrog.pronoun, direct object of ποιήσωμεν, direct question) 281.

ποιήσωμεν (1st.per.pl.aor.act.subj.of ποιέω, deliberative subjunctive, direct question) 127.

ἄνδρες (voc.pl.masc.of ἀνήρ, address) 63.

ἀδελφοί (voc.pl.masc.of ἀδελφός, address) 15.

Translation - "And when (because) they heard this they were stabbed to the heart and said both to Peter and to the other apostles, 'Why shall we do, men and brethren?' "

Comment: Here in᾽Ακούσαντες we have another adverbial participle which is both temporal and causal. Since result always follows cause a causal participle must also be temporal if the cause of the result is in the context. It is idle to argue whether the cause of the conviction in the hearts of the people was Peter's sermon or the work of the Holy Spirit. Of course both the sermon and the Holy Spirit were involved. Certainly if Peter had not been filled with the Holy Spirit, his sermon, however logical, scriptural and forcefully delivered would have had no spiritual effect upon the audience. But the Holy Spirit convicts the unsaved through the preaching of the Word which Peter expounded. Thus we have the function of the Holy Spirit, the direct agent working through the sermon of Peter, the indirect agent, who expounded the Word. Note the direct question and compare with Acts 16:30, where the Philippian jailor put it in a different form.

Thus did Peter witness (Acts 2:14-36), and so also did the Holy Spirit (Acts 5:32) with the results described. Perhaps some of the same Jews who had stood in Pilate's courtyard and cried out, "Crucify him" were now asking how to be saved.

Verse 38 - "Then Peter said unto them, Repent and be baptized every one of you in the name of Jesus Christ for the remission of sins, and ye shall receive the gift of the Holy Ghost."

Πέτρος δὲ πρὸς αὐτούς, Μετανοήσατε, καὶ βαπτισθήτω ἕκαστος ὑμῶν ἐπὶ τῷ ὀνόματι Ἰησοῦ Χριστοῦ εἰς ἄφεσιν τῶν ἁμαρτιῶν ὑμῶν καὶ λήμφεσθε τὴν δωρεὰν τοῦ ἁγίου πνεύματος.

Πέτρος (nom.sing.masc.of Πέτρος, subject of εἶπεν understood) 387.

δὲ (continuative conjunction) 11.

πρὸς (preposition with the accusative of extent after a very of speaking) 197.

αὐτούς (acc.pl.masc.of αὐτός, extent after a verb of speaking) 16.

Μετανοήσατε (2d.per.pl.aor.act.impv.of μετανοέω, command) 251.

καὶ (adjunctive conjunction joining verbs) 14.

βαπτισθήτω (2d.per.pl.aor.pass.impv.of βαπτίζω, command) 273.

ἕκαστος (nom.sing.masc.of ἕκαστος, nominative absolute) 1217.

ὑμῶν (gen.pl.masc.of σύ, partitive genitive) 104.

ἐπὶ (preposition with the locative, cause) 47.

τῷ (loc.sing.neut.of the article in agreement with ὀνόματι) 9.

ὀνόματι (loc.sing.neut.of ὄνομα, cause) 108.

Ἰησοῦ (gen.sing.masc.of Ἰησοῦς, possession) 3.

Χριστοῦ (gen.sing.masc.of Χριστός, apposition) 4.

εἰς (preposition with the accusative, cause) 140.

ἄφεσιν (acc.sing.fem.of ἄφεσις, cause) 1576.

τῶν (gen.pl.fem. of the article in agreement with ἁμαρτιῶν) 9.

ἁμαρτιῶν (gen.pl.fem.of ἁμαρτία, description) 111.

ὑμῶν (gen.pl.masc.of σύ, possession) 104.

καὶ (continuative conjunction) 14.

λήμφεσθε (2d.per.pl.fut.mid.ind.of λαμβάνω, predictive) 533.

τὴν (acc.sing.fem.of the article in agreement with δωρεὰν) 9.

δωρεὰν (acc.sing.fem.of δωρεά, direct object of λήμφεσθε) 2004.

τοῦ (gen.sing.neut.of the article in agreement with πνεύματος) 9.

ἁγίου (gen.sing.neut.of ἅγιος, in agreement with πνεύματος) 84.

πνεύματος (gen.sing.neut.of πνεῦμα, description) 83.

Translation - "And Peter (said) to them, 'Repent and be immersed, each one of you, in the name of Jesus Christ, because of forgiveness of your sins, and you will receive the gift of the Holy Spirit.' "

Comment: Billions of words have been uttered at decibel ratios that threatened tympanic membranes while blood pressures soared as this verse has been discussed, applied, misapplied, exegeted, tortured, defended, attacked - in and out of context — and all in the name of Christian orthodoxy, over the question of baptismal regeneration. A little girl, five years old is said to have reported to her grandfather that the preacher said during his sermon that he was going to get an axe and two thirty-eights and rid the county of all of the Baptist preachers!

ἐπὶ τῷ ὀνόματι can be a locative of sphere, an instrumental of cause or manner or a dative of personal advantage or reference. Peter meant that he wanted them publicly to identify with Jesus Christ by submitting to immersion in water in a ceremony for all to see. If they did they would be moving theologically into a new and different sphere of religious thinking and identification, because they would then be known as followers of Jesus Christ. An instrumental of manner could refer to the spoken formula of Matthew 28:19. Cause, with the instrumental is also possible. *Because* of the name of Jesus

Christ and all that His name had come to stand for, they were to be immersed publicly. If the phrase is dative it can mean that for the personal advantage of Jesus Christ or in reference to Him the ordinance was to be enacted. These ideas are by no means severally and mutually exclusive. There is little difference between sphere and reference. In all cases the candidate is being identified with a name, a Person, a theology, a cause, an organism and an organization. Secrecy is to be ruled out. Peter was demanding that there be no secret believers there in Jerusalem that day " for fear of the Jews." Jesus had been openly crucified for all to see and to scoff. His followers must now openly associate with Him. In the light of this fact, εἰς ἄφεσιν τῶν ἁμαρτιῶν ὑμῶν may indeed mean purpose - "be immersed *in order to receive forgiveness of sins."* But this does not mean that the water was in any sense sacerdotal. We must view the passage with the *zeitgeist* without which nothing written or spoken can properly be interpreted. The "spirit of the times" demands that when we interpret Acts 2:38 we must evaluate the circumstances under which it was spoken so thoroughly that it is as though we ourselves had been the speaker or one in the audience. Let the reader imagine himself in Peter's position and that it was he, not Peter, who had made this demand. Or let the reader imagine himself in the position of one of those Jews, under deep conviction and willing to do whatever was necessary to be saved, although not anxious to do something that would bring the wrath of Jersualem society down upon his head. *On that day and in that particular social and political milieu* it would have been impossible to believe sincerely upon Christ and keep the fact a secret, thus to avoid persecution. The act of repentance cannot be observed since repentance is a change of mind and attitude that goes on internally in the nervous system. But repentance also has an emotional side (*Cf.*#1371) which affects our sense of loyalty to that or to whom we are now committed. True repentance on that day in Jerusalem would certainly be followed by public immersion in water, despite the social cost. There would be every reason to suspect that the motive of the secret believer was adulterated by self interest. Peter and the other apostles may have suspected that some would slip quietly away from the meeting, believing in his heart that Jesus Christ was indeed the Messiah and resolved to follow Him, but not in Jerusalem and among friends and acquaintances where discipleship with Jesus would mean carrying His cross. Jesus had said something about secret discipleship (Luke 14:27; Matthew 10:38).

What we are suggesting here is completely different from the position of those who teach baptismal regeneration. That doctrine says that true repentance and genuine faith must be supplemented by water baptism or the candidate is not saved - a view that condemns to the eternal burnings far more than 99% of all professing Christians of all ages, without regard to their faith and Christian works - a view that is notable for its lack of charity and tolerance. Such a view is not supported by the fact that εἰς with the accusative can in certain contexts be telic. Indeed εἰς with the accusative is often found in a purpose clause where the translation is properly rendered "in order that" or "in order to" as in 2 Cor.2:12 - ἐλθὼν εἰς τὴν Τρῳάδα εἰς τὸ εὐαγγέλιον, where the second εἰς suggests that Paul was coming to Troas "in order to preach the gospel" or "for the purpose of preaching the gosel." *Cf.*also 1 Cor.11:24 which says that we are to eat the bread of the communion for the purpose of reminding us of Him. Thus εἰς ἄφεσιν τῶν ἁμαρτιῶν ὑμῶν in Acts 2:38 can be translated " for the purpose of having your sins forgiven" with complete grammatical and syntactical support and even, in this passage with contextual support, as I have indicated. Because the time and place when and where Peter said that, and the circumstances under which he said it were such that the genuineness of the candidate's repentance and true desire to accept Christ could be demonstrated only by the publicity which he would be certain to receive when he was immersed - a publicity that would be unfavorable to him and mark him for the persecution which was imposed upon the Christians in Jerusalem soon after Pentecost.

Syntax cannot always have the last word. Robertson says, "After all is done, instances remain where syntax cannot say the last word, where theological bias will inevitably determine how one interprets the Greek idiom. Take ὕδατι in Acts 1:5, for instance. In itself the word can be either locative or instrumental with βαπτίζω. So in Ac.2:38 εἰς does not of itself express design (Mt.10:41), but it may be so used. When the grammarian has finished, the theologian steps in, and sometimes before the grammarian is through." (Robertson, *Grammar*, 389). Speaking of Acts 2:38, Robertson adds, ". . . only the context and tenor of N.T. teaching can determine whether "into" "unto" or merely "in" or "on" (upon) is the right translation, a task for the interpreter, not the grammarian." (*Ibid.,* 592).

Just as εἰς with the accusative can be telic when the context demands it can also be causal, as we have translated it in Acts 2:38. The men of Nineveh repented εἰς τὸ κήρυγμα Ἰωνᾶ - "because of the preaching of Jonah" (Mt.12:41). Let the Campbellites try that one in a telic sense - "the men of Nineveh repented in order to get Jonah to preach"!

Let us keep in mind that Peter's superb evangelistic preaching at Pentecost was the result of the filling of the Holy Spirit Who directed his every word, gesture, facial expression and tonal inflection. The results were also superb, since it was the Holy Spirit Who stung 3000 people in their hearts with a conviction that they could not resist. When they cried out to the Apostles, "What shall we do?" they meant it and they were willing to do anything to escape the wrath of God. They proved it by a public ceremony in which they were immersed in water in the name which they had previously despised, despite the fact that they were certain to be marked as religious fanatics worthy only of public censure and even death. Such true believers, made thus by the supernatural ministry of the Holy Spirit, who have truly repented and who have definitely made the leap of faith to Christ are immersed *because* their sins are forgiven, not *in order that* their sins may be forgiven. Yet we have suggested that there may very well be cases where the only way to show true repentance and faith (for certainly insincere commitments are unavailing) is to submit to the public act of being immersed in water. It is extremely likely that Pentecost on that day in Jerusalem was one of those times. It might possibly be true in certain parts of the world in 1981 where an open commitment to Christ would invite persecution if not martyrdom. But there is a vast difference between the situation in which Peter preached this sermon and gave this invitation and a peaceful God honoring community, dominated by Presbyterians, Baptists, Methodists, *et al*, where no persecution for the Christian could be expected and would not be tolerated. For a preacher of baptismal regeneration to move into such a community and preach   that they were all damned because they had not been dipped in water on the authority of his church organization, which is less than 200 years old and comprises only a small percentage of all professing Christians, is preposterous. We enhance the degree of curiosity with which such a view is endowed when we add that the validity of the administration of baptism in water is also made contingent upon whether the congregational singing is *a cappella* or accompanied on a piano, or, in cases where a modicum of tolerance is permitted by a tuning fork.

Peter added that following repentance and faith as indicated by immersion in water, the candidates would receive the gift of the Holy Spirit, just as the disciples had on resurrection evening (John 20:22). That faith in Christ is antecedent to water baptism and not to be confused with it, is clear from Acts 8:35-39 and Acts 16:30-33, *q.v.en.loc.* Indeed the story of the conversion of the Philippian jailor clearly presents a situation counterpart to that of Peter and his converts at Pentecost. In Philippi, a jailor, 750 miles from Jerusalem, with nothing to fear from persecutors if he became a Christian was told that in order to be saved he need only "believe on the Lord Jesus Christ" (Acts 16:31). The two passages (Acts 2:38 and Acts 16:31), each viewed in context and with due regard to *zeitgeist* teach the same thing. Immersion in water, following repentance and faith is a matter of Christian obedience to a divine command and should be practised by all true believers, but it is not prerequisite to salvation. Otherwise we must conclude that the Holy Spirit was guilty of giving conflicting advice by Peter to the Jews in Jerusalem and by Paul to a gentile in Philippi. Are we to conclude that Peter was a Campbellite and that Paul was a Baptist?

Verse 39 - "For the promise is unto you, and to your children, and to all that are afar off, even as many as the Lord our God shall call."

ὑμῖν γάρ ἐστιν ἡ ἐπαγγελία καὶ τοῖς τέκνοις ὑμῶν καὶ πᾶσιν τοῖς εἰς μακρὰν ὅσους ἂν προσκαλέσηται κύριος ὁ θεὸς ἡμῶν.

ὑμῖν (dat.pl.masc.of σύ, personal advantage) 104.

γάρ (causal conjunction) 105.

ἐστιν (3d.per.sing.pres.ind.of εἰμί, static) 86.

ἡ (nom.sing.fem.of the article in agreement with ἐπαγγελία) 9.

ἐπαγγελία (nom.sing.fem.of ἐπαγγελία, subject of ἐστιν) 2929.

καὶ (adjunctive conjunction joining a pronoun and a noun) 14.

τοῖς (dat.pl.neut.of the article in agreement with τέκνοις) 9.

τέκνοις (dat.pl.neut.of τέκνον, personal advantage) 229.

ὑμῶν (gen.pl.masc.of σύ, relationship) 104.

καὶ (adjunctive conjunction joining a noun with a substantive) 14.

πᾶσιν (dat.pl.masc.of πᾶς in agreement with τοῖς) 67.

τοῖς (dat.pl.masc.of the article, personal advantage) 9.

εἰς (preposition with the adverb in a predicate accustive construction, original static use, like a locative of place) 140.

μακράν (adverb, predicate accusative with εἰς in an original static use, like a locative) 768.

ὅσους (acc.pl.masc.of the indefinite pronoun with the subjunctive in a more probable condition) 660.

ἄν (contingent particle with the subjunctive in a more probable condition) 206.

προσκαλέσηται (3d.per.sing.aor.mid.subj.of προσκαλέω, more probable condition) 842.

κύριος (nom.sing.masc.of κύριος, subject of προσκαλέσηται) 97.

ὁ (nom.sing.masc.of the article in agreement with θεὸς) 9.

θεὸς (nom.sing.masc.of θεός, apposition) 124.

ἡμῶν (gen.pl.masc.of ἐγώ, relationship) 123.

Translation - "Because the promise is for you and for your children and for all those in distant places whoever they may be whom the Lord our God will call."

Comment: We may call ὑμῖν, τοῖς τέκνοις and πᾶσιν τοῖς datives of possession as Robertson does, or we can get the same concept with the dative of personal advantage. Note the unusual original static use of εἰς with the accusative in a locative of place construction, in this case, joined to the adverb μακράν, which can mean philosophical and cultural aloofness as well as geographical isolation. Here Peter is suggesting something that he himself did not understand perfectly until his experience in the home of Cornelius, the gentile (Acts 10:9-35. One wonders if the thought crossed his mind when he said this if this could possibly mean that a gentile could also be saved? But Peter did not mean that all who are afar off, or even all those who were near were to be saved. The promise was not to all of the people in Peter's audience, nor to all of their children, nor to all who were afar off. It is limited by the indefinite relative clause and its more probable condition, with the subjunctive and ἄν. The promise is to those, whoever they may prove to be, whom the Lord will call. Peter may have remembered this bit of theology, later to be written into the New Testament by Paul and expounded by Augustine, Calvin, Luther and the Reformed theologians, from Jesus' statements in John 6:44; 6:37, *et al.* Salvation will not be denied because of race, color, national origin, social, economic or political status, corruption of blood or geographic or philosophical isolation (Rev.5:9). But the individual, lost in Adam and totally unwilling to come to God, must wait until he is called - another flash of prescience on Peter's part which he later wrote into his own contribution to the New Testament literature (1 Peter.1:2). *Cf.*Romans 8:29-30; Acts 13:48; Eph.2:1-3, *et al.*This is the doctrine of election and effectual call. Those who dislike it and therefore choose to dismiss it in the hope of explaining it away, so as to make Christian theology palatable to depraved human reason, either end up denying it altogether or they accept it by faith as they should have done in the first place. The fact that should amaze every Christian is not that God should be selective, but that God should have chosen him. Peter's statement here goes far beyond the limits of Jewish nationalism as conceived by Jewish legalists, of whom Peter himself, when he was not filled by the Holy Spirit, was one. He was preaching what Jesus did in John 6 and what Paul later preached. *Cf.*#842 for other passages in the sense of calling for salvation. Peter's sermon is not finished, but we have all of that which Luke chose to report except for one more statement in

Verse 40 - "And with many other words did he testify and exhort, saying, Save yourselves from this untoward generation."

ἑτέροις τε λόγοις πλείοσιν διεμαρτύρατο, καί παρεκάλει αὐτοὺς λέγων, Σώθητε ἀπὸ τῆς γενεᾶς τῆς σκολιᾶς ταύτης.

ἑτέροις (instru.pl.masc.of ἕτερος, in agreement with λόγοις) 605.

τε (correlative conjunction) 1408.

λόγοις (instru.pl.masc.of λόγος, means) 510.

πλείοσιν (instru.pl.masc.of πλείων, in agreement with λόγοις) 474.

διεμαρτύρατο (3d.per.sing.1st.aor.mid.ind.of διαμαρτύρομαι, constative) 2589.

καὶ (adjunctive conjunction joining verbs) 14.

παρεκάλει (3d.per.sing.imp.act.ind.of παρακαλέω, iterative) 230.

αὐτοὺς (acc.pl.masc.of αὐτός, direct object of παρεκάλει) 16.

λέγων (pres.act.part.nom.sing.masc.of λέγω, recitative) 66.

Σώθητε (2d.per.pl.1st.aor.pass.impv.of σώζω, entreaty) 109.

ἀπὸ (preposition with the ablative of separation) 70.

τῆς (abl.sing.fem.of the article in agreement with γενεᾶς) 9.

γενεᾶς (abl.sing.fem.of γενεά, separation) 922.

τῆς (abl.sing.fem.of the article in agreement with σκολιᾶς) 9.

σκολιᾶς (abl.sing.fem.of σκολιά, in agreement with γενεᾶς) 1939.

ταύτης (abl.sing.fem.of οὗτος, in agreement with γενεᾶς) 93.

Translation - "With many other statements he both earnestly gave his testimony and begged them again and again - 'Be saved from this perverted generation.'"

Comment: There is no ablative of comparison with πλείοσιν, a comparative adjective, but the context provides the basis for comparison. Peter spoke many more words than he had spoken in his formal presentation of vss. 14-39. *Cf.*#2589 to appreciate the earnestness and intensity of Peter's plea. The idea of intensity is heightened by the iterative imperfect in παρεκάλει as Peter begged them again and again to repent. Spirit filled Christians have a burden for the lost that they cannot dismiss easily.

Early evangelism on the American frontier in the late 18th and early 19th centuries, was characterized by the formal presentation of the preacher, followed by a long "invitation" to come to the altar, repent, believe and confess Christ. This invitation period was generally prolonged and interspersed by what was called "exhorting." This is what Peter did at Pentecost, although his performance, directed by the Holy Spirit, was free from emotional excesses which emanated more from carnality than from the Spirit, in the frontier meetings.* Peter's sermon was a reasoned exposition of Scripture, which, of course, in his case, meant the Old Testament, since the New Testament was not

*Cf.*Frances Trollope, *Domestic Manners of the Americans,* 167-175. Trollope's description is somewhat marred by her prejudice against Americans derived perhaps from the failure of her business venture in Cincinnati.

yet written. He demonstrated the unity that existed between the prophecies of the Old Testament and their fulfillment in the historic events of the life and death of Jesus, thus to show that the gospel was not a new religion in opposition to the Jewish faith in the Old Testament, but rather a logical extension of it, without which the Old Testament was incomplete. The ἑτέροις . . . λόγοις πλείοσσιν were devoted more to an emotional plea to the audience. Its intensity depended upon the zeal, moral sincerity and intellectual balance of the speaker. In Peter's case of course, it was superb, since it was directed by the Holy Spirit. Long invitations, with much singing and fervent exhortations, sometimes accompanied by "personal work" by various members of the congregation, has become taboo with many modern congregations which may be more interested in their reputations for decorum than for spiritual results.Indeed, if the Holy Spirit is not present, such extended efforts are ineffectual in any case and therefore in poor taste. As a matter of fact they are counterproductive, since they tend to discourage repeat attendance. How often have modern evangelists, more interested in their track record than in permanent results, "killed their crowds" on the first night with an extended invitation, to which the unsaved did not respond, and during which the congregation was asked to continue to stand and sing. But Peter used this method at Pentecost because (1) he was filled with the Holy Spirit, (2) he was speaking with wisdom not his own (vs.14, ἀπεφθέξατο), (3) he had expounded the Scripture faithfully, and (4) he was earnestly burdened about the dreadful state of things, theological, philosophical and moral in the nation's status quo and totally convinced that Christ was the only answer. Peter believed that those in his audience were lost, that Jerusalem was doomed, that the Jewish Establishment was "crooked"(*cf.*#1939) and perverted because their basic assumption about God's plan for national Israel was false and hence that the only thing that could save them was a turn of 180 degrees in their thinking (μετανοέω #251) and supernatural faith in their resurrected and glorified Messiah, Jesus Christ.

Society in the 20th century is also "crooked" - σκολιά. Guided by a deistic or atheistic premise with an evolutionary view of life, there exists an exaggerated emphasis upon pragmatism and consequent undue repudiation of reason (philosophy) and faith (revealed theology). The world has accepted a logical positivism and environmental determinism, accompanied by an unwarranted optimism that assumes that since change is inevitable it is always associated with progress. Thus, we leave the old landmarks behind because, if for no other reason, they are old, and rush forward to embrace the new frontiers of change, which, since they represent the progeny of determinism, include situation ethics, ethical relativism and the permissive toleration that has disarmed law enforcement and will return society to the jungle where the law of claw and fang prevails. There are two hopes — one that the Holy Spirit fills Christians as He did at Pentecost and we have a worldwide revival. The other is the second coming of our Lord.

Verse 41 - "Then they that gladly received his word were baptized: and the same day there were added unto them about three thousand souls."

οἱ μὲν οὖν ἀποδεξάμενοι τὸν λόγον αὐτοῦ ἐβαπτίσθησαν, καὶ προσετέθησαν ἐν τῇ ἡμέρᾳ ἐκείνῃ ψυχαὶ ὡσεὶ τρισχίλιαι.

οἱ (nom.pl.masc.of the article in agreement with ἀποδεξάμενοι) 9.

μὲν (particle of affirmation) 300.

οὖν (continuative conjunction) 68.

ἀποδεξάμενοι (aor.mid.part.nom.pl.masc.of ἀποδχομαι, substantival,
subject of ἐβαπτίσθησαν) 2245.

τὸν (acc.sing.masc.of the article in agreement with λόγον) 9.

λόγον (acc.sing.masc.of λόγος, direct object of ἀποδεξάμενοι) 510.

αὐτοῦ (gen.sing.masc.of αὐτός, possession) 16.

ἐβαπτίσθησαν (3d.per.pl.aor.pass.ind.of βαπτίζω, constative) 273.

καὶ (continuative conjunction) 14.

προσετέθησαν (3d.per.pl.aor.pass.ind.of προστίθημι, constative) 621.

ἐν (preposition with the locative of time point) 80.

τῇ (loc.sing.fem.of the article in agreement with ἡμέρᾳ) 9.

ἡμέρᾳ (loc.sing.fem.of ἡμέρα, time point) 135.

ἐκείνῃ (loc.sing.fem.of ἐκεῖνος, in agreement with ἡμέρᾳ) 246.

ψυχαὶ (nom.pl.fem.of ψυχή, subject of προσετέθησαν) 233.

ὡσεὶ (conjunction in a comparison) 325.

#3000 τρισχίλιαι (nom.pl.fem.of τρισχίλιος, in agreement with ψυχαὶ).

three thousand - Acts 2:41.

Meaning: A combination of τρίς (#1582) and χίλιοι (#5278). Hence, three
thousand - Acts 2:41.

*Translation - "Then those who received his message were immersed and about
three thousand souls were added on that day."*

Comment: The μὲν οὖν sequence is sometimes used to show contrast. *Cf.*#300,
but here it is only resumptive. ἀποδέχομαι (#2245) means more than δέχομαι
without ἀπό in prefix. To receive from someone is to welcome. The King James
"gladly" goes a little too far. Three thousand people (or thereabout) gave
attention to Peter's message, believed and received it. The genuineness of their
sincerity and faith is attested by the fact that they did not hesitate to give public
testimony to the change in their allegiance from the Judaism of the status quo,
which had the blood of Jesus Christ upon its hands, to the new Christianity
which had the blood of Jesus Christ applied in expiation for sin. The blood
applied to the church spoke better things than the blood of Abel (Heb.12:24).
Abel's blood cried out from the ground to God for vengeance (Gen.4:10) against
his brother who had murdered him. Cain was "of that wicked one, and slew his
brother" (1 John 3:12) "because his own works were evil, and his brother's
righteous." Christ's blood also cried out from the ground at the foot of the cross
to God for vengeance against the current generation of Satan's progeny (John
8:44) who had murdered Him for the same reason that Cain killed Abel - it is the
difference between righteous works and evil. Any man who does always and only

"the things that please Him" (John 8:29) will be the target of those "every imagination of the thoughts of whose hearts are only evil continually" (Genesis 6:5).

What the 3000 people did that day took courage as the story of persecution which follows reveals.

They received the Holy Spirit (1 Cor.12:13), but the record does not say that the new converts were given the ability to speak languages other than their own. Indeed there was no need for the miracle to be repeated, since the visitors in Jerusalem had already heard the gospel message from the Apostles in the language which they could understand. The signs did not always follow those who accepted Christ, nor does the Word of God promise that they will, which may be why some later scribe, without authorization from the Holy Spirit added that in Mark 16:20, a passage eight verses too late to be included in the category of "God-breathed" scripture (2 Tim.3:16).

It is important that we distinguish between the *baptism/filling* of the Holy Spirit on the one hand and the *reception* of the Holy Spirit on the other. The Holy Spirit regenerates when we receive Him as we receive Christ and by the miracle of regeneration we are submerged (immersed into, buried within) into the Body of Christ. There is a baptism mentioned in 1 Cor.12:13 but it is our baptism into the Body, which is effected by the Holy Spirit, not the baptism of the Holy Spirit. What happened at Pentecost in the experience of the 120 Christians who had already received the Holy Spirit, can happen to any Christian who asks God for His filling, but there is no promise that the necessary result of such baptism/filling of the Holy Spirit will be the miracle of linguistic communication beyond our natural talents. If any Christian in the exercise of his duty to preach the gospel is ever placed in a situation in which he is the only Christian present with a group whose language he cannot speak, it would be completely Scriptural and proper for the Holy Spirit again to grant the gift of language capability which He gave to the Christians at Pentecost. If no one is available to preach the good news to the people in eastern Africa except me, and if they can understand nothing except Swahili, then the Holy Spirit is perfectly capable of giving me the ability to speak Swahili long enough for me to tell them that God loves them and that Christ died for their sins, but I do not expect to understand a word I say.

Three thousand new Christians were baptized into the Body of Christ, but the miracle of regeneration which incorporates another member of Christ into His mystical body does not necessarily carry the "sign gifts" with it as a concomitant. There are gifts for all the saints (1 Cor.12:7), but those that are excitingly and strikingly different or unusual are reserved for those Christians who are given the intellectual and emotional balance to exercise them without a demonstration of carnal pride.

The miracle of regeneration for 3000 people that day was evident, not because of unusual manifestations of miracle working prowess but in their steadfast adherence to the doctrinal views of the Apostles, with whom they came to fellowship at the Lord's table and in the prayer meetings. This is the story of the next verse.

Verse 42 - "And they continued steadfastly in the apostles' doctrines and fellowship, and in breaking of bread, and in prayers."

ἦσαν δὲ προσκαρτεροῦντες τῇ διδαχῇ τῶν ἀποστόλων καὶ τῇ κοινωνίᾳ, τῇ κλάσει τοῦ ἄρτου καὶ ταῖς προσευχαῖς.

ἦσαν (3d.per.pl.imp.ind.of εἰμί, imperfect periphrastic) 86.
δὲ (continuative conjunction) 11.
προσκαρτεροῦντες (pres.act.part.nom.pl.masc.of προσκαρτερέω, imperfect periphrastic) 2113.
τῇ (loc.sing.fem.of the article in agreement with διδαχῇ) 9.
διδαχῇ (loc.sing.fem.of διδαχή, sphere) 706.
τῶν (gen.pl.masc.of the article in agreement with ἀποστόλων) 9.
ἀποστόλων (gen.pl.masc.of ἀπόστολος, description) 844.
καὶ (adjunctive conjunction joining nouns) 14.
τῇ (loc.sing.fem.of the article in agreement with κοινωνίᾳ) 9.

#3001 κοινωνίᾳ (loc.sing.fem.of κοινωνία, sphere).

communication - Philemon 6.
communion - 1 Cor.10:16,16; 2 Cor.6:14; 13:14.
contribution - Romans 15:26.
distribution - 2 Cor.9:13.
fellowship - Acts 2:42; 1 Cor.1:9; 2 Cor.8:4; Gal.2:9; Phil.1:5; 2:1; 3:10; 1 John 1:3,3,6,7.
to communicate - Heb.13:16.

Meaning: Cf. κοινωνέω (#4026), κοινωνικός (#4795), κοινωνός (#1470), κοινωνόω (#1152) and κοινός (#2295). I. A share, part or participation which one has in something - followed by a genitive of description - τῆς πίστεως - Phm.6; τοῦ αἵματος - 1 Cor.10:16a; τοῦ σώματος - 1 Cor.10:16b; τοῦ υἱοῦ αὐτοῦ - 1 Cor.1:9; πνεύματος - 2 Cor.13:14; Phil.2:1; παθημάτων αὐτοῦ - Phil.3:10. II. the psychological feeling of intimacy, fellowship, rapport: with πρός and the accusative - "light and darkness' - 2 Cor.6:14; with a locative of sphere - Acts 2:42; Phil.1:5 (causal). In a genitive of description - Gal.2:9; as subject - 1 John 1:3b; as a direct object - 1 John 1:3a,6,7. III. a jointly contributed collection of money, food, clothing, etc. - material gifts - Rom.15:26; as a genitive of description - 2 Cor.9:13; Heb.13:16; direct object - 2 Cor.8:4.

τῇ (loc.sing.fem.of the article in agreement with κλάσει) 9.
κλάσει (loc.sing.fem.of κλάσις, sphere) 2912.
τοῦ (gen.sing.masc.of the article in agreement with ἄρτου) 9.
ἄρτου (gen.sing.masc.of ἄρτος, description) 338.
καὶ (adjunctive conjunction joining nouns) 14.
ταῖς (loc.pl.fem.of the article in agreement with προσευχαῖς) 9.
προσευχαῖς (loc.pl.fem.of προσευχή, sphere) 1238.

Translation - "And they began to participate regularly in programs in which they

*studied the Apostles' teachings, fellowshipped with them, and ate and prayed
with them."*

Comment: The imperfect periphrastic ἦσαν προσκαρτεροῦντες with its decided
durative character speaks of the consistency with which the new Christians
pursued their programs of Christian development. Peter later stressed the
necessity for babes in Christ to "grow in grace, and in the knowledge of our Lord
and Saviour, Jesus Christ" (2 Pet.3:18). No doubt he remembered that he had a
special commission from the Lord to "strengthen his brethren" (Luke 22:32).
Their program included all of the necessary elements for Christian development.
It involved Christian Education. They studied the doctrines of the Apostles.
How this great Bible College was conducted we are not told. There were eleven
instructors - perhaps others also of the disciples, who, though not Apostles, were
familiar with the teachings of Jesus and met with the students. They had no text
book except their copies of the Old Testament. All New Testament teaching was
provided from the memories of the teachers who told the stories about Jesus and
His words and works and expounded His theology.

They enjoyed the Christian fellowship of each other. Their social life was not
neglected. This phase of their development no doubt was pursued on a more
informal basis, as they visited in each other's homes. They probably drank a lot
of coffee together. Wherever these people who numbered more than 3120 and
were soon to increase in number to more than 5000, met they talked Christian
theology. New and enduring friendships were formed. It is probable that the
young people fell in love. They shared one another's burdens and so learned to
fulfill the law of Christ (Gal.6:2). Christians who fail to develop social
relationships with other Christians are not going to grow in grace as rapidly as if
they made new Christian friends and became involved in new social activities
with others of like mind.

In addition to their theological education and their social development, they
learned self discipline. The personal introspection by which every Christian
takes a long and honest look at himself before he eats the bread and drinks the
wine at the Lord's table is a necessary part of Christian growth. Honest
evaluation of personal attitudes and behavior will contribute to humility and a
heightened sense of the need for more complete dependence upon the Holy
Spirit. As the early Christians broke bread together they probably confessed
their "faults one to another and prayed one for another" (James 5:16).

Finally they prayed together and for each other.

The new way of life in Christ was so thrilling that they could do little else than
occupy themselves in these four spheres of activity that are so important in the
development of the victorious life. The intellectual stimulus of the classes in
theology, the rapport of Christian fellowship as like minds communicated and
shared burdens and blessings, the joyous communion services as each sought to
measure his own record of achievement against the divine standard and the
prayer sessions - And these were the people who only 52 days before had
applauded the murder of the Son of God.

Verse 43 - "And fear came upon every soul: and many wonders and signs were done by the apostles."

Ἐγίνετο δὲ πάσῃ ψυχῇ φόβος, πολλά τε τέρατα καὶ σημεῖα διὰ τῶν ἀποστόλων ἐγίνετο.

Ἐγίνετο (3d.per.sing.imp.ind.of γίνομαι, inceptive) 13.

δὲ (continuative conjunction) 11.

πάσῃ (loc.sing.fem.of πᾶς, in agreement with ψυχῇ) 67.

ψυχῇ (loc.sing.fem.of ψυχή, place) 233.

φόβος (nom.sing.masc.of φόβος, subject of ἐγίνετο) 1131.

πολλά (nom.pl.neut.of πολύς, in agreement with τέρατα and σημεῖα) 228.

τε (correlative conjunction) 1408.

τέρατα (nom.pl.neut.of τέρας, subject of ἐγίνετο) 1500.

καὶ (adjunctive conjunction joining nouns) 14.

σημεῖα (nom.pl.neut.of σημεῖα, subject of ἐγίνετο) 1005.

διὰ (preposition with the genitive, indirect agency) 118.

τῶν (gen.pl.masc.of the article in agreement with ἀποστόλων) 9.

ἀποστόλων (gen.pl.masc.of ἀπόστολος, direct agency) 844.

ἐγίνετο (3d.per.sing.imp.ind.of γίνομαι, iterative) 113.

Translation - "And reverential awe filled every soul and many both of wonders and signs were being performed by the Apostles."

Comment: We have not often found ἐγίνετο, the imperfect indicative. The aorist ἐγένετο usually occurs. Everyone began to feel a deep sense of awe in the presence of God. φόβος in this sense, not terror. There was deep conviction throughout the Christian community that God was present. There are several variant readings. "It is exceedingly difficult to ascertain the original text of this passage. It can be argued, as Ropes does, that the words ἐν Ἰερουσαλήμ, φόβος τε ἦν μέγας ἐπὶ πάντας καί were omitted because they seem to repeat ver.43a. On the other hand, Haenchen supposes that the words are an expansion smoothing the way for ver.44. A majority of the Committee preferred to follow B (D) 614 1739 itd,gig,p*,57 syrh copsa al." (Metzger, *A Textual Commentary on the Greek New Testament*, 302). If the disputed words are included they add nothing to the message which is not already there in the portion that is not in dispute.

Verse 44 - "And all that believed were together, and had all things common."

πάντες δὲ οἱ πιστεύσαντες ἦσαν ἐπὶ τὸ αὐτὸ καὶ εἶχον ἄπαντα κοινά.

πάντες (nom.pl.masc.of πᾶς, in agreement with πιστεύσαντες) 67.

δὲ (continuative conjunction) 11.

οἱ (nom.pl.masc.of the article in agreement with πιστεύσαντες) 9.

πιστεύσαντες (aor.act.part.nom.pl.masc.of πιστεύω, substantival, subject of ἦσαν and εἶχον) 734.

ἦσαν (3d.per.pl.imp.ind.of εἰμί, progressive description) 86.

ἐπὶ (preposition with the accusative of place) 47.

τό (acc.sing.neut.of the article in agreement with αὐτό) 9.
αὐτό (acc.sing.neut.of αὐτός, place where, intensive) 16.
καί (continuative conjunction) 14.
εἶχον (3d.per.pl.imp.ind.of ἔχω, inceptive) 82.
ἅπαντα (acc.pl.neut.of ἅπας, direct object of εἶχον) 639.
κοινά (acc.pl.neut.of κοινός, predicate accusative, adverbial) 2295.

Translation - "And all the believers were living in the same neighborhood and they introduced a system of communal property ownership."

Comment: ἦσαν is progressive description, but εἶχον is inceptive. We must call in the facts of the context in order to interpret the grammar here. There were 3120 believers and that many people could not have lived in the same house. So we must stretch ἐπὶ τὸ αὐτό to mean the same neighbourhood. They all lived "in the same place" which probably means that the Christians, who now had so much in common as a result of their recent wonderful experience, now found it profitable to find living quarters in the same section of the city. It was also imperative that they be near the Apostles whose theology classes they were attending (vs.42). A similar situation developed in the 17th, 18th and early 19th centuries in the United States, when Catholics immigrated and congregated in the eastern seaboard cities because at that time few Catholic priests had penetrated into the Ohio valley. Roman Catholic sacerdotalism demands that the penitent be close enough to the clergy to avail himself of the priestly absolution. The early Christians did not need that, but they did need to be near the Apostles for their spiritual and intellectual guidance. (*Cf.*Oscar Handlin, *Immigration as a Factor in American History,* 77*ff* and W.P.A. Federal Art Project, *The Italians of New York,* 86-91 *et passim*). The social life suggested in verse 42 was the result of spiritual and intellectual propinquity which could be served only with proximity. ἐπὶ τὸ αὐτό indicates proximity but it does not tell us how big the place was. It is likely that most of the Christians lived within walking distance of all of the others.

Verse 43 tells of many signs and wonders but it is careful to say that these miracles were performed only by the Apostles. Mark 16:20, which is a spurious and much later addition to the inspired text,and therefore need command no respect from the exegete suggests that every Christian is to be enabled to perform miracles and many Christians since have assumed that this is so. But the Scriptures are silent about miracle working powers to be dispensed on a wholesale basis to every Christian believer. The Apostles had been given special powers by Christ upon the occasion when they were first called (Matthew 10:1) and that was for a special reason. Their message required authentication which was provided by the services they were able to render through the powers which Jesus had given to them. The Apostles after Pentecost still needed these powers, as they were charged with the responsibility of establishing the churches throughout the Roman world upon a solid theological, ecclessiological and ethical basis, while Matthew, John, Paul and Peter, who were Apostles, and Mark, Luke, James and Jude would be chosen as the authors of the New

Testament. Had the Apostles not had the power to perform miracles it is not likely that their teachings would have been accepted nor their advice sought in the vital questions of church administration which needed solution during the crucial formative years. The experience of Simon, the sorcerer, who was converted in Philip's revival in Samaria serves to illustrate the point. In league with Satan before he heard Philip preach he was able to command a following among the people,but when he saw the apostolic power to perform miracles in the name of Christ, he realized that his own occult powers were insufficient to maintain his position with the people. Thus, when Peter and John came to Samaria to pray for Philip's converts, he tried to buy their apostolic gifts. Peter's response to Simon reveals how dangerous "sign gift" powers would be in the hands of any except the Apostles. (Acts 8:9-24). Note also the story of Elymas the sorcerer (Acts 13:7-12) and that of the demon possessed girl in Philippi (Acts 16:16-18). Bible students of discrimination who have spent years in painstaking and prayerful consideration of the total message of the Old and New Testaments are often struck with the shallow, misguided and even heretical views that are taught by modern miracle workers after whom "the signs have followed." It can not be doubted that they are being followed by some signs, although one may properly question the source of these signs. Why the Holy Spirit has not chosen to reveal sounder Christian theology to those who profess to be honored most with His ability to perform miracles is not explained. In view of the pessimistic evaluation of P. T. Barnum with reference to the intelligence of certain whom he said could be counted on to be "born every minute" it would be most unwise if the Holy Spirit gave every Christian the apostolic powers which he gave to the first century Apostles. Antichrist's ability to seduce the unsaved - a power which if it were possible would even deceive the elect, will be given to him by Satan to perform the incredible feats for which people now pay good money to witness. (Rev.13:11-17). The rich man in Hades was told that unsaved men on earth who will not consult Moses and the prophets in search for spiritual help, will not believe even if Lazarus is raised from the dead (Luke 16:31) and Jesus said that the generation that can be impressed only by signs is thereby demonstrated to be "evil and adulterous" (Mt.12:39).

The experiment in communal ownership of property was begun, not by a directive from the Apostles but by someone else who acted without authority. It was probably the result of the perfect rapport which the early Christians enjoyed for a time. That communism, even among Christians is not the economic plan by which society should be ordered, is clear from Acts 5:4 and Eph.4:28, upon which see comment. The New Testament order is private ownership of the means of production accompanied by a voluntary Christian stewardship in the field of distribution. There was no need for a governmentally sponsored "welfare state" program in the early church, nor would there be now if the church in the 20th century lived up to her ethical responsibilities.

Verse 45 - "And sold their possessions and goods and parted them to all men, as every man had need."

καὶ τὰ κτήματα καὶ τὰς ὑπάρξεις ἐπίπρασκον καὶ διεμέριζον αὐτὰ πᾶσιν καθότι ἄν τις χρείαν εἶχεν.

καὶ (continuative conjunction) 14.
τὰ (acc.pl.neut.of the article in agreement with κτήματα) 9.
κτήματα (acc.pl.neut.of κτῆμα, direct object of ἐπίπρασκον) 1305.
καὶ (adjunctive conjunction joining nouns) 14.
τὰς (acc.pl.fem.of the article in agreement with ὑπάρξεις) 9.

#3002 ὑπάρξεις (acc.pl.fem.of ὕπαρξις, direct object of ἐπίπρασκον).

goods - Acts 2:45.
substance - Heb.10:34.

Meaning: Cf.ὑπάρχω (#1303) Possessions, goods, property. Distributed in the early church - Acts 2:45. With reference to eternal wealth in heaven - Heb.10:34.

ἐπίπρασκον (3d.per.pl.imp.act.ind.of πιπράσκω, inceptive) 1088.
καὶ (adjunctive conjunction joining verbs) 14.
διεμέριζον (3d.per.pl.imp.act.ind.of διαμερίζω, inceptive) 1647.
αὐτὰ (acc.pl.neut.of αὐτός, direct object of διεμέριζον) 16.
πᾶσιν (dat.pl.masc.of πᾶς, indirect object of διεμέριζον) 67.
καθότι (for καθ' ὅτι, in a relative clause in a second-class condition) 1783.
ἄν (contingent particle in a second-class condition) 205.
τις (nom.sing.masc.of τις, indefinite pronoun, subject of εἶχεν) 486.
χρείαν (acc.sing.fem.of χρεία, direct object of εἶχεν) 317.
εἶχεν (3d.per.sing.imp.act.ind.of ἔχω, second-class condition) 82.

Translation - "And they began to sell their property and goods and to divide them to all accordingly if anyone had a need."

Comment: The distinction between κτήματα (#1305) and ὑπάρξεις (#3002) is probably that of real property in the former and personal effects in the latter case. Note the imperfect tenses in ἐπίπρασκον καὶ διεμέριζον, which can be taken either as inceptive or iterative. The beginning of their action (inceptive) is certainly in view, and the context indicates that their action was not progressive (continuous) but iterative. From time to time as they discovered that someone in the fellowship had a need that he could not provide from his own resources, more selling of property and more distribution of wealth was effected. Note the relative clause in the second-class condition. Every time a need arose from anyone in the fellowship, whoever it might be and whatever the need, it was supplied. Thus the church was practising Eph.4:28 before Paul had written it. This is private ownership coupled with Christian stewardship. Their practice reveals (a) a great love for each other, and (b) an other worldly attitude material wealth. This is certainly not Adam Smith's *homo economicus* or Bernard Mandeville's *Fable of the Bees* where the "invisible hand" dictates that every man serves society best when he is the most selfish. If the church had always followed the example set by this verse, the problem of mal-distribution of wealth which results in a failure of the consumption function and its result in terms of inventory glut would be avoided. When inventories cannot be sold business men, unwilling to make new investments, retrench and unemployment increases, which only exacerbates the maldistribution of the wealth which started the downward cycle in the first place. Thus social problems are created and human rights are denied to the dispossessed. Economies which are immune from exogenous factors must generate within their own systems the purchasing power necessary to buy back all that is produced. The rich who have too much money will not spend beyond the dictates of their own diminishing marginal utility, and the poor who do not have enough, although they spend all the money which they have, are not able to generate enough consumption to prevent downswings in the cycle. Thus the basic problem of cyclical fluctuations which generate so much human misery and demonstrate the failure of the *laissez faire* system is a moral one. For a time the Christians in the early church in Jerusalem proved that their love for God and for each other overcame their lust for material wealth. If the pattern of distribution developed within the confines of the Christian community in Jerusalem could have spread throughout the entire economy, stable production/consumption activities would have kept the price level constant and growth would have occurred *pari passu* the increase in population. This coordination of the production and consumption function could go on indefinitely unless it was upset by the failure of supply of raw material or power resources or by exogenous factors.

That what happened in Jerusalem among the early Christians was not Marxian communism is clear from the fact that the Christians were private owners before they chose voluntarily to sell their possessions and give the proceeds to others less fortunate than themselves. The means of production were not owned by the group as a whole. But if it was not Marxian communism, neither was it the cutthroat impersonal capitalism of the Ricardo-Marshallian model in which the psychology of individual differences dictated that the market degenerated into a jungle ruled only by the law of claw and fang, in which the strong only survived and the weak perished. Nor, indeed was it the Welfare-State policy of the Keynesian model which must depend upon spending in the public sector to supplement investment in the private sector. The Christians were doing on a voluntary basis what they wished to do because they loved each other and wished to bear the burdens of one another and thus fulfill the law of Christ. They were not economists and could not have analyzed why they were doing the right thing. For them, the right thing was the moral thing, dictated by Christian love and compassion, and they were willing to leave the economic results up to economic principles of which they had never heard. Filled with the Holy Spirit they were doing then what they wanted to do, not what they were told to do by the legislative enactments of the architects of the welfare state. We will discover in the story of Ananias and Sapphira (Acts 5:1-11) that though they were saved, they were not free from the cupidity which has always wrought havoc in society.

Verse 46 - "And they, continuing daily with one accord in the temple and breaking bread from house to house, did eat their meat with gladness and singleness of heart."

καθ' ἡμέραν τε προσκαρτεροῦντες ὁμοθυμαδὸν ἐν τῷ ἱερῷ, κλῶντές τε κατ' οἶκον ἄρτον, μετελάμβανον τροφῆς ἐν ἀγαλλιάσει καὶ ἀφελότητι καρδίας.

καθ' (preposition with the accusative, distributive) 98.
ἡμέραν (acc.sing.fem.of ἡμέρα, distributive) 135.
τε (correlative particle) 1408.
προσκαρτεροῦντες (pres.act.part.nom.pl.masc.of προσκαρτερέω, adverbial, temporal) 2113.
ὁμοθυμαδὸν (adverbial) 2942.
ἐν (preposition with the locative of place) 80.
τῷ (loc.sing.neut.of the article in agreement with ἱερῷ) 9.
ἱερῷ (loc.sing.neut.of ἱερον, place where) 346.
κλῶντες (pres.act.part.nom.pl.masc.of κλάω, adverbial, modal) 1121.
τε (adjunctive conjunction joining participles) 1408.
κατ' (preposition with the accusative, distributive) 98.
οἶκον (acc.sing.masc.of οἶκος, distributive) 784.
ἄρτον (acc.sing.masc.of ἄρτος, direct object of κλῶντες) 338.

#3003 μετελάμβανον (3d.per.pl.imp.act.ind.of μεταλαμβάνω, iterative).

be partaker of - 2 Tim.2:6; Heb.12:10.

eat - Acts 2:46.
have - Acts 24:25.
receive - Heb.6:7.
take - Acts 27:33,34.

Meaning: A combination of μετά (#50) and λαμβάνω (#533). To take with; to partake; to take unto oneself; to be made a partaker. With a genitive of description - Heb.12:10 (his holiness); 2 Tim.2:6 - "of the harvest." Followed by a direct object - Acts 24:25. With a subjective genitive - Heb.6:7; with objective genitive - Acts 2:46; 27:33. To receive something physical - food - Acts 2:46; 27:33,34; produce from the ground - 2 Tim.2:6; time - Acts 24:25; God holiness - Heb.12:10; blessing from God - Heb.6:7.

τροφῆς (gen.sing.fem.of τροφή, subjective genitive) 266.
ἐν (preposition with the instrumental of manner) 80.
ἀγαλλιάσει (instru.sing.fem.of ἀγαλλίασις, manner) 1797.
καὶ (adjunctive conjunction joining nouns) 14.

#3004 ἀφελότητι (instru.sing.masc.of ἀφελότης, manner).

singleness - Acts 2:46.

Meaning: α privative and φελλεύς - "rocky land." Hence ἀφελής means "without rocks; smooth," "plain." Thus ἀφελότης - simplicity, undeviating, singleness, sincerity, without duplicity. Followed by καρδίας - Acts 2:46.

καρδίας (gen.sing.fem.of καρδία, description) 432.

Translation - *"Day by day they went together to the temple, and they broke their bread together in their homes and with sincere hearts filled with gladness they ate their food."*

Comment: Note the two interesting uses of κατά and the accusative in a distributive sense - "day by day" or "one day after another" and "from house to house." So the early Christians gathered for the fellowship that is possible when there is unity of purpose, feeling and doctrinal agreement. Note that they went to the temple, and apparently at first they were not molested by the temple authorities. It was only when they grew in numbers that they aroused the opposition of the Establishment. The larger meetings in the temple were supplemented by meetings of smaller numbers as they went from one home to another. The "breaking of bread" probably refers to the communion services, while the "taking of food" refers to the social interaction which they enjoyed. All of this was carried on with hearts that overflowed with gladness and complete lack of the duplicity which later, at least in the case of Ananias and Sapphira marred their fellowship. Complete egalitarianism in Christ is seen in this picture. A process of economic and social levelling had taken place. There is no ground for discrimination of any sort within the Body of Christ. The ground at the foot of the cross is level. *Cf.*#2113 for the intense and consistent effort of their service, and #2942 for a description of their unity, a result of the filling of the Holy Spirit as He enthroned Christ in every heart.

Two more characteristics of their life style are added in

Verse 47 - *"Praising God and having favor with all the people. And the Lord added to the church daily such as should be saved."*

αἰνοῦντες τὸν θεὸν καὶ ἔχοντες χάριν πρὸς ὅλον τὸν λαόν. ὁ δὲ κύριος προσετίθει τοὺς σωζομένους καθ᾽ ἡμέραν ἐπὶ τὸ αὐτό.

αἰνοῦντες (pres.act.part.nom.pl.masc.of αἰνέω, adverbial, complementary) 1881.

τὸν (acc.sing.masc.of the article in agreement with θεόν) 9.

θεόν (acc.sing.masc.of θεός, direct object of αἰνοῦντες) 124.

καὶ (adjunctive conjunction joining participles) 14.

ἔχοντες (pres.act.part.nom.pl.masc.of ἔχω, adverbial, complementary) 82.

χάριν (acc.sing.masc.of χάρις, direct object of ἔχοντες) 1700.

πρὸς (preposition with the accusative of extent, with persons, metaphorical) 197.

ὅλον (acc.sing.masc.of ὅλος, in agreement with λαόν) 112.

τὸν (acc.sing.masc.of the article in agreement with λαόν) 9.

λαόν (acc.sing.masc.of λαός, extent, with persons, metaphorical) 110.

ὁ (nom.sing.masc.of the article in agreement with κύριος) 9.

δὲ (continuative conjunction) 11.

κύριος (nom.sing.masc.of κύριος, subject of προσετίθει) 97.

προσετίθει (3d.per.sing.imp.act.ind.of προστίθημι, iterative) 621.

τοὺς (acc.pl.masc.of the article in agreement with σωζομένους) 9.

σωζομένους (pres.pass.part.acc.pl.masc.of σώζω, substantival, direct object of προσετίθει) 109.
καθ' (preposition with the accusative, distributive) 98.
ἡμέραν (acc.sing.fem.of ἡμέρα, distributive) 135.
ἐπὶ (preposition with the accusative of extent) 47.
τό (acc.sing.neut.of the article in agreement with αὐτό) 9.
αὐτό (acc.sing.neut.of αὐτός, extent) 16.

Translation - ". . .they were always praising God and they were favorably regarded by all the people. And the Lord continued every day to add to their number those who were saved."

Comment: The present participle is timeless and durative, just as the aorist participle is timeless and punctiliar. They were always praising God and they continued to receive the approbation of all of the people, who could find nothing in their behavior to which they could object. The imperfect tense in προσετίθει is iterative, an idea that is supported by the distributive καθ' ἡμέραν. "Every day" - it all speaks of the consistency of the performance of the early church. ἐπὶ τὸ αὐτό (*cf.* Acts 2:44) does not mean "to the church" but to the fellowship of like minded saints.

The Lame Man Healed at the Gate of the Temple

(Acts 3:1-10)

Acts 3:1 - "*Now Peter and John went up together into the temple at the hour of prayer, being the ninth hour.*"

Πέτρος δὲ καὶ Ἰωάννης ἀνέβαινον εἰς τὸ ἱερὸν ἐπὶ τὴν ὥραν τῆς προσευχῆς τὴν ἐνάτην.

Πέτρος (nom.sing.masc.of Πέτρος, subject of ἀνέβαινον) 387.
δὲ (explanatory conjunction) 11.
καὶ (adjunctive conjunction joining nouns) 14.
Ἰωάννης (nom.sing.masc.of Ἰωάννης, subject of ἀνέβαινον) 399.
ἀνέβαινον (3d.per.pl.imp.act.ind.of ἀναβαίνω, inceptive) 323.
εἰς (preposition with the accusative of extent) 140.
τό (acc.sing.neut.of the article in agreement with ἱερὸν) 9.
ἱερὸν (acc.sing.neut.of ἱερόν, extent) 346.
ἐπὶ (preposition with the accusative with a time expression) 47.
τὴν (acc.sing.fem.of the article in agreement with ὥραν) 9.
ὥραν (acc.sing.fem.of ὥρα, time expression) 735.
τῆς (gen.sing.fem.of the article in agreement with προσευχῆς) 9.
προσευχῆς (gen.sing.fem.of προσευχή, description) 1238.
τὴν (acc.sing.fem.of the article in agreement with ἐνάτην) 9.
ἐνάτην (acc.sing.fem.of ἔννατος, in agreement with ὥραν) 1318.

Translation - "Now Peter and John started up to the temple at three o'clock in the afternoon, the hour of prayer."

Comment: We can think of ἀνέβαινον as progressive description and translate, "were on their way up to the temple." The inceptive and progressive description uses of the imperfect give us the full picture.   Note the temporal use of ἐπί with the accusative. There has been no record of active opposition from the temple authorities up to this point, despite the fact that the Christians had been going there every day in great numbers, witnessing the gospel of Christ. They were much bolder now, as a result of the filling of the Holy Spirit, than they were before Pentecost when they feared persecution and tooks steps to stay out of trouble (John 20:19). The miracle which was about to be performed and Peter's sermon in Solomon's Porch was soon to end the period of relative quiet. That Peter and John should still go up to the temple at the three o'clock prayer hour, even though their prayers would be offered along new-found lines of approach to the throne of God, indicates that they were not yet completely free from Judaistic tendencies. Indeed there was a small group of Judaic Christians who for five hundred years resisted the trend. introduced by Peter and Paul, that offered the gospel to the Gentiles. They practised Christian poverty but clung to observance of the full Jewish law. They did not yield to the new revelation (Eph.3:3-6; Acts 10:34,35) which transformed Christianity into a religion more in conformity to the eclectic Mid-Eastern thought, although resisting the dualism of Zoroaster, Mani, Plotinus, Philo, the Neo-Pythagoreans, the Neo-Platonists and the Alexandrian Gnostics. These Syriac Christians who were known as *Ebionim* ("the poor") were condemned as heretics by the Church at the end of the second century. (Will Durant, *Caesar and Christ,* 577). Traces of this stubborn determination to cling to Judaism at the expense of Christian freedom as expounded by Paul in his Colossian epistle, are still found in the ban on pork by the Seventh Day Adventists and the sabbatarian views of many Christians who refuse to "work on Sunday." The author remembers a godly deacon who confessed that before he came to understand Paul's message on Christian freedom from the law, his conscience was troubled every time he threw a fork full of hay into the manger for his horses on Sunday.

Verse 2 - "And a certain man, lame from his mother's womb, was carried, whom they laid daily at the gate of the temple which is called Beautiful, to ask alms of them that entered into the temple."

καί τις ανὴρ χωλὸς ἐκ κοιλίας μητρὸς αὐτοῦ ὑπάρχων ἐβαστάζετο, ὃν ἐτίθουν καθ' ἡμέραν πρὸς τὴν θύραν τοῦ ἱεροῦ τὴν λεγομένην Ὡραίαν τοῦ αἰτεῖν ἐλεημοσύνην παρὰ τῶν εἰσπορευομένων εἰς τὸ ἱερόν.

καί (continuative conjunction) 14.
τις (nom.sing.masc.of τις, in agreement with ἀνήρ) 486.
ἀνὴρ (nom.sing.masc.of ἀνήρ, subject of ἐβαστάζετο) 63.
χωλὸς (nom.sing.masc.of χωλός, predicate adjective) 908.
ἐκ (preposition with the ablative of time separation) 19.

κοιλίας (abl.sing.fem.of κοιλία, time separation) 1008.

μητρὸς (gen.sing.fem.of μήτηρ, possession) 76.

αὐτοῦ (gen.sing.masc.of αὐτός, relationship) 16.

ὑπάρχων (pres.part.nom.sing.masc.of ὑπάρχω, adjectival, in agreement with ἀνὴρ) 1303.

ἐβαστάζετο (3d.per.sing.imp.pass.ind.of βαστάζω, iterative) 306.

ὃν (acc.sing.masc.of ὅς, direct object of ἐτίθουν) 65.

ἐτίθουν (3d.per.pl.imp.act.ind.of τίθημι, iterative) 455.

καθ' (preposition with the accusative, distributive) 98.

ἡμέραν (acc.sing.fem.of ἡμέρα, distributive) 135.

πρὸς (preposition with the accusative of extent) 197.

τὴν (acc.sing.fem.of the article in agreement with θύραν) 9.

θύραν (acc.sing.fem.of θύρα, extent) 571.

τοῦ (gen.sing.neut.of the article in agreement with ἱεροῦ) 9.

ἱεροῦ (gen.sing.neut.of ἱερόν, description) 346.

τὴν (acc.sing.fem.of the article in agreement with λεγομένην) 9.

λεγομένην (pres.pass.part.acc.sing.fem.of λέγω, substantival, apposition) 66.

Ὡραίαν (acc.sing.fem.of ὡραῖος, appellation) 1465.

τοῦ (gen.sing.neut.of the article, with an infinitive of purpose) 9.

αἰτεῖν (pres.act.inf.of αἰτέω, purpose) 537.

ἐλεημοσύνην (acc.sing.fem.of ἐλεημοσύνη, direct object of αἰτεῖν) 558.

παρὰ (preposition with the ablative of source) 154.

τῶν (abl.pl.masc.of the article in agreement with εἰσπορευομένων) 9.

εἰσπορευομένων (pres.mid.part.abl.pl.masc.of εἰσπορεύομαι, substantival, source) 1161.

εἰς (preposition with the accusative of extent) 140.

τὸ (acc.sing.neut.of the article in agreement with ἱερόν) 9.

ἱερόν (acc.sing.neut.of ἱερόν, extent) 346.

Translation - "And a certain man who had been lame since birth was always carried in, whom they placed every day near the door of the temple called 'Beautiful', so that he might beg from those who were coming into the temple, ...
"

Comment: The man who is not named, but rather identified by the indefinite pronoun as one who had been lame since birth, who was carried there periodically (iterative imperfect in ἐβαστάζετο). ἐκ κοιλίας μητρὸς αὐτοῦ - literally "from his mother's womb," hence, lame since birth. He is further identified by the relative clause as the one who was placed (iterative imperfect again) on a day by day basis (καθ' ἡμέραν) near the temple door. Why? The telic infinitive in the genitive case τοῦ αἰτεῖν tells us that it was done in order that he might beg. τοῦ with the genitive infinitive to indicate purpose is also found, though rarely in the New Testament in Mt.2:13; 13:3; Lk.21:22; 24:29; 5:31; 26:18; 1 Cor.10:7; Gal.3:10; Heb.10:7. These and others. Votaw (*The Infinitive in Biblical Greek*, 21) counts 33 instances. There is no subject for ἐτίθουν, though the context makes clear that the subject, omitted here and implicit in the 3rd.per.pl.ending, is the man's family and/or friends. Thus Luke sets the stage in verses 1 and 2 for the miracle about to be performed. A cripple since birth carried every day by friends to the Gate Beautiful. He was a familiar figure, as he lay there every day begging from those who passed by. The two Apostles, Peter and John, enroute to the temple to pray in mid-afternoon approached the spot. The story continues in

Verse 3 - "who seeing Peter and John about to go into the temple asked an alms."

ὃς ἰδὼν Πέτρον καὶ Ἰωάννην μέλλοντας εἰσιέναι εἰς τὸ ἱερὸν ἠρώτα ἐλεημοσύνην (λαβεῖν).

ὅς (nom.sing.masc.of ὅς, subject of ἠρώτα) 65.
ἰδὼν (aor.act.part.nom.sing.masc.of ὁράω, adverbial, temporal/causal) 144.
Πέτρον (acc.sing.masc.of Πέτρος, direct object of ἰδὼν) 387.
καὶ (adjunctive conjunction joining nouns) 14.
Ἰωάννην (acc.sing.masc.of Ἰωάννης, direct object of ἰδὼν) 399.
μέλλοντας (pres.act.part.acc.pl.masc.of μέλλω, adverbial, temporal) 206.

#3005 εἰσιέναι (pres.inf.of εἴσειμί, complementary).

go in - Acts 21:18.
enter - Acts 21:26.
go into - Acts 3:3; Heb.9:6.

Meaning: A combination of εἰς (#140) and εἰμί, (#86). To be in; to enter. Followed by εἰς and the accusative of extent - Acts 3:3; 21:26; followed by πρός and the accusative - Acts 21:18. Joined with εἰς and the accusative in Heb.9:6.

εἰς (preposition with the accusative of extent) 140.
τὸ (acc.sing.neut.of the article in agreement with ἱερὸν) 9.
ἱερὸν (acc.sing.neut.of ἱερόν, extent) 346.
ἠρώτα (3d.per.sing.imp.act.ind.of ἐρωτάω, inceptive) 1172.
ἐλεημοσύνην (acc.sing.fem.of ἐλεημοσύνη, direct object of λαβεῖν) 558.
(λαβεῖν) (2d.aor.act.inf.of λαμβάνω, object of ἠρώτα) 533.

Translation - ". . . who, when he saw Peter and John about to enter into the temple, began to ask them to give him some money."

Comment: The participle ἰδὼν is both temporal and causal. "When (because) he saw Peter and John. . . κ.τ.λ." Verbs which are composed of εἰς and the copula regularly repeat εἰς. Cf.#3005. The iterative imperfect is clear in ἠρώτα, with its object in the infinitive λαβεῖν. A lifetime of practice at the art of begging had made the man insistent. It is a moving picture. The rugged fishermen approach. The emaciated cripple stirs with outstretched hands and piteous cry, "Alms, Alms, Alms."
He was about to receive something far better than money.

Verse 4 - "And Peter, fastening his eyes upon him with John, said, Look on us."

ἀτενίσας δὲ Πέτρος εἰς αὐτὸν σὺν τῷ Ἰωάννῃ εἶπεν, Βλέφον εἰς ἡμᾶς.

ἀτενίσας (aor.act.part.nom.sing.masc.of ἀτενίζω, adverbial, temporal) 2028.
δὲ (continuative conjunction) 11.
Πέτρος (nom.sing.masc.of Πέτρος, subject of εἶπεν) 387.
εἰς (preposition with the accusative of extent) 140.
αὐτὸν (acc.sing.masc.of αὐτός, extent) 16.
σὺν (preposition with the instru.of association) 1542.
τῷ (instru.sing.masc.of the article in agreement with Ἰωάννῃ) 9.
Ἰωάννῃ (instru.sing.masc.of Ἰωάννης, association) 399.
εἶπεν (3d.per.sing.aor.act.ind.of εἶπον, constative) 155.
Βλέφον (2d.per.sing.aor.act.impv.of βλέπω, command) 499.
εἰς (preposition with the accusative of extent) 140.
ἡμᾶς (acc.pl.masc.of ἐγώ, extent) 123.

Translation - "And Peter along with John looked at him intently and said, 'Look at us.' "

Comment: Peter and John secured the cripple's undivided attention after which came the order with a strong tone of apostolic authority.

Verse 5 - "And he gave heed unto them, expecting to receive something of them."

ὁ δὲ ἐπεῖχεν αὐτοῖς προσδοκῶν τι παρ' αὐτῶν λαβεῖν.

ὁ (nom.sing.masc.of the article, subject of ἐπεῖχεν) 9.
δὲ (inferential conjunction) 11.
ἐπεῖχεν (3d.per.sing.imp.act.ind.of ἐπέχω, progressive description) 2522.
αὐτοῖς (dat.pl.masc.of αὐτός, indirect object of ἐπεῖχεν) 16.
προσδοκῶν (pres.act.part.nom.sing.masc.of προσδοκάω, adverbial, causal) 906.
τι (acc.sing.neut.of τις, direct object of λαβεῖν) 486.
παρ' (preposition with the ablative of source) 154.
αὐτῶν (abl.pl.masc.of αὐτός, source) 16.
λαβεῖν (2d.aor.act.inf.of λαμβάνω, epexegetical) 533.

Translation - "So he continued to pay close attention to them, because he expected to receive something from them."

Comment: Cf.#2522 and note the influence of ἐπί upon ἔχω in the compound verb. The cripple, who had concentrated his attention upon Peter and John from the moment he first saw them approaching continued to watch them intently. προσδοκῶν is causal. He expected to receive some money from them. This was natural as money was the usual gratuity which he received. Hence his great surprized delight prefaced for a brief moment by a stab of disappointment, as Peter first said that he and John were temporarily without funds, but that they had something of far greater value.

Verse 6 - *"Then Peter said, Silver and gold have I none; but such as I have give I to thee: in the name of Jesus Christ of Nazareth rise up and walk."*

εἶπεν δὲ Πέτρος,'Αργύριον καὶ χρυσίον οὐχ ὑπάρχει μοι, ὃ δὲ ἔχω τοῦτό σοι δίδωμι, ἐν τῷ ὀνόματι Ἰησοῦ Χριστοῦ τοῦ Ναζωραίου περιπάτει.

εἶπεν (3d.per.sing.aor.act.ind.of εἶπον, constative) 155.
δὲ (adversative conjunction) 11.
Πέτρος (nom.sing.masc.of Πέτρος, subject of εἶπεν, ἔχω and δίδωμι) 387.
'Αργύριον (nom.sing.neut.of ἀργύριον, subject of ὑπάρχει) 1535.
καὶ (adjunctive conjunction joining nouns) 14.

#3006 χρυσίον (nom.sing.neut.of ὑπάρχει).

gold - Acts 3:6; 20:33; Heb.9:4; 1 Peter 1:7,18; 3:3; Rev.3:18; 21:18,21; 1 Tim.2:9; Rev.17:4.

Meaning: Gold. In a monetary sense - Acts 3:6; 20:33; 1 Peter 1:7,18. In an ornamental sense - 1 Peter 3:3; Heb.9:4; 1 Tim.2:9; Rev.21:18,21. In metaphorical contrast between human and divine values - Rev.3:18.

οὐχ (summary negative conjunction with the indicative) 130.
ὑπάρχει (3d.per.sing.pres.act.ind.of ὑπάρχω, aoristic) 1303.
μοι (dat.sing.masc.of ἐγώ, personal advantage) 123.
ὃ (acc.sing.neut.of ὅς, direct object of ἔχω) 65.
δὲ (adversative conjunction) 11.
ἔχω (1st.per.sing.pres.act.ind.of ἔχω, aoristic) 82.
τοῦτο (acc.sing.neut.of οὗτος, resumptive, direct object of δίδωμι) 93.
σοι (dat.sing.masc.of σύ, indirect object of δίδωμι) 104.
δίδωμι (1st.per.sing.pres.act.ind.of δίδωμι, futuristic) 362.
ἐν (preposition with the instrumental of cause) 80.
τῷ (instru.sing.neut.of the article in agreement with ὀνόματι) 9.
ὀνόματι (instru.sing.neut.of ὄνομα, cause) 108.
Ἰησοῦ (gen.sing.masc.of Ἰησοῦς, possession) 3.
Χριστοῦ (gen.sing.masc.of Χριστός, apposition) 4.
τοῦ (gen.sing.masc.of the article in agreement with Ναζωραίου) 9.
Ναζωραίου (gen.sing.masc.of Ναζωραῖος, apposition) 245.
περιπάτει (2d.per.sing.pres.act.impv.of περιπατέω, command) 384.

Translation - *"But Peter said, 'Silver and gold are not available to me at present, but I will give you what I have. In the name of Jesus Christ, the Nazarene, start walking.' "*

Comment: I have called the first δὲ adversative, because the last clause of verse 5 says that the cripple was expecting to receive some money from them. But (adversative δὲ) that is not what he got. Rather (adversative δὲ again) he got something that he did not expect.'Αργύριον . . . μοι is an interesting way to put it. ὑπάρχω (#1303) means "to exercise authority or control over" something or somebody. Peter did not say that he had no money at all. He did say that at the moment there was no silver or gold which could be used to his advantage. This is why μοι is the dative of personal advantage and not the dative of possession. Peter was saying in effect, "Silver and gold do not, at the moment, fall within the purview of my authority and control" or "I do not at the moment command any control over silver and gold." He may have had some at home, but that could serve no good purpose, now that he stood before the crippled beggar. τοῦτο is resumptive, as it points to the relative pronoun ὅ. δίδωμι is futuristic, although the time span into the future was very short. Yet δίδωμι is not strictly aoristic. It was in the next moment that Peter redeemed his promise. He did it in the name that had turned the nation upside down and inside out only a short time before. Note that Peter took no credit for the miracle. It was because and by the authority of a Nazarene carpenter, whom the sophisticated Jews in Jerusalem had despised, that the cripple walked for the first time in his life. Jesus was present in the temple again, as surely as if He had been there in the flesh.

Verse 7 - "And he took him by the right hand and lifted him up: and immediately his feet and ankle bones received strength."

καὶ πιάσας αὐτὸν τῆς δεξιᾶς χειρὸς ἤγειρεν αὐτόν, παραχρῆμα δὲ ἐστερεώθησαν αἱ βάσεις αὐτοῦ καὶ τὰ σφυδρά.

καὶ (continuative conjunction) 14.
πιάσας (aor.act.part.nom.sing.masc.of πιάζω, adverbial, modal) 2371.
αὐτὸν (acc.sing.masc.of αὐτός, direct object of πιάσας) 16.
τῆς (gen.sing.fem.of the article in agreement with χειρὸς) 9.
δεξιᾶς (gen.sing.fem.of δεξιός, in agreement with χειρὸς) 502.
χειρὸς (gen.sing.fem.of χείρ, description after a verb of touching) 308.
ἤγειρεν (3d.per.sing.aor.act.ind.of ἐγείρω, constative) 125.
αὐτόν (acc.sing.masc.of αὐτός, direct object of ἤγειρεν) 16.
παραχρῆμα (adverbial) 1369.
δὲ (continuative conjunction) 11.

#3007 ἐστερεώθησαν (3d.per.pl.aor.pass.ind.of στερεόω, constative).

establish - Acts 16:5.
make strong - Acts 3:16.
receive strength - Acts 3:7.

Meaning: Cf. στερέωμα (#4612), στερεός (# 4827), στηριγμός (#5287) and στηρίζω (#2359). To make firm; to make steadfast; to strengthen - In a physical sense - the body - Acts 3:7,16; followed by a locative of sphere - τῇ πίστει - Acts 16:5.

αἱ (nom.pl.fem.of the article in agreement with βάσεις) 9.

#3008 βάσεις (nom.pl.fem.of βάσις, subject of ἐστερεώθησαν).

foot - Acts 3:7.

Meaning: Cf. βαίνω - "to walk." Hence, the foot. With reference to the cripple at the Gate Beautiful - Acts 3:7.

αὐτοῦ (gen.sing.masc.of αὐτός, possession) 16.
τά (nom.pl.neut.of the article in agreement with σφυδρά) 9.

#3009 σφυδρά (nom.pl.neut.of σφυδρόν, subject of ἐστερεώθησαν).

anklebone - Acts 3:7.

Meaning - the anklebone of the cripple of Acts 3:7.

Translation - "And by taking his right hand he lifted him up, and immediately his feet and anklebones were made strong, . . . "

Comment: There was no delay as παραχρῆμα (#1369) indicates. The miracle was as instantaneous as if Jesus had been present personally. His feet and anklebones were strengthened enough for his performance of verse 8.

The authority with which Peter spoke in the sermon which followed (vss. 12-26) was greatly enhanced by the prestige which was his as a result of this notable miracle. Thus is demonstrated the purpose for which the sign gifts were given to the Apostles and to no one else in the early church. Peter and John, since they were Apostles, chosen personally by Jesus to represent Him, supervise the early activities of the church and write their parts of the New Testament, could speak with authority about Jesus and the terms of the new gospel. They had travelled with Him for three years and could personally attest to the fact of His resurrection and ascension. The current effort on the part of some to show that the powers which our Lord gave to the Apostles in the first century were also given to all who believe and that "the signs follow" while it may not be a conscious effort to assume apostolic authority, thus to rewrite, modify and change Christian theology, is having that effect in some quarters. There is a remarkable reluctance to engage in serious exegesis of the New Testament on the part of those who are less interested in what the Holy Spirit said in the first century of the Christian era than in what He may now say, as if He had not finished the revelation of truth and included all of it within the pages of the New Testament. A Pentecostalist who is looking for new and different light from God, in addition to that which has been revealed in the Bible as the church has had it for 1900 years is little different from the Mormon elder who declares that his "revelations" are superior to those of former prophets and that his directives are therefore to take precedence over what has gone before.

Verse 8 - "And he leaping up stood, and walked, and entered with them into the temple, walking and leaping and praising God."

καὶ ἐξαλλόμενος ἔστη καὶ περιεπάτει, καὶ εἰσῆλθεν σὺν αὐτοῖς εἰς τὸ ἱερὸν περιπατῶν καὶ ἀλλόμενος καὶ αἰνῶν τὸν θεόν.

καὶ (inferential conjunction) 14.

#3010 ἐξαλλόμενος (pres.mid.part.nom.sing.masc.of ἐξάλλομαι, adverbial, temporal).

leap up - Acts 3:8.

Meaning: A combination of ἐκ (#19) and ἄλλομαι (#2009). Hence, to leap up. Of the cripple at the Beautiful Gate - Acts 3:8.

ἔστη (3d.per.sing.2d.aor.act.ind.of ἵστημι, constative) 180.
καὶ (adjunctive conjunction joining verbs) 14.
περιεπάτει (3d.per.sing.imp.act.ind.of περιπατέω, inceptive) 384.
καὶ (adjunctive conjunction joining verbs) 14.
εἰσῆλθεν (3d.per.sing.aor.mid.ind.of εἰσέρχομαι, constative) 234.
σὺν (preposition with the instrumental of association) 1542.
αὐτοῖς (instru.pl.masc.of αὐτός, association) 16.
εἰς (preposition with the accusative of extent) 140.
τὸ (acc.sing.neut.of the article in agreement with ἱερὸν) 9.
ἱερὸν (acc.sing.neut.of ἱερόν, extent) 346.
περιπατῶν (pres.act.part.nom.sing.masc.of περιπατέω, adverbial, complementary) 384.
καὶ (adjunctive conjunction joining participles) 14.
ἀλλόμενος (pres.mid.part.nom.sing.masc.of ἄλλομαι, adverbial, complementary) 2009.
καὶ (adjunctive conjunction joining participles) 14.
αἰνῶν (pres.act.part.nom.sing.masc.of αἰνέω, adverbial, complementary) 1881.
τὸν (acc.sing.masc.of the article in agreement with θεόν) 9.
θεόν (acc.sing.masc.of θεός, direct object of αἰνῶν) 124.

Translation - "And he leaped up and stood, and he began to walk around, and he went into the temple with them, walking around, and leaping and praising God."

Comment: It is a dramatic picture, skillfully portrayed by the inceptive imperfect in περιεπάτει and the complementary participles. The action began as Peter took the man's right hand and pulled him to a standing position. As the strength flowed into feet and anklebones which had since his birth been useless, the man leaped up and then stood erect, without Peter's help, as if to test the reality of the healing. At that point he began to walk around - here and there he went, in the area outside the temple gate. After several exploratory excursions he returned to the gate where the Apostles were standing and together the three of them entered the temple, whereupon the man resumed his walking - round and round in ever widening circles he went, punctuating his progress with leaps, high into the air and shouting his praises to God from the top of his lungs. It was the first time in his life that he had ever walked.

His performance attracted the attention of all of the people in the temple, and Peter and John had their crowd.

Verse 9 - "And all the people saw him walking and praising God."

καὶ εἶδεν πᾶς ὁ λαὸς αὐτὸν περιπατοῦντα καὶ αἰνοῦντα τὸν θεόν.

καὶ (continuative conjunction) 14.

εἶδεν (3d.per.sing.aor.act.ind.of ὁράω, constative) 144.

πᾶς (nom.sing.masc.of πᾶς, in agreement with λαὸς) 67.

ὁ (nom.sing.masc.of the article in agreement with λαὸς) 9.

λαὸς (nom.sing.masc.of λαός, subject of εἶδεν) 110.

αὐτὸν (acc.sing.masc.of αὐτός, direct object of εἶδεν) 16.

περιπατοῦντα (pres.act.part.acc.sing.masc.of περιπατέω, adverbial, circumstantial) 384.

καὶ (adjunctive conjunction joining participles) 14.

αἰνοῦντα (pres.act.part.acc.sing.masc.of αἰνέω, adverbial, circumstantial) 1881.

τὸν (acc.sing.masc.of the article in agreement with θεόν) 9.

θεόν (acc.sing.masc.of θεός, direct object of αἰνοῦντα) 124.

Translation - "And all the people saw him walking around and praising God."

Comment: Thus the miracle and the healed man's reaction to it attracted the attention of a great number of people who were present in the temple court at the time. *Cf.*#384 for the list of verses where περιπατέω is used of the Christian's walk in the world. If we walk worthily of the vocation to which we have been called (Eph.4:1) and praise God as we walk, as this man did, all of the people will notice. Unfortunately they will also notice if we do not walk worthy of Him Who called us.

Verse 10 - "And they knew that it was he which sat for alms at the Beautiful gate of the temple: and they were filled by wonder and amazement at that which had happened unto him."

ἐπεγίνωσκον δὲ αὐτὸν ὅτι αὐτὸς ἦν ὁ πρὸς τὴν ἐλεημοσύνην καθήμενος ἐπὶ τῇ Ὡραίᾳ Πύλῃ τοῦ ἱεροῦ, καὶ ἐπλήσθησαν θάμβους καὶ ἐκστάσεως ἐπὶ τῷ συμβεβηκότι αὐτῷ.

ἐπεγίνωσκον (3d.per.pl.imp.act.ind.of ἐπιγινώσκω, inceptive) 675.

δὲ (continuative conjunction) 11.

αὐτὸν (acc.sing.masc.of αὐτός, direct object of ἐπεγίνωσκον) 16.

ὅτι (conjunction introducing an object clause in indirect discourse) 211

αὐτὸς (nom.sing.masc.of αὐτός, subject of ἦν) 16.

ἦν (3d.per.sing.imp.ind.of εἰμί, progressive description) 86.

ὁ (nom.sing.masc.of the article in agreement with καθήμενος) 9.

πρὸς (preposition with the accusative, purpose) 197.

τὴν (acc.sing.fem.of the article in agreement with ἐλεημοσύνην) 9.

ἐλεημοσύνην (acc.sing.fem.of ἐλεημοσύνη, purpose) 558.

καθήμενος (pres.mid.part.nom.sing.masc.of κάθημαι, substantival, predicate nominative) 377.

ἐπί (preposition with the locative of place) 47.

τῇ (loc.sing.fem.of the article in agreement with Πύλη) 9.

Ὡραίᾳ (loc.sing.fem.of ὡραῖος, in agreement with Πύλη) 1465.

Πύλη (loc.sing.fem.of πύλη, place where) 662.

τοῦ (gen.sing.neut.of the article in agreement with ἱεροῦ) 9.

ἱεροῦ (gen.sing.neut.of ἱερόν, description) 346.

καί (adjunctive conjunction joining verbs) 14.

ἐπλήσθησαν (3d.per.pl.aor.pass.ind.of πλήθω, constative) 1409.

θάμβους (abl.sing.masc.of θάμβος, source) 2053.

καί (adjunctive conjunction joining nouns) 14.

ἐκστάσεως (abl.sing.fem.of ἔκστασις, source) 2083.

ἐπί (preposition with the instrumental of cause) 47.

τῷ (instru.sing.neut.of the article in agreement with συμβεβηκότι) 9.

συμβεβηκότι (perf.act.part.instru.sing.neut.of συμβαίνω, substantival, cause) 2642.

αὐτῷ (dat.sing.masc.of αὐτός, reference) 16.

Translation - "And they recognized him (and realized) that he was the one who sat by the Beautiful Gate of the temple in order to beg, and they were filled with wonder and amazement because of what had happened to him."

Comment: *Cf.*#675. This is a heightened perception - stronger than γινώσκω (#131). It is inceptive. It dawned upon them, or "they began to realize" that it was he. They had seen him often and should have known at once that it was he, except for the amazing fact that the former cripple was running, leaping and shouting all over the temple court. Note the indirect discourse in the object clause after ὅτι. πρός with the accusative here in a telic sense. *Cf.*#197 for other instances. ἐπί with the locative for place where is normal. Also ἐπί with the instrumental to indicate cause.

The cripple's request for alms resulted in Peter's miracle, which produced the man's reaction which the Lord used to attract the attention of the people in order that Peter might have an audience to whom he would now preach his second great sermon after Pentecost.

Verse 11 - "And as the lame man which was healed held Peter and John, all the people ran together unto them in the porch that is called Solomon's greatly wondering."

Κρατοῦντος δὲ αὐτοῦ τὸν Πέτρον καὶ Ἰωάννην συνέδραμεν πᾶς ὁ λαὸς πρὸς αὐτοὺς ἐπὶ τῇ στοᾷ τῇ καλουμένῃ Σολομῶντος ἔκθαμβοι.

Κρατοῦντος (pres.act.part.gen.sing.masc.of κρατέω, genitive absolute) 828.

δέ (continuative conjunction) 11.

αὐτοῦ (gen.sing.masc.of αὐτός, genitive absolute) 16.

τόν (acc.sing.masc.of the article in agreement with Πέτρον) 9.

Πέτρον (acc.sing.masc.of Πέτρος, direct object of κρατοῦντος) 387.

καί (adjunctive conjunction joining nouns) 14.

τὸν (acc.sing.masc.of the article in agreement with Ἰωάννην) 9.
Ἰωάννην (acc.sing.masc.of Ἰωάννης, direct object of κρατοῦντος) 399.
συνέδραμεν (3d.per.sing.2d.aor.act.ind.of συντρέχω, constative) 2264.
πᾶς (nom.sing.masc.of πᾶς, in agreement with λαὸς) 67.
ὁ (nom.sing.masc.of the article in agreement with λαὸς) 9.
λαὸς (nom.sing.masc.of λαός, subject of συνέδραμεν) 110.
πρὸς (preposition with the accusative of extent) 197.
αὐτοὺς (acc.pl.masc.of αὐτός, extent) 16.
ἐπὶ (preposition with the locative of place) 47.
τῇ (loc.sing.fem.of the article in agreement with στοᾷ) 9.
στοᾷ (loc.sing.fem.of στοά, place) 2096.
τῇ (loc.sing.fem.of the article in agreement with καλουμένῃ) 9.
καλουμένῃ (pres.pass.part.loc.sing.fem.of καλέω, substantival, apposition) 107.
Σολομῶντος (gen.sing.masc.of Σολομών, description) 32.

#3011 ἔκθαμβοι (nom.pl.masc.of ἔκθαμβος,predicate adjective).

greatly wondering - Acts 3:11.

Meaning: A combination of ἐκ (#19) and θάμβος (#2053), *Cf.*ἔκφοβος (#2323). ἐκ serves to intensify the meaning. With reference to the amazement of the people in the temple as a result of Peter's miracle - Acts 3:11.

Translation - "And as he was hugging Peter and John all the people, greatly excited, came running to them into Solomon's Porch."

Comment: In Matthew 28:9 we have κρατέω in the same sense in which I conceive it here. The translation "clung to" (Goodspeed, Williams), while not denoting it, connotes the idea of weakness or helplessness, which is out of harmony with the man's ecstatic physical activity of vss.8,9. Rather it is a picture of loving gratitude and worship as in Mt.28:9. Thus our translation. As he embraced the Apostles and poured out his gratitude to them, all of the people came running. The predicate adjective ἔκθαμβοι is plural, yet joined to the singular λαὸς. This need cause no confusion since λαός, a collective noun is singular, but composed of many individuals in the single group. "People" is made up of "persons." "The term (*i.e.* "construction according to sense") is unobjectionable, providing we remember that constructions, according to the meaning are generally older than those in which meaning is overridden by idiom or grammatical analogy." (Monro, *Homeric Greek*, 118, as cited in Robertson, *Grammar*, 655). So we need not worry about ἔκθαμβοι with ὁ λαὸς in Acts 3:11, nor πλῆθος κράζοντες in Acts 21:36. The grammar is "wrong" but the sense is clear, thanks to the context. Peter now has an audience, a boon that he had not expected and he was quick to take advantage of it and quite equal to the occasion, thanks to the filling of the Holy Spirit. His sermon follows essentially the same plan as his first, though he used a different set of Old Testament Scriptures for support.

Verse 12 - *"And when Peter saw it, he answered unto the people, Ye men of Israel, why marvel ye at this? Or why look ye so earnestly on us, as though by our own power or holiness we had made this man to walk?"*

ἰδὼν δὲ ὁ Πέτρος ἀπεκρίνατο πρὸς τὸν λαόν, Ἄνδρες Ἰσραηλῖται, τί θαυμάζετε ἐπὶ τούτῳ, ἢ ἡμῖν τί ἀτενίζετε ὡς ἰδίᾳ δυνάμει ἢ εὐσεβείᾳ πεποιηκόσιν τοῦ περιπατεῖν αὐτόν;

ἰδὼν (aor.act.part.nom.sing.masc.of ὁράω, adverbial, temporal/causal) 144.

δὲ (continuative conjunction) 11.

ὁ (nom.sing.masc.of the article in agreement with Πέτρος) 9.

Πέτρος (nom.sing.masc.of Πέτρος, subject of ἀπεκρίνατο) 387.

ἀπεκρίνατο (3d.per.sing.1st.aor.mid.ind.of ἀποκρίνομαι, constative) 318.

πρὸς (preposition with the accusative of extent, after a verb of speaking) 197.

τὸν (acc.sing.masc.of the article in agreement with λαόν) 9.

λαόν (acc.sing.masc.of λαός, extent after a verb of speaking) 110.

Ἄνδρες (voc.pl.masc.of ἀνήρ, address) 63.

Ἰσραηλῖται (voc.pl.masc.of Ἰσραηλείτης, apposition) 1967.

τί (acc.sing.neut.of τίς, cause) 281.

θαυμάζετε (2d.per.pl.pres.act.ind.of θαυμάζω, direct question) 726.

ἐπὶ (preposition with the instrumental, cause) 47.

τούτῳ (instru.sing.neut.of οὗτος, cause) 93.

ἢ (disjunctive particle) 465.

ἡμῖν (dat.pl.masc.of ἐγώ, indirect object of ἀτενίζετε) 123.

τί (acc.sing.neut.of τίς, cause, direct question) 281.

ἀτενίζετε (2d.per.pl.pres.act.ind.of ἀτενίζω, direct question) 2028.

ὡς (concessive particle) 128.

ἰδίᾳ (instru.sing.fem.of ἴδιος, in agreement with δυνάμει) 778.

δυνάμει (instru.sing.fem.of δύναμις, means) 687.

ἢ (disjunctive particle) 465.

#3012 εὐσεβείᾳ (instru.sing.fem.of εὐσέβεια, means).

godliness - 1 Tim.2:2; 3:16; 4:7,8; 6:3,5,6,11; 2 Tim.3:5; Titus 1:1; 2 Pet.1:3,6,7; 3:11.

holiness - Acts 3:12.

Meaning: A combination of εὐ and σέβω (#1149). Cf. also σέβασμα (#3411), σεβάζομαι (#3806), σεβαστός (#3644). Reverance and respect for God. It is associated and therefore not to be confused with σεμνότης (#4715) in 1 Tim.2:2; with δικαιοσύνη (#322), πίστις (#728), ἀγάπη (#1490), ὑπομένη (#2204) and πραϋπάθεια (#4787) in 1 Tim.6:11; with ἐπίγνωσις (#3817) in Titus 1:1, with δύναμις (#687) in Acts 3:12. It is included in the heirarchy of virtues in 2 Peter 1:5-7, as being contingent upon ὑπομόνη and prerequisite to φιλαδελφεία (#5324). That which pertains to life also pertains to godliness - 2 Peter 1:3. It is consistent with holy converstion - 2 Peter 3:11; it is powerful - 2 Tim.3:5. It cannot be disassociated from the theology of Jesus Christ - 1 Tim.6:3. It is not necessarily equated with financial prosperity - 1 Tim.6:5, but is itself a great asset - 1 Tim.6:6. It is antithetical to profane and old wives' tales - 1 Tim.4:7, unlike physical conditioning, which is profitable to a small degree, godliness is profitable in all spheres - 1 Tim.4:8.

It is essentially mysterious - 1 Tim.3:16, but must be associated with the theistic theology of Christian faith. All of the other virtues mentioned in this article are fruits from the tree of godliness.

πεποιηκόσιν (perf.act.part.instru.pl.masc.of ποιέω, adverbial, concessive) 127.

τοῦ (gen.sing.neut.of the article, with the infinitive, subjective genitive) 9.

περιπατεῖν (pres.act.inf.of περιπατέω, subjective genitive) 384.

αὐτόν (acc.sing.masc.of αὐτός, general reference) 16.

Translation - "And when Peter saw it he said to the people, 'Men, Israelites, why are you wondering about this, or why are you staring at us as though by our own power or godliness we have made him walk?'"

Comment: Note ἡμῖν in prolepsis, *i.e.* out of place. Peter saw the situation - a grateful man, leaping for joy and loudly proclaiming his gratitude both to God and to Peter and John. The people, once they came to realize that it was the same man whom they had seen every day for years begging outside the Beautiful Gate, now crowd into Solomon's Porch in amazement. Peter preached. Again as at Pentecost, he began by correcting a wrong impression in the minds of the people. Then it was that the disciples were intoxicated. Now it was that Peter and John themselves had healed the cripple by their own powers. Good preaching always corrects wrong impressions, of which there is a spate, in the minds of the people. That is why repentance (a change of the mind) is prerequisite to saving faith. Two causal clauses in direct question and a causal construction with ἐπί and the instrumental in τούτῳ are found in Peter's question. We supply διά with τί in each case. "On account of what?" therefore, "Why?" Why were they amazed? And why were they staring at Peter and John? What was the cause of this - *i.e.* the healing miracle. ὡς here is concessive, introducing the concessive participle.

Thus Peter first disclaimed any credit, either for himself or John, for the miracle. He used this disclaimer as a means of introducing Christ to the Jewish audience. If Peter and John didn't do it, who did? For obviously somebody had enabled a grown man who had never walked before a single day in his life to walk run and leap about for joy.

Note that Peter again appeals to the national history of Israel as he did at Pentecost. Good teaching always begins with something that the student knows, from which he is carried into areas of which he does not know. Observe also, as in the first sermon, that Peter reveals the continuity and consistency that exists between the Old and New Testaments, thus to show the Jews that Christianity is not a different religion from their own, but a logical extension of it.

Verse 13 - "The god of Abraham and of Isaac, and of Jacob, the god of our fathers, hath glorified His Son, Jesus; whom ye delivered up, and denied him in the presence of Pilate, when he was determined to let him go."

ὁ θεὸς Ἀβραὰμ καὶ (ὁ θεὸς) Ἰσαὰκ καὶ (ὁ θεὸς) Ἰακώβ, ὁ θεὸς τῶν πατέρων
ἡμῶν, ἐδόξασεν τὸν παῖδα αὐτοῦ Ἰησοῦν, ὃν ὑμεῖς μὲν παρεδώκατε καὶ
ἠρνήσασθε κατὰ πρόσωπον Πιλάτου, κρίναντος ἐκείνου ἀπολύειν,

ὁ (nom.sing.masc.of the article in agreement with θεὸς) 9.
θεὸς (nom.sing.masc.of θεός, subject of ἐδόξασεν) 124.
Ἀβραὰμ (indeclin.gen.sing.masc.of Ἀβραάμ, relationship) 7.
καὶ (adjunctive conjunction joining nouns) 14.
(ὁ (nom.sing.masc.of the article in agreement with θεὸς) 9.
θεὸς) (nom.sing.masc.of θεός, subject of ἐδόξασεν) 124.
Ἰσαὰκ (indeclin.gen.sing.masc.of Ἰσαάκ, relationship) 10.
καὶ (adjunctive conjunction joining nouns) 14.
(ὁ (nom.sing.masc.of the article in agreement with θεὸς) 9.
θεὸς) (nom.sing.masc.of θεός, subject of ἐδόξασεν) 124.
Ἰακώβ (indeclin.gen.sing.masc.of Ἰακώβ, relationship) 12.
ὁ (nom.sing.masc.of the article in agreement with θεὸς) 9.
θεὸς (nom.sing.masc.of θεός, apposition) 124.
τῶν (gen.pl.masc.of the article in agreement with πατέρων) 9.
πατέρων (gen.pl.masc.of πατήρ, relationship) 238.
ἡμῶν (gen.pl.masc.of ἐγώ, relationship) 123.
ἐδόξασεν (3d.per.sing.aor.act.ind.of δοξάζω, culminative) 461.
τὸν (acc.sing.masc.of the article in agreement with παῖδα) 9.
παῖδα (acc.sing.masc.of παῖς, direct object of ἐδόξασεν) 217.
αὐτοῦ (gen.sing.masc.of αὐτός, relationship) 16.
Ἰησοῦν (acc.sing.masc.of Ἰησοῦς, apposition) 3.
ὃν (acc.sing.masc.of ὅς, direct object of παρεδώκατε and ἠρνήσασθε) 65.
ὑμεῖς (nom.pl.masc.of σύ, subject of παρεδώκατε and ἠρνήσασθε) 104.
μὲν (concessive particle) 300.
παρεδώκατε (2d.per.pl.aor.act.ind.of παραδίδωμι, constative) 368.
καὶ (adjunctive conjunction joining verbs) 14.
ἠρνήσασθε (2d.per.pl.aor.mid.ind.of ἀρνέομαι, constative) 895.
κατὰ (preposition with the accusative, general reference) 98.
πρόσωπον (acc.sing.neut.of πρόσωπον, general reference) 588.
Πιλάτου (gen.sing.masc.of Πιλᾶτος, possession) 1616.
κρίναντος (1st.aor.act.part.gen.sing.masc.of κρίνω, genitive absolute) 531.
ἐκείνου (gen.sing.masc.of ἐκεῖνος, genitive absolute) 246.
ἀπολύειν (pres.act.inf.of ἀπολύω, complementary) 92.

Translation - "*The God of Abraham and the God of Isaac and the God of Jacob,
the God of our Fathers has glorified His child Jesus, although you betrayed and
denied Him before Pilate when he had decided to set Him free, . . .* "

Comment: Peter began his sermon by appealing to their nationalism. The God
of the patriarchs is the God of the everlasting covenants which mean so much to
the Jewish people. Peter then identified himself and John with his audience.
Everyone present was a descendant of Abraham, Isaac and Jacob, through one
of his twelve sons. Peter then reminded them that Jesus of Nazareth was also one

of the sons of Israel, and that He was the son (παῖδα) of God, a fact which Jesus had affirmed for which they had condemned Him as a blasphemer.

Peter then pointed to the death, burial, resurrection and ascension of Jesus which he calls evidence that God had glorified Him. Note the culminative aorist in ἐδόξασεν and the glorification of Jesus in Heb.5:5; John 7:39; 8:45b; 12:16,23; 13:31,32,32; Acts 3:13. Of course the audience could not have connected the death, resurrection and ascension of Jesus with the verb δοξάζω as we have just done, because the New Testament had not yet been written, although some in the audience may have heard Jesus use the word in this connection. It is more likely that Peter alluded more to the fact that it was in the name of Jesus, the Nazarene that he had performed the miracle upon the lame man (vs.6).

It is interesting to see Peter's method of presentation of his material. It is a study in contrasts. God glorified Jesus. The Jews had betrayed and denied Him. Pilate, a complete outsider, an uncircumcised Gentile, an alien from the commonwealth of Israel, a worshipper of idols, if indeed he worshipped anything at all had decided to set Jesus free. Even a pagan Gentile had a more positive attitude toward the incarnate Son of God than those in Peter's audience had. Note the contrast between ὑμεῖς and ἐκείνου. "You" betrayed Jesus. Pilate determined to set "that One" free. Israel wanted Him dead. Rome decreed that He was not guilty. God decreed that He was His eternal Son and proved it by resurrection (Rom.1:4; Ps.2:7) and ascension (Psalm 110:1; Eph.1:19-23; Phil.2:9-11) and then, only moments before God had glorified Jesus again by healing the cripple. μὲν *solitarium* is concessive. The concessive idea carries over into verse 14 where δὲ is continuative, not adversative.

Verse 14 - ". . . but ye denied the Holy One and the Just, and desired a murderer to be granted unto you,. . . "

ὑμεῖς δὲ τὸν ἅγιον καὶ δίκαιον ἠρνήσασθε, καὶ ἠτήσασθε ἄνδρα φονέα χαρισθῆναι ὑμῖν,

ὑμεῖς (nom.pl.masc.of σύ, subject of ἠρνήσασθε and ἠτήσασθε) 104.
δὲ (continuative conjunction) 11.
τὸν (acc.sing.masc.of the article in agreement with ἅγιον) 9.
ἅγιον (acc.sing.masc.of ἅγιος, direct object of ἠρνήσασθε) 84.
καὶ (adjunctive conjunction joining nouns) 14.
δίκαιον (acc.sing.masc.of δίκαιος, direct object of ἠρνήσασθε) 85.
ἠρνήσασθε (2d.per.pl.aor.mid.ind.of ἀρνέομαι, constative) 895.
καὶ (adjunctive conjunction joining verbs) 14.
ἠτήσασθε (2d.per.pl.aor.mid.ind.of αἰτέω, constative) 537.
ἄνδρα (acc.sing.masc.of ἀνήρ, general reference) 63.
φονέα (acc.sing.masc.of φονεύς, apposition) 1405.
χαρισθῆναι (aor.pass.inf.of χαρίζομαι, direct object of ἠτήσασθε) 2158.
ὑμῖν (dat.pl.masc.of σύ, indirect object of χαρισθῆναι) 104.

Translation - "and although you denied the Holy and Just One and asked that a murderer be granted to you, . . .

Comment: We have another contrast, as Peter arrays τὸν ἅγιον καὶ δίκαιον against ἄνδρα φονέα. God offered them a Holy and Righteous King and they chose a robber/killer instead, and then demanded that their King be crucified. "The use of ἀνήρ, ἄνθρωπος, γυνή with words in apposition seems superfluous, though it is perfectly intelligible. The word in apposition conveys the main idea, as ἀνὴρ προφήτης (Lu.24:19)." (Robertson, *Grammar*, 399). *Cf.* other examples in Mt.21:33; Acts 1:16; 2:22; 17:22 and in Acts 3:14, the verse under discussion. If Israel had chosen the best man in the nation instead of Jesus - someone like Nicodemus or Joseph of Arimathaea, it would have been a mistake, but they decreed that Barabbas was less a threat to society than Jesus. Thus the choice of a depraved nation is held up for ridicule by Peter within the confines of their own holy temple, the place where God was supposed to come down and visit them.

Note how Peter continues to play upon this concessive idea which he introduced with μὲν in verse 13. "Although you betrayed and denied a Holy and Just embodiment of God incarnate and chose a murderer instead, and (continuative δὲ, verse 15) although you killed the ἀρχηγὸν τῆς ζωῆς (vs.15), yet God glorified Him and raised Him from the dead and by the faith which the lame man had in the name of Jesus, performed the miracle which you must admit has indeed been performed." The long sentence finally closes at the end of verse 15.

Verse 15 - ". . . and killed the Prince of Life, whom God hath raised from the dead, whereof we are witnesses."

τὸν δὲ ἀρχηγὸν τῆς ζωῆς ἀπεκτείνατε, ὃν ὁ θεὸς ἤγειρεν ἐκ νεκρῶν, οὗ ἡμεῖς μάρτυρές ἐσμεν.

τὸν (acc.sing.masc.of the article in agreement with ἀρχηγὸν) 9.
δὲ (continuative conjunction) 11.

#3013 ἀρχηγὸν (acc.sing.masc.of ἀρχηγός, direct object of ἀπεκτείνατε).

    author - Heb.12:2.
    captain - Heb.2:10.
    prince - Acts 3:15; 5:31.

Meaning: A combination of ἄρχω (#383) and ἄγω (#876). The leading first cause. The originator, creator, first example (ἄρχω). But also the one who delivers (ἄγω). With reference to Christ the source of all life - Acts 3:15; 5:31 (abiogenesis to the contrary notwithstanding); faith - Heb.12:2; salvation - Heb.2:10. None of the three words used in the JKV to translate this Greek word is adequate, and two of them, "captain" and "prince" are totally misleading. "Author" comes closer than either of the other two, but also is inadequate.

τῆς (gen.sing.fem.of the article in agreement with ζωῆς) 9.
ζωῆς (gen.sing.fem.of ζωή, description) 668.
ἀπεκτείνατε (2d.per.pl.aor.act.ind.of ἀποκτείνω, constative) 889.
ὃν (acc.sing.masc.of ὅς, direct object of ἤγειρεν) 65.

ὁ (nom.sing.masc.of the article in agreement with θεός) 9.

θεός (nom.sing.masc.of θεός, subject of ἤγειρεν) 124.

ἤγειρεν (3d.per.sing.aor.act.ind.of ἐγείρω, culminative) 125.

ἐκ (preposition with the ablative of separation) 19.

νεκρῶν (abl.pl.masc.of νεκρός, separation) 749.

οὗ (gen.sing.neut.of ὅς, reference) 65.

ἡμεῖς (nom.pl.masc.of ἐγώ, subject of ἐσμεν) 123.

μάρτυρές (nom.pl.masc.of μάρτυς , predicate nominative) 1263.

ἐσμεν (1st.per.pl.pres.ind.of εἰμί, aoristic) 86.

Translation - "... *and although you killed the Source of Life, God raised Him from the dead, with reference to which we are witnesses.*

Comment: Israel not only made a grossly immoral choice when they chose Barabbas instead of Jesus Christ, but they also did something incredibly stupid. They killed the Originator (First Cause, Producer, Deliverer) of Life. Peter was speaking of course in an accommodated sense. No one can kill the Originator of Life, but they hated Him and they wanted and tried to kill Him. Thus Peter was not wrong in charging them with the moral responsibility of His death. (Mt.5:21-22; 1 John 2:9-11). Peter had not hesitated to charge the Jews with the murder of Jesus in his sermon at Pentecost (Acts 2:23). Again he fearlessly accuses them.

It is important to understand the full significance of the word ἀρχηγός (#3013). Jesus Christ is the One in Whom life has always been, from all eternity (John 1:4; 11:25, *et al.*). He alone gave life to a material creation which was otherwise inert. *Cf.*#668 for all the references in which ζωή is associated with Jesus Christ. Life is supernatural. No man can produce it without using previous existing life. Abiogenesis, which is popularly called spontaneous generation, which, if it existed would produce life from inert material, has never been accomplished. Pasteur's formula *omne vivum e vivo* "all life from life" was the result of his research in which he disproved abiogenesis. Redi, an Italian biologist pioneered in the research which disproved spontaneous generation. In 1668 he proved that maggots were baby flies which had hatched from the eggs laid by flies upon meat which he had placed in the sun at their disposal. When he screened the flies away from the meat no maggots were produced. The invention of the microscope carried the research further. In 1683, the Dutch scientist A van Leeuwenhoek discovered bacteria and faith in abiogenesis revived to some extent. Louis Pasteur is chiefly responsible for the final refutation. "It may now be stated definitely that all known living organisms arise only from preexisting living organisms... It must be noted, however, that this statement relates only to known existing organisms. It may be that in the progress of science it may yet become possible to construct living protoplasm from non-living material." (*Encyclopedia Britannica,* I, 48). Biologists reserve the words "archebiosis" and "archegenesis" for the theory "... that protoplasm in the remote past has developed from non-living matter by a series of steps, and many of those, notably T. H. Huxley, who took a large share in the process of refuting contemporary abiogenesis, have stated their belief in a priordial archebiosis.

(*Ibid.*) In the article on *Life*, Encyclopedia Britannica (XIV, 42) says, "Thus life is an activity of organisms which requires for its description concepts transcending those of mechanism." So it is not a mechanical process and the concept that the Eternal Son of god, who has been life from all eternity, is needed to explain the fact that life exists on earth today. Then the writer reverses himself in the next sentence with, "This view does not in any way contradict the theory that living organisms may have arisen on the earth from non-living materials. When the materials were complex enough and in an appropriate collocation, living organisms may have emerged." Of course, a scientist, speaking about life purely from his scientific point of view could say no more. To speak of God and postulating Him as the One Who has always lived falls within the purview of theology, which is based upon faith in an *a priori* premise, but that is beyond the pale for the empiricist. The view, held by atheists or deists, neither of whom dare say that God has ever had anything to do with the universe since creation must be that life today is the result of an evolutionary development that began without the aid of non-resident influences - a view that expresses its faith in spontaneous generation, something that no scientist today has ever seen and which they reject. Unless we conclude that there is no such thing as life (!) and that nothing or anybody has ever lived, we must either say that God is life and that He has always lived or we must say that spontaneous generation is a fact. Thus by faith the atheist supports his view that faith in Jesus Christ is fallacious. Either abiogenesis is true or life has always existed, since few will doubt that life exists now. It seems clear that if spontaneous generation of life should ever take place, the event would be a death blow to Christianity with its faith in Christ as the ἀρχηγὸς τῆς ζωῆς (Acts 3:15).

Since He is the ἀρχηγὸς τῆς ζωῆς, it was obviously impossible for Him to remain dead (Ps.16:8-11; John 10:16-18). Did He in fact rise from the dead? Once again, as upon the day of Pentecost, Peter and John add ἡμεῖς μάρτυρές ἐσμεν (Act.2:32). Thus Peter has pointed out that Israel was indulging a gigantic death wish, individually and nationally, when the mob cried out, "Crucify Him." When one kills the source of life he is asking for universal and permanent death, but fortunately man's attempt to kill the Son of God was as futile as all of his other attempts at universal *coup d' etat*. (Psalm 2:1-4).

Verse 16 - "And his name, through faith in his name hath made this man strong, whom ye see and know; yes, the faith which is by him hath given him this perfect soundness in the presence of you all."

καὶ ἐπὶ τῇ πίστει τοῦ ὀνόματος αὐτοῦ τοῦτον ὃν θεωρεῖτε, καὶ οἴδατε ἐστερέωσεν τὸ ὄνομα αὐτοῦ, καὶ ἡ πίστις ἡ δι' αὐτοῦ ἔδωκεν αὐτῷ τὴν ὁλοκληρίαν ταύτην ἀπέναντι πάντων ὑμῶν.

καὶ (continuative conjunction) 14.

ἐπὶ (preposition with the instrumental, cause) 47.

τῇ (instru.sing.fem.of the article in agreement with πίστει) 9.

πίστει (instru.sing.fem.of πίστις, cause) 728.

τοῦ (gen.sing.neut.of the article in agreement with ὀνόματος) 9.

ὀνόματος (gen.sing.neut.of ὄνομα, reference) 108.
αὐτοῦ (gen.sing.masc.of αὐτός, possession) 16.
τοῦτον (acc.sing.masc.of οὗτος, direct object of ἐστερέωσεν) 93.
ὅν (acc.sing.neut.of ὅς, direct object of θεωρεῖτε and οἴδατε) 65.
θεωρεῖτε (2d.per.pl.pres.act.ind.of θεωρέω, aoristic) 1667.
καὶ (adjunctive conjunction joining verbs) 14.
οἴδατε (2d.per.pl.pres.act.ind.of οἶδα, aoristic) 144.
ἐστερέωσεν (3d.per.sing.aor.act.ind.of στερεόω, culminative) 3007.
τὸ (nom.sing.neut.of the article in agreement with ὄνομα) 9.
ὄνομα (nom.sing.neut.of ὄνομα, subject of ἐστερέωσεν) 108.
αὐτοῦ (gen.sing.masc.of αὐτός, possession) 16.
καὶ (emphatic conjunction) 14.
ἡ (nom.sing.fem.of the article in agreement with πίστις) 9.
πίστις (nom.sing.fem.of πίστις, subject of ἔδωκεν) 728.
ἡ (nom.sing.fem.of the article in agreement with πίστις) 9.
δι' (preposition with the ablative, source) 118.
αὐτοῦ (abl.sing.masc.of αὐτός, source) 16.
ἔδωκεν (3d.per.sing.aor.act.ind.of δίδωμι, culminative) 362.
αὐτῷ (dat.sing.masc.of αὐτός, indirect object of ἔδωκεν) 16.
τὴν (acc.sing.fem.of the article in agreement with ὁλοκληρίαν) 9.

#3014 ὁλοκληρίαν (acc.sing.fem.of ὁλοκλρία, direct object of ἔδωκεν).

perfect soundness - Acts 3:16.

Meaning: Cf.ὁλόκληρος (#4672). A combination of ὅλος (#112) and κλῆρος (#1648). Hence, the result of being whole or complete. Total soundness - Acts 3:16.

ταύτην (acc.sing.fem.of οὗτος, in agreement with ὁλοκληρίαν) 93.
ἀνέναντι - (improper preposition with the ablative of separation) 1679.
πάντων (abl.pl.masc.of πᾶς, place) 67.
ὑμῶν (gen.pl.masc.of σύ, description) 104.

Translation - "And because of faith in His name, it has made this man whom you see and know strong. In fact the faith of which He is the source has given to him this total recovery in the presence of all of you."

Comment: The miracle was accomplished by faith, no thanks either to the lame men or to Peter and John, because Peter adds that the faith was δι' αὐτοῦ - an ablative of source construction. Thus the faith to believe with reference to the Name of Jesus in order to be healed by the power of Jesus had its source in Jesus, Who is not only the ἀρχηγὸς τῆς ζωῆς (Acts 3:15), but also ὁ ἀρχηγὸς τῆς πίστεως (Heb.12:2). And it also brought salvation, both physical, from the trials of lifelong lameness and also from the curse of lifelong sin to both the lame man, now healed, and also to about 5000 others, for the Source and Deliverer of Life and Faith is also ὁ ἀρχηγὸς τῆς σωτηρίας (Heb.2:10). Peter was careful to point out that he and John had very little indeed to do with the miracle. It was the man's faith in a name which had only shortly before been a reproach in the temple. He also emphasized that the object was a man whom they both saw and knew well as a lifelong cripple and beggar. The healing itself was then emphasized, although Peter did not need to point to that which they could not doubt. Then Peter adds that the faith did not originate with the patient, nor with the Apostles. It came from Him Who has the name which is above every name (Heb.12:2; Phil.2:9-11). Salvation is the "gift of God, not of works" (Eph.2:8,9).

A quick review of Peter's approach in this sermon will help us understand what Spirit filled preaching is. First, he appealed to their national pride of origin (vs.13), but not until he had disclaimed any personal credit for the healing (vs.12). Next he contrasted God's treatment of Jesus with their own, to their manifest discredit and shame (vs.13). God glorified Jesus, despite the fact that they betrayed and denied Him in the court of a pagan Gentile whose sense of rectitude was such that he made every effort to set Him free. They also rejected Jesus in favor of a bandit who was a killer (vs.14) and they killed the Source and Deliverer of all life (vs.15) after which God raised Him from the dead. Finally he and John declared that they were witnesses to the fact that Jesus Christ had risen from the dead. It was time now for Peter to be conciliatory, but not in any way that would lessen their sense of great need for repentance and faith. If he had excused them there would have been no repentance. It was true that they did it because they were ignorant, but that fact did not exculpate them. They were involved in that which God had decreed and they did it in ignorance, but they also did it because they willed to do it. Thus they were guilty. But they came to understand that though they stood at the foot of His cross and joined in laughter and derision as He died, they also were nailed to His cross and joined in His suffering and death (Gal.2:20) and that is why they would be saved when they received the gift of salvation through the faith which has its source solely in Him.

Verse 17 - "And now, brethren, I wot that through ignorance ye did it, as did also your rulers."

καὶ νῦν, ἀδελφοί, οἶδα ὅτι κατὰ ἄγνοιαν ἐπράξατε, ὥσπερ καὶ οἱ ἄρχοντες ὑμῶν.

καὶ (continuative conjunction) 14.
νῦν (adverbial) 1497.
ἀδελφοί (voc.pl.masc.of ἀδελφός, address) 15.
οἶδα (1st.per.sing.pres.act.ind.of οἶδα, aoristic) 144.
ὅτι (conjunction introducing an object clause in indirect discourse) 211.
κατὰ (preposition with the accusative, standard rule) 98.

#3015 ἄγνοιαν (acc.sing.fem.of ἄγνοια, standard rule).

ignorance - Acts 3:17; 17:30; Eph.4:18; 1 Pet.1:14.

Meaning: Cf.ἀγνοέω (#2345); ἀγνωσία (#4249); ἄγνωστος (#3413). Ignorance; lack of knowledge. In the New Testament with special reference to divine matters. The intellectual blindness that caused Israel's rejection of Christ - Acts

3:17; the ignorance of Gentiles who lack spiritual perception - Eph.4:18; the ignorance of Christian Jews before and after they were saved - 1 Pet.1:14.

ἐπράξατε (2d.per.pl.aor.act.ind.of πράσσω, culminative) 1943.
ὥσπερ (intensive particle in a comparative clause) 560.
καὶ (adjunctive conjunction joining substantives) 14.
οἱ (nom.pl.masc.of the article in agreement with ἄρχοντες) 9.
ἄρχοντες (nom.pl.masc.of ἄρχων, subject of ἐποίησαν, understood) 816.
ὑμῶν (gen.pl.masc.of σύ, relationship) 104.

Translation - "But now, brethren, I realize that you did it in ignorance, just as your rulers also did."

Comment: The indirect discourse retains the tense of the direct. Since the crucifixion some in Jerusalem may have been excusing themselves on the ground that they did not know any better. They were saying, "We did it in ignorance." Peter is now agreeing with them. God once overlooked ignorance (Acts 17:30,31) for those who had no opportunity to hear the gospel and repent, but not any more. He added that the Establishment might also plead but no more. Peter added that the Establishment might also plead ignorance. It being preached, ignorance is no longer an extenuating circumstance. Repentance is demanded. Peter is not preaching environmental determinism as a means to escape moral responsibility. This is not the situation ethics of ethical relativism.

Peter intended to hold them to strict moral account, even though what they did was a part of that which God had ordained and foretold.

Verse 18 - "But those things which God before had showed by the mouth of all his prophets, that Christ should suffer, he hath so fulfilled."

ὁ δὲ θεὸς ἃ προκατήγγειλεν διὰ στόματος πάντων τῶν προφητῶν παθεῖν τὸν Χριστὸν αὐτοῦ ἐπλήρωσεν οὕτως.

ὁ (nom.sing.masc.of the article in agreement with θεός) 9.
δὲ (adversative conjunction) 11.
θεὸς (nom.sing.masc.of θεός, subject of προκατήγγειλεν and ἐπλήρωσεν) 124.
ἃ (acc.pl.neut.of ὅς, direct object of προκατήγγειλεν and ἐπλήρωσεν) 65.

#3016 προκατήγγειλεν (3d.per.sing.1st.aor.act.ind.of προκαταγγέλλω, culminative).

foretell - Acts 3:24.
show before - Acts 3:18; 7:52.

Meaning: A combination of πρό (#442), κατά (#98) and ἀγγέλλω - "to announce." Hence to announce before the time. To predict. Followed by an infinitive - the suffering of Christ - Acts 3:18; followed by περί and the genitive with reference to the coming of Christ - Acts 7:52.

διά (preposition with the ablative of agent) 118.
στόματος (abl.sing.neut.of στόμα, agent) 344.
πάντων (gen.pl.masc.of πᾶς, in agreement with προφητῶν) 67.
τῶν (gen.pl.masc.of the article in agreement with προφητῶν) 9.
προφητῶν (gen.pl.masc.of προφήτης, description) 119.
παθεῖν (2d.aor.act.inf.of πάσχω, direct object of προκατήγγειλεν) 1208.
τὸν (acc.sing.masc.of the article in agreement with Χριστὸν) 9.
Χριστὸν (acc.sing.masc.of Χριστός, general reference) 4.
αὐτοῦ (gen.sing.masc.of αὐτός, relationship) 16.
ἐπλήρωσεν (3d.per.sing.aor.act.ind.of πληρόω, culminative) 115.
οὕτως (demonstrative adverb) 74.

Translation - "But that is how God fulfilled that which He predicted by the mouth of the Prophets, that His Anointed would suffer."

Comment: Israel, both at the official level and among the rank and file, acted in ignorance when they crucified Jesus, but God had predicted the events that culminated in His death in the Old Testament. Note the aorist (timeless) infinitive παθεῖν in reference to an future event at the time that the prophecy was spoken. διά στόματος πάντων τῶν προφητῶν is a Hebraism. οὕτως depends for meaning on previous action, *viz.* that described in vss.13,14,15,17. They were ignorant of the significance of their action and of its results. They had fulfilled God's prophecy. Now the door of salvation was opened to them. Whether they would be saved or not depended upon how they reacted to the total story, now that they understood it.

Every elect member of the Body of Christ sustains the same relationship to the crucifixion of our Lord as did those to whom Peter preached that day. They were present at the cross and it was their demand that He be impaled there before them, the object of their hatred and contempt. But the sins of all for whom He died nailed Him there as surely as did the spikes of the Roman soldiers. It is only because of the accident of history that they were there and that we were not. If we had been there we would have reacted as they did. Only those present at the cross who had already repented and believed upon Him were grieved at His suffering and death. In fact, even the Apostles and His mother and other loyal disciples did not understand it as well as we do now, that we have the full revelation of God's plan written in the New Testament. Since "all have sinned and continue to come short of the glory of God" (Rom.3:23) all must accept responsibility for His death. It is those of us, who, by the grace of God alone, have accepted our responsibility, repented of our past attitude and accepted Him by faith, who are saved. This is what Peter made plain to his audience in

Verse 19 - "Repent ye therefore and be converted, that your sins may be blotted out . . . " (The remainder of verse 19 in the KJV is associated with verse 20 in the Greek text).

μετανοήσατε οὖν καὶ ἐπιστρέψατε εἰς τὸ ἐξαλειφθῆναι ὑμῶν τὰς ἁμαρτίας,

μετανοήσατε (2d.per.pl.aor.act.impv.of μετανοέω, entreaty) 251.
οὖν (inferential conjunction) 68.
καὶ (adjunctive conjunction joining verbs) 14.
ἐπιστρέψατε (2d.per.pl.aor.act.impv.of ἐπιστρέφω, entreaty) 866.
εἰς (preposition with the accusative, purpose) 140.
τὸ (acc.sing.neut.of the article in agreement with ἐξαλειφθῆναι) 9.

#3017 ἐξαλειφθῆναι (aor.pass.inf.of ἐξαλείφω, purpose).

blot out - Acts 3:19; Col.2:14; Rev.3:5.
wipe away - Rev.7:17; 21:4.

Meaning: A combination of ἐκ (#19) and λείπω (#2636). Hence, to eliminate, obliterate, erase, wipe away, blot out, leave out. With reference to the sin record obliterated on the Book of Eternal Justice - Acts 3:19. With reference to the elimination of legaisms in Judaism by the death of Christ - Col.2:14. With reference to the erasure of a name from the Book of Life - Rev.3:5. Tears will be wiped away - Rev.7:17; 21:4.

ὑμῶν (gen.pl.masc.of σύ, possession) 104.
τὰς (acc.pl.fem.of the article in agreement with ἁμαρτίας) 9.
ἁμαρτίας (acc.pl.fem.of ἁμαρτία, general reference) 111.

Translation - "So change your minds and turn around in order that your sins may be blotted out, . . . "

Comment: οὖν is inferential. "In view of what was said in vss.17,18. . ." *Cf.*#'s 251 and 866. μετανοήσατε is a plea for a change in their attitude, while ἐπιστρέψατε pleads for a change in behavior. Repentance is an intellectual process and only incidentally emotional. Conversion is related to regeneration and spiritual reversal only when the context demands it. Note that it is applied to a sick dog in 2 Peter 2:22; also to Jesus - Mk.5:30. It refers to an intellectual change and is thus synonymous with μετανοέω in 1 Thess.1:9. In Acts 3:19 it does refer to regeneration, but this is the demand of the context, not of the meaning of the word. Note that in Acts 2:38 Peter demanded immersion in water in connection with repentance, while here he demands, not water baptism (though they were immersed) but a new ethical policy which demanded new and indeed opposite institutional alignments. Thus the idea of a secret faith is precluded as before. If immersion in water were essential to regeneration the Apostles should have mentioned it in every invitation. Repentance and faith are essential to salvation (actually they are heads and tails of the same coin) and they are always mentioned, either in explicit terms or by implication. *Contra* Acts 16:31, which says nothing about repentance because the jailor had already repented. Happier times are ahead for those who repent and believe, as we see in

Verse 20 - ". . . when the times of refreshing shall come, from the presence of the

Lord; and he shall send Jesus Christ, which before was preached unto you."

ὅπως ἄν ἔλθωσιν καιροὶ ἀναφύξεως ἀπὸ προσώπου τοῦ κυρίου καὶ ἀποστείλῃ τὸν προκεχειρισμένον ὑμῖν Χριστόν Ἰησοῦν.

ὅπως (conjunction introducing a purpose clause with the subjunctive) 177.
ἄν (contingent particle with the subjunctive in a purpose clause) 205.
ἔλθωσιν (3d.per.pl.aor.subj.of ἔρχομαι, purpose) 146.
καιροὶ (nom.pl.masc.of καιρός, subject of ἔλθωσιν) 767.

#3018 ἀναφύξεως (gen.sing.fem.of ἀνάφυξις, description).

refreshing - Acts 3:19.

Meaning: A combination of ἀνά (#1059) and φύχω (#1489). *Cf.* ἀναφύχω (#4812). The experience of being cooled and refreshed. In the New Testament of the improvement upon earth brought about by the second coming of Christ - Acts 3:20 (vs.19 in the KJV).

ἀπὸ (preposition with the ablative of source) 70,
προσώπου (abl.sing.neut.of πρόσωπον, source) 588.
τοῦ (gen.sing.masc.of the article in agreement with κυρίου) 9.
κυρίου (gen.sing.masc.of κύριος, possession/description) 97.
καὶ (adjunctive conjunction joining verbs) 14.
ἀποστείλῃ (3d.per.sing.aor.act.subj.of ἀποστέλλω, purpose) 215.
τὸν (acc.sing.masc.of the article in agreement with προκεχειρισμένον) 9.

#3019 προκεχειρισμένον (perf.pass.part.acc.sing.masc.of προκηρύσσω, substantival, direct object of ἀποστείλῃ).

preach before - Acts 3:20.
preach first - Acts 13:24.

Meaning: A combination of πρό (#442) and κηρύσσω (#249). To preach before in a chronological sense; to announce ahead of time; to predict. With reference to the prior announcement that Jesus Christ would come to earth to sit on David's throne - Acts 3:20. Of John the Baptist's ministry before Jesus appeared - Acts 13:24.

ὑμῖν (dat.pl.masc.of σύ, indirect object of προκεχειρισμένον) 104.
Χριστόν (acc.sing.masc.of Χριστός, apposition) 4.
Ἰησοῦν (acc.sing.masc.of Ἰησοῦς, apposition) 3.

Translation - "*In order that seasons of refreshment may come from the presence of the Lord, and that He may send to you Jesus, the Messiah, who was previously promised.*

Comment: ὅπως with ἄν and the two subjunctives, ἔλθωσιν and ἀποστείλῃ are telic. ἄν introduces a temporal element also. There is no doubt that the refreshing time will come and that God will send the Messiah, but ἄ introduces the element of doubt as to when that time will come. καιροὶ ἀναφύξεως - the refreshment season. It is an apt figure. An overheated, feverish world, at the close of man's day (1 Cor.4:3), after seven years of great tribulation during which all of the calamities described in Revelation 6:1-17; 8:7-9:21; 11:15-19; 16:1-21 will occur, will have lost its way completely and plunged into the war at Armageddon. Every pessimistic picture of the end-time Gentile dominated world emphasizes how great the need for cool refreshment will be. The seventh seal will open to bring a short period of utter silence - what a refreshment now that the storm will be over. In connection with this season of refreshment will be the coming of the Messiah, Whose coming to earth is the theme of the Old Testament Prophets. Note how Peter identifies Jesus, Whom they had crucified, but Whom God had raised from the dead, as the Messiah.

All of this will occur when the time is right. The time depends upon the completion of the missionary enterprise (*cf.* Acts 15:14; Eph.3:3-6; Rev.10:7), which began, as far as that audience was concerned that day in Solomon's Porch. "Change your minds and turn around . . . in order than when the time comes, as some day it certainly shall, He may send Messiah to you, namely Jesus to bring everlasting refreshment and blessing to a world that will have been cursed by the results of sin far too long."

The prophetic pictures of moral, social, political, economic, physical, human and animal conditions during the millenium and, after that, in a new heaven and a new earth, throughout eternity, give us some small idea about how refreshing those times will be. *Cf.* Isa.2:1-4; 9:6,7; 11:1-10; 35:1-10; 60:1-12; Jer.23:3-8; 31:7-14, 31-40; Ezek.36:22-38; 37:21-28; 39:25-29; Hosea 3:4,5; Joel 3:1-8, 15-20; Zech.10:6-12; Isa.4:1-6; 7:14; 9:6,7; 24:23; 32:1-2, 14-18; 33:17-22; 40:9-11; 62:10-12; 65:25; Jer.16:12-16; 30:7-9; 33:14-17; Ezek.11:14-20; 20:33-44; 34:11-15, 22-25; 37:21-28; Daniel 2:34-45; Hosea 3:4,5; Joel 3:16-20; Amos 9:11-15; Micah 4:1-3.

Thus the Prophets, speaking as they were motivated by the Holy Spirit, sang of happier days for the nation, which God had called from the loins of Abraham, Isaac and Jacob. In the moments of their wildest imagination they could not have painted a more beautiful picture. In fact they did not grasp the full significance of that which came from their hearts, minds and pens (1 Peter 1:10-12).

But Peter then told his audience that before that great day other things on the divine agenda must be attended to, in

Verse 21 - "Whom the heavens must receive until the times of restitution of all things which God hath spoken by the mouth of all his holy prophets since the world began."

ὃν δεῖ οὐρανὸν μὲν δέξασθαι ἄρχι χρόνων ἀποκαταστάσεως πάντων ὧν ἐλάησεν ὁ θεὸς διὰ στόματος τῶν ἁγίων ἀπ' αἰῶνος αὐτοῦ προφητῶν.

ὃν (acc.sing.masc.of ὅς, direct object of δέξασθαι) 65.
δεῖ (3d.per.sing.pres.ind.of δέω, static) 1207.
οὐρανὸν (acc.sing.masc.of οὐρανός, general reference) 254.
μὲν (concessive particle) 300.
δέξασθαι (aor.mid.inf.of δέχομαι, complementary) 867.

ἄχρι (improper preposition with the genitive of time description) 1517.
χρόνων (gen.pl.masc.of χρόνος, time description) 168.

#3020 ἀποκαταστάσεως (gen.sing.fem.of ἀποκατάστασις, description).

restitution - Acts 3:21.

Meaning: A combination of ἀπό (#70), κατά (#98) and ἵστημι (#180).
*Cf.*ἀποκαθιστάνω (#2938); ἀποκαθίστημι (#978). The restoration. With
reference to the Davidic theocracy in Israel, at which time also the perfect state
of society upon earth before the fall will be restored - Acts 3:21.

πάντων (gen.pl.masc.of πᾶς, description) 67.
ὧν (gen.pl.neut.of ὅς, attracted in case to πάντων) 65.
ἐλάλησεν (3d.per.sing.aor.act.ind.of λαλέω, culminative) 815.
ὁ (nom.sing.masc.of the article in agreement with θεός) 9.
θεὸς (nom.sing.masc.of θεός, subject of ἐλάλησεν) 124.
διὰ (preposition with the genitive of agent) 118.
στόματος (gen.sing.neut.of στόμα, agent) 344.
τῶν (gen.pl.masc.of the article in agreement with προφητῶν) 9.
ἁγίων (gen.pl.masc.of ἅγιος, in agreement with προφητῶν) 84.
ἀπ' (preposition with the ablative of time separation) 70.
αἰῶνος (abl.sing.masc.of αἰών, time separation) 1002.
αὐτοῦ (gen.sing.masc.of αὐτός, possession) 16.
προφητῶν (gen.pl.masc.of προφήτης, possession) 119.

*Translation - "Although heaven must receive Him until the times when all things
from the beginning of time will be restored, about which God spoke through the
mouth of His holy prophets."*

Comment: μὲν *solitarium* has a restrictive or concessive force here. Peter had
just promised them that if they would repent and be saved, God would send to
them the refreshing times as Messiah would come back to earth. But, lest they
get the impression that the second coming was imminent, as the rumor which
was passing about among the Christians had it, Peter now enters a concessive
caveat. Messiah will remain at the right hand of God until an event will occur
which he describes as the restoration of all things. He added that this restoration
was also described in the Old Testament, and further that it included everything
since the beginning of time. This is the force of the ablative time phrase ἀπ'
αἰῶνος. The eternal ages were interrupted by what men call χρόνος - "time" at
the creation, soon after which the fall of man occurred and God's earthly
creation passed under the curse of sin. That curse will be removed and the Edenic
state, which Adam and Eve enjoyed, and over which they were completely
dominant, will be restored. This is the picture that we get from reading the Old
Testament prophecies listed *supra*. Included in the restoration of all things, of
course, is the completion of the "mystery" defined by Paul in Eph.3:3-6. The
Body of Christ must be completed before this restoration can take place and
Messiah can return. This passage fits perfectly with the time point mentioned in

Rev.10:7. The "mystery of Christ, which in other ages was not made known unto the sons of men, as it is now revealed unto his holy apostles and prophets by the Spirit, that the Gentiles should be fellowheirs, and of the same body, and partakers of his promise in Christ by the gospel," (Eph.3:4-6) will be completed on the day indicated by Rev.11:15. That is the day when the seventh angel will sound his trumpet. On that day the last elect soul for whom Christ died, will be convicted by the Holy Spirit, drawn to Christ through the preaching of the gospel and baptized by the Holy Spirit into the Body of Christ. The Holy Spirit will finish on that day His task of taking out from the Gentiles a people for His name (Acts 15:14). There will be no further need for delay. On that day Christ's enemies will all have been made His footstool (Psalm 110:1). That "last trump' time (1 Cor.15:52) is the day when the dead in Christ will rise first, after which and together with whom we, the living will be caught up to meet the Lord in the air, as He descends to stand upon the Mount of Olives, judge His enemies and take His place upon the throne that only He of all the human race is legally entitled to occupy. That is also the day when the saints will be arrayed before the judgment seat of Christ for rewards (2 Cor.5:10,11; 1 Cor.3:11-15; Luke 14:14; Mt.16:27). All of this events, with their respective time points correlate precisely and clearly. Peter taught a great deal of eschatology in this sermon. Some eschatologists think that it is an evidence of their intellectual humiltiy to say that though they are premillenial/amillenial/promillenial (!), they are whatever they are (it is chiefly a matter of taste and the opinions which they formed earlier in life) "without a program." One wonders why they have no notion of the correlation of these events, since the Bible makes them clear. This is not to say, however, that those who think that their present views are correct views, should not continue with great humility to search the Scriptures for new light on a fascinating subject that Peter (and the Holy Spirit) thought important enough for him to include in this sermon in Solomon's Porch. Peter could not, at that time, outline events and dates as we have done, since the literature of the New Testament had not yet been written.

The necessity of which δεῖ speaks if that which grows out of God's eternal decree. *Cf.*#1207, 5, b. When the great day comes, all of Christ's enemies will be put under the feet (Psalm 110:1) of the Judge (John 5:22).

During "man's day" (1 Cor.4:3), when no man can work constructively (John 9:4) it pleases God to allow fallen man to govern the portion of the globe over which he happens at the moment to have jurisdiction which whatever sort of government he thinks best. Some are willing to abdicate all personal responsibility for government and live under the rule of a dictator. Others, with unwarranted confidence in the goodness of man, sing the praises of democracy and speak of the "freedom" which is his. It makes little difference to God, since His only concern with the world at this time is that from it He is busy selecting the personnel of His church, for whom He died and rose again. God is not on the side of any apologist in political science, although He did endorse private ownership of the means of production and the profit motive (Eph.4:28). Since the day that man snuffed out the life of the "Light of the World" (John 8:12) unsaved men have walked upon this earth in darkness (John 12:35), with his soul within as dark as his environment without (Mt.6:23). That is because evil men love darkness rather than light (John 3:19). They try often successfully to hide from society, but always unsuccessfully from God when they indulge their evil propensities. But this does not mean that God's purpose is frustrated in world history. He is doing now, as He has always done, and as He always will do, precisely what pleases Him. When the proper time comes it will be apparent to men, angels and demons that He is God and that there is none else (Isa.45:22). The greatest possible offer to the greatest possible number by the greatest possible authority was made when Isaiah's vision transcended the narrow conceptions of nationalism and he saw that God would redeem by His blood men out of "every kindren, tongue, people and nation and make them unto Himself a kingdom of priests who would dwell forever upon the   earth" (Rev.5:9,10).

It has been 1900 years since Peter preached this sermon. And the heavens are still entertaining Him at the Father's right hand (Heb.1:3; 12:2). Obviously the missionary enterprise is nearer completion now than when Peter promised the restoration of all things. The effectual call of the Holy Spirit that brings one more sinner home to the foot of the cross shortens the time that we must wait. In the meantime ". . . we have need of patience, that after we have done the will of God, we might receive the promise, for yet a little while, and he that shall come will come, and will not tarry." (Heb.10:36,37).

Peter now cites another passage, contained in the Old Testament but explained only in the New Testament, in

Verse 22 - "For Moses truly said unto the fathers, A prophet shall the Lord your God raise up unto you of your brethren, like unto me; him shall ye hearken in all things whatsoever he shall say unto you."

Μωϋσῆς μὲν εἶπεν ὅτι Προφήτην ὑμῖν ἀναστήσει κύριος ὁ θεὸς ὑμῶν ἐκ τῶν ἀδελφῶν ὑμῶν ὡς ἐμέ, αὐτοῦ ἀκούεσθε κατὰ πάντα ὅσα ἂν λαλήσῃ πρὸς ὑμᾶς.

Μωϋσῆς (nom.sing.masc.of Μωϋσῆς, subject of εἶπεν) 715.
μὲν (affirmative particle) 300.
εἶπεν (3d.per.sing.aor.act.ind.of εἶπον, constative) 155.
ὅτι (recitative) 211.
Προφήτην (acc.sing.masc.of προφήτης, direct object of ἀαστήσει) 119.
ὑμῖν (dat.pl.masc.of σύ, indirect object of ἀναστήσει) 104.
ἀναστήσει (3d.per.sing.fut.act.ind.of ἀνίστημι, predictive) 789.
κύριος (nom.sing.masc.of κύριος, subject of ἀναστήσει) 97.
ὁ (nom.sing.masc.of the article in agreement with θεὸς) 9.
θεὸς (nom.sing.masc.of θεός, apposition) 124.
ὑμῶν (gen.pl.masc.of σύ, relationship) 104.
ἐκ (preposition with the partitive genitive) 19.
τῶν (gen.pl.masc.of the article in agreement with ἀδελφῶν) 9.
ἀδελφῶν (gen.pl.masc.of ἀδελφός, partitive) 15.
ὑμῶν (gen.pl.masc.of σύ, relationship) 104.

ὡς (particle in a comparative phrase) 128.

ἐμέ (acc.sing.masc.of ἐγώ, in agreement with Προφήτην) 123.

αὐτοῦ (gen.sing.masc.of αὐτός, description after a verb of hearing) 16.

ἀκούσεσθε (2d.per.pl.fut.mid.ind.of ἀκούω, imperative) 148.

κατὰ (preposition with the accusative of extent) 98.

πάντα (acc.pl.neut.of πᾶς, extent) 67.

ὅσα (acc.pl.neut.of ὅσος, relative pronoun with the subjunctive in a more probable condition) 660.

ἀν (contingent particle with the subjunctive in a more probable condition) 205.

λαλήσῃ (3d.per.sing.aor.act.ind.of λαλέω, more probable condition) 815.

πρὸς (preposition with the accusative of extent, after a verb of speaking) 197.

ὑμᾶς (acc.pl.masc.of σύ, extent, after a verb of speaking) 104.

Translation - "Moses, in fact said, 'The Lord your God will raise up for you from among your brothers a Prophet like me. You will listen to Him with reference to everything he may say to you.' "

Comment: μὲν, is the affirmative particle and it correlates with δὲ in verse 23. One of God's prophets mentioned in verse 21 was Moses. Peter is saying, "Take Moses as a case in point." Then he quotes Deuteronomy 18:15. ὡς ἐμέ is not adjectival, but adverbial. Jesus was not like Moses, for Moses gave the law, but grace and truth came by Jesus Christ (John 1:17). But He was resurrected as Moses was - He from a grave, and Moses from a life of luxury in Pharaoh's court where he posed as the son of his daughter, after which he fled for his life to the backside of a lonely desert. That the Jews understood that, although that prophecy was fulfilled in Joshua, after the death of Moses, it was to have a greater and more significant fulfillment at some later time is clear from John 1:21. When He came Israel was ordered to listen to and obey everything that He said. Note the imperatival use of the future in ἀκούεσθε and the indefinite relative clause with the subjunctive and ἀν to indicate that the disciples of this Prophet, Whoever He might be and whenever He might come, were to hear Him whatever He might say. The doubt is not that He would say something, but rather in what that might be. Little did they expect Him to say, "I and my Father are one" (John 10:30) and "And I, if I be lifted up from the earth will draw all men unto me" (John 12:32). They did not expect Him to offer salvation to a Samaritan women or to predict that "many shall come from the east and west, and shall sit down with Abraham, and Isaac, and Jacob, in the kingdom of heaven, but the children of the kingdom shall be cast into outer darkness: there shall be weeping and gnashing of teeth" (Mt.8:11,12).

But whoever the Lord God of Israel sent to His chosen people was authorized to speak with the authority of heaven and heaven and earth will pass away before one of His words can be safely ignored. A dire warning follows for those in Israel who refused to hear that Prophet.

Verse 23 - "And it shall come to pass, that every soul which will not hear that prophet, shall be destroyed from among the people."

ἔσται δὲ πᾶσα ψυχὴ ἥτις ἐὰν μὴ ἀκούσῃ τοῦ προφήτου ἐκείνου ἐξολεθρευθήσεται ἐκ τοῦ λαοῦ.

ἔσται (3d.per.sing.fut.ind.of εἰμί, predictive) 86.
δὲ (continuative conjunction) 11.
πᾶσα (nom.sing.fem.of πᾶς, in agreement with ψυχὴ) 67.
ψυχὴ (nom.sing.fem.of ψυχή, subject of ἐξολεθρευθήσεται) 233.
ἥτις (nom.sing.fem.of ὅστις, subject of ἀκούσῃ, in a more probable
condition) 163.
ἐὰν (conditional particle in a third-class condition) 363.
μὴ (qualified negative conjunction with the subjunctive) 87.
ἀκούσῃ (3d.per.sing.aor.act.subj.of ἀκούω, third-class condition) 148.
τοῦ (gen.sing.masc.of the article in agreement with προφήτου) 9.
προφήτου (gen.sing.masc.of προφήτης, description after a verb of hearing)
119.
ἐκείνου (gen.sing.masc.of ἐκεῖνος, in agreement with προφήτου) 246.

#3021 ἐξολεθρευθήσεται (3d.per.sing.fut.pass.ind.of ἐξολοθρεύω, predictive).

destroy - Acts 3:23.

Meaning: A combination of ἐκ (#19) and ὀλοθρεύω (#5038). Hence, to destroy
utterly. To remove from its place. To extirpate. Followed by an ablative of
separtion - ἐκ τοῦ λαοῦ - Acts 3:23.

ἐκ (preposition with the ablative of separation) 19.
τοῦ (abl.sing.masc.of the article in agreement with λαοῦ) 9.
λαοῦ (abl.sing.masc.of λαός, separation) 110.

*Translation - "And it will be that every soul who does not hear that Prophet will
be extirpated from among his people."*

Comment: The indefinite relative in the conditional clause leaves no doubt that
the Jew who refuses to hear the Lord Jesus will be removed, root and branch
from the religious heritage of his people, but it says nothing about who that
unbeliever might be. There is no assertion that anyone would, in fact, refuse to
hear the Prophet when He came, although of course there were. They not only
refused to listen to Him - they took up stones to stone Him.

Here is the evidence that a mere genetic connection with Abraham is not to be
equated with salvation. "Birthright Jews, Quakers, Lutherans or Presbyterians"
is a concept conceived by someone who has overlooked Paul's statement that ". .
. he is not a Jew, which is one outwardly; neither is that circumcision, which is
outward in the flesh: but he is a Jew, which is one inwardly; and circumcision is
that of the heart, in the spirit, and not in the letter; whose praise is not of men, but
of God." If a Jew professes to hear Moses but refuses to hear the Prophet Whom
Moses predicted, his genetic connection with the Jewish race is worthless.

Verse 24 - "Yea, and all the prophets from Samuel and those that follow after, as many have spoken, have likewise foretold these days."

καὶ πάντες δὲ οἱ προφῆται ἀπὸ Σαμουὴλ καὶ τῶν καθεξῆς ὅσοι ἐλάλησαν κατήγγειλαν τὰς ἡμέρας ταύτης.

καὶ (emphatic conjunction) 14.
πάντες (nom.pl.masc.of πᾶς, in agreement with προφῆται) 67.
δὲ (continuative conjunction) 11.
οἱ (nom.pl.masc.of the article in agreement with προφῆται) 9.
προφῆται (nom.pl.masc.of προφήτης, subject of κατήγγειλαν) 119.
ἀπὸ (preposition with the ablative of time separation) 70.

#3022 Σαμουὴλ (gen.sing.masc.indeclin.of Σαμουήλ, time description).

Samuel - Acts 3:24; 13:20; Heb.11:32.

Meaning: Samuel - last of the Judges. A prophet who anointed Saul - Acts 3:23; 13:20; Heb.11:32.

καὶ (adjunctive conjunction joining substantives) 14.
τῶν (abl.pl.masc.of the article, time separation) 9.
καθεξῆς (adverbial) 1711.
ὅσοι (nom.pl.masc.of ὅσος, subject of ἐλάλησαν) 660.
ἐλάλησαν (3d.per.pl.aor.act.ind.of λαλέω, culminative) 815.
καὶ (adjunctive conjunction joining substantives) 14.

#3023 κατήγγειλαν (3d.per.pl.aor.act.ind.of καταγγέλλω, culminative).

foretell - Acts 3:24.

shew - 1 Cor.11:26; Acts 13:38; 16:17; 26:23.
speak of - Rom.1:8.
declare - 1 Cor.2:1; Acts 17:23.
teach - Acts 16:21.   Acts 13:38.
preach - Acts 13:5; 15:36; 17:3,13; 1 Cor.9:14; Acts 4:2; Phil.1:17,18; Col.1:28;

Meaning: A combination of κατά (#98) and ἀγγέλλω - "to tell." Hence, to announce, declare, promulgate, make known, proclaim, publish. With reference to the preaching of the word of the Lord in some one of its phases - Acts 13:5; 15:36; 17:3,13; 16:21; 1 Cor.9:14; Acts 4:2; 3:24; 17:23; Phil.1:17,18; Col.1:28; Acts 13:38; 16:17; 26:23; 1 Cor.2:1. To pass along a rumor - Romans 1:8. Symbolically - to demonstrate, as in the elements of the Lord's Supper - 1 Cor.11:26.

τὰς (acc.pl.fem.of the article in agreement with ἡμέρας) 9.
ἡμέρας (acc.pl.fem.of ἡμέρα, direct object of κατήγγειλαν) 135.
ταύτας (acc.pl.fem.of οὗτος, in agreement with ἡμέρας) 93.

Translation - "*And, in fact, all the Prophets from (the time of) Samuel and (from the time of) those who have spoken since have told about these days.*"

Comment: There is considerable breviloquence here. We have enclosed in parentheses those parts which must be supplied in order to fit Peter's thought with the grammar. Goodspeed's translation is an admirable piece of condensation which faithfully says it all - "Why, all the prophets from Samuel down, who have spoken, have also foretold these days." Not only Moses,the author of Deut.18:15, but also Samuel and the prophets who had spoken since had foretold the coming of the Messiah and the events which would accompany His visit to earth and the promise of His second coming. Samuel received special mention because he reported the Davidic covenant, delivered by the prophet Nathan in 2 Samuel 7:12-17. Peter's statement here is similar to Jesus' statement to the Emmaus disciples in Luke 24:27.

Peter has clearly connected the resurrected Jesus Whom God glorified and in Whose name the cripple was healed, with the national hopes of Israel. Now he must remind his listeners that they personally are a part of that nation, just as he did in his Pentecost sermon (Acts 2:39).

Verse 25 - "Ye are the children of the prophets, and of the covenant which God made with our fathers, saying unto Abraham, And in thy seed shall all the kindreds of the earth be blessed."

ὑμεῖς ἐστε οἱ υἱοὶ τῶν προφητῶν καὶ τῆς διαθήκης ἧς διέθετο ὁ θεὸς πρὸς τοὺς πατέρας ὑμῶν, λέγων πρὸς Ἀβραάμ, Καὶ ἐν τῷ σπέρματί σου ἐνευλογηθήσονται πᾶσαι αἱ πατριαὶ τῆς γῆς.

ὑμεῖς (nom.pl.masc.of σύ, subject of ἐστε) 104.
ἐστε (2d.per.pl.pres.ind.of εἰμί, aoristic) 86.
οἱ (nom.pl.masc.of the article in agreement with υἱοί) 9.
υἱοὶ (nom.pl.masc.of υἱός, predicate nominative) 5.
τῶν (gen.pl.masc.of the article in agreement with προφητῶν) 9.
προφητῶν (gen.pl.masc.of προφήτης, relationship) 119.
καὶ (adjunctive conjunction joining substantives) 14.
τῆς (gen.sing.fem.of the article in agreement with διαθήκης) 9.
διαθήκης (gen.sing.fem.of διαθήκη, description) 1575.
ἧς (gen.sing.fem.of ὅς, attracted to διαθήκης) 65.
διέθετο (3d.per.sing.aor.mid.of διατίθεμαι, culminative) 2779.
ὁ (nom.sing.masc.of the article in agreement with θεός) 9.
θεὸς (nom.sing.masc.of θεός, subject of διέθετο) 124.
πρὸς (preposition with the accusative after a verb of speaking) 197.
τοὺς (acc.pl.masc.of the article in agreement with πατέρας) 9.
πατέρας (acc.pl.masc.of πατήρ, extent after a verb of speaking) 238.
ὑμῶν (gen.pl.masc.of σύ, relationship) 104.
λέγων (pres.act.part.nom.sing.masc.of λέγω, adverbial, modal) 66.
πρὸς (preposition with the accusative of extent, after a verb of speaking) 197.
Ἀβραάμ (acc.sing.masc.of Ἀβραάμ, extent after a verb of speaking) 7.
Καὶ (continuative conjunction) 14.
ἐν (preposition with the instrumental of means) 80.
τῷ (instru.sing.neut.of the article in agreement with σπέρματί) 9.

σπέρματί (instru.sing.neut.of σπέρμα, means) 1056.

σου (gen.sing.masc.of σύ, relationship) 104.

#3024 ἐνευλογηθήσονται (3d.per.pl.fut.pass.ind.of ἐνευλογέομαι, predictive).

be blessed - Acts 3:25; Gal.3:8.

Meaning: A combination of ἐν (#80) and εὐλογέω (#1120) To be blessed by means (ἐν) of something or someone. By virtue of one's relation with the "seed of Abraham" *i.e.* Jesus Christ - Acts 3:25; Gal.3:8.

πᾶσαι (nom.pl.fem.of πᾶς, in agreement with πατριαὶ) 67.

αἱ (nom.pl.fem.of the article in agreement with πατριαὶ) 9.

πατριαὶ (nom.pl.fem.of πατριά, subject of ἐνευλογηθήσονται) 1870.

τῆς (gen.sing.fem.of the article in agreement with γῆς) 9.

γῆς (gen.sing.fem.of γῆ, description) 157.

Translation - "You are the sons of the Prophets and of the covenant which God made with your fathers by saying to Abraham, '. . . and in your seed shall all the families of the earth be blessed.' "

Comment: Note ὑμεῖς in emphasis, since it is otherwise unnecessary being derived from the 2d.per.pl.of ἐστε. Perhaps Peter pointed his finger at his audience and emphasized it with the voice. The Prophets to whom God gave this message were their ancestors and the blood of Abraham, with whom God made an everlasting covenant, flowed in their veins. The covenant (Gen.12:3) was unconditional, *i.e.* its fulfillment was not contingent upon anything that Abraham did, and therefore could not be abrogated by anything which he failed to do. Its fulfillment is certain since God cannot lie. The "seed of Abraham" is Christ (Gal.3:16). In Him all the families of the earth, which includes the Jews as they believed, but also all others, which they did not believe, would be blessed. (John 10:16; Eph.3:3-6; Col.1:21,22,26; 3:11,12; Eph.2:11-22; Rev.5:9; Acts 10:34,35; 15:14-18). Thus all who call upon the name of the Lord will be saved (Acts 2:21; Rom.10:13) without prejudice to genetic or cultural background, color, sex or national origin.

In his final statement, Peter added that they were first in line for the blessing, but by no means the only ones to whom the offer of the gospel would be made.

Verse 26 - "Unto you first God, having raised up his Son Jesus, sent him to bless you, in turning away everyone of you from his iniquities."

ὑμῖν πρῶτον ἀναστήσας ὁ θεὸς τὸν παῖδα αὐτοῦ ἀπέστειλεν αὐτὸν εὐλογοῦντα ὑμᾶς ἐν τῷ ἀποστρέφειν ἕκαστον ἀπὸ τῶν πονηριῶν ὑμῶν.

ὑμῖν (dat.pl.masc.of σύ, indirect object of ἀπέστειλεν) 104.

πρῶτον (acc.sing.neut.of πρῶτος, adverbial) 487.

ἀναστήσας (aor.act.part.nom.sing.masc.of ἀνίστημι, adverbial, temporal) 789.

ὁ (nom.sing.masc.of the article in agreement with θεὸς) 9.

θεός (nom.sing.masc.of θεός, subject of ἀπέστειλεν) 124.

τόν (acc.sing.masc.of the article in agreement with παῖδα) 9.

παῖδα (acc.sing.masc.of παῖς, direct object of ἀναστήσας) 217.

αὐτοῦ (gen.sing.masc.of αὐτός, relationship) 16.

ἀπέστειλεν (3d.per.sing.aor.act.ind.of ἀποστέλλω, culminative) 215.

αὐτόν (acc.sing.masc.of αὐτός, direct object of ἀπέστειλεν) 16.

εὐλογοῦντα (pres.act.part.acc.sing.masc.of εὐλογέω, adverbial, telic) 1120.

ὑμᾶς (acc.pl.masc.of σύ, direct object of εὐλογοῦντα) 104.

ἐν (preposition with the instrumental of manner) 80.

τῷ (instru.sing.neut.of the article, manner) 9.

ἀποστρέφειν (pres.act.inf.of ἀποστρέφω, noun use, instrumental of manner) 539.

ἕκαστον (acc.sing.masc.of ἕκαστος, direct object of ἀποστρέφειν) 1217.

ἀπό (preposition with the ablative of separation) 70.

τῶν (abl.pl.fem.of the article in agreement with πονηριῶν) 9.

πονηριῶν (abl.pl.fem.of πονηρία, separation) 1419.

ὑμῶν (gen.pl.masc.of σύ, possession) 104.

Translation - "God raised up His Son and sent Him to you first, in order to bless you by turning each one of you from his evil ways."

Comment: The main point here is that the Jews were the first to whom God sent His Son, after the resurrection (Rom.1:16). Jesus came to Israel first when He presented Himself to them as their Messiah. The emphasis of His ministry during the first months was such as to convince them beyond reasonable doubt that He was in fact their Messiah. *Cf.* our discussion of this problem in *The Renaissance New Testament*, I, 189-193. But even in His first coming He gradually revealed to the Jews that His redemptive ministry was to have a wider application than they supposed. After His resurrection His commission directed their witness first to Jerusalem and Judea, and only after that to Samaria and unto the rest of the earth (Acts 1:8).

The Jews had crucified Him. Now they were to be the first to have the opportunity to repent and accept Him, not only as Messiah, Who ultimately would come to fulfill the Messianic office, but also as Saviour, which He was prepared to fulfill immediately, contingent only upon their repentance and faith. He was being offered to Israel in order to bless them (telic participle in εὐλογοῦντα) and the manner in which this blessing would come is indicated by the articular infinitive τῷ ἀποστρέφειν, joined with the preposition ἐν. This is the repentance which Peter had demanded at Pentecost (Acts 2:38).

This sermon, like the one at Pentecost tied the prophecies of the Old Testament to the events which would later become the subject matter of the New Testament. Just as he had expounded for them the Prophet Joel and the Psalmist David to show that the events at Pentecost were the fulfillment of the former and that the resurrection of Jesus was the fulfillment of the latter, so now he says that Jesus is the fulfillment of the Abrahamic covenant. In the opening statement of each sermon Peter reminded them that they had murdered Jesus

(Acts 2:23; 3:13,14). Now in Solomon's Porch Peter introduced Jesus in a new way. He is the Originator and Deliverer of Life (Acts 3:15). This is the first use of the noun ἀρχηγός, which occurs only three more times in the New Testament - in Acts 5:31; Heb.2:10; 12:2, where He is also presented as the Originator and Deliverer of salvation (Heb.2:10) and faith (Heb.12:2). Then, having introduced the term and having associated it only with Jesus Christ, Peter illustrates all three functions. In Acts 3:15 the ἀρχγὸς τῆς ζωῆς arose from the dead. In Acts 3:16 the ἀρχηγὸς τῆς πίστεως is the Source of the faith with which the cripple believed. This is clear from καὶ ἡ πίστις ἡ δι' αὐτοῦ - "the faith, the from Him faith" where διά with the ablative indicates source. And Jesus is also the ἀρχγὸς τῆς σωτηρίας, for the cripple was saved both physically and spiritually. Each of these functions of Jesus will be discussed in greater depth elsewhere. Here we suggest that life, faith and salvation are supernatural in their origin and function and can never be produced by natural means. There could have been no life if Jesus Christ, Ὁ Λόγος had not had life in Himself (John 1:4). There can be no faith except as it comes from him. What unsaved men carelessly refer to as "faith" is only human confidence in statistical probability. And there can be no salvation except as a gift of God (Eph.2:8,9). What men call "salvation" can never mean anything more than the efforts of inert depravity to achieve an ethical standard that someone, somewhere in the world calls acceptable. In other words Jesus Christ is unique in that He has a monopoly on life, faith and salvation and those who share these wondrous gifts with Him do so only by His grace.

Peter's second sermon, which began with God's promise to Abraham describes the course of history, including Messiah's death and resurrection and ends with the eschatology without which no theological system can be complete. Thus he promises that Messiah will return to bring the "refreshing times." Finally, he calls in Moses to add to the prophecies about the Son of God and warns that those who do not heed the Prophet whom Moses foresaw would be cut off from the covenant, and adds that the blessings of Abraham are not to be denied to the Gentiles, although God, in deference to His chosen people, has decreed that this gospel should be offered first in Jerusalem to the Jews.

Once again, therefore it is demonstrated that the kind of preaching which is done when the Holy Spirit directs the preacher as He did in Peter's case on both occasions is expository and that it acquaints the audience as much with the supernatural character of the Written Word of God as it does the deity of the Living Word. This is the only preaching that is sure to enjoy the blessings of the promise of Isaiah 55:8-11.

Peter and John Before the Council

(Acts 4:1-22)

Acts 4:1 - "And as they spoke unto the people, the priests, and the captain of the temple, and the Sadducees, came upon them."

Λαλούντων δὲ αὐτῶν πρὸς τὸν λαὸν ἐπέστησαν αὐτοῖς οἱ ἱερεῖς καὶ ὁ στρατηγὸς τοῦ ἱεροῦ καὶ οἱ Σαδδουκαῖοι,

Λαλούντων (pres.act.part.gen.pl.masc.of λαλέω, genitive absolute) 815.
δὲ (adversative conjunction) 11.
αὐτῶν (gen.pl.masc.of αὐτός, genitive absolute) 16.
πρὸς (preposition with the accusative of extent, after a verb of speaking) 197.
τὸν (acc.sing.masc.of the article in agreement with λαὸν) 9.
λαὸν (acc.sing.masc.of λαός, accusative of extent, after a verb of speaking) 110.
ἐπέστησαν (3d.per.pl.aor.act.ind.of ἐφίστημι, constative) 1877.
αὐτοῖς (loc.pl.masc.of αὐτός, after ἐπί in composition, place) 16.
οἱ (nom.pl.masc.of the article in agreement with ἱερεῖς) 9.
ἱερεῖς (nom.pl.masc.of ἱερεύς, subject of ἐπέστησαν) 714.
καὶ (adjunctive conjunction joining nouns) 14.
ὁ (nom.sing.masc.of the article in agreement with στραγηγὸς) 9.
στρατηγὸς (nom.sing.masc.of στρατηγός, subject of ἐπέστησαν) 2754.
τοῦ (gen.sing.neut.of the article in agreement with ἱεροῦ) 9.
ἱεροῦ (gen.sing.neut.of ἱερόν, description) 346.
καὶ (adjunctive conjunction joining nouns) 14.
οἱ (nom.pl.masc.of the article in agreement with Σαδδουκαῖοι) 9.
Σαδδουκαῖοι (nom.pl.masc.of Σαδδουκαῖος, subject of ἐπέστησαν) 277.

Translation - "But as they were speaking to the people the priests and the police officer of the temple and the Sadducees swooped down upon them. . . "

Comment: δὲ is adversative. Peter was preaching a resurrected Jesus to the people but the Establishment, from whom we have not heard since the crucifixion had opposite ideas. The present participle in the genitive absolute indicates simultaneous action with that of the main verb. The compound verb (#1877) is picturesque. The priests, the temple policeman on duty and the Sadducees "stood against them" (confronted, stood up to). The picture is one of precipitate haste and impulse. "Bore down upon" pictures a battleship with loaded guns bearing down on a smaller craft. We are about to see the beginning of the persecution of the early church at the hands of the same people who crucified Christ.

That Peter had the insight to connect their sacred Scriptures from the Pentateuch, History, Poetry and Prophecy sections with their national heritage in terms of a Nazarene carpenter is evidence both of the fact that he was filled with the Holy Spirit and that partial blindness is to be their lot until "the fulness of the Gentiles be come in" (Rom.11:25).

Verse 2 - ". . . being grieved that they taught the people and preached through Jesus, the resurrection from the dead."

διαπονούμενοι διὰ τὸ διδάσκειν αὐτοὺς τὸν λαὸν καὶ καταγγέλλειν ἐν τῷ Ἰησοῦ τὴν ἀνάστασιν τὴν ἐκ νεκρῶν.

#3025 καιπονούμενοι (pres.pass.part.nom.pl.masc.of διαπονέομαι, adverbial, causal).

be grieved - Acts 4:2; 16:18.

Meaning: A combination of διά (#118) and πονέω - "to work hard" (exert oneself, take pains to do a thorough job, etc.) In the middle voice, to be thoroughly unhappy or agitated about something or someone. With reference to the temple officials who were upset about Peter's preaching - Acts 4:2. Of Paul's displeasure with the demented girl in Philippi - Acts 16:18.

διά (preposition with the accusative, cause) 118.
τὸ (acc.sing.neut.of the article, cause) 9.
διδάσκειν (pres.act.inf.of διδάσκω, accusative, cause) 403.
αὐτοὺς (acc.pl.masc.of αὐτός, general reference) 16.
τὸν (acc.sing.masc.of the article in agreement with λαὸν) 9.
λαὸν (acc.sing.masc.of λαός, direct object of διδάσκειν) 110.
καὶ (adjunctive conjunction joining infinitives) 14.
καταγγέλλειν (pres.act.inf.of καταγγέλλω, articular infinitive, cause, after διά) 3023.
ἐν (preposition with the instrumental, manner) 80.
τῷ (instru.sing.masc.of the article in agreement with Ἰησοῦ) 9.
Ἰησοῦ (instru.sing.masc.of Ἰησοῦς, manner) 3.
τὴν (acc.sing.fem.of the article in agreement with ἀνάστασιν) 9.
ἀνάστασιν (acc.sing.fem.of ἀνάστασις, direct object of καταγγέλλειν) 1423.
τὴν (acc.sing.fem.of the article in agreement with ἀνάστασιν) 9.
ἐκ (preposition with the ablative of separation) 19.
νεκρῶν (abl.pl.masc.of νεκρός, separation) 749.

Translation - ". . .for they were upset because they were teaching the people and preaching in the case of Jesus the resurrection from the dead."

Comment: ἐν τῷ Ἰησοῦ can be taken as an instrumental of manner or to illustrate Robertson's comment, "A frequent use is where a single case is selected as a specimen or striking illustration. Here the resultant notion is 'in the case of,' which does not differ greatly from the metaphorical use of ἐν with soul, mind, etc." (*Grammar*, 587). The former interpretation is that because, or by means of the merits of Jesus, the resurrection will occur. *Cf.* John 14:19. That the N.T. teaches this is clear and such an interpretation of Acts 4:2 is not heresy, though it is bad exegesis. Robertson cites Lk.24:38; Gal.1:16 and John 6:61 as examples. Peter was certainly teaching that, in the case of Jesus, He was alive, which probably fits the context better. It is a case where both interpretations are possible and the acceptance of one does not preclude the acceptance of the other, though one may be closer to the context than the other. διά τὸ and the infinitive in a causal construction "is common in the N.T., occurring thirty-two times according to Votaw as compared with thirty-five for the O.T. and twenty-six for the Apocrypha. It is particularly frequent in Luke." (Blass, *Grammar of New Testament Greek*, 236, as cited in Robertson, *Ibid.*, 966). The priests were unhappy, not because Peter was preaching the resurrection for they believed in that, but that he was saying that Jesus had risen. The Sadducees, who rejected the idea of a bodily resurrection were upset because he was preaching the resurrection at all, particularly that of Jesus.

Verse 3 - "And they laid hands on them, and put them in hold unto the next day; for it was now eventide."

καὶ ἐπέβαλον αὐτοῖς τάς χεῖρας καὶ ἔθεντο εἰς τήρησιν εἰς τὴν εὔριον, ἦν γὰρ ἑσπέρα ἤδη.

καὶ (inferential conjunction) 14.
ἐπέβαλον (3d.per.pl.aor.act.ind.of ἐπιβάλλω, constative) 800.
αὐτοῖς (loc.pl.masc.of αὐτός, place, after ἐπί in composition) 16.
τὰς (acc.pl.fem.of the article in agreement with χεῖρας) 9.
χεῖρας (acc.pl.fem.of χείρ, direct object of ἐπέβαλον) 308.
καὶ (adjunctive conjunction joining verbs) 14.
ἔθεντο (3d.per.pl.2d.aor.mid.ind.of τίθημι, constative) 455.
εἰς (preposition with the accusative of extent) 140.

#3026 τήρησιν (acc.sing.fem.of τήρησις, extent).

   hold - Acts 4:3.
   keeping - 1 Cor.7:19.
   prison - Acts 5:18.

Meaning: Cf. τηρέω (#1297). Properly, an observance of a rule. With reference to the commandments of God - 1 Cor.7:19. With reference to a jail where prisoners are kept - Acts 4:3; 5:18.

εἰς (preposition with the accusative, time extent) 140.
τὴν (acc.sing.fem.of the article in agreement with αὔριον) 9.
αὔριον (acc.sing.fem.of αὔριον, time extent) 633.
ἦν (3d.per.sing.imp.ind.of εἰμί, progressive duration) 86.
γὰρ (causal conjunction) 105.
ἑσπέρα (nom.sing.fem.of ἑσπέρα, predicate nominative) 2909.
ἤδη (adverbial) 291.

Translation - "So they laid their hands on them and put them into jail until the next day, because it was already evening."

Comment: Thus to give variety to their experiences, Peter and John, who had gone up to the temple to pray, as orthodox Jews should, healed a lifelong cripple, preached a sermon and landed in jail. But the Holy Spirit, Who cannot be incarcerated, witnessed in power and the sermon was not without results.

Verse 4 - "Howbeit many of them which heard the word believed; and the number of the men was about five thousand."

πολλοὶ δὲ τῶν ἀκουσάντων τὸν λόγον ἐπίστευσαν, καὶ ἐγενήθη ἀριθμὸς τῶν ἀνδρῶν (ὡς) χιλιάδες πέντε.

πολλοὶ (nom.pl.masc.of πολύς, subject of ἐπίστευσαν) 228.

δὲ (adversative conjunction) 11.

τῶν (gen.pl.masc.of the article in agreement with ἀκουσάντων) 9.

ἀκουσάντων (aor.act.part.gen.pl.masc.of ἀκούω, substantival, partitive genitive) 148.

τὸν (acc.sing.masc.of the article in agreement with λόγον) 9.

λόγον (acc.sing.masc.of λόγος, direct object of ἀκουσάντων) 510.

ἐπίστευσαν (3d.per.pl.aor.act.ind.of πιστεύω, ingressive) 734.

καὶ (continuative conjunction) 14.

ἐγενήθη (3d.per.sing.aor.pass.ind.of γίνομαι, culminative) 113.

ἀριθμὸς (nom.sing.masc.of ἀριθμός, subject of ἐγενήθη) 2278.

τῶν (gen.pl.masc.of the article in agreement with ἀνδρῶν) 9.

ἀνδρῶν (gen.pl.masc.of ἀνήρ, description) 63.

(ὡς) (comparative particle) 128.

χιλιάδες (numeral) 2536.

πέντε (numeral) 1119.

Translation - "But many of those who had heard the message began to believe, and the final count of the men was about five thousand."

Comment: δὲ is adversative. Despite the fact that the authorities removed the preachers they could not remove their message. δέ also points to the difference between the reaction of the people and that of the Establishment. The police could break up the meeting and throw Peter and John into jail, but they could not prevent the Holy Spirit from generating faith in the hearts of about five thousand men. It is pure eisegesis to say that since Luke uses ἀνήρ and not λαός, women were not being saved. The only thing that can be said is that five thousand men were saved and that Luke did not mention how many women came to Christ. While it is possible to say that ἐγενήθη - ("came to be") means that the five thousand figure includes the 3120 who were already saved and therefore that the results of this day's evangelism was about 2000, a view which Meyer accepts and in reference to which "St. Luke does not say that five thousand of St. Peter's hearers were converted, in addition to those already converted at Pentecost" (*The Expositors' Greek Testament*, II, 124), others make the total number to date at about eight thousand. "Dr. Hort, following Chrysostom, Augustine and Jerome takes this view." (*Judaistic Christianity*, 47, ac cited in *Ibid.*). If we take ἐπίστευσαν as ingressive, ἐγενήθη can mean that as Peter and John were carried off to jail and the people continued to think about what Peter had said, they "began to believe" and accept Christ and that before the Holy Spirit had finished His work, about five thousand men (in addition to women and children) were saved that day.

Verse 5 - "And it came to pass on the morrow, that their rulers, and elders and scribes, . . . "

Ἐγένετο δὲ ἐπὶ τὴν αὔριον συναχθῆναι αὐτῶν τοὺς ἄρχοντας καὶ τοὺς πρεσβυτέρους καὶ τοὺς γραμματεῖς ἐν Ἰερουσαλήμ. . .

Ἐγένετο (3d.per.sing.2d.aor.ind.of γίνομαι, constative) 113.
δὲ (continuative conjunction) 11.
ἐπὶ (preposition with the accusative in a time expression) 47.
τὴν (acc.sing.fem.of the article in agreement with αὔριον) 9.
αὔριον (acc.sing.fem.of αὔριον, time expression) 633.
συναχθῆναι (1st.aor.pass.inf.of συνάγω, noun use, subject of ἐγένετο) 150.
αὐτῶν (gen.pl.masc.of αὐτός, designation) 16.
τοὺς (acc.pl.masc.of the article in agreement with ἄρχοντας) 9.
ἄρχοντας (acc.pl.masc.of ἄρχων, general reference) 816.
καὶ (adjunctive conjunction joining nouns) 14.
τοὺς (acc.pl.masc.of the article in agreement with πρεσβύτερους) 9.
πρεσβύτερους (acc.pl.masc.of πρεσβύτερος, general reference) 1141.
καὶ (adjunctive conjunction joining nouns) 14.
τοὺς (acc.pl.masc.of the article in agreement with γραμματεῖς) 9.
γραμματεῖς (acc.pl.masc.of γραμματεύς, general reference) 152.
ἐν (preposition with the locative of place) 80.
Ἰερουσαλήμ (loc.sing.masc.of Ἰεροσολύμων, place) 141.

Translation - "And on the next day as the rulers and the elders and the scribes in Jerusalem assembled . . . "

Comment: *Cf.* comment at end of verse 6.

Verse 6 - "And Annas, the high priest, and Caiaphas, and John, and Alexander, and as many as were of the kindred of the high priests were gathered together at Jerusalem."

(καὶ Ἄννας ὁ ἀρχιερεὺς καὶ Καϊάφας καὶ Ἰωάννης καὶ Ἀλέξανδρος καὶ ὅσοι ἦσαν ἐκ γένους ἀρχιερατικοῦ)

(καὶ (adjunctive conjunction joining nouns) 14.
Ἄννας (nom.sing.masc.of Ἄννας, subject of ἐπυνθάνοντο) 1936.
ὁ (nom.sing.masc.of the article in agreement with ἀρχιερεὺς) 9.
ἀρχιερεὺς (nom.sing.masc.of ἀρχιερεύς, apposition) 151.
καὶ (adjunctive conjunction joining nouns) 14.
Καϊάφας (nom.sing.masc. of Καϊάφας, subject of ἐπυνθάνοντο) 1555.
καὶ (adjunctive conjunction joining nouns) 14.

#3027 Ἰωάννης (nom.sing.masc.of Ἰωάννης, subject of ἐπυνθάνοντο).

John - Acts 4:6.

Meaning: A member of the San Hedrin - Acts 4:6.

καὶ (adjunctive conjunction joining nouns) 14.

#3028 Ἀλέξανδρος (nom.sing.masc.of Ἀλέξανδρος, subject of ἐπυνθάνοντο).

Alexander - Acts 4:6.

Meaning: a member of the San Hedrin - Acts 4:6.

καί (adjunctive conjunction joining substantives) 14.
ὅσοι (nom.pl.masc.of ὅσος, subject of ἦσαν) 660.
ἦσαν (3d.per.pl.imp.ind.of εἰμί, progressive description) 86.
ἐκ (preposition with the partitive genitive) 19.
γένους (gen.sing.neut.of γένος, partitive) 1090.

#3029 ἀρχιερατικοῦ) (gen.sing.neut.of ἀρχιερατικός, in agreement with γένους).

of the high priest - Acts 4:6.

Meaning: Cf. ἀρχιερεύς (#151). An adjective. Pertaining to the high priest. High Priestly - Acts 4:6.

Translation - ". . . and Annas, the high priest, and Caiaphas and John and Alexander, and some others who belonged to the high priest's clan . . . "

Comment: The episode in Solomon's Porch called for a special meeting of the Board! Subjects of the institutional church are always alerted that something untoward has happened when the Board meets. There was not time to assemble the entire San Hedrin, but they gathered as many as they could find in a hurry. John and Alexander owe the distinction of having their names recorded in the New Testament to the fact that they were members of the Board. Others in the high priest's familial entourage were so insignificant as to be cast among the anonymous.

Annas and Caiaphas probably thought that they had disposed of the Jesus affair. It had been almost two months since He died and little had been heard from His followers since. Now they were rudely awakened to the fact that one cannot dismiss τὸν ἀρχηγὸν τῆς ζωῆς by crucifixion. They were soon to be dispossessed of another false notion. The true followers τοῦ ἀρχηγοῦ τῆς ζωῆς cannot be controlled by anyone except the Holy Spirit, when they have His fulness. Neither civil nor ecclesiastical tribunals are going to silence a Christian who is filled with the Holy Spirit. At the end of the church age, when Antichrist gains control of the world for forty-two months we will know who is filled with the Holy Spirit and who is not.

Verse 7 - "And when they had set them in the midst, they asked, By what power, or by what name, have ye done this?"

καὶ στήσαντες αὐτοὺς ἐν τῷ μέσῳ ἐπυνθάνοντο, Ἐν ποίᾳ δυνάμει ἢ ποίᾳ ὀνόματι ἐποιήσατε τοῦτο ὑμεῖς.

καί (continuative conjunction) 14.
στήσαντες (aor.act.part.nom.pl.masc.of ἵστημι, adverbial, temporal) 180.
αὐτούς (acc.pl.masc.of αὐτός, direct object of στήσαντες) 16.

ἐν (preposition with the locative of place) 80.
τῷ (loc.sing.masc.of the article in agreement with μέσῳ) 9.
μέσῳ (loc.sing.masc.of μέσος, place) 873.
ἐπυνθάνοντο (3d.per.pl.imp.mid.ind.of πυνθάνομαι, inceptive) 153.
ἐν (preposition with the instrumental of means) 80.
ποίᾳ (instru.sing.fem.of ποῖος, in agreement with δυνάμει) 1298.
δυνάμει (instru.sing.fem.of δύναμις, means) 687.
ἤ (disjunctive particle) 465.
ἐν (preposition with the instrumental of agency) 80.
ποίῳ (instru.sing.neut.of ποῖος, in agreement with ὀνόματι,) 1298.
ὀνόματι (instru.sing.neut.of ὄνομα, agency) 108.
ἐποιήσατε (2d.per.pl.aor.act.ind.of ποιέω, constative) 127.
τοῦτο (acc.sing.neut.of οὗτος, direct object of ἐποιήσατε) 93.
ὑμεῖς (nom.pl.masc.of σύ, subject of ἐποιήσατε) 104.

Translation - "*And when they had brought them into the room, they began to demand by what power or in what name they did this.*"

Comment: The arbitrary treatment which the Establishment dealt out to Peter and John is typical of the exaggerated conception which these men had of their own importance and the dignity and jurisdiction of their court. The inceptive imperfect in ἐπυνθάνοντο indicates that they asked the question more than once. It implies that Galilean fishermen, of all people, were not to be expected to perform miracles - a function to be left to the proper dignitaries.It is the qualatative use of ποῖος (#1298) in both phrases.

If Annas and Caiaphas had known that their question would result in another one of Peter's sermons, they probably would not have asked it. First, at Pentecost, then in Solomon's Porch and now in court before Israel's highest authorities - thus the Holy Spirit opened the door for Peter to preach. Here we go again!

Verse 8 - "*Then Peter, filled with the Holy Ghost, said unto them, Ye rulers of the people and elders of Israel, . . . *"

τότε Πέτρος πλησθεὶς πνεύματος ἁγίου εἶπεν πρὸς αὐτούς, Ἄρχοντες τοῦ λαοῦ καὶ πρεσβύτεροι,

τότε (adverbial) 166.
Πέτρος (nom.sing.masc.of Πέτρος, subject of εἶπεν) 387.
πλησθεὶς (aor.pass.part.nom.sing.masc.of πίμπλημι, adverbial, modal) 1409.
πνεύματος (abl.sing.neut.of πνεῦμα, source) 83.
ἁγίου (abl.sing.neut.of ἅγιος, in agreement with πνεύματος) 84.
εἶπεν (3d.per.sing.aor.act.ind.of εἶπον, constative) 155.
πρὸς (preposition with the accusative of extent after a verb of speaking) 197.
αὐτούς (acc.pl.masc.of αὐτός, extent after a verb of speaking) 16.
Ἄρχοντες (voc.pl.masc.of ἄρχων, address) 816.

τοῦ (gen.sing.masc.of the article in agreement with λαοῦ) 9.
λαοῦ (gen.sing.masc.of λαός, relationship) 110.
καὶ (adjunctive conjunction joining nouns) 14.
πρεσβύτεροι (voc.pl.masc.of πρεσβύτερος, address) 1141.

Translation - "Then Peter, filled with the Holy Spirit, said to them, 'Rulers of the people and Elders . . . ' "

Comment: Note how faithfully the Holy Spirit equipped Peter to speak when the occasion demanded. It is the fulfillment of the promise of Luke 21:12-15. The filling of the Holy Spirit is available to every Christian. Our Heavenly Father is more ready to give Him to us when we ask Him than an earthly parent is to give bread, fish, eggs or other good gifts to their children (Luke 11:9-13).

We are now afforded another opportunity to study the preaching methods of the Apostles. This sermon was even shorter than the others. It required only thirty seconds, but it contained all the elements of the other two. Peter again accused the Jews of murdering Jesus. Again he said that Jesus had risen from the dead. He declared that it was in the name of Jesus that the miracle had been performed, and he quoted again from the Hebrew Scriptures, this time from the Psalms and tied current history to previous prophecy. Finally he said that the name of the man they had crucified alone provided access to salvation.

Verse 9 - "If we this day be examined of the good deed done to the impotent man, by what means he is made whole, . . . "

εἰ ἡμεῖς σήμερον ἀνακρινόμεθα ἐπὶ εὐεργεσίᾳ ἀνθρώπου ἀσθενοῦς, ἐν τίνι οὗτος σέσωσται,

εἰ (conditional particle in a first-class condition) 337.
ἡμεῖς (nom.pl.masc.of ἐγώ, subject of ἀνακρινόμεθα) 123.
σήμερον (temporal adverb) 579.
ἀνακρινόμεθα (1st.per.pl.pres.pass.ind.of ἀνακρίνω, aoristic, first-class condition) 2837.
ἐπὶ (preposition with the dative of reference) 47.

#3030 εὐεργεσίᾳ (dat.sing.fem.of εὐεργασία, reference).

benefit - 1 Tim.6:2.
good deed done - Acts 4:9.

Meaning: A combination of εὖ and ἔργον (#460). Hence, good work, good deed, benefit. *Cf.*εὐεργετέω (#3231) and εὐεργέτης (#2778). With reference to the healing of the cripple - Acts 4:9. Of the benefit of salvation shared alike by a Christian master and his Christian slave - 1 Tim.6:2.

ἀνθρώπου (gen.sing.masc.of ἄνθρωπος, objective genitive) 341.
ἀσθενοῦς (gen.sing.masc.of ἀσθενής, in agreement with ἀνθρώπου) 1551.
ἐν (preposition with the instrumental of means) 80.
τίνι (instru.sing.neut.of τίς, interrogative pronoun, indirect question) 281.

οὗτος (nom.sing.masc.of οὗτος, subject of σέσωσται) 93.
σέσωσται (3d.per.sing.perf.pass.ind.of σώζω, intensive) 109.

Translation - "In view of the fact that today we are being questioned with reference to the manner by which a good deed was performed upon a crippled man, by which he was healed, . . . "

Comment: This is the protasis of a first-class condition. The premise was true. Peter and John were indeed being questioned that day. In reference to what? The good deed conferred upon a cripple. What about it? How was it done? How was he healed? The apodosis is an emphatic indicative assertion in verse 10. The resultant idea is, "Very well. You gentlemen asked for it and you are going to get it." The court opened the door for Peter to talk about a name and about the power which the name carries. One shares vicariously some of the thrill of the Holy Spirit which must have surged through Peter as, with holy boldness he threw the information that they sought back into their teeth, in

Verse 10 - "Be it known unto you all, and to all the people of Israel, that by the name of Jesus Christ of Nazareth, whom ye crucified, whom God raised from the dead, even by him doth this man stand here before you whole."

γνωστὸν ἔστω πᾶσιν ὑμῖν καὶ παντὶ τῷ λαῷ Ἰσραὴλ ὅτι ἐν τῷ ὀνόματι Ἰησοῦ Χριστοῦ τοῦ Ναζωραίου, ὃν ὑμεῖς ἐσταυρώσατε, ὃν ὁ θεὸς ἤγειρεν ἐκ νεκρῶν, ἐν τούτῳ οὗτος παρέστηκεν ἐνώπιον ὑμῶν ὑγιής.

γνωστὸν (acc.sing.neut.of γνωστός, predicate adjective) 1917.
ἔστω (3d.per.sing.pres.impv.of εἰμί, command) 86.
πᾶσιν (dat.pl.masc.of πᾶς, in agreement with ὑμῖν) 67.
ὑμῖν (dat.pl.masc.of σύ, indirect object of ἔστω) 104.
καὶ (adjunctive conjunction joining substantives) 14.
παντὶ (dat.sing.masc.of πᾶς, in agreement with λαῷ) 67.
τῷ (dat.sing.masc.of the article in agreement with λαῷ) 9.
λαῷ (dat.sing.masc.of λαός, indirect object of ἔστω) 110.
Ἰσραὴλ (gen.sing.masc.of Ἰσραήλ, description) 165.
ὅτι (conjunction introducing an object clause in indirect discourse) 211.
ἐν (preposition with the instrumental of agency) 80.
τῷ (instru.sing.neut.of the article in agreement with ὀνόματι) 9.
ὀνόματι (instru.sing.neut.of ὄνομα, agency) 108.
Ἰησοῦ (gen.sing.masc.of Ἰησοῦς, possession) 3.
Χριστοῦ (gen.sing.masc.of Χριστός, apposition) 4.
τοῦ (gen.sing.masc.of the article in agreement with Ναζωραίου) 9.
Ναζωραίου (gen.sing.masc.of Ναζωραῖος, apposition) 245.
ὃν (acc.sing.masc.of ὅς, direct object of ἐσταυρώσατε) 65.
ὑμεῖς (nom.pl.masc.of σύ, subject of ἐσταυρώσατε) 104.
ἐσταυρώσατε (2d.per.pl.aor.act.ind.of σταυρόω, constative) 1328.
ὃν (acc.sing.masc.of ὅς, direct object of ἤγειρεν) 65.
ὁ (nom.sing.masc.of the article in agreement with θεὸς) 9.

θεὸς (nom.sing.masc.of θεός, subject of ἤγειρεν) 124.
ἤγειρεν (3d.per.sing.aor.act.ind.of ἐγείρω, culminative) 125.
ἐκ (preposition with the ablative of separation) 19.
νεκρῶν (abl.pl.masc.of νεκρός, separation) 749.
ἐν (preposition with the instrumental of means) 80.
τούτῳ (instru.sing.neut.of οὗτος, resumptive) 93.
οὗτος (nom.sing.masc.of οὗτος, subject of παρέστηκεν, deictic) 93.
παρέστηκεν (3d.per.sing.perf.act.ind.of παρίστημι, intensive) 1596.
ἐνώπιον (improper preposition with the genitive of place description) 1798.
ὑμῶν (gen.pl.masc.of σύ, place description) 104.
ὑγιής (nom.sing.masc.of ὑγιής, predicate adjective) 979.

Translation - "Be it known to you and to all the Israeli people that by the authority of the name of Jesus Christ, the Nazarene, whom you crucified, whom God raised from the dead - by that name, this man is standing before you in good health."

Comment: γνωστὸν ἔστω is like an official announcement of great authority - "Let it be known. . . " as in the United States Congress, "Ladies and Gentlemen, the President of the United States," or as in the Olympic Games, "Let the games begin," or at the Indianapolis Motor Speedway, "Ladies and Gentlemen, start your motors." ἔστω is intransitive, but we have πᾶσιν ὑμῖν and παντὶ τῷ λαῷ as indirect object - "let it be said to . . . κ.τ.λ." In the gospels the idiom would probably have been λέγω ὑμῖν. ὅτι introduces indirect discourse. "By the name of Jesus Christ, the Nazarene. . . " This is the third time in three sermons that Peter has spoken in "the name that is above every name" (Phil.2:9-11; Acts 2:22; 3:16). It is the name that the Father gave to Him (John 17:11,12). Having mentioned His name to those who had desecrated it, Peter quickly follows it with two relative clauses, in the first of which he reminded them that they had murdered Jesus, and in the second of which he boasted that God had raised Him from the dead. Thus in three sermons, Peter has accused them three times of Jesus' murder (Acts 2:23; 3:13-15; 4:10) and three times he has declared that Jesus had risen from the dead. The killer need fear no retribution from his victim so long as he stays dead, but suppose the victim should arise from the dead? We remember how Herod felt about that (Mt.14:2). ἐν τούτῳ is resumptive, as Peter points again to the name and then to the man who was healed. οὗτος is deictic. We now learn that the patient was also in court, as Peter points to him still standing before them (intensive perfect in παρέστηκεν), a living and healthy testimony to the fact that Jesus Christ is sovereign.

When a Christian witness is filled with the Holy Spirit (verse 8) his message is straightforward, positive and delivered for all to hear. So with Peter's statement. Jesus Christ got all the credit for the miracle. Peter's audience got all the blame for murdering Him. God got all the credit for raising Him from the dead. There was no temporizing here. Peter did not try to soft-pedal the charge. He was not thinking of diplomacy. "You killed the incarnate Son of God, whom you thought only to be an obscure Galilean carpenter. You, who are so highly touted as guides in religious matters, were so out of step with God that you killed Him,

Whom God raised up." A timid preacher, without the Holy Spirit's help would have tried to approach the subject diplomatically so as not to offend his audience! It is not probable that Peter had read Dale Carnegie's book. The seminary bred preacher with a relativistic philosophy that "finds tongues in trees, books in the running brooks, Sermons in stones, and good in everything" and who, like Duke Senior, ". . . would not change it" (William Shakespeare, *As You Like It*, II, 1, 16-18) is not likely to be as unequivocal as Peter was. A more diplomatic approach would be, "If you do not repent as it were, and be converted so to speak, you may go to hell in a measure." But let modern evangelistic fire-eaters understand that a macho pulpit pose, a roaring voice and a threatening visage is not a substitute for the fulness of the Holy Spirit. When preachers are under the control of the Holy Spirit, as Peter was, they may speak as Peter did. If they are not, perhaps they should remember Falstaff's observation that "The better part of valour is discretion; in the which better part I have saved my life." (William Shakespeare, *King Henry IV*, Part I, 5, iv.,120). No God-called preacher of the gospel need speak without the Holy Spirit's power. He is available for the asking (Luke 11:9-13).

Verse 11 - "This is the stone which was set at nought of you builders, which is become the head of the corner."

οὗτός ἐστιν ὁ λίθος ὁ ἐξουθενηθεὶς ὑφ᾽ ὑμῶν τῶν οἰκοδόμων, ὁ γενόμενος εἰς κεφαλὴν γωνίας.

οὗτός (nom.sing.masc.of οὗτος, subject of ἐστιν) 93.

ἐστιν (3d.per.sing.pres.ind.of εἰμί, static) 86.

ὁ (nom.sing.masc.of the article in agreement with λίθος) 9.

λίθος (nom.sing.masc.of λίθος, predicate nominative) 290.

ὁ (nom.sing.masc.of the article in agreement with ἐξουθενηθεὶς) 9.

ἐξουθενηθεὶς (1st.aor.pass.part.nom.sing.masc.of ἐξουθενέω, substantival, in apposition) 2628.

ὑφ᾽ (preposition with the ablative of agency) 117.

ὑμῶν (abl.pl.masc.of σύ, agency) 104.

τῶν (abl.pl.masc.of the article in agreement with οἰκοδόμων) 9.

οἰκοδόμων (pres.act.part.abl.pl.masc.of οἰκοδομέω, substantival, in apposition) 694.

ὁ (nom.sing.masc.of the article in agreement with γενόμενος) 9.

γενόμενος (aor.mid.part.nom.sing.masc.of γίνομαι, in apposition with λίθος) 113.

εἰς (preposition with the predicate accusative) 140.

κεφαλὴν (acc.sing.fem.of κεφαλή, predicate accusative) 521.

γωνίας (gen.sing.fem.of γωνία, description) 567.

Translation - "This man is the Stone, disdained by you who are the builders, the One Who has become the Cornerstone."

Comment: οὗτος is resumptive. Peter had momentarily turned their attention to the healed man. Now, with resumptive οὗτος he turned their thoughts back to

Christ. With a skillful use of the Psalms which they knew well, he related Jesus to Psalm 118:22. He scorned them with their lack of discrimination. A good builder should be able to select the best materials. Peter was saying, in effect, "You builders (!) are building a society in Israel. God sent His Son. You examined Him and repudiated Him as being unfit. Indeed He did not fit into your blueprint, but that was the fault of the blueprint, which you had designed and which you are still determined to follow. You killed Him, but God, contrary to your cynical evaluation of His merit, has raised Him from the dead and He has become, indeed, as He always has been, the most important part of God's building - the Cornerstone with the lines of which every other part of the building, those parts already in place and those parts yet to be added, must conform. How far from God's value system you self-appointed builders are!"

The student should run the references under #'s 694, 521 and 567 for all the allusions to Christ as the Cornerstone. Did Paul and Peter discuss this sermon, as a result of which Paul copied Peter's reference to Psalm 118:22 in Eph.2:20 or did Paul think of this with the help of the Holy Spirit alone. Perhaps both things are true. Peter used it again in 1 Peter 2:7.

Any builder who could not use building material like Jesus Christ in his construction is not a safe guide to salvation. True biblical Judaism points the sinner to the foot of the cross of Jesus Christ, the Messiah and then to the door of His empty tomb. Finally it directs his attention to the right hand of the throne of God in heaven where Messiah sits awaiting the day when He will fulfill all of God's promises to the nation. This is the true message of the Old Testament. The law of Moses and the messages of the prophets pointed forward to the righteousness of Jesus Christ (Romans 3:21,22). Moses, representative of the law and Elijah, speaking for the Prophets, appeared with Jesus on the Transfiguration Mountain. Each had tried to redeem Israel and had failed. Moses could lead Israel out of Egyptian bondage, but he could not lead them into the promised land. Elijah could behead 450 false prophets, the priests of Baal, but he could not turn the hearts of his people back to the God of righteousness. Each having failed in his mission, came to Jesus Who was standing in transfiguration glory on the mount, to be sure, but also within the shadow of a Roman cross, and admonished Him not to fail in τὴν ἔξοδον αὐτοῦ ἣν ἤμελλεν πληροῦν ἐν Ἰερουσαλήμ (Luke 9:31). God called many Jews during the Old Testament period to salvation. They looked beyond the trappings and the symbols of the Mosaic law and the rituals of the Aaronic Priesthood and, by the grace of God and the illumination of the Holy Spirit, they understood that these things were fingers pointing them forward to the Lamb of God whose blood, unlike the blood of bulls and goats, could indeed cleanse from sin. These were the true members of the Body of Christ, whose Judaism, unlike that of Annas and Caiaphas, was perceived in its proper light. But the Judaism which demanded the death at the hands of the Romans for their Messiah could never provide salvation. Thus Christianity has a unique place among the religions of the world. It is the only one that has a gospel that can save. This Peter says in

Verse 12 - "Neither is there salvation in any other; for there is none other name

under heaven given among men, whereby we must be saved."

καὶ οὐκ ἔστιν ἐν ἄλλῳ οὐδενὶ ἡ σωτηρία, οὐδὲ γὰρ ὄνομά ἐστιν ἕτερον ὑπὸ τὸν οὐρανὸν τὸ δεδομένον ἐν ἀνθρώποις ἐν ᾧ δεῖ σωθῆναι ὑμᾶς.

καὶ (adversative conjunction) 14.

οὐκ (summary negative conjunction with the indicative) 130.

ἔστιν (3d.per.sing.pres.ind.of εἰμί, static) 86.

ἐν (preposition with the instrumental of agent) 80.

ἄλλῳ (instru.sing.masc.of ἄλλος, in agreement with οὐδενὶ) 198.

οὐδενὶ (instru.sing.masc.of οὐδείς, agent) 446.

ἡ (nom.sing.fem.of the article in agreement with σωτηρία) 9.

σωτηρία, (nom.sing.fem.of σωτηρία, subject of ἔστιν) 1852.

οὐδὲ (disjunctive particle) 452.

γὰρ (causal conjunction) 105.

ὄνομα (nom.sing.neut.of ὄνομα, subject of ἐστιν) 108.

ἐστιν (3d.per.sing.pres.ind.of εἰμί, static) 86.

ἕτερον (nom.sing.neut.of ἕτερος, in agreement with ὄνομα) 605.

ὑπὸ (preposition with the accusative of extent) 117.

τὸν (acc.sing.masc.of the article in agreement with οὐρανὸν) 9.

οὐρανὸν (acc.sing.masc.of οὐρανός, extent) 254.

τὸ (nom.sing.neut.of the article in agreement with δεδωμένον) 9.

δεδωμένον (perf.pass.part.nom.sing.neut.of δίδωμι, adjectival restrictive) 362.

ἐν (preposition with the locative with persons) 80.

ἀνθρώποις (loc.pl.masc.of ἄνθρωπος, place, "among") 341.

ἐν (preposition with the instrumental of agent) 80.

ᾧ (instru.sing.neut.of ὅς, agent) 65.

δεῖ (3d.per.sing.imper.pres.ind.of δέω, static) 1207.

σωθῆναι (aor.pass.inf.of σώζω, complementary) 109.

ἡμᾶς (acc.pl.masc.of ἐγώ, general reference) 123.

Translation - "*But there is no salvation in any other, because there is not another name under heaven which has been given among men, by which it is possible for us to be saved.*"

Comment: In Acts 2 at Pentecost, Peter developed the basic idea that all of God's covenant promises to Israel as a nation were fulfilled in Jesus Christ. Hence to reject Him is to leave no alternative but condemnation. In Acts 3, the same idea comes through. The killed the ἀρχηγὸς τῆς ζωῆς (Acts 3:15). Jesus Christ is the Jewish Messiah or no one is (Acts 2). Christ alone can give life. No one else can (Acts 3). Now, in Acts 4:12 Christ alone can give salvation on a personal basis. No one else can. It follows then that in killing Him, Israel destroyed her only hope for a national king, her only hope for life beyond the grave and her only hope for personal salvation. The crime at Calvary dashed all hope for mankind. But God intervened and raised Him from the dead. Hence Israel's Messiah is restored, life is still available, and salvation can be had. But only if they repent and accept Him Whom they betrayed to death. This is evangelistic preaching at its Spirit-filled best. The message must deny to the audience all avenues of approach to God, eternal life and salvation except Jesus Christ, Who died and rose again. Jesus is not *a* way of salvation. He is *the* way. (John 14:6; Rom.4:1-6; Eph.2:8,9). It was given to the Apostle Paul to develop this concept of salvation by grace in a most thorough fashion, but his development is only a more extended treatment of that which Jesus and the other Apostles clearly taught.

Verse 13 - "Now when they saw the boldness of Peter and John, and perceived that they were unlearned and ignorant men, they marvelled; and they took knowledge of them, that they had been with Jesus."

Θεωροῦντες δὲ τὴν τοῦ Πέτρου παρρησίαν καὶ Ἰωάννου, καὶ καταλαβόμενοι ὅτι ἄνθρωποι ἀγράμματοί εἰσιν καὶ ἰδιῶται, ἐθαύμαζον ἐπεγίνωσκόν τε αὐτοὺς ὅτι σὺν τῷ Ἰησοῦ ἦσαν.

Θεωροῦντες (pres.act.part.nom.pl.masc.of θεωρέω, adverbial, causal) 1667.
δὲ (explanatory conjunction) 11.
τὴν (acc.sing.fem.of the article in agreement with παρρησίαν) 9.
τοῦ (gen.sing.masc.of the article in agreement with Πέτρου) 9.
Πέτρου (gen.sing.masc.of Πέτρος, possession) 387.
παρρησίαν (acc.sing.fem.of παρρησία, direct object of θεωροῦντες) 2319.
καὶ (adjunctive conjunction joining nouns) 14.
Ἰωάννου (gen.sing.masc.of Ἰωάννης, possession) 399.
καὶ (adjunctive conjunction joining participles) 14.
καταλαβόμενοι (2d.aor.mid.part.nom.pl.masc.of καταλαμβάνω, temporal-causal) 1694.
ὅτι (conjunction introducing an object clause in indirect discourse) 211.
ἄνθρωποι (nom.pl.masc.of ἄνθρωπος, predicate nominative) 341.

#3031 ἀγράμματοί (nom.pl.masc.of ἀγράμματος, in agreement with ἄνθρωποι).

unlearned - Acts 4:13.

Meaning: A combination of α privative and γράμμα (#2100). Unlearned; without formal education; illiterate - Acts 4:13.

εἰσιν (3d.per.pl.pres.ind.of εἰμί, indirect discourse) 86.
καὶ (adjunctive conjunction joining adjectives) 14.

#3032 ἰδιῶται (nom.pl.masc.of ἰδιώτης, in agreement with ἄνθρωποι).

ignorant - Acts 4:13.
rude - 2 Cor.11:6.
unlearned - 1 Cor.14:16,23,24.

Meaning: In classical Greek, a private individual as opposed to a public official or officer. A writer of common prose as opposed to a poet. In the New Testament, an unlearned man; illiterate relative to one well educated. Not as low on the IQ scale as an idiot, in terms of modern psychology and intelligence testing. Followed by a locative of sphere - 2 Cor.11:6. In 1 Cor.14:16,23,24 of a Christian who is not able to translate a foreign language. With reference to Peter and John, who were less well educated than members of the San Hedrin - Acts 4:13.

ἐθαύμαζον (3d.per.pl.imp.act.ind.of θαυμάζω, inceptive) 726.
ἐπεγίνωσκόν (3d.per.pl.imp.act.ind.of ἐπιγινώσκω, inceptive) 675.
τε (correlative conjunction) 1408.
αὐτοὺς (acc.pl.masc.of αὐτός, direct object of ἐπεγίνωσκόν) 16.
ὅτι (conjunction introducing an object clause in indirect discourse) 211.
σὺν (preposition with the instrumental of association) 1542.
τῷ (instru.sing.masc.of the article in agreement with Ἰησοῦ) 9.
Ἰησοῦ (instru.sing.masc.of Ἰησοῦς, association) 3.
ἦσαν (3d.per.pl.imp.ind.of εἰμί, progressive duration) 86.

Translation - "Now because they saw the boldness of Peter and John, and after they became aware that they were ignorant and illiterate men, they were seized with amazement and they began to realize that they had been associated with Jesus, . . . "

Comment: It was unusual for uneducated men to speak so boldly to the San Hedrin. Peter and John seemed devoid of the tact and diplomacy that one would expect in a salon. *Cf.*#2319 for the basic meaning of the word. The San Hedrin also observed that these men were not university bred. ἀγράμματοί - "unskilled in Greek rhetoric." We need read only 2 Peter and the Revelation to agree that both Peter and John, for all of their Spirit-filled zeal and devotion to Christ, could have used a refresher course in Greek syntax. The word ἰδιώτης - means an individualist. Obviously Peter and John were not marching to the cadence of the Establishment drum. As a result the officials were filled with amazement (imperfect tense in ἐθαύμαζον) and it began to dawn upon them that Peter and John were two of Jesus' disciples who had spent the past three years with Him. John and Annas were acquainted (John 18:15), but Luke does not indicate that Annas recognized him. He may not have remembered him or if he did he made no mention of the fact.

Once the San Hedrin realized that Peter and John were disciples of Jesus, their course should have been clear. Here were two of those subversive Galileans. Crucify them! But they were experienced politicians who did not want another round with Pilate.

The complete absence of any visible impact of the Holy Spirit, through the Word which Peter preached, upon these reprobate men is to be noted. Without the slightest indication that they felt that they were lost in sin and destined to face this Jesus Whom they had crucified in judgment, they came to grips with the situation immediately, like the practical political animals that they were. There was a problem. A notable miracle had been performed by these ignorant Jesus fanatics and that was not the worst of it. The public knew about it. Indeed there were about 8000 Jews in Jerusalem who were eternally committed to the gospel which Peter preached.

Verse 14 - "And beholding the man which was healed standing with them, they could say nothing against it."

τόν τε ἄνθρωπον βλέποντες σὺν αὐτοῖς ἑστῶτα τὸν τεθεραπευμένον οὐδὲν εἶχον ἀντειπεῖν.

τόν (acc.sing.masc.of the article in agreement with ἄνθρωπον) 9.
τε (adversative conjunction) 1408.
ἄνθρωπον (acc.sing.masc.of ἄνθρωπος, direct object of βλέποντες) 341.
σὺν (preposition with the instrumental of association) 1542.
αὐτοῖς (instru.pl.masc.of αὐτός, association) 16.
ἑστῶτα (perf.act.part.acc.sing.masc.of ἵστημι, adverbial, circumstantial) 180.
τὸν (acc.sing.masc.of the article in agreement with τεθεραπευμένον) 9.
τεθεραπευμένον (perf.pass.part.acc.sing.masc.of θεραπεύω, adjectival, restrictive) 406.
οὐδὲν (acc.sing.neut.of οὐδείς, direct object of εἶχον) 446.
εἶχον (3d.per.pl.imp.act.ind.of ἔχω, progressive description) 82.
ἀντειπεῖν (aor.act.inf.of ἀντεῖπον, epexegetical) 2713.

Translation - "And because they saw the man who had been healed and who was still standing with them, they had nothing to say against it."

Comment: The two perfect participles ἑστῶτα and τεθεραπευμένον make the picture clear. The former is an adverb used circumstantially. The latter is an adjective to define ἄνθρωπον. He had been healed, with a completed action in the past, and as a result he was still standing there in court listening to the procedings. His presence made it impossible for the court to say anything against what Peter and John had done. Why, then had they arrested them and held them overnight in jail? An apology was in order and the case should have been dismissed. Of course there was no apology. The San Hedrin acted like typical politicians. They sent the defendants out of the room in order that they could discuss their problem like politicians.

Verse 15 - "But when they had commanded them to go aside out of the council, they conferred among themselves."

κελεύσαντες δὲ αὐτοὺς ἔξω τοῦ συνεδρίου ἀπελθεῖν συνέβαλλον πρὸς ἀλλήλους.

κελεύσαντες (aor.act.part.nom.pl.masc.of κελεύω, adverbial, temporal) 741.
δὲ (inferential conjunction) 11.
αὐτοὺς (acc.pl.masc.of αὐτός, direct object of κελεύσαντες) 16.
ἔξω (adverbial) 449.
τοῦ (abl.sing.neut.of the article in agreement with συνεδρίου) 9.
συνεδρίου (abl.sing.neut.of συνέδριον, separation) 481.
ἀπελθεῖν (aor.mid.inf.of ἀπέρχομαι, epexegetical) 239.
συνέβαλλον (3d.per.pl.imp.act.ind.of συνβάλλω, inceptive) 1885.

πρὸς (preposition with the accusative of extent after a verb of speaking) 197.
ἀλλήλους (acc.pl.masc.of ἀλλήλων, extent, after a verb of speaking) 1487.

Translation - "So they ordered them to step out of the council chamber and began to discuss it among themselves."

Comment: It is possible to take δὲ here inferentially, although it is a rare use. It was because they had nothing to say against the healing that they ordered the Apostles to leave. The San Hedrin was hard pressed for a policy that was consistent with their own great desire - to survive, which was the only consistency that they were interested in. The action of the court is typical. The honest thing to do can be done only if it is also politically feasible. If they were determined to silence Peter and John why ask them to leave while they discuss it? Honest men are not afraid to discuss their problems in the presence of all concerned. So Peter and John waited outside the door while their fate was being discussed.

We have a case here where the context provides a noun to serve as the object of a verb. συνέβαλλον means that they were throwing something around among themselves. What? Obviously we supply λογούς.

Verse 16 - "Saying, what shall we do to these men? for that indeed a notable miracle hath been done by them is manifest to all them that dwell in Jerusalem; and we cannot deny it."

λέγοντες, Τί ποιήσωμεν τοῖς ἀνθρώποις τούτοις; ὅτι μὲν γὰρ γνωστὸν σημεῖον γέγονεν δι' αὐτῶν πᾶσιν τοῖς κατοικοῦσιν Ἱερουσαλὴμ φανερόν, καὶ οὐ δυνάμεθα ἀρνεῖσθαι.

λέγοντες (pres.act.part.nom.pl.masc.of λέγω, recitative) 66.
Τί (acc.sing.neut.of τίς, interrogative pronoun, in direct question) 281.
ποιήσωμεν (1st.per.pl.aor.act.subj.of ποιέω, deliberative) 127.
τοῖς (dat.pl.masc.of the article in agreement with ἀνθρώποις) 9.
ἀνθρώποις (dat.pl.masc.of ἄνθρωπος, reference) 341.
τούτοις (dat.pl.masc.of οὗτος, in agreement with ἀνθρώποις) 93.
ὅτι (conjunction introducing an object clause in indirect discourse) 211.
μὲν (affirmative particle) 300.
γὰρ (causal conjunction) 105.
γνωστὸν (nom.sing.neut.of γνωστός, in agreement with σημεῖον) 1917.
σημεῖον (nom.sing.neut.of σημεῖον, subject of γέγονεν) 1005.
γέγονεν (3d.per.sing.2d.perf.ind.of γίνομαι, consummative) 113.
δι' (preposition with the ablative of agency) 118.
αὐτῶν (abl.pl.masc.of αὐτός, agency) 16.
πᾶσιν (dat.pl.masc.of πᾶς, in agreement with κατοικοῦσιν) 67.
τοῖς (dat.pl.masc.of the article in agreement with κατοικοῦσιν) 9.
κατοικοῦσιν (pres.act.part.dat.pl.masc.of κατοικέω, substantival, personal interest) 242.
φανερόν (acc.sing.neut.of φανερός, predicate adjective) 981.

καὶ (continuative conjunction) 14.
οὐ (summary negative conjunction with the indicative) 130.
δυνάμεθα (1st.per.pl.pres.mid.ind.of δύναμαι, customary) 289.
ἀρνεῖσθαι (pres.mid.inf.of ἀρνέομαι, epexegetical) 895.

Translation - ". . . *saying, 'What are we going to do about these men? Because that in fact a well publicized miracle has been performed by them is obvious to all who live in Jerusalem, and we cannot deny it.'* "

Comment: Deliberative subjunctive in ποιήσωμεν followed by a dative of reference. "What are we to do about (with, to, with reference to) these men?" ὅτι introduces the object clause in indirect discourse, since we hace causal γὰρ also. μὲν, the affirmative particle is joined with ἀλλ', the adversative in verse 17.

The implication is that they would have denied it, even though they knew that it was true, but for the fact that everyone in Jerusalem also knew that it was true. Five thousand people had witnessed the miracle, heard Peter's sermon in Solomon's Porch, come to accept Christ, and had gone out telling it. A story like that would blanket the city in a matter of minutes. We can be sure that the healed cripple would have spread the word all over the city even if the others had not. He is the one who publicized it in the first place, with his joyous capers as he leaped all over the court, praising God with every jump. It is impossible to imagine him having been quiet about this. He had not taken a step in forty years and now he was ready to enter the Olympic games. Otherwise the San Hedrin could have suppressed the story. Why indeed should good men wish to keep such good news secret in any case? But these were not good men. They were the murderers of the one Good Man in Whose name the miracle had been performed. The decision to which the council came reveals how naive these men were.

Verse 17 - "*But that it spread no further among the people, let us straitly threaten them, that they speak henceforth to no man in this name.*"

ἀλλ' ἵνα μὴ ἐπὶ πλεῖον διανεμηθῇ εἰς τὸν λαόν, ἀπειλησώμεθα αὐτοῖς μηκέτι λαλεῖν ἐπὶ τῷ ὀνόματι τούτῳ μηδενὶ ἀνθρώπων.

ἀλλ' (adversative conjunction) 342.
ἵνα (conjunction with the subjunctive, negative purpose) 114.
μὴ (qualified negative conjunction with the subjunctive) 87.
ἐπὶ (preposition with the accusative of extent) 47.
πλεῖον (acc.sing.neut.of πλείων, extent) 474.

#3033 διανεμηθῇ (3d.per.sing.aor.pass.subj.of διανέμω, negative purpose).

spread - Acts 4:17.

Meaning: A combination of διά (#118) and νέμω - "to deal out, dispense, distribute, divide." With reference to a rumor spreading among the people. Followed by εἰσ τὸν λαόν - Acts 4:17.

εἰς (preposition with the accusative of extent) 140.
τὸν (acc.sing.masc.of the article in agreement with λαόν) 9.
λαόν (acc.sing.masc.of λαός, extent) 110.

#3034 ἀπειλησώμεθα (1st.per.pl.aor.mid.subj.of ἀπειλέω, hortatory).

threaten - Acts 4:17; 1 Peter 2:23.

Meaning: To threaten; to speak with menace. With reference to the threat of the San Hedrin to Peter and John - Acts 4:17. Jesus did not threaten his persecutors at Calvary - 1 Peter 2:23.

αὐτοῖς (dat.pl.masc.of αὐτός, indirect object of ἀπειλησώμεθα) 16.
μηκέτι (negative temporal adverb) 1368.
λαλεῖν (pres.act.inf.of λαλέω, epexegetical) 815.
ἐπὶ (preposition with the instrumental of agency) 47.
τῷ (instru.sing.neut.of the article in agreement with ὀνόματι) 9.
ὀνόματι (instru.sing.neut.of ὄνομα, agency) 108.
τούτῳ (instru.sing.neut.of οὗτος, in agreement with ὀνόματι) 93.
μηδενὶ (dat.sing.masc.of μηδείς, indirect object of λαλεῖν) 713.
ἀνθρώπων (gen.pl.masc.of ἄνθρωπος, partitive genitive) 341.

Translation - "But in order that it does not spread further among the people, let us sternly order them to speak further in this name to no man."

Comment: ἀλλ' is antithetical to μὲν in verse 16 - "in fact a well known miracle .. . but in order that . . . κ.τ.λ." The negative purpose clause explains their suggestion in the hortatory subjunctive. ἐπὶ πλεῖον is interesting. *Cf.* Acts 24:4; 2 Tim.3:9 for the other two examples. The Greek piles up the negatives for emphasis - "no more (longer) . . to no man. . . " Thus the San Hedrin decided. They were assured of the righteousness of their case. Why were they so afraid of the man, who, in their view was dead and buried? Yet they forbade the exercise of free speech in His name, despite the fact that they had just admitted that in His name a great miracle had been performed - a fact which they could not gainsay. A lame man, more than forty years old, who had never walked a step in his life was now walking and leaping about the temple and up and down the streets of the city. But the Apostles were ordered never again to speak to any man in this name.

Apparently they would rather that all of Israel be lame and blind, except themselves, of course, than that their own religious and political position be threatened. This is depravity the depths of which no man can plumb. When one is that possessed with evil, his ability to make realistic assumptions is gone. Did anyone, except those men in the San Hedrin, think for a moment that Peter and John would obey their order to desist?

Verse 18 - "And they called them, and commanded them not to speak at all nor teach in the name of Jesus."

καὶ καλέσαντες αὐτοὺς παρήγγειλαν τὸ καθόλου μὴ φθέγγεσθαι μηδὲ διδάσκειν ἐπὶ τῷ ὀνόματι τοῦ Ἰησοῦ.

καὶ (continutiave conjunction) 14.
καλέσαντες (aor.act.part.nom.pl.masc.of καλέω, adverbial, temporal) 107.
αὐτοὺς (acc.pl.masc.of αὐτός, direct object of καλέσαντες) 16.
παρήγγειλαν (3d.per.pl.aor.act.ind.of παραγγέλλω, constative) 855.
τὸ (acc.sing.neut.of the article in agreement with φθέγγεσθαι) 9.

#3035 καθόλου (adverbial).

at all - Acts 4:18.

Meaning: A combination of κατά (#98) and ὅλος (#112). According to (at) all. With μή - Acts 4:18.

μὴ (qualified negative conjunction with the infinitive) 87.

#3036 φθέγγεσθαι (pres.inf.of φθέγγομαι, acc.sing.neut., object of παρήγγειλαν)

speak - Acts 4:18; 2 Peter 2:16,18.

Meaning: To give vent to a sound, noise or cry. Used in classic Greek of any kind of sound or voice, whether of man, animal or even of an inanimate object, such as a musical instrument or thunder. Sound in relation to the hearer, not in relation to the cause. To preach or proclaim a message - Acts 4:18; of the voice of Balaam's ass - 2 Peter 2:16. With references to the great speeches of end-time apostates - 2 Peter 2:18.

μηδὲ (negative continuative particle) 612.
διδάσκειν (pres.act.inf.of διδάσκω, accusative case, object of παρήγγειλαν) 403.

ἐπὶ (preposition with the instrumental of agent) 47.
τῷ (instru.sing.neut.of the article in agreement with ὀνόματι) 9.
ὀνόματι (instru.sing.neut.of ὄνομα, agency) 108.
τοῦ (gen.sing.masc.of the article in agreement with Ἰησοῦ) 9.
Ἰησοῦ (gen.sing.masc.of Ἰησοῦς, possession) 3.

Translation - "*And when they had called them they ordered them not to speak at all, nor to teach in the name of Jesus.*"

Comment: The verb παρήγγειλαν has two objects. The Apostles were ordered to desist from any further speaking or teaching in the name of Jesus. Thus the Establishment admitted that they could not compete with the all powerful weapon - the name which is above every name (Phil.2:9-11). The opponent who is invincible was not to be permitted to enter the game. That is like one football coach saying to his opponent before the game, "You may not play that halfback because our defense cannot stop him." The order of the San Hedrin was an exercise in futility. How could an order from an institution which had just been totally discredited in the opinion of the Apostles have been enforced? What sanctions could Caiaphas impose? He could have cast Peter and John out of the temple. It is not likely that they would have regarded that punishment very great. The Jewish court had little jurisdiction to enforce other penalties, and it had none in cases that involved Roman citizens. Whatever the punishment might have been, it was proved later to be ineffective against the surge of the Holy Spirit filled church in Jerusalem, the members of which were on fire with the message of a resurrected Christ.

Verse 19 - "But Peter and John answered and said unto them, Whether it be right in the sight of God to hearken unto you more than unto God, judge ye."

ὁ δὲ Πέτρος καὶ Ἰωάννης ἀποκριθέντες εἶπον πρὸς αὐτούς, Εἰ δίκαιόν ἐστιν ἐνώπιον τοῦ θεοῦ ἡμῶν ἀκούειν μᾶλλον ἢ τοῦ θεοῦ, κρίνατε,

ὁ (nom.sing.masc.of the article in agreement with Πέτρος) 9.

δὲ (adversative conjunction) 11.

Πέτρος (nom.sing.masc.of Πέτρος subject of εἶπον) 387.

καὶ (adjunctive conjunction joining nouns) 14.

Ἰωάννης (nom.sing.masc.of Ἰωάννης, subject of εἶπον) 399.

ἀποκριθέντες (aor.part.nom.pl.masc.of ἀποκρίνομαι, adverbial, modal) 318.

εἶπον (3d.per.pl.aor.act.ind.of εἶπον, constative) 155.

πρὸς (preposition with the accusative of extent, after a verb of speaking) 197.

αὐτούς (acc.pl.masc.of αὐτός, extent after a verb of speaking) 16.

Εἰ (conditional particle in an indirect question) 337.

δίκαιόν (acc.sing.neut.of δίκαιος, predicate accusative) 85.

ἐστιν (3d.per.sing.pres.ind.of εἰμί, static) 86.

ἐνώπιον (improper preposition with the genitive of place description) 1798.

τοῦ (gen.sing.masc.of the article in agreement with θεοῦ) 9.

θεοῦ (gen.sing.masc.of θεός, description) 124.

ὑμῶν (gen.pl.masc.of σύ, objective genitive) 104.

ἀκούειν (pres.act.inf.of ἀκούω, subject of ἐστιν) 148.

μᾶλλον (comparative adverb) 619.

ἢ (disjunctive particle) 465.

τοῦ (gen.sing.masc.of the article in agreement with θεοῦ) 9.

θεοῦ (gen.sing.masc.of θεός, objective genitive) 124.

κρίνατε (2d.per.pl.1st.aor.act.impv.of κρίνω, command) 531.

Translation - "But Peter and John said to them in reply, 'If it is right before God to listen to you rather than to God, you must hand down a decision to that effect."

Comment: Peter and John with tongue in cheek threw themselves upon the mercy of the court and asked the judge for his opinion. Εἰ is here in indirect question, or we can call it a first-class conditional sentence, as I have translated.

The Apostles were daring Caiaphas to say that the judgment of the court was superior to the judgment of God. Of course the issue between them concerned which one was listening to the voice of God and which was not. Peter and John had very good evidence that they were on the right side of that question. Jesus, Who had said that He was the Son of God and that He and the Father were one (John 10:30), had died and risen from the dead. And His name, through the cripple's faith in it had made him healthy. What evidence did Caiaphas have to support his contention? Thus they asked, "What does the court think? Is it right to obey God or you?" Obviously they could not do both since they were getting orders from God to speak and had just had an order from the court to remain silent. That the San Hedrin could be on a side opposed to God was a thought totally foreign to Annas and Caiaphas. But it was clear to Peter and John. Then they appealed to experience, in

Verse 20 - "For we cannot but speak the things which we have seen and heard."

οὐ δυνάμεθα γὰρ ἡμεῖς ἃ εἴδαμεν καὶ ἠκούσαμεν μὴ λαλεῖν.

οὐ (summary negative conjunction with the indicative) 130.
δυνάμεθα (1st.per.pl.pres.mid.ind.of δύναμαι, aoristic) 289.
γὰρ (causal conjunction) 105.
ἡμεῖς (nom.pl.masc.of ἐγώ, subject of δυνάμεθα) 123.
ἃ (acc.pl.neut.of ὅς, direct object of λαλεῖν) 65.
εἴδαμεν (1st.per.pl.aor.act.ind.of ὁράω, culminative) 144.
καὶ (adjunctive conjunction, joining verbs) 14.
ἠκούσαμεν (1st.per.pl.aor.act.ind.of ἀκούω, culminative) 148.
μὴ (qualified negative conjunction with the infinitive) 87.
λαλεῖν (pres.act.inf.of λαλέω, complementary) 815.

Translation - "Because we are unable to refrain from speaking of the things which we have seen and heard."

Comment: οὐ δυνάμεθα . . . μὴ λαλεῖν is not redundant. "We are not able not to speak" means "We are unable to refrain from speaking. . . " ἡμεῖς is in strong contrast to ὑμῶν in verse 19. "As for us, despite what judgment you arrive at with reference to the question, we cannot help but speak, because we are talking about what we have seen and heard." Peter and John were not saying that they could speak *only* of what they saw and heard, but that they *must* speak of that which they saw and heard. They could also speak of matters which, though neither seen nor heard, nor perceived in any sensory fashion, could logically be inferred from what they knew by sense perception. The radical empiricists can derive no support from this passage for their notion that certitude is derived only from sense perception. Peter and John had indeed seen and heard a great deal, on the basis of which they went on, with complete validity, to infer the truth of the remainder of Christian theology, insofar as they understood it at that time. Their conceptual theological schema was due to be greatly enriched and expanded in the future, but the inferences which Peter drew from his empirical experiences with Jesus, as well as those experiences which he had had since the ascension - Pentecost, supernatural language capability, miracles in Jesus' name, etc., were valid. Sense perception, holism and logic adds up to truth. The rationalist who infers everything from his *a priori* assumptions and eschews historical evidence is no further astray than the empiricist who refuses all approaches to truth except sense perception. Peter and John had God given faith, but they also had the advantage of some experiences and they were determined to go on talking about them. The San Hedrin could do nothing more than repeat their threats.

Verse 21 - "So when they had further threatened them, they let them go, finding nothing how they might punish them, because of the people: for all men glorified God for that which was done."

οἱ δὲ προσαπειλησάμενοι ἀπέλυσαν αὐτούς, μηδὲν εὑρίσκοντες τὸ πῶς κολάσωνται αὐτούς, διὰ τὸν λαόν, ὅτι πάντες ἐδόξαζον τὸν θεὸν ἐπὶ τῷ γεγονότι.

οἱ (nom.pl.masc.of the article, subject of ἀπέλυσαν) 9.
δὲ (continuative conjunction) 11.

#3037 προσαπειλησάμενοι (aor.mid.part.nom.pl.masc.of προσαπειλέω, adverbial, temporal).

threaten further - Acts 4:21.

Meaning: A combination of πρός (#197) and ἀπειλέω (#3034). To add to (πρός) threats already issued. To emphasize previous warnings of reprisal. The San Hedrin's threat to Peter and John - Acts 4:21.

ἀπέλυσαν (3d.per.pl.aor.act.ind.of ἀπολύω, constative) 92.
αὐτούς (acc.pl.masc.of αὐτός, direct object of ἀπέλυσαν) 16.
μηδὲν (acc.sing.neut.of μηδείς, direct object of εὑρίσκοντες) 713.
εὑρίσκοντες (pres.act.part.nom.pl.masc.of εὑρίσκω, adverbial, causal) 79.
τὸ (acc.sing.neut.of the article to introduce indirect question) 9.
πῶς (interrogative adverb in indirect question) 627.

#3038 κολάσωνται (3d.per.pl.aor.mid.subj.of κολάζω, indirect question).

punish - Acts 4:21; 2 Peter 2:9.

Meaning: Cf.κόλος - "lopped." Hence, to cut, prune, restrain. Generally to punish. With reference to the Peter, John and the San Hedrin - Acts 4:21. Of final punishment for apostates - 2 Peter 2:9.

αὐτούς (acc.pl.masc.of αὐτός, direct object of κολάσωνται) 16.
διὰ (preposition with the accusative, cause) 118.
τὸν (acc.sing.masc.of the article in agreement with λαόν) 9.
λαόν (acc.sing.masc.of λαός, cause) 110.

ὅτι (conjunction introducing a subordinate causal clause) 211.

πάντες (nom.pl.masc.of πᾶς, subject of ἐδόξαζον) 67.

ἐδόξαζον (3d.per.pl.imp.act.ind.of δοξάζω, iterative) 461.

τὸν (acc.sing.masc.of the article in agreement with θεόν) 9.

θεόν (acc.sing.masc.of θεός, direct object of ἐδόξαζον) 124.

ἐπὶ (preposition with the instrumental, cause) 47.

τῷ (instru.sing.neut.of the article in agreement with γεγονότι) 9.

γεγονότι (perf.part.instru.sing.neut.of γίνομαι, substantival, cause) 113.

Translation - *"And after they had threatened them further they let them go, because they found no way to punish them on account of the people, because everyone was glorifying God because of what had happened."*

Comment: The statement of Peter and John that they had no intention of complying with the order of the court to remain silent about Jesus, only intensified the wrath of the high priests. But they were in an impossible position. There was no other reason to hold the Apostles. The only rational thing for them to do was to repent, accept Christ and join the witnesses. Since they would not do that, everything else that they did was irrational. They threatened them further, as if that did any good. Peter and John had already rejected their order to desist, and the former threats were unavailing. They released them, which, from their point of view, was irrational, because they had been told that as soon as Peter and John walked out of their court room they would continue as occasion presented itself to witness in the name of Jesus. Since Peter and John were heretics, who constituted a distinct threat to the Judaism which the San Hedrin was pledged to protect, they should have imprisoned or killed them. Why then did they release them? The causal participle εὑρίσκοντες tells us. They found no reason to hold them. Note the article τὸ introducing the indirect question, πῶς κολάσωνται αὐτούς. The verb is subjunctive because it was subjunctive in direct question. The direct question had the deliberative subjunctive - πῶς κολάσωμεν αὐτούς - "How can we punish them?" The article with indirect question is classical usage, found only in Luke and Paul. There is much argument among the grammarians about it. ". . . at least it makes clearer the substantival idea of the indirect question and its relation to the principal clause" (Robertson, *Grammar,* 766).

There was another reason why the San Hedrin did not punish Peter and John. It was because of the people - διὰ τὸν λαόν. What had the people to do with it? Another causal construction, this time introduced by ὅτι - the people were glorifying God (iterative imperfect in ἐδόξαζον). Why? Still another causal construction, with ἐπί and the instrumental in the substantival participle γεγονότι. The public reaction to the miracle of healing for the cripple was so great that the court did not dare to arouse the people by punishing the men who had performed the healing. The court was not interested in a legal justification for punishment. He was interested in the reaction of the people, which he discerned would be distinctly unfavorable. Thus the court, totally devoid of any sense of propriety or legal rectitude was thinking only of its own survival. What the court did it would do, not because of any inherent right or wrong, but only because of expediency.

Verse 22 - "For the man was above forty years old, on whom this miracle of healing was shewed."

ἐτῶν γὰρ ἦν πλειόνων τεσσαράκοντα ὁ ἄνθρωπος ἐφ᾽ ὃν γενόνει τὸ σημεῖον τοῦτο τῆς ἰάσεως.

ἐτῶν (abl.pl.neut.of ἔτος, comparison) 821.

γὰρ (causal conjunction) 105.

ἦν (3d.per.sing.imp.ind.of εἰμί, progressive description) 86.

πλειόνων (abl.pl.neut.of πλειών, comparison) 474.

τεσσαράκοντα (numeral) 333.

ὁ (nom.sing.masc.of the article in agreement with ἄνθρωπος) 9.

ἄνθρωπος (nom.sing.masc.of ἄνθρωπος, subject of ἦν) 341.

ἐπ᾽ (preposition with the accusative, reference) 47.

ὃν (acc.sing.masc.of ὅς, reference) 65.

γεγόνει (3d.per.sing.pluperfect ind.of γίνομαι, consummative) 113.

τὸ (nom.sing.neut.of the article in agreement with σημεῖον) 9.

σημεῖον (nom.sing.neut.of σημεῖον, subject of γεγόνει) 1005.

τοῦτο (nom.sing.neut.of οὗτος, in agreement with σημεῖον) 93.

τῆς (gen.sing.fem.of the article in agreement with ἰάσεως) 9.

ἰάσεως (gen.sing.fem.of ἴασις, description) 2514.

Translation - "Because the man for whom this miracle of healing had been performed was more than forty years old."

Comment: γὰρ is causal. Such a notable miracle could not be explained away by the San Hedrin. ἐφ᾽ ὃν γεγόνει is a construction a little hard to see after ἐπί with the accusative. There is a personal relation expressed here. "In whose behalf" or "for whom" is the idea, but such a translation should use the dative case. Mk.9:12 - γέγραπται ἐπὶ τὸν υἱὸν τοῦ ἀνθρώπου is a similar construction - "about" or "with reference to."

The shabby performance of the San Hedrin, which grew out of the utter poverty of intellectual honesty and bitter prejudice against the Truth, is only characteristic of the unregenerate politician who has been entrusted with a position of leadership. Unfortunately many have greater police powers of enforcement than were available to Annas and Caiaphas.

We have studied three of Peter's sermons. We now have a chance to study the prayers of the early Christians.

The Believers Pray for Boldness

(Acts 4:23-31)

Verse 23 - "And being let go, they went to their own company, and reported all that the chief priests and elders had said unto them."

'Απολυθέντες δὲ ἦλθον πρὸς τοὺς ἰδίους καὶ ἀπήγγειλαν ὅσα πρὸς αὐτοὺς
οἱ ἀρχιερεῖς καὶ οἱ πρεσβύτεροι εἶπαν.

'Απολυθέντες (1st.aor.pass.part.nom.pl.masc.of ἀπολύω, adverbial,
temporal) 92.

δὲ (continuative conjunction) 11.

ἦλθον (3d.per.pl.aor.mid.ind.of ἔρχομαι, constative) 146.

πρὸς (preposition with the accusative of extent) 197.

τοὺς (acc.pl.masc.of the article in agreement with ἰδίους) 9.

ἰδίους (acc.pl.masc.of ἴδιος, extent) 778.

καὶ (adjunctive conjunction joining verbs) 14.

ἀπήγγειλαν (3d.per.pl.aor.act.ind.of ἀπαγγέλλω, constative) 176.

ὅσα (acc.pl.neut.of ὅσος, direct object of εἶπαν) 660.

πρὸς (preposition with the accusative of extent, after a verb of speaking) 197.

αὐτοὺς (acc.pl.masc.of αὐτός, extent after a verb of speaking) 16.

οἱ (nom.pl.masc.of the article in agreement with ἀρχιερεῖς) 9.

ἀρχιερεῖς (nom.pl.masc.of ἀρχιερεύς, subject of εἶπαν) 151.

καὶ (adjunctive conjunction joining nouns) 14.

οἱ (nom.pl.masc.of the article in agreement with πρεσβύτεροι) 9.

πρεσβύτεροι (nom.pl.masc.of πρεσβύτερος, subject of εἶπαν) 1141.

εἶπαν (3d.per.pl.aor.act.ind.of εἶπον, constative) 155.

Translation - *"And when they were released, they came to their own people and
reported to them that which the chief priests and elders said to them."*

Comment: Released they came and reported to their Christian friends, who may
have been concerned about them as Peter and John had left the afternoon before
at the hour of prayer and had not been seen since. It is probable that the
Christians had heard about the miracle, since the story had circulated all over the
city. Faced with the ultimatum from the San Hedrin not to preach again in Jesus'
name, the church resorted to prayer.

Verse 24 - *"And when they heard that, they lifted up their voice to God with one
accord, and said, Lord, thou art God, which has made heaven, and earth, and the
sea, and all that in them is."*

οἱ δὲ ἀκούσαντες ὁμοθυμαδὸν ἦραν φωνὴν πρὸς τὸν θεὸν καὶ εἶπαν,
Δέσποτα, σὺ ὁ ποιήσας τὸν οὐρανὸν καὶ τὴν γῆν καὶ τὴν θάλασσαν καὶ πάντα
τὰ ἐν αὐτοῖς,

οἱ (nom.pl.masc.of the article, subject of ἦραν and εἶπαν) 9.

δὲ (continuative conjunction) 11.

ἀκούσαντες (aor.act.part.nom.pl.masc.of ἀκούω, adverbial, temporal/caus-
al) 148.

ὁμοθυμαδὸν (adverbial) 2942.

ἦραν (3d.per.pl.aor.act.ind.of αἴρω, ingressive) 350.

φωνὴν (acc.sing.fem.of φωνή, direct object of ἦραν) 222.

πρὸς (preposition with the accusative of extent after a verb of speaking) 197.

τὸν (acc.sing.masc.of the article in agreement with θεὸν) 9.

θεὸν (acc.sing.masc.of θεός, extent after a verb of speaking) 124.

καὶ (adjunctive conjunction joining verbs) 14.

εἶπαν (3d.per.sing.aor.act.ind.of εἶπον, constative) 155.

Δέσποτα (voc.sing.masc.of δεσπότης, address) 1900.

σὺ (voc.sing.masc.of σύ, address) 104.

ὁ (nom.sing.masc.of the article in agreement with ποιήσας) 9.

ποιήσας (aor.act.part.voc.sing.masc.of ποιέω, apposition) 127.

τὸν (acc.sing.masc.of the article in agreement with οὐρανὸν) 9.

οὐρανὸν (acc.sing.masc.of οὐρανός, direct object of ποιήσας) 254.

καὶ (adjunctive conjunction joining nouns) 14.

τὴν (acc.sing.fem.of the article in agreement with γῆν) 9.

γῆν (acc.sing.fem.of γῆ, direct object of ποιήσας) 157.

καὶ (adjunctive conjunction joining nouns) 14.

τὴν (acc.sing.fem.of the article in agreement with θάλασσαν) 9.

θάλασσαν (acc.sing.fem.of θάλασσα, direct object of ποιήσας) 374.

καὶ (adjunctive conjunction joining substantives) 14.

πάντα (acc.pl.neut.of πᾶς, in agreement with τὰ) 67.

τὰ (acc.pl.neut.of the article, direct object of ποιήσας) 9.

ἐν (preposition with the locative of place) 80.

αὐτοῖς (loc.pl.masc.of αὐτός, place) 16.

Translation - "*And when they heard with one mind and heart they began to raise their voices to God and said, 'Lord, you Who made the heaven and the earth and the sea and everything in them, . . . "*

Comment: They prayed ὁμοθυμαδόν. *Cf.*#2942 for its meaning of emotional as well as intellectual unanimity. They prayed with one heart and mind.

The first lesson we can learn is that when Christians are faced with a problem that they cannot solve the first resort is to prayer. There is not a line in the text to indicate that when they heard the story of possible persecution they became frightened or that they worried about it. A sign on a church bulletin board said, "Why Pray When You Can Worry?" The Christians in the Jerusalem church prayed. The second lesson is that when they prayed they were united in their view of God and also in what they wanted Him to do for them. (Mt.18:19,20). Goodspeed's translation "with one impulse they all raised their voice to God and said, . . . " is good, since "impulse" carries the idea of motivation which springs both from mind and heart, intellect and emotion. *Cf.* Acts 1:14; 2:46; 4:24; 5:12; 15:25 for this unity in the early church in Jerusalem.

Note that they began their prayer by telling the Lord that they knew that He is sovereign. When Satan and the world system which he owns and operates temporarily, presses upon the Christian, his first thought should be of the sovereignty of God. (John 16:33; 1 John 4:4). What comfort they derived from knowing that although the Jewish Establishment had threatened, they were personally and intimately related to One Whom they call δέσποτα ὁ ποιήσας . . . ἐν αὐτοῖς. The Creator of heaven, earth, sea and everything in all three can help His saints out of any difficulty. Successful prayer brings peace to the heart of the Christian, because it begins with the recognition that our God is sovereign by right of creation. Christians in the late 20th century have the same connection with the δέσποτα as did Peter, John and the other first century saints.

Verse 25 - "Who by the mouth of thy servant David hast said, Why did the heathen rage, and the people imagine vain things?"

ὁ τοῦ πατρὸς ἡμῶν διὰ πνεύματος ἁγίου στόματος Δαυὶδ παιδός σου εἰπών, Ἱνατί ἐφρύαξαν ἔθνη καὶ λαοὶ ἐμελέτησαν κενά;

ὁ (nom.sing.masc.of the article in agreement with εἰπών) 9.

τοῦ (gen.sing.masc.of the article in agreement with πατρὸς) 9.

πατρὸς (gen.sing.masc.of πατήρ, in apposition with Δαυὶδ) 238.

ἡμῶν (gen.pl.masc.of ἐγώ, relationship) 123.

διὰ (preposition with the ablative of agent) 118.

πνεύματος (abl.sing.neut.of πνεῦμα, agent) 83.

ἁγίου (abl.sing.neut.of ἅγιος, in agreement with πνεύματος) 84.

στόματος (abl.sing.neut.of στόμα, indirect agent) 344.

Δαυὶδ (gen.sing.masc.of Δαυίδ, possession) 6.

παιδός (gen.sing.masc.of παῖς, in apposition with Δαυὶδ) 217.

σου (gen.sing.masc.of σύ, relationship) 104.

εἰπών (aor.act.part.voc.sing.masc.of εἶπον, substantival, in apposition with Δέσποτα) 155.

#3039 Ἱνατί (Crasis - ἵνα plus τί, where τί is the subject of γένηται in ellipsis).

Why? - Acts 4:25; 7:26; 1 Cor.10:29.

Meaning: A combination of ἵνα (#114) and τί, the acc.sing.neut.of τίς (#281), where τί is the subject of γένηται, the aor.subjunctive of γίνομαι, in direct question. "For what purpose does it happen that. . . " or "in order for what?" Hence, "Why?" It is written ἵνα τί in W/H in Mt.9:4; 27:46 and Lk.13:7. (*Note:* The Gospels in RNT are based upon W/H — Acts through Revelation upon the text of the United Bible Society).

#3040 ἐφρύαξαν (3d.per.pl.aor.act.ind.of φρυάσσω, direct question).

rage - Acts 4:25.

Meaning: In profane Greek, to neigh, paw the ground, prance, snort, to be high spirited. Properly of horses. With reference to men, to be arrogant, to assume a lofty attitude, behave arrogantly. To be tumultuous; to rant, rave and rage - of the Gentile nations rebelling against God's authority - Acts 4:25.

ἔθνη (nom.pl.neut.of ἔθνος, subject of ἐφρύαξαν) 376.

καὶ (continuative conjunction) 14.

λαοὶ (nom.pl.masc.of λαός, subject of ἐμελέτησαν) 110.

#3041 ἐμελέτησαν (3d.per.pl.aor.act.ind.of μελετάω, constative).

imagine - Acts 4:25.
meditate upon - 1 Tim.4:15.

Meaning: Cf. μελέτη - "care, practice." To care for, practise, give careful attention to, meditate upon, think about - 1 Tim.4:15; to plan, scheme - Acts 4:25. Used by the Greeks of meditative ponderings of orators and authors. With reference to the godless plans of nations for supremacy - Acts 4:25. Of Timothy's preparation for the ministry - 1 Tim.4:15.

κενά (acc.pl.neut.of κενός, direct object of ἐμελέτησαν) 1836.

Translation - "Who, through the mouth of David, our father and your servant, by the Holy Spirit said, 'Why did the Gentile nations rage and people contemplate irrational things?' "

Comment: We are still in apposition to Δέσποτα as was ὁ ποιήσας in verse 24. Between the article ὁ and the participial substantive εἰπών we have two ablatives and two appositions. The student should keep in mind that Greek is an inflected language (*i.e.* the grammatical and syntactical relationships are determined by case and verb form endings) and that the word order means nothing except for emphasis.

The quotation is from Psalm 2:1-2. Ἱνατί, here, written together, needs γένηται supplied, since τί is its subject. "Why have the Gentile nations pawed the ground and snorted their rage and impatience like wild horses?" And "why have the Jewish people devised stupid and irrational schemes? Thus the prayer which begins with praise to the God of creation who is utterly sovereign, procedes to a contemplation upon the stupid, totally irrational and ultimately futile attacks of puny men against Him. David, speaking by inspiration, had all human rebellion against God's divinely constituted authority, both Jewish and Gentile, in mind, but it is probable that the Christians in Jerusalem who were praying this prayer were thinking of Annas, Caiaphas and their compatriots in the San Hedrin. The quotation from Psalm 2:1-2 goes on in

Verse 26 - "The kings of the earth stood up, and the rulers were gathered together against the Lord, and against His Christ."

παρέστησαν οἱ βασιλεῖς τῆς γῆς καὶ οἱ ἄρχοντες συνήχθησαν ἐπὶ τὸ αὐτὸ κατὰ τοῦ κυρίου καὶ κατὰ τοῦ Χριστοῦ αὐτοῦ.

παρέστησαν (3d.per.pl.aor.act.ind.of παρίστημι, constative) 1596.
οἱ (nom.pl.masc.of the article in agreement with βασιλεῖς) 9.
βασιλεῖς (nom.pl.masc.of βασιλεύς, subject of παρέστησαν) 31.
τῆς (gen.sing.fem.of the article in agreement with γῆς) 9.
γῆς (gen.sing.fem.of γῆ, description) 157.
καὶ (adjunctive conjunction joining nouns) 14.
οἱ (nom.pl.masc.of the article in agreement with ἄρχοντες) 9.

ἄρχοντες (nom.pl.masc.of ἄρχων, subject of συνήχθησαν) 150.

ἐπὶ (preposition with the accusative of extent, adverbial) 47.

τὸ (acc.sing.neut.of the article in agreement with αὐτό) 9.

αὐτὸ (acc.sing.neut.of αὐτός, adverbial) 16.

κατὰ (preposition with the genitive, opposition) 98.

τοῦ (gen.sing.masc.of the article in agreement with κυρίου) 9.

κυρίου (gen.sing.masc.of κύριος, opposition) 97.

καὶ (adjunctive conjunction joining prepositional phrases) 98.

κατὰ (preposition with the genitive, opposition) 98.

τοῦ (gen.sing.masc.of the article in agreement with Χριστοῦ) 9.

Χριστοῦ (gen.sing.masc.of Χριστός, opposition) 4.

αὐτοῦ (gen.sing.masc.of αὐτός, relationship) 16.

Translation - "*The kings of the earth and the rulers were gathered together to one place against the Lord and against His Messiah, . . .* "

Comment: The verse presents a picture of military mobilization and battle array, preparatory to the battle of Armageddon. The Hebrew parallelism is evident - the thought of the first clause is repeated in slightly different form in the second clause. *Cf.*Luke 17:35 for ἐπὶ τὸ αὐτό as here - "to the same place." κατά with the genitive can express opposition or hostility. *Cf.*#98. Heaven's reaction to this irrational revolution follows in Ps.2:;4,5, and that is followed by a picture of Messiah's earthly reign with an invitation to repentance and faith in verse 12. Thus the Christians, by alluding to this Psalm in their prayer, were expressing their faith in the ultimate victory of Jesus over His enemies, some of whom they specify in

Verse 27 - "*For of a truth against thy holy child Jesus, whom thou hast anointed, both Herod and Pontius Pilate, with the Gentiles, and the people of Israel, were gathered together.*"

συνήχθησαν γὰρ ἐπ' ἀληθείας ἐν τῇ πόλει ταύτῃ, ἐπὶ τὸν ἅγιον παῖδά σου Ἰησοῦν, ὃν ἔχρισας, Ἡρῴδης τε καὶ Πόντιος Πιλᾶτος σὺν ἔθνεσιν καὶ λαοῖς Ἰσραήλ,

συνήχθησαν (3d.per.pl.aor.pass.ind.of συνάγω, constative) 150.

γὰρ (inferential conjunction) 105.

ἐπ' (preposition with the genitive, adverbial) 47.

ἀληθείας (gen.sing.fem.of ἀλήθεια, adverbial) 1416.

ἐν (preposition with the locative of place where) 80.

τῇ (loc.sing.fem.of the article in agreement with πόλει) 9.

πόλει (loc.sing.fem.of πόλις, place where) 243.

ταύτῃ (loc.sing.fem.of οὗτος, in agreement with πόλει) 93.

ἐπὶ (preposition with the accusative, hostility) 47.

τὸν (acc.sing.masc.of the article in agreement with παῖδά) 9.

ἅγιον (acc.sing.masc.of ἅγιος, in agreement with παῖδά) 84.

παῖδά (acc.sing.masc.of παῖς, hostility) 217.

σου (gen.sing.masc.of σύ, relationship) 104.

'Ιησοῦν (acc.sing.masc.of 'Ιησοῦς, apposition) 3.
ὅν (acc.sing.masc.of ὅς, direct object of ἔχρισας) 65.
ἔχρισας (2d.per.sing.aor.act.ind.of χρίω, culminative) 2021.
'Ηρῴδης (nom.sing.masc.of 'Ηρῴδης, subject of συνήχθησαν) 136.
τε (correlative conjunction) 1408.
καὶ (adjunctive conjunction joining nouns) 14.
Πόντιος (nom.sing.masc.of Πόντιος, subject of συνήχθησαν) 1930.
Πιλᾶτος (nom.sing.masc.of Πιλᾶτος, apposition) 1616.
σὺν (preposition with the instrumental of association) 1542.
ἔθνεσιν (instru.pl.neut.of ἔθνος, association) 376.
καὶ (adjunctive conjunction joining nouns) 14.
λαοῖς (instru.pl.masc.of λαός, association) 110.
'Ισραήλ (genitive, indeclin.masc.of 'Ισραήλ, description) 165.

Translation - *"Thus truthfully there were gathered together in this city against your holy Son, Jesus, Whom you anointed, both Herod and Pilate with the Gentiles and people of Israel."*

Comment: We have taken γὰρ as inferential, as the events described were thought to be in fulfillment of the prophecy of Psalm 2, as verse 28 implies. For ἐπ' ἀληθείας in the adverbial sense, *cf.* Acts 10:34; Luke 4:25; 22:59. Again we see the contrast between God's evaluation of Jesus and man's view of Him. The Gentiles and Jews, otherwise cultural and social enemies unite in opposition to the Son of God, just as Herod and Pontios Pilate did (Luke 23:12).

Just as the gospel of Christ, with its unifying power to blot out the ordinances which divide Jew from Gentile was first preached in Jerusalem, so the opposition to the gospel also united Gentile and Jew in the same city. Thus the only real divider in human society is Jesus Christ. Both Jew and Gentile have accepted Him, and they are arrayed against Jew and Gentile who reject Him. Why did they reject? Gentiles rage. Jews plot foolishness. Kings of earth assemble in battle array. Jewish rulers come together in the same way. Herod, an apostate Jewish king and Pilate, a Roman governor unite. What unites these otherwise totally disunited social, theological and political forces? It is mutual hatred for God and His Anointed Messiah. Why did they do this? In verse 28 we have a statement of the theological interpretation of history.

Verse 28 - *"For to do whatsoever thy hand and thy counsel determined before to be done."*

ποιῆσαι ὅσα ἡ χείρ σου καὶ ἡ βουλή σου προώρισεν γενέσθαι.

ποιῆσαι (aor.act.inf.of ποιέω, purpose) 127.
ὅσα (acc.pl.neut.of ὅσος, direct of προώρισεν) 660.
ἡ (nom.sing.fem.of the article in agreement with χείρ) 9.
χείρ (nom.sing.fem.of χείρ, subject of προώρισεν) 308.
σου (gen.sing.masc.of σύ, possession) 104.
καὶ (adjunctive conjunction joining nouns) 14.

ἥ (nom.sing.fem.of the article in agreement with βουλῇ) 9.

βουλή (nom.sing.fem.of βουλή, subject of προώρισεν) 2163.

σου (gen.sing.masc.of σύ, possession) 104.

#3042 προώρισεν (3d.per.sing.aor.act.ind.of προορίζω, constative).

determine before - Acts 4:28.
ordain - 1 Cor.2:7.
predestinate - Rom.8:29,30; Eph.1:5,11.

Meaning: A combination of πρό (#442) and ὁρίζω - "to determine." Hence to predetermine; to foreordain; to declare that the events involved shall be. With reference to the death of Christ and related events which were carried out by His enemies at the crucifixion - Acts 4:28; of the elect or "foreknown" whom He also called, justified and will glorify - Rom.8:29,30; Eph.1:5,11. Of the hidden wisdom which Christians speak "in a mystery" - 1 Cor.2:7.

γενέσθαι (aor.inf.of γίνομαι, complementary) 113.

Translation - ". . . to do whatever your hand and your plan of operation predetermined to be done."

Comment: We have here the conclusion of the sentence begun in verse 27. "Herod and Pilate, Gentiles and Jews gathered together in Jerusalem in opposition to Jesus (vs.27)." Why? A purpose clause follows in verse 28. They were to do all that God had determined should happen. ποιῆσαι completes συνήχθησαν and γενέσθαι completes προώρισεν. They did not know that they were fulfilling an eternal plan. All but Pilate revelled in it because what they did reflected how they felt about Jesus. Pilate tried to escape the circumstances with which he was surrounded, because he did not wish to crucify Jesus, but finally yielded to uncontrollable circumstances, but not until he had asked God for mercy. *Cf.* our comment on Mt.27:24-25. *Cf.*#2163 for βουλή as an expression of God's eternal decrees. This verse further supports the sovereignty of God. The prayer opened with a recognition of God's sovereignty as Creator (vs.24) and now it suggests that God makes even the wrath of men to bring about the events of His counselled plan of operation. How could the early Christians lose? The worship in the prayer is finished and in verses 29-30 they made their request. The prayer reveals that they believed fully in the ultimate triumph of the divine program, because they recognized in God the creator of the universe and therefore the One able to control everything that occurred in the course of history to the end that His own name would be glorified. The Christian who believes that need be concerned only with one other thing: he must ask only for that which is the will of the sovereign, because only with such a request can he have the confidence that it will be heard. And if it is heard, "we know that we have the petitions that we desired of him." (1 John 5:14,15).

Verse 29 - "And now, Lord, behold their threatenings: and grant unto thy servants that with all boldness they may speak thy word."

καὶ τὰ νῦν, κύριε, ἔπιδε ἐπὶ τὰς ἀπειλὰς αὐτῶν, καὶ δὸς τοῖς δούλοις σου
μετὰ παρρησίας πάσης λαλεῖν τὸν λόγον σου.

καὶ (continuative conjunction) 14.
τὰ (acc.pl.neut.of the article with the adverb) 9.
νῦν (adverbial) 1497.
κύριε (voc.sing.masc.of κύριος, address) 97.
ἔπιδε (2d.per.sing.aor.act.impv.of ἐπεῖδον, entreaty) 1810.
ἐπὶ (preposition with the accusative of extent) 47.
τὰς (acc.pl.fem.of the article in agreement with ἀπειλὰς) 9.

#3043 ἀπειλὰς (acc.pl.fem.of ἀπειλή, direct object of ἔπιδε).

threatening - Acts 4:29; 9:1; Eph.6:9.

Meaning: Cf.ἀπειλέω (#3034). A threat; a threatening statement. With reference
to the threat of the San Hedrin against Peter and John - Acts 4:29. Saul's threats
against the Christians - Acts 9:1. Something forbidden to masters of slaves -
Eph.6:9.

αὐτῶν (gen.pl.masc.of αὐτός, possession) 16.
καὶ (adjunctive conjunction joining verbs) 14.
δὸς (2d.per.sing.2d.aor.act.impv.of δίδωμι, entreaty) 362.
τοῖς (dat.pl.masc.of the article in agreement with δούλοις) 9.
δούλοις (dat.pl.masc.of δοῦλος, indirect object of δὸς) 725.
σου (gen.sing.masc.of σύ, relationship) 104.
μετὰ (preposition with the ablative of manner) 50.
παρρησίας (abl.sing.fem.of παρρησία, manner) 2319.
πάσης (abl.sing.fem.of πᾶς, in agreement with παρρησίας) 67.
λαλεῖν (pres.act.inf.of λαλέω, direct object of δὸς) 815.
τὸν (acc.sing.masc.of the article in agreement with λόγον) 9.
λόγον (acc.sing.masc.of λόγος, direct object of λαλεῖν) 510.
σου (gen.sing.masc.of σύ, possession) 104.

Translation - "And now, Lord, take note of their threats and give to your
servants the courage to deliver your message without reservation."

Comment: τὰ with the adverb νῦν is good κοινή Greek, though not used often in
the New Testament except by Luke and Paul. Note the repetition of ἐπί with the
same preposition in composition in the verb. They need not have asked the Lord
for this because we may be certain that He already knew all about them. As a
matter of fact He knew about the threats before they were uttered. And yet it is
good for the saints to discuss matters with the Lord like this. The request for
courage follows. The object of δὸς is the infinitive λαλεῖν. They wanted to speak
His message fearlessly and without equivocation.We can supply some other
noun - opportunity, eloquence, courage, Holy Spirit enabling - all that is
required to preach the message of the gospel. Most of all they were asking that
God would save them from what some have called tact and diplomacy, but

what is really a defensive mechanism designed to insulate them from the offense of the cross. *Cf.*#2319 for the meaning of παρρησία.

Verse 30 - "By stretching forth thy hand to heal; and that signs and wonders may be done by the name of thy holy child Jesus."

ἐν τῷ τὴν χεῖρά σου ἐκτείνειν σε εἰς ἴασιν καὶ σημεῖα καὶ τέρατα γίνεσθαι διὰ τοῦ ὀνόματος τοῦ ἀγίου παιδός σου Ἰησοῦ.

ἐν (preposition with the instrumental of manner) 80.
τῷ (instru.sing.neut.of the article, manner) 9.
τὴν (acc.sing.fem.of the article in agreement with χεῖρά) 9.
χεῖρά (acc.sing.fem.of χείρ, direct object of ἐκτείνειν) 308.
σου (gen.sing.masc.of σύ, possession) 104.
ἐκτείνειν (pres.act.inf.of ἐκτείνω, articular infinitive, manner) 710.
σε (acc.sing.masc.of σύ, general reference) 104.
εἰς (preposition with the accusative, purpose) 140.
ἴασιν (acc.sing.fem.of ἴασις, purpose) 2514.
καὶ (adjunctive conjunction joining infinitives) 14.
σημεῖα (acc.pl.neut.of σημεῖον, general reference) 1005.
καὶ (adjunctive conjunction joining nouns) 14.
τέρατα (acc.pl.neut.of τέρας, general reference) 1500.
γίνεσθαι (pres.mid.inf.of γίνομαι, articular infinitive, manner) 113.
διὰ (preposition with the ablative of direct agent) 118.
τοῦ (abl.sing.neut.of the article in agreement with ὀνόματος) 9.
ὀνόματος (abl.sing.neut.of ὄνομα, direct agent) 108.
τοῦ (gen.sing.masc.of the article in agreement with παιδός) 9.
ἀγίου (gen.sing.masc.of ἅγιος, in agreement with παιδός) 84.
σου (gen.sing.masc.of σύ, relationship) 104.
Ἰησοῦ (gen.sing.masc.of Ἰησοῦς, apposition) 3.d

Translation - ". . . by stretching out your hand to heal and by performing signs and wonder by the name of your holy child, Jesus."

Comment: ἐν introduces the two articular infinitives in the instrumental case, indicating the manner in which they were praying that God would give to them the courage to speak His message boldly. ἐν τῷ serves both ἐκτείνειν and γίνεσθαι. Thus the prayer asks for opportunities to be given to them to witness and also that the sign gifts, which were then needed to authenticate their message would be forthcoming. After the New Testament literature was written, the sign gifts would be phased out, since the total authority of God through the Holy Spirit is in the Word. The desire of the early Christians for the performance of miracles of healing, signs and wonders, therefore, was not primarily for the miracles *per se* , but because they resulted in the gathering of large crowds to whom the Christians could witness and gave authority to what they said. In early Apostolic days the church had no social status, no buildings and no regularly advertized meetings. They cannot be compared to the current situation in which society suggests, albeit without much success, that people should attend church to hear the Word of God. The desire of the church for miracles and signs, since the New Testament canon has been completed, must be examined in the light of the basic reasons for wanting them. When there is an authoritative message from God, such as we have in the New Testament, which the Holy Spirit is pledged to bless and use when it is expounded, it is sufficient to bring the elect to Christ. The rich man in Hades was told that if his brothers who were still alive would not hear Moses and the Prophets, which they had readily available to them, they would not have repented even if Lazarus rose from the dead and warned them of their dead brother's fate. It is significant that the groups in modern churchianity who major in the ecstatic method of presentation of the gospel are notable for their heretical theological views and superficial approach to the study of the New Testament. Where emotional manifestations are regarded as evidences of piety and exotic gibberish, popularly referred to as "unknown tongues" are advanced as evidence that the Christian witness is genuine, there is little need for Bible exposition. The miracle worker today is in a strong position to mislead the public in theological matters, since the untaught are impressed with unusual evidences of supernatural power. It seems strange that there is not at least one or two scholarly Reformed theologians in the world to whom the Holy Spirit has given the "sign gifts" if indeed they are still to be given to the church. There is no evidence in Scripture that Timothy was a miracle worker, although God could have given him these gifts if it had been His policy, and that is why Paul told him to "preach the Word."

The elements that made up the prayer are as follows: United in mind and heart they began by worshipping the God of creation, Who by virtue of His role as Creator is sovereign in His universe. Then they quoted Psalm 2 to the Lord and pointed out to Him the threats which had come to Peter and John, as an indication that antichristian movements would characterize human history, as both Jew and Gentile would rebel against God and seek to suppress the preaching of His gospel. However, they added that the course of this age was not something which God had not foreseen. On the contrary what was happening was only the outworking of the plan of the ages. In view, therefore, that they were confident of victory in Christ, they prayed for the opportunities to witness for Christ with the same boldness and unequivocation with which Peter had preached at Pentecost, in Solomon's Porch and before the San Hedrin, and that their preaching might be accompanied by the supernatural evidences that what they said was endorsed by the God of heaven. Such a prayer was certain to receive favorable attention from heaven, and we are not surprized to learn in verse 31 that their prayer was answered.

Verse 31 - "And when they had prayed, the place was shaken where they were assembled together; and they were all filled with the Holy Ghost, and they spake the word of God with boldness."

καὶ δεηθέντων αὐτῶν ἐσαλεύθη ὁ τόπος ἐν ᾧ ἦσαν συνηγμένοι, καὶ ἐπλήσθησαν ἅπαντες τοῦ ἁγίου πνεύματος, καὶ ἐλάλουν τὸν λόγον τοῦ θεοῦ μετὰ παρρησίας.

καὶ (continuative conjunction) 14.

δεηθέντων (1st.aor.pass.part.gen.pl.masc.of δέομαι, genitive absolute) 841.

αὐτῶν (gen.pl.masc.of αὐτός, genitive absolute) 16.

ἐσαλεύθη (3d.per.sing.aor.pass.ind.of σαλεύω, ingressive) 911.

ὁ (nom.sing.masc.of the article in agreement with τόπος) 9.

τόπος (nom.sing.masc.of τόπος, subject of ἐσαλεύθη) 1019.

ἐν (preposition with the locative of place) 80.

ᾧ (loc.sing.masc.of ὅς, place where) 65.

ἦσαν (3d.per.pl.imp.ind.of εἰμί, pluperfect periphrastic) 86.

συνηγμένοι (perf.pass.part.nom.pl.masc.of συνάγω, pluperfect periphrastic) 150.

καὶ (continuative conjunction) 14.

ἐπλήσθησαν (3d.per.pl.aor.pass.ind.of πληρόω, constative) 115.

ἅπαντες (nom.pl.masc.of ἅπας, subject of ἐπλήσθησαν) 639.

τοῦ (abl.sing.neut.of the article in agreement with πνεύματος) 9.

ἁγίου (abl.sing.neut.of ἅγιος, in agreement with πνεύματος) 84.

πνεύματος (abl.sing.neut.of πνεῦμα, source) 83.

καὶ (adjunctive conjunction joining verbs) 14.

ἐλάλουν (3d.per.pl.imp.act.ind.of λαλέω, inceptive) 815.

τὸν (acc.sing.masc.of the article in agreement with λόγον) 9.

λόγον (acc.sing.masc.of λόγος, direct object of ἐλάλουν) 510.

τοῦ (gen.sing.masc.of the article in agreement with θεοῦ) 9.

θεοῦ (gen.sing.masc.of θεός, description) 124.

μετὰ (preposition with the ablative of manner) 50.

παρρησίας (abl.sing.fem.of παρρησία, manner) 2319.

Translation - *"And after they had prayed the place in which they had been assembled began to shake, and all were filled with the Holy Spirit and they began to speak the message of God with boldness."*

Comment: The genitive absolute δεηθέντων αὐτῶν is aorist, indicating antecedent action to that of the main verbs ἐσαλεύθη and ἐπλήσθησαν. A church that will not pray together as they did is not going to shake the place, or will its members be filled with the Holy Spirit. Note the precision of the Greek in the pluperfect periphrastic ἦσαν συνηγμένοι in the relative local clause - "in which they *had been assembled,* thus pointing to their meeting time as somewhat earlier. The church had not come together in order to meet Peter and John, but were assembled before the two Apostles arrived with their story. There was a physical and a spiritual manifestation of the filling of the Holy Spirit. The room (building) shook. At Pentecost the physical manifestation was the sound that resembled the tornado. God's voice shakes the earth (Heb.12:26,27). Some things can be shaken; our glorified Lord at the Father's right hand cannot (Acts 2:25). It is well for us to distinguish accurately between persons and things that can and cannot be shaken. He Who sits in glory can shake heaven and earth and a building in Jerusalem, but He Himself cannot be shaken. But it requires a church in perfect unity in a prayer meeting, where prayer is offered scripturally to effect miracles. Unfortunately most modern churches witness no miracles because they do not meet prerequisite conditions. The second answer to their prayer was another filling of the Holy Spirit, about which two observations are in order: (1) although the indwelling Holy Spirit, once He has taken up His residence in the body of the believer at regeneration, never leaves it (1 Cor.6:19,20; John 14:17; 20:22), the *filling* of the Holy Spirit is not a continuous experience. It is iterative. He is always resident in the believer. He is periodically regnant. This is the second time that His filling is recorded, although there may have been other times when they were filled. (2) The second observation is that *all of them* were filled. The word is the intensive ἅπας (#639), not πᾶς (#67). The Holy Spirit's filling is not a gift to be bestowed exclusively upon the twelve Apostles, but the privilege of every member of the Body of Christ.

It is also to be noted that there was no mention of a linguistic miracle, and for a very good reason. No one was present who needed to hear what was being said in any other language than that which was being spoken, whether it was Aramaic or Greek. In our comments upon the Pentecost experience (Acts 2:1-11) we pointed out that the langague miracle was necessary for there were those present who would not have understood otherwise. The socalled "gift of tongues" as indulged in now is alleged to occur whether foreigners are present or not, and in most cases when they are not. Further, if a German who understood no English visited such a meeting and the "gift of tongues" was given, the speaker would not speak German, nor any other language to be understood by any except one who said that his gift of interpretation of the "heavenly language" was such that he could tell the rest of the congregation what was said. If the interpreter should say that the message was something contrary to the New Testament, it is likely that his message would take precedence over the New Testament. However, some apologists for the "tongues movement" say that there is always a check in the New Testament against what the interpreter says, to which argument, an adequate reply is that if the New Testament is the final arbiter about the truth of the message, there is no reason for the supernaturally given message in the first place, unless one wants to join the Mormons in their view that the message of the New Testament is not the last word. Nothing like that happened in the story under discussion. All were filled with the Holy Spirit, the least accomplished saint, no less than the Apostles, but no one performed any miracles. They did begin (inceptive imperfect in ἐλάλουν) to speak the message of God without fear.

How futile the vain imagination of the Establishment, that they should suppose that a threat of reprisal would or could shut the mouths of Spirit-filled Christians who *knew* that Jesus Christ was alive! (Acts 4:13-22,25). Thus in fulfillment of Psalm 2 the "people" think up stupidity in their attack upon God and His Messiah.

We also note that the church in Jerusalem, totally dedicated to God's perfect will, filled with the Holy Spirit and faithful in her witness, despite the threat of persecution, put into practice a "welfare state" program without governmental orders and bureaucratic regulations. What they did was strictly on a personal and voluntary basis - a program of Christian stewardship in relation to wealth sharing.

The theological gospel, properly presented and thoroughly absorbed by the saints will produce the ameliorating results sought by the social gospel. The "first and greatest commandment" if it is obeyed will lead to obedience to the second which is "like unto it." When we love the Lord our God with heart, soul, mind and strength, we will also love our neighbour as we love ourselves. *Cf.* our discussion of this on Matthew 22:37-40; Luke 19:1-10. The first thing that Zacchaeus thought of when he was saved was his obligation to divide his wealth with the poor and as a result the richest man in Jericho gave some of his money to the poorest man in Jericho who only moments before had been a blind beggar.

The theological altitude of our equilaterial triangle is directly related to the sociological base. Cain had a stunted conception of God (1 John 3:12) and a vicious attitude toward his brother. Ahab, seduced by his pagan wife, worshipped so long at the altars of Baal, that he and she had Naboth murdered and took his vineyard. The German school of Higher Criticism taught the German preachers, and through them, the German people that God was a puppet and thus they concluded that Adoplf Hitler was *der fuhrer* of the Master Race, authorized by Thor and Woden to rid the earth of Jews, Slavs, Blacks and any others who were brunettes or who happened to disagree with anything that Hitler said. This is why some of us are not impressed when the Ku Klux Klan displays the Bible and the American flag at the same meeting where they burn a cross.

The early Christians loved God and they loved each other so much that they could not endure the misfortunes of others. Thus their division of property.

A Voluntary Experiment in Christian Communism

(Acts 4:32-27)

Verse 32 - "And the multitude of them that believed were of one heart and one soul: neither said any of them that ought of the things which he possessed was his own; but they had all things common."

Τοῦ δὲ πλήθους τῶν πιστευσάντων ἦν καρδία καὶ ψυχὴ μία, καὶ οὐδὲ εἷς τι τῶν ὑπαρχόντων αὐτῷ ἔλεγεν ἴδιον εἶναι, ἀλλ᾽ ἦν αὐτοῖς πάντα κοινά.

Τοῦ (gen.sing.neut.of the article in agreement with πλήθους) 9.

δὲ (explanatory conjunction) 11.

πλήθους (gen.sing.neut.of πλῆθος, possession) 1792.

τῶν (gen.pl.masc.of the article in agreement with πιστευσάντων) 9.

πιστευσάντων (aor.act.part.gen.pl.masc.of πιστεύω, substantival, partitive) 734.

ἦν (3d.per.sing.imp.ind.of εἰμί, progressive description) 86.

καρδία (nom.sing.fem.of καρδία, subject of ἦν) 432.

καὶ (adjunctive conjunction, joining nouns) 14.

ψυχή (nom.sing.fem.of ψυχή, subject of ἦν) 233.

μία (nom.sing.fem.of εἷς, predicate adjective) 469.

καὶ (continuative conjunction) 14.

οὐδὲ (disjunctive particle) 452.

εἷς (nom.sing.masc.of εἷς, subject of ἔλεγεν) 469.

τι (acc.sing.neut.of τις, general reference) 486.

τῶν (gen.pl.neut.of the article in agreement with ὑπαρχόντων) 9.

ὑπαρχόντων (pres.act.part.gen.pl.neut.of ὑπάρχω, substantival, partitive) 1303.

αὐτῷ (dat.sing.masc.of αὐτός, possession) 16.

ἔλεγεν (3d.per.sing.imp.act.ind.of λέγω, progressive description) 66.

ἴδιον (acc.sing.masc.of ἴδιος, predicate adjective) 778.

εἶναι (pres.inf.of εἰμί, direct of ἔλεγεν in indirect discourse) 86.

ἀλλ' (alternative conjunction) 342.

ἦν (3d.per.sing.imp.ind.of εἰμί, progressive description) 86.

αὐτοῖς (dat.pl.masc.of αὐτός, possession) 16.

πάντα (nom.pl.neut.of πᾶς, subject of ἦν) 67.

κοινά (nom.pl.neut.of κοινός, predicate adjective) 2295.

Translation - *"Now heart and soul of a great number of the believers was as one, and not a single one was saying that any of his possession were his private property; rather everything was held in common for them."*

Comment: Although Luke tells us that not one of them was saying that what he had was his own, he does not tell us that everyone of the believers had his heart and soul in this plan. πλήθους - "a large number" is followed by a partitive genitive in τῶν πισστευσάντων. Thus the Greek reads that the heart and soul of a great number (not necessarily all) of the believers was as one. To be sure all of them gave lip service to the idea. We mention this because at least two, Ananias and Sapphira (Acts 5:1-11) were not in favor of this communistic distribution of the wealth, although social control forced them to say that they agreed with the policy.

It is important to note that this policy of wealth distribution was not a directive from the Apostles or from the Holy Spirit. It was a voluntary program. Those who wished to follow it did so. No compulsion was involved as Peter told Ananias in Acts 5:4. What each possessed was in fact his own property. It was just that some felt the desire to share what was theirs with others less fortunate. When heart and soul are one, earthly wealth is also one. Note the proper order. Imposed distribution of wealth by governmental decree, in opposition to private wishes, can never be successful. Rational citizens pay taxes to the governments, without significant protest, at municipal, county, state and federal levels, because they are convinced that the benefits they derive from the services in the public sector are sufficient to counter the pain of paying their tax dollars. As long as they believed that public services (fire and police protection, public education, national defense, mail service, etc.) are worth the tax cost they acquiesce in the policy. We can do some things collectively through government cheaper than we can do for ourselves on an individual basis. There may be objections when a redistribution of wealth occurs as a result of progressive taxation, funds from which are used to support some whom the tax payers may regard as unworthy of support. Economists will point out that such redistribution of wealth, even if it is not even-handed, is necessary to sustain the consumption function, which in turn maintains investment at a high level, thus to prevent unemployment, from which the tax payer himself may suffer. But this kind of Keynesian economics which emphasizes the demand side of the market is little understood by the layman, and is regarded by other economists who emphasize supply and production, as did Adam Smith and Alfred Marshall, as an insult to the intelligence of Adam Smith's *homo economicus.* Keynesians who are also at home in Christian theology will retort that no Calvinist can believe that the consumer is rational enough to spend his money with strict regard to cost/benefit analysis, and therefore that the *laissez faire* system, since it assumes that man is bascily rational cannot work since it is incorrect in its premise.

However these matters may or may not be, the fact is that the Holy Spirit did not say in the New Testament that the communistic system which many of the early Christians in Jerusalem were led to follow was to be imposed upon those who did not agree with the policy. What the individual Christian wishes to do with his money he is free to do and that which the individual Christian would rather not do is not to be demanded of him in terms of an arbitrary command from heaven. When heart and soul dictates the share-and-share-alike policy the plan is viable. The enthusiam for the plan among a great number of Christians created a form of social control to which Ananias and Sapphira yielded by misrepresenting the facts in their case. The distribution of wealth taught in the New Testament is always a voluntary movement among the saints. The Protestant Ethic, which stressed hard work, self denial and thrift, forbade charity to the poor on the ground that poverty was evidence that the poor were at worst, non-elect and at best, backslidden. Proverbs 13:15, which says, "the way of transgressors is hard" was often cited by Calvinists in 17th century New England. Thus for a Christian to give a dime to a beggar in the street was regarded as seeking to mitigate punishment which had been imposed by the Lord. Cotton Mather did not wish to be found in opposition to the divine policy. This philosophy, which cannot be squared with Matthew 7:12; 22:39, when adopted on a nationwide basis resulted in a maldistribution of wealth and consequent failure of effective demand and new investment, without which abundant production cannot be achieved. Wide fluctuations of the business cycle with their attendant unemployment, poverty and social disintegration, particularly in the inner city areas resulted. If the modern church possessed the unity of heart and mind, with its willingness to distribute wealth on a voluntary basis, as the Jerusalem church demonstrated, governmental invasions of regulation and stimulation into the private sector would be unnecessary. Christians, who, in the name of orthodoxy, attack the Welfare State are ignoring the fact that the Church is not a Welfare Church. The early church in Jerusalem was such a church. Everyone worked who was able. Those who truly could not work, either for lack of skill or lack of opportunity, suffered no lack. As we shall see, after the early church lost some of its pristine purity and zeal, the program broke down, and it has never been restored. So the government must do by law what the modern church will not do by grace.

Verse 33 - "And with great power gave the apostles witness of the resurrection of the Lord Jesus: and great grace was upon them all."

καὶ δυνάμει μεγάλῃ ἀπεδίδουν τὸ μαρτύριον οἱ ἀπόστολοι τῆς ἀναστάσεως τοῦ κυρίου Ἰησοῦ, χάρις τε μεγάλη ἦν ἐπὶ πάντας αὐτούς.

καὶ (continuative conjunction) 14.
δυνάμει (instru.sing.fem.of δύναμις, means) 687.
μεγάλῃ (instru.sing.fem.of μέγας, in agreement with δυνάμει) 184.
ἀπεδίδουν (3d.per.pl.imp.act.ind.of ἀποδίδωμι, iterative) 495.
τὸ (acc.sing.neut.of the article in agreement with μαρτύριον) 9.
μαρτύριον (acc.sing.neut.of μαρτύριον, direct object of ἀπεδίδουν) 716.
οἱ (nom.pl.masc.of the article in agreement with ἀπόστολοι) 9.
ἀπόστολοι (nom.pl.masc.of ἀπόστολος, subject of ἀπεδίδουν) 844.
τῆς (gen.sing.fem.of the article in agreement with ἀναστάσεως) 9.
ἀναστάσεως (gen.sing.fem.of ἀνάστασις, reference) 1423.
τοῦ (gen.sing.masc.of the article in agreement with κυρίου) 9.
κυρίου (gen.sing.masc.of κύριος, possession) 97.
Ἰησοῦ (gen.sing.masc.of Ἰησοῦς, apposition) 3.
χάρις (nom.sing.fem.of χάρις, subject of ἦν) 1700.
τε (continuative conjunction) 1408.
μεγάλη (nom.sing.fem.of μέγας, in agreement with χάρις) 184.
ἦν (3d.per.sing.imp.ind.of εἰμί, progressive description) 86.
ἐπὶ (preposition with the accusative of extent, metaphorical) 47.
πάντας (acc.pl.masc.of πᾶς, in agreement with αὐτούς) 67.
αὐτούς (acc.pl.masc.of αὐτός, extent, after ἐπὶ, metaphorical) 16.

Translation - "And with great power the Apostles continued to preach about the resurrection of the Lord Jesus, and great grace was upon them all."

Comment: The intellectual and emotional unity in the church (vs.32), the fervent and scriptural prayer and the fullness of the Holy Spirit resulted in great power in the preaching of the Apostles. Lay persons often fail to realize that a lack of power in the pulpit often results from a lack of unity in the pew. There was little lack, either in pew or pulpit in the early church. The Apostles were everlastingly at it (iterative imperfect in ἀπεδίδουν). They were men with only one message. Everything they preached centered around and depended for validity upon the fact of the bodily resurrection of Jesus - a fact to which they could give personal witness. All of the saints enjoyed the bountiful favor of God. The church, living under the worst of sociological, economic and political conditions was operating under ideal spiritual conditions. One wonders if the inverse relation is mandatory? Many modern congregations maintain such favorable social relations with the enemy that the Lord Jesus is on the outside (Rev.3:20). Such an institution is not a church at all in the New Testament sense.

Verse 34 - "Neither was there any of them that lacked: for as many as were possessors of lands or houses, sold them, and brought the prices of the things that were sold."

οὐδὲ γὰρ ἐνδεής τις ἦν ἐν αὐτοῖς, ὅσοι γὰε κτήτορες χωρίων ἢ οἰκιῶν
ὑπῆρχον, πωλοῦντες ἔφερον τὰς τιμὰς τῶν πιπρασκομένων

οὐδὲ (disjunctive particle) 452.
γὰρ (inferential conjunction) 105.

#3044 ἐνδεής (nom.sing.masc.of ἐνδεής, predicate adjective).

that lack - Acts 4:34.

Meaning: Cf.ἐνδέω - "to be needy" "to be destitute." Hence, poverty strcken,
destitute - Acts 4:34.

τις (nom.sing.masc.of τις, subject of ἦν) 486.
ἦν (3d.per.sing.imp.ind.of εἰμί, progressive description) 86.
ἐν (preposition with the locative of place, with pronouns) 80.
αὐτοῖς (loc.pl.masc.of αὐτός, place) 16.
ὅσοι (nom.pl.masc.of ὅσος, relative pronoun, subject of ὑπῆρχον) 660.
γὰρ (causal conjunction) 105.

#3045 κτήτορες (nom.pl.masc.of κτήτωρ, predicate nominative).

possessor - Acts 4:34.

Meaning: Cf. κτάομαι (#859). Hence, a possessor, owner. Followed by a genitive
of description) - Acts 4:34.

χωρίων (gen.pl.neut.of χωρίον, description) 583.
ἢ (disjunctive particle) 465.
οἰκιῶν (gen.pl.fem.of οἰκία, description) 186.
ὑπῆρχον (3d.per.pl.imp.act.ind.of ὑπάρχω, progressive description) 1303.
πωλοῦντες (pres.act.part.nom.pl.masc.of πωλέω, adverbial, temporal) 892.
ἔφερον (3d.per.pl.imp.act.ind.of φέρω, iterative) 693.
τὰς (acc.pl.fem.of the article in agreement with τιμὰς) 9.
τιμὰς (acc.pl.fem.of τιμή, direct object of ἔφερον) 1619.
τῶν (gen.pl.masc.of the article in agreement with πιπρασκομένων) 9.
πιπρασκομένων (pres.pass.part.gen.pl.masc.of πιπράσκω, substantival,
description) 1088.

*Translation - "Nor was there one destitute among them, because those who were
owners of farms or houses were selling them and bringing the proceeds of the
sales. . . "*

Comment: The first γὰρ is inferential, since the fact that no one in the church
was in want was contingent upon the great grace which the church was enjoying
(vs.33). When Christians are happy in the Lord they are gracious to each other.
The second γὰρ is causal. It introduces the explanation for their distribution of
the wealth in practical terms. The joy, grace and peace in the church (vs.33)
contributed to the fact that no one suffered financially because those with

property liquidated it and brought the money to the Apostles. God's grace produces Christian attitudes, which in turn produce Christian actions which, in their turn generate happy social, economic and political results. Only thus can utility be maximized in society. πωλοῦντες, the present participle if of course timeless, getting its time from ἔφερον, the main verb. The context provides the knowledge of course that before the money could be brought to the Apostles the sale had to be negotiated and closed.

This simple statement of fact tends to obscure the extent of the activity in the church, until we remember that there were more than 8000 Christians at this time. How many of them held real assets is not known, but the economic activity must be been great as the cash proceeds from the sales poured into the Apostles' hands for the direction in distribution.

Verse 35 - "... and laid them down at the apostles' feet: and distribution was made unto every man according as he had need."

καὶ ἐτίθουν παρὰ τοὺς πόδας τῶν ἀποστόλων, διεδίδετο δὲ ἑκάστῳ καθότι ἄν τις χρείαν εἶχεν.

καὶ (adjunctive conjunction joining verbs) 14.
ἐτίθουν (3d.per.pl.imp.act.ind.odf τίθημι, iterative) 455.
παρὰ (preposition with the accusative of extent, place) 154.
τοὺς (acc.pl.masc.of the article in agreement with πόδας) 9.
πόδας (acc.pl.masc.of πούς, place where) 353.
τῶν (gen.pl.masc.of the article in agreement with ἀποστόλων) 9.
ἀποστόλων (gen.pl.masc.of ἀπόστολος, possession) 844.
διεδίδετο (3d.per.sing.imp.pass.ind.of διαδίδωμι, iterative) 2279.
δὲ (continuative conjunction) 11.
ἑκάστῳ (dat.sing.masc.of ἕκαστος, indirect object of διεδίδετο) 1217.
καθότι (particle in a comparative clause) 1783.
ἄν (contingent particle in a comparative clause, in an iterative sense) 205.
τις (nom.sing.masc.of τις, subject of εἶχεν) 486.
χρείαν (acc.sing.fem.of χρεία, direct object of εἶχεν) 317.
εἶχεν (3d.per.sing.imp.act.ind.of ἔχω, iterative) 82.

Translation - "... and they were laying them down at the feet of the Apostles, and a distribution was made to each as he from time to time had need."

Comment: The sustained action continues as the present and imperfect tenses indicate. They were selling and from time to time bringing the money and laying it down at the Apostles' feet. They in turn were in charge of the distribution. καθότι here in a comparative clause with ἄν in an iterative sense. It expresses contingency. The distribution was made from time to time (iterative imperfect in εἶχεν) on the basis of the need which might occur from time to time for each person. "Καθότι in a comparative sense ... occurs only twice (Ac.2:45; 4:35) and the same idiom precisely each time, καθότι ἄν τις χρείαν εἶχεν. Here ἄν seems to particularize each case from time to time (imperfect tense), the iterative use of ἄν. (Moulton, *Prolegomena*, 167, as cited in Robertson, *Grammar*, 967). This usage approaches the temporal in idea." (*Ibid.*). The verbs indicate a continuing round of liquidation of real estate assets, delivery of money to the Apostles and distribution, for διεδίδετο is also an iterative imperfect. The giving continued as long as the need existed. Thus five imperfect tense verbs give us the moving picture of 8000 Christians in love with each other because each was in love with the Lord Jesus and filled with His Spirit. There is no specification of person or type of need. Anyone with any need could have funds to meet the needs. The church put into practice the production and distribution formula for which communism has become well known - "From each according to his ability" (verse 34) and "to each according to his need" (verse 35). The vast difference between 20th century Russian communism and 1st century Christian communism is that the motivation in Russia is widespread fear of the power of a dictator to exact reprisals for nonconformity, while the early Christians were doing it voluntarily as they were led by the Holy Spirit, because they loved each other, and they recognized that all of the law in a moral universe and the realization of the dreams of all the prophets were realized when we love God with our entire personality and our neighbour as ourselves. Godless and materialistic communism must work with selfish, unregenerate human nature, lost in Adam, while the Holy Spirit was leading those, who before He brought them to Christ were lost, but who now were loving born again children of God through faith in Jesus Christ. The church was demonstrating what Jesus told the rich young ruler to do (Luke 18:22).

It is likely that a part of the motivation for this policy from a purely human point of view, was the widespread belief among the early Christians that the church age would be quite short and that Christ would return to earth in their lifetime. The New Testament had not yet been written, although the church had the advantage of the guidance of those Apostles who would write it. Jesus had not encouraged such a belief, but in the absence of guidelines which were inspired *after* this period, it is easy to suspect that they thought that there was no need to provide for economic security in any case, since Messiah would soon return. Similarly, it will be quite logical for endtime Christians, living on earth during Daniel's 70th week and who will know that Antichrist will soon impose his mark - a mark which they will refuse to take - and thus drive them from the market, to liquidate their assets while they can and give the money away. Money will be of no value to a Christian on earth during the last three and one half years of the church age. As the notion that the second coming of Christ might be delayed, the early church lost much of its communistic character, but still retained the practice of a Christian stewardship, based upon private ownership of the means of production (Eph.4:28; Jam.5:1-4; 2:15-16; 1 John 3:17).

Verse 36 - "And Joses who by the Apostles was surnamed Barnabas, (which is, being interpreted, the Son of Consolation), a Levite, and of the country of Cyprus, . . . "

Ἰωσὴφ δὲ ὁ ἐπικληθεὶς Βαρναβᾶς ἀπὸ τῶν ἀποστόλων, ὅ ἐστιν μεθερμηνευόμενον υἱὸς παρακλήσεως, Λευίτης, Κύπριος τῷ γένει,

#3046 Ἰωσήφ (nom.sing.masc.of Ἰωσήφ, subject of ἤνεγκεν and ἔθηκεν).

Joseph - Acts 4:36.

Meaning: Joseph, a Christian in the early church in Jerusalem - Acts 4:36.

δὲ (continuative conjunction) 11.
ὁ (nom.sing.masc.of the article in agreement with ἐπικληθεὶς) 9.
ἐπικληθεὶς (aor.pass.part.nom.sing.masc.of ἐπικαλέω, substantival, in apposition) 884.

#3047 Βαρναβᾶς (nom.sing.masc.of Βαρναβᾶς, appellation).

Barnabas - Acts 4:36; 9:27; 11:;22,30; 12:25; 13:1,2,7,43,46,50; 14:12,14,20; 15:2,2,12,22,25,35,36,37,39; 1 Cor.9:6; Gal.2:1,9,13; Col.4:10

Meaning: A member of the Jerusalem, a Levite from Cyprus, who accompanied Paul on his first missionary journey - Acts 4:36; 9:27; 11:22,30; 12:25; 13:1,2,7,43,46,50; 14:12,14,20; 15:2,2,12,22,25,35,36,37,39; 1 Cor.9:6; Gal.2:1,9,13; Col.4:10.

ἀπὸ (preposition with the ablative of agent) 70.
τῶν (abl.pl.masc.of the article in agreement with ἀποστόλων) 9.
ἀποστόλων (abl.pl.masc.of ἀπόστολος, agent) 844.
ὁ (nom.sing.neut.of ὅς subject of ἐστιν) 65.
μεθερμηνευόμενον (perf.pass.part.nom.sing.neut.of μεθερμηνεύω, adverbial, modal) 122.
υἱὸς (nom.sing.masc.of υἱός, predicate nominative) 5.
παρακλήσεως (gen.sing.fem.of παράκλησις, definition) 1896.
Λευίτης (nom.sing.masc.of Λευίτης, apposition) 1955.

#3048 Κύπριος (nom.sing.masc.of Κύριος, apposition).

Cyrpus - Acts 4:36; 11:20; 21:16.

Meaning: A native or inhabitant of Cyprus - Acts 4:36; 11:20; 21:16.

τῷ (instrumental sing. neut.of the article in agreement with γένει) 9.
γένει (instru.sing.neut.of γένος, cause) 1090.

Translation - *"And Joseph, the one who was nicknamed Barnabas by the Apostles, which in translation means 'Son of Consolation,' a Levite and a Cyprian by birth."*

Comment: We get an introduction to Barnabas, who accompanied Paul on the first part of his first missionary journey. A series of appositions follow his name. Nicknamed Barnabas, he was a Levite born on the island of Cyprus. We shall see much of him in the future.

Verse 37 - "... having land, sold it, and brought the money, and laid it at the apostles' feet."

ὑπάρχοντος αὐτῷ ἀγροῦ πωλήσας ἤνεγκεν τὸ χρῆμα καὶ ἔθηκεν παρὰ τοὺς πόδας τῶν ἀποστόλων.

ὑπάρχοντος (pres.act.part.gen.sing.masc.of ὑπάρχω, genitive absolute) 1303.

αὐτῷ (dat.sing.masc.of αὐτός, possession) 16.

ἀγροῦ (gen.sing.masc.of ἀγρός, genitive absolute) 626.

πωλήσας (aor.act.part.nom.sing.masc.of πωλέω, adverbial, temporal) 892.

ἤνεγκεν (3d.per.sing.aor.act.ind.of φέρω, constative) 683.

τὸ (acc.sing.neut.of the article in agreement with χρῆμα) 9.

χρῆμα (acc.sing.neut.of χρῆμα, direct object of ἤνεγκεν) 2637.

καὶ (adjunctive conjunction joining verbs) 14.

ἔθηκεν (3d.per.sing.aor.act.ind.of τίθημι, constative) 455.

παρὰ (preposition with the accusative of extent, place) 154.

τοὺς (acc.pl.masc.of the article in agreement with πόδας) 9.

πόδας (acc.pl.masc.of πούς, locative usage) 353.

τῶν (gen.pl.masc.of the article in agreement with ἀποστόλων) 9.

ἀποστόλων (gen.pl.masc.of ἀπόστολος, possession) 844.

Translation - "... owning a piece of land sold it and brought the money and laid it down at the feet of the Apostles."

Comment: In verse 34 we had πωλοῦντες ἔφερον, a present timeless participle with an iterative imperfect in ἔφερον. Here we have an aorist participle, also timeless with ἤνεγκεν, the constative aorist of φέρω ἤνεγκεν. Again the sale of the property preceded the bringing of the money, but that idea is gathered from the context, as much as from the grammar. We must not think that the most important factor in translating the participle is time, although in most cases the temporal element is important - antecedent time for the aorist and contemporary time for the present. But the context is always the overriding arbiter of the interpretation and translation. All the Christians who owned real estate are in view in verse 34. In verse 37 a single individual is singled out for discussion, perhaps because later Barnabas was selected to travel with Paul (Acts 13:2), shared his preaching and teaching ministry, suffered with him (Acts 13:5), whom the people of Lystra worshipped because they thought he was Jupiter (Acts 14:12), who argued with Paul about his nephew, John Mark (Col.4:10; Acts 15:37-39) and took Mark back with him to his native island (Acts 15:39). Barnabas and Paul were ordained at the same time by Peter, James and John (Gal.2:9), although a little later he was temporarily influenced by the Judaic Christians to discriminate against Gentile saints (Gal.2:13). Nevertheless he had an illustrious career as a great witness for Christ, which he began by liquidating a valuable asset in real estate and contributing the money to the common fund in Jerusalem.

Ananias and Sapphira

(Acts 5:1-11)

Acts 5:1 - *"But a certain man named Ananias, with Sapphira, his wife, sold a possession, . . .*

Ἀνὴρ δέ τις Ἀνανίας ὀνόματι σὺν Σαπφείρῃ τῇ γυναικὶ αὐτοῦ ἐπώλησεν κτῆμα . . . "

Ἀνὴρ (nom.sing.masc.of ἀνήρ, subject of ἐπώλησεν) 63.
δέ (adversative conjunction) 11.
τις (nom.sing.masc.of τις, in agreement with ἀνήρ) 486.

#3049 Ἀνανίας (nom.sing.masc.of Ἀνανίας, appellation).

Ananias - Acts 5:1,3,5.

Meaning: A Christian in the Jerusalem church; husband of Sapphira - Acts 5:1,3,5.

ὀνόματι (dat.sing.neut.of ὄνομα, possession) 108.
σὺν (preposition with the instrumental of association) 1542.

#3050 Σαπφείρῃ (instru.sing.fem.of Σαπφείρῃ, association).

Sapphira - Acts 5:1.

Meaning: Wife of Ananias. Member of the Jerusalem church - Acts 5:1.

τῇ (instru.sing.fem.of the article in agreement with γυναικὶ) 9.
γυναικὶ (instru.sing.fem.of γυνή, apposition) 103.
αὐτοῦ (gen.sing.masc.of αὐτός, relationship) 16.
ἐπώλησεν (3d.per.sing.aor.act.ind.of πωλέω, constative) 892.
κτῆμα (acc.sing.neut.of κυῆμα, direct object of ἐπώλησεν) 1305.

Translation - *"But a certain man named Anaias, with Sapphira, his wife, sold a possession . . . "*

Comment: δέ is adversative as Luke introduces the story of two members of the church whose behavior was contrary to that previously described. Ananias and Sapphira acted from motives that were derived from social control through peer pressure, rather than from personal conviction that what was being done by others should also be done by them. There was no formal directive from the Apostles that this share-the-wealth activity should be engaged in by all. Those who wished to do it, did so out of sincere hearts. Those who did not wish to do it were not compelled to do so except by the compulsion which came from others. What they did was self-serving. They wished to appear unselfish. We are not told that others in the fellowship urged Ananias and his wife to conform to the pattern being set by others. Such pressure may have been applied, and if so, it was a mistake. Christ, the Head over all things to His church (Eph.1:22) directs her activities through the ministry of the Holy Spirit. It is not reasonable to suppose that He wishes every member of His body to do exactly the same thing at exactly the same time. If all are led by the Holy Spirit to sing in the choir, who is left to listen? It has been noted that some who feel "led" to "speak in tongues" are not happy and satisfied until they have urged all others to seek to be "slain by the Spirit." Those who do are accepted into the inner circle of high level Christian activity, while those who do not are placed upon prayer lists, generally at or near the top of the list. Whether there were people like that in the Jerusalem church or not we are not told. Perhaps the peer pressure was felt by Ananias and Sapphira although no conscious effort was made by anyone to impose it. Some inner insecurity may have been present in their makeup which developed into incipient paranoia. It may or may not have been true that if they had not sold their property they would have been criticized by those who did. It is certain that no Christian who is genuinely dominated by the Holy Spirit will preempt the position of Him, to Whom all judgment has been given (John 5:22) and even think negative thoughts about others, much less express them.

Whatever the facts of the case, the details of which are not given in the text, may have been, Ananias and Sapphira devised a plan which would preserve their reputation with their peers and still provide for their own financial security.

Verse 2 - ". . . and kept back part of the price, his wife also being privy to it, and brought a certain part, and laid it at the apostles' feet."

καὶ ἐνοσφίσατο ἀπὸ τῆς τιμῆς, συνειδθίης καὶ τῆς γυναικός, καὶ ἐνέγκας μέρος τι παρὰ τοὺς πόδας τῶν ἀποστόλων ἔθηκεν.

καὶ (continuative conjunction) 14.

#3051 ἐνοσφίσατο (3d.per.sing.aor.mid.inf.of νοσφίζω, constative).

keep back - Acts 5:2,3.
purloin - Titus 2:10.

Meaning: Cf.νόσφι - "afar," "apart." Hence to withhold; in the middle to retain for oneself - Acts 5:2,3. To embezzle - Titus 2:10. The word occurs in the secular κοινή sources generally to indicate dishonest dealings.

ἀπὸ (preposition with the ablative of source) 70.
τῆς (abl.sing.fem.of the article in agreement with τιμῆς) 9.
τιμῆς (abl.sing.fem.of τιμή, source) 1619.

#3052 συνειδθίης (perf.part.gen.sing.fem.of συνείδον, genitive absolute).

be privy to - Acts 5:2.
beware of - Acts 14:6.
consider - Acts 12:12.
know by - 1 Cor.4:4.

Meaning: A combination of σύν (#1542) and οἶδα (#144). Hence, to share knowledge with another; to be aware of the plan of another. With reference to Sapphira, who knew about her husband's scheme - Acts 5:2; to consider all of the factors in a problem; to think holistically - Acts 12:12; to be acquainted with a given situation - Acts 14:6. With reference to Paul's declaration that he had a clear conscience about his ministry - 1 Cor.4:4.

καὶ (adjunctive conjunction joining nouns) 14.

τῆς (gen.sing.fem.of the article in agreement with γυναικός) 9.

γυναικός (gen.sing.fem.of γυνή, genitive absolute) 103.

καὶ (adjunctive conjunction joining verbs) 14.

ἐνέγκας (1st.aor.act.part.nom.sing.masc.of φέρω, adverbial, modal) 683.

μέρος (acc.sing.neut.of μέρος, direct object of ἐνέγκας) 240.

τι (acc.sing.neut.of τις, indefinite pronoun, in agreement with μέρος) 486.

παρὰ (preposition with the accusative in a locative usage) 154.

τοὺς (acc.pl.masc.of the article in agreement with πόδας) 9.

πόδας (acc.pl.masc.of πούς, in a locative usage) 353.

τῶν (gen.pl.masc.of the article in agreement with ἀποστόλων) 9.

ἀποστόλων (gen.pl.masc.of ἀπόστολος, possession) 844.

ἔθηκεν (3d.per.sing.aor.act.ind.of τίθημι, constative) 455.

Translation - "And he kept for himself some of the price, his wife also having been told about it, and brought a certain part and laid it at the feet of the Apostles."

Comment: The genitive absolute in the perfect tense tells us that Ananias and his wife had discussed the plan and that she was fully aware of all that was going on (verse 8). It is not difficult to understand why they wished to do this. Society demands individual conformity to the set pattern of group behavior. The pattern set by the church was one of voluntary distribution of the wealth. Only the strong individualist will dare to be different. If Ananias had possessed more moral courage he might have said that he thought that the policy was ill-advised. It is desirable that Christians be charitable, but Christian charity need not go to extremes. What they were doing was extremely unwise from a long-range economic point of view. If they understood this we could conclude that they did it nevertheless because they were convinced that the Lord was to return soon - within their lifetime. They could have given all or, at least, large portions of the capital flow of production, to the poor and been in a position to repeat the gifts at a later time. But they divested themselves of the capital stock - the producers goods capital which yields the flow of consumers goods. A farmer can give the corn that grows on his farm every year, but when he surrenders his farm he will have no corn to give at the next harvest. If Ananias understood this kind of economics he should have said so and justified his own reluctance to follow the lead of others who were generous in the short-run, but unwise in the long-run. If he had done this he would have served his Christian brethren well. His sin was not that he was reluctant to reduce himself and his wife to a poverty level. His sin was that he lied about it. It is probable that others gave grudgingly but did not articulate their reservations about it. Often it is fear of criticism that prevents us from being intellectually honest.

Verse 3 - "But Peter said, Ananias, why hath Satan filled thine heart to lie to the Holy Ghost, to keep back part of the price of the land?"

εἶπεν δὲ ὁ Πέτρος, Ἀνανία, διὰ τί ἐπλήρωσεν ὁ Σατανᾶς τὴν καρδίαν σου ψεύσασθαί σε τὸ πνεῦμα τὸ ἅγιον καὶ νοσφίσασθαι ἀπὸ τῆς τιμῆς τοῦ χωρίου;

εἶπεν (3d.per.sing.aor.act.ind.of εἶπον, constative) 155.
δὲ (adversative conjunction) 11.
ὁ (nom.sing.masc.of the article in agreement with Πέτρος) 9.
Πέτρος (nom.sing.masc.of Πέτρος, subject of εἶπεν) 387.
Ἀνανία (voc.sing.masc.of Ἀνανίας, address) 3049.
διὰ (preposition with the accusative, cause) 118.
τί (acc.sing.neut.of τίς, interrogative pronoun, cause) 281.
ἐπλήρωσεν (3d.per.sing.aor.act.ind.of πληρόω, culminative) 115.
ὁ (nom.sing.masc.of the article in agreement with Σατανᾶς) 9.
Σατανᾶς (nom.sing.masc.of Σατανᾶς, subject of ἐπλήρωσεν) 365.
τὴν (acc.sing.fem.of the article in agreement with καρδίαν) 9.
καρδίαν (acc.sing.fem.of καρδία, direct object of ἐπλήρωσεν) 432.
σου (gen.sing.masc.of σύ, possession) 104.
ψεύσασθαι (aor.mid.inf.of ψεύδομαι, sub-final clause) 439.
σε (acc.sing.masc.of σύ, general reference) 104.
τὸ (acc.sing.neut.of the article in agreement with πνεῦμα) 9.
πνεῦμα (acc.sing.neut.of πνεῦμα, direct object of ψεύσασθαι) 83.
τὸ (acc.sing.neut.of the article in agreement with ἅγιον) 9.
ἅγιον (acc.sing.neut.of ἅγιος, in agreement with πνεῦμα) 84.
καὶ (adjunctive conjunction joining infinitives) 14.
νοσφίσασθαι (aor.mid.inf.of νοσφίζω, sub-final clause) 3051.
ἀπὸ (preposition with the ablative of source) 70.
τῆς (abl.sing.fem.of the article in agreement with τιμῆς) 9.
τιμῆς (abl.sing.fem.of τιμή, source) 1619.
τοῦ (gen.sing.neut.of the article in agreement with χωρίον) 9.
χωρίον (gen.sing.neut.of χωρίον, description) 1583.

Translation - "But Peter said, 'Ananias, why did Satan fill your heart in order (and with the result) that you lied to the Holy Spirit and kept for yourself some of the proceeds of the land?' "

Comment: The Holy Spirit filled the other Christians with the results recorded (Acts 2:2). Satan filled the heart of Ananias. The two evil results followed. The two infinitives are sub-final - both purpose and result. Purpose is "intended result" (Burton, *Moods and Tenses*, 148). The censure was not for keeping back some of the money, but for lying about it.

Verse 4 - "Whiles it remained, was it not thine own? And after it was sold, was it not in thine own power? Why hast thou conceived this thing in thine heart? Thou hast not lied unto men but unto God."

οὐχὶ μένον σοὶ ἔμενεν καὶ πραϑὲν ἐν τῇ σῇ ἐξουσίᾳ ὑπῆρχεν; τί ὅτι ἔϑου ἐν τῇ καρδίᾳ σου τὸ πρᾶγμα τοῦτο; οὐκ ἐφεύσω ἀνϑρώποις ἀλλὰ τῳ ϑεῷ.

οὐχὶ (summary negative conjunction with the indicative in rhetorical question, expecting an affirmative reply) 130.

μένον (pres.act.part.nom.sing.neut.of μένω, adverbial, circumstantial) 864.

σοὶ (dat.sing.masc.of σύ, possession) 104.

ἔμενεν (3d.per.sing.imp.act.ind.of μένω, customary) 864.

καὶ (continuative conjunction) 14.

πραϑὲν (1st.aor.pass.part.nom.sing.neut.of πιπράσκω, adverbial, temporal) 1088.

ἐν (preposition with the locative of sphere) 80.

τῇ (loc.sing.fem.of the article in agreement with ἐξουσίᾳ) 9.

σῇ (loc.sing.fem.of σός, in agreement with ἐξουσίᾳ) 646.

ἐξουσίᾳ (loc.sing.fem.of ἐξουσία, sphere) 707.

ὑπῆρχεν (3d.per.sing.imp.act.ind.of ὑπάρχω, customary) 1303.

τί (nom.sing.neut.of τίς, subject of γέγονεν understood, direct question) 281.

ὅτι (conjunction introducing an object clause after γέγονεν understood) 211.

ἔϑου (2d.per.sing.2d.aor.mid.ind.of τίϑημι, constative) 455.

ἐν (preposition with the instrumental of means) 80.

τῇ (instru.sing.fem.of the article in agreement with καρδίᾳ) 9.

καρδίᾳ (instru.sing.fem.of καρδία, means) 432.

σου (gen.sing.masc.of σύ, possession) 104.

τὸ (acc.sing.neut.of the article in agreement with πρᾶγμα) 9.

πρᾶγμα (acc.sing.neut.of πρᾶγμα, direct object of ἔϑου) 1266.

τοῦτο (acc.sing.neut.of οὗτος, in agreement with πρᾶγμα) 93.

οὐκ (summary negative conjunction with the indicative) 130.

ἐφεύσω (2d.per.sing.aor.mid.ind.of φεύδω, culminative) 439.

ἀνϑαρώποις (dat.pl.masc.of ἄνϑρωπος, direct object of ἐφεύσω) 341.

ἀλλὰ (antithetical conjunction) 342.

τῷ (dat.sing.masc.of the article in agreement with ϑεῷ) 9.

ϑεῷ (dat.sing.masc.of ϑεός, direct object of ἐφεύσω) 124.

Translation - "While you owned it, it was yours, was it not? And after you sold it, it was still under your authority wasn't it? What happened that in your heart you decided to do this? You have lied, not to men but to God!"

Comment: The text does not reveal how Peter knew about the plot. One of the gifts of the Holy Spirit is the "discerning of spirits" (1 Cor.12:10) - the Spirit directed intuitive ability to detect fraud.This writer has few gifts, but seldom fails to detect the identity of the publisher of certain books, pamphlets and tracts, which propagate Watch Tower Bible and Tract Society and/or Seventh Day Adventist heresy. If Peter had not detected the fraud we would not have his statement for the record and might thus have been led to believe that the policy which many in the church was following at that time was a directive for the time to come.

The rhetorical questions expect an affirmative reply. Note the customary imperfect tenses in ἔμενεν and ὑπάρχεν. After the land was sold the money was still under Ananias' control (locative of sphere in ἐξουσίᾳ). Here is the evidence that the Apostles had not issued an order that the Christians do what they were doing. What they did was purely voluntary. Ananaias and Sapphira could liquidate this asset and give the money away if they wished to do so. They were not ordered to do so. But they were forced to do so by their own fear that if they did not they would be criticized. Thus both their decisions were self-serving - the decision to sell and the decision to withhold some of the money. τί ὅτι is for τί γέγονεν ὅτι as we have it in a parallel construction in John 14:22. Peter was asking, "What has happened that caused this?" *Cf.#*455 for τίθημι in this same sense. *cf.* Lk.1:66; Acts 19:21; Lk.21:14; Acts 27:12. ἐν τῇ σῇ ἐξουσίᾳ - "Did it not lie within the sphere of your own jurisdiction?" The obvious answer is that it did. Thus the concept of private ownership was never denied by the early church. Note οὐκ . . . ἀλλά "where one thing is denied that another may be established," (Thayer, *A Greek-English Lexicon of the New Testament*, 461).The dative of direct object of a transitive verb is possible, with verbs of confessing, lying, helping, etc. There are many such verbs, but only such as emphasize close personal relationships like trusting, distrusting, envying, pleasing, satisfying, serving, etc. take the dative. Actually Ananias had already lied to God and was prepared to lie to Peter if he were asked any questions. The οὐκ . . . ἀλλά sequence is Peter's way of emphasizing how heinous the sin was, since Ananias had tried to mislead God - a very difficult feat to perform. Hence the incredibility in Peter's third question, which is not rhetorical - τί ὅτι ἔθου ἐν τῇ καρδίᾳ σου τὸ πρᾶγμα τοῦτο; *Cf.*τίς ὑμᾶς ἐβάσκαμεν in Gal.3:1 - the modern idiom is "What's got into you?" It was a totally irrational act. No one could have inspired it but Satan, who was suggesting to Ananias how he might withstand the social pressure and still keep his money. What a threat to the victorious life the desire for conformity can be, even when we try to conform to something good that others are doing, because we think that since the Holy Spirit is leading them to do it, we must do it also. How much better it would have been if Ananias had simply done nothing at all, or had announced his decision that, while he did not question the wisdom of what others were doing, he and Sapphira were going to keep their farm. He might have added, "in order that we will have something to give the poor next year."

Verse 5 - "And Ananias, hearing these words fell down, and gave up the ghost: and great fear came on all them that heard these things."

ἀκούων δὲ ὁ Ἀνανίας τοὺς λόγους τούτους πεσὼν ἐξέφυξεν, καὶ ἐγένετο φόβος μέγας ἐπὶ πάντας τοὺς ἀκούοντας.

ἀκούων (pres.act.part.nom.sing.masc.of ἀκούω, adverbial, temporal/causal) 148.

δὲ (continuative conjunction) 11.

ὁ (nom.sing.masc.of the article in agreement with Ἀνανίας) 9.

'Ανανίας (nom.sing.masc.of 'Ανανίας, subject of ἐξέφυξεν) 3049.
τοὺς (acc.pl.masc.of the article in agreement with λόγους) 9.
λόγους (acc.pl.masc.of λόγος, direct object of ἀκούων) 510.
τούτους (acc.pl.masc.of οὗτος, in agreement with λόγους) 93.
πεσὼν (aor.act.part.nom.sing.masc.of πίπτω, adverbial, timeless) 187.

#3052 A ἐξέφυξεν (3d.per.sing.aor.act.ind.of ἐκφύχω, constative).

give up the ghost - Acts 5:5; 12:23.
yield up the ghost - Acts 5:10.

Meaning: A combination of ἐκ (#19) and φύχω (#1489). Hence, to breathe out; to expire; to die. With reference to Ananias - Acts 5:5; Sapphira - Acts 5:10; Herod - Acts 12:23.

καὶ (continuative conjunction) 14.
ἐγένετο (3d.per.sing.aor.ind.of γίνομαι, constative) 113.
φόβος (nom.sing.masc.of φόβος, subject of ἐγένετο) 1131.
μέγας (nom.sing.masc.of μέγας, in agreement with φόβος) 184.
ἐπὶ (preposition with the accusative of extent, metaphorical) 47.
πάντας (acc.pl.masc.of πᾶς, in agreement with ἀκούοντας) 67.
τοὺς (acc.pl.masc.of the article in agreement with ἀκούοντας) 9.
ἀκούοντας (pres.act.part.acc.pl.masc.of ἀκούω, substantival, metaphorical place) 148.

Translation - "*And when Ananias heard these remarks he fell down and died, and all who heard about it were seized with great fear.*"

Comment: πεσὼν before ἐξέφυξεν is another example of a timeless aorist participle. Ananias fell down and died, although the actual order may have been that he died and fell down. Note the grammatical contrast between this passage and Mt.27:50, where the KJV translation is the same. *cf.* our comment on Mt.27:50. Jesus died in a sovereign act. Ananias was overtaken by an attack, perhaps heart, stroke, seizure - Dr. Luke, greatly interested in the story, probably asked Peter to describe the symptoms, so that he could tell us the cause of death, but if so, Peter was unable to tell him. It really isn't important. If we assume that Ananias and Sapphira were saved (and there is no reason to assume otherwise) their deaths illustrate 1 Cor.5:5 and 1 John 5:16, *q.v.*

Verse 6 - "*And the young men arose, wound him up, and carried him out, and buried him.*"

ἀναστάντες δὲ οἱ νεώτεροι συνέστειλαν αὐτὸν καὶ ἐξενέγκαντες ἔθαψαν.

ἀναστάντες (aor.act.part.nom.pl.masc.of ἀνίστημι, adverbial, timeless) 789.
δὲ (continuative conjunction) 11.
οἱ (nom.pl.masc.of the article in agreement with νεώτεροι) 9.
νεώτεροι (nom.pl.masc.of νεώτερος, subject of συνέστειλαν and ἔθαψαν) 2543.

#3053 συνέστειλαν (3d.per.pl.aor.act.ind.of συστέλλω, constative).

    wind up - Acts 5:6.
    short - 1 Cor.7:29.

Meaning: A combination of σύν (#1542) and στέλλω (#4342). To draw together. Contract, compress. Physically, of the wrapping of the body of Ananias - Acts 5:6. Metaphorically, of compressing time into a short period - 1 Cor.7:29.

    αὐτὸν (acc.sing.masc.of αὐτός, direct object of συνέστειλαν) 16.
    καὶ (adjunctive conjunction joining verbs) 14.
    ἐξενέγκαντες (aor.act.part.nom.pl.masc.of ἐκφέρω, adverbial, temporal) 2551.
    ἔθαψαν (3d.per.pl.aor.act.ind.of θάπτω, constative) 748.

Translation - "*And the young men arose, wrapped up the body, carried it out and buried it.*"

Comment: The disposition of the body was abrupt and simple. There were no ceremonies and no comment from the Apostles or any other of the company.

Verse 7 - "*And it was about the space of three hours after, when his wife, not knowing what was done, came in.*"

Ἐγένετο δὲ ὡς ὡρῶν τριῶν διάστημα καὶ ἡ γυνὴ αὐτοῦ μὴ εἰδυῖα τὸ γεγονὸς εἰσῆλθεν.

    Ἐγένετο (3d.per.sing.aor.ind.of γίνομαι, constative) 113.
    δὲ (continuative conjunction) 11.
    ὡς (particle introducing a comparative phrase) 128.
    ὡρῶν (gen.pl.fem.of ὥρα, time description) 735.
    τριῶν (gen.pl.fem.of τρεῖς, in agreement with ὡρῶν) 1010.

#3054 διάστημα (nom.sing.neut.of διάστημα, parenthetic nominative).

    space - Acts 5:7.

Meaning: An interval, distance between, of two (διά) - depending upon adjuncts. In Acts 5:7 joined with a genitive of time. Hence a time interval between two events.

    καὶ (continuative conjunction) 14.
    ἡ (nom.sing.fem.of the article in agreement with γυνὴ) 9.
    γυνὴ (nom.sing.fem.of γυνή, subject of εἰσῆλθεν) 103.
    αὐτοῦ (gen.sing.masc.of αὐτός, relationship) 16.
    μὴ (qualified negative conjunction with the participle) 87.
    εἰδυῖα (perf.part.nom.sing.fem.of οἶδα, adverbial, circumstantial) 144.
    τὸ (acc.sing.neut.of the article in agreement with γεγονὸς) 9.
    γεγονὸς (2d.perf.part.acc.sing.neut.of γίνομαι, substantival, direct object of εἰδυῖα) 113.

εἰσῆλθεν (3d.per.sing.aor.ind.of εἰσέρχομαι, constative) 234.

Translation - *"And it happened that about three hours later his wife, not knowing what had occurred, came in."*

Comment: Cf.ὡς ὡρῶν τριῶν διάστημα with the parenthetic nominative in Lk.9:38 - ὡσεὶ ἡμέραι ὀκτώ. The idea of division between two events, inherent in διὰ is seen in διάστημα - an interval of time between two events. The perfect participle εἰδυῖα indicates that Sapphira had not heard the news of her husband's death. She happened to come into the room unaware of the fact that the deception had been exposed and that her husband was dead and buried. Peter assumes the role of an investigator in

Verse 8 - *"And Peter answered unto her, Tell me whether ye sold the land for so much? And she said, Yea, for so much."*

ἀπεκρίθη δὲ πρὸς αὐτὴν Πέτρος, Εἰπέ μοι, εἰ τοσούτου τὸ χωρίον ἀπέδοσθε; ἡ δὲ εἶπεν, Ναί, τοσούτου.

ἀπεκρίθη (3d.per.sing.aor.mid.ind.of ἀποκρίνομαι, constative) 318.
δὲ (continuative conjunction) 11.
πρὸς (preposition with the accusative of extent, after a verb of speaking) 197.
αὐτὴν (acc.sing.fem.of αὐτός, extent after a verb of speaking) 16.
Πέτρος (nom.sing.masc.of Πέτρος, subject of ἀπεκρίθη) 387.
Εἰπέ (2d.per.sing.aor.act.impv.of εἶπον, command) 155.
μοι (dat.sing.masc.of ἐγώ, indirect object of εἰπέ) 123.
εἰ (conditional particle in a first-class condition) 337.
τοσούτου (gen.sing.neut.of τοσοῦτος, demonstrative of quality) 727.
τὸ (acc.sing.neut.of the article in agreement with χωρίον) 9.
χωρίον (acc.sing.neut.of χωρίον, direct object of ἀπέδοσθε) 1583.
ἀπέδοσθε (2d.per.pl.2d.aor.mid.ind.of ἀποδίδωμι, indirect middle) 495.
ἡ (nom.sing.fem.of the article, subject of εἶπεν) 9.
δὲ (continuative conjunction) 11.
εἶπεν (3d.per.sing.aor.act.ind.of εἶπον, constative) 155.
Ναί (affirmative particle) 524.
τοσούτου (gen.sing.neut.of τοσοῦτος, demonstrative of quality) 727.

Translation - *"And Peter said to her, 'If you sold the farm for such and such, tell me.' And she said, 'Yes, that was the price.' "*

Comment: τοσοῦτος, the qualitative demonstrative has the genitive with a verb of selling. Note the indirect middle in ἀπέδοσθε by which is indicated that "the subject is represented as doing something for, to or by himself." (Robertson, *Grammar*, 809). Thus ἀπέδοσθε means "ye gave away for your own interest" ("sold"). (*Ibid.*,810). Note that τοσούτου lacks a substantive. "For such and such an amount of money." Peter's question, in the form of a first-class condition, implies that there was some question about the sale price for the land. Had Sapphira known about the judgment that fell upon her husband, no doubt she would have told the truth. The only thing for her to do was to carry on the deception by sticking to the story that she and Ananias had agreed to tell.

Vese 9 - "Then Peter said to her, How is it that ye have agreed together to tempt the spirit of the Lord? behold, the feet of them which have buried thy husband are at the door, and shall carry thee out."

ὁ δὲ Πέτρος πρὸς αὐτήν, Τί ὅτι συνεφωνήθη ὑμῖν πειράσαι τὸ πνεῦμα κυρίου; ἰδοὺ οἱ πόδες τῶν θαφάντων τὸν ἄνδρα σου ἐπὶ τῇ θύρᾳ καὶ ἐξοίσουσίν σε.

ὁ (nom.sing.masc.of the article in agreement with Πέτρος) 9.

δὲ (continuative conjunction) 11.

Πέτρος (nom.sing.masc.of Πέτρος, subject of εἶπεν understood) 387.

πρὸς (preposition with the accusative of extent after a verb of speaking) 197.

αὐτήν (acc.sing.fem.of αὐτός, extent after a verb of speaking) 16.

Τί (nom.sing.neut.of τίς, interrogative pronoun in direct question, subject of γέγονεν understood) 281.

ὅτι (conjunction introducing an object clause after γέγονεν understood) 211.

συνεφωνήθη (2d.per.sing.1st.aor.pass.ind.of συμφωνέω, culminative) 1265.

ὑμῖν (instru.pl.masc.of σύ, agent) 104.

πειράσαι (aor.act.inf.of πειράζω, epexegetical) 330.

τὸ (acc.sing.neut.of the article in agreement with πνεῦμα) 9.

πνεῦμα (acc.sing.neut.of πνεῦμα, direct object of πειράσαι) 83.

κυρίου (gen.sing.masc.of κύριος, possession) 97.

ἰδοὺ (exclamation) 95.

οἱ (nom.pl.masc.of the article in agreement with πόδες) 9.

πόδες (nom.pl.masc.of πούς, subject of εἰσί, understood) 353.

τῶν (gen.pl.masc.of the article in agreement with θαφάντων) 9.

θαφάντων (aor.act.part.gen.pl.masc.of θάπτω, substantival, possession) 748.

τὸν (acc.sing.masc.of the article in agreement with ἄνδρα) 9.

ἄνδρα (acc.sing.masc.of ἀνήρ, direct object of θαφάντων) 63.

σου (gen.sing.masc.of σύ, relationship) 104.

ἐπὶ (preposition with the locative of place) 47.

τῇ (loc.sing.fem.of the article in agreement with θύρᾳ) 9.

θύρᾳ (loc.sing.fem.of θύρα, place where) 571.

καὶ (continuative conjunction) 14.

ἐξοίσουσιν (3d.per.pl.fut.act.ind.of ἐκφέρω, predictive) 2551.

σε (acc.sing.fem.of σύ, direct object of ἐξοίσουσιν) 104.

Translation - "And Peter (said) to her, 'How did it happen that you two agreed to tempt the Spirit of the Lord? Listen! The feet of those who buried your husband are at the door, and they will carry you out.' "

Comment: We have Τί ὅτι here as we did in verse 4, with the same exegesis. Note the plural in ὑμῖν- "you two." ἰδού is an attention getter. It can mean "Listen!"

Verse 10 - "Then fell she down straightway at his feet, and yielded up the ghost:

and the young men came in, and found her dead, and, carrying her forth, buried her by her husband."

ἔπεσεν δὲ παραχρῆμα πρὸς τοὺς πόδας αὐτοῦ καὶ ἐξέφυξεν. εἰσελθόντες δὲ οἱ νεανίσκοι εὗρον αὐτὴν νεκράν, καὶ ἐξενέγκαντες ἔθαψαν πρὸς τὸν ἄνδρα αὐτῆς.

ἔπεσεν (3d.per.sing.aor.act.ind.of πίπτω, constative) 187.
δὲ (continuative conjunction) 11.
παραχρῆμα (adverbial) 1369.
πρὸς (preposition with the accusative of extent) 197
τοὺς (acc.pl.masc.of the article in agreement with πόδας) 9.
πόδας (acc.pl.masc.of πούς, place) 353.
αὐτοῦ (gen.sing.masc.of αὐτός, possession) 16.
καὶ (adjunctive conjunction joining verbs) 14.
ἐξέφυξεν (3d.per.sing.act.ind.of ἐκφύκω, constative) 3052.
εἰσελθόντες (aor.mid.part.nom.pl.masc.of εἰσέρχομαι, constative) 234.
δὲ (continuative conjunction) 11.
οἱ (nom.pl.masc.of the article in agreement with νεανίσκοι) 9.
νεανίσκοι (nom.pl.masc.of νεανίσκος, subject of εὗρον) 1300.
εὗρον (3d.per.pl.aor.act.ind.of εὑρίσκω, constative) 79.
αὐτὴν (acc.sing.fem.of αὐτός, direct object of εὗρον) 16.
νεκράν (acc.sing.fem.of νεκρός, predicate adjective) 749.
καὶ (adjunctive conjunction joining verbs) 14.
ἐξενέγκαντες (aor.act.part.nom.pl.masc.of ἐκφέρω, adverbial, temporal) 2551.
ἔθαψαν (3d.per.pl.aor.act.ind.of θάπτω, constative) 748.
πρὸς (preposition with the accusative of extent, place) 197.
τὸν (acc.sing.masc.of the article in agreement with ἄνδρα) 9.
ἄνδρα (acc.sing.masc.of ἀνήρ, place where) 63.
αὐτῆς (gen.sing.fem.of αὐτός, relationship) 16.

Translation - "And immediately she fell down at his feet and died. And the young men came in, found her dead, carried her out and buried her beside her husband."

Comment: Note the basic idea of πρός - "near to." Thus two Christians, of whom we know nothing evil except this story, made the mistake of feeling that they were being compelled to conform to a social pattern of their peers, even though they did not wish to do so, and even though they found it necessary to be dishonest. Other Christians since have comitted this sin and have not been stricken as they were. The question which no mortal can answer is that of the degree to which each of us can tempt the Holy Spirit without calling down divine judgment of this kind. The safe thing for all of us is to stay far over on the safe side. And when we disagree with a policy followed by others, we should say so.

Verse 11 - "And great fear came upon all the church, and upon as many as heard these things."

καὶ ἐγένετο φόβος μέγας ἐφ' ὅλην τὴν ἐκκλησίαν καὶ ἐπὶ πάντας τοὺς ἀκούοντας ταῦτα.

καὶ (inferential conjunction) 14.

ἐγένετο (3d.per.sing.aor.ind.of γίνομαι, ingressive) 113.

φόβος (nom.sing.masc.of φόβος, subject of ἐγένετο) 1131.

μέγας (nom.sing.masc.of μέγας, in agreement with φόβος) 184.

ἐφ' (preposition with the accusative of extent, metaphorical place) 47.

ὅλην (acc.sing.fem.of ὅλος, in agreement with ἐκκλησίαν) 112.

τὴν (acc.sing.fem.of the article in agreement with ἐκκλησίαν) 9.

ἐκκλησίαν (acc.sing.fem.of ἐκκλησία, metaphorical extent) 1204.

καὶ (adjunctive conjunction joining substantives) 14.

ἐπὶ (preposition with the accusative of metaphorical extent) 47.

πάντας (acc.pl.masc.of πᾶς, in agreement with ἀκούοντας) 67.

τοὺς (acc.pl.masc.of the article in agreement with ἀκούοντας) 9.

ἀκούοντας (pres.act.part.acc.pl.masc.of ἀκούω, substantival, metaphorical extent) 148.

ταῦτα (acc.pl.neut.of οὗτος, direct object of ἀκούοντας) 93.

Translation - "And great fear began to seize upon the entire church and spread to all those who heard about these things."

Comment: φόβος must be interpreted in terms of those who experienced it. For all of the Christians it meant reverential awe and perhaps fright because of the wrath of outraged deity upon the unfaithful believer. The degree to which physical fear of punishment was felt would depend upon the spiritual state of the individual. But the Christians were not the only ones who feared. As the story spread throughout the communitity many of those who heard about it also feared, in most cases in the physical sense. God's wrath was exhausted at Calvary, but He deals sternly with the disobedient Christian. No loss of salvation is involved, but the disobedient Christian is sacrificing his opportunity to fulfill his destiny (Eph.2:10).

It is interesting to note that Luke uses ὅλην to describe the church, but only πάντας to describe others, outside the church, who were unregenerate. Not all of the unsaved who heard about the incident became afraid, though some did. But *all* of the members of the church were seized with this fear. Cf.#'s 67 and 112 for the difference between these two words. Here we have an example of the precision with which the Holy Spirit has inspired the writing, when it is His purpose to give us precise information on a given point.

This is the first time in the Acts that the organization of Christians in Jerusalem are referred to as a church (ἐκκλησία, #1204).

Many Signs and Wonders Performed
(Acts 5:12-16)

Verse 12 - "And by the hands of the apostles were many signs and wonders wrought among the people; (and they were all with one accord in Solomon's porch).

Διὰ δὲ τῶν χειρῶν τῶν ἀποστόλων ἐγίνετο σημεῖα καὶ τέρατα πολλὰ ἐν τῷ λαῷ, καὶ ἦσαν ὁμοθυμαδὸν ἅπαντες ἐν τῇ Στοᾷ Σολομῶντος.

Διὰ (preposition with the ablative of agent) 118.
δὲ (continuative conjunction) 11.
τῶν (abl.pl.fem.of the article in agreement with χειρῶν) 9.
χειρῶν (abl.pl.fem.of χείρ, agent) 308.
τῶν (gen.pl.masc.of the article in agreement with ἀποστόλων) 9.
ἀποστόλων (gen.pl.masc.of ἀπόστολος, possession) 844.
ἐγίνετο (3d.per.sing.imp.mid.ind.of γίνομαι, iterative) 113.
σημεῖα (nom.pl.neut.of σημεῖον, subject of ἐγίνετο) 1005.
καὶ (adjunctive conjunction joining nouns) 14.
τέρατα (nom.pl.neut.of τέρας, subject of ἐγίνετο) 1500.
πολλὰ (nom.pl.neut.of πολύς, in agreement with σημεῖα and τέρατα) 228.
ἐν (preposition with the locative of place, with persons) 80.
τῷ (loc.sing.masc.of the article in agreement with λαῷ) 9.
λαῷ (loc.sing.masc.of λαός, place, with persons - "among") 110.
καὶ (continuative conjunction) 14.
ἦσαν (3d.per.pl.imp.ind.of εἰμί, progressive description) 86.
ὁμοθυμαδὸν (adverbial) 2942.
ἅπαντες (nom.pl.masc.of ἅπας, subject of ἦσαν) 639.
ἐν (preposition with the locative of place) 80.
τῇ (loc.sing.fem.of the article in agreement with Στοᾷ) 9.
Στοᾷ (loc.sing.fem.of στοά, place where) 2096.
Σολομῶντος (gen.sing.masc.of Σολομῶν, designation) 32.

Translation - "And from time to time many signs and wonders were being performed among the people by the Apostles, and all enthusiastically assembled in Solomon's Portico."

Comment: Note the iterative imperfect in ἐγίνετο. Obviously the Apostles were performing miracles not continuously but continually. Again and again the apostolic power, given to the Apostles to establish and maintain their authority over the church and to prove to the world that they were speaking with the voice of God was displayed. This was particularly necessary now as it is likely that Peter's action in the cases of Ananias and Sapphira was looked upon, even by some Christians as unnecessarily severe. This is not to say that Peter killed Ananias and Sapphira. If it had not been God's will tor them to sutter death, they would have lived. But it was God's will for Peter to say what he did to them. The decisions of deity have already been made and are not contingent upon human decisions on earth in time - not even those of an Apostle.

It is not possible, insofar as I can determine, to tell whether the plural ἅπαντες refers to τῷ λαῷ or to τῶν ἀποστόλων. To be sure there must be agreement of gender and number, but λαῷ is a collective noun and can be considered plural.

Since we have the intensive ἅπαντες (#639), rather than πᾶς (#67), we must rule out hyperbole. If it refers to λαῷ, there were more than 8000 people assembled in Solomon's Portico. One wonders whether the place was large enough to accommodate that many people? The contextual picture as presented through verse 16 seems not to support the idea that all the Christians were there. The Apostles were likely to return to Solomon's Portico to perform their miracles as that was the scene of the previous meeting when Peter and John had witnessed to the people following the healing of the cripple. It was a good place to get a crowd.

It is important to point out again that the text does not say that all of the believers performed miracles, a significant omission in the light of Mark 16:20 which Pentecostalists cite for support for their view that *all* believers are miracle workers. It has already been pointed out that Mark 16:9-20 are not regarded by textual critics as a part of the inspired record. The Apostles, armed with apostolic sign gifts, devoid of fear of persecution which they were certain to suffer and filled with the Holy Spirit gathered in the temple. Christians who are filled with the Holy Spirit need not fear the police power of unbelievers, even when they suffer from it.

Verse 13 - "And of the rest durst no man join himself to them: but the people magnified them."

τῶν δὲ λοιπῶν οὐδεὶς ἐτόλμα κολλᾶσθαι αὐτοῖς, ἀλλ' ἐμεγάυνεν αὐτοὺς ὁ λαός.

τῶν (gen.pl.masc.of the article in agreement with λοιπῶν) 9.
δὲ (adversative conjunction) 11.
λοιπῶν (gen.pl.masc.of λοιπός, partitive) 1402.
οὐδεὶς (nom.sing.masc.of οὐδείς, subject of ἐτόλμα) 446.
ἐτόλμα (3d.per.sing.imp.act.ind.of τολμάω, inceptive) 1430.
κολλᾶσθαι (pres.mid.inf.of κολλάω, epexegetical) 1288.
αὐτοῖς (instru.pl.masc.of αὐτός, association) 16.
ἀλλ' (adversative conjunction) 342.
ἐμεγάλυνεν (3d.per.sing.imp.act.ind.of μεγαλύνω, inceptive) 1438.
αὐτοὺς (acc.pl.masc.of αὐτός, direct object of ἐμεγάλυνεν) 16.
ὁ (nom.sing.masc.of the article in agreement with λαός) 9.
λαός (nom.sing.masc.of λαός, subject of ἐμεγάλυνεν) 110.

Translation - "But not one of the others began to dare to join them; however the people began to make much ado about them."

Comment: This language seems to indicate that it was the Apostles, not all of the other Christians who assembled in Solomon's Portico. τῶν λοιπῶν is seems must refer to the other Christians. Not one of them dared to be identified with the Apostles, who by common consent went to the danger zone, where the possibility of arrest, imprisonment and even death might await them. Others in the church were less courageous. Not one of them was going to be seen in public with the Apostles. Apparently ὁ λαός refers to the unsaved people in Jerusalem.

The current idiom in popular use for the attitude of the rank and file of the Christians has it that "not one of the others was about to join himself with the Apostles."

But great crowds gathered around the Apostles in the temple, hoping to see other miracles of healing like the one that restored a forty year cripple to health. And they were not disappointed. In fact they became so laudatory that they attracted the attention of the officials. This is how Peter and John got arrested on the previous occasion (Acts 3:11). There is no reason to be secretive about a resurrected Saviour. Indeed there is every reason to advertize Him, but the Apostles were beginning to learn that they could not have kept it a secret even if they had wished to do so. Thus, while the Christians judiciously avoided the place, multitudes of Jews from all over the city gathered in Solomon's Portico to look, listen and applaud all that the Apostles said and did. The result was another ingathering into the sheepfold over which our Lord is the good, great and chief Shepherd (John 10:11; Heb.13:20; 1 Peter 5:4).

Verse 14 - "And believers were the more added to the Lord, multitudes both of men and women."

μᾶλλον δὲ προσετίθεντο πιστεύοντες τῷ κυρίῳ πλήθη ἀνδρῶν τε καὶ γυναικῶν.

μᾶλλον (comparative adverb) 619.

δὲ (continuative conjunction) 11.

προσετίθεντο (3d.per.pl.imp.pass.ind.of προστίθημι, iterative) 621.

πιστεύοντες (pres.act.part.nom.pl.masc.of πιστεύω, substantival, subject of προσετίθεντο) 734.

τῷ (instru.sing.masc.of the article in agreement with κυρίῳ) 9.

κυρίῳ (instru.sing.masc.of κύριος, association) 97.

πλήθη (nom.pl.masc.of πλῆθος, in apposition) 1792.

ἀνδρῶν (gen.pl.masc.of ἀνήρ, description) 63.

τε (correlative particle) 1408.

καὶ (adjunctive conjunction joining nouns) 14.

γυναικῶν (gen.pl.masc.of γυνή, description) 103.

Translation - "And, what is more, believers were being added to the Lord, multitudes both of men and women."

Comment: The favorable publicity that the unsaved people gave the Apostles (verse 13) was not all of the story. Not only did many in Jerusalem regard the Apostles and the work that they were doing with great respect and admiration, but, what is more (μᾶλλον) great numbers of them believed and were being saved. The iterative imperfect in προσετίθεντο indicates that again and again the miracle of regeneration occurred and the Body of Christ grew as individual members became identified with Christ and the Father (John 17:21). That these men and women were more than intellectual believers is clear from the fact that they were added τῷ κυρίῳ. In Acts 2:47 the new believers were added ἐπὶ τὸ αὐτό - "to the same group." The Church, filled with the Spirit, powerful in prayer, courageous in witnessing, with supernatural powers granted to the Apostles, was having phenomenal success in evangelism. No more statistics as to the number saved are given. The Lord has not stopped counting, but Luke has stopped reporting the results. We may be sure that He Who keeps account of dead birds and the hairs on your head also knows how many elect members of His Body there are and how many of them have been incorporated into it by the Holy Spirit at any given moment in time. The number before the ingathering of verse 14 was in excess of 8000.

It will soon be necessary to use the word church with a designating genitive to distinguish it from other churches in other localities. The New Testament knows nothing of a universal organization spread throughout the world to which all believers belong. However the organism of the Body of Christ, which comprises all of the individual regenerates of both Old and New Testament periods, as distinct from a single ecclessiastical organization, is called the "Church" (singular) in a few places in the New Testament. Note the plural form in some one of the cases in Acts 15:41; 16:5; 1 Cor.14:33; 1 Thess.2:14; Rev.1:4,11; 2:7,11,17,29; 3:6,13,22; 2:23; 22:16. When a single church organization is in view, it is identified either by context or by a genitive of designation as in 1 Thess.1:1 where we have Παῦλος . . . τῇ ἐκκλησίᾳ Θεσσαλονικέων - "Paul to the Thessalonian church."

The church in Jerusalem made no special efforts. There were so commissions on evangelism or Sunday School promotion who felt impelled to give unasked advice about how the Lord's work should be done. There were no "retreats" since the church was not retreating. All they did was witness to the death and resurrection of their Lord on an iterative basis, with the help of the Holy Spirit.

The enthusiasm of the public in Jerusalem knew virtually no bounds as the unregenerate in the city pushed the matter to within an approximation of fanaticism, although there is no evidence that the Christians were fanatical.

Verse 15 - "Isomuch that they brought forth the sick into the streets, and laid them on beds and couches, that at the least the shadow of Peter passing by might overshadow some of them."

ὥστε καὶ εἰς τὰς πλατείας ἐκφέρειν τοὺς ἀσθενεῖς καὶ τιθέναι ἐπὶ κλιναρίων καὶ κραβάττων, ἵνα ἐρχομένου Πέτρου κἂν ἡ σκιὰ ἐπισκιάσῃ τινὶ αὐτῶν.

ὥστε (conjunction with the infinitive, ecbatic) 752.
καὶ (ascensive conjunction) 14.
εἰς (preposition with the accusative of extent) 140.
τὰς (acc.pl.fem.of the article in agreement with πλατείας) 9.
πλατείας (acc.pl.fem.of πλατεῖα, extent) 568.
ἐκφέρειν (pres.act.inf.of ἐκφέρω, result) 2551.
τοὺς (acc.pl.masc.of the article in agreement with ἀσθενεῖς) 9.
ἀσθενεῖς (acc.pl.masc.of ἀσθενής, direct object of ἐκφέρειν) 1551.
καὶ (adjunctive conjunction joining infinitives) 14.
τιθέναι (pres.act.inf.of τίθημι, result) 455.

ἐπὶ (preposition with the genitive of place description) 47.

#3055 κλιναρίων (gen.pl.neut.of κλινάριον, place description).

beds - Acts 5:15.

Meaning: Cf.κλίνη (#779). A small pallet. A bedroll - Acts 5:15.

καὶ (adjunctive conjunction joining nouns) 14.

κραββάτων (gen.pl.masc.of κράββατος, place description) 2077.

ἵνα (conjunction with the subjunctive in a telic clause) 114.

ἐρχομένου (pres.part.gen.sing.masc.of ἔρχομαι, genitive absolute) 146.

Πέτρου (gen.sing.masc.of Πέτρος, genitive absolute) 387.

κἄν (ascensive particle) 1370.

ἡ (nom.sing.fem.of the article in agreement with σκιὰ) 9.

σκιὰ (nom.sing.fem.of σκιά, subject of ἐπισκιάσῃ) 380.

ἐπισκιάσῃ (3d.per.sing.aor.act.subj.of ἐπισκίαζω, purpose) 1226.

τινὶ (loc.sing.masc.of τις, the indefinite pronoun, place where) 486.

αὐτῶν (gen.pl.masc.of αὐτός, partitive genitive) 16.

Translation - "So that they were even bringing the sick into the streets and laying them upon bedrolls and cots in the hope that when Peter came along at least his shadow might overshadow some of them."

Comment: ὥστε, the ecbatic conjunction is ὡς plus τε and means "and so." It introduces two consecutive infinitives to show the result of the great spiritual movement of verse 14 in which men and women in great numbers were born from above. Their first thought seems to be of their sick friends and neighbours. As a result they went and got them and brought them out into the streets and laid them on bedrolls or cots. Why? The ἵνα clause has the subjunctive of purpose. κἄν here, which is a result of crasis (καί plus ἄν) is ascensive (καί) and contingent (ἄν). The hope was that even (ascensive καί) the shadow perhaps (contingent ἄν) of Peter might fall upon the sick as he went by. Note the genitive absolute in the present tense in ἐρχομένου Πέτρου. In Mark 6:56 we have the only other instance of ἵνα and κἄν used together with the subjunctive - "they were begging Him for permission even to touch the hem of His garment."

There is something emotionally affecting about this scene. The downtrodden masses, exploited by a religious system, which not only offered them no help but lived at their expense, poverty stricken and disease ridden by ghetto conditions in a city that had just crucified her Messiah, they suddenly sensed the fact that there might be hope. That their first thought after salvation was for others indicates the genuine character of their new experience. They did not expect that Peter or the other Apostles would be able to meet their sick loved ones personally but if *even his shadow* might possibly fall upon some of those who were brought . . . ! The text does not say that any healings occurred as a result of this stratagem. The incident may reveal what was perhaps the misplaced zeal of a new convert. The incident also goes along with verse 16 to explain the reaction of the Establishment in Jerusalem in verses 17 and 18.

Verse 16 - "There came also a multitude out of the cities round about unto Jerusalem, bringing sick folks, and them which were vexed with unclean spirits: and they were healed every one."

συνήρχετο δὲ καὶ τὸ πλῆθος τῶν πέριξ πόλεων Ἰερουσαλήμ, φέροντες ἀσθενεῖς καὶ ὀχλουμένους ὑπὸ πνευμάτων ἀκαθάρτων, οἵτινες ἐθεραπεύοντο ἅπαντες.

συνήρχετο (3d.per.sing.imp.mid.ind.of συνέρχομαι, inceptive) 78.
δὲ (continuative conjunction) 11.
καὶ (adjunctive conjunction) 14.
τὸ (nom.sing.neut.of the article in agreement with πλῆθος) 9.
πλῆθος (nom.sing.neut.of πλῆθος, subject of συνήρχετο) 1792.
τῶν (abl.pl.fem.of the article in agreement with πόλεων) 9.

#3056 πέριξ (adverbial).

round about - Acts 5:16.

Meaning: Cf.περί (#173). Round about. τῶν πέριξ πόλεων - "the circumjacent cities" - Acts 5:16.

πόλεων (abl.pl.fem.of πόλις, source) 243.
Ἰερουσαλήμ (indeclin., extent) 141.
φέροντες (pres.act.part.nom.pl.masc.of φέρω, adverbial, circumstantial) 683.
ἀσθενεῖς (acc.pl.masc.of ἀσθενής, direct object of φέροντες) 1551.
καὶ (adjunctive conjunction joining substantives) 14.

#3057 ὀχλουμένους (pres.pass.part.acc.pl.masc.of ὀχλέω, substantival, direct object of φέροντες).

vex - Acts 5:16.

Meaning: Cf. ὄχλος (#418). To excite a mob against one; to trouble, molest, cause to be in confusion. With reference to those under pressure from unclean spirits - Acts 5:16.

ὑπο (preposition with the ablative of agent) 117.
πνευμάτων (abl.pl.neut.of πνεῦμα, agent) 83.
ἀκαθάρτων (abl.pl.neut.of ἀκάθαρτος, in agreement with πνευμάτων) 843.
οἵτινες (nom.pl.masc.of ὅστις, subject of ἐθεραπεύοντο) 163.
ἐθεραπεύοντο (3d.per.pl.imp.pass.ind.of θεραπεύω, progressive description) 406.
ἅπαντες (nom.pl.masc.of ἅπας, in agreement with οἵτινες) 639.

Translation - "And also the crowds from the cities round about Jerusalem began to come together, bringing sick people and those who were under pressure from unclean spirits, all of whom were healed."

Comment: The news spread to the outlying districts as a result of which people from suburbia came bringing those who needed help. No one was disappointed. General debility and demon possession are specified. Luke does not tell us how far from the city the news travelled. Bethlehem, directly south, Bethphage and Bethany to the southeast, the Mount of Olives area on the east extending eastward to En-shemesh and Birel Kot, Nob and Anathoth to the northeast, Ramah on the north, Beth Hanina and Mizpeh to the northwest and Nephtoah, Lifta, Ain-Karim and Ain-Yalo to the west and southwest all lie within a radius of five English miles from the heart of Jerusalem. One wonders if Lazarus and his sisters, Mary and Martha were present. Lazarus had a real story to tell.

Such a mass movement would be certain to attract the attention of the authorities. The remainder of the chapter is devoted to the fascinating story that has in it elements of a comic opera, including the frustration of the court, the miraculous jail break, the advice of a true liberal and joy of Christian believers who had been counted worthy to suffer shame for His name.

Persecution of the Apostles

(Acts 5:17-42)

Verse 17 - "Then the high priest rose up, and all they that were with him, (which is the sect of the Sadducees,) and were filled with indignation."

Ἀναστὰς δὲ ὁ ἀρχιερεὺς καὶ πάντες οἱ σὺν αὐτῷ, ἡ οὖσα αἵρεσις τῶν Σαδδουκαίων, ἐπλήσθησαν ζήλου . . .

Ἀναστὰς (aor.act.part.nom.sing.masc.of ἀνίστημι, adverbial, causal) 789.
δὲ (continuative conjunction) 11.
ὁ (nom.sing.masc.of the article in agreement with ἀρχιερεὺς) 9.
ἀρχιερεὺς (nom.sing.masc.of ἀρχιερεύς, subject of ἐπλήσθησαν) 151.
καὶ (adjunctive conjunction joining substantives) 14.
πάντες (nom.pl.masc.of πᾶς, in agreement with οἱ) 67.
οἱ (nom.pl.masc.of the article, subject of ἐπλήσθησαν) 9.
σὺν (preposition with the instrumental of association) 1542.
αὐτῷ (instru.sing.masc.of αὐτός, association) 16.
ἡ (nom.sing.fem.of the article in agreement with οὖσα) 9.
οὖσα (pres.part.nom.sing.fem.of εἰμί, in apposition to οἱ σὺν αὐτῷ) 86.

#3058 αἵρεσις (nom.sing.fem.of αἵεσις, predicate nominative).

heresy - Acts 24:14; 1 Cor.11:19; Gal.5:20; 2 Peter 2:1.
sect - Acts 5:17; 15:5; 24:5; 26:5; 28:22.

Meaning: Cf. αἱρέομαι (#4546). Hence, choice. That which is chosen; one's choice, tenet or opinion. With reference to the heresy against the Christian faith - 2 Peter 2:1, where it is followed by a genitive of description - ἀπωλείας. Any heresy - Gal.5:20; in the Corinthian church - 1 Cor.11:19; in general reference to the Christian faith - Acts 24:14; 28:22. Of the Sadducees - Acts 5:17; Pharisees -

Acts 15:5; 26:5; Nazarenes - Acts 24:5.

τῶν (gen.pl.masc.of the article in agreement with Σαδδουκαῖος) 9.
Σαδδουκαίων (gen.pl.masc.of Σαδδουκαῖος, description) 277.
ἐπλήσθησαν (3d.per.pl.aor.pass.ind.of πληρόω, constative) 115.
ζήλου (abl.sing.masc.of ζῆλος, source) 1985.

Translation - "But the high priest and all those with him, who were of the heresy of the Sadducees, were aroused and filled with zeal . . . "

Comment: So much favorable prominence for the cause of Christ was certain to arouse the opposition. ἀναστάς refers, not to physical but to emotional uprising. The high priest was filled with consternation when he heard what was happening in the streets and immediately filled with zealous and jealous determination to do something about it. From his point of view it was righteous indignation. From the point of view of the Christians it was diabolical fanaticism. The Sadducees were with him in this action, especially since the Christians were preaching the resurrection of the body, - a doctrine which they denied (Mt.22:23). *Cf.*#1985 for the uses of ζῆλος.

J.A.Robinson says that in Acts the articular participle ὁ ὤν "introduces some technical phrase, or some term which it marks out as having a technical sense (cf.Acts 5:17; 13:1; 28:17), and is almost equivalent to τοῦ ὀνομαζομένου." (as cited by W.M.Ramsay, *The Church in the Roman Empire*, 52, as cited by Robertson, *Grammar*, 1107).It can be thought of as appellation as in Exodus 3:14, LXX, where in response to Moses' demand to know the name of the Lord, He said, Ἐγώ εἰμι ὁ ὤν, where ὁ ὤν, the articular participle is an additional name, in apposition to Ἐγώ εἰμι. Those who were with the high priest are identified technically, to use Robinson's term, as "the heresy of the Sadducees."

Verse 18 - ". . . and laid their hands on the apostles, and put them in the common prison."

καὶ ἐπέβαλον τὰς χεῖρας ἐπὶ τοὺς ἀποστόλους καὶ ἔθεντο αὐτοὺς ἐν τηρήσει δημοσίᾳ.

καὶ (continuative conjunction) 14.
ἐπέβαλον (3d.per.pl.2d.aor.act.ind.of ἐπιβάλλω, constative) 800.
τὰς (acc.pl.fem.of the article in agreement with χεῖρας) 9.
χεῖρας (acc.pl.fem.of χείρ, direct object of ἐπέβαλον) 308.
ἐπὶ (preposition with the accusative of extent, place) 47.
τοὺς (acc.pl.masc.of the article in agreement with ἀποστόλους) 9.
ἀποστόλους (acc.pl.masc.of ἀπόστολος, extent, place) 844.
καὶ (adjunctive conjunction joining verbs) 14.
ἔθεντο (3d.per.pl.2d.aor.mid.ind.of τίθημι, indirect) 455.
αὐτοὺς (acc.pl.masc.of αὐτός, direct object of ἔθεντο) 16.
ἐν (preposition with the locative of place where) 80.
τηρήσει (loc.sing.fem.of τήρησις, place where) 3026.

#3059 δημοσίᾳ (loc.sing.fem.of δημόσιος, in agreement with πηρήσει).

    common - Acts 5:18.
    publicly - Acts 18:28; 20:20.
    openly - Acts 16:37.

Meaning: Cf.δῆμος (#3264). Hence, belonging to the people or to the state. Public as opposed to ἴδιος (#778) - "one's own" or "private." As an adjective - "the public jail" - Acts 5:18; adverbially in Acts 16:37; 18:28; 20:20.

Translation - " . . . and laid hands upon the Apostles and put them in a public jail."

Comment: Thus Peter and John are back in jail and with them the other Apostles. It would be interesting to know whether or not Matthias was among them.

    George Colman The Younger entitled his play "Love Laughs at Locksmiths" The same can be said for truth. Annas and Caiaphas turned the lock designed to keep the Apostles in. They never knew who turned it to let them out.

    "Truth is often eclipsed, but never extinguished," (Livy, *History of Rome,* XXII, *c.*10).

    "It is as hard to tell the truth as to hide it." (Baltasar Gracian, *The Art of Worldly Wisdom,* CLXXI).

    An English proverb of the 18th century says, "Truth will out." The Russians added, ". . . even if buried in a golden coffin." The Germans put it this way, "It takes a great many shovelfuls to bury the truth."

    A legal maxim says, "*Suppressio veri, expressio falsi*" - "Suppression of the truth is a false representation."

> *Truth crushed to earth shall rise again:*
> *Th' eternal years of God are hers;*
> *But error, wounded, writhes in pain,*
> *And dies among his worshippers."*

William Cullen Bryant, *The Battlefield,* 1839.

    "The truth. . . shall always prevail above lies, as the oil above the water." (Thomas Shelton: Tr.of Cervantes, *Don Quixote,* II.)

    "It is error alone which needs the support of government. Truth can stand by itself." (Thomas Jefferson, *Notes on Virginia,* 1782).

    Annas and Caiaphas could neither tell the truth nor hide it, and they were quite willing to lend governmental support to error.

Verse 19 - "But the angel of the Lord by night opened the prison doors, and brought them forth, and said, . . . "

ἄγγελος δὲ κυρίου διὰ νυκτὸς ἤνοιξε τὰς θύρας τῆς φυλακῆς ἐξαγαγών τε αὐτοὺς εἶπεν, . . .

ἄγγελος (nom.sing.masc.of ἄγγελος, subject of ἤνοιξε and εἶπεν) 96.

δὲ (adversative conjunction) 11.

κυρίου (gen.sing.masc.of κύριος, descriptive) 97.

διὰ (preposition with the genitive of time description) 118.

νυκτὸς (gen.sing.fem.of νύξ, time description) 209.

ἤνοιξε (3d.per.sing.aor.act.ind.of ἀνοίγω, constative) 188.

τὰς (acc.pl.fem.of the article in agreement with θύρας) 9.

θύρας (acc.pl.fem.of θύρα, direct object of ἤνοιξε) 571.

τῆς (gen.sing.fem.of the article in agreement with φυλακῆς) 9.

φυλακῆς (gen.sing.fem.of φυλακή, description) 494.

ἐξαγαγών (aor.act.part.nom.sing.masc.of ἐξάγω, adverbial, temporal) 2316.

τε (adjunctive conjunction joining verbs) 1408.

αὐτοὺς (acc.pl.masc.of αὐτός, extent with a verb of speaking) 16.

εἶπεν (3d.per.sing.aor.act.ind.of εἶπον, constative) 155.

Translation - "*But a lordly angel opened the doors of the prison during the night, led them out and said to them, . . .* "

Comment: δὲ is adversative. Apparently Annas and Caiaphas forgot about the "lordly angel" or, if they thought about him, they assumed that he was on their side - an assumption totally unwarranted. κυρίου without the article is descriptive, not substantival. The translation is not "an angel of the Lord," but "a lordly angel." Did the San Hedrin think that they could stop the witness of the Christians by locking up eleven Apostles? Perhaps not, but they could not throw 10,000 people into jail.

If any of the other prisoners escaped while the jail doors were opened, it is not recorded. Luke is careful to tell us how the escape of the Apostles was carried out. They were not transformed, temporarily, into immateriality, thus to escape between the bars or through them. The angel had a key and the doors were opened. His instructions to the Apostles, once he had them safely outside the prison are recorded in

Verse 20 - "*Go, stand and speak in the temple to the people all the words of this life.*"

Πορεύεσθε καὶ σταθέντες λαλεῖτε ἐν τῷ ἱερῷ τῷ λαῷ πάντα τὰ ῥήματα τῆς ζωῆς ταύτης.

Πορεύεσθε (2d.per.pl.pres.mid.impv.of πορεύομαι, direct) 170.

καὶ (adjunctive conjunction joining verbs) 14.

σταθέντες (aor.mid.part.nom.pl.masc.of ἵστημι, direct, adverbial, temporal) 180.

λαλεῖτε (2d.per.pl.pres.act.impv.of λαλέω, command) 815.

ἐν (preposition with the locative of place where) 80.

τῷ (loc.sing.neut.of the article in agreement with ἱερῷ) 9.

ἱερῷ (loc.sing.neut.of ἱερόν, place where) 346.

τῷ (dat.sing.masc.of the article in agreement with λαῷ) 9.

λαῷ (dat.sing.masc.of λαός, indirect object of λαλεῖτε) 110.

πάντα (acc.pl.neut.of πᾶς, in agreement with ῥήματα) 67.

πὰ (acc.pl.neut.of the article in agreement with ῥήματα) 9.

ῥήματα (acc.pl.neut.of ῥῆμα, direct object of λαλεῖτε) 343.

τῆς (gen.sing.fem.of the article in agreement with ζωῆς) 9.

ζωῆς (gen.sing.fem.of ζωή, description) 668.

ταύτης (gen.sing.fem.of οὗτος, in agreement with ζωῆς) 93.

Translation - "Go, take your stand and go on speaking in the temple to the people all the words of this life."

Comment: The angel told the Apostles to "take their stand," which has become a way of saying that people with strong convictions should not hesitate to speak out on controversial issues, particularly if the threat of persecution is present. There is something thrilling about "Then Paul stood up" (Acts 13:16) as he began his sermon at Antioch.Of course the Apostles obeyed the angel's command.If they had followed Falstaff's advice they would have said that "the better part of valor is discretion." Had they not gone to the temple the day before to preach they would not have gone to jail.But who is afraid of jail if he has an angel to let him out? There were occasions later when the Apostles fell into the hands of their persecutors and were not rescued by the angel as they had been this time (Acts 24:27).

The pronoun ταύτης, in gender agreement with ζωῆς, seems awkward - "speak all the words *of this life.*" Goodspeed, sensing this awkwardness as I did, translated, "tell the people all about this *new* life." I toyed with the idea of translating, "tell the people all the words of *this philosophy of* life," but rejected it as an unwarranted addition of a word that is not in the text. Winer (Winer-Thayer, 237) ". . . says that in τὰ ῥήματα τῆς ζωῆς ταύτης . . . the demonstrative goes in sense in ῥήματα" (Robertson, *Grammar*, 497). "In sense" perhaps it does but a genitive feminine singular pronoun does not normally adjoin an accusative, neuter plural noun. We have the same problem in Acts 13:26 and Romans 7:24. Robertson says that "It is possible that in Ac.5:20 . . . a slight change in sense has occurred, ταύτης more naturally going with ῥήματα" and then adds lamely that ". . . the point is not very material." (*Ibid.,*706). By "this life" the angel meant the kind of life which the Apostles had in Christ, which was characterized by love, joy, peace and the desire to preach about a resurrected Saviour, and which was, upon occasion, spiced up by such small items as having an angel get you out of jail. At the moment when the angel said this to the Apostles "this life" was more in view than the words which they would use to preach about it. Thus Goodspeed's translation is better, not only because it fits the context better but also because it is true to the grammatical rule involved.

Verse 21 - "And when they heard that, they entered into the temple, early in the morning, and taught. But the high priest came, and they that were with him, and called the council together, and all the senate of the children of Israel, and sent to the prison to have them brought."

ἀκούσαντες δὲ εἰσῆλθον ὑπὸ τὸν ὄρθρον εἰς τὸ ἱερὸν καὶ ἐδίδασκον.
Παραγενόμενος δὲ ὁ ἀρχιερεὺς καὶ οἱ σὺν αὐτῷ συνεκάλεσαν τὸ συνέδριον καὶ
πᾶσαν τὴν γερουσίαν τῶν υἱῶν Ἰσραήλ, καὶ ἀπέστειλαν εἰς τὸ δεσμωτήριον
ἀχθῆναι αὐτούς.

ἀκούσαντες (aor.act.part.nom.pl.masc.of ἀκούω, adverbial, temporal, causal) 148.

δὲ (inferential conjunction) 11.

εἰσῆλθον (3d.per.pl.aor.ind.of εἰσέρχομαι, constative) 234.

ὑπὸ (preposition with the accusative in a time expression) 117.

τὸν (acc.sing.masc.of the article in agreement with ὄρθρον) 9.

ὄρθρον (acc.sing.masc.of ὄρθρος, time expression, adverbial) 2375.

εἰς (preposition with the accusative of extent) 140.

τὸ (acc.sing.neut.of the article in agreement with ἱερὸν) 9.

ἱερὸν (acc.sing.neut.of ἱερόν, extent) 346.

καὶ (adjunctive conjunction joining verbs) 14.

ἐδίδασκον (3d.per.pl.imp.act.ind.of διδάσκω, inceptive) 403.

Παραγενόμενος (aor.part.nom.sing.masc.of παραγίνομαι, adverbial, temporal) 139.

δὲ (explanatory conjunction) 11.

ὁ (nom.sing.masc.of the article in agreement with ἀρχιερεὺς) 9.

ἀρχιερεὺς (nom.sing.masc.of ἀρχιερεύς, subject of συνεκάλεσαν and ἀπέστειλαν) 151.

καὶ (adjunctive conjunction joining substantives) 14.

οἱ (nom.pl.masc.of the article, subject of συνεκάλεσαν and ἀπέστειλαν) 9.

σὺν (preposition with the instrumental of association) 1542.

αὐτῷ (instru.sing.masc.of αὐτός, association) 16.

συνεκάλεσαν (3d.per.pl.aor.act.ind.of συγκαλέω, constative) 2251.

τὸ (acc.sing.neut.of the article in agreement with συνέδριον) 9.

συνέδριον (acc.sing.neut.of συνέδριον, direct object of συνεκάλεσαν) 481.

καὶ (adjunctive conjunction joining nouns) 14.

πᾶσαν (acc.sing.fem.of πᾶς, in agreement with γερουσίαν) 67.

τὴν (acc.sing.fem.of the article in agreement with γερουσίαν) 9.

#3060 γερουσίαν (acc.sing.fem.of γερουσία, direct object of ἐκάλεσαν).

senate - Acts 5:21.

Meaning: Cf. γέρων (#1987). A council of old men. Used with συνέδριον, the San Hedrin, to indicate that τὸ συνέδριον was the younger working group of the entire body, of which ἡ γερουσία was the older group of men, now living in retirement or upon a limited service basis - Acts 5:21.

τῶν (gen.pl.masc.of the article in agreement with υἱῶν) 9.

υἱῶν (gen.pl.masc.of υἱός, partitive) 5.

Ἰσραήλ (gen.sing.masc.indeclin. description) 165.

καὶ (adjunctive conjunction joining verbs) 14.

ἀπέστειλαν (3d.per.pl.aor.act.ind.of ἀποστέλλω, constative) 215.
εἰς (preposition with the accusative of extent) 140.
τό (acc.sing.neut.of the article in agreement with δεσμωτήριον) 9.
δεσμωτήριον (acc.sing.neut.of δεσμωτήριον, extent) 905.
ἀχθῆναι (aor.pass.inf.of ἄγω, purpose) 876.
αὐτούς (acc.pl.masc.of αὐτός, general reference) 16.

Translation - "And when they heard (the Apostles) came into the temple at daybreak and began to teach. Now when the high priest arrived at the office in company with those associated with him, they called together the San Hedrin and all the old men of the sons of Israel, and they sent (an officer) to the jail to have them brought."

Comment: The aorist participle ἀκούσαντες refers to the Apostles who had just been let out of jail. Under orders from the angel they went at daybreak to the temple and began to teach (inceptive imperfect in ἐδίδασκον). The imperfect in ἐδίδασκον with its linear action is in keeping with λαλεῖτε in verse 20 - "continue to speak." I have found no other instance in the New Testament of ὑπό with the accusative in a temporal sense.

διὰ νυκτός in verse 19 only tells us that it was sometime during the night that the Apostles were liberated. Thus there may have been some time between their liberation and the time when they went to the temple and began to teach, if it was also true that there was nobody in the temple area during the night, except perhaps the guards. In this case, they would have waited until dawn to go.

With παραγενόμενος the scene shifts from the Apostles and their angelic liberator to the high priest and his colleagues. He did not know that the Apostles were free until the officers returned from their mission (verse 22). But he knew that he had another crisis on his hands, the dimensions of which were greater than he feared. Something had to be done to arrest the growth of the Christian movement. He and his associates summoned not only the entire San Hedrin of seventy members, but the older men, now retired, who had previously served in the government. Caiaphas' report to his assembled advisors probably reviewed the miracle Peter and John had performed for the cripple, the sermon that Peter preached in Solomon's Portico, the response of 5000 Jews who deserted the temple worship in favor of Christianity, the demand of the court that the Apostles desist, their refusal and overnight imprisonment. Of course he and Annas did not know about the prayer meeting the following morning, but they certainly knew about the events described in Acts 5:12-16 as the streets of Jerusalem were filled with Jews, both men and women, seeking healing for themselves and their friends and salvation for their souls.

Such was the pessimistic report of Caiaphas to the San Hedrin and the Senate. They agreed that they must begin by sending the police to the prison to bring the Apostles back in their custody to face the charges of contempt of court. That was one thing with which the Apostles were well supplied - contempt for the court. It is difficult to imagine the consternation of the court when the officers returned with their story as recorded in

Verse 22 - "But when the officers ame and found them not in the prison, they returned, and told, . . . "

οἱ δὲ παραγενόμενοι ὑπηρέται οὐχ εὗρον αὐτοὺς ἐν τῇ φυλακῇ, ἀναστρέψαντες δὲ ἀπήγγειλαν . . .

οἱ (nom.pl.masc.of the article in agreement with ὑπηρέται) 9.

δὲ (adversative conjunction) 11.

παραγενόμενοι (aor.part.nom.pl.masc.of παραγίνομαι, adverbial, temporal) 139.

ὑπηρέται (nom.pl.masc.of ὑπητέτης, subject of εὗρον and ἀπήγγειλαν) 493.

οὐχ (summary negative conjunction with the indicative) 130.

εὗρον (3d.per.pl.aor.act.ind.of εὑρίσκω, constative) 79.

αὐτοὺς (acc.pl.masc.of αὐτός, direct object of εὗρον) 16.

ἐν (preposition with the locative of place where) 80.

τῇ (loc.sing.fem.of the article in agreement with φυλακῇ) 9.

φυλακῇ (loc.sing.fem.of φυλακή, place where) 494.

#3061 ἀναστρέψαντες (aor.act.part.nom.pl.masc.of ἀναστρέφω, adverbial, temporal).

return - Acts 5:22; 15:16.
be used - Heb.10:33.
behave self - 1 Tim.3:15.
have one's conversation - 2 Cor.1:12; Eph.2:3.
live - Heb.13:18; 2 Peter 2:18.
pass - 1 Peter 1:17.

Meaning: A combination of ἀνά (#1059) and στρέφω (#530). To turn back; to return in a physical sense - of the police from the prison - Acts 5:22; with reference to the Second Coming of the Messiah - Acts 15:16; to behave one's self ἐν οἴκῳ θεοῦ - 1 Tim.3:15; ἐν τῷ κόσμῳ - 2 Cor.1:12; ἐν οἷς - Eph.2:3; ἐν πλάνῃ - 2 Peter 2:18; ἐν φόβῳ - 1 Pet.1:17; with καλῶς - Heb.13:18. *Cf.* also Heb.10:33 in the passive.

δὲ (continuative conjunction) 11.

ἀπήγγειλαν (3d.per.pl.aor.act.ind.of ἀπαγγέλλω, constative) 176.

Translation - "But when the officers came and found them not in the prison, they returned, and told . . . . "

Comment: δὲ is adversative. The police, under orders from the court to fetch the Apostles did not find them in the jail. They returned and reported to the court, although they offered no explanation.

Verse 23 - "Saying, the prison truly found we shut with all safety, and the keepers standing without before the doors: but when we had opened, we found no man within."

λέγοντες ὅτι Τὸ δεσμωτήριον εὕρομεν κεκλεισμένον ἐν πάσῃ ἀσφαλείᾳ καὶ τοὺς φύλακας ἑστῶτας ἐπὶ τῶν θυρῶν, ἀνοίξαντες δὲ ἔσω, οὐδένα εὕρομεν.

λέγοντες (pres.act.part.nom.pl.masc.of λέγω, adverbial, modal) 66.

ὅτι (recitative) 211.

τὸ (acc.sing.neut.of the article in agreement with δεσμωτήριον) 9.

δεσμωτήριον (acc.sing.neut.of δεσμωτήριον, direct object of εὕρομεν) 905.

εὕρομεν (1st.per.pl.aor.act.ind.of εὑρίσκω, constative) 79.

κεκλεισμένον (perf.pass.part.acc.sing.neut.of κλείω, adverbial, circumstantial) 570.

ἐν (preposition with the instrumental of manner) 80.

πάσῃ (instru.sing.fem.of πᾶς, in agreement with ἀσφαλείᾳ) 67.

ἀσφαλείᾳ (instru.sing.fem.of ἀσφάλεια, manner) 1715.

καὶ (adjunctive conjunction joining nouns) 14.

τοὺς (acc.pl.masc.of the article in agreement with φύλακας) 9.

#3062 φύλακας (acc.pl.masc.of φύλαξ, direct object of εὕρομεν).

keeper - Acts 5:23; 12:6,19.

Meaning: Cf.φυλάσσω (#1301); φυλακή (#494); φυλακίζω (#3581). A prison guard - Acts 5:23; 12:6,19.

ἑστῶτας (perf.act.part.acc.pl.masc.of ἵστημι, adverbial, circumstantial) 180.

ἐπὶ (preposition with the genitive of place description) 47.

τῶν (gen.pl.fem.of the article in agreement with θυρῶν) 9.

θυρῶν (gen.pl.fem.of θύρα, place description) 571.

ἀνοίξαντες (aor.act.part.nom.pl.masc.of ἀνοίγω, adverbial, temporal) 188.

δὲ (adversative conjunction) 11.

ἔσω (adverbial) 1601.

οὐδένα (acc.sing.masc.of οὐδείς, direct object of εὕρομεν) 446.

εὕρομεν (1st.per.pl.2d.aor.act.ind.of εὑρίσκω, constative) 79.

Translation - ". . . saying, 'We found the prison as secure as they could make it, and we found the guards standing before the doors, but when we opened we found nobody inside."

Comment: The two circumstantial participles tell the story. The police found the prison in its usual condition of security - ἐν πάσῃ ἀσφαλείᾳ - "with every precaution taken." The perfect tense tells us that the condition of the prison when the officers arrived was the same as that which had been maintained throughout the night. The guards had been standing at their places before the doors all night and they were still there when the officers found them. They had nothing to report. This is what the police reported, for they had nothing else to tell. We know from verse 19 what had happened, but the guards had seen and heard nothing. We stil do not know whether there were other prisoners in the jail when the Apostles were brought. If there were, they too escaped, since there was no one in there when the police opened the doors and made a search. What about that?!

Verse 24 - "Now when the high priest and the captain of the temple and the chief priests heard these things, they doubted of them whereunto this would grow."

ὡς δὲ ἤκουσαν τοὺς λόγους τούτους ὅ τε στρατηγὸς τοῦ ἱεροῦ καὶ οἱ ἀρχιερεῖς, διηπόρουν περὶ αὐτῶν τί ἀν γένοιτο τοῦτο.

ὡς (particle with the indicative, introducing a definite temporal clause) 128.

δὲ (continuative conjunction) 11.

ἤκουσαν (3d.per.pl.aor.act.ind.of ἀκούω, in a definite temporal clause) 148.

τοὺς (acc.pl.masc.of the article in agreement with λόγους) 9.

λόγους (acc.pl.masc.of λόγος, direct object of ἤκουσαν) 510.

τούτους (acc.pl.masc.of οὗτος, in agreement with λόγους) 93.

ὅ (nom.sing.masc.of the article in agreement with στρατηγὸς) 9.

τε (correlative particle) 1408.

στρατηγὸς (nom.sing.masc.of στρατηγός, subject of ἤκουσαν and διηπόρουν) 2754.

τοῦ (gen.sing.neut.of the article in agreement with ἱεροῦ) 9.

ἱεροῦ (gen.sing.neut.of ἱερόν, description) 346.

καὶ (adjunctive conjunction joining nouns) 14.

οἱ (nom.pl.masc.of the article in agreement with ἀρχιερεῖς) 9.

ἀρχιερεῖς (nom.pl.masc.of ἀρχιερεύς, subject of ἤκουσαν and διηπόρουν) 151.

διηπόρουν (3d.per.pl.imp.act.ind.of διαπορέω, inceptive) 2262.

περὶ (preposition with the genitive of reference) 173.

αὐτῶν (gen.pl.neut.of αὐτός, reference) 16.

τί (nom.sing.neut.of τίς, interrogative pronoun, in indirect question) 281.

ἀν (contingent particle with the optative in indirect question) 205.

γένοιτο (3d.per.sing.aor.optative of γίνομαι, indirect question) 113.

τοῦτο (nom.sing.neut.of οὗτος, subject of γένοιτο) 93.

Translation - "And when both the captain of the temple and the high priest heard these reports they began to be in great doubt as to what might develop."

Comment: The indirect question has the optative mode with ἀν, which speaks of the greatest possible doubt. It may be significant that there is no evidence in the text that either the high priest or the temple police had any doubts about the veracity of the officers who came back and told their story. After having seen the miraculous events which had occurred through the ministry of the Christians, they may have come to expect anything. If the christians had raided the jail, overpowered the guards and rescued the Apostles, the guards would have told the story. The only possible explanation was the truth of what happened, although they did not have the details. So they began (inceptive imperfect in διηπόρουν) to have the greatest doubts as to what would come of it all. The less vivid future in an indirect question with the optative speaks of a remote prospect of determination (Robertson, *Grammar*, 1020). "The context shows great doubt and perplexity in the indirect questions which have ἀν and the opt.in the N.T. (Lu.1:62; 6:11; 9:46; 15:26; Ac.5:24; 10:17)" (*Ibid.*, 940). There was no way for them to predict what would happen if the supernatural results of the Apostles' witness to a resurrected Jesus continued. The remainder of the revelation in the New Testament reveals that what was happening then was the beginning of the worldwide missionary enterprise through which God would take out from among the Gentiles a people for His name (Acts 15:14). As for Annas, Caiaphas, their San Hedrin and the aged Senate, Jesus had told the disciples what was in their future (Mt.23:37-39; 24:1-2). In only thirty-seven years Jerusalem would be sacked, the temple would be taken apart, piece by piece, the area would be sown in salt, hundreds of Jews would be crucified on crosses surrounding the burning city and the Jews would be scattered to the four corners of the earth. From an intellectual and spiritual point of view, "blindness in part would happen to Israel until the fulfness of the Gentiles be come in" (Romans 11:25) and "they (would) fall by the edge of the sword, and be led away captive into all nations: and Jerusalem (would) be trodden down of the Gentiles, until the times of the Gentiles be fulfilled" (Luke 21:24).

While the high priest and his colleagues were debating policy, they received more bad news, in

Verse 25 - "Then came one and told them, saying, Behold, the men whom ye put in prison are standing in the temple, and teaching the people."

παραγενόμενος δέ τις ἀπήγγειλεν αὐτοῖς ὅτι Ἰδοὺ οἱ ἄνδρες οὓς ἔθεσθε ἐν τῇ φυλακῇ εἰσὶν ἐν τῷ ἱερῷ ἑστῶτες καὶ διδάσκοντες τὸν λαόν.

παραγενόμενος (aor.part.nom.sing.masc.of παραγίνομαι, adverbial, temporal) 139.

δὲ (continuative conjunction) 11.

τις (nom.sing.masc.of τις, indefinite pronoun, subject of ἀπήγγειλεν) 486.

ἀπήγγειλεν (3d.per.sing.aor.act.ind.of ἀπαγγέλλω, constative) 176.

αὐτοῖς (dat.pl.masc.of αὐτός, indirect object of ἀπήγγειλεν) 16.

ὅτι (recitative) 211.

ἰδοὺ (exclamation) 95.

οἱ (nom.pl.masc.of the article in agreement with ἄνδρες) 9.

ἄνδρες (nom.pl.masc.of ἀνήρ, subject of εἰσὶν) 63.

οὓς (acc.pl.masc.of ὅς, direct object of ἔθεσθε) 65.

ἔθεσθε (2d.per.pl.2d.aor.mid.ind.of τίθημι, indirect) 455.

ἐν (preposition with the locative of place where) 80.

τῇ (loc.sing.fem.of the article in agreement with φυλακῇ) 9.

φυλακῇ (loc.sing.fem.of φυλακή, place where) 494.

εἰσὶν (3d.per.pl.pres.ind.of εἰμί, perfect and present periphrastic) 86.

ἐν (preposition with the locative of place where) 80.

τῷ (loc.sing.neut.of the article in agreement with ἱερῷ) 9.

ἱερῷ (loc.sing.neut.of ἱερόν, place where) 346.

ἑστῶτες (perf.act.part.nom.pl.masc.of ἵστημι, perfect periphrastic) 180.

καὶ (adjunctive conjunction joining participles) 14.

διδάσκοντες (pres.act.part.nom.pl.masc.of διδάσκω, present periphrastic0 403.

τὸν (acc.sing.masc.of the article in agreement with λαόν) 9.

λαόν (acc.sing.masc.of λαός, direct object of διδάσκοντες) 110.

Translation - "And a certain man came by and announced to them, 'Look! The men whom you threw into jail have been standing in the temple and they are teaching the people.' "

Comment: The identity of the man who came to the court to report is not important. He was excited. "Look!" (ἰδού). We have an interesting example of εἰσιν with two participles, the one (ἑστῶτες) in the perfect to form a perfect periphrastic and the other (διδάσκοντες) in the present for a present periphrastic. The difference is that in the former we have a past completed action resulting in a present linear performance, while in the latter we have only a linear performance. The Apostles had taken their place in the temple as the angel had ordered them to do (verse 20) and when the crowds gathered they began to teach. Thus while the enemies of Christ were having their futile meeting, God's messengers were teaching His Word to the people.

One can well imagine the reaction of Annas, Caiaphas, the San Hedrin and the Senate upon hearing this announcement. So there was no doubt about the report of the police. The Apostles were not only out of jail, but they were back in the temple doing precisely what they had been ordered only yesterday never to do again. The captain of the temple is now ordered to serve the Apostles with a *subpoena ad testificandum,* but the court entered a *caveat* to the officer - "Bring them in here, but be diplomatic. Don't get rough with them. Do you want to get yourself stoned?!"

Verse 26 - "Then went the captain with the officers and brought them without violence: for they feared the people, lest they should have been stoned."

τότε ἀπελθὼν ὁ στρατηγὸς σὺν τοῖς ὑπηρέταις ἦγεν αὐτούς, οὐ μετὰ βίας, ἐφοβοῦντο γὰρ τὸν λαόν, μὴ λιθασθῶσιν.

τότε (continuative conjunction) 166.

ἀπελθὼν (aor.mid.part.nom.sing.masc.of ἀπέρχομαι, adverbial, temporal, direct, 239).

ὁ (nom.sing.masc.of the article in agreement with στρατηγὸς) 9.

στρατηγὸς (nom.sing.masc.of στρατηγός, subject of ἦγεν) 2754.

σὺν (preposition with the instrumental of association) 1542.

τοῖς (instru.pl.masc.of the article in agreement with ὑπηρέταις) 9.

ὑπηρέταις (instru.pl.masc.of ὑπηρέτης, accompaniment) 493.

ἦγεν (3d.per.sing.2d.aor.act.ind.of ἄγω, ingressive) 876.

αὐτούς (acc.pl.masc.of αὐτός, direct object of ἦγεν) 16.

οὐ (summary negative conjunction with the indicative) 130.

μετὰ (preposition with the ablative of manner) 50.

#3063 βίας (abl.sing.fem.of βία, manner).

violence - Acts 5:26; 21:35; 27:41.

Meaning: - Strength, whether physical or mental. In the New Testament contexts physical force is always in view. Physical coercion by the police - Acts 5:26; with reference to the crush of a large crowd - Acts 21:35; of the violence of the waves of the sea - Acts 27:41.

ἐφοβοῦντο (3d.per.pl.imp.mid.ind.of φοβέομαι, progressive description) 101.
γάρ (causal conjunction) 105.
τόν (acc.sing.masc.of the article in agreement with λαόν) 9.
λαόν (acc.sing.masc.of λαός, direct object of ἐφοβοῦντο) 110.
μή (qualified negative conjunction with the subjunctive in an object clause, the object of ἐφοβοῦντο) 87.
λιθασθῶσιν (3d.per.pl.aor.pass.subj.of λιθάζω, object of ἐφοβοῦντο) 2377.

Translation - *"Then the captain went away with the officers and began to try to bring them in, but without violence, because they were afraid that they should be stoned by the people."*

Comment: I have taken ἤγεν here as ingressive, to show how gingerly the police approached the Apostles in the temple. They did indeed bring them in, - a fact that is shown by the constative use ἤγεν, but they did so only after they began (ingressive) to make the effort, without knowing whether it would succeed or not. The police were under orders from the court not to use force. Thus if the Apostles had refused to go with them peacefully they would have returned without them. One can imagine the scene. Eleven Apostles are standing in the temple, each with an audience. The people have gathered about them. They are asking questions. The Apostles are witnessing - preaching the gospel, telling what they know about Jesus, explaining what it all means, relating prophecies of the Old Testament to facts in the life of Jesus, admonishing the people to repent and believe. The crowds of people are fascinated, not only by their miracles which the Apostles have performed, but also by the lilt of their voices, the expressions on their faces and their dynamic gestures. These are uneducated Galileans, but they have something vital to say and they hold their audiences like Demosthenes. The captain of the temple and his squad of police approach timorously. As they elbow their way through the crowd to approach their prey they are greeted with scowls and muttered imprecations from the people, who understand perfectly why the police are there. The captain speaks to Peter or John or to one of the others, as soon as he is able to get in a word, "Pardon me, Sir. I apologize for the interruption, but would you mind too much if I ask you to come with us?" Let us suppose that the Apostles had said, "No!" In that case the police would have been forced to submit and retire with whatever grace they could muster, with the taunts of the audience ringing in their ears. "Get lost, flatfoot. Hit the road!" So the captain brought the Apostles in, but only because when he tried to do so they were quite willing to cooperate.

Why should they not? If they were ordered again to discontinue their preaching, they would refuse. If they were thrown into jail, there was always an angel ready to set them free. If they were beaten, it was an occasion for joy that they were accounted worthy to suffer shame for His name. If they were killed a martyr's crown awaited them at the judgment seat of Christ (2 Cor.5:10). Besides if they went with the police back to the court they would have another opportunity to preach the gospel to a most distinguished audience - the high priest, the San Hedrin and the Senate. What do you do with people like that? Obviously the wisest thing to do is to let them talk, as Gamaliel was soon to suggest (verse 34). It is a sad indication of human stupidity that it took the human race 1700 years of wandering through the jungles of bigotry before someone finally wrote down the concept of freedom of speech in a constitution, and even then it was an afterthought to correct an unfortunate oversight. But Gamaliel understood our first amendment freedoms and enunciated them to a court that was planning public assassination.

τὸν λαόν is proleptic, ". . . τὸν λαόν denoting the persons feared, and μὴ λιθασθῶσιν the thing feared (cf.the familiar idiom with οἶδα illustrated in Mark 1:24; see also Gal.4:11), so that the meaning would be expressed in English by translating, *for they were afraid that they should be stoned by the people;* or ἐφοβοῦντο . . . λαόν may be taken as parenthetical, and μὴ λιθασθῶσιν made to limit ἦγεν αὐτούς, οὐ μετὰ βίας." (Burton, *New Testament Moods and Tenses*, 95,96).

We have here a dramatic demonstration of the power of the gospel of Christ upon public opinion. Not long before the same Jewish authorities who are now cowering in abject fear before the menacing growl of a mob with stones in their hands, had incited that same mob to threaten a Roman Governor with death if he did not crucify the Man Whom they now worshipped. Why had the public changed sides in this struggle?   They had not forgotten that the Jewish Establishment murdered Jesus. But they also remembered that God raised Him from the dead. And how did they know this? They did not see Jesus after His resurrection. They knew it because the Apostles witnessed to the fact, with a boldness and clarity, born of the filling of the Holy Spirit, that dared the police to do their worst, even if it meant their death. If the 20th century church ever again preaches the gospel of Christ with the power of the Apostolic church, the public again will accept Christ on the terms of His gospel.

Verse 27 - "And when they had brought them, they set them before the council: and the high priest asked them, . . . "

Ἀγαγόντες δὲ αὐτοὺς ἔστησαν ἐν τῷ συνεδρίῳ, καὶ ἐπηρώτησεν αὐτους ὁ ἀρχιερεὺς . . .

Ἀγαγόντες (aor.act.part.nom.pl.masc.of ἄγω, adverbial, temporal) 876.
δὲ (continuative conjunction) 11.
αὐτοὺς (acc.pl.masc.of αὐτός, direct object of ἀγαγόντες and ἔστησαν) 16.
ἔστησαν (3d.per.pl.aor.act.ind.of ἵστημι, constative) 180.
ἐν (preposition with the locative of place where) 80.
τῷ (loc.sing.neut.of the article in agreement with συνεδρίῳ) 9.
συνεδρίῳ (loc.sing.neut.of συνέδριον, place where) 481.
καὶ (continuative conjunction) 14.
ἐπηρώτησεν (3d.per.sing.aor.act.ind.of ἐπερωτάω, constative) 973.

αὐτοὺς (acc.pl.masc.of αὐτός, direct object of ἐπηρώτησεν) 16.
ὁ (nom.sing.masc.of the article in agreement with ἀρχιερεύς) 9.
ἀρχιερεύς (nom.sing.masc.of ἀρχιερεύς, subject of ἐπηρώτησεν) 151.

Translation - "And they brought them and stood them before the San Hedrin. And the high priest asked them, . . . "

Comment: The high priest asked a question totally different from what we would expect. The first question that a normal person would have asked was, "How did you get out of jail?" But he did not ask it because he did not want to know. He was afraid to find out. Had Caiaphas asked it, Peter probably would have said, "If we told you you wouldn't believe it." But Caiaphas was confused - very confused. All that he could think to ask was a rhetorical question the answer to which was already well known to all of them.

Verse 28 - ". . . saying, Did not we straitly command you that ye should not teach in this name? and, behold, ye have filled Jerusalem with your doctrine, and intend to bring this man's blood upon us."

λέγων, Παραγγελίᾳ παρηγγείλαμεν ὑμῖν μὴ διδάσκειν ἐπὶ τῷ ὀνόματι τούτῳ, καὶ ἰδοὺ πεπληρώκατε τὴν Ἰερουσαλὴμ τῆς διδαχῆς ὑμῶν, καὶ βούλεσθε ἐπαγαγεῖν ἐφ' ἡμᾶς τὸ αἷμα τοῦ ἀνθρώπου τούτου.

λέγων (pres.act.part.nom.sing.masc.of λέγω, recitative) 66.

#3064 παραγγελίᾳ (instrumental sing. fem.of παραγελία, cognate instrumental).

charge - Acts 16:24; 1 Tim.1:18.
commandment - 1 Thess.4:2; 1 Tim.1:5.
straitly - Acts 5:28.

*Meaning: Cf.*παραγγέλλω (#855). An order, commandment, charge to do or not to do something. To the Apostles not to preach in a cognate instrumental - Acts 5:28; to the Philippian jailor to secure Paul and Silas - Acts 16:24; with reference to the commission to preach the Word of God - 1 Tim.1:5,18. With reference to Paul's message to the Thessalonians - 1 Thess.4:2.

παρηγγείλαμεν (1st.per.pl.aor.act.ind.of παραγγέλλω, rhetorical question. *Cf.* comment *infra*).
ὑμῖν (dat.pl.masc.of σύ, indirect object of παρηγγείλαμεν) 104.
μὴ (qualified negative conjunction with the infinitive) 87.
διδάσκειν (pres.act.inf.of διδάσκω, object of παρηγγείλαμεν) 403.
ἐπὶ (preposition with the locative of sphere) 47.
τῷ (loc.sing.neut.of the article in agreement with ὀνόματι) 9.
ὀνόματι (loc.sing.neut.of ὄνομα, sphere) 108.
τούτῳ (loc.sing.neut.of οὗτος, in agreement with ὀνόματι) 93.
καὶ (adversative conjunction) 14.
ἰδοὺ (exclamation) 95.

πεπληρώκατε (2d.per.pl.perf.act.ind.of πληρόω, intensive) 115.

τὴν (acc.sing.fem.of the article in agreement with Ἱερουσαλήμ) 9.

Ἱερουσαλήμ (acc.sing.fem.of Ἱερουσαλήμ, direct object of πεπληρώκατε) 141.

τῆς (gen.sing.fem.of the article in agreement with διδαχῆς) 9.

διδαχῆς (gen.sing.fem.of διδαχή, description) 706.

ὑμῶν (gen.pl.masc.of σύ, possession) 104.

καὶ (adjunctive conjunction joining verbs) 14.

βούλεσθε (2d.per.pl.pres.mid.ind.of βούλομαι, aoristic) 953.

#3065 ἐπαγαγεῖν (aor.act.inf.of ἀπάγω, epexegetical).

bring in upon - 2 Peter 2:5.
bring upon - Acts 5:28; 2 Peter 2:1.

Meaning: A combination of ἐπί (#47) and ἄγω (#876). Hence, to bring upon; to cause some result to be imposed upon someone or something. To induce. Followed by a double accusative - the blood of Christ upon the San Hedrin, *i.e.* to make the Jews morally responsible for the death of Christ - Acts 5:28. Followed by a dative of indirect object and an accusative of direct object - false teachers bring upon themselves swift retribution - 2 Peter 2:1. Noah's preaching brought a flood (accusative) upon the world (dative of personal disadvantage) - 2 Peter 2:5.

ἐφ' (preposition with the accusative of extent, metaphorical) 47.

ἡμᾶς (acc.pl.masc.of ἐγώ, extent, metaphorical) 123.

τὸ (acc.sing.neut.of the article in agreement with αἷμα) 9.

αἷμα (acc.sing.neut.of αἷμα, direct object of ἐπαγαγεῖν) 1203.

τοῦ (gen.sing.masc.of the article in agreement with ἀνθρώπου) 9.

ἀνθρώπου (gen.sing.masc.of ἄνθρωπος, possession) 341.

τούτου (gen.sing.masc.of οὗτος, contemptuous use, in agreement with ἀνθρώπου) 93.

Translation - "... saying, 'Did we not strictly order you not to teach in this name? But, Look! You have filled the (city of) Jerusalem with your teaching and you are planning to bring upon us the blood of this fellow.' "

Comment: There is controversy with reference to the presence or absence of Οὐ before παραγγελίᾳ. Metzger's personal opinion is that it does not belong. In a personal note, following the report of the decision of the United Bible Societies' Committee, he says, "From the standpoint of transcriptional probability, it appears that οὐ is a scribal addition, occasioned by the influence of the verb ἐπηρώτησεν in ver.27 (compare 4.17). For this reason, as well as the strong combination of p74 Sinaiticus * A B itd,gig vg copsa ms,bo geo Lucifer *al*, the word should be omitted from the text. B.M.M." (Metzger, *Textual Commentary*, 331).

"A majority of the Committee interpreted the absence of οὐ from several witnesses as due to their copyist's desire to transform thereby the high priest's question into a rebuke. In view, however, of the weight of the external evidence supporting the shorter reading, it was decided to print οὐ within square brackets." (*Ibid.*).

If οὐ belongs in the text we have rhetorical question. If not we have a statement. Why should Luke have used ἐπηρώτησεν is verse 27 if the high priest made a statement? "The high priest *asked* them saying, ' . . . κ.τ.λ." If οὐ does not belong in the text Luke should have written, "The high priest *said* to them. . . κ.τ.λ." The interpretation of the passage is not affected by the resolution of this question. In either case, the high priest pointed out, whether by statement or by rhetorical question, that the Apostles had been ordered before not to teach in Jesus' name. The text does not tell us how the Apostles reponded to Caiaphas, whether he put it in the form of a question or not. Rhetorical question is only an emphatic way of making a statement. We can be sure that the Apostles at this point were not overcome with fear or awe in the court's presence, and they may have been so confident as to manifest a lack of respect for the court. It would have been highly amusing if in response to his question, "Did we not forbid you to speak again in Jesus' name?", Peter or James and John, who were noted for their belligerence (Mk.3:17) had responded, "That is correct, Rabbi Smell Fungus. That is what you told us. Now just what do you intend to do about it?" What could he do? There wasn't a jail in Jerusalem that could hold them, what with the lordly angel on the loose with his key of liberation. If they killed them they would only secure for them a special reward in heaven, and there were still thousands of others to carry on the work of Christ and His church.

It is interesting that Caiaphas used the same word for *fill* that is used for the filling of the Holy Spirit. Because the Christians were filled with the Holy Spirit (πληρόω, Acts 2:2; 4:31) they had filled Jerusalem with their teaching (Acts 5:28). The Apostles had spread the gospel until everyone in Jerusalem had heard it. Then the priest plumbed the depths of depravity from the bottom of his rotten heart when he added, like a whimpering child, "You are plotting to bring upon us the blood of this fellow." Note the contemptuous use of τούτου. What if they did? It would be nothing more than they had asked for as they stood before Pilate and cried, "Let His blood be on us and on our children." (Mt.27:25). Now Caiaphas was pouting as though he had had nothing to do with the crucifixion of Jesus. Thus politicians disclaim personal responsibility for past blunders. Statesmen who make mistakes admit it and try not to make them again. Politicians never admit past sins.

But there is a sense in which Caiaphas' statement was true, though not in the sense in which he meant it. The Apostles would have been very happy to bring upon the Jews the blood of the Son of God as it was shed in redemptive payment for their sins. The blood of Christ spoke better things than the blood of Abel (Heb.12:24) which had cried out from the ground to God for vengeance (Gen.4:10). Jesus' blood cried out to God, not for vengeance. This was Caiaphas' idea. It cried out from the ground at the foot of the cross and from the mercy seat in heaven to God for forgiveness. And if Caiaphas had been called by the Holy

Spirit he could have been forgiven just as were the Roman soldiers who nailed Him to a cross. (Lk.23:34).

Verse 29 - "Then Peter and the other apostles answered and said, We ought to obey God rather than men."

ἀποκριθεὶς δὲ Πέτρος καὶ οἱ ἀπόστολοι εἶπαν, Πειθαρχεῖν δεῖ θεῷ μᾶλλον ἢ ἀνθρώποις.

ἀποκριθεὶς (aor.mid.part.nom.sing.masc.of ἀποκρίνομαι, constative) 318.
δὲ (adversative conjunction) 11.
Πέτρος (nom.sing.masc.of Πέτρος, subject of εἶπαν) 387.
καὶ (adjunctive conjunction joining nouns) 14.
οἱ (nom.pl.masc.of the article in agreement with ἀπόστολοι) 9.
ἀπόστολοι (nom.pl.masc.of ἀπόστολος, subject of εἶπαν) 844.
εἶπαν (3d.per.pl.aor.act.ind.of εἶπον, constative) 144.

#3066 πειθαρχεῖν (pres.act.inf.of πειθαρχέω, epexegetical).

hearken - Acts 27:21.
obey - Acts 5:29,32.
obey a magistrate - Titus 3:1.

Meaning: A combination of πείθω (#1629) and ἀρχή (#1285). Hence, to be persuaded to follow a ruler; to obey. To obey God - Acts 5:29,32; to follow Paul's suggestion about navigation of a ship - Acts 27:21; to obey public law officials - Titus 3:1.

δεῖ (3d.per.sing.pres.ind.of δέω, customary) 1207.
θεῷ (dat.sing.masc.of θεός, dative of person) 124.
μᾶλλον (comparative adverb) 619.
ἢ (disjunctive particle) 465.
ἀνθρώποις (dat.pl.masc.of ἄνθρωπος, dative of person) 341.

Translation - "But Peter and the Apostles said, 'It is necessary that we obey God rather than men.' "

Comment: δεῖ here in the moral necessity of the case. (#1207, (I) (f). There should have been no argument in that Jewish court that obedience to God takes precedence over obedience to man. The Apostles were about to declare that the court was on the wrong side of a moral question, something which was far from Caiaphas' mind. Christians, placed in this dilemma must always answer as the Apostles did. Magistrates who expect obedience must issue only orders in keeping with the will of God. The days will come again, as they often have in the past, when Christians will be faced with this dilemma. When that time comes, our course will be clear. All the court got from the Apotles was anothing sermon, with the same theme - Jesus' life, death, Jewish guilt and the resurrection.

Verse 30 - "The God of our fathers raised up Jesus, whom ye slew and hanged on a tree.

ὁ θεὸς τῶν πατέρων ἡμῶν ἤγειρεν Ἰησοῦν, ὃν ὑμεῖς διεχειρίσασθε κρεμάσαντες ἐπὶ ξύλον.

ὁ (nom.sing.masc.of the article in agreement with θεὸς) 9.
θεὸς (nom.sing.masc.of θεός, subject of ἤγειρεν) 124.
τῶν (gen.pl.masc.of the article in agreement with πατέρων) 9.
πατέρων (gen.pl.masc.of πατήρ, relationship) 238.
ἡμῶν (gen.pl.masc.of ἐγώ, relationship) 123.
ἤγειρεν (3d.per.sing.aor.act.ind.of ἐγείρω, culminative) 125.
Ἰησοῦν (acc.sing.masc.of Ἰησοῦς, direct object of ἤγειρεν) 3.
ὃν (acc.sing.masc.of ὅς, direct object of διεχειρίσασθε) 65.

#3067 διεχιερίσασθε (2d.per.pl.aor.mid.ind.of διαχειρίζομαι, indirect, constative).

kill - Acts 26:21.
slay - Acts 5:30.

Meaning: A combination of διά (#118) and χειρίζω - "to take in hand" The preposition διά is perfective; hence to take in hand thoroughly. To dominate. In the New Testament, to kill - With reference to Jesus - Acts 5:30; with reference to Paul - Acts 26:21.

κρεμάσαντες (aor.act.part.nom.pl.masc.of κρεμάννομι, adverbial, modal) 1249.
ἐπὶ (preposition with the genitive of place description) 47.
ξύλου (gen.sing.neut.of ξύλος, place description) 1590.

Translation - "The God of our father raised up Jesus, Whom you killed by hanging Him upon a cross."

Comment: Note our translation of ξύλου as something that had been sawn, shaped and planed. *Cf.*#1590. The New Testament nowhere uses δένδρον (#294) - "a living tree" - with reference to the stake upon which Jesus died. *Cf.* also σταυρός (#899). There is no clear evidence in the New Testament that the stake was also in the shape of a cross, but ξύλος indicates that it had undergone some change at the hands of a carpenter. Note the indirect middle in διεχιερίσασθε. - "You took Him into your hands for your own benefit." This is precisely correct. *Cf.* John 11:47-53. Jesus' death was planned with deliberation by the San Hedrin for the express benefit of the nation, *viz.,* in order to avoid a public riot and the possible intervention of the Romans who might have taken away the jurisdictional authority of the Jewish court in the areas where it still existed. Note that Peter again openly accused the Jews of murdering Jesus, as he had done on every other occasion (Acts 2:23; 3:13-15; 4:10). And in each case he immediately followed his accusation that they had killed Him with his statement that God had raised Him from the dead.

Verse 31 - "Him hath God exalted with his right hand to be a Prince and a

Saviour for to give repentance to Israel, and forgiveness of sins."

τοῦτον ὁ θεὸς ἀρχηγὸν καὶ σωτῆρα ὕφωσεν τῇ δεξιᾷ αὐτοῦ, δοῦναι
μετάνοιαν τῷ Ἰσραὴλ καὶ ἄφεσιν ἁμαρτιῶν.

τοῦτον (acc.sing.masc.of οὗτος, direct object of ὕφωσεν) 93.
ὁ (nom.sing.masc.of the article in agreement with θεὸς) 9.
θεὸς (nom.sing.masc.of θεός, subject of ὕφωσεν) 124.
ἀρχηγὸν (acc.sing.masc.of ἀρχηγός, predicate accustive) 3013.
καὶ (adjunctive conjunction joining nouns) 14.
σωτῆρα (acc.sing.masc.of σωτήρ, predicate accusative) 1824.
ὕφωσεν (3d.per.sing.aor.act.ind.of ὑφόω, culminative) 946.
τῇ (loc.sing.fem.of the article in agreement with δεξιᾷ) 9.
δεξιᾷ (loc.sing.fem.of δεξιός, place where) 502.
αὐτοῦ (gen.sing.masc.of αὐτός, possession) 16.
δοῦναι (aor.act.inf.of δίδωμι, purpose) 362.
μετάνοιαν (acc.sing.fem.of μετάνοια, direct object of δοῦναι) 286.
τῷ (dat.sing.masc.of the article in agreement with Ἰσραήλ) 9.
Ἰσραὴλ (dat.sing.masc.of Ἰσραήλ, indirect object of δοῦναι) 165.
καὶ (adjunctive conjunction joining nouns) 14.
ἄφεσιν (acc.sing.fem.of ἄφεσις, direct object of δοῦναι) 1576.
ἁμαρτιῶν (gen.pl.fem.of ἁμαρτία, description) 111.

*Translation - "God has lifted this Man up to His right hand, as a Pioneer and a
Saviour, to give to Israel repentance and forgiveness of sins."*

Comment: τοῦτον is in the position of emphasis, pointing back to Ἰησοῦν in
verse 30, where He was the victim of a murder. Thus Peter focused again on the
contrast between Israel's evaluation of Jesus and that of God. *Cf.*Acts 3:14,15
where we have the same contrast. "You killed Him but God raised Him up.
Cf.#946 for the play on the word ὑφόω. In John 3:14b; 8:28; 12:32,34, it is used of
the crucifixion of Jesus, whereas in Acts 2:33; 5:31 it is used of His resurrection.
Israel lifted Jesus up to die. God lifted Him up to live. Why? The purpose of the
resurrection and ascension of Jesus is that He may give repentance and the
forgiveness of sins to Israel. Exalted to the Father's right hand, He is both
ἀρχηγός and σωτήρ. Study #3013 again for the full meaning of ἀρχηγός - "an
Originator and a Deliverer" of life (Acts 3;15), salvation (Heb.2:10) and faith
(Heb.12:2). Since life, salvation and faith can originate only in Him and in no
other, and since He alone can deliver these valuable possessions, He is indeed the
only Saviour. Peter had emphasized this in Acts 4:12. Although Peter charges
Israel again with the death of Christ, he hastens to assure them that God's plan of
redemption is greater than their hatred and that God is willing to grant
repentance and faith to the nation with the blood of the Son of God upon her
hands. But their forgiveness is contingent upon a change in their thinking
(*Cf.*#286).

Verse 32 - "And we are his witnesses of these things; and so is also the Holy

Ghost, whom God hath given to them that obey him."

καὶ ἡμεῖς ἐσμεν μάρτυρες τῶν ῥημάτων τούτων, καὶ τὸ πνεῦμα τὸ ἅγιον ὃ
ἔδωκεν ὁ θεὸς τοῖς πειθαρχοῦσιν αὐτῷ.

καὶ (continuative conjunction) 14.

ἡμεῖς (nom.pl.masc.of ἐγώ, subject of ἐσμεν) 123.

ἐσμεν (1st.per.pl.pres.ind.of εἰμί, aoristic) 86.

μάρτυρες (nom.pl.masc.of μάρτυς, predicate nominative) 1263.

τῶν (gen.pl.neut.of the article in agreement with ῥημάτων) 9.

ῥημάτων (gen.pl.neut.of ῥῆμα, reference) 343.

τούτων (gen.pl.neut.of οὗτος, in agreement with ῥημάτων) 93.

καὶ (adjunctive conjunction joining substantives) 14.

τὸ (nom.sing.neut.of the article in agreement with πνεῦμα) 9.

πνεῦμα (nom.sing.neut.of πνεῦμα, subject of ἐσμεν) 83.

τὸ (nom.sing.neut.of the article in agreement with ἅγιον) 9.

ἅγιον (nom.sing.neut.of ἅγιος, in agreement with πνεῦμα) 84.

ὃ (acc.sing.neut.of ὅς, direct object of ἔδωκεν) 65.

ἔδωκεν (3d.per.sing.aor.act.ind.of δίδωμι, culminative) 362,

ὁ (nom.sing.masc.of the article in agreement with θεὸς) 9.

θεὸς (nom.sing.masc.of θεός, subject of ἔδωκεν) 124.

τοῖς (dat.pl.masc.of the article in agreement with πειθαρχοῦσιν) 9.

πειθαρχοῦσιν (pres.act.part.dat.pl.masc.of πειθαρχέω, substantival, indirect object of ἔδωκεν) 3066.

αὐτῷ (dat.sing.masc.of αὐτός, dative of personal advantage) 16.

Translation - "*And we and the Holy Spirit, Whom God has given to those who are obeying Him, are witnesses with reference to these words.*"

Comment: A double witness as to the truth of the words spoken is offered. Peter and the other Apostles were the human witnesses to the fact that Jesus was raised from the dead. So also was the Holy Spirit present to add His witness to the fact of the resurrection.

The human witness, even though true is ineffectual without the witness of the Holy Spirit. For the task of convincing the unsaved of the sin of rejecting Jesus, of convincing them that Jesus has gone back to the Father, which is why we see Him no more, and, thirdly, the task of convincing them that the prince of this world has been judged at the cross, is too great for the human witness. The preacher does not live who is eloquent, scholarly, sincere and convincing enough to bring the lost to Christ. That is the function of the Holy Spirit (John 16:7-11). No man can call Jesus his Lord without the movement of the Holy Spirit upon his will, his intellect and his emotions (1 Cor.12:3). The lost are held in the grip of Satan (Eph.2:1-3). The darkness of that bondage is too great to be dispelled by human wisdom alone, however attractively presented.

But although it is true that the human witness, without the witness of the Holy Spirit is ineffective, it is equally true that the Holy Spirit will not witness until the preacher does. "Faith comes by hearing, and hearing by the exposition of the

Word of God" (Rom.10:17). The sower who went forth to sow was a human being. It was God who performed the miracle of germination, growth and maturation (Mt.13:3-9). It was Paul who planted; it was Apollos who watered, but it was God who gave the increase (1 Cor.3:6-7). Paul added that neither he nor Apollos were anything, but he meant that they were nothing in comparison to God. If Paul and Apollos had not sown and watered the seed there would have been no increase. And if the Apostles had not witnessed to the resurrection of Jesus before the San Hedrin the Holy Spirit could not have witnessed either, since without the Apostles there would have been nothing to witness. This analysis is sufficient to answer the critics of Calvinism, who suffer from an overdose of Gnosticism (any Gnosticism is too much), when they say that if God has elected to save some He will do it with or without human cooperation. To be sure God has chosen to save the elect, but He has also ordained the manner in which they are to be effectually called by the Holy Spirit, and that is through the preaching of the Word of God.

There are many faithful preachers of the Word who witness as the Apostles did and do not see the results that they saw. This can be partially explained by the fact that the Holy Spirit is sometimes limited in His work because of known sin in the lives of believers, but it is not always God's will to reap a harvest. There must be a sowing and watering time. After Paul has sown the seed and Apollos has watered it, some other witness comes along, and it is under his ministry that God gives the increase. It is well for preachers who do not see converts streaming down the aisles at the close of every sermon to remember that God did not say, "Well done thou good and successful servant."

Verse 33 - "When they heard that they were cut to the heart, and took counsel to slay them."

Οἱ δὲ ἀκούσαντες διεπρίοντο καὶ ἐβουλεύοντο ἀνελεῖν αὐτούς.

Οἱ (nom.pl.masc.of the article, subject of διεπρίοντο and ἐβουλεύοντο) 9.
δὲ (continuative conjunction) 11.
ἀκούσαντες (aor.act.part.nom.pl.masc.of ἀκούω, adverbial, temporal/ causal) 148.

#3068 διεπρίοντο (3d.per.pl.imp.pass.ind.of διαπρίομαι).

be cut - Acts 5:33; 7:54.

Meaning: A combination of διά (#118) and πρίω - "to saw into pieces; to cut." Hence to cut asunder. In the psychological sense in Acts 5:33 in reaction to Peter's message. In reaction to the message of Stephen - Acts 7:54.

καὶ (adjunctive conjunction joining verbs) 14.
ἐβουλεύοντο (3d.per.pl.imp.mid.ind.of βουλεύομαι, indirect, inceptive) 90.
ἀνελεῖν (2d.aor.act.inf.of ἀναιρῶ, epexegetical) 216.
αὐτούς (acc.pl.masc.of αὐτός, direct object of ἀνελεῖν) 16.

Translation - *"And when they heard they became enraged and began to plot to kill them."*

Comment: διαπρίζω equals διαπρίω (#3068). The word means "to saw into two pieces" and is applied in a variety of contexts, both physical and psychological. In Luc.*Cal.*24 (Liddell & Scott, 409) we have δ. τοὺς ὀδόντας - "to gnash the teeth," in much the same sense in which it is used here. In Acts 2:37 sinners were "pricked in the heart" and repented. The word there is κατανύσσω (#2999). Both verbs in their respective contexts indicate psychological distress, the former however led to repentance, while the latter brought insane rage. Goodspeed's "furious" is well chosen, although he misses the inchoative force of the imperfect. Caiaphas and his colleagues were seized with an insane rage that led them without further analysis of their feelings to a policy which was totally irrational, as one of them, perhaps the only exception to the rule, was soon to point out.

Caiaphas and his court had a great deal at stake.. They were the political leaders of the nation, with a great deal of jurisdictional liberty under the Romans, so long as they were able to maintain a reasonable degree of social and political stability. If things got out of hand, the Romans would come (or so they thought) and take away their jurisdiction (John 11:48) and they would be forced to make an honest living! All that they had stood for had been challenged by Jesus. They had killed Him, but now they realize that they have not got rid of Him. *Au contraire*, even as He had predicted, His disciples were now doing works greater than His (John 14:12). Once there was only Jesus, with His revolutionary preaching and His fantastic miracles. Now there were thousands of Christians, in each of whom the resurrected Christ dwelt (1 Cor.6:19,20), and they were all filled with the Holy Spirit. Eleven of them were apparently empowered to perform the same miracles that Jesus had performed. Thus the problem that faced the court was thousands of times greater now than before. It is scant wonder, therefore, that the San Hedrin was upset — so upset in fact that they assumed that the way to stop Christianity was to kill Christians! There were three choices before them. (1) They could repent, admit their guilt, confess Christ and be saved, in keeping with the slogan, "If you can't lick 'em, join 'em." or (2) they could die and go to hell — a choice that they looked upon with scant favor, or (3) they could stamp out Christianity and prove that it was false. The success of this policy, of course would depend upon the fundamental point of disagreement between the Apostles and the court. Was Christianity the truth or not? What evidence did the Apostles have? They had seen Jesus dead on a cross. Later they saw Him alive. He invited them to examine the scars in His body. He ate in their presence. They saw Him periodically for the next forty days. More than 500 could testify to that effect. What evidence did Caiaphas have that Jesus was only a misguided Galilean carpenter and that if the Christians could be liquidated the movement would soon be forgotten? He had no evidence at all, and that is probably why he was so insanely angry. The thought of being hoisted upon his own petard was maddening. Note that the apostolic message and the witness of the Holy Spirit had no reaction upon these men except to drive them further into the pit. They knew only how to kill (John 5:44). The same sun that melts wax hardens clay. And yet the difference in the reaction of those who were saved and those who were lost was not in them, but in the sovereign will of God (2 Cor.2:14-17). The Gnostics will demand an explanation for this outrageous Calvinism, but only another misguided Gnostic would attempt to give it.

> *Who can explain it? Who can tell you why?*
> *Fools give you reasons; wise men never try.*

South Pacific

Verse 34 - "Then stood there up one in the council, a Pharisee, named Gamaliel, a doctor of the law, had in reputation among all the people, and commanded to put the apostles forth a little space."

ἀναστὰς δέ τις ἐν τῷ συνεδρίῳ Φαρισαῖος ὀνόματι Γαμαλιήλ, νομοδιδάσκαλος τίμιος παντὶ τῷ λαῷ, ἐκέλευσεν ἔξω βραχὺ τοὺς ἀνθρώπους ποιῆσαι,

ἀναστὰς (aor.act.part.nom.sing.masc.of ἀνίστημι, adverbial, temporal) 789.
δέ (adversative conjunction) 11.
τις (nom.sing.masc.of τις, in agreement with Φαρισαῖος) 486.
ἐν (preposition with the locative of place where) 80.
τῷ (loc.sing.neut.of the article in agreement with συνεδρίῳ) 9.
συνεδρίῳ (loc.sing.neut.of συνέδριον, place where) 481.
Φαρισαῖος (nom.sing.masc.of φαρισαῖος, subject of ἐκέλευσεν) 276.
ὀνόματι (dat.sing.neut.of ὄνομα, reference) 108.

#3069 Γαμαλιήλ (nom.sing.masc.of Γαμαλιήλ, appellation).

Gamaliel - Acts 5:34; 22:3.

Meaning: A Pharisee, Doctor of Jewish Law, grandson of Hillel, Paul's law professor. He had great influence in the San Hedrin. A man of permanent renown among the Jews. Died in A.D. 52. - Acts 5:34; 22:3.

νομοδιδάσκαλος (nom.sing.masc.of νομοδιδάσκαλος, in apposition) 2078.

#3070 τίμιος (nom.sing.masc.of τίμιος, in agreement with Γαμαλιήλ).

dear - Acts 20:24.
had in reputation - Acts 5:3,4.
honorable - Heb.13:4.
precious - 1 Cor.3:12; James 5:7; 1 Peter 1:19; 2 Peter 1:4; Rev.17:4; 18:12,12,16; 21:11,19.
much more precious - 1 Peter 1:7.

Meaning: precious; highly valued; of a good reputation; renowned. With reference to Gamaliel - Acts 5:34; the value one places upon his life - Acts 20:24; in high repute as an institution - Heb.13:4. With reference to inanimate objects of great value - 1 Cor.3:12; James 5:7; Rev.17:4; 18:12a, 12b (superlative degree),16; 21:11,19. Of the trial of the Christian faith (comparative degree) 1

Peter 1:7. Of the promises in God's Word - 2 Peter 1:4.

παντὶ (loc.sing.masc.of πᾶς, in agreement with λαῷ) 67.
τῷ (loc.sing.masc.of the article in agreement with λαῷ) 9.
λαῷ (loc.sing.masc.of λαός, place where, with persons) 110.
ἐκέλευσεν (3d.per.sing.aor.act.ind.of κελεύω, constative) 741.
ἔξω (adverbial) 449.
βραχὺ (acc.sing.neut.of βραχύς, adverbial) 2274.
τοὺς (acc.pl.masc.of the article in agreement with ἀνθρώπους) 9.
ἀνθρώπους (acc.pl.masc.of ἄνθρωπος, direct object of ποιῆσαι) 341.
ποιῆσαι (aor.act.inf.of ποιέω, epexegetical) 127.

Translation - "But a certain Pharisee, named Gamaliel, a law professor of great reputation among all the people stood up and demanded that the men be put outside for a short time."

Comment: δὲ is adversative. The San Hedrin wanted to plot the death of the Apostles, but Gamaliel had other ideas. He was a prominent scholar in the field of Jewish jurisprudence, the grandson of the famous Hillel, and the mentor of Saul of Tarsus, a fact of which student was justifiably proud (Acts 22:3). His word was heeded.

Verse 35 - "And said unto them, Ye men of Israel, take heed to yourselves what ye intend to do as touching these men."

εἶπέν τε πρὸς αὐτούς, Ἄνδρες Ἰσραηλῖται, προσέχετε ἑαυτοῖς ἐπὶ τοῖς ἀνθρώποις τούτοις τί μέλλετε πράσσειν.

εἶπέν (3d.per.sing.aor.act.ind.of εἶπον, constative) 155.
τε (continuative conjunction) 1408.
πρὸς (preposition with the accusative of extent, after a verb of speaking) 197.
αὐτούς (acc.pl.masc.of αὐτός, extent, after a verb of speaking) 16.
Ἄνδρες (voc.pl.masc.of ἀνήρ, address) 63.
Ἰσραηλῖται (voc.pl.masc.of Ἰσραηλίτης, in agreement with Ἄνδρες) 1967.
προσέχετε (2d.per.pl.pres.act.impv.of προσέχω, entreaty) 555.
ἑαυτοῖς (dat.pl.masc.of ἑαυτός, reference) 288.
ἐπὶ (preposition with the dative of reference) 47.
τοῖς (dat.pl.masc.of the article in agreement with ἀνθρώποις) 9.
ἀνθρώποις (dat.pl.masc.of ἄνθρωπος, reference) 341.
τούτοις (dat.pl.masc.of οὗτος, in agreement with ἀνθρώποις) 93.
τί (acc.sing.neut.of τίς, general reference) 281.
μέλλετε (2d.per.pl.pres.act.ind.of μέλλω, aoristic) 206.
πράσσειν (pres.act.inf.of πράσσω, epexegetical) 1943.

Translation - "And he said to them, 'Men of Israel, think carefully about what you are planning to do with reference to these men. . . .

Comment: ἐπί with the dative of reference is an unusual usage. Gamaliel followed his warning to the San Hedrin against precipitate action with two examples from Israel's history in verses 36 and 37.

Verse 36 - "For before these days rose up Theudas, boasting himself to be somebody; to whom a number of men, about four hundred, joined themselves: who was slain, and all as many as obeyed him, were scattered, and brought to nought."

πρὸ γὰρ τούτων τῶν ἡμερῶν ἀνέστη Θευδᾶς, λέγων εἶναί τινα ἑαυτόν, ᾧ προσεκλίθη ἀνδρῶν ἀριθμὸς ὡς τετρακοσίων, ὃς ἀνῃρέθη, καὶ πάντες ὅσοι ἐπείθοντο αὐτῷ διελύθησαν καὶ ἐγένοντο εἰς οὐδέν.

πρὸ (preposition with the genitive of time description) 442.
γὰρ (causal conjunction) 105.
τούτων (gen.pl.fem.of οὗτος, in agreement with ἡμερῶν) 93.
τῶν (gen.pl.fem.of the article in agreement with ἡμερῶν) 9.
ἡμερῶν (gen.pl.fem.of ἡμέρα, time description) 135.
ἀνέστη (3d.per.sing.aor.act.ind.of ἀνίστημι, constative) 789.

#3071 Θευδᾶς (nom.sing.masc.of Θευδᾶς, subject of ἀνέστη).

Theudas - Acts 5:36.

Meaning: An imposter in Israel during the reign of Augustus - Acts 5:36.

λέγων (pres.act.part.nom.sing.masc.of λέγω, adverbial, modal) 66.
εἶναί (pres.inf.of εἰμί, in an object clause in indirect discourse) 86.
τινα (acc.sing.masc.of τις, predicate accusative, emphatic) 486.
ἑαυτόν (acc.sing.masc.of ἑαυτός, general reference) 288.
ᾧ (instrumental sing.masc.of ὅς, association) 65.

#3072 προσεκλίθη (3d.per.sing.aor.pass.ind.of προσκλίνω, constative).

join one's self - Acts 5:36.

Meaning: A combination of πρός (#197) and κλίνω (#746). Used intransitively, with a middle voice significance - to join oneself to another - Acts 5:36.

ἀνδρῶν (gen.pl.masc.of ἀνήρ, partitive genitive) 63.
ἀριθμὸς (nom.sing.masc.of ἀριθμός, subject of προσεκλίθη) 2278.
ὡς (particle in a comparative clause) 128.

#3073 τετρακοσίων (gen.pl.masc.of τετρακόσιοι, description).

four hundred - Acts 5:36; 7:6; 13:20; Gal.3:17.

Meaning: Four hundred. Men - Acts 5:36; years - Acts 7:6; 13:20; Gal.3:17.

ὃς (nom.sing.masc.of ὅς, subject of ἀνῃρέθη) 65.
ἀνῃρέθη (3d.per.sing.aor.pass.ind.of ἀναιρέω, constative) 216.
καὶ (continuative conjunction) 14.

πάντες (nom.pl.masc.of πᾶς, subject of διελύθησαν) 67.
ὅσοι (nom.pl.masc.of ὅσος, subject of ἐπείθοντο) 660.
ἐπείθοντο (3d.per.pl.imp.mid.ind.of πείθω, progressive description) 1629.
αὐτῷ (dat.sing.masc.of αὐτός, personal advantage) 16.

#3074 διελύθησαν (3d.per.pl.aor.pass.ind.of διαλύω, constative).

scatter - Acts 5:36.

Meaning: A combination of διά (#118) and λύω (#471). Hence, to loose or separate thoroughly. To scatter. Intensive διά. With reference to a band of men in an attempted *coup d'etat* - Acts 5:36.

καὶ (continuative conjunction) 14.
ἐγένοντο (3d.per.pl.aor.mid.ind.of γίνομαι, culminative) 113.
εἰς (preposition with the accusative of extent, metaphorical) 140.
οὐδέν (acc.sing.neut.of οὐδείς, metaphorical extent) 446.

Translation - "Because some time ago Theudas attempted a revolt, claiming that he was someone special, with whom a number of men, about four hundred, aligned themselves, who was killed and all who were following his orders were scattered, and it came to nothing."

Comment: Thus Gamaliel reminded the San Hedrin of an attempted *coup d'etat* of former days that was abortive. He cited another case in

Verse 37 - "After this man rose up Judas of Galilee in the days of the taxing, and drew many people after him: he also perished; and all, even as many as obeyed him were dispersed."

μετὰ τοῦτον ἀνέστη Ἰούδας ὁ Γαλιλαῖος ἐν ταῖς ἡμέραις τῆς ἀπογραφῆς καὶ ἀπέστησεν λαὸν ὀπίσω αὐτοῦ, κἀκεῖνος ἀπώλετο, καὶ πάντες ὅσοι ἐπείθοντο αὐτῷ διεσκορπίσθησαν.

μετὰ (preposition with the accusative of time extent) 50.
τοῦτον (acc.sing.neut.of οὗτος, time extent) 93.
ἀνέστη (3d.per.sing.aor.act.ind.of ἀνίστημι, constative) 789.

#3075 Ἰούδας (nom.sing.masc.of Ἰούδας, subject of ἀνέστη and ἀπέστησεν).

Judas - Acts 5:37.

Meaning: Judas, a Galilean who, at the time of the census of Quirinus staged a revolt in Galilee - Acts 5:37.

ὁ (nom.sing.masc.of the article in agreement with Γαλιλαῖος) 9.
Γαλιλαῖος (nom.sing.masc.of Γαλιλαῖος, in apposition) 2016.
ἐν (preposition with the locative of time point) 80.
ταῖς (loc.pl.fem.of the article in agreement with ἡμέραις) 9.
ἡμέραις (loc.pl.fem.of ἡμέρα, time point) 135.

τῆς (gen.sing.fem.of the article in agreement with ἀπογραφῆς) 9.

ἀπογραφῆς (gen.sing.fem.of ἀπογραφή, description) 1867.

καὶ (adjunctive conjunction joining verbs) 14.

ἀπέστησεν (3d.per.sing.aor.act.ind.of ἀφίστημι, ingressive) 1912.

λαὸν (acc.sing.masc.of λαός, direct object of ἀπέστησεν) 110.

ὀπίσω (improper preposition with the ablative of separation) 302.

αὐτοῦ (abl.sing.masc.of αὐτός, separation) 16.

κἀκεῖνος (nom.sing.masc.of κἀκεῖνος, subject of ἀπώλετο, crasis, adversative καί and ἐκεῖνος) 1164.

ἀπώλετο (3d.per.sing.2d.aor.mid.ind.of ἀπόλλυμι, constative) 208.

καὶ (continuative conjunction) 14.

πάντες (nom.pl.masc.of πᾶς, subject of διεσκορπισθήσαν) 67.

ὅσοι (nom.pl.masc.of ὅσος, subject of ἐπείθοντο) 660.

ἐπείθοντο (3d.per.pl.imp.mid.ind.of πείθω, progressive description) 1629.

αὐτῷ (instrumental sing.masc.of αὐτός, association) 16.

διεσκορπίσθησαν (3d.per.pl.aor.pass.ind.of διασκορπίζω, culminative) 1538.

Translation - *"After that Judas, the Galilean appeared at the time of the census, and he enlisted people to follow him, but he perished and all who were obeying him were dispersed."*

Comment: μετὰ τοῦτον in a temporal sense. *Cf.#50*. The stories of verses 36,37 are parallel. Both Theudas and Judas were demagogues who seduced some people to follow them in revolt. But both died, their followers were scattered and the revolutions failed. Gamaliel does not go on to predict that the Christian movement will fail. He does predict that events will determine whether or not Christianity is a system of truth. If it is not, it will fail. If it is, the attempt of the San Hedrin to stop it will be an exercise in futility.

Did William Cullen Bryant get his inspiration from Gamaliel, or did both the Jewish lawyer and the poet get it from Plato or some other friend of truth? *Cf. supra*, 222.

Verse 38 - *"And now I say unto you, Refrain from these men, and let them alone: for if this counsel or this work be of men, it will come to nought. . . "*

καὶ τὰ νῦν λέγω ὑμῖν, ἀπόστητε ἀπὸ τῶν ἀνθρώπων τούτων καὶ ἄφετε αὐτούς, ὅτι ἐὰν ᾖ ἐξ ἀνθρώπων ἡ βουλὴ αὕτη ἢ τὸ ἔργον τοῦτο, καταλυθήσεται, . . . "

καὶ (inferential conjunction) 14.

τὰ (acc.pl.neut.of the article, joined to νῦν) 9.

νῦν (adverbial) 1497.

λέγω (1st.per.sing.pres.act.ind.of λέγω, aoristic) 66.

ὑμῖν (dat.pl.masc.of σύ, indirect object of λέγω) 104.

ἀπόστητε (2d.per.pl.aor.act.impv.of ἀφίστημι, entreaty) 1912.

ἀπὸ (preposition with the ablative of separation) 70.

τῶν (abl.pl.masc.of the article in agreement with ἀνθρώπων) 9.

ἀνθρώπων (abl.pl.masc.of ἄνθρωπος, separation) 341.

τούτων (abl.pl.masc.of οὗτος, in agreement with ἀνθρώπων) 93.

καί (adjunctive conjunction joining verbs) 14.

ἄφετε (2d.per.pl.aor.act.impv.of ἀφίημι, entreaty) 319.

αὐτούς (acc.pl.masc.of αὐτός, direct object of ἄφετε) 16.

ὅτι (conjunction introducing a subordinate causal clause) 211.

ἐάν (conditional particle in a third-class condition) 363.

ᾖ (3d.per.sing.pres.subj.of εἰμί, third-class condition) 86.

ἐξ (preposition with the ablative of source) 19.

ἀνθρώπων (abl.pl.masc.of ἄνθρωπος, source) 341.

ἡ (nom.sing.fem.of the article in agreement with βουλή) 9.

βουλή (nom.sing.fem.of βουλή, subject of ᾖ) 2163.

ἤ (disjunctive particle) 465.

τό (nom.sing.neut.of the article in agreement with ἔργον) 9.

ἔργον (nom.sing.neut.of ἔργον, subject of ᾖ) 460.

τοῦτο (nom.sing.neut.of οὗτος, in agreement with ἔργον) 93.

καταλυθήσεται (3d.per.sing.fut.pass.ind.of καταλύω, predictive) 463.

Translation - *"So now I am telling you, 'Withdraw from these men and let them alone, because if this counsel or this work is of men, it will collapse.' "*

Comment: Note the article τά joined to the adverb νῦν to give substantival character to the temporal phrase. ἀπόστητε (#1912) means "to stand away from" whereas ἄφετε (#319) means "to be away from." Thus, though both are aorist, Gamaliel was saying, "Withdraw from and stay away from" as though ἄφετε were in the present tense. Gamaliel was advocating a complete *laissez faire* policy for the San Hedrin with reference to the Christian movement. Why should they? The ὅτι clauses are causal, the first (vs.38) is a third-class condition and the second (vs.39) is a first-class condition. It is interesting that Gamaliel introduced the element of doubt into the former, not the latter. He seems to have had some doubts that Christianity was merely a human scheme, like the efforts of Theudas and Judas. In verse 39 he assumes as true the statement of the premise. Did Gamaliel, with his superior grasp of Jewish law and the message of the Old Testament prophets, believe that the empirical evidence for Christianity as displayed in Jerusalem since Pentecost, was conclusive? Would he have counselled the same in the cases of Theudas and Judas? Robertson warns against the conclusion from this grammar that Gamaliel had become a Christian (Robertson, *Grammar*, 1018). And I agree. But he did give "the benefit of the doubt to Christianity. He assumes that Christianity is of God and puts the alternative that it is of men in the third class. . . . He was merely willing to score a point against the Sadducees." Gamaliel, a Pharisee, seemed gratified that the Christians were offering public testimony to the reality of the resurrection of the body, something that Pharisees believed and that Sadducees denied (Mt.22:23). At least we can say that Gamaliel was entertaining the idea that the Apostles might be correct.

Verse 39 - "But if it be of God, ye cannot overthrow it; lest haply ye be found even to fight against God."

εἰ δε ἐκ θεοῦ ἐστιν, οὐ δυνήσεσθε καταλῦσαι αὐτούς — μήποτε καὶ θεομάχοι εὑρεθῆτε. ἐπείσθησαν δὲ αὐτῷ,

εἰ (conditional particle in a first-class condition) 337.
δὲ (adversative conjunction) 11.
ἐκ (preposition with the ablative of source) 19.
θεοῦ (abl.sing.masc.of θεός, source) 124.
ἐστιν (3d.per.sing.pres.ind.of εἰμί, aoristic) 86.
οὐ (summary negative conjunction with the indicative) 130.
δυνήσεσθε (2d.per.pl.fut.mid.ind.of δύναμαι,] predictive) 289.
καταλῦσαι (aor.act.inf.of καταλύω, epexegetical) 463.
αὐτούς (acc.pl.masc.of αὐτός, direct object of καταλῦσαι) 16.
μήποτε (prohibitory conjunctive particle in a negative result clause) 351.
καὶ (ascensive conjunction) 14.

#3076 θεομάχοι (nom.pl.masc.of θεομάχος, predicate nominative).

to fight against God - Acts 5:39.

Meaning: A combination of θεός (#124) and μάχομαι (#2291). One who fights against God. With reference to the San Hedrin in Acts 5:39.

εὑρεθῆτε (2d.per.pl.aor.pass.subj.of εὑρίσκω, negative result) 79.
ἐπείσθησαν (3d.per.pl.aor.act.ind.of πείθω, constative) 1629.
δὲ (continuative conjunction) 11.
αὐτῷ (dat.sing.masc.of αὐτός, dative of person) 16.

Translation - "But if it is of God you will not be able to overthrow them — lest you be found to be fighting against God.' And they obeyed him."

Comment: The Greek text places ἐπείσθησαν δὲ αὐτῷ in verse 39, though the KJV has it in verse 40. Here Gamaliel puts his observation in a simple first-class condition. In neither of these conditional sentences is he dogmatizing about the premise, though in both he is dogmatic about the conclusion. However, he expresses some doubt (subjunctive mode) about his assumption in verse 38 and no doubt in verse 39. Thus Gamaliel implies that he is more inclined to believe that Christianity is genuine, than that it is of only human origin. Certainly if it is false, and of that he has some doubt - it will collapse as did the movements of Theudas and Judas (vss.36,37). Of that he has no doubt. But if it is genuine (and Gamaliel expressed no opinion, one way or the other), he is sure that the San Hedrin would not be able to stop it. As a matter of fact, in their position they would not wish to stop it, since their attempt to silence the Apostles would put them in a position as "God fighters." Gamaliel's logic was unassailable. The San Hedrin was persuaded and they obeyed him.

Verse 40 - "And to him they agreed: and when they had called the apostles, and beaten them, they commanded that they should not speak in the name of Jesus, and let them go."

καὶ προσκαλεσάμενοι τοὺς ἀποστόλους δείραντες παρήγγειλαν μὴ λαλεῖν ἐπὶ τῷ ὀνόματι τοῦ Ἰησοῦ καὶ ἀπέλυσαν.

καὶ (continuative conjunction) 14.
προσκαλεσάμενοι (aor.mid.part.nom.pl.masc.of προσκαλέω, adverbial, temporal) 842.
τοὺς (acc.pl.masc.of the article in agreement with ἀποστόλους) 9.
ἀποστόλους (acc.pl.masc.of ἀπόστολος, direct object of προσκαλεσάμενοι) 844.
δείραντες (aor.act.part.nom.pl.masc.of δέρο, adverbial, temporal) 1383.
παρήγγειλαν (3d.per.pl.aor.act.ind.of παραγγέλλω, constative) 855.
μὴ (qualified negative conjunction with the infinitive) 87.
λαλεῖν (pres.act.inf.of λαλέω, object of παρήγγειλαν, indirect discourse) 815.
τῷ (dat.sing.neut.of the article in agreement with ὀνόματι) 9.
ὀνόματι (dat.sing.neut.of ὄνομα, reference) 108.
τοῦ (gen.sing.masc.of the article in agreement with Ἰησοῦ) 9.
Ἰησοῦ (gen.sing.masc.of Ἰησοῦς, possession) 3.
καὶ (adjunctive conjunction joining verbs) 14.
ἀπέλυσαν (3d.per.pl.aor.act.ind.of ἀπολύω, constative) 92.

Translation - "And they called the Apostles back, beat them and ordered them not to speak with reference to the name of Jesus, and they let them go."

Comment: The San Hedrin did not obey Gamaliel completely. If they wanted to avoid being found in opposition to God, why did they order His servants flogged? It is worth noting that they did not tell the Apostles to stop talking about the resurrection, but they did order them to stop saying that Jesus had risen. Thus Gamaliel had carried his point against the Sadducees.

They rejected Gamaliel's advice in another way. If the work of God cannot be stopped, then the best policy is to let God's servant alone. Instead they flogged the Apostles and gave the order. Did they suppose that a fear of further punishment would stop their mouths? If so, they were quite mistaken as we see in

Verse 41 - "And they departed from the presence of the council, rejoicing that they were counted worthy to suffer shame for his name."

Οἱ μὲν οὖν ἐπορεύοντο χαίροντες ἀπὸ προσώπου τοῦ συνεδρίου ὅτι κατηξιώθησαν ὑπὲρ τοῦ ὀνόματος ἀτιμασθῆναι.

Οἱ (nom.pl.masc.of the article, subject of ἐπορεύοντο) 9.
μὲν (correlative affirmative particle) 300.
οὖν (resumptive conjunction) 68.
ἐπορεύοντο (3d.per.pl.imp.mid.ind.of πορεύομαι, progressive description) 170

χαίροντες (pres.act.part.nom.pl.masc.of χαίρω, adverbial, circumstantial) 182.

ἀπό (preposition with the ablative of separation) 70.

προσώπου (abl.sing.neut.of πρόσωπον, separation) 588.

τοῦ (gen.sing.neut.of the article in agreement with συνεδρίου) 9.

συνεδρίου (gen.sing.neut.of συνέδριον, description) 481.

ὅτι (conjunction introducing a subordinate causal clause) 211.

κατηξιώθησαν (3d.per.pl.aor.pass.ind.of καταξιόω, constative) 2698.

ὑπέρ (preposition with the ablative, "for the sake of") 545.

τοῦ (abl.sing.neut.of the article in agreement with ὀνόματος) 9.

ὀνόματος (abl.sing.neut.of ὄνομα, "for the sake of") 108.

ἀτιμασθῆναι (aor.pass.inf.of ἀτιμάζω, epexegetical) 2390.

Translation - "*And they went on their way from the presence of the San Hedrin rejoicing because they had been accounted worthy to suffer shame for the Name.*"

Comment: μέν is correlated with τε in verse 42. οὖν is resumptive. Note the force of the μέν . . . τε sequence. The Apostles were under orders from the court to desist from any further preaching and teaching in the name of Jesus. "And (μέν) they went out . . . and (τε) they did not cease to teach and preach. . . κ.τ.λ." The imperfect tense in ἐπορεύοντο is linear as is the present participle χαίροντες, showing simultaneity of action. They had just been beaten. How did they react? They went out the door rejoicing, not because of sore backs, but because they had had the opportunity to take some of the same punishment which Jesus had taken. Thus they identified with Him. Paul and Silas reacted to their beating in the same way (Acts 16:23-25). They were accounted worthy (Luke 20:35). "To be disgraced because of their connection with and for the sake of Jesus' name." The enemy had dishonored Jesus (John 8:49) and He had predicted that the world would also dishonor His disciples (John 15:18,19,23). Their rejoicing was in obedience to an earlier order from Jesus (Mt.5:12). James and Peter incorporated this thought into their writings (James 1:2; 1 Peter 4:12,13).

The utter futility of the effort of the San Hedrin to stop the Apostles from preaching is clear in

Verse 42 - "And daily in the temple and in every house, they ceased not to teach and preach Jesus Christ."

πᾶσάν τε ἡμέραν ἐν τῷ ἱερῷ καὶ κατ' οἶκον οὐκ ἐπαύοντο διδάσκοντες καὶ εὐαγγελιζόμενοι τὸν Χριστόν Ἰησοῦν.

πᾶσάν (acc.sing.fem.of πᾶς, in agreement with ἡμέραν) 67.

τε (correlative particle, with μέν) 1408.

ἡμέραν (acc.sing.fem.of ἡμέρα, distributive) 135.

ἐν (preposition with the locative of place) 80.

τῷ (loc.sing.neut.of the article in agreement with ἱερῷ) 9.

ἱερῷ (loc.sing.neut.of ἱερόν, place where) 346.

καὶ (adjunctive conjunction joining prepositional phrases) 14.

κατ' (preposition with the accusative, distributive) 98.

οἶκον (acc.sing.masc.of οἶκος, distributive) 784.

οὐκ (summary negative conjunction with the indicative) 130.

ἐπαύοντο (3d.per.pl.imp.act.ind.of παύω, progressive description) 2044.

διδάσκοντες (pres.act.part.nom.pl.masc.of διδάσκω, adverbial, complementary) 403.

καὶ (adjunctive conjunction joining participles) 14.

εὐαγγελιζόμενοι (pres.mid.part.nom.pl.masc.of εὐαγγελίζομαι, adverbial, complementary) 909.

τὸν (acc.sing.masc.of the article in agreement with Χριστόν) 9.

Χριστόν (acc.sing.masc.of Χριστός, direct object of εὐαγγελιζόμενοι) 4.

Ἰησοῦν (acc.sing.masc.of Ἰησοῦς, apposition) 3.

Translation - "And both in the temple and from house to house, every day they did not stop teaching and preaching Jesus, the Messiah."

Comment: Always in the temple and/or from house to house. Some Apostles in one place; others in another. There was no day of rest. They did not cease to teach and to tell the good news that Jesus, the Galilean carpenter was the Messiah. Crucified for Israel's sins, He was the Lamb of God (John 1:29). But He was alive and He would never die again. The ban on the activities of the Apostles imposed by the San Hedrin had exactly the opposite effect from that which they intended. The early church, filled with the Holy Spirit, was aflame with zeal. Such activitiy was certain to bring persecution, the beginnings of which we have already seen. The first Christian martyr of record is not an Apostle, however but one of the first deacons, whom we will meet in Chapter 6.

Note that ἐπαύοντο is followed here, not by the infintive, but by the participles. In the New Testament παύομαι "occurs only with the participle as in Lu.5:4, ἐπαύσατο λαλῶν. Cf. Acts 5:42; 6:13; Eph.1:16; Col.1:9; Heb.10:2. But in Ac.14:18 note κατέπαυσαν τοῦ μὴ θύειν, which well illustrates the difference between the infintive and the participle." (Robertson, *Grammar*, 1102). Participles and infinitives "are closely allied in use, though different in origin. Both are verbal nouns; both are infinitival; both are participial. But the participle so-called in inflected always, while the infinitive so-called has lost its proper inflection. The infinitive, besides, expresses the action in relation to the verb, while the participle expresses the action in relation to the subject of the object of the verb (or some other substantive or pronoun)." (Schoemann, *Die Lehre von den Redet. nach den Alten*, 34, as cited in Robertson, *Ibid.,*1102). The distinction between the participle and the infinitive thus becomes quite important" (*Ibid.*). διδάσκοντες and εὐαγγελιζόμενοι describes the action in relation to the Apostles. They were everlastingly at it. Doing what? Teaching and preaching.

The Appointment of the Seven
(Acts 6:1-7)

Acts 6:1 - "And in those days, when the number of the disciples was multiplied, there arose a murmering of the Grecians against the Hebrews because their widows were neglected in the daily ministration."

'Εν δὲ ταῖς ἡμέραις ταύταις πληθυνόντων τῶν μαθητῶν ἐγένετο γογγυσμὸς τῶν Ἑλληνιστῶν πρὸς τοὺς Ἑβραίους, ὅτι παρεθεωροῦντο ἐν τῇ διακονίᾳ τῇ καθημερινῇ αἱ χῆραι αὐτῶν.

'Εν (preposition with the locative of time point) 80.

δὲ (explanatory conjunction) 11.

ταῖς (loc.pl.fem.of the article in agreement with ἡμέραις) 9.

ἡμέραις (loc.pl.fem.of ἡμέρα, time point) 135.

ταύταις (loc.pl.fem.of οὗτος, in agreement with ἡμέραις) 93.

πληθυνόντων (pres.act.part.gen.pl.masc.of πληθύνω, genitive absolute) 1488.

τῶν (gen.pl.masc.of the article in agreement with μαθητῶν) 9.

μαθητῶν (gen.pl.masc.of μαθητής, genitive absolute) 421.

ἐγένετο (3d.per.sing.aor.ind.of γίνομαι, ingressive) 113.

γογγυσμὸς (nom.sing.masc.of γογγυσμός, subject of ἐγένετο) 2364.

τῶν (gen.pl.masc.of the article in agreement with Ἑλληνιστῶν) 9.

#3077 Ἑλληνιστῶν (gen.pl.masc.of Ἑλληνιστής, description).

Grecian - Acts 6:1; 9:29.

Meaning: Cf. ἑλληνίζω - "to act like a Greek." Hence, one who copies the manner or worship of the Greeks or uses the Greek language. A Hellenist. A Jew born in foreign lands and speaking Greek. Opposed to Ἑβραῖοι in Acts 6:1; 9:29. With reference to the Hebrew Christians in the early Jerusalem church who were culturally oriented around Greek culture - Acts 6:1; 9:29.

πρὸς (preposition with the accusative of extent, after a verb of speaking) 197.

τοὺς (acc.pl.masc.of the article in agreement with Ἑβραίους) 9.

#3078 Ἑβραίους (acc.pl.masc.of ἑβραῖος, extent, after a verb of speaking).

Hebrews - Acts 6:1; 2 Cor.11:22; Phil.3:5,5.

Meaning: A member of the Jewish or Israelitish nation - 2 Cor.11:22; Phil.3:5,5. Hebrew Christians in the early Jerusalem church, in distinction from Ἑλληνιστής (#3077) - Acts 6:1.

ὅτι (conjunction introducing a subordinate causal clause) 211.

#3079 παρεθεωροῦντο (3d.per.pl.imp.pass.ind.of παραθεωρέω, progressive description).

neglect - Acts 6:1.

Meaning: A combination of παρά (#154) and θεωρέω (#1667). Hence, to look past, beside or beyond; hence to overlook; to neglect. With reference to the Grecian widows in the Jerusalem church who were being neglected in the welfare program - Acts 6:1.

ἐν (preposition with the locative of sphere) 80.
τῇ (loc.sing.fem.of the article in agreement with διακονίᾳ) 9.
διακονίᾳ (loc.sing.fem.of διακονία, sphere) 2442.
τῇ (loc.sing.fem.of the article in agreement with καθημερινῇ) 9.

#3080 καθημερινῇ (loc.sing.fem.of καθημεράνος, in agreement with διακονίᾳ).

daily - Acts 6:1.

Meaning: A combination of κατά (#98) and ἡμέρα (#135). According to the day. Daily. Day by day - Acts 6:1.

αἱ (nom.pl.fem.of the article in agreement with χῆραι) 9.
χῆραι (nom.pl.fem.of χῆρα, subject of παρεθεωροῦντο) 1910.
αὐτῶν (gen.pl.masc.of αὐτός, relationship) 16.

Translation - "Now at that time, when the number of disciples was increasing, there developed a complaint from the Grecians against the Hebrews because their widows were always being overlooked in the daily food service."

Comment: The genitive absolute tells us that the number of disciples was increasing in the period in question. This is probably the reason for the breakdown in the administration of the food service. Apparently this work was being done by the Apostles,for it was to them that the people brought they proceeds from the sale of their property (Acts 4:35,37). There is nothing in the text to indicate that the oversight was the result of deliberate discrimination. The evangelistic work being done by the Christians (Acts 5:42), energized by the Holy Spirit (Acts 5:32) brought many converts into the church. They were all Hebrew Christians, but some were Hellenists (#3077), while others were Hebrews (#3078). The work was growing so fast that the Apostles could not keep up with the problem, which had begun to be noticed a short time before (imperfect tense in παρεθεωροῦντο). The first rift in the church came, not along theological, but along ethnic and cultural lines. All were Jewish, but the Hellenists came from a different background and displayed some cultural variations.

It was a serious problem and the Apostles moved quickly to solve it.

Verse 2 - "Then the twelve called the multitude of the disciples unto them and said, it is not reason that we should leave the word of God and serve tables."

προσκαλεσάμενοι δὲ οἱ δώδεκα τὸ πλῆθος τῶν μαθητῶν εἶπαν, Οὐκ ἀρεστόν ἐστιν ἡμᾶς καταλείψαντας τὸν λόγον τοῦ θεοῦ διακονεῖν τραπέζαις.

προσκαλεσάμενοι (aor.mid.part.nom.pl.masc.of προσκαλέω, adverbial, temporal) 842.
δὲ (inferential) 11.

οἱ (nom.pl.masc.of the article in agreement with δώδεκα) 9.

δώδεκα (nom.pl.masc.of δώδεκα, subject of εἶπαν) 820.

τό (acc.sing.neut.of the article in agreement with πλῆθος) 9.

πλῆθος (acc.sing.neut.of πλῆθος, direct object of προσκαλεσάμενοι) 1792.

τῶν (gen.pl.masc.of the article in agreement with μαθητῶν) 9.

μαθητῶν (gen.pl.masc.of μαθητής, definition) 421.

εἶπαν (3d.per.pl.aor.act.ind.of εἶπον, constative) 155.

οὐκ (summary negative conjunction with the indicative) 130.

ἀρεστόν (nom.sing.neut.of ἀρεστός, predicate adjective) 2384.

ἡμᾶς (acc.pl.masc.of ἐγώ, general reference) 123.

καταλείψαντας (aor.act.part.acc.pl.masc.of καταλείπω, adverbial, telic) 369.

τὸν (acc.sing.masc.of the article in agreement with λόγον) 9.

λόγον (acc.sing.masc.of λόγος, direct object of καταλείψαντας) 510.

τοῦ (gen.sing.masc.of the article in agreement with θεοῦ) 9.

θεοῦ (gen.sing.masc.of θεός, description) 124.

διακονεῖν (pres.act.inf.of διακονέω, noun use, nom.sing.neut., subject of ἐστιν) 367.

τραπέζαις (loc.pl.fem.of πράπεζα, sphere) 1176.

Translation - "Therefore the Twelve called the multitude of the disciples together and said, 'For us to abandon the Word of God in order to serve tables is not acceptable.' "

Comment: The problem was brought to the Apostles, as a result of which they called the meeting. Thus δὲ is inferential.

This is the first indication that we have had that Matthias, selected by the 120 as a successor to Judas Iscariot (Acts 1:15-26) was still reckoned among the Apostles. He is not called an Apostle in this passage. It is impossible to tell whether he is among the Apostles of verse 6.

Cf.#2384 for the meaning of ἀρεστός - it is a general adjective that can fit into many contexts. It was not proper, wise, desirable or efficient for the Apostles who were carrying on the most important work of the church to abandon their teaching and preaching, in order to do the welfare work that others, who were not endowed as they were, could do just as well. For the Apostles to have spent their time distributing to the necessities of the saints (Romans 12:13) and seeing to it that the Grecian widows were getting their fair share, would have been a serious misallocation of valuable and scarce resources. The Apostles revealed deep insight into the problem of the production function. They were not suggesting that the welfare work was not important. Nor were they suggesting that they thought that such work was beneath their dignity - a carnal idea. It was a matter of the most efficient allocation of scarce human resources. Men with less personal endowment to preach and teach could serve the food. This is not to say, however, that those chosen to serve in this menial capacity could not also bear this witness to the gospel, as is clear in Acts 6:8-7:60.

Verse 3 - "Wherefore, brethren, look ye out among you seven men of honest report, full of the Holy Ghost and wisdom, whom we may appoint over this business."

ἐπισκέφασθε δέ, ἀδελφοί, ἄνδρας ἐξ ὑμῶν μαρτυρουμένους ἑπτὰ πλήρεις
πνεύματος καὶ σοφίας, οὓς καταστήσομεν ἐπὶ τῆς χρείας ταύτης,

ἐπισκέφασθε (2d.per.pl.aor.mid.impv.of ἐπισκέπτομαι, command, indirect)
1549.

δέ (inferential conjunction) 11.

ἀδελφοί (voc.pl.masc.of ἀδελφός, address) 15.

ἄνδρας (acc.pl.masc.of ἀνήρ, direct object of ἐπισκέφασθε) 63.

ἐξ (preposition with the partitive genitive) 19.

ὑμῶν (gen.pl.masc.of σύ, partitive) 104.

μαρτυρουμένους (pres.pass.part.acc.pl.masc.of μαρτυρέω, adjectival,
ascriptive, in agreement with ἄνδρας) 1471.

ἑπτὰ (numeral, indeclin., in agreement with ἄνδρας) 1024.

πλήρεις (acc.pl.masc.of πλήρης, in agreement with ἄνδρας) 1124.

πνεύματος (gen.sing.neut.of πνεῦμα, description) 83.

καὶ (adjunctive conjunction joining nouns) 14.

σοφίας (gen.sing.fem.of σοφία, description) 934.

οὓς (acc.pl.masc.of ὅς, direct object of καταστήσομεν) 65.

καταστήσομεν (1st.per.pl.fut.act.ind.of καθίστημι, gnomic) 1523.

ἐπὶ (preposition with the genitive of reference) 47.

τῆς (gen.sing.fem.of the article in agreement with χρείας) 9.

χρείας (gen.sing.fem.of χρεία, reference) 317.

ταύτης (gen.sing.fem.of οὗτος, in agreement with χρείας) 93.

*Translation - "Therefore, brethren, select from your number seven men who are
regarded as full of the Spirit and wisdom whom we will appoint with reference to
this need."*

Comment: δέ is inferential, as it introduces the suggestion of the Apostles, which
was based upon their decision in verse 2 that, though they realized that there was
a problem which must be solved, they did not have the time to do it. The D mss.
(Codex Bezae) has τί οὖν εστιν, ἀδελφοί; - "what therefore is to be done,
brethren. . . " "The reading οὖν is so appropriate in the context that, if it were
original, there would have been no reason why the other readings should have
arisen. The Committee agreed with Tischendorf (*ad loc.*) that the presence of δέ
in both the preceding and following sentences prompted scribes to alter δέ in this
verse (Sinaiticus, B cop_sa) to either δή (A) or οὖν (C E P Ψ 33 614 1739 *Byz*,
followed by the Textus Receptus), or to omit it entirely (p74 cop_sa ms arm eth geo
al).The conflation δὲ οὖν is read by 1175." Metzger, *Textual Commentary,*337).

Thus the first deacons were to be selected for a specific purpose, *viz.* to attend
to the administration of the social and economic welfare of the church, thus to
release the Apostles from the time consuming task, in order that they might
devote all of their time to the Word of God. In view of the problem that had
arisen, where there may have been some feeling that discrimination was present,
and also in view of the fact that large amounts of money were involved, it was
important that the men selected should be of good repute and wise in matters of

public relations. In no sense did they constitute a church "Board", except within the limited jurisdiction for which they were selected. They were to relieve the Apostles of the tasks of administering the welfare program so that the Apostles could devote all of their time to their duties, as they suggested in

Verse 4 - "But we will give ourselves continually to prayer and to the ministry of the word."

ἡμεῖς δὲ τῇ προσευχῇ καὶ τῇ διακονίᾳ τοῦ λόγου προσκαρτερήσομεν.

ἡμεῖς (nom.pl.masc.of ἐγώ, subject of προσκαρτερήσομεν) 123.
δὲ (continuative conjunction) 11.
τῇ (loc.sing.fem.of the article in agreement with προσευχῇ) 9.
προσευχῇ (loc.sing.fem.of προσευχή, sphere) 1238.
καὶ (adjunctive conjunction joining nouns) 14.
τῇ (loc.sing.fem.of the article in agreement with διακονίᾳ) 9.
διακονίᾳ (loc.sing.fem.of διακονία, sphere) 2442.
τοῦ (gen.sing.masc.of the article in agreement with λόγου) 9.
λόγου (gen.sing.masc.of λόγος, description) 510.
προσκαρτερήσομεν (1st.per.pl.fut.act.ind.of προσκαρτερέω, predictive) 2113.

Translation - "And we will continue to give all of our time to prayer and to the ministry of the Word."

Comment: The view of Tischendorf (*cf. supra,* p.256) that the copyists were disturbed by the presence of δέ in vss.2,3,4, and that they changed δέ in verse 3 to δή or οὖν, is to be noted. If we take δὲ in verses 2 and 3 as inferential and in verse 4 as continuative, the passage translates smoothly and logically. Thus the Apostles dictated the division of labor within the church. The deacons were to wait on tables, and see that the welfare funds given by some for the good of all were distributed on an equitable basis, with particular attention to the needs of the Grecian widows. The Apostles were to pray and teach and preach the Word. The Apostles (Ἀπόστολοι) were also Deacons (διάκονοι), for all who are "sent forth" are also to "serve." *Cf.*#2442 for various types of administration covered by the word. To be an Apostle was also to be a Deacon, but the reverse is not necessarily true. Deacons are not Apostles and should not be given authority to make decisions that belong now to Bishops (Ἐπίσκοποι), who in church bodies with the congregational form of church government are also called Pastors. Deacons should not "think of (themselves) more highly than (they) ought to think; but to think soberly, according as God hath dealt to every man the measure of faith" (Rom.12:3). *Cf.*#2113. Concentration is the concept. Preachers should pray hard and preach hard, while the deacons feed the poor.

Verse 5 - "And the saying pleased the whole multitude: and they chose Stephen, a man full of faith and of the Holy Ghost, and Philip, and Prochorus, and Nicanor, and Timon, and Parmenas, and Nicolas a proselyte of Antioch."

καὶ ἤρεσεν ὁ λόγος ἐνώπιον παντὸς τοῦ πλήθους, καὶ ἐξελέξαντο Στέφανον, ἄνδρα πλήρης πίστεως καὶ πνεύματος ἁγίου, καὶ Φίλιππον καὶ Πρόχορον καὶ Νικάνορα καὶ Τίμωνα καὶ Παρμενᾶν καὶ Νικόλαον προσήλυτον Ἀντιοχέα,

καὶ (continuative conjunction) 14.

ἤρεσεν (3d.per.sing.aor.act.ind.of ἀρέσκω, constative) 1110.

ὁ (nom.sing.masc.of the article in agreement with λόγος) 9.

λόγος (nom.sing.masc.of λόγος, subject of ἤρεσεν) 510.

ἐνώπιον (improper preposition with the genitive of place description) 1798.

παντὸς (gen.sing.neut.of πᾶς, in agreement with πλήθους) 67.

τοῦ (gen.sing.neut.of the article in agreement with πλήθους) 9.

πλήθους (gen.sing.neut.of πλῆθος, place description) 1792.

καὶ (continuative conjunction) 14.

ἐξελέξαντο (3d.per.pl.aor.mid.ind.of ἐκλέγω, constative, indirect) 2119.

#3081 Στέφανον (acc.sing.masc.of Στέφανος, direct object of ἐξελέξαντο).

Stephen - Acts 6:5,8,9; 7:59; 8:2; 11:19; 22:20.

Meaning: One of the seven deacons. The first Christian martyr - Acts 6:5,8,9; 7:59; 8:2; 11:19; 22:20.

ἄνδρα (acc.sing.masc.of ἀνήρ, in apposition) 63.

πλήρης (acc.sing.masc.of πλήρης, predicate adjective) 1124.

πίστεως (gen.sing.fem.of πίστις, description) 728.

καὶ (adjunctive conjunction joining nouns) 14.

πνεύματος (gen.sing.neut.of πνεῦμα, description) 83.

ἁγίου (gen.sing.neut.of ἅγιος, in agreement with πνεύματος) 84.

καὶ (adjunctive conjunction joining nouns) 14.

#3082 Φίλιππον (acc.sing.masc.of Φίλιππος, direct object of ἐξελέξαντο).

Philip - Acts 6:5; 8:5,6,12,13,26,29,30,31,34,35,38,39,40; 21:8.

Meaning: One of the first deacons - Acts 6:5. Also the evangelist of Acts 8:5,6,12,13,26,29,30,31,34,35, 37*, 38,39,40; 21:8. Literally, "a lover of horses." *in D mss. (Codex Bezae).

καὶ (adjunctive conjunction joining nouns) 14.

#3083 Πρόχορον (acc.sing.masc.of Πρόχορος, direct object of ἐξελέξαντο).

Prochorus - Acts 6:5.

Meaning: literally "leader of the dance." One of the seven deacons - Acts 6:5.

καὶ (adjunctive conjunction joining nouns) 14.

#3084 Νικάνορα (acc.sing.masc.of Νικάνωρ, direct object of ἐξελέξαντο).

Nicanor - Acts 6:5.

Meaning: literally "conqueror." One of the seven deacons, thought by some to have come from Antioch - Acts 6:5.

καί (adjunctive conjunction joining nouns) 14.

#3085 Τίμωνα (acc.sing.masc.of Τίμων, direct object of ἐξελέξαντο).

Timon - Acts 6:5.

Meaning: One of the seven deacons - Acts 6:5.

καί (adjunctive conjunction joining nouns) 14.

#3086 Παρμενᾶν (acc.sing.masc.of Παρμενᾶς, direct object of ἐξελέξαντο).

Parmenas - Acts 6:5.

Meaning: contracted from Παρμενίδης. Literally "steadfast." One of the seven deacons - Acts 6:5.

καί (adjunctive conjunction joining nouns) 14.

#3087 Νικόλαον (acc.sing.masc.of Νικόλαος, direct object of ἐξελέξαντο).

Nicolas - Acts 6:5.

Meaning: A combination of νίκη (#5293) and λαός (#110). "Conqueror of the people." One of the seven deacons, a proselyte from Antioch - Acts 6:5.

προσήλυτον (acc.sing.masc.of προσήλυτος, in apposition) 1445.

#3088 Ἀντιοχέα (acc.sing.masc.of Ἀντιοχεύς, in agreement with προσήλυτον).

Antioch - Acts 6:5.

Meaning: A native of Antioch. An Antiocean - Acts 6:5.

Translation - "And the suggestion was acceptable to all the multitude and they chose Stephen, a man full of faith and of the Holy Spirit, and Philip and Prochorus and Nicanor and Timon and Parmenas and Nicolas, an Antiochean proselyte."

Comment: Five of these men are mentioned by name only here, but Stephen and Philip had illustrious careers in the first century of church history.

Verse 6 - "... whom they set before the apostles; and when they had prayed, they laid their hands on them."

οὓς ἔστησαν ἐνώπιον τῶν ἀποστόλων, καὶ προσευξάμενοι ἐπέθηκαν αὐτοῖς τὰς χεῖρας.

οὕς (acc.pl.masc.of ὅς, direct object of ἔστησαν) 65.
ἔστησαν (3d.per.pl.aor.act.ind.of ἵστημι, constative) 180.
ἐνώπιον (improper preposition with the genitive of place description) 1798.
τῶν (gen.pl.masc.of the article in agreement with ἀποστόλων) 9.
ἀποστόλων (gen.pl.masc.of ἀπόστολος, place description) 844.
καὶ (continuative conjunction) 14.
προσευξάμενοι (aor.mid.part.nom.pl.masc.of προσεύχομαι, indirect, adverbial, temporal) 544.

ἐπέθηκαν (3d.per.pl.aor.act.ind.of ἐπιτίθημι, constative) 818.
αὐτοῖς (loc.pl.masc.of αὐτός, place where, after ἐπί in composition) 16.
τὰς (acc.pl.fem.of the article in agreement with χεῖρας) 9.
χεῖρας (acc.pl.fem.of χείρ, direct object of ἐπέθηκαν) 308.

Translation - "... *whom they stood before the Apostles, and after they had prayed they laid their hands upon them.*"

Comment: οὕς has the seven men mentioned in verse 5 as its antecedent. The service, now popularly known as ordination, was simple. Prayer for God's blessing was followed by the ceremony in which the Apostles laid their hands upon the deacons, thus formally to set them apart for the specific service of seeing that the physical needs of all of the people in the church were met, without discrimination against anyone. It is interesting, and it may be significant that the Scripture nowhere refers to this act as an ordination. "Ordained" deacons may be preempting a position that the first deacons did not occupy.

Verse 7 - "*And the word of God increased; and the number of the disciples multiplied in Jerusalem greatly; and a great company of the priests were obedient to the faith.*"

Καὶ ὁ λόγος τοῦ θεοῦ ηὔξανεν, καὶ ἐπληθύνετο ὁ ἀριθμὸς τῶν μαθητῶν ἐν Ἰερουσαλὴμ σφόδρα, πολύς τε ὄχλος τῶν ἱερέων ὑπήκουον τῇ πίστει.

Καὶ (continuative conjunction) 14.
ὁ (nom.sing.masc.of the article in agreement with λόγος) 9.
λόγος (nom.sing.masc.of λόγος, subject of ηὔξανεν) 510.
τοῦ (gen.sing.masc.of the article in agreement with θεοῦ) 9.
θεοῦ (gen.sing.masc.of θεός, description) 124.
ηὔξανεν (3d.per.sing.imp.act.ind.of αὐξάνω, progressive duration) 628.
καὶ (continuative conjunction) 14.
ἐπληθύνετο (3d.per.sing.imp.pass.ind.of πληθύνω, progressive duration) 1488.
ὁ (nom.sing.masc.of the article in agreement with ἀριθμὸς) 9.
ἀριθμὸς (nom.sing.masc.of ἀριθμός, subject of ἐπληθύνετο) 2278.
τῶν (gen.pl.masc.of the article in agreement with μαθητῶν) 9.
μαθητῶν (gen.pl.masc.of μαθητής, description) 421.
ἐν (preposition with the locative of place where) 80.
Ἰερουσαλὴμ (loc.sing.masc.of Ἰεροσολύμων, place where) 141.

σφόδρα (adverbial) 185.
πολὺς (nom.sing.masc.of πολύς, in agreement with ὄχλος) 228.
τε (continuative conjunction) 1408.
ὄχλος (nom.sing.masc.of ὄχλος, subject of ὑπήκουον) 418.
τῶν (gen.pl.masc.of the article in agreement with ἱερέων) 9.
ἱερέων (gen.pl.masc.of ἱερεύς, partitive genitive) 714.
ὑπήκουον (3d.per.pl.imp.act.ind.of ὑπακούω,inceptive) 760.
τῇ (loc.sing.fem.of the article in agreement with πίστει) 9.
πίστει (loc.sing.fem.of πίστις, sphere) 728.

Translation - "And the message of God continued to spread and the number of the disciples continued to multiply greatly in Jerusalem; and a great number of the priests began to comply with the tenets of the faith."

Comment: αὐξάνω here (#628) in the sense that a knowledge of the Christian message spread throughout Jerusalem as a result of widespread dissemination. *Cf*.Acts 5:42. Results followed, as they always do when the witness of the Holy Spirit accompanies that of the preacher (Acts 5:32). Converts increased in number, including a large number of priests of the tribe of Levi.

Just as the Holy Spirit opened the mind of John the Baptist to understand the significance of the first coming of Messiah after he had immersed Jesus, so that on "the next day" (John 1:29) he could announce that Messiah, in His first coming, was to be "the Lamb of God" Who would die to bear the sins, not only of the Jews, but also of the entire world, so He convinced (John 16:7-11) a great many priests that their functions in the Aaronic priesthood were only typical of blood, which, unlike that of bulls and goats, could indeed take away sin (Heb.10:4). They came to see that the law, which they had previously trusted as a means to salvation was only "a shadow of good things to come, not the very image of the things. . . " (Heb.10:1). The blindness which "in part" still obscures the perceptions of Israel (Romans 11:25) and will continue until the "fullness of the Gentiles be come in," was lifted from their eyes.

The Arrest of Stephen

(Acts 6:8-15)

Verse 8 - "And Stephen, full of faith and power, did great wonders and miracles among the people."

Στέφανος δὲ πλήρης χάριτος καὶ δυνάμεως ἐποίει τέρατα καὶ σημεῖα μεγάλα ἐν τῷ λαῷ.

Στέφανος (nom.sing.masc.of Στέφανος, subject of ἐποίει) 3081.
δὲ (continuative conjunction) 11.
πλήρης (nom.sing.masc.of πλήρης, predicate adjective) 1124.
χάριτος (gen.sing.fem.of χάρις, description) 1700.
καὶ (adjunctive conjunction joining nouns) 14.
δυνάμεως (gen.sing.fem.of δύναμις, description) 687.

ἐποίει (3d.per.sing.imp.act.ind.of ποιέω, inceptive) 127.
τέρατα (acc.pl.neut.of τέρας, direct object of ἐποίει) 1500.
καὶ (adjunctive conjunction joining nouns) 14.
σημεῖα (acc.pl.neut.of σημεῖον, direct object of ἐποίει) 1005.
μεγάλα (acc.pl.neut.of μέγας, in agreement with σημεῖα) 184.
ἐν (preposition with the locative of place, with persons) 80.
τῷ (loc.sing.masc.of the article in agreement with λαῷ) 9.
λαῷ (loc.sing.masc.of λαός, place where) 110.

Translation - "And Stephen, full of grace and power, began to perform wonders and mighty signs among the people."

Comment: Though deacons were selected by the church and appointed by the Apostles for a less prestigious task than the ministry of prayer and preaching, which was primarily delegated to the Apostles at the beginning, we now learn that God also works through deacons and other Christians who are elevated to no particular position of authority. The filling of the Holy Spirit results in His bestowing of gifts severally as He wills to do so (1 Cor. 12:11). Perhaps because Stephen was willing to be a deacon, serving food at the tables, God gave to him the more spectacular ministry also. Conversely perhaps the reason why modern deacons are so powerless and such dreadful blights upon the spiritual life of the church is that they have misconstrued the office of deacon, as being one of dictatorship. God will bless the deacon who, like Stephen was, is full of grace and power as a result of the filling of the Holy Spirit, though, now that the canon of New Testament Scripture is complete, and the Holy Spirit has completed His message to the church in this age, there will be no further miracle working. Stephen's gifts gave to him the prestige which was required to authenticate the gospel which he was about to preach. It was the only time he was privileged to preach it. There is no record of souls saved, but God used Stephen's sermon, which he sealed with his own blood, under an avalanche of murderous stones, to open the eyes of Saul of Tarsus whose ministry was then used to take the gospel to the Gentile world throughout the Mediterranean world.

The student should note the reason why sign gifts were given, whether to the Apostles, who guided the early church in her faith and practice or to others. All "sign-gift" theology should be evaluated in the light of 1 Corinthians 13. Signs and wonders are not performed by the Holy Spirit since He closed the pages of the New Testament, but Satan empowers the working of miracles among his own false prophets, in order to gain for them the prestige needed for the acceptance of their "additions" to the Word of God. It is not surprizing that those who emphasize the ecstatic are not known for their work in New Testament exegesis, and in recent years have begun a systematic attack, through press and pulpit upon it. The preacher who has heard the voice of God in a physically audible sense or has performed or witnessed a mighty miracle need not bother to find out what the New Testament teaches. Anything he says, however fanatical will find believers among the evil and adulterous generation who characteristically seeks a sign (Mt. 12:39). Stephen's activities involved him in controversy that led to his magniloquent sermon and his death. His tenure in the diaconate was short but among the most distinguished.

Verse 9 - "Then there arose certain of the synagogue which is called the synagogue of the Libertines, and Cyrenians, and Alexandrians, and of them of Cilicia and of Asia, disputing with Stephen."

ἀνέστησαν δέ τινες τῶν ἐκ τῆς συναγωγῆς τῆς λεγομένης Λιβερτίνων καὶ Κυρηναίων καὶ Ἀλεξανδρέων καὶ τῶν ἀπὸ Κιλικίας καὶ Ἀσίας συζητοῦντες τῷ Στεφάνῳ,

ἀνέστησαν (3d.per.pl.aor.act.ind.of ἀνίστημι, constative) 789.
δέ (continuative conjunction) 11.
τινες (nom.pl.masc.of τις, subject of ἀνέστησαν) 486.
τῶν (gen.pl.masc.of the article, partitive genitive) 9.
ἐκ (preposition with the partitive genitive) 19.
τῆς (gen.sing.fem.of the article in agreement with συναγωγῆς) 9.
συναγωγῆς (gen.sing.fem.of συναγωγή, partitive) 404.
τῆς (gen.sing.fem.of the article in agreement with λεγομένης) 9.
λεγομένης (pres.pass.part.gen.sing.fem.of λέγω, substantival, in apposition with συναγωγῆς) 66.

#3090 Λιβερτίνων (nom.pl.masc.of Λιβερτῖνος, appellation).

Libertines - Acts 6:9.

Meaning: Conflicting views exist as to the identity of these people: (1) They were manumitted Roman slaves who became proselytes and had their own synagogue in Jerusalem. (2) They were citizens of Libertum, a city or region in proconsular North Africa. (3) They were Jews, made captive by Pompey, the Roman, but later set free, who lived in Rome but came often to Jerusalem where they had their own synagogue. They were enemies of Stephen - Acts 6:9.

(Note: When the longhand manuscript of *The Renaissance New Testament* was being prepared, the word Στέφανος was inadvertently given two numbers, viz. #'s 3081 and 3089, the latter of which is in error. Before the error was discovered I had gone on to subsequent new words and their respective numbers. In order not to disrupt the numbering of the remaining 2355 words, which will be encountered between Acts 6:9 and Revelation 22:11, I have omitted #3089).

καὶ (adjunctive conjunction joining nouns) 14.
Κυρηναίων (gen.pl.masc.of Κυρηναῖος, partitive) 1641.
καὶ (adjunctive conjunction, joining nouns) 14.

#3091 Ἀλεχανδρέων (gen.pl.masc.of Ἀλεξανδρεύς, partitive).

Alexandrians - Acts 6:9; 18:24.

Meaning: A native or a resident of Alexandria, a prominent city in Egypt - Acts

6:9; 18:24.

καὶ (adjunctive conjunction joining substantives) 14.
τῶν (gen.pl.masc.of the article, partitive) 9.
ἀπὸ (preposition with the ablative of source) 70.

#3092 Κιλικίας (abl.sing.fem.of Κιλικία, source).

Cilicia - Acts 6:9; 15:23,41; 21:39; 22:3; 23:34; 27:5; Gal.1:21.

Meaning: An Asia Minor province, bounded by Cappadocia, Lycaonia and Isayria on the North, by the Mediterranean Sea on the South, on the East by Syria and on the West by Pamphylia. Tarsus, its capital city was Paul's birthplace - Acts 6:9; 15:23,41; 21:39; 22:3; 23:34; 27:5; Gal.1:21.

καὶ (adjunctive conjunction joining nouns) 14.
'Ασίας (gen.sing.fem.of'Ασία, partitive) 2968.
συζητοῦντες (pres.act.part.nom.pl.masc.of συζητέω, adverbial, circumstantial) 2060.
τῷ (dat.sing.masc.of the article in agreement with Στεφάνῳ) 9.
Στεφάνῳ (dat.sing.masc.of Στέφανος, indirect object of συζητοῦντες) 3081.

Translation - "And there arose some men from the synagogue known as the Synagogue of the Libertines, and from the Cyrenians and Alexandrians and those from Cilicia and Asia, arguing with Stephen."

Comment: This group of Hellenistic Jews, some of whom were proselytes, were probably infected with the Gnostic heresy which had been introduced into the Mediterranean world after the conquest of Alexander the Great. Although Alexander did not return to Asia Minor, but died and was buried in Babylon in 323 B.C., the political unity which his conquests brought to the Middle East and which was continued by the Romans resulted in a cultural, philosophical and theological mix which plagued the early church during the period when the Christological controversies raged. The dispute over the hypostatic union of the divine and human in'Ο ΛΟΓΟΣ was not settled until the Council of Chalcedon in A.D.451, when the theologians adopted the statement with reference to the person and work of Christ which has been the standard for Christian theology since. The text does not tell us the nature of the controversy, but it is very likely that Stephen's opponents were infected with the views of Zoroaster, with reference to the eternity of matter, which, when applied to Jesus would mean that He could not be the divine ΛΟΓΟΣ if in the incarnation He took real humanity, as John was later to declare in John 1:14. Whatever the issues in the debate, Stephen's adversaries were unable to reply to his words of wisdom, as we learn in

Verse 10 - "And they were not able to resist the wisdom and the spirit by which he spoke."

καὶ οὐκ ἴσχυον ἀντιστῆναι τῇ σοφίᾳ καὶ τῷ πνεύματι ᾧ ἐλάλει.

καί (adversative conjunction) 14.

οὐκ (summary negative conjunction with the indicative) 130.

ἴσχυον (3d.per.pl.imp.act.ind.of ἰσχύω, progressive description) 447.

ἀντιστῆναι (aor.act.inf.of ἀνθίστημι, epexegetical) 527.

τῇ (instru.sing.fem.of the article in agreement with σοφίᾳ) 9.

σοφίᾳ (instru.sing.fem.of σοφία, cause) 934.

καί (adjunctive conjunction joining nouns) 14.

τῷ (instru.sing.neut.of the article in agreement with πνεύματι) 9.

πνεύματι (instru.sing.neut.of πνεῦμα, cause) 83.

ᾧ (instru.sing.neut.of ὅς, manner) 65.

ἐλάλει (3d.per.sing.imp.act.ind.of λαλέω, progressive description) 815.

Translation - "But they were never able to stand against him because of the wisdom and the spirit, with which he was speaking."

Comment: καί is adversative. The Jews from out of town were disputing with Stephen but (adversative καί) to no avail. They were not strong enough to "stand up against" (refute) his arguments. Why? The instrumental of cause in τῇ σοφίᾳ καί τῷ πνεύματι tells us why? It is not necessary to believe that πνεύματι here means the Holy Spirit, though, of course He had filled Stephen and it was by His power that Stephen was able to defend the faith against the heretics. Stephen was naturally animated and totally fearless as his sermon which follows indicates. Thus they were no match for the deacon.

They reacted like losers, who lose with ill grace. They adopted illicit strategy.

Verse 11 - "Then they suborned men, which said, We have heard him speak blasphemous words against Moses, and against God."

τότε ὑπέβαλον ἄνδρας λέγοντας ὅτι᾽Ακηκόαμεν αὐτοῦ λαλοῦντος ῥήματα βλάσφημα εἰς Μωϋσῆν καὶ τὸν θεόν.

τότε (continuative conjunction) 166.

#3093 ὑπέβαλον (3d.per.pl.aor.act.ind.of ὑποβάλλω, constative).

suborn - Acts 6:11.

Meaning: A combination of ὑπό (#117) and βάλλω (#299). Hence, to throw or to cast under. To suggest to the mind. To infiltrate the mind of another without his knowledge. To introduce thoughts subliminally. - "To brainwash." With reference to the tactics used by Stephen's antagonists. The word "suborn" or "bribe" does not indicate that the victim is unaware of the process. It is not clear whether the men who misquoted Stephen were aware of the methods of his enemies or not. - Acts 6:11.

ἄνδρας (acc.pl.masc.of ἀνήρ, direct object of ὑπέβαλον) 63.

λέγοντας (pres.act.part.acc.pl.masc.of λέγω, adverbial, modal) 66.

ὅτι (recitative) 211.

᾽Ακηκόαμεν (1st.per.pl.2d.perf.act.ind. (Atttic) of ἀκούω, intensive) 148.

αὐτοῦ (gen.sing.masc.of αὐτός, description after a verb of sensation) 16.

λαλοῦντος (pres.act.part.gen.sing.masc.of λαλέω, adverbial, circumstantial) 815.

ῥήματα (acc.pl.neut.of ῥῆμα, direct object of λαλοῦντος) 3431.

#3094 βλάσφημα (acc.pl.neut.of βλασφημός, in agreement with ῥήματα).

    blasphemous - Acts 6:11.
    railing - 2 Peter 2:11.
    blasphemer - 1 Tim.1:13; 2 Tim.3:2.

*Meaning: Cf.*βλασφημέω (#781); βλασφημία (#1001). As an adjective - Acts 6:11; 2 Peter 2:11. As a substantive - 1 Tim.1:13; 2 Tim.3:2.

εἰς (preposition with the accusative, hostility, like a dative) 140.
Μωϋσῆν (acc.sing.masc.of Μωϋσῆς, hostility) 715.
καὶ (adjunctive conjunction joining nouns) 14.
τὸν (acc.sing.masc.of the article in agreement with θεόν) 9.
θεόν (acc.sing.masc.of θεός, hostility, like a dative) 124.

Translation - "Then with subtle suggestion they induced men to say, 'We have heard him utter blasphemous words against Moses and against God.' "

Comment: It is difficult to find a formal English word for ὑποβάλλω (#3093). In some underhanded manner they suggested to witnesses that they give the damaging testimony against Stephen which is recorded. It is doubtful that the witnesses were aware of the fact that they were being used. "Brainwash" comes close to the idea, except that it implies that the witnesses were favorably disposed toward Stephen before and that the Libertines *et al* had changed their minds. Goodspeed has "instigate." Whether the false witnesses were consciously involved in the conspiracy to defame Stephen or not, the main point is that they did in fact accuse him falsely. My impression is that ὑποβάλλω means to impose subliminal provocation.

The method used by the enemies of Stephen to attack him had ". . . degenerated much from the primitive simplicity, and the true rules of controversy." Apparently these men ". . . had been educated in the schools of the rhetoricians and sophists (and) rashly employed the arts and evasions of their subtile (*sic.*) masters . . . and, intent only upon defeating the enemy, they were too little attentive to the means of victory, indifferent whether they acquired it by artifice or plain dealing. This method of disputing, which the ancients called *oeconomical,* and which had victory for its object, rather than truth, was in consequence of the prevailing taste for rhetoric and sophistry, almost universally approved. The Platonists contributed to the support and encouragement of this ungenerous method of disputing, by that maxim which asserted the innocence of defending the truth by artifice and falsehood. This will appear manifest to those who have read, with any manner of penetration and judgment, the arguments of Origen against Celsus, and those of the other Christian disputants against the idolatrous Gentiles. . . . *To do a thing,* i.e. *oeconomically,* was the phrase applied to this devious and adroit method. It was indicated by the Greek prepositional phrase κατ' οἰκονομίαν - "in the cheapest (easiest, most efficient, shortest) manner." (John Laurence Mosheim, *An Ecclesiastical History, Ancient and Modern,* Book I, Part II, Chapter III, X). Thus we see the Gnostic influence, a result of the Hellenistic penetration into the West after the cultural and political consolidation of Alexander the Great. The Jews used it against the Christians and the Christian doctors, of whom Origen is a prime example, later used it against the infidels.

The stratagem worked, as we see in

Verse 12 - "And they stirred up the people, and the elders, and the scribes, and came upon him, and caught him, and brought him to the council."

συνεκίνησάν τε τὸν λαὸν καὶ τοὺς πρεσβυτέρους καὶ τοὺς γραμματεῖς, καὶ ἐπιστάντες συνήρπασαν αὐτὸν καὶ ἤγαγον εἰς τὸ συνέδριον,

#3095 συνεκίνησαν (3d.per.pl.aor.act.ind.of συνκινέω, constative).

stir up - Acts 6:12.

Meaning: A combination of σύν (#1542) and κινέω (#1435). Hence to move (κινέω) together with others (σύν). In an evil sense, to excite, stir up, cause commotion, incite to violence. With reference to the Jews' action against Stephen - Acts 6:12.

τε (correlative particle) 1408.
τὸν (acc.sing.masc.of the article in agreement with λαὸν) 9.
λαὸν (acc.sing.masc.of λαός, direct object of συνεκίνησαν) 110.
καὶ (adjunctive conjunction joining verbs) 14.
τοὺς (acc.pl.masc.of the article in agreement with πρεσβυτέρους) 9.
πρεσβυτέρους (acc.pl.masc.of πρεσβύτερος, direct object of συνεκίνησαν) 1141.
καὶ (adjunctive conjunction joining nouns) 14.
τοὺς (acc.pl.masc.of the article in agreement with γραμματεῖς) 9.
γραμματεῖς (acc.pl.masc.of γραμματεύς, direct object of συνεκίνησαν) 152.
αδξθντιωε ψονξθνψτιον ξοινινγ ωερβσ)".
ἐπιστάντες (aor.act.part.nom.pl.masc.of ἐφίστημι, adverbial, temporal) 1877.
συνήρπασαν (3d.per.pl.aor.act.ind.of συναρπάζω, constative) 2228.
αὐτὸν (acc.sing.masc.of αὐτός, direct object of συνήρπασαν) 16.
καὶ (adjunctive conjunction joining verbs) 14.
ἤγαγον (3d.per.pl.aor.act.ind.of ἄγω, constative) 876.
εἰς (preposition with the accusative of extent) 140.
τὸ (acc.sing.neut.of the article in agreement with συνέδριον) 9.
συνέδριον (acc.sing.neut.of συνέδριον, extent) 481.

Translation - "And they incited the people and the elders and the scribes, and confronted and arrested him and brought him to the San Hedrin.

Comment: Once again the Devil has painted himself into a corner. God makes the wrath of man to praise Him (Psalm 76:10). "He that sitteth in the heavens shall laugh" (Psalm 2:4). Unable to refute Stephen's arguments, his enemies stirred up a riot, returned, arrested and brought him before the San Hedrin. The kangeroo court sat and the false witnesses were sworn. As in all other cases they only gave Stephen a chance to preach.

Verse 13 - "And set up false witnesses, which said, This man ceaseth not to speak blasphemous words against this holy place and the law."

ἐστησάν τε μάρτυρας ψευδεῖς λέγοντας, Ὁ ἄνθρωπος οὗτος οὐ παύεται λαλῶν ῥήματα κατὰ τοῦ τόπου τοῦ ἁγίου (τούτου) καὶ τοῦ νόμου.

ἐστησαν (3d.per.pl.aor.act.ind.of ἵστημι, constative) 180.
τε (continuative conjunction) 1408.
μάρτυρας (acc.pl.masc.of μάρτυς, direct object of ἐστησαν) 1263.

#3096 ψευδεῖς (acc.pl.masc.of ψεῦδος, in agreement with μάρτυρας).

false - Acts 6:13.
liars - Rev.2:2; 21:8.

Meaning: false, lying, deceitful. As an adjective - Acts 6;13; as a noun - Rev.2:2; 21:8.

λέγοντας (pres.act.part.acc.pl.masc.of λέγω, adjectival, restrictive) 66.
Ὁ (nom.sing.masc.of the article in agreement with ἄνθρωπος) 9.
ἄνθρωπος (nom.sing.masc.of ἄνθρωπος, subject of παύεται) 341.
οὗτος (nom.sing.masc.of οὗτος, in agreement with ἄνθρωπος, contemptuous use) 93.
οὐ (summary negative conjunction with the indicative) 130.
παύεται (3d.per.sing.pres.act.ind.of παύω, progressive duration) 2044.
λαλῶν (pres.act.part.nom.sing.masc.of λαλέω, adverbial, complementary) 815.
ῥήματα (acc.pl.neut.of ῥῆμα, direct object of λαλῶν) 343.
κατὰ (preposition with the genitive, opposition) 98.
τοῦ (gen.sing.masc.of the article in agreement with τόπου) 9.
τόπου (gen.sing.masc.of τόπος, opposition) 1019.
τοῦ (gen.sing.masc.of the article in agreement with ἁγίου) 9.
ἁγίου (gen.sing.masc.of ἅγιος, in agreement with τόπου) 84.
(τούτου) (gen.sing.masc.of οὗτος, in agreement with τόπου) 93.
καὶ (adjunctive conjunction joining prepositional phrases) 14.
τοῦ (gen.sing.masc.of the article in agreement with νόμου) 9.
νόμου (gen.sing.masc.of νόμος, opposition) 464.

Translation - "And they put false witnesses upon the stand who said, 'This fellow is always saying things against this holy place and the law.'"

Comment: In a context describing a courtroom scene, ἐστησαν can be translated "sworn" or "put on the witness stand." Note the contemptuous use of οὗτος. Here again we have παύω, followed by a participle. *Cf.* our discussion of it *supra*, p.252. κατά with the genitive to indicate opposition or hostility is common enough. The accusation was general. Stephen was said to be speaking against the temple and the Mosaic law. In verse 14, they got specific.

Verse 14 - "For we have heard him say that this Jesus of Nazareth shall destroy this place, and shall change the customs which Moses delivered us."

ἀκηκόαμεν γὰρ αὐτοῦ λέγοντας ὅτι Ἰησοῦς ὁ Ναζωραῖος οὗτος καταλύσει τὸν τόπον τοῦτον καὶ ἀλλάξει τὰ ἔθη ἃ παρέδωκεν ἡμῖν Μωϋσῆς

ἀκηκόαμεν (1st.per.pl.2d.perf.act.ind. (Attic) of ἀκούω, iterative) 148.
γὰρ (causal conjunction) 105.
αὐτοῦ (gen.sing.masc.of αὐτός, after a verb of sensation) 16.
λέγοντος (pres.act.part.gen.sing.masc.of λέγω, adverbial, circumstantial) 66.
ὅτι (conjunction introducing an object clause in indirect discourse) 211.
Ἰησοῦς (nom.sing.masc.of Ἰησοῦς, subject of καταλύσει and ἀλλάξει) 3.
ὁ (nom.sing.masc.of the article in agreement with Ναζωραῖος) 9.
Ναζωραῖος (nom.sing.masc.of Ναζωραῖος, in apposition with Ἰησοῦς) 245.
οὗτος (nom.sing.masc.of οὗτος, in agreement with Ναζωραῖος, contemptuous use) 93.
καταλύσει (3d.per.sing.fut.act.ind.of καταλύω, predictive) 463.
τὸν (acc.sing.masc.of the article in agreement with τόπον) 9.
τόπον (acc.sing.neut.of τόπος, direct object of καταλύσει) 1019.
τοῦτον (acc.sing.masc.of οὗτος, in agreement with τόπον) 93.
καὶ (adjunctive conjunction joining verbs) 14.

#3097 ἀλλάξει (3d.per.sing.fut.act.ind.of ἀλλάσσω, predictive).

change - Acts 6;14; Rom.1:23; 1 Cor.15:51,52; Gal.4:20; Heb.1:12.

Meaning: To change; to alter. Customs - Acts 6;14; the glory of God into something less glorious - Rom.1:23; the physical bodies of the dead - 1 Cor.15:51,52; Paul's voice, *i.e.* his method of dealing with the Galatian Christians - Gal.4:20; the heavenly bodies - Heb.1:12.

τὰ (acc.pl.neut.of the article in agreement with ἔθη) 9.
ἔθη (acc.pl.neut.of ἔθος, direct object of ἀλλάξει) 1788.
ἃ (acc.pl.neut.of ὅς, direct object of παρέδωκεν) 65.
παρέδωκεν (3d.per.sing.aor.act.ind.of παραδίδωμι, culminative) 368.
ἡμῖν (dat.pl.masc.of ἐγώ, indirect object of παρέδωκεν) 123.
Μωϋσῆς (nom.sing.masc.of Μωϋσῆς, subject of παρέδωκεν) 715.

Translation - "For we have heard him repeatedly saying that Jesus, this Nazarene is going to destroy this place and change the customs which Moses has handed down to us."

Comment: The witnesses were trying to support their false accusations of verse 13. Whether contemptuous οὗτος is joined to Ἰησοῦς or Ναζωραῖος, the result is the same. This is the same accusation that was brought against Jesus (Mt.26:61). Jesus did not say that He would destroy the Temple of Solomon, although He did predict that it would be destroyed (Mt.24:2), as indeed it was by Titus in A.D.70. Nor did Stephen say that Jesus would do this. In rebuttal to the last part of the charge *cf.* Mt.5:17. It was a matter of interpretation. Jesus was in fact opposed to the customs which the Jews said had been handed down to them from Moses. He disagreed with their interpretation of the law of Moses, as indeed did Stephen.

Verse 15 - "And all that sat in the council, looking steadfastly on him, saw his face as it had been the face of an angel."

καὶ ἀτενίσαντες εἰς αὐτὸν πάντες οἱ καθεζόμενοι ἐν τῷ συνεδρίῳ εἶδον τὸ πρόσωπον αὐτοῦ ὡσεὶ πρόσωπον ἀγγέλου.

καὶ (continuative conjunction) 14.
ἀτενίσαντες (aor.act.part.nom.pl.masc.of ἀτενίζω, adverbial, modal) 2028.
εἰς (preposition with the accusative of extent) 140.
αὐτὸν (acc.sing.masc.of αὐτός, extent) 16.
πάντες (nom.pl.masc.of πᾶς, in agreement with καθεζόμενοι) 67.
οἱ (nom.pl.masc.of the article in agreement with καθεζόμενοι) 9.
καθεζόμενοι (pres.mid.part.nom.pl.masc.of καθέζομαι, substantival, subject of εἶδον) 1599.
ἐν (preposition with the locative of place where) 80.
τῷ (loc.sing.neut.of the article in agreement with συνεδρίῳ) 9.
συνεδρίῳ (loc.sing.neut.of συνέδριον, place where) 481.
εἶδον (3d.per.pl.aor.ind.of ὁράω, constative) 144.
τὸ (acc.sing.neut.of the article in agreement with πρόσωπον) 9.
πρόσωπον (acc.sing.neut.of πρόσωπον, direct object of εἶδον) 588.
αὐτοῦ (gen.sing.masc.of αὐτός, possession) 16.
ὡσεὶ (conjunction introducing a comparative phrase) 325.
πρόσωπον (nom.sing.neut.of πρόσωπον, subject of a verb understood) 588.
ἀγγέλου (gen.sing.masc.of ἄγγελος, possession) 96.

Translation - "And when those who were sitting in the San Hedrin riveted their gaze upon him they saw his face as if it were angelic."

Comment: *Cf.* Luke 9:29. A special filling of the Holy Spirit prepared Stephen for the great sermon which follows.

Stephen's Sermon

(Acts 7:1-53)

Acts 7:1 - "Then said the high priest, Are these things so?"

Εἶπεν δὲ ὁ ἀρχιερεύς Εἰ ταῦτα οὕτως ἔχει;

Εἶπεν (3d.per.sing.aor.act.ind.of εἶπον, constative) 155.
δὲ (continuative conjunction) 11.
ὁ (nom.sing.masc.of the article in agreement with ἀρχιερεύς) 9.
ἀρχιερεύς (nom.sing.masc.of ἀρχιερεύς, subject of εἶπεν) 151.
Εἰ (particle in a first-class elliptical condition, direct question) 337.
ταῦτα (nom.pl.neut.of οὗτος, subject of ἔχει) 93.
οὕτως (demonstrative adverb) 74.
ἔχει (3d.per.sing.pres.act.ind.of ἔχω, aoristic) 82.

Translation - "And the high priest said, 'Are these things true?' "

Comment: With reference to οὕτως, the predicate adverb with ἔχει, instead of a predicate adjective, as we would put it in English, Robertson says, "One must be willing for the Greek to have his standpoint" (*Grammar*, 546). *Cf.*our comment on Mark 7:6 (*The Renaissance New Testament*, 5, 528). When we have εἰ in a direct question it is elliptical. The apodosis is omitted. The entire conditional sentence would read, "If these things are true, tell me." Otherwise it is indirect question. In English we would use the predicate adjective, in which case it would be "Does he (*i.e.* the witness) have it correct?" With the predicate adverb, a literal translation would read, "Does he have it in conformity with (οὕτως) the truth?"

Caiaphas' question opened the door of opportunity for Stephen to preach. After Stephen had begun to preach it is probable that the high priest muttered to himself, "I wish I hadn't asked!" Stephen had been accused of subverting Judaism. His rebuttal is in terms of a detailed history of Israel, beginning with Abraham, and following with a detailed description of the period of Egyptian bondage and God's deliverance under the direction of Moses, the shabby treatment which their fathers visited upon Moses and Aaron and closing with his castigation of them for their murder of the Messiah. Thus Stephen asks and give a devastating answer to the question, "Who is guilty of violating the moral standards and customs handed down by Moses." Caiaphas and his colleagues rejected God's counsel by murdering their Messiah, just as their fathers had rejected God's counsel by rebelling against Moses and Aaron.

Verse 2 - "And he said, 'Men, brethren, and fathers, hearken: The God of glory appeared unto our father Abraham, when he was in Mesopotamia, before he dwelt in Charran."

ὁ δὲ ἔφη, Ἄνδρες ἀδελφοὶ καὶ πατέρες, ἀκούσατε. Ὁ θεὸς τῆς δόξης ὤφθη τῷ πατρὶ ἡμῶν Ἀβραὰμ ὄντι ἐν τῇ Μεσοποταμίᾳ πρὶν ἢ κατοικῆσαι αὐτὸν ἐν Χαρράν,

ὁ (nom.sing.masc.of the article, subject of ἔφη) 9.
δὲ (continuative conjunction) 11.
ἔφη (3d.per.sing.aor.act.ind.of φημί, constative) 354.
Ἄνδρες (voc.pl.masc.of ἀνήρ, address) 63.
ἀδελφοὶ (voc.pl.masc.ofd ἀδελφός, address) 15.

καὶ (adjunctive conjunction joining nouns) 14.

πατέρες (voc.pl.masc.of πατήρ, address) 238.

ἀκούσατε (2d.per.pl.aor.act.impv.of ἀκούω, command) 148.

Ὁ (nom.sing.masc.of the article in agreement with θεὸς) 9.

θεὸς (nom.sing.masc.of θεός, subject of ὤφθη) 124.

τῆς (gen.sing.fem.of the article in agreement with δόξης) 9.

δόξης (gen.sing.fem.of δόξα, description) 361.

ὤφθη (3d.per.pl.aor.mid.ind.of ὁράω, direct, constative) 144.

τῷ (dat.sing.masc.of the article in agreement with πατρὶ) 9.

πατρὶ (dat.sing.masc.of πατήρ, indirect object of ὤφθη) 238.

ἡμῶν (gen.pl.masc.of ἐγώ, relationship) 123.

Ἀβραὰμ (dat.sing.masc.indeclin., in apposition) 7.

ὄντι (pres.part.dat.sing.masc.of εἰμί, adverbial, temporal) 86.

ἐν (preposition with the locative of place) 80.

τῇ (loc.sing.fem.of the article in agreement with Μεσοποταμίᾳ) 9.

Μεσοποταμίᾳ (loc.sing.fem.of Μεσοποταμία, place where) 2965.

πρὶν (adverbial preposition in a temporal clause with the infinitive) 77.

ἤ (disjunctive conjunction) 465.

κατοικῆσαι (aor.act.inf.of κατοικέω, in a temporal clause, antecedent time) 242.

ἐν (preposition with the locative of place where) 80.

#3098 Χαρράν (loc.sing.of Χαρράν, place where).

Charran - Acts 7:2,4.

Meaning: A city in Mesopotamia of great antiquity. Made famous by the defeat of Crassus. Abraham stopped there enroute to the Promised Land - Acts 7:2,4.

Translation - "And he said, 'Men, brethren and fathers, Listen! The God of glory appeared to our father, Abraham when he was still in Mesotamia before he took his residence in Charran."

Comment: The revelation of the "God of glory" to Abraham occurred while he was still in Mesopotamia, and before he lived at Charran. The present participle ὄντι and πρὶν and the infinitive give us two temporal clauses. *Cf.* Gen.11:27-12:1. God appeared to Abraham before he moved to Charran (Haran). Note Gen.12:1 - "Now the Lord *had* said to Abram, . . . "

Verse 3 - ". . . and said unto him, Get thee out of thy country and from thy kindred, and come into the land which I shall show thee."

καὶ εἶπεν πρὸς αὐτόν, Ἔξελθε ἐκ τῆς γῆς σου καὶ ἐκ τῆς συγγενείας σου, καὶ δεῦρο εἰς τὴν γῆν ἣν ἄν σοι δείξω.

καὶ (adjunctive conjunction joining verbs) 14.

εἶπεν (3d.per.sing.aor.act.ind.of εἶπον, constative) 155.

πρὸς (preposition with the accusative of extent, after a verb of speaking) 197.

αὐτόν (acc.sing.masc.of αὐτός, extent after a verb of speaking) 16.

Ἔξελθε (2d.per.sing.aor.impv.of ἐξέρχομαι, command) 161.

ἐκ (preposition with the ablative of separation) 19.

τῆς (abl.sing.fem.of the article in agreement with γῆς) 9.

γῆς (abl.sing.fem.of γῆ, separtion) 157.

σου (gen.sing.masc.of σύ, possession) 104.

καὶ (adjunctive conjunction joining prepositional phrases) 14.

ἐκ (preposition with the ablative of separation) 19.

τῆς (abl.sing.fem.of the article in agreement with συγγενείας) 9.

συγγενείας (abl.sing.fem.of συγγένεια, separation) 1843.

σου (gen.sing.masc.of σύ, relationship) 104.

καὶ (adjunctive conjunction joining verbs) 14.

δεῦρο (2d.per.sing.impv., command) 1304.

εἰς (preposition with the accusative of extent) 140.

τὴν (acc.sing.fem.of the article in agreement with γῆν) 9.

γῆν (acc.sing.fem.of γῆ, extent) 157.

ἥν (acc.sing.fem.of ὅς, direct object of δείξω) 65.

ἄν (contingent modal particle in a relative clause) 205.

σοι (dat.sing.masc.of σύ, indirect object of δείξω) 104.

δείξω (1st.per.sing.fut.act.ind.of δείκνυμι, predictive) 359.

Translation - ". . . and he said to him, 'Come out of your country and away from your relatives and come into the land which I am going to show you."

Comment: The quotation is from Gen.12:1. The LXX also has καὶ ἐκ τοῦ οἴκου τοῦ πατρός σου. Instead of that Abraham took his father with him and, as a result, he was delayed in Haran by the death of Terah. Abraham was told to leave his native land, his relatives and his immediate family. The relative clause is indefinite, made so by ἄν. It indicates that though Abraham could be sure that God would show some land to him, he could not be certain in advance about its specific location.

Verse 4 - *"Then came he out of the land of the Chaldreans, and dwelt in Charran: and from thence when his father was dead, he removed him into this land, wherein ye now dwell."*

τότε ἐξελθὼν ἐκ γῆς Χαλδαίων κατῴκησεν ἐν Χαρράν. κἀκεῖθεν μετὰ τὸ ἀποθανεῖν τὸν πατέρα αὐτοῦ μετῴκισεν αὐτὸν εἰς τὴν γῆν ταύτην εἰς ἣν ἡμεῖς νῦν κατοικεῖτε.

τότε (continuative conjunction) 166.

ἐξελθὼν (aor.part.nom.sing.masc.of ἐξέρχομαι, adverbial, temporal) 161.

ἐκ (preposition with the ablative of separation) 19.

γῆς (abl.sing.fem.of γῆ, separation) 157.

#3099 Χαλδαίων (abl.pl.fem.of Χαλδαῖος, description).

Chaldean - Acts 7:4.

Meaning: The land of the Chaldreans. Chaldea. It seems to refer to southern Armenia. The country of the ancient city of Ur. Abraham's native country - Act 7:4. The Euphrates River flows southeastward from Syria, through Chaldea and joins the Tigris on its southeastern border 100 miles north of the northern end of the Persian Gulf.

κατῴκησεν (3d.per.sing.aor.act.ind.of κατοικέω, ingressive) 242.

ἐν (preposition with the locative of place) 80.

Χαρράν (loc.sing.of Χαρράν, place where) 3098.

κἀκεῖθεν (local adverb. Crasis - καί plus ἐκεῖθεν).

μετά (preposition with the accusative of time extent) 50.

τό (acc.sing.neut.of the article in an articular infinitive, time extent) 9.

ἀποθανεῖν (aaor.act.inf.of ἀποθνήσκω, noun use, accusative sing.neut, time expression) 774.

τὸν (acc.sing.masc.of the article in agreement with πατέρα) 9.

πατέρα (acc.sing.masc.of πατήρ, general reference) 238.

αὐτοῦ (gen.sing.masc.of αὐτός, relationship) 16.

#3100 μετῴκισεν (3d.per.sing.aor.act.ind.of μετοικίζω, constative).

carry away - Acts 7:43.
removed into - Acts 7:4.

Meaning: A combination of μετά (#50) and οἰκίζω - "to establish a new settlement." Hence, to transfer settlers. To cause to move to another location. Followed by the accusative of direct object and extent - Acts 7;4. Followed by an accusative of direct object and a genitive of description - Acts 7:43.

αὐτὸν (acc.sing.masc.of αὐτός, direct object of μετῴκισεν) 16.

εἰς (preposition with the accusative of extent) 140.

τὴν (acc.sing.fem.of the article in agreement with γῆν) 9.

γῆν (acc.sing.fem.of γῆ, extent) 157.

ταύτην (acc.sing.fem.of οὗτος, in agreement with γῆν) 93.

εἰς (preposition with the accusative in the original use, like a locative) 140.

ἣν (acc.sing.fem.of ὅς, like a locative) 65.

ὑμεῖς (nom.pl.masc.of σύ, subject of κατοικεῖτε) 104.

νῦν (adverbial) 1497.

κατοικεῖτε (2d.per.pl.pres.act.ind.of κατοικέω, aoristic) 242.

Translation - "*Then after he left Chaldean country he settled in Haran. And from there, after the death of his father, (God) moved him into this land in which you now live.*"

Comment: μετά τό with a temporal infinitive is rare in the New Testament. Cf.#50. The subject of μετῴκισεν may be ὁ θεὸς τῆς δόξης (vs.2), or it can refer to Abraham. If the former, then αὐτὸν, the object of μετῴκισεν refers to Abraham. If the latter, then αὐτὸν means the corpse of Abraham's father, Terah. Gen. 12:4 seems to favor view. If that is correct, Terah, who died in Haran was buried there. From Haran, Abraham came to Palestine where Stephen's audience was still living. Thus Stephen skillfully relates Abraham, the patriarch, to his audience, - an appeal to their nationalism.

Verse 5 - "And he gave him none inheritance in it, no, not so much as to set his foot on: yet he promised that he would give it to him for a possession, and to his seed after him, when as yet he had no child."

καὶ οὐκ ἔδωκεν αὐτῷ κληρονομίαν ἐν αὐτῇ οὐδὲ βῆμα ποδός, καὶ ἐπηγγείλατο δοῦναι αὐτῷ εἰς κατάσχεσιν αὐτὴν καὶ τῷ σπέρματι αὐτοῦ μετ' αὐτόν, οὐκ ὄντος αὐτῷ τέκνον.

καὶ (adversative conjunction) 14.
οὐκ (summary negative conjunction with the indicative) 130.
ἔδωκεν (3d.per.sing.aor.act.ind.of δίδωμι, constative) 362.
αὐτῷ (dat.sing.masc.of αὐτός, indirect object of ἔδωκεν) 16.
κληρονομίαν (acc.sing.fem.of κληρονομία, direct object of ἔδωκεν) 1387.
ἐν (preposition with the locative of place where) 80.
αὐτῇ (loc.sing.fem.of αὐτός, place where) 16.
οὐδὲ (disjunctive particle) 452.
βῆμα (acc.sing.neut.of βῆμα, direct object of ἔδωκεν) 1628.
ποδός (gen.sing.masc.of πούς, description) 353.
καὶ (adversative conjunction) 14.
ἐπηγγείλατο (3d.per.sing.aor.mid.ind.of ἐπαγγέλλω, indirect middle, constative) 2752.
δοῦναι (aor.act.inf.of δίδωμι, epexegetical) 362.
αὐτῷ (dat.sing.masc.of αὐτός, indirect object of δοῦναι) 16.
εἰς (preposition with the accusative, purpose) 140.

#3101 κατάσχεσιν (acc.sing.fem.of κατάσχεσις, purpose).

possession - Acts 7:5,45.

Meaning: A combination of κατά (#98) and ἔχω (#82). Hence, something held down; a possession. An inheritance. God's gift to Abraham - Acts 7;5,45.

αὐτὴν (acc.sing.fem.of αὐτός, direct object of δοῦναι) 16.
καὶ (adjunctive conjunction joining substantives) 14.
τῷ (dat.sing.masc.of the article in agreement with σπέρματι) 9.
σπέρματι (dat.sing.masc.of σπέρμα, indirect object of δοῦναι) 1056.
αὐτοῦ (gen.sing.masc.of αὐτός, relationship) 16.
μετ' (preposition with the accusative of time extent) 50.
αὐτόν (acc.sing.masc.of αὐτός, time extent, after) 16.
οὐκ (summary negative conjunction with the participle) 130.
ὄντος (pres.part.gen.sing.neut.of εἰμί, genitive absolute) 86.
αὐτῷ (dat.sing.masc.of αὐτός, possession) 16.
τέκνου (gen.sing.neut.of τέκνον, genitive absolute) 229.

Translation - "But He did not give him an inheritance in it, not even a place to put his foot, but, although he had no children, He promised to give it to him and to his posterity as a possession."

Comment: The genitive absolute ὄντος αὐτῷ τέκνου has the participle which can be taken both as temporal and concessive. The promise was given to Abraham at a time when (temporal) and despite the fact that (concessive) he and Sarah had no children. When Abraham arrived in Canaan, having made the journey from Ur to Haran, and then, after a delay and the death of his father, on to the land of Canaan (Gen.11:31 - 12:5), he made the trip on the promise that God would show him the land which was to be his to convey at death to his posterity forever. But since they had no child, Abraham could realize the fulfillment of this promise only by faith. Paul discusses this in Romans 4:1-25 and Galatians 4:21-31.

Verse 6 - "And God spake on this wise, That his seed should sojourn in a strange land; and that they should bring them into bondage, and entreat them evil four hundred years."

ἐλάλησεν δὲ οὕτως ὁ θεὸς ὅτι ἔσται τὸ σπέρμα αὐτοῦ πάροικον ἐν γῇ ἀλλοτρίᾳ, καὶ δουλώσουσιν αὐτὸ καὶ κακώσουσιν ἔτη τετρακόσια.

ἐλάλησεν (3d.per.sing.aor.act.ind.of λαλέω, constative) 815.

δὲ (adversative conjunction) 11.

οὕτως (demonstrative adverb) 74.

ὁ (nom.sing.masc.of the article in agreement with θεὸς) 9.

θεὸς (nom.sing.masc.of θεός, subject of ἐλάλησεν) 124.

ὅτι (conjunction introducing indirect discourse) 211.

ἔσται (3d.per.sing.fut.ind.of εἰμί, predictive) 86.

τὸ (nom.sing.neut.of the article in agreement with σπέρμα) 9.

σπέρμα (nom.sing.neut.of σπέρμα, subject of ἔσται) 1056.

αὐτοῦ (gen.sing.masc.of αὐτός, relationship) 16.

#3102 πάροικον (nom.sing.neut.of πάροικος, predicate nomintive).

foreigner - Eph.2:19.
stranger - Acts 7:29; 1 Peter 2:11.
sojourn - Acts 7:6.

Meaning: A combination of παρά (#154) and οἰκέω (#3926). One who has moved in by your side. Hence, a stranger, foreigner, sojourner, temporary resident. With reference to Israel in Egypt - Acts 7:6. Moses in Midian - Acts 7:29; metaphorically, the elect from among the Gentiles who are brought into covenant blessings - Eph.2:19; the Jewish Christians - 1 Peter 2:11.

ἐν (preposition with the locative of place) 80.

γῇ (loc.sing.fem.of γῆ, place where) 157.

ἀλλοτρίᾳ (loc.sing.fem.of ἀλλότριος, in agreement with γῇ) 1244.

καὶ (continuative conjunction) 14.

#3103 δουλώσουσιν (3d.per.pl.fut.act.ind.of δουλόω, predictive).

bring into bondage - Acts 7:6.
make servant - 1 Cor.9:19.
be brought into bondage - 2 Peter 2:19.
become servant - Romans 6:18,22.
be under bondage - 1 Cor.7:15.
given to Titus 2:3.
in bondage - Gal.4:3.

Meaning: Cf.δοῦλος (#725), δουλεύω (#604). To enslave; to reduce to bondage. With reference to Israel in Egypt - Acts 7:6; figuratively to be in bondage to a rule, *i.e.* under obligation - 1 Cor.7:15; 9:19. To assume the obligation to live a righteous life - Rom.6:18,22. With reference to the bondage of the alcoholic - Titus 2:3; with reference to other habits - 2 Peter 2:19.

αὐτὸ (acc.sing.neut.of αὐτός, direct object of δουλώσουσιν) 16.
καὶ (adjunctive conjunction joining verbs) 14.

#3104 κακώσουσιν (3d.per.pl.fut.act.ind.of κακόω, predictive).

evil entreat - Acts 7:6,19.
harm - 1 Peter 3:13.
hurt - Acts 18:10.
make evil affected - Acts 14:2.
vex - Acts 12:1.

Meaning: Cf. κακός (#1388); κακῶς (#411). To maltreat, oppress, harm, afflict. With reference to the treatment given the Jews in Egypt - Acts 7:6,19; Herod's persecution of the church - Acts 12:1. The Jews in Iconium prejudiced the Gentiles against the Christians - Acts 14:2; generally of the sufferings of Paul - Acts 18:10; 1 Peter 3:13.

ἔτη (acc.pl.neut.of ἔτος, time extent) 821.
τετρακόσια (acc.pl.neut.of τετρακόσιοι, in agreement with ἔτη) 3073.

Translation - "But God put it like this: that his descendants would be strangers in another country and that they (those of the host country) would enslave them and afflict them for four hundred years."

Comment: Stephen's use of the third personal pronoun αὐτοῦ instead of σοῦ, makes the statement of God in verse 6 indirect discourse, although in verse 7 the quotation can become direct discourse. Burton calls the future tenses "progressive future" denoting a continuing action for some time - in this case, four hundred years. (Burton, *Moods and Tenses,* 32). It is, of course, also predictive. The prophecy was given to Abraham in Genesis 15:13,14. God also told Abraham of His future judgment upon the Egyptians and of the Exodus in

Verse 7 - "And the nation to whom they shall be in bondage will I judge, said

God: and after that shall they come forth, and serve me in this place."

καὶ τὸ ἔθνος ᾧ ἐὰν δουλεύσουσιν κρινῶ ἐγώ, ὁ θεὸς εἶπεν, καὶ μετὰ ταῦτα
ἐξελεύσονται καὶ λατρεύσουσίν μοι ἐν τῷ τόπῳ τούτῳ.

καὶ (continuative conjunction) 14.
τὸ (acc.sing.neut.of the article in agreement with ἔθνος) 9.
ἔθνος (acc.sing.neut.of ἔθνος, direct object of κρινῶ) 376.
ᾧ (dat.sing.neut.of ὅς,in a relative clause, personal advantage) 65.
ἐὰν (conditional particle with the subjunctive in a relative clause) 363.
δουλεύσουσιν (3d.per.pl.aor.act.subj.of δουλεύω, Thessalian dialect) 604.
κρινῶ (1st.per.sing.fut.act.ind.of κρίνω, predictive) 531.
ἐγώ (nom.sing.masc.of ἐγώ, subject of κρινῶ) 123.
ὁ (nom.sing.masc.of the article in agreement with θεὸς) 9.
θεὸς (nom.sing.masc.of θεός, subject of εἶπεν) 124.
εἶπεν (3d.per.sing.aor.act.ind.of εἶπον) 155.
καὶ (continuative conjunction) 14.
μετὰ (preposition with the accusative of time extent) 50.
ταῦτα (acc.pl.neut.of οὗτος, time extent) 93.
ἐξελεύσονται (3d.per.pl.fut.mid.ind.of ἐξέρχομαι, predictive) 161.
καὶ (adjunctive conjunction joining verbs) 14.
λατρεύσουσίν (3d.per.pl.fut.act.ind.of λατρεύω, predictive) 366.
μοι (dat.sing.masc.of ἐγώ, personal advantage) 123.
ἐν (preposition with the locative of place) 80.
τῷ (loc.sing.masc.of the article in agreement with τόπῳ) 9.
τόπῳ (loc.sing.masc.of τόπος, place where) 1019.
τούτῳ (loc.sing.masc.of οὗτος, in agreement with τόπῳ) 93.

Translation - " 'And I will judge the nation which they will serve,' God said, 'and after that they will come out and they will serve me in this place.' "

Comment: The relative clause ᾧ ἐὰν δουλεύσουσιν is indefinite. The conditional particle ἐὰν is here with δουλεύσουσιν, which is really aorist subjunctive, not future indicative, as a result of a vowel-interchange. "The Thessalian dialect changed ω to ου as in τοῦ κοινοῦ for τῷ κοινῷ. This change reappears in Rhodes and the AEolic-Doric. Buresch finds the change between ω and ου common in the Egyptian vernacular, as in the Sahidic dialect οο is often used for ω. It is, of course, possible . . . that some indicatives in ου may really be subjunctive as a result of the vowel-interchange." (Robertson, *Grammar,* 202,203). "The use οι ἐάν like ἄν has been shown to be very common with relatives in this period, (*i.e.* in Doric, *my comment*).It is immaterial which is found." (*Ibid,* 959). There is nothing indefinite about the fact that some nation would enslave Israel, nor, indeed anything indefinite about God's foreknowledge of which nation it would be. But God did not choose to tell Abraham definitely that it would be the Egyptians. "The nation, whichever one it may turn out to be, (indefinite) I will judge (definite)" Then God added that after 400 years of bondage the Exodus would occur and the children of Abraham, 3,500,000 strong, would serve Him at Bethel. *Cf.* Exodus 3:12; Gen.15:14.

The predicted Egyptian bondage which would occupy Israel for 400 years is the reason why God did not give any land to Abraham when he first arrived in Canaan (verse 5), although He promised that after the Egyptian ordeal was past and the wilderness wanderings were over, He would give the land, which He was, at that time, showing to Abraham, to his descendants for an everlasting possession. So Abraham got to see it, but he was not privileged to own it, although he knew that someday his grandchildren would own it, and that one of them, King David's Greater Son, the Messiah would sit upon David's throne and rule over it, and the entire world, forever. If God had given Palestine to Abraham personally, to convey at his death to Isaac and he to Jacob, Jacob could not have held it, since, in his old age he and his family of sons, daughter and grandchildren, seventy in number, left Palestine and went to Egypt to see Joseph, there to remain until the Exodus, rougly 400 years later.

Abraham's faith, the gift to him from the ἀρχηγὸς τῆς πίστεως (Heb.12:2), enabled him to look about him in Palestine, as far as his eye could reach and beyond and say, "Some day all of this land will belong to my children and grandchildren." And yet at the time that he was told all of this he was 86 years old, his wife was 76 and they had no children. That is what the next part of Stephen's story is about in

Verse 8 - "And he gave him the covenant of circumcision: and so Abraham begat Isaac, and circumcised him the eighth day: and Isaac begat Jacob, and Jacob begat the twelve patriarchs."

καὶ ἔδωκεν αὐτῷ διαθήκην περιτομῆς καὶ οὕτως ἐγέννησεν τὸν Ἰσαὰκ καὶ περιέτεμεν αὐτὸν τῇ ἡμέρᾳ τῇ ὀγδόῃ καὶ Ἰσαὰκ τὸν Ἰακώβ, καὶ Ἰακὼβ τοὺς δώδεκα πατριάρχας.

καὶ (continuative conjunction) 14.
ἔδωκεν (3d.per.sing.aor.act.ind.of δίδωμι, constative) 362.
αὐτῷ (dat.sing.masc.of αὐτός, indirect object of ἔδωκεν) 16.
διαθήκην (acc.sing.fem.of διαθήκη, direct object of ἔδωκεν) 1575.
περιτομῆς (gen.sing.fem.of περιτομή, description) 2368.
καὶ (continuative conjunction) 14.
οὕτως (demonstrative adverb) 74.
ἐγέννησεν (3d.per.sing.aor.act.ind.of γεννάω, constative) 9.
τὸν (acc.sing.masc.of the article in agreement with Ἰσαὰκ) 9.
Ἰσαὰκ (acc.sing.masc.of Ἰσαάκ, direct object of ἐγέννησεν) 10.
καὶ (adjunctive conjunction joining verbs) 14.
περιέτεμεν (3d.per.sing.2d.aor.act.ind.of περιτέμνω, constative) 1842.
αὐτὸν (acc.sing.masc.of αὐτός, direct object of περιέτεμεν) 16.
τῇ (loc.sing.fem.of the article in agreement with ἡμέρᾳ) 9.
ἡμέρᾳ (loc.sing.fem.of ἡμέρα, time point) 135.
τῇ (loc.sing.fem.of the article in agreement with ὀγδόῃ) 9.
ὀγδόῃ (loc.sing.fem.of ὄγδοος, in agreement with ἡμέρᾳ) 1841.

καὶ (continuative conjunction) 14.

Ἰσαὰκ (nom.sing.masc.of Ἰσαάκ, subject of ἐγέννησεν understood) 10.

τὸν (acc.sing.masc.of the article in agreement with Ἰακώβ) 9.

Ἰακώβ (acc.sing.masc.of Ἰακώβ, direct object of ἐγέννησεν understood) 12.

καὶ (continuative conjunction) 14.

Ἰακὼβ (nom.sing.masc.of Ἰακώβ, subject of ἐγέννησεν understood) 12.

τοὺς (acc.pl.masc.of the article in agreement with πατριάρχας) 9.

δώδεκα (numeral) 820.

πατριάρχας (acc.pl.masc.of πατριάρχης, direct object of ἐγέννησεν understood) 2998.

Translation - "And He gave to him a covenant of circumcision: and thus he became the father of Isaac and circumcised him on the eighth day; and Isaac fathered Jacob and Jacob the twelve patriarchs."

Comment: Stephen omitted any mention of Abraham's lapse in faith which resulted in the birth of Ishmael (Gen.16:1-16). Nor did he allude to the element of the miraculous in the birth of Isaac to his aged parents (Gen.17:1-27), or to the test of Abraham's faith in the sacrifice of Isaac (Gen.22; Heb.11:17-19; Rom.4:17-22).

God gave Abraham orders to circumcise his son at a time when he had no son and at an age at which the birth of a son would clearly come within the realm of the miraculous. But faith in the promises of God is measured in reverse ratio to confidence in our own ability. It was when Abraham realized that he had passed beyond the age when paternity could reasonably be expected (Rom.4:19,20) that he was strong in faith and gave glory to God, knowing full well that what God had promised "He was able also to perform." If Caiaphas and his colleagues on the San Hedrin had possessed the faith of Abraham, descent from whom they so proudly proclaimed, they would have recognized Jesus, the Galilean as the ultimate fulfillment of God's covenant promise to their father.

Stephen went on with his story, the details of which were already well known to those in his audience, but the spiritual significance of which they had not the perspicacity to grasp.

Verse 9 - "And the patriarchs, moved with envy, sold Joseph into Egypt: but God was with him."

Καὶ οἱ πατριάρχαι ζηλώσαντες τὸν Ἰωσὴφ ἀπέδοντο εἰς Αἴγυπτον, καὶ ἦν ὁ θεὸς μετ' αὐτοῦ.

Καὶ (continuative conjunction) 11.

οἱ (nom.pl.masc.of the article in agreement with πατριάρχαι) 9.

πατριάρχαι (nom.pl.masc.of πατριάρχης, subject of ἀπέδοντο) 2998.

#3105 ζηλώσαντες (aor.act.part.nom.pl.masc.of ζηλόω, adverbial, causal).

affect - Gal.4:17.
be jealous over - 2 Cor.11:2.

be moved with envy - Acts 7:9.
be zealous - Rev.3:19.
covet - 1 Cor.14:39.
covet earnestly - 1 Cor.12:31.
desire - 1 Cor.14:1.
desire to have - James 4:2.
envy - Acts 17:5; 1 Cor.13:4.
zealously affect - Gal.4:17,18.

Meaning: To be consumed with zeal, or to instil zeal in others. In an evil sense, to inspire others to a wrong attitude - Gal.4:17; in a good sense - Gal.4:18. With reference to Paul's zeal for the best for the Corinthian church - 2 Cor.11:2; to be moved to do evil: - Joseph's brothers - Acts 7:9; Jews - Acts 17:5; in a good sense, to desire something good - Rev.3:19; the best gifts - 1 Cor.12:31; 14:1; to prophesy - 1 Cor.14:39; James 4:2. To envy in an evil sense - 1 Cor.13:4. To support another financially - Gal.4:17b.

τὸν (acc.sing.masc.of the article in agreement with Ἰωσήφ) 9.
Ἰωσήφ (acc.sing.masc.of Ἰωσήφ, direct object of ἀπέδοντο) 2000.
ἀπέδοντο (3d.per.pl.2d.aor.mid.ind.of ἀποδίδωμι, indirect middle, constative) 495.
εἰς (preposition with the accusative of extent) 140.
Αἴγυπτον (acc.sing.masc.of Αἴγυπτον, extent) 203.
καὶ (adversative conjunction) 14.
ἦν (3d.per.sing.imp.ind.of εἰμί, progressive duration) 86.
ὁ (nom.sing.masc.of the article in agreement with θεός) 9.
θεὸς (nom.sing.masc.of θεός, subject of ἦν) 124.
μετ' (preposition with the genitive of accompaniment) 50.
αὐτοῦ (gen.sing.masc.of αὐτός, accompaniment) 16.

Translation - "And because they were jealous the patriarchs sold Joseph into slavery in Egypt, but God was always with him."

Comment: ζηλώσαντες is a causal participle. It provides the motive. Note the indirect middle in ἀπέδοντο - "they sold him for themselves" - *i.e.* for the desired end to rid themselves of his presence, and also for the money.

Stephen is trying to show the San Hedrin that since the day when the covenant was originally given to Abraham, God, Who predicted the course of events in Israel's history, overrode every trial and overcame every obstacle. Joseph was delivered to Egyptian bondage but not without God's knowledge and continual watchcare over him. *Cf.*Gen.37:1-36. If Joseph had not been sold, the it likely that Jacob and his family would have starved to death in the famine which followed and the promise of God to Abraham would not have been fulfilled. (Gen.45:4-8). Stephen's speech is an exposition of the theological interpretation of history, such as Paul delivered on Mars Hill (Acts 17).

Verse 10 - ". . . and delivered him out of all his afflictions, and gave him favour

*and wisdom in the sight of Pharaoh king of Egypt; and he made him governor
over Egypt and all his house."*

καὶ ἐξείλατο αὐτὸν ἐκ πασῶν τῶν θλίφεων αὐτοῦ, καὶ ἔδωκεν αὐτῷ χάριν
καὶ σοφίαν ἐναντίον Φαραὼ βασιλέως Αἰγύπτου, καὶ κατέστησεν αὐτὸν
ἡγούμενον ἐπ' Αἴγυπτον καὶ (ἐφ') ὅλον τὸν οἶκον αὐτοῦ.

καὶ (continuative conjunction) 14.
ἐξείλατο (3d.per.sing.1st.aor.mid.ind.of ἐξαιρέω, constative) 504.
αὐτὸν (acc.sing.masc.of αὐτός, direct object of ἐξείλατο) 16.
ἐκ (preposition with the ablative of separation) 19.
πασῶν (abl.pl.fem.of πᾶς, in agreement with θλίφεων) 67.
τῶν (abl.pl.fem.of the article in agreement with θλίφεων) 9.
θλίφεων (abl.pl.fem.of θλίφις, separation) 1046.
αὐτοῦ (gen.sing.masc.of αὐτός, possession) 16.
καὶ (adjunctive conjunction joining verbs) 14.
ἔδωκεν (3d.per.sing.aor.act.ind.of δίδωμι, constative) 362.
αὐτῷ (dat.sing.masc.of αὐτός, indirect object of ἔδωκεν) 16.
χάριν (acc.sing.fem.of χάρις, direct object of ἔδωκεν) 1700.
καὶ (adjunctive conjunction joining nouns) 14.
σοφίαν (acc.sing.fem.of σοφία, direct object of ἔδωκεν) 934.
ἐναντίον (improper preposition with the genitive of place description) 1780.

#3106 Φαραὼ (gen.sing.masc.of Φαραώ, place description).

Pharaoh - Acts 7;10,13,21; Rom.9;17; Heb.11:24.

Meaning: Pharaoh, the common title of the ancient rulers of Egypt - Acts
7:10,13,21; Rom.9:17; Heb.11:24.

βασιλέως (gen.sing.masc.of βασιλεύς, in apposition) 31.
Αἰγύπτου (gen.sing.masc.of Αἴγυπτον, designation) 203.
καὶ (adjunctive conjunction joining verbs) 14.
κατέστησεν (3d.per.sing.aor.act.ind.of καθίστημι, constative) 1523.
αὐτὸν (acc.sing.masc.of αὐτός, direct object of κατέστησεν) 16.
ἡγούμενον (pres.mid.part.acc.sing.masc.of ἡγέομαι, substantival, predicate
nominative) 162.
ἐπ' (preposition with the accusative, general reference) 47.
Αἴγυπτον (acc.sing.masc.of Αἴγυπτον, general reference) 203.
καὶ (adjunctive conjunction joining prepositional phrases) 14.
ἐφ' (preposition with the accusative of general reference) 47.
ὅλον (acc.sing.masc.of ὅλος, in agreement with οἶκον) 112.
τὸν (acc.sing.masc.of the article in agreement with οἶκον) 9.
οἶκον (acc.sing.masc.of οἶκος, general reference) 784.
αὐτοῦ (gen.sing.masc.of αὐτός, possession) 16.

*Translation - "And He delivered him out of all his oppressions and gave to him
grace and wisdom in the presence of Pharaoh, King of Egypt, and he appointed
him Governor over Egypt and over his entire household."*

Comment: The ϑλίφεων referred to are recorded in Gen.39:7-20. His deliverance and elevation to a high post in the Egyptian government occupy the remainder of the book of Genesis. The story is rich in detail. It reveals clearly the manner in which the sovereign God manipulates and uses the events of human history to effect His purpose. Specifically, in the Joseph story, God was circumventing the effects of the famine, which, of course He foresaw, upon the people to whom He had committed Himself in an unconditional covenant. Of course He could have used other means to rescue them if He had chosen, in His wisdom to do so. Stephen was trying to impress the San Hedrin with the fact that each of them was a part of a redemptive program for the nation, the key figure in which is their Messiah, Whom they crucified, but Whom God raised from the dead. Thus the Jew who is granted repentance and salvation sees the events surrounding the death of Jesus as a part of the divine scheme of redemption, which is his only means of escape from eternal judgment. The wisdom and personal traits which He gave to Joseph, by which he commended himself to the Pharaoh were all part of God's guidance for His chosen people. That Stephen did not describe in detail the story of Joseph in Egypt was not necessary since those in his audience were familiar with it, and he knew that they would get the point.

The famine came and starvation faced Jacob and his family in Canaan. This is the next step in the story in

Verse 11 - "Now there came a dearth over all the land of Egypt and Chanaan, and great affliction; and our fathers found no sustenance."

ἦλθεν δὲ λιμὸς ἐφ' ὅλην τὴν Αἴγυπτον καὶ Χανάαν καὶ ϑλῖφις μεγάλη, καὶ οὐχ ηὕρισκον χορτάσματα οἱ πατέρες ἡμῶν.

ἦλθεν (3d.per.sing.aor.ind.of ἔρχομαι, ingressive) 146.
δὲ (explanatory conjunction) 11.
λιμὸς (nom.sing.masc.of λιμός, subject of ἦλθεν) 1485.
ἐφ' (preposition with the accusative of extent) 47.
ὅλην (acc.sing.fem.of ὅλος, in agreement with Αἴγυπτον) 112.
τὴν (acc.sing.fem.of the article in agreement with Αἴγυπτον) 9.
Αἴγυπτον (acc.sing.fem.of Αἴγυπτον, extent) 203.
καὶ (adjunctive conjunction joining nouns) 14.

#3107 Χανάαν (acc.sing.fem.of Χανάαν, extent)/

Chanaan - Acts 7;11; 13:19.

Meaning: That part of Palestine lying west of the Jordan River - Acts 7:11. Of all Palestine - Acts 13:19.

καὶ (adjunctive conjunction joining nouns) 14.
ϑλῖφις (nom.sing.fem.of ϑλῖφις, subject of ἦλθεν) 1046.
μεγάλη (nom.sing.fem.of μέγας, in agreement with ϑλῖφις) 184.
καὶ (inferential conjunction) 14.
οὐχ (summary negative conjunction with the indicative) 130.

ηὕρισκον (3d.per.pl.imp.act.ind.of εὑρίσκω, progressive description) 79.

#3108 χορτάσματα (acc.pl.neut.of χόρτασμα, direct object of ηὕρισκον).

sustenance - Acts 7:11.

Meaning: Cf. χορτάζω (#428); χόρτος (#632). Hence, sustenance, food. With reference to the famine in Israel - Acts 7:11.

οἱ (nom.pl.masc.of the article in agreement with πατέρες) 9.
πατέρες (nom.pl.masc.of πατήρ, subject of ηὕρισκον) 238.
ἡμῶν (gen.pl.masc.of ἐγώ, relationship) 123.

Translation - "Now a famine began to spread throughout all of Egypt and Canaan and with it great distress; therefore our fathers could not find anything to eat."

Comment: δὲ is explanatory. The imperfect tense in ηὕρισκον indicates repeated searches for food by Jacob and his sons, but without success.

Verse 12 - "But when Jacob heard that there was corn in Egypt, he sent out our fathers first."

ἀκούσας δὲ Ἰακὼβ ὄντα σιτία εἰς Αἴγυπτον ἐξαπέστειλεν τοὺς πατέρας ἡμῶν πρῶτον.

ἀκούσας (aor.act.part.nom.sing.masc.of ἀκούω, adverbial, temporal/causal) 148.
δὲ (inferential conjunction) 11.
Ἰακὼβ (nom.sing.masc.of Ἰακώβ, subject of ἐξαπέστειλεν) 12.
ὄντα (pres.part.acc.sing.neut.of εἰμί, adjectival, in agreement with σιτία, restrictive, indirect discourse) 86.

#3109 σιτία (acc.pl.neut.of σιτίον, general reference).

corn - Acts 7:12.

Meaning: Corn, wheat, grain. Dimin.of σῖτος (#311). Available in Egypt during the famine - Acts 7:12.

εἰς (preposition with the accusative, like a locative) 140.
Αἴγυπτον (acc.sing.fem.of Αἴγυπτον, like a locative, place) 203.
ἐξαπέστειλεν (3d.per.sing.aor.act.ind.of ἐξαποστέλλω, constative) 1835.
τοὺς (acc.pl.masc.of the article in agreement with πατέρας) 9.
πατέρας (acc.pl.masc.of πατήρ, direct object of ἐξαπέστειλεν) 238.
ἡμῶν (gen.pl.masc.of ἐγώ, relationship) 123.
πρῶτον (acc.sing.neut.of πρῶτος, adverbial) 487.

Translation - "And when Jacob heard that there was grain in Egypt he sent out our fathers first."

Comment: The participle ἀκούσας is both temporal and causal. When/because Jacob heard about the grain available in Egypt he sent his sons. Here we have the participle ὄντα, after ἀκούσας in an object clause in indirect discourse. It is joined to σιτία, an accusative of general reference, which it modifies as a participial adjective. Jacob heard about (indirect discourse) the corn. What corn? That which was in Egypt. *Cf.*Acts 14:9; 3 John 4 and 2 Thess.3:11, among others for a participle in indirect discourse. *Cf.* Luke 4:23 for another adjectival participle in an indirect discourse construction. *Cf.*Gen.42:1-3 for the story.

Verse 13 - "And at the second time Joseph was made known to his brethren; and Joseph's kindred was made known to Pharaoh."

καὶ ἐν τῷ δευτέρῳ ἀνεγνωρίσθη Ἰωσὴφ τοῖς ἀδελφοῖς αὐτοῦ, καὶ φανερὸν ἐγένετο τῷ Φαραὼ τὸ γένος (τοῦ) Ἰωσήφ.

καὶ (continuative conjunction) 14.
ἐν (preposition with the locative of time point) 80.
τῷ (loc.sing.masc.of the article in agreement with καιρῷ understood) 9.
δευτέρῳ (loc.sing.masc.of δεύτερος, in agreement with καιρῷ understood) 1371.

#3110 ἀνεγνωρίσθη (3d.per.sing.aor.pass.ind.of ἀναγνωρίζω, constative).

be made known - Acts 7:13.

Meaning: A combination of ἀνά (#1059) and γνωρίζω (#1882). Hence, to be recognized. With reference to Joseph and his brothers in Egypt - Acts 7:13.

Ἰωσὴφ (nom.sing.masc.of Ἰωσήφ, subject of ἀνεγνωρίσθη) 2000.
τοῖς (instru.pl.masc.of the article in agreement with ἀδελφοῖς) 9.
ἀδελφοῖς (instru.pl.masc.of ἀδελφός, agent) 15.
αὐτοῦ (gen.sing.masc.of αὐτός, relationship) 16.
καὶ (continuative conjunction) 14.
φανερὸν (nom.sing.neut.of φανερός, predicate adjective) 981.
ἐγένετο (3d.per.sing.aor.ind.of γίνομαι, constative) 113.
τῷ (dat.sing.masc.of the article in agreement with Φαραώ) 9.
Φαραὼ (dat.sing.masc.of Φαραώ, personal interest) 3106.
τὸ (nom.sing.neut.of the article in agreement with γένος) 9.
γένος (nom.sing.neut.of γένος, subject of ἐγένετο) 1090.
(τοῦ) (gen.sing.masc.of the article in agreement with Ἰωσφ) 9.
Ἰωσήφ (gen.sing.masc.of Ἰησώφ, relationship) 2000.

Translation - "And on the second occasion Joseph was recognized by his brothers, and the family relationship was made known to the Pharaoh."

Comment: The passive voice in ἀνεγνωρίσθη creates a contradiction between the record in Gen.45:3 and the statement of Stephen. Joseph introduced himself to his brothers. He was not recognized by his brothers. Stephen should have used the middle voice - "Joseph made himself known to his brothers." It is a small error which did not affect Stephen's purpose which was to emphasize the fact that God, in faithful observance of His covenant promises to Abraham, Isaac and Jacob, protected His children at every step.

Verse 14 - "Then sent Joseph, and called his father Jacob to him, and all his kindred, threescore and fifteen souls."

ἀποστείλας δὲ Ἰωσὴφ μετεκαλέσατο Ἰακὼβ τὸν πατέρα αὐτοῦ καὶ πᾶσαν τὴν συγγένειαν ἐν ψυχαῖς ἑβδομήκοντα πέντε,

ἀποστείλας (1st.aor.act.part.nom.sing.masc.of ἀποστέλλω, adverbial, temporal) 215.

δὲ (continuative conjunction) 11.

Ἰωσὴφ (nom.sing.masc.of Ἰωσήφ, subject of μετεκαλέσατο) 2000.

#3111 μετεκαλέσατο (3d.per.sing.aor.mid.ind.of μετακαλέω, constative, indirect middle).

call - Acts 20:17.
call for - Acts 24:25.
call hither - Acts 10:32.
call to one's self - Acts 7:14.

Meaning: A combination of μετα (#50) and καλέω (#107). Hence, to summon, call. In the indirect middle - "to call to or for oneself." Joseph called his father to Egypt - Acts 7;14; Cornelius is told to call Peter - Acts 10:32; Paul called the elders of the church at Ephesus - Acts 20:17. Felix promised to call for Paul - Acts 24:25.

Ἰακὼβ (acc.sing.masc.of Ἰακώβ, direct object of μετεκαλέσατο) 12.
τὸν (acc.sing.masc.of the article in agreement with πατέρα) 9.
πατέρα (acc.sing.masc.of πατήρ, in apposition) 238.
αὐτοῦ (gen.sing.masc.of αὐτός, relationship) 16.
καὶ (adjunctive conjunction joining nouns) 14.
πᾶσαν (acc.sing.fem.of πᾶς, in agreement with συγγένειαν) 67.
τὴν (acc.sing.fem.of the article in agreement with συγγένειαν) 9.
συγγένειαν (acc.sing.fem.of συγγενής, direct object of μετεκαλέσατο) 1815.
ἐν (preposition with the locative - "amounting to" or "numbering") 80.
ψυχαῖς (loc.pl.fem.of ψυχή, sphere) 233.
ἑβδομήκοντα (numeral) 2410.
πέντε - (numeral) 1119.

Translation - "And Joseph sent (his brothers) and summoned Jacob, his father and all his relatives — numbering seventy-five."

Comment: *Cf.*Genesis 45:25 - 46:34.

Verse 15 - "So Jacob went down into Egypt, and died, he, and our fathers."

καὶ κατέβη Ἰακὼβ εἰς Αἴγυπτον. καὶ ἐτελεύτησεν αὐτὸς καὶ οἱ πατέρες ἡμῶν,

καὶ (inferential conjunction) 14.

κατέβη (3d.per.sing.aor.act.ind.of καταβαίνω, constative) 324.

Ἰακὼβ (nom.sing.masc.of Ἰακώβ, subject of κατέβη and ἐτελεύτησεν) 12.

εἰς (preposition with the accusative of extent) 140.

Αἴγυπτον (acc.sing.fem.of Αἴγυπτον, extent) 203.

καὶ (adjunctive conjunction joining verbs) 14.

ἐτελεύτησεν (3d.per.sing.aor.act.ind.of τελευτάω, constative) 231.

αὐτὸς (nom.sing.masc.of αὐτός, subject of ἐτελεύτησεν) 16.

καὶ (adjunctive conjunction joining nouns) 14.

οἱ (nom.pl.masc.of the article in agreement with πατέρες) 9.

πατέρες (nom.pl.masc.of πατήρ, subject of ἐτελεύτησαν, understood) 238.

ἡμῶν (gen.pl.masc.of ἐγώ, relationship) 123.

Translation - "*So Jacob went down to Egypt and he died — and our fathers died.*"

Comment: *Cf.* Genesis 49:1 - 50:3. In verse 14 we have ἐν with the locative idea meaning "amounting to" or "numbering." "It is needless to multiply unduly the various uses of ἐν, which are "innumerable" in the LXX. (Conybears and Stock, *Selections From the LXX*, 82, as cited in Robertson, *Grammar,* 588). "H. St. Thackeray,(*A Grammar of the Old Testament in Greek*, I, 47) calls attention to the frequent use of ἐν of accompanying circumstance in the LXX. . . . its chief extension is due to the imitation of the Hebrew *beth.*" (Blass, *Grammatik d.neut. Griech,* 130, as cited in *Ibid.)* But by no means all these uses are Hebraic. Thus ἐν for the idea of accompanying circumstance is classical enough (*cf.* ἐν ὅπλοις εἶναι, Xen. *Anab.* 5.9, like English "The people are up in arms"), though the LXX abounds with it. It occurs also in the papyri." (*Ibid.*). *Cf.* Luke 14:31; Jude 14; Eph.6:16; Mark 12:38; Mt.7:15; John 20:12; Heb.9:25 *et al.*

Verse 16 - "And were carried over into Sychem, and laid in the sepulchre that Abraham bought for a sum of money of the Sons of Emmor, the father of Sychem."

καὶ μετετέθησαν εἰς Συχὲμ καὶ ἐτέθησαν ἐν τῷ μνήματι ᾧ ὠνήσατο Ἀβραὰμ τιμῆς ἀργυρίου παρὰ τῶν υἱῶν Ἐμμὼρ ἐν Συχέμ.

καὶ (continuative conjunction) 14.

#3112 μετετέθησαν (3d.per.pl.aor.pass.ind.of μετατίθημι, direct middle).

carry over - Acts 7:16.
change - Heb.7:12.
remove - Gal.1:6.
translate - Heb.11:5,5.
turn - Jude 4.

Meaning: A combination of μετά (#50) and τίθημι (#180). To transpose, transfer, change from one place to another; to desert one view for another. With reference to the transfer of bodies from Egypt to Sychem for burial - Acts 7:16; to forsake the gospel of Christ for an opposing theology - Gal.1:6; Jude 4; With reference to a change in the priesthood from the Aaronic to the Melchisedek - Heb.7:12. Of Enoch's translation without death from earth to heaven - Heb.11:5,5.

εἰς (preposition with the accusative of extent) 140.

#3113 Συχὲμ (acc.sing.masc.of Συχέμ, extent).

Sychem - Acts 7:16,16.

Meaning: The Son of Emmor, from whom Abraham bought a burial ground - Gen.23:1-20; 50:1-26. Also the area by the same name - 1 Kings 12:25. Where Jacob and the Patriarchs were buried - Acts 7:16,16.

καὶ (continuative conjunction) 14.
ἐτέθησαν (3d.per.pl.1st.aor.pass.ind.of τίθημι, direct middle) 455.
ἐν (preposition with the locative of place where) 80.
τῷ (loc.sing.neut.of the article in agreement with μνήματι) 9.
μνήματι (loc.sing.neut.of μνήμα, place where) 2876.
ᾧ (loc.sing.neut.of ὅς, attracted in case to μνήματι) 65.

#3114 ὠνήσατο (3d.per.sing.aor.mid.ind.of ὠνέομαι, indirect middle).

buy - Acts 7:16.

Meaning: to buy. Followed by the genitive - Acts 7:16.

Ἀβραὰμ (nom.sing.masc.of Ἀβραάμ, subject of ὠνήσατο) 7.
τιμῆς (gen.sing.fem.of τιμή, price description, after a verb of buying) 1619.
ἀργυρίου (gen.sing.neut.of ἀργύιον, description) 1535.
παρὰ (preposition with the ablative of source) 154.
τῶν (abl.pl.masc.of the article in agreement with υἱῶν) 9.
υἱῶν (abl.pl.masc.of υἱός, source) 5.

#3115 Ἐμμὼρ (gen.sing.masc.of Ἐμμόρ, relationship).

Emmor - Acts 7:16.

Meaning: Called Hamor in Genesis 33:19; 34:2. Jacob also bought some land there, as did Abraham - Acts 7:16.

ἐν (preposition with the locative of place) 80.
Συχέμ (loc.sing.masc.of Συχέμ, place) 3113.

Translation - "And they were taken to Sychem and buried in the tomb which Abraham bought for a price of silver from the sons of Hamor in Sychem."

Comment: Dead in Egypt, the Patriarchs and Jacob, their father were nevertheless buried in the covenanted land of promise to await resurrection. God made the covenant first to Abraham and then confirmed it both to Isaac and his son, Jacob. There was no direct confirmation to the twelve sons of Jacob, whom Stephen calls the Patriarchs. Jacob, on his deathbed (Gen.49) spoke to each of his sons and reminded them of the value of the estate which he conveyed to them. God later reconfirmed the covenant, with the throne rights to David (2 Samuel 7:10-17), which had come down in inheritance to him from Judah, in whom they were vested in Genesis 49:10-12. Thus Stephen is emphasizing the fact that God's eternal purpose for Israel is that she will own the land of Canaan as a permanent possession. The Egyptian bondage of four hundred years was only an interlude in her history.

The sanctity with which the American Indian regards the burial grounds of his forefathers is an example of how the descendants of Abraham felt about their inheritance. It was theirs only in contemplation of God's promise to Abraham, Isaac and Jacob, since He had not yet allowed them to possess any of it. When Abraham needed a burial plot for Sarah he was forced to buy it (Gen.25:9,10), just as Jacob had later done (Gen.33:19). We are indebted to Stephen for the information that Abraham had also bought land in Sychem. There is no record of this transaction in the Old Testament.

Verse 17 - "But when the time of the promise drew nigh, which God had sworn to Abraham, the people grew and multiplied in Egypt."

Καθὼς δὲ ἤγγιζεν ὁ χρόνος τῆς ἐπαγγελίας ἧς ὡμολόγησεν ὁ θεὸς τῷ Ἀβραάμ, ηὔξησεν ὁ λαὸς καὶ ἐπληθύνη ἐν Αἰγύπτῳ,

Καθὼς (conjunction in a definite temporal clause) 1348.

δὲ (explanatory conjunction) 11.

ἤγγιζεν (3d.per.sing.imp.act.ind.of ἐγγίζω, inceptive) 252.

ὁ (nom.sing.masc.of the article in agreement with χρόνος) 9.

χρόνος (nom.sing.masc.of χρόνος, subject of ἤγγιζεν) 168.

τῆ (gen.sing.fem.of the article in agreement with ἐπαγγελίας) 9.

ἐπαγγελίας (gen.sing.fem.of ἐπαγγελία, description) 2929.

ἧς (gen.sing.fem.of ὅς, attraction to ἐπαγγελίας) 65.

ὡμολόγησεν (3d.per.sing.aor.act.ind.of ὁμολογέω, culminative) 688.

ὁ (nom.sing.masc.of the article in agreement with θεὸς) 9.

θεὸς (nom.sing.masc.of θεός, subject of ὡμολόγησεν) 124.

τῷ (dat.sing.masc.of the article in agreement with Ἀβραάμ) 9.

Ἀβραάμ (dat.sing.masc.of Ἀβραάμ, indirect object of ὡμολόγησεν) 7.

ηὔξησεν (3d.per.sing.aor.act.ind.of αὐξάνω, ingressive) 628.

ὁ (nom.sing.masc.of the article in agreement with λαὸς) 9.

λαὸς (nom.sing.masc.of λαός, subject of ηὔξησεν and ἐπληθύνθη) 110.

καὶ (adjunctive conjunction joining verbs) 14.

ἐπληθύνθη (3d.per.sing.aor.pass.ind.of πληθύνω, direct middle) 1488.

ἐν (preposition with the locative of place) 80.

Αἰγύπτῳ (loc.sing.fem.of Αἴγυπτον, place) 203.

Translation - *"Now as the time for the fulfillment of the promise which God had given to Abraham drew near, the population began to increase and multiplied in Egypt."*

Comment: καθώς in introduction of a definite temporal clause is unusual in the New Testament, but here that is clearly its force. It is noteworthy that Stephen did not specify how long it would be before Israel was to be liberated. Nor did he specify by whom Abraham and his family would be oppressed. When God made the covenant with Abraham, He said that he and his children would be strangers in territory not theirs for four hundred years, and that these would be four hundred years of affliction. We may not read into this statement (Gen.15:13) that they would spend four hundred years in Egyptian bondage. The following chronological chart measures the accuracy of God's prediction. It also show the accuracy of Paul's statement in Galatians 3:17 that it was 430 years from the Abrahamic Covenant to the Mosaic Covenant at Mount Sinai. It is not possible to account for every day within this period, and the gaps which occur, of undetermined duration are sufficient to explain the slight discrepancies.

Abraham

	Abraham	Isaac	Jacob	Joseph
Abrahamic Covenant (Gen.15:4-18)	85			
Birth of Ishmael (Gen.16:16)	86			
The Covenant Confirmed (Gen.17:1)	99			
Birth of Isaac (Gen.21:5)	100	0		
Death of Sarah (Gen.23:1)	137	37		
Marriage of Isaac (Gen.25:20)	140	40		
Birth of Jacob (Gen.25:26)	160	60	0	
Death of Abraham (Gen.25:7)	175	75	15	
Death of Isaac (Gen.35:28)	280	180	120	
Marriages of Jacob (Gen.29:15-28)	287		127	
Birth of Joseph (Gen.30:22-24)	300		140	0
Joseph is sold into bondage (Gen.37:2-28)	317		157	17
Joseph is imprisoned (Gen.41:1)	328		168	28
Joseph becomes Prime Minister (Gen.41:46)	330		170	30
Jacob goes to Egypt (Gen.45:6,11)	339		179	39
Death of Jacob (Gen.47:28)	356		196	56
Death of Joseph (Gen.50:26)	410			110
		Moses		
Birth of Moses (Exod.2:2)		0?		
The Exodus (Exod.3:14-14:31)	490	80?		

85 plus 430 equals 515 (Gal.3:17). A discrepancy of 25 years.
85 plus 400 equals 485 (Gen.15:13). A discrepancy of 5 years.

We do not know precisely how long after Isaac died that Jacob married Leah and Rachel. It was something more than seven years, nor do we know the precise age of Jacob when Joseph was born. Joseph was in prison something more than two years. Nor do we know how long after the death of Joseph the Exodus took place. It was 80 years plus the time between the death of Joseph and the birth of Moses. These gaps of imprecise duration account for the discrepancies.

"The number four hundred and thirty is evidently derived by the apostle from Exod.12:40, where, though according to the Hebrew text, "the time that the children of Israel dwelt in Egypt was four hundred and thirty years," the Vatican ms.of the Lxx, with which agrees, also the Samaritan Pentateuch, reads: ἡ δὲ κατοίκησις τῶν υἱῶν Ἰσραὴλ ἥν κατῴκησαν ἐν γῇ Αἰγύπτον καὶ ἐν γῇ Χανάαν ἔτη τετρακοσία τριάκοντα πέντε, but AF, perhaps also the second hand of B, omit πέντε (so Tdf.), and A adds αὐτοὶ καὶ οἱ πατέρες αὐτῶν. The expression καὶ ἐν γῇ Χανάαν, for which there is no equivalent in Hebrew, evidently refers to the residence in Canaan previous to that in Egypt, so that the whole period covered is, roughly speaking, from Abraham to Moses. On the comparison between this datum and Gen.15:13, quoted in the speech of Stephen, *cf.* Alf.on Gal.*ad hoc.* For the apostle's argument the length of the period has, of course, no significance, save that the longer the covenant had been in force, the more impressive is his statement." (Ernest De Witt Burton, *A Critical and Exegetical Commentary on The Epistle to the Galatians," 183, 184).*

The KJV has "Now the sojourning of the children of Israel, *who dwelt in Egypt,* was four hundred and thirty years" (Exod.12:40) and thus avoids saying that the entire 430 years was spent in Egypt. Thus the time period from Gen.15:13 until Jacob and his family went to Egypt is included, as they were then living on land which, although promised in the covenant to become theirs at some future time, was not yet theirs.

God moved in keeping with natural law to bring about the fulfillment of His prophecy. His method was a population explosion among the Israelis in Egypt. *Cf.* Exodus 1:7. Note that the two verbs which Stephen used to describe the demographic increase indicate both arithmetic (ηὔξησεν) and exponential (ἐπληθύνθη) progression. The population not only increased arithmetically, but also exponentially. The geometric increase of the "swarm" (Exod.1:7) in Egypt brought increased pressure upon the productive capacity of the land to support the population. Egypt's productive potential was pushed into the area of diminishing returns. Thus while total production increased as population grew, at the point of diminishing returns, it increased at a slower rate than population until marginal production became negative, at which point total production actually declined and approached the vanishing point. Thus per capita production fell and inflation occurred, particularly in the food market. Everyone in Egypt would feel the pinch and the Egyptians reacted as we might expect. As standards of living declined it was to be the Jews who would suffer first.

There is a hint here that relates the divine foreknowledge to His prediction of coming events, and also to the manner in which the predicted events occur. God only allowed the natural laws of economic supply and demand to run their course in terms of the principles which were established in creation. As the time for Israel's deliverance from Egypt approached (430 years from Abraham to Sinai) the Egyptian government acted to stem the population flood, with the edict that Jewish male babies should be destroyed. In the long run Israel's population would decline to the vanishing point or the Jewish blood line would be amalgamated with the Egyptian and the divine program of redemption would fail.

The Jewish population explosion not only threatened the economy of Egypt, as we have seen but also its culture. Judaism was a spiritual monotheism, while the Egyptians worshipped a variety of deities modeled chiefly on the animal kingdom and the ethical system that resulted was what one might expect.

A similar threat faces the Soviet Union in the closing decades of the twentieth century.

"During the next two decades, the Soviet Union will face special problems that have never before afflicted a major industrialized nation during peacetime. Simply stated, the European part of the population is not replacing itself, while the non-Russian, non-Slavic, non- European people of the Soviet Union — most of whom are of Muslin origin — are experiencing a strong growth in numbers. By the year 2000, ethnic Russians will be a clear minority in the country that most Americans call "Russia."

From this simple fact flow consequences that may, over the next two decades, lead the Soviet Union into peculiar economic, military, and political difficulties.

The USSR's annual rate of economic growth now stands at a low 2 percent; shortages of skilled labor caused by the slowdown in the ethnic Russian rate of increase could trim that to zero or even induce a decline. Barring some unforeseen change in the Kremlin's world view, the Soviet military will continue to require hundreds of thousands of conscripts each year through the 1980s and '90s — but in 15 years, the Red Army may well find itself with large numbers of soldiers who turn toward Mecca at sunset. In short, between now and the end of the century, the ethnic Russian primacy long taken for granted by both tsars and Bolsheviks will be challenged — not by individuals but by inescapable demographic trends.

. . . The demographic shift will magnify the effects of a general demographic *slump*. Overall, death rates are up, and birth rates are down. Since 1964, the Soviet death rate has jumped by 40 percent; by the end of the century, it is expected to hit 10.6 annually per 1,000 population, nearly the same rate as China's is now. Meanwhile, the national birth rate has fallen by 30 percent since 1950; two decades from now, the rate likely will be down to 16.1 per 1,000. Labor is already short, and the available supply will tighten further over the next few years as the annual net increase in the size of the working-age population sags from its 1976 high of 2.7 million to a projected 1986 low of 285,000. For a variety of reasons, the 1980s should also bring a long-term decline in Soviet capital formation — just when more investment in machinery will be needed to help offset labor shortages by boosting productivity.

How did the Soviet Union get caught in this bind?

The past is partly to blame. Stalin's purges of the 1930s took many millions of lives. Battlefield losses during World War II claimed another 15 million Soviet *males* alone. The Soviet Union is still feeling the "demographic echo" of both events. To policymakers in the Kremlin, the phrase "generation gap" has a special gruesome reality.

But the continuing climb in the Soviet death rate indicates that whatever the other problems of the past were, many of them are still around. Indeed, during the last few years the mortality rate for 20- to 44-year-olds has shot up so fast that male life expectancy has dropped from 66 to 63 years, a full decade less than the life span for females. (The only nation with a larger gap is Gabon). The chief villain here is, in two words, rampant alcoholism. Among its well-known effects are ill health, malnutrition, and accidential death.

. . . Soviet babies are also dying in shockingly large numbers. During the past decade, the USSR became the first industrialized nation to experience a long-term rise in infant mortality, which grew, according to the Soviet definition, from 22.9 per 1,000 live births in 1971 to 31.1 per 1,000 in 1976. (The Soviets consider infant losses with a week of delivery as miscarriages, not deaths. If calculated by American methods, the 1976 figure would be 35.6 per 1,000, more than twice the U.S. rate).

One reason for the rise in infant mortality is that abortion has apparently become the USSR's principal means of "contraception," with a present average of six abortions per woman per lifetime, 12 times the U.S. rate. When used repeatedly, abortion may induce premature delivery in subsequent pregnancies, and premature infants are 25 times more likely to die during their first year than full-term infants. Another baby-killer is female alcoholism, which weakens the fetus.

. . . the Muslims of the borderlands reportedly taunt the Russians with the warning: "Wait until the Chinese come."

The Chinese may never come, but the year 2000 will, and it might bring a Muslim "victory in the bedroom." At century's end, the population of the Central Asian repulbics will have grown by one-half, from 40 to 60 million. These five republics, populated mainly by ethnic Turks sharing a common religion and culture, will then account for more than 20 percent of the entire Soviet population. If one adds the three Transcaucasian republics of Armenia, Azerbaijan, and Georgia, then the turn-of-the-century total for the "Soviet sunbelt" climbs to almost 30 percent. In 1970, only 1 out of 7 persons in the Soviet Union was of Muslim origin. By the turn of the century, the ratio will be at least 1 out of 5, and perhaps 1 out of 4. Of the Soviet population as a whole, ethnic Russians will be a minority - 48 percent." (Murray Feshbach, *The Soviet Future — A Different Crisis," The Wilson Quarterly,* Winter, 1981, 117-120).

Such are the problems that powerful nations have always faced when they failed to deal with their minorities on an equitable basis. God had promised Abraham that the nation that oppressed his family would be judged (Acts 7:7). Not all of the woes that beset the Egyptians were the result of the ten plagues with which God, through the agency of Moses, smote the land. Pharaoh was ambivalent about Moses' demand that Israel be set free. He was loath to lose a large free labor supply, but he was also heartily glad to be rid of them, before they, with their amazing fecundity took over the land. Twentieth century Russians will either use their Muslim subjects as "cannon fodder" or ship them to Siberia.

Verse 18 - "Till another king arose, which knew not Joseph."

ἄχρι οὗ ἀνέστη βασιλεὺς ἕτερος (ἐπ' Αἴγυπτον) ὃς οὐκ ᾔδει τὸν Ἰωσήφ.

ἄχρι (conjunction introducing a definite relative temporal clause) 1517.
οὗ (gen.sing.neut.of ὅς, time description in a relative temporal clause) 65.
ἀνέστη (3d.per.sing.aor.act.ind.of ἀνίστημι, definite temporal clause, constative) 789.
βασιλεὺς (nom.sing.masc.of βασιλεύς, subject of ἀνέστη) 31.
ἕτερος (nom.sing.masc.of ἕτερος, in agreement with βασιλεὺς) 605.
(ἐπ' (preposition with the accusative, general reference) 47.
Αἴγυπτον) (acc.sing.masc.of Αἴγυπτον, general reference) 203.
ὃς (nom.sing.masc.of ὅς, subject of ᾔδει) 65.
οὐκ (summary negative conjunction with the indicative) 130.
ᾔδει (3d.per.sing.pluperf.ind.of οἶδα, intensive) 144.
τὸν (acc.sing.masc.of the article in agreement with Ἰωσήφ) 9.
Ἰωσήφ (acc.sing.masc.of Ἰωσήφ, direct object of ᾔδει) 2000.

Translation - ". . . until another king arose in Egypt who had never known Joseph."

Comment: ἄχρι οὗ with the indicative introduces a definite relative temporal clause. "Until such time had elapsed, after which another king. . . κ.τ.λ." There is a hint here that some time elapsed after the death of Joseph before the king who ordered the suppression of the Jews came to power. Joseph was a well known man in Egypt, by virtue of his service to the former Pharaoh, by which he had saved the entire nation from starvation. The new king had never met him (pluperf. in ᾔδει).. Joseph's prestige and influence with the government could no longer be counted upon to protect his people. God was moving to fulfill His promise to Abraham. When the economic situation in Egypt worsened, as a result of the exploding Jewish population, the obvious solution was to suppress the growth of population by decreeing the death of all first-born sons, a fact to which Stephen alludes in

Verse 19 - "*The same dealt subtilly with our kindred, and evil entreated our fathers, so that they cast out their young children, to the end they might not live.*"

οὗτος κατασοφισάμενος τὸ γένος ἡμῶν ἐκάκωσεν τοὺς πατέρας τοῦ ποιεῖν τὰ βρέφη ἔκθετα αὐτῶν εἰς τὸ μὴ ζῳογονεῖσθαι.

οὗτος (nom.sing.masc.of οὗτος, subject of ἐκάκωσεν, deictic) 93.

#3116 κατασοφισάμενος (aor.mid.part.nom.sing.masc.of κατασοφίζομαι, adverbial, modal).

deal subtilly with - Acts 7:19.

Meaning: A combination of κατά (#98) and σοφίζω (#4856). To circumvent by fraud; trick; outwit; deal with in a crafty manner. With reference to Pharaoh's treatment of the Jews in Egypt - Acts 7:19.

τό (acc.sing.neut.of the article in agreement with γένος) 9.
γένος (acc.sing.neut.of γένος, direct object of κατασοφισάμενος) 1090.
ἡμῶν (gen.pl.masc.of ἐγώ, relationship) 123.
ἐκάκωσεν (3d.per.sing.aor.act.ind.of κακόω, ingressive) 3104.
τούς (acc.pl.masc.of the article in agreement with πατέρας) 9.
πατέρας (acc.pl.masc.of πατήρ, direct object of ἐκάκωσεν) 238.
τοῦ (gen.sing.neut.of the article, designed result with the infinitive) 9.
ποιεῖν (pres.act.inf.of ποιέω, designed result) 127.
τά (acc.pl.neut.of the article in agreement with βρέφη) 9.
βρέφη (acc.pl.neut.of βρέφοε, general reference) 1821.

#3117 ἔκθετα (acc.pl.neut.of ἔκθετος, predicate adjective).

cast out - Acts 7:19.

Meaning: A combination of ἐκ (#19) and τίθημι (#455). Hence, cast out; rejected; thrown away. With reference to the abandonment of the children of the Jews in Egypt - Acts 7:29. *Cf.*ἐκτίθημι (#3120).

αὐτῶν (gen.pl.masc.of αὐτός, relationship) 16.
εἰς (preposition with the accusative , with the infinitive of hypothetical result) 140.

τό (acc.sing.neut.of the article, with the infinitive, hypothetical result) 9.
μή (qualified negative conjunction with the infinitive) 87.
ζωογονεῖσθαι (pres.pass.inf.of ζωογονέω, acc.sing.neut., hypothetical result) 2621.

Translation - "By deceiving our people, this man began to mistreat our fathers and made them abandon their babies so that they would not survive."

Comment: οὗτος is deictic, referring to βασιλεύς in verse 18. The participle is modal. By deceiving the people the Pharaoh mistreated them. κατασοφισάμεν-ος may refer to his demand for more bricks per day, even though no straw was provided. The evil treatment has reference to the infanticide. τοῦ and the infinitive indicates designed result, while εἰς τό and the infinitive is hypothetical result. *Cf.* Ex.1:7-16. If the order had been carried out all the male children would have been wiped out and the seed line from Abraham, through Isaac, Jacob, Judah and David to Jesus Christ would have been broken. God's plan of redemption would have been foiled. Again we stress the fact that this is Stephen's main point in the sermon. He will conclude (vss.52,53) that the Jerusalem Establishment sought to interdict the eternal plan of God in the same way that Pharaoh did, *viz.,* by the slaughter of the first-born.

Verse 20 - "In which time Moses was born, and was exceeding fair, and nourished up in his father's house three months."

ἐν ᾧ καιρῷ ἐγεννήθη Μωϋσῆς, καὶ ἦν ἀστεῖος τῷ θεῷ, ὅς ἀνετράφη μῆνας τρεῖς ἐν τῷ οἴκῳ τοῦ πατρός.

ἐν (preposition with the locative, time period) 80.
ᾧ (loc.sing.masc.of ὅς, relative time phrase) 65.
καιρῷ (loc.sing.masc.of καιρός, time period) 767.
ἐγεννήθη (3d.per.sing.aor.pass.ind.of γεννάω, constative) 8.
Μωϋσῆς (nom.sing.masc.of Μωϋσῆς, subject of ἐγεννήθη) 715.
καὶ (adjunctive conjunction joining verbs) 14.
ἦν (3d.per.sing.imp.ind.of εἰμί, progressive description) 86.

#3118 ἀστεῖος (nom.sing.masc.of ἀστεῖος, predicate adjective).

fair - Acts 7:20.
proper - Heb.11:23.

Meaning: Cf. ἄστυ - "a city." Hence, one of polished and sophisticated demeanor. Urbane. In the New Testament, of Moses. Followed by τῷ θεῷ in Acts 7:20. *Cf.* also Heb.11:23.

τῷ (dat.sing.masc.of the article in agreement with θεῷ) 9.
θεῷ (dat.sing.masc.of θεός, reference) 124.
ὅς (nom.sing.masc.of ὅς, subject of ἀνετράφη) 65.

#3119 ἀνετράφη (3d.per.sing.2d.aor.pass.ind.of ἀνατρέφω, constative).

bring up - Acts 22:3.
nourish up - Acts 7:20.
nourish - Acts 7:21.

Meaning: A combination of ἀνά (#1059) and τρέφω (#618). To bring up; to nourish. Physically - Acts 7:20; both physically and culturally - Moses in Pharaoh's house - Acts 7:21. With reference to Paul in Jerusalem - Acts 22:3.

μῆνας (acc.pl.fem.of μήν, time extent) 1809.
τρεῖς (numeral) 1010.
ἐν (preposition with the locative of place) 80.
τῷ (loc.sing.masc.of the article in agreement with οἴκῳ) 9.
οἴκῳ (loc.sing.masc.of οἶκος, place) 784.
τοῦ (gen.sing.masc.of the article in agreement with πατρός) 9.
πατρός (gen.sing.masc.of πατήρ, possession) 238.

Translation - "During which time Moses was born; and he was acceptable to God. He was cared for three months in the house of his father."

Comment: ἦν ἀστεῖος τῷ θεῷ - "beautiful by divine standards." *Cf.* Ex.2:1,2. Note that Stephen makes the point that Moses was acceptable to God when he was born. Later (vss.39-41) he was to show that he, whom God thought acceptable, was rejected by Israel, just as Israel later rejected and murdered God's only begotten Son, Who was totally acceptable to God, and totally unacceptable to Israel.

Verse 21 - "And when he was cast out, Pharaoh's daughter took him up, and nourished him for her own son."

ἐκτεθέντος δὲ αὐτοῦ ἀνείλατο αὐτὸν ἡ θυγάτηρ Φαραὼ καὶ ἀνεθρέψατο αὐτὸν ἑαυτῇ εἰς υἱόν.

#3120 ἐκτεθέντος (perf.pass.part.gen.sing.masc.of ἐκτίθημι, genitive absolute, temporal).

    cast out - Acts 7:21.
    expound - Acts 11:4; 18:26; 28:23.

Meaning: A combination of ἐκ (#19) and τίθημι (#455). Hence, to place or lay out, but not with force or violence. With reference to the action of Moses' parents in placing Moses in the bullrushes - Acts 7:21. In an intellectual sense, to expound. Peter's explanation of the experience of Cornelius - Acts 11:4; Aquila and Priscilla explain theology to Apollos - Acts 18:26; with reference to Paul's preaching in Rome - Acts 28:23.

    δὲ (continuative conjunction) 11.
    αὐτοῦ (gen.sing.masc.of αὐτός, genitive absolute) 16.
    ἀνείλατο (3d.per.sing.aor.mid.ind.of ἀναιρέω, constative, indirect) 216.
    αὐτὸν (acc.sing.masc.of αὐτός, direct object of ἀνείλατο) 16.
    ἡ (nom.sing.fem.of the article in agreement with θυγάτηρ) 9.
    θυγάτηρ (nom.sing.fem.of θυγάτηρ, subject of ἀνείλατο and ἀνεθρέψατο) 817.
    Φαραὼ (gen.sing.masc.indeclin.relationship) 3106.
    καὶ (adjunctive conjunction joining verbs) 14.
    ἀνεθρέψατο (3d.per.sing.aor.mid.ind.of ἀνατρέφω, ingressive, indirect) 3119.
    αὐτὸν (acc.sing.masc.of αὐτός, direct object of ἀνεθρέψατο) 16.
    ἑαυτῇ (dat.sing.fem.of ἑαυτός, possession) 288.
    εἰς (preposition with the accusative, in a predicative amplification) 140.
    υἱόν (acc.sing.masc.of υἱός, predicative amplification) 5.

Translation - "And after he was put out, Pharaoh's daughter took him up and began to rear him for herself as a son."

Comment: Moses' parents obeyed Pharaoh's edict to the letter. The order was to put the baby in the river. And that is what they did. Pharaoh did not say that they could not put Moses into a basket first. For their act of faith Amram and Jochebed (Ex.6:20) were awarded a place in "Faith's Hall of Fame" (Heb.11:23) as was their famous son also (Heb.11:24-29). Note the indirect middle in ἀνείλατο - "to lift him up for herself." ἀνεθρέψατο is a redundant indirect middle since it is followed by ἑαυτῇ. εἰς υἱόν amplifies the meaning. Pharaoh's daughter took the baby from the river and into the castle, with his mother as his nurse, "for herself." We need not be told what is added in εἰς υἱόν - "as a son." Winer (Winer-Thayer, p.527, as cited in Robertson, *Grammar*, 401) calls this a predicative amplification. Robertson cites 1 Tim.2:7 and Romans 3:25 as other examples.

God's overruling watchcare in behalf of His covenant people is still the dominant theme of Stephen's message.

Verse 22 - "And Moses was learned in all the wisdom of the Egyptians, and was mighty in words and deeds."

καὶ ἐπαιδεύθη Μωϋσῆς (ἐν) πάσῃ σοφίᾳ Αἰγυπτίων, ἦν δὲ δυνατὸς ἐν λόγοις καὶ ἔργοις αὐτοῦ.

καὶ (continuative conjunction) 14.
ἐπαιδεύθη (3d.per.sing.1st.aor.pass.ind.of παιδεύω, constative) 2838.
Μωϋσῆς (nom.sing.masc.of Μωϋσῆς, subject of ἐπαιδεύθη and ἦν) 715.
ἐν (preposition with the locative of sphere) 80.
πάσῃ (loc.sing.fem.of πᾶς, in agreement with σοφίᾳ) 67.
σοφίᾳ (loc.sing.fem.of σοφία, sphere) 934.
Αἰγυπτίων (gen.pl.masc.of Αἰγύπτιος, description) 3568.
ἦν (3d.per.sing.imp.ind.of εἰμί, progressive description) 86.
δὲ (continuative conjunction) 11.
δυνατὸς (nom.sing.masc.of δυνατός, predicate adjective) 1311.
ἐν (preposition with the locative of sphere) 80.
λόγοις (loc.pl.masc.of λόγος, sphere) 510.
καὶ (adjunctive conjunction joining nouns) 14.
ἔργοις (loc.pl.neut.of ἔργον, sphere) 460.
αὐτοῦ (gen.sing.masc.of αὐτός, possession) 16.

Translation - "And Moses was tutored in all Egyptian philosophy and he was a great speaker and worker."

Comment: Here we have excellent examples of the locative of sphere. Moses majored in Egyptian philosophy, religion, art, etc., and both in his public speaking and in the things that he was able to accomplish he was outstanding. With the best of education he succeeded in excelling in all that he said and did. Apparently he was suffering from an overdose of false humility when he told the Lord that he was not a good speaker (Ex.4:10). Once again Stephen glorifies Moses, with a view to demonstrating the criminality and stupidity of Israel's rejection of him. Jesus was also mighty in philosophy and in the things He said and did, yet the Jerusalem Establishment rejected Him as their forefathers had rejected Moses.

Verse 23 - "And when he was full forty years old, it came into his heart to visit his breathren the children of Israel."

Ὡς δὲ ἐπληροῦτο αὐτῷ τεσσαρακονταετὴς χρόνος, ἀνέβη ἐπὶ τὴν καρδίαν αὐτοῦ ἐπισκέψασθαι τοὺς ἀδελφοὺς αὐτοῦ τοὺς υἱοὺς Ἰσραήλ.

Ὡς (conjunction with the indicative introducing a definite temporal clause) 128.

δέ (continuative conjunction) 11.
ἐπληροῦτο (3d.per.sing.imp.pass.ind.of πληρόω, inceptive) 115.
αὐτῷ (dat.sing.masc.of αὐτός, reference) 16.

#3121 τεσσαρακονταετής (nom.sing.masc.of τεσσαρακονταετής, predicate adjective).

of forty years - Acts 13:18.
forty years old - Acts 7:23.

Meaning: forty years old - as a predicate adjective with χρόνος - of Moses' age - Acts 7:23; with χρόνον, of time spent in the wilderness - Acts 13:18.

χρόνος (nom.sing.masc.of χρόνος, subject of ἐπληροῦτο) 168.
ἀνέβη (3d.per.sing.aor.act.ind.of ἀναβαίνω, ingressive) 323.
ἐπί (preposition with the accusative of extent) 47.
τὴν (acc.sing.fem.of the article in agreement with καρδίαν) 9.
καρδίαν (acc.sing.fem.of καρδία, extent) 432.
αὐτοῦ (gen.sing.masc.of αὐτός, possession) 16.
ἐπισκέψασθαι (1st.aor.mid.inf.of ἐπισκέπτομαι, noun use, subject of ἀνέβη) 1549.
τούς (acc.pl.masc.of the article in agreement with ἀδελφούς) 9.
ἀδελφούς (acc.pl.masc.of ἀδελφός, direct object of ἐπισκέψασθαι) 15.
αὐτοῦ (gen.sing.masc.of αὐτός, relationship) 16.
τούς (acc.pl.masc.of the article in agreement with υἱούς) 9.
υἱούς (acc.pl.masc.of υἱός, in apposition) 5.
Ἰσραήλ (gen.sing.masc.of Ἰσραήλ, description) 165.

Translation - "And when he became forty years old he began to feel a desire to visit his brothers, the sons of Israel."

Comment: Literally "When the time span of his life began to be forty years." Note the inceptive imperfect in ἐπληροῦτο. On the first day that it could be said that he had lived forty years - on his 40th birthday. *Cf.* 1 Cor.2:9 for ἐπὶ καρδίαν ... οὐκ ἀνέβη. "The idea *began* to occur to Moses" (ingressive aorist in ἀνέβη). Though the infinitive ἐπισκέψασθαι in its use as a noun is the subject of ἀνέβη, it also has a verbal use, as all infinitives do. As a verb it has an object in τούς ἀδελφούς. Thus it is clear that Moses, though reared in Pharaoh's court and widely regarded as the son of Pharaoh's daughter, knew of his Jewish origin. (Heb.11:24). It was natural for the public to think that he was indeed the grandson of Pharaoh, as the story of his daughter that while she was bathing she found him in the river was not likely to have been believed.

Just as God raised up Joseph to save His covenant people from famine, so now He raises up another Jew, Moses, to save them from slavery and from ultimate extinction. *Cf.*Ex.2:11.

Verse 24 - "And seeing one of them suffer wrong, he defended him, and avenged him that was oppressed, and smote the Egyptian."

καὶ ἰδών τινα ἀδικούμενον ἠμύνατο καὶ ἐποίησεν ἐκδίκησιν τῷ καταπονουμένῳ πατάξας τὸν Αἰγύπτιον.

καὶ (continuative conjunction) 14.

ἰδών (aor.act.part.nom.sing.masc.ofd ὁράω, adverbial, temporal/causal) 144.

τινα (acc.sing.masc.of τις, direct object of ἰδών) 486.

ἀδικούμενον (pres.pass.part.acc.sing.masc.of ἀδικέω, adverbial, circumstantial) 1327.

#3122 ἠμύνατο (3d.per.sing.1st.aor.mid.ind.of ἀμύνω, indirect).

defend - Acts 7:24.

Meaning: to ward off blows. Defend. With reference to Moses' defense of the Jew from the attack of the Egyptian - Acts 7:24.

καὶ (adjunctive conjunction joining verbs) 14.
ἐποίησεν (3d.per.sing.aor.act.ind.of ποιέω, constative) 127.
ἐκδίκησιν (acc.sing.fem.of ἐκδίκησις, direct object of ἐποίησεν) 2625.
τῷ (dat.sing.masc.of the article in agreement with καταπονουμένῳ) 9.

#3123 καταπονουμένῳ (pres.pass.part.dat.sing.masc.of καταπονέω, substantival, personal advantage).

oppress - Acts 7:24.
vex - 2 Peter 2:7.

Meaning: A combination of κατά (#98) and πονέω - "to exhaust." Hence to wear down with fatigue; exhaust with labor; treat roughly; oppress. With reference to the Jew in Egypt - Acts 7:24; of Lot in Sodom, in a psychological sense - 2 Peter 2:7.

πατάξας (aor.act.part.nom.sing.masc.of πατάσσω, adverbial, modal) 1579.
τὸν (acc.sing.masc.of the article in agreement with Αἰγύπτιον) 9.
Αἰγύπτιον (acc.sing.masc.of Αἰγύπτιος, direct object of πατάξας) 3568.

Translation - "*And when (because) he saw one being beaten he joined in the fight himself and secure revenge for the man who was exhausted, by smiting the Egyptian.*"

Comment: When we read the account of the fight which Stephen here described in Ex.2:11 we note that ἀδικούμενον here means "to be beaten." The LXX uses τύπτω (#1526) for the treatment which the Egyptian was inflicting upon the Jew. *Cf.* Lk.18:7,8 for the ἐποίησεν ἐκδίκησιν idiom. *Cf.*#3123 for a word picture of the condition of the Jew when Moses involved himself (middle voice) in the fight. The victim, almost totally exhausted, had little more energy with which to defend himself, and probably would have been killed had Moses not defended him. Stephen does not say that Moses killed the Egyptian but Ex.2:12 says that he did.

Verse 25 - "For he supposed his brethren would have understood how that God by his hand would deliver them: but they understood not."

ἐνόμιζεν δὲ συνιέναι τοὺς ἀδελφοὺς αὐτοῦ ὅτι ὁ θεὸς διὰ χειρὸς αὐτοῦ δίδωσιν σωτηρίαν αὐτοῖς, οἱ δὲ οὐ συνῆκαν.

ἐνόμιζεν (3d.per.sing.imp.act.ind.of νομίζω, inceptive) 462.
δὲ (continuative conjunction) 11.
συνιέναι (pres.inf.of συνίημι, noun use, object of ἐνόμιζεν, in indirect discourse) 1039.
τοὺς (acc.pl.masc.of the article in agreement with ἀδελφοὺς) 9.
ἀδελφοὺς (acc.pl.masc.of ἀδελφός, general reference) 15.
αὐτοῦ (gen.sing.masc.of αὐτός, relationship) 16.
ὅτι (conjunction introducing an object clause in indirect discourse) 211.
ὁ (nom.sing.masc.of the article in agreement with θεὸς) 9.
θεὸς (nom.sing.masc.of θεός, subject of δίδωσιν) 124.
διὰ (preposition with the ablative of means) 118.
χειρὸς (abl.sing.fem.of χείρ, means) 308.
αὐτοῦ (gen.sing.masc.of αὐτός, possession) 16.
δίδωσιν (3d.per.sing.pres.act.ind.of δίδωμι, indirect discourse) 362.
σωτηρίαν (acc.sing.fem.of σωτηρία, direct object of δίδωσιν) 1852.
αὐτοῖς (dat.pl.masc.of αὐτός, indirect object of δίδωσιν) 16.
οἱ (nom.pl.masc.of the article, subject of συνῆκαν) 9.
δὲ (adversative conjunction) 11.
οὐ (summary negative conjunction with the indicative) 130.
συνῆκαν (3d.per.pl.aor.act.ind.of συνίημι, ingressive) 1039.

Translation - "And he assumed that his brothers would understand that God was using him to deliver them, but the thought did not occur to them."

Comment: Two forms of indirect assertion are found here. ἐνόμιζεν, an inceptive imperfect is followed by the present infinitive, the same tense in indirect discourse as in the direct.συνιέναι in turn is followed by ὅτι and an object clause in indirect discourse, again with δίδωσιν, present tense, the same as in direct. When Moses intervened, rescued the Jew and killed the Egyptian who had been beating him, he began to assume (inceptive imperfect) that the Jew would understand that God had raised up, in the house of Pharaoh, one of their own number, to deliver them from bondage. This deliverance would be in keeping with God's promise to Abraham in Genesis 15:13,14. This promise the Lord reiterated to Moses on Mount Sinai, forty years later (Exod.3:4-10). But his action was misinterpreted by the Jews. They did not begin to understand (ingressive aorist in συνῆκαν).

The next day Moses intervened in another fight - this time between two Jews, in

Verse 26 - "And the next day he shewed himself unto them as they strove, and would have set them at one again, saying, Sirs, ye are brethren; why do ye wrong

one to another?"

τῇ τε ἐπιούσῃ ἡμέρᾳ ὤφθη αὐτοῖς μαχομένοις καὶ συνήλλασεν αὐτοὺς εἰς εἰρήνην εἰπών, Ἄνδρες, ἀδελφοί ἐστε, ἱνατί ἀδεικεῖτε ἀλλήλους;

τῇ (loc.sing.fem.of the article in agreement with ἡμέρᾳ) 9.
τε (correlative conjunction) 1408.

#3124 ἐπιούσῃ (pres.part.loc.sing.fem.of ἔπειμι, adjectival, ascriptive, in agreement with ἡμέρᾳ).

following - Acts 23:11.
next - Acts 7:26.
the day following - Acts 21:18.
the next day - Acts 16:11; 20:15.

Meaning: A combination of ἐπί (#47) and εἰμί (#86); to be upon; to be added to; therefore, as an adjectival participle - next. In a temporal phrase, with the locative of time point, with ἡμέρᾳ in Acts 7:26; with ἡμέρᾳ supplied in Acts 16:11; 20:15; 21:18. Followed by νυκτί in Acts 23:11.

ἡμέρᾳ (loc.sing.fem.of ἡμέρα, time point) 135.
ὤφθη (3d.per.sing.aor.mid.ind.of ὁράω, direct middle, constative) 144.
αὐτοῖς (dat.pl.masc.of αὐτός, indirect object of ὤφθη) 16.
μαχομένοις (pres.mid.part.dat.pl.masc.of μάχομαι, adjectival, restrictive) 2291.
καί (adjunctive conjunction joining verbs) 14.

#3125 συνήλλασεν   (3d.per.sing.imp.act.ind.of συναλλάσσω, inceptive).

set them at one - Acts 7:26.

Meaning: A combination of σύν (#1542) and ἀλλάσσω (#3097). To change, with a view to reconciliation. To change a hostile situation into a friendly one. With reference to Moses' attempt to make peace between two Jews - Acts 7:26, followed by an accusative of purpose - εἰς εἰρήνην.

αὐτούς (acc.pl.masc.of αὐτός, direct object of συνήλλασσεν) 16.
εἰς (preposition with the accusative, purpose) 140.
εἰρήνην (acc.sing.fem.of εἰρήνη, purpose) 865.
εἰπών (pres.act.part.nom.sing.masc.of εἶπον, adverbial, modal) 155.
Ἄνδρες (voc.pl.masc.of ἀνήρ, address) 63.
ἀδελφοί (nom.pl.masc.of ἀδελφός, predicate nominative) 15.
ἐστε (2d.per.pl.pres.ind.of εἰμί, aoristic) 86.
ἱνατί (conjunction in direct question) 3039.
ἀδικεῖτε (2d.per.pl.pres.act.ind.of ἀδικέω, direct question) 1327.
ἀλλήλους (acc.pl.masc.of ἀλλήλων, direct object of ἀδικεῖτε) 1487.

Translation - "And the next day he appeared and tried to stop a fight by saying,

'Men, you are brothers. Why are you hurting each other?' "

Comment: *Cf.* Ex.2:13. συνήλασσεν is in inceptive imperfect, and thus the word "tried" in our translation. He began to make the effort to change fighting men into men of peace. Note the adjectival use of μαχομένοις. His method (modal εἰπών) was to appeal to their nationalism. "You are brothers." Jewish brethren alike under a yoke of slavery imposed by the Egyptians. Why should they fight each other? Why not fight the Egyptians as he had done the day before? Here we have Moses, at age 40, trying in his own strength and wisdom, to do what God accomplished through him, after 40 years of seasoning and communion with God in the desert. Apparently Moses believed that his position in the court (Heb.11:24,25) with the advantages of his education (Acts 7:22) was enough to contest Pharaoh's policy toward this growing minority which had the potential for a major threat to the government. He would discover, 40 years later, that only God could accomplish the liberation of His covenant people.

Verse 27 - "But he that did his neighbour wrong thrust him away, saying, Who made thee a ruler and a judge over us?"

ὁ δὲ ἀδικῶν τὸν πλησίον ἀπώσατο αὐτὸν εἰπών, Τίς σε κατέστησεν ἄρχοντα καὶ δικαστὴν ἐφ' ἡμῶν;

ὁ (nom.sing.masc.of the article in agreement with ἀδικῶν) 9.

δὲ (adversative conjunction) 11.

ἀδικῶν (pres.act.part.nom.sing.masc.of ἀδικέω, substantival, subject of ἀπώσατο) 1327.

τὸν (acc.sing.masc.of the article in agreement with πλησίον) 9.

πλησίον (acc.sing.masc.of πλησίον, direct object of ἀδικῶν) 541.

#3126 ἀπώσατο (3d.per.sing.aor.mid.ind.of ἀπωθέομαι, indirect middle).

cast away - Rom.11:1,2.
put away - 1 Tim.1:19.
put from - Acts 13:46.
thrust away - Acts 7:27.
thrust from - Acts 7:39.

Meaning: A combination of ἀπό (#70) and ὠθέω - "to push" - hence, to push away from one, in the direct middle; to push another away in the indirect middle. Physically - Acts 7:27; to reject mentally and emotionally. Israel rejected Moses' attempt to help them - Acts 7:39. The Jews rejected the gospel message of Paul and Barnabas - Acts 13:46. To reject the faith, as an apostate - 1 Tim.1:19. With reference to the possibility that God will repudiate His promise to Israel and reject the seed of Abraham nationally - Rom.11:;1,2.

αὐτὸν (acc.sing.masc.of αὐτός, direct object of ἀπώσατο) 16.

εἰπών (pres.act.part.nom.sing.masc.of εἶπον, adverbial, temporal) 155.

Τίς (nom.sing.masc.of τίς, interrogative pronoun in direct question) 281.

σε (acc.sing.masc.of σύ, direct object of κατέστησεν) 104.

κατέστησεν (3d.per.sing.aor.act.ind.of καθίστημι, culminative) 1523.

ἄρχοντα (acc.sing.masc.of ἄρχων, predicate accusative) 816.

καὶ (adjunctive conjunction, joining nouns) 14.

#3127 δικαστὴν (acc.sing.fem.of δικαστής, predicate accusative).

judge - Acts 7:27,35.

Meaning: Cf.δικαιόω (#933), δικαιοσύνη (#322), δίκαιος (#85), δικαίως (#2855). A judge - Acts 7:27,35. Cf.κριτής (#492), which refers more to the mental process than the formal action of judging as a magistrate. κριτής need not be a judge on a bench, while δικαστής must judge in the κριτής sense, and also serve formally on the bench. δικαστής is the more dignified term.

ἐφ' (preposition with the genitive of reference) 47.

ἡμῶν (gen.pl.masc.of ἐγώ, reference) 123.

Translation - "*But the one injuring his neighbour pushed him away, as he said, 'Who authorized you to be a ruler and judge over us?'* "

Comment: Moses' attempt to stop the fight between the Jewish slaves was misunderstood. He was repulsed. The indirect middle voice in ἀπώσατο indicates the actor acting for his own advantage. The stronger of the two fighters, who was inflicting damage upon the weaker, turned away from the fight long enough to repulse Moses. As he pushed him away he asked the question. His direct question (verse 27) is followed by a rhetorical question in

Verse 28 - "*Wilt thou kill me, as thou didst the Egyptian yesterday?*"

μὴ ἀνελεῖν με σὺ θέλεις ὃν τρόπον ἀνεῖλες ἐχθὲς τὸν Αἰγύπτιον;

μὴ (qualified negative conjunction with the indicative in rhetorical question) 87.

ἀνελεῖν (aor.act.inf.of ἀναιρέω, epexegetical) 216.

με (acc.sing.masc.of ἐγώ, direct object of ἀνελεῖν) 123.

σὺ (nom.sing.masc.of σύ, subject of θέλεις) 104.

θέλεις (2d.per.sing.pres.act.ind.of θέλω, direct question) 88.

ὃν (acc.sing.neut.of ὅς, adverbial accusative in a comparative clause) 65.

τρόπον (acc.sing.neut.of τρόπος, adverbial accusative in a comparative clause) 1477.

ἀνεῖλες (2d.per.sing.aor.act.ind.of ἀναιρέω, constative) 216.

ἐχθὲς (adverbial) 2019.

τὸν (acc.sing.masc.of the article in agreement with Αἰγύπτιον) 9.

Αἰγύπτιον (acc.sing.masc.of Αἰγύπτιος, direct object of ἀνεῖλες) 3568.

Translation - "*You do not want to kill me as you killed the Egyptian yesterday, do you?*"

Comment: Note the emphatic οὐ. μὴ with direct question expects a negative reply. *Cf.* ὃν τρόπον in introduction of a comparative clause - #1477. The rhetorical question was probably sarcastic. At any rate Moses interpreted it negatively. *Cf.* Ex.2:14.

Verse 29 - "Then fled Moses at this saying, and was a stranger in the land of Midian, where he begat two sons."

ἔφυγεν δὲ Μωϋσῆς ἐν τῷ λόγῳ τούτῳ, καὶ ἐγένετο πάροικος ἐν γῇ Μαδιάμ, οὗ ἐγέννησεν υἱοὺς δύο.

ἔφυγεν (3d.per.sing.2d.aor.act.ind.of φεύγω, constative) 202.
δὲ (inferential conjunction) 11.
Μωϋσῆς (nom.sing.masc.of Μωϋσῆς,subject of ἔφυγεν, ἐγένετο and ἐγέννησεν) 715.
ἐν (preposition with the instru.of cause) 80.
τῷ (instru.sing.masc.of the article in agreement with λόγῳ) 9.
λόγῳ (instru.sing.masc.of λόγος, cause) 510.
τούτῳ (instru.sing.masc.of οὗτος, in agreement with λόγῳ) 93.
καὶ (adjunctive conjunction joining verbs) 14.
ἐγένετο (3d.per.sing.aor.ind.of γίνομαι, constative) 113.
πάροικος (nom.sing.masc.of πάροικος, predicate nominative) 3102.
ἐν (preposition with the locative of place) 80.
γῇ (loc.sing.fem.of γῆ, place where) 157.

#3128 Μαδιάμ (indeclin., genitive of description).

Midian - Acts 7:29.

Meaning: Territory of the Midianites in Arabia, named after Midian, a son of Abraham and Keturah (Gen.25:1,2). The place of Moses' sojourn - Acts 7:29.

οὗ (gen.sing.neut.of ὅς, place description) 65.
ἐγέννησεν (3d.per.sing.aor.act.ind.of γεννάω, constative) 8.
υἱοὺς (acc.pl.masc.of υἱός, direct object of ἐγέννησεν) 5.
δύο (numeral) 385.

Translation - "And Moses fled because of that remark and he became a stranger in Midianite country where he fathered two sons."

Comment: ἐν τῷ λόγῳ τούτῳ - an instrumental of cause. Robertson calls it "occasion." Stephen passes over the details of these forty years in Moses' life with only a brief word. *Cf.* Ex.2:14-22.

Verse 30 - "And when forty years were expired, there appeared to him in the wilderness of Mount Sina an angel of the Lord in a flame of fire in a bush."

Καὶ πληρωθέντων ἐτῶν τεσσαράκοντα ὤφθη αὐτῷ ἐν τῇ ἐρήμῳ τοῦ ὄρους Σινᾶ ἄγγελος ἐν φλογὶ πυρὸς βάτου.

Καὶ (continuative conjunction) 14.

πληρωθέντων (aor.pass.part.gen.pl.neut.of πληρόω, genitive absolute) 115.

ἐτῶν (gen.pl.neut.of ἔτος, genitive absolute) 821.

τεσσαράκοντα (numeral) 333.

ὤφθη (3d.per.sing.aor.pass.ind.of ὁράω, constative) 144.

αὐτῷ (dat.sing.masc.of αὐτός, indirect object of ὤφθη) 16.

ἐν (preposition with the locative of place) 80.

τῇ (loc.sing.fem.of the article in agreement with ἐρήμῳ) 9.

ἐρήμῳ (loc.sing.fem.of ἔρημος, place where) 250.

τοῦ (gen.sing.neut.of the article in agreement with ὄρους) 9.

ὄρους (gen.sing.neut.of ὄρος, description) 357.

#3129 Σινᾶ (gen.sing.,indecl., description).

Sinai - Acts 7:30,38; Gal.4:24,25.

Meaning: Sinai. The mountain approximately 100 miles southwest of the point where the Jordan River flows into the Gulf of Aqabah. It is about 25 miles north of the northern coast line of the Red Sea. Moses received the law here - Acts 7:30,38; Gal.4:24,25.

ἄγγελος (nom.sing.masc.of ἄγγελος, subject of ὤφθη) 96.

ἐν (preposition with the locative of place) 80.

φλογὶ (loc.sing.fem.of φλόξ, place where) 2586.

πυρὸς (gen.sing.neut.of πῦρ, description) 298.

βάτου (gen.sing.fem.of βάτος, description) 2138.

Translation - "And after forty years, an angel appeared to him in the desert of Mount Sinai, in the flame of a burning bush."

Comment: When? After 40 years. Where? At Sinai. How? In a bush that appeared to be on fire.

Verse 31 - "When Moses saw it, he wondered at the sight: and as he drew near to behold it, the voice of the Lord came unto him."

ὁ δὲ Μωϋσῆς ἰδὼν ἐθαύμαζεν τὸ ὅραμα προσερχομένον δὲ αὐτοῦ κατανοῆσαι ἐγένετο φωνὴ κυρίου,

ὁ (nom.sing.masc.of the article in agreement with Μωϋσῆς) 9.

δὲ (continuative conjunction) 11.

Μωϋσῆς (nom.sing.masc.of Μωϋσῆς, subject of ἐθαύμαζεν) 715.

ἰδὼν (aor.act.part.nom.sing.masc.of ὁράω, adverbial, temporal/causal) 144.

ἐθαύμαζεν (3d.per.sing.imp.act.ind.of θαυμάζω, inceptive) 726.

τὸ (acc.sing.neut.of the article in agreement with ὅραμα) 9.

ὅραμα (acc.sing.neut.of ὅραμα, accusative of the thing, with ἐθαύμαζεν) 1228.

προσερχομένου (pres.mid.part.gen.sing.masc.of προσέρχομαι, genitive absolute) 336.

δὲ (continuative conjunction) 11.

αὐτοῦ (gen.sing.masc.of αὐτός, genitive absolute) 16.
κατανοῆσαι (aor.act.inf.of κατανοέω, purpose) 648.
ἐγένετο (3d.per.sing.aor.ind.of γίνομαι, constative) 113.
φωνή (nom.sing.fem.of φωνή, subject of ἐγένετο) 222.
κυρίου (gen.sing.masc.of κύριος, description) 97.

Translation - *"And when Moses saw it he was seized with amazement at the sight, and as he came near in order to examine it, a lordly voice sounded out ... "*

Comment: The sight of a bush on fire, but without being consumed attracted Moses' curiosity, after he had recovered from the first shock of amazement (inceptive imperfect in ἐθαύμαζεν). He came closer in order to investigate. *Cf.*#648 for the exact meaning. As he did (present tense in the participle προσερχομένου) the lordly voice was heard. θαυμάζω is one of those verbs which takes the accusative of the thing. *Cf.* also Luke 7:9 and Jude 16. There is an element of cause in the construction. *Cf.* Ex.3:3,4.

Verse 32 - *". . . saying, I am the God of thy fathers, the God of Abraham, and the God of Isaac, and the God of Jacob. Then Moses trembled and durst not behold."*

Ἐγὼ ὁ θεὸς τῶν πατέρων σου, ὁ θεὸς Ἀβραὰμ καὶ Ἰσαὰκ καὶ Ἰακώβ. ἔντρομος δὲ γενόμενος Μωϋσῆς οὐκ ἐτόλμα κατανοῆσαι.

Ἐγὼ (nom.sing.masc.of ἐγώ, subject of εἰμί understood) 123.
ὁ (nom.sing.masc.of the article in agreement with θεός) 9.
θεὸς (nom.sing.masc.of θεός, predicate nominative) 124.
τῶν (gen.pl.masc.of the article in agreement with πατέρων) 9.
πατέρων (gen.pl.masc.of πατήρ, relationship) 238.
σου (gen.sing.masc.of σύ, relationship) 104.
ὁ (nom.sing.masc.of the article in agreement with θεός) 9.
θεὸς (nom.sing.masc.of θεός, in apposition) 124.
Ἀβραὰμ (gen.sing.masc.indeclin., relationship) 7.
καὶ (adjunctive conjunction joining nouns) 14.
Ἰσαὰκ (gen.sing.masc.indeclin., relationship) 10.
καὶ (adjunctive conjunction joining nouns) 14.
Ἰακώβ (gen.sing.masc.indeclin., relationship) 12.

#3130 ἔντρομος (nom.sing.masc.of ἔντρομος, predicate adjective).

tremble - Acts 7:32; 16:29.
quake - Heb.12:21.

Meaning: A combination of ἐν (#80) and τρόμος (#2889). Trembling, terrified. With γενόμενος - "being made to tremble" - with reference to Moses at the bush - Acts 7:32; Heb.12:21. The Philippian jailor - Acts 16:29.

δὲ (continuative conjunction) 11.
γενόμενος (aor.mid.part.nom.sing.masc.of γίνομαι, adverbial, causal) 113.
Μωϋσῆς (nom.sing.masc.of Μωϋσῆς, subject of ἐτόλμα) 715.

οὐκ (summary negative conjunction with the indicative) 130.
ἐτόλμα (3d.per.sing.imp.ind.of τολμάω, progressive description) 1430.
κατανοῆσαι (aor.act.inf.of κατανοέω, complementary) 648.

Translation - "I am the God of your fathers, the God of Abraham and Isaac and Jacob.' But Moses, seized with trepidation, did not dare to look."

Comment: The Lord introduced Himself in terms of the covenant making God Who had promised Abraham, Isaac and Jacob that, though their children would be enslaved by the Egyptians, He would bring them out and give them the land of Canaan for an everlasting possession. Stephen is about to show that God is determined to keep His promise, despite Israel's unfaithfulness, both in rejecting Moses and in their rejection of Jesus, the crime of which his audience was personally guilty.

Moses' reaction to the voice of the Lord was one of fear and trembling. His earlier curiosity to investigate the phenomenon of a burning bush was overcome by his awestricken reverential fear. *Cf.* Ex.3:4.

Verse 33 - "Then said the Lord to him, Put off thy shoes from thy feet: for the place where thou standest is holy ground."

εἶπεν δὲ αὐτῷ ὁ κύριος, Λῦσον τὸ ὑπόδημα τῶν ποδῶν σου, ὁ γὰρ τόπος ἐφ' ᾧ ἕστηκας γῆ ἁγία ἐστίν.

εἶπεν (3d.per.sing.aor.act.ind.of εἶπον, constative) 155.
δὲ (continuative conjunction) 11.
αὐτῷ (dat.sing.masc.of αὐτός, indirect object of εἶπεν) 16.
ὁ (nom.sing.masc.of the article in agreement with κύριος) 9.
κύριος (nom.sing.masc.of κύριος, subject of εἶπεν) 97.
Λῦσον (2d.per.sing.aor.act.impv.of λύω, command) 471.
τὸ (acc.sing.neut.of the article in agreement with ὑπόδημα) 9.
ὑπόδημα (acc.sing.neut.of ὑπόδημα, direct object of λῦσον) 305.
τῶν (abl.pl.masc.of the article in agreement with ποδῶν) 9.
ποδῶν (abl.pl.masc.of πούς, separation, after ὑπό in composition) 353.
σου (gen.sing.masc.of σύ, possession) 104.
ὁ (nom.sing.masc.of the article in agreement with τόπος) 9.
γὰρ (causal conjunction) 105.
τόπος (nom.sing.masc.of τόπος, subject of ἐστίν) 1019.
ἐφ' (preposition with the locative of place, in a relative clause) 47.
ᾧ (loc.sing.masc.of ὅς, place where) 65.
ἕστηκας (2d.per.sing.perf.act.ind.of ἵστημι, intensive) 180.
γῆ (nom.sing.fem.of γῆ, predicate nominative) 157.
ἁγία (nom.sing.fem.of ἅγιος, in agreement with γῆ) 84.
ἐστίν (3d.per.sing.pres.ind.of εἰμί, aoristic) 86.

Translation - "And the Lord said to him, 'Take off your shoe from your feet, because the spot where you have been standing is holy ground.' "

Comment: Note the intensive perfect in ἔστηκας. The ground was holy because of the identity of the One Who was speaking (verse 32) and because of what He was about to say (verse 34).

Verse 34 - "I have seen, I have seen the affliction of my people which is in Egypt, and I have heard their groaning, and am come down to deliver them. And now come, I will send thee into Egypt."

ἰδὼν εἶδον τὴν κάκωσιν τοῦ λαοῦ μου τοῦ ἐν Αἰγύπτῳ, καὶ τοῦ στεναγμοῦ αὐτῶν ἤκουσα, καὶ κατέβην ἐξελέσθαι αὐτούς, καὶ νῦν δεῦρο ἀποστείλω σε εἰς Αἴγυπτον.

ἰδὼν (aor.act.part.nom.sing.masc.of ὁράω, adverbial, redundant) 144.
εἶδον (1st.per.sing.aor.act.ind.of ὁράω, culminative) 144.
τὴν (acc.sing.fem.of the article in agreement with κάκωσιν) 9.

#3131 κάκωσιν (acc.sing.fem.of κάκωσις, direct object of εἶδον).

affliction - Acts 7:34.

Meaning: Cf.κακόω (#3104). Ill treatment; abuse. With reference to the treatment received by Israel in Egypt - Acts 7:34.

τοῦ (gen.sing.masc.of the article in agreement with λαοῦ) 9.
λαοῦ (gen.sing.masc.of λαός, description) 110.
μου (gen.sing.masc.of ἐγώ, relationship) 123.
ἐν (preposition with the locative of place) 80.
Αἰγύπτῳ (loc.sing.fem.of Αἴγυπτος, place where) 203.
καὶ (adjunctive conjunction joining verbs) 14.
τοῦ (gen.sing.masc.of the article in agreement with στεναγμοῦ) 9.

#3132 στεναγμοῦ (gen.sing.masc.of στεναγμός, objective genitive).

groaning - Acts 7:34.

Meaning: Cf.στενάζω (#2310). A groan; a sign. Cf.ἀλάλητος (#3949) in Romans 8:26. The audible groans of Israel in Egypt - Acts 7:34. Of the unexpressed spiritual agony of the Holy Spirit, Who intercedes for the believer - Romans 8:26.

αὐτῶν (gen.pl.masc.of αὐτός, possession) 16.
ἤκουσα (1st.per.sing.aor.act.ind.of ἀκούω, culminative) 148.
καὶ (adjunctive conjunction joining verbs) 14.
κατέβην (1st.per.sing.2d.aor.act.ind.of καταβαίνω, culminative) 324.
ἐξελέσθαι (2d.aor.mid.inf.of ἐξαιρέω, purpose) 504.
αὐτούς (acc.pl.masc.of αὐτός, direct object of ἐξελέσθαι) 16.
καὶ (continuative conjunction) 14.
νῦν (adverbial, non-temporal, inferential) 1497.
δεῦρο (imperatival interjection) 1304.

ἀποστείλω (1st.per.sing.aor.act.subj.of ἀποστέλλω, hortatory) 215.
σε (acc.sing.masc.of σύ, direct object of ἀποστείλω) 104.
εἰς (preposition with the accusative of extent) 140.
Αἴγυπτον (acc.sing.fem.of Αἴγυπτος, extent) 203.

Translation - "I have been aware of the ill treatment of my people in Egypt, and I have heard their groaning and I have come down to take them out. So now, come. Let me send you to Egypt."

Comment: ἰδών is really a redundant adverbial participle, as in Mt.13:14 and Heb.6:14. These follow the Hebrew idiom in the LXX. (*Cf.*Ex.3:7; Gen.22:17; Isa.6:9). God had never been unmindful of the fortunes of Israel, His covenant people. (Mt.10:29; Lk.21:18). The infinitive of purpose completes κατέβην. ἀποστείλω is hortatory - "Let me send you to Egypt." The 400 years of subordination to Gentile powers are over for Israel. She would not be subjected to their rule again for another 900 years, after which she has suffered under Gentile rule until A.D.1948. God's promise to Abraham must be honored (Gen.15:13). Note the dramatic verb (ἐξαιρέω) which the Lord used to refer to His rescue of His people. He would pick them up and take them out of Egypt.

Stephen goes on with his story in

Verse 35 - "This Moses whom they refused, saying, Who made thee a ruler and a judge? the same did God send to be a ruler and a deliverer by the hand of the angel which appeared to him in the bush."

Τοῦτον τὸν Μωϋσῆν, ὃν ἠρνήσαντο εἰπόντες, Τίς σε κατέστησεν ἄρχοντα καὶ δικαστήν; τοῦτον ὁ θεὸς (καὶ) ἄρχοντα καὶ λυτρωτὴν ἀπέσταλκεν σὺν χειρὶ ἀγγέλου τοῦ ὀφθέντος αὐτῷ ἐν τῇ βάτῳ.

Τοῦτον (acc.sing.masc.of οὗτος, in agreement with Μωϋσῆν, deictic) 93.
τὸν (acc.sing.masc.of the article in agreement with Μωϋσῆν) 9.
Μωϋσῆν (acc.sing.masc.of Μωϋσῆς, direct object of ἀπέσταλκεν) 715.
ὃν (acc.sing.masc.of ὅς, direct object of ἠρνήσαντο) 65.
ἠρνήσαντο (3d.per.pl.aor.mid.ind.of ἀρνέομαι, indirect middle) 895.
εἰπόντες (pres.act.part.nom.pl.masc.of εἶπον, adverbial, modal) 155.
Τίς (nom.sing.masc.of τίς, interrogative pronoun, subject of κατέστησεν, in direct question) 281.
σε (acc.sing.masc.of σύ, direct object of κατέστησεν) 104.
κατέστησεν (3d.per.sing.aor.act.ind.of καθίστημι, constative) 1523.
ἄρχοντα (acc.sing.masc.of ἄρχων, direct object of κατέστησεν, double accusative) 816.
καὶ (adjunctive conjunction joining nouns) 14.
δικαστήν (acc.sing.masc.of δικαστής, direct object of κατέστησεν, double accusative) 3127.
τοῦτον (acc.sing.masc.of οὗτος, resumptive, direct object of ἀπέσταλκεν) 93.
ὁ (nom.sing.masc.of the article in agreement with θεὸς) 9.
θεὸς (nom.sing.masc.of θεός, subject of ἀπέσταλκεν) 124.

(καί) (correlative conjunction) 14.

ἄρχοντα (acc.sing.masc.of ἄρχων, predicate accusative) 816.

καί (adjunctive conjunction joining nouns) 14.

#3133 λυτρωτὴν (acc.sing.masc.of λυτρωτής, predicate accusative).

deliverer - Acts 7:35.

Meaning: Cf. λυτρόω (#2902). Hence, a redeemer, one who delivers by paying a price. With reference to Moses, who delivered Israel - Acts 7:35.

ἀπέσταλκεν (3d.per.sing.perf.act.ind.of ἀποστέλλω, dramatic historical present perfect) 215.

σὺν (preposition with the instrumental of means) 1542.

χειρὶ (instru.sing.fem.of χείρ, means) 308.

ἀγγέλου (gen.sing.masc.of ἄγγελος, description) 96.

τοῦ (gen.sing.masc.of the article in agreement with ὀφθέντος) 9.

ὀφθέντος (aor.pass.part.gen.sing.masc.of ὁράω, adjectival, restrictive) 144.

αὐτῷ (dat.sing.masc.of αὐτός, personal interest) 16.

ἐν (preposition with the locative of place) 80.

τῇ (loc.sing.fem.of the article in agreement with βάτῳ) 9.

βάτῳ (loc.sing.fem.of βάτος, place) 2138.

Translation - "This man Moses, whom they rejected, saying, 'Who appointed you a ruler and a judge?' — this one God sends to be both a ruler and a deliverer by the hand of a messenger who appeared to him at the bush."

Comment: Note Stephen's striking use of deictic οὗτος to refer to Moses in vss.35,36,37,38. The same man whom they had rejected (verse 27) is the one whom God sent, not only as a ruler and a judge, but also, and first of all, as a deliverer. Moses would have had no moral right to rule over and judge them if he had not first of all delivered them. To this extent, the man of verse 27 was correct. What had Moses at that time done for his people? The pampered adopted son of Pharaoh's daughter, he had grown up in the royal palace and had had all of the advantages of education that Egypt could give (vs.22), while his brothers and sisters were being exploited by the Pharaoh. It is as though the Jew had said to Moses, "If you want to be our ruler and judge, deliver us first from this bondage, and we will be happy to follow and obey you." And this is precisely what God intended to do. He who ransoms, redeems and delivers from bondage has a moral right to lead and judge. Thus Jesus Christ, without whose sacrifice at Calvary all would be enslaved by sin, has the right to lead us in His ways and judge us when we stray from His paths.

Stephen is emphasizing the same point that Peter made in Acts 3:14,15, to show the diametrically opposed points of view of God and the nation Israel. They chose Barabbas (Acts 3:14) and murdered the Originator and Deliverer of Life (Acts 3:15), Whom God, of course, raised up. Now, in Stephen's story, Israel rejects as deliverer the same man whom God selects. Thus Israel was always wrong from God's point of view (*cf.* verse 51).

Note the dramatic historical present perfect in ἀπέσταλκεν. "Here an action completed in the past is conceived in terms of the present time for the sake of vividness." (Robertson, *Grammar,* 896). John may have used κέκραγεν in this sense in John 1:15, since he used the historical present in μαρτυρεῖ in the same clause. The historical present perfect is used like the historical present, as though the speaker or writer were actually witnessing what he describes. Burton describes the idiom as " . . . a Perfect which expresses a past completed action, the result of which the speaker conceives himself to be witnessing (as in the case of the Historical Present he conceives himself to be witnessing the action itself)." (*Moods and Tenses,* 38). He doubts that we have a clear New Testament example, although he lists Mt.13:46; Lk.9:36; 2 Cor.12:17; James 1:24 as "Possible instances" and adds that "This idiom is perhaps rather rhetorical than strictly grammatical." (*Ibid.*). With reference to John 1:15, Burton comments, "κέκραγεν in John 1:15 is a Perfect expressing a past fact vividly conceived of as if present to the speaker. But since the Perfect of the verb had already in classical Greek come to be recognized as functionally a Present, it is from the point of view of the current usage a Historical Present rather than a Historical Perfect." (*Ibid.,*39). Robertson counters by saying that κέκραγεν in John 1:15 "is a vivid historical tense even if only intensive in sense. . . . But by the term "historical" it is not meant that this use of the perfect is common in all narrative. But the Vedic Sanskrit has it often in narrative.It is a matter of personal equation after all.Thus Xenophon, who "affects naivete" uses the present perfect much more frequently than Herodotus and Thucydides. It is rather the tense of the orator or the dramatist and is often rhetorical." (Gildersleeve, *American Journal of Philology,* XXIX, p.396 and F.E.Thompson, *A Syntax of Attic Greek,* p.216, as cited in *Ibid.,* 896). Stephen's use in Acts 7:35 is for forensic effect. Often when public speakers get excited about their subject matter they refer to events which the audience clearly recognizes as having occurred in the past as though they were current.

It was in company with the angel who had appeared to Moses at the bush, that he went back to Egypt to carry out his commission of deliverance. He had tried forty years before in his own strength and had failed. Now, forty years later, he was aware of his own lack of ability and undertook the task only because he was promised that God would be at his side. (Ex.3:7 — 4:17).

Verse 36 - "He brought them out after that he had shewed wonders and signs in the land of Egypt, and in the Red Sea, and in the wilderness forty years."

οὗτος ἐξήγαγεν αὐτοὺς ποιήσας τέρατα καὶ σημεῖα ἐν γῇ Αἰγύπτῳ καὶ ἐν Ἐρυθρᾷ Θαλάσσῃ καὶ ἐν τῇ ἐρήμῳ ἔτη τεσσαράκοντα.

οὗτος (nom.sing.masc.of οὗτος, subject of ἐξήγαγεν, continuative) 93.
ἐξήγαγεν (3d.per.sing.aor.act.ind.of ἐξάγω, constative) 2316.
αὐτοὺς (acc.pl.masc.of αὐτός, direct object of ἐξήγαγεν) 16.
ποιήσας (aor.act.part.nom.sing.masc.of ποιέω, adverbial, modal) 127.
τέρατα (acc.pl.neut.of τέρας, direct object of ποιήσας) 1500.
καὶ (adjunctive conjunction joining nouns) 14.

σημεῖα (acc.pl.neut.of σημεῖον, direct object of ποιήσας) 1005.
ἐν (preposition with the locative of place) 80.
γῆ (loc.sing.fem.of γῆ, place where) 157.
Αἰγύπτῳ (loc.sing.fem of Αἴγυπτος, in agreement with γῆ) 203.
καὶ (adjunctive conjunction joining prepositional phrases) 14.
ἐν (preposition with the locative of place where) 80.

#3134 Ἐρυθρᾷ (loc.sing.fem.of Ιἐρυθρός, in agreement with θαλάσσῃ).

red - Acts 7:36; Heb.11:29.

Meaning: Red. With θάλασσα in Acts 7:36; Heb.11:29. In modern geography, the Gulf of Suez.

θαλάσσῃ (loc.sing.fem.of θάλασσα, place where) 3743.
καὶ (adjunctive conjunction joining prepositional phrases) 80.
ἐν (preposition with the locative of place where) 80.
τῇ (loc.sing.fem.of the article in agreement with ἐρήμῳ) 9.
ἐρήμῳ (loc.sing.fem.of ἔρημος, place where) 250.
ἔτη (acc.pl.neut.of ἔτος, time extent) 821.
τεσσαράκοντα (numeral) 333.

Translation - "This man led them out by performing wonders and signs in Egyptian country, in the Red Sea and in the wilderness for forty years."

Comment: Again we have deictic οὗτος, as in verses 35 and 37. Stephen's purpose is to spotlight Moses as God's messenger, armed with miracle working power and charged with a divine commission of national rescue, who, aided only by God, led Israel out of bondage. By playing Moses up as God's hero, Stephen played Israel down as Satan's heel, because they rejected Moses just as they later crucified God's Son Who came with a more glorious mission even than that of Moses (the entire argument of Hebrews 2-10). Moses came to save them from political bondage, but Jesus came to save them from the spiritual bondage of Satan, who is even a harder taskmaster than Pharaoh. Moses offered them only the law, but Jesus, Who fulfilled the Mosaic law perfectly and then died as though He had broken every commandment of it, offered them grace (John 1:17).

Signs and wonders were performed by Moses in Egypt, at the Red Sea and for the next forty years in the wilderness. If Israel could not believe what Moses said, they should have believed him "for the works' sake" just as Jesus challenged His disciples (John 14:11). Moses (his name is Egyptian - *Mosheth*, and means "to lead out") led them out of Egypt, but he could not lead them into Canaan. Only Joshua ("Yahweh is the Saviour") could do that. Even so, "what the law could not do, in that it was weak through the flesh, God, sending His own Son (Joshua, Jesus - Mt.1:21), in the likeness of sinful flesh, and for sin, condemned sin in the flesh, that the righteousness of the law might be fulfilled in us, who walk not after the flesh, but after the Spirit" (Rom.8:3,4).

The entire time span from God's call to Moses at the burning bush to his death on Mount Nebo was forty years. (Deut.34:7). We are indebted to Stephen for the chronological division of the life of Moses. He was forty years old when he killed the Egyptian (Acts 7:23). He was eighty at the burning bush (vs.30) and he was one hundred twenty when he died (vs.36,42; Deut.34:7). He spent the first forty years in Egypt, the second forty years in the Midian desert and the last forty years in the same desert as he led Israel to Canaan.

We cannot call ποιήσας a temporal participle, even though, being aorist it represents antecedent action in relation to the contest with Pharaoh in Egypt and simultaneity with the Exodus at the Red Sea, both of which relationships are within the scope of the aorist participle. But Stephen relates it also to the period of wilderness wandering. If it were temporal it would represent the miracles during the last forty years of Moses' life as subsequent to the verb ἐξήγαγεν. Its action is antecedent to the verb in relation to the miracles of the contest and simultaneous in relation to the action at the Red Sea, but it cannot be subsequent to the verb in relation to the wilderness miracles. So we have called it modal, which is proper, since it was certainly by means of his miracles that Moses accomplished all three missions. The plagues with which Moses fought Pharaoh were miraculous, as was the Red Sea passage and the miraculous provision of food, water and leadership during the last forty years.

Having pictured Moses as their great national hero - a picture with which they had no disagreement, Stephen next pictures him as the one who prophesied the coming of their Messiah, in

Verse 37 - "This is that Moses, which said unto the children of Israel, A prophet shall the Lord your God raise up unto you of your brethren, like unto me; him shall ye hear."

οὗτός ἐστιν ὁ Μωϋσῆς ὁ εἴπας τοῖς υἱοῖς Ἰσραήλ, Προφήτην ὑμῖν ἀναστήσει ὁ θεὸς ἐκ τῶν ἀδελφῶν ὑμῶν ὡς ἐμέ.

οὗτός (nom.sing.masc.of οὗτος, in agreement with Μωϋσῆς, deictic) 93.

ἐστιν (3d.per.sing.pres.ind.of εἰμί, aoristic) 86.

ὁ (nom.sing.masc.of the article in agreement with Μωϋσῆς) 9.

Μωϋσῆς (nom.sing.masc.of Μωϋσῆς, subject of ἐστιν) 715.

ὁ (nom.sing.masc.of the article in agreement with εἴπας) 9.

εἴπας (aor.act.part.nom.sing.masc.of εἶπον, substantival, predicate nominative) 155.

τοῖς (dat.pl.masc.of the article in agreement with υἱοῖς) 9.

υἱοῖς (dat.pl.masc.of υἱός, indirect object of εἴπας) 5.

Ἰσραήλ (gen.sing.indeclin. relationship) 165.

Προφήτην (acc.sing.masc.of προφήτης, direct object of ἀναστήσει) 119.

ὑμῖν (dat.pl.masc.of σύ, personal advantage) 104.

ἀναστήσει (3d.per.sing.fut.act.ind.of ἀνίστημι, predictive) 789.

ὁ (nom.sing.masc.of the article in agreement with θεὸς) 9.

θεὸς (nom.sing.masc.of θεός, subject of ἀναστήσει) 124.

ἐκ (preposition with the ablative of source) 19.

τῶν (abl.pl.masc.of the article in agreement with ἀδελφῶν) 9.

ἀδελφῶν (abl.pl.masc.of ἀδελφός, source) 15.
ὑμῶν (gen.pl.masc.of σύ, relationship) 104.
ὡς (particle introducing a comparative clause) 128.
ἐμέ (acc.sing.masc.of ἐγώ, in agreement with προφήτην, comparative clause) 123.

Translation - *"This man Moses is the one who said to the sons of Israel, 'A Prophet will God raise up for you, from among your brothers, just as He raised up me.' "*

Comment: Once again as in verses 35 and 36 and as he will again in verse 38, Stephen points to Moses with οὗτος. It was Moses whom God sent to deliver them from bondage (vs.35). It was Moses who performed the miracles and led them through the Red Sea and the wilderness for forty years (vs.36). It was Moses who, at the end of his life, spoke locally of Joshua (Deut.18:15) but prophetically of Jesus. Israel was to look for another Prophet, raised up supernaturally as he had been for them, who would do for them what he could not do. Moses could lead them out of Egyptian bondage, but he could not take them into Canaan land - the land which God had promised to Abraham. So the law cannot save us (Acts 13:38,39), although it can point out to us the drudgery of our bondage unto sin, just as Moses pointed out to Israel their bondage to Pharaoh. Thus Joshua ("Yahweh is the Saviour") becomes a type of Jesus ("Yahweh is the Saviour").Ἰησοῦς is the Greek for which *Jehoshua* is the English transliteration of the Hebrew word which means "Yahweh is the Saviour." (Deut.31:3, LXX; Mt.1:21). When their new Deliverer came they were to regard him as having been sent by God, just as Moses had been. He would be God's Prophet and they were to listen to Him. That Moses meant Joshua in the local sense is clear from Acts 7:45. That he meant Jesus, the Messiah is clear from the fact that God raised Jesus from the dead. *Cf.*#789. The student should run the references and note where ἀνίστημι is used to refer to the resurrection of Jesus Christ - Acts 2:24,32; 3:26; 13:33,34, and where it is used to refer to the resurrection of the saints at the second coming of Messiah.

Once again the theme in Stephen's sermon emerges - Israel rejected a supernaturally commissioned and authenticated Moses. They also rejected the counsel of another supernaturally commissioned deliverer, *viz.* Joshua (Joshua 1:1-9; 24:14,15). Finally, having rejected Moses and the counsel of Joshua, they crucified their Heavenly Joshua.

Once more Stephen points to Moses in

Verse 38 - *"This is he that was in the church in the wilderness with the angel which spake to him in the mount Sina, and with our fathers: who received the lively oracles to give unto us."*

οὗτός ἐστιν ὁ γενόμενος ἐν τῇ ἐκκλησίᾳ ἐν τῇ ἐρήμῳ μετὰ τοῦ ἀγγέλου τοῦ λαλοῦντος αὐτῷ ἐν τῷ ὄρει Σινᾶ καὶ τῶν πατέρων ἡμῶν, ὃς ἐδέξατο λόγια ζῶντα δοῦναι ἡμῖν.

οὗτός (nom.sing.masc.of οὗτος, subject of ἐστιν) 93.

ἐστιν (3d.per.sing.pres.ind.of εἰμί, aoristic) 86.

ὁ (nom.sing.masc.of the article in agreement with γενόμενος) 9.

γενόμενος (aor.mid.part.nom.sing.masc.of γίνομαι, substantival, predicate nominative) 113.

ἐν (preposition with the locative of place) 80.

τῇ (loc.sing.fem.of the article in agreement with ἐκκλησίᾳ) 9.

ἐκκλησίᾳ (loc.sing.fem.of ἐκκλησία, place) 1204.

ἐν (preposition with the locative of place) 80.

τῇ (loc.sing.fem.of the article in agreement with ἐρήμῳ) 9.

ἐρήμῳ (loc.sing.fem.of ἔρημος, place) 250.

μετὰ (preposition with the genitive of accompaniment) 50.

τοῦ (gen.sing.masc.of the article in agreement with ἀγγέλου) 9.

ἀγγέλου (gen.sing.masc.of ἄγγελος, accompaniment) 96.

τοῦ (gen.sing.masc.of the article in agreement with λαλοῦντος) 9.

λαλοῦντος (pres.act.part.gen.sing.masc.of λαλέω, adjectival, in agreement with ἀγγέλου) 815.

αὐτῷ (dat.sing.masc.of αὐτός, indirect object of λαλοῦντος) 16.

ἐν (preposition with the locative of place) 80.

τῷ (loc.sing.neut.of the article in agreement with ὄρει) 9.

ὄρει (loc.sing.neut.of ὄρος, place) 357.

Σινᾶ (loc.sing.masc.of Σινᾶ, indeclin., in apposition) 3129.

καὶ (adjunctive conjunction joining nouns) 14.

τῶν (gen.pl.masc.of the article in agreement with πατέρων) 9.

πατέρων (gen.pl.masc.of πατήρ, accompaniment) 238.

ἡμῶν (gen.pl.masc.of ἐγώ, relationship) 123.

ὅς (nom.sing.masc.of ὅς, subject of ἐδέξατο) 65.

ἐδέξατο (3d.per.sing.aor.mid.ind.of δέχομαι, indirect middle) 867.

#3135 λόγια (acc.pl.neut.of λόγιον, direct object of ἐδέξατο).

oracle - Acts 7:38; Rom.3:2; Heb.5:12; 1 Peter 4:11.

Meaning. Cf.λόγος (#510). Saying, pronouncement, statement. Written on tablets of stone - the Mosaic law - Acts 7:38; Rom.3:2 (including also the remainder of the law, given orally to Moses and written by him). With reference to the entire message of salvation - Heb.5:12. The inspired utterances of saints with the gift of teaching - 1 Peter 4:11.

ζῶντα (pres.act.part.acc.pl.neut.of ζάω, adjectival, ascriptive) 340.

δοῦναι (aor.act.inf.of δίδωμι, purpose) 362.

ἡμῖν (dat.pl.masc.of ἐγώ, indirect object of δοῦναι) 123.

Translation - "This is the man who was assembled in the desert with the messenger who spoke to him on Mount Sinai, and to our forefathers who received the messages of life to give to us."

Comment: For the last time Stephen emphasizes Moses as the one to whom he refers with deictic οὗτος. It goes back in reference to σε in verse 34. God sent him. This Moses, although sent by God as their leader and deliverer (verse 35) they rejected. This Moses, who led them out of Egypt by performing miracles in Egypt, by whose faith the Red Sea parted, and who fed and guided them through the wilderness for forty years (verse 36), they were ready on one occasion to stone. This Moses who in the long run predicted the Messiah, while pointing locally to His type, Joshua (vs.37), assembled them on the eastern shore of the Red Sea and watched with them as the waves, returning to their channels, overwhelmed the Egyptians. He watched and listened while his sister Miriam and the other women danced upon the sands and sang. He joined them in praise to the God of Israel Who had delivered them

I will sing unto the Lord,
for He hath triumphed gloriously.
The horse and his rider hath He thrown into the sea.
The Lord is my strength and song,
And He has become my salvation.
He is my God, and I will prepare Him an habitation;
My father's God, and I will exalt Him.
The Lord is a man of war: the Lord is His name.
Pharaoh's chariots and his host hath He cast into the sea:
His chosen captains also are drowned in the Red Sea.
The depths have covered them: they sank into the bottom as a stone.
Thy right hand, O Lord, is become glorious in power:
Thy right hand, O Lord, hath dashed in pieces the enemy.
And in the greatness of thine excellency
Thou hast overthrown them that rose up against thee.
Thou sentest forth thy wrath, which consumed them as stubble.
And with the blast of thy nostrils the waters were gathered together;
The floods stood upright as an heap,
And the depths were congealed in the heart of the sea.
The enemy said, I will pursue, I will overtake,
I will divide the spoil.
My lust shall be satisfied upon them.
I will draw my sword, my hand shall destroy them.
Thou didst blow with thy wind,
The sea covered them;
They sank as lead in the mighty waters.
Who is like unto thee, O Lord, among the gods?
Who is like thee, glorious in holiness,
Fearful in praises, doing wonders?
Thou stretchest out thy right hand, the earth swallowed them.
Thou in thy mercy hast led forth the people which thou hast redeemed:
Thou hast guided them in thy strength unto thy holy habitation.
The people shall hear, and be afraid:
Sorrow shall take hold on the inhabitants of Palestina.
Then the dukes of Edom shall be amazed;

The mighty men of Moab, trembling shall take hold upon them;
All the inhabitants of Canaan shall melt away.
Fear and dread shall fall upon them.
By the greatness of thine arm they shall be as still as a stone;
Till thy people pass over, O Lord, till the people pass over,
Which thou hast purchased.
Thou shalt bring them in and plant them in the mountain of thine inheritance,
In the place, O Lord, which thou hast made for thee to dwell in,
In the Sanctuary, O Lord, which thy hands have established.
The Lord shall reign forever and ever.
For the horse of Pharaoh went in with his chariots
and with his horsemen into the sea,
And the Lord brought again the waters of the sea upon them;
But the children of Israel went on dry land in the midst of the sea.

Exodus 15:1-19

The saints in Heaven will sing this song of Moses as they rejoice in Him Who has given them the victory over another dictator more diabolical even than Pharaoh (Rev.15:3).

Stephen's story continues: Moses led them south, along the eastern shore of the Red Sea to the southern tip of the Sinai peninsula. There they camped, while Moses climbed into the mountain, there to meet the God of Israel, whom he had met before at the bush on fire and there to receive, written with the finger of God upon stone, the moral law of His universe, by which Israel was to be guided. There Moses descended from the mount to find them in violation of every one of the commandments which he held in his hands. There he dashed the stones in pieces in frustration and destroyed the golden calf. Again he ascended into the mountain for the second edition of the law.

God had offered to carry Israel on the wings of His grace, as the eagle carried her young (Ex.19:4). There their forefathers, unmindful of the wickedness of their hearts and their inability to keep God's moral law, had rashly promised, "All that the Lord hath spoken we will do" (Ex.19:8).

With this buildup Stephen now accuses Israel of disobeying Moses (vss.39-41). Note the present participle ζῶντα in description of λόγια. God's Word, given to Moses to be given in turn to the people at the foot of the mountain, is permanently alive.

Stephen has shown that a covenant keeping God has sprinkled the pages of Jewish national history with evidences of His faithfulness, and the Jews have cluttered the same pages with evidences of their infidelity.

Verse 39 - "To whom our fathers would not obey, but thrust him from them, and in their hearts turned back again into Egypt."

ᾧ οὐκ ἠθέλησαν ὑπήκοοι γενέσθαι οἱ πατέρες ἡμῶν ἀλλὰ ἀπώσαντο καὶ ἐστράφησαν ἐν ταῖς καρδίαις αὐτῶν εἰς Αἴγυπτον,

ᾧ (dat.sing.masc.of ὅς, dative of person) 65.

οὐκ (summary negative conjunction with the indicative) 130.
ἠθέλησαν (3d.per.pl.aor.act.ind.of θέλω, constative) 88.

#3136 ὑπήκοοι (nom.pl.masc.of ὑπήκοος, predicate adjective).

obedient - 2 Cor.2:9; Phil.2:8.
obey - Acts 7:39.

Meaning: Cf. ὑπακούω (#760), ἀκοή (#409). Adjective - obedient; giving ear to - with a dative of person - Moses - Acts 7:39. Followed by μέχρι θανάτου - Phil.2:8. With εἰς πάντα - 2 Cor.2:9.

γενέσθαι (aor.mid.inf.of γίνομαι, complementary) 113.
οἱ (nom.pl.masc.of the article in agreement with πατέρες) 9.
πατέρες (nom.pl.masc.of πατήρ, subject of ἠθέλησαν) 238.
ἡμῶν (gen.pl.masc.of ἐγώ, relationship) 123.
ἀλλὰ (alternative conjunction) 342.
ἀπώσαντο (3d.per.pl.aor.mid.ind.of ἀπωθέομαι, indirect middle) 3126.
καὶ (adjunctive conjunction joining verbs) 14.
ἐστράφησαν (3d.per.pl.aor.act.ind.of στρέφω, constative) 530.
ἐν (preposition with the locative of sphere) 80.
ταῖς (loc.pl.fem.of the article in agreement with καρδίαις) 9.
καρδίαις (loc.pl.fem.of καρδία, sphere) 432.
αὐτῶν (gen.pl.masc.of αὐτός, possession) 16.
εἰς (preposition with the accusative of extent) 140.
Αἴγυπτον (acc.sing.fem.of Αἴγυπτος, extent) 203.

Translation - ". . . to whom our forefathers did not wish to be obedient. Instead they pushed him aside and in their hearts they turned to Egypt."

Comment: The antecedent of ᾧ is οὗτος of verse 38, which is turn refers to Moses in verse 34. The Jews to whom Stephen was speaking were the descendants of those who came with Moses out of Egypt. Their forefathers had seen the miracluous manner in which God sustained Moses and his demands upon Pharaoh. The plagues upon the Egyptians, the miraculous escape from them through the Red Sea and God's judgment upon Pharaoh and his troops had been the subject matter of their song and dance. In the wilderness of Shur they longed for water. With an oasis in sight three and one half million people rushed to the wells of Marah, only to find to their bitter disappointment that the water was unfit for drinking, possibly as a result of chemical pollution in the surrounding desert. By the miracle of Marah (Ex.15:25) the waters were made sweet, suggesting perhaps that the bitter waters of life are made sweet because of the tree upon which Jesus bore our sins (Gal.3:13). Again the Lord promised that if they would obey His voice, He would visit none of the diseases upon them which He had brought upon the Egyptians (Ex.15:26). They marched onward to the southeast and came to Elim with its twelve wells of water and seventy palm trees. After a much needed rest, they marched onward to the southeast into the Wilderness of Sin, where again they longed for the flesh pots of Egypt (Ex.16:3).

Divine justice dictated their death in the desert, but divine grace provided quails and their introduction to the manna which was to sustain them for the next thirty-eight years. Our Lord alluded to this episode in the nation's history in His discourse on the Bread of Life (John 6:48-51). They moved on southeastward and again suffered for water at Rephidim. But water from the smitten Rock in Horeb (Ex.17:6) suggested "that spiritual Rock that followed them - Christ" (1 Cor.10:1-4). Food and water for 3,500,000 people was no problem of course for the God of Abraham, Isaac and Jacob Who was as sovereign as He was gracious. The God of battles gave victory to the sword of Joshua over Amalek (Ex.17:8-16), who would have murdered or enslaved them all and brought the divine program of redemption to a disastrous end.

Thus they came to Sinai. They had not returned to Egypt , but in their hearts they did, intellectually and emotionally. Manna, the heavenly food, which defied analysis, but was more nutricious than anything they had ever eaten was considered inferior to the fare they would have eaten if they could only go back to Egypt and take up their tasks at making bricks without straw.

Thus Stephen made his point that Israel had always spurned God's genuine salvation with its blessings for human wisdom. He then reminded them of the behavior of their forefathers at the foot of Mount Sinai in verses 40 - 43.

Verse 40 - "Saying unto Aaron, Make us gods to go before us: for as for this Moses, which brought us out of the land of Egypt, we wot not what is become of him."

εἰπόντες τῷ Ἀαρών, Ποίησον ἡμῖν θεοὺς οἳ προπορεύσονται ἡμῶν, ὁ γὰρ Μωϋσῆς οὗτος, ὃς ἐξήγαγεν ἡμᾶς ἐκ γῆς Αἰγύπτου, οὐκ οἴδαμεν τί ἐγένετο αὐτῷ.

εἰπόντες (pres.act.part.nom.pl.masc.of εἶπον, recitative) 155.

τῷ (dat.sing.masc.of the article in agreement with Ἀαρών) 9.

Ἀαρών (dat.sing.masc.of Ἀαρών, indeclin.ind.object of εἰπόντες) 1778.

Ποίησον (2d.per.sing.aor.act.impv.of ποιέω, command) 127.

ἡμῖν (dat.pl.masc.of ἐγώ, dative of person) 123.

θεοὺς (acc.pl.masc.of θεός, direct object of Ποίησον) 124.

οἳ (nom.pl.masc.of ὅς, subject of προπορεύσονται, in a relative purpose clause) 65.

προπορεύσονται (3d.per.pl.fut.mid.ind.of προπορεύομαι, purpose) 1855.

ἡμῶν (abl.pl.masc.of ἐγώ, separation after πρό in composition) 123.

ὁ (nom.sing.masc.of the article in agreement with Μωϋσῆς) 9.

γὰρ (causal conjunction) 105.

Μωϋσῆς (nom.sing.masc. of Μωϋσῆς, nominative absolute, suspended subject) 715.

οὗτος (nom.sing.masc.of οὗτος, in agreement with Μωϋσῆς, contemptuous use) 93.

ὃς (nom.sing.masc.of ὅς, subject of ἐξήγαγεν, adjectival relative clause, in agreement with Μωϋσῆς) 65.

ἐξήγαγεν (3d.per.sing.aor.act.ind.of ἐξάγω, culminative) 2316.

ἡμᾶς (acc.pl.masc.of ἐγώ, direct object of ἐξήγαγεν) 123.

ἐκ (preposition with the ablative of separation) 19.

τῆς (abl.sing.fem.of the article in agreement with Αἰγύπτου) 9.

Αἰγύπτου (abl.sing.fem.of Αἴγυπτος, separation) 203.

οὐκ (summary negative conjunction with the indicative) 130.

οἴδαμεν (1st.per.pl.pres.act.ind.of οἶδα, aoristic) 144.

τί (acc.sing.neut.of τίς, direct object of οἴδαμεν, indirect question) 281.

ἐγένετο (3d.per.sing.aor.ind.of γίνομαι, constative) 113.

αὐτῷ (dat.sing.masc.of αὐτός, dative of person, with an intransitive verb) 16.

Translation - ". . . *saying to Aaron, 'Make gods for us, who will go before us, because as for this fellow Moses, who has led us out of Egypt — we do not know what has happened to him.'* "

Comment: γάρ is causal. Note the contemptuous use of οὗτος. The first relative clause is purpose. The second is adjectival, in definition of Μωϋσῆς. In ὁ γὰρ Μωϋσῆς οὗτος we have *nominatus pendens* - the nominative absolute. Some grammarians call it a suspended subject. The sentence structure is broken. There is no verb to go with Μωϋσῆς.

This request by the people for Aaron to provide them with a god or gods (note how they had become accustomed to polytheism during their stay in Egypt) was made while Moses, the only benefactor who had done anything constructive for them in 80 years of Egyptian slavery, was up in the mountain receiving the oracles of God for them to follow. Meanwhile they, the recipients of all of His miraculous power in deliverance, were down on the slopes of Sinai, preparing to transgress every one of the ten commandments. Read the story in Ex.32:1-35.

Luke quotes from the LXX (Ex.32:1,23). The quotation is accurate except that the LXX has ὁ ἄνθρωπος after οὗτος and the perfect γέγονεν instead of the aorist ἐγένετο.

Aaron yielded to the demand of the people as we see in

Verse 41 - *"And they made a calf in those days, and offered sacrifice unto the idol, and rejoiced in the works of their own hands."*

καὶ ἐμοσχοποίησαν ἐν ταῖς ἡμέραις ἐκείναις καὶ ἀνήγαγον θυσίαν τῷ εἰδώλῳ, καὶ εὐφραίνοντο ἐν τοῖς ἔργοις τῶν χειρῶν αὐτῶν.

καὶ (continuative conjunction) 14.

#3137 ἐμοσχοποίησαν (3d.per.pl.aor.act.ind.of μοσχοποιέω, constative).

make a calf - Acts 7:41.

Meaning: A combination of μόσχος (#2554) and ποιέω (#127). To make an image of a calf - Acts 7:41.

ἐν (preposition with the locative of time point) 80.

ταῖς (loc.pl.fem.of the article in agreement with ἡμέραις) 9.

ἡμέραις (loc.pl.fem.of ἡμέρα, time point) 135.

ἐκείναις (loc.pl.fem.of ἐκεῖνος, in agreement with ἡμέραις) 246.

καὶ (adjunctive conjunction joining verbs) 14.
ἀνήγαγον (3d.per.pl.aor.act.ind.of ἀνάγω, constative) 329.
θυσίαν (acc.sing.fem.of θυσία, direct object of ἀνήγαγον) 796.
τῷ (dat.sing.neut.of the article in agreement with εἰδώλῳ) 9.

#3138 εἰδώλῳ (dat.sing.neut.of εἴδωλον, indirect object of ἀνήγαγον).

idol - Acts 7:41; 15:20; Rom.2:22; 1 Cor.8:4,7; 10:19; 12:2; 2 Cor.6:16; 1 Thess.1:9; 1 John 5:21; Rev.9:20.

Meaning: an image to a heathen god - Acts 7:4; Rev.9:20; 1 Cor.12:2. False gods - Acts 15:20; Rom.2:22; 1 Cor.8:4,7; 10:19; 2 Cor.6:16; 1 Thess.1:9; 1 John 5:21.

καὶ (adjunctive conjunction joining verbs) 14.
εὐφραίνοντο (3d.per.pl.imp.mid.ind.of εὐφραίνω, inceptive) 2479.
ἐν (preposition with the instrumental, cause) 80.
τοῖς (instru.pl.neut.of the article in agreeement with ἔργοις) 9.
ἔργοις (instru.pl.neut.of ἔργον, cause) 460.
τῶν (gen.pl.fem.of the article in agreement with χειρῶν) 9.
χειρῶν (gen.pl.fem.of χείρ, description) 308.
αὐτῶν (gen.pl.masc.of αὐτός, possession) 16.

Translation - "*And they made a calf at that time, and offered a sacrifice to the idol, and they began to celebrate because of the works of their hands.*"

Comment: *Cf.* Ex.32:2-25. All of this was going on at the foot of Mount Sinai while Moses was getting the living message from the Lord that forbade everything that they were doing. *Cf.*#2479 for other uses of εὐφραίνω in this same evil sense.

The divine reaction to the sins of Israel is noted in

Verse 42 - "*Then God turned and gave them up to worship the host of heaven; as it is written in the book of the prophets, O ye house of Israel, have ye offered to me slain beasts and sacrifices by the space of forty years in the wilderness.*"

ἔστρεφεν δὲ ὁ θεὸς καὶ παρέδωκεν αὐτοὺς λατρεύειν τῇ στρατιᾷ τοῦ οὐρανοῦ, καθὼς γέγραπται ἐν βίβλῳ τῶν προφητῶν, Μὴ σφάγια καὶ θυσίας προσηνέγκατέ μοι ἔτη τεσσαράκοντα ἐν τῇ ἐρήμῳ, οἶκος Ἰσραήλ;

ἔστρεφεν (3d.per.sing.aor.act.ind.of στρέφω, constative) 530.
δὲ (continuative conjunction) 11.
ὁ (nom.sing.masc.of the article in agreement with θεὸς) 9.
θεὸς (nom.sing.masc.of θεός, subject of ἔστρεφεν and παρέδωκεν) 124.
καὶ (adjunctive conjunction joining verbs) 14.
παρέδωκεν (3d.per.sing.aor.act.ind.of παραδίδωμι, constative) 368.
αὐτοὺς (acc.pl.masc.of αὐτός, direct object of παρέδωκεν) 16.
λατρεύειν (pres.act.inf.of λατρεύω, epexegetical, dative case) 366.
τῇ (dat.sing.fem.of the article in agreement with στρατιᾷ) 9.
στρατιᾷ (dat.sing.fem.of στρατιά, indirect object of λατρεύειν) 1880.

τοῦ (gen.sing.masc.of the article in agreement with οὐρανοῦ) 9.
οὐρανοῦ (gen.sing.masc.of οὐρανός, description) 254.
καθὼς (particle introducing a comparative clause) 1348.
γέγραπται (3d.per.sing.perf.pass.ind.of γράφω, intensive) 156.
ἐν (preposition with the locative of place) 80.
βίβλῳ (loc.sing.masc.of βίβλος, place) 1.
τῶν (gen.pl.masc.of the article in agreement with προφητῶν) 9.
προφητῶν (gen.pl.masc.of προφήτης, description) 119.
Μὴ (qualified negative conjunction with the indicative in rhetorical question) 87.

#3139 σφάγια (acc.pl.neut.of σφάγιον, direct object of προσηνέγκατέ).

slain beast - Acts 7:42.

Meaning: Cf. σφάζω (#5292), σφαγή (#3175). That which is earmarked for slaughter. A victim. Slain beasts in pagan sacrifice - Acts 7:42.

καὶ (adjunctive conjunction joining nouns) 14.
θυσίας (acc.pl.fem.of θυσία, direct object of προσηνέγκατέ) 796.
προσηνέγκατέ (2d.per.pl.1st.aor.act.ind.of προσφέρω, culminative, direct question) 190.
μοι (dat.sing.masc.of ἐγώ, indirect object of προσηνέγκατέ) 123.
ἔτη (acc.pl.neut.of ἔτος, time extent) 821.
τεσσαράκοντα (numeral) 333.
ἐν (preposition with the locative of place) 80.
τῇ (loc.sing.fem.of the article in agreement with ἐρήμῳ) 9.
ἐρήμῳ (loc.sing.fem.of ἔρημος, place) 250.
οἶκος (voc.sing.masc.of οἶκος, address) 784.
Ἰσραήλ (voc.sing.masc.of Ἰσραήλ, indecl., in agreement with οἶκος) 165.

Translation - "*And God turned and gave them up to serve the host of heaven, just as it is written in a book of the prophets, 'You have offered dead animals and sacrifices to me for forty years in the wilderness, have you not, O House of Israel?'* "

Comment: Stephen's quotation is a composite of Amos 5:25-27 and Jeremiah 7:18; 8:2; 19:13. Luke follows the LXX faithfully except for minor changes; *e.g.* he adds Βαβυλῶνος at the end of verse 43 for Amos' Δαμασκοῦ. Because Stephen was quoting both Jeremiah and Amos, he does not specify his sources except to say that it was written ἐν βίβλῳ τῶν προφηστῶν - "in a book of the Prophets." Israel did not turn back to Egypt physically, but they did in their hearts (verse 39) and God turned away from them. ἐστρέφεν is intransitive here. He turned away and left them at the mercy of their own evil hearts, with the result that they worshipped the sun, moon and stars which are defined as the army of heaven (Jer.8:2). The entire Jewish family was involved in this idolatry. The children gathered the wood; the father kindled the fire and the mother kneaded the dough and baked the cakes which were then offered in sacrifice to their pagan deity who is described as τῇ στρατιᾷ τοῦ οὐρανοῦ - "the queen of heaven" (Jer.7:18). λατρεύειν is epexegetical. It explains παρέδωκεν. God did not turn them over to their pagan proclivities "in order that they might serve the queen of heaven" (purpose), but the result was that they did so. For forty years they ate the bread from heaven and enjoyed God's guidance, protection and provision and during the same forty years they refused to offer the Levitical offerings commanded by Moses and Aaron. It is interesting that at least they did not try to offer the manna which God provided to the pagan gods — a fact which indicates the insincerity of their worship. They needed the manna to eat. Instead they gathered wood, built a fire and baked cakes from the limited resources of the wilderness as they passed through. One wonders where they got the ingredients for the cakes?

The enormities of their pagan worship are described in

Verse 43 - "Yea, ye took up the tabernacle of Moloch, and the star of your god Remphan, figures which ye made to worship them: and I will carry you away before Babylon."

καὶ ἀνελάβετε τὴν σκηνὴν τοῦ Μολὸχ καὶ τὸ ἄστρον τοῦ θεοῦ (ὑμῶν) Ῥαιφάν, τοὺς τύπους οὓς ἐποιήσατε προσκυνεῖν αὐτοῖς. καὶ μετοικιῶ ὑμᾶς ἐπέκεινα Βαβυλῶνος.

καὶ (ascensive conjunction) 14.
ἀνελάβετε (2d.per.pl.2d.aor.act.ind.of ἀναλαμβάνομαι, indirect middle) 2930.
τὴν (acc.sing.fem.of the article in agreement with σκηνὴν) 9.
σκηνὴν (acc.sing.fem.of σκηνή, direct object of ἀνελάβετε) 1224.
τοῦ (gen.sing.masc.of the article in agreement with Μολὸχ) 9.

#3140 Μολὸχ (gen.sing.masc.indecl.of Μολόχ, description).

Moloch - Acts 7:43.

Meaning: an idol god of the Ammonites, to which human victims, particularly young children, were offered in sacrifice. Its image was that of a hollow brazen figure, with the head of an ox and outstretched human arms. It was heated to red-hot intensity by a fire built in its interior and the children were placed in the outstretched arms to be slowly burned. To prevent the parents from hearing the dying cries of the children the sacrificing priests beat drums - Acts 7:43.

καὶ (continuative conjunction) 14.
τὸ (acc.sing.neut.of the article in agreement with ἄστρον) 9.
ἄστρον (acc.sing.neut.of ἀστήρ, direct object of ἐποιήσατε) 145.
τοῦ (gen.sing.masc.of the article in agreement with θεοῦ) 9.
θεοῦ (gen.sing.masc.of θεός, description) 124.
ὑμῶν (gen.pl.masc.of σύ, relationship) 104.

#3141 Ῥαιφάν (gen.sing.masc.of Ῥαιφάν, indeclin., in apposition).

Remphan - Acts 7:43.

Meaning: Chiun, for the Arabic *Chevan*, the name of the planet Saturn, which as well as Mars was worshipped by the Semite nations as a source of evil. Remphan is the Coptic name of Saturn. "(Ρομφά, Westcott and Hort). The writer is quoting the Septuagint of Amos v. 26 (Ραιφάν), where the Hebrew has *Kiyyun*. This is probably a mistake for *Kewan*, the Babylonian name for the planet Saturn. The Greek form may be an error of the transliterator" (*Encyclopaedia Britannica*, 19, 121).

τοὺς (acc.pl.masc.of the article in agreement with τύπους) 9.
τύπους (acc.pl.masc.of τύπος, in apposition) 2917.
οὓς (acc.pl.masc.of ὅς, direct object of ἐποιήσατε) 65.
ἐποιήσατε (2d.per.pl.aor.act.ind.of ποιέω, constative) 127.
προσκυνεῖν (pres.act.inf.of προσκυνέω, purpose) 147.
αὐτοῖς (dat.pl.masc.of αὐτός, dative of person) 16.
καὶ (inferential conjunction) 14.
μετοικιῶ (1st.per.sing.fut.act.ind.of μετοικίζω, predictive) 3100.
ὑμᾶς (acc.pl.masc.of σύ, direct object of μετοικιῶ) 104.

#3142 ἐπέκεινα (improper preposition with the ablative of separation).

beyond - Acts 7:43.

Meaning: A combination of ἐπί (#47) and ἐκεῖνος (#246). Hence, "added to that" - "beyond." With the ablative of separation in a spatial sense - Acts 7:43.

Βαβυλῶνος (abl.sing.fem.of Βαβυλών, separation) 49.

Translation - "You even built the tabernacle of Moloch, and you made the star of your god, Remphan, the figure you produced in order to worship them. Therefore I am going to carry you away beyond Babylon."

Comment: καὶ is ascensive. They had not offered what God asked, but they even went further and substituted pagan worship, the worst of which was the worship of Moloch with its heartrending sacrifices of little children. The tabernacle of Moloch and the star of Remphan were the idols which Josiah destroyed (2 Kings 23:10). In verse 41 Stephen said that they were proud of their handicraft. Now he describes it. They made figures (τύπους) of the idols in order to worship them (purpose infinitive in προσκυνεῖν). Thus God announced through His prophet Amos that they would be carried away into Babylon.

It is a wretched picture of Israel's idolatry, as they turned away from the pure ethical monotheism to which Moses had introduced them, and reverted to the paganism which they and their forefathers had learned during their long stay in Egypt. And they did this despite the miraculous way in which Moses had delivered them from Egypt, provided for them, in terms of water, food and guidance to the promised land. The sons and daughters of those Jews who had placed their babies in the red-hot arms of Moloch were destined to see the Nazis incinerate themselves and their little children.

Verse 44 - "Our fathers had the tabernacle of witness in the wilderness, as he had appointed, speaking unto Moses, that he should make it according to the fashion he had seen."

Ἡ σκηνὴ τοῦ μαρτυρίου ἦν τοῖς πατράσιν ἡμῶν ἐν τῇ ἐρήμῳ, καθὼς διετάξατο ὁ λαλῶν τῷ Μωϋσῇ ποιῆσαι αὐτὴν κατὰ τὸν τύπον ὃν ἑωράκει,

Ἡ (nom.sing.fem.of the article in agreement with σκηνὴ) 9.

σκηνὴ (nom.sing.fem.of σκηνή, subject of ἦν) 1224.

τοῦ (gen.sing.neut.of the article in agreement with μαρτυρίου) 9.

μαρτυρίου (gen.sing.neut.of μαρτύριον, description) 716.

ἦν (3d.per.sing.imp.ind.of εἰμί, progressive description) 86.

τοῖς (dat.pl.masc.of the article in agreement with πατράσιν) 9.

πατράσιν (dat.pl.masc.of πατήρ, personal advantage) 238.

ἡμῶν (gen.pl.masc.of ἐγώ, relationship) 123.

ἐν (preposition with the locative of place) 80.

τῇ (loc.sing.fem.of the article in agreement with ἐρήμῳ) 9.

ἐρήμῳ (loc.sing.fem.of ἔρημος, place) 250.

καθὼς (particle introducing a comparative clause) 1348.

διετάξατο (3d.per.sing.aor.mid.ind.of διατάσσω, indirect middle, constative) 904.

ὁ (nom.sing.masc.of the article in agreement with λαλῶν) 9.

λαλῶν (pres.act.part.nom.sing.masc.of λαλέω, substantival, subject of διετάξατο) 815.

τῷ (dat.sing.masc.of the article in agreement with Μωϋσῇ) 9.

Μωϋσῇ (dat.sing.masc.of Μωϋσῆς, indirect object of διετάξατο) 715.

ποιῆσαι (aor.act.inf.of ποιέω, epexegetical) 127.

αὐτὴν (acc.sing.fem.of αὐτός, direct object of ποιῆσαι) 16.

κατὰ (preposition with the accusative, standard of measurement) 98.

τὸν (acc.sing.masc.of the article in agreement with τύπον) 9.

τύπον (acc.sing.masc.of τύπος, standard of measurement) 2917.

ὃν (acc.sing.masc.of ὅς, adjectival relative clause, in agreement with τύπον) 65.

ἑωράκει (3d.per.sing.pluferfect active indicative of ὁράω, Attic, intensive) 144.

Translation - "The tabernacle of the testimony was for the benefit of our forefathers in the wilderness, just as He Who spoke ordered Moses to build it according to the pattern which he had seen."

Comment: Luke, one of the three more sophisticated literary writers of the New Testament (Paul and the writer of Hebrews being the other two) reveals in this verse the Atticistic influence, in addition to the influence of the LXX. ἑωράκει is the Attic accidence for the pluperfect indicative. He followed the LXX, as he normally did, in the orthography of Μωϋσῇ. The κοινή spells it Μωϋσεῖ. The

Attiticists were a group of literary Greek writers who deplored the Hellenistic tendencies to "corrupt" the classic dialects (*i.e.* the Doric of Pindar, the Ionic of Herodotus, the Attic of Xenophon, the Aeolic of Sappho) into the κοινή, either literary or vernacular. Plutarch was a leading Purist who tried in vain to reestablish the Attic dialect as the only proper form. Of the New Testament writers, probably Luke, Paul and the writer of Hebrews were the only ones who would have had any sympathy with this movement.

Stephen's point here is that Israel's idolatry described in verses 42 and 43 was not the result of their lack of any other mode of worship. They built Moloch a temple and fashioned objects of worship to Saturn, even though they had available to them the Tabernacle of Witness which God ordered Moses to build in accord with the pattern which Moses had seen on Mount Sinai. Israel made her choice between God's temple and her own.

The Tabernacle is described as one designed to be a witness. To whom? Its furnishings and the offerings which were prescribed all point forward to the Lamb of God, Whose blood, unlike that of bulls and goats, could redeem from sin. (Heb.9:13-15). The righteousness of God, which is available only by faith in Jesus Christ was witnessed in the Old Testament age by the law and the prophets (Rom.3: 21). Stephen perhaps did not grasp the full significance of what he was saying. Only after the Holy Spirit spelled it out in detail to the writer of Hebrews did we know how completely the Tabernacle of Witness in the wilderness pointed the sinning Hebrew forward to the cross. (Hebrews 5-10). God not only provided manna and quail for their food and water from rock of Horeb for their thirst, guidance for their feet and footwear that resisted the desert sands for thirty-eight years, but He also provided that which was infinitely more important - salvation for their souls. Though they did not understand all that the Tabernacle worship of the Aaronic Priesthood meant, any more than Christians today understand all that Christian theology means to us, yet when they came in faith and obedience, they were looking forward in a monotheistic way to a God Who was Spirit and Who ruled supremely in a moral universe. Their God who insisted that He was unique and thus demanded all of their devotion was the God of history. Israel's future, like her past history, was tied up closely with the promises of a covenant keeping God. He had maneuvered history to preserve them. Joseph's bondage in Egypt was the factor that saved them from starvation in Canaan, a land in which, at that time, they owned not a single square foot of real estate. They rejected Moses in Egypt whom God had appointed to be their ruler and deliverer. They rejected the manna in the desert and longed to return to the flesh pots of Egypt, even though their return entailed slavery under a pagan power. Then came their supreme insult to the God of their covenant — they turned their backs upon the Tabernacle of Witness, which was designed and built exactly like the one which God has in heaven and which spoke to them of love and grace, pardon, redemption and everlasting life, and sacrificed their children to the fiery god Moloch. The offerings which should have been brought to Aaron in the Tabernacle were offered to Remphan. When He came, of whom the Tabernacle of Witness spoke in anticipation, they chose Barabbas and murdered Him. Thus Stephen was building up to the climax of his bitter denunciation of verse 51.

The generation of Jews who came out of Egypt at the Red Sea died in the wilderness, except for Joshua and Caleb. Even Moses did not enter Canaan, but died and was buried on Mt. Nebo (Deut.34:1-8). Except for Joshua and Caleb the entire population that crossed the Jordan and occupied the land, as recorded in the book of Joshua was thirty-eight years old or less. Although their fathers largely ignored the Aaronic priesthood and its worship in the Tabernalce of Witness, they had carried it with them. And when they crossed the Jordan to occupy their national home land, they brought the Tabernacle with them, only to ignore it again in Canaan as they had done in the wilderness. This is the thought in

Verse 45 - "Which also our fathers that came after brought in with Jesus into the possession of the Gentiles, whom God drove out before the face of our fathers, unto the days of David."

ἣν καὶ εἰσήγαγον διαδεξάμενοι οἱ πατέρες ἡμῶν μετὰ Ἰησοῦ ἐν τῇ κατασχέσει τῶν ἐθνῶν ωῖν ἐξῶσεν ὁ θεὸς ἀπὸ προσώπου τῶν πατέρων ἡμῶν ἕως τῶν ἡμερῶν Δαυίδ,

ἣν (acc.sing.fem.of ὅς, direct object of εἰσήγαγον, in an adjectival relative clause, in agreement with σκηνή) 65.

καὶ (adjunctive conjunction joining verbs) 14.

εἰσήγαγον (3d.per.pl.aor.act.ind.of εἰσάγω, constative) 1897.

#3143 διαδεξάμενοι (1st.aor.mid.part.nom.pl.masc.of διαδέχομαι, adjectival, restrictive).

came after - Acts 7:45.

Meaning: A combination of διά (#118) and δέχομαι (#867). To receive through another; to succeed to; in Acts 7:45, to inherit, with reference to the inheritance of the land of Canaan, by the children of the generation that came out of Egypt.

οἱ (nom.pl.masc.of the article in agreement with πατέρες) 9.

πατέρες (nom.pl.masc.of πατήρ, subject of εἰσήγαγον) 238.

ἡμῶν (gen.pl.masc.of ἐγώ, relationship) 123.

μετὰ (preposition with the genitive of accompaniment) 50.

Ἰησοῦ (gen.sing.masc.of Ἰησοῦ, accompaniment) 3.

ἐν (preposition with the locative of place) 80.

τῇ (loc.sing.fem.of the article in agreement with κατασχέσει) 9.

κατασχέσει (loc.sing.fem.of κατάσχεσις, place) 3101.

τῶν (gen.pl.neut.of the article in agreement with ἐθνῶν) 9.

ἐθνῶν (gen.pl.neut.of ἔθνος, possession) 376.

ὧν (gen.pl.neut.of ὅς, direct attraction to ἐθνῶν, relative adjectival clause) 65.

#3144 ἐξῶσεν (3d.per.sing.aor.act.ind.of ἐξωθέω, constative).

drive out - Acts 7:45.

thrust out - Acts 27:39

Meaning: A combination of ἐκ (#19) and ὠθέω - "to push" hence, to push out; to displace. Israel's armies, under the direction of Joshua and by the power of God displaced the inhabitants of Palestine - Acts 7:45. With reference to propelling a ship out of the dangerous waves into a safe harbor - Acts 27:39.

ὁ (nom.sing.masc.of the article in agreement with θεός) 9.
θεός (nom.sing.masc.of θεός, subject of ἐξῶσεν) 124.
ἀπό (preposition with the ablative of separation) 70.
προσώπου (abl.sing.neut.of πρόσωπον, separation) 588.
τῶν (gen.pl.masc.of the article in agreement with πατέρων) 9.
πατέρων (gen.pl.masc.of πατήρ, possession) 238.
ἡμῶν (gen.pl.masc.of ἐγώ, relationship) 123.
ἕως (adverb introducing a definite temporal clause) 71.
τῶν (gen.pl.fem.of the article in agreement with ἡμέρων) 9.
ἡμέρων (gen.pl.fem.of ἡμέρα, time description) 135.
Δαυίδ (gen.sing.masc.indeclin., of Δαυίδ, description) 6.

Translation - ". . . which (the Tent of Testimony) our forefathers, who inherited it, with (the leadership of) Joshua, brought into the land of the Gentiles, whom God drove out from before the attack of our forefathers, until David's time."

Comment: ἥν refers to ἡ σκηνή of verse 44. διά in composition is perfective. The generation that followed those who died in the wilderness inherited the Tabernacle of Witness which God designed, the model of which He showed to Moses at Sinai, which Moses built and which the Levites carried with them through the wilderness for thirty-eight years. When they crossed the Jordan under the leadership of Joshua, after the death and burial of Moses on Mount Nebo, they did not abandon the Tabernacle. They brought it with them into Canaan, which until that time had been the possession of Gentiles tribes, who fled from before the ark of the covenant as God gave supernatural help to Israel's armies. Note ἐν with the locative where we normally expect εἰς with the accusative, particularly in view of the fact that we already have εἰς in composition in the verb.

Despite Israel's long and miserable record of idolatry God drove the Gentiles out of Canaan to make room for His chosen people. This He did because He was under covenant obligations to Abraham, Isaak and Jacob, not because Israel deserved it. Had He not done so He would have been guilty of failing to fulfill His promise which was given in an unconditional covenant. The Tabernacle, with its Holy of Holies, in which the ark of the covenant rested was the battle weapon which God used, even though Israel had forsaken its services to worship Moloch and Remphan.

Once established in Canaan Israel set up the Tabernacle and gave it the same halfhearted attention that she had given in the wilderness.

Moses, who died on Mount Nebo (Deut.34:1-8) led them out of Egypt, but he could not take them into Canaan. This became the privilege of Joshua (Ιησοῦ -

"Yahweh is the Saviour"). The law "given by Moses" cannot do what grace and truth which "comes by Jesus Christ" can (John 1:17). Moses did not die because of old age or ill health (Deut.34:7). He died, short of the accomplishment for which he had contended with Pharaoh and led his people through the wilderness for thirty-eight years because of his own disobedience. The full discussion of this matter will be given in comment on 1 Cor.10:4, *q.v.*, but here we can say that Moses destroyed a wonderful type which God had planned for Israel. The Rock of Horeb, once smitten, had yielded water for Israel when the people were ready to die of thirst (Ex.17:1-7), suggesting that when Christ was smitten upon the cross, the water of everlasting life might be ours. Years later Israel was back at Horeb. Again there was no water and again they thirsted. God told Moses and Aaron to assemble the people at the Rock. However, this time Moses was ordered to "speak . . . unto the rock before their eyes" and the promise was that "it shall give forth his water, and thou shalt bring forth to them water out of the rock: so thou shalt give the congregation and their beasts drink" (Numbers 20:1-13). What a beautiful way for God to say in type that the Rock Christ Jesus (Mt.16:18; 1 Cor.10:4), need be smitten only once. After that we need only to speak to Him to receive the water of everlasting life (John 4:13,14; 7:37-39). Moses, now comparatively speaking, an old man, eighty years older than any of the people of Israel, except Joshua and Caleb, and understandingly irritated by their continual complaints and lack of faith, lost his temper and, instead of speaking to the rock as he had been told to do, he struck it twice. The water came from the rock to refresh the thirsty people, for God could not punish the people for Moses' disobedience, but the Lord told Moses that he would never lead the nation across the Jordan into Canaan (Numbers 20:12). It is significant that Moses did not forget the costly lesson which he had learned. In his last message to the nation he alluded to the Rock five times (Deut.32:4,15,18,31,37) after which the Lord again reminded him why he was not permitted to lead the nation which he had led so many years, across the Jordan into Canaan land (Deut.32:51,52).

Thus Moses, successful in leading Israel out of Egyptian bondage, and through the wilderness, failed to lead them into the promise land. Fifteen hundred years later the writer of Hebrews observed that "The law (Moses) made nothing perfect, but the bringing in of a better hope did." (Joshua, Jesus and the covenant of grace, Heb.7:19; 10:1).

Stephen has now brought his audience all the way from the day that God called Abraham in Mesopotamia, to Haran, to Bethel, in and out of Egypt, through the wilderness, into Canaan and to the establishment of David upon his throne (Acts 7:2-45). He will now show that David, who wished to replace the Tabernacle of Witness with a permanent temple was forbidden to do so and promised an heir, King David's Greater Son, who would sit upon his throne forever. This King, promised to David was Jesus, the Nazarene carpenter, whom Caiaphas and his colleagues had murdered.

Verse 46 - "Who found favor before God, and desired to find a tabernacle for the God of Jacob."

ὃς εὗρεν χάριν ἐνώπιον τοῦ θεοῦ καὶ ᾐτήσατο εὑρεῖν σκήνωμα τῷ οἴκῳ
Ἰακώβ.

ὃς (nom.sing.masc.of ὅς, subject of εὗρεν, adjectival relative clause, in
agreement with Δαυίδ) 65.
εὗρεν (3d.per.sing.aor.act.ind.of εὑρίσκω, constative) 79.
χάριν (acc.sing.fem.of χάρις, direct object of εὗρεν) 1700.
ἐνώπιον (improper preposition with the genitive of reference) 1798.
τοῦ (gen.sing.masc.of the article in agreement with θεοῦ) 9.
θεοῦ (gen.sing.masc.of θεός, reference) 124.
καὶ (adjunctive conjunction joining verbs) 14.
ᾐτήσατο (3d.per.sing.aor.mid.ind.of αἰτέω, constative) 537.
εὑρεῖν (aor.act.inf.of εὑρίσκω, epexegetical) 79.

#3145 σκήνωμα (acc.sing.neut.of σκήνωμα, direct object of εὑρεῖν).

tabernacle - Acts 7:46; 2 Peter 1:13,14.

Meaning: Cf. σκηνή (#1224), σκηνόω (#1698), σκηνοπηγία (#2357),
σκηνοποιός (#3436) and σκῆνος (#4304). With reference to the permanent
temple which David wanted to build to replace the Aaronic Tabernacle - Acts
7:46. Metaphorically of the human body of a Christian - 2 Peter 1:13,14.

τῷ (dat.sing.masc.of the article in agreement with οἴκῳ) 9.
οἴκῳ (dat.sing.masc.of οἶκος, personal advantage) 784.
Ἰακώβ (gen.sing.masc.indeclin. of Ἰακώβ, description) 12.

*Translation - ". . . who found favor before God and sought to build a temple for
the House of Jacob."*

Comment: ὃς introduces the relative clause which serves like an adjective to
describe Δαυίδ of verse 45. He found himself in God's favor, and he hoped to
build a permanent place of worship to replace the Tabernacle of Testimony
which had been built by Moses at Sinai and carried by the Levites through the
desert for thirty-eight years. The priests, under the protection of Joshua's army,
carried it across the Jordan and set it up in Canaan where it had housed the
ministry of the Aaronic priesthood since. *Cf.* 2 Sam.7:1-17.
     The favor which David found before God was due above all to the fact that he
was the first man in the line of Judah who was free from the curse of Deut.23:2,
which was cast upon Judah's line by his adultery with his daughter-in-law,
Tamar, and her conception by him of the bastards, Pharez and Zara. Read the
shameful story in Genesis 38.
     The throne rights of God's unconditional covenant with Abraham descended
from him through Isaac and Jacob to Judah (Gen.49:8-12). But Judah's
adultery, although it did not abrogate God's promise that Messiah, when He
came, would be one of Judah's descendants, did make it impossible for Judah or
any of his line to serve with God's blessing as King of Israel until the tenth
generation. The genealogical register of the kings in Mt.1:3-6 lists Judah,
Pharez, Esrom, Aram, Aminadab, Naason, Salmon, Boaz, Obed, Jesse and

David. If we count Judah, whose sin brought the curse upon his line, Jesse was his son of the tenth generation and David was the eleventh. Hence David was the first in Judah's line who was not under the ban of Deut.23:2. Thus he was the first who could "find favor with God" - ὃς εὗρεν χάριν ἐνώπιον τοῦ θεοῦ.

If the gentlemen who sat in the San Hedrin were as great students of the Old Testament as they professed to be this exposition by Stephen was nothing new. They should have known what he meant when he spoke of the favor which David found before the Lord.

Joshua, who was commander in chief of Israel's army, led the nation across the Jordan and, though not all of the Gentile tribes were driven from the land, most of them were and the people were settled upon the land which was divided among all of the tribes except the tribe of Levi, which was given land scattered throughout the nation, in order that they could carry on the priestly functions. The governmental functions were carried out by Joshua until his death, at age 110, and after that by the elders of Israel, "who had seen all the great works of the Lord, that He did for Israel" (Judges 2:7,8) The generation which had been born during the thirty-eight years of wilderness wandering died and the succeeding generation "after them . . . knew not the Lord, nor yet the works which He had done for Israel" (Judges 2:10,11), as a result of which Israel "did evil in the sight of the Lord, and served Baalim." Although God was angry with His people for their idolatry, as He had been with their parents and grandparents in the wilderness, He was bound by His promise to Abraham, Isaac and Jacob not to destroy them. They needed a king who would lead them back to the Tabernacle of the Testimony, but Judah's adultery made that impossible until the birth of David. Therefore, as a temporary expedient "the Lord raised up judges, which delivered them out of the hand of those that spoiled them" (Judges 2:16).During the life of each judge the nation returned to the worship of the God of the covenant and observed the rituals of the Tabernacle of the Testimony as administered by the priests of Levi. With the death of the judge, the nation backslid again (Judges 2:19), and each time, as punishment for their idolatry the Lord allowed their pagan neighbours to oppress them, until the next judge arose. Thus Othniel, the younger brother of Caleb, delivered them from the Mesopotamians (Judges 3:10), Ehud rescued them from the Moabites (Judges 3:12-30), Shamgar defeated the Philistines (Judges 3:31), Deborah and Barak defeated the forces of Sisera, who was killed by Jael (Judges 4:1-5:31).). Then came Gideon, who defeated the Midianites (Judges 6:1- 8:32), after whose death the nation again ". . . went a whoring after Baalim"(Judges 8:33).Then in order came Abimelech, Tola, Jair, Jephtha, Ibzan, Elon, Abdon, Samson and Samuel, the last of the judges. In this period of more than three hundred years, from the death of Joshua to the anointing of Saul, as Israel's first king, there were seven apostasies, six servitudes and a Civil War. The nation was enslaved by the Mesopotamians, the Moabites, the Canaanites, the Midianites and twice by the Philistines, after which came a period of confusion and anarchy.All, or at least some of this might have been avoided if the line of the royal house of Judah could have been installed when they entered in upon possession of their land.

The anarchy became so great that the nation came to Samuel and demanded he give them a king who would govern them as their neighbour nations were governed. Samuel was aware of the corruption in the courts of his two sons, Joel and Abiah, whom he had named to succeed him, and he was probably sympathetic with the elders' desire for better government. His lack of sympathy with their demand was probably based upon other grounds. The text does not tell us whether or not Samuel was familiar with the line of thought that we have presented in relation to Judah's adultery and the curse of Deut.23:2. It is more than likely that he was, as he must have been a good student of the Pentateuch. He prayed about it and the Lord told him to acquiesce in their request, but not before he had warned the elders that their king, if they got him, would be a tyrant. Despite Samuel's warning to Israel she persisted in her request for a king, and Samuel reported the decision to the Lord and was told to go ahead with the inauguration of the monarchy (1 Samuel 8:1-22).

The story illustrates how the misguided plans of man, however sincere and, on human grounds, well intentioned they may be, can put God in the dilemma, the horns of which arose, on the one hand from his unconditional covenant with Jacob and Judah and on the other from the enforcement of His moral law.

His promise to Jacob, which he in turn gave to his son, Judah was that the family of Judah was to be the regal line. The LXX has Jacob's statement to Judah in these terms: οὐκ ἐκλείψει ἄρχων ἐξ Ἰούδα, καὶ ἡγούμενος ἐκ τῶν μηρῶν αὐτοῦ, ἕως ἂν ἔλθῃ τὰ ἀποκείμενα αὐτῷ, καὶ αὐτὸς προσδοκία ἐθνῶν. The Oxford Revised Standard Version translates, "The scepter shall not depart from Judah, nor the ruler's staff from between his feet, until he comes *to whom it belongs;* and to him shall be the obedience of the peoples." This is the Syriac for the Hebrew which translates *"until Shiloh comes"* or *"until he comes to Shiloh."* The Revised Version, newly edited by the American Revision Committee in 1901, has "The sceptre shall not depart from Judah, nor the ruler's staff (margin, *a lawgiver)* from between his feet, until Shiloh come . . . κ.τ.λ." This language clearly means that Israel's kings must always be from the tribe of Judah and that "the one to whom it belongs" is the Messiah, Who, when He comes will occupy the throne forever as "the Lion of the tribe of Juda," (Rev.5:5), Who was also destined to be called "the Root of David" (Rev.5:5) after the events of 2 Samuel 7:1-17, which events, of course were future to Jacob on his deathbed in Egypt when he vested the throne rights of the kingdom in his son Judah.

The other horn of the dilemma which confronted God when the elders demanded a king consisted of the moral obligation which He could not fail to honor to enforce the rule of Deut.23:2. Judah's adultery had made it impossible for the nation to have a king until the birth of David, the son of Jesse, who, since he would represent the eleventh generation from Judah, would be free from the ban.

It is difficult to tell whether or not David was born at the time that Israel demanded a king. Ussher's chronology which is not too far wrong has the anointing of Saul and Samuel's proclamation of the kingdom in 1095 B.C. At the end of his second year as king, he went to war with the Philistines (1 Sam.13:1). We do not know how long the war lasted, but the impression is that it was not long. Following Jonathan's great victory over the Philistines (1 Samuel 14) Saul was ordered by Samuel to attack Amalek (1 Samuel 15:3). His victory over the Amalekites was followed by his incomplete obedience as he spared Agag, as a result of which the Lord told Samuel to strip the king of his power. This the aged Samuel did when he met the king at Gilgal and uttered his famous speech - "Hath the Lord as great delight in burntofferings and sacrifice, as in obeying the voice of the Lord? Behold, to obey is better than sacrifice, and to hearken than the fat of rams.For rebellion is as the sin of witchcraft and stubbornness is as iniquity and idolatry.Because thou hast rejected the word of the Lord, he hath also rejected thee from being king. . . The Lord hath rent the kingdom of Israel from thee this day, and hath given it to a neighbour of thine, that is better than thou. And also the Strength of Israel will not lie nor repent: for he is not a man, that he should repent." (1 Sam.15:22-23, 28-29).

It is important to note that while God's covenant with Jacob and Judah with reference to throne rights in the nation was unconditional, his covenant with Saul was conditioned upon Saul's obedience (1 Sam.15:23b). God did not promise Judah that he would be the king, but he did promise him that when Messiah came, He would be from the tribe of Judah. Thus, although Judah's sin of adultery kept him from the throne, and extended the ban down his line to include Jesse, the father of David, it did not abrogate the promise of God that the Lord Jesus Christ would occupy the throne of Israel forever.

Although Saul, a Benjamite (1 Samuel 9:1,2) was officially relieved of his duties after his victory over Amalek, he was still with the army in the Valley of Elah when the Philistine giant challenged the camp. In the meantime Samuel, under orders from the Lord, had gone to Bethlehem and anointed David.Ussher dates this event at B.C.1063, which is 32 years after Saul was anointed. We are not told how long after Saul was removed from office that David was anointed, but that David was not yet born in 1095 seems clear from his description in 1 Samuel 16:12, and also from Saul's estimate of his age, when the young man came to visit the army on the day that he killed Goliath. When David appeared before Saul before he went out to fight the giant, the former king, now deposed, called him παιδάριον (#2275), which is the diminutive form of παῖς (#217). *Cf.* 1 Samuel 17:33. παῖς was defined by Hippocrates in these terms: παῖς δὲ ἄχρι γονῆς ἐκφύσεως εἰς τὰ δὶς ἑπτα - "He is a παῖς until puberty, until twice seven." Soranus, a Greek physician, born at Ephesus in A.D.98, is the author of the *Life of Hippocrates.* He says that Hippocrates was born on the island of Cos in about 460 B.C. The great physician thus wrote in the latter half of the fifth century before Christ, and about one hundred years before the Hellenistic revolution following the death of Alexander the Great (323 B.C.), had begun to change the idiom and etymology of the Greek language. Hippocrates was defining παῖς as the Greeks in the period of post-Epic Greek did, and we are applying his definition to a young man who lived 600 years before Hippocrates was born.

Thus we cannot say with certainty whether David had been born at the time that the elders of Israel forced God to go to the Tribe of Benjamin and "borrow" a king from a tribe with no throne rights, or not. Saul may have been exaggerating his youth when he called him a παιδάριον - "a little παῖς," If, in fact, David was only 14 or less when he fought Goliath it is clear that when Saul was anointed by Samuel and proclaimed king David was not yet born. Thus God could not have ordered Samuel to anoint Jesse who was the tenth generation in Judah's line and therefore banned from the kingship, because of Deut.23:2.

We will return to this line of thought to show that neither Solomon nor any of his line had a right to the throne and that, although Nathan, Solomon's brother, was in the line, he, too could not have occupied the throne, even if he had been named by David, because both he and Solomon were illegitimate. Thus the same curse that fell upon the line of Judah because of his adultery, also fell upon the line of David because of his adultery with Bathsheba, from which illicit union came the heads both of the Solomonic and Nathanic families, the former of which leads to Joseph the carpenter and the latter to Mary, the mother of Jesus.

An understanding of the circumstances that led to the selection of Saul as the King of Israel will generate some sympathy for him. He did not want the job. Read the story in 1 Samuel 9:1-10:27. Saul was busy looking for his father's livestock. He and his servant, unsuccessful in the search, spent so much time that he suggested to the servant that they ought to give up the search and go home, lest his father Kish, be more worried over his lost son than over the lost asses, whereupon the servant suggested that they visit Samuel and get supernatural help in their search. Meanwhile God had told Samuel that Saul was coming to see him. When Saul arrived, Samuel assured him that the animals had already been found, and then said, "And on whom is all the desire of Israel? Is it not on thee, and on all thy father's house?" (1 Sam.9:20). Whereupon Saul immediately protested that he was a Benjamite and that Samuel was looking for a king in the wrong tribe (vs.21). It may be significant that Samuel did not use the word "king." In the anointing ceremony (1 Sam.10:1) he called Saul a "captain." The LXX has Οὐχὶ κέχρικέν σε Κύριος εἰς ἄρχοντα ἐπὶ τὸν λαὸν αὐτοῦ, ἐπὶ Ἰσραήλ;It is true that when Samuel presented Saul to the people they said, Ζήτω ὁ βασιλεύς (1 Sam.10:24) - "may the *king* be saved." There is a difference between ἄρχων and βασιλεύς. *Kings* are, by virtue of their position also *leaders*, but the reverse is not true. It is not likely that many of the common people in Israel knew enough about their law to realize that Saul was not eligible for kingship. Samuel, who may have understood it better, was really saying that Saul was to be a *leader* for the nation until such time that a *king* could be anointed. When Samuel called the nation together to comply with their demand that they be given a king, the process of selection was carried out by lot. The tribe of Benjamin was selected. Within the tribe, the family of Matri was taken, and within that family group Saul, the son of Kish was taken. He could not be found, until a search revealed that he had hidden himself "among the stuff" (1 Sam.10:22). The young man, taller than all others in the kingdom, was dragged reluctantly from his hiding place and the responsibility of leadership was forced upon him.

His performance in the office was no worse than David's. He was disobedient to the Lord's order to kill Agag, the Amalakite - a lapse in obedience but he did not seduce another man's wife and then plot to have her husband killed, as David later did. The difference is that Saul's tenure depended upon his obedience under a conditional covenant, while David's kingship was the result of God's unconditional promise to Jacob and Judah. Since Messiah must be Son of Man as well as Son of God (1 Tim.2:5) if He is to be both Prophet, Priest and Potentate, His incarnation must be from *some* family line of the human race. Therefore, since "all have sinned and come short of the glory of God" (Rom.3:23), God's covenant promise must be unconditionally made to the nation, tribe and family that produced Him. Otherwise God could never have found a line from which to produce the "seed of the woman" whom He promised from the beginning would bruise the serpent's head and redeem the race (Gen.3:15).

Stephen passed over the period of the Judges and the reign of Saul, without comment. It has been presented here for the benefit of the student who may not have understood as well as his audience his point when he said that David "found favor before God." David was the King of Israel by God's appointment, and his ascent to the throne, first in Hebron over the house of Judah and then, seven and one-half years later in Jerusalem, over the united nation of Israel and Judah (2 Samuel 5:4,5), was proof that God was determined to follow His divine scenario for Israel, His chosen people, and for the entire human race, despite the follies and failures of men. Though David was anointed by Samuel when he was only a boy, his reign over Judah did not begin until he was thirty and his rule of the entire nation came when he was thirty-six. Until he died, at age seventy, he elevated the nation to a position of preeminence among the neighbouring Gentile powers. Indeed he was so certain that Israel's position in the world was secure that he planned to build a permanent temple of worship to replace the Tabernacle of the Testimony, which had served the nation during the wilderness wanderings and since the day that they entered Canaan under Joshua.

That David was ill advised in this plan is clear to us who have the advantage of the hindsight of history and the revelation of the New Testament. He could not have known the future of Israel as we know it now. That Israel would crucify her Messiah, that He would rise from the dead and go back to heaven for two thousand years, during which the Holy Spirit, through the preaching of the gospel would select from the Gentile nations "a people for His name" (Acts 15:14) and that only after the Church Age is past and the Bride of Christ, consisting of regenerate sinners, both Jew and gentile, is complete, Messiah would return to give to Israel the eternal permanence which David thought was theirs in his day - all of this was unclear to David, and we could not expect that it would be otherwise.

That is why the prophet Nathan was ordered by the Lord to tell David to forget his plan to build a permanent temple. Though God forbade him to build it, he did not tell him all the reason why he should not do so. But he did promise David that someday his throne would be permanent. This Davidic covenant (2 Samuel 7:10-17) is unconditional. It will never be abrogated as a result of failure from the human side. The key to its fulfillment is God's promise that God would "set up thy seed after thee, which shall proceed out of thy bowels, and I will establish his kingdom. He shall build an house for my name, and I will stablish his kingdom for ever. I will be his father and he shall be my son." (2 Samuel 7:12-14). The prophecy goes on in verses 14,15 to foretell the redemptive work of King

David's Greater Son upon the cross and His resurrection from the dead. The prophecy does not say that its promises would be fulfilled during the reign of David's immediate successor, Solomon, although it was natural for David and his court to think so. This is why there was so much interest in the selection of Solomon when King David lay upon his deathbed - an interest that was not wholly free from sinful ambition. Read the story in 1 Kings 1:1-31. That the choice which Bathsheba, the Queen Mother, suggested to the dying King was not within the will of God is clear for the same reason that Judah was not permitted to take his throne after the death of Jacob. For David's adultery with Bathsheba, as a result of which both Solomon and his brother Nathan were born, cast the curse of Deut.23:2 upon the line of David just as it had kept every generation of Judah's line from the throne, until the birth of David. In other words Israel has had only one legitimate reigning king in all of her history. Others have been eligible but they have not reigned. Judah was eligible (Gen. 49:10) but he forfeited his throne with his adultery (Gen. 38). David was eligible and he reigned for forty years, during which time God gave him His unconditional promise that some day Israel would have a King Who would rule forever. Neither Solomon nor Nathan were eligible for the same reason that Pharez, the illegitimate son of Judah was not. The descendants of Solomon and Nathan, in their respective family lines were not eligible until ten generations had been born and by that time Israel was under the domination of Gentile powers - Babylon, Media-Persia, Greece, Rome. Scattered by the Romans in A.D.70 after the destruction of Jerusalem they have been individually subject to Gentile powers since, except for those who, since 1948, have returned to Palestine and established, not a monarchy but a democracy. The Nathanic line, listed in inverse order in Luke 3:23-29, from Heli, the father of Mary, the Virgin, down to Levi (verse 29), were eligible so far as we know (unless there was some adultery in that part of the line!), but they had no chance to be king since they lived and died at a time when Israel was subject to Gentile powers. Mary, the mother of Jesus, had a legal right to the throne of David, but she could not exercise it because she was a woman, but she could and did pass it down to her firstborn son, Jesus, Who also was not permitted to take His place upon David's throne on earth, since His part in the divine scenario was to take His place upon a cross, after which He ascended to heaven to take His place upon His throne at the right hand of God. So we cannot count Jesus of Nazareth, along with David, as one of Israel's *reigning* kings, although He is eminently eligible for the position and will indeed become the Second and Last reigning King of Israel.

Amillenialists fall into error when they assume that the throne which Jesus Christ occupies now, since His ascension and before His second coming, is David's throne of 2 Samuel 7:12,13. David's throne was not in heaven. It was in Jerusalem.

That God did not mean Solomon in 2 Samuel 7:14 is clear from Hebrews 1:5 where the writer says that "I will be to him a Father, and he shall be to me a Son" refers to Jesus Christ. Which ought to settle the question.

Verse 47 - "But Solomon built him an house."

Σολομῶν δὲ οἰκοδόμησεν αὐτῷ οἶκον.

Σολομῶν (nom.sing.masc.of Σολομῶν, subject of οἰκοδόμησεν) 32.
δὲ (adversative conjunction) 11.
οἰκοδόμησεν (3d.per.sing.aor.act.ind.of οἰκοδομέω, constative) 694.
αὐτῷ (dat.sing.masc.of αὐτός, personal advantage) 16.
οἶκον (acc.sing.masc.of οἶκος, direct object of οἰκοδόμησεν) 784.

Translation - "But Solomon built a house for Him."

Comment: The first mistake that Solomon made was that he assumed that he was the fulfillment of God's promise to David, his father in 2 Samuel 7:12-14. God had said, "I will set up thy seed after thee. . ." but He did not say *immediately after*. God did not establish the Solomonic kingdom except temporarily. After his death the kingdom divided and then both the houses of Judah and Israel were carried away to Babylonian captivity. The second mistake that Solomon made was that he was to build the house for the Lord which David had been forbidden to build. The same reasons why David should not have built it are those that would forbid Solomon to build it. But (adversative δὲ) Solomon built it, ostensibly because he thought that his kingdom was permanent, but probably for vainglory. God permitted the king to build it, and on dedication day Solomon prayed his long dedication prayer in which he indicated that he misunderstood the Davidic covenant (1 Kings 8:1 - 9:9). Note also that God's promise to Solomon (1 Kings 9:1-9) was conditioned upon Israel's faithfulness which was not forthcoming, whereas God's promise to David (2 Samuel 7:10-17) was unconditional. Israel failed and divine judgment fell. Nebuchadnezzar, the king of Babylon and his army came and took Jehoiachin, the king of Judah in the eighth year of his reign, and violated the sanctity of the temple and carried out the gold treasures which Solomon had placed there (2 Kings 24:11-13. The Babylonians established Zedekiah, the uncle of Jehoiachin, as the Babylonian puppet in Jerusalem. For eleven years Zedekiah reigned in Jerusalem, under the aegis of the Babylonians. His corrupt administration ended when Nebuchadnezzar came and laid seige to Jerusalem for more than a year. Famine prevailed within the walls of the city. The siege ended in the eleventh year of Zedekiah's reign. The city walls were breached, the sons of Zedekiah were killed and the king's eyes were gouged out. He was bound in fetters and carried away to Babylon. The Babylonians burned the temple which Solomon had built and carried the remainder of its treasures to the banks of the Euphrates. (2 Kings 24,25).

Again we provide the details of the history of the period - details which Stephen did not discuss because his audience already knew the outcome of the Solomonic story.

But though Solomon was wrong in his grandiose assumptions and plans, the destruction of the temple and the captivity of Israel did not affect the outcome of the divine scenario which the God of Israel had written. This we see in

Verse 48 - "Howbeit the most high dwelleth not in temples made with hands, as

saith the prophet."

ἀλλ' οὐχ ὁ ὕφιστος ἐν χειροποιήτοις κατοικεῖ, καθὼς ὁ προφήτης λέγει,

ἀλλ' (adversative conjunction) 342.

οὐχ (summary negative conjunction with the indicative, joined to κατοικεῖ) 130.

ὁ (nom.sing.masc.of the article in agreement with ὕφιστος) 9.

ὕφιστος (nom.sing.masc.of ὕφιστος, subject of κατοικεῖ) 1353.

ἐν (preposition with the locative of place) 80.

χειροποιήτοις (loc.pl.masc.of χειροποίητος, place) 2809.

κατοικεῖ (3d.per.sing.pres.act.ind.of κατοικέω, customary) 242.

καθὼς (particle introducing a comparative clause) 1348.

ὁ (nom.sing.masc.of the article in agreement with προφήτης) 9.

προφήτης (nom.sing.masc.of προφήτης, subject of λέγει) 119.

λέγει (3d.per.sing.pres.act.ind.of λέγω, historical) 66.

Translation - "But it is not customary for the Most High to live in buildings made with human hands, just as the prophet said, . . . "

Comment: ἀλλά is the strong adversative. Thus Stephen expressed his strong disapproval of Solomon's presumptive and grandiose building program which called forth from God nothing more than His conditional promise to bless Solomon and regard him as the fulfillment of the promise that God had made to David in 2 Samuel 7:10-13. At the dedication ceremony of the Solomonic temple, after Solomon's long prayer, the Lord agreed to "hallow this house" (1 Kings 9:3), but He followed this promise with two conditional promises, each with its *if clause*. The first (vss.4-5) was the carrot; the second (vss.6-9). *If* Solomon would "walk before me, as David thy father walked, in integrity of heart, and in uprightness, to do all that I have commanded thee, and wilt keep my statutes and judgments, . . ." then God promised the same perpetuity for the throne of Solomon which He had promised to David. But the stick followed - "But if ye shall at all turn from following me . . . " the results of such apostasy is then described in vss.7-9.

The Lord was grateful that Solomon had tried to please Him, but it is not likely that the divine Architect and Creator of the universe would be favourably impressed with anything that Solomon, his architects and contractors could build. What pleases Him more is obedience, which is much better than "burnt offerings and sacrifices" (1 Samuel 15:22,23) as Samuel had once reminded Saul.

The fact that Israel failed God under the Solomonic covenant did not abrogate His promise to David, because the former was unconditional, while His promise to Solomon was contingent upon human compliance with the terms of the agreement, which was not forthcoming. Indeed David had placed the same ban upon his line, under the terms of Deut.23:2, that Judah placed upon his. Thus neither Solomon nor his younger brother Nathan could occupy the throne legally. The Nathanic line was God's choice as is clear from the genealogy of Luke 3:23-31, as compared with Jer.22:28-30. Thus Mary, the mother of Jesus was the only person in Israel who had a legal right to David's throne - a right which she could not exercise because she was a woman. But there was no reason why she could not pass it down to her firstborn son, subject only to the provision that when she married, she gave her hand to a man within her own tribe. Mary met this condition as the Matthew genealogy (Mt.1:1-16) attests. Joseph, the carpenter to whom she was engaged, was a descendant of David through the Solomonic line, as she was through the Nathanic line. *Cf.* our discussion of this problem in *The Renaissance New Testament*, I, 4.

Thus Stephen makes his point. When Caiaphas and his colleagues in the San Hedrin demanded the death of Jesus, they killed the only man in Israel who had the right to sit on David's throne. He died without issue, and if it were not for the fact that God had raised Him from the dead, Israel's hopes for the position of world leadership which God had promised to Abraham, would have been forever dashed. That King David himself understood this is clear from his statements in the Psalms which the Holy Spirit inspired him to sing, *e.g.* Psalm 2, 8, 16, 22, 23, 24, 40, 41, 45, 68, 69, 72, 89, 102, 110, 118.

With the quotation of Isaiah's prophecy in verses 49 and 50, Stephen concluded his witness with his excoriation of the San Hedrin, who, blinded to the true message of the prophets, who had pointed forward to the Just One, their Messiah, had killed the prophets and crucified Him Who alone could fulfill for them the promises which God made to Abraham and David.

Verse 49 - "Heaven is my throne, and earth is my footstool: what house will ye build me? saith the Lord: or what is the place of my rest?"

'Ο οὐρανός μοι θρόνος, ἡ δὲ γῆ ὑποπόδιον τῶν ποδῶν μου. ποῖον οἶκον οἰκοδομήσετέ μοι, λέγει κύριος, ἢ τίς τόπος τῆς καταπαύσεώς μου;

'Ο (nom.sing.masc.of the article in agreement with οὐρανός) 9.

οὐρανός (nom.sing.masc.of οὐρανός, subject of ἐστιν, understood) 254.

μοι (dat.sing.masc.of ἐγώ, possession) 123.

θρόνος (nom.sing.masc.of θρόνος, predicate nominative) 519.

ἡ (nom.sing.fem.of the article in agreement with γῆ) 9.

δὲ (continuative conjunction) 11.

γῆ (nom.sing.fem.of γῆ, subject of ἐστιν, understood) 157.

ὑποπόδιον (nom.sing.neut.of ὑποπόδιον, predicate nominative) 520.

τῶν (gen.pl.masc.of the article in agreement with ποδῶν) 9.

ποδῶν (gen.pl.masc.of πούς, description) 353.

μου (gen.sing.masc.of ἐγώ, possession) 123.

ποῖον (acc.sing.masc.of ποῖος, in agreement with οἶκον) 1298.

οἶκον (acc.sing.masc.of οἶκος, direct object of οἰκοδομήσετε) 784.

οἰκοδομήσετε (2d.per.pl.fut.act.ind.of οἰκοδομέω, deliberative) 694.

μοι (dat.sing.masc.ofd ἐγώ, dative of person) 123.

λέγει (3d.per.sing.pres.act.ind.of λέγω, aoristic) 66.

κύριος (nom.sing.masc.of κύριος, subject of λέγει) 97.

ἢ (disjunctive particle) 465.

τίς (nom.sing.masc.of τίς, in agreement with τόπος, direct question) 281.

τόπος (nom.sing.masc.of τόπος, subject of ἐστιν, understood) 1019.

τῆς (gen.sing.fem.of the article in agreement with καταπαύσεώς) 9.

#3146 καταπαύσεώς (gen.sing.fem.of κατάπαυσις, predicate description).

rest - Acts 7:49; Heb.3:11,18; 4:1,3,3,5,10,11.

Meaning: A combination of κατά (#98) and παύω (#2044). *Cf.* also καταπαύω (#3329). Rest. A place where God may dwell for rest, in a metaphorical sense - Acts 7:49. With reference to Israel's rest from wilderness wandering in Canaan - Heb.3:11,18; 4:1*, 3a*, 3b, 5*, 10*, 11*.

* The rest of salvation which results from trusting in a finished work.

μου (gen.sing.masc.of ἐγώ, possession) 123.

Translation - "The heaven is my throne, and the earth is the footstool of my feet. What kind of a house will you build for me, says the Lord, or what sort of place as my rest?"

Comment: ποῖον οἶκον is qualatative. What kind of a house? What quality? How can you build a house good enough for me? What sort of place of good enough for my rest? The quotation is from Isa.66:1,2. The questions are rhetorical. They emphasize the fact that no man can build a house good enough for God. The Jews in Stephen's audience were as proud of the temple in Jerusalem, which Herod was building for them, as Solomon had been of his. Stephen's false accusers had accused him of plotting to detroy it (Acts 6:14). They said that Stephen said that Jesus would destroy the temple. He had predicted that the Romans would destroy it (Mt.24:2). Isaiah made it clear that Solomon could not glorify God by building a temple, regardless of its earthly splendor. The true Jewish conception of God, which Moses and the prophets had preached was far above their interpretation of it, perhaps as a result of their association with the pagan deities of their neighbours. God cannot be made dependent upon material things since He created matter. This is the thought in

Verse 50 - "Hath not my hand made all these things?"

οὐχὶ ἡ χείρ μου ἐποίησεν ταῦτα πάντα;

οὐχὶ (summary negative conjunction with the indicative in rhetorical question, which expects an affirmative reply) 130.
    ἡ (nom.sing.fem.of the article in agreement with χείρ) 9.
    χείρ (nom.sing.fem.of χείρ, subject of ἐποίησεν) 308.
    μου (gen.sing.masc.of ἐγώ, possession) 123.
    ἐποίησεν (3d.per.sing.aor.act.ind.of ποιέω, culminative) 127.
    ταῦτα (acc.pl.neut.of οὗτος, direct object of ἐποίησεν) 93.
    πάντα (acc.pl.neut.of πᾶς, in agreement with ταῦτα) 67.

Translation - "My hand has made all these things, has it not?"

Comment: The question is rhetorical. Of course God's hand made everything.

All of the raw materials which Solomon used, the human labor, the transport and the architechtural and artistic genius which it displayed were the products of His creative genius and power. This applies of course to all of the idolatrous trappings with which man has sought to impress the deity. Man cannot by his own devices glorify God.

Stephen's speech is finished except for his denunciation of his audience and his excoriation of their forefathers. A quick review of his remarks reveals the underlying truth that runs throughout. He began by describing the God of Israel who made an unconditional covenant with an old man. He directed Abraham to leave his native land and travel to an unannounced destination, where he would personally never own a square foot of it, but which God promised to give as an everlasting possession to Abraham's unborn descendants. This unconditional covenant was given to Abraham when he was 85 years old, with a wife who was 75, and still childless (Acts 7:1-5). God also foretold the Egyptian bondage for Abraham's children. It was to continue for 400 years, after which God would redeem His promise to the patriarch and bring them out of bondage (vss.6-7). He also gave to Abraham a covenant of circumcision, which Abraham observed upon his miracle child, Isaac, who in turn fathered Jacob. The next generation consisted of the twelve patriarchs (vs.8) of the twelve tribes that became the demographic divisions of the nation. Israel's sons repudiated Joseph their younger brother and plotted to kill him. God overruled and Joseph became the one who rescued them from starvation. Thus their moral judgments were opposed to God (vss.9-16). At the end of the 400 years, God redeemed His promise to Abraham and raised up Moses as a leader and deliverer, but again Israel rejected God's man (vss.17-39). Kept alive by God's miraculous manna in the desert, they rejected it and, in their hearts, longed to return to the flesh pots of Egyptian bondage (vs.40). While God was giving to Moses His living law, they were engaged in transgressing it at the foot of the mountain (vss.40-41). And though they had God's Tabernacle of Testimony and the Levitical offerings which He prescribed for them, all of which pointed forward to the perfect sacrifice of their ultimate Redeemer, they built their own temples to Moloch and Remphan and fashioned heathen idols as substitutes for God's worship (vss.42-43). Finally God gave them a king whom He could bless, who, when he planned to build a permanent temple, was forbidden to build it, but promised that His seed, Jesus Christ;, would some day establish a literal earthly throne and build a spiritual temple (the Body of Christ, Acts 15:13-17) that would remain forever. Despite this they rejected God's promise to David and brought to the throne David's illegitimate son who built the temple, and at its dedication was committed to a *conditional* covenant, with the terms of which Israel failed to comply and as a result saw the temple destroyed and were themselves carried into Babylonian captivity. Their latest and greatest crime was the muder upon a cross of King David's Greater Son, the Lord Jesus Christ, the only man who had a legal right to sit upon David's throne. At every step in Israel's history she had been unfaithful to a totally faithful God, Who would not permit His chosen people, for all of their disobedience to frustrate His eternal purpose. Though they crucified their Messiah, God raised Him from the dead. Stephen was abundantly justified in his thunderous denunciation in verse 51.

Verse 51 - *"Ye stiffnecked and uncircumcised in hearts and ears, ye do always resist the Holy Ghost: as your fathers did, so do ye."*

Σκληροτράχηλοι καὶ ἀπερίτμητοι καρδίαις καὶ τοῖς ὠσίν, ὑμεῖς ἀεὶ τῷ πνεύματι τῷ ἁγίῳ ἀντιπίπτετε, ὡς οἱ πατέρες ὑμῶν καὶ ὑμεῖς.

#3147 Σκληροτράχηλοι (voc.pl.masc.of σκληροτράχηλος, address).

stiff-necked - Acts 7:51.

Meaning: A combination of σκληρός (#1537) and τράχηλος (#1252). Stiff-necked, stubborn, obstinate, unrelenting, unrepentant - with reference to Israel - Acts 7:51.

καὶ (adjunctive conjunction, joining adjectives) 14.

#3148 ἀπερίτμητοι (voc.pl.masc.of ἀπερίτμητος, address).

uncircumcised - Acts 7:51.

Meaning: α privative and περιτομή (#2368). Uncircumcised. Metaphorically - not subject to God's covenant and moral law - followed by a locative of sphere - Acts 7:51.

καρδίαις (loc.pl.fem.of καρδία, sphere) 432.
καὶ (adjunctive conjunction joining nouns) 14.
τοῖς (loc.pl.neut.of the article in agreement with ὠσίν) 9.
ὠσίν (loc.pl.neut.of οὖς, sphere) 887.
ὑμεῖς (nom.pl.masc.of σύ, emphatic, subject of ἀντιπίπτετε) 104.

#3149 ἀεὶ (adverb of time).

alway - 2 Cor.4:11; 6:10; Heb.3:10.
always - Acts 7:51; 1 Pet.3:15; 2 Pet.1:12; Tit.1:12.

Meaning: cf.αἰών (#1002). Perpetually, invariably, always, at any and every time. Israel always resisted God - Acts 7:51; Heb.3:10; the believer is subject to martyrdom at any time - 2 Cor.4:11; always rejoicing, despite earthly sorrow - 2 Cor.6:10; always ready to speak for Christ - 1 Pet.3:15. Peter always reminded the saints of their spiritual obligations - 2 Pet.1:12. Cf.πάντοτε (#1567).

τῷ (dat.sing.neut.of the article in agreement with πνεύματι) 9.
πνεύματι (dat.sing.neut.of πνεῦμα, dative of disadvantage, after ἀντί in composition) 83.
τῷ (dat.sing.neut.of the article in agreement with ἁγίῳ) 9.
ἁγίῳ (dat.sing.neut.of ἅγιος, in agreement with πνεύματι) 84.

#3150 ἀντιπίπτετε (2d.per.pl.pres.act.ind.of ἀντιπίπτω, customary).

resist - Acts 7:51.

Meaning: A combination of ἀντί (#237) and πίπτω (#187). To fall against; to resist. Israel always resisted the Holy Spirit - Acts 7:51.

ὡς (particle introducing a comparative clause) 128.

οἱ (nom.pl.masc.of the article in agreement with πατέρες) 9.

πατέρες (nom.pl.masc.of πατήρ, subject of ἐποίησαν, understood) 238.

ὑμῶν (gen.pl.masc.of σύ, relationship) 104.

καὶ (adjunctive conjunction joining verbs ((supplied)) in a comparative clause) 14.

ὑμεῖς (nom.pl.masc.of σύ, subject of ποίετε, understood) 104.

Translation - "You stiff-necked Gentiles, with pagan hearts and ears! You are always resisting the Holy Spirit, just as your forefathers did."

Comment: Here is an example of the locative of sphere with adjectives. τῷ πνεύματι τῷ ἁγίῳ is a dative of personal disadvantage after ἀντί in composition. The translation indicates that Stephen was calling Caiaphas and his colleagues pagans - ἀπερίτμητοι, being a Jew's way of saying it. "You are no better than the Gentiles." They were indeed circumcised in the flesh, but emotionally (καρδίαις) and intellectually (τοῖς ὠσίν) they were not. In verse 39 he had said that "in their hearts" - ἐν ταῖς καρδίαις, they had wanted to return to Egypt. Genetically speaking, they were God's chosen people, for they were the seed of Abraham, but in fact, they were not. They and their forefathers had a long record of resistance to the Holy Spirit Who had always helped them. Not everyone with ears can hear (Mt.13:43). *Cf.* Rom.2:28,29.

Verse 52 - "Which of the prophets have not your fathers persecuted? And they have slain them which shewed before of the coming of the Just One: of whom ye have been now the betrayers and murderers."

τίνα τῶν προφητῶν οὐκ ἐδίωξαν οἱ πατέρες ὑμῶν; καὶ ἀπέκτειναν τοὺς προκαταγγείλαντας περὶ τῆς ἐλεύσεως τοῦ δικαίου οὗ νῦν ὑμεῖς προδόται καὶ φονεῖς ἐγένεσθε,

τίνα (acc.sing.masc.of τίς, interrogative pronoun, direct object of ἐδίωξαν, in direct question) 281.

τῶν (gen.pl.masc.of the article in agreement with προφητῶν) 9.

προφητῶν (gen.pl.masc.of προφήτης, partitive genitive) 119.

οὐκ (summary negative conjunction with the indicative) 130.

ἐδίωξαν (3d.per.pl.aor.act.ind.of διώκω, culminative) 434.

οἱ (nom.pl.masc.of the article in agreement with πατέρες) 9.

πατέρες (nom.pl.masc.of πατήρ, subject of ἐδίωξαν) 238.

ὑμῶν (gen.pl.masc.of σύ, relationship) 104.

καὶ (emphatic conjunction) 14.

ἀπέκτειναν (3d.per.pl.aor.act.ind.of ἀποκτείνω, culminative) 889.
τοὺς (acc.pl.masc.of the article in agreement with προκαταγγείλαντας) 9.
προκαταγγείλαντας (aor.act.part.acc.pl.masc.of προκαταγγέλλω, substantival, direct object of ἀπέκτειναν) 3016.
περὶ (preposition with the genitive of reference) 173.
τῆς (gen.sing.fem.of the article in agreement with ἐλεύσεως) 9.

#3151 ἐλεύσεως (gen.sing.fem.of ἔλευσις, reference).

coming - Acts 7:52.

Meaning: Cf. ἔρχομαι (#146). Coming, advent. The prophets foretold both the first and second advents of Christ - Acts 7:52.

τοῦ (gen.sing.masc.of the article in agreement with δικαίου) 9.
δικαίου (gen.sing.masc.of δίκαιος, description) 85.
οὗ (gen.sing.masc.of ὅς, case attraction to the antecedent, description) 65.
νῦν (temporal adverb) 1497.
προδόται (nom.pl.masc.of προδότης, predicate nominative) 2123.
καὶ (adjunctive conjunction joining nouns) 14.
φονεῖς (nom.pl.masc.of φονεύς, predicate nominative) 1405.
ἐγένεσθε (2d.per.pl.aor.ind.of γίνομαι, culminative) 113.

Translation - "Which one of the prophets have your forefathers not persecuted? They even killed those who foretold of the coming of the Just One, of Whom you have now become the betrayers and killers."

Comment: The rhetorical question is a challenge. "Name one prophet whom your forefathers did not persecute?" Then with ascensive καὶ he added, "They *even* killed . . . κ.τ.λ." The only "crime" that the prophets committed was that of foretelling the coming of the Messiah, Whom God had promised to Abraham and David, Who would liberate them forever from the bondage of the Gentiles. Every time the prophets mentioned the Messiah they aroused opposition from the Jewish Establishment of their day. Finally the Messiah Himself came and the descendants of those who killed the prophets who predicted Messiah's coming, betrayed and murdered Him when He came. Thus the story of Israel's infidelity is complete from the day that the patriarchs sold Joseph, their future benefactor into **Egyptian bondage to the day that their descendants murdered** the Son of God, in Whom the Abrahamic covenant was to be fulfilled.

In closing, Stephen now adds that this sad story of apostasy is not the behavior of ignorant heathen, but rather that of the recipients of God's law which was delivered by the angels.

Verse 53 - "Who have received the law by the disposition of angels and have not kept it."

οἵτινες ἐλάβετε τὸν νόμον εἰς διαταγὰς ἀγγέλων, καὶ οὐκ ἐφυλάξατε.

οἵτινες (nom.pl.masc.of ὅστις, subject of ἐλάβετε and ἐφυλάξετε) 163.

ἐλάβετε (2d.per.pl.aor.act.ind.of λαμβάνω, constative) 533.

τὸν (acc.sing.masc.of the article in agreement with νόμον) 9.

νόμον (acc.sing.masc.of νόμος, direct object of ἐλάβετε) 464.

εἰς (preposition with the predicate accusative, like ἐν and the instrumental) 140.

#3152 διαταγὰς (acc.pl.fem.of διαταγή, predicate accusative).

disposition - Acts 7:53.
ordinance - Rom.13:2.

Meaning: Cf.διατάσσω (#904), which is from διά (#118) and τάσσω (#722). Hence, administration, superitendence. The angels supervised the giving of the law to Moses at Sinai - Acts 7:53. The police power of the state, whether established upon democratic, monarchical or other grounds is God's present means of maintaining order in society (Rom.13:1). Hence it is called the *ordinance* or *supervision* of God (Rom.13:2).

ἀγγέλλων (gen.pl.masc.of ἄγγελος, description) 96.

καὶ (adversative conjunction) 14.

οὐκ (summary negative conjunction with the indicative) 130.

ἐφυλάξατε (2d.per.pl.aor.mid.ind.of φυλάσσω, culminative) 1301.

Translation - *"Because you received the law, under the supervision of angels, but you did not keep it."*

Comment: Here we have a causal use of ὅστις. *Cf.* John 8:53; Acts 10:47; Rom.2:15; 6:2; Heb.8:6; 10:35; Eph.3:13; Phil.4:3; Col.3:5; Jam.4:14; 1 Pet.2:11. Why did they kill the Messiah? Because, although they had received the law under auspicious and even ostentatious circumstances, they had not kept it. One would normally think that a moral code handed down with the heavenly fanfare that occurred at Sinai, would have commanded respect and obedience, if not because of its ethical merit, at least because of the manner in which it was given. But Israel did not keep it. As a matter of fact, even before they had it given to them, written by the finger of God upon tablets of stone, and after they had been warned not to approach too close to the holy ground of the mountain, they had thrown a party and transgressed every precept of it. The Just One, Whom the law prefigured and Who said that He came not to destroy but to fulfill the law (Mt.5:17) kept the law so perfectly that they killed Him. Stephen's indictment is complete. Only one element is needed to complete the story - the resurrection and glorification of Messiah. He added these in verses 55,56.

We have εἰς introducing a predicate accusative in an idiom similar to ἐν with the instrumental. Robertson, (*Grammar*, 482) admits that there is ". . . some Hebrew influence here because of its frequency." *Cf.* Mt.21:46; Acts 7:21; 13:22,47.

Caiaphas and his crowd of worthies (!) had heard enough. When one cannot answer an argument, he can always kill the one who gave it.

The Stoning of Stephen
(Acts 7:54-60)

Verse 54 - "When they heard these things, they were cut to the heart, and they gnashed on him with their teeth."

Ἀκούοντες δὲ ταῦτα διεπρίοντο ταῖς καρδίαις αὐτῶν καὶ ἔβρυχον τοὺς ὀδόντας ἐπ' αὐτόν.

Ἀκούοντες (pres.act.part.nom.pl.masc.of ἀκούω, adverbial, temporal/causal) 148.

δὲ (continuative conjunction) 11.

ταῦτα (acc.pl.neut.of οὗτος, direct object of ἀκούοντες) 93.

διεπρίοντο (3d.per.pl.imp.pass.ind.of διαπρίομαι, progressive description) 3068.

ταῖς (loc.pl.fem.of the article in agreement with καρδίαις) 9.

καρδίαις (loc.pl.fem.of καρδία, sphere) 432.

αὐτῶν (gen.pl.masc.of αὐτός, possession) 16.

καὶ (adjunctive conjunction joining verbs) 14.

#3153 ἔβρυχον (3d.per.pl.imp.act.ind.of βρύχω, inceptive).

gnash - Acts 7:54.

Meaning: To bite; to gnash the teeth. Followed by τοὺς ὀδόντας in Acts 7:54.

τοὺς (acc.pl.masc.of the article in agreement with ὀδόντας) 9.

ὀδόντας (acc.pl.masc.of ὀδούς, direct object of ἔβρυχον) 526.

ἐπ' (preposition with the accusative of extent) 47.

αὐτόν (acc.sing.masc.of αὐτός, extent) 16.

Translation - "And when they heard these things they were cut to pieces with rage and they began to gnash their teeth at him."

Comment: The participle is in the present tense. As they listened what they heard caused their emotional reaction described by διεπρίοντο ταῖς καρδίαις - "emotionally cut to pieces" or "cut in two." As Stephen finished they *began* (inceptive imperfect in ἔβρυχον) to grind their teeth at him. Their reaction is interesting from a psychological point of view. *Cf.*#3068 for its basic meaning. These people were on the verge of insane rage. The message of Stephen contained history which they could not deny. Every word he said was true, and they knew it. Their intellects demanded that they agree. Their wills demanded that they disagree. When the will strongly rejects what the mind is forced to accept a sort of emotional schizophrenia takes place. Stephen, with the help of the Holy Spirit, Who also witnessed (Acts 5:32), almost drove the audience insane. Teeth grinding as an evidence of great emotional disturbance, is a symptom of insanity. Thus Jesus Christ, the Eternal Truth, demands acceptance and worship or the rational mind loses its moorings. They were ready to tear him limb from limb. He who cannot be answered must be silenced. They needed only one more stimulus before their rage turned to murder. This Stephen provided in the next two verses.

Verse 55 - "But he, being full of the Holy Ghost, looked up steadfastly into heaven, and saw the glory of God, and Jesus standing on the right hand of God."

ὑπάρχων δὲ πλήρης πνεύματος ἁγίου ἀτενίσας εἰς τὸν οὐρανὸν εἶδεν δόξαν θεοῦ καὶ Ἰησοῦν ἑστῶτα ἐκ δεξιῶν τοῦ θεοῦ,

ὑπάρχων (pres.act.part.nom.sing.masc.of ὑπάρχω, adverbial, causal) 1303.

δὲ (continuative conjunction) 11.

πλήρης (nom.sing.masc.of πλήρης, predicate adjective) 1124.

πνεύματος (gen.sing.neut.of πνεῦμα, descriptive with the adjective) 83.

ἁγίου (gen.sing.neut.of ἅγιος, in agreement with πνεύματος) 84.

ἀτενίσας (aor.act.part.nom.sing.masc.of ἀτενίζω, adverbial, temporal) 2028.

εἰς (preposition with the accusative of extent, with a verb of motion) 140.

τὸν (acc.sing.masc.of the article in agreement with οὐρανὸν) 9.

οὐρανὸν (acc.sing.masc.of οὐρανός, extent) 254.

εἶδεν (3d.per.sing.aor.act.ind.of ὁράω, constative) 144.

δόξαν (acc.sing.fem.of δόξα, direct object of εἶδεν) 361.

θεοῦ (gen.sing.masc.of θεός, description) 124.

καὶ (adjunctive conjunction joining nouns) 14.

Ἰησοῦν (acc.sing.masc.of Ἰησοῦς, direct object of εἶδεν) 3.

ἑστῶτα (perf.act.part.acc.sing.masc.of ἵστημι, adjectival, ascriptive, predicate) 180.

ἐκ (preposition with the ablative of separation) 19.

δεξιῶν (abl.pl.masc.of δεξιός, place) 19.

τοῦ (gen.sing.masc.of the article in agreement with θεοῦ) 9.

θεοῦ (gen.sing.masc.of θεός, description) 124.

Translation - "And because he was full of the Holy Spirit when he gazed intently into heaven he saw divine glory and Jesus standing at the right hand of God."

Comment: ὑπάρχων, the causal participle in the present tense is completed by πλήρης πνεύματος ἁγίου. It was because Stephen was full of the Holy Spirit that he saw in heaven what others, who might have looked did not see. The present tense in the participle makes it simultaneous with the time of ἀτενίσας. Stephen had been full of the Holy Spirit from the beginning of his speech (Acts 6:15). His experience was the fulfillment of the promise of Mark 13:11. It is doubtful that Stephen could have delivered such a masterful address without the Holy Spirit's direction. He saw "divine glory" - θεοῦ without the article is descriptive. Note the genitive in πνεύματος when joined to an adjective. Stephen saw the same glory that Moses saw at the bush. He also saw Jesus, not seated (Ps.110:1; Heb.1:3) but in a standing posture, as if to give a standing ovation to His servant for his faithful witness. Note that ἑστῶτα is an intensive perfect. Perhaps Jesus had stood up when Stephen began his sermon with its masterful survey of the theological interpretation of the history of Israel. All that God did for Israel from the days of Abraham was in contemplation of the coming of their Messiah, in Whom the only hope for their future rested. Stephen said the last word on the subject. God's case against the Jewish Establishment was complete. There would be no further remedy but the judgment which came in A.D. 70, at the hands of Titus and his troops. Yet God's grace would rescue individual Jews, as He had Stephen, the Apostles and the rest of the deacons and other Christians, and add them to the Body of Christ. In fact one of His greatest preachers was present and witnessed the stoning of Stephen.

And, since God's promise to Abraham, Isaac, Jacob, Judah and David was unconditional, no amount of infidelity on Israel's part can abrogate it, and it will yet be fulfilled at the end of the church age, when Messiah returns again.

Stephen's remark of verse 56 triggered the violent reaction of the mob, described in the remainder of the chapter.

Verse 56 - "And said, Behold I see the heavens opened, and the Son of Man standing on the right hand of God."

καὶ εἶπεν, Ἰδοὺ θεωρῶ τοὺς οὐρανοὺς διηνοιγμένους καὶ τὸν υἱὸν τοῦ ἀνθρώπου ἐκ δεξιῶν ἑστῶτα τοῦ θεοῦ.

καὶ (continuative conjunction) 14.

εἶπεν (3d.per.sing.aor.act.ind.of εἶπον, constative) 155.

Ἰδοὺ (exclamation) 95.

θεωρῶ (1st.per.sing.pres.act.ind.of θεωρέω, aoristic) 1667.

τοὺς (acc.pl.masc.of the article in agreement with οὐρανοὺς) 9.

οὐρανοὺς (acc.pl.masc.of οὐρανός, direct object of θεωρῶ) 254.

διηνοιγμένους (perf.pass.part.acc.pl.masc.of διαωοίγω, adjectival, predicate, ascriptive) 1888.

καὶ (adjunctive conjunction joining nouns) 14.

τὸν (acc.sing.masc.of the article in agreement with υἱὸν) 9.

υἱὸν (acc.sing.masc.of υἱός, direct object of θεωρῶ) 5.

τοῦ (gen.sing.masc.of the article in agreement with ἀνθρώπου) 9.

ἀνθρώπου (gen.sing.masc.of ἄνθρωπος, description) 341.

ἐκ (preposition with the ablative of separation) 19.

δεξιῶν (abl.pl.masc.of δεξιός, separation, after ἐκ) 502.

ἑστῶτα (perf.act.part.nom.sing.masc.of ἵστημι, adverbial, circumstantial) 180.

τοῦ (gen.sing.masc.of the article in agreement with θεοῦ) 9.

θεοῦ (gen.sing.masc.of θεός, description) 124.

Translation - "And he said, 'Look! I see the heavens opened and the Son of Man standing at the right hand of God.'"

Comment: The two participles are perfect, with intensive force, indicating past action that persists to the moment of speaking. Heaven had opened and Jesus had stood before Stephen looked up to see. When he looked the heavens were already open for him to see Jesus, Who was already standing. Note comment on verse 55. In this statement Stephen added the one main element of the Christian message which he had not yet mentioned, *viz.* the resurrection and ascension of the Just One. The Apostles never failed to mention the fact that Jesus rose from the dead and went back to the glory. Nor did Stephen. Thus the Jewish Establishment was made to understand that their murder of the Son of God did not frustrate, but rather fulfilled the eternal purpose of God. These were Stephen's last words to his audience. Two more significant requests are directed to heaven.

Verse 57 - "Then they cried out with a loud voice, and stopped their ears, and ran upon him with one accord."

κράξαντες δὲ φωνῇ μεγάλῃ συνέσχον τὰ ὦτα αὐτῶν, καί ὥρμησαν ὁμοθυμαδὸν ἐπ᾽ αὐτόν,

κράξαντες (aor.act.part.nom.pl.masc.of κράζω, adverbial, temporal) 765.
δὲ (adversative conjunction) 11.
φωνῇ (instru.sing.fem.of φωνή, means) 222.
μεγάλῃ (instru.sing.fem.of μέγας, in agreement with φωνῇ) 184.
συνέσχον (3d.per.pl.2d.aor.act.ind.of συνέχω, constative) 414.
τὰ (acc.pl.neut.of the article in agreement with ὦτα) 9.
ὦτα (acc.pl.neut.of οὖς, direct object of συνέσχον) 887.
αὐτῶν (gen.pl.masc.of αὐτος, possession) 16.
καὶ (adjunctive conjunction joining verbs) 14.
ὥρμησαν (3d.per.pl.aor.act.ind.of ὁρμάω, constative) 772.
ὁμοθυμαδὸν (acc.sing.neut.of ὁμοθυμαδός, adverbial) 2942.
ἐπ᾽ (preposition with the accusative of extent) 47.
αὐτόν (acc.sing.masc.of αὐτός, extent) 16.

Translation - "But when they had cried out with a loud voice, they stopped their ears and all at once they rushed at him."

Comment: The frustrated heart and the gnashing, grinding teeth of verse 54 are now joined by the outraged cry, the stopped ears and the concerted rush at Stephen, all of which clearly indicates that he had driven these Jews temporarily insane. Notice that as long as he continued to speak they listened. Only when he stopped speaking, did they stop their ears! Men who are immoral may, upon provocation become irrational. *cf.* comment on Acts 3:15. Stupidity generally accompanies immorality. *cf.*#772 - the same word used for the insane pigs is used here for the insane men!

Verse 58 - "And cast him out of the city, and stoned him: and the witnesses laid down their clothes at a young man's feet, whose name was Saul."

καὶ ἐκβαλόντες ἔξω τῆς πόλεως ἐλιθοβόλουν. καὶ οἱ μάρτυρες ἀπέθεντο τὰ ἱμάτια αὐτῶν παρὰ τοὺς πόδας νεανίου καλουμένου Σαύλου.

καὶ (adjunctive conjunction joining verbs) 14.

ἐκβαλόντες (2d.aor.act.part.nom.pl.masc.of ἐκβάλλω, adverbial, temporal) 649.

ἔξω (an adverb of place) 449.

τῆς (abl.sing.fem.of the article in agreement with πόλεως) 9.

πόλεως (abl.sing.fem.of πόλις, separation) 243.

ἐλιθοβόλουν (3d.per.pl.imp.act.ind.of λιθοβολέω, inceptive) 1384.

καὶ (continuative conjunction) 14.

οἱ (nom.pl.masc.of the article in agreement with μάρτυρες) 9.

μάρτυρες (nom.pl.masc.of μάρτυς, subject of ἀπέθεντο) 1263.

ἀπέθεντο (3d.per.pl.2d.aor.mid.ind.of ἀποτίθεμαι, redundant) 1106.

τὰ (acc.pl.neut.of the article in agreement with ἱμάτια) 9.

ἱμάτια (acc.pl.neut.of ἱμάτιον, direct object of ἀπέθεντο) 534.

αὐτῶν (gen.pl.masc.of αὐτός, possession) 16.

παρὰ (preposition with the accusative of extent after a verb of rest) 154.

τοὺς (acc.pl.masc.of the article in agreement with πόδας) 9.

πόδας (acc.pl.masc.of πούς, extent, after a verb of rest) 353.

#3154 νεανίου (gen.sing.masc.of νεανίας, possession).

young man - Acts 7:58; 20:9; 23:17.

Meaning: young man. Cf.νεανίσκος (#1300). Thayer thinks that νεανίας means a man up to about 40 years old, the age also covered by ἀνήρ (#63). With reference to Saul - Acts 7:58; Eutychus - Acts 20:9; Paul's nephew - Acts 23:17.

καλουμένου (pres.pass.part.gen.sing.masc.of καλέω, adjectival, predicate, restrictive) 107.

#3155 Σαύλου (gen.sing.masc.of Σαῦλος, apposition).

Saul - Acts 7:58; 8:1,3; 9:1,4,4,8,11,17,22,24; 11:25,30; 12:25; 13:1,2,7,9,21; 22:7,7,13; 26:14,14.

Meaning: Saul, the Jewish name of the Apostle Paul. Present at the stoning of Stephen - Acts 7:58; 8:1. Persecutor of the early church - Acts 8:3; 9:1. Converted on the Damascus road - Acts 9:4,4,8,11,17,22,24; 11:25,30; 22:7,7,13; 26:14,14. Christian missionary - Acts 12:25; 13:1,2,7,9, after which Luke uses his Greek name Παῦλος. Saul, the first king of Israel - Acts 13:21.

Translation - "And when they had dragged him out of the city, they began to stone him. And the witnesses laid down their garments at the feet of a young man named Saul."

Comment: ἐκβάλλω (#649) means "to throw out." The distance from the temple, where the action began, to the edge of the city makes "dragged out" a necessary translation. Note the inceptive action in the imperfect ἐλιθοβόλουν. "they began to stone him." The same form in verse 59 is progressive description. Here we have an excellent example of the manner in which the context dictates the translation and exegesis of the idiom. The middle voice form ἀπέθεντο is redundant. Note the possessive genitive of the personal pronoun αὐτῶν instead of the reflexive. The witnesses whose false testimony was recorded in Acts 6:13,14 laid aside their outer garments to assist in the stoning. The Apostle Paul, who was to be used of God to build up the Christian faith, was present to see the death of the first Christian martyr.

Verse 59 - "And they stoned Stephen, calling upon God, and saying, Lord Jesus, receive my spirit."

καὶ ἐλιθοβόλουν τὸν Στέφανον ἐπικαλούμενον καὶ λέγοντα, Κύριε Ἰησοῦ, δέξαι τὸ πνεῦμά μου.

καὶ (adjunctive conjunction joining verbs) 14.
ἐλιθοβόλουν (3d.per.pl.imp.act.ind.of λιθοβολέω, progressive description) 1384.
τὸν (acc.sing.masc.of the article in agreement with Στέφανον) 9.
Στέφανον (acc.sing.masc.of Στέφανος, direct object of ἐλιθοβόλουν) 3081.
ἐπικαλούμενον (pres.mid.part.acc.sing.masc.of ἐπικαλέω, adjectival, predicate, ascriptive) 884.
καὶ (adjunctive conjunction joining participles) 14.
λέγοντα (pres.act.part.acc.sing.masc.of λέγω, adjectival, predicate, ascriptive) 66.
Κύριε (voc.sing.masc.of κύριος, address) 97.
Ἰησοῦ (voc.sing.masc.of Ἰησοῦς, apposition) 3.
δέξαι (2d.per.sing.1st.aor.mid.impv.of δέχομαι, entreaty) 867.
τὸ (acc.sing.neut.of the article in agreement with πνεῦμα) 9.
πνεῦμά (acc.sing.neut.of πνεῦμα, direct object of δέξαι) 83.
μου (gen.sing.masc.of ἐγώ, possession) 123.

Translation - "And they continued to stone Stephen as he called upon God, saying, 'Lord Jesus, receive my spirit.' "

Comment: All of the action is linear. The mob began to stone Stephen (verse 58). They continued to stone him (verse 59) as he prayed. The two adjectival participles are present tense, denoting simultaneous action. Note the difference between the death of Stephen and that of Jesus (Mt.27:50; Lk.23:46). Stephen did not send his spirit into God's care as Jesus did. Stephen could not die as Jesus did. Stephen was overtaken by death - a death which he was powerless to delay or prevent. But, although he was helpless as his body succumbed to the torture of the falling stones, he had the perfect assurance that his spirit was in good hands.

Verse 60 - "And he kneeled down, and cried with a loud voice, Lord, lay not this sin to their charge. And when he had said this, he fell asleep."

θεὶς δὲ τὰ γόνατα ἔκραξεν φωνῇ μεγάλῃ, Κύριε, μὴ στήσῃς αὐτοῖς ταύτην τὴν ἁμαρτίαν. καὶ τοῦτο εἰπὼν ἐκοιμήθη.

θείς (aor.act.part.nom.sing.masc.of τίθημι, adverbial, temporal) 455.

δέ (continuative conjunction) 11.

τὰ (acc.pl.neut.of the article in agreement with γόνατα) 9.

γόνατα (acc.pl.neut.of γόνυ, direct object of θείς) 2052.

ἔκραξεν (3d.per.sing.aor.act.ind.of κράζω, constative) 765.

φωνῇ (instrumental sing. fem.of φωνή, means, with ἔκραξεν) 222.

μεγάλῃ (instrumental sing.fem.of μέγας, in agreement with φωνῇ) 184.

Κύριε (voc.sing.masc.of κύριος, address) 97.

μή (qualified negative conjunction with the subjunctive in a negative entreaty) 87.

στήσῃς (2d.per.sing.aor.act.subj.ingressive, negative entreaty) 180.

αὐτοῖς (dat.pl.masc.of αὐτός, with στήσῃς, personal disadvantage) 16.

ταύτην (acc.sing.fem.of οὗτος, in agreement with ἁμαρτίαν) 93.

τὴν (acc.sing.fem.of the article in agreement with ἁμαρτίαν) 9.

ἁμαρτίαν (acc.sing.fem.of ἁμαρτία, direct object of στήσῃς) 111.

καὶ (continuative conjunction) 14.

τοῦτο (acc.sing.neut.of οὗτος, direct object of εἰπών) 93.

εἰπών (aor.act.part.nom.sing.masc.of εἶπον, adverbial, temporal) 155.

ἐκοιμήθη (3d.per.sing.aor.pass.ind.of κοιμάω, ingressive) 1664.

Translation - "And he knelt and cried out with a loud voice, 'Lord, do not charge this sin against them.' And when he had said this he fell asleep."

Comment: The idiom θείς τὰ γόνατα, which literally translates, "having placed the knees" means "to kneel." *Cf.*#2052 for similar instances of this idiom. The aorist subjunctive in the second person, with μή can be used in prohibitions or (in this case) in negative entreaty. Note that στήσῃς is ingressive. "do not enter this sin on the books against them." Thus Stephen prayed for his murderers as Jesus did for His (Luke 23:34). ἐκοιμήθη is also ingressive. Stephen "fell asleep" which is a beautiful way to say that he was dead. He was the first of the early Christians whose martyr death is recorded. We have in his sermon a most devastating review of Jewish history which serves as a stern indictment, but, since the Abrahamic and David covenants are unconditional the infidelity of the Jews, either individually or collectively does not abrogate them. Individuals will pay individually for their rejection of their Messiah, but the nation will live to see the fulfillment of all of God's promises to Abraham and David.

Saul Persecutes the Church
(Acts 8:1-3)

Acts 8:1 - "And Saul was consenting unto his death. And at that time there was a great persecution against the church which was at Jerusalem: and they were all scattered abroad throughout the regions of Judea and Samaria, except the apostles."

Σαῦλος δὲ ἦν συνευδοκῶν τῇ ἀναιρέσει αὐτοῦ.Ἐγένετο δὲ ἐν ἐκείνῃ τῇ ἡμέρᾳ διωγμὸς μέγας ἐπὶ τὴν ἐκκλησίαν τὴν ἐν Ἰεροσολύμοις. πάντες δὲ διεσπάρησαν κατὰ τὰς χώρας τῆς Ἰουδαίας καὶ Σαμαρείας πλὴν τῶν ἀποστόλων.

Σαῦλος (nom.sing.masc.of Σαῦλος, subject of ἦν) 3155.

δὲ (continuative conjunction) 11.

ἦν (3d.per.sing.imp.ind.of εἰμί, imperfect periphrastic) 86.

συνευδοκῶν (pres.act.part.nom.sing.masc.of συνευδοκέω, imperfect periphrastic) 2468.

τῇ (dat.sing.fem.of the article in agreement with ἀναιρέσει) 9.

#3156 ἀναιρέσει (dat.sing.fem.of ἀναίρεσις, reference with an intransitive verb).

death - Acts 8:1.

Meaning: Cf. ἀναιρέω (#216). Death by murder. Stephen - Acts 8:1.

αὐτοῦ (gen.sing.masc.of αὐτός, description) 16.

ἐγένετο (3d.per.sing.aor.ind.of γίνομαι, ingressive) 113.

δὲ (continuative conjunction) 11.

ἐν (preposition with the locative of time point) 80.

ἐκείνῃ (loc.sing.fem.of ἐκεῖνος, in agreement with ἡμέρᾳ) 246.

τῇ (loc.sing.fem.of the article in agreement with ἡμέρᾳ) 9.

ἡμέρᾳ (loc.sing.fem.of ἡμέρα, time point) 135.

διωγμὸς (nom.sing.masc.of διωγμός, subject of ἐγένετο) 1047.

μέγας (nom.sing.masc.of μέγας, in agreement with διωγμὸς) 184.

ἐπὶ (preposition with the accusative, hostility) 47.

τὴν (acc.sing.fem.of the article in agreement with ἐκκλησίαν) 9.

ἐκκλησίαν (acc.sing.fem.of ἐκκλησία, hostility) 1204.

τὴν (acc.sing.fem.of the article in agreement with ἐκκλησίαν) 9.

ἐν (preposition with the locative of place) 80.

Ἰεροσολύμοις (loc.sing.masc.of Ἰεροσολύμων, place) 141.

πάντες (nom.pl.masc.of πᾶς, subject of διεσπάρησαν) 67.

δὲ (continuative conjunction) 11.

#3157 διεσπάρησαν (3d.per.pl.aor.act.ind.of διασπείρω, ingressive).

scatter abroad - Acts 8:1,4; 11:19.

Meaning: A combination of διά (#118) and σπείρω (#616). To be scattered thoroughly. With reference to the early Christians who fled for their lives from Jerusalem - Acts 8:1,4; 11:19.

κατὰ (preposition with the accusative, spatial distribution) 98.

τὰς (acc.pl.fem.of the article in agreement with χώρας) 9.

χώρας (acc.pl.fem.of χώρα, spatial distribution) 201.

τῆς (gen.sing.fem.of the article in agreement with Ἰουδαίας) 9.

Ἰουδαίας (gen.sing.fem.of Ἰουδαία, description) 134.

καὶ (adjuntive conjunction joining nouns) 14.
Σαμαρείας (gen.sing.fem.of Σαμάρεια, description) 1998.
πλὴν (adversative conjunction) 944.
τῶν (abl.pl.masc.of the article in agreement with ἀποστόλων) 9.
ἀποστόλων (abl.pl.masc.of ἀπόστολος, exception) 844.

Translation - "And Saul agreed that he should be killed. And a great persecution against the church in Jerusalem began that day, and all except the Apostles began to be dispersed throughout the regions of Judea and Samaria."

Comment: ἦν συνευδοκῶν, the imperfect periphrastic is durative. Saul had no doubts about the justice and the wisdom of the action of the mob as he stood and watched them stone Stephen to death. This intensive construction serves to point up the depth of Saul's prejudice against Christianity at this time, and thus, by contrast, the dramatic character of his conversion in chapter 9. The pursuit (with a view to punishment/death) perhaps continued for several days. The locative in ἐν ἐκείνη τῇ ἡμέρᾳ, indicates a time point within the longer period. This day was the first day of the persecution, as the ingressive in ἐγένετο indicates. It is not necessary to push πάντες to mean that every layman left town, and that only the Apostles stayed. The word is πᾶς (#67), not ἅπας (#639). Most of those who fled for their lives went only to the surrounding countryside in Judea and Samaria, though some travelled as far as Phenice, Cyprus and Antioch (Acts 11:19).

Verse 2 - "And devout men carried Stephen to his burial, and made great lamentation over him."

συνεκόμισαν δὲ τὸν Στέφανον ἄνδρες εὐλαβεῖς καὶ ἐποίησαν κοπετὸν μέγαν ἐπ' αὐτῷ.

#3158 συνεκόμισαν (3d.per.pl.aor.act.ind.of συγκομίζω, constative).

carry to one's burial - Acts 8:2.

Meaning: A combination of σύν (#1542) and κομίζω (#1541). To bring or carry together/into one place. Used in Sophocles, *Aj.,*1048 and Plutarch, *Sull.,*38, in the sense of "to bury." But "Souter (*Lex. s.v.*) suggests that in Ac 8:2 the verb may mean not "take up" for burial (see Field *Notes,* p.116 f.) but "get back," "recover"; " (Moulton & Milligan, *The Vocabulary of the Greek Testament,* 609). There need be no conflict between the two ideas.

δὲ (continuative conjunction) 11.
τὸν (acc.sing.masc.of the article in agreement with Στέφανον) 9.
Στέφανον (acc.sing.masc.of Στέφανος, direct object of συνεκόμισαν) 3081.
ἄνδρες (nom.pl.masc.of ἀνήρ, subject of συνεκόμισαν and ἐποίησαν) 63.
εὐλαβεῖς (nom.pl.masc.of εὐλαβής, in agreement with ἄνδρες) 1894.
καὶ (adjunctive conjunction joining verbs) 14.
ἐποίησαν (3d.per.pl.aor.act.ind.of ποιέω, constative) 127.

#3159 κοπετὸν (acc.sing.masc.of κοπετός, direct object of ἐποίησαν).

lamentation - Acts 8:2.

Meaning: Cf.κοπιάω (#629), κόπτω (#929). Grief, lamentation, an outcry of grief. Cf. also κόπος (#1565). For Stephen at his death - Acts 8:2.

μέγαν (acc.sing.masc.of μέγας, in agreement with κοπετὸν) 184.
ἐπ' (preposition with the dative of person) 47.
αὐτῷ (dat.sing.masc.of αὐτός, person) 16.

Translation - "And men of good conscience recovered the body and buried Stephen and expressed their great sorrow over him."

Comment: ἐπ' αὐτῷ here seems a clear case of the pure dative. Cf. 2 Cor.9:14; 1 Thess.3:7; Rom.16:19. The personal concept is present. The thought seems close to being causal. Cf.#1894. These men were Christians who took their Christian duties very seriously. The fact that they gave Stephen a decent burial in the presence of the spirit of persecution against the Christians which pervaded the city adds to the glory of their act. If Souter is correct (cf.#3158, *Meaning)*, it would appear that the mob may have sought to prevent the burial, perhaps in order to desecrate the body. These Christian men hazarded their lives in order to remain in the city long enough to bury Stephen, while others were fleeing the city. Note also that there was no attempt at secrecy. They made a great outcry of grief over him.

The death of Stephen seems to have been the factor that ignited the fury of Saul against the Christians, and he took a leading part in their persecution, as we see in
Verse 3 - "As for Saul, he made havock of the church, entering into every house, and haling men and women, committed them to prison."

Σαῦλος δὲ ἐλυμαίνετο τὴν ἐκκλησίαν κατὰ τοὺς οἴκους εἰσπορευόμενος, σύρων τε ἄνδρας καὶ γυναῖκας παρεδίδου εἰς φυλακήν.

Σαῦλος (nom.sing.masc.of Σαῦλος, subject of ἐλυμαίνετο and παρεδίδου) 3155.
δὲ (adversative conjunction) 11.

#3160 ἐλαυμαίνετο (3d.per.sing.imp.mid.ind.of λυμαίνομαι, indirect middle, inceptive imperfect).

make havoc of - Acts 8:3.

Meaning: Cf. λύμη - "injury." Hence, to injure, inflict injury upon, ruin devastate, dishonor, treat shamefully, persecute. The manner in which Saul persecuted the church is described, in part, in Acts 8:3.

τὴν (acc.sing.fem.of the article in agreement with ἐκκλησίαν) 9.
ἐκκλησίαν (acc.sing.fem.of ἐκκλησία, direct object of ἐλυμαίνεταο) 1204.
κατὰ (preposition with the accusative, spatial distribution) 98.
τοὺς (acc.pl.masc.of the article in agreemt with οἴκους) 9.
οἴκους (acc.pl.masc.of οἶκος, spatial distribution) 784.

εἰσπορευόμενος (pres.mid.part.nom.sing.masc.of εἰσπορεύομαι, adverbial, modal) 1161.

σύρων (pres.act.part.nom.sing.masc.of σύρω, adverbial, modal) 2922.

τε (correlative conjunction, with καί) 1408.

ἄνδρας (acc.pl.masc.of ἀνήρ, direct object of σύρων) 63.

καί (adjunctive conjunction joining nouns) 14.

γυναῖκας (acc.pl.fem.of γυνή, direct object of σύρων) 103.

παρεδίδου (3d.per.sing.imp.act.ind.of παραδίδωμι, iterative) 368.

εἰς (preposition with the accusative of extent, with παρεδίδου) 140.

φυλακήν (acc.sing.fem.of φυλακή, extent with a verb of motion) 494.

Translation - "And Saul was devastating the church by entering house after house and dragging out both men and women and committing them to prison."

Comment: *Cf.* #3160 - "harass," "make havoc of," "devastate" - these words carry the idea of Saul's violence against the church. Note ἐκκλησία, here in the generic sense. Luke uses the word here in a corporate sense to denote all of the Christians, who, in a spiritual sense, were called out from the world, even though, when arrested, they were not physically called out of their homes to meet together in a single assembly. Saul did not enter every house, but only those where the Christians were living. Thus κατά in a distributive sense. A study of #2922 reveals that Paul himself later received the same treatment from his persecutors (Acts 14:19). Note the iterative imperfect in παρεδίδου. Saul's zeal was unrelenting, albeit misplaced. We think of this often when we see the Jehovah's Witnesses, Mormons, "Moonies," and representatives of other Christless cults patiently (some doggedly) walking the streets with their literature, ringing doorbells or standing in the airport lobbies. It is unfortunate that Christians are not as zealous to spread the Gospel of Christ.

Verse 4 - "Therefore they that were scattered abroad went everywhere preaching the word."

Οἱ μὲν οὖν διασπαρέντες διῆλθον εὐαγγελιζόμενοι τὸν λόγον.

Οἱ (nom.pl.masc.of the article in agreement with διασπαρέντες) 9.

μὲν (particle of affirmation) 300.

οὖν (inferential conjunction) 68.

διασπαρέντες (2d.aor.pass.part.nom.pl.masc.of διασπείρω, substantival, subject of διῆλθον) 3157.

διῆλθον (3d.per.pl.aor.mid.ind.of διέρχομαι, constative) 1017.

εὐαγγελιζόμενοι (pres.mid.part.nom.pl.masc.of εὐαγγελίζομαι, adverbial, complementary) 909.

τὸν (acc.sing.masc.of the article in agreement with λόγον) 9.

λόγον (acc.sing.masc.of λόγος, direct object of εὐαγγελιζόμενοι) 510.

Translation - "Therefore in fact those who were dispersed went everywhere proclaiming the message."

Comment: οἱ μὲν οὖν is demonstrative, joined with the participle διασπαρέντες, as the subject of διῆλθον. Thus God made the wrath of Saul to praise Him. Any fire fighter knows that the way to put out a fire is to contain, not scatter it. In his zeal to stamp out "heresy" Saul forgot about this principle. Before the dispersion the Christians concentrated their witness upon Jerusalem. Afterward it was scattered fire, and every ember ignited new fires which raged on and on to the glory of God. As we shall see shortly, Philip, one of the deacons, driven from Jerusalem by Saul, went north into Samaria and started a great revival.

Cf. Acts 11:19 to learn that though they preached the word in every place, they still restricted its message to a Jewish audience. This was to be expected, since Peter had not yet had his experience of Acts 10, and Paul, the apostle to the Gentiles, had not yet been called.

The persecution and dispersion caused by the witness and death of one deacon, Stephen, served to bring another deacon, Philip, into the spotlight.

The Gospel Preached in Samaria

(Acts 8:4-25)

Verse 5 - "Then Philip went down to the city of Samaria, and preached Christ unto them."

Φίλιππος δὲ κατελθὼν εἰς (τὴν) πόλιν τῆς Σαμαρείας ἐκήρυσσεν αὐτοῖς τὸν Χριστόν.

Φίλιππος (nom.sing.masc.of Φίλιππος, subect of ἐκήρυσσεν) 3082.
δὲ (continuative conjunction) 11.
κατελθὼν (aor.mid.part.nom.sing.masc.of κατέρχομαι, adverbial, temporal) 2037.
εἰς (preposition with the accusative of extent, after a verb of motion) 140.
(τὴν) (acc.sing.fem.of the article in agreement with πόλιν) 9.
πόλιν (acc.sing.fem.of πόλις, extent after a verb of motion) 243.
τῆς (gen.sing.fem.of the article in agreement with Σαμαρείας) 9.
Σαμαρείας (gen.sing.fem.of Σαμάρεια, designation) 1998.
ἐκήρυσσεν (3d.per.sing.imp.act.ind.of κηρύσσω, inceptive) 249.
αὐτοῖς (dat.pl.masc.of αὐτός, indirect object of ἐκήρυσσεν) 16.
τὸν (acc.sing.masc.of the article in agreement with Χριστόν) 9.
Χριστόν (acc.sing.masc.of Χριστός, direct object of ἐκήρυσσεν) 4.

Translation - "And Philip went down to a city of Samaria and began to preach Christ to them."

Comment: κατελθὼν (#2037), because the road from Jerusalem up in the mountains descends to the Samaritan plane "up north." Note the inchoative imperfect in ἐκήρυσσεν. As soon as Philip arrived he began to preach the gospel of Christ. Note the absence of an antecedent for αὐτοῖς - obviously a reference to the residents of the city. Philip acted in obedience to our Lord's orders of Acts 1:8. He took two steps away from Jerusalem - From Judea to Samaria is a geographical step, and one-half step in the genetic sense, since the Samaritans were hybrid Jews (John 4:9,20-22). To be sure, Jesus had ordered the church to include Samaria in their preaching schedules, after Jerusalem and Judea, but the offer of the gospel of Christ even to the Samaritans, much less to the Gentiles was to create problems in the mind of many Jewish Christians, as we shall see in Paul's controveries with the Judaizers, in the conduct of which he wrote the Epistle to the Galatians. Philip did not read about Jesus' conversation with the woman at the well near Sychar, since John had not yet written it (John 4). Did John or perhaps one of the other disciples who were with Jesus that day tell Philip about it, or did he preach the good news solely on the basis of the authority of Acts 1:8? Or was he so full of the Holy Spirit that he could not refrain from telling the good news? Whatever the reason, a great revival swept the city.

Verse 6 - "And the people with one accord gave heed unto those things which Philip spoke, hearing and seeing the miracles which he did."

προσεῖχον δὲ οἱ ὄχλοι τοῖς λεγομένοις ὑπὸ τοῦ Φιλίππου ὁμοθυμαδὸν ἐν τῷ ἀκούειν αὐτοὺς καὶ βλέπειν τὰ σημεῖα ἃ ἐποίει.

προσεῖχον (3d.per.pl.imp.act.ind.of προσέχω, progressive description) 555.
δὲ (continuative conjunction) 11.
οἱ (nom.pl.masc.of the article in agreement with ὄχλοι) 9.
ὄχλοι (nom.pl.masc.of ὄχλος, subject of προσεῖχον) 418.
τοῖς (dat.pl.masc.of the article in agreement with λεγομένοις) 9.
λεγομένοις (pres.pass.part.dat.pl.masc.of λέγω, substantival, dative of reference, after πρός in composition) 66.
ὑπὸ (preposition with the ablative of agent) 117.
τοῦ (abl.sing.masc.of the article in agreement with Φιλίππου) 9.
Φιλίππου (abl.sing.masc.of φίλιππος, agent) 3082.
ὁμοθυμαδὸν (accusative adverb with the verb προσεῖχον) 2942.
ἐν (preposition with the locative of time point, with the infinitive in a temporal clause) 80.
τῷ (loc.sing.neut.of the article, time point in a temporal clause) 9.
ἀκούειν (pres.act.inf.of ἀκούω, noun use, loc.sing.neut., time point in a temporal clause) 148.
αὐτοὺς (acc.pl.masc.of αὐτός, direct object of ἀκούειν) 16.
καὶ (adjunctive conjunction joining infinitives) 14.
βλέπειν (pres.act.inf.of βλέπω, articular infinitive, loc.sing.neut., in a temporal clause, after ἐν) 499.
τὰ (acc.pl.neut.of the article in agreement with σημεῖα) 9.
σημεῖα (acc.pl.neut.of σημεῖον, direct object of βλέπειν) 1005.
ἃ (acc.pl.neut.of ὅς, direct object of ἐποίει) 65.
ἐποίει (3d.per.sing.imp.act.ind.of ποιέω, iterative) 127.

Translation - "And the crowds gave their undivided attention to the things being said by Philip, when they heard them and saw the miracles which he performed from time to time."

Comment: The linear action in the imperfect προσεῖχον, with its progressive description is strengthened by the accusative adverb ὁμοθυμαδὸν. It really makes the adverb redundant. The crowds of people were always giving their undivided attention. The dative of reference in the participial substantive τοῖς λεγομένοις results from πρός in composition in the verb. We have a double articular infinitive (note that τῷ occurs only once, thus indicating that ἀκούειν .. . καὶ βλέπειν are to be taken as a unit), in the temporal clause with ἐν and the locative of time point. As Philip said the things which he said and performed the miracles which from time to time (iterative imperfect in ἐποίει) he performed, - at those time points (ἐν τῷ) the Samaritans gave him their undivided attention. I have taken αὐτοὺς as the object of ἀκούειν, just as τὰ σημεῖα is the object of βλέπειν. As such it has its antecedent in τοῖς λεγομένοις. They heard the things which were being said by Philip and saw the miracles being done by Philip. It is also possible to take αὐτοὺς as an accusative of general reference, joined to the infinitive, in which case the translation would be essentiallythe same. "They gave their undivided attention to what was being said by Philip when they heard and saw . . . κ.τ.λ."

The Samaritans near Sychar once before had been eager to hear the words of eternal life from Jesus (John 4:39-42). Now they listen eagerly to Philip.

Here we have a deacon to whom the Holy Spirit has given the gifts of prophecy (forthtelling in preaching), healing and discerning of spirits (1 Cor.12:10). These gifts which Philip exercised served to give authenticity to the message which he preached. He preached in Samaria before the canon of New Testament scripture had been written and compiled. The sign gifts of this period in the first century of the Christian era substituted for the New Testament and provided the authority which Christians now derive, not from the performing of miracles, but from consistent exposition of the perfect revelation of the New Testament. When the perfect revelation came (1 Cor.13:10) the sign gifts were no longer needed and were phased out. *Cf.* our discussion of this important matter in 1 Corinthians 13:8-13. Charismatics who point to scriptures which show that first century Christians had the sign gifts and conclude that the same gifts are available now, since the New Testament literature is complete, are overlooking the fact that sign gifts were needed by Philip in Samaria, since he could not point to inspired scripture to support what he had to say. Modern charismatics have their Bibles which comprise "all the writings that are God-breathed" and they are profitable "for doctrine, for reproof, for correction, for instruction in righteousness, so that the man of God may be perfect, thoroughly furnished unto all good works." (2 Timothy 3:16,17). Thus Paul told Timothy that all he needed was his New Testament, and that with it he was "thoroughly equipped unto *all good works.*" If modern charismatics would pay more attention to their New Testaments and less to their psychic seizures they would be more useful to the Lord. It is totally invidious to compare ourselves in the twentieth century with Philip in Samaria in the first century. He did not own a New Testament. We do, although some of the charismatics would rather be "slain by the Spirit" than study their Bibles.

Verse 7 - "For unclean spirits, crying with loud voice, came out of many that were possessed with them, and many taken with palsies, and that were lame, were healed."

πολλοὶ γὰρ τῶν ἐχόντων πνεύματα ἀκάθαρτα βοῶντα φωνῇ μεγάλῃ ἐξήρχοντο, πολλοὶ δὲ παραλελυμένοι καὶ χωλοὶ ἐθεραπεύθησαν.

πολλοὶ (nom.pl.masc.of πολύς, in agreement with παραλελυμένοι) 228.
γὰρ (causal conjunction) 105.
τῶν (gen.pl.masc.of the article in agreement with ἐχόντων) 9.
ἐχόντων (pres.act.part.gen.pl.masc.of ἔχω, substantival, partitive genitive) 82.
πνεύματα (acc.pl.neut.of πνεῦμα, direct object of ἐχόντων) 83.
ἀκάθαρτα (acc.pl.neut.of ἀκάθαρτος, in agreement with πνεύματα) 843.
βοῶντα (pres.act.part.acc.pl.neut.of βοάω, adverbial, complementary) 256.
φωνῇ (instru.sing.fem.of φωνή, manner) 222.
μεγάλῃ (instru.sing.fem.of μέγας, in agreement with φωνῇ) 184.
ἐξήρχοντο (3d.per.pl.imp.ind.of ἐξέρχομαι, iterative) 161.
πολλοὶ (nom.pl.masc.of πολύς, subject of ἐθεραπεύθησαν) 228.
δὲ (continuative conjunction) 11.
παραλελυμένοι (perf.pass.part.nom.pl.masc.of παραλύω, substantival, subject of ἐθεραπεύθησαν) 2079.
καὶ (adjunctive conjunction joining substantives) 14.
χωλοὶ (nom.pl.masc.of χωλός, subject of ἐθεραπεύθησαν) 908.
ἐθεραπεύθησαν (3d.per.pl.aor.pass.ind.of θεραπεύω, direct middle, constative) 406.

Translation - "Because many of those having unclean spirits were coming out, crying with a loud voice, and many who had been paralyzed and lame were healed."

Comment: The first πολλοὶ is the subject of ἐξήρχοντο. The second is an adjective joined to παραλελυμένοι καὶ χωλοὶ. Not all those who were possessed with evil spirits were healed, but many of them were. The demons cried out with a loud voice as they were exorcised. Paralytics who had been in that condition for some time (intensive perfect tense in the participle) and were therefore lame (χωλοὶ) were also healed. The Holy Spirit was using Philip as He had used Stephen, though in a different way. The result of the revival was joy. Revivals of genuine religion always are accompanied by joy.

Verse 8 - "And there was great joy in that city."

ἐγένετο δὲ πολλὴ χαρὰ ἐν τῇ πόλει ἐκείνῃ.

ἐγένετο (3d.per.sing.aor.ind.of γίνομαι, constative) 113.

δὲ (continuative conjunction) 11.

πολλή (nom.sing.fem.of πολύς, in agreement with χαρὰ) 228.

χαρὰ (nom.sing.fem.of χαρά, subject of ἐγένετο) 183.

ἐν (preposition with the locative of place) 80.

τῇ (loc.sing.fem.of the article in agreement with πόλει) 9.

πόλει (loc.sing.fem.of πόλις, place where) 243.

ἐκείνῃ (loc.sing.fem.of ἐκεῖνος, in agreement with πόλει) 246.

Translation - *"And there was great joy in that city."*

Comment: Obviously. *Cf.* Gal.5:22. The Samaritans had reacted to Jesus in the same way (John 4:40).

But when revival fires burn brightly, the insects come crawling out of the woodwork. Enter, Simon Magus in

Verse 9 - *"But there was a certain man, called Simon, which beforetime in the same city, used sorcery, and bewitched the people of Samaria, giving out that himself was some great one."*

Ἀνὴρ δέ τις ὀνόματι Σίμων προϋπῆρχεν ἐν τῇ πόλει μαγεύων καὶ ἐξιστάνων τὸ ἔθνος τῆς Σαμαρείας, λέγων εἶναί τινα ἑαυτὸν μέγαν,

Ἀνὴρ (nom.sing.masc.of ἀνήρ, subject of προϋπῆρχεν) 63.

δέ (explanatory conjunction) 11.

τις (nom.sing.masc.of τις, indefinite pronoun, in agreement with Ἀνηρ) 486.

ὀνόματι (dat.sing.neut.of ὄνομα, person) 108.

#3161 Σίμων (nom.sing.masc.of Σίμων, appellation).

Simon - Acts 8:9,13,18,24.

Meaning: Simon Magus, the Samaritan sorcerer - Acts 8:9,13,18,24.

προϋπῆρχεν (3d.per.sing.imp.act.ind.of προϋπάρχω, progressive duration) 2833.

ἐν (preposition with the locative of place) 80.

τῇ (loc.sing.fem.of the article in agreement with πόλει) 9.

πόλει (loc.sing.fem.of πόλις, place) 243.

#3162 μαγεύων (pres.act.part.nom.sing.masc.of μαγεύω, adverbial, circumstantial).

use sorcery - Acts 8:9.

*Meaning: Cf.*μάγος (#137). To be a magician; to practise magical arts - with reference to Simon Magus - Acts 8:9.

καὶ (adjunctive conjunction joining verbs) 14.

ἐξιστάνων (pres.act.part.nom.sing.masc.of ἐξιστάνω, adverbial, circumstantial) 992.

τό (acc.sing.neut.of the article in agreement with ἔθνος) 9.
ἔθνος (acc.sing.neut.of ἔθνος, direct object of ἐξιστάνων) 376.
τῆς (gen.sing.fem.of the article in agreement with Σαμαρείας) 9.
Σαμαρείας (gen.sing.fem.of Σαμαρεία, description) 1998.
λέγων (pres.act.part.nom.sing.masc.of λέγω, adverbial, modal) 66.
εἶναι (pres.inf.of εἰμί, in indirect declaration) 86.
τινα (acc.sing.masc.of τις, with the adjective for rhetorical effect) 486.
ἑαυτὸν (acc.sing.masc.of ἑαυτός, general reference) 288.
μέγαν (acc.sing.masc.of μέγας, predicate adjective) 184.

Translation - "Now a certain man named Simon had formerly been in the city, using sorcery and bewitching the people of Samaria by declaring that he was a very great man himself."

Comment: μαγεύων and ἐξιστάνων are circumstantial participles. λέγων is modal. The infinitive clause is indirect discourse. Indefinite τινα in the predicate is emphatic indicating an attempt for rhetorical effect. This insecure demagogue was destined to create problems for the Apostles as we shall see in verses 18-24.

Verse 10 - "To whom they all gave heed, from the least to the greatest, saying, This man is the great power of God."

ᾧ προσεῖχον πάντες ἀπὸ μικροῦ ἕως μεγάλου λέγοντες, Οὗτός ἐστιν ἡ δύναμις τοῦ θεοῦ ἡ καλουμένη Μεγάλη.

ᾧ (dat.sing.masc.of ὅς, indirect object) 65.
προσεῖχον (3d.per.pl.imp.act.ind.of προσέχω, progressive description) 555.
πάντες (nom.pl.masc.of πᾶς, subject of προσεῖχον) 67.
ἀπὸ (preposition with the ablative of comparison) 70.
μικροῦ (abl.sing.masc.of μικρός, comparison) 901.
ἕως (preposition with the ablative of comparison) 71.
μεγάλου (abl.sing.masc.of μέγας, comparison) 184.
λέγοντες (pres.act.part.nom.pl.masc.of λέγω, adverbial, temporal) 66.
Οὗτός (nom.sing.masc.of οὗτος, subject of ἐστιν) 93.
ἐστιν (3d.per.sing.pres.ind.of εἰμί, aoristic) 86.
ἡ (nom.sing.fem.of the article in agreement with δύναμις) 9.
δύναμις (nom.sing.fem.of δύναμις, predicate nominative) 687.
τοῦ (gen.sing.masc.of the article in agreement with θεοῦ) 9.
θεοῦ (gen.sing.masc.of θεός, description) 124.
ἡ (nom.sing.fem.of the article in agreement with καλουμένη) 9.
καλουμένη (pres.pass.part.nom.sing.fem.of καλέω, in apposition) 107.
Μεγάλη (nom.sing.fem.of μέγας, appellation) 184.

Translation - ". . . to whom everybody had been listening, from small to great, saying, 'This man is the one who is called the Great Power of God.' "

Comment: Thus Simon's reputation in the city had been established. Everyone paid attention to him and recognized in him the medium of the power of God.

"The awkward καλουμένη is omitted by the later Byzantine text; it is replaced by λεγομένη is several minuscules. Klostermann thought that Μεγάλη was a transliteration of the Samaritan (word or words) meaning "he who reveals, the revealer," in which case καλουμένη apologizes for the foreign term (compare 1:12; 3:2,11; 6:9)." (Metzger, *A Textual Commentary on the Greek New Testament*, 358).

Verse 11 - "And to him they had regard, because of long time he had bewitched them with sorceries."

προσεῖχον δὲ αὐτῷ διὰ τὸ ἱκανῷ χρόνῳ ταῖς μαγείαις ἐξεστακέναι αὐτούς.

προσεῖχον (3d.per.pl.imp.act.ind.of προσέχω, progressive description) 555.

δὲ (continuative conjunction) 11.

αὐτῷ (dat.sing.masc.of αὐτός, indirect object) 16.

διὰ (preposition with the articular infinitive in the accusative, cause) 118.

τὸ (acc.sing.neut.of the article in agreement with ἐξεστακέναι, cause) 9.

ἱκανῷ (instru.sing.masc.of ἱκανός, in agreement with χρόνῳ) 304.

χρόνῳ (instru.sing.masc.of χρόνος, associative-instrumental, in a time expression) 168.

ταῖς (instru.pl.fem.of the article in agreement with μαγείαις) 9.

#3163 μαγείαις (instru.pl.fem.of μαγεία, means).

sorcery - Acts 8:11.

Meaning: magic, magic arts, sorcery - Acts 8:11.

ἐξεστακέναι (perf.act.inf.of ἐξίστημι, accusative singular, after διὰ, cause) 992.

αὐτούς (acc.pl.masc.of αὐτός, general reference) 16.

Translation - "And they had been paying attention to him because for a long time he had been bewitching them with witchcraft."

Comment: The imperfect tense in προσεῖχον, as in verse 10, indicates the unbrokaen tide of popularity which Simon had enjoyed with the public. διὰ with the articular infinitive in the accusative tells us why. In a series of demonstrations he had titillated his audiences with his sleight of hand performances. Note the perfect tense in the infinitive. It indicates unbroken continuity. Not all of the time, but across a long period of time at intervals spaced with sufficient frequence to maintain his hold upon the people. "Man is by his constitution a religious animal." (Edmund Burke, *Reflections on the Revolution in France.)* The Samaritans were no different from modern Americans, as the frequent appearances of magicians and alleged psychics on television attest. Those who reject Christ must have something to worship. Now another miracle worker comes to the city to challenge Simon's monopoly.

Verse 12 - "But when they believed Philip preaching the things concerning the kingdom of God, and the name of Jesus Christ, they were baptized, both men and women."

ὅτε δὲ ἐπίστευσαν τῷ Φιλίππῳ εὐαγγελιζομένῳ περὶ τῆς βασιλείας τοῦ θεοῦ καὶ τοῦ ὀνόματος Ἰησοῦ Χριστοῦ, ἐβαπτίζοντο ἄνδρες τε καὶ γυναῖκες.

ὅτε (conjunction with the indicative in a definite temporal clause, contemporaneous time) 703.

δὲ (adversative conjunction) 11.

ἐπίστευσαν (3d.per.pl.aor.act.ind.of πιστεύω, definite temporal clause, constative) 734.

τῷ (dat.sing.masc.of the article in agreement with Φιλίππῳ) 9.

Φιλίππῳ (dat.sing.masc.of Φίλιππος, direct object of ἐπίστευσαν) 3082.

εὐαγγελιζομένῳ (pres.mid.part.dat.sing.masc.of εὐαγγελίζω, adjectival, predicate, ascriptive) 909.

περὶ (preposition with the genitive of reference) 173.

τῆς (gen.sing.fem.of the article in agreement with βασιλείας) 9.

βασιλείας (gen.sing.fem.of βασιλεία, reference) 253.

τοῦ (gen.sing.masc.of the article in agreement with θεοῦ) 9.

θεοῦ (gen.sing.masc.of θεός, description) 124.

καὶ (adjunctive conjunction joining nouns) 14.

τοῦ (gen.sing.neut.of the article in agreement with ὀνόματος) 9.

ὀνόματος (gen.sing.neut.of ὄνομα, reference) 108.

Ἰησοῦ (gen.sing.masc.of Ἰησοῦς, possession) 3.

Χριστοῦ (gen.sing.masc.of Χριστός, apposition) 4.

ἐβαπτίζοντο (3d.per.pl.imp.pass.ind.of βαπτίζω, inceptive) 273.

ἄνδρες (nom.pl.masc.of ἀνήρ, subject of ἐβαπτίζοντο) 63.

τε (correlative conjunction, with καὶ) 1408.

καὶ (adjunctive conjunction joining nouns) 14.

γυναῖκες (nom.pl.fem.of γυνή, subject of ἐβαπτίζοντο) 103.

Translation - *"But when they believed Philip who was preaching about the kingdom of God and the name of Jesus Christ, both men and women began to be immersed."*

Comment: δὲ is adversative. Formerly the people had given their attention to Simon and his magic. But (adversative δὲ) no more. Now they shift their allegiance to Philip, his message and his miracles. His message associated Jesus Christ, Who had visited them once before (John 4) and Who had at that time introduced Himself as their Messiah (John 4:25,26) with the coming kingdom of God. The result was an intellectual assent to the things which Philip taught and the signifying of their assent by their submission to immersion in water. The immersions began (inceptive imperfect) and continued as many men and women were immersed. As the story unfolds it becomes apparent that their faith was in Jesus as their Messiah, but not in Him as their Redeemer. They were not yet regenerate.

Verse 13 - "Then Simon himself believed also; and when he was baptized, he continued with Philip, and wondered, beholding the miracles and signs which were done."

ὁ δὲ Σίμων καὶ αὐτὸς ἐπίστευσεν, καὶ βαπτισθεὶς ἦν προσκαρτερῶν τῷ Φιλίππῳ, θεωρῶν τε σημεῖα καὶ δυνάμεις μεγάλας γινομένας ἐξίστατο.

ὁ (nom.sing.masc.of the article in agreement with Σίμων) 9.
δὲ (continuative conjunction) 11.
Σίμων (nom.sing.masc.of Σίμων, subject of ἐπίστευσεν) 3161.
καὶ (adjunctive conjunction joining nouns) 14.
αὐτὸς (nom.sing.masc.of αὐτός, intensive) 16.
ἐπίστευσεν (3d.per.sing.aor.act.ind.of πιστεύω, constative) 734.
καὶ (adjunctive conjunction joining verbs) 14.
βαπτισθεὶς (aor.pass.part.nom.sing.masc.of βαπτίζω, adverbial, temporal) 273.
ἦν (3d.per.sing.imp.ind.of εἰμί, imperfect periphrastic) 86.
προσκαρτερῶν (pres.act.part.nom.sing.masc.of προσκαρτερέω, imperfect periphrastic) 2113.
τῷ (instru.sing.masc.of the article in agreement with Φιλίππῳ) 9.
Φιλίππῳ (instru.sing.masc.of Φίλιππος, association) 3082.
θεωρῶν (pres.act.part.nom.sing.masc.of θεωρέω, adverbial, temporal, causal) 1667.
τε (correlative conjunction with καὶ) 1408.
σημεῖα (acc.pl.neut.of σημεῖον, direct object of θεωρῶν) 1005.
καὶ (adjunctive conjunction joining nouns) 14.
δυνάμεις (acc.pl.fem.of δύναμις, direct object of θεωρῶν) 687.
μεγάλας (acc.pl.fem.of μέγας, in agreement with δυνάμεις) 184.
γινομένας (pres.pass.part.acc.pl.fem.of γίνομαι, adjectival, in agreement with σημεῖα and δυνάμεις, predicate, restrictive) 113.
ἐξίστατο (3d.per.sing.aor.pass.ind.of ἐξίστημι, constative) 992.

Translation - "And Simon himself also believed and after he was immersed he remained by Philip's side and when he saw the great signs and demonstrations of power which were being performed he was amazed."

Comment: Simon, the sorcerer, who had manipulated his own Samaritan audiences for so long a time, and had been enriched with the obvious financial advantages available to one with his popularity, now saw the advantage of appearing to be in league with Philip. The text is not clear as to whether or not Simon ever became truly regenerate. The language of verses 20 - 23 weighs against it. On the surface it would seem to indicate that Simon's motives were self-serving. Demagogues determine the direction in which the crowd is going and then get out and front and beckon them to follow. That his "miracles" were not in the same category as those which Philip, by the power of the Holy Spirit, performed is indicated by his own reaction to the signs and wonders which Philip performed. His constant attendance upon Philip, after his immersion, is indicated by the imperfect periphrastic, which is decidedly durative. Simon stuck to Philip like a leech. He did not let the deacon out of his sight. He may have been studying Philip's technique with a view to copying him. Unable to discover how Philip performed his miracles, Simon was finally reduced to the attempt to buy the power. For him it would have been a good investment. His interest in the magic arts explains his great interest in Philip's ministry. There is no evidence that he had a felt need for the salvation which the Samaritans manifested. Note that the same word used to describe the reaction of the Samaritans to Simon's magic (verse 11) is used to describe his reaction to Philip's ministry (verse 13). Simon had the tables turned on him. The mystifier is mystified. The treatment that he had dealt out to the Samaritans Philip is now dealing out to him.

We leave Simon for a moment to return to him in verse 18. Meanwhile the story turns to Jerusalem and to Peter and John, in

Verse 14 - "Now when the apostles which were at Jerusalem heard that Samaria had received the word of God, they sent unto them Peter and John."

Ἀκούσαντες δὲ οἱ ἐν Ἱεροσολύμοις ἀπόστολοι ὅτι δέδεκται ἡ Σαμάρεια τὸν λόγον τοῦ θεοῦ ἀπέστειλαν πρὸς αὐτοὺς Πέτρον καὶ Ἰωάννην,

Ἀκούσαντες (aor.act.part.nom.pl.masc.of ἀκούω, adverbial, temporal) 148.
δὲ (explanatory conjunction) 11.
οἱ (nom.pl.masc.of the article in agreement with ἀπόστολοι) 9.
ἐν (preposition with the locative of place) 80.
Ἱεροσολύμοις (loc.pl.masc.of Ἱεροσολύμων, place) 141.
ἀπόστολοι (nom.pl.masc.of ἀπόστολος, subject of ἀπέστειλαν) 844.
ὅτι (conjunction introducing an object clause in indirect discourse) 211.
δέδεκται (3d.per.sing.perf.mid.ind.of δέχομαι, consummative) 867.
ἡ (nom.sing.fem.of the article in agreement with Σαμαρεία) 9.
Σαμαρεία (nom.sing.fem.of Σαμαρεία, subject of δέδεκται) 1998.
τὸν (acc.sing.masc.of the article in agreement with λόγον) 9.
λόγον (acc.sing.masc.of λόγος, direct object of δέδεκται) 510.
τοῦ (gen.sing.masc.of the article in agreement with θεοῦ) 9.
θεοῦ (gen.sing.masc.of θεός, designation) 124.
ἀπέστειλαν (3d.per.pl.aor.act.ind.of ἀποστέλλω, constative) 215.
πρὸς (preposition with the accusative of extent) 197.
αὐτοὺς (acc.pl.masc.of αὐτός, extent) 16.
Πέτρον (acc.sing.masc.of Πέτρος, direct object of ἀπέστειλαν) 387.
καὶ (adjunctive conjunction joining nouns) 14.
Ἰωάννην (acc.sing.masc.of Ἰωάννης, direct object of ἀπέστειλαν) 399.

Translation - "Now when the Apostles in Jerusalem heard that Samaria had received the Word of God, they sent to them Peter and John."

Comment: δὲ is explanatory as Luke introduces a new element into the story. In the opinion of the Apostles in Jerusalem the situation in Samaria needed supervision. Philip was only a Deacon, not an Apostle. The Samaritans were half Jewish, half Gentile. The local populace had a reputation for a superstitious interest in magic and wizardry, with particular prominence having been given to their local "medicine man" - a man named Simon, who was reported to have believed Philip's message and submitted to immersion in water. The Apostles were not necessarily in doubt about the purity of Philip's motives. He had received the approbation of the church when he was elected to the diaconate. But they were not certain that he was well enough acquainted with the gospel to present it clearly. And in this they were correct, for Philip, for all of his sincerity had preached only that Jesus was the Jewish Messiah. He had not told the story of His redemption upon the cross. His message was the same as that of John the Baptist at the beginning of his ministry, before, at the baptism of Jesus, John found that the Messiah was also "the Lamb of God that takes away the sins of the world" (John 1:29). So it is fortunate that Peter and John went down to Samaria to see what was going on.

This is the first time since Pentecost that the gospel of Christ had been offered to anyone except Jews. Note the indirect discourse in the object clause introduced by ὅτι, using the same tense as in the direct. The rumor, as heard in Jerusalem was, "Samaria has received the Word of God."

This supervision by the Apostles looks like episcopacy, which indeed it was, but only because the Apostles were specifically appointed by the Lord to serve in a supervisory capacity, and endowed with special gifts and powers until the New Testament message in its completed form could be committed to a written record. Episcopal forms of church government now are not justified in pointing to this supervisory visit by Peter and John to Samaria as precedent for their assumed powers. They are comparing apples and oranges. Philip in Samaria did not have a New Testament. We do.

Verse 15 - "Who, when they were come down, prayed for them, that they might receive the Holy Ghost."

οἵτινες καταβάντες προσηύξαντο περὶ αὐτῶν ὅπως λάβωσιν πνεῦμα ἅγιον,

οἵτινες (nom.pl.masc.of ὅστις, subject of προσηύξαντο) 163.
καταβάντες (aor.act.part.nom.pl.masc.of καταβαίνω, adverbial, temporal) 324.
προσηύξαντο (3d.per.pl.aor.mid.ind.of προσεύχομαι, constative) 544.
περὶ (preposition with the genitive of reference) 173.
αὐτῶν (gen.pl.masc.of αὐτός, reference) 16.
ὅπως (conjunction with the subjunctive in a purpose clause) 177.
λάβωσιν (3d.per.pl.aor.act.subj.of λαμβάνω, purpose) 533.
πνεῦμα (acc.sing.neut.of πνεῦμα, direct object of λάβωσιν) 83.
ἅγιον (acc.sing.neut.of ἅγιος, in agreement with πνεῦμα) 84.

Translation - "Who, when they arrived, prayed for them that they might receive the Holy Spirit."

Comment: We have here a weakened use of ὅστις - like ὅς. The distinction between the two (#'s 65, 163) wears thin in the κοινή. *Cf.*#163 for other definite uses of ὅστις. καταβάντες is adverbial and temporal. ὅπως introduces the subjunctive clause of purpose. Due to the long story about Simon, αὐτῶν in verse 15 must go back to verse 9 for its antecedent - the people of Samaria.

In verse 16 we have the explanation of the fact that though the Samaritans had accepted Philip's message and had been immersed, they had not yet received the Holy Spirit.

Verse 16 - ("For as yet he was fallen upon none of them: only they were baptized in the name of the Lord Jesus.")

οὐδέπω γὰρ ἦν ἐπ' οὐδενὶ αὐτῶν ἐπιπεπτωκός, μόνον δὲ βεβαπτισμένοι ὑπῆρχον εἰς τὸ ὄνομα τοῦ κυρίου Ἰησοῦ.

οὐδέπω (negative temporal adverb) 2885.
γὰρ (causal conjunction) 105.
ἦν (3d.per.sing.imp.ind.of εἰμί, pluperfect periphrastic) 86.
ἐπ' (preposition with the locative of place) 47.
οὐδενὶ (loc.sing.masc.of οὐδείς, place) 446.
αὐτῶν (gen.pl.masc.of αὐτός, partitive genitive) 16.
ἐπιπεπτωκός (perf.act.part.nom.sing.masc.of ἐπιπίπτω, pluperfect periphrastic) 1794.
μόνον (acc.sing.neut.of μόνος, adverbial, joined to the verb) 339.
δὲ (causal conjunction) 11.
βεβαπτισμένοι (perf.pass.part.nom.pl.masc.of βαπτίζω, pluperfect periphrastic) 273.
ὑπῆρχον (3d.per.pl.imp.ind.of ὑπάρχω, pluperfect periphrastic) 1303.
εἰς (preposition with the accusative, general reference) 140.
τὸ (acc.sing.neut.of the article in agreement with ὄνομα) 9.
ὄνομα (acc.sing.neut.of ὄνομα, general reference) 108.
τοῦ (gen.sing.masc.of the article in agreement with κυρίου) 9.
κυρίου (gen.sing.masc.of κύριος, possession) 97.
Ἰησοῦ (gen.sing.masc.of Ἰησοῦς, apposition) 3.

Translation - "Because He had not yet fallen upon any of them, because they had been immersed only in the name of the Lord Jesus."

Comment: The prayer of Peter and John of verse 15 is explained by the causal clause introduced by γὰρ, which, in turn is explained by the second causal clause introduced by δὲ. Note that in each clause we have the pluperfect periphrastic, which points backward in time to a point where something happened (or did not happen) as a result of which a present condition prevails. The Holy Spirit did not fall upon the believers in Samaria when they accepted Philip's message. Thus, they did not have Him when Peter and John arrived from Jerusalem. The reason? **Because, although they had believed and then been immersed in water, their faith and the baptism which symbolized it was only (adverbial μόνον)**

in contemplation of Jesus as their long expected Messiah. Philip's message to them had been correct, so far as it went, but it was truncated. Jesus indeed is the Lord Messiah. When Philip told them this, they may have remembered His visit to Sychar and His conversation with the woman at the well and the excitement which followed (John 4:4-42). But apparently Philip did not tell them, at least not with sufficient unction and clarity, of the significance of His redemption upon the cross. The situation here is similar to that which occurred in Ephesus when twelve men were converted, though not regenerated, under the ministry of Apollow, the Alexandrian, before he was set straight theologically by Aquila and Priscilla. *Cf.* our comments on Acts 18:24 - 19:7. *Cf.*#1794 and note that ἐπιπίπτω, when it is used with reference to the Holy Spirit and the believer, is used only in Acts 8:16; 10:44 and 11:15 - in all three verses with reference to the first presentation of the gospel to (a) the Samaritans (Acts 8:16), and to (b) the Gentiles (Cornelius and his household) (Acts 10:44; 11:15). In both cases, the Holy Spirit "fell upon" believers only when the Apostles were present to authenticate the genuineness of the experience. *Cf.* also Acts 19:5,6, where, in a similar situation, Paul was present to explain the gospel more fully and where the language is ἦλθε τὸ πνεῦμα τὸ ἅγιον ἐπ᾽ αὐτούς - "the Holy Spirit came upon them." If there was no deficiency in Philip's message to the Samaritans, at least there was in their acceptance of it. The entire personality must experience confrontation with the Holy Spirit on the terms of the Gospel of Christ, before regeneration can take place. The intellect must have a minimal understanding of Who Jesus Christ is and what He came to earth to do, on the basis of which understanding there is a change of the mind, which is indicated by repentance (μετανοέω, #251). The emotion must also be affected as a result of which there is genuine sorrow for sin, a state indicated by μεταμέλλομαι #1371 . With intellect and emotion in compliance with the Holy Spirit, there remains the will, which must also comply (John 7:17). Something was missing in the Samaritan experience, a lack that was supplied by the ministry of Peter and John when they arrived, just as Paul supplied the missing material in the case of the Ephesian twelve. It is possible that the Samaritans were reacting to Philip's ministry as they had been conditioned to react to the sorcery of Simon Magus, which may serve, in part, to explain why Peter rebuked Simon so strongly (vss.20-23), although he had done enough to merit Peter's rebuke in any case.

The deficiency, whatever it may have been, was corrected by Peter and John, as we see in

Verse 17 - "Then laid they their hands on them, and they received the Holy Ghost."

τότε ἐπετίθουν τὰς χεῖρας ἐπ᾽ αὐτούς, καὶ ἐλάμβανον πνεῦμα ἅγιον.

τότε (temporal adverb) 166.
ἐπετίθουν (3d.per.pl.imp.act.ind.of ἐπιτίθημι, inceptive) 818.
τὰς (acc.pl.fem.of the article in agreement with χεῖρας) 9.
χεῖρας (acc.pl.fem.of χείρ, direct object of ἐπετίθουν) 308.
ἐπ᾽ (preposition with the accusative of extent) 47.

αὐτούς (acc.pl.masc.of αὐτός, extent) 16.
καί (continuative conjunction) 14.
ἐλάμβανον (3d.per.pl.imp.act.ind.of λαμβάνω, inceptive) 533.
πνεῦμα (acc.sing.neut.of πνεῦμα, direct object of ἐλάμβανον) 83.
ἅγιον (acc.sing.neut.of ἅγιος, in agreement with πνεῦμα) 84.

Translation - "Then they began to place their hands on them and they began to receive the Holy Spirit."

Comment: We should not ignore the imperfect tenses in the verbs, both of which are inceptive. They present a thrilling picture. Peter and John did not perform this function collectively, but individually. They could not lay their hands upon each of the believing Samarians at the same time. They moved in and out among the believers, and placed their hands upon each, in turn, and as a result the recipient received the Holy Spirit. No mention is made of specific results, such as special gifts, but we may be certain that the fruits of the Holy Spirit (Gal.5:22,23) were much in evidence. There was no need for anyone present to be endowed with the special ability to speak in any foreign language, as there is no record that there was anyone present who did not understand Greek or Aramaic, both languages of which were current in the vicinity.

Philip's work of evangelism in Samaria was thus rendered official and authentic by Peter and John, both of whom had seen the Lord and were made original recipients of His commission and instructions. We may be certain that any theological vagaries in the minds of the Samaritans that would have rendered Philip's efforts nugatory, were dispelled by Peter and John. There was also no doubt that the gospel of Christ was to be proclaimed, both to Samaritans, who were hybrids between Jew and Gentile and to the Gentiles as well, as this was made clear in the commissions to preach (Mt.28:18-20; Acts 1:8). Philip's next soul winning experience was with a Gentile.

Verse 18 - "And when Simon saw that through laying on of the Apostles' hands, the Holy Ghost was given, he offered them money."

ἰδὼν δὲ ὁ Σίμων ὅτι διὰ τῆς ἐπιθέσεως τῶν χειρῶν τῶν ἀποστόλων δίδοται τὸ πνεῦμα, προσήνεγκεν αὐτοῖς χρήματα,

ἰδών (aor.act.part.nom.sing.masc.of ὁράω, adverbial, temporal) 144.
δέ (continuative conjunction) 11.
ὁ (nom.sing.masc.of the article in agreement with Σίμων) 9.
Σίμων (nom.sing.masc.of Σίμων, subject of προσήνεγκεν) 3161.
ὅτι (conjunction introducing an object clause in indirect discourse) 211.
διά (preposition with the genitive of descriptive agency) 118.
τῆς (gen.sing.fem.of the article in agreement with ἐπιθέσεως) 9.

#3164 ἐπιθέσεως (gen.sing.fem.of ἐπίθεσις, descriptive agency).

laying on - Acts 8:18; 1 Tim.4:14; Heb.6:2.
putting on - 2 Tim.1:6.

Meaning: A combination of ἐπί (#47) and τίθημι (#455). *Cf.* also ἐπιτίθημι (#818). An imposition; a laying on - followed by τῶν χειρῶν in Acts 8:18; 1 Tim.4:14; 2 Tim.1:6; Heb.6:2. *Cf.* Mt.19:13; Mk.16:18; Acts 6:6; 13:3, etc. A symbolic act by which spiritual blessing, bodily healing, or reception of the Holy Spirit was bestowed.

τῶν (gen.pl.fem.of the article in agreement with χειρῶν) 9.

χειρῶν (gen.pl.fem.of χείρ, description) 308.

τῶν (gen.pl.masc.of the article in agreement with ἀποστόλων) 9.

ἀποστόλων (gen.pl.masc.of ἀπόστολος, possession) 844.

δίδοται (3d.per.sing.pres.pass.ind.of δίδωμι, static) 362.

τὸ (nom.sing.neut.of the article in agreement with πνεῦμα) 9.

πνεῦμα (nom.sing.neut.of πνεῦμα, subject of δίδοται) 83.

προσήνεγκεν (3d.per.sing.aor.act.ind.of προσφέρω, constative) 190.

αὐτοῖς (dat.pl.masc.of αὐτός, indirect object of προσήνεγκεν) 16.

χρήματα (acc.pl.neut.of χρῆμα, direct object of προσήνεγκεν) 2637.

Translation - "And when Simon saw that by the laying on of the hands of the Apostles the Spirit was given, he offered them money,"

Comment: Simon, who had followed Philip around so persistently (verse 13), in an effort to learn his *modus operandi*, was now more interested in Peter and John, whom he regarded as having greater prestige than Philip. He observed the effect of their symbolic act. The ὅτι clause is the object of ἰδών, in indirect discourse, with δίδοται in the present tense, the same as in direct discourse. διά with the genitive of description of the act by which the object was attained. Simon saw that his control over the people, which had been so complete before Philip came, would diminish if he could not do for them what Philip, Peter and John were doing. Hence his offer in monetary terms. "How much will it cost me to find out how you did that?"

Verse 19 - "Saying, Give me also this power that on whomsoever I lay hands, he may receive the Holy Ghost."

λέγων, Δότε κἀμοὶ τὴν ἐξουσίαν ταύτην ἵνα ᾧ ἐὰν ἐπιθῶ τὰς χεῖρας λαμβάνῃ πνεῦμα ἅγιον.

λέγων (pres.act.part.nom.sing.masc.of λέγω, recitative) 66.

Δότε (2d.per.sing.aor.act.impv.of δίδωμι, entreaty) 362.

κἀμοὶ (dat.sing.masc.of κἀγώ, indirect object of Δότε) 178.

τὴν (acc.sing.fem.of the article in agreement with ἐξουσίαν) 9.

ἐξουσίαν (acc.sing.fem.of ἐξουσία, direct object of Δότε) 707.

ταύτην (acc.sing.fem.of οὗτος, in agreement with ἐξουσίαν) 93.

ἵνα (conjunction with the subjunctive in a sub-final clause) 114.

ᾧ (loc.sing.masc.of ὅς, place, with ἐπί in composition) 65.

ἐὰν (conditional particle in a third-class condition) 363.

ἐπιθῶ (1st.per.sing.aor.act.subj.of ἐπιτίθημι, third-class condition) 818.

τὰς (acc.pl.fem.of the article in agreement with χεῖρας) 9.

χεῖρας (acc.pl.fem.of χείρ, direct object of ἐπιθῶ) 308.
λαμβάνῃ (3d.per.sing.pres.act.subj.of λαμβάνω, sub-final) 533.
πνεῦμα (acc.sing.neut.of πνεῦμα, direct object of λαμβάνῃ) 83.
ἅγιον (acc.sing.neut.of ἅγιος, in agreement with πνεῦμα) 84.

Translation - ". . . saying, 'Give to me also this authority, in order (and with the result) that he upon whom I lay my hands may receive the Holy Spirit.' "

Comment: The ἵνα clause is sub-final - both purpose and result. Note the ellipsis. We must supply οὗτος before ᾧ, as its antecedent, which then serves as the subject of λαμβάνῃ. ἐάν and the subjunctive ἐπιθῶ indicates that Simon had no one in particular in mind, but that he, upon whomever he might lay hands, might receive the Holy Spirit. With this power Simon could maintain his position as spiritual leader of the city, after the Apostles and Philip had gone - a position which he enjoyed before they came. Simon assumed that he would encounter no opposition from the Christians who would remain in town after the Apostles and Philip had gone. That Peter understood the situation is clear from his response in verses 20 - 23.

Verse 20 - "*But Peter said unto him, Thy money perish with thee, because thou hast thought that the gift of God may be purchased with money.*"

Πέτρος δὲ εἶπεν πρὸς αὐτόν, Τὸ ἀργύριόν σου σὺν σοὶ εἴη εἰς ἀπώλειαν, ὅτι τὴν δωρεὰν τοῦ θεοῦ ἐνόμισας διὰ χρημάτων κτᾶσθαι.

Πέτρος (nom.sing.masc.of Πέτρος, subject of εἶπεν) 387.
δὲ (adversative conjunction) 11.
εἶπεν (3d.per.sing.aor.act.ind.of εἶπον, constative) 155.
πρὸς (preposition with the accusative, after a verb of speaking) 197.
αὐτόν (acc.sing.masc.of αὐτός, extent after a verb of speaking) 16.
τὸ (nom.sing.neut.of the article in agreement with ἀργύριόν) 9.
ἀργύριόν (nom.sing.neut.of ἀργύριον, subject of εἴη) 1535.
σου (gen.sing.masc.of σύ, possession) 104.
σὺν (preposition with the instrumental of association) 1542.
σοὶ (instru.sing.masc.of σύ, association) 104.
εἴη (3d.per.sing.pres.opt.of εἰμί, voluntative) 86.
εἰς (preposition with the accusative, predicative usage) 140.
ἀπώλειαν (acc.sing.fem.of ἀπώλεια, predicate usage) 666.
ὅτι (conjunction introducing a causal clause) 211.
τὴν (acc.sing.fem.of the article in agreement with δωρεὰν) 9.
δωρεὰν (acc.sing.fem.of δωρεά, general reference) 2004.
τοῦ (gen.sing.masc.of the article in agreement with θεοῦ) 9.
θεοῦ (gen.sing.masc.of θεός, description) 124.
ἐνόμισας (2d.per.sing.aor.act.ind.of νομίζω, constative) 462.
διὰ (preposition with the genitive of descriptive means) 118.
χρημάτων (gen.pl.neut.of χρῆμα, descriptive means) 2637.
κτᾶσθαι (pres.mid.inf.of κράομαι, epexegetical) 859.

Translation - "But Peter said to him, 'You and your money be damned, because you thought that the gift of God can be had for money. . . "

Comment: Peter's imprecation comes very close to what prudes would call profanity. *Cf.*#666 for the various uses of ἀπώλεια. The present optative in εἴη is seen in imprecation here and in Mark 11:4. It carries a great deal of strong feeling, which is characteristic of Peter upon occasion. He was deeply offended because of the obvious insult to the Holy Spirit involved in Simon's offer. The more intimate association which the Apostles enjoyed with the Holy Spirit established for them certain bounds of propriety which could not be violated with impunity. Some may think of Peter's outburst as intemperance, and perhaps it was, but he explains his feeling about the matter in verses 21-23.

Verse 21 - "Thou hast neither part nor lot in this matter, for thy heart is not right in the sight of God."

οὐκ ἔστιν σοι μερὶς οὐδὲ κλῆρος ἐν τῷ λόγῳ τούτῳ, ἡ γὰρ καρδία σου οὐκ ἔστιν εὐθεῖα ἔναντι τοῦ θεοῦ.

οὐκ (summary negative conjunction with the indicative) 130.
ἔστιν (3d.per.sing.pres.ind.of εἰμί, aoristic) 86.
σοι (dat.sing.masc.of σύ, possession) 104.
μερὶς (nom.sing.fem.of μερίς, subject of ἔστιν) 2445.
οὐδὲ (disjunctive particle) 452.
κλῆρος (nom.sing.masc.of κλῆρος, subject of ἔστιν) 1648.
ἐν (preposition with the locative of sphere) 80.
τῷ (loc.sing.masc.of the article in agreement with λόγῳ) 9.
λόγῳ (loc.sing.masc.of λόγος, sphere) 510.
τούτῳ (loc.sing.masc.of οὗτος, in agreement with λόγῳ) 93.
ἡ (nom.sing.fem.of the article in agreement with καρδία) 9.
γὰρ (causal conjunction) 105.
καρδία (nom.sing.fem.of καρδία, subject of ἔστιν) 432.
σου (gen.sing.masc.of σύ, possession) 104.
οὐκ (summary negative conjunction with the indicative) 130.
ἔστιν (3d.per.sing.pres.ind.of εἰμί, aoristic) 86.
εὐθεῖα (nom.sing.fem.of εὐθύς, predicate adjective, in agreement with καρδία) 258.
ἔναντι (preposition with the genitive of place description) 1787.
τοῦ (gen.sing.masc.of the article in agreement with θεοῦ) 9.
θεοῦ (gen.sing.masc.of θεός, place description) 124.

Translation - "There is neither a share nor a vote for you in this crusade, because your heart is not right in the sight of God."

Comment: "Your motive is not honest (pure, sincere, in line with)" would be an equally good translation. Peter's use of κλῆρος (#1648) is a pun. "You are not in this game!" or "You do not have your name in the pot!" By ἐν τῷ λόγῳ τούτῳ, Peter meant the movement built around the word (message, concept) of the gospel of Christ. Simon Magus was the first type on record of the unregenerate preacher who tries to enter the gospel ministry for the financial benefits which he imagines are to be derived therefrom. Anyone who seeks the gospel ministry as a source of financial security indicates by that decision that he is intellectually incapable of being a preacher. In ἔναντι we have we have a clear example of how this compound preposition (ἐν plus ἀντί) is used with the genitive of place description. Simon's heart (motives, attitudes, desires) was *in a place* (ἐν) *opposite from* and therefore *face to face with* God, and thus in a place where God could get a good look at him. As a result Simon failed the test. He was not "lined up" with God. No one will be given a part in the ministry of the gospel of Christ until his heart has been brought into line with the divine ethic. This miracle takes place only when regeneration comes, and that is contingent upon repentance. It was quite logical therefore for Peter to demand that Simon change his mind (repentance) and pray for forgiveness in

Verse 22 - "Repent therefore of this thy wickedness, and pray God, if perhaps the thought of thine heart may be forgiven thee."

μετανόησον οὖν ἀπὸ τῆς κακίας σου ταύτης, καὶ δεήθητι τοῦ κυρίου εἰ ἄρα ἀφεθήσεταί σοι ἡ ἐπίνοια τῆς καρδίας σου.

μετανόησον (2d.per.sing.aor.act.impv.of μετανοέω, entreaty) 251.

οὖν (inferential conjunction) 68.

ἀπὸ (preposition with the ablative of separation) 70.

τῆς (abl.sing.fem.of the article in agreement with κακίας) 9.

κακίας (abl.sing.fem.of κακία, separation) 641.

σου (gen.sing.masc.of σύ, possession) 104.

ταύτης (abl.sing.fem.of οὗτος, in agreement with κακίας) 93.

καὶ (adjunctive conjunction joining verbs) 14.

δεήθητι (2d.per.sing.1st.aor.impv.of δέομαι, entreaty) 841.

τοῦ (gen.sing.masc.of the article in agreement with κυρίου) 9.

κυρίου (gen.sing.masc.of κύριος, objective genitive) 97.

εἰ (conditional particle in an elliptical first-class condition) 337.

ἄρα (illative particle in the first-class elliptical condition) 995.

ἀφεθήσεταί (3d.per.sing.fut.pass.ind.of ἀφίημι, deliberative, in a first-class condition) 319.

σοι (dat.sing.masc.of σύ, personal advantage) 104.

ἡ (nom.sing.fem.of the article in agreement with ἐπίνοια) 9.

#3165 ἐπίνοια (nom.sing.fem.of ἐπίνοια, subject of ἀφεθήσεταί).

thought - Acts 8:22.

Meaning: A combination of ἐπί (#47) and νοέω (#1160). Thought, purpose. The ground meaning of ἐπί - "resting upon" with νοέω "to think" thus becomes "that which rests upon (is the result of) your thinking." Thus ἐπίνοια is not the act of thinking, but the product of it. Followed by the genitive of description in Acts 8:22 - the idea in the heart of Simon was the result of his thought about the advantage which would be his if he had the power which the Apostles displayed.

τῆς (gen.sing.fem.of the article in agreement with καρδίας) 9.
καρδίας (gen.sing.fem.of καρδία, description) 432.
σου (gen.sing.masc.of σύ, possession) 104.

Translation - *"Repent therefore of this wickedness of yours and ask the Lord that perhaps this scheme of yours may be forgiven you."*

Comment: In ἀπὸ τῆς κακίας σου ταύτης we have the original idea of ἀπό with the ablative, *viz.* the starting point (ἀπό) from which to separate (the ablative case). Peter was telling Simon to change his mind (μετανόησον) and thus separate himself from the evil scheme which his covetous heart had suggested. After repentance comes the prayer for forgiveness for having entertained the thought in the first place. Peter's entreaty to Simon is for both the repentance and the prayer for forgiveness. εἰ here introduces an elliptical first-class condition, with illative ἄρα added for emphasis. "If therefore, and in fact, the ... may be forgiven for you." Simon's thought was that with the gift which he tried to buy from Peter and John, he might retain his position in the city among the Samaritans and thus realize the lucrative benefits which would flow from it. If Peter and John had acquiesced in his scheme, no doubt the payment which he would have made would have been a good investment. Simon may have been the first sorcerer to seek to use the gospel of the grace of God for selfish reasons, but he was certainly not the last. On the present religious scene the divine healer and the miracle worker usually has a collection plate handy and some of his books for sale. The incurable religiosity of unregenerate man provides a willing base for this lucrative traffic in spiritual prostitution. Thanks to Peter's perception the Samaritan believers were spared this exploitation. Peter concludes his rebuke to Simon in

Verse 23 - *"For I perceive that thou art in the gall of bitterness, and in the bond of iniquity."*

εἰς γὰρ χολὴν πικρίας καὶ σύνδεσμον ἀδικίας ὁρῶ σε ὄντα.

εἰς (preposition with the predicate accusative) 140.
γὰρ (causal conjunction) 105.
χολὴν (acc.sing.fem.of χολή, predicate accusative) 1645.

#3166 πικρίας (gen.sing.fem.of πικρία, description).

bitterness - Acts 8:23; Rom.3:14; Eph.4:31; Heb.12:15.

Meaning: Cf. πικρός (#5135). Bitterness. χολὴν πικρίας - Acts 8:23, *i.e.* a poisonous influence; bitter speech (Rom.3:14); bitter hatred (Eph.4:31) ῥίζα πικρίας, *i.e.* a root that would produce bitterness - Heb.12:15.

καὶ (adjunctive conjunction joining nouns) 14.

#3167 σύνδεσμον (acc.sing.masc.of σύνδεσμος, predicate accusative).

bond - Col.2:19; Acts 8:23; Eph.4:3; Col.3:14.

Meaning: Cf. συνδέω (#5084). A combination of σύν (#1542) and δεσμός (#2229). That which binds together. When followed by the genitive of description, a bundle. Charity is σύνδεσμος τῆς τελειότητος - "a bundle of perfection." (Col.3:14). With ἅφη in Col.2:19, by which the body of Christ is knit together. Thus it is the wrapping by which something is held together. The unity of the Spirit is kept by τῷ συνδέσμῳ τῆς εἰρήνης - Eph.4:3. Simon the sorcerer was a bundle of ἀδικίας ("a bundle of iniquity") - Acts 8:23.

ἀδικίας (gen.sing.fem.of ἀδικία, description) 2367.

ὁρῶ (1st.per.sing.pres.act.ind.of ὁράω, aoristic) 144.

σε (acc.sing.masc.of σύ, direct object of ὁρῶ) 104.

ὄντα (pres.part.acc.sing.masc.of εἰμί, adverbial, circumstantial) 86.

Translation - "Because I see you as bitter poison and a bundle of iniquity."

Comment: Peter's advice to Simon was based upon his observation of his behavior and analysis of his psychology. He was indeed very perceptive. That is why (causal γὰρ) he told him to repent and ask for forgiveness. *Cf.*#1645. Since χολή was considered soporofic to some extent, it is possible that Peter was saying that Simon was drugged on bitterness, which produced his attempt to buy the apostolic gifts. It can also produce evil speech (Rom.3:14) and hatred (Eph.4:31). Simon's bitter attitude had put to sleep the angels of his better nature and induced him to stoop to the depths of trying to buy God's power. This is as irrational as it is presumptuous and wicked. A sermon on the evils of bitterness can be developed here. What made Simon bitter? Was it not the fact that he saw his Samaritan audiences, over whom he had exercised so much demagogic power in the past and from whom he had received such great financial rewards, slip away from him as they listened with even greater interest to Philip's preaching and marvelled even more at Philip's miracles. Thus Simon was jealous of Philip and his jealousy turned to the bitterness that put him in an intellectual stupor and an ethical cesspool.

He also became a "bundle of unrighteousness" - a wicked bombshell, tied up with and compacted by evil, and ready to explode with a detonation that would create immoral and godless fallout and infest the entire community. There is no doubt that sinful attitudes, words and actions are the bitter fruitage of previous attitudes of bitterness. Simon the sorcerer demonstrated this. But Peter, with his apostolic gift from the Holy Spirit, called by Paul "discerning of spirits" (1 Cor.12:10) was able to detect in Simon the danger, expose it and counsel his repentance and prayer for forgiveness.

We cannot be certain how the matter ended. Peter's rebuke registered with Simon at least to the extent that he asked the Apostles to pray for him.

Verse 24 - "Then answered Simon and said, Pray ye to the Lord for me, that none of these things which ye have spoken come upon me."

ἀποκριθεὶς δὲ ὁ Σίμων εἶπεν, Δεήθητε ὑμεῖς ὑπὲρ ἐμοῦ πρὸς τὸν κύριον ὅπως μηδὲν ἐπέλθῃ ἐπ' ἐμὲ ὧν εἰρήκατε.

ἀποκριθεὶς (aor.part.nom.sing.masc.of ἀποκρίνομαι, adverbial, modal) 318.

δὲ (continuative conjunction) 11.

ὁ (nom.sing.masc.of the article in agreement with Σίμων) 9.

Σίμων (nom.sing.masc.of Σίμων, subject of εἶπεν) 3161.

εἶπεν (3d.per.sing.aor.act.ind.of εἶπον, constative) 155.

δεήθητε (2d.per.pl.aor.mid.impv.of δέομαι, entreaty) 841.

ὑμεῖς (nom.pl.masc.of σύ, subject of δεήθητε) 104.

ὑπὲρ (preposition with the ablative, "in behalf of.") 545.

ἐμοῦ (abl.sing.masc.of ἐγώ, "in behalf of") 123.

πρὸς (preposition with the accusative of extent after a verb of speaking) 197.

τὸν (acc.sing.masc.of the article in agreement with κύριον) 9.

κύριον (acc.sing.masc.of κύριος, extent, after a verb of speaking) 97.

ὅπως (conjunction with the subjunctive in a purpose clause) 177.

μηδὲν (nom.sing.neut.of μηδείς, subject of ἐπέλθῃ) 713.

ἐπέλθῃ (3d.per.sing.aor.mid.subj.of ἐπέρχομαι, purpose) 1814.

ἐπ' (preposition with the accusative of extent) 47.

ἐμὲ (acc.sing.masc.of ἐγώ, extent) 123.

ὧν (gen.pl.neut.of ὅς, in attraction to τούτων, supplied) 65.

εἰρήκατε (2d.per.pl.perf.act.ind.(Attic) of ῥέω, consummative) 116.

Translation - "And in reply Simon said, 'Pray for me to the Lord in order that not one of these things of which you have spoken come upon me.' "

Comment: Note the pleonasm, not common in Acts in ἀποκριθεὶς δὲ ὁ Σίμων εἶπεν . Simon emphasized ὑμεῖς, in his request for prayer and directed it both to Peter and John, as the plural pronoun and the 2d.per.pl.in δεήθητε makes clear. There is debate among the grammarians as to whether ὑπέρ here is genitive of ablative. The context demands the sense of "in my behalf." If genitive, we can call it the genitive of reference - "Pray with reference to me" or "Pray about me" which is not quite as close as "Pray for me." The purpose clause specifies what Simon wished to avoid. τούτων, a partitive genitive is supplied after μηδὲν, to which genitive case the relative ὧν is attracted.

This is the last word on Simon. He disappears from the New Testament. Whether his request for prayer was sincere or sarcastic and whether it was answered or not we have no way of knowing.

Verse 25 - "And they, when they had testified and preached the word of the Lord, returned to Jerusalem, and preached the gospel in many villages of the Samaritans."

Οἱ μέν οὖν διαμαρτυράμενοι καὶ λαλήσαντες τὸν λόγον τοῦ κυρίου ὑπέστρεφον εἰς Ἱεροσόλυμα, πολλάς τε κώμας τῶν Σαμαριτῶν εὐηγγελίζοντο.

Οἱ (nom.pl.masc.of the article, subject of ὑπέστρεφον) 9.

μὲν (affirmative particle) 300.

οὖν (continuative conjunction) 68.

διαμαρτυράμενοι (aor.mid.part.nom.pl.masc.of διαμαρτύρομαι, adverbial, temporal) 2589.

καὶ (adjunctive conjunction joining participles) 14.

λαλήσαντες (aor.act.part.nom.pl.masc.of λαλέω, adverbial, temporal) 815.

τὸν (acc.sing.masc.of the article in agreement with λόγον) 9.

λόγον (acc.sing.masc.of λόγος, direct object of λαλήσαντες) 510.

τοῦ (gen.sing.masc.of the article in agreement with κυρίου) 9.

κυρίου (gen.sing.masc.of κύριος, description) 97.

ὑπέστρεφον (3d.per.pl.aor.act.ind.of ὑποστρέφω, ingressive) 1838.

εἰς (preposition with the accusative of extent) 140.

Ἱεροσόλυμα (acc.sing.masc.of Ἱεροσολύμων, extent) 141.

πολλάς (acc.pl.fem.of πολύς, in agreement with κώμας) 228.

τε (affirmative particle) 1408.

κώμας (acc.pl.fem.of κώμη, accusative of person, object of εὐηγγελίζοντο) 834.

τῶν (gen.pl.masc.of the article in agreement with Σαματιτῶν) 9.

Σαμαριτῶν (gen.pl.masc.of Σαμαρειτῶν,, description) 856.

εὐηγγελίζοντο (3d.per.pl.imp.act.ind.of εὐαγγελίζω, progressiv description) 909.

Translation - "Then, after having given their testimonies and spoken the message of the Lord they started back to Jerusalem, preaching the good news in many villages of the Samaritans along the way."

Comment: μὲν and τε each add affirmative emphasis to their respective clauses. οὖν is continuative. Peter and John took full advantage of the situation in Samaria. They had gone down to check on the story of Philip's ministry and had made the theological adjustments of verses 15-17, after which they exposed the evil machinations of Simon Magus. They found the Samaritans as receptive to their message as had Philip and Jesus (John 4) and, inasmuch as they were in the territory already they did not start back to Jerusalem (ingressive aorist in ὑπέστρεφον) before taking full advantage of the opportunity to give their testimonies (perfective διά in διαμαρτυράμενοι) after which they expounded the theology of the Christian message. On the way back to Jerusalem, as they toiled southward, up the mountain trails to the city in the heights, they preached the good news of the gospel of Christ is many of the Samaritan villages - many, not all, because to have visited all would have made necessary side trips to those which were not directly on the way. Apparently Peter and John did not have sufficient time to preach in the entire area. We have the accusative of person addressed in κώμας, after a verb of speaking.

Thus Peter and John had a profitable trip to Samaria. They confirmed the sincerity of Philip's ministry, set his theology straight, put the stamp of Apostolic approval upon the missionary enterprise among the hybrid Samaritans (Acts 1:8), rebuked and exposed a bitter, wicked and insincere would-be exploiter of the grace of God, and themselves witnessed to the truth of the gospel, both in the village in which the revival began and in many others on their way back to Jerusalem.

Meanwhile, Philip, the deacon, who now understood Christian theology better (Acts 18:26) and was therefore qualified for his next assignment, was to have a new experience.

Philip and the Ethiopian Eunuch

(Acts 8:26-40)

Verse 26 - "And the angel of the Lord spoke unto Philip saying, Arise, and go toword the south unto the way that goeth down from Jerusalem, unto Gaza, which is desert."

Ἄγγελος δὲ κυρίου ἐλάλησεν πρὸς Φίλιππον λέγων,᾿Ανάστηθι καὶ πορεύου κατὰ μεσημβρίαν ἐπὶ τὴν ὁδὸν τὴν καταβαίνουσαν ἀπὸ Ἱερουσαλὴμ εἰς Γάζαν, αὕτη ἐστὶν ἔρημος.

Ἄγγελος (nom.sing.masc.of ἄγγελος, subject of ἐλάλησεν) 96.
δὲ (continuative conjunction) 11.
κυρίου (gen.sing.masc.of κύριος, description) 97.
ἐλάλησεν (3d.per.sing.aor.act.ind.of λαλέω, constative) 815.
πρὸς (preposition with the accusative of extent, after a verb of speaking) 197.
Φίλιππον (acc.sing.masc.of Φίλιππος, extent after a verb of speaking) 3082.
λέγων (pres.act.part.nom.sing.masc.of λέγω, recitative) 66.
᾿Ανάστηθι (2d.per.sing.2d.aor.act.impv.of ἀνίστημι, command) 789.
καὶ (adjunctive conjunction joining verbs) 14.
πορεύου (2d.per.sing.pres.impv.of πορεύομαι, command) 170.
κατὰ (preposition with the accusative of extent in a local use) 98.

#3168 μεσημβρίαν (acc.sing.fem.of μεσημβρία, extent).

noon - Acts 22:6.
south - Acts 8:26.

Meaning: A combination of μέσος (#873) and ἡμέρα (#135). Hence, midday. In that latitude the word also came to refer to the southern part of the zodiac in Acts 8:26 where it is introduced by κατά. With περί in Acts 22:6 - "around noon."

ἐπὶ (preposition with the accusative, in an expression of place) 47.
τὴν (acc.sing.fem.of the article in agreement with ὁδόν) 9.
ὁδὸν (acc.sing.fem.of ὁδός, place) 199.
τὴν (acc.sing.fem.of the article in agreement with καταβαίνουσαν) 9.
καταβαίνουσαν (pres.act.part.acc.sing.fem.of καταβαίνω, adjectival, restrictive, in agreement with ὁδόν) 324.
ἀπὸ (preposition with the ablative, separation) 70.

Ἰερουσαλήμ (abl.sing.masc.of Ἰεροσολύμων, separation) 141.

εἰς (preposition with the accusative of extent) 140.

#3169 Γάζαν (acc.sing.fem.of Γάζα, extent).

Gaza - Acts 8:26.

Meaning: A former celebrated Philistine city, near the southern border of Israel, between Raphia and Ascalon. It is near the coast, about 45 miles southwest of Jerusalem. Modern Gaza has more than 20,000 inhabitants. Philip was directed to take the Gaza road - Acts 8:26.

αὕτη (nom.sing.fem.of οὗτος, anaphoric, with reference to ὁδόν, subject of ἐστὶν) 93.

ἐστὶν (3d.per.sing.pres.ind.of εἰμί, aoristic) 86.

ἔρημος (nom.sing.fem.of ἔρημος, predicate nominative) 250.

Translation - "And an angel of the Lord said to Philip, 'Get up and be on your way south on the road that goes down from Jerusalem to Gaza. The road goes through the desert.' "

Comment: αὕτη is anaphoric and it can refer either to ὁδόν or Γάζαν. If the former the last clause describes the country through which the road runs, as in my translation. If the latter it refers to the town and Goodspeed's translation is better - "the town is now deserted."

δὲ can be either continuative or adversative. Philip was in the midst of a great revival in Samaria and would not normally wish to leave it to make a long trip into desert country, without at least being told why he should go and whom he would meet. This information was not provided. The trip would be long and taxing. Gaza is 45 miles southwest of Jerusalem and to that distance would be added the distance north of Jerusalem in Samaria. The word ἔρημος does not necessarily denote aridity. Indeed the area was not totally arid (verse 36). It was however, an area of low population density, with relatively few prospects for evangelism, in contrast to Samaritan country where the crowds were large. Note the pleonasm in Ἀνάστηθι, when joined with πορεύου. The presence of Ἀνάστηθι may indicate that Philip was asleep at the time that the angel spoke to him.

Despite any reservations which Philip may have had about the angelic orders, he obeyed and was soon to discover the wisdom of the move.

Verse 27 - "And he arose and went: and, behold a man of Ethiopia, an eunuch of great authority under Candace, queen of the Ethiopians, who had the charge of all her treasure, and had come to Jerusalem for to worship."

καὶ ἀναστὰς ἐπορεύθη, καὶ ἰδοὺ ἀνὴρ Αἰθίοψ εὐνοῦχος δυνάστης Κανδάκης βασιλίσσης Αἰθιόπων, ὅς ἦν ἐπὶ πάσης τῆς γάζης αὐτῆς, ὅς ἐληλύθει προσκυνήσων εἰς Ἰερουσαλήμ,

καὶ (inferential conjunction) 14.

ἀναστάς (aor.act.part.nom.sing.masc.of ἀνίστημι, adverbial, temporal) 789.
ἐπορεύθη (3d.per.sing.aor.mid.ind.of πορεύομαι, constative) 170.
καὶ (continuative conjunction) 14.
ἰδοὺ (exclamation) 95.
ἀνήρ (nom.sing.masc.of ἀνήρ, subject of ἦν . . . ὑποστρέφων) 63.

#3170 Αἰθίοφ (nom.sing.masc.of Αἰθίοφ, in agreement with ἀνήρ).

Ethiopia - Acts 8:27,27.

Meaning: Cf.αἴθω - "to burn" and ὤφ - "face." Hence "to burn the face."
Sunburn, swarthy, black, dark skinned. Upper Ethiopia - a region called Habesh
or Abyssinia, in Africa, adjoining Egypt and including Meroe, an island - Acts
8:27,27.

εὐνοῦχος (nom.sing.masc.of εὐνοῦχος, apposition) 1294.
δυνάστης (nom.sing.masc.of δυνάστης, in agreement with εὐνοῦχος) 1832.

#3171 Κανδάκης (gen.sing.fem.of Κανδάκη, relationship).

Candace - Acts 8:27.

Meaning: A name common to the queens of the Ethiopian country, whose
capital was Napata. The title Candace relates to the queen of Ethiopia as
Ptolemy relates to the Egyptian kings and Henry to the Reuss princes.

βασιλίσσης (gen.sing.fem.of βασίλισσα, apposition) 1014.
Αἰθιόπων (gen.pl.masc.of Αἰθίοφ, relationship) 3170.
ὅς (nom.sing.masc.of ὅς, subject of ἦν, anaphoric, relative to ἀνήρ) 65.
ἦν (3d.per.sing.imp.ind.of εἰμί, progressive description) 86.
ἐπὶ (preposition with the genitive, metaphorical use - indicating administrative authority) 47.
πάσης (gen.sing.fem.of πᾶς, in agreement with γάζης) 67.
τῆς (gen.sing.fem.of the article in agreement with γάζης) 9.

#3172 γάζης (gen.sing.fem.of γάζα, reference).

treasure - Acts 8:27.

Meaning: a Persian word, adopted by Greeks and Latins. The roygal treasury;
riches; "crown jewels" and other treasures - Acts 8:27.

αὐτῆς (gen.sing.fem.of αὐτός, possession) 16.
ὅς (nom.sing.masc.of ὅς, subject of ἐληλύθει, anaphoric, relative to ἀνήρ)
65.
ἐληλύθει (3d.per.sing.pluperfect ind.of ἔρχομαι, consummative) 146.
προσκυνήσων (fut.act.part.nom.sing.masc.of προσκυνέω, adverbial, telic)
147.
εἰς (preposition with the accusative of extent) 140.
Ἰερουσαλήμ (acc.sing.masc.of Ἰεροσόλυμων, extent) 141.

Translation - *"So he got up and started. And behold a man of Ethiopia, a powerful eunuch of Candace, Queen of the Ethiopians, who was her Secretary of the Treasury, who had come to Jerusalem to worship. . . "*

Comment: καὶ may very well be inferential here. It was because of the angelic order to leave Samaria that Philip got up and went - perhaps against his own desires, for he probably did not expect to meet anyone in the desert. But God's direction had a purpose. It always does. A Christian deacon, a converted Jew, who, before he became a Christian had been reared in a religious culture that denied salvation to all except Jews had just been treated to evidence that God would also save half-breed Samaritans. He is now about to learn that the gospel of Christ is also to be preached to a black Gentile. He is about to meet a black man, a black Gentile, a politically powerful administrative authority charged with the responsibility of conducting fiscal and monetary affairs for the queen of the Ethiopians. This man had come to Jerusalem in order to worship. There are not many future participles in the New Testament. This one is telic. For other future participles of purpose *cf.* Mt.27:49; Acts 22:5; 24:11,17 and Heb.13:17 which also has an element of cause in it.

The pluperfect ἐληλύθει points backward to the time when the man was on his way to Jerusalem for purposes of worship. We learn in verse 28 that his visit to Jerusalem was over and that, at the time of our story, he was enroute back to Ethiopia. The fact that he had gone to Jerusalem to worship indicates that he was probably a prosylyte Jew. That he was one of God's elect and that the Holy Spirit had already begun to prepare his heart and mind for Philip's message is clear as we see in

Verse 28 - ". . . was returning, and sitting in his chariot read Esaias the prophet."

ἦν τε ὑποστρέφων καὶ καθήμενος ἐπὶ τοῦ ἅρματος αὐτοῦ καὶ ἀνεγίνωσκεν τὸν προφήτην Ἡσαΐαν.

ἦν (3d.per.sing.imp.ind.of εἰμί, imperfect periphrastic) 86.

τε (affirmative particle) 1408.

ὑποστρέφων (pres.act.part.nom.sing.masc.of ὑποστρέφω, imperfect periphrastic) 1838.

καὶ (adjunctive conjunction joining participles) 14.

καθήμενος (pres.mid.part.nom.sing.masc.of κάθημαι, imperfect periphrastic) 377.

ἐπὶ (preposition with the genitive of place description) 47.

τοῦ (gen.sing.neut.of the article in agreement with ἅρματος) 9.

#3173 ἅρματος (gen.sing.neut.of ἅρμα, place description).

chariot - Acts 8:28,29,38; Rev.9:9.

Meaning: Cf. ἄρω - "to join or to fit to a team." Chariot. In Rev.9:9, a war chariot drawn by ἵππων πολλῶν. Of the vehicle of the Ethiopian eunuch - Acts 8:28,29,38.

αὐτοῦ (gen.sing.masc.of αὐτός, possession) 16.
καὶ (adjunctive conjunction, joining verbs) 14.
ἀνεγίνωσκεν (3d.per.sing.imp.act.ind.of ἀναγινώσκω, progressive description) 967.
τὸν (acc.sing.masc.of the article in agreement with προφήτην) 9.
προφήτην (acc.sing.masc.of προφήτης, direct object of ἀνεγίνωσκεν) 119.
Ἡσαΐαν (acc.sing.masc.of Ἡσαΐας, apposition) 255.

Translation - ". . . and was returning and sitting in his chariot, and he was reading the prophet Isaiah."

Comment: We have a double imperfect periphrastic - ἦν with two present participles - ὑποστρέφων and καθήμενος. The man was on his way back home and sitting in his chariot. Note ἐπί and the genitive here where normally we would expect ἐν with the locative, although, if we knew precisely the shape and form of the chariot we might find that ἐπί ("upon") with the genitive is more accurate than ἐν ("in") with the locative.

The Holy Spirit, Who knew in advance where the Ethiopian was, and what he was doing, arranged the "chance" meeting and gave Philip instruction accordingly. Had Philip interposed his own wisdom and refused to leave a revival in a populous area for a trip into a desert, he would have missed his assignment with its glorious opportunity, not only to lead a hungry soul to Christ, but also be instrumental in introducing the gospel story to the Ethiopians. There is little doubt that the government official witnessed to his new faith among his colleagues in Ethiopia. One wonders whether the Neo-Platonists who established their brand of Christianity in Alexandria, following the death of Alexander the Great (323 B.C.) found Christianity already established in Ethiopia among the Copts? Did the Eunuch become a gospel missionary to his people? If so, did his work have permanent results?

As Philip toiled southward along the deserted road he saw the chariot and got further orders from the Holy Spirit.

Verse 29 - "Then the Spirit said unto Philip, Go near, and join thyself to this chariot."

εἶπεν δὲ τὸ πνεῦμα τῷ Φιλίππῳ, Πρόσελθε καὶ κολλήθητι τῷ ἅρματι τούτῳ.

εἶπεν (3d.per.sing.aor.act.ind.of εἶπον, constative) 155.
δὲ (continuative conjunction) 11.
τὸ (nom.sing.neut.of the article in agreement with πνεῦμα) 9.
πνεῦμα (nom.sing.neut.of πνεῦμα, subject of εἶπεν) 83.
τῷ (dat.sing.masc.of the article in agreement with Φιλίππῳ) 9.
Φιλίππῳ (dat.sing.masc.of Φίλιππος, indirect object of εἶπεν) 3082.
Πρόσελθε (2d.per.sing.aor.mid.impv.of προσέρχομαι, command) 336.
καὶ (adjunctive conjunction joining verbs) 14.
κολλήθητι (2d.per.sing.1st.aor.mid.impv.of κολλάομαι, command) 1288.

τῷ (loc.sing.neut.of the article in agreement with ἅρματι) 9.

ἅρματι (loc.sing.nmeut.of ἅρμα, place with verbs) 3173.

τούτῳ (loc.sing.neut.of οὗτος, in agreement with ἅρματι) 93.

Translation - "And the Spirit said to Philip, 'Go up and get on that chariot.' "

Comment: Note ἅγγελος (vs.26) as the speaker and τὸ πνεῦμα (vs.29). ἅγγελος (#96) means "messenger" and could have been a human being, an angel or the Holy Spirit. Some agent of communication told Philip to go south. We know only that he was κυρίου - "from the Lord." Now that Philip is in place, the Holy Spirit gives him further instruction - "go near" - "approach." Cf.#1288 - "glue yourself to that car." Thus Philip may have become the first hitchhiking evangelist. Φίλιππος (#3082) means "a lover of horses." It derives from φιλέω (#566) and ἵππος (#5121). It may be that the deacon was attracted at first, not so much to the distinguished Ethiopian and his chariot, but to the horses that were pulling it.

Note that when God leads us (1) He leads us often in ways that seem to us irrational. Why leave a revival to take a desert trip? (2) He leads us by different messengers: - ἅγγελος κυρίου in verse 26 and τὸ πνεῦμα in verse 29. (3) He leads us a step at a time. We do not need to know His will for us tomorrow. Only for the present moment. (4) Often He leads us in keeping with our personal interests. Philip loved horses. (5) Wherever and whenever He leads us it is always in order to glorify His name. The Eunuch was saved and (6) He leads us in keeping with His long range plan. The gospel of Christ was carried into Northeast Africa, perhaps to lay the foundation for what later became the Coptic Church.

Verse 30 - "And Philip ran thither to him, and heard him read the prophet Esaias, and said, Understandest thou what thou readest?"

προσδραμὼν δὲ ὁ Φίλιππος ἤκουσεν αὐτοῦ ἀναγινώσκοντος Ἡσαῖαν τὸν προφήτην, καὶ εἶπεν, Ἀρά γε γινώσκεις ἃ ἀναγινώσκεις;

προσδραμὼν (aor.act.part.nom.sing.masc.of προστρέχω, adverbial, temporal) 2333.

δὲ (inferential conjunction) 11.

ὁ (nom.sing.masc.of the article in agreement with Φίλιππος) 9.

Φίλιππος (nom.sing.masc.of Φίλιππος, subject of ἤκουσεν and εἶπεν) 3082.

ἤκουσεν (3d.per.sing.aor.act.ind.of ἀκούω, constative) 148.

αὐτοῦ (gen.sing.masc.of αὐτός, designation) 16.

ἀναγινώσκοντος (pres.act.part.gen.sing.masc.of ἀναγινώσκω, adverbial, circumstantial) 967.

Ἡσαῖαν (acc.sing.masc.of Ἡσαίας, direct object of ἀναγινώσκοντος) 255.

τὸν (acc.sing.masc.of the article in agreement with προφήτην) 9.

προφήτην (acc.sing.masc.of προφήτης, apposition) 119.

καὶ (adjunctive conjunction joining verbs) 14.

εἶπεν (3d.per.sing.aor.act.ind.of εἶπον, constative) 155.

Ἀρά (interrogative particle in rhetorical question expecting a negative reply) 2627.

γε (intensive particle, crescendo effect) 2449.

γινώσκεις (2d.per.sing.pres.act.ind.of γινώσκω, aoristic) 131.

ἅ (acc.pl.neut.of ὅς, direct object of γινώσκεις) 65.

ἀναγινώσκεις (2d.per.sing.pres.act.ind.of ἀναγινώσκω, aoristic) 967.

Translation - *"So when Philip ran up and heard him reading the prophet Isaiah he said, 'You don't really understand what you are reading do you?' "*

Comment: δὲ is inferential. Philip's action was the result of the Holy Spirit's order of verse 29. Whether it was necessary for Philip to run in order to catch the chariot the text does not tell us. We are not informed about the relative positions of the deacon and the chariot when he first saw it. His haste may have been the result of his alacrity in obeying the Spirit's order. He now began to see some reason for the previous order that he should leave Samaria and go south into the desert. He may also have been anxious to get a closer look at the horses. In any event his trip to the desert has not been totally in vain. He will have the opportunity to talk with someone. He overtook (intercepted) the chariot and came close enough to hear the man reading - obviously aloud. There is no record that the eunuch had a companion. The fact that he was reading aloud probably indicates his intense interest in what he was reading and perhaps a concentrated effort to understand Isaiah's prophecy. ἆρα introduces a rhetorical question that expects a negative reply and γε, the enclitic postpositive intensifies the force of ἆρα. Hence our translation. Philip may have noted from the fact that he was reading aloud that he understood little of what he read. Robertson admits that "it is not clear" how the preposition ἀνά turns γινώσκω from "to know" to "to read" (*Grammar*, 571). *Cf.*#131 with #976. Literally to "read up." We say "I will look it up" which means more intensive research that a casual reading. This play on words indicates that the man was deeply interested in what he read and that he did not understand it fully, as his own statement attests in verse 31. Hence our translation of verse 30. In modern parlance we often say, "I do not understand all that I know about it."

There is nothing in the text to say that before the eunuch invited Philip into the chariot he stopped it, although verses 36 - 38 make it clear that as they discussed the Scripture the chariot was moving. Perhaps the eunuch had become so engrossed in his study before he met Philip that he had allowed the horses to stop. If so, this would explain how Philip was able to catch up with the chariot. All of this is conjecture, and it is harmless as long as we recognize it as such. There is nothing wrong with making an effort to reconstruct the scene. It may be the Luke omitted the statement that when Philip ran alongside the chariot and asked his question the man called the horses to a halt.

The eunuch's reply in verse 31 is evidence that Philip's rhetorical question was not in bad taste.

Verse 31 - *"And he said, How can I except some man should guide me? And he desired Philip that he would come up and sit with him."*

ὁ δὲ εἶπεν, Πῶς γὰρ ἂν δυναίμην ἐὰν μή τις ὁδηγήσει με; παρεκάλεσέν τε τὸν Φίλιππον ἀναβάντα καθίσαι σὺν αὐτῷ.

ὁ (nom.sing.masc.of the article, subject of εἶπεν) 9.

δὲ (continuative conjunction) 11.

εἶπεν (3d.per.sing.aor.act.ind.of εἶπον, constative) 155.

Πῶς (interrogative conjunction in direct question) 627.

γὰρ (emphatic conjunction) 105.

ἄν (particle with the potential optative in a mixed condition, fourth-class apodosis) 205.

δυναίμην (1st.per.sing.pres.optative of δύναμαι, in a mixed condition, fourth-class apodosis, in direct question) 289.

ἐὰν (conditional particle in a mixed condition, first-class protasis) 363.

μὴ (qualified negative conjunction with the future indicative in a first-class protasis of a mixed condition) 87.

τις (nom.sing.masc.of τις, subject of ὁδηγήσει) 486.

ὁδηγήσει (3d.per.sing.fut.act.ind.of ὁδηγέω, first-class protasis in a mixed condition, direct question) 1156.

με (acc.sing.masc.of ἐγώ, direct object of ὁδηγήσει) 123.

παρεκάλεσέν (3d.per.sing.aor.act.ind.of παρακαλέω, constative) 230.

τε (continuative particle) 1408.

τὸν (acc.sing.masc.of the article in agreement with Φίλιππον) 9.

Φίλιππον (acc.sing.masc.of Φίλιππος, direct object of παρεκάλεσεν) 3082.

ἀναβάντα (aor.act.part.acc.sing.masc.of ἀναβαίνω, adverbial, temporal) 323.

καθίσαι (aor.act.inf.of καθίζω, epexegetical) 420.

σὺν (preposition with the instrumental, accompaniment) 1542.

αὐτῷ (associative-instrumental sing.masc.of αὐτός, accompaniment) 16.

Translation - "*And he said, 'How indeed can I ever, if someone does not guide me?' And he invited Philip to step up and sit with him.*"

Comment: In πῶς γὰρ ἄν δυναίμην ἐὰν μή τις ὁδηγήσει με, we have a direct question and a mixed condition. The protasis is of the first class and the apodosis of the fourth class. This assumes that ὁδηγήσει is not itacistic — η.

There is a good deal of feeling - perhaps even asperity, in the man's retort to Philip's question, which implies that he really wanted to understand what he read. Thus γὰρ is emphatic. *Cf.* ἄν with the optative in direct question also in Acts 17:18. ἐὰν μή also expresses his doubt that anyone in the future could be found capable of explaining the passage to him. He seems to imply that there is some doubt that Philip can help him, but he is willing to give him the chance. Thus he was polite enough to ask Philip to step up into the chariot and sit with him. Note the epexegetical infinitive καθίσαι which explains παρεκάλεσεν.

The eunuch's skepticism was not without some foundation. He had just been to Jerusalem to worship. Asking for the Bread of Life he had been given only a religious stone by the Jewish Establishment in the Temple. They knew no more about Isaiah's message than he. He faced the prospect of questions from his colleagues back in Ethiopia and was trying to understand Isaiah's message for their sake as well as for his own. His modern counterpart is the hungry worshipper who leaves a modern church service where the stones of modern agnosticism are dispensed instead of the Bread of Life. In the eunuch's case, fortunately, the Holy Spirit had arranged for a Spirit-filled deacon to expound the passage to him, although Philip himself had not understood it until Peter and John came down to Samaria to help.

Verse 32 - "The place of the scripture which he read was this, He was led as a sheep to the slaughter; and like a lamb dumb before his shearers, so opened he not his mouth."

ἡ δὲ περιοχὴ τῆς γραφῆς ἣν ἀνεγίνωσκεν ἦν αὕτη, Ὡς πρόβατον ἐπὶ σφαγὴν ἤχθη, καὶ ὡς ἀμνὸς ἐναντίον τοῦ κείραντος αὐτὸν ἄφωνος, οὕτως οὐκ ἀνοίγει τὸ στόμα αὐτοῦ.

ἡ (nom.sing.fem.of the article in agreement with περιοχῆ) 9.
δὲ (explanatory conjunction) 11.

#3174 περιοχὴ (nom.sing.fem.of περιοχή, subject of ἦν).

place - Acts 8:32.

Meaning: Cf. περιέχω (#2054). Hence, an encompassing. That which is contained within a given place. Followed by a genitive of description - τῆς γραφῆς - "the place of the scripture" - the passage being read - Acts 8:32.

τῆς (gen.sing.fem.of the article in agreement with γραφῆς) 9.
γραφῆς (gen.sing.fem.of γραφή, description) 1389.
ἣν (acc.sing.fem.of ὅς, direct object of ἀνεγίνωσκεν) 65.
ἀνεγίνωσκεν (3d.per.sing.imp.act.ind.of ἀναγινώσκω, progressive duration) 967.
ἦν (3d.per.sing.imp.ind.of εἰμί, progressive description) 86.
αὕτη (nom.sing.fem.of οὗτος, predicate nominative, deictic) 93.
Ὡς (particle introducing a comparative clause) 128.
πρόβατον (nom.sing.neut.of πρόβατον, predicate nominative) 671.
ἐπὶ (preposition with the accusative of extent) 47.

#3175 σφαγὴν (acc.sing.fem.of σφαγή, extent).

slaughter - Acts 8:32; Rom.8:36; Jam.5:5.

Meaning: Cf. σφάζω (#5292). Slaughter. Sheep, destined to slaughter - Acts 8:32; Rom.8:36. As a genitive of description of an era of slaughter; an era characterized by man's inhumanity to man. Man's day - from Calvary to the Second Coming.

ἤχθη (3d.per.sing.aor.pass.ind.of ἄγω, constative) 876.
καὶ (adjunctive conjunction joining comparative clauses) 14.
ὡς (particle introducing a comparative clause) 128.

ἀμνὸς (nom.sing.masc.of ἀμνός, predicate nominative) 1959.
ἐναντίον (preposition with the genitive) 1780.
τοῦ (gen.sing.masc.of the article in agreement with κείραντος) 9.

#3176 κείραντος (aor.act.part.gen.sing.masc.of κείρω, substantival, genitive of place description).

shear - Acts 18:18; 1 Cor.11:6,6.
shearer - Acts 8:32.

Meaning: To shear a sheep - Acts 8:32. To cut the hair of a human head - Acts 18:18; 1 Cor.11:6,6.

αὐτὸν (acc.sing.masc.of αὐτός, direct object of κείραντος) 16.

#3177 ἄφωνος (nom.sing.masc.of ἄφωνος, predicate adjective).

without signification - 1 Cor.14:10.
dumb - Acts 8:32; 1 Cor.12:2; 2 Pet.2:16.

Meaning: α privative plus φωνή (#222). Hence, without voice; silent; dumb; speechless. Figuratively, like a lamb - Acts 8:32. Without powers of articulation like an idol - 1 Cor.12:2; 14:10; without the power of human speech - 2 Pet.2:16.

οὕτως (demonstrative adverb) 74.
οὐκ (summary negative conjunction with the indicative) 130.
ἀνοίγει (3d.per.sing.pres.act.ind.of ἀνοίγω, customary) 188.
τὸ (acc.sing.neut.of the article in agreement with στόμα) 9.
στόμα (acc.sing.neut.of στόμα, direct object of ἀνοίγει) 344.
αὐτοῦ (gen.sing.masc.of αὐτός, possession) 16.

Translation - *"Now the passage of scripture which he was reading was this: 'He was led to slaughter like a sheep, and as a lamb before him who shears him is speechless, so He never opens His mouth.'"*

Comment: δὲ is explanatory. We have a double comparison. Note the ὡς ... καὶ ὡς ... οὕτως sequence. ἐναντίον (#1780) - "before" for purposes of examination. Cf. John 19:9; Lk.23:9. He was the speechless Christ who needed no defense and refused to cast pearls before swine. The passage is a quotation from Isaiah 53:7-8, LXX.

Verse 33 - *"In his humiliation his judgment was taken away: and who shall declare his generation? for his life is taken from the earth."*

Ἐν τῇ ταπεινώσει ἡ κρίσις αὐτοῦ ἤρθη, τὴν γενεὰν αὐτοῦ τίς διηγήσεται; ὅτι αἴρεται ἀπὸ τῆς γῆς ἡ ζωὴ αὐτοῦ.

Ἐν (preposition with the locative of accompanying circumstance) 80.
τῇ (loc.sing.fem.of the article in agreement with ταπεινώσει) 9.
ταπεινώσει (loc.sing.fem.of ταπείνωσις, accompanying circumstance) 1826.

ἡ (nom.sing.fem.of the article in agreement with κρίσις) 9.

κρίσις (nom.sing.fem.of κρίσις, subject of ἤρθη) 478.

αὐτοῦ (gen.sing.masc.of αὐτός, possession) 16.

ἤρθη (3d.per.sing.aor.pass.ind.of αἴρω, constative) 350.

τὴν (acc.sing.fem.of the article in agreement with γενεὰν) 9.

γενεὰν (acc.sing.fem.of γενεά, direct object of διηγήσεται) 922.

αὐτοῦ (gen.sing.masc.of αὐτός, possession) 16.

τίς (nom.sing.masc.of τίς, interrogative pronoun, subject of διηγήσεται) 281.

διηγήσεται (3d.per.sing.fut.mid.ind.of διηγέομαι, deliberative) 2225.

ὅτι (conjunction introducing a causal clause) 211.

αἴρεται (3d.per.sing.pres.pass.ind.of αἴρω, aoristic) 350.

ἀπὸ (preposition with the ablative of separation) 70.

τῆς (abl.sing.fem.of the article in agreement with γῆς) 9.

γῆς (abl.sing.fem.of γῆ, separation) 157.

ἡ (nom.sing.fem.of the article in agreement with ζωή) 9.

ζωὴ (nom.sing.fem.of ζωή, subject of αἴρεται) 668.

αὐτοῦ (gen.sing.masc.of αὐτός, possession) 16.

Translation - "Because He lacked prestige He was denied a fair trial. Who will list His descendants since His life is taken from the earth?"

Comment: Jesus did not belong to the Jewish Establishment in Jerusalem. That is why He did not get a fair trial. He was, from the viewpoint of His prosecutors, an uneducated Galilean carpenter from Nazareth, of all places, whose preaching and behavior had alienated Him from the "smart set" in Jerusalem. ἐν ταπεινώσει is the locative of accompanying circumstance. The lowly estate of our Lord was a part of his κένόσις (Phil.2:6-8), without which there would have been no redemption. The rhetorical question does not require an answer, which is "No one." Who could trace the genealogical register of Jesus to its conclusion (#2225), since Jesus was not married and died without issue? He was the end of that line. ὅτι supports the question by introducing the causal clause. Thus Isaiah forepictures Jesus at His trial and subsequent murder. Of course the eunuch would never have heard from the religious authorities in Jerusalem, whom he had just visited, that the prophet was talking about Jesus.

In fact, it is not likely that Philip would have understood the prophecy well enough to connect it with Jesus' life, death and resurrection, had it not been for the visit of Peter and John to his Samaritan revival. For it was there that they performed for Philip the same function that Aquila and Priscilla performed for Apollos, when they explained to him the way of God "more perfectly." Apollos in Ephesus and Philip in Samaria had preached only that Jesus was the Jesus Messiah. They had not understood His redemptive function. That is why their converts, who had repented, had not also believed to the saving of their souls. But now Philip was thoroughly prepared to tell the eunuch what he needed to know in order to assure his regeneration.

Verse 34 - "And the eunuch answered Philip, and said, I pray thee, of whom speaketh the prophet this? of himself, or of some other man?"

'Αποκριθεὶς δὲ ὁ εὐνοῦχος τῷ Φιλίππῳ εἶπεν, Δέομαί σου, περὶ τίνος ὁ
προφήτης λέγει τοῦτο; περὶ ἑαυτοῦ ἢ περὶ ἑτέρου τινός;

'Αποκριθεὶς (aor.pass.part.nom.sing.masc.of ἀποκρίνομαι, adverbial,
modal, pleonastic) 318.

δὲ (continuative conjunction) 11.

ὁ (nom.sing.masc.of the article in agreement with εὐνοῦχος) 9.

εὐνοῦχος (nom.sing.masc.of εὐνοῦχος, subject of εἶπεν) 1294.

τῷ (dat.sing.masc.of the article in agreement with Φιλίππῳ) 9.

Φιλίππῳ (dat.sing.masc.of Φίλιππος, indirect object of εἶπεν) 3082.

εἶπεν (3d.per.sing.aor.act.ind.of εἶπον, constative) 155.

δέομαί (1st.per.sing.pres.mid.ind.of δέομαι, aoristic) 841.

σου (gen.sing.masc.of σύ, descriptive) 104.

περὶ (preposition with the genitive of reference) 173.

τίνος (gen.sing.masc.of τίς, interrogative pronoun, direct question) 281.

ὁ (nom.sing.masc.of the article in agreement with προφήτης) 9.

προφήτης (nom.sing.masc.of προφήτης, subject of λέγει) 119.

λέγει (3d.per.sing.pres.act.ind.of λέγω, aoristic) 66.

τοῦτο (acc.sing.neut.of οὗτος, direct object of λέγει) 93.

περὶ (preposition with the genitive of reference) 173.

ἑαυτοῦ (gen.sing.masc.of ἑαυτοῦ, reference) 288.

ἢ (disjunctive particle) 465.

περὶ (preposition with the genitive of reference) 173.

ἑτέρου (gen.sing.masc.of ἕτερος, in agreement with τινός) 605.

τινός (gen.sing.masc.of τις, indefinite pronoun, reference) 486.

*Translation - "And the eunuch said to Philip, 'I pray you, of whom is the prophet
saying this? Of himself or of somebody else?'"*

Comment: 'Αποκριθεὶς is pleonastic, unless Philip made some further
comment after his question in verse 30 which the text does not record. Even if he
did the participle is still pleonastic. We often find it with εἶπεν or ἔλεξεν. Note
ἕτερος here with a substantive. *Cf.* Rom.13:9. In Luke 14:19 it is used absolutely.

When the Holy Spirit sends a christian on a soul-winning mission, as He did in
Philip's case, He also prepares the heart of the prospect and puts the right
questions into his mouth. The eunuch could not have set a better stage for
Philip's performance. To ask who is the subject of Isaiah 53 is to ask for a sermon
about Jesus Christ, the suffering substitute for sinners and the sin-bearing Lamb
of God. If Philip had not been visited by Peter and John in Samaria and made to
understand more clearly what the gospel message was (vss.14-17) he would not
have been able to answer the eunuch's question properly. When the Holy Spirit
prepares the heart of the prospect He also prepares the heart and mind of the
preacher. The deacon was ready with the right answer.

*Verse 35 - "Then Philip opened his mouth, and began at the same scripture, and
preached unto him Jesus."*

ἀνοίξας δὲ ὁ Φίλιππος τὸ στόμα αὐτοῦ καὶ ἀρξάμενος ἀπὸ τῆς γραφῆς ταύτης εὐηγγελίσατο αὐτῷ τὸν Ἰησοῦν.

ἀνοίξας (aor.act.part.nom.sing.masc.of ἀνοίγω, adverbial, temporal) 188.

δὲ (continuative conjunction) 11.

ὁ (nom.sing.masc.of the article in agreement with Φίλιππος) 9.

Φίλιππος (nom.sing.masc.of Φίλιππος, subject of εὐηγγελίσατο) 3082.

τὸ (acc.sing.neut.of the article in agreement with στόμα) 9.

στόμα (acc.sing.neut.of στόμα, direct object of ἀνοίξας) 344.

αὐτοῦ (gen.sing.masc.of αὐτός, possession) 16.

καὶ (adjunctive conjunction joining participles) 14.

ἀρξάμενος (aor.mid.part.nom.sing.masc.ofd ἄρχω, adverbial, modal) 383.

ἀπὸ (preposition with the ablative of source) 70.

τῆς (abl.sing.fem.of the article in agreement with γραφῆς) 9.

γραφῆς (abl.sing.fem.of γράφη, source) 1389.

ταύτης (abl.sing.fem.of οὗτος, in agreement with γραφῆς) 93.

εὐηγγελίσατο (3d.per.sing.aor.mid.ind.of εὐαγγελίζομαι, ingressive) 909.

αὐτῷ (dat.sing.masc.of αὐτός, indirect object of εὐηγγελίσατο) 16.

τὸν (acc.sing.masc.of the article in agreement with Ἰησοῦν) 9.

Ἰησοῦν (acc.sing.masc.of Ἰησοῦς, direct object of εὐηγγελίσατο) 3.

Translation - *"And with that scripture as a starting point Philip began to tell him the good news about Jesus."*

Comment: ἀνοίξας (a Hebraism) and ἀρξάμενος are aorist participles. ἀνοίξας is redundant. ἀρξάμενος is modal. It reveals how Philip preached. His point of departure was the passage in Isaiah 53, which the eunuch had been reading, in which he was interested and about which he had asked. Luke has not told us the precise points that Philip made, but other New Testament passages abound which expound clearly Isaiah 53 as it relates to the person and work of Christ. The basic fact of the Christian gospel is the substitutionary death of Jesus Christ and His subsequent resurrection and ascension. This the eunuch heard, understood, accepted, and carried with him to his court in Abyssinia.

Verse 36 - *"And as they went on their way they came unto a certain water: and the eunuch said, See, here is water; what doth hinder me to be baptized?"*

ὡς δὲ ἐπορεύοντο κατὰ τὴν ὁδόν, ἦλθον ἐπί τι ὕδωρ, καί φησιν ὁ εὐνοῦχος, Ἰδοὺ ὕδωρ. τί κωλύει με βαπτισθῆναι;

ὡς (conjunction introducing a definite temporal clause, contemporaneous time) 128.

δὲ (continuative conjunction) 11.

ἐπορεύοντο (3d.per.pl.imp.mid.ind.of πορεύομαι, progressive description) 170.

κατὰ (preposition with the accusative, distributive) 98.

τὴν (acc.sing.fem.of the article in agreement with ὁδόν) 9.

ὁδόν (acc.sing.fem.of ὁδός, distributive) 199.

ἦλθον (3d.per.pl.aor.mid.ind.of ἔρχομαι, constative) 146.

ἐπί (preposition with the accusative of extent) 47.

τι (acc.sing.neut.of τις, indefinite pronoun, in agreement with ὕδωρ) 486.

ὕδωρ (acc.sing.neut.of ὕδωρ, extent) 301.

καί (continuative conjunction) 14.

φησιν (3d.per.sing.pres.act.ind.of φημί, historical) 354.

ὁ (nom.sing.masc.of the article in agreement with εὐνοῦχος) 9.

εὐνοῦχος (nom.sing.masc.of εὐνοῦχος, subject of φησιν) 1294.

Ἰδού (exclamation) 95.

ὕδωρ (nom.sing.neut.of ὕδωρ, nominative absolute) 301.

τί (nom.sing.neut.of τίς, interrogative pronoun, subject of κωλύει, direct question) 281.

κωλύει (3d.per.sing.pres.act.ind.of κωλύω, static) 1296.

με (acc.sing.masc.of ἐγώ, direct object of κωλύει) 123.

βαπτισθῆναι (aor.pass.inf.of βαπτίζω, epexegetical) 273.

Translation - "And as they were going down the road they came to some body of water, and the eunuch said, 'Look. Water! What is there to prevent me from being immersed?' "

Comment: ὡς introduces the definite temporal clause indicating contemporaneous time with ἦλθον. The indefinite pronoun τι serves to show that Luke is not interested in identifying the place or describing it in terms of pond, lake, brook, river etc. The place is not important. We may be sure that the water was deep enough to allow immersion, since βαπτισθῆναι is used. The uses of κατά with the accusative and ἐπί also with the accusative are regular. Note the historical present in φησιν, and the nominative absolute in the eunuch's excited exclamation.

The eunuch's interest had been excited by the reading of Isaiah before he met Philip. Indeed the Holy Spirit had directed him to the passage. Philip, only recently prepared to expound it properly had given an interpretation which resulted in the eunuch's salvation. Apparently he knew enough about Christianity, possibly as a result of his recent visit to Jerusalem, to know that immersion in water was appropriate for those who wished to confess faith in Jesus Christ. Now the opportunity presented itself. The Holy Spirit had it all planned. Note κωλύω (#1296) also in Acts 10:47 where the question of immersion for another Gentile convert is in view. There Peter directed his question to other Christians present. Here the eunuch directs his question to Philip in order to determine whether or not he was ready for this step. He seemed to be saying that if he had not yet done that which was prerequisite for immersion he was willing to do it.

Verse 37 - "And Philip said, if thou believest with all thine heart, thou mayest. And he answered and said, I believe that Jesus Christ is the Son of God."

εἶπε δὲ ὁ Φίλιππος, Εἰ πιστεύεις ἐξ ὅλης τῆς καρδίας, ἔξεστιν. ἀποκριθεὶς δὲ εἶπε, Πιστεύω τὸν υἱὸν τοῦ θεοῦ εἶναι τὸν Ἰησοῦν Χριστόν.

Comment: Only a few minor textual authorities include verse 37 in the original text. p45,74, Sinaiticus, A, B, C, P Φ 049,056,0142, 33?, 81, 88*, 104, 181, 326, 330, 436, 451, 614, 1241, 1505, 2127, 2412, 2492, 2495 Byz., Lect. vgww, syr91 hl, copsa bo, eth, Chrysostom, Theophlylact all omit it. It is the opinion of Aland, Black, Martini, Metzger and Wikgren that it is not a part of the original text, which opinion they express with an A degree of certitude.

"There is no reason why scribes should have omitted the material, if it had originally stood in the text. It should be noted too that τὸν᾽Ιησοῦν Χριστόν is not a Lukan expression. The formula πιστεύω. . . Χριστόν was doubtless used by the early church in baptismal ceremonies, and may have been written in the margin of a copy of Acts. Its insertion into the text seems to have been due to the feeling that Philip could not have baptized the Ethiopian without securing a confession of faith, which needed to be expressed in the narrative. Although the earliest known New Testament manuscript which contains the words dates from the sixth century (ms. E), the tradition of the Ethiopian's confession of faith in Christ was current as early as the latter part of the second century, for Irenaeus quotes part of it (*Against Heresies*, III. xii.8). Although the passage does not appear in the late medieval manuscript on which Erasmus chiefly depended for his edition (ms.2), it stands in the margin of another (ms.4), from which he inserted it into his text because he "judged that it had been omitted by the carelessness of scribes (*arbitror omissum librariorum incuria*)." (Metzger, *A Textual Commentary on the Greek New Testament*, 359, 360).

The omission need not upset the conservative theologian as there is plenty of scripture elsewhere in the New Testament to establish the fact that immersion in water as a Christian ordinance was administered only after the candidate had made the commitment of verse 37. What should concern all of us is the fact that scribes have thought it proper to *add* their own inventions to that which the Holy Spirit permitted the original authors to write. We destroy the authority of the Word of God as much when we add to it as when we take from it.

Charismatics, Mormons, the Reverend Mr. Moon, Ellen White and other cultists may or may not be disturbed when textual difficulties occur in the Greek New Testament, but they are quite willing to supplement the New Testament with alleged translations of inarticulate gibberish from an emotionally overwrought psychic, with alleged divine revelations which came from a plagarized novel, such as Joseph Smith's contribution to religious literature, with the psychic pronouncements of Ellen White who suffered a severe concussion when she was a child or from the propaganda of a Korean fanatic who suffers from delusions of grandeur.

Despite all these attempts to divert the attention of the sincere Christian from the Word of God, we have its assurance that "The law (testimony, statutes, commandment, fear, judgments) of the Lord is perfect, sure, right, pure, clean, true and righteous altogether" (Ps.19:7-9).

Verse 38 - "And he commanded the chariot to stand still: and they went down both into the water, both Philip and the eunuch, and he baptized him."

καὶ ἐκέλευσεν στῆναι τὸ ἅρμα, καὶ κατέβησαν ἀμφότεροι εἰς τὸ ὕδωρ ὅ τε Φίλιππος καὶ ὁ εὐνοῦχος, καὶ ἐβάπτισεν αὐτόν.

καὶ (continuative conjunction) 14.

ἐκέλευσεν (3d.per.sing.aor.act.ind.of κελεύω, constative) 741.

στῆναι (2d.aor.act.inf.of ἵστημι, epexegetical) 180.

τὸ (acc.sing.neut.of the article in agreement with ἅρμα) 9.

ἅρμα (acc.sing.neut.of ἅρμα, general reference) 3173.

καὶ (continuative conjunction) 14.

κατέβησαν (3d.per.pl.aor.act.ind.of καταβαίνω, constative) 324.

ἀμφότεροι (nom.pl.masc.of ἀμφότεροι, subject of κατέβησαν) 813.

εἰς (preposition with the accusative, extent) 140.

τὸ (acc.sing.neut.of the article in agreement with ὕδωρ) 9.

ὕδωρ (acc.sing.neut.of ὕδωρ, extent) 301.

ὅ (nom.sing.masc.of the article, in agreement with Φίλιππος) 9.

τε (affirmative particle) 1408.

Φίλιππος ꞌ (nom.sing.masc.of Φίλιππος, in apposition to ἀμφότεροι) 3082.

καὶ (adjunctive conjunction joining nouns) 14.

ὁ (nom.sing.masc.of the article in agreement with εὐνοῦχος) 9.

εὐνοῦχος (nom.sing.masc.of εὐνοῦχος, in apposition with ἀμφότεροι) 1294.

καὶ (continuative conjunction) 14.

ἐβάπτισεν (3d.per.sing.aor.act.ind.of βαπτίζω, constative) 273.

αὐτόν (acc.sing.masc.of αὐτός, direct object of ἐβάπτισεν, anaphoric) 16.

Translation - *"And he ordered the chariot to halt and both Philip and the eunuch went down into the water and Philip immersed him."*

Comment: Three paratactic clauses are joined here, joined by continuative καὶ. The chariot was brought to a halt; they walked down into the water; Philip immersed the eunuch. We assume that the eunuch gave the order for the car to stop, since it was his chariot. We do not need the material of verse 37 to make out the story. It can safely be inferred that since the eunuch asked the question of verse 36 there would have been no immersion if Philip had objected, or if the eunuch had not qualified for the immersion. Certainly the eunuch needed Philip's cooperation. He could not have baptized himself. Thus the fact that the car was brought to a halt indicates (a) that Philip had no objection, given the confession of the candidate, and (b) that the candidate made whatever confession was needed to satisfy the deacon that the ceremony should procede. The infinitive στῆναι explains the verb ἐκέλευσεν with τὸ ἅρμα in general reference. The dual ἀμφότεροι here means two and only two, as the context makes clear, as it should, but in Acts 19:16 it means seven people. τε emphasizes the fact that *both* Philip and the eunuch walked down the bank and into the water. Note εἰς τὸ ὕδωρ in verse 38 and ἐκ τοῦ ὕδατος in verse 39. It is εἰς not πρός and ἐκ not ἀπό. They went *into* not *near to* the water and the came *out from within* not *away from* the water. Yet the argument for baptism by immersion cannot stand on the use of the prepositions, the former with the accusative of extent and the latter with the ablative of separation. Pedobaptists can contend that they walked down into the water, where Philip sprinkled him, after which they waded out of the water. The case for immersion is based principally upon the meaning of βαπτίζω (#273). If it were not for the presence of the verb in the passage immersionists would need the text to say that the eunuch was placed "under" the water - a thought conveyed by ὑπό and the accusative. ὑπό τὸ ὕδωρ would mean that the eunuch came "up from under the water." But that is not what the text says. It need not say it since the immersionist idea is found in ἐβάπτισεν. Also Philip's body did not go "into the water" in the same sense in which the body of the eunuch did. The lower part of his body went "into" in the sense of "under" the water as did the eunuch. But the candidate's entire body went "into" the water. The baptizer need not be immersed as he immerses the baptized! There is a danger that immersionists will be so pleased with themselves because they are correct with reference to the mode of baptism that they will neglect the weightier ethical demands of the Gospel of Christ.

A thornier question is whether or not Philip considered water baptism so necessary as to identify obedience in this ordinance with the equation of salvation. There is little doubt that most of those in the early church whose repentance and faith in Christ was the result of the supernatural operation of the Holy Spirit, and not the result of social pressure or some other naturalistic cause, confessed Him openly by submitting to immersion in water, though the text does not say in every case that believers were immersed in water. Verse 37, added no doubt, by a later hand, has Philip saying that sincere faith, personal commitment and open confession are prerequisite to water baptism. However, this is not to state that those who are not baptized are thereby lost because of their not having been immersed. Philip preached Jesus unto him from Isaiah 53. To argue that he did or did not also talk to him about water baptism is to argue from silence. Paul did not tell the Philippian jailor that baptism was necessary for salvation, and this is not an argument from silence (Acts 16:31).

Another question that has bothered some who place great stress on ecclesiological authority for the ordinances, is in reference to the source of the authority by which Philip baptized the eunuch. Did the local church to which Philip belonged (presumably the church in Jerusalem) specifically authorize Philip to baptize his converts in the Samaritan revival (or elsewhere) and if so, were they baptized into Philip's church, and if so, were they later given letters of dismissal in order that, with the authority of the Jerusalem church, they might establish their own church?! Peter and John approved Philip's work in Samaria. Did this approbation extend to their recognition that Philip was empowered by the church in Jerusalem to baptize his converts and set new churches in order? On these points the scriptures are silent, but we know that Philip preached, not only in Samaritan country and in the Gaza desert, but also in Azotus and Caesarea (vs.40) and several other places. It is not likely that the Sovereign God was unduly disturbed about Philip's ecclessiology when he immersed a black Ethiopian government official, without local church authority.

This is not to say that we ought not to be concerned about ecclesiological correctitude, but it is to say that those who major on minor issues are neglecting the weightier matters of Christian doctrine and practice.

Verse 39 - "And when they were come up out of the water, the Spirit of the Lord caught away Philip, that the eunuch saw him no more; and he went on his way rejoicing."

ὅτε δὲ ἀνέβησαν ἐκ τοῦ ὕδατος, πνεῦμα κυρίου ἥρπασεν τὸν Φίλιππον, καὶ οὐκ εἶδεν αὐτὸν οὐκέτι ὁ εὐνοῦχος, ἐπορεύετο γὰρ τὴν ὁδὸν αὐτοῦ χαίρων.

ὅτε (conjunction introducing a definite temporal clause, contemporaneous time) 703.

δὲ (continuative conjunction) 11.

ἀνέβησαν (3d.per.pl.aor.act.ind.of ἀναβαίνω, culminative) 323.

ἐκ (preposition with the ablative of separation) 19.

τοῦ (abl.sing.neut.of the article in agreement with ὕδατος) 9.

ὕδατος (abl.sing.neut.of ὕδωρ, separation) 301.

πνεῦμα (nom.sing.neut.of πνεῦμα, subject of ἥρπασεν) 83.

κυρίου (gen.sing.masc.of κύριος, description) 97.

ἥρπασεν (3d.per.sing.aor.act.ind.of ἁρπάζω, constative) 920.

τὸν (acc.sing.masc.of the article in agreement with Φίλιππον) 9.

Φίλιππον (acc.sing.masc.of Φίλιππος, direct object of ἥρπασεν) 3082.

καὶ (continuative conjunction) 14.

οὐκ (summary negative conjunction with the indicative) 130.

εἶδεν (3d.per.sing.aor.act.ind.of ὁράω, constative) 144.

αὐτὸν (acc.sing.masc.of αὐτός, direct object of εἶδεν) 16.

οὐκέτι (adverb of denial) 1289.

ὁ (nom.sing.masc.of the article in agreement with εὐνοῦχος) 9.

εὐνοῦχος (nom.sing.masc.of εὐνοῦχος, subject of ἐπορεύετο) 1294.

ἐπορεύετο (3d.per.sing.imp.mid.ind.of πορεύομαι, inceptive) 170.

γὰρ (inferential conjunction) 105.

τὴν (acc.sing.fem.of the article in agreement with ὁδὸν) 9.

ὁδὸν (acc.sing.fem.of ὁδός, analogous cognate accusative) 199.

αὐτοῦ (gen.sing.masc.of αὐτός, possession) 16.

χαίρων (pres.act.part.nom.sing.masc.of χαίρω, adverbial, complementary) 182.

Translation - "And when they had come up out of the water, the Spirit of the Lord took Philip away and the eunuch never saw him again, so he resumed his journey rejoicing."

Comment: Note ὅτε with the definite temporal clause indicating contemporaneity, instead of the aorist temporal participle. ἐκ τοῦ ὕδατος in contrast to εἰς τὸ ὕδωρ in verse 38 - "out of" and "into" the water, with nothing in the prepositions to permit a translation of "into the inside of" for εἰς or "out of from within" for ἐκ. The eunuch came ἐκ τοῦ ὕδατος in a more complete sense than did Philip, for he was totally surrounded by the water, whereas Philip was in the water only perhaps waist deep. But this depends, not upon the prepositions but upon the verb ἐβάπτισεν in verse 38. The context always makes the grammar clear.

Philip had his own personal "rapture" - not into heaven, as all of the saints will experience at the second coming (1 Thess.4:17) and as Paul experienced (2 Cor.12:2), but to other fields upon earth where he could continue to preach the gospel. The eunuch, unable to find Philip, therefore (inferential γὰρ) resumed his return trip homeward (inceptive imperfect in ἐπορεύετο). The complementary participle adds a delightful touch. As he travelled along the desert road he was filled with joy. He had great cause for rejoicing. A sincere seeker had found the Light of the World. He was **SAVED!** The Holy Spirit, Who had led him to Jerusalem, where his curiosity about the Jewish religion was aroused, and had directed him to read the prophecy of Isaiah at its 53rd chapter, had also directed Philip to leave a great revival in Samaria and meet him on the deserted road. As a result the eunuch had been effectually called to salvation through the preaching of Philip and the Holy Spirit, having "breathed upon" him (John 3:8) had regenerated him and taken up a permanent abode in his body (1 Cor.6:19). As a result the fruits of the Holy Spirit (Gal.5:22,23), one of which is joy, immediately became evident.

We hear nothing further about the Ethiopian eunuch, but we assume that he became a witness for Christ in Northeast Africa.

Note the analogous cognate accusative in ἐπορεύετο . . . τὴν ὁδόν. For other examples, cf. *1 Peter 3:6; 4:2.*

Cf.#920 for a study of ἁρπάζω. There is nothing in the meaning to suggest that Philip's exit from the scene was sudden or miraculous. The Holy Spirit directed him to the next field of gospel service, just as He had directed him from Samaria, down to Gaza. We find him next up the coast at Azotus, twenty miles northeast of Gaza where he began a coastal city revival that reached Caesarea.

Verse 40 - "But Philip was found at Azotus: and passing through he preached in all the cities, till he came to Caesarea."

Φίλιππος δὲ εὑρέθη εἰς Ἄζωτον, καὶ διερχόμενος εὐηγγελίζετο τὰς πόλεις πάσας ἕως τοῦ ἐλθεῖν αὐτὸν εἰς Καισάρειαν.

Φίλιππος (nom.sing.masc.of Φίλιππος, subject of εὑρέθη and εὐηγγελίζετο) 3082.

δὲ (continuative conjunction) 11.

εὑρέθη (3d.per.sing.aor.mid.ind.of εὑρίσκω, constative) 79.

εἰς (preposition with the accusative, static use, like the locative) 140.

#3178 Ἄζωτον (acc.sing.fem.of Ἄζωτος, original static use of εἰς, like ἐν and the locative).

Azotus - Acts 8:40.

Meaning: Azotus. Also called Ashdod. One of the five chief cities of the Philistines, lying near the Mediterranean, between Ashkelon and Jamnia. Philip visited there on his preaching mission - Acts 8:40.

καὶ (continuative conjunction) 14.

διερχόμενος (pres.mid.part.nom.sing.masc.of διέρχομαι, adverbial, temporal) 1017.

εὐηγγελίζετο (3d.per.sing.imp.mid.ind.of εὐαγγελίζομαι, inceptive) 909.
τὰς (acc.pl.fem.of the article in agreement with πόλεις) 9.
πόλεις (acc.pl.fem.of πόλις, direct object of εὐηγγελίζετο) 243.
πάσας (acc.pl.fem.of πᾶς, in agreement with πόλεις) 67.
ἕως (preposition with the infinitive, time description) 71.
τοῦ (gen.sing.neut.of the article, time description) 9.
ἐλθεῖν (aor.mid.inf.gen.sing.neut., time description) 146.
αὐτὸν (acc.sing.masc.of αὐτός, general reference) 16.
εἰς (preposition with the accusative of extent) 140.

Καισάρειαν (acc.sing.fem.of Καισαρίας, extent) 1200.

Translation - "And Philip found himself in Azotus, and as he passed through he began to evangelize all the cities until he came to Caesarea."

Comment: This is the only place in the New Testament where the preposition ἕως occurs with the articular infinitive in the genitive case in a temporal sense. Philip's evangelistic ministry continued until he reached Caesarea. The middle voice in εὑρέθη indicates that Philip found himself at Azotus (Ashdod), a city up the northeast coast from Gaza about twenty miles. When any Christian, be he an Apostle or only a deacon is willing to be used by the Lord he is going to be kept busy. We do not know the circumstances that led Philip to leave Jerusalem for his visit northward into Samaria, but his ministry from that time on was characterized by the leadership of the Holy Spirit. He was ordered into the desert (vs.26). He was then ordered by the Holy Spirit to "hitchhike" a ride with the eunuch (vs.29). After his work of leading the eunuch to Christ and immersing him, the Holy Spirit "caught him away" and set him down in Ashdod, where he resumed his ministry that was not finished until he had preached the gospel in all of the cities between Ashdod and Caesarea, a distance up the northeast coast of about 55 miles. Luke has not given us the details of this series of encounters in which Philip was privileged to tell the story of the gospel of Christ. His account, which we will hear, when we get to heaven, is something to look forward to. His trip to Ashdod was a thrilling experience. He hardly knew how he got there - a manifest blessing, in view of the heat of the desert. It was almost as though he awoke to find himself in this ancient Philistine city. Note the original static use of εἰς with the accusative, like ἐν with the locative. As he passed through (present participle) he began a new series of meetings (inceptive imperfect).

The gospel has now been preached first to the Jews, at Pentecost, then to the Samaritans in Philip's revival and finally to a black Gentile, in the desert. It is time to introduce the Apostle to the gentiles.

The Conversion of Saul

(Acts 9:1-19; 22:6-16; 26:12-18)

Acts 9:1 - "And Saul, yet breathing out threatenings and slaughter against the disciples of the Lord, went unto the high priest."

'Ο δὲ Σαῦλος, ἔτι ἐμπνέων ἀπειλῆς καὶ φόνου εἰς τοὺς μαθητάς τοῦ κυρίου, προσελθὼν τῷ ἀρχιερεῖ

'Ο (nom.sing.masc.of the article in agreement with Σαῦλος) 9.

δὲ (adversative conjunction) 11.

Σαῦλος (nom.sing.masc.of Σαῦλος, subject of ᾐτήσατο) 3155.

ἔτι (temporal adverb, with the participle) 448.

#3179 ἐμπνέων (pres.act.part.nom.sing.masc.of ἐμπνέω, adverbial, complementary).

breathe out - Acts 9:1.

Meaning: A combination of ἐν (#80) and πνέω (#697). Hence, to inhale; to breathe in; to take a breath. With the genitive in Acts 9:1.

ἀπειλῆς (gen.sing.fem.of ἀπειλή, description) 3043.

καὶ (adjunctive conjunction joining nouns) 14.

φόνου (gen.sing.masc.of φόνος, description, with a verb of emotion) 1166.

εἰς (preposition with the accusative, like a dative, hostility) 140.

τοὺς (acc.pl.masc.of the article in agreement with μαθητάς) 9.

μαθητὰς (acc.pl.masc.of μαθητής, hostility) 421.

τοῦ (gen.sing.masc.of the article in agreement with κυρίου) 9.

κυρίου (gen.sing.masc.of κύριος, relationship) 97.

προσελθὼν (aor.mid.part.nom.sing.masc.of προσέρχομαι, adverbial, temporal) 336.

τῷ (loc.sing.masc.of the article in agreement with ἀρχιερεῖ) 9.

ἀρχιερεῖ (loc.sing.masc.of ἀρχιεραεύς, place) 151.

Translation - "But Saul, all the while threatening murder against the disciples of the Lord, went to the high priest, . . . "

Comment: δὲ is adversative. While Philip was preaching the glorious gospel of the grace of God in Samaria, in the desert and up the Mediterranean coast in every city, Saul had other ideas for the Christians. Note the adverb ἔτι with the participle. *Cf.* Acts 24:26; 23:15; John 19:33. Here it is temporal and indicates a sustained rage as Luke describes this passionate series of outbursts from this outraged bigot. It had been going on for some time. Indeed we first met Saul of Tarsus at the stoning of Stephen, which was some time before, as the evangelism of Philip in Chapter 8 had intervened. Robertson somewhat lamely suggests that the genitive in ἀπειλῆς and φόνου follows ἐμπνέων, like we find the genitive with verbs of sensation. He says that it is "certainly analogous" to a "verb of smelling." (*Grammar,* 507). It seems more appropriate to regard ἐμπνέων as a verb of emotion, with εἰς and the accusative like a dative "where disposition or attitude of mind is set forth" (*Ibid.,*594). If, as in this case, the attitude is hostile, the translation is "against" although εἰς does not mean "against." The hostile idea comes from the context as in Luke 12:10 - εἰς τὸν υἱὸν τοῦ ἀνθρώπου. Cf. the parallel passage in Matthew 12:32, where κατά and the genitive case is used to convey the same idea.

Saul had gone to law school under Gamaliel and he recognized the need for a warrant. He knew who could issue it and he went to the high priest.

Verse 2 - "And desired of him letters to Damascus to the synagogues, that if he found any of this way, whether they were men or women, he might bring them bound unto Jerusalem."

ᾐτήσατο παρ' αὐτοῦ ἐπιστολὰς εἰς Δαμασκὸν πρὸς τὰς συναγωγάς, ὅπως ἐάν τινας εὕρῃ τῆς ὁδοῦ ὄντας, ἄνδρας τε καὶ υθναῖκας, δεδεμένους ἀγάγῃ εἰς Ἰερουσαλήμ.

ᾐτήσατο (3d.per.sing.aor.mid.ind.of αἰτέω, constative) 537.
παρ' (preposition with the ablative, source) 154.
αὐτοῦ (abl.sing.masc.of αὐτός, source) 16.

#3180 ἐπιστολὰς (acc.pl.fem.of ἐπιστολή, direct object of ᾐτήσατο).

epistle - Acts 15:30; 23:33; Rom.16:22; 1 Cor.5:9; 2 Cor.3:1,2,3; 7:8; Col.4:16; 1 Thess.5:27; 2 Thess.2:15; 3:14,17; 2 Pet.3:1,16.
letter - Acts 9:2; 22:5; 23:25; 1 Cor.16:3; 2 Cor.7:8; 10:9,10,11;1 2 Thess.2:2.

Meaning: A letter; written communication. A subpoena from the high priest in Jerusalem to synagogue officials in Damascus authorizing Saul to arrest Christians and bring them to Jerusalem - Acts 9:2; 22:5. Claudius Lysias to Felix, *in re* Paul - Acts 23:25,33; a letter of instruction to the church at Antioch - Acts 15:30; an unknown letter, Paul to the Corinthians, written before First Corinthians - 1 Cor.5:9; the first and/or second recorded letter(s) of Paul to Corinth - 1 Cor.7:8; 2 Cor.7:8; 10:9,10,11; Paul to the Roman church - Rom.16:22; to the Colossians - Col.4:16; to the Thessalonians (1st letter) - 1 Thess.5:27; 2 Thess.2:15; (2d.letter) - 2 Thess.3:14. The second epistle of Peter to the dispersed Christian Jews - 2 Pet.3:1; a letter of recommendation, Corinth to Paul - 1 Cor.16:3; a forgery, purporting to be Paul to the Thessalonians - 2 Thess.2:2. All of Paul's letters generally - 2 Thess.3:17; 2 Pet.3:16; letters of commendation *in re* Paul to Corinth - 2 Cor.3:1. Metaphorically, the Corinthian Christians in their Christian life and witness are letters of commendation - 2 Cor.3:2,3.

εἰς (preposition with the accusative, original static use, like a locative) 140.

#3181 Δαμασκὸν (acc.sing.fem.of Δαμασκός, place where).

Damascus - Acts 9:2,3,8,10,19,22,27; 22:5,6,10,11; 26:12,20; 2 Cor.11:32; Gal.1:17.

Meaning: Cf. Gen.14:15. An ancient flourishing city in Syria, at the eastern base of Antilibanus. It has always had a large Jewish population. Paul was taken there after his conversion - Acts 9:2,3,8,10,19,22,27; 22:5,6,10,11; 26:12,20. He later returned there in his early ministry - Gal.1:17. Later ministry - 2 Cor.11:32.

πρός (preposition with the accusative of extent in a context of communication) 197.

τάς (acc.pl.fem.of the article in agreement with συναγωγάς) 9.

συναγωγάς (acc.pl.fem.of συναγωγή, extent) 404.

ὅπως (relative indefinite adverb with the subjunctive in a purpose clause) 177.

ἐάν (conditional particle in a third-class condition) 363.

τινας (acc.pl.masc.of τις, direct object of εὕρῃ) 486.

εὕρῃ (3d.per.sing.aor.act.subj.of εὑρίσκω, third-class condition) 79.

τῆς (gen.sing.fem.of the article in agreement with ὁδοῦ) 9.

ὁδοῦ (gen.sing.fem.of ὁδός, predicate genitive) 199.

ὄντας (pres.part.acc.pl.masc.of εἰμί, adjectival, in agreement with τινας) 86.

ἄνδρας (acc.pl.masc.of ἀνήρ, double accusative, object of εὕρῃ) 63.

τε (correlative particle, with καί) 1408.

καί (adjunctive conjunction joining nouns) 14.

γυναῖκας (acc.pl.fem.of γυνή, double accusative, object of εὕρῃ) 103.

δεδεμένους (perf.pass.part.acc.pl.masc.of δέω, adverbial, complementary) 998.

ἀγάγῃ (3d.per.sing.2d.aor.act.subj.of ἄγω, purpose) 876.

εἰς (preposition with the accusative of extent) 140.

Ἰερουσαλήμ (acc.sing.masc.of Ἰεροσολύμων, extent) 141.

Translation - ". . . he requested warrants from him to the synagogues in Damascus in order that if he found anyone of the way, whether they be men or women, he could bring them in chains to Jerusalem."

Comment: παρά with the ablative of source is used only with persons. *Cf.* Mk.8:11; 12:2; John 1:40; 8:38; Acts 10:22; John 6:45; 16:27; Rom.11:27. This letter was of a special type (used in this sense only here and in Acts 22:5). It was a court order, or authorization to arrest persons not specifically named. We call it a "John Doe Warrant." In modern law a John Doe warrant has until recently been considered illegal, since a legal warrant must specify individuals or object to be apprehended. The indefinite pronoun τινας and the third-class condition with ἐάν and the subjunctive εὕρῃ make it clear that neither Saul nor the high priest could have had any specific person in mind. Hence, Saul, a lawyer, trained in Jewish jurisprudence and the high priest were, by modern standards of justice acting without legal warrant. The letter was directed πρός τάς συναγωγάς - "to the synagogues" εἰς Δαμασκόν - "in Damascus" where we have the original static use of εἰς with the accusative like ἐν with the locative. The purpose clause with ὅπως and the subjunctive ἀγάγῃ. The third-class condition indicates doubt that any such person could be found, but no doubt about what Saul would do if he did find a Christian. τε καί normally means "both and" but here "either or." τῆς ὁδοῦ is a predicate genitive. The participle ὄντας is adjectival, modifying τινας. The participle δεδεμένους is adverbial. Arrested for being committed to "the Way" they were to be returned to Jerusalem in chains. Thus Saul's fanatical theo/Christophobia, with its bigoted intolerance manifested itself. This is in line with verse 1 which describes him as muttering to himself his murderous hatred and threatening to kill Christians. *Cf.* Heb.11:37; Phil.3:6; 1 Tim.1:13,16. But the sovereign Christ had other plans for Saul.

Verse 3 - "And as he journeyed, he came near Damascus: and suddenly there shined round about him a light from heaven."

ἐν δὲ τῷ πορεύεσθαι ἐγένετο αὐτὸν ἐγγίζειν τῇ Δαμασκῷ, ἐξαίφνης τε αὐτὸν περιήστραφεν φῶς ἐκ τοῦ οὐρανοῦ,

ἐν (preposition with the locative of time point) 80.

δὲ (adversative conjunction) 11.

τῷ (loc.sing.neut.of the article, time point in an articular infinitive) 9.

πορεύεσθαι (pres.mid.infinitive of πορεύομαι, articular infinitive, time point) 170.

ἐγένετο (3d.per.sing.aor.ind.of γίνομαι, constative) 113.

αὐτὸν (acc.sing.masc.of αὐτός, general reference) 16.

ἐγγίζειν (pres.act.inf.of ἐγγίζω, noun use, subject of ἐγένετο) 252.

τῇ (loc.sing.fem.of the article in agreement with Δαμασκῷ) 9.

Δαμασκῷ (loc.sing.fem.of Δαμασκός, place where) 3181.

ἐξαίφνης (adverbial) 1879.

τε (affirmative particle) 1408.

αὐτὸν (acc.sing.masc.of αὐτός, direct object of περιήστραφεν) 16.

#3182 περιήστραφεν (3d.per.sing.aor.act.ind.of περιαστράπτω, ingressive).

shine round about - Acts 9:3; 22:6.

Meaning: A combination of περί (#173) and ἀστράπτω (#2617). Hence, to shine around. To surround one with light. With reference to Paul's conversion experience on the Damascus road - Acts 9:3; in his account of it - Acts 22:6.

φῶς (nom.sing.neut.of φῶς, subject of περιήστραφεν) 379.

ἐκ (preposition with the ablative of source) 19.

τοῦ (abl.sing.masc.of the article in agreement with οὐρανοῦ) 9.

οὐρανοῦ (abl.sing.masc.of οὐρανός, source) 254.

Translation - "But when on the trip he approached Damascus, suddenly a light out of heaven began to shine around him."

Comment: δὲ here is one of the most significant adversatives in the Scripture. It served to turn an intolerant religious bigot into the greatest evangelist for Christ of the first century. ἐν introduces a locative of time point double articular infinitive. Note that the article τῷ occurs only once, but it serves both infinitives. The light from heaven surrounded Saul while he was on his way to Damascus and, more specifically, at the point on his journey when he drew near the city. ἐγγίζειν serves as the subject of ἐγένετο. The flashing light came suddenly. It came out of heaven and surrounded Saul. The coming of our Lord to earth again will also be sudden (Mk.13:36). God's power was abundantly displayed, but His abundant grace was also manifested. Christ could have smitten him into blindness at the beginning of the journey in which case he probably would have returned to Jerusalem. But God wanted this blind Pharisee in Damascus where He was prepared to provide the Christian who would lead him to Christ (vss. 10-18). If the Lord had not waited until Saul came near the end of the trip, the blind man would have had a long way to stumble along in the dark.

Verse 4 - "And he fell to the earth, and heard a voice saying unto him, Saul, Saul, why persecutest thou me?"

καὶ πέσων ἐπὶ τὴν γῆν ἤκουσεν φωνὴν λέγουσαν αὐτῷ, Σαοὺλ Σαούλ, τί με διώκεις;

καὶ (continuative conjunction) 14.
πέσων (aor.act.part.nom.sing.masc.of πίπτω, adverbial, temporal) 187.
ἐπὶ (preposition with the accusative of extent) 47.
τὴν (acc.sing.fem.of the article in agreement with γῆν) 9.
γῆν (acc.sing.fem.of γῆ, extent) 157.
ἤκουσεν (3d.per.sing.aor.act.ind.of ἀκούω, constative) 148.
φωνὴν (acc.sing.fem.of φωνή, direct object of ἤκουσεν) 222.
λέγουσαν (pres.act.part.acc.sing.fem.of λέγω, adjectival, restrictive) 66.
αὐτῷ (dat.sing.masc.of αὐτός, indirect object of λέγουσαν) 16.
Σαοὺλ (voc.sing.masc.of Σαῦλος, address) 3155.
Σαοὺλ (voc.sing.masc.of Σαῦλος, address) 3155.
τί (acc.sing.neut.of τίς, cause) 281.
με (acc.sing.masc.of ἐγώ, direct object of διώκεις) 123.
διώκεις (2d.per.sing.pres.act.ind.of διώκω, aoristic, direct question) 434.

Translation - "And he fell to the ground and heard a voice saying to him, 'Saul, Saul, why are you persecuting me?' "

Comment: ἤκουσεν, followed by the accusative of extent in φωνὴν indicates more than that Saul heard the sound of our Lord's voice. He also heard it intellectually, *i.e.* he understood what Jesus said. *Cf.* comment on Acts 22:7,9; 26:14. Everyone in the party heard the sound of the voice. Saul's companions did not understand what was said, but Saul did. The precise distinction between ἀκούω with the genitive and ἀκούω with the accusative is thus illustrated. Only those who are ignorant of this fine point in Greek grammar will contend for a contradiction in the stories.

Note τί without διά in the causal construction.

Christ, in resurrection glory is so intimately identified with the saints on earth through the miracle of regeneration and the baptism of the Holy Spirit, which results in the mystic incorporation of the believer into His body (John 17:21), that persecution of the saints on earth is looked upon by Him as persecution of Jesus Christ Himself (John 17:14,21; 1 Cor.12:13). The unsaved world with its arrogant and cynical attack upon the Christian is really directing his hatred at the resurrected Head of the body, whose members are still upon the earth.

Verse 5 - "And he said, Who art thou, Lord? And the Lord said, I am Jesus whom thou persecutest: it is hard for thee to kick against the pricks."

εἶπεν δέ, Τίς εἶ, κύριε; ὁ δὲ Ἐγώ εἰμι Ἰησοῦς ὅν σὺ διώκεις.

εἶπεν (3d.per.sing.aor.act.ind.of εἶπον, constative) 155.

δέ (continuative conjunction) 11.

Τίς (nom.sing.masc.of τίς, predicate nominative, in direct question) 281.

εἶ (2d.per.sing.pres.ind.of εἰμί, aoristic, direct question) 86.

κύριε (voc.sing.masc.of κύριος, address) 97.

ὁ (nom.sing.masc.of the article, subject of εἶπεν understood) 9.

δέ (continuative conjunction) 11.

Ἐγώ (nom.sing.masc.of ἐγώ, subject of εἰμί) 123.

εἰμι (1st.per.sing.pres.ind.of εἰμί, aoristic) 86.

Ἰησοῦς (nom.sing.masc.of Ἰησοῦς, predicate nominative) 3.

ὅν (acc.sing.masc.of ὅς, relative pronoun, direct object of διώκεις) 65.

σὺ (nom.sing.masc.of σύ, subject of διώκεις) 104.

διώκεις (2d.per.sing.pres.act.ind.of διώκω, customary) 434.

Translation - "And he said, 'Who are you, Sir?' And He said, 'I Am, Jesus, whom you persecute.' "

Comment: The absence of the verb εἶπεν in Jesus' reply heightens the dramatic impact. "Who, Sir?" And He — "I Am, Jesus, whom you persecute" - as a policy. Note the customary present. We can translate "Whom you are always persecuting" or "Whom you persecute from time to time." Thus Jesus introduced Himself to Saul as He did to Moses (Ex.3:14). Thus we have another proof that the Jesus of the New Testament record is the I AM of the Bush on Fire Who gave the law to Moses. Saul, a trained lawyer, a Pharisee, who was thoroughly acquainted with Jewish history felt the tremendous impact of the encounter. The light from heaven flashed about the prostrate form of this Jewish lawyer as once the Shekinah from the bush had attracted Moses, the first lawgiver. Then the introduction. Ἐγώ εἰμι. That was the name of the God of Abraham, Isaac and Jacob (Ex.3:14). *Cf.* comment on John 8:58. Any orthodox Jew had great reverence for the Great I AM. Now He is identified with Jesus of Nazareth and also identified as the One Whom Saul was pursuing to the death. It is no wonder that this proud Pharisee was stricken blind! So Stephen had been correct in his speech that had resulted in his death? So the Christians, of whom there were now thousands in Jerusalem were in the proper Judeo tradition! So Saul of Tarsus had been guilty of fighting against the God of his fathers!

The earliest manuscripts omit the last sentence of verse 5 and the first portion of verse 6.

Verse 6 - "And he trembling and astonished, said, Lord, What wilt thou have me to do? And the Lord said unto him, Arise, and go into the city, and it shall be told thee what thou must do."

ἀλλὰ ἀνάστηθι καὶ εἴσελθε εἰς τὴν πόλιν, καὶ λαληθήσεταί σοι ὅ τί σε δεῖ ποιεῖν.

ἀλλά (adversative conjunction) 342.

ἀνάστηθι (2d.per.sing.aor.act.impv.of ἀνίστημι, command) 789.

καί (adjunctive conjunction joining verbs) 14.

εἴσελθε (2d.per.sing.aor.mid.impv.of εἰσέρχομαι, command) 234.

εἰς (preposition with the accusative of extent) 140.

τήν (acc.sing.fem.of the article in agreement with πόλιν) 9.

πόλιν (acc.sing.fem.of πόλις, extent) 243.

καί (continuative conjunction) 14.

λαληθήσεταί (3d.per.sing.fut.pass.ind.of λαλέω, predictive) 815.

σοι (dat.sing.masc.of σύ, indirect object of λαληθήσεταί) 104.

ὅ (acc.sing.neut.of ὅς, attracted to τί) 65.

τί (acc.sing.neut.of the interrogative pronoun, direct object of λαληθήσεταί, in indirect question) 281.

σε (acc.sing.masc.of σύ, general reference) 104.

δεῖ (3d.per.sing.pres.ind.impersonal, of δεῖ) 1207.

ποιεῖν (pres.act.inf.of ποιέω, epexegetical) 127.

Translation - "*But stand up and go into the city and that which you must do will be told to you.*"

Comment: Metzger offers the following explanation *in re* the deleted material:

"After διώκεις (and omitting ἀλλά of ver.6) the Textus Receptus adds σκληρόν σοι πρὸς κέντρα λακτίζειν. (6) τρέμων τε καὶ θαμβῶν εἶπε, Κύριε, τί με θέλεις ποιῆσαι; καὶ ὁ κύριος πρὸς αὐτόν, which is rendered in the AV as follows: 'it is hard for thee to kick against the pricks. (6) And he trembling and astonished said, Lord, what wilt thou have me to do? And the Lord said unto him." So far as is known, no Greek witness reads these words at this place; they have been taken from 26.14 and 22.10, and are found here in codices of the Vulgate, with which ith,p syrh with * copG67 substantially agree (all except the Vulgate add after θαμβῶν the words ἐπὶ τῷ γεγονότι αὐτῷ, taken from 3.10). The spurious passage came into the Textus Receptus when Erasmus translated it from the Latin Vulgate into Greek and inserted it in his first edition of the Greek New Testament (Basel, 1516)." (Metzger, *A Textual Commentary on the Greek New Testament*, 362).

The Great Ἐγώ Εἰμι is now giving the orders and Saul of Tarsus, soon to become Paul the Apostle to the Gentiles is obedient. *Cf.* τίς in indirect questions in Mt.6:25; Lk.9:46; John 2:25; Acts 19:32.

Just as the Holy Spirit had directed Philip to go down to the Gaza desert, where he would find a man whose heart was being prepared to receive the gospel message, so now the Lord directs Saul, once proud and committed to a collision course with Almighty God, but now blind, humble and repentant, to go into Damascus where He has prepared the preacher. God can either send the preacher to the prospective convert or He can send the prospective convert to the preacher.

Verse 7 - "*And the men which journeyed with him stood speechless, hearing a voice, but seeing no man."*

οἱ δὲ ἄνδρες οἱ συνοδεύοντες αὐτῷ εἰστήκεισαν ἐνεοί, ἀκούοντες μὲν τῆς φωνῆς μηδένα δὲ θεωροῦντες.

οἱ (nom.pl.masc.of the article in agreement with ἄνδρες) 9.
δὲ (continuative conjunction) 11.
ἄνδρες (nom.pl.masc.of ἀνήρ, subject of εἰστήκεισαν) 63.
οἱ (nom.pl.masc.of the article in agreement with συνοδεύοντες) 9.

#3183 συνοδεύοντες (pres.act.part.nom.pl.masc.of συνοδεύω, substantival, in apposition with ἄνδρες).

journey with - Acts 9:7.

Meaning: A combination of σύν (#1542) and ὁδεύω - "to travel." Hence, one who travels with - fellow traveller. With reference to those who accompanied Saul enroute to Damascus - Acts 9:7.

αὐτῷ (instrumental sing.masc.of αὐτός, association, after σύν in composition) 16.
εἰστήκεισαν (3d.per.pl.pluperfect act.ind.of ἵστημι, consummative) 180.

#3184 ἐνεοί (nom.pl.masc.of ἐννεός, predicate adjective).

speechless - Acts 9:7.

Meaning: more correctly ἐνεός equals ἄνεως, from ἄω, αὔω, hence, without sound; mute; speechless; unable to speak; stricken dumb. With reference to Saul's travelling companions - Acts 9:7.

ἀκούοντες (pres.act.part.nom.pl.masc.of ἀκούω, adverbial, concessive) 148.
μὲν (particle of affirmation) 300.
τῆς (gen.sing.fem.of the article in agreement with φωνῆς) 9.
φωνῆς (gen.sing.fem.of φωνή, description) 222.
μηδένα (acc.sing.masc.of μηδείς, direct object of θεωροῦντες) 713.
δὲ (adversative conjunction) 11.
θεωροῦντες (pres.act.part.nom.pl.masc.of θεωρέω, adverbial, complementary) 1667.

Translation - "And the men who were travelling with him had stood speechless. Although they heard the voice yet they saw nobody."

Comment: Note the pluperfect in εἰστήκεισαν. When the brilliant flashing light first appeared from heaven Saul's companions had stood still, frightened into silence. The participle ἀκούοντες is concessive; θεωροῦντες is complementary. φωνῆς after a verb of sensation is descriptive. The genitive after a verb of hearing means this and no other. The accusative after a verb of hearing means this and no more. They heard the sound of the voice of the Lord. That was all. They did not understand what He said, although Saul did. In Acts 22:9 ἀκούω is followed by the accusative of extent, thus indicating that what was said was heard and also understood. There is no contradiction between the account in Acts 9 and those of Acts 22 and Acts 26. Saul's companions saw nothing. This verse guards against the canard that Saul was the victim of a seizure of some sort - possibly epilepsy or a stroke brought on by his rage against the Christians, and that all that he thought he saw and heard was subjective. Such an explanation does not account for the experiences of Saul's companions.

Verse 8 - "And Saul arose from the earth; and when his eyes were opened, he saw no man: but they led him by the hand, and brought him into Damascus."

ἠγέρθη δὲ Σαῦλος ἀπὸ τῆς γῆς, ἀνεῳγμένων δὲ τῶν ὀφθαλμῶν αὐτοῦ οὐδὲν ἔβλεπεν. χειραγωγοῦντες δὲ αὐτὸν εἰσήγαγον εἰς Δαμασκόν.

ἠγέρθη (3d.per.sing.aor.pass.ind.of ἐγείρω, culminative) 125.
δὲ (continuative conjunction) 11.
Σαῦλος (nom.sing.masc.of Σαῦλος, subject of ἠγέρθη and ἔβλεπεν) 3155.
ἀπὸ (preposition with the ablative of separation) 70.
τῆς (abl.sing.fem.of the article in agreement with γῆς) 9.
γῆς (abl.sing.fem.of γῆ, separation) 157.
ἀνεῳγμένων (perf.pass.part.gen.pl.masc.of ἀνοίγω , genitive absolute, concessive) 188.
δὲ (adversative conjunction) 11.
τῶν (gen.pl.masc.of the article in agreement with ὀφθαλμῶν) 9.
ὀφθαλμῶν (gen.pl.masc.of ὀφθαλμός, genitive absolute) 501.
αὐτοῦ (gen.sing.masc.of αὐτός, possession) 16.
οὐδὲν (acc.sing.neut.of οὐδείς, direct object of ἔβλεπεν) 446.
ἔβλεπεν (3d.per.sing.imp.act.ind.of βλέπω, progressive description) 499.

#3185 χειραγωγοῦντες (pres.act.part.nom.pl.masc.of χειραγωγέω, adverbial, modal).

lead by the hand - Acts 9:8; 22:11.

Meaning: A combination of χείρ (#308) and ἄγω (#876). Hence, to lead by the hand. As a modal participle - Acts 9:8; as a passive participle followed by ὑπό with the ablative - Acts 22:11.

δὲ (continuative conjunction) 11.
αὐτὸν (acc.sing.masc.of αὐτός, direct object of εἰσήγαγον) 16.
εἰσήγαγον (3d.per.pl.2d.aor.act.ind.of εἰσάγω, ingressive) 1897.
εἰς (preposition with the accusative of extent, repeated after εἰς in composition) 140.
Δαμασκόν (acc.sing.fem.of Δαμασκός, extent) 3181.

Translation - "And Saul was picked up from the ground, and although he opened his eyes, he saw nothing. And leading him by the hand they escorted him into Damascus."

Comment: Some one of Saul's companions, although frightened speechless, was still capable of action. He picked him up only to find that Saul was blind. There is no explanation for his blindness - possibly the brightness of the light, which only Saul saw. (Exodus 33:20). In any case his companions took him by the hand and began (ingressive aorist) to escort him into the city which was not far away, where he remained for three days, with sight, food or drink, as we learn in

Verse 9 - "And he was three days without sight, and neither did eat nor drink."

καὶ ἦν ἡμέρας τρεῖς μὴ βλέπων, καὶ οὐκ ἔφαγεν οὐδὲ ἔπιεν.

καὶ (continuative conjunction) 14.
ἦν (3d.per.sing.imp.ind.of εἰμί, progressive description) 86.
ἡμέρας (acc.pl.fem.of ἡμέρα, time extent) 135.
τρεῖς (numeral) 1010.
μὴ (negative qualified conjunction with the participle) 87.
βλέπων (pres.act.part.nom.sing.masc.of βλέπω, imperfect periphrastic) 499.
καὶ (emphatic conjunction) 14.
οὐκ (summary negative conjunction with the indicative) 130.
ἔφαγεν (3d.per.sing.aor.act.ind.of ἐσθίω, constative) 610.
οὐδὲ (disjunctive particle) 452.
ἔπιεν (3d.per.sing.aor.act.ind.of πίνω, constative) 611.

Translation - "And for three days he was blind. In fact he neither ate nor drank."

Comment: καί is first continuative, then either emphatic ("in fact") or ascensive ("even"). The imperfect periphrastic ἦν . . . βλέπων describes his blindness for a period of three days. Note μή with the participle βλέπων. Homer always used οὐ with the participle except in Odyssey, IV, 684, where we have μὴ μνηστεύσαν-τες. In Attic Greek μή gradually replaced οὐ with the participle.

Saul, blinded and humbled by his encounter with the great Ἐγώ Εἰμι, Whom he was pursuing with murder on his mind, neither ate nor drank during those three days. Of course he could not kill the resurrected and ascended Lord (Rom.6:9). But he had been making every effort. None of the stupidity and wickedness of his past policy of persecution was lost upon this sophisticated Jewish scholar of the law. When we get to heaven it will be interesting to talk with Paul about his thoughts during those three days when, with no desire to eat or even drink, he groped about his quarters, awaiting the good pleasure of His Lord, to Whom he was now totally willing to surrender.

The Lord's servant who was to lead Saul to Christ is now introduced into the story, in

Verse 10 - "And there was a certain disciple at Damascus, named Ananias; and to him said the Lord in a vision, Ananias, And he said, Behold I am here, Lord."

Ἦν δέ τις μαθητὴς ἐν Δαμασκῷ ὀνόματι Ἀνανίας, καὶ εἶπεν πρὸς αὐτὸν ἐν ὁράματι ὁ κύριος, Ἀνανία. ὁ δὲ εἶπεν, Ἰδοὺ ἐγώ, κύριε.

Ἦν (3d.per.sing.imp.ind.of εἰμί, progressive description) 86.
δέ (explanatory conjunction) 11.

τις (nom.sing.masc.of τις, indefinite pronoun, in agreement with μαθητὴς) 486.

μαθητὴς (nom.sing.masc.of μαθητής, subject of ἦν) 421.

ἐν (preposition with the locative of place) 80.

Δαμασκῷ (loc.sing.fem.of Δαμασκός, place) 3181.

ὀνόματι (dat.sing.neut.of ὄνομα, possession) 108.

#3186 Ἀνανίας (nom.sing.masc.of Ἀνανίας, predicate nominative).

Ananias - Acts 9:10,10,12,13,17; 22:12.

Meaning: A christian of Damascus who first visited Saul - Acts 9:10,10,12,13,17; 22:12. Not to be confused with #3049 or the man of Acts 23:2; 24:1 (#3592).

καὶ (continuative conjunction) 14.

εἶπεν (3d.per.sing.aor.act.ind.of εἶπον, constative) 155.

πρὸς (preposition with the accusative of extent, after a verb of speaking) 197.

αὐτὸν (acc.sing.masc.of αὐτός, extent, after a verb of speaking) 16.

ἐν (preposition with the locative, instrumental use) 80.

ὁράματι (loc.sing.neut.of ὅραμα, instrumental use) 1228.

ὁ (nom.sing.masc.of the article in agreement with κύριος) 9.

κύριος (nom.sing.masc.of κύριος, subject of εἶπεν) 97.

Ἀνανία (voc.sing.masc.of Ἀνανίας, address) 3186.

ὁ (nom.sing.masc.of the article, subject of εἶπεν) 9.

δὲ (continuative conjunction) 11.

εἶπεν (3d.per.sing.aor.act.ind.of εἶπον, constative) 155.

Ἰδοὺ (exclamation) 95.

ἐγώ (nom.sing.masc.of ἐγώ, nominative absolute) 123.

κύριε (voc.sing.masc.of κύριος, address) 97.

Translation - "*Now there was a certain disciple in Damascus named Ananias; and the Lord said to him in a dream, 'Ananias!' And he said, 'Present, Lord!'* "

Comment: δὲ is explanatory as Luke moves the narrative along. We have a blind, hungry, thirsty and distressed former bigot who needs help. He has been granted repentance and he is in sore need of faith which will give direction to his life - a life that, three days before was set on a course, the wisdom of which was for him beyond all doubt. Now he has come to understand that the Jesus Whom he was determined to destroy is none other than the Ἐγώ Εἰμι of Exodus 3:14, the God of Abraham, Isaac and Jacob.

It is time to introduce a new character into the story. Ananias dared not answer the Lord with Ἐγώ εἰμι, since that is the high, holy and exclusive designation for Almighty God. Ananias replied with Ἰδοὺ ἐγώ, κύριε. Goodspeed has, "Yes, Lord" and Montgomery has "I am here." Either of these, or mine, will serve to indicate the ready response of this faithful disciple.

Robertson insists that when we view ἐν historically we must conclude that it is used only with the locative case in the New Testament, although he concedes that in some cases it looks like an instrumental. There is a long list of which ἐν ὁράματι is representative. *Cf.* also Rev.17:16; 1 Cor.3:13; Mt.3:11; 5:13; 7:2, and even Luke 22:49, with reference to which Robertson says, "But even so one must observe that all the N.T. examples of ἐν can be explained from the point of view of the locative. The possibility of this point of view is the reason why ἐν was so used in the beginning. I pass by examples like βαπτίζω ἐν ὕδατι, βαπτίσει ἐν πνεύματι ἁγίῳ καὶ πυρί (Mt.3:11) as probably not being instances of the instrumental usage at all. But there are real instances enough. Take Lu.22:49 εἰ πατάξομεν ἐν μαχαίρῃ; Here the smiting can be regarded as located in the sword." (Robertson, *Grammar*, 590). In Acts 9:10 ἐν ὁράματι can be regarded as a locative of time point and translated "during a dream." However the grammarians may argue about it, the concept is clear enough. It was during and by means of a dream that Ananias got his orders from the Lord to visit Saul.

The story reveals, as did the story of Philip and the eunuch, how God in glory, Who knows the events of earth and manipulates them in order to bring about a fulfillment of His purpose, directs the course of history. (Eph.1:11). If the normal course of events, dictated by cause and result relations, in obedience to natural law, suffice, God need not intervene. He is still the Doer of it, since in creation He ordained the workings of the natural order. When special divine action is needed it is available. The strongest evidence for the sovereignty of God is revealed in these stories. Having brought Saul of Tarsus down in defeat, God now arranges to lift him up.

Verse 11 - "And the Lord said unto him, Arise, and go into the street which is called Straight, and enquire in the house of Judas for one called Saul, of Tarsus: for, behold he prayeth."

ὁ δὲ κύριος πρὸς αὐτόν, Ἀναστὰς πορεύθητι ἐπὶ τὴν ῥύμην τὴν καλουμένην Εὐθεῖαν καὶ ζήτησον ἐν οἰκίᾳ Ἰούδα Σαῦλον ὀνόματι Ταρσέα; ἰδοὺ γὰρ προσεύχεται,

ὁ (nom.sing.masc.of the article in agreement with κύριος) 9.
δὲ (continuative conjunction) 11.
κύριος (nom.sing.masc.of κύριος, subject of εἶπεν understood) 97.
πρὸς (preposition with the accusative of extent, after a verb of speaking) 197.
αὐτόν (acc.sing.masc.of αὐτός, extent after a verb of speaking) 16.
Ἀναστὰς (aor.act.part.nom.sing.masc.of ἀνίστημι, verbal, temporal) 789.
πορεύθητι (2d.per.sing.aor.mid.impv.of πορεύομαι, command) 170.
ἐπὶ (preposition with the accusative of extent) 47.
τὴν (acc.sing.fem.of the article in agreement with ῥύμην) 9.
ῥύμην (acc.sing.fem.of ῥύμη, extent) 562.
τὴν (acc.sing.fem.of the article in agreement with καλουμένην) 9.
καλουμένην (pres.pass.part.acc.sing.fem.of καλέω, adjectival, restrictive, in agreement with ῥύμην) 107.
Εὐθεῖαν (acc.sing.fem.of εὐθύς, appellation, in agreement with ῥύμην) 258.
καὶ (adjunctive conjunction joining verbs) 14.
ζήτησον (2d.per.sing.aor.act.impv.of ζητέω, command) 207.
ἐν (preposition with the locative of place) 80.
οἰκίᾳ (loc.sing.fem.of οἰκία, place where) 186.

#3187 Ἰούδα (gen.sing.masc.indeclin., possession).

Judas - Acts 9:11.

Meaning: The resident in Damascus in whose house on Straight Street Ananias found Saul of Tarsus - Acts 9:11.

Σαῦλον (acc.sing.masc.of Σαῦλος, direct object of ζήτησον) 3155.
ὀνόματι (dat.sing.neut.of ὄνομα, possession) 108.

#3188 Ταρσέα (gen.sing.masc.of Ταρσεύς, local description).

Tarsus - Acts 9:11; 21:39.

Meaning: ". . . a maritime city, the capital of Cilicia during the Roman period, . . . situated on the river Cydnus, which divided it into two parts (hence the plural Ταρσοί). It was not only large and populous, but also renowned for its Greek learning and its numerous schools of philosophers. . . . Moreover it was a free city . . . and exempt alike from the jurisdiction of a Roman governor, and the maintenance of a Roman garrison, although it was not a Roman 'colony.' It had received its freedom from Anthony . . . on the condition that it might retain its own magistrates and laws, but should acknowledge the Roman sovereignty and furnish auxiliaries in time of war. . . It was the birthplace of the apostle Paul." (Thayer, 615). This word (#3198) occurs in Acts 9:30; 11:25; 22:3. Ταρσεύς (#3188) means one belonging to Tarsus; one who lives in Tarsus. - Acts 9:11; 21:39.

ἰδού (exclamation) 95.
γὰρ (causal conjunction) 105.
προσεύχεται (3d.per.sing.pres.mid.ind.of προσεύχομαι, progressive) 544.

Translation - "And the Lord (said) to him, 'Get up and go to Straight Street and, in the house of Judas, look for a man named Saul of Tarsus, because he is praying.' "

Comment: We must supply εἶπεν in the first clause. The directions are specific. The street in question is called Straight. The house on Straight Street is that of Judas. The man whom Ananias is to find is named Saul. He is a citizen of Tarsus. Ananias was told that he would find Saul in prayer. Thus does God maneuver in human history. The causal γὰρ shows that God's instructions to Ananias are contingent upon the circumstances surrounding Saul of Tarsus. The prayers of Saul were the result of all that had happened to him within the past three days. There is no rational way to avoid the conclusion that a sovereign God is active in human history.

The Lord continues to acquaint Ananias with the details of the scenario in

Verse 12 - "And hath seen in a vision a man named Ananias coming in and putting his hand on him, that he might receive his sight."

καὶ εἶδεν ἄνδρα (ἐν ὁράματι) Ἀνανίαν ὀνόματι εἰσελθόντα καὶ ἐπιθέντα αὐτῷ (τὰς) χεῖρας ὅπως ἀναβλέψῃ.

καὶ (continuative conjunction) 14.

εἶδεν (3d.per.sing.aor.act.ind.of ὁράω, culminative) 144.

ἄνδρα (acc.sing.masc.of ἀνήρ, direct object of εἶδεν) 63.

(ἐν (preposition with the locative, instrumental use) 80.

ὁράματι) (loc.sing.neut.of ὅραμα, instrumental use) 1228.

Ἀνανίαν (acc.sing.masc.of Ἀνανίας, appellation, in agreement with ἄνδρα) 3186.

ὀνόματι (dat.sing.neut.of ὄνομα, possession) 108.

εἰσελθόντα (aor.mid.part.acc.sing.masc.of εἰσέρχομαι, adverbial, complementary, in indirect discourse) 234.

καὶ (adjunctive conjunction joining participles) 14.

ἐπιθέντα (2d.aor.act.part.acc.sing.masc.of ἐπιτίθημι, adverbial, complementary, in indirect discourse) 818.

αὐτῷ (loc.sing.masc.of αὐτός, place, after ἐπί in composition) 16.

(τὰς) (acc.pl.fem.of the article in agreement with χεῖρας) 9.

χεῖρας (acc.pl.fem.of χείρ, direct object of ἐπιθέντα) 308.

ὅπως (conjunction with the subjunctive in a purpose clause) 177.

ἀναβλέψῃ (3d.per.sing.aor.act.subj.of ἀναβλέπω, purpose) 907.

Translation - ". . . and he has seen in a vision a man named Ananias, coming in and laying his hands upon him in order that he might recover his sight."

Comment: The adverbial complementary participles εἰσελθόντα and ἐπιθέντα, in indirect discourse are timeless. *Cf.*the difference between these aorists and the present participle in Mt.16:28, where ἐρχόμενον, a present participle follows ἴδωσιν. Here we have two aorist participles after εἶδεν, in a similar situation. Thus we see that the tense of the participle in indirect discourse, refers not to time relations, but to type of action.

The sovereign God, Who orchestrated the entire episode struck Saul to the ground, blinded him, arranged for his safe conduct to Damascus, provided him with housing in Straight Street, heard his prayers, took note of his fast and sent the message to Ananias in order that he could perform his part of the scenario. Saul's choice was between great faith in blind, impersonal chance or in an intelligent, sovereign, holy and loving Christ. And that is the same choice that is open to unbelievers of all ages.

Verse 13 - "Then Ananias answered, Lord, I have heard by many of this man, how much evil he hath done to thy saints at Jerusalem."

ἀπεκρίθη δὲ Ἀνανίας, Κύριε, ἤκουσα ἀπὸ πολλῶν περὶ τοῦ ἀνδρὸς τούτου, ὅσα κακὰ τοῖς ἁγίους σου ἐποίησεν ἐν Ἰερουσαλήμ.

ἀπεκρίθη (3d.per.sing.aor.mid.ind.of ἀποκρίνομαι, constative) 318.

δὲ (adversative conjunction) 11.

Ἀνανίας (nom.sing.masc.of Ἀνανίας, subject of ἀπεκρίθη) 3186.

Κύριε (voc.sing.masc.of κύριος, address) 97.

ἤκουσα (1st.per.sing.aor.act.ind.of ἀκούω, culminative) 148.

ἀπὸ (preposition with the ablative, source) 70.

πολλῶν (abl.pl.masc.of πολύς, source) 228.

περὶ (preposition with the genitive of reference) 173.

τοῦ (gen.sing.masc.of the article in agreement with ἀνδρὸς) 9.

ἀνδρὸς (gen.sing.masc.of ἀνήρ, reference) 63.

τούτου (gen.sing.masc.of οὗτος, in agreement with ἀνδρὸς) 93.

ὅσα (acc.pl.neut.of ὅσος, in a relative clause, incorporation with κακὰ) 660.

κακὰ (acc.pl.neut.of κακός, direct object of ἐποίησεν) 1388.

τοῖς (dat.pl.masc.of the article in agreement with ἁγίοις) 9.

ἁγίοις (dat.pl.masc.of ἅγιος, dative of the person) 84.

σου (gen.sing.masc.of σύ, possession) 104.

ἐποίησεν (3d.per.sing.aor.act.ind.of ποιέω, culminative) 127.

ἐν (preposition with the locative of place) 80.

Ἰερουσαλήμ (loc.sing.masc.of Ἰεροσολύμων, place) 141.

Translation - *"But Ananias replied, 'Lord, I have heard from many people about this man with reference to the evil which he has inflicted upon your saints in Jerusalem.' "*

Comment: δὲ is adversative, as Ananias implied that he was not too happy about the assignment which the Lord was about to give him. He was objecting on grounds of his desire for self-preservation. For Ananias, discretion was the better part of valor. Note κακὰ with the relative ὅσα incorporated in case with it. *Cf.*ὅσον χρόνον in Mk.2:19. Also Rom.7:1; 1 Cor.7:39; Gal.4:1. ὅσα here in the sense of quantity, measure and degree. *Cf.*#660, (4).

The news of Saul's depredations upon the Jerusalem saints had spread by many mouths even to Damascus. This passage gives us a better knowledge of the extent of Saul's persecution of the christians than can be gained from Acts 7:58; 8:1,3; 9:1. His name had become a source of terror to the christians, not only in Jerusalem, but even in Damascus, and, no doubt, in other places. The greater the enormity of his reputation as an antiChrist the greater the glory of God when the news of his conversion spread throughout the territory.

Note the possessive σου. Ananias understood that the christians were the personal possessions of Christ, a thought in line with Jesus' statement to Saul that in persecuting the christians he was in reality persecuting Him (vs.4).

The news that Saul was armed with "John Doe" writs of assistance from the high priest in Jerusalem to facilitate his pogrom against the christians in Damascus had preceded him, as we learn in

Verse 14 - *"And here he hath authority from the chief priests to bind all that call on thy name."*

καὶ ὧδε ἔχει ἐξουσίαν παρὰ τῶν ἀρχιερέων δῆσαι πάντας τοὺς ἐπικαλουμένους τὸ ὄνομά σου.

καὶ (emphatic conjunction) 14.

ὧδε (an adverb of place) 766.

ἔχει (3d.per.sing.pres.act.ind.of ἔχω, aoristic) 82.

ἐξουσίαν (acc.sing.fem.of ἐξουσία, direct object of ἔχει) 707.

παρὰ (preposition with the ablative of source) 154.

τῶν (abl.pl.masc.of the article in agreement with ἀρχιερέων) 9.

ἀρχιερέων (abl.pl.masc.of ἀρχιερεύς, source) 151.

δῆσαι (aor.act.inf.of δέω, in apposition with ἐξουσίαν) 998.

πάντας (acc.pl.masc.of πᾶς, in agreement with ἐπικαλουμένους) 67.

τοὺς (acc.pl.masc.of the article in agreement with ἐπικαλουμένους) 9.

ἐπικαλουμένους (pres.mid.part.acc.pl.masc.of ἐπικαλέω, substantival, direct object of δῆσαι) 884.

τὸ (acc.sing.neut.of the article in agreement with ὄνομά) 9.

ὄνομά (acc.sing.neut.of ὄνομα, direct object of ἐπικαλουμένους) 108.

σου (gen.sing.masc.of σύ, possession) 104.

Translation - "*And here he has authority from the priests to put in chains all who call upon your name.*"

Comment: Saul had been in Damascus for three days, and the circumstances under which he came into the city, and the purpose for which he had begun the trip were well known by this time. *Cf.*#998 - Acts 21:11,11,13,33; 24:27; Col.4:3 for evidence that Paul himself, later was to suffer the same persecutions which he had planned for the saints.

Ananias was unduly alarmed, as we find in

Verse 15 - "But the Lord said unto him, Go thy way: for he is a chosen vessel unto me, to bear my name before the Gentiles, and kings, and the children of Israel."

εἶπεν δὲ πρὸς αὐτὸν ὁ κύριος, Πορεύου, ὅτι σκεῦος ἐκλογῆς ἐστίν μοι οὗτος τοῦ βαστάσαι τὸ ὄνομά μου ἐνώπιον ἐθνῶν τε καὶ βασιλέων υἱῶν τε Ἰσραήλ.

εἶπεν (3d.per.sing.aor.act.ind.of εἶπον, constative) 155.

δὲ (adversative conjunction) 11.

πρὸς (preposition with the accusative after a verb of speaking) 197.

αὐτὸν (acc.sing.masc.of αὐτός, extent, after a verb of speaking) 16.

ὁ (nom.sing.masc.of the article in agreement with κύριος) 9.

κύριος (nom.sing.masc.of κύριος, subject of εἶπεν) 97.

Πορεύου (2d.per.sing.pres.act.impv.of πορεύομαι, command) 170.

ὅτι (conjunction introducing a causal clause) 211.

σκεῦος (nom.sing.masc.of σκεῦος, predicate nominative) 997.

#3189 ἐκλογῆς (gen.sing.fem.of ἐκλογή, attributive genitive).

election - Rom.9:11; 11:5,7,28; 1 Thess.1:4; 2 Pet.1:10.
chosen - Acts 9:15.

*Meaning: Cf.*ἐκλέγω (#2119). The act of God whereby He chooses, for reasons solely sufficient unto Himself, and without regard to human merit, to save some

Rom.9:11; followed by χάριτος - Rom.11:5. Of the person or group of persons elected - Rom.11:7,28; 1 Thess.1:4.Used with τὴν κλῆσιν in 2 Pet.1:10. As an attributive genitive, like an adjective in Acts 9:15.

ἐστίν (3d.per.sing.pres.ind.of εἰμί, aoristic) 86.

μοι (dat.sing.masc.of ἐγώ, person) 123.

οὗτος (nom.sing.masc.of οὗτος, subject of ἐστίν, deictic) 93.

τοῦ (gen.sing.neut.of the article, articular infinitive of purpose) 9.

βαστάσαι (aor.act.inf.of βαστάζω, purpose) 306.

τὸ (acc.sing.neut.of the article in agreement with ὄνομά) 9.

ὄνομά (acc.sing.neut.of ὄνομα, direct object of βαστάσαι) 108.

μου (gen.sing.masc.of ἐγώ, possession) 123.

ἐνώπιον (preposition with the genitive, place description, before persons) 1798.

ἐθνῶν (gen.pl.masc.of ἔθνος, place description) 376.

τε (correlative particle) 1408.

καὶ (adjunctive conjunction joining nouns) 14.

βασιλέων (gen.pl.masc.of βασιλεύς, place description) 31.

υἱῶν (gen.pl.masc.of υἱός, place description) 5.

τε (adjunctive particle, joining nouns) 1408.

Ἰσραήλ (gen.sing.masc.indeclin., relationship) 165.

Translation - "But the Lord said to him, 'Go, because this man is a chosen agent of mine to carry my name before both Gentiles and kings and the sons of Israel.'"

Comment: Our Lord now uses His own adversative, in response to that of Ananias (verse 13), as He insists that Ananias carry out the divine commission, despite his fears. Πορεύου sounds peremptory - "Go! On your way!" and no more argument. However the Lord went on to tell Ananias why his mission was

so important. ὅτι introduces the causal clause. Note deictic οὗτος. Saul of Tarsus was an agent of the Lord with a specific mission to perform.

The doctrine of election, the stumbling block over which the unregenerate rationalist falls flat on his epistemic face, is nevertheless accepted, though not without some confusion, by the child of God because it is clearly taught in Scripture. Jesus chose Paul (whom we will now call by his new name) as He chose all of the true Apostles (John 15:16) and as He did all of the elect (Eph.1:4). This doctrine is rejected by the unsaved, as well as by many carnal and untaught christians because it runs counter to human standards of reason and impartial fair play. What must be understood and accepted is that God is truly God and therefore unique. He has His own standards and He is under no obligation to conform his standards to ours or to explain to us. God is not on the witness stand testifying in His own defense and no mortal, be he saved or unsaved is in the role of the prosecuting attorney. Our place before the throne of God is one of abject humility. The hiss of the serpent is easily detected in the criticism one often hears of the doctrine of election.

Paul was chosen for a special as well as for a general task. He was specially commissioned to preach Christ both before the Gentiles and their kings.

Generally, of course, he would on occasion preach to the Jews as opportunity presented itself, being careful always to observe the order of the great commission (Acts 1:8; Rom.1:16; Acts 13:46). This arrangement was understood also by Peter, James and John (Gal.2:8,9).

The blueprint of Christian service was marked out, not for Paul, the Apostle to the Gentiles, only, but also for all of the elect (Eph.2:10). Every Christian should fight the good fight and "finish the course" (2 Tim. 4:7,8). Every Christian who lives his life under the direction of the Holy Spirit is in fact immortal until his work on earth is finished (Rev.3:2). Pope John Paul II, after the unsuccessful attempt upon his life responded to the suggestion that he needed better body guards by saying that the man of God who is doing God's will needs no more protection than that provided by Providence. This is true, but no christian should presume upon it. It may be that a part of the will of God for the christian life is that we should take reasonable precaution to remain alive so that we can do all that He has marked out for us to do.

To do the will of God in a world that has never expressed regret that it crucified Jesus Christ is certain to involve the faithful witness in suffering, as we learn in

Verse 16 - "For I will shew him how great things he must suffer for my name's sake."

ἐγὼ γὰρ ὑποδείξω αὐτῷ ὅσα δεῖ ὑπὲρ τοῦ ὀνόματός μου παθεῖν.

ἐγὼ (nom.sing.masc.of ἐγώ, subject of ὑποδείξω, emphatic) 123.
γάρ (inferential conjunction) 105.
ὑποδείξω (1st.per.sing.fut.act.ind.of ὑποδείκνυμι, predictive) 282.
αὐτῷ (dat.sing.masc.of αὐτός, indirect object of ὑποδείξω) 16.
ὅσα (acc.pl.neut.of ὅσος, direct object of ὑποδείξω) 660.
δεῖ (3d.per.sing.pres.ind.impersonal of δεῖ) 1207.
αὐτὸν (acc.sing.masc.of αὐτός, general reference) 16.
ὑπὲρ (preposition with the ablative, "for the sake of") 545.
τοῦ (abl.sing.neut.of the article in agreement with ὀνόματος) 9.
ὀνόματός (abl.sing.neut.of ὄνομα, "for the sake of") 108.
μου (gen.sing.masc.ofd ἐγώ, possession) 123.
παθεῖν (aor.act.inf.of πάσχω, epexegetical) 1208.

Translation - "Therefore I will show him that which he must suffer for the sake of my name."

Comment: γὰρ is inferential. Since Jesus has chosen Paul and marked out his course of action (2 Tim.4:7) that will occupy him throughout the remainder of his life, it was necessary to show Paul what the cost would be. He should have known this quite well, as he had been busy dealing out punishment for those who called upon Jesus' name. He had played the game in the role of the hunter. Now he would be the object of the chase. *Cf.*#1207, II, b. Paul, who was destined to suffer much for the sake of the name which he was later to say was "the name

. . . above every name" (Phil.2:9), was in a strong position to understand his persecutions as he needed only to remember how he persecuted Christians before he was saved. When a persecutor becomes the persecuted he should at least understand his persecutors. Paul's perils were destined to become manifold. *Cf.* 2 Cor.11:23-33. He was not surprized. Our Lord told him that he must suffer these things. But He also told him of the glory which would follow (Rom.8:18; 2 Tim.4:8).

Reassured by the explanation offered him by his sovereign Lord, Ananias hastened to obey as we see in

Verse 17 - "And Ananias went his way, and entered into the house; and putting his hands on him said, Brother Saul, the Lord, even Jesus, that appeared unto thee in the way as thou camest, hath sent me, that thou mightest receive thy sight, and be filled with the Holy Ghost."

Ἀπῆλθεν δὲ Ἀνανίας καὶ εἰσῆλθεν εἰς τὴν οἰκίαν, καὶ ἐπιθεὶς ἐπ᾽ αὐτὸν τὰς χεῖρας εἶπεν, Σαοὺλ ἀδελφέ, ὁ κύριος ἀπέσταλκέν με, Ἰησοῦς ὁ ὀφθείς σοι ἐν τῇ ὁδῷ ᾗ ἤρχου, ὅπως ἀναβλέψῃς καὶ πλησθῇς πνεύματος ἁγίου.

Ἀπῆλθεν (3d.per.sing.aor.mid.ind.of ἀπέρχομαι, constative) 239.

δὲ (inferential conjunction) 11.

Ἀνανίας (nom.sing.masc.of Ἀνανίας, subject of ἀπῆλθεν, εἰσῆλθεν and εἶπεν) 3186.

καὶ (adjunctive conjunction joining verbs) 14.

εἰσῆλθεν (3d.per.sing.aor.mid.ind.of εἰσέρχομαι, constative) 234.

εἰς (preposition with the accusative of extent, repeated after εἰς in composition) 140.

τὴν (acc.sing.fem.of the article in agreement with οἰκίαν) 9.

οἰκίαν (acc.sing.fem.of οἰκία, extent) 186.

καὶ (adjunctive conjunction joining verbs) 14.

ἐπιθεὶς (aor.act.part.nom.sing.masc.of ἐπιτίθημι, adverbial, temporal) 818.

ἐπ᾽ (preposition with the accusative of extent, place) 47.

αὐτὸν (acc.sing.masc.of αὐτός, place) 16.

τὰς (acc.pl.fem.of the article in agreement with χεῖρας) 9.

χεῖρας (acc.pl.fem.of χείρ, direct object of ἐπιθεὶς) 308.

εἶπεν (3d.per.sing.aor.act.ind.of εἶπον, constative) 155.

Σαοὺλ (voc.sing.masc.of Σαῦλος, address) 3155.

ἀδελφέ (voc.sing.masc.of ἀδελφός, apposition) 15.

ὁ (nom.sing.masc.of the article in agreement with κύριος) 9.

κύριος (nom.sing.masc.of κύριος, subject of ἀπέσταλκέν) 97.

ἀπέσταλκέν (3d.per.sing.aor.act.ind.of ἀποστέλλω, culminative) 215.

με (acc.sing.masc.of ἐγώ, direct object of ἀπέσταλκέν) 123.

Ἰησοῦς (nom.sing.masc.of Ἰησοῦς, in apposition with κύριος) 3.

ὁ (nom.sing.masc.of the article in agreement with ὀφθείς) 9.

ὀφθείς (1st.aor.pass.part.nom.sing.masc.of ὁράω, substantival, in apposition with Ἰησοῦς) 144.

σοι (dat.sing.masc.of σύ, indirect object of ὀφθείς) 104.

ἐν (preposition with the locative of place) 80.
τῇ (loc.sing.fem.of the article in agreement with ὁδῷ) 9.
ὁδῷ (loc.sing.fem.of ὁδός, place where) 199.
ᾗ (loc.sing.fem.of ὅς, the relative pronoun, place where) 65.
ἤρχου (2d.per.sing.imp.mid.ind.of ἔρχομαι, progressive duration) 146.
ὅπως (conjunction with the subjunctive in a double purpose clause) 177.
ἀναβλέψῃς (2d.per.sing.aor.act.subj.of ἀναβλέπω, purpose) 907.
καὶ (adjunctive conjunction joining verbs) 14.
πλησθῇς (2d.per.sing.aor.pass.subj.of πληρόω, purpose) 115.
πνεύματος (abl.sing.neut.of πνεῦμα, source) 83.
ἁγίου (abl.sing.neut.of ἅγιος, in agreement with πνεύματος) 84.

*Translation - "And Ananias left and entered the house, and after laying his
hands on him, he said, 'Brother Saul, the Lord Jesus, Who was made visible to
you on the road by which you were coming has sent me in order that you might
see again and be filled with the Holy Spirit.' "*

Comment: Ananias walked in and laid his hands upon Paul before he spoke.
Then he called him, 'Brother Saul.' Note that he identified ὁ κύριος
unmistakably with the two substantives in apposition,Ἰησοῦς and ὁ ὀφθείς σοι.
Jesus had formerly introduced Himself to Paul as Ἐγὼ Εἰμι (vs.5). Paul must be
made to understand that Jesus, the Nazarene carpenter is the Great Ἐγὼ Εἰμι ὁ
κύριος ὁ ὤν (Exodus 3:14), the One Who appeared to Him and the One Whom
he had been persecuting. But He is also the One Who has sent Ananias to restore
his sight and see that he is filled with the Holy Spirit. Thus what Saul saw in
vision, Paul experienced in reality.

Often the article alone is sufficient to express the relation normally conveyed
by the possessive pronoun in the first and/or second persons, or by
αὐτοῦ/αὐτῶν. Cf. Mt.8:3; Mk.14:46,47; 2 Cor.12:18; Acts 9:17 et al.

The issue has recently been raised to the level of heated controversy in the
media with reference to whether or not God will hear prayer not offered in the
name of Jesus Christ. It is said by some that God, being sovereign, can do
anything He wishes to do and therefore that He can be approached in prayer
apart from the mediatorial agency of Jesus Christ, His Son. Saul of Tarsus and
Cornelius, the Roman army officer are cited as examples. Each prayed to God
and each was answered. It should be remembered that God answered Cornelius'
prayer by sending to him Peter who told him about the gospel of Jesus Christ
and offered him salvation through the Lord Jesus. In the case of Saul of Tarsus,
Jesus had already appeared to him and identified Himself as the God of the
Jewish patriarchs. Whatever Saul may have prayed during his three days of
blindness as he waited in Damascus for the visit of Ananias, his prayer was
answered by Ananias in the same way that Peter was used to answer the prayer of
Cornelius. Neither of these men found their way into the grace of God apart
from the mediation of the person of Jesus Christ. The real question is whether or
not one who cognitively rejects Jesus Christ as the incarnate Son of God can gain
audience with God in prayer. To affirm that is to place Jesus on the same level
with Moses, Mohammed, Ellen White, Joseph Smith, Buddha and the Reverend
Moon, and to insult the God of the Bible.

Verse 18 - *"And immediately there fell from his eyes as it had been scales: and he received sight forthwith, and arose, and was baptized."*

καὶ εὐθέως ἀπέπεσαν αὐτοῦ ἀπὸ τῶν ὀφθαλμῶν ὡς λεπίδες, ἀνέβλεψέν τε, καὶ ἀναστὰς ἐβαπτίσθη,

καὶ (continuative conjunction) 14.
εὐθέως (temporal adverb) 392.

#3190 ἀπέπεσαν (3d.per.pl.aor.act.ind.of ἀποπίπτω, constative).

fall from - Acts 9:18.

Meaning: A combination of ἀπό (#70) and πίπτω (#187). To fall away from; to fall from. With the ablative of separation and with the preposition repeated in Acts 9:18.

αὐτοῦ (gen.sing.masc.of αὐτός, possession) 16.
ἀπό (preposition with the ablative of separation, repeated after ἀπό in composition) 70.
τῶν (abl.pl.masc.of the article in agreement with ὀφθαλμῶν) 9.
ὀφθαλμῶν (abl.pl.masc.of ὀφθαλμός, separation) 501.
ὡς (particle in a comparative clause) 128.

#3191 λεπίδες (nom.pl.masc.of λεπίς, predicate nominative in a comparative clause).

scale - Acts 9:18.

Meaning: Cf. λέπω - "to strip off the rind or husk; to peel; to scale." Hence, scales, fleshly portions. That which had blinded Saul - Acts 9:18.

ἀνέβλεψέν (3d.per.sing.aor.act.ind.of ἀναβλέπω, ingressive) 907.
τε (adjunctive particle) 1408.
καὶ (adjunctive conjunction joining verbs) 14.
ἀναστὰς (aor.act.part.nom.sing.masc.of ἀνίστημι, adverbial, temporal) 789.
ἐβαπτίσθη (3d.per.sing.aor.pass.ind.of βαπτίζω, constative) 273.

Translation - "And immediately something like cataracts fell away from his eyes and he began to see again, and he stood up and was immersed."

Comment: Whatever had blinded Saul of Tarsus now fell away from his eyes and he began to see again. Nothing was said to him about immersion in water being prerequisite to salvation, as indeed it is not. It is essential to total obedience which God has a right to expect from all His children. Paul was immersed in water in obedience to the divine command, as a matter of course. He had already been declared by a sovereign Christ to be an elect agent of God to carry His word. All he needed now was a good meal.

Verse 19 - *"And when he had received meat he was strengthened. Then was Saul certain days with the disciples which were at Damascus."*

καὶ λαβὼν τροφὴν ἐνίσχυσεν.

καὶ (continuative conjunction) 14.
λαβὼν (aor.act.part.nom.sing.masc.of λαμβάνω, adverbial, temporal) 533.
τροφὴν (acc.sing.fem.of τροφή, direct object of λαβὼν) 266.
ἐνίσχυσεν (3d.per.sing.aor.act.ind.of ἐνισχύω, constative) 2793.

Comment: Paul, the Apostle to the Gentiles, had not eaten for three days. His stomach was as devoid of food as his heart was full of joy. It is for the ascetics, deluded as they are by the Gnostic contempt for and fear of the material, to explain why the first thing that Paul did after he was saved and immersed was eat!

Paul Preaches at Damascus

(Acts 9:19b - 22)

Ἐγένετο δὲ μετὰ τῶν ἐν Δαμασκῷ μαθητῶν ἡμέρας τινάς.

Ἐγένετο (3d.per.sing.aor.mid.ind.of γίνομαι, constative) 113.
δὲ (continuative conjunction) 11.
μετὰ (preposition with the genitive of accompaniment) 50.
τῶν (gen.pl.masc.of the article in agreement with μαθητῶν) 9.
ἐν (preposition with the locative of place where) 80.
Δαμασκῷ (loc.sing.fem.of Δαμασκός, place where) 3181.
μαθητῶν (gen.pl.masc.of μαθητής, accompaniment) 421.
ἡμέρας (acc.pl.fem.of ἡμέρα, time extent) 135.
τινάς (acc.pl.fem.of τις, in agreement with ἡμέρας) 486.

Translation - "And after he had eaten he regained his strength, and he stayed with the disciples in Damascus for some time."

Comment: Spiritual fellowship with the other christians in Damascus followed naturally. As his body was strengthened by the food his spirit and soul were refreshed and strengthened by the spiritual food which was his during this period. Paul, no doubt, was an apt student. Already familiar with the Judeo tradition, he needed only to be shown how the Christian message of the New Testament, much of which he was destined to write, supplemented and fulfilled it. His giant intellect was greatly stimulated and his soul burned with the desire to preach the gospel message of Christ, which he had been so zealous to destroy.

Verse 20 - "And straightway he preached Christ in the synagogues, that he is the Son of God."

καὶ εὐθέως ἐν ταῖς συναγωγαῖς ἐκήρυσσεν τὸν Ἰησοῦν ὅτι οὗτός ἐστιν ὁ υἱὸς τοῦ θεοῦ.

καὶ (continuative conjunction) 14.

εὐθέως (temporal adverb) 392.
ἐν (preposition with the locative of place where) 80.
ταῖς (loc.pl.fem.of the article in agreement with συναγωγαῖς) 9.
συναγωγαῖς (loc.pl.fem.of συναγωγή, place where) 404.
ἐκήρυσσεν (3d.per.sing.imp.act.ind.of κηρύσσω, inceptive) 249.
τὸν (acc.sing.masc.of the article in agreement with Ἰησοῦν) 9.
Ἰησοῦν (acc.sing.masc.of Ἰησοῦς, direct object of ἐκήρυσσεν) 3.
ὅτι (conjunction introducing an object clause in indirect discourse) 211.
οὗτός (nom.sing.masc.of οὗτος, deictic, subject of ἐστιν) 93.
ἐστιν (3d.per.sing.pres.ind.of εἰμί, aoristic) 86.
ὁ (nom.sing.masc.of the article in agreement with υἱὸς) 9.
υἱὸς (nom.sing.masc.of υἱός, predicate nominative) 5.
τοῦ (gen.sing.masc.of the article in agreement with θεοῦ) 9.
θεοῦ (gen.sing.masc.of θεός, relationship) 124.

Translation - *"And immediately he began to preach in the synagogues that this man Jesus was the Son of God."*

Comment: ἐκήρυσσεν is an inchoative (inceptive) imperfect with the emphasis upon the beginning of a continued action. Paul wasted no time. He began immediately (εὐθέως) and he continued until he died. Note τὸν Ἰησοῦν before the ὅτι clause. This is prolepsis - "He began to preach Jesus — that He is the Son of God." This is sometimes called the epexegetic use of ὅτι. It explains what Paul said about Jesus. In this construction the case changes from the accusative in τὸν Ἰησοῦν to nominative in οὗτός. How well Paul knew the truth of his message. He had just had a dramatic personal encounter with Jesus. All effective witnessing of the saving power of Christ begins with the witness's personal conviction that what he says is true.

After we leave chapter nine of Luke's account in the Acts we do not hear of Paul again until chapter thirteen, after which his ministry occupies the center of the stage until Acts 28. The details of Paul's life in the intervening period are recorded by him in Galatians 1 and 2.

It is not strange that Paul's ministry in Damascus attracted great attention, as verse 21 explains.

Verse 21 - *"But all that heard him were amazed, and said, Is not this he that destroyed them which called on this name in Jerusalem, and came hither for that intent, that he might bring them bound unto the chief priests?"*

ἐξίσταντο δὲ πάντες οἱ ἀκούοντες καὶ ἔλεγον, Οὐχ οὗτός ἐστιν ὁ πορθήσας ἐν Ἰερουσαλὴμ τοὺς ἐπικαλουμένους τὸ ὄνομα τοῦτο, καὶ ὧδε εἰς τοῦτο ἐληλύθει ἵνα δεδεμένους αὐτοὺς ἀγάγη ἐπὶ τοὺς ἀρχιερεῖς;

ἐξίσταντο (3d.per.pl.imp.mid.ind.of ἐξίστημι, progressive description) 992.
δὲ (continuative conjunction) 11.
πάντες (nom.pl.masc.of πᾶς, in agreement with ἀκούοντες) 67.
οἱ (nom.pl.masc.of the article in agreement with ἀκούοντες) 9.

ἀκούοντες (pres.act.part.nom.pl.masc.of ἀκούω, substantival, subject of ἐξίσταντο and ἔλεγον) 148.

καὶ (adjunctive conjunction joining verbs) 14.

ἔλεγον (3d.per.pl.imp.act.ind.of λέγω, iterative) 66.

Οὐχ (summary negative conjunction with the indicative, in rhetorical question, expecting an affirmative reply) 130.

οὗτός (nom.sing.masc.of οὗτος, deictic, predicate nominative) 93.

ἐστιν (3d.per.sing.pres.ind.of εἰμί, aoristic) 86.

ὁ (nom.sing.masc.of the article in agreement with πορθήσας) 9.

#3192 πορθήσας (aor.act.part.nom.sing.masc.of πορθέω, substantival, subject of ἐστιν).

destroy - Acts 9:21; Gal.1:23.
waste - Gal.1:13.

Meaning: Cf. πέρθω - "to lay waste." To destroy, overthrow, make havok of - with reference to Saul's attempt to overthrow Christianity by persecuting christians - Acts 9:21; Gal.1:13,23.

ἐν (preposition with the locative of place where) 80.

Ἰερουσαλήμ (loc.sing.masc.of Ἱεροσολύμων, place where) 141.

τοὺς (acc.pl.masc.of the article in agreement with ἐπικαλουμένους) 9.

ἐπικαλουμένους (pres.mid.part.acc.pl.masc.of ἐπικαλέω, substantival, direct object of πορτήσας) 884.

τὸ (acc.sing.neut.of the article in agreement with ὄνομα) 9.

ὄνομα (acc.sing.neut.of ὄνομα, direct object of ἐπικαλουμένους) 108.

τοῦτο (acc.sing.neut.of οὗτος, in agreement with ὄνομα, anaphoric) 93.

καὶ (continuative conjunction) 14.

ὧδε (local adverb) 766.

εἰς (preposition with the accusative, purpose) 140.

τοῦτο (acc.sing.neut.of οὗτος, purpose) 93.

ἐληλύθει (3d.per.sing.pluperfect mid.ind.of ἔρχομαι, consummative) 146.

ἵνα (conjunction with the subjunctive in a purpose clause) 114.

δεδεμένους (perf.pass.part.acc.pl.masc.of δέω, adjectival, in agreement with αὐτοὺς) 998.

αὐτοὺς (acc.pl.masc.of αὐτός, direct object of ἀγάγη) 16.

ἀγάγη (3d.per.sing.aor.act.subj.of ἄγω, purpose) 876.

ἐπὶ (preposition with the accusative of extent) 47.

τοὺς (acc.pl.masc.of the article in agreement with ἀρχιερεῖς) 9.

ἀρχιερεῖς (acc.pl.masc.of ἀρχιερεύς, extent) 151.

Translation - "*And all who heard him were astounded and they were saying, 'Is not this the man who in Jerusalem destroyed those who called upon this name, and had he not come here for this purpose - in order to bring to the priests those who were in chains?'* "

Comment: The first reaction to Paul's preaching apparently was not widespread acceptance of his message, but astonishment in all who heard him. They went about Damascus spreading the story and repeating their rhetorical question (iterative imperfect in ἔλεγον). The question is clearly rhetorical. They expected an affirmative reply. Such rhetorical question is a strong form of affirmation. There was little doubt about it. Saul the persecutor had become Paul the preacher. Note εἰς τοῦτο in a purpose construction with the ἵνα clause in apposition. "For this purpose." What purpose? "In order that .. κ.τ.λ." Note the pluperfect in ἐληλύθει. Paul had arrived in Damascus three days before. Contrast the intensive force of the perfect participle δεδεμένους - "those who having been bound were still in chains." Apparently Saul had made arrangements with the Jewish authorities in Damascus, before he left Jerusalem, to arrest and place in irons the Damascus christians and to hold them there until he arrived with warrants to take them to Jerusalem for trial. The text does not tell us whether the authorities in Damascus had complied with Saul's order. We may be sure that if they had, the christians were released, as a result of Saul's conversion.

The stories that circulated in Damascus served only to increase the size of Paul's crowds.

Verse 22 - "But Saul increased the more in strength, and confounded the Jews which dwelt at Damascus, proving that this is very Christ."

Σαῦλος δὲ μᾶλλον ἐνεδυναμοῦτο καὶ συνέχυννεν (τοὺς) Ἰουδαίους τοὺς κατοικοῦντας ἐν Δαμασκῷ, συμβιβάζων ὅτι οὗτός ἐστιν ὁ Χριστός.

Σαῦλος (nom.sing.masc.of Σαῦλος, subject of ἐνεδυναμοῦτο and συνέχυννεν) 3155.

δὲ (continuative conjunction) 11.

μᾶλλον (adverbial) 619.

#3193 ἐνεδυναμοῦτο (3d.per.sing.imp.pass.ind.of ἐνδυναμόω, inchoative).

enable - 1 Tim.1:12.
strengthen - Phil.4:13; 2 Tim.4:17.
be made strong - Heb.11:34.
be strong - Rom.4:20; Eph.6:10; 2 Tim.2:1.
increase in strength - Acts 9:22.

Meaning: A combination of ἐν (#80) and δυναμόω (#4601). To gain strength; in the passive, to be strengthened. To grow in grace, *i.e.* to become more proficient in Christian service - Acts 9:22; 2 Tim.4:17. Followed by a locative of sphere and an instrumental of means in Eph.6:10; by a locative of sphere - 1 Tim.2:1; Rom.4:20; as a participial substantive in Phil.4:13; 1 Tim.1:12. Joined with ἀπὸ ἀσθενείας in Heb.11:34.

καὶ (adjunctive conjunction joining verbs) 14.

συνέχυννεν (3d.per.sing.imp.act.ind.of συγχέω, progressive description) 2961.

(τοὺς) (acc.pl.masc.of the article in agreement with Ἰουδαίους) 9.

'Ιουδαίους (acc.pl.masc.of 'Ιουδαῖος, direct object of συνέχυννεν) 143.
τοὺς (acc.pl.masc.of the article in agreement with κατοικοῦντας) 9.
κατοικοῦντας (pres.act.part.acc.pl.masc.of κατοικέω, adjectival, restrictive, in agreement with 'Ιουδαίους) 242.
ἐν (preposition with the locative of place where) 80.
Δαμασκῷ (loc.sing.masc.of Δαμασκός, place where) 3181.

#3194 συμβιβάζων (pres.act.part.nom.sing.masc.of συμβιβάζω, modal).

gather assuredly - Acts 16:10.
instruct - 1 Cor.2:16.
knit together - Col.2:2,19.
draw - Acts 19:33.
prove - Acts 9:22.
be compacted - Eph.4:16.

Meaning: A combination of σύν (#1542) and βιβάζω - "to breed," "bring together for mating purposes. Hence, metaphorically, in an intellectual sense, to bring all elements in an argument together to produce a desired result or conclusion. To "put it all together." Paul in Damascus wove together a scriptural argument that resulted in a given conclusion - ὅτι οὗτός ἐστιν ὁ Χριστός - Acts 9:22. Who can argue with God? - 1 Cor.2:16. Paul interpreted certain events to conclude that God had called him to Macedonia - Acts 16:10. The body of Christ is brought together in a tighter spiritual union by spiritual inbreeding. (Here the basic idea of βιβάζω comes out) - Col.2:2,19; Eph.4:16. To conclude from circumstances that a man is guilty and pick him out of a crowd - Acts 19:22.

ὅτι (conjunction introducing an object clause in indirect discourse) 211.
οὗτός (nom.sing.masc.of οὗτος, predicate nominative) 93.
ἐστιν (3d.per.sing.pres.ind.of εἰμί, aoristic) 86.
ὁ (nom.sing.masc.of the article in agreement with Χριστός) 9.
Χριστός (nom.sing.masc.of Χριστός, subject of ἐστιν) 4.

Translation - "But Saul was beginning to grow in grace more and more, and he continued to confuse the Jews living in Damascus by proving logically that this man is the Messiah."

Comment: As the Jews opposed Paul he increased more and more in strength. He began and continued to grow in grace (inchoative imperfect in ἐνεδυναμοῦ-το). His remarkable growth in grace, under fire from the local Jewish theologians, is not surprizing. First of all, he was the chosen agent of the Lord to preach the gospel of Christ, first to the Jews, that they might be convinced from their own Old Testament scriptures that Jesus is their Messiah, and then, to the Gentiles, that they might come to understand that the Jewish Messiah is also the Good Shepherd Who must bring other sheep as well into the fold (John 10:16). It was to Paul that the "mystery" would be revealed more completely than it had been revealed to the Old Testament prophets (Eph.3:3-8). We may be sure that the Holy Spirit would begin the theological education of this "chosen vessel"

The Renaissance New Testament

without delay.

Secondly, Paul was endowed with a superior intellect. The superior intellectual tone of his writings indicates this. He was exceptionally perceptive. His intuitive powers enabled him quickly to sense, lay hold upon and organize ideas, which in the average mind would present themselves, if at all, only as discordant elements.

Thirdly, among all of the Apostles, Paul was without doubt the best educated. Matthew, the tax collector, may have had a little education, but the others were only fishermen. Some of them may have been above the average in intellectual power, but none had the education that Paul had gained. He was a lawyer - a student of Gamaliel and, as such, thoroughly acquainted with Old Testament law. It quickly became apparent to him that Jesus of Nazareth was the only man in Israel who had a legal right to occupy the throne of David. *Cf.* our discussion of this matter in *The Renaissance New Testament*, I, 4. Israel's only hope for the future therefore was in Jesus Christ, whom they had murdered, but whom God had raised from the dead. Thus Paul saw the close connection between the theological foundation for the Christian faith and the national hope of the Jewish people. He grasped this concept very quickly and as he began to explain it to his audiences the idea developed to even greater lengths in his mind. Nothing advances one's thought on a complex subject like the intellectual and spiritual exercise of articulating it. Spirit filled preachers of the Word of God will testify that often we learn more theology in the pulpit than out of it as we pore over some weighty tome written by another. This was Paul's experience in the synagogues of Damascus.

There is a fourth explanation for his sudden growth in grace. A lofty intelligence quotient and a broad education, while they are prerequisite to comprehensive grasp of any subject, will avail nothing in Christian Education without a deep sense of intellectual humility. Thanks to his recent harrowing experiences enroute to Damascus and during the three days that followed, Paul was thoroughly humbled before the feet of Jesus Christ, his Messiah, Saviour and new Friend. A religious bigot, enflamed with a hatred that had no rational basis, he had been engaged in an exercise of total futility. Now he was in a position to realize how incredibly stupid he had been. This is especially difficult to bear for one as brilliant as he knew he was. Smitten to the ground and blinded by the brilliance of the Shekinah glory of the Great Ἐγώ Εἰμι Ὁ ὤν, the Lord God of his fathers, and confronted with Jesus' question for which there was no sensible answer, Paul was now ready to learn from Him Who had promised the propositional revelation which we now call the New Testament.

Thus Paul was in a position to learn. He stood at the moment at the first level of Christian growth beyond faith in the sequence that Peter was later to contribute (2 Peter 1:5-7). A full exposition of Peter's formula for Christian growth will come at the proper time. *Cf.* our discussion *en loc.* Here we only point out that the intellectual humility which is the outgrowth of faith is prerequisite for the acquisition of knowledge. The virtue (ἀρετή) of the passage is clearly demonstrated by the context to be humility. Paul had come to *believe* in order that he might *understand*. Thus his epistemic development was in keeping with the philosophy of Anselm, *viz.* "that faith provides conclusions which reason, assured of their truth, can often prove necessary." (*The Encyclopedia of Philosophy*, I, 128). Anselm defended his epistemology by saying, *"Credo ut intelligam"* - "I believe in order that I may understand." "The fear of the Lord is the beginning of wisdom" (Psalm 111:10; Proverbs 9:10) and ". . . the knowledge of the holy is understanding." Given faith and with a little illumination from the Holy Spirit, an intellect like Paul could put his theological gestalt together. This is what happened during the first thrilling days of his Christian experience in the synagogues of Damascus.

He *began* to grow stronger. Another imperfect in συνέχυννεν indicates Paul's impact upon the Jewish theologians in Damascus. He was continuing to "mix them up" in their thinking. *Cf.* #2961 for the basic meaning. He "poured their brains together." They were thoroughly confused when Paul confronted them with the inherent inconsistencies in their own position. Note all of the contexts where the word occurs. Paul gave his Jewish antagonists the same treatment that the evangelical epistemologists have given to the logical positivists since the days of Auguste Comte, as a result of which positivism has collapsed like the house of cards it always was. (Cf.Carl F.H.Henry, *God, Revelation and Authority*, I, 96-111). One who values logic and intellectual consistency may not be confused in holding a false position until someone points out the inconsistency. Then the desire to be logical is in conflict with the unwillingness to admit error. The Damascus Jews could resolve their problem and rid themselves of their confusion by admitting that Jesus was their Messiah - a confession that they did not wish to make. Or they could avoid confusion by not thinking about the problem. This Paul would not permit. Or they could give battle and prove him wrong in his interpretation of their scriptures, and thus turn the tables upon him by involving him in an intellectual tangle. But this third alternative was not open to them, since Paul was "putting it all together" with concrescence and consistency which they could not refute. Besides Paul also preached a gospel that also corresponded with reality, as there was plenty of empirical evidence in Jerusalem that Jesus had risen from the dead and demonstrated the fact with "many infallible proofs" (Acts 1:3). When one has the three C's of epistemology - consistency, coherence and correspondance to reality - on his side he is in a strong position and need not fear successful rebuttal. Paul was in a strong position and the Jews in Damascus knew it, but were unwilling to admit it. After all one does not call Jesus Lord ". . . but by the Holy Spirit" (1 Cor.12:3). It was only because of the regeneration of the Holy Spirit that Saul of Tarsus was now Paul the Evangelist preaching that "Jesus is the Lord."

The Damascus rabbis, though perhaps not as sophisticated as Paul, were not totally ignorant of the Old Testament Law and Prophets. His advantage was that, by the grace of God, he had a frame of reference - a conceptual schema which united all of the disparate passages in closure to provide a logical gestalt. Why could he not have done this before? For the same reason that his opponents could not yet do it. Because "the fear of the Lord" - something that Saul of Tarsus never had until three days before, "is the beginning of (both) knowledge" (Proverbs 1:7) and "wisdom" (Psalm 111:10). Christ now reigned within the heart of this brilliant lawyer - the Christ Who is the Source of all "wisdom and knowledge" (Col.2:3). Paul had just enrolled, by the grace of God, in a University with an infinite curriculum! No wonder he was excited. No wonder he was growing in grace (2 Peter 3:18). Suddenly everything came into clear focus in his mind. It was an example of insight learning. If Chica, Kohler's ape, had the "insight" to climb the scaffold and catch the basket of food as it swung by, while Grande and Tercera, two less perceptive simians languished in malnutrition, could not Saul of Tarsus, whom Gamaliel had taught to think, under the guidance of the Holy Spirit learn that Christ, Who is the Light of the world (John 8:12) was the Jewish Messiah? He could because Christ had turned the light on in his brain, while the minds of his Jewish colleagues were still "blinded" by "the god of this world" (2 Cor.4:4).

The participle συμβιβάζων, is modal. It tells us how Paul argued with the Jews in Damascus and how he confused them. It implies that there was a great deal of scripture exposition. Luke has not given us the outline of Paul's argument. We may be certain that it was exhaustive. By putting "precept upon precept, precept upon precept; line upon line, line upon line; here a little and there a little" (Isa.28:10) Paul presented to them Jesus of Nazareth, Messiah of Israel and Saviour of the world, and as a result they fell backward and were "broken, and snared and taken" (Isa.28:13). Thus συνέχυννεν is the negative counterpart of the participle συμβιβάζων.

Paul was later to receive personal instruction from his ascended Lord (2 Cor.12:1-4), but as a result of his ministry in Damascus, soon after he was saved and filled with the Holy Spirit, he was already on the way to becoming the great theologian of the New Testament.

The Jewish Establishment in Damascus was no different from Caiaphas and his worthies in Jerusalem. When one cannot win an argument, he can always plot to kill the other fellow. They they did in Damascus.

Saul Escapes From the Jews

(Acts 9:23-25)
Verse 23 - "And after that many days were fulfilled, the Jews took counsel to kill him."

Ὡς δὲ ἐπληροῦντο ἡμέραι ἱκαναί, συνεβουλεύσαντο οἱ Ἰουδαῖοι ἀνελεῖν αὐτόν.

Ὡς (adverb in a temporal clause) 128.
δὲ (adversative conjunction) 11.
ἐπληροῦντο (3d.per.pl.imp.pass.ind.of πληρόω, progressive duration) 115.
ἡμέραι (nom.pl.fem.of ἡμέρα, subject of ἐπληροῦντο) 135.
ἱκαναί (nom.pl.fem.of ἱκανός, in agreement with ἡμέραι) 304.
συνεβουλεύσαντο (3d.per.pl.aor.mid.ind.of συνβουλεύομαι, ingressive) 1556.

οἱ (nom.pl.masc.of the article in agreement with Ἰουδαῖοι) 9.

Ἰουδαῖοι (nom.pl.masc.of Ἰουδαῖος, subject of συνεβουλεύσαντο) 143.

ἀνελεῖν (2d.aor.act.inf.of ἀναιρέω, epexegetical) 216.

αὐτόν (acc.sing.masc.of αὐτός, direct object of ἀνελεῖν) 16.

Translation - "But during the course of the next few days the Jews began to plot to kill him."

Comment: The temporal clause with ὡς indicates contemporaneity with the time of the main verb. ἐπληροῦντο is imperfect, not aorist. Hence we cannot translate "after some days" but "during the course of some days." The main verb συνεβουλεύσαντο is an ingressive aorist. The Jews *began* to discuss their plot to kill Paul. This is typical bigotry. It represents the desperate measure of the Establishment, poverty stricken for scholarship and thus unable to meet its foes in rational discussion, but in possession of police power. He who cannot be answered must be killed. The Jews were old hands at this. *Cf.* Mt.26:14; John 18:14. All dictators are. As they had plotted to kill Jesus, the Messiah, now they plot to kill Paul, who has proved that Jesus is the Messiah. They were powerless to turn back the pages of history and obliterate the fact, but they thought that they still had the power to prevent the propagation of the fact. They were as powerless to stop Paul's preaching as they had been powerless to prevent the history that was the basis for his message. The sovereign God had already told Ananias that Paul had been chosen to carry the gospel message to the Gentiles and their kings and to the children of Israel (vs.15). What God has planned, He will bring to fruition and no "hit squad" in Damascus will stop Him.

From the point of view of the Jews, it was a matter of institutional survival. The days went by - each one witnessing Paul in one of their local synagogues presenting his brilliant expositions of their own scriptures, as he gave overwhelming proof to his audiences that official Jewry in Jerusalem had crucified their King and that the Christian churches were on solid Old Testament ground for proclaiming Him as Risen and Ascended - superior to the Old Testament prophets (Heb.1:1,2), to angels (Heb.1:4-14), to Moses (Heb.3:3) and to Aaron (Heb.7:1-28).

Since Paul could not be refuted he must be killed. They felt that the alternative was to see every Jew in Damascus forsake the synagogue and unite with the local Christian church. In this, if they believed it, they were unduly alarmed. Not every Jew in Damascus would be saved - only ". . . as many as the Lord our God shall call" (Acts 2:39: 13:48)

Verse 24 - "But their laying await was known to Saul. And they watched the gate day and night to kill him."

ἐγνώσθη δὲ τῷ Σαύλῳ ἡ ἐπιβουλὴ αὐτῶν. παρετηροῦντο δὲ καὶ τὰς πύλας ἡμέρας τε καὶ νυκτὸς ὅπως αὐτὸν ἀνέλωσιν.

ἐγνώσθη (3d.per.sing.aor.pass.ind.of γινώσκω, constative) 131.

δὲ (adversative conjunction) 11.

τῷ (dat.sing.masc.of the article in agreement with Σαύλῳ) 9.
Σαύλῳ (dat.sing.masc.of Σαῦλος, personal advantage) 3155.
ἡ (nom.sing.fem.of the article in agreement with ἐπιβουλή) 9.

#195 ἐπιβουλή (nom.sing.fem.of ἐπιβουλή, subject of ἐγνώσθη).

laying await - Acts 9:24.
lying in wait - Acts 20:19.
lay wait - Acts 20:3; 23:30.

Meaning: A combination of ἐπί (#47) and βουλή (#2163). A plot or plan against someone. With reference to the Jews in Damascus and their plot against Paul - Acts 9:24; the Jews in Ephesus - Acts 20:3,19; the Jews in Jerusalem - Acts 23:30.

αὐτῶν (gen.pl.masc.of αὐτός, description) 16.
παρετηροῦντο (3d.per.pl.imp.mid.ind.of παρατηρέω, progressive description) 2104.
δὲ (adversative conjunction) 11.
καὶ (emphatic conjunction) 14.
τὰς (acc.pl.fem.of the article in agreement with πύλας) 9.
πύλας (acc.pl.fem.of πύλη, direct object of παρετηροῦντο) 662.
ἡμέρας (gen.sing.fem.of ἡμέρα, time description) 135.
τε (correlative particle) 1408.
καὶ (adjunctive conjunction joining nouns) 14.
νυκτὸς (gen.sinbg.fem.of νύξ, time description) 209.
ὅπως (conjunction with the subjunctive in a purpose clause) 177.
αὐτὸν (acc.sing.masc.of αὐτός, direct object of ἀνέλωσιν) 16.
ἀνέλωσιν (3d.per.pl.2d.aor.act.ind.of ἀναιρέω, purpose) 216.

Translation - *"But Saul found out about it. But they were in fact watching the gates both by day and night, in order that they might kill him."*

Comment: Literally "Their plot was made known to Saul." Note the dative case with the passive voice. Just how Saul discovered the plot to kill him, Luke does not tell us. The sovereign God intervened to spare the life of His Apostle.The story has the elements of a comic opera. The police kept a constant vigil at the gates of the city. They watched around the clock - ἡμέρας τε καὶ νυκτὸς - "both a day and a night watch." The genitive describes the watches that were kept.Not "throughout the day and night," but "day watches" and "night watches." One wonders why the police did not go to the house where Paul stayed and arrest him. Perhaps they did not have sufficient manpower to take him from his friends by force. Perhaps they feared a popular demonstration in Paul's favor, as Caiphas has feared the people in Jerusalem. They plotted to take Paul secretly when he tried to leave the city. *Cf.* 2 Cor.11:32. In verse 25 we see Paul, with some loss to his dignity, lowered over the wall in a basket. The child of God need not worry about his dignity, so long as he is in the will of the Heavenly Father.

Verse 25 - "Then the disciples took him by night, and let him down by the wall in a basket."

λαβόντες δὲ οἱ μαθηταὶ αὐτοῦ νυκτὸς διὰ τοῦ τείχους καθῆκαν αὐτὸν χαλάσαντες ἐν σπυρίδι.

λαβόντες (aor.act.part.nom.pl.masc.of λαμβάνω, adverbial, temporal) 533.
δὲ (adversative conjunction) 11.
οἱ (nom.pl.masc.of the article in agreement with μαθηταὶ) 9.
μαθηταὶ (nom.pl.masc.of μαθητής, subject of καθῆκαν) 421.
αὐτοῦ (gen.sing.masc.of αὐτός, relationship) 16.
νυκτὸς (gen.sing.fem.of νύξ, time description) 209.
διὰ (preposition with the ablative of agent) 118.
τοῦ (abl.sing.neut.of the article in agreement with τείχους) 9.

#3196 τείχους (abl.sing.neut.of τεῖχος, agent).

wall - Acts 9:25; 2 Cor.11:33; Heb.11:30; Rev.21:12,14,15,17,18,19.

Meaning: Cf. θιγγάνω (#4625). Compared with it are the English "dike" or "ditch." Cf. Den Hagg, Holland. A city wall; a wall around a city. Damascus - Acts 9:25; 2 Cor.11:33; Jericho - Heb.11:30; New Jerusalem - Rev.21:12,14,15, 17,18,19.

καθῆκαν (3d.per.pl.1st.aor.act.ind.of καθίημι, constative) 2081.
αὐτὸν (acc.sing.masc.of αὐτός, direct object of καθῆκαν) 16.
χαλάσαντες (aor.act.part.nom.pl.masc.of χαλάω, adverbial, modal) 2045.
ἐν (preposition with the locative of place where) 80.
σπυρίδι (loc.sing.fem.of σπυρίς, place where, instrumental use) 1186.

Translation - *"But his disciples took him at night and let him down at the wall, lowering him in a basket."*

Comment: δὲ is adversative to counter the adversaive action of the city authorities in verse 24. They plotted to kill Paul, *but* Paul learned of the plot, *but* the police were guarding the gates day and night, *but* Paul's disciples let him down by the wall in a basket. Point and counterpoint. Plot and counterplot. Because Paul and his disciples had the Lord on their side, the plot to kill the Apostle failed. It is interesting to note that even though Paul had had but a brief ministry in Damascus, he had already gained some converts who became his students. They are called "his" disciples, which leads to the idea that these were people who had not been saved before Paul came to the city. We may be sure that the Christians in Damascus who were saved before he arrived were greatly strengthened by his teaching ministry. Both #'s 2081 and 2045 mean "to let down." καθῆκαν stresses the fact. χαλάσαντες stresses the method. σπυρίδι - the same type used to collect the fragments of the loaves and fishes. Cf. 2 Cor.11:33.

As Paul breathlessly held to the sides of the swaying basket and finally stepped out at the foot of the wall and fled stealthfully into the darkness, he perhaps reflected upon the fact that the persecutor of Christians, who only a short time before had journeyed to Damascus to arrest Christians was now fleeing from

Damascus as a persecuted Christian. This was not a surprize to Paul. He had been forewarned (vs.16).

One of the evils of democracy with its built-in tolerance for free expression of the Christian gospel is that the modern Christian seldom suffers for the cause of Christ, and thus has less stimulus for Christian growth. "If we suffer, we shall also reign with him." (2 Tim.2:12). The Apostle Paul has certainly earned his right to reign with Christ. (Rom.8:18; 2 Cor.4:16-18).

Paul at Jerusalem
(Acts 9:26-31)

Verse 26 - "And when Saul was come to Jerusalem, he assayed to join himself to the disciples: but they were all afraid of him, and believed not that he was a disciple."

Παραγενόμενος δὲ εἰς Ἰερουσαλὴμ ἐπείραζεν κολλᾶσθαι τοῖς μαθηταῖς. καὶ πάντες ἐφοβοῦντο αὐτόν, μὴ πιστεύοντες ὅτι ἐστὶν μαθητής.

Παραγενόμενος (aor.mid.part.nom.sing.masc.of παραγίνομαι, adverbial, temporal) 139.

δὲ (continuative conjunction) 11.

εἰς (preposition with the accusative of extent) 140.

Ἰερουσαλήμ (acc.sing.masc.of Ἰεροσολύμων, extent) 141.

ἐπείραζεν (3d.per.sing.imp.act.ind.of πειράζω, inchoative) 330.

κολλᾶσθαι (pres.mid.inf.of κολλάω, epexegetical) 1288.

τοῖς (instru.pl.masc.of the article in agreement with μαθηταῖς) 9.

μαθηταῖς (instru.pl.masc.of μαθητής, association) 421.

καὶ (adversative conjunction) 14.

πάντες (nom.pl.masc.of πᾶς, subject of ἐφοβοῦντο) 67.

ἐφοβοῦντο (3d.per.pl.imp.mid.ind.of φοβέομαι, inchoative) 101.

αὐτόν (acc.sing.masc.of αὐτός, direct object of ἐφοβοῦντο) 16.

μὴ (qualified negative conjunction with the participle) 87.

πιστεύοντες (pres.act.part.nom.pl.masc.of πιστεύω, adverbial, causal) 734.

ὅτι (conjunction introducing an object clause in indirect discourse) 211.

ἐστὶν (3d.per.sing.pres.ind.of εἰμί, aoristic) 86.

μαθητής (nom.sing.masc.of μαθητής, predicate nominative) 421.

Translation - "And when he got back into Jerusalem, he began to try to associate himself with the disciples, but they were all afraid of him because they did not believe that he was a disciple."

Comment: *Cf.* Acts 5:13. Some of the early christians were afraid publicly to associate with the Apostles in Jerusalem, because of their fear of reprisal from the Establishment. Now Paul tries to "glue himself to the disciples" (same word, κολλάω, #1288, in Acts 5:13; 9:26) in Jerusalem, despite the fact that he already knew from his own pre-regenerate experience as a persecutor (Acts 8:3), as well as from his post-regenerate experience as a persecuted Christian (Acts 9:23) that to be publicly associated with the Christians, either in Jerusalem or in Damascus was to invite persecution and even death. This did not deter Paul. However (adversative καὶ) the Jerusalem saints continued to fear him (imperfect tense in ἐφοβοῦντο) with good reason. The causal participle tells us why. μὴ πιστεύοντες - "because they did not believe that he was a disciple." The ὅτι clause is indirect discourse. This was a perfectly natural reaction for the Jerusalem Christians. The news from Damascus had not yet reached Jerusalem. In view of Saul's last actions in Jerusalem they quite understandably concluded that he was posing as a Christian in order to infiltrate their ranks and gather evidence against them, thus serving as a spy for the Jerusalem Establishment. Paul's efforts to convince the Christians that he was sincere were to no avail. But Barnabas came to his rescue.

Verse 27 - "But Barnabas took him, and brought him to the apostles, and declared unto them how he had seen the Lord in the way, and that he had spoken to him, and how he had preached boldly at Damascus in the name of Jesus."

Βαρναβᾶς δὲ ἐπιλαβόμενος αὐτὸν ἤγαγεν πρὸς τοὺς ἀποστόλους, καὶ διηγήσατο αὐτοῖς πῶς ἐν τῇ ὁδῷ εἶδεν τὸν κύριον καὶ ὅτι ἐλάλησεν αὐτῷ, καὶ πῶς ἐν Δαμασκῷ ἐπαρρησιάσατο ἐν τῷ ὀνόματι Ἰησοῦ.

Βαρναβᾶς (nom.sing.masc.of Βαρναβᾶς, subject of ἤγαγεν and διηγήσατο) 3047.

δὲ (adversative conjunction) 11.

ἐπιλαβόμενος (2d.aor.mid.part.nom.sing.masc.of ἐπιλαμβάνω, adverbial, temporal) 1133.

αὐτὸν (acc.sing.masc.of αὐτός, direct object of ἐπιλαβόμενος) 16.

ἤγαγεν (3d.per.sing.aor.act.ind.of ἄγω, constative) 876.

πρὸς (preposition with the accusative of extent) 197.

τοὺς (acc.pl.masc.of the article in agreement with ἀποστόλους) 9.

ἀποστόλους (acc.pl.masc.of ἀπόστολος, extent) 844.

καὶ (adjunctive conjunction joining verbs) 14.

διηγήσατο (3d.per.sing.aor.mid.ind.of διηγέομαι, constative) 2225.

αὐτοῖς (dat.pl.masc.of αὐτός, indirect object of διηγήσατο) 16.

πῶς (interrogative adverb introducing indirect question) 627.

ἐν (preposition with the locative of place where) 80.

τῇ (loc.sing.fem.of the article in agreement with ὁδῷ) 9.

ὁδῷ (loc.sing.fem.of ὁδός, place where) 199.

εἶδεν (3d.per.sing.aor.act.ind.of ὁράω, constative) 144.

τὸν (acc.sing.masc.of the article in agreement with κύριον) 9.

κύριον (acc.sing.masc.of κύριος, direct object of εἶδεν) 97.

καὶ (adjunctive conjunction joining indirect question with indirect assertion) 14.

ὅτι (conjunction introducing a declarative clause in indirect assertion) 211.

ἐλάλησεν (3d.per.sing.aor.act.ind.of λαλέω, constative) 815.

αὐτῷ (dat.sing.masc.of αὐτός, indirect object of ἐλάλησεν) 16.

καὶ (adjunctive conjunction joining indirect assertion with indirect question) 14.

πῶς (interrogative adverb introducing indirect question) 627.

ἐν (preposition with the locative of place where) 80.

Δαμασκῷ (loc.sing.fem.of Δαμασκός, place where) 3181.

#3197 ἐπαρρησιάσατο (3d.per.sing.aor.mid.ind.of παρρησιάζομαι, constative).

be bold - 1 Thess.2:2.
preach boldly - Acts 9:27.
speak boldly - Acts 14:3; 18:26; 19:8; Eph.6:20.
wax bold - Acts 13:46.
freely - Acts 26:26.

Meaning: To conduct oneself in a free, fearless and bold manner; to speak fearlessly and without reservation. With reference to the ministry of Apollos in Acts 18:26. Elsewhere of Paul's ministry in 1 Thess.2:2; Acts 9:27; 13:46; 14:3; 19:8; 26:26; Eph.6:20.

ἐν (preposition with the locative, instrumental use) 80.

τῷ (loc.sing.neut.of the article in agreement with ὀνόματι) 9.

ὀνόματι (loc.sing.neut.of ὄνομα, instrumental) 108.

Ἰησοῦ (gen.sing.masc.of Ἰησοῦς, possession) 3.

Translation - "But Barnabas took him in hand and brought him to the Apostles and told the entire story to them, how he saw the Lord on the road, and that He spoke to him, and how in Damascus he spoke boldly in the name of Jesus."

Comment: Barnabas moved to correct the situation by allaying the suspicion in the minds of the saints and introducing Paul to the Apostles. We have met Barnabas before (Acts 4:36,37) and will have occasion to meet him again. He must have been prominent in the Jerusalem church, since, among many who sold their possession, he alone (except Ananias and Sapphira, for a different reason) received special mention in Luke's account. Now he asserts his leadership again to correct what could have become a bad situation. Note the full account which Barnabas gave to the Apostles. *Cf.* #2225. "He led them through the story to the end." We have indirect question, followed by indirect assertion, and that followed by another indirect question. There is no indirect discourse since Barnabas did not tell the Apostles *what* Jesus said to Paul, but only that He spoke to him. Note the instrumental use of ἐν with the locative. Paul spoke boldly about and by the authority of Jesus despite the danger which he faced in Damascus. Thanks to Barnabas, Paul's record of service, following his dramatic encounter with Jesus was laid before the Apostles and they endorsed their new ally in the cause of Christ. The text does not tell us how Barnabas found out about the story which he related to the Apostles.

There is nothing in Barnabas' account to indicate that Paul was commissioned especially to carry the gospel of Christ to the Gentiles. Paul, of course knew of this (verse 15), although he may not at that time have understood fully the character of that which he later called "the mystery" (Eph.3:3-7). It was to create some difficulty a little later, though not of insuperable nature (Acts 15:1-31).

Verse 28 - "And he was with them coming in and going out at Jerusalem."

καὶ ἦν μετ' αὐτῶν εἰσπορευόμενος καὶ ἐκπορευόμενος εἰς Ἰερουσαλήμ, παρρησιαζόμενος ἐν τῷ ὀνόματι τοῦ κυρίου,

καὶ (continuative conjunction) 14.

ἦν (3d.per.sing.imp.ind.of εἰμί imperfect periphrastic) 86.

μετ' (preposition with the genitive of accompaniment) 50.

αὐτῶν (gen.pl.masc.of αὐτός, accompaniment) 16.

εἰσπορευόμενος (pres.mid.part.nom.sing.masc.of εἰσπορεύομαι, imperfect periphrastic) 1161.

καὶ (adjunctive conjunction joining participles) 14.

ἐκπορευόμενος (pres.mid.part.nom.sing.masc.of ἐκπορεύομαι, imperfect periphrastic) 270.

εἰς (preposition with the accusative, original static use, like a locative) 140.

Ἰερουσαλήμ (acc.sing.masc.of Ἱεροσολύμων, place where) 141.

παρρησιαζόμενος (pres.mid.part.nom.sing.masc. of παρρησιάζομαι, imperfect periphrastic) 3197.

ἐν (preposition with the locative, instrumental use) 80.

τῷ (loc.sing.neut.of the article in agreement with ὀνόματι) 9.

ὀνόματι (loc.sing.neut.of ὄνομα, instrumental use) 108.

τοῦ (gen.sing.masc.of the article in agreement with κυρίου) 9.

κυρίου (gen.sing.masc.of κύριος, possession) 97.

Translation - "And he remained with them in Jerusalem, coming in and going out and speaking boldly in the name of the Lord."

Comment: The first clause of verse 29 in the KJV is a part of verse 28 in the Greek text. ἦν is joined by three present participles for a triple imperfect periphastic, with a decidedly durative thrust. They speak of the consistent effort of Paul to serve the Lord in Jerusalem. In day by day association with the other Christians in Jerusalem, he came and went, always witnessing for Christ as he had done in Damascus. Paul made no effort to conceal his associations with the other members of the local Jerusalem congregation. He was as bold in speaking for Christ now as he had been in speaking against him before.

Verse 29 - "And he spake boldly in the name of the Lord Jesus, and disputed against the Grecians: but they went about to slay him."

ἐλάλει τε καὶ συνεζήτει πρὸς τοὺς Ἑλληνιστάς. οἱ δὲ ἐπεχείρουν ἀνελεῖν αὐτόν.

ἐλάλει (3d.per.sing.imp.act.ind.of λαλέω, progressive description) 815.

τε (correlative particle) 1408.

καὶ (adjunctive conjunction joining verbs) 14.

συνεζήτει (3d.per.sing.imp.act.ind.of συζητέω, progressive description) 2060.

πρὸς (preposition with the accusative of extent, after a verb of speaking) 197.

τοὺς (acc.pl.masc.of the article in agreement with Ἑλληνιστάς) 9.

Ἑλληνιστάς (acc.pl.masc.of Ἑλληνιστής, extent, after a verb of speaking) 3077.

οἱ (nom.pl.masc.of the article, subject of ἐπεχείρουν) 9.

δὲ (adversative conjunction) 14.

ἐπεχείρουν (3d.per.pl.imp.act.ind.of ἐπιχειρέω, progressive description) 1705.

ἀνελεῖν (aor.act.inf.of ἀναιρέω, epexegetical) 216.

αὐτόν (acc.sing.masc.of αὐτός, direct object of ἀνελεῖν) 16.

Translation - *"He continued both to speak and to argue with the Greek speaking Jews. But they were going about to kill him."*

Comment: παρρησιαζόμενος (verse 28) probably refers to Paul's public preaching on the streets, in the temple, or wherever the occasion demanded and the opportunity presented itself. The word means more than that Paul's manner of speaking was unequivocal. It was always that. When he was in private converstion he spoke unequivocally. Just as Jesus had spoken openly in the Temple for the entire world to hear (John 18:20) so also did Peter, John, the other Apostles and Paul. ἐλάλει τε καὶ συνεζήτει πρὸς τοὺς Ἑλληνιστάς may refer to private converstions which he had with the Greek speaking Jews. *Cf.*#2060 for the precise meaning of the verb. He was "seeking with them" - exploring, asking questions, posing dilemmas, inviting rebuttal, exposing inconsistencies and leading them into damaging commitments, from which they could not retreat. It is the technique of a skilled trial lawyer. It is the same technique which he had used in Damascus, where his approach was described as "mixing up" the opposition and "putting it all together" (*cf.*συνέχυννεν and συμβιβάζων in verse 22). The Hellenists were unable to stay in the conversation with Paul and could only resort to plots to waylay and kill him. They reacted as did his frustrated opponents in Damascus (verse 23).

Paul's method of preaching at that time was always to show the connection between the claims of the gospel of Christ and the prophetic writings of the Old Testament, since at that time none of the New Testament literature had yet been written. The message of the New Testament in no way contradicts that of the Old Testament (Mt.5:17; Rom.3:21). "The New is in the Old contained; the Old is in the New explained." The Holy Spirit Who is the author of both is incapable of inconsistency (2 Peter 1:20,21; 2 Tim.3:16,17). Paul was later to write that his message smelled like death to some and like life to others, but that whatever the result among his listeners his ministry smelled good to God, as long as he did not corrupt the Word of God, but was preaching it in sincerity and in truth (2 Cor.2:15-17).

Just as the Christians in Damascus took steps to save Paul from his assassins, so the Jerusalem saints thought it best to get him out of town.

Verse 30 - *"Which when the brethren knew they brought him down to Caesarea, and sent him forth to Tarsus."*

ἐπιγνόντες δὲ οἱ ἀδελφοὶ κατήγαγον αὐτὸν εἰς Καισάρειαν καὶ
ἐξαπέστειλαν αὐτὸν εἰς Ταρσόν.

ἐπιγνόντες (2d.aor.act.part.nom.pl.masc.of ἐπιγινώσκω, adverbial,
temporal) 675.

δὲ (inferential conjunction) 11.

οἱ (nom.pl.masc.of the article in agreement with ἀδελφοὶ) 9.

ἀδελφοὶ (nom.pl.masc.of ἀδελφός, subject of κατήγαγον and ἐξαπέστειλαν)
15

κατήγαγον (3d.per.pl.aor.act.ind.of κατάγω, constative) 2056.

αὐτὸν (acc.sing.masc.of αὐτός, direct object of κατήγαγον) 16.

εἰς (preposition with the accusative of extent) 140.

Καισάρειαν (acc.sing.fem.of Καισαρίας, extent) 1200.

καὶ (adjunctive conjunction joining verbs) 14.

ἐξαπέστειλαν (3d.per.pl.aor.act.ind.of ἐξαποστέλλω, constative) 1835.

αὐτὸν (acc.sing.masc.of αὐτός, direct object of ἐξαπέστειλαν) 16.

εἰς (preposition with the accusative of extent) 140.

#3198 Ταρσόν (acc.sing.fem.of Ταρσός, extent).

Tarsus - Acts 9:30; 11:25; 22:3.

Meaning: Tarsus, the birthplace of Paul. A maritime city, capital of Cilicia
during the Roman period. It was noted for its Greek learning with many
philosophical schools. It was not a Roman "colony" but a free city. Now called
Tarso or Tersus. Paul was proud of his citizenship in this favored Roman city -
Acts 22:3; 9:30; 11:25.

*Translation - "Therefore when the brethren learned about it they took him down
to Caesarea and sent him away to Tarsus."*

Comment: δὲ here can be considered inferential or adversative, as the Christian
brothers in Jerusalem took steps to frustrate the murderous plans of the enemies
of the cross. They got Paul out of town. *Cf.#675* for a study of ἐπιγινώσκω. It is
perfective knowledge. That the Jews were trying to kill Paul was no rumor. They
were really going to kill him. So they escorted Paul down the mountain road to
the coastal city of Caesarea and put him on a ship bound for Tarsus, his home
town, on the southern coast of Asia Minor. Thus the second time the Christians
have taken steps to frustrate the efforts of the enemy to kill Paul (vss.25, 30).

It is idle to speculate whether or not Paul would have been killed if he had
remained, either in Damascus or in Jerusalem. Perhaps the intervention of the
brethren on both occasions was the manner in which the sovereign God
contrived to keep him alive. We may be sure that Paul was destined to live until
he could write 2 Tim.4:6-8. A view of predestination which assures us that what
God has determined to do He will do, and thus that He will keep alive those
whom He has determined to use for His glory, until His purpose is fulfilled, is
proper. But such a view does not justify a presumptuous policy of failing to
observe ordinary standards of precaution. The Christian most devoted to the

fulfillment of the perfect will of God for his life will not indiscriminately cross the street against the light. It is presumptuous to put God to the test.

Verse 31 - "Then had the churches rest throughout all Judea and Galilee and Samaria, and were edified, walking in the fear of the Lord, and in the comfort of the Holy Ghost, were multiplied."

Ἡ μὲν οὖν ἐκκλησία καθ' ὅλης τῆς Ἰουδαίας καὶ Γαλιλαίας καὶ Σαμαρείας εἶχεν εἰρήνην, οἰκοδομουμένη καὶ πορευομένη τῷ φόβῳ τοῦ κυρίου, καὶ τῇ παρακλήσει τοῦ ἁγίου πνεύματος ἐπληθύνετο.

Ἡ (nom.sing.fem.of the article in agreement with ἐκκλησία) 9.

μὲν (particle of affirmation) 300.

οὖν (continuative conjunction) 68.

ἐκκλησία (nom.sing.fem.of ἐκκλησία, subject of εἶχεν) 1204.

καθ' (preposition with the genitive, place description - "throughout") 98.

ὅλης (gen.sing.fem.of ὅλος, in agreement with Ἰουδαίας) 112.

τῆς (gen.sing.fem.of the article in agreement with Ἰουδαίας) 9.

Ἰουδαίας (gen.sing.fem.of Ἰουδαίας, place description, "throughout") 134.

καὶ (adjunctive conjunction joining nouns) 14.

Γαλιλαίας (gen.sing.fem.of Γαλιλαίας, place description - "throughout") 241.

καὶ (adjunctive conjunction joining nouns) 14.

Σαμαρείας (gen.sing.fem.of Σαμάρεια, place description, - "throughout") 1998.

εἶχεν (3d.per.sing.imp.act.ind.of ἔχω, inchoative) 82.

εἰρήνην (acc.sing.fem.of εἰρήνη, direct object of εἶχεν) 865.

οἰκοδομουμένη (pres.pass.part.nom.sing.fem.of οἰκοδομέω, adverbial, circumstantial) 694.

καὶ (adjunctive conjunction joining participles) 14.

πορευομένη (pres.mid.part.nom.sing.fem.of πορεύομαι, adverbial, circumstantial) 170.

τῷ (instrumental sing.masc.of the article in agreement with φόβῳ) 9.

φόβῳ (instrumental sing.masc.of φόβος, means) 1131.

τοῦ (gen.sing.masc.of the article in agreement with κυρίου) 9.

κυρίου (gen.sing.masc.of κύριος, description) 97.

καὶ (adjunctive conjunction joining nouns) 14.

τῇ (instru.sing.fem.of the article in agreement with παρακλήσει) 9.

παρακλήσει (instru.sing.fem.of παράκλησις, means) 1896.

τοῦ (abl.sing.neut.of the article in agreement with πνεύματος) 9.

ἁγίου (abl.sing.neut.of ἅγιος, in agreeement with πνεύματος) 84.

πνεύματος (abl.sing.neut.of πνεῦμα, source) 83.

ἐπληθύνετο (3d.per.sing.imp.pass.ind.of πληθύνω, progressive description) 1488.

Translation - "Then in fact the church throughout all of Judea and Galilee and Samaria began to have peace, being built up and walking in the fear of the Lord and it grew in numbers with the help of the Holy Spirit."

Comment: μὲν seems to emphasize the contrast between the difficulty which the church had while Paul was in Jerusalem and the peace that prevailed after he left. This in no way denigrates Paul. Consumed with the zeal of the Lord he was, from an intellectual point of view, by far the best qualified to press the claims of Jesus Christ against the opposition of the Jewish scholars in the Jerusalem Establishment. Once he had gone to Tarsus, things got quiet. The church was given a period of quiet which continued for some time. The durative time in the imperfect εἶχεν is supported by the present participles οἰκοδομουμένη and πορευομένη and the imperfect tense in ἐπληθύνετο. Everything is durative. They were continuing to have peace; they were being built up in the faith; they were always walking in the fear of the Lord and they were growing in numbers, thanks to the support, stimulation, comfort and encouragement of the Holy Spirit.

The time is approximately two years after Pentecost - about A.D. 35.

The Healing of Aeneas

(Acts 9:32 - 35)

Verse 32 - "And it came to pass, as Peter passed throughout all quarters he came down also to the saints which dwelt at Lydda."

Ἐγένετο δὲ Πέτρον διερχόμενον διὰ πάντων κατελθεῖν καὶ πρὸς τοὺς ἁγίους τοὺς κατοικοῦντας Λύδδα.

Ἐγένετο (3d.per.sing.aor.ind.of γίνομαι, with the infinitive in indirect discourse) 113.

δὲ (continuative conjunction) 11.

Πέτρον (acc.sing.masc.of Πέτρος, general reference) 387.

διερχόμενον (pres.mid.part.acc.sing.masc.of διέρχομαι, adverbial, temporal) 1017.

διὰ (preposition with the ablative, physically through, repeated after διά in composition) 118.

πάντων (abl.pl.masc.of πᾶς, physically through) 67.

κατελθεῖν (aor.mid.inf.of κατέρχομαι, in a temporal clause) 2037.

καὶ (adjunctive conjunction joining prepositional phrases) 14.

πρὸς (preposition with the accusative of extent, with persons) 197.

τοὺς (acc.pl.masc.of the article in agreement with ἁγίους) 9.

ἁγίους (acc.pl.masc.of ἅγιος, extent) 84.

τοὺς (acc.pl.masc.of the article in agreement with κατοικοῦντας) 9.

κατοικοῦντας (pres.act.part.acc.pl.masc.of κατοικέω, adjectival, restrictive, in agreement with ἁγίους) 242.

#3199 Λύδδα (loc.sing.fem.of Λύδδα, place).

Lydda - Acts 9:32,35,38.

Meaning: A Benjamite town near Joppa, about eleven miles inland from the Mediterranean coast - Acts 9:32,35,38.

Translation - "And as Peter was going throughout all the area he went down also to the saints living in Lydda."

Comment: Peter was taking advantage of the period of peace to go here and there throughout the area to visit the Christians. He had a special commission from the Lord to "strengthen (his) brethren" (Luke 22:32). It is interesting to reflect upon the possibility that it was through his experiences in this pastoral ministry, that he developed the material which he later wrote into his epistles, especially those portions that relate to spiritual development (1 Peter 2:1-3; 2 Peter 1:1-13). These visits were probably made in the homes of the people as it is unlikely at this time that the local congregations had acquired real estate and built formal places of worship.

There is doubt about the singular form ἐκκλησία in verse 31. If, in fact, the true text reads the singular it need not point to an episcopal form of church government which was to prevail. It was still very early in the life of the saints after Pentecost and all of the Christians looked to the Apostles for guidance in matters of faith and practice. It is not likely that at this early date the Apostles had had time to appoint local pastors in local congregations. This being true, if indeed it is, it would be proper to think of all of the Christians as belonging to the same church, *viz.* the one in Jerusalem.

"The range and age of the witnesses which read the singular number are superior to those that read the plural. The singular can hardly be a scribal modification in the interest of expressing the idea of the unity of the church, for in that case we should have expected similar modifications in 15.41 and 16.5, where there is no doubt that the plural number ἐκκλησίαι is the original text. More probably the singular number here has been altered to the plural in order to conform to the two later passages." (Metzger, *Textual Commentary on the Greek New Testament*,367).

There is no doubt that as Christianity spread throughout the Mediterranean world, as a result of the missionary work of the Apostle Paul, autonomous *churches* were formed by the Apostles, and that after the New Testament literature became available, it became their sole guide to faith and practice. This is not to say, however, that a church could not have, nor did not profit from the counsel to be derived from the exposition of the Scriptures by visiting preachers.

It is possible that the Christians whom Peter visited in Lydda were the converts of Philip, who had only shortly before visited all of the towns in the coastal area between Azotus and Caesarea (Acts 8:40).

Verse 33 - "And there he found a certain man named Aeneas which had kept his bed eight years, and was sick of the palsy."

εὗρεν δὲ ἐκεῖ ἄνθρωπόν τινα ὀνόματι Αἰνέαν ἐξ ἐτῶν ὀκτὼ κατακείμενον ἐπὶ κραβάττου, ὃς ἦν παραλελυμένος.

εὗρεν (3d.per.sing.aor.act.ind.of εὑρίσκω, constative) 79.

δέ (continuative conjunction) 11.

ἐκεῖ (local adverb) 204.

ἄνθρωπόν (acc.sing.masc.of ἄνθρωπος, direct object of εὗρεν) 341.

τινα (acc.sing.masc.of τις, in agreement with ἄνθρωπόν) 486.

ὀνόματι (dat.sing.neut.of ὄνομα, possession) 108.

#3200 Αἰνέαν (acc.sing.masc.of Αἰνέας, appellation, in agreement with ἄνθρωπόν).

Aeneas - Acts 9:33,34.

Meaning: The paralytic of Lydda whom Peter healed - Acts 9:33,34.

ἐξ (preposition with the ablative of time separation) 19.

ἐτῶν (abl.pl.neut.of ἔτος, time separation) 821.

ὀκτώ (numeral) 1886.

κατακείμενον (pres.pass.part.acc.sing.masc.of κατάκειμαι, adjectival, ascriptive, in agreement with ἄνθρωπόν) 2065.

ἐπί (preposition with the genitive of place description) 47.

κραββάττου (gen.sing.masc.of κράββατος, place description) 2077.

ὅς (nom.sing.masc.of ὅς, definite relative pronoun in an adjectival clause) 65.

ἦν (3d.per.sing.imp.ind.of εἰμί, pluperfect periphrastic) 86.

παραλελυμένος (perf.pass.part.nom.sing.masc.of παραλύω, pluperfect periphrastic) 2079.

Translation - "And he found there some man named Aeneas, who for the past eight years had been confined to his bed with paralysis."

Comment: ἐξ with the ablative of time, gives the point of departure - "since a day eight years ago" or "for the past eight years." He is defined by the adjectival participle κατακείμενον and also by the adjectival relative clause with the pluperfect periphrastic. For eight years he had been paralyzed,never able to get out of bed.

Verse 34 - "And Peter said unto him, Aeneas, Jesus Christ maketh thee whole: arise, and make thy bed. And he arose immediately."

καὶ εἶπεν αὐτῷ ὁ Πέτρος, Αἰνέα, ἰᾶταί σε Ἰησοῦς Χριστός. ἀνάστηθι καὶ στρῶσον σεαυτῷ, καὶ εὐθέως ἀνέστη.

καί (continuative conjunction) 14.

εἶπεν (3d.per.sing.aor.act.ind.of εἶπον, constative) 155.

αὐτῷ (dat.sing.masc.of αὐτός, indirect object of εἶπεν) 16.

ὁ (nom.sing.masc.of the article in agreement with Πέτρος) 9.

Πέτρος (nom.sing.masc.of Πέτρος, subject of εἶπεν) 387.

Αἰνέα (voc.sing.masc.of Αἰνέας, address) 3200.

ἰᾶταί (3d.per.sing.pres.ind.mid.of ἰάομαι, aoristic) 721.

σε (acc.sing.masc.of σύ, direct object of ἰᾶταί) 104.

Ἰησοῦς (nom.sing.masc.of Ἰησοῦς, subject of ἰᾶταί) 3.

Χριστός (nom.sing.masc.of Χριστός, apposition) 4.

ἀνάστηθι (2d.per.sing.2d.aor.act.impv.of ἀνίστημι, command) 789.

καὶ (adjunctive conjunction joining verbs) 14.

στρῶσον (2d.per.sing.aor.act.ind.of στρώννυμι, command) 1351.

σεαυτῷ (dat.sing.masc.of σεαυτοῦ, person) 347.

καὶ (continuative conjunction) 14.

εὐθέως (adverbial) 392.

ἀνέστη (3d.per.sing.aor.act.ind.of ἀνίστημι, constative) 789.

Translation - "And Peter said to him, 'Aeneas, Jesus Christ heals you. Get up and get dressed.' And immediately he arose."

Comment: Gildersleeve calls ἰαταί a "specific present" because it is aoristic, instead of the universal present with intensive force. Jannaris thinks that "effective present" is a better name, since the present can also have ingressive and constative force. As an ingressive present it could mean "Jesus Christ begins to heal you." The constative force would only mean the healing, without reference to when it would be accomplished, whereas the context makes it clear that the man was healed forthwith, as is evidenced by the fact that immediately he arose. στρῶσον σεαυτῷ can mean "make the bed yourself" or it can also mean "dress yourself." Let the student study #1351 and decide. The question has nothing to do with the thrust of the passage, which is to the effect that when Peter arrived in Lydda he found and, by the power of Jesus Christ, he healed Aeneas. The reaction of the people in Lydda and the residents of the coastal plane of Sharon is recorded in verse 35

We must keep in mind that the man who called upon the Lord Jesus Christ to heal Aeneas was Peter, one of the twelve Apostles who along with his eleven colleagues, was commissioned by the Lord, Who is the Head of His church, to write the New Testament literature and see that the churches were established. The new movement, as yet had nothing to commend it to the people, except the eye witness accounts of those who had been with Jesus and who witnessed His miracles, His death and His resurrection and ascension. The New Testament, which is the source of authority for Christian witnesses since the first century, was not available to them. Hence they were given the gifts which served to authenticate the message which they preached. The revival recorded to verse 35 occurred because the people saw the evidence of supernatural power in the total recovery of a paralytic who had been in bed for eight years. It was because of this that they listened to what Peter had to say. Once the New Testament canon of Scripture was completed the Apostolic sign gifts were phased out. They are not available to preachers today, nor have they been since the New Testament was completed. It is noteworthy that those who claim to have supernatural powers to heal, to the same degree as did the Apostles, convince some who are easily convinced because they lack the skepticism which is the mark of mental maturity, and are then in a position to preach other false views which are accepted readily by their disciples for the same reason that the people of Lydda believed Peter's message. Modern "charismatics" point to Mark 16:20 for support for the notion that the "signs follow" those who witness for purposes of confirmation of what is witnessed, apparently not realizing that Mark 16:9-20 are not a part of the inspired text. These same verses support snake handling, the practice of drinking poison, exorcism of demons, glossalalia and baptismal regeneration (Mk.16:16-18). It is significant that preachers who appeal to their audiences on the evidence of their miracles, rather than on the evidence of New Testament exegesis propagate heresies which have long been rejected by those in the mainstream of evangelical orthodoxy. Witness the unitarianism of the so-called "Jesus Only" people.

It should be added that the New Testament does not teach that *all* of the gifts of the Holy Spirit to the Body of Christ ceased in the first century of the Christian era. *Au contraire* 1 Corinthians 12:1-13 seems clear that the Holy Spirit enriches every member of the Body of Christ with some gift. It is nowhere said that the gift of "tongues" is the ability to utter sounds other than those classified as languages which are understood somewhere upon the earth. There are no "unknown" languages. All tongues (languages) are understood and recognized as native by someone on earth. No incomprehensible gibberish was uttered at Pentecost. Paul was an accomplished linguist who could preach in more than one language if the occasion demanded. A French Christian who is giving his witness for Christ in French is not speaking in an "unknown" tongue, nor is his performance miraculous, anymore than it would be if an Englishman witnessed for Christ in English, although what they had to say would not be understood without translation by some others.

It is incumbent upon the miracle workers of the 20th century to reproduce *in kind* and *to the same degree* the miracles which the Apostles performed in the first century.

No one doubts that the sovereign God is able to heal the sick if He finds it consistent with His will to do so. The question involves the purpose for the sign gifts, the time period in which they were properly in force, and the relation that they bear to the finality of God's message to man. If the New Testament is not the perfect and final message of God to man, but must be supplemented by what He wishes to add in charismatics meetings, as interpreted by other charismatics, then it follows that we had better wait until God has finished speaking to us before we make the effort to decide what He had to say. All who claim to be the messengers of supernaturally transmitted messages from God imply that the New Testament is not the final word. Indeed Mormon "prophets" openly state that what they have to say is as important as what the Biblical writers wrote. To say, as some do, that what is said in a "tongues" meeting is always checked against the New Testament is to say that what they had to say was unnecessary. If it is already in the New Testament the Holy Spirit need not say it again. He would be better advised to induce Christians to read their Bibles. If what is said is contrary or supplemental to the New Testament message, then either the Holy Spirit has given us an incomplete message or He is contradicting Himself. If the New Testament is His final word He need not supplement it. If it is wholly correct in all of its parts, He dare not contradict it. Thus the "charismatics" qualify as cultists for the same reason as did Joseph Smith, Ellen White and the Reverend Moon.

Verse 35 - "And all that dwelt at Lydda and Saron saw him, and turned to the Lord."

καὶ εἶδαν αὐτὸν πάντες οἱ κατοικοῦντες Λύδδα καὶ τὸν Σαρῶνα, οἵτινες ἐπέστρεφαν ἐπὶ τὸν κύριον.

καὶ (continuative conjunction) 14.
εἶδαν (3d.per.pl.aor.act.ind.of ὁράω, constative) 144.
αὐτὸν (acc.sing.masc.of αὐτός, direct object of εἶδαν) 16.
πάντες (nom.pl.masc.of πᾶς, in agreement with κατοικοῦντες) 67.
οἱ (nom.pl.masc.of the article in agreement with κατοικοῦντες) 9.
κατοικοῦντες (pres.act.part.nom.pl.masc.of κατοικέω, substantival, subject of εἶδαν) 242.
Λύδδα (loc.sing.fem.of Λύδδα, indeclin., place) 3199.
καὶ (adjunctive conjunction joining nouns) 14.
τὸν (acc.sing.masc.of the article in agreement with Σαρῶνα) 9.

#3201 Σαρῶνα (acc.sing.masc.of Σαρών, place).

Sharon - Acts 9:35.

Meaning: a plain reaching from Caesarea of Palestine south to Joppa about thirty miles. Famous for its fertility - Acts 9:35.

οἵτινες (nom.pl.masc.of ὅστις, subject of ἐπέστρεφαν) 163.
ἐπέστρεφαν (3d.per.pl.aor.act.ind.of ἐπιστρέφω, constative) 866.
ἐπὶ (preposition with the accusative of extent, metaphorical) 47.
τὸν (acc.sing.masc.of the article in agreement with κύριον) 9.
κύριον (acc.sing.masc.of κύριος, metaphorical extent) 97.

Translation - "And all those living at Lydda and in the plain of Sharon saw him and they turned to the Lord."

Comment: It is doubtful that everyone in Lydda and all of the inhabitants of the plain of Sharon, which was a long fertile valley extending southward from Caesarea, down the coast to Joppa, was saved. But all those who saw Aeneas and knew of his healing turned to the Lord. Note ἐπί with the accusative of extent in a metaphorical usage involving some emotional decision. *Cf.* Rom.4:24; 1 Pet.1:13; Mt.15:32. They were not saved because they saw the miracle of healing. They were saved because the miracle gave to Peter's ministry the prestige which he needed in order to secure an audience that would listen seriously to his gospel message. Faith comes by hearing the Word of God (Rom.10:17), not by observing supernatural events.

Dorcas Restored to Life

(Acts 9:36 - 43)

Verse 36 - "Now there was at Joppa a certain disciple named Tabitha, which by interpretation is called Dorcas; this woman was full of good works and almsdeeds which she did."

Ἐν Ἰόππῃ δέ τις ἦν μαθήτρια ὀνόματι Ταβιθά, ἣ διερμηνευομένη λέγεται Δορκάς. αὕτη ἦν πλήρης ἔργων ἀγαθῶν καὶ ἐλεημοσυνῶν ὧν ἐποίει.

Ἐν (preposition with the locative, place where) 80.

#3202 Ἰόππῃ (loc.sing.fem.of Ἰοππη, place where).

Joppa - Acts 9:36,38,42,43; 10:5,8,23,32; 11:5,13.

Meaning: A Palestine city on the Mediterranean; on the border of Dan and Ephraim. A celebrated, though dangerous port, where a flourishing trade developed. It is the modern Jappa, just south of Tel Aviv. The home of Dorcas - Acts 9:36,38,42,43. The home of Simon, the tanner, where the servant of Cornelius found Peter - Acts 10:5,8,23,32; 11:5,13.

δέ (explanatory conjunction) 11.
τις (nom.sing.fem.of τις, in agreement with μαθήτρια) 486.
ἦν (3d.per.sing.imp.ind.of εἰμί, progressive description) 86.

#3203 μαθήτρια (nom.sing.fem.of μαθήτρια, subject of ἦν).

disciple - Acts 9:36.

Meaning: the feminine form of μαθητής (#421). A female disciple; a Christian woman. With reference to Tabitha (Dorcas) of Joppa - Acts 9:36.

ὀνόματι (dat.sing.neut.of ὄνομα, possession) 108.

#3204 Ταβιθά (nom.sing.fem.of Ταβιθά, appellation).

Tabitha - Acts 9:36,40.

Meaning: A Christian woman of Joppa - Acts 9:36,40.

ἣ (nom.sing.fem.of ὅς, subject of λέγεται) 65.
διερμηνευομένη (pres.pass.part.nom.sing.fem.of διερμηνεύω, adverbial, conditional) 2906.
λέγεται (3d.per.sing.pres.pass.ind.of λέγω, static) 66.

#3205 Δορκάς (nom.sing.fem.of Δορκάς, appellation).

Dorcas - Acts 9:36,39.

Meaning: Properly, a wild she-goat; a gazelle. A certain Christian woman of Joppa - Acts 9:36,39. *Cf.* #3204.

αὕτη (nom.sing.fem.of οὗτος, subject of ἦν) 93.
ἦν (3d.per.sing.imp.ind.of εἰμί, progressive description) 86.

πλήρης (nom.sing.fem.of πλήρης, predicate adjective) 1124.

ἔργων (abl.pl.neut.of ἔργον, source) 460.

αγαθῶν (abl.pl.neut.of ἀγαθός, in agreement with ἔργων) 547.

καὶ (adjunctive conjunction joining nouns) 14.

ἐλεημοσυνῶν (abl.pl.fem.of ἐλεημοσύνη, source) 558.

ὧν (abl.pl.fem.of ὅς, in a relative adjectival clause, case attraction to the antecedent) 65.

ἐποίει (3d.per.sing.imp.act.ind.of ποιέω, iterative) 127.

Translation - *"Now in Joppa there was a certain Christian woman named Tabitha, which, if translated into Greek means Dorcas. This woman was full of good works and philanthropies which she did frequently."*

Comment: δὲ is explanatory as Luke introduces a new element in the story of Peter's ministry in this area. The Aramaic "Tabitha" is the Greek "Dorcas" and the English "Gazelle. If her name is significant she must have been a beautiful and graceful woman. Spiritually she was as her works attest. Note the emphatic αὕτη and the iterative imperfect in ἐποίει. Note the attraction of the relative pronoun ὧν to the ablative case of its antecedent. *Cf.*Mt.18:19; John 15:20; Acts 1:1; 3:21; 22:10; 3:25; 7:17,45; Tit.3:6; 1 Cor.6:19; 2 Cor.10:8,13; Eph.1:8; Heb.6:10; 9:20; James 2:5.

Dorcas sickened and died as we learn in

Verse 37 - *"And it came to pass in those days, that she was sick and died: whom when they had washed, they laid her in an upper chamber."*

ἐγένετο δὲ ἐν ταῖς ἡμέραις ἐκείναις ἀσθενήσασαν αὐτὴν ἀποθανεῖν. λούσαντες δὲ (αὐτὴν) ἔθηκαν ἐν ὑπερῴῳ.

ἐγένετο (3d.per.sing.aor.ind.of γίνομαι, constative) 113.

δὲ (continuative conjunction) 11.

ἐν (preposition with the locative of time point) 80.

ταῖς (loc.pl.fem.of the article in agreement with ἡμέραις) 9.

ἡμέραις (loc.pl.fem.of ἡμέρα, time point) 135.

ἐκείναις (loc.pl.fem.of ἐκεῖνος, in agreement with ἡμέραις) 246.

ἀσθενήσασαν (1st.aor.act.part.acc.sing.fem.of ἀσθενέω, adverbial, temporal) 857.

αὐτὴν (acc.sing.fem.of αὐτός, general reference) 16.

ἀποθανεῖν (2d.aor.inf.of ἀποθνήσκω, noun use, subject of ἐγένετο) 774.

λούσαντες (aor.act.part.nom.pl.masc.of λούω, adverbial, temporal) 2761.

δὲ (continuative conjunction) 11.

αὐτὴν (acc.sing.fem.of αὐτός, direct object of ἔθηκαν) 16.

ἔθηκαν (3d.per.pl.aor.act.ind.of τίθημι, constative) 455.

ἐν (preposition with the locative of place where) 80.

ὑπερῴῳ (loc.sing.masc.of ὑπερῷος, place where) 2940.

Translation - *"And at that time she got sick and died. And when they had bathed her they laid her in the upper room."*

Comment: δὲ is adversative. This good and beautiful woman sickened and died. Loving hands tenderly bathed her body and she lay in state in the upper room, while other Christian disciples in Joppa sent for Peter. Rumor had it that he was in Lydda, not far away. *Cf.* #2940 for this interesting word. The scene is set for Peter's appearance and the miracle which occupies the remainder of the chapter.

Verse 38 - "And forasmuch as Lydda was nigh to Joppa, and the disciples had heard that Peter was there, they sent unto him two men, desiring him that he would not delay to come to them."

ἐγγὺς δὲ οὔσης Λύδδας τῇ Ἰόππῃ οἱ μαθηταὶ ἀκούσαντες ὅτι Πέτρος ἐστὶν ἐν αὐτῇ ἀπέστειλαν δύο ἄνδρας πρὸς αὐτὸν παρακαλοῦντες, Μὴ ὀκνήσῃς διελθεῖν ἕως ἡμῶν.

ἐγγὺς (nom.sing.neut.of ἐγγύς, predicate adjective) 1512.

δὲ (explanatory conjunction) 11.

οὔσης (pres.part.gen.sing.fem.of εἰμί) 86.

Λύδδας (gen.sing.fem.of Λύδδα, genitive absolute) 3199.

τῇ (dat.sing.fem.of the article in agreement with Ἰόππῃ) 9.

Ἰόππῃ (dat.sing.fem.of Ἰόππη, reference) 3202.

οἱ (nom.pl.masc.of the article in agreement with μαθηταὶ) 9.

μαθηταὶ (nom.pl.masc.of μαθητής, subject of ἀπέστειλαν) 421.

ἀκούσαντες (aor.act.part.nom.pl.masc.of ἀκούω, adverbial, temporal/-causal) 148.

ὅτι (conjunction introducing an object clause in indirect discourse) 211.

Πέτρος (nom.sing.masc.of Πέτρος, subject of ἐστὶν) 387.

ἐστὶν (3d.per.sing.pres.ind.of εἰμί, aoristic, indirect discourse) 86.

ἐν (preposition with the locative of place) 80.

αὐτῇ (loc.sing.fem.of αὐτός, place) 16.

ἀπέστειλαν (3d.per.pl.aor.act.ind.of ἀποστέλλω, constative) 215.

δύο (numeral) 385.

ἄνδρας (acc.pl.masc.of ἀνήρ, direct object of ἀπέστειλαν) 63.

πρὸς (preposition with the accusative of extent) 197.

αὐτὸν (acc.sing.masc.of αὐτός, extent) 16.

παρακαλοῦντες (pres.act.part.nom.pl.masc.of παρακαλέω, adverbial, telic) 230.

μὴ (qualified negative conjunction with the subjunctive in a purpose clause) 87.

#3206 ὀκνήσῃς (2d.per.sing.aor.act.subj.of ὀκνέω, purpose).

delay - Acts 9:38.

Meaning: Cf. ὄκνος - "shrinking, reluctance, hesitation." Hence, to delay, to be reticent, to be hesitant. With reference to Peter's desire to go to Joppa - Acts 9:38, followed by an epexegetical infinitive)

διελθεῖν (aor.mid.inf.of διέρχομαι, epexegetical) 1017.

ἕως (preposition with the genitive of place description with persons) 71.
ἡμῶν (gen.pl.masc.of ἐγώ, place description, with persons) 123.

Translation - "Now since Lydda was not far from Joppa, when the disciples heard that Peter was there, they sent two men to him to beg him not to hesitate to come to them at once."

Comment:δὲ is explanatory as Luke continues his narrative. Dorcas is dead in Joppa. Lydda is not far away - less than fifteen miles. The Christians in Joppa learn that Peter is there. They need his help and they send for him. Note the dative here with ἐγγύς, only one of four places where it occurs with the dative, if we count the indeclinable Ἰερουσαλήμ in Luke 19:11 and Acts 1:12. The other two are Acts 9:38; 27:8. Lydda is near *in reference to* Joppa. The participle ἀκούσαντες is adverbial, both temporal and causal. Causal participles are always temporal also, since cause must precede result. The ὅτι clause is objective in indirect discourse, with the tense of ἐστίν the same as in direct discourse. They were saying in Joppa, "Peter is in Lydda." The text does not tell us that the Christians in Joppa expected Peter to perform a miracle and raise Dorcas from the dead. It does tell us that they were very eager for him to come. Perhaps they wanted him only for the comfort and consolation that he could bring, perhaps with an assurance that Dorcas would rise again in the resurrection at the last day. The participle παρακαλοῦντες is telic and is followed by the telic clause with μὴ and the subjunctive in ὀκνήσῃς, which, in turn is followed by the epexegetical infinitive διελθεῖν. The preposition ἕως here with the genitive of place description with persons, completes the sentence. *Cf.* ἕως αὐτοῦ in Luke 4:42.

The subjunctive with μὴ indicates that there was some hope in Joppa that Peter would accept their urgent invitation to visit them. "You will not hesitate to come to us, will you?" They hoped that Peter would say, "Of course not," which is equivalent to "Yes, I will come." There was no great need for haste. Dorcas was already dead. Peter's function in Joppa, whatever it might be, whether to comfort the mourners or to raise the dead could wait until he got there.

Consistent with the hopeful expectations of the Christians in Joppa, Peter complied with their request as we learn in

Verse 39 - "Then Peter arose and went with them. When he was come, they brought him into the upper chamber: and all the widows stood by him weeping, and shewing the coats and garments which Dorcas made, while she was with them."

ἀναστὰς δὲ Πέτρος συνῆλθεν αὐτοῖς. ὃν παραγενόμενον ἀνήγαγον εἰς τὸ ὑπερῷον, καὶ παρέστησαν αὐτῷ πᾶσαι αἱ χῆραι κλαίουσαι καὶ ἐπιδεικνύμεναι χιτῶνας καὶ ἱμάτια ὅσα ἐποίει μετ' αὐτῶν οὖσα ἡ Δορκάς.

ἀναστὰς (aor.act.part.nom.sing.masc.of ἀνίστημι, adverbial, temporal) 789.
δὲ (continuative conjunction) 11.
Πέτρος (nom.sing.masc.of Πέτροςl, subject of συνῆλθεν) 387.
συνῆλθεν (3d.per.sing.aor.mid.ind.of συνέρχομαι, constative) 78.

αὐτοῖς (instru.pl.masc. of αὐτός, association after σύν in composition) 16.

ὅν (acc.sing.masc.of ὅς, direct object of ἀνήγαγον,) 65.

παραγενόμενον (aor.mid.part.acc.sing.masc.of παραγίνομαι, adverbial, temporal) 139.

ἀνήγαγον (3d.per.pl.aor.act.ind.of ἀνάγω, constative) 329.

εἰς (preposition with the accusative of extent) 140.

τό (acc.sing.neut.of the article in agreement with ὑπερῷον) 9.

ὑπερῷον (acc.sing.neut.of ὑπερῷος, extent) 2940.

καί (continuative conjunction) 14.

παρέστησαν (3d.per.pl.aor.act.ind.of παρίστημι, constative) 1596.

αὐτῷ (loc.sing.masc.of αὐτός, place where, after παρά

πᾶσαι (nom.pl.fem.of πᾶς, in agreement with χῆραι) 67.

αἱ (nom.pl.fem.of the article in agreement with χῆραι) 9.

χῆραι (nom.pl.fem.of χήρα, subject of παρέστησαν) 1910.

κλαίουσαι (pres.act.part.nom.pl.fem.of κλαίω, adverbial, circumstantial) 225.

καί (adjunctive conjunction joining participles) 14.

ἐπιδεικνύμεναι (pres.mid.part.nom.pl.fem.of ἐπιδείκνυμι, adverbial, circumstantial) 1189.

χιτῶνας (acc.pl.masc.of χιτών, direct object of ἐπιδεικνύμεναι) 532.

καί (adjunctive conjunction joining nouns) 14.

ἱμάτια (acc.pl.neut.of ἱμάτιον, direct object of ἐπιδεικνύμεναι) 534.

ὅσα (acc.pl.neut.of ὅσος, direct object of ἐποίει, in an adjectival relative clause) 660.

ἐποίει (3d.per.sing.imp.act.ind.of ποιέω, tendential) 127.

μετ' (preposition with the genitive of accompaniment) 50.

αὐτῶν (gen.pl.masc.of αὐτός, accompaniment) 16.

οὖσα (pres.part.nom.sing.fem.of εἰμί, adverbial, temporal) 86.

ἡ (nom.sing.fem.of the article in agreement with Δορκάς) 9.

Δορκάς (nom.sing.fem.of Δορκάς, subject of ἐποίει) 3205.

Translation - "*And Peter got up and went with them, whom, when he arrived they conducted up to the upper room, and all the widows stood by his side, weeping and displaying the slips and dresses which Dorcas had intended to finish when she was still with them.*"

Comment: Dorcas' friends provided the evidence of the truth of verse 36b. Note the tendential imperfect in ἐποίει. Mantey (*Manual*, 189) defines it as "The lack of a sense of attainment . . . emphasized to the point of a positive implication that the end was not attained, but was only attempted, or that action tended toward realization." *Cf.* Luke 1:59; Mt.3:14; Acts 7:26, which are more clearly tendential than inceptive or descriptive as I have called them. Goodspeed's "that Dorcas *had made* when she was still with them" is wrong, as the imperfect never indicates the culminative result of completed action. The time frame for ἐποίει is set by the present participle οὖσα, which is temporal. During the time that Dorcas was still alive she had planned to make the garments involved, but did not live to finish them. The fact that they are mentioned in terms of specific types of garments - χιτῶνας καὶ ἱμάτια - indicates that either the women showed to Peter the material which had already been cut out, or, at least, the patterns. An uncut bolt of cloth would not indicate what type of garment Dorcas had in mind. I have assumed that the garments were designed for women, perhaps for the widows who were showing them, although the words used can apply to any garment, whether designed for men or women.

The scene is typical. A group of poverty stricken widows who had been clothed by the industry of Dorcas' needle are now weeping that she is dead. What happened in verse 40 is atypical.

Verse 40 - "But Peter put them all forth and kneeled down, and prayed; and turning him to the body said, Tabitha, arise. And she opened her eyes: and when she saw Peter, she sat up."

ἐκβαλὼν δὲ ἔξω πάντας ὁ Πέτρος καὶ θεὶς τὰ γόνατα προσηύξατο, καὶ ἐπιστρέψας πρὸς τὸ σῶμα εἶπεν, Ταβιθά, ἀνάστηθι. ἡ δὲ ἤνοιξεν τοὺς ὀφθαλμοὺς αὐτῆς, καὶ ἰδοῦσα τὸν Πέτρον ἀνεκάθισεν.

ἐκβαλὼν (aor.act.part.nom.sing.masc.of ἐκβάλλω, adverbial, temporal) 649.
δὲ (adversative conjunction) 11.
ἔξω (local adverb) 449.
πάντας (acc.pl.fem.of πᾶς, direct object of ἐκβαλὼν) 67.
ὁ (nom.sing.masc.of the article in agreement with Πέτρος) 9.
Πέτρος (nom.sing.masc.of Πέτρος, subject of προσηύξατο) 387.
καὶ (adjunctive conjunction joining participles) 14.
θεὶς (aor.act.part.nom.sing.masc.of τίθημι, adverbial, temporal) 455.
τὰ (acc.pl.neut.of the article in agreement with γόνατα) 9.
γόνατα (acc.pl.neut.of γόνυ, direct object of θεὶς) 2052.
προσηύξατο (3d.per.sing.aor.mid.ind.of προσεύχομαι, ingressive) 455.
καὶ (adjunctive conjunction joining verbs) 14.
ἐπιστρέψας (aor.act.part.nom.sing.masc.of ἐπιστρέφω, adverbial, temporal) 866.
πρὸς (preposition with the accusative of extent) 197.
τὸ (acc.sing.neut.of the article in agreement with σῶμα) 9.
σῶμα (acc.sing.neut.of σῶμα, extent) 507.
εἶπεν (3d.per.sing.aor.act.ind.of εἶπον, constative) 155.
Ταβιθά (voc.sing.fem.of Ταβιθά, address) 3204.
ἀνάστηθι (2d.per.sing.aor.act.impv.of ἀνίστημι, command) 789.
ἡ (nom.sing.fem.of the article, subject of ἤνοιξεν and ἀνεκάθισεν) 9.
δὲ (continuative conjunction) 11.
ἤνοιξεν (3d.per.sing.aor.act.ind.of ἀνοίγω, constative) 188.
τοὺς (acc.pl.masc.of the article in agreement with ὀφθαλμοὺς) 9.
ὀφθαλμοὺς (acc.pl.masc.of ὀφθαλμός, direct object of ἤνοιξεν) 501.
αὐτῆς (gen.sing.fem.of αὐτός, possession) 16.
καὶ (adjunctive conjunction joining verbs) 14.
ἰδοῦσα (aor.act.part.nom.sing.fem.of ὁράω, adverbial, temporal) 144.
τὸν (acc.sing.masc.of the article in agreement with Πέτρον) 9.

Πέτρον (acc.sing.masc.of Πέτρος, direct object of ἰδοῦσα) 387.
ἀνεκάθισεν (3d.per.sing.aor.act.ind.of ἀνακαθίζω, constative) 2157.

Translation - *"But Peter asked them all to step out, knelt and began to pray. And he turned toward the body and said, 'Tabitha, get up!' And she opened her eyes, and when she saw Peter, she sat up."*

Comment: δὲ is adversative as Peter prepared to do something more constructive than weep and speculate about what might have been. Literally, the text says that he threw them all out, but we need not think of this in any hostile or physically violent sense. He probably politely asked the women to step out of the room for a moment. Then he knelt and began to pray. Note the usual idiom for kneeling - θεὶς τὰ γόνατα - "he placed his knees." *Cf.* #2052 for the complete list. Luke does not tell us what Peter said. After all he was not speaking to anyone but God. The imperative is preemptory. There is a ring of heavenly authority in the Apostle's voice. God performed the miracle, not Peter. She opened her eyes, saw Peter and sat up. Thus Peter fulfilled Jesus' prophecy of John 14:12. *Cf.* #2157 - The son of the widow of Nain also sat up when Jesus raised him from death. Note the genitive of possession αὐτῆς after ὀφθαλμοὺς, but not αὐτοῦ after γόνατα. Thus the article often serves for the third personal pronoun in possession when the context allows. Note also the article ἡ serving as subject of ἤνοιξεν and ἀνεκάθισεν.

Verse 41 - *"And he gave her his hand, and lifted her up, and when he had called the saints and widows, presented her alive."*

δοὺς δὲ αὐτῇ χεῖρα ἀνέστησεν αὐτήν, φωνήσας δὲ τοὺς ἁγίους καὶ τὰς χήρας παρέστησεν αὐτὴν ζῶσαν.

δοὺς (aor.act.part.nom.sing.masc.of δίδωμι, adverbial, temporal/modal) 362.1
δὲ (continuative conjunction) 11.
αὐτῇ (dat.sing.fem.of αὐτός, indirect object of δοὺς) 16.
χεῖρα (acc.sing.neut.of χείρ, direct object of δοὺς) 308.
ἀνέστησεν (3d.per.sing.aor.act.ind.of ἀνίστημι, constative) 789.
αὐτήν (acc.sing.fem.of αὐτός, direct object of ἀνέστησεν) 16.
φωνήσας (aor.act.part.nom.sing.masc.of φωνέω, adverbial, temporal) 1338.
δὲ (continuative conjunction) 11.
τοὺς (acc.pl.masc.of the article in agreement with ἁγίους) 9.
ἁγίους (acc.pl.masc.of ἅγιος, direct object of φωνήσας) 94.
καὶ (adjunctive conjunction joining nouns) 14.
χήρας (acc.pl.fem.of χήρα, direct object of φωνήσας) 1910.
παρέστησεν (3d.per.sing.aor.act.ind.of παρίστημι, constative) 1596.
αὐτὴν (acc.sing.fem.of αὐτός, direct object of παρέστησεν) 16.
ζῶσαν (pres.act.part.acc.sing.fem.of ζάω, adverbial, circumstantial) 340.

Translation - *"And he gave her a hand and raised her up, and when he had called the saints and the widows, he presented her alive."*

Comment: The aorist participles δούς and φωνήσας are antecedent to their main verbs, ἀνέστησεν and παρέστησεν respectively. Peter "stood her up" and "stood her beside" her friends. ζῶσαν, the circumstantial participle tells us that she was alive. She had opened her eyes, she had seen Peter and she had sat up on the side of the bed. The action described is completely natural. Peter reached out his hand, which she grasped and he pulled her up on her feet. Then he called in her friends and presented her to them. And she was alive! It is a dramatic scene. Intuitionists, rationalists and empircists who reject the propositional revelation of evangelical Christianity will of course demythologize all elements of the supernatural in the Biblical account. To demythologize, as Bultmann, with his existentialism, has done, is only to replace what one calls a myth with another myth. Since no myth can be said to convey cognitive reality, what difference does it make which myth we believe, if indeed the story that Luke tells us in this passage is untrue?

The sovereign God of creation and redemption raised Dorcas from the dead. People who do not believe that He did this do not have the kind of faith that the New Testament associates with Christianity.

Just as the healing of Aeneas in Lydda had resulted in a revival in which all who saw it "turned to the Lord" (vs.35), so in Joppa Peter's miracle that restored the life of Dorcas was used by the Holy Spirit to bring many to Christ.

Verse 42 - "And it was known throughout all Joppa; and many believed in the Lord."

γνωστὸν δὲ ἐγένετο καθ' ὅλης (τῆς)'Ιόππης, καὶ ἐπίστευσαν πολλοὶ ἐπὶ τὸν κύριον.

γνωστὸν (acc.sing.neut.of γνωστός, predicate adjective) 1917.
δὲ (continuative conjunction) 11.
ἐγένετο (3d.per.sing.aor.ind.of γίνομαι, culminative) 113.
καθ' (preposition with the genitive, distributive - "throughout") 98.
ὅλης (gen.sing.fem.of ὅλος, in agreement with 'Ιόππης) 112.
(τῆς) (gen.sing.fem.of the article in agreement with 'Ιόππης) 9.
'Ιόππης (gen.sing.fem.of 'Ιόππη, distributive) 3202.
καὶ (continuative conjunction) 14.
ἐπίστευσαν (3d.per.pl.aor.act.ind.of πιστεύω, constative) 734.
πολλοὶ (nom.pl.masc.of πολύς subject of ἐπίστευσαν) 228.
ἐπὶ (preposition with the accusative, after ἐπίστευσαν to express emotion) 47.
τὸν (acc.sing.masc.of the article in agreement with κύριον) 9.
κύριον (acc.sing.masc.of κύριος, to express emotion) 97.

Translation - "And it came to be known all over Joppa, and many believed on the Lord."

Comment: Note that γνωστὸν and ἐπίστευσαν are emphasized, each in its own clause. Thus the revival continued, supported by the faithful witnessing of the early Christians and the gift of miracles which the Holy Spirit bestowed upon the

Apostles. Thus the Holy Spirit gave to His chosen Apostles the prestige essential to the authentication of their message, until they could commit it to the parchment that became the written New Testament. Once that document was complete there was no further need for miracles and accordingly they ceased. With the pages of the New Testament open before it, it is only a wicked and adulterous generation that would seek for any other sign. If they will not believe Moses, the prophets and the New Testament accounts of the person and work of Jesus Christ, of whom Moses and the prophets spoke, they will not believe though one rose from the dead. Faith comes by hearing and hearing by the Word of God, not by witnessing the titillative performances of mob psychologists, who should be out in the market making an honest living.

The incident in Joppa is closed and the final verse of the chapter sets the stage for the story of chapter ten.

Verse 43 - "And it came to pass that he tarried many days in Joppa with one Simon a tanner."

Ἐγένετο δὲ ἡμέρας ἱκανὰς μεῖναι ἐν Ἰόππῃ παρά τινι Σίμωνι βυρσεῖ.

Ἐγένετο (3d.per.sing.aor.ind.of γίνομαι, constative) 113.
δὲ (continuative conjunction) 11.
ἡμέρας (acc.pl.fem.of ἡμέρα, time extent) 135.
ἱκανὰς (acc.pl.fem.of ἱκανός, in agreement with ἡμέρας) 304.
μεῖναι (1st.aor.act.inf.of μένω, noun use, subject of ἐγένετο) 864.
ἐν (preposition with the locative of place) 80.
Ἰόππῃ (loc.sing.fem.of Ἰόππη, place where) 3202.
παρά (preposition with the locative of place, with persons) 154.
τινι (loc.sing.masc.of τις, indefinite pronoun, in agreement with Σίμωνι) 486.

#3207 Σίμωνι (loc.sing.masc.of Σίμωνι, place where, with persons).

Simon - Acts 9:43; 10:6,17,32.

Meaning: la tanner who lived in Joppa - Acts 9:43; 10:6,17,32.

#3208 βυρσεῖ (loc.sing.masc.of βυρσεύς, apposition).

tanner - Acts 9:43; 10:6,32.

Meaning: Cf. βύρσα - "a skin of an animal. A hide." Hence, a tanner - Simon, of Joppa - Acts 9:43; 10:6,32.

Translation - "And he stayed several days in Joppa with a certain tanner, named Simon."

Comment: Thus we find Simon Peter, the Apostle, a guest in the home of Simon, a tanner in Joppa, where he will be prepared by the Holy Spirit for his next adventure.

Peter and Cornelius
(Acts 10:1-33)

Acts 10:1 - "There was a certain man in Caesarea called Cornelius, a centurion of the band called the Italian band."

'Ανὴρ δέ τις ἐν Καισαρείᾳ ὀνόματι Κορνήλιος, ἑκατοντάρχης ἐκ σπείρης τῆς καλουμένης Ἰταλικῆς,

'Ανὴρ (nom.sing.masc.of ἀνήρ, subject of εἶδεν) 63.
δέ (explanatory conjunction) 11.
τις (nom.sing.masc.of τις, indefinite pronoun, in agreement with ἀνήρ) 486.
ἐν (preposition with the locative of place) 80.
Καισαρείᾳ (loc.sing.fem.of Καισαρίας, place where) 1200.
ὀνόματι (dat.sing.neut.of ὄνομα, possession) 108.

#3209 Κορνήλιος (nom.sing.masc.of Κορνήλιος, appellation).

Cornelius - Acts 10:1,3,17,22,24,25,30,31.

Meaning: A Roman Centurion, living at Caesarea, who was converted to Christianity - Acts 10:1,3,17,22,24,25,30,31.

#3210 ἑκατοντάρχης (nom.sing.masc.of ἑκατοντάρχης, apposition).

centurion - Acts 10:1,22; 21:32; 22:26; 24:23; 27:1,6,11,31,43.

Meaning: Cf. #717. A Roman military officer, presumably in charge of 100 men. Cornelius of Caesarea - Acts 10:1,22. An officer under Felix - Acts 24:23. Julius of Augustus band - Acts 27:1,31; In Jerusalem - Acts 21:32; 22:26; 27:6,11,31,43.

ἐκ (preposition with the ablative of source) 19.
σπείρης (abl.sing.fem.of σπεῖρα, source) 1635.
τῆς (abl.sing.fem.of the article in agreement with καλουμένης) 9.
καλουμένης (pres.pass.part.abl.sing.fem.of καλέω, adjectival, restrictive, in agreement with σπείρης) 107.

#3211 Ἰταλικῆς (abl.sing.fem.of Ἰταλικός, in apposition, in agreement with σπείρης).

Italian - Acts 10:1.

Meaning: σπεῖρα Ἰταλικ. - the Italian cohort. One of ten divisions of an ancient Roman legion, composed of Italian soldiers, not of local provincials - Acts 10:1.

Translation - "Now a certain man in Caesarea, named Cornelius, a centurion of the cohort known as the Italian . . . "

Comment: The verb of which 'Ανὴρ is the subject is εἶδεν of verse 3. Verse 2 is occupied with further description of Cornelius. Thus far we have his name, his residence city, his rank in the Roman army and the outfit to which he is attached. We learn something about his religion and social ideals in

Verse 2 - "A devout man, and one that feared God with all his house, which gave much alms to the people, and prayed to God alway."

εὐσεβὴς καὶ φοβούμενος τὸν θεὸν σὺν παντὶ τῷ οἴκῳ αὐτοῦ, ποιῶν ἐλεημοσύνας πολλὰς τῷ λαῷ καὶ δεόμενος τοῦ θεού διὰ παντός.

#3212 εὐσεβὴς (nom.sing.masc.of εὐσεβὴς, predicate adjective).

    devout - Acts 10:2,7.
    godly - 2 Pet.2:9.

Meaning: A combination of εὐ and σέβω (#1149). *Cf.* also σέβασμα (#3411) and σεβάζομαι (#3806). Hence devoted; devout. One who worships - Cornelius - Acts 10:2; one of his soldiers - Acts 10:7; the saints generally - 2 Pet.2:9.

    καὶ (adjunctive conjunction joining adjectives) 14.
φοβούμενος (pres.mid.part.nom.sing.masc.of φοβέομαι, adjectival, ascriptive, in agreement with ἀνήρ) 101.
    τὸν (acc.sing.masc.of the article in agreement with θεὸν) 9.
    θεὸν (acc.sing.masc.of θεός, direct object of φοβούμενος) 124.
    σὺν (preposition with the instrumental of association) 1542.
    παντὶ (instru.sing.masc.of πᾶς, in agreement with οἴκῳ) 67.
    τῷ (instru.sing.masc.of the article in agreement with οἴκῳ) 9.
    οἴκῳ (instru.sing.masc.of οἴκος, association) 784.
    αὐτοῦ (gen.sing.masc.of αὐτός, relationship) 16.
    ποιῶν (pres.act.part.nom.sing.masc.of ποιέω, adjectival, ascriptive, in agreement with ἀνήρ) 127.
ἐλεημοσύνας (acc.pl.fem.of ἐλεημοσύνη, direct object of ποιῶν) 558.
    πολλὰς (acc.pl.fem.of πολύς, in agreement with ἐλεημοσύνας) 228.
    τῷ (dat.sing.masc.of the article in agreement with λαῷ) 9.
    λαῷ (dat.sing.masc.of λαός, indirect object of ποιῶν) 110.
    καὶ (adjunctive conjunction joining participles) 14.
δεόμενος (pres.mid.part.nom.sing.masc.of δέομαι, adjectival, ascriptive, in agreement with ἀνήρ) 841.
    τοῦ (gen.sing.masc.of the article in agreement with θεοῦ) 9.
    θεοῦ (gen.sing.masc.of θεός, with a verb of emotion) 124.
    διὰ (preposition with the genitive of time description) 118.
    παντός (gen.sing.neut.of πᾶς, time description) 67.

Translation - " . . . devout and one who, with all of his family had great reverence for God, who gave many gifts to the people and who prayed to God always."

Comment: We still do not have a main verb, until we come to verse 3. Luke is still describing ἀνήρ of verse 1. The adjective εὐσεβής is in the predicate as are the adjectival participles φοβούμενος, ποιῶν and δεόμενος, all of which are present tense participles indicating durative action. Cornelius was consistent in his reverence for God, his charities and his prayer life. Accustomed to maintaining a strict discipline in the military, he exercised the same control over his household. One is reminded of Joshua, the military chieftain of Israel (Joshua 24:15). *Cf.*#67 for other examples of διὰ παντός, indicating an extended period of time, "always" or "continually." We say, "through thick and thin."

Verse 1 points to Cornelius' social and political prestige. Verse 2 describes his consistent religious life.

Cornelius is often cited as an evidence from Scripture that one need not approach the throne of God in prayer in the name of Jesus Christ in order to secure an audience. But it is important to see that Cornelius did not become a Christian until he came to God for salvation in the name of Jesus Christ. His prayers gained for him a visit from Peter who preached the gospel of Christ to him and resulted in his prayer of faith in the mediator Christ Jesus. The revelation of God to man is Christocentric   God is known by man only through the divine Logos. Cornelius is representative of a great many people who have a deep sense of need and longing for something better and who reach out in the darkness for more light. These people are not knowlingly rejecting the claims of the gospel of Jesus Christ. When a sinner sincerely seeks for more light, God is under moral obligation to give him more light until he comes to Christ.

God cannot and will not hear the prayer of one who has a full knowledge of the mediatorial work of His Son and who with deliberation seeks to bypass Jesus Christ in his approach to the throne of God.

Few who come to God for the first time to seek salvation are well acquainted with the theological issues involved. If the Holy Spirit is calling the sinner, and granting to him repentance and faith his prayer, though perhaps not clearly perceptive in reference to the person and work of Christ, is nevertheless not contemptuous of it. Cornelius prayed earnestly before he became a Christian, and in answer to his prayer, God sent His Apostle who spelled out for Cornelius the plan of salvation.

Verse 3 - "He saw in a vision evidently about the ninth hour of the day an angel of God coming in to him, and saying to him, Cornelius, . . . "

εἶδεν ἐν ὁράματι φανερῶς ὡσεὶ περὶ ὥραν ἐνάτην τῆς ἡμέρας ἄγγελον τοῦ θεοῦ εἰσελθόντα πρὸς αὐτὸν καὶ εἰπόντα αὐτῷ, Κορνήλιε,

εἶδεν (3d.per.sing.aor.act.ind.of ὁράω, constative) 144.
ἐν (preposition with the locative, instrumental use) 80.
ὁράματι (locative sing.neut.of ὅραμα, instrumental use) 1228.
φανερῶς (adverbial) 2072.
ὡσεὶ (conjunction in a comparative clause) 325.
περὶ (preposition with the accusative of time extent) 173.
ὥραν (acc.sing.fem.of ὥρα, time extent) 735.
ἐνάτην (acc.sing.fem.of ἔννατος, in agreement with ὥραν) 1318.
τῆς (gen.sing.fem.of the article in agreement with ἡμέρας) 9.

ἡμέρας (gen.sing.fem.of ἡμέρα, time description) 135.

ἄγγελον (acc.sing.masc.of ἄγγελος, direct object of εἶδεν) 96.

τοῦ (gen.sing.masc.of the article in agreement with θεοῦ) 9.

θεοῦ (gen.sing.masc.of θεός, description) 124.

εἰσελθόντα (aor.mid.part.acc.sing.masc.of εἰσέρχομαι, adjectival, ascriptive, in agreement with ἄγγελον) 234.

πρὸς (preposition with the accusative of extent) 197.

αὐτὸν (acc.sing.masc.of αὐτός, extent) 16.

καὶ (adjunctive conjunction joining participles) 14.

εἰπόντα (aor.act.part.acc.sing.masc.of εἶπον, adjectival, ascriptive, in agreement with ἄγγελον) 155.

αὐτῷ (dat.sing.masc.of αὐτός, indirect object of εἰπόντα) 16.

Κορνήλιε (voc.sing.masc.of Κορνήλιος, address) 3209.

Translation - ". . . at about three o'clock in the afternoon, he clearly saw in a vision an angel of God coming in to him and saying to him, 'Cornelius. . . ' "

Comment: φανερῶς (#2072) is the opposite of ἐν κρύπτῳ - "clearly" or "distinctly" are satisfactory translations. ὡσεὶ περὶ is rare in the New Testament. The participles εἰσελθόντα and εἰπόντα, though aorist participles, do not express time. They are coincident participles in indirect discourse. *Cf.* Acts 9:12; 26:13; 2 Peter 1:18 - in Acts 10:3 after εἶδεν; in 2 Pet.1:18 after ἀκούω.

The vision which Cornelius saw and the instructions which he is about to receive do not prove that he is a Christian. There is evidence that God is about to reward his sincere search for the truth by sending Peter to him in order that he can hear the gospel of Christ and approach God through the mediatorial agency of His Son, the Divine Logos.

Verse 4 - "And when he looked on him, he was afraid, and said, What is it, Lord? And he said unto him, Thy prayers and thine alms are come up for a memorial before God."

ὁ δὲ ἀτενίσας αὐτῷ καὶ ἔμφοβος γενόμενος εἶπεν, Τί ἐστιν, κύριε; εἶπεν δὲ αὐτῷ, Αἱ προσευχαί σου καὶ αἱ ἐλεημοσύναι σου ἀνέβησαν εἰς μνημόσυνον ἔμπροσθεν τοῦ θεοῦ.

ὁ (nom.sing.masc.of the article, subject of εἶπεν) 9.

δὲ (continuative conjunction) 11.

ἀτενίσας (aor.act.part.nom.sing.masc.of ἀτενίζω, adverbial, temporal) 2028.

αὐτῷ (dat.sing.masc.of αὐτός, person) 16.

καὶ (adjunctive conjunction joining participles) 14.

ἔμφοβος (nom.sing.masc.of ἔμφοβος, predicate adjective) 2890.

γενόμενος (aor.mid.part.nom.sing.masc.of γίνομαι, adverbial, temporal) 113.

εἶπεν (3d.per.sing.aor.act.ind.of εἶπον, constative) 155.

Τί (nom.sing.neut.of τίς, interrogative pronoun, subject of ἐστιν, direct question) 281.

ἐστιν (3d.per.sing.pres.ind.of εἰμί, aoristic) 86.

κύριε (voc.sing.masc.of κύριος, address) 97.

εἶπεν (3d.per.sing.aor.act.ind.of εἶπον, constative) 155.

δὲ (continuative conjunction) 11.

αὐτῷ (dat.sing.masc.of αὐτός, indirect object of εἶπεν) 16.

Αἱ (nom.pl.fem.of the article in agreement with προσευχαί) 9.

προσευχαί (nom.pl.fem.of προσευχή, subject of ἀνέβησαν) 1238.

σου (gen.sing.masc.of σύ, possession) 104.

καὶ (adjunctive conjunction joining nouns) 14.

αἱ (nom.pl.fem.of the article in agreement with ἐλεημοσύναι) 9.

ἐλεημοσύναι (nom.pl.fem.of ἐλεημοσύνη, subject of ἀνέβησαν) 558.

σου (gen.sing.masc.of σύ, possession) 104.

ἀνέβησαν (3d.per.pl.aor.act.ind.of ἀναβαίνω, culminative) 323.

εἰς (preposition with the accusative, purpose) 140.

μνημόσυνον (acc.sing.neut.of μνημόσυνον, purpose) 1569.

ἔμπροσθεν (preposition with the genitive, with persons, place description) 459.

τοῦ (gen.sing.masc.of the article in agreement with θεοῦ) 9.

θεοῦ (gen.sing.masc.of θεός, place description) 124.

Translation - "And he stared at him, seized with fear and said, 'What is it, Lord?' And he said to him, 'Your prayers and charities have risen as a matter of record before God.' "

Comment: *Cf.*#'s 2028 and 2890. Cornelius was rooted to the spot as he riveted his gaze upon the heavenly messenger and he was seized with terror. εἰς with the accusative denotes purpose. A soldier would understand this, as the record of service of a military man is always on file for purposes of evaluation and possible promotion. That Cornelius was not justified by works (Acts 13:39) is clear from the thrust of the entire passage. If God could have accepted his prayers and charitable acts in lieu of faith, and given him salvation in exchange, it would not have been necessary for God to instruct him to send for Peter to preach the gospel to him. What the passage does teach is clear - if a sinner sincerely follows whatever light he has, it is incumbent upon a moral God to see that he gets more light. God, of course, knows what the unsaved think and do and how they respond to the light of conscience. If and when He finds sincerity He must reward that by offering the light of the gospel of Christ.

A missionary in French Equatorial Africa says that at the close of his sermon in a village of disc-lipped women, where he had preached the gospel for the first time, an old woman came to him and said, "I have believed since I was a little girl that there was a God in heaven like that." It is not the fault of people like that, that for hundreds of years the Western church neglected the missionary enterprise in much of the heathen world. Those who, like the old woman, but who never had the opportunity to hear the gospel, as she did, will be judged on the basis of Romans 2:6-16. It is comforting to note that demographic studies make clear the fact that the vast majority of those born in uncivilized parts of the world have died in infancy. Were this not true there would not be standing room upon the planet now, 4400 years after the flood and the land/man ratio, which translates to the food/population ratio, would long since have starved the human race to death. Those who die in infancy, though sinners by birth, are not transgressors of God's law. They "had not sinned after the similitude of Adam's transgression" (Rom.5:14). "Adam was not deceived" (1 Tim.2:14). He sinned after full deliberation of the consequences of his act. Thus his sin was also transgression. Those who die before they have reached the age of discretion, therefore are not transgressors. Little babies, who died in infancy are not saved because they have never been *lost*. They are *safe*.

This analysis will help us to conclude that heaven will be far more heavily populated then hell. A discussion of the saved/lost ratio must take into account only those who survived infancy - a number which is a very small percentage of the total number of sons and daughters born to Adam's race. The story of Cornelius touches this matter only obliquely. He lived in a culture and at a time when the church was active in the missionary enterprise. He lived at the time when the Christians still did not understand as well as they later came to understand that the gospel of Christ is for the Gentile as well as for the Jew. He was the object lesson, designed by the Lord, to make Peter and his Apostolic colleagues understand this. Now Cornelius gets instructions to send men to Joppa and invite a man named Simon Peter to visit him.

Verse 5 - "And now send men to Joppa, and call for one Simon, whose surname is Peter."

καὶ νῦν πέμφον ἄνδρας εἰς Ἰόππην καὶ μετάπεμφαι Σίμωνά τινα ὃς ἐπικαλεῖται Πέτρος,

καὶ (continuative conjunction) 14.
νῦν (temporal adverb) 1497.
πέμφον (2d.per.sing.aor.act.impv.of πέμπω, command) 169.
ἄνδρας (acc.pl.masc.of ἀνήρ, direct object of πέμφον) 63.
εἰς (preposition with the accusative of extent) 140.
Ἰόππην (acc.sing.fem.of Ἰόππη, extent) 3202.
καὶ (adjunctive conjunction joining verbs) 14.

#3213 μετάπεμφαι (2d.per.sing.1st.aor.mid.impv.of μεταπέμπω, command).

call for - Acts 10:5; 11:13.
send for - Acts 10:22,29,29; 20:1; 24:24,26; 25:3.

Meaning: A combination of μετά (#50) and πέμπω (#169). Hence, to send after: to send for. With reference to Cornelius' men who came to summon Peter - Acts 10:5,22,29,29; 11:13. Felix sent for Paul - Acts 24:24,26; Festus is requested to summon Paul to Jerusalem - Acts 25:3. Paul sent for his disciples - Acts 20:1.

Σίμωνά (acc.sing.masc.of Σίμων, direct object of μετάπεμφαι) 386.
τινα (acc.sing.masc.of τις, in agreement with Σίμωνά) 486.

ὅς (nom.sing.masc.of ὅς, subject of ἐπικαλεῖται, in an adjectival relative clause) 65.

ἐπικαλεῖται (3d.per.sing.pres.pass.ind.of ἐπικαλέω, customary) 884.

Πέτρος (nom.sing.masc.of Πέτρος, appellation) 387.

Translation - "*And now send men to Joppa and call for a certain man - Simon, who is nicknamed Peter.*"

Comment: Note the repetition of πέμπω, combined with μετά in #3213. - "Send and send after. . . " The Lord's directions are specific so that there will be no mistake. This man Simon is defined by the relative adjectival clause as the Simon who is known also by his nickname, Peter. The Lord's directions continue in

Verse 6 - "*He lodgeth with one Simon, a tanner, whose house is by the sea side: he shall tell thee what thou oughtest to do.*"

οὗτος ξενίζεται παρά τινι Σίμωνι βυρσεῖ, ᾧ ἐστιν οἰκία παρὰ θάλασσαν.

οὗτος (nom.sing.masc.of οὗτος, subject of ξενίζεται) 93.

#3214 ξενίζεται (3d.per.sing.pres.mid.ind.of ξενίζω, aoristic).

    entertain - Heb.13:2.
    lodge - Acts 10:6,18,23,32; 21:16; 28:7.
    strange thing - Acts 17:20.
    think strange - 1 Pet.4:4,12.

Meaning: To receive and entertain as a guest. In the passive, to be entertained. To give/receive hospitality. With reference to Abraham who entertained angels - Heb.13:2. *Cf.* Gen.18:1-33. With reference to Peter in the house of Simon the Tanner - Acts 10:6,18,32. Cornelius' servants in the house of Simon - Acts 10:23. Paul and Luke in the home of Mnason - Acts 21:16; with Publius on Malta - Acts 28:7. In an accommodated meaning, to consider something strange, new, unprecedented or unusual - as an adjective - Acts 17:20; the attitude of the unregenerate who think the behavior of the saints is strange - 1 Pet.4:4. Christians should not regard persecution from the world a strange thing - 1 Pet.4:12.

    παρὰ (preposition with the locative of place, with persons) 154.
    τινι (loc.sing.masc.of τις, indefinite pronoun, in agreement with Σίμωνι) 486.
    Σίμωνι (loc.sing.masc.of Σίμων, association) 3207.
    βυρσεῖ (loc.sing.masc.of βυρσεύς, apposition) 3208.
    ᾧ (dat.sing.masc.of ὅς, possession) 65.
    ἐστιν (3d.per.sing.pres.ind.of εἰμί, aoristic) 86.
    οἰκία (nom.sing.fem.of οἰκία, subject of ἐστιν) 186.
    παρὰ (preposition with the accusative, "near to") 154.
    θάλασσαν (acc.sing.fem.of θάλασσα, "near to.") 374.

Translation - "*This man is the guest of a certain Simon, a tanner, who has a house by the sea.*"

Comment: οὗτος is deictic, pointing with emphasis to Σίμων Πέτρος, who must be carefully distinguished from Σίμων βυρσεύς. παρά with the locative of place, with persons, and παρά with the accusative with a verb of rest, where its basic idea - "parallel to" is seen. It is interesting that the Lord's instructions to Cornelius and his messengers are so specific. The problem of avoiding confusion between the two Simons is handled by telling that the first has a nickname and that the second is a tanner who lives by the seashore. Thus Cornelius' messengers lost no time in Joppa looking for Simon the tanner. He was the only tanner in Joppa named Simon who also lived by the sea. One wonders whether he chose his home site with a view to having the salt water and sunshine on the beach for his hide tanning business. Thus God directed Cornelius, not only to the city and the man, but also to his host and the location of the house where they would find him.

We are delighted to challenge the existentialists to tell us how the angel of the Lord knew that at that particular time Simon Peter, having been called from Lydda to Joppa, for the miracle that restored Dorcas to life, was staying in the home of Simon the tanner, who lived by the seaside. Let Bultmann demythologize that one! There is no problem for one who accepts on an *a priori* basis the "given" that the New Testament is an inspired book that has for its subject matter propositional revelation. We expect novelists to write scenarios like this, but they do not expect their readers to believe what they write. This is not a novel. It is history, and it really happened. The omniscience that is required for God to know where Peter was and how he could be found is not unusual for the God of the Bible.

Verse 7 - "And when the angel which spoke unto Cornelius was departed, he called two of his household servants, and a devout soldier of them that waited on him continually."

ὡς δὲ ἀπῆλθεν ὁ ἄγγελος ὁ λαλῶν αὐτῷ, φωνήσας δύο τῶν οἰκετῶν καὶ στρατιώτην εὐσεβῆ τῶν προσκαρτερούντων αὐτῷ,

ὡς (conjunction with the indicative in a definite temporal clause) 128.

δὲ (continuative conjunction) 11.

ἀπῆλθεν (3d.per.sing.aor.mid.ind.of ἀπέρχομαι, culminative) 239.

ὁ (nom.sing.masc.of the article in agreement with ἄγγελος) 9.

ἄγγελος (nom.sing.masc.of ἄγγελος, subject of ἀπῆλθεν) 96.

ὁ (nom.sing.masc.of the article in agreement with λαλῶν) 9.

λαλῶν (pres.act.part.nom.sing.masc.of λαλέω, substantival, in apposition with ἄγγελος) 815.

αὐτῷ (dat.sing.masc.of αὐτός, indirect object of λαλῶν) 16.

φωνήσας (aor.act.part.nom.sing.masc.of φωνέω, adverbial, temporal) 1338.

δύο (numeral) 385.

τῶν (gen.pl.masc.of the article in agreement with οἰκετῶν) 9.

οἰκετῶν (gen.pl.masc.of οἰκέτης, partitive genitive) 2572.

καὶ (adjunctive conjunction joining nouns) 14.

στρατιώτην (acc.sing.masc.of στρατιώτης, direct object of φωνήσας) 724.

εὐσεβῆ (acc.sing.masc.of εὐσεβής, in agreement with στρατιώτην) 3212.

τῶν (gen.pl.masc.of the article in agreement with προσκαρτερούντων) 9.

προσκαρτερούντων (pres.act.part.gen.pl.masc.of προσκαρτερέω, substantival, partitive genitive) 2113.

αὐτῷ (dat.sing.masc.of αὐτός, person) 16.

Translation - "*And when the angel who had been speaking to him had gone away, he called two of his house servants and a devoted soldier of his bodyguard. . .*"

Comment: ὡς introduces a definite temporal clause. Once the angel had departed, Cornelius acted. He chose two house servants and a devout aide-de-camp. The sentence goes on through verse eight, where we have one more temporal participle before we reach the main verb, ἀπέστειλεν, in verse 8.

Verse 8 - "*And when he had declared all these things unto them, he sent them to Joppa.*"

καὶ ἐξηγησάμενος ἅπαντα αὐτοῖς ἀπέστειλεν αὐτοὺς εἰς τὴν Ἰόππην.

καὶ (continuative conjunction) 14.

ἐξηγησάμενος (aor.mid.part.nom.sing.masc.of ἐξηγέομαι, adverbial, temporal) 1703.

ἅπαντα (acc.pl.neut.of ἅπας, direct object of ἐξηγησάμενος) 639.

αὐτοῖς (dat.pl.masc.of αὐτός, indirect object of ἐξηγησάμενος) 16.

ἀπέστειλεν (3d.per.sing.aor.act.ind.of ἀποστέλλω, constative) 215.

αὐτοὺς (acc.pl.masc.of αὐτός, direct object of ἀπέστειλεν) 16.

εἰς (preposition with the accusative of extent) 140.

τὴν (acc.sing.fem.of the article in agreement with Ἰόππην) 9.

Ἰόππην (acc.sing.fem.of Ἰόππη, extent) 3202.

Translation - "*And when he had explained it all to them fully, he sent them to Joppa.*"

Comment: The three men got a full review of events - the vision, the visit of the angel, what he said and the orders he gave, together with clear directions. They were to look for a man named Simon, whom most people called Peter, who was a guest in the house by the sea side where another man named Simon who was a tanner lived. Joppa was down the coast from Caesarea a distance of about thirty miles. The vision came to Cornelius at three in the afternoon. It was now near the close of the day, and the three men waited until the following morning to begin their journey.

Verse 9 - "*On the morrow, as they went on their journey, and drew nigh unto the city, Peter went up upon the housetop to pray about the sixth hour.*"

Τῇ δὲ ἐπαύριον ὁδοιπορούντων ἐκείνων καὶ τῇ πόλει ἐγγιζόντων ἀνέβη Πέτρος ἐπὶ τὸ δῶμα προσεύξασθαι περὶ ὥραν ἑκτήν.

τῇ (loc.sing.fem.of the article, time point) 9.

δὲ (continuative conjunction) 11.

ἐπαύριον (temporal adverb) 1680.

#3215 ὁδοιπορούντων (pres.mid.part.gen.pl.masc.of ὁδοιπορέω, genitive absolute).

go on one's journey - Acts 10:9.

Meaning: Cf.ὁδοιπόρος - "traveller" and ὁδοιπορία (#2002). Hence, to make a journey; to travel. With reference to Cornelius' servants who travelled from Caesarea to Joppa - Acts 10:9.

ἐκείνων (gen.pl.masc.of ἐκεῖνος, genitive absolute) 246.

καὶ (adjunctive conjunction joining participles) 14.

τῇ (loc.sing.fem.of the article in agreement with πόλει) 9.

πόλει (loc.sing.fem.of πόλις, place where) 243.

ἐγγιζόντων (pres.act.part.gen.pl.masc.of ἐγγίζω, genitive absolute) 252.

ἀνέβη (3d.per.sing.aor.act.ind.of ἀναβαίνω, constative) 323.

Πέτρος (nom.sing.masc.of Πέτρος, subject of ἀνέβη) 387.

ἐπὶ (preposition with the accusative of extent, place) 47.

τὸ (acc.sing.neut.of the article in agreement with δῶμα) 9.

δῶμα (acc.sing.neut.of δῶμα, place where) 888.

προσεύξασθαι (aor.mid.inf.of προσεύχομαι, purpose) 544.

περὶ (preposition with the accusativen, time approximation) 173.

ὥραν (acc.sing.fem.of ὥρα, accusative of time approximation) 735.

ἕκτην (acc.sing.fem.of ἕκτος, in agreement with ὥραν) 1317.

Translation - "And the next day, while they were on their way and as they approached the city, Peter went up about noon on the rooftop to pray."

Comment: ἐπαύριον (#1680) always has τῇ, the locative of time point, meaning "the next day" — "next" in relation to the previous day indicated by the context. In this case it means the day after that on which Cornelius saw the vision and gave the order to his servants. The genitive absolutes are in the present tense and indicate simultaneous time with Peter's prayer meeting on the rooftop in Joppa. More specifically, the time was "about noon." The main verb is ἀνέβη and refers to Peter's climb to the rooftop where he went for the purpose of prayer. The timing is right, directed by the sovereign God who "works all things after the counsel of his own will" (Eph.1:11). If Cornelius' servants had left Caesarea the evening before they would have arrived in Joppa, after a walk of about five or six hours (thirty miles) in the middle of the night. They waited until early morning, the next day and arrived in Joppa about noon. God timed Peter's prayer meeting and vision so that when he awoke and pondered its meaning, the answer to his problem was knocking at the gate of his host. Note that it was as the men were approaching Joppa that Peter went up to pray. We saw this principle at work in chapter 8 as God brought Philip and the eunuch together in the desert, as if by chance, and also in chapter 9, as God arranged the events that transpired between Saul and Ananias in Damascus. The three men from Caesarea are on the outskirts of Joppa, asking for directions to the house of Simon, a tanner, who lives by the seashore. Simon Peter, the Apostle, is praying atop that house. It is noon. Freud should have been interested in what we have in

Verse 10 - "And he became very hungry, and would have eaten: but while they made ready, he fell into a trance."

ἐγένετο δὲ πρόσπεινος καὶ ἤθελεν γεύσασθαι. παρασκευαζόντων δὲ αὐτῶν ἐγένετο ἐπ' αὐτὸν ἔκστασις,

ἐγένετο (3d.per.sing.aor.ind.of γίνομαι, ingressive) 113.
δὲ (adversative conjunction) 11.

#3216 πρόσπεινος (nom.sing.masc.of πρόσπεινος, predicate adjective).

very hungry - Acts 10:10.

Meaning: Cf. πεῖνα - "hunger" and πεινάω (#335), plus πρός (#197) in a perfective sense - "hunger besides" *i.e.* very hungry. With reference to Peter in Joppa - Acts 10:10.

καὶ (inferential conjunction) 14.
ἤθελεν (3d.per.sing.imp.act.ind.of θέλω, inchoative) 88.
γεύσασθαι (aor.mid.inf.of γεύομαι, epexegetical) 1219.

#3217 παρασκευαζόντων (pres.act.part.gen.pl.masc.of παρασκευάζω, genitive absolute).

make ready - Acts 10:10.
be ready - 2 Cor.9:2.
prepare one's self - 1 Cor.14:8.
ready - 2 Cor.9:3.

Meaning: A combination of παρά (#154) and σκευάζω - "to prepare" - "to make ready." παρά in a perfective sense. In the Acts 10:10 context "to prepare food." Followed by εἰς πόλεμον in 1 Cor.14:8; to prepare to make a finanicial offering - 2 Cor.9:2,3.

δὲ (adversative conjunction) 11.
αὐτῶν (gen.pl.masc.of αὐτός, genitive absolute) 16.
ἐγένετο (3d.per.sing.aor.ind.of γίνομαι, ingressive) 113.
ἐπ' (preposition with the accusative of extent, metaphorica place) 47.
αὐτὸν (acc.sing.masc.of αὐτός, metaphorical extent) 16.
ἔκστασις (nom.sing.fem.of ἔκστασις, subject of ἐγένετο) 2083.

Translation - "But he became very hungry and (therefore) he began to want to eat. But while they were preparing lunch he fell into a trance."

Comment: Peter went up to pray but (adversative δὲ) he became very hungry (ingressive aorist in ἐγένετο) and he began to want to eat (inchoative imperfect in ἤθελεν and an epexegetical infinitive in γεύσασθαι). Peter was so hungry that he could not keep his mind on his praying. But (another adversative δὲ) lunch was not yet ready. This is clear from the present tense in the genitive absolute. The cook was getting lunch as fast as she could. Peter was going to be forced to wait, but he was too hungry to pray. The Lord apparently was not interested in listening to Peter pray anyway, as He had something to tell him that was very important.

Note the perfective force of πρός in composition. *Cf.* Acts 1:14, and also the perfective force of παρά. *Cf.* Acts 17:16; Heb.3:16; Acts 28:11 Gal.4:10; Luke 14:1; 2 Cor.11:23; Heb.6:6; Acts 15:19.

Unable to pray because of the intensity of hunger pangs and unable to eat because lunch was not yet ready, Peter was treated to an experience that may have been to some extent the result of his hunger, and certainly was to his benefit, as he was to learn a lesson that he and his brethren, to the strengthening of whom he was committed by a divine commission (Luke 22:31,32), would never forget. What Peter saw in the trance fits his desire for food before he fell asleep. If Sigmund Freud can derive any comfort from that, he is welcome to it, though it is not likely that Freud would suggest that God had anything to do with it.

Verse 11 - "And saw heaven opened, and a certain vessel descending unto him, as it had been a great sheet knit at the four corners, and let down to the earth."

καὶ θεωρεῖ τὸν οὐρανὸν ἀνεῳγμένον καὶ καταβαῖνον σκεῦός τι ὡς ὀθόνην μεγάλην τέσσαρσιν ἀρχαῖς καθιέμενον ἐπὶ τῆς γῆς,

καὶ (continuative conjunction) 11.

θεωρεῖ (3d.per.sing.pres.act.ind.of θεωρέω, historical) 1667.

τὸν (acc.sing.masc.of the article in agreement with οὐρανὸν) 9.

οὐρανὸν (acc.sing.masc.of οὐρανός, direct object of θεωρεῖ) 254.

ἀνεῳγμένον (perf.pass.part.acc.sing.masc.of ἀνοίγω, adjectival, ascriptive, in agreement with οὐρανὸν) 188.

καὶ (adjunctive conjunction joining nouns) 14.

καταβαῖνον (pres.act.part.acc.sing.neut.of καταβαίνω, adjectival ascriptive, in agreement with σκεῦος) 324.

σκεῦός (acc.sing.neut.of σκεῦος, direct object of θεωρεῖ) 997.

τι (acc.sing.neut.of τις, indefinite pronoun, in agreement with σκεῦος) 486.

ὡς (conjunction in a comparative clause) 128.

#3218 ὀθόνην (acc.sing.fem.of ὀθόνη, in agreement with σκεῦος).

sheet - Acts 10:11; 11:5.

Meaning: linen cloth, such as was used for women's clothing. Sail cloth; a linen sheet - Acts 10:11; 11:5.

μεγάλην (acc.sing.fem.of μέγας, in agreement with ὀθόνην) 184.

τέσσαρσιν (instru.pl.fem.of τέσσαρες, in agreement with ἀρχαῖς) 1508.

ἀρχαῖς (instrumental pl.fem.of ἀρχή, means) 1285.

καθιέμενον (pres.pass.part.acc.sing.neut.of καθίημι, adjectival, ascriptive, in agreement with σκεῦός) 2081.

ἐπὶ (preposition with the genitive, physical place description) 47.

τῆς (gen.sing.fem.of the article in agreement with γῆς) 9.

γῆς (gen.sing.fem.of γῆ, physical place description) 157.

Translation - "And he saw the opened sky and a certain object like a large sheet on its way down, being let down to the ground by the four corners."

Comment: Luke did not often use the historical present as he did here in θεωρεῖ. The perfect passive participle ἀνεῳγμένον, with its intensive force (present condition because of past completed action) is adjectival, as are καταβαῖνον and καθιέμενον which modify σκεῦός. The ὡς comparative clause helps us to define σκεῦος (#997), which in this context means some sort of container. It looked to Peter like a large linen sheet or piece of sail cloth, caught up by the four corners, so as not to spill the contents. It was on its way down, being lowered by the four corners.

Peter must have watched with great interest as the sheet descended, and then with gladness when he saw that it contained food, only to be disappointed when he saw upon closer examination that the food was off limits to a Jew who was under the dietary regulations of Leviticus 11.

What a cruel jest! To torture an orthodox Jew, currently under siege by the imperious pangs of unrelenting hunger, with a collection of animals, birds, insects and snakes, indiscriminately assembled in a sheet let down before him. He saw a cow, but he also saw a pig. He saw a deer, but he also saw a cat. He saw a locust. If John the Baptist could eat them, so could he, but he also saw an owl and a stork. He saw a bass, but he also saw a snake. If only lunch had been ready and he had eaten before he came up to the rooftop! Then he could have had his prayer meeting and lay down for an afternoon nap. But it was not to be.

His frustration is equalled only by his amazement when, after seeing the contents of the sheet in verse 12, Peter hears the suggestion of the Lord in verse 13.

Verse 12 - "Wherein were all manner of fourfooted beasts of the earth, and wild beasts, and creeping things, and fowls of the air."

ἐν ᾧ ὑπῆρχεν πάντα τὰ τετράποδα καὶ ἑρπετὰ τῆς γῆς καὶ πετεινὰ τοῦ οὐρανοῦ.

ἐν (preposition with the locative of place where) 80.

ᾧ (loc.sing.neut.of ὅς, place where, in an adjectival relative clause) 65.

ὑπῆρχεν (3d.per.sing.imp.ind.of ὑπάρχω, progressive description) 1303.

πάντα (nom.pl.neut.of πᾶς, in agreement with τετράποδα) 67.

τὰ (nom.pl.neut.of the article in agreement with τετράποδα) 9.

#3219 τετράποδα (nom.pl.neut.of τετράπους, subject of ὑπῆρχεν).

four footed beast - Acts 10:12; 11:6; Rom.1:23.

Meaning: A combination of τέτρα - "four" and πούς (#353). Hence, four footed beast. In Peter's sheet - Acts 10:12; 11:6. In Paul's analysis of man's depravity - Rom.1:23.

καὶ (adjunctive conjunction joining nouns) 14.

#3220 ἑρπετὰ (nom.pl.neut.of ἑρπετόν, subject of ὑπῆρχεν).

creeping things - Acts 10:12; 11:6; Rom.1:23.
serpent - James 3:7.

Meaning: Cf. ἕρπτω - "to creep, crawl." Hence, crawling thing. Serpent - In Peter's sheet - Acts 10:12; 11:6; in Paul's analysis - Rom.1:23. Properly in James 3:7.

τῆς (gen.sing.fem.of the article in agreement with γῆς) 9.
γῆς (gen.sing.fem.of γῆ, description) 157.
καὶ (adjunctive conjunction joining nouns) 14.
πετεινὰ (nom.pl.neut.of πετεινόν, subject of ὑπῆρχεν) 615.
τοῦ (gen.sing.masc.of the article in agreement with οὐρανοῦ) 9.
οὐρανοῦ (gen.sing.masc.of οὐρανός, description) 254.

Translation - ". . . in which were all the four-footed beasts and crawling things of the earth and birds of the air."

Comment: The point is that a hungry Jew sees a presentation from heaven of every conceivable species of animal, snake, worm and bird. To one committed to the taboos of Leviticus 11 it was a revolting sight, but the real problem comes when Peter heard the Lord's instructions in

Verse 13 - "And there came a voice to him, Rise, Peter; kill and eat."

καὶ ἐγένετο φωνὴ πρὸς αὐτόν, Ἀναστάς, Πέτρε, θῦσον καὶ φάγε.

καὶ (continuative conjunction) 14.
ἐγένετο (3d.per.sing.aor.ind.of γίνομαι, constative) 113.
φωνὴ (nom.sing.fem.of φωνή, subject of ἐγένετο) 222.
πρὸς (preposition with the accusative of extent, in a context of speaking) 197.
αὐτόν (acc.sing.masc.of αὐτός, extent, in a context of speaking) 16.
Ἀναστάς (aor.act.part.nom.sing.masc.of ἀνίστημι, adverbial, temporal) 789.
Πέτρε (voc.sing.masc.of πέτρος, address) 387.
θῦσον (2d.per.sing.aor.act.impv.of θύω, command) 1398.
καὶ (adjunctive conjunction joining verbs) 14.
φάγε (2d.per.sing.aor.act.impv.of ἐσθίω, command) 610.

Translation - "And a voice came to him, 'Stand up, Peter. Kill and eat."

Comment: The heavenly command was clear. The problem was that many of the creatures which Peter had seen in the sheet are on the taboo list of Leviticus 11. Peter's reaction is what we would expect from a Hebrew Christian whose values were still deeply rooted in Hebrew tradition and who needed the lesson from the Lord which he was about to receive. He is not to be condemned for his strict adherence to the dietary code of Leviticus, since the items on the list which the Jews were forbidden to eat were deleterious to health, while many of them still are, despite the progress in the science of nutrition which we now enjoy. Peter did not know that the Lord's object lesson was being given for another purpose.

Verse 14 - "But Peter said, Not so, Lord; for I have never eaten anything that is common or unclean."

ὁ δέ Πέτρος εἶπεν, Μηδαμῶς, κύριε, ὅτι οὐδέποτε ἔφαγον πᾶν κοινὸν καὶ ἀκάθαρτον.

ὁ (nom.sing.masc.of the article in agreement with Πέτρος) 9.
δέ (adversative conjunction) 11.
Πέτρος (nom.sing.masc.of Πέτρος, subject of εἶπεν) 387.
εἶπεν (3d.per.sing.aor.act.ind.of εἶπον, constative) 155.

#3221 Μηδαμῶς (negative interjectional adverb, ablative analogy).

not so - Acts 10:14; 11:8.

Meaning: An intensifying particle from μηδαμός from μηδέ and ἀμός - "someone." Hence, "by no means." "not at all." Following the imperative in Acts 10;14; 11:8.

κύριε (voc.sing.masc.of κύριος, address) 97.
ὅτι (conjunction introducing a causal clause) 211.
οὐδέποτε (intensifying negative compound) 689.
ἔφαγον (1st.per.sing.aor.act.ind.of ἐσθίω, culminative) 610.
πᾶν (acc.sing.neut.of πᾶς, in agreement with κοινὸν) 67.
κοινὸν (acc.sing.neut.of κοινός, direct object of ἔφαγον) 2295.
καὶ (adjunctive conjunction joining substantives) 14.
ἀκάθαρτον (acc.sing.neut.of ἀκάθαρτος, direct object of ἔφαγον) 843.

Translation - "But Peter said, 'Not so, Lord, because I have never yet eaten any common or unclean thing.'"

Comment: δέ is clearly adversative. Peter is about to refuse the Lord's offer of food. The ὅτι clause is causal. He tells us why he will not eat. The negative οὐδέποτε goes with the verb ἔφαγον, not with πᾶν. The statement is a negative statement about πᾶν κοινὸν καὶ ἀκάθαρτον. Peter is not saying that he has not eaten all of the unclean food, implying that he has eaten some of it, and will eat some more. He is saying that his boycott extends to all food that is common and unclean. Although when Peter said this he was not aware that his gospel boycott against the Gentiles offended God and disobeyed the terms of the Great Commission (Mt.28:18-20; Acts 1:8), he was soon to be told that this was true. It must be remembered that the idea of including the Gentiles in the Body of Christ was a new concept to the Jews, despite Jesus' previous teaching. *Cf.* Mt.28:18-20; Acts 1:8; John 10:16; Mt.8:11,12.

Verse 15 - "And the voice spake unto him again the second time, What God hath cleansed, that call not thou common."

καί φωνὴ πάλιν ἐκ δευτέρου πρὸς αὐτόν,ͺA ὁ θεὸς ἐκαθάρισεν σὺ μὴ κοίνου.

καὶ (adversative conjunction) 14.
φωνὴ (nom.sing.fem.of φωνή, subject of εἶπεν understood) 222.
πάλιν (adverbial) 355.
ἐκ (preposition with the ablative, point of departure in succession) 19.
δευτέρου (abl.sing.neut.of δεύτερος, point of departure in succession) 1371.
πρὸς (preposition with the accusative of extent, in a context of speaking) 197.
αὐτόν (acc.sing.masc.of αὐτός, extent in a context of speaking) 16.
ʹA (acc.pl.neut.of ὅς, direct object of κοίνου,) 65.
ὁ (nom.sing.masc.of the article in agreement with θεὸς) 9.
θεὸς (nom.sing.masc.of θεός, subject of ἐκαθάρισεν) 124.
ἐκαθάρισεν (3d.per.sing.aor.act.ind.of καθαρίζω, culminative) 709.
σὺ (nom.sing.masc.of σύ, subject of κοίνου) 104.
μὴ (qualified negative conjunction with the imperative, in a prohibition) 87.
κοίνου (2d.per.sing.pres.act.impv.of κοινόω, prohibition) 1152.

Translation - "And the voice said to him again the second time, 'Stop calling unclean those things which God has cleansed.' "

Comment: καὶ is adversative as God seeks to teach Peter the lesson. We have pleonasm in πάλιν ἐκ δευτέρου. *Cf.*#355 for other examples. ἐκ with the ablative where succession is in view speaks of a point of departure. *Cf.* John 9:24; Mt.26:44; 2 Pet.2:8; 1 Cor.12:27; John 3:34; 2 Cor.9:7; 1 Cor.7:5. σὺ is emphatic as God gives Peter a sharp rebuke. Nothing is unclean, despite Peter's orthodox interpretation of Leviticus 11, if God chooses to cleanse it. Peter was soon to realize that God was not talking about clean and unclean food, but clean and unclean people. *Cf.*#709 for the list of passages where καθαρίζω refers to the spiritual cleansing of the blood of Christ. Those for whom Christ died are cleansed and the result is a purity infinitely greater than any purity to be gained from society or the business, educational or philosophical worlds. There is no greater prestige than that which is connected with membership in the Body of Christ. A Roman army officer who lived up the coast, thirty miles from Joppa, was one who had been cleansed by the blood of Christ. Peter, who until this moment had regarded him as a member of an outcast race, was to learn that Cornelius was destined to occupy a place in the Body of Christ equal to his own. Racists deny the efficacy of the blood of Jesus Christ when they indulge in the bigoted discrimination that seeks to elevate one social group above another. Before the Christian evaluates the worth and dignity of another, he had better find out what Christ thought of him when He was hanging on the cross.

Verse 16 - "This was done thrice: and the vessel was received up again into heaven."

τοῦτο δὲ ἐγένετο ἐπὶ τρίς, καὶ εὐθὺς ἀνελήμφθη τὸ σκεῦος εἰς τὸν οὐρανόν.

τοῦτο (nom.sing.neut.of οὗτος, subject of ἐγένετο) 93.
δὲ (continuative conjunction) 11.
ἐγένετο (3d.per.sing.aor.ind.of γίνομαι, constative) 113.
ἐπὶ (preposition with the adverb) 47.
τρίς (adverbial) 1582.
καὶ (continuative conjunction) 14.
εὐθὺς (adverbial) 258.
ἀνελήμφθη (3d.per.sing.aor.pass.ind.of ἀναλαμβάνω, constative) 2930.
τὸ (nom.sing.neut.of the article in agreement with σκεῦος) 9.
σκεῦος (nom.sing.neut.of σκεῦος, subject of ἀνελήμφθη) 997.
εἰς (preposition with the accusative of extent) 140.
τὸν (acc.sing.masc.of the article in agreement with οὐρανόν) 9.
οὐρανόν (acc.sing.masc.of οὐρανός, extent) 254.

Translation - "This occurred three times and immediately thereafter the sheet was taken up into heaven."

Comment: ἐπὶ τρίς - the preposition with the adverb. *Cf.* Acts 11:10. The lesson was repeated twice in order to make the impression upon Peter so that he would not forget. When he emerged from the trance, he tried to analyze what it all meant. He did not have long to wait.

Verse 17 - "Now while Peter doubted in himself what this vision which he had seen should mean, behold, the men which were sent from Cornelius had made enquiry for Simon's house, and stood before the gate."

Ὡς δὲ ἐν ἑαυτῷ διηπόρει ὁ Πέτρος τί ἂν εἴη τὸ ὅραμα ὃ εἶδεν, ἰδοὺ οἱ ἄνδρες οἱ ἀπεσταλμένοι ὑπὸ τοῦ Κορνηλίου διερωτήσαντες τὴν οἰκίαν τοῦ Σίμωνος ἐπέστησαν ἐπὶ τὸν πυλῶνα,

Ὡς (conjunction with the indicative in a definite temporal clause) 128.
δὲ (continuative conjunction) 11.
ἐν (preposition with locative , place) 80.
ἑαυτῷ (loc.sing.masc.of ἑαυτοῦ, place) 288.
διηπόρει (3d.per.sing.imp.act.ind.of διαπορέω, progressive description) 2262.
ὁ (nom.sing.masc.of the article in agreement with Πέτρος) 9.
Πέτρος (nom.sing.masc.of Πέτρος, subject of διηπόρει) 387.
τί (nom.sing.neut.of τίς, predicate nominative, in indirect question) 281.
ἂν (particle with the optative in deliberative question) 205.
εἴη (3d.per.sing.pres.optative of εἰμί, deliberative indirect question) 86.
τὸ (nom.sing.neut.of the article in agreement with ὅραμα) 9.
ὅραμα (nom.sing.neut.of ὅραμα, subject of εἴη) 1228.
ὃ (nom.sing.neut.of ὅς, subject of εἶδεν) 65.
εἶδεν (3d.per.sing.aor.act.ind.of ὁράω, culminative) 144.
ἰδοὺ (exclamation) 95.

οἱ (nom.pl.masc.of the article in agreement with ἄνδρες) 9.

ἄνδρες (nom.pl.masc.of ἀνήρ, subject of ἐπέστησαν) 63.

οἱ (nom.pl.masc.of the article in agreement with ἀπεσταλμένοι) 9.

ἀπεσταλμένοι (perf.pass.part.nom.pl.masc.of ἀποστέλλω, substantival, in apposition with ἄνδρες) 215.

ὑπὸ (preposition with ablative of agent) 117.

τοῦ (abl.sing.masc.of the article in agreement with Κορνηλίου) 9.

Κορνηλίου (abl.sing.masc.of Κορνήλιος, agent) 3209.

#3222 διερωτήσαντες (aor.act.part.nom.pl.masc.of διερωτάω, adverbial, temporal).

make enquiry for - Acts 10:17.

Meaning: A combination of διά (#118) and ἐρωτάω (#1172). Hence, to make a thorough search. διά is perfective. To ask repeatedly. Cornelius' servants apparently had some difficulty finding the home of Simon the tanner in Joppa - Acts 10:17.

τὴν (acc.sing.fem.of the article in agreement with οἰκίαν) 9.

οἰκίαν (acc.sing.fem.of οἰκία, direct object of διερωτήσαντες) 186.

τοῦ (gen.sing.masc.of the article in agreement with Σίμωνος) 9.

Σίμωνος (gen.sing.masc.of Σίμων, possession) 3207.

ἐπέστησαν (3d.per.pl.aor.act.ind.of ἐφίστημι, constative) 1877.

ἐπὶ (preposition with the accusative of place) 47.

τὸν (acc.sing.masc.of the article in agreement with πυλῶνα) 9.

πυλῶνα (acc.sing.masc.of πυλών, place) 1610.

Translation - "And while Peter was wondering within himself as to what the vision which he had seen might mean, behold the men who were sent by Cornelius, having made a thorough search for the house of Simon, stood at the gate."

Comment: The temporal clause with ὡς and the imperfect tense in διηπόρει, tells us that while Peter was pondering the question in his own mind as to what possible significance the vision which he had seen could have, the servants of Cornelius had been searching for the house, and, having found it, were now standing before the gate. They had made exhaustive enquiry (#3222) and had been directed to Simon's house. The optative indicates the deliberation of the indirect question. There was great doubt in Peter's mind about what it all meant. εἴη here in its futuristic or potential use. Though Peter was in grave doubt about the meaning of this twice repeated vision, God had planned to enlighten him very soon indeed. At that very moment there stood at his host's gate the men who would take him to Caesarea where he would find a man whom God had "cleansed" but who Peter, but for the new light, would call unclean.

Verse 18 - ". . . and called, and asked whether Simon, which was surnamed Peter, were lodged there."

καὶ φωνήσαντες ἐπυνθάνοντο εἰ Σίμων ὁ ἐπικαλούμενος Πέτρος ἐνθάδε
ξενίζεται.

καὶ (adjunctive conjunction joining verbs) 14.
φωνήσαντες (aor.act.part.nom.pl.masc.of φωνέω, adverbial, temporal) 1338.
ἐπυνθάνοντο (3d.per.pl.imp.mid.ind.of πυνθάνομαι, progressive description) 153.
εἰ (particle in indirect question) 337.
Σίμων (nom.sing.masc.of Σίμων, subject of ξενίζεται) 386.
ὁ (nom.sing.masc.of the article in agreement with ἐπικαλούμενος) 9.
ἐπικαλούμενος (pres.pass.part.nom.sing.masc.of ἐπικαλέω, attributive articular participle in apposition with Σίμων) 884.
Πέτρος (nom.sing.masc.of Πέτρος, appellation) 387.
ἐνθάδε (local adverb) 2010.
ξενίζεται (3d.per.sing.pres.pass.ind.of ξενίζω, indirect question) 3214.

Translation - "... *and after they had called, they were asking if Simon, the man called Peter, was being entertained there.*"

Comment: Cornelius servants first called out. Someone, perhaps Simon the tanner or a servant responded to the call. Then the men asked, "Is Simon whose nickname is Peter your guest?" εἰ introduces indirect question, in which the tense is retained as in direct question. It is probably not proper to push the imperfect tense in ἐπυνθάνοντο too much. They began to ask the question. It is not likely that they continued to ask it. This would indicate a little more anxiety than they probably felt, although they may have had some difficulty in finding the house. The articular attributive participle ὁ ἐπικαλούμενος is in apposition to Σίμων.

It is time for the Holy Spirit to give Peter some light on the course of events. This we have in

Verse 19 - "While Peter thought on the vision, the Spirit said unto him, Behold, three men seek thee."

τοῦ δὲ Πέτρου διενθυμουμένου περὶ τοῦ ὁράματος εἶπεν (αὐτῷ) τὸ πνεῦμα, Ἰδοὺ ἄνδρες (δύο) ζητοῦσίν σε.

τοῦ (gen.sing.masc.of the article in agreement with Πέτρου) 9.
δὲ (continuative conjunction) 11.
Πέτρου (gen.sing.masc.of Πέτρος, genitive absolute) 387.

#3223 διενθυμουμένου (pres.mid.part.gen.sing.masc.of διενθυμέομαι, genitive absolute).

think on - Acts 10:19.

Meaning: A combination of διά (#118) and ἐνθυμέομαι (#94). Hence, to weigh in the mind thoroughly. With reference to Peter's thoughts about the visions of Acts 10:19.

περὶ (preposition with the genitive of reference) 173.

τοῦ (gen.sing.neut.of the article in agreement with δράματος) 9.

δράματος (gen.sing.neut.of δραμα, reference) 1228.

εἶπεν (3d.per.sing.aor.act.ind.of εἶπον, constative) 155.

αὐτῷ (dat.sing.masc.of αὐτός, indirect object of εἶπεν) 16.

τό (nom.sing.neut.of the article in agreement with πνεῦμα) 9.

πνεῦμα (nom.sing.neut.of πνεῦμα, subject of εἶπεν) 83.

Ἰδού (exclamation) 95.

ἄνδρες (nom.pl.masc.of ἀνήρ, subject of ζητοῦσιν) 63.

(δύο) (numeral) 385.

ζητοῦσίν (3d.per.pl.pres.act.ind.of ζητέω, aoristic) 207.

σε (acc.sing.masc.of σύ, direct object of ζητοῦσίν) 104.

Translation - "*And while Peter continued to ponder about the vision, the Spirit said to him, 'Look, two men are looking for you.'*"

Comment: τοῦ Πέτρος διενθυμουμένου is a genitive absolute in the present tense. Its action is simultaneous with the action of the main verb, εἶπεν, which has direct discourse with the verb in the Holy Spirit's statement in the present tense. Thus the grammar makes it clear that the two men at the gate arrived and asked for Peter while he was mulling over the meaning of the vision. God's timing is perfect. Cornelius had a vision at three o'clock in the afternoon the day before, and on the basis of his instructions he sent men to Joppa, thirty miles away. They remained in Caesarea until the next morning and set out for Joppa where they arrived a little before noon and began to enquire about the house of Simon the tanner. As they approached the city, Peter, the man they were seeking, went up on the housetop to pray, fell into a trance and had his vision which was twice repeated. When he awoke and as he sat trying to fathom the significance of the vision of the sheet the men from Caesarea arrive and ask for him. Three men made the trip (Acts 10:7; 11:11). Two men called for Peter at the gate (Acts 10:19). Some manuscripts read τρεῖς instead of δύο in Acts 10:19. Metzger explains:

The evidence for and against each of the three variant readings is curiously kaleidescopic, and a case can be made for each of them. (1) The reading of codex Vaticanus assumes that only the two servants, mentioned in ver.7, need be mentioned as messengers, the soldier serving as guard. It is possible that scribes, not observing the reason lying behind the use of δύο, corrected what they supposed was an error either by deleting the word or by substituting τρεῖς (in accord with 11.11).

(2) The reading τρεῖς is strongly supported by diversified external evidence. Assuming this reading to be original, one can explain the origin of δύο as the work of a discriminating scribe and the absence of the word as an accidental omission after ἄνδρες (— ΔΡΕΣΤΡΕΙΣ).

(3) If, as is usual in similar cases, the shortest reading is regarded as original (compare ἄνδρας, ver.5), recollection of ver.7 or 11.11 would have induced scribes to include a numeral with ἄνδρες.

On balance, it seemed to the Committee that the least unsatisfactory solution was to adopt the reading supported by the broadest spectrum of external evidence. (Metzger, *A Textual Commentary on the Greek New Testament*, 373).

The thrust of the passage is not lessened, whether two or three men were asking for Peter at the gate. No manuscript says that only two of the three men who left Caesarea for Joppa arrived. If δύο is the original reading, the explanation that one of the three men was engaged in other activities at the time is plausible. He may in fact have been standing there with his colleagues before the gate in silence.

The Holy Spirit continued his orders to Peter in

Verse 20 - "Arise therefore, and get thee down, and go with them, doubting nothing: for I have sent them."

ἀλλὰ ἀναστὰς κατάβηθι καὶ πορεύου σὺν αὐτοῖς μηδὲν διακρινόμενος, ὅτι ἐγὼ ἀπέσταλκα αὐτούς.

ἀλλὰ (adversative conjunction) 342.
ἀναστὰς (aor.act.part.nom.sing.masc.of ἀνίστημι, adverbial, temporal) 789.
κατάβηθι (2d.per.sing.aor.mid.impv.of καταβαίνω, command) 324.
καὶ (adjunctive conjunction joining verbs) 14.
πορεύου (2d.per.sing.pres.mid.impv.of πορεύομαι, command) 170.
σὺν (preposition with the instrumental of association) 1542.
αὐτοῖς (instru.pl.masc.of αὐτός, association) 16.
μηδὲν (acc.sing.neut.of μηδείς, direct object of διακρινόμενος) 713.
διακρινόμενος (pres.mid.part.nom.sing.masc.of διακρίνομαι, adverbial, complementary) 1195.
ὅτι (conjunction introducing a causal clause) 211.
ἐγὼ (nom.sing.masc.of ἐγώ, subject of ἀπέσταλκα, emphatic) 123.
ἀπέσταλκα (1st.per.sing.perf.act.ind.of ἀποστέλλω, intensive) 215.
αὐτούς (acc.pl.masc.of αὐτός, direct object of ἀπέσταλκα) 16.

Translation - "But get up and go downstairs and go with them with no reservations, because I have sent them."

Comment: The Holy Spirit knew what Peter was thinking and how he would react when he saw that the men downstairs were Gentiles who would ask him to come with them to preach the gospel to a Roman soldier and his family. To forestall any further doubt in Peter's mind, the Holy Spirit forbids it - μηδὲν διακρινόμενος, the complementary participle. Why should Peter not doubt? Because (the ὅτι clause) the Holy Spirit had sent them. Note the emphatic ἐγὼ, emphatic because unnecessary, since it is implicit in the verb. Peter had already questioned God's judgment in this episode. He had refused to eat what God told him to eat, as though the Lord had forgotten about Leviticus 11. Peter assumed that his standards were higher than God's. Now the Holy Spirit warns Peter not to make the same mistake again. God has sent the men. He has told them what to say. Peter is forbidden to question it.

Verse 21 - "Then Peter went down to the men which were sent unto him from Cornelius and said, Behold, I am he whom ye seek: what is the cause wherefore ye are come?"

καταβὰς δὲ Πέτρος πρὸς τοὺς ἄνδρας εἶπεν, Ἰδοὺ ἐγώ εἰμι ὃν ζητεῖτε. τίς ἡ αἰτία δι' ἣν πάρεστε;

καταβὰς (aor.act.part.nom.sing.masc.of καταβαίνω, adverbial, temporal) 324.

δὲ (inferential conjunction) 11.

Πέτρος (nom.sing.masc.of Πέτρος, subject of εἶπεν) 387.

πρός (preposition with the accusative of extent after a verb of speaking) 197.

τοὺς (acc.pl.masc.of the article in agreement with ἄνδρας) 9.

ἄνδρας (acc.pl.masc.of ἀνήρ, extent, after a verb of speaking) 63.

εἶπεν (3d.per.sing.aor.act.ind.of εἶπον, constative) 155.

Ἰδοὺ (exclamation) 95.

ἐγώ (nom.sing.masc.of ἐγώ, subject of εἰμι, emphatic) 123.

εἰμι (1st.per.sing.pres.ind.of εἰμί, aoristic) 86.

ὃν (acc.sing.masc.of ὅς, the relative pronoun, in an adjectival relative clause) 65.

ζητεῖτε (2d.per.pl.pres.act.ind.of ζητέω, aoristic) 207.

τίς (nom.sing.masc.of τίς, interrogative pronoun, in direct question, predicate nominative) 281.

ἡ (nom.sing.fem.of the article in agreement with αἰτία) 9.

αἰτία (nom.sing.fem.of αἰτία, subject of ἐστίν, understood) 1283.

δι' (preposition with the accusative of cause) 118.

ἣν (acc.sing.fem.of ὅς, relative pronoun, causal) 65.

πάρεστε (2d.per.pl.pres.ind.of πάρειμί, aoristic, direct question) 1592.

Translation - "So Peter went down and said to the men, 'Look! I am the man for whom you are looking. Why are you here?' "

Comment: We can translate, "Peter went down to the men and said, . . . " or "Peter went down and said to the men. . . " The grammar permits either translation. There may be a little impertinence in Peter's Ἰδού and the crisp manner in which he introduced himself and his demand that they tell him why they had come, as though they were not likely to have told him otherwise. After all Peter had been awakened from a troubled nap in which he had seen a terrifying vision and heard some confusing orders. And he was still hungry. He never had had the chance to have his lunch. To add to all of this, he was under orders from the Holy Spirit to go with these Gentiles, although he did not know why he should except that the Lord had ordered it. At this point he was not yet sure that God had included Gentiles in the covenant of salvation, despite passages like John 10:16; Mt.28:18-20; Acts 1:8 *et al.*

Verse 22 - "And they said, Cornelius the centurion, a just man, and one that feareth God, and of good report among all the nation of the Jews, was warned from God by an holy angel to send for thee into his house, and to hear words of thee."

οἱ δὲ εἶπαν, Κορνήλιος ἑκατοντάρχης, ἀνὴρ δίκαιος καὶ φοβούμενος τὸν θεὸν μαρτυρούμενός τε ὑπὸ ὅλου τοῦ ἔθνους τῶν Ἰουδαίων, ἐχρηματίσθη ὑπὸ ἀγγέλου ἁγίου μεταπέμψασθαί σε εἰς τὸν οἶκον αὐτοῦ καὶ ἀκοῦσαι ῥήματα παρὰ σοῦ.

οἱ (nom.pl.masc.of the article, subject of εἶπαν) 9.

δὲ (continuative conjunction) 11.

εἶπαν (3d.per.pl.aor.act.ind.of εἶπον, constative) 155.

Κορνήλιος (nom.sing.masc.of Κορνήλιος, subject of ἐχρηματίσθη) 3209.

ἑκατοντάρχης (nom.sing.masc.of ἑκατοντάρχης, in apposition) 3210.

ἀνὴρ (nom.sing.masc.of ἀνήρ, in apposition) 63.

δίκαιος (nom.sing.masc.of δίκαιος, in agreement with ἀνήρ) 85.

καὶ (adjunctive conjunction joining substantives) 14.

φοβούμενος (pres.mid.part.nom.sing.masc.of φοβέομαι, substantival, in apposition) 101.

τὸν (acc.sing.masc.of the article in agreement with θεὸν) 9.

θεὸν (acc.sing.masc.of θεός, direct object of φοβούμενος) 124.

μαρτυρούμενος (pres.pass.part.nom.sing.masc.of μαρτυρέω, substantival, in apposition) 1471.

τε (emphatic particle) 1408.

ὑπὸ (preposition with the ablative of agent) 117.

ὅλου (abl.sing.neut.of ὅλος, in agreement with ἔθνους) 112.

τοῦ (abl.sing.neut.of the article in agreement with ἔθνους) 9.

ἔθνους (abl.sing.neut.of ἔθνος, agent) 376.

τῶν (gen.pl.masc.of the article in agreement with Ἰουδαίων) 9.

Ἰουδαίων (gen.pl.masc.of Ἰουδαῖος, description) 143.

ἐχρηματίσθη (3d.per.sing.aor.pass.ind.of χρηματίζω, constative) 195.

ὑπὸ (preposition with the ablative of agent) 117.

ἀγγέλου (abl.sing.masc.of ἄγγελος, agent) 96.

ἁγίου (abl.sing.masc.of ἅγιος, in agreement with ἀγγέλου) 84.

μεταπέμψασθαί (1st.aor.mid.inf.of μεταπέμπω, epexegetical) 3213

σε (acc.sing.masc.of σύ, direct object of μεταπέμψασθαι) 104.

εἰς (preposition with the accusative of extent) 140.

τὸν (acc.sing.masc.of the article in agreement with οἶκον) 9.

οἶκον (acc.sing.masc.of οἶκος, extent) 784.

αὐτοῦ (gen.sing.masc.of αὐτός, possession) 16.

καὶ (adjunctive conjunction joining infinitives) 14.

ἀκοῦσαι (aor.act.inf.of ἀκούω, epexegetical) 148.

ῥήματα (acc.pl.neut.of ῥῆμα, direct object of ἀκοῦσαι) 343.

παρὰ (preposition with the ablative of source, with persons) 154.

σοῦ (abl.sing.masc.of σύ, source, with persons) 104.

Translation - "And they said, 'Cornelius, a centurion, a righteous man and one who fears God, as reported by all of the tribes of Israel, has been ordered by a holy angel to invite you to his house and to hear what you have to say."

Comment: The messengers of Cornelius were good salesmen. Apparently they anticipated from Peter the usual reaction that a Jew would customarily give when a Gentile was mentioned. Note the order of the emphases in their statement: first they quickly listed the assets and achievements of the man. He was a Roman army officer of some distinction. He was a righteous man. He feared God, and he had a good reputation among Peter's Jewish colleagues. The entire Jewish nation thought well of him. Second, Cornelius would not have been so bold as to send his servants to Peter with an invitation to come to his house, were it not for the fact that he was ordered by an holy angel to do so. Third, the purpose of the invitation was not that Cornelius could then tell Peter something, but that he might have the opportunity and privilege to listen to what Peter might wish to say to him. They did not know that the Holy Spirit had just confirmed to Peter the fact that they were there by divine appointment (verse 20).

Peter's response to all of this was considerably more civil that he had been prepared to be when he first met the men, as we see in

Verse 23 - "Then called he them in, and lodged them. And on the morrow Peter went away with them, and certain brethren from Joppa accompanied him."

εἰσκαλεσάμενος οὖν αὐτοὺς ἐξένισεν. Τῇ δὲ ἐπαύριον ἀναστὰς ἐξῆλθεν σὺν αὐτοῖς, καί τινες τῶν ἀδελφῶν τῶν ἀπὸ Ἰόππης συνῆλθον αὐτῷ.

#3224 εἰσκαλεσάμενος (aor.mid.part.nom.sing.masc.of εἰσκαλέω, adverbial, temporal).

call in - Acts 10:23.

Meaning: A combination of εἰς (#140) and καλέω (#107). Hence to call in; to invite a caller to come in. With reference to Peter's invitation to the servants of Cornelius to come into the house of Simon, of Joppa - Acts 10:23.

οὖν (continuative conjunction) 68.
αὐτοὺς (acc.pl.masc.of αὐτός, direct object of εἰσκαλεσάμενος and ἐξένισεν) 16.
ἐξένισεν (3d.per.sing.aor.act.ind.of ξενίζω, constative) 3214.
Τῇ (loc.sing.fem.of the article, time point) 9.
δὲ (continuative conjunction) 11.
ἐπαύριον (temporal adverb) 1680.
ἀναστὰς (aor.act.part.nom.sing.masc.of ἀνίστημι, adverbial, temporal) 789.
ἐξῆλθεν (3d.per.sing.aor.mid.ind.of ἐξέρχομαι, ingressive) 161.
σὺν (preposition with the instrumental of association) 1542.
αὐτοῖς (instru.pl.masc.of αὐτός, association) 16.
καὶ (continuative conjunction) 14.
τινες (nom.pl.masc.of τις, indefinite pronoun, subject of συνῆλθον) 486.
τῶν (gen.pl.masc.of the article in agreement with ἀδελφῶν) 9.

ἀδελφῶν (gen.pl.masc.of ἀδελφός, partitive genitive) 15.
ἀπό (preposition with the ablative of source) 70.
Ἰόππης (abl.sing.fem.of Ἰόππη, source) 3202.
συνῆλθον (3d.per.pl.aor.mid.ind.of συνέρχομαι, ingressive) 78.
αὐτῷ (instru.sing.masc.of αὐτός, association, after σύν in composition) 16.

Translation - "Then he invited them in and gave them lodging. And the next day he got up and started out with them, and some of the brethren from Joppa went along them him."

Comment: It was probably early enough in the afternoon that they could have reached Caesarea before dark if they had left Joppa immediately, but the men had already travelled the distance once that day and there was no great urgency about the matter. There was another reason. Peter had not yet had his lunch. He was hungry at noon. It may have been an hour later. So Simon the tanner's hospitality was indulged at the suggestion of Peter and the men remained in Joppa until the next morning.

Peter probably suspected that something was going to happen in Caesarea for which he would need confirmation from Christian witnesses when he returned to face the other Apostles in Jerusalem. This is probably the reason why other Christian brethren from Joppa went along with him to Caesarea.

Verse 24 - "And the morrow after they entered into Caesarea. And Cornelius waited for them, and had called together his kinsmen and near friends."

τῇ δὲ ἐπαύριον εἰσῆλθεν εἰς τὴν Καισάρειαν. ὁ δὲ Κορνήλιος ἦν προσδοκῶν αὐτούς, συγκαλεσάμενος τοὺς συγγενεῖς αὐτοῦ καὶ τοὺς ἀναγκαίους φίλους.

τῇ (loc.sing.fem.of the article, time point) 9.
δὲ (continuative conjunction) 11.
ἐπαύριον (temporal adverb) 1680.
εἰσῆλθεν (3d.per.sing.aor.mid.ind.of εἰσέρχομαι, constative) 234.
εἰς (preposition with the accusative of extent) 140.
τὴν (acc.sing.fem.of the article in agreement with Καισάρειαν) 9.
Καισάρειαν (acc.sing.fem.of Καισαρίας, extent) 1200.
ὁ (nom.sing.masc.of the article in agreement with Κορνήλιος) 9.
δὲ (continuative conjunction) 11.
Κορνήλιος (nom.sing.masc.of Κορνήλιος, subject of ἦν) 3209.
ἦν (3d.per.sing.imp.ind.of εἰμί, imperfect periphrastic) 86.
προσδοκῶν (pres.act.part.nom.sing.masc.of προσδοκάω, imperfect periphrastic) 906.
αὐτούς (acc.pl.masc.of αὐτός, direct object of προσδοκῶν) 16.
συγκαλεσάμενος (aor.mid.part.nom.sing.masc.of συγκαλέω, adverbial, temporal) 2251.
τοὺς (acc.pl.masc.of the article in agreement with συγγενεῖς) 9.
συγγενεῖς (acc.pl.masc.of συγγενής, direct object of συγκαλεσάμενος) 1815.
αὐτοῦ (gen.sing.masc.of αὐτός, relationship) 16.

καὶ (adjunctive conjunction joining nouns) 14.

τοὺς (acc.pl.masc.of the article in agreement with φίλους) 9.

#3225 ἀναγκαίους (acc.pl.masc.of ἀναγκαῖος, in agreement with φίλους).

near - Acts 10:24.
necessary - Acts 13:46; 1 Cor.12:22; 2 Cor.9:5; Phil.2:25; Tit.3:14.
needful - Phil.1:24.
of necessity - Heb.8:3.

Meaning: Cf. ἀνάγκη (#1254). As an attributive adjective defining φίλους - "close friends" - "intimate friends" - Acts 10:24. Elsewhere, meaning "necessary." As an attributive adjective - Tit.3:14; predicate adjective - 1 Cor.12:22; followed by an infinitive - Acts 13:46; 2 Cor.9:5; Phil.1:24; 2:25; Heb.8:3. That which is indispensable - 1 Cor.12:22; Tit.3:14. That which, though not indispensable, ought to be done - Phil.1:24; Acts 13:46; Heb.8;3; Phil.2:25; 2 Cor.9:5.

φίλους (acc.pl.masc.of φίλος, direct object of συγκαλεσάμενος) 932.

Translation - "And the following day he entered into Caesarea. And Cornelius had been expecting them, having called together his relatives and intimate friends."

Comment: I take it that τῇ . . . ἐπαύριον of verse 24 is in relation to the first clause of verse 23, not to the second. Otherwise, Peter and his friends spent an entire day and a night on the road. The distance is only thirty miles. The men had made the trip down from Caesarea in the morning of the day before.

Cornelius had been waiting for them (imperfect periphrastic in ἦν προσδοκῶν) having previously called together his relative and close friends, with whom he wished to share his own experience of meeting Peter and hearing the message which the Lord had promised that he would bring. This is the behavior of a man who was under the deep convicting ministry of the Holy Spirit as Jesus had outlined His work in John 16:7-11. Since the entire episode was directed by the Lord, who visited both Cornelius and Peter with preparatory visions, there was no doubt in the Roman's mind that Peter would come.

That God should have chosen Peter for this experience, rather than one of the other Apostles, comports with His commission which He gave to Peter on the night that He was arrested. It was Peter who was to "strengthen the brethren." It was time for the early church to understand clearly that salvation was to be given on an international basis in a way that would cross racial, ethnic and cultural lines. To be sure, Paul was the special Apostle to the Gentiles, but at this time Paul did not enjoy the prestige with the early church that Peter did. It was Peter, on the basis of the experience which he was about to have in the case of Cornelius, who defended Paul's ministry to the Gentiles in the council of Jerusalem (Acts 15:1-18) as he had successfully defended his own action in a previous discussion of the question (Acts 11:1-18).

Verse 25 - "And as Peter was coming in, Cornelius met him, and fell down at his feet, and worshipped him."

ὡς δὲ ἐγένετο τοῦ εἰσελθεῖν τὸν Πέτρον, συναντήσας αὐτῷ ὁ Κορνήλιος πεσὼν ἐπὶ τοὺς πόδας προσεκύνησεν.

ὡς (conjunction introducing a temporal clause) 128.

δὲ (continuative conjunction) 11.

ἐγένετο (3d.per.sing.aor.ind.of γίνομαι, constative) 113.

τοῦ (gen.sing.neut.of the article, articular infinitive of time description) 9.

εἰσελθεῖν (aor.mid.inf.of εἰσέρχομαι, noun use, time description) 234.

τὸν (acc.sing.masc.of the article in agreement with Πέτρον) 9.

Πέτρον (acc.sing.masc.of Πέτρος, general reference) 387.

συναντήσας (aor.act.part.nom.sing.masc.of συναντάω, adverbial, temporal) 2340.

αὐτῷ (dat.sing.masc.of αὐτός, person) 16.

ὁ (nom.sing.masc.of the article in agreement with Κορνήλιος) 9.

Κορνήλιος (nom.sing.masc.of Κορνήλιος, subject of προσεκύνησεν) 3209.

πεσὼν (aor.act.part.nom.sing.masc.of πίπτω, adverbial, temporal) 187.

ἐπὶ (preposition with the accusative of place) 47.

τοὺς (acc.pl.masc.of the article in agreement with πόδας) 9.

πόδας (acc.pl.masc.of πούς, place) 353.

προσεκύνησεν (3d.per.sing.aor.act.ind.of προσκυνέω, ingressive) 147.

Translation - "*And when Peter came in Cornelius met him, fell at his feet and began to worship him.*"

Comment: τοῦ εἰσελθεῖν, though an articular infinitive in the genitive case, in the temporal clause, introduced by ὡς, is nevertheless the subject of ἐγένετο. Robertson (*Grammar*, 98) calls it "an awkward . . . imitation of the Hebrew infinitive construct." Literally "as Peter's entrance happened. . . " The two temporal participles συναντήσας and πεσὼν, both aorist, are antecedent in time to the action of the main verb, προσεκύνησεν, which is an ingressive aorist. Peter walked in, Cornelius came forward and met him and promptly fell down at his feet and began an act of obeisance. It is a dramatic scene. Cornelius, for all of his godly piety and sincere search for the truth, was nevertheless a product of his culture. Pagans worshipped many gods and godesses and were addicted to the esoteric and unusual. When Cornelius experienced his vision and received his instructions from the angel, it was natural that he should think that he was in touch with the supernatural and should act accordingly. His action is an evidence of his humility - not a bad condition of mind for one who wishes to become a Christian.

Verse 26 - "*But Peter took him up, saying, Stand up; I myself also am a man.*"

ὁ δὲ Πέτρος ἤγειρεν αὐτὸν λέγων,'Ανάστηθι. καὶ ἐγὼ αὐτὸς ἄνθρωπός εἰμι.

ὁ (nom.sing.masc.of the article in agreement with Πέτρος) 9.

δὲ (adversative conjunction) 11.

Πέτρος (nom.sing.masc.of Πέτρος, subject of ἤγειρεν) 387.

ἤγειρεν (3d.per.sing.imp.act.ind.of ἐγείρω, inceptive) 125.

αὐτὸν (acc.sing.masc.of αὐτός, direct object of ἤγειρεν) 16.
λεγὼν (pres.act.part.nom.sing.masc.of λέγω, adverbial, temporal) 66.
'Ανάστηθι (2d.per.sing.aor.act.impv.of ἀνίστημι, command) 789.
καὶ (adjunctive conjunction joining substantives) 14.
ἐγὼ (nom.sing.masc.of ἐγώ, subject of εἰμι, emphatic) 123.
αὐτὸς (nom.sing.masc.of αὐτός, intensive) 16.
ἄνθρωπος (nom.sing.masc.of ἄνθρωπος, predicate nominative) 341.
εἰμι (1st.per.sing.pres.ind.of εἰμί, aoristic) 86.

Translation - *"But as Peter lifted him up he said, 'Stand up! I also myself am a man.' "*

Comment: The inceptive imperfect in ἤγειρεν and the continuous action of the participle λεγὼν combine to give us the picture. As Peter reached down and laid hold of Cornelius and began to lift him up he was making the emphatic and intensive statement of the text. The emphatic use of ἐγὼ and the intensive use of αὐτὸς in the predicate should be noted. We have already commented on the background of Cornelius and his attitude in relation to Peter. Peter's reaction indicates that he well understood that his power and status as a Christian Apostle were only results of God's grace. We understand Cornelius' action, but we would be greatly surprized and disappointed if Peter had accepted the Roman soldier's adulation. Peter's remark here is all the more to be admired when we recall that he had just come from Lydda where he healed a man who had been paralyzed for eight years and from Joppa where he had raised a dead woman and given back her life to her.

Verse 27 - *"And as he talked with him, he went in, and found many that were come together."*

κ021ι συνομιλῶν αὐτῷ εἰσῆλθεν, καὶ εὑρίσκει συνεληλυθότας πολλούς,

καὶ (continuative conjunction) 14.

#3226 συνομιλῶν (pres.act.part.nom.sing.masc.of συνομιλέω, adverbial, temporal).

Meaning: A combination of σύν (#1542) and ὁμιλέω - "to fellowship with." To consort, or be in company with; hence to talk and fellowship together. With reference to Peter and Cornelius - Acts 10:27.

αὐτῷ (instrumental sing.masc.of αὐτός, association, after σύν in composition) 16.
εἰσῆλθεν (3d.per.sing.aor.mid.ind.of εἰσέρχομαι, constative) 234.
καὶ (adjunctive conjunction joining verbs) 14.
εὑρίσκει (3d.per.sing.pres.act.ind.of εὑρίσκω, historical) 79.
συνεληλυθότας (perf.pass.part.acc.pl.masc.of συνέρχομαι, adjectival, ascriptive, in agreement with πολλούς) 78.
πολλούς (acc.pl.masc.of πολύς, direct object of εὑρίσκει) 228.

Translation - *"And as he chatted with him, he walked in and found many who had come together."*

Comment: The behavior of each man at their first meeting enhanced the appreciation of each for the other. Peter may have expected a haughty reception from this proud Roman military officer, which would only have increased the contempt which he, as a Jew, had been conditioned to feel for the Gentiles generally and the Romans particularly. Cornelius, at first unsure of his protocol, since he did not know with certainty what powers this famous Christian Apostle might possess, nevertheless was perceptive enough to sense at once that Christianity did not elevate Christians to the realm of the untouchable. This situation paves the way for Luke's use of the participle συνομιλῶν, which indicates a state of close fellowship - even camaraderie. Peter and Cornelius immediately became good friends, even before Cornelius became a Christian. Peter was happy to find a humble and respectful Roman army officer and Cornelius was glad that Peter did not accept his worship, because he was looking for something of a higher order to worship. It was with a high degree of rapport, therefore, that they walked into the room, chatting together, where Peter found (note the historical present in εὑρίσκει) Cornelius' friends and relatives ready to listen to his gospel.

Before Peter began to preach (verse 33) both he and Cornelius made explanatory statements. Peter's first words to the people assembled were in the nature of a confession of his past misunderstanding of the sweep and scope of the gospel missionary enterprise.

Verse 28 - "And he said unto them, Ye know how that it is an unlawful thing for a man that is a Jew to keep company, or come unto one of another nation; but God hath shewed me that I should not call any man common or unclean."

ἔφη τε πρὸς αὐτούς, Ὑμεῖς ἐπίστασθε ὡς ἀθέμιτόν ἐστιν ἀνδρὶ Ἰουδαίῳ κολλᾶσθαι ἢ προσέρχεσθαι ἀλλοφύλῳ. κἀμοὶ ὁ θεὸς ἔδειξεν μηδένα κοινὸν ἢ ἀκάθαρτον λέγειν ἄνθρωπον.

ἔφη (3d.per.sing.aor.act.ind. of φημί, constative) 354.
τε (continuative conjunction) 1408.
πρὸς (preposition with the accusative of extent, after a verb of speaking) 197.
αὐτούς (acc.pl.masc.of αὐτός, extent after a verb of speaking) 16.
Ὑμεῖς (nom.pl.masc.of σύ, subject of ἐπίστασθε) 104.
ἐπίστασθε (2d.per.pl.pres.ind.of ἐπίσταμαι, aoristic) 2814.
ὡς (conjunction in indirect question) 128.

#3227 ἀθέμιτόν (acc.sing.neut.of ἀθέμιτός, predicate adjective).

abominable - 1 Pet.4:3.
unlawful thing - Acts 10:28.

Meaning: α privative plus θεμιτός - "law" or "right." Hence unlawful, not right, illegal, against presribed rules of procedure. With reference to the Jewish restriction against Jewish association with Gentiles - Acts 10:28. With reference to idolatry - 1 Pet.4:3.

ἐστιν (3d.per.sing.pres.ind.of εἰμί, static) 86.

ἀνδρὶ (dat.sing.masc.of ἀνήρ, with adjectives) 63.

Ἰουδαίῳ (dat.sing.masc.of Ἰουδαῖος, in agreement with ἀνδρὶ, apposition) 143.

κολλᾶσθαι (pres.mid.inf.of κολλάω, noun use, subject of ἐστιν) 1288.

ἢ (disjunctive particle) 465.

προσέρχεσθαι (pres.mid.inf.of προσέρχομαι, noun use, subject of ἐστιν) 336.

#3228 ἀλλοφύλῳ (loc.sing.masc.of ἀλλόφυλος, place).

one of another nation - Acts 10:28.

Meaning: A combination of ἄλλος (#198) and φῦλον - "race." Hence, another race; of a different genetic extraction. When used in a Jewish context, it means a Gentile. With reference to Peter's comment to Cornelius and his guests - Acts 10:28.

κἀμοὶ (dat.sing.masc.of κἀγώ, indirect object of ἔδειξεν) 178.

ὁ (nom.sing.masc.of the article in agreement with θεὸς) 9.

θεὸς (nom.sing.masc.of θεός, subject of ἔδειξεν) 124.

ἔδειξεν (3d.per.sing.aor.act.ind.of δείκνυμι, culminative) 359.

μηδένα (acc.sing.masc.of μηδείς, in agreement with ἄνθρωπον) 713.

κοινὸν (acc.sing.masc.of κοινός, predicate adjective) 2295.

ἢ (disjunctive particle) 465.

ἀκάθαρτον (acc.sing.masc.of ἀκάθαρτος, predicate adjective) 843.

λέγειν (pres.act.inf.of λέγω, epexegetical) 66.

ἄνθρωπον (acc.sing.masc.of ἄνθρωπος, direct object of λέγειν) 341.

Translation - "And he said to them, 'You are aware that it is considered improper for a man who is a Jew to be closely associated or to enter into intimate fellowship with one of another race; but God has taught me to call no man common or unclean.'"

Comment: Direct discourse here as Luke gives us Peter's exact words. We have ὡς used like ὅτι in indirect question. "There is no clear instance of ὡς in this sense" (indirect assertion) "in the N.T. It was common in the ancient Greek" (Goodwin, *Moods and Tenses*, 258, as cited in Robertson, *Grammar*, 1032). "Just as final ὅπως retreated before ἵνα, so declarative ὡς did before ὅτι." (Janneris, *History of Greek Grammar*, 571, as cited in *Ibid.*). "In late Greek ἵνα monopolized the field as a final particle and divided it with ὅτι as a declarative conjunction. We do have ὡς in indirect questions a few times. . . . This is more likely the meaning even in Ac.10:28, ἐπίστασθε ὡς ἀθέμιτον. Reeb (*De Particulorum ὅτι et ὡς apud Demosthenum Usu*, 1890, 38, as cited in *Ibid.*) points out that Demosthenes uses ὡς for what is false and ὅτι for what is true." With verbs of reading, narrating and testifying ". . . ὡς is more than just ὅτι ('that'). Ὅτι expresses the thing itself and ὡς the mode or quality of the thing (Thayer). With this explanation it is possible to consider it as declarative, though really meaning 'how.'" (*Ibid.*).

The two infinitives, both of which are nouns more than verbs are the subject of ἐστιν, and ἀθέμιτόν is the predicate adjective. "To κολλ. or to προσέρχ. is unlawful." For whom? For a man who is a Jew. ἀνδρὶ is an example of the dative with adjectives. *Cf.* Acts 26:19; John 8:29; Mt.10:25, *et al. Cf.*#359 for δείκνυμι in the sense of demonstration as well as by spoken word. God had given Peter an object lesson before He had administered His rebuke (verse 15). μηδένα, the adjective joined to ἄνθρωπον is emphasized. No man is common, (vulgar, beneath one's notice) or unclean any more than are all other men. In fact, all men, including Peter and the Jews, Cornelius and the Roman soldiers, all Gentiles, the writer of these lines and the reader, are vulgar and unclean, no one more or less than any other. Paul was later to write, "What then? Are we (Jews) better than they? (Gentiles). No, in no wise: for we have before proved both Jews and Gentiles, that they are all under sin." (Rom.3:9)

Peter seems to have learned his lesson, at least in part. See Gal. 2:11-14 for the story of his later lapse. Though he was not the Apostle to the Gentiles, yet he was made to understand that Paul's special ministry to the Gentiles was in conformity to the will of God - indeed it was at His direction. Peter is about to use the "keys" the second time - the first occasion being at Pentecost, when he first preached the gospel of the grace of God to the Jews. He will now open the door of salvation to the Gentiles. This does not mean that Peter is the only one who has the key to the door of salvation. Every Christian witness who tells the story of the cross of Christ is using the key. No man or religious institution has monopolized its use.

Having confessed to his audience that he has learned a valuable lesson - a lesson that places bigotry forever beyond the purview of the Christian, Peter than told his audience that his new light on the subject was the reason why he had come to Caesarea when he was invited, and he proceded to ask them what they wanted. As though he did not know.

Verse 29 - "Therefore came I unto you without gainsaying, as soon as I was sent for: I ask therefore for what intent ye have sent for me?"

διὸ καὶ ἀναντιρρήτως ἦλθον μεταπεμφθείς. πυνθάνομαι οὖν τίνι λόγῳ μετεπέμφασθέ με;

διὸ (inferential conjunction introducing a clause in explanation) 1622.
καὶ (continuative conjunction) 14.

#3229 ἀναντιρρήτως (adverbial, manner).

without gainsaying - Acts 10:29.

Meaning: Cf. ἀναντίρρητος (#3492) in Acts 19:36. A combination of α privative plus ἀντί (#237) and ῥητός from ῥέω (#116). Hence, "not to speak against." Without debate; without gainsaying - with reference to Peter's acquiesence in the suggestion of Cornelius's servants - Acts 10:29.

ἦλθον (1st.per.sing.aor.mid.ind.of ἔρχομαι, culminative) 146.

μεταπεμφθείς (aor.pass.part.nom.sing.masc.of μεταπέμπω, adverbial, temporal/causal) 3213.

πυνθάνομαι (1st.per.sing.pres.mid.ind.of πυνθάνομαι, aoristic) 153.

οὖν (inferential conjunction) 68.

τίνι (instrumental sing.masc.of τίς, in agreement with λόγῳ) 281.

λόγῳ (instru.sing.masc.of λόγος, cause) 510.

μετεπέμφασθέ (2d.per.pl.aor.mid.ind. of μεταπέμπω, indirect question) 3213.

με (acc.sing.masc.of ἐγώ, direct object of μετεπέμφασθέ) 123.

Translation - "And therefore I came without objection when I was invited. So I am asking for what reason you have sent for me."

Comment: διό depends for its thrust upon what God showed Peter in verse 28. Since God had taught him to be more discerning with his discrimination, he had come when he was invited, and he came along peaceably, with grace enough to spare his companions his diatribe about racial superiority, as they trudged along the road to Caesarea. The Ku Klux Klan and Adolf Hitler's Hegelian superman of the Master Race have not yet learned Peter's lesson. Peter did not yet understand fully why he had been wrong before, but he clearly understood God's order of verse 20 and was not disposed to argue with God, even though he began to wonder if his own standards were not superior to God's. He was soon to be set straight on that score also.

In τίνι λόγῳ, in indirect question we have an excellent illustration of the basic meaning of λόγος (#510). "What rationale have you to support your invitation to me to come here?"

Verse 30 - "And Cornelius said, Four days ago I was fasting until this hour; and at the ninth hour I prayed in my house, and, behold, a man stood before me in bright clothing."

καὶ ὁ Κορνήλιος ἔφη, Ἀπὸ τετάρτης ἡμέρας μέχρι ταύτης τῆς ὥρας ἤμην τὴν ἐνάτην προσευχόμενος ἐν τῷ οἴκῳ μου, καὶ ἰδοὺ ἀνὴρ ἔστη ἐνώπιόν μου ἐν ἐσθῆτι λαμπρᾷ

καὶ (continuative conjunction) 14.

ὁ (nom.sing.masc.of the article in agreement with Κορνήλιος) 9.

Κορνήλιος (nom.sing.masc.of Κορνήλιος, subject of ἔφη) 3209.

ἔφη (3d.per.sing.aor.act.ind.of φημί, ingressive) 354.

Ἀπὸ (preposition with the ablative of time description) 70.

τετάρτης (abl.sing.fem.of τέταρτος, in agreement with ἡμέρας) 1129.

ἡμέρας (abl.sing.fem.of ἡμέρα, time separation) 135.

μέχρι (preposition with the genitive of time description) 948.

ταύτης (gen.sing.fem.of οὗτος, in agreement with ὥρας) 93.

τῆς (gen.sing.fem.of the article in agreement with v4raw) 9.

ὥρας (gen.sing.fem.of ὥρα, time description) 735.

ἤμην (1st.per.sing.imp.ind.of εἰμί, imperfect periphrastic) 86.

τὴν (acc.sing.fem.of the article in agreement with ἐνάτην) 9.

ἐνάτην (acc.sing.fem.of ἔννατος, time extent) 1318.

προσευχόμενος (pres.mid.part.nom.sing.masc.of προσεύχομαι, imperfect periphrastic) 544.

ἐν (preposition with the locative of place) 80.

τῷ (loc.sing.masc.of the article in agreement with οἴκῳ) 9.

οἴκῳ (loc.sing.masc.of οἶκος, place where) 784.

μου (gen.sing.masc.of ἐγώ, possession) 123.

καὶ (continuative conjunction) 14.

ἰδοὺ (exclamation) 95.

ἀνὴρ (nom.sing.masc.of ἀνήρ, subject of ἔστη) 63.

ἔστη (3d.per.sing.aor.act.ind.of ἵστημι, constative) 180.

ἐνώπιόν (preposition with the genitive of place description) 1798.

μου (gen.sing.masc.of ἐγώ, place description) 123.

ἐν (preposition with the locative, instrumental use) 80.

ἐσθῆτι (loc.sing.fem.of ἐσθής, means) 2831.

λαμπρᾷ (loc.sing.fem.of λαμπρός, in agreement with ἐσθῆτι) 2832.

Translation - "And Cornelius began, 'Four days ago until this hour, three in the afternoon, I was praying in my house, and a man stood before me in shining apparel.' "

Comment: *Cf.* our comment on verse 24. Rather than revise it, I will let it stand and present the reader with the problem. If Cornelius was correct then Peter met him at his home four days, not three, after the afternoon at three o'clock when Cornelius had his vision. Somewhere in the story we have lost a day. His vision with its instructions to send men to summon Peter was seen on the first day. The next day (the second) his men set out for Joppa, and arrived at noon, met Peter in the afternoon, and remained until the next (the third) day, when they started back to Caesarea. According to Cornelius they arrived at his home on the fourth day. This must mean that either they stayed in Joppa an extra day before starting back, or they spent the third day and the following night before they reached Cornelius' house. What time did they leave Joppa? How long did the trip of only thirty miles require? It had taken Cornelius' servants only half a day. What time did they reach Caesarea? Was it too late in the evening for Peter to call on Cornelius? Goodspeed, without textual authority, resolves the difficulty by translating "Three days ago. . . " ! Meyer attempts to explain it by saying that Cornelius was counting backwards from the day when he was speaking. This does not help. Assume that his vision was seen on Monday. If so, his men left for Joppa on Tuesday, arrived that day, delivered their message and were invited to remain overnight. On Wednesday they started back to Caesarea. Cornelius and Peter met on Thursday, the fourth day. If we count Thursday as the first day, then Monday was the fourth. It is not important for us to know what happened to the extra day. If it had been the Holy Spirit would have directed Luke to fill in the explanatory details.

Note that τὴν ἐνάτην,the phrase to define ταύτης τῆς ὥρας is in the accusative case, whereas the former phrase is in the genitive of time description. The accusative of time extent indicates that the prayer extended throughout the whole hour. This comports with the imperfect periphrastic ἤμην προσευχόμεν-ος. It was three o'clock when the Lord's messenger appeared to Cornelius.

Verse 31 - "... and said, Cornelius, thy prayer is heard, and thine alms are had in remembrance in the sight of God."

καὶ φησίν, Κορνήλιε, εἰσηκούσθη σου ἡ προσευχὴ καὶ αἱ ἐλεημοσύναι σου ἐμνήσθησαν ἐνώπιον τοῦ θεοῦ.

καὶ (adjunctive conjunction joining verbs) 14.

φησίν (3d.per.sing.pres.act.ind.of φημί, historical) 354.

Κορνήλιε (voc.sing.masc.of Κορνήλιος, address) 3209.

εἰσηκούσθη (3d.per.sing.1st.aor.pass.ind.of εἰσακούω, culminative) 574.

σου (gen.sing.masc.of σύ, possession) 104.

ἡ (nom.sing.fem.of the article in agreement with προσευχή) 9.

προσευχή (nom.sing.fem.of προσευχή, subject of εἰσηκούσθη) 1238.

καὶ (continuative conjunction) 14.

αἱ (nom.pl.fem.of the article in agreement with ἐλεημοσύναι) 9.

ἐλεημοσύναι (nom.pl.fem.of ἐλεημοσύνη, subject of ἐμνήσθησαν) 558.

σου (gen.sing.masc.of σύ, possession) 104.

ἐμνήσθησαν (3d.per.pl.aor.pass.ind.of μιμνήσκομαι, culminative) 485.

ἐνώπιον (preposition with the genitive of place description, with persons) 1798.

τοῦ (gen.sing.masc.of the article in agreement with θεοῦ) 9.

θεοῦ (gen.sing.masc.of θεός, place description) 124.

Translation - "... and he said, 'Cornelius, your prayer has been heard and your charities were noted and recorded before God."

Comment: Again, lest the uninitiated misunderstand, the point must be made that though God was aware of the prayers and charitable contributions of Cornelius, they did not suffice to save him. They only prompted God to send Peter to him with the gospel, in order that he might be saved, through the preaching of the gospel and the hearing by faith. There is nothing in this passage to teach salvation by works. No man, however sincere, is saved because he prayed or scattered his wealth about among the needy. When God chose to open the door of salvation to the Gentiles in a formal way, through Peter's ministry, He chose Corelius, a sincerely devout Gentile. If Cornelius had lived in a part of the world in which it would have been impossible for him to hear the gospel, God would have judged him on the basis of Romans 2:6-16, *q.v.* comment, *en loc.*

Verse 32 - "Send therefore to Joppa, and call hither Simon, whose surname is Peter; he is lodged in the house of one Simon a tanner by the sea side: who, when he cometh, shall speak unto thee."

πέμφον οὖν εἰς Ἰόππην καὶ μετακάλεσαι Σίμωνα ὃς ἐπικαλεῖται Πέτρος. Οὗτος ξενίζεται ἐν οἰκίᾳ Σίμωνος βυρσέως παρὰ θάλασσαν.

πέμφον (2d.per.sing.aor.act.impv.of πέμπω, command) 169.
οὖν (inferential conjunction) 68.
εἰς (preposition with the accusative of extent) 140.
Ἰόππην (acc.sing.fem.of Ἰόππη, extent) 3202.
καὶ (adjunctive conjunction joining verbs) 14.
μετακάλεσαι (2d.per.sing.1st.aor.mid.impv.of μετακαλέω, command) 3111.
Σίμωνα (acc.sing.masc.of Σίμων, direct object of μετακάλεσαι) 386.
ὃς (nom.sing.masc.of ὅς, subject of ἐπικαλεῖται, in a relative adjectival clause) 65.
ἐπικαλεῖται (3d.per.sing.pres.pass.ind.of ἐπικαλέω, customary) 884.
Πέτρος (nom.sing.masc.of Πέτρος, appellation) 387.
Οὗτος (nom.sing.masc.of οὗτος, subject of ξενίζεται, deictic) 93.
ξενίζεται (3d.per.sing.pres.pass.ind.of ξενίζω, aoristic) 3214.
ἐν (preposition with the locative of place) 80.
οἰκίᾳ (loc.sing.fem.of οἰκία, place where) 186.
Σίμνος (gen.sing.masc.of Σίμων, possession) 3207.
βυρσέως (gen.sing.masc.of βυρσεύς, apposition) 3208.
παρὰ (preposition with the accusative with a verb of rest) 154.
θάλασσαν (acc.sing.fem.of θάλασσα, with a verb of rest) 374.

Translation - *"Therefore you must send to Joppa and call for Simon who is nicknamed Peter. This man is a guest in a house owned by Simon, a tanner, by the sea."*

Comment: *Cf.* Acts 10:18 where we have Σίμων ὁ ἐπικαλούμενος Πέτρος, instead of Σίμωνα ὃς ἐπικαλεῖται Πέτρος. Note the absence of the articles in the last clause.

Thus the angel of the Lord spoke to Cornelius. He continues to relate what he did, congratulates Peter for his willingness to come and urges him to say whatever he wishes to say.

Verse 33 - "Immediately therefore I sent to thee; and thou hast well done that thou art come. Now therefore are we all here present before God, to hear all things that are commanded thee of God."

ἐξαυτῆς οὖν ἔπεμφα πρὸς σέ, σύ τε καλῶς ἐποίησας παραγενόμενος. νῦν οὖν πάντες ἡμεῖς ἐνώπιον τοῦ θεοῦ πάρεσμεν ἀκοῦσαι πάντα τὰ προστεταγμένα σοι ὑπὸ τοῦ κυρίου.

ἐξαυτῆς (adverbial, manner) 2260.
οὖν (inferential conjunction) 68.
ἔπεμφα (1st.per.sing.aor.act.ind.of πέμπω, constative) 169.
πρὸς (preposition with the accusative of extent) 197.
σέ (acc.sing.masc.of σύ, extent) 104.
σύ (nom.sing.masc.of σύ subject of ἐποίησας) 104.

τε (affirmative particle) 1480.

καλῶς (adverbial, manner) 977.

ἐποίησας (2d.per.sing.aor.act.ind.of ποιέω, culminative) 127.

παραγενόμενος (pres.mid.part.nom.sing.masc.of παραγίνομαι, adverbial, modal) 139.

νῦν (temporal adverb) 1497.

οὖν (continuative conjunction) 68.

πάντες (nom.pl.masc.of πᾶς, in agreement with ἡμεῖς) 67.

ἡμεῖς (nom.pl.masc.of ἐγώ, subject of πάρεσμεν) 123.

ἐνώπιον (preposition with the genitive of place description, with persons) 1798.

τοῦ (gen.sing.masc.of the article in agreement with θεοῦ) 9.

θεοῦ (gen.sing.masc.of θεός, place description) 124.

πάρεσμεν (1st.per.pl.pres.ind.of πάρειμι, aoristic) 1592.

ἀκοῦσαι (aor.act.inf.of ἀκούω, purpose) 148.

πάντα (acc.pl.neut.of πᾶς, in agreement with προστεταγμένα) 67.

τὰ (acc.pl.neut.of the article in agreement with προστεταγμένα) 9.

προστεταγμένα (perf.pass.part.acc.pl.neut.of προστάσσω, substantival, direct object of ἀκοῦσαι) 129.

σοι (dat.sing.masc.of σύ, indirect object of προστεταγμένα) 104.

ὑπὸ (preposition with the ablative of agent) 117.

τοῦ (abl.sing.masc.of the article in agreement with κυρίου) 9.

κυρίου (abl.sing.masc.of κύριος, agent) 97.

Translation - "Therefore I sent to you forthwith, and you indeed have been kind to be present. And now we are all here before God to hear all the things which have been ordered you by the Lord."

Comment: The first οὖν is inferential. Pursuant to God's instructions in verse 32, Cornelius sent for Peter. A military man has been trained to obey orders without delay. Hence the adverb ἐξαυτῆς. Literally, "you did well to be present" which probably means "you were kind enough to come." Peter did indeed do well to come, since he was under orders from the Lord to accept Cornelius' invitation, just as Cornelius was under orders from the same Lord to invite him. Note προστεταγμένα, a military word with which Cornelius a Roman army officer understood well. It is interesting that Cornelius understood that although Peter was an Apostle who had seen the Lord and had heard Him preach many times, yet he was not the source of the message which he was about to give. Cornelius wants to hear only what the Lord had ordered Peter to say. And this is what he and his relatives and friends heard with the results that are recorded in the remainder of the chapter.

INDEX